Praise for the First Edition of *TCP/IP Illustrated, Volume 1: The Protocols*

"This is sure to be the bible for TCP/IP developers and users. Within minutes of picking up the text, I encountered several scenarios that had tripped up both my colleagues and myself in the past. Stevens reveals many of the mysteries once held tightly by the ever-elusive networking gurus. Having been involved in the implementation of TCP/IP for some years now, I consider this by far the finest text to date."

—Robert A. Ciampa, network engineer, Synernetics, division of 3COM

"While all of Stevens' books are readable and technically excellent, this new opus is awesome. Although many books describe the TCP/IP protocols, Stevens provides a level of depth and real-world detail lacking from the competition. He puts the reader inside TCP/IP using a visual approach and shows the protocols in action."

—Steven Baker, networking columnist, *Unix Review*

"*TCP/IP Illustrated, Volume 1*, is an excellent reference for developers, network administrators, or anyone who needs to understand TCP/IP technology. *TCP/IP Illustrated* is comprehensive in its coverage of TCP/IP topics, providing enough details to satisfy the experts while giving enough background and commentary for the novice."

—Bob Williams, vice president, Marketing, NetManage, Inc.

". . . [T]he difference is that Stevens wants to show as well as tell about the protocols. His principal teaching tools are straightforward explanations, exercises at the ends of chapters, byte-by-byte diagrams of headers and the like, and listings of actual traffic as examples."

—Walter Zintz, *UnixWorld*

"Much better than theory only. . . . W. Richard Stevens takes a multihost-based configuration and uses it as a travelogue of TCP/IP examples with illustrations. *TCP/IP Illustrated, Volume 1*, is based on practical examples that reinforce the theory—distinguishing this book from others on the subject, and making it both readable and informative."

—Peter M. Haverlock, consultant, IBM TCP/IP Development

"The diagrams he uses are excellent and his writing style is clear and readable. In sum, Stevens has made a complex topic easy to understand. This book merits everyone's attention. Please read it and keep it on your bookshelf."

—Elizabeth Zinkann, sys admin

"W. Richard Stevens has produced a fine text and reference work. It is well organized and very clearly written with, as the title suggests, many excellent illustrations exposing the intimate details of the logic and operation of IP, TCP, and the supporting cast of protocols and applications."

—Scott Bradner, consultant, Harvard University OIT/NSD

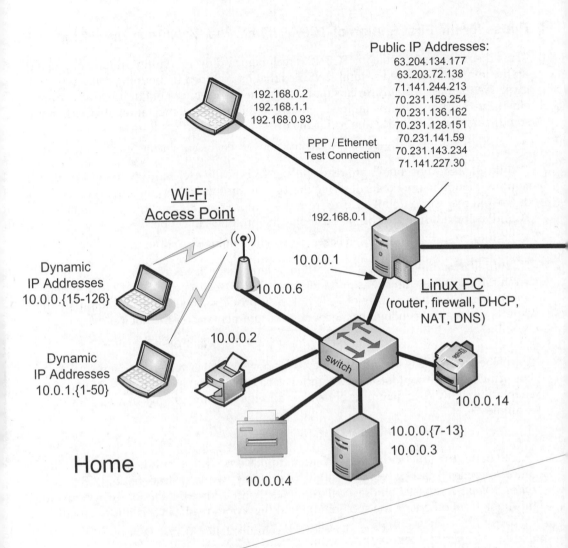

Public IP Addresses:
63.204.134.177
63.203.72.138
71.141.244.213
70.231.159.254
70.231.136.162
70.231.128.151
70.231.141.59
70.231.143.234
71.141.227.30

192.168.0.2
192.168.1.1
192.168.0.93

PPP / Ethernet
Test Connection

Wi-Fi
Access Point

192.168.0.1

10.0.0.1

10.0.0.6

Linux PC
(router, firewall, DHCP,
NAT, DNS)

Dynamic
IP Addresses
10.0.0.{15-126}

10.0.0.2

Dynamic
IP Addresses
10.0.1.{1-50}

switch

10.0.0.14

10.0.0.{7-13}
10.0.0.3

Home

10.0.0.4

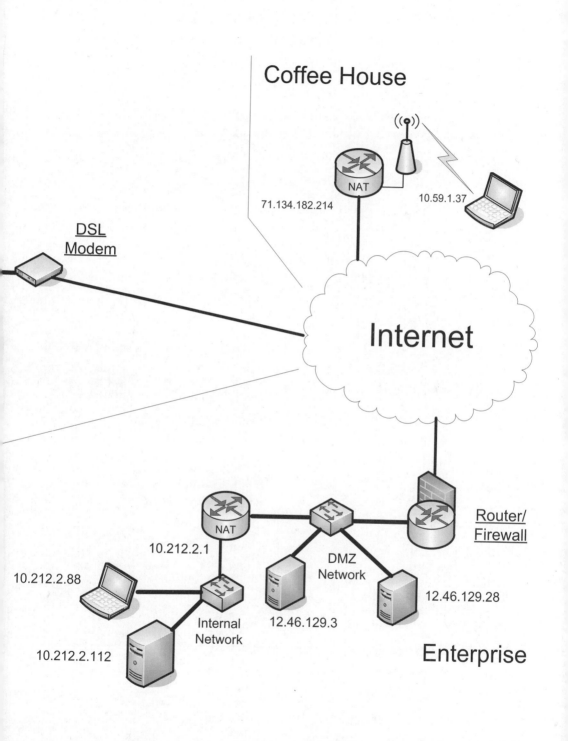

TCP/IP Illustrated, Volume 1

The Protocols

Second Edition

Kevin R. Fall
W. Richard Stevens

Originally written by Dr. W. Richard Stevens.
Revised by Dr. Kevin R. Fall.

PEARSON

Original Edition entitled *TCP/IP Illustrated Volume 1: The Protocols International Edition, Second Edition,* by Fall, Kevin R., published by Pearson Education, Inc, Copyright © 2012.

Indian edition published by Dorling Kindersley India Pvt. Ltd. Copyright © 2014

ISBN 978-93-325-3595-4

First Impression
Second Impression, 2015

This edition is manufactured in India and is authorized for sale only in India, Bangladesh, Bhutan, Pakistan, Nepal, Sri Lanka and the Maldives. Circulation of this edition outside of these territories is UNAUTHORIZED.

Published by Pearson India Education Services Pvt Ltd, CIN: U72200TN2005PTC057128, formerly known as TutorVista Global Pvt Ltd, licensee of Pearson Education in South Asia.

Head Office: 7th Floor, knowledge Boulevard, A-8(A) Sector-62, Noida (U.P) 201309, India
Registered Office: Module G4, Ground Floor, Elnet Software City, TS-140,Block 2 and 9, Rajiv Gandhi Salai, Taramani, Chennai 600 113, Tamil Nadu, India.Fax: 080-30461003,
Phone: 080-30461060, www.pearson.co.in, Email: companysecretary.india@pearson.com

Printed in India by Pushp Print Services.

To Vicki, George, Audrey, Maya, Dylan, and Jan,
for their insight, tolerance, and support
through the long nights and weekends.

—Kevin

Contents

Foreword   xxv

Preface to the Second Edition   xxvii

Adapted Preface to the First Edition   xxxiii

Chapter 1   Introduction   1

    1.1   Architectural Principles   2

           1.1.1 Packets, Connections, and Datagrams   3

           1.1.2 The End-to-End Argument and Fate Sharing   6

           1.1.3 Error Control and Flow Control   7

    1.2   Design and Implementation   8

           1.2.1 Layering   8

           1.2.2 Multiplexing, Demultiplexing, and Encapsulation in Layered
                 Implementations   10

    1.3   The Architecture and Protocols of the TCP/IP Suite   13

           1.3.1 The ARPANET Reference Model   13

           1.3.2 Multiplexing, Demultiplexing, and Encapsulation in TCP/IP   16

           1.3.3 Port Numbers   17

           1.3.4 Names, Addresses, and the DNS   19

    1.4   Internets, Intranets, and Extranets   19

    1.5   Designing Applications   20

           1.5.1 Client/Server   20

           1.5.2 Peer-to-Peer   21

           1.5.3 Application Programming Interfaces (APIs)   22

1.6   Standardization Process   22
       1.6.1 Request for Comments (RFC)   23
       1.6.2 Other Standards   24
1.7   Implementations and Software Distributions   24
1.8   Attacks Involving the Internet Architecture   25
1.9   Summary   26
1.10   References   28

Chapter 2   The Internet Address Architecture   31

2.1   Introduction   31
2.2   Expressing IP Addresses   32
2.3   Basic IP Address Structure   34
       2.3.1 Classful Addressing   34
       2.3.2 Subnet Addressing   36
       2.3.3 Subnet Masks   39
       2.3.4 Variable-Length Subnet Masks (VLSM)   41
       2.3.5 Broadcast Addresses   42
       2.3.6 IPv6 Addresses and Interface Identifiers   43
2.4   CIDR and Aggregation   46
       2.4.1 Prefixes   47
       2.4.2 Aggregation   48
2.5   Special-Use Addresses   50
       2.5.1 Addressing IPv4/IPv6 Translators   52
       2.5.2 Multicast Addresses   53
       2.5.3 IPv4 Multicast Addresses   54
       2.5.4 IPv6 Multicast Addresses   57
       2.5.5 Anycast Addresses   62
2.6   Allocation   62
       2.6.1 Unicast   62
       2.6.2 Multicast   65
2.7   Unicast Address Assignment   65
       2.7.1 Single Provider/No Network/Single Address   66
       2.7.2 Single Provider/Single Network/Single Address   67
       2.7.3 Single Provider/Multiple Networks/Multiple Addresses   67
       2.7.4 Multiple Providers/Multiple Networks/Multiple Addresses
              (Multihoming)   68

2.8   Attacks Involving IP Addresses   70
2.9   Summary   71
2.10   References   72

Chapter 3   Link Layer   79

3.1   Introduction   79
3.2   Ethernet and the IEEE 802 LAN/MAN Standards   80
        3.2.1 The IEEE 802 LAN/MAN Standards   82
        3.2.2 The Ethernet Frame Format   84
        3.2.3 802.1p/q: Virtual LANs and QoS Tagging   89
        3.2.4 802.1AX: Link Aggregation (Formerly 802.3ad)   92
3.3   Full Duplex, Power Save, Autonegotiation, and 802.1X Flow Control   94
        3.3.1 Duplex Mismatch   96
        3.3.2 Wake-on LAN (WoL), Power Saving, and Magic Packets   96
        3.3.3 Link-Layer Flow Control   98
3.4   Bridges and Switches   98
        3.4.1 Spanning Tree Protocol (STP)   102
        3.4.2 802.1ak: Multiple Registration Protocol (MRP)   111
3.5   Wireless LANs—IEEE 802.11(Wi-Fi)   111
        3.5.1 802.11 Frames   113
        3.5.2 Power Save Mode and the Time Sync Function (TSF)   119
        3.5.3 802.11 Media Access Control   120
        3.5.4 Physical-Layer Details: Rates, Channels, and Frequencies   123
        3.5.5 Wi-Fi Security   129
        3.5.6 Wi-Fi Mesh (802.11s)   130
3.6   Point-to-Point Protocol (PPP)   130
        3.6.1 Link Control Protocol (LCP)   131
        3.6.2 Multilink PPP (MP)   137
        3.6.3 Compression Control Protocol (CCP)   139
        3.6.4 PPP Authentication   140
        3.6.5 Network Control Protocols (NCPs)   141
        3.6.6 Header Compression   142
        3.6.7 Example   143
3.7   Loopback   145
3.8   MTU and Path MTU   148
3.9   Tunneling Basics   149
        3.9.1 Unidirectional Links   153

3.10   Attacks on the Link Layer   154
3.11   Summary   156
3.12   References   157

Chapter 4   ARP: Address Resolution Protocol   165

4.1   Introduction   165
4.2   An Example   166
        4.2.1 Direct Delivery and ARP   167
4.3   ARP Cache   169
4.4   ARP Frame Format   170
4.5   ARP Examples   171
        4.5.1 Normal Example   171
        4.5.2 ARP Request to a Nonexistent Host   173
4.6   ARP Cache Timeout   174
4.7   Proxy ARP   174
4.8   Gratuitous ARP and Address Conflict Detection (ACD)   175
4.9   The `arp` Command   177
4.10   Using ARP to Set an Embedded Device's IPv4 Address   178
4.11   Attacks Involving ARP   178
4.12   Summary   179
4.13   References   179

Chapter 5   The Internet Protocol (IP)   181

5.1   Introduction   181
5.2   IPv4 and IPv6 Headers   183
        5.2.1 IP Header Fields   183
        5.2.2 The Internet Checksum   186
        5.2.3 *DS Field* and *ECN* (Formerly Called the *ToS Byte* or IPv6 *Traffic Class*)   188
        5.2.4 IP Options   192
5.3   IPv6 Extension Headers   194
        5.3.1 IPv6 Options   196
        5.3.2 Routing Header   200
        5.3.3 Fragment Header   203
5.4   IP Forwarding   208
        5.4.1 Forwarding Table   208
        5.4.2 IP Forwarding Actions   209

5.4.3 Examples   210
5.4.4 Discussion   215
5.5   Mobile IP   215
5.5.1 The Basic Model: Bidirectional Tunneling   216
5.5.2 Route Optimization (RO)   217
5.5.3 Discussion   220
5.6   Host Processing of IP Datagrams   220
5.6.1 Host Models   220
5.6.2 Address Selection   222
5.7   Attacks Involving IP   226
5.8   Summary   226
5.9   References   228

Chapter 6   System Configuration: DHCP and Autoconfiguration   233

6.1   Introduction   233
6.2   Dynamic Host Configuration Protocol (DHCP)   234
6.2.1 Address Pools and Leases   235
6.2.2 DHCP and BOOTP Message Format   236
6.2.3 DHCP and BOOTP Options   238
6.2.4 DHCP Protocol Operation   239
6.2.5 DHCPv6   252
6.2.6 Using DHCP with Relays   267
6.2.7 DHCP Authentication   271
6.2.8 Reconfigure Extension   273
6.2.9 Rapid Commit   273
6.2.10 Location Information (LCI and LoST)   274
6.2.11 Mobility and Handoff Information (MoS and ANDSF)   275
6.2.12 DHCP Snooping   276
6.3   Stateless Address Autoconfiguration (SLAAC)   276
6.3.1 Dynamic Configuration of IPv4 Link-Local Addresses   276
6.3.2 IPv6 SLAAC for Link-Local Addresses   276
6.4   DHCP and DNS Interaction   285
6.5   PPP over Ethernet (PPPoE)   286
6.6   Attacks Involving System Configuration   292
6.7   Summary   292
6.8   References   293

Chapter 7   Firewalls and Network Address Translation (NAT)   299

7.1   Introduction   299
7.2   Firewalls   300
    7.2.1 Packet-Filtering Firewalls   300
    7.2.2 Proxy Firewalls   301
7.3   Network Address Translation (NAT)   303
    7.3.1 Traditional NAT: Basic NAT and NAPT   305
    7.3.2 Address and Port Translation Behavior   311
    7.3.3 Filtering Behavior   313
    7.3.4 Servers behind NATs   314
    7.3.5 Hairpinning and NAT Loopback   314
    7.3.6 NAT Editors   315
    7.3.7 Service Provider NAT (SPNAT) and Service Provider IPv6
        Transition   315
7.4   NAT Traversal   316
    7.4.1 Pinholes and Hole Punching   317
    7.4.2 UNilateral Self-Address Fixing (UNSAF)   317
    7.4.3 Session Traversal Utilities for NAT (STUN)   319
    7.4.4 Traversal Using Relays around NAT (TURN)   326
    7.4.5 Interactive Connectivity Establishment (ICE)   332
7.5   Configuring Packet-Filtering Firewalls and NATs   334
    7.5.1 Firewall Rules   335
    7.5.2 NAT Rules   337
    7.5.3 Direct Interaction with NATs and Firewalls: UPnP, NAT-PMP,
        and PCP   338
7.6   NAT for IPv4/IPv6 Coexistence and Transition   339
    7.6.1 Dual-Stack Lite (DS-Lite)   339
    7.6.2 IPv4/IPv6 Translation Using NATs and ALGs   340
7.7   Attacks Involving Firewalls and NATs   345
7.8   Summary   346
7.9   References   347

Chapter 8   ICMPv4 and ICMPv6: Internet Control Message Protocol   353

8.1   Introduction   353
    8.1.1 Encapsulation in IPv4 and IPv6   354
8.2   ICMP Messages   355
    8.2.1 ICMPv4 Messages   356

8.2.2 ICMPv6 Messages   358

8.2.3 Processing of ICMP Messages   360

8.3   ICMP Error Messages   361

8.3.1 Extended ICMP and Multipart Messages   363

8.3.2 Destination Unreachable (ICMPv4 Type 3, ICMPv6 Type 1)
and Packet Too Big (ICMPv6 Type 2)   364

8.3.3 Redirect (ICMPv4 Type 5, ICMPv6 Type 137)   372

8.3.4 ICMP Time Exceeded (ICMPv4 Type 11, ICMPv6 Type 3)   375

8.3.5 Parameter Problem (ICMPv4 Type 12, ICMPv6 Type 4)   379

8.4   ICMP Query/Informational Messages   380

8.4.1 Echo Request/Reply (`ping`) (ICMPv4 Types 0/8, ICMPv6 Types
129/128)   380

8.4.2 Router Discovery: Router Solicitation and Advertisement
(ICMPv4 Types 9, 10)   383

8.4.3 Home Agent Address Discovery Request/Reply (ICMPv6 Types
144/145)   386

8.4.4 Mobile Prefix Solicitation/Advertisement (ICMPv6 Types 146/147)   387

8.4.5 Mobile IPv6 Fast Handover Messages (ICMPv6 Type 154)   388

8.4.6 Multicast Listener Query/Report/Done (ICMPv6 Types
130/131/132)   388

8.4.7 Version 2 Multicast Listener Discovery (MLDv2) (ICMPv6
Type 143)   390

8.4.8 Multicast Router Discovery (MRD) (IGMP Types 48/49/50,
ICMPv6 Types 151/152/153)   394

8.5   Neighbor Discovery in IPv6   395

8.5.1 ICMPv6 Router Solicitation and Advertisement (ICMPv6 Types
133, 134)   396

8.5.2 ICMPv6 Neighbor Solicitation and Advertisement (IMCPv6 Types
135, 136)   398

8.5.3 ICMPv6 Inverse Neighbor Discovery Solicitation/Advertisement
(ICMPv6 Types 141/142)   401

8.5.4 Neighbor Unreachability Detection (NUD)   402

8.5.5 Secure Neighbor Discovery (SEND)   403

8.5.6 ICMPv6 Neighbor Discovery (ND) Options   407

8.6   Translating ICMPv4 and ICMPv6   424

8.6.1 Translating ICMPv4 to ICMPv6   424

8.6.2 Translating ICMPv6 to ICMPv4   426

8.7   Attacks Involving ICMP   428

8.8   Summary   430
8.9   References   430

Chapter 9   Broadcasting and Local Multicasting (IGMP and MLD)   435

9.1   Introduction   435
9.2   Broadcasting   436
      9.2.1 Using Broadcast Addresses   437
      9.2.2 Sending Broadcast Datagrams   439
9.3   Multicasting   441
      9.3.1 Converting IP Multicast Addresses to 802 MAC/Ethernet Addresses   442
      9.3.2 Examples   444
      9.3.3 Sending Multicast Datagrams   446
      9.3.4 Receiving Multicast Datagrams   447
      9.3.5 Host Address Filtering   449
9.4   The Internet Group Management Protocol (IGMP) and Multicast Listener
      Discovery Protocol (MLD)   451
      9.4.1 IGMP and MLD Processing by Group Members ("Group
            Member Part")   454
      9.4.2 IGMP and MLD Processing by Multicast Routers ("Multicast
            Router Part")   457
      9.4.3 Examples   459
      9.4.4 Lightweight IGMPv3 and MLDv2   464
      9.4.5 IGMP and MLD Robustness   465
      9.4.6 IGMP and MLD Counters and Variables   467
      9.4.7 IGMP and MLD Snooping   468
9.5   Attacks Involving IGMP and MLD   469
9.6   Summary   470
9.7   References   471

Chapter 10   User Datagram Protocol (UDP) and IP Fragmentation   473

10.1 Introduction   473
10.2 UDP Header   474
10.3 UDP Checksum   475
10.4 Examples   478
10.5 UDP and IPv6   481
      10.5.1 Teredo: Tunneling IPv6 through IPv4 Networks   482

10.6   UDP-Lite   487
10.7   IP Fragmentation   488
        10.7.1 Example: UDP/IPv4 Fragmentation   488
        10.7.2 Reassembly Timeout   492
10.8   Path MTU Discovery with UDP   493
        10.8.1 Example   493
10.9   Interaction between IP Fragmentation and ARP/ND   496
10.10   Maximum UDP Datagram Size   497
        10.10.1 Implementation Limitations   497
        10.10.2 Datagram Truncation   498
10.11   UDP Server Design   498
        10.11.1 IP Addresses and UDP Port Numbers   499
        10.11.2 Restricting Local IP Addresses   500
        10.11.3 Using Multiple Addresses   501
        10.11.4 Restricting Foreign IP Address   502
        10.11.5 Using Multiple Servers per Port   503
        10.11.6 Spanning Address Families: IPv4 and IPv6   504
        10.11.7 Lack of Flow and Congestion Control   505
10.12   Translating UDP/IPv4 and UDP/IPv6 Datagrams   505
10.13   UDP in the Internet   506
10.14   Attacks Involving UDP and IP Fragmentation   507
10.15   Summary   508
10.16   References   508

Chapter 11   Name Resolution and the Domain Name System (DNS)   511

11.1   Introduction   511
11.2   The DNS Name Space   512
        11.2.1 DNS Naming Syntax   514
11.3   Name Servers and Zones   516
11.4   Caching   517
11.5   The DNS Protocol   518
        11.5.1 DNS Message Format   520
        11.5.2 The DNS Extension Format (EDNS0)   524
        11.5.3 UDP or TCP   525
        11.5.4 Question (Query) and Zone Section Format   526
        11.5.5 Answer, Authority, and Additional Information Section Formats 526
        11.5.6 Resource Record Types   527

	11.5.7 Dynamic Updates (DNS UPDATE)	555
	11.5.8 Zone Transfers and DNS NOTIFY	558
11.6	Sort Lists, Round-Robin, and Split DNS	565
11.7	Open DNS Servers and DynDNS	567
11.8	Transparency and Extensibility	567
11.9	Translating DNS from IPv4 to IPv6 (DNS64)	568
11.10	LLMNR and mDNS	569
11.11	LDAP	570
11.12	Attacks on the DNS	571
11.13	Summary	572
11.14	References	573

Chapter 12   TCP: The Transmission Control Protocol (Preliminaries)   579

12.1	Introduction	579
	12.1.1 ARQ and Retransmission	580
	12.1.2 Windows of Packets and Sliding Windows	581
	12.1.3 Variable Windows: Flow Control and Congestion Control	583
	12.1.4 Setting the Retransmission Timeout	584
12.2	Introduction to TCP	584
	12.2.1 The TCP Service Model	585
	12.2.2 Reliability in TCP	586
12.3	TCP Header and Encapsulation	587
12.4	Summary	591
12.5	References	591

Chapter 13   TCP Connection Management   595

13.1	Introduction	595
13.2	TCP Connection Establishment and Termination	595
	13.2.1 TCP Half-Close	598
	13.2.2 Simultaneous Open and Close	599
	13.2.3 Initial Sequence Number (ISN)	601
	13.2.4 Example	602
	13.2.5 Timeout of Connection Establishment	604
	13.2.6 Connections and Translators	605
13.3	TCP Options	605
	13.3.1 Maximum Segment Size (MSS) Option	606

13.3.2 Selective Acknowledgment (SACK) Options   607

13.3.3 Window Scale (WSCALE or WSOPT) Option   608

13.3.4 Timestamps Option and Protection against Wrapped
        Sequence Numbers (PAWS)   608

13.3.5 User Timeout (UTO) Option   611

13.3.6 Authentication Option (TCP-AO)   612

13.4   Path MTU Discovery with TCP   612

13.4.1 Example   613

13.5   TCP State Transitions   616

13.5.1 TCP State Transition Diagram   617

13.5.2 TIME_WAIT (2MSL Wait) State   618

13.5.3 Quiet Time Concept   624

13.5.4 FIN_WAIT_2 State   625

13.5.5 Simultaneous Open and Close Transitions   625

13.6   Reset Segments   625

13.6.1 Connection Request to Nonexistent Port   626

13.6.2 Aborting a Connection   627

13.6.3 Half-Open Connections   628

13.6.4 TIME-WAIT Assassination (TWA)   630

13.7   TCP Server Operation   631

13.7.1 TCP Port Numbers   632

13.7.2 Restricting Local IP Addresses   634

13.7.3 Restricting Foreign Endpoints   635

13.7.4 Incoming Connection Queue   636

13.8   Attacks Involving TCP Connection Management   640

13.9   Summary   642

13.10   References   643

Chapter 14 TCP Timeout and Retransmission   647

14.1   Introduction   647

14.2   Simple Timeout and Retransmission Example   648

14.3   Setting the Retransmission Timeout (RTO)   651

14.3.1 The Classic Method   651

14.3.2 The Standard Method   652

14.3.3 The Linux Method   657

14.3.4 RTT Estimator Behaviors   661

14.3.5 RTTM Robustness to Loss and Reordering   662

14.4   Timer-Based Retransmission   664
        14.4.1 Example   665
14.5   Fast Retransmit   667
        14.5.1 Example   668
14.6   Retransmission with Selective Acknowledgments   671
        14.6.1 SACK Receiver Behavior   672
        14.6.2 SACK Sender Behavior   673
        14.6.3 Example   673
14.7   Spurious Timeouts and Retransmissions   677
        14.7.1 Duplicate SACK (DSACK) Extension   677
        14.7.2 The Eifel Detection Algorithm   679
        14.7.3 Forward-RTO Recovery (F-RTO)   680
        14.7.4 The Eifel Response Algorithm   680
14.8   Packet Reordering and Duplication   682
        14.8.1 Reordering   682
        14.8.2 Duplication   684
14.9   Destination Metrics   685
14.10   Repacketization   686
14.11   Attacks Involving TCP Retransmission   687
14.12   Summary   688
14.13   References   689

Chapter 15   TCP Data Flow and Window Management   691

15.1   Introduction   691
15.2   Interactive Communication   692
15.3   Delayed Acknowledgments   695
15.4   Nagle Algorithm   696
        15.4.1 Delayed ACK and Nagle Algorithm Interaction   699
        15.4.2 Disabling the Nagle Algorithm   699
15.5   Flow Control and Window Management   700
        15.5.1 Sliding Windows   701
        15.5.2 Zero Windows and the TCP Persist Timer   704
        15.5.3 Silly Window Syndrome (SWS)   708
        15.5.4 Large Buffers and Auto-Tuning   715
15.6   Urgent Mechanism   719
        15.6.1 Example   720
15.7   Attacks Involving Window Management   723

15.8 Summary   723

15.9 References   724

Chapter 16 TCP Congestion Control   **727**

16.1 Introduction   727

   16.1.1 Detection of Congestion in TCP   728

   16.1.2 Slowing Down a TCP Sender   729

16.2 The Classic Algorithms   730

   16.2.1 Slow Start   732

   16.2.2 Congestion Avoidance   734

   16.2.3 Selecting between Slow Start and Congestion Avoidance   736

   16.2.4 Tahoe, Reno, and Fast Recovery   737

   16.2.5 Standard TCP   738

16.3 Evolution of the Standard Algorithms   739

   16.3.1 NewReno   739

   16.3.2 TCP Congestion Control with SACK   740

   16.3.3 Forward Acknowledgment (FACK) and Rate Halving   741

   16.3.4 Limited Transmit   742

   16.3.5 Congestion Window Validation (CWV)   742

16.4 Handling Spurious RTOs—the Eifel Response Algorithm   744

16.5 An Extended Example   745

   16.5.1 Slow Start Behavior   749

   16.5.2 Sender Pause and Local Congestion (Event 1)   750

   16.5.3 Stretch ACKs and Recovery from Local Congestion   754

   16.5.4 Fast Retransmission and SACK Recovery (Event 2)   757

   16.5.5 Additional Local Congestion and Fast Retransmit Events   759

   16.5.6 Timeouts, Retransmissions, and Undoing *cwnd* Changes   762

   16.5.7 Connection Completion   766

16.6 Sharing Congestion State   767

16.7 TCP Friendliness   768

16.8 TCP in High-Speed Environments   770

   16.8.1 HighSpeed TCP (HSTCP) and Limited Slow Start   770

   16.8.2 Binary Increase Congestion Control (BIC and CUBIC)   772

16.9 Delay-Based Congestion Control   777

   16.9.1 Vegas   777

   16.9.2 FAST   778

	16.9.3 TCP Westwood and Westwood+	779
	16.9.4 Compound TCP	779
16.10	Buffer Bloat	781
16.11	Active Queue Management and ECN	782
16.12	Attacks Involving TCP Congestion Control	785
16.13	Summary	786
16.14	References	788

Chapter 17   TCP Keepalive   **793**

17.1	Introduction	793
17.2	Description	795
	17.2.1 Keepalive Examples	797
17.3	Attacks Involving TCP Keepalives	802
17.4	Summary	802
17.5	References	803

Chapter 18   Security: EAP, IPsec, TLS, DNSSEC, and DKIM   **805**

18.1	Introduction	805
18.2	Basic Principles of Information Security	806
18.3	Threats to Network Communication	807
18.4	Basic Cryptography and Security Mechanisms	809
	18.4.1 Cryptosystems	809
	18.4.2 Rivest, Shamir, and Adleman (RSA) Public Key Cryptography	812
	18.4.3 Diffie-Hellman-Merkle Key Agreement (aka Diffie-Hellman or DH)	813
	18.4.4 Signcryption and Elliptic Curve Cryptography (ECC)	814
	18.4.5 Key Derivation and Perfect Forward Secrecy (PFS)	815
	18.4.6 Pseudorandom Numbers, Generators, and Function Families	815
	18.4.7 Nonces and Salt	816
	18.4.8 Cryptographic Hash Functions and Message Digests	817
	18.4.9 Message Authentication Codes (MACs, HMAC, CMAC, and GMAC)	818
	18.4.10 Cryptographic Suites and Cipher Suites	819
18.5	Certificates, Certificate Authorities (CAs), and PKIs	821
	18.5.1 Public Key Certificates, Certificate Authorities, and X.509	822
	18.5.2 Validating and Revoking Certificates	828
	18.5.3 Attribute Certificates	831

18.6	TCP/IP Security Protocols and Layering	832
18.7	Network Access Control: 802.1X, 802.1AE, EAP, and PANA	833
	18.7.1 EAP Methods and Key Derivation	837
	18.7.2 The EAP Re-authentication Protocol (ERP)	839
	18.7.3 Protocol for Carrying Authentication for Network Access (PANA)	839
18.8	Layer 3 IP Security (IPsec)	840
	18.8.1 Internet Key Exchange (IKEv2) Protocol	842
	18.8.2 Authentication Header (AH)	854
	18.8.3 Encapsulating Security Payload (ESP)	858
	18.8.4 Multicast	864
	18.8.5 L2TP/IPsec	865
	18.8.6 IPsec NAT Traversal	865
	18.8.7 Example	867
18.9	Transport Layer Security (TLS and DTLS)	876
	18.9.1 TLS 1.2	877
	18.9.2 TLS with Datagrams (DTLS)	891
18.10	DNS Security (DNSSEC)	894
	18.10.1 DNSSEC Resource Records	896
	18.10.2 DNSSEC Operation	902
	18.10.3 Transaction Authentication (TSIG, TKEY, and SIG(0))	911
	18.10.4 DNSSEC with DNS64	915
18.11	DomainKeys Identified Mail (DKIM)	915
	18.11.1 DKIM Signatures	916
	18.11.2 Example	916
18.12	Attacks on Security Protocols	918
18.13	Summary	919
18.14	References	922
Glossary of Acronyms		**933**
Index		**963**

Foreword

Rarely does one find a book on a well-known topic that is both historically and technically comprehensive and remarkably accurate. One of the things I admire about this work is the "warts and all" approach that gives it such credibility. The TCP/IP architecture is a product of the time in which it was conceived. That it has been able to adapt to growing requirements in many dimensions by factors of a million or more, to say nothing of a plethora of applications, is quite remarkable. Understanding the scope and limitations of the architecture and its protocols is a sound basis from which to think about future evolution and even revolution.

During the early formulation of the Internet architecture, the notion of "enterprise" was not really recognized. In consequence, most networks had their own IP address space and "announced" their addresses in the routing system directly. After the introduction of commercial service, Internet Service Providers emerged as intermediaries who "announced" Internet address blocks on behalf of their customers. Thus, most of the address space was assigned in a "provider dependent" fashion. "Provider independent" addressing was unusual. The net result (no pun intended) led to route aggregation and containment of the size of the global routing table. While this tactic had benefits, it also created the "multi-homing" problem since users of provider-dependent addresses did not have their own entries in the global routing table. The IP address "crunch" also led to Network Address Translation, which also did not solve provider dependence and multi-homing problems.

Reading through this book evokes a sense of wonder at the complexity that has evolved from a set of relatively simple concepts that worked with a small number of networks and application circumstances. As the chapters unfold, one can see the level of complexity that has evolved to accommodate an increasing number of requirements, dictated in part by new deployment conditions and challenges, to say nothing of sheer growth in the scale of the system.

The issues associated with securing "enterprise" users of the Internet also led to firewalls that are intended to supply perimeter security. While useful, it has become clear that attacks against local Internet infrastructure can come through internal compromises (e.g., an infected computer is put onto an internal network or an infected thumb-drive is used to infect an internal computer through its USB port).

It has become apparent that, in addition to a need to expand the Internet address space through the introduction of IP version 6, with its 340 trillion trillion trillion addresses, there is also a strong need to introduce various security-enhancing mechanisms such as the Domain Name System Security Extension (DNSSEC) among many others.

What makes this book unique, in my estimation, is the level of detail and attention to history. It provides background and a sense for the ways in which solutions to networking problems have evolved. It is relentless in its effort to achieve precision and to expose remaining problem areas. For an engineer determined to refine and secure Internet operation or to explore alternative solutions to persistent problems, the insights provided by this book will be invaluable. The authors deserve credit for a thorough rendering of the technology of today's Internet.

Woodhurst   Vint Cerf
June 2011

Preface to the Second Edition

Welcome to the second edition of *TCP/IP Illustrated, Volume 1*. This book aims to provide a detailed, current look at the TCP/IP protocol suite. Instead of just describing how the protocols operate, we show the protocols in operation using a variety of analysis tools. This helps you better understand the design decisions behind the protocols and how they interact with each other, and it simultaneously exposes you to implementation details without your having to read through the implementation's software source code or set up an experimental laboratory. Of course, reading source code or setting up a laboratory will only help to increase your understanding.

Networking has changed dramatically in the past three decades. Originally a research project and object of curiosity, the Internet has become a global communication fabric upon which governments, businesses, and individuals depend. The TCP/IP suite defines the underlying methods used to exchange information by every device on the Internet. After more than a decade of delay, the Internet and TCP/IP itself are now undergoing an evolution, to incorporate IPv6. Throughout the text we will discuss both IPv6 and the current IPv4 together, but we highlight the differences where they are important. Unfortunately, they do not directly interoperate, so some care and attention are required to appreciate the impact of the evolution.

The book is intended for anyone wishing to better understand the current set of TCP/IP protocols and how they operate: network operators and administrators, network software developers, students, and users who deal with TCP/IP. We have included material that should be of interest to both new readers as well as those familiar with the material from the first edition. We hope you will find the coverage of the new and older material useful and interesting.

Comments on the First Edition

Nearly two decades have passed since the publication of the first edition of *TCP/IP Illustrated, Volume 1*. It continues to be a valuable resource for both students and professionals in understanding the TCP/IP protocols at a level of detail difficult to obtain in competing texts. Today it remains among the best references for detailed information regarding the operation of the TCP/IP protocols. However, even the best books concerned with information and communications technology become dated after a time, and the TCP/IP Illustrated series is no exception. In this edition, I hope to thoroughly update the pioneering work of Dr. Stevens with coverage of new material while maintaining the exceptionally high standard of presentation and detail common to his numerous books.

The first edition covers a broad set of protocols and their operation, ranging from the link layer all the way to applications and network management. Today, covering this breadth of material comprehensively in a single volume would produce a very lengthy text indeed. For this reason, the second edition focuses specifically on the *core* protocols: those relatively low-level protocols used most frequently in providing the basic services of configuration, naming, data delivery, and security for the Internet. Detailed discussions of applications, routing, Web services, and other important topics are postponed to subsequent volumes.

Considerable progress has been made in improving the robustness and compliance of TCP/IP implementations to their corresponding specifications since the publication of the first edition. While many of the examples in the first edition highlight implementation bugs or noncompliant behaviors, these problems have largely been addressed in currently available systems, at least for IPv4. This fact is not terribly surprising, given the greatly expanded use of the TCP/IP protocols in the last 18 years. Misbehaving implementations are a comparative rarity, which attests to a certain maturity of the protocol suite as a whole. The problems encountered in the operation of the core protocols nowadays often relate to intentional exploitation of infrequently used protocol features, a form of security concern that was not a primary focus in the first edition but one that we spend considerable effort to address in the second edition.

The Internet Milieu of the Twenty-first Century

The usage patterns and importance of the Internet have changed considerably since the publication of the first edition. The most obvious watershed event was the creation and subsequent intense commercialization of the World Wide Web starting in the early 1990s. This event greatly accelerated the availability of the Internet to large numbers of people with various (sometimes conflicting) motivations. As such, the protocols and systems originally implemented in a small-scale environment of academic cooperation have been stressed by limited availability of addresses and an increase of security concerns.

In response to the security threats, network and security administrators have introduced special control elements into the network. It is now common practice to place a *firewall* at the point of attachment to the Internet, for both large enterprises as well as small businesses and homes. As the demand for IP addresses and security has increased over the last decade, *Network Address Translation* (NAT) is now supported in virtually all current-generation routers and is in widespread use. It has eased the pressure on Internet address availability by allowing sites to obtain a comparatively small number of routable Internet addresses from their service providers (one for each simultaneously online user), yet assign a very large number of addresses to local computers without further coordination. A consequence of NAT deployment has been a slowing of the migration to IPv6 (which provides for an almost incomprehensibly large number of addresses) and interoperability problems with some older protocols.

As the users of personal computers began to demand Internet connectivity by the mid-1990s, the largest supplier of PC software, Microsoft, abandoned its original policy of offering only proprietary alternatives to the Internet and instead undertook an effort to embrace TCP/IP compatibility in most of its products. Since then, personal computers running their Windows operating system have come to dominate the mix of PCs presently connected to the Internet. Over time, a significant rise in the number of Linux-based systems means that such systems now threaten to displace Microsoft as the frontrunner. Other operating systems, including Oracle Solaris and Berkeley's BSD-based systems, which once represented the majority of Internet-connected systems, are now a comparatively small component of the mix. Apple's OS X (Mach-based) operating system has risen as a new contender and is gaining in popularity, especially among portable computer users. In 2003, portable computer (laptop) sales exceeded desktop sales as the majority of personal computer types sold, and their proliferation has sparked a demand for widely deployed, high-speed Internet access supported by wireless infrastructure. It is projected that the most common method for accessing the Internet from 2012 and beyond will be smartphones. Tablet computers also represent an important growing contender.

Wireless networks are now available at a large number of locations such as restaurants, airports, coffeehouses, and other public places. They typically provide short-range free or pay-for-use (flat-rate) high-speed wireless Internet connections using hardware compatible with commonly used office or home local area network installations. A set of alternative "wireless broadband" technologies based on cellular telephone standards (e.g., LTE, HSPA, UMTS, EV-DO) are becoming widely available in developed regions of the world (and some developing regions of the words that are "leapfrogging" to newer wireless technology), offering longer-range operation, often at somewhat reduced bandwidths and with volume-based pricing. Both types of infrastructure address the desire of users to be mobile while accessing the Internet, using either portable computers or smaller devices. In either case, mobile end users accessing the Internet over wireless networks pose two significant technical challenges to the TCP/IP protocol architecture. First, mobility affects the Internet's routing and addressing structure by breaking the assumption that hosts have addresses assigned to them based upon the identity of their nearby router. Second, wireless links may experience outages and therefore cause data to be lost for reasons other than those typical of wired links (which generally do not lose data unless too much traffic is being injected into the network).

Finally, the Internet has fostered the rise of so-called peer-to-peer applications forming "overlay" networks. Peer-to-peer applications do not rely on a central server to accomplish a task but instead determine a set of *peer* computers with which they can communicate and interact to accomplish a task. The peer computers are operated by other end users and may come and go rapidly compared to a fixed server infrastructure. The "overlay" concept captures the fact that such interacting peers themselves form a network, overlaid atop the conventional TCP/IP-based network (which, one may observe, is itself an overlay above the underlying physical links). The development of peer-to-peer applications, while of intense interest to those who study traffic flows and electronic commerce, has not had a profound impact on the core protocols described in *Volume 1* per se, but the concept of overlay networks has become an important consideration for networking technology more generally.

Content Changes for the Second Edition

Regarding content in the text, the most important changes from the first edition are a restructuring of the scope of the overall text and the addition of significant material on security. Instead of attempting to cover nearly all common protocols in use at every layer in the Internet, the present text focuses in detail first on the non-security core protocols in widespread use, or that are expected to be in widespread use in the near future: Ethernet (802.3), Wi-Fi (802.11), PPP, ARP, IPv4, IPv6, UDP, TCP, DHCP, and DNS. These protocols are likely to be encountered by system administrators and users alike.

In the second edition, security is covered in two ways. First, in each appropriate chapter, a section devoted to describing known attacks and their countermeasures relating to the protocol described in the chapter is included. These descriptions are not presented as a recipe for constructing attacks but rather as a practical indication of the kinds of problems that may arise when protocol implementations (or specifications, in some cases) are insufficiently robust. In today's Internet, incomplete specification or lax implementation practice can lead to mission-critical systems being compromised by even relatively unsophisticated attacks.

The second important discussion of security occurs in Chapter 18, where security and cryptography are studied in some detail, including protocols such as IPsec, TLS, DNSSEC, and DKIM. These protocols are now understood to be important for implementing any service or application expected to maintain integrity or secure operation. As the Internet has increased in commercial importance, the need for security (and the number of threats to it) has grown proportionally.

Although IPv6 was not included in the first edition, there is now reason to believe that the use of IPv6 may increase significantly with the exhaustion of unallocated IPv4 address groups in February 2011. IPv6 was conceived largely to address the problems of IPv4 address depletion and, and while not nearly as common as IPv4 today, is becoming more important as a growing number of small devices (such as cellular telephones, household devices, and environmental sensors) become attached to the Internet. Events such as the World IPv6 Day (June 8, 2011) helped to demonstrate that the Internet can continue to work even as the underlying protocols are modified and augmented in a significant way.

A second consideration for the structure of the second edition is a deemphasis of the protocols that are no longer commonly used and an update of the descriptions of those that have been revised substantially since the publication of the first edition. The chapters covering RARP, BOOTP, NFS, SMTP, and SNMP have been removed from the book, and the discussion of the SLIP protocol has been abandoned in favor of expanded coverage of DHCP and PPP (including PPPoE). The function of IP forwarding (described in Chapter 9 in the first edition) has been integrated with the overall description of the IPv4 and IPv6 protocols in Chapter 5 of this edition. The discussion of dynamic routing protocols (RIP, OSPF, and BGP) has been removed, as the latter two protocols alone could each conceivably merit a book-long discussion. Starting with ICMP, and continuing through IP, TCP, and UDP, the impact of operation using IPv4 versus IPv6 is discussed in any cases where the difference in operation is significant. There is no specific chapter devoted solely to IPv6; instead, its impact relative to each existing core protocol is described where appropriate. Chapters 15 and 25–30 of the first edition, which are devoted to Internet applications and their supporting protocols, have been largely removed; what remains only illustrates the operation of the underlying core protocols where necessary.

Several chapters covering new material have been added. The first chapter begins with a general introduction to networking issues and architecture, followed by a more Internet-specific orientation. The Internet's addressing architecture is covered in Chapter 2. A new chapter on host configuration and how a system "gets on" the network appears as Chapter 6. Chapter 7 describes firewalls and Network Address Translation (NAT), including how NATs are used in partitioning address space between routable and nonroutable portions. The set of tools used in the first edition has been expanded to include Wireshark (a free network traffic monitor application with a graphical user interface).

The target readership for the second edition remains identical to that of the first edition. No prior knowledge of networking concepts is required for approaching it, although the advanced reader should benefit from the level of detail and references. A rich collection of references is included in each chapter for the interested reader to pursue.

Editorial Changes for the Second Edition

The general flow of material in the second edition remains similar to that of the first edition. After the introductory material (Chapters 1 and 2), the protocols are presented in a bottom-up fashion to illustrate how the goal of network communication presented in the introduction is realized in the Internet architecture. As in the first edition, actual packet traces are used to illustrate the operational details of the protocols, where appropriate. Since the publication of the first edition, freely available packet capture and analysis tools with graphical interfaces have become available, extending the capabilities of the `tcpdump` program used in the first edition. In the present text, `tcpdump` is used when the points to be illustrated are easily conveyed by examining the output of a text-based packet capture tool. In most other cases, however, screen shots of the Wireshark tool are used. Please be aware that some output listings, including snapshots of `tcpdump` output, are wrapped or simplified for clarity.

The packet traces shown typically illustrate the behavior of one or more parts of the network depicted on the inside of the front book cover. It represents a broadband-connected "home" environment (typically used for client access or peer-to-peer networking), a "public" environment (e.g., coffee shop), and an enterprise environment. The operating systems used for examples include Linux, Windows, FreeBSD, and Mac OS X. Various versions are used, as many different OS versions are in use on the Internet today.

The structure of each chapter has been slightly modified from the first edition. Each chapter begins with an introduction to the chapter topic, followed in some cases by historical notes, the details of the chapter, a summary, and a set of references. A section near the end of most chapters describes security concerns and attacks. The per-chapter references represent a change for the second edition. They should make each chapter more self-contained and require the reader to perform fewer "long-distance page jumps" to find a reference. Some of the references are now enhanced with WWW URLs for easier access online. In addition, the reference format for papers and books has been changed to a somewhat more compact form that includes the first initial of each author's last name followed by the last two digits of the year (e.g., the former [Cerf and Kahn 1974] is now shortened to [CK74]). For the numerous RFC references used, the RFC number is used instead of the author names. This follows typical RFC conventions and has the side benefit of grouping all the RFC references together in the reference lists.

On a final note, the typographical conventions of the TCP/IP Illustrated series have been maintained faithfully. However, the present author elected to use an editor and typesetting package other than the Troff system used by Dr. Stevens and some other authors of the Addison-Wesley Professional Computing Series collection. Thus, the particular task of final copyediting could take advantage of the significant expertise of Barbara Wood, the copy editor generously made available to me by the publisher. We hope you will be pleased with the results.

Berkeley, California   Kevin R. Fall
September 2011

Adapted Preface
to the First Edition

Introduction

This book describes the TCP/IP protocol suite, but from a different perspective than other texts on TCP/IP. Instead of just describing the protocols and what they do, we'll use a popular diagnostic tool to watch the protocols in action. Seeing how the protocols operate in varying circumstances provides a greater understanding of how they work and why certain design decisions were made. It also provides a look into the implementation of the protocols, without having to wade through thousands of lines of source code.

When networking protocols were being developed in the 1960s through the 1980s, expensive, dedicated hardware was required to see the packets going "across the wire." Extreme familiarity with the protocols was also required to comprehend the packets displayed by the hardware. Functionality of the hardware analyzers was limited to that built in by the hardware designers.

Today this has changed dramatically with the ability of the ubiquitous workstation to monitor a local area network [Mogul 1990]. Just attach a workstation to your network, run some publicly available software, and watch what goes by on the wire. While many people consider this a tool to be used for *diagnosing* network problems, it is also a powerful tool for *understanding* how the network protocols operate, which is the goal of this book.

This book is intended for anyone wishing to understand how the TCP/IP protocols operate: programmers writing network applications, system administrators responsible for maintaining computer systems and networks utilizing TCP/IP, and users who deal with TCP/IP applications on a daily basis.

Typographical Conventions

When we display interactive input and output we'll show our typed input in a **bold font**, and the computer output `like this`. *Comments are added in italics.*

```
bsdi % telnet svr4 discard
Trying 140.252.13.34...
Connected to svr4.
```
connect to the discard server
this line and next output by Telnet client

Also, we always include the name of the system as part of the shell prompt (`bsdi` in this example) to show on which host the command was run.

Note

Throughout the text we'll use indented, parenthetical notes such as this to describe historical points or implementation details.

We sometimes refer to the complete description of a command on the Unix manual as in `ifconfig(8)`. This notation, the name of the command followed by a number in parentheses, is the normal way of referring to Unix commands. The number in parentheses is the section number in the Unix manual of the "manual page" for the command, where additional information can be located. Unfortunately not all Unix systems organize their manuals the same, with regard to the section numbers used for various groupings of commands. We'll use the BSD-style section numbers (which is the same for BSD-derived systems such as SunOS 4.1.3), but your manuals may be organized differently.

Acknowledgments

Although the author's name is the only one to appear on the cover, the combined effort of many people is required to produce a quality text book. First and foremost is the author's family, who put up with the long and weird hours that go into writing a book. Thank you once again, Sally, Bill, Ellen, and David.

The consulting editor, Brian Kernighan, is undoubtedly the best in the business. He was the first one to read various drafts of the manuscript and mark it up with his infinite supply of red pens. His attention to detail, his continual prodding for readable prose, and his thorough reviews of the manuscript are an immense resource to a writer.

Technical reviewers provide a different point of view and keep the author honest by catching technical mistakes. Their comments, suggestions, and (most importantly) criticisms add greatly to the final product. My thanks to Steve Bellovin, Jon Crowcroft, Pete Haverlock, and Doug Schmidt for comments on the entire manuscript. Equally valuable comments were provided on portions of the manuscript by Dave Borman for his thorough review of all the TCP chapters, and to Bob Gilligan who should be listed as a coauthor for Appendix E.

An author cannot work in isolation, so I would like to thank the following persons for lots of small favors, especially by answering my numerous e-mail questions: Joe Godsil, Jim Hogue, Mike Karels, Paul Lucchina, Craig Partridge, Thomas Skibo, and Jerry Toporek.

This book is the result of my being asked lots of questions on TCP/IP for which I could find no quick, immediate answer. It was then that I realized that the easiest way to obtain the answers was to run small tests, forcing certain conditions to occur, and just watch what happens. I thank Peter Haverlock for asking the probing questions and Van Jacobson for providing so much of the publicly available software that is used in this book to answer the questions.

A book on networking needs a real network to work with along with access to the Internet. My thanks to the National Optical Astronomy Observatories (NOAO), especially Sidney Wolff, Richard Wolff, and Steve Grandi, for providing access to their networks and hosts. A special thanks to Steve Grandi for answering lots of questions and providing accounts on various hosts. My thanks also to Keith Bostic and Kirk McKusick at the U.C. Berkeley CSRG for access to the latest 4.4BSD system.

Finally, it is the publisher that pulls everything together and does whatever is required to deliver the final product to the readers. This all revolves around the editor, and John Wait is simply the best there is. Working with John and the rest of the professionals at Addison-Wesley is a pleasure. Their professionalism and attention to detail show in the end result.

Camera-ready copy of the book was produced by the author, a Troff die-hard, using the Groff package written by James Clark.

Tucson, Arizona
October 1993   W. Richard Stevens

1

Introduction

Effective communication depends on the use of a common language. This is true for humans and other animals as well as for computers. When a set of common behaviors is used with a common language, a *protocol* is being used. The first definition of a protocol, according to the *New Oxford American Dictionary*, is

> The official procedure or system of rules governing affairs of state or diplomatic occasions.

We engage in many protocols every day: asking and responding to questions, negotiating business transactions, working collaboratively, and so on. Computers also engage in a variety of protocols. A collection of related protocols is called a *protocol suite*. The design that specifies how various protocols of a protocol suite relate to each other and divide up tasks to be accomplished is called the *architecture* or *reference model* for the protocol suite. TCP/IP is a protocol suite that implements the Internet architecture and draws its origins from the *ARPANET Reference Model* (ARM) [RFC0871]. The ARM was itself influenced by early work on packet switching in the United States by Paul Baran [B64] and Leonard Kleinrock [K64], in the U.K. by Donald Davies [DBSW66], and in France by Louis Pouzin [P73]. Other protocol architectures have been specified over the years (e.g., the ISO protocol architecture [Z80], Xerox's XNS [X85], and IBM's SNA [I96]), but TCP/IP has become the most popular. There are several interesting books that focus on the history of computer communications and the development of the Internet, such as [P07] and [W02].

It is worth mentioning that the TCP/IP architecture evolved from work that addressed a need to provide interconnection of multiple *different* packet-switched computer networks [CK74]. This was accomplished using a set of *gateways* (later called *routers*) that provided a translation function between each otherwise incompatible network. The resulting "concatenated" network or *catenet* (later called *internetwork*) would be much more useful, as many more nodes offering a wide variety of services could communicate. The types of uses that a global network might offer were envisioned years before the protocol architecture was fully developed.

In 1968, for example, J. C. R. Licklider and Bob Taylor foresaw the potential uses for a global interconnected communication network to support "supercommunities" [LT68]:

> Today the on-line communities are separated from one another functionally as well as geographically. Each member can look only to the processing, storage and software capability of the facility upon which his community is centered. But now the move is on to interconnect the separate communities and thereby transform them into, let us call it, a supercommunity. The hope is that interconnection will make available to all members of all the communities the programs and data resources of the entire supercommunity . . . The whole will constitute a labile network of networks—ever-changing in both content and configuration.

Thus, it is apparent that the global network concept underpinning the ARPA-NET and later the Internet was designed to support many of the types of uses we enjoy today. However, getting to this point was neither simple nor obvious. The success resulted from paying careful attention to design and engineering, innovative users and developers, and the availability of sufficient resources to move from concept to prototype and, eventually, to commercial networking products.

This chapter provides an overview of the Internet architecture and TCP/IP protocol suite, to provide some historical context and to establish an adequate background for the remaining chapters. Architectures (both protocol and physical) really amount to a set of design decisions about what features should be supported and where such features should be logically implemented. Designing an architecture is more art than science, yet we shall discuss some characteristics of architectures that have been deemed desirable over time. The subject of network architecture has been undertaken more broadly in the text by Day [D08], one of few such treatments.

1.1   Architectural Principles

The TCP/IP protocol suite allows computers, smartphones, and embedded devices of all sizes, supplied from many different computer vendors and running totally different software, to communicate with each other. By the turn of the twenty-first century it has become a necessity for modern communication, entertainment, and commerce. It is truly an *open system* in that the definition of the protocol suite and many of its implementations are publicly available at little or no charge. It forms the basis for what is called the *global Internet*, or the *Internet*, a wide area network (WAN) of about two billion users that literally spans the globe (as of 2010, about 30% of the world's population). Although many people consider the Internet and the *World Wide Web* (WWW) to be interchangeable terms, we ordinarily refer to the Internet in terms of its ability to provide basic communication of messages between computers. We refer to WWW as an application that uses the Internet for communication. It is perhaps the most important Internet application that brought Internet technology to world attention in the early 1990s.

Several goals guided the creation of the Internet architecture. In [C88], Clark recounts that the primary goal was to "develop an effective technique for multiplexed utilization of existing interconnected networks." The essence of this statement is that the Internet architecture should be able to interconnect multiple distinct networks and that multiple activities should be able to run simultaneously on the resulting interconnected network. Beyond this primary goal, Clark provides a list of the following second-level goals:

- Internet communication must continue despite loss of networks or gateways.
- The Internet must support multiple types of communication services.
- The Internet architecture must accommodate a variety of networks.
- The Internet architecture must permit distributed management of its resources.
- The Internet architecture must be cost-effective.
- The Internet architecture must permit host attachment with a low level of effort.
- The resources used in the Internet architecture must be accountable.

Many of the goals listed could have been supported with somewhat different design decisions from those ultimately selected. However, a few design options were gaining momentum when these architectural principles were being formulated that influenced the designers in the particular choices they made. We will mention some of the more important ones and their consequences.

1.1.1   Packets, Connections, and Datagrams

Up to the 1960s, the concept of a network was based largely on the telephone network. It was developed to connect telephones to each other for the duration of a call. A call was normally implemented by establishing a *connection* from one party to another. Establishing a connection meant that a circuit (initially, a physical electrical circuit) was made between one telephone and another for the duration of a call. When the call was complete, the connection was cleared, allowing the circuit to be used by other users' calls. The call duration and identification of the connection endpoints were used to perform billing of the users. When established, the connection provided each user a certain amount of *bandwidth* or *capacity* to send information (usually voice sounds). The telephone network progressed from its analog roots to digital, which greatly improved its reliability and performance. Data inserted into one end of a circuit follows some preestablished path through the network switches and emerges on the other side in a predictable fashion, usually with some upper bound on the time (*latency*). This gives predictable service, as long as a circuit is available when a user needs one. Circuits allocate a pathway through the network that is reserved for the duration of a call, even if they are not entirely busy. This is a common experience today with the phone network—as long as a call is taking place, even if we are not saying anything, we are being charged for the time.

One of the important concepts developed in the 1960s (e.g., in [B64]) was the idea of *packet switching*. In packet switching, "chunks" (packets) of digital information comprising some number of bytes are carried through the network somewhat independently. Chunks coming from different sources or senders can be mixed together and pulled apart later, which is called *multiplexing*. The chunks can be moved around from one switch to another on their way to a destination, and the path might be subject to change. This has two potential advantages: the network can be more resilient (the designers were worried about the network being physically attacked), and there can be better utilization of the network links and switches because of *statistical multiplexing*.

When packets are received at a packet switch, they are ordinarily stored in *buffer memory* or *queue* and processed in a *first-come-first-served* (FCFS) fashion. This is the simplest method for *scheduling* the way packets are processed and is also called *first-in-first-out* (FIFO). FIFO buffer management and on-demand scheduling are easily combined to implement statistical multiplexing, which is the primary method used to intermix traffic from different sources on the Internet. In statistical multiplexing, traffic is mixed together based on the arrival statistics or timing pattern of the traffic. Such multiplexing is simple and efficient, because if there is any network capacity to be used and traffic to use it, the network will be busy (high utilization) at every bottleneck or choke point. The downside of this approach is limited predictability—the performance seen by any particular application depends on the statistics of other applications that are sharing the network. Statistical multiplexing is like a highway where the cars can change lanes and ultimately intersperse in such a way that any point of constriction is as busy as it can be.

Alternative techniques, such as *time-division multiplexing* (TDM) and *static multiplexing*, typically reserve a certain amount of time or other resources for data on each connection. Although such techniques can lead to more predictability, a feature useful for supporting constant bit rate telephone calls, they may not fully utilize the network capacity because reserved bandwidth may go unused. Note that while circuits are straightforwardly implemented using TDM techniques, *virtual circuits* (VCs) that exhibit many of the behaviors of circuits but do not depend on physical circuit switches can be implemented atop connection-oriented packets. This is the basis for a protocol known as X.25 that was popular until about the early 1990s when it was largely replaced with Frame Relay and ultimately *digital subscriber line* (DSL) technology and cable modems supporting Internet connectivity (see Chapter 3).

The VC abstraction and connection-oriented packet networks such as X.25 required some information or *state* to be stored in each switch for each connection. The reason is that each packet carries only a small bit of overhead information that provides an index into a state table. For example, in X.25 the 12-bit *logical channel identifier* (LCI) or *logical channel number* (LCN) serves this purpose. At each switch, the LCI or LCN is used in conjunction with the *per-flow state* in each switch to determine the next switch along the path for the packet. The per-flow state is established prior to the exchange of data on a VC using a signaling protocol that supports connection establishment, clearing, and status information. Such networks are consequently called *connection-oriented*.

Connection-oriented networks, whether built on circuits or packets, were the most prevalent form of networking for many years. In the late 1960s, another option was developed known as the *datagram*. Attributed in origin to the CYCLADES [P73] system, a datagram is a special type of packet in which all the identifying information of the source and final destination resides inside the packet itself (instead of in the packet switches). Although this tends to require larger packets, per-connection state at packet switches is no longer required and a *connectionless* network could be built, eliminating the need for a (complicated) signaling protocol. Datagrams were eagerly embraced by the designers of the early Internet, and this decision had profound implications for the rest of the protocol suite.

One other related concept is that of *message boundaries* or *record markers*. As shown in Figure 1-1, when an application sends more than one chunk of information into the network, the fact that more than one chunk was written may or

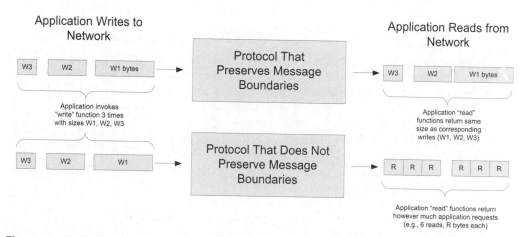

Figure 1-1   Applications write messages that are carried in protocols. A message boundary is the position or byte offset between one write and another. Protocols that preserve message boundaries indicate the position of the sender's message boundaries at the receiver. Protocols that do not preserve message boundaries (e.g., streaming protocols like TCP) ignore this information and do not make it available to a receiver. As a result, applications may need to implement their own methods to indicate a sender's message boundaries if this capability is required.

may not be preserved by the communication protocol. Most datagram protocols preserve message boundaries. This is natural because the datagram itself has a beginning and an end. However, in a circuit or VC network, it is possible that an application may write several chunks of data, all of which are read together as one or more different-size chunks by a receiving application. These types of protocols do not preserve message boundaries. In cases where an underlying protocol fails to preserve message boundaries but they are needed by an application, the application must provide its own.

1.1.2 The End-to-End Argument and Fate Sharing

When large systems such as an operating system or protocol suite are being designed, a question often arises as to where a particular feature or function should be placed. One of the most important principles that influenced the design of the TCP/IP suite is called the *end-to-end argument* [SRC84]:

> The function in question can completely and correctly be implemented only with the knowledge and help of the application standing at the end points of the communication system. Therefore, providing that questioned function as a feature of the communication itself is not possible. (Sometimes an incomplete version of the function provided by the communication system may be useful as a performance enhancement.)

This argument may seem fairly straightforward upon first reading but can have profound implications for communication system design. It argues that correctness and completeness can be achieved *only* by involving the application or ultimate user of the communication system. Efforts to correctly implement what the application is "likely" to need are doomed to incompleteness. In short, this principle argues that important functions (e.g., error control, encryption, delivery acknowledgment) should usually not be implemented at low levels (or layers; see Section 1.2.1) of large systems. However, low levels may provide capabilities that make the job of the endpoints somewhat easier and consequently may improve performance. A nuanced reading reveals that this argument suggests that low-level functions should not aim for perfection because a perfect guess at what the application may require is unlikely to be possible.

The end-to-end argument tends to support a design with a "dumb" network and "smart" systems connected to the network. This is what we see in the TCP/IP design, where many functions (e.g., methods to ensure that data is not lost, controlling the rate at which a sender sends) are implemented in the end hosts where the applications reside. The selection of which functions are implemented together in the same computer or network or software stack is the subject of another related principle known as fate sharing [C88].

Fate sharing suggests placing all the necessary state to maintain an active communication association (e.g., virtual connection) at the same location with the communicating endpoints. With this reasoning, the only type of failure that destroys communication is one that also destroys one or more of the endpoints, which obviously destroys the overall communication anyhow. Fate sharing is one of the design philosophies that allows virtual connections (e.g., those implemented by TCP) to remain active even if connectivity within the network has failed for a (modest) period of time. Fate sharing also supports a "dumb network with smart end hosts" model, and one of the ongoing tensions in today's Internet is what functions reside in the network and what functions do not.

1.1.3 Error Control and Flow Control

There are some circumstances where data within a network gets damaged or lost. This can be for a variety of reasons such as hardware problems, radiation that modifies bits while being transmitted, being out of range in a wireless network, and other factors. Dealing with such errors is called *error control*, and it can be implemented in the systems constituting the network infrastructure, or in the systems that attach to the network, or some combination. Naturally, the end-to-end argument and fate sharing would suggest that error control be implemented close to or within applications.

Usually, if a small number of bit errors are of concern, a number of mathematical codes can be used to detect and repair the bit errors when data is received or while it is in transit [LC04]. This task is routinely performed within the network. When more severe damage occurs in a packet network, entire packets are usually resent or *retransmitted*. In circuit-switched or VC-switched networks such as X.25, retransmission tends to be done inside the network. This may work well for applications that require strict in-order, error-free delivery of their data, but some applications do not require this capability and do not wish to pay the costs (such as connection establishment and potential retransmission delays) to have their data reliably delivered. Even a reliable file transfer application does not really care in what order the chunks of file data are delivered, provided it is eventually satisfied that all chunks are delivered without errors and can be reassembled back into the original order.

As an alternative to the overhead of reliable, in-order delivery implemented within the network, a different type of service called *best-effort delivery* was adopted by Frame Relay and the Internet Protocol. With best-effort delivery, the network does not expend much effort to ensure that data is delivered without errors or gaps. Certain types of errors are usually detected using error-detecting codes or *checksums*, such as those that might affect where a datagram is directed, but when such errors are detected, the errant datagram is merely discarded without further action.

If best-effort delivery is successful, a fast sender can produce information at a rate that exceeds the receiver's ability to consume it. In best-effort IP networks, slowing down a sender is achieved by *flow control* mechanisms that operate outside the network and at higher levels of the communication system. In particular,

TCP handles this type of problem, and we shall discuss it in detail in Chapters 15 and 16. This is consistent with the end-to-end argument: TCP, which resides at the end hosts, handles rate control. It is also consistent with fate sharing: the approach allows some elements of the network infrastructure to fail without necessarily affecting the ability of the devices outside the network to communicate (as long as some communication path continues to operate).

1.2   Design and Implementation

Although a protocol architecture may suggest a certain approach to implementation, it usually does not include a mandate. Consequently, we make a distinction between the protocol architecture and the *implementation architecture*, which defines how the concepts in a protocol architecture may be rendered into existence, usually in the form of software.

Many of the individuals responsible for implementing the protocols for the ARPANET were familiar with the software structuring of operating systems, and an influential paper describing the "THE" multiprogramming system [D68] advocated the use of a hierarchical structure as a way to deal with verification of the logical soundness and correctness of a large software implementation. Ultimately, this contributed to a design philosophy for networking protocols involving multiple *layers* of implementation (and design). This approach is now called *layering* and is the usual approach to implementing protocol suites.

1.2.1   Layering

With layering, each layer is responsible for a different facet of the communications. Layers are beneficial because a layered design allows developers to evolve different portions of the system separately, often by different people with somewhat different areas of expertise. The most frequently mentioned concept of protocol layering is based on a standard called the *Open Systems Interconnection* (OSI) model [Z80] as defined by the International Organization for Standardization (ISO). Figure 1-2 shows the standard OSI layers, including their names, numbers, and a few examples. The Internet's layering model is somewhat simpler, as we shall see in Section 1.3.

Although the OSI model suggests that seven logical layers may be desirable for modularity of a protocol architecture implementation, the TCP/IP architecture is normally considered to consist of five. There was much debate about the relative benefits and deficiencies of the OSI model, and the ARPANET model that preceded it, during the early 1970s. Although it may be fair to say that TCP/IP ultimately "won," a number of ideas and even entire protocols from the ISO protocol suite (protocols standardized by ISO that follow the OSI model) have been adopted for use with TCP/IP (e.g., IS-IS [RFC3787]).

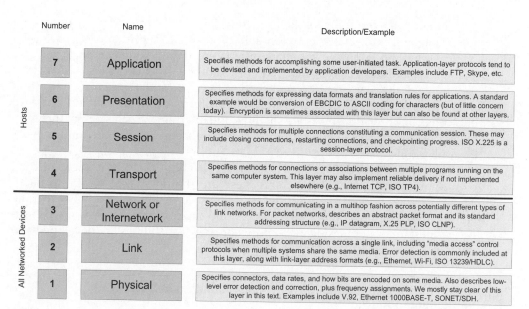

Number	Name	Description/Example
7	Application	Specifies methods for accomplishing some user-initiated task. Application-layer protocols tend to be devised and implemented by application developers. Examples include FTP, Skype, etc.
6	Presentation	Specifies methods for expressing data formats and translation rules for applications. A standard example would be conversion of EBCDIC to ASCII coding for characters (but of little concern today). Encryption is sometimes associated with this layer but can also be found at other layers.
5	Session	Specifies methods for multiple connections constituting a communication session. These may include closing connections, restarting connections, and checkpointing progress. ISO X.225 is a session-layer protocol.
4	Transport	Specifies methods for connections or associations between multiple programs running on the same computer system. This layer may also implement reliable delivery if not implemented elsewhere (e.g., Internet TCP, ISO TP4).
3	Network or Internetwork	Specifies methods for communicating in a multihop fashion across potentially different types of link networks. For packet networks, describes an abstract packet format and its standard addressing structure (e.g., IP datagram, X.25 PLP, ISO CLNP).
2	Link	Specifies methods for communication across a single link, including "media access" control protocols when multiple systems share the same media. Error detection is commonly included at this layer, along with link-layer address formats (e.g., Ethernet, Wi-Fi, ISO 13239/HDLC).
1	Physical	Specifies connectors, data rates, and how bits are encoded on some media. Also describes low-level error detection and correction, plus frequency assignments. We mostly stay clear of this layer in this text. Examples include V.92, Ethernet 1000BASE-T, SONET/SDH.

Hosts: layers 5–7 (and 4). All Networked Devices: layers 1–3.

Figure 1-2 The standard seven-layer OSI model as specified by the ISO. Not all protocols are implemented by every networked device (at least in theory). The OSI terminology and layer numbers are widely used.

As described briefly in Figure 1-2, each layer has a different responsibility. From the bottom up, the *physical* layer defines methods for moving digital information across a communication medium such as a phone line or fiber-optic cable. Portions of the Ethernet and Wireless LAN (Wi-Fi) standards are here, although we do not delve into this layer very much in this text. The *link* or *data-link* layer includes those protocols and methods for establishing connectivity to a neighbor sharing the same medium. Some link-layer networks (e.g., DSL) connect only two neighbors. When more than one neighbor can access the same shared network, the network is said to be a *multi-access* network. Wi-Fi and Ethernet are examples of such multi-access link-layer networks, and specific protocols are used to mediate which stations have access to the shared medium at any given time. We discuss these in Chapter 3.

Moving up the layer stack, the *network* or *internetwork* layer is of great interest to us. For packet networks such as TCP/IP, it provides an interoperable packet format that can use different types of link-layer networks for connectivity. The layer also includes an addressing scheme for hosts and routing algorithms that choose where packets go when sent from one machine to another. Above layer 3 we find protocols that are (at least in theory) implemented only by end hosts, including the *transport* layer. Also of great interest to us, it provides a flow of data between sessions and can be quite complex, depending on the types of services it provides (e.g., reliable delivery on a packet network that might drop data). *Sessions* represent ongoing interactions between applications (e.g., when "cookies" are used with a Web browser during a Web login session), and session-layer protocols may provide capabilities such as connection initiation and restart, plus *checkpointing* (saving work that has been accomplished so far). Above the session layer we find the *presentation* layer, which is responsible for format conversions and standard encodings for information. As we shall see, the Internet protocols do not include a formal session or presentation protocol layer, so these functions are implemented by applications if needed.

The top layer is the *application* layer. Applications usually implement their own application-layer protocols, and these are the ones most visible to users. There is a wide variety of application-layer protocols, and programmers are constantly inventing new ones. Consequently, the application layer is where there is the greatest amount of innovation and where new capabilities are developed and deployed.

1.2.2 Multiplexing, Demultiplexing, and Encapsulation in Layered Implementations

One of the major benefits of a layered architecture is its natural ability to perform *protocol multiplexing*. This form of multiplexing allows multiple different protocols to coexist on the same infrastructure. It also allows multiple instantiations of the same protocol object (e.g., connections) to be used simultaneously without being confused.

Multiplexing can occur at different layers, and at each layer a different sort of *identifier* is used for determining which protocol or stream of information belongs together. For example, at the link layer, most link technologies (such as Ethernet and Wi-Fi) include a *protocol identifier* field value in each packet to indicate which protocol is being carried in the link-layer frame (IP is one such protocol). When an object (packet, message, etc.), called a *protocol data unit* (PDU), at one layer is carried by a lower layer, it is said to be *encapsulated* (as opaque data) by the next layer down. Thus, multiple objects at layer N can be multiplexed together using encapsulation in layer N - 1. Figure 1-3 shows how this works. The identifier at layer N - 1 is used to determine the correct receiving protocol or program at layer N during demultiplexing.

In Figure 1-3, each layer has its own concept of a message object (a PDU) corresponding to the particular layer responsible for creating it. For example, if a layer 4 (transport) protocol produces a packet, it would properly be called a layer 4 PDU or *transport PDU* (TPDU). When a layer is provided a PDU from the layer above it, it usually "promises" to not look into the contents of the PDU. This is the essence of encapsulation—each layer treats the data from above as opaque, uninterpretable information. Most commonly a layer prepends the PDU with its own header, although trailers are used by some protocols (not TCP/IP). The header is used for multiplexing data when sending, and for the receiver to perform demultiplexing,

Layer Number   Encapsulated Object

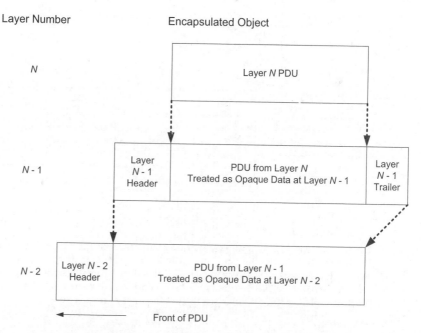

Figure 1-3   Encapsulation is usually used in conjunction with layering. Pure encapsulation involves taking the PDU of one layer and treating it as opaque (uninterpreted) data at the layer below. Encapsulation takes place at each sender, and decapsulation (the reverse operation) takes place at each receiver. Most protocols use headers during encapsulation; a few also use trailers.

based on a demultiplexing (demux) identifier. In TCP/IP networks such identifiers are commonly hardware addresses, IP addresses, and port numbers. The header may also include important state information, such as whether a virtual circuit is being set up or has already completed setup. The resulting object is another PDU.

One other important feature of layering suggested by Figure 1-2 is that in pure layering not all networked devices need to implement all the layers. Figure 1-4 shows that in some cases a device needs to implement only a few layers if it is expected to perform only certain types of processing.

In Figure 1-4, a somewhat idealized small internet includes two end systems, a switch, and a router. In this figure, each number corresponds to a type of protocol at a particular layer. As we can see, each device implements a different subset of the layer stack. The host on the left implements three different link-layer protocols (D, E, and F) with corresponding physical layers and three different transport-layer protocols (A, B, and C) that run on a single type of network-layer protocol. End hosts implement all the layers, switches implement up to layer 2 (this switch implements D and G), and routers implement up to layer 3. Routers are capable of interconnecting different types of link-layer networks and must implement the link-layer protocols for each of the network types they interconnect.

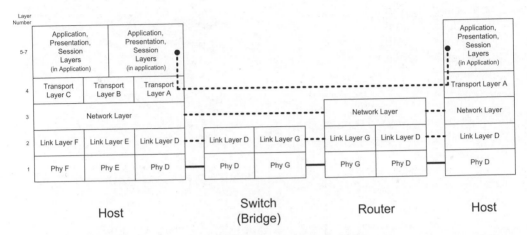

Figure 1-4   Different network devices implement different subsets of the protocol stack. End hosts tend to implement all the layers. Routers implement layers below the transport layer, and switches implement link-layer protocols and below. This idealized structure is often violated because routers and switches usually include the ability to act as a host (e.g., to be managed and set up) and therefore need an implementation of all of the layers even if they are rarely used.

The internet of Figure 1-4 is somewhat idealized because today's switches and routers often implement more than the protocols they are absolutely required to implement for forwarding data. This is for a number of reasons, including management. In such circumstances, devices such as routers and switches must sometimes act as hosts and support services such as remote login. To do this, they usually must implement transport and application protocols.

Although we show only two hosts communicating, the link- and physical-layer networks (labeled as D and G) might have multiple hosts attached. If so, then communication is possible between any pair of systems that implement the appropriate higher-layer protocols. In Figure 1-4 we can differentiate between an *end system* (the two hosts on either side) and an *intermediate system* (the router in the middle) for a particular protocol suite. Layers above the network layer use *end-to-end* protocols. In our picture these layers are needed only on the end systems. The network layer, however, provides a *hop-by-hop* protocol and is used on the two end systems and every intermediate system. The switch or bridge is not ordinarily considered an intermediate system because it is not addressed using the internetworking protocol's addressing format, and it operates in a fashion that is largely transparent to the network-layer protocol. From the point of view of the routers and end systems, the switch or bridge is essentially invisible.

A router, by definition, has two or more network interfaces (because it connects two or more networks). Any system with multiple interfaces is called *multihomed*. A host can also be multihomed, but unless it specifically forwards packets from one interface to another, it is not called a router. Also, routers need not be special hardware boxes that only move packets around an internet. Most TCP/IP implementations, for example, allow a multihomed host to act as a router also, if properly configured to do so. In this case we can call the system either a host (when an application such as *File Transfer Protocol* (FTP) [RFC0959] or the Web is used) or a router (when it is forwarding packets from one network to another). We will use whichever term makes sense given the context.

One of the goals of an internet is to hide all of the details of the physical layout (the topology) and lower-layer protocol heterogeneity from the applications. Although this is not obvious from our two-network internet in Figure 1-4, the application layers should not care (and do not care) that even though each host is attached to a network using link-layer protocol D (e.g., Ethernet), the hosts are separated by a router and switch that use link-layer G. There could be 20 routers between the hosts, with additional types of physical interconnections, and the applications would run without modification (although the performance might be somewhat different). Abstracting the details in this way is what makes the concept of an internet so powerful and useful.

1.3   The Architecture and Protocols of the TCP/IP Suite

So far we have discussed architecture, protocols, protocol suites, and implementation techniques in the abstract. In this section, we discuss the architecture and particular protocols that constitute the *TCP/IP suite*. Although this has become the established term for the protocols used on the Internet, there are many protocols beyond TCP and IP in the collection or family of protocols used with the Internet. We begin by noting how the ARPANET reference model of layering, which ultimately formed the basis for the Internet's protocol layering, differs somewhat from the OSI layering discussed earlier.

1.3.1   The ARPANET Reference Model

Figure 1-5 depicts the layering inspired by the ARPANET reference model, which was ultimately adopted by the TCP/IP suite. The structure is simpler than the OSI model, but real implementations include a few specialized protocols that do not fit cleanly into the conventional layers.

Starting from the bottom of Figure 1-5 and working our way up the stack, the first layer we see is 2.5, an "unofficial" layer. There are several protocols that operate here, but one of the oldest and most important is called the *Address Resolution Protocol* (ARP). It is a specialized protocol used with IPv4 and only with multi-access link-layer protocols (such as Ethernet and Wi-Fi) to convert between the addresses used by the IP layer and the addresses used by the link layer. We examine this protocol in Chapter 4. In IPv6 the address-mapping function is part of ICMPv6, which we discuss in Chapter 8.

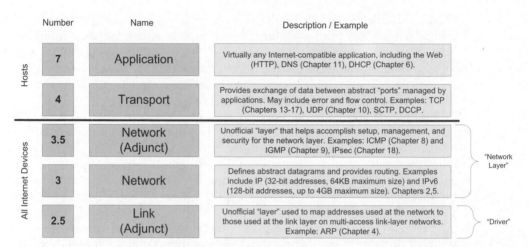

Figure 1-5 Protocol layering based on the ARM or TCP/IP suite used in the Internet. There are no official session or presentation layers. In addition, there are several "adjunct" or helper protocols that do not fit well into the standard layers yet perform critical functions for the operation of the other protocols. Some of these protocols are not used with IPv6 (e.g., IGMP and ARP).

At layer number 3 in Figure 1-5 we find IP, the main network-layer protocol for the TCP/IP suite. We discuss it in detail in Chapter 5. The PDU that IP sends to link-layer protocols is called an *IP datagram* and may be as large as 64KB (and up to 4GB for IPv6). In many cases we shall use the simpler term *packet* to mean an IP datagram when the usage context is clear. Fitting large packets into link-layer PDUs (called *frames*) that may be smaller is handled by a function called *fragmentation* that may be performed by IP hosts and some routers when necessary. In fragmentation, portions of a larger datagram are sent in multiple smaller datagrams called *fragments* and put back together (called *reassembly*) when reaching the destination. We discuss fragmentation in Chapter 10.

Throughout the text we shall use the term IP to refer to both IP versions 4 and 6. We use the term IPv6 to refer to IP version 6, and IPv4 to refer to IP version 4, currently the most popular version. When discussing architecture, the details of IPv4 versus IPv6 matter little. When we delve into the way particular addressing and configuration functions work (Chapter 2 and Chapter 6), for example, these details will become more important.

Because IP packets are datagrams, each one contains the address of the layer 3 sender and recipient. These addresses are called *IP addresses* and are 32 bits long for IPv4 and 128 bits long for IPv6; we discuss them in detail in Chapter 2. This difference in IP address size is the characteristic that most differentiates IPv4 from IPv6. The destination address of each datagram is used to determine where each datagram should be sent, and the process of making this determination and sending the datagram to its next hop is called *forwarding*. Both routers and hosts perform forwarding, although routers tend to do it much more often. There are three types of IP addresses, and the type affects how forwarding is performed: *unicast* (destined for a single host), *broadcast* (destined for all hosts on a given network), and *multicast* (destined for a set of hosts that belong to a multicast group). Chapter 2 looks at the types of addresses used with IP in more detail.

The *Internet Control Message Protocol* (ICMP) is an adjunct to IP, and we label it as a layer 3.5 protocol. It is used by the IP layer to exchange error messages and other vital information with the IP layer in another host or router. There are two versions of ICMP: ICMPv4, used with IPv4, and ICMPv6, used with IPv6. ICMPv6 is considerably more complex and includes functions such as address autoconfiguration and Neighbor Discovery that are handled by other protocols (e.g., ARP) on IPv4 networks. Although ICMP is used primarily by IP, it is also possible for applications to use it. Indeed, we will see that two popular diagnostic tools, `ping` and `traceroute`, use ICMP. ICMP messages are encapsulated within IP datagrams in the same way transport layer PDUs are.

The *Internet Group Management Protocol* (IGMP) is another protocol adjunct to IPv4. It is used with multicast addressing and delivery to manage which hosts are members of a *multicast group* (a group of receivers interested in receiving traffic for a particular multicast destination address). We describe the general properties of broadcasting and multicasting, along with IGMP and the *Multicast Listener Discovery* protocol (MLD, used with IPv6), in Chapter 9.

At layer 4, the two most common Internet transport protocols are vastly different. The most widely used, the *Transmission Control Protocol* (TCP), deals with problems such as packet loss, duplication, and reordering that are not repaired by the IP layer. It operates in a connection-oriented (VC) fashion and does not preserve message boundaries. Conversely, the *User Datagram Protocol* (UDP) provides little more than the features provided by IP. UDP allows applications to send datagrams that preserve message boundaries but imposes no rate control or error control.

TCP provides a reliable flow of data between two hosts. It is concerned with things such as dividing the data passed to it from the application into appropriately sized chunks for the network layer below, acknowledging received packets, and setting timeouts to make certain the other end acknowledges packets that are sent, and because this reliable flow of data is provided by the transport layer, the application layer can ignore all these details. The PDU that TCP sends to IP is called a *TCP segment*.

UDP, on the other hand, provides a much simpler service to the application layer. It allows datagrams to be sent from one host to another, but there is no guarantee that the datagrams reach the other end. Any desired reliability must be added by the application layer. Indeed, about all that UDP provides is a set of port numbers for multiplexing and demultiplexing data, plus a data integrity checksum. As we can see, UDP and TCP differ radically even though they are at the same layer. There is a use for each type of transport protocol, which we will see when we look at the different applications that use TCP and UDP.

There are two additional transport-layer protocols that are relatively new and available on some systems. As they are not yet very widespread, we do not devote much discussion to them, but they are worth being aware of. The first is the *Datagram Congestion Control Protocol* (DCCP), specified in [RFC4340]. It provides a type of service midway between TCP and UDP: connection-oriented exchange of unreliable datagrams but with congestion control. Congestion control comprises a number of techniques whereby a sender is limited to a sending rate in order to avoid overwhelming the network. We discuss it in detail with respect to TCP in Chapter 16.

The other transport protocol available on some systems is called the *Stream Control Transmission Protocol* (SCTP), specified in [RFC4960]. SCTP provides reliable delivery like TCP but does not require the sequencing of data to be strictly maintained. It also allows for multiple streams to logically be carried on the same connection and provides a message abstraction, which differs from TCP. SCTP was designed for carrying signaling messages on IP networks that resemble those used in the telephone network.

Above the transport layer, the application layer handles the details of the particular application. There are many common applications that almost every implementation of TCP/IP provides. The application layer is concerned with the details of the application and not with the movement of data across the network. The lower three layers are the opposite: they know nothing about the application but handle all the communication details.

1.3.2 Multiplexing, Demultiplexing, and Encapsulation in TCP/IP

We have already discussed the basics of protocol multiplexing, demultiplexing, and encapsulation. At each layer there is an identifier that allows a receiving system to determine which protocol or data stream belongs together. Usually there is also addressing information at each layer. This information is used to ensure that a PDU has been delivered to the right place. Figure 1-6 shows how demultiplexing works in a hypothetical Internet host.

Although it is not really part of the TCP/IP suite, we shall begin bottom-up and mention how demultiplexing from the link layer is performed, using Ethernet as an example. We discuss several link-layer protocols in Chapter 3. An arriving Ethernet frame contains a 48-bit destination address (also called a link-layer or MAC—Media Access Control—address) and a 16-bit field called the *Ethernet type*. A value of 0x0800 (hexadecimal) indicates that the frame contains an IPv4 datagram. Values of 0x0806 and 0x86DD indicate ARP and IPv6, respectively. Assuming that the destination address matches one of the receiving system's addresses, the frame is received and checked for errors, and the *Ethernet Type* field value is used to select which network-layer protocol should process it.

Assuming that the received frame contains an IP datagram, the Ethernet header and trailer information is removed, and the remaining bytes (which constitute the frame's *payload*) are given to IP for processing. IP checks a number of items, including the destination IP address in the datagram. If the destination

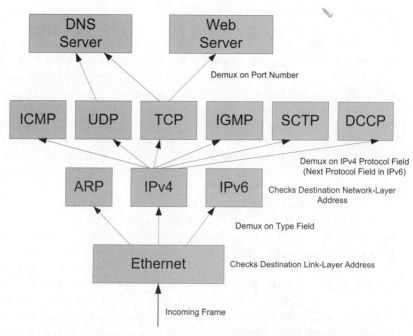

Figure 1-6 The TCP/IP stack uses a combination of addressing information and protocol demultiplexing identifiers to determine if a datagram has been received correctly and, if so, what entity should process it. Several layers also check numeric values (e.g., checksums) to ensure that the contents have not been damaged in transit.

address matches one of its own and the datagram contains no errors in its header (IP does not check its payload), the 8-bit IPv4 *Protocol* field (called *Next Header* in IPv6) is checked to determine which protocol to invoke next. Common values include 1 (ICMP), 2 (IGMP), 4 (IPv4), 6 (TCP), and 17 (UDP). The value of 4 (and 41, which indicates IPv6) is interesting because it indicates the possibility that an IP datagram may appear inside the payload area of an IP datagram. This violates the original concepts of layering and encapsulation but is the basis for a powerful technique known as tunneling, which we discuss more in Chapter 3.

Once the network layer (IPv4 or IPv6) determines that the incoming datagram is valid and the correct transport protocol has been determined, the resulting datagram (reassembled from fragments if necessary) is passed to the transport layer for processing. At the transport layer, most protocols (including TCP and UDP) use port numbers for demultiplexing to the appropriate receiving application.

1.3.3 Port Numbers

Port numbers are 16-bit nonnegative integers (i.e., range 0–65535). These numbers are abstract and do not refer to anything physical. Instead, each IP address has 65,536 associated port numbers for each transport protocol that uses port numbers (most do), and they are used for determining the correct receiving application. For client/server applications (see Section 1.5.1), a server first "binds" to a port number, and subsequently one or more clients establish connections to the port number using a particular transport protocol on a particular machine. In this sense, port numbers act more like telephone number extensions, except they are usually assigned by standards.

Standard port numbers are assigned by the Internet Assigned Numbers Authority (IANA). The set of numbers is divided into special ranges, including the *well-known* port numbers (0–1023), the *registered* port numbers (1024–49151), and the *dynamic/private* port numbers (49152–65535). Traditionally, servers wishing to bind to (i.e., offer service on) a well-known port require special privileges such as administrator or "root" access.

The range of well-known ports is used for identifying many well-known services such as the *Secure Shell Protocol* (SSH, port 22), FTP (ports 20 and 21), *Telnet* remote terminal protocol (port 23), e-mail/*Simple Mail Transfer Protocol* (SMTP, port 25), *Domain Name System* (DNS, port 53), the *Hypertext Transfer Protocol* or Web (HTTP and HTTPS, ports 80 and 443), *Interactive Mail Access Protocol* (IMAP and IMAPS, ports 143 and 993), *Simple Network Management Protocol* (SNMP, ports 161 and 162), *Lightweight Directory Access Protocol* (LDAP, port 389), and several others. Protocols with multiple ports (e.g., HTTP and HTTPS) often have different port numbers depending on whether *Transport Layer Security* (TLS) is being used with the base application-layer protocol (see Chapter 18).

Note

If we examine the port numbers for these standard services and other standard TCP/IP services (Telnet, FTP, SMTP, etc.), we see that most are odd numbers. This is historical, as these port numbers are derived from the NCP port numbers. (NCP, the Network Control Protocol, preceded TCP as a transport-layer protocol for the ARPANET.) NCP was simplex, not full duplex, so each application required two connections, and an even-odd pair of port numbers was reserved for each application. When TCP and UDP became the standard transport layers, only a single port number was needed per application, yet the odd port numbers from NCP were used.

The registered port numbers are available to clients or servers with special privileges, but IANA keeps a reserved registry for particular uses, so these port numbers should generally be avoided when developing new applications unless an IANA allocation has been procured. The dynamic/private port numbers are essentially unregulated. As we will see, in some circumstances (e.g., on clients) the value of the port number matters little because the port number being used is transient. Such port numbers are also called *ephemeral* port numbers. They are considered to be temporary because a client typically needs one only as long as the user running the client needs service, and the client does not need to be found by the server in order to establish a connection. Servers, conversely, generally require names and port numbers that do not change often in order to be found by clients.

1.3.4 Names, Addresses, and the DNS

With TCP/IP, each link-layer interface on each computer (including routers) has at least one IP address. IP addresses are enough to identify a host, but they are not very convenient for humans to remember or manipulate (especially the long addresses used with IPv6). In the TCP/IP world, the DNS is a distributed database that provides the mapping between host names and IP addresses (and vice versa). Names are set up in a hierarchy, ending in *domains* such as .com, .org, .gov, .in, .uk, and .edu. Perhaps surprisingly, DNS is an application-layer protocol and thus depends on the other protocols in order to operate. Although most of the TCP/IP suite does not use or care about names, typical users (e.g., those using Web browsers) use names frequently, so if the DNS fails to function properly, normal Internet access is effectively disabled. Chapter 11 looks into the DNS in detail.

Applications that manipulate names can call a standard API function (see Section 1.5.3) to look up the IP address (or addresses) corresponding to a given host's name. Similarly, a function is provided to do the reverse lookup—given an IP address, look up the corresponding host name. Most applications that take a host name as input also take an IP address. Web browsers support this capability. For example, the *Uniform Resource Locators* (URLs) http://131.243.2.201/index. html and http://[2001:400:610:102::c9]/index.html can be typed into a Web browser and are both effectively equivalent to http://ee.lbl.gov/index.html (at the time of writing; the second example requires IPv6 connectivity to be successful).

1.4 Internets, Intranets, and Extranets

As suggested previously, the Internet has developed as the aggregate network resulting from the interconnection of constituent networks over time. The lower-case *internet* means multiple networks connected together, using a common proto-col suite. The uppercase *Internet* refers to the collection of hosts around the world that can communicate with each other using TCP/IP. The Internet is an internet, but the reverse is not true.

One of the reasons for the phenomenal growth in networking during the 1980s was the realization that isolated groups of stand-alone computers made little sense. A few stand-alone systems were connected together into a *network*. Although this was a step forward, during the 1990s we realized that separate networks that could not interoperate were not as valuable as a bigger network that could. This notion is the basis for the so-called Metcalfe's Law, which states roughly that the value of a computer network is proportional to the square of the number of connected endpoints (e.g., users or devices). The Internet idea, and its supporting protocols, would make possible the interconnection of different net-works. This deceptively simple concept turns out to be remarkably powerful.

The easiest way to build an internet is to connect two or more networks with a router. A router is often a special-purpose device for connecting networks. The nice thing about routers is that they provide connections to many different types of physical networks: Ethernet, Wi-Fi, point-to-point links, DSL, cable Internet service, and so on.

Note

These devices are also called *IP routers*, but we will use the term router. Historically these devices were called *gateways*, and this term is used throughout much of the older TCP/IP literature. Today the term gateway is used for an *application-layer gateway* (ALG), a process that connects two different protocol suites (say, TCP/IP and IBM's SNA) for one particular application (often electronic mail or file transfer).

In recent years, other terms have been adopted for different configurations of internets using the TCP/IP protocol suite. An *intranet* is the term used to describe a private internetwork, usually run by a business or other enterprise. Most often, the intranet provides access to resources available only to members of the particular enterprise. Users may connect to their (e.g., corporate) intranet using a *virtual private network* (VPN). VPNs help to ensure that access to potentially sensitive resources in an intranet is made available only to authorized users, usually using the tunneling concept we mentioned previously. We discuss VPNs in more detail in Chapter 7.

In many cases an enterprise or business wishes to set up a network containing servers accessible to certain partners or other associates using the Internet. Such networks, which also often involve the use of a VPN, are known as *extranets* and consist of computers attached outside the serving enterprise's firewall (see Chapter 7). Technically, there is little difference between an intranet, an extranet, and the Internet, but the usage cases and administrative policies are usually different, and therefore a number of these more specific terms have evolved.

1.5   Designing Applications

The network concepts we have touched upon so far provide a fairly simple service model [RFC6250]: moving bytes between programs running on different (or, occasionally, the same) computers. To do anything useful with this capability, we need networked applications that use the network for providing services or performing computations. Networked applications are typically structured according to a small number of design patterns. The most common of these are *client/server* and *peer-to-peer*.

1.5.1   Client/Server

Most network applications are designed so that one side is the client and the other side is the server. The server provides some type of service to clients, such as access to files on the server host. We can categorize servers into two classes: *iterative* and *concurrent*. An iterative server iterates through the following steps:

I1. Wait for a client request to arrive.

I2. Process the client request.

I3. Send the response back to the client that sent the request.

I4. Go back to step I1.

The problem with an iterative server occurs when step I2 takes a long time. During this time no other clients are serviced. A concurrent server, on the other hand, performs the following steps:

C1. Wait for a client request to arrive.

C2. Start a new server instance to handle this client's request. This may involve creating a new process, task, or thread, depending on what the underlying operating system supports. This new server handles one client's entire request. When the requested task is complete, the new server terminates. Meanwhile, the original server instance continues to C3.

C3. Go back to step C1.

The advantage of a concurrent server is that the server just spawns other server instances to handle the client requests. Each client has, in essence, its own server. Assuming that the operating system allows multiprogramming (essentially all do today), multiple clients are serviced concurrently. The reason we categorize servers, and not clients, is that a client normally cannot tell whether it is talking to an iterative server or a concurrent server. As a general rule, most servers are concurrent.

Note that we use the terms *client* and *server* to refer to applications and not to the particular computer systems on which they run. The very same terms are sometimes used to refer to the pieces of hardware that are most often used to execute either client or server applications. Although the terminology is thus somewhat imprecise, it works well enough in practice. As a result, it is common to find a server (in the hardware sense) running more than one server (in the application sense).

1.5.2   Peer-to-Peer

Some applications are designed in a more distributed fashion where there is no single server. Instead, each application acts both as a client and as a server, sometimes as both at once, and is capable of forwarding requests. Some very popular applications (e.g., Skype [SKYPE], BitTorrent [BT]) are of this form. These applications are called *peer-to-peer* or *p2p* applications. A concurrent p2p application may receive an incoming request, determine if it is able to respond to the request, and if not forward the request on to some other peer. Thus, the set of p2p applications together form a network among applications, also called an *overlay network*. Such overlays are now commonplace and can be extremely powerful. Skype, for example, has grown to be the largest carrier of international telephone calls. According to some estimates, BitTorrent was responsible for more than half of all Internet traffic in 2009 [IPIS].

One of the primary problems in p2p networks is called the *discovery problem*. That is, how does one peer find which other peer(s) can provide the data or service it wants in a network where peers may come and go? This is usually handled by a bootstrapping procedure whereby each client is initially configured with the addresses and port numbers of some peers that are likely to be operating. Once connected, the new participant learns of other active peers and, depending on the protocol, what services or files they provide.

1.5.3 Application Programming Interfaces (APIs)

Applications, whether p2p or client/server, need to express their desired network operations (e.g., make a connection, write or read data). This is usually supported by a host operating system using a networking *application programming interface* (API). The most popular API is called *sockets* or *Berkeley sockets,* indicating where it was originally developed [LJFK93].

This text is not a programming text, but occasionally we refer to a feature of TCP/IP and whether that feature is provided by the sockets API or not. All of the programming details with examples for sockets can be found in [SFR04]. Modifications to sockets intended for use with IPv6 are also described in a number of freely available online documents [RFC3493][RFC3542][RFC3678][RFC4584] [RFC5014].

1.6   Standardization Process

Newcomers to the TCP/IP suite often wonder just who is responsible for specifying and standardizing the various protocols and how they operate. A number of organizations represent the answer to this question. The group with which we will most often be concerned is the Internet Engineering Task Force (IETF) [RFC4677]. This group meets three times each year in various locations around the world to develop, discuss, and agree on standards for the Internet's "core" protocols. Exactly what constitutes "core" is subject to some debate, but common protocols such as IPv4, IPv6, TCP, UDP, and DNS are clearly in the purview of IETF. Attendance at IETF meetings is open to anyone, but it is not free.

IETF is a forum that elects leadership groups called the Internet Architecture Board (IAB) and the Internet Engineering Steering Group (IESG). The IAB is chartered to provide architectural guidance to activities in IETF and to perform a number of other tasks such as appointing liaisons to other *standards-defining organizations* (SDOs). The IESG has decision-making authority regarding the creation and approval of new standards, along with modifications to existing standards. The "heavy lifting" or detailed work is generally performed by IETF working groups that are coordinated by working group chairs who volunteer for this task.

In addition to the IETF, there are two other important groups that interact closely with the IETF. The Internet Research Task Force (IRTF) explores protocols, architectures, and procedures that are not deemed mature enough for standardization. The chair of the IRTF is a nonvoting member of IAB. The IAB, in turn, works with the Internet Society (ISOC) to help influence and promote worldwide policies and education regarding Internet technologies and usage.

1.6.1   Request for Comments (RFC)

Every official standard in the Internet community is published as a *Request for Comments*, or RFC. RFCs can be created in a number of ways, and the publisher of RFCs (called the *RFC editor*) recognizes multiple document streams corresponding to the way an RFC has been developed. The current streams (as of 2010) include the IETF, IAB, IRTF, and independent submission streams. Prior to being accepted and published (permanently) as an RFC, documents exist as temporary *Internet drafts* while they receive comments and progress through the editing and review process.

All RFCs are not standards. Only so-called *standards-track* category RFCs are considered to be official standards. Other categories include *best current practice* (BCP), *informational, experimental,* and *historic.* It is important to realize that just because a document is an RFC does not mean that the IETF has endorsed it as any form of standard. Indeed, there exist RFCs on which there is significant disagreement.

The RFCs range in size from a few pages to several hundred. Each is identified by a number, such as RFC 1122, with higher numbers for newer RFCs. They are all available for free from a number of Web sites, including http://www.rfc-editor.org. For historical reasons, RFCs are generally delivered as basic text files, although some RFCs have been reformatted or authored using more advanced file formats.

A number of RFCs have special significance because they summarize, clarify, or interpret particular sets of other standards. For example, [RFC5000] defines the set of all other RFCs that are considered official standards as of mid-2008 (the most recent such RFC at the time of writing). An updated list is available at the current standards Web site [OIPSW]. The *Host Requirements* RFCs ([RFC1122] and [RFC1123]) define requirements for protocol implementations in Internet IPv4 hosts, and the *Router Requirements* RFC [RFC1812] does the same for routers. The *Node Requirements* RFC [RFC4294] does both for IPv6 systems.

1.6.2   Other Standards

Although the IETF is responsible for standardizing most of the protocols we discuss in this text, other SDOs are responsible for defining protocols that merit our attention. The most important of these groups include the Institute of Electrical and Electronics Engineers (IEEE), the World Wide Web Consortium (W3C), and the International Telecommunication Union (ITU). In their activities relevant to this text, IEEE is concerned with standards below layer 3 (e.g., Wi-Fi and Ethernet), and W3C is concerned with application-layer protocols, specifically those related to Web technologies (e.g., HTML-based syntax). ITU, and more specifically ITU-T (formerly CCITT), standardizes protocols used within the telephone and cellular networks, which is becoming an ever more important component of the Internet.

1.7   Implementations and Software Distributions

The historical de facto standard TCP/IP implementations were from the Computer Systems Research Group (CSRG) at the University of California, Berkeley. They were distributed with the 4.x BSD (Berkeley Software Distribution) system and with the BSD Networking Releases until the mid-1990s. This source code has been the starting point for many other implementations. Today, each popular operating system has its own implementation. In this text, we tend to draw examples from the TCP/IP implementations in Linux, Windows, and sometimes FreeBSD and Mac OS (both of which are derived from historical BSD releases). In most cases, the particular implementation matters little.

Figure 1-7 shows a chronology of the various BSD releases, indicating the important TCP/IP features we cover in later chapters. It also shows the years when Linux and Windows began supporting TCP/IP. The BSD Networking Releases shown in the second column were freely available public source code releases containing all of the networking code, both the protocols themselves and many of the applications and utilities (e.g., the Telnet remote terminal program and FTP file transfer program).

By the mid-1990s, the Internet and TCP/IP were well established. All subsequent popular operating systems support TCP/IP natively. Research and development of new TCP/IP features, previously found first in BSD releases, are now typically found first in Linux releases. Windows has recently implemented a new TCP/IP stack (starting with Windows Vista) with many new features and native IPv6 capability. Linux, FreeBSD, and Mac OS X also support IPv6 without setting any special configuration options.

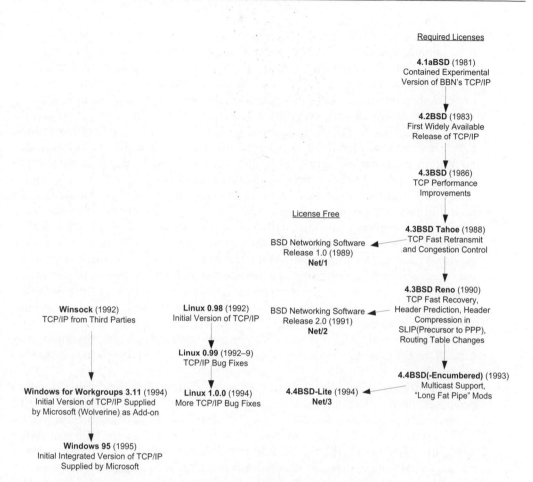

Figure 1-7   The history of software releases supporting TCP/IP up to 1995. The various BSD releases pioneered the availability of TCP/IP. In part because of legal uncertainties regarding the BSD releases in the early 1990s, Linux was developed as an alternative that was initially tailored for PC users. Microsoft began supporting TCP/IP in Windows a couple of years later.

1.8   Attacks Involving the Internet Architecture

Throughout the text we shall briefly describe attacks and vulnerabilities that have been discovered in the design or implementation of the topic we are discussing. Few attacks target the Internet architecture as a whole. However, it is worth observing that the Internet architecture delivers IP datagrams based on destination IP addresses. As a result, malicious users are able to insert whatever IP address they choose into the source IP address field of each IP datagram they send, an activity called *spoofing*. The resulting datagrams are delivered to their destinations, but it is difficult to perform *attribution*. That is, it may be difficult or impossible to determine the origin of a datagram received from the Internet.

Spoofing can be combined with a variety of other attacks seen periodically on the Internet. *Denial-of-service* (DoS) attacks usually involve using so much of some important resource that legitimate users are denied service. For example, sending so many IP datagrams to a server that it spends all of its time just processing the incoming packets and performing no other useful work is a type of DoS attack. Other DoS attacks may involve clogging the network with so much traffic that no other packets can be sent. This is often accomplished by using many sending computers, forming a *distributed DoS* (DDoS) attack.

Unauthorized access attacks involve accessing information or resources in an unauthorized fashion. This can be accomplished with a variety of techniques such as exploiting protocol implementation bugs to take control of a system (called *Owning* the system and turning it into a *zombie* or *bot*). It can also involve various forms of masquerading such as an attacker's agent impersonating a legitimate user (e.g., by running with the user's credentials). Some of the more pernicious attacks involve taking control of many remote systems using malicious software (*malware*) and using them in a coordinated, distributed fashion (called *botnets*). Programmers who intentionally develop malware and exploit systems for (illegal) profit or other malicious purposes are generally called *black hats*. So-called *white hats* do the same sorts of technical things but notify vulnerable parties instead of exploit them.

One other concern with the Internet architecture is that the original Internet protocols did not perform any encryption in support of authentication, integrity, or confidentiality. Consequently, malicious users could usually ascertain private information by merely observing packets in the network. Those with the ability to modify packets in transit could also impersonate users or alter the contents of messages. Although these problems have been reduced significantly thanks to encryption protocols (see Chapter 18), old or poorly designed protocols are still sometimes used that are vulnerable to simple eavesdropping attacks. Given the prevalence of wireless networks, where it is relatively easy to "sniff" the packets sent by others, such older or insecure protocols should be avoided. Note that while encryption may be enabled at one layer (e.g., on a link-layer Wi-Fi network), only host-to-host encryption (IP layer or above) protects information across the multiple network segments an IP datagram is likely to traverse on its way to its final destination.

1.9   Summary

This chapter has been a whirlwind tour of concepts in network architecture and design in general, plus the TCP/IP protocol suite in particular that we discuss in detail in later chapters. The Internet architecture was designed to interconnect different existing networks and provide for a wide range of services and protocols operating simultaneously. Packet switching using datagrams was chosen for its robustness and efficiency. Security and predictable delivery of data (e.g., bounded latency) were secondary concerns.

Based on their understanding of layered and modular software design in operating systems, the early implementers of the Internet protocols adopted a layered design that employs encapsulation. The three main layers in the TCP/IP protocol suite are the network layer, transport layer, and application layer, and we mentioned the different responsibilities of each. We also mentioned the link layer because it relates so closely with the TCP/IP suite. We shall discuss each in more detail in subsequent chapters.

In TCP/IP, the distinction between the network layer and the transport layer is critical: the network layer (IP) provides an unreliable datagram service and must be implemented by all systems addressable on the Internet, whereas the transport layers (TCP and UDP) provide an end-to-end service to applications running on end hosts. The primary transport layers differ radically. TCP provides in-ordered reliable stream delivery with flow control and congestion control. UDP provides essentially no capabilities beyond IP except port numbers for demultiplexing and an error detection mechanism. Unlike TCP, however, it supports multicast delivery.

Addresses and demultiplexing identifiers are used by each layer to avoid confusing protocols or different associations/connections of the same protocol. Link-layer multi-access networks often use 48-bit addresses; IPv4 uses 32-bit addresses and IPv6 uses 128-bit addresses. The TCP and UDP transport protocols use distinct sets of port numbers. Some port numbers are assigned by standards, and others are used temporarily, usually by client applications when communicating with servers. Port numbers do not represent anything physical; they are merely used as a way for applications that want to communicate to rendezvous.

Although port numbers and IP addresses are usually enough to identify the location of a service on the Internet, they are not very convenient for humans to remember or use (especially IPv6 addresses). Consequently, the Internet uses a hierarchical system of host names that can be converted to IP addresses (and back) using DNS, a distributed database application running on the Internet. DNS has become an essential component of the Internet infrastructure, and efforts are under way to make it more secure (see Chapter 18).

An internet is a collection of networks. The common building block for an internet is a router that connects the networks at the IP layer. The "capital-I" Internet is an internet that spans the globe and interconnects nearly two billion users (as of 2010). Private internets are called intranets and are usually connected to the Internet using special devices (firewalls, discussed in Chapter 10) that attempt to prevent unauthorized access. Extranets usually consist of a subset of an institution's intranet that is designed to be accessed by partners or affiliates in a limited way.

Networked applications are usually designed using a client/server or peer-to-peer design pattern. Client/server is more popular and traditional, but peer-to-peer designs have also seen tremendous success. Whatever the design pattern, applications invoke APIs to perform networking tasks. The most common API for TCP/IP networks is called sockets. It was provided with BSD UNIX distributions, software releases that pioneered the use of TCP/IP. By the late 1990s the TCP/IP protocol suite and sockets API were available on every popular operating system.

Security was not a major design goal for the Internet architecture. Determining where packets originate can be difficult for a receiver, as end hosts can easily spoof source IP addresses in unsecured IP datagrams. Distributed DoS attacks also remain an ongoing challenge because victim end hosts can be collected together to form botnets that can carry out DDoS and other attacks, sometimes without the system owners' knowledge. Finally, early Internet protocols did little to ensure privacy of sensitive information, but most of those protocols are now deprecated, and modern replacements use encryption to provide confidential and authenticated communications between hosts.

1.10 References

[B64] P. Baran, "On Distributed Communications: 1. Introduction to Distributed Communications Networks," RAND Memorandum RM-3420-PR, Aug. 1964.

[BT] http://www.bittorrent.com

[C88] D. Clark, "The Design Philosophy of the DARPA Internet Protocols," *Proc. ACM SIGCOMM*, Aug. 1988.

[CK74] V. Cerf and R. Kahn, "A Protocol for Packet Network Intercommunication," *IEEE Transactions on Communications*, COM-22(5), May 1974.

[D08] J. Day, *Patterns in Network Architecture: A Return to Fundamentals* (Prentice Hall, 2008).

[D68] E. Dijkstra, "The Structure of the 'THE'-Multiprogramming System," *Communications of the ACM*, 11(5), May 1968.

[DBSW66] D. Davies, K. Bartlett, R. Scantlebury, and P. Wilkinson, "A Digital Communications Network for Computers Giving Rapid Response at Remote Terminals," *Proc. ACM Symposium on Operating System Principles*, Oct. 1967.

[I96] IBM Corporation, *Systems Network Architecture—APPN Architecture Reference*, Document SC30-3422-04, 1996.

[IPIS] Ipoque, *Internet Study 2008/2009*, http://www.ipoque.com/resources/internet-studies/internet-study-2008_2009

[K64] L. Kleinrock, *Communication Nets: Stochastic Message Flow and Delay* (McGraw-Hill, 1964).

[LC04] S. Lin and D. Costello Jr., *Error Control Coding, Second Edition* (Prentice Hall, 2004).

[LJFK93] S. Leffler, W. Joy, R. Fabry, and M. Karels, "Networking Implementation Notes—4.4BSD Edition," June 1993.

[LT68] J. C. R. Licklider and R. Taylor, "The Computer as a Communication Device," *Science and Technology*, Apr. 1968.

[OIPSW] http://www.rfc-editor.org/rfcxx00.html

[P07] J. Pelkey, *Entrepreneurial Capitalism and Innovation: A History of Computer Communications 1968–1988*, available at http://historyofcomputercommunications.info

[P73] L. Pouzin, "Presentation and Major Design Aspects of the CYCLADES Computer Network," NATO Advanced Study Institute on Computer Communication Networks, 1973.

[RFC0871] M. Padlipsky, "A Perspective on the ARPANET Reference Model," Internet RFC 0871, Sept. 1982.

[RFC0959] J. Postel and J. Reynolds, "File Transfer Protocol," Internet RFC 0959/ STD 0009, Oct. 1985.

[RFC1122] R. Braden, ed., "Requirements for Internet Hosts—Communication Layers," Internet RFC 1122/STD 0003, Oct. 1989.

[RFC1123] R. Braden, ed., "Requirements for Internet Hosts—Application and Support," Internet RFC 1123/STD 0003, Oct. 1989.

[RFC1812] F. Baker, ed., "Requirements for IP Version 4 Routers," Internet RFC 1812, June 1995.

[RFC3493] R. Gilligan, S. Thomson, J. Bound, J. McCann, and W. Stevens, "Basic Socket Interface Extensions for IPv6," Internet RFC 3493 (informational), Feb. 2003.

[RFC3542] W. Stevens, M. Thomas, E. Nordmark, and T. Jinmei, "Advanced Sockets Application Program Interface (API) for IPv6," Internet RFC 3542 (informational), May 2003.

[RFC3678] D. Thaler, B. Fenner, and B. Quinn, "Socket Interface Extensions for Multicast Source Filters," Internet RFC 3678 (informational), Jan. 2004.

[RFC3787] J. Parker, ed., "Recommendations for Interoperable IP Networks Using Intermediate System to Intermediate System (IS-IS)," Internet RFC 3787 (informational), May 2004.

[RFC4294] J. Loughney, ed., "IPv6 Node Requirements," Internet RFC 4294 (informational), Apr. 2006.

[RFC4340] E. Kohler, M. Handley, and S. Floyd, "Datagram Congestion Control Protocol (DCCP)," Internet RFC 4340, Mar. 2006.

[RFC4584] S. Chakrabarti and E. Nordmark, "Extension to Sockets API for Mobile IPv6," Internet RFC 4584 (informational), July 2006.

[RFC4677] P. Hoffman and S. Harris, "The Tao of IETF—A Novice's Guide to the Internet Engineering Task Force," Internet RFC 4677 (informational), Sept. 2006.

[RFC4960] R. Stewart, ed., "Stream Control Transmission Protocol," Internet RFC 4960, Sept. 2007.

[RFC5000] RFC Editor, "Internet Official Protocol Standards," Internet RFC 5000/STD 0001 (informational), May 2008.

[RFC5014] E. Nordmark, S. Chakrabarti, and J. Laganier, "IPv6 Socket API for Source Address Selection," Internet RFC 5014 (informational), Sept. 2007.

[RFC6250] D. Thaler, "Evolution of the IP Model," Internet RFC 6250 (informational), May 2011.

[SFR04] W. R. Stevens, B. Fenner, and A. Rudoff, *UNIX Network Programming, Volume 1, Third Edition* (Prentice Hall, 2004).

[SKYPE] http://www.skype.com

[SRC84] J. Saltzer, D. Reed, and D. Clark, "End-to-End Arguments in System Design," *ACM Transactions on Computer Systems*, 2(4), Nov. 1984.

[W02] M. Waldrop, *The Dream Machine: J. C. R. Licklider and the Revolution That Made Computing Personal* (Penguin Books, 1992).

[X85] Xerox Corporation, *Xerox Network Systems Architecture—General Information Manual*, XNSG 068504, 1985.

[Z80] H. Zimmermann, "OSI Reference Model—The ISO Model of Architecture for Open Systems Interconnection," *IEEE Transactions on Communications*, COM-28(4), Apr. 1980.

2

The Internet Address Architecture

2.1 Introduction

This chapter deals with the structure of network-layer addresses used in the Internet, also known as IP addresses. We discuss how addresses are allocated and assigned to devices on the Internet, the way hierarchy in address assignment aids routing scalability, and the use of special-purpose addresses, including broadcast, multicast, and anycast addresses. We also discuss how the structure and use of IPv4 and IPv6 addresses differ.

Every device connected to the Internet has at least one IP address. Devices used in private networks based on the TCP/IP protocols also require IP addresses. In either case, the forwarding procedures implemented by IP routers (see Chapter 5) use IP addresses to identify where traffic is going. IP addresses also indicate where traffic has come from. IP addresses are similar in some ways to telephone numbers, but whereas telephone numbers are often known and used directly by end users, IP addresses are often shielded from a user's view by the Internet's DNS (see Chapter 11), which allows most users to use names instead of numbers. Users are confronted with manipulating IP addresses when they are required to set up networks themselves or when the DNS has failed for some reason. To understand how the Internet identifies hosts and routers and delivers traffic between them, we must understand the role of IP addresses. We are therefore interested in their administration, structure, and uses.

When devices are attached to the global Internet, they are assigned addresses that must be coordinated so as to not duplicate other addresses in use on the network. For private networks, the IP addresses being used must be coordinated to avoid similar overlaps within the private networks. Groups of IP addresses are *allocated* to users and organizations. The recipients of the allocated addresses then *assign* addresses to devices, usually according to some network "numbering plan." For global Internet addresses, a hierarchical system of administrative entities helps in allocating addresses to users and service providers. Individual users typically receive address allocations from *Internet service providers* (ISPs) that provide both the addresses and the promise of routing traffic in exchange for a fee.

2.2   Expressing IP Addresses

The vast majority of Internet users who are familiar with IP addresses understand the most popular type: IPv4 addresses. Such addresses are often represented in so-called dotted-quad or dotted-decimal notation, for example, 165.195.130.107. The dotted-quad notation consists of four decimal numbers separated by periods. Each such number is a nonnegative integer in the range [0, 255] and represents one-quarter of the entire IP address. The dotted-quad notation is simply a way of writing the whole IPv4 address—a 32-bit nonnegative integer used throughout the Internet system—using convenient decimal numbers. In many circumstances we will be concerned with the binary structure of the address. A number of Internet sites, such as http://www.subnetmask.info and http://www.subnet-calculator.com, now contain calculators for converting between formats of IP addresses and related information. Table 2-1 gives a few examples of IPv4 addresses and their corresponding binary representations, to get started.

Table 2-1   Example IPv4 addresses written in dotted-quad and binary notation

Dotted-Quad Representation	Binary Representation
0.0.0.0	00000000 00000000 00000000 00000000
1.2.3.4	00000001 00000010 00000011 00000100
10.0.0.255	00001010 00000000 00000000 11111111
165.195.130.107	10100101 11000011 10000010 01101011
255.255.255.255	11111111 11111111 11111111 11111111

In IPv6, addresses are 128 bits in length, four times larger than IPv4 addresses, and generally speaking are less familiar to most users. The conventional notation adopted for IPv6 addresses is a series of four hexadecimal ("hex," or base-16) numbers called *blocks* or *fields* separated by colons. An example IPv6 address containing eight blocks would be written as 5f05:2000:80ad:5800:0058:0800:2023:1d71. Although not as familiar to users as decimal numbers, hexadecimal numbers make the task of converting to binary somewhat simpler. In addition, a number of agreed-upon simplifications have been standardized for expressing IPv6 addresses [RFC4291]:

1. Leading zeros of a block need not be written. In the preceding example, the address could have been written as 5f05:2000:80ad:5800:58:800:2023:1d71.

2. Blocks of all zeros can be omitted and replaced by the notation ::. For example, the IPv6 address 0:0:0:0:0:0:0:1 can be written more compactly as ::1. Similarly, the address 2001:0db8:0:0:0:0:0:2 can be written more compactly as 2001:db8::2. To avoid ambiguities, the :: notation may be used only once in an IPv6 address.

3. Embedded IPv4 addresses represented in the IPv6 format can use a form of hybrid notation in which the block immediately preceding the IPv4 portion of the address has the value ffff and the remaining part of the address is formatted using dotted-quad. For example, the IPv6 address ::ffff:10.0.0.1 represents the IPv4 address 10.0.0.1. This is called an *IPv4-mapped IPv6 address*.

4. A conventional notation is adopted in which the low-order 32 bits of the IPv6 address can be written using dotted-quad notation. The IPv6 address ::0102:f001 is therefore equivalent to the address ::1.2.240.1. This is called an *IPv4-compatible IPv6 address*. Note that IPv4-compatible addresses are not the same as IPv4-mapped addresses; they are compatible only in the sense that they can be written down or manipulated by software in a way similar to IPv4 addresses. This type of addressing was originally required for transition plans between IPv4 and IPv6 but is now no longer required [RFC4291].

Table 2-2 presents some examples of IPv6 addresses and their binary representations.

Table 2-2   Examples of IPv6 addresses and their binary representations

Hex Notation	Binary Representation
5f05:2000:80ad:5800:58:800:2023:1d71	0101111100000101 0010000000000000 1000000010101101 0101100000000000 0000000001011000 0000100000000000 0010000000100011 0001110101110001
::1	0000000000000000 0000000000000000 0000000000000000 0000000000000000 0000000000000000 0000000000000000 0000000000000000 0000000000000001
::1.2.240.1 or ::102:f001	0000000000000000 0000000000000000 0000000000000000 0000000000000000 0000000000000000 0000000000000000 0000000100000010 1111000000000001

In some circumstances (e.g., when expressing a URL containing an address) the colon delimiter in an IPv6 address may be confused with another separator such as the colon used between an IP address and a port number. In such circumstances, bracket characters, [and], are used to surround the IPv6 address. For example, the URL

```
http://[2001:0db8:85a3:08d3:1319:8a2e:0370:7344]:443/
```

refers to port number 443 on IPv6 host 2001:0db8:85a3:08d3:1319:8a2e:0370:7344 using the HTTP/TCP/IPv6 protocols.

The flexibility provided by [RFC4291] resulted in unnecessary confusion due to the ability to represent the same IPv6 address in multiple ways. To remedy this situation, [RFC5952] imposes some rules to narrow the range of options while remaining compatible with [RFC4291]. They are as follows:

1. Leading zeros must be suppressed (e.g., 2001:0db8::0022 becomes 2001:db8::22).

2. The :: construct must be used to its maximum possible effect (most zeros suppressed) but not for only 16-bit blocks. If multiple blocks contain equal-length runs of zeros, the first is replaced with ::.

3. The hexadecimal digits a through f should be represented in lowercase.

In most cases, we too will abide by these rules.

2.3   Basic IP Address Structure

IPv4 has 4,294,967,296 possible addresses in its address space, and IPv6 has 340,282,366,920,938,463,463,374,607,431,768,211,456. Because of the large number of addresses (especially for IPv6), it is convenient to divide the address space into chunks. IP addresses are grouped by type and size. Most of the IPv4 address chunks are eventually subdivided down to a single address and used to identify a single network interface of a computer attached to the Internet or to some private intranet. These addresses are called *unicast* addresses. Most of the IPv4 address space is unicast address space. Most of the IPv6 address space is not currently being used. Beyond unicast addresses, other types of addresses include broadcast, multicast, and anycast, which may refer to more than one interface, plus some special-purpose addresses we will discuss later. Before we begin with the details of the current address structure, it is useful to understand the historical evolution of IP addresses.

2.3.1   Classful Addressing

When the Internet's address structure was originally defined, every unicast IP address had a *network* portion, to identify the network on which the interface using the IP address was to be found, and a *host* portion, used to identify the particular host on the network given in the network portion. Thus, some number of contiguous bits in the address became known as the *net number*, and remaining bits were known as the *host number*. At the time, most hosts had only a single network interface, so the terms *interface address* and *host address* were used somewhat interchangeably.

With the realization that different networks might have different numbers of hosts, and that each host requires a unique IP address, a partitioning was devised wherein different-size allocation units of IP address space could be given out to different sites, based on their current and projected number of hosts. The partitioning of the address space involved five *classes*. Each class represented a different trade-off in the number of bits of a 32-bit IPv4 address devoted to the network number versus the number of bits devoted to the host number. Figure 2-1 shows the basic idea.

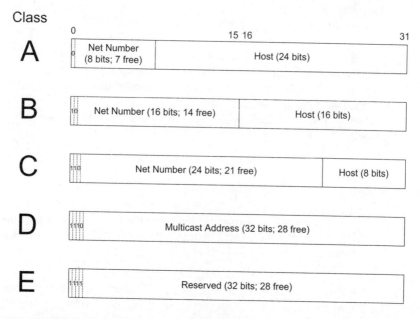

Figure 2-1 The IPv4 address space was originally divided into five classes. Classes A, B, and C were used for assigning addresses to interfaces on the Internet (unicast addresses) and for some other special-case uses. The classes are defined by the first few bits in the address: 0 for class A, 10 for class B, 110 for class C, and so on. Class D addresses are for multicast use (see Chapter 9), and class E addresses remain reserved.

Here we see that the five classes are named A, B, C, D, and E. The A, B, and C class spaces were used for unicast addresses. If we look more carefully at this addressing structure, we can see how the relative sizes of the different classes and their corresponding address ranges really work. Table 2-3 gives this class structure (sometimes called *classful addressing* structure).

Table 2-3   The original ("classful") IPv4 address space partitioning

Class	Address Range	High-Order Bits	Use	Fraction of Total	Number of Nets	Number of Hosts
A	0.0.0.0–127.255.255.255	0	Unicast/special	1/2	128	16,777,216
B	128.0.0.0–191.255.255.255	10	Unicast/special	1/4	16,384	65,536
C	192.0.0.0–223.255.255.255	110	Unicast/special	1/8	2,097,152	256
D	224.0.0.0–239.255.255.255	1110	Multicast	1/16	N/A	N/A
E	240.0.0.0–255.255.255.255	1111	Reserved	1/16	N/A	N/A

The table indicates how the classful addressing structure was used primarily to have a way of allocating unicast address blocks of different sizes to users. The partitioning into classes induces a trade-off between the number of available network numbers of a given size and the number of hosts that can be assigned to the given network. For example, a site allocated the class A network number 18.0.0.0 (MIT) has 2^{24} possible addresses to assign as host addresses (i.e., using IPv4 addresses in the range 18.0.0.0–18.255.255.255), but there are only 127 class A networks available for the entire Internet. A site allocated a class C network number, say, 192.125.3.0, would be able to assign only 256 hosts (i.e., those in the range 192.125.3.0–192.125.3.255), but there are more than two million class C network numbers available.

Note

These numbers are not exact. Several addresses are not generally available for use as unicast addresses. In particular, the first and last addresses of the range are not generally available. In our example, the site assigned address range 18.0.0.0 would really be able to assign as many as $2^{24} - 2 = 16,777,214$ unicast IP addresses.

The classful approach to Internet addressing lasted mostly intact for the first decade of the Internet's growth (to about the early 1980s). After that, it began to show its first signs of scaling problems—it was becoming too inconvenient to centrally coordinate the allocation of a new class A, B, or C network number every time a new network segment was added to the Internet. In addition, assigning class A and B network numbers tended to waste too many host numbers, whereas class C network numbers could not provide enough host numbers to many new sites.

2.3.2   Subnet Addressing

One of the earliest difficulties encountered when the Internet began to grow was the inconvenience of having to allocate a new network number for any new network segment that was to be attached to the Internet. This became especially cumbersome with the development and increasing use of local area networks (LANs) in the early 1980s. To address the problem, it was natural to consider a way that a site attached to the Internet could be allocated a network number centrally that could then be subdivided locally by site administrators. If this could be accomplished without altering the rest of the Internet's core routing infrastructure, so much the better.

Implementing this idea would require the ability to alter the line between the network portion of an IP address and the host portion, but only for local purposes at a site; the rest of the Internet would "see" only the traditional class A, B, and C partitions. The approach adopted to support this capability is called *subnet addressing* [RFC0950]. Using subnet addressing, a site is allocated a class A, B, or C network number, leaving some number of remaining host bits to be further allocated and assigned within a site. The site may further divide the host portion of its base address allocation into a *subnetwork* (subnet) number and a host number. Essentially, subnet addressing adds one additional field to the IP address structure, but without adding any bits to its length. As a result, a site administrator is able to trade off the number of subnetworks versus the number of hosts expected to be on each subnetwork without having to coordinate with other sites.

In exchange for the additional flexibility provided by subnet addressing, a new cost is imposed. Because the definition of the *Subnet* and *Host* fields is now site-specific (not dictated by the class of the network number), all routers and hosts at a site require a new way to determine where the *Subnet* field of the address and the *Host* field of the address are located within the address. Before subnets, this information could be derived directly by knowing whether a network number was from class A, B, or C (as indicated by the first few bits in the address). As an example, using subnet addressing, an IPv4 address might have the form shown in Figure 2-2.

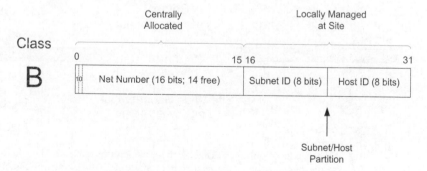

Figure 2-2   An example of a subnetted class B address. Using 8 bits for the subnet ID provides for 256 subnets with 254 hosts on each of the subnets. This partitioning may be altered by the network administrator.

Figure 2-2 is an example of how a class B address might be "subnetted." Assume that some site in the Internet has been allocated a class B network number. The first 16 bits of every address the site will use are fixed at some particular number because these bits have been allocated by a central authority. The last 16 bits (which would have been used only to create host numbers in the class B network without subnets) can now be divided by the site network administrator as needs may dictate. In this example, 8 bits have been chosen for the subnet number, leaving 8 bits for host numbers. This particular configuration allows the site to support 256 subnetworks, and each subnetwork may contain up to 254 hosts (now the first and last addresses for each subnetwork are not available, as opposed to losing only the first and last addresses of the entire allocated range). Recall that the subnetwork structure is known only by hosts and routers where the subnetting is taking place. The remainder of the Internet still treats any address associated with the site just as it did prior to the advent of subnet addressing. Figure 2-3 shows how this works.

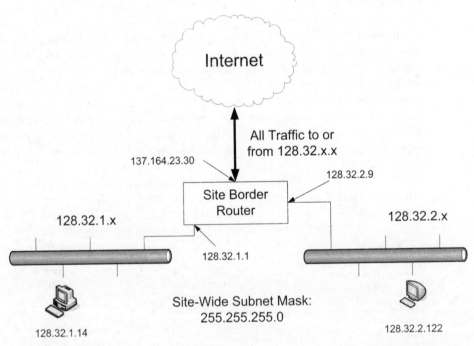

Figure 2-3   A site is allocated the classical class B network number 128.32. The network administrator decides to apply a site-wide subnet mask of 255.255.255.0, giving 256 subnetworks where each subnetwork can hold 256 − 2 = 254 hosts. The IPv4 address of each host on the same subnet has the subnetwork number in common. All of the IPv4 addresses of hosts on the left-hand LAN segment start with 128.32.1, and all of those on the right start with 128.32.2.

This figure shows a hypothetical site attached to the Internet with one border router (i.e., one attachment point to the Internet) and two internal local area networks. The value of x could be anything in the range [0, 255]. Each of the Ethernet networks is an IPv4 subnetwork of the overall network number 128.32, a class B address allocation. For other sites on the Internet to reach this site, all traffic with destination addresses starting with 128.32 is directed by the Internet routing system to the border router (specifically, its interface with IPv4 address 137.164.23.30). At this point, the border router must distinguish among different subnetworks within the 128.32 network. In particular, it must be able to distinguish and separate traffic destined for addresses of the form 128.32.1.x from those destined for addresses of the form 128.32.2.x. These represent subnetwork numbers 1 and 2, respectively, of the 128.32 class B network number. In order to do this, the router must be aware of where the subnet ID is to be found within the addresses. This is accomplished by a configuration parameter we will discuss next.

2.3.3 Subnet Masks

The *subnet mask* is an assignment of bits used by a host or router to determine how the network and subnetwork information is partitioned from the host information in a corresponding IP address. Subnet masks for IP are the same length as the corresponding IP addresses (32 bits for IPv4 and 128 bits for IPv6). They are typically configured into a host or router in the same way as IP addresses—either statically (typical for routers) or using some dynamic system such as the *Dynamic Host Configuration Protocol* (DHCP; see Chapter 6). For IPv4, subnet masks may be written in the same way an IPv4 address is written (i.e., dotted-decimal). Although not originally required to be arranged in this manner, today subnet masks are structured as some number of 1 bits followed by some number of 0 bits. Because of this arrangement, it is possible to use a shorthand format for expressing masks that simply gives the number of contiguous 1 bits in the mask (starting from the left). This format is now the most common format and is sometimes called the *prefix length*. Table 2-4 presents some examples for IPv4.

Table 2-4   IPv4 subnet mask examples in various formats

Dotted-Decimal Representation	Shorthand (Prefix Length)	Binary Representation
128.0.0.0	/1	10000000 00000000 00000000 00000000
255.0.0.0	/8	11111111 00000000 00000000 00000000
255.192.0.0	/10	11111111 11000000 00000000 00000000
255.255.0.0	/16	11111111 11111111 00000000 00000000
255.255.254.0	/23	11111111 11111111 11111110 00000000
255.255.255.192	/27	11111111 11111111 11111111 11100000
255.255.255.255	/32	11111111 11111111 11111111 11111111

Table 2-5   IPv6 subnet mask examples in various formats

Hex Notation	Shorthand (Prefix Length)	Binary Representation
ffff:ffff:ffff:ffff::	/64	1111111111111111 1111111111111111 1111111111111111 1111111111111111 0000000000000000 0000000000000000 0000000000000000 0000000000000000
ff00::	/8	1111111100000000 0000000000000000 0000000000000000 0000000000000000 0000000000000000 0000000000000000 0000000000000000 0000000000000000

Table 2-5 presents some examples for IPv6.

Masks are used by routers and hosts to determine where the network/sub-network portion of an IP address ends and the host part begins. A bit set to 1 in the subnet mask means the corresponding bit position in an IP address should be considered part of a combined network/subnetwork portion of an address, which is used as the basis for forwarding datagrams (see Chapter 5). Conversely, a bit set to 0 in the subnet mask means the corresponding bit position in an IP address should be considered part of the host portion. For example, in Figure 2-4 we can see how the IPv4 address 128.32.1.14 is treated when a subnet mask of 255.255.255.0 is applied to it.

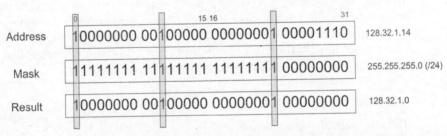

Figure 2-4   An IP address can be combined with a subnet mask using a bitwise AND operation in order to form the network/subnetwork identifier (prefix) of the address used for routing. In this example, applying a mask of length 24 to the IPv4 address 128.32.1.14 gives the prefix 128.32.1.0/24.

Here we see how each bit in the address is ANDed with each corresponding bit in the subnet mask. Recalling the bitwise AND operation, a result bit is only ever a 1 if the corresponding bits in both the mask and the address are 1. In this example, we see that the address 128.32.1.14 belongs to the subnet 128.32.1.0/24. In Figure 2-3, this is precisely the information required by the border router to determine to which subnetwork a datagram destined for the system with address 128.32.1.14 should be forwarded. Note again that the rest of the Internet routing system does not require knowledge of the subnet mask because routers outside the site make routing decisions based only on the network number portion of an address and not the combined network/subnetwork or host portions. Consequently, subnet masks are purely a local matter at the site.

2.3.4 Variable-Length Subnet Masks (VLSM)

So far we have discussed how a network number allocated to a site can be subdivided into ranges assigned to multiple subnetworks, each of the same size and therefore able to support the same number of hosts, based on the operational expectations of the network administrator. We now observe that it is possible to use a different-length subnet mask applied to the same network number in different portions of the same site. Although doing this complicates address configuration management, it adds flexibility to the subnet structure because different subnetworks may be set up with different numbers of hosts. *Variable-length subnet masks* (VLSM) are now supported by most hosts, routers, and routing protocols. To understand how VLSM works, consider the network topology illustrated in Figure 2-5, which extends Figure 2-3 with two additional subnetworks using VLSM.

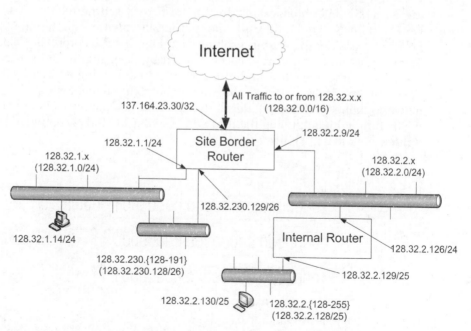

Figure 2-5   VLSM can be used to partition a network number into subnetworks with a differing number of hosts on each subnet. Each router and host is configured with a subnet mask in addition to its IP address. Most software supports VLSM, except for some older routing protocols (e.g., RIP version 1).

In the more complicated and realistic example shown in Figure 2-5, three different subnet masks are used within the site to subnet the 128.32.0.0/16 network: /24, /25, and /26. Doing so provides for a different number of hosts on each subnet. Recall that the number of hosts is constrained by the number of bits remaining in the IP address that are not used by the network/subnet number. For IPv4 and a /24 prefix, this allows for 32 − 24 = 8 bits (256 hosts); for /25, half as many (128 hosts); and for /26, half further still (64 hosts). Note that each interface on each host and router depicted is now given both an IP address and a subnet mask, but the mask differs across the network topology. With an appropriate dynamic routing protocol running among the routers (e.g., OSPF, IS-IS, RIPv2), traffic is able to flow correctly among hosts at the same site or to/from the outside of the site across the Internet.

Although it may not seem obvious, there is a common case where a subnetwork contains only two hosts. When routers are connected together by a point-to-point link requiring an IP address to be assigned at each end, it is common practice to use a /31 network prefix with IPv4, and it is now also a recommended practice to use a /127 prefix for IPv6 [RFC6164].

2.3.5   Broadcast Addresses

In each IPv4 subnetwork, a special address is reserved to be the *subnet broadcast address*. The subnet broadcast address is formed by setting the network/subnetwork portion of an IPv4 address to the appropriate value and all the bits in the *Host* field to 1. Consider the left-most subnet from Figure 2-5. Its prefix is 128.32.1.0/24. The subnet broadcast address is constructed by inverting the subnet mask (i.e., changing all the 0 bits to 1 and vice versa) and performing a bitwise OR operation with the address of any of the computers on the subnet (or, equivalently, the network/subnetwork prefix). Recall that the result of a bitwise OR operation is 1 if either input bit is 1. Using the IPv4 address 128.32.1.14, this computation can be written as shown in Figure 2-6.

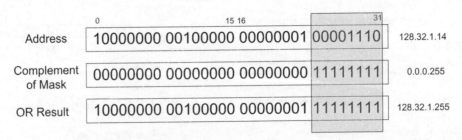

Figure 2-6   The subnet broadcast address is formed by ORing the complement of the subnet mask with the IPv4 address. In this case of a /24 subnet mask, all of the remaining 32 − 24 = 8 bits are set to 1, giving a decimal value of 255 and the subnet broadcast address of 128.32.1.255.

As shown in the figure, the subnet broadcast address for the subnet 128.32.1.0/24 is 128.32.1.255. Historically, a datagram using this type of address as its destination has also been known as a *directed broadcast*. Such a broadcast can, at least theoretically, be routed through the Internet as a single datagram until reaching the target subnetwork, at which point it becomes a collection of broadcast datagrams that are delivered to all hosts on the subnetwork. Generalizing this idea further, we could form a datagram with the destination IPv4 address 128.32.255.255 and launch it into the Internet attached to the network depicted in Figure 2-3 or Figure 2-5. This would address all hosts at the target site.

Note

Directed broadcasts were found to be such a big problem from a security point of view that they are effectively disabled on the Internet today. [RFC0919] describes the various types of broadcasts for IPv4, and [RFC1812] suggests that support for forwarding directed broadcasts by routers should not only be available but enabled by default. This policy was reversed by [RFC2644] so that by default routers must now disable the forwarding of directed broadcasts and are even free to omit support for the capability altogether.

In addition to the subnet broadcast address, the *special-use* address 255.255.255.255 is reserved as the *local net broadcast* (also called *limited broadcast*), which is never forwarded by routers. (See Section 2.5 for more detail on special-use addresses.) Note that although routers may not forward broadcasts, subnet broadcasts and local net broadcasts destined for the same network to which a computer is attached should be expected to work unless explicitly disabled by end hosts. Such broadcasts do not require action by a router; link-layer broadcast mechanisms, if available, are used for supporting them (see Chapter 3). Broadcast addresses are typically used with protocols such as UDP/IP (Chapter 10) or ICMP (Chapter 8) because these protocols do not involve two-party conversations as in TCP/IP. IPv6 lacks any broadcast addresses; for places where broadcast addresses might be used in IPv4, IPv6 instead uses exclusively multicast addresses (see Chapter 9).

2.3.6   IPv6 Addresses and Interface Identifiers

In addition to being longer than IPv4 addresses by a factor of 4, IPv6 addresses also have some additional structure. Special prefixes used with IPv6 addresses indicate the *scope* of an address. The scope of an IPv6 address refers to the portion of the network where it can be used. Important examples of scopes include *node-local* (the address can be used only for communication on the same computer), *link-local* (used only among nodes on the same network link or IPv6 prefix), or *global* (Internet-wide). In IPv6, most nodes have more than one address in use, often on the same network interface. Although this is supported in IPv4 as well, it is not nearly as common. The set of addresses required in an IPv6 node, including multicast addresses (see Section 2.5.2), is given in [RFC4291].

Note

Another scope level called *site-local* using prefix fec0::/10 was originally supported by IPv6 but was deprecated for use with unicast addressing by [RFC3879]. The primary problems include how to handle such addresses given that they may be reused in more than one site and a lack of clarity on precisely how to define a "site."

Link-local IPv6 addresses (and some global IPv6 addresses) use *interface identifiers* (IIDs) as a basis for unicast IPv6 address assignment. IIDs are used as the low-order bits of an IPv6 address in all cases except where the address begins with the binary value 000, and as such they must be unique within the same network prefix. IIDs are ordinarily 64 bits long and are formed either directly from the underlying link-layer MAC address of a network interface using a *modified EUI-64 format* [EUI64], or by another process that randomizes the value in hopes of providing some degree of privacy against address tracking (see Chapter 6).

In IEEE standards, EUI stands for *extended unique identifier*. EUI-64 identifiers start with a 24-bit *Organizationally Unique Identifier* (OUI) followed by a 40-bit *extension identifier* assigned by the organization, which is identified by the first 24 bits. The OUIs are maintained and allocated by the IEEE registration authority [IEEERA]. EUIs may be "universally administered" or "locally administered." In the Internet context, such addresses are typically of the universally administered variety.

Many IEEE standards-compliant network interfaces (e.g., Ethernet) have used shorter-format addresses (48-bit EUIs) for years. The only significant difference between the EUI-48 and EUI-64 formats is their length (see Figure 2-7).

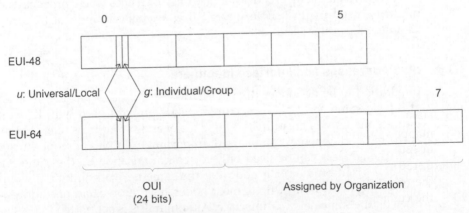

Figure 2-7   The EUI-48 and EUI-64 formats defined by the IEEE. These are used within IPv6 to form interface identifiers by inverting the *u* bit.

The OUI is 24 bits long and occupies the first 3 bytes of both EUI-48 and EUI-64 addresses. The low-order 2 bits of the first bytes of these addresses are designated the *u* and *g* bits, respectively. The *u* bit, when set, indicates that the address is locally administered. The *g* bit, when set, indicates that the address is a group or multicast-type address. For the moment, we are concerned only with cases where the *g* bit is not set.

An EUI-64 can be formed from an EUI-48 by copying the 24-bit OUI value from the EUI-48 address to the EUI-64 address, placing the 16-bit value 1111111111111110 (hex FFFE) in the fourth and fifth bytes of the EUI-64 address, and then copying the remaining organization-assigned bits. For example, the EUI-48 address 00-11-22-33-44-55 would become 00-11-22-FF-FE-33-44-55 in EUI-64. This mapping is the first step used by IPv6 in constructing its interface identifiers when such underlying EUI-48 addresses are available. The modified EUI-64 used to form IIDs for IPv6 addresses simply inverts the *u* bit.

When an IPv6 interface identifier is needed for a type of interface that does not have an EUI-48-bit address provided by its manufacturer, but has some other type of underlying address (e.g., AppleTalk), the underlying address is left-padded with zeros to form the interface identifier. Interface identifiers created for interfaces that lack any form of other identifier (e.g., tunnels, serial links) may be derived from some other interface on the same node (that is not on the same subnet) or from some identifier associated with the node. Lacking any other options, manual assignment is a last resort.

2.3.6.1 Examples

Using the Linux `ifconfig` command, we can investigate the way a link-local IPv6 address is formed:

```
Linux% ifconfig eth1
eth1      Link encap:Ethernet  HWaddr 00:30:48:2A:19:89
          inet addr:12.46.129.28  Bcast:12.46.129.127
          Mask:255.255.255.128
          inet6 addr: fe80::230:48ff:fe2a:1989/64 Scope:Link
          UP BROADCAST RUNNING MULTICAST  MTU:1500  Metric:1
          RX packets:1359970341 errors:0 dropped:0 overruns:0 frame:0
          TX packets:1472870787 errors:0 dropped:0 overruns:0 carrier:0
          collisions:0 txqueuelen:1000
          RX bytes:4021555658 (3.7 GiB)  TX bytes:3258456176 (3.0 GiB)
          Base address:0x3040 Memory:f8220000-f8240000
```

Here we can see how the Ethernet's hardware address 00:30:48:2A:19:89 is mapped to an IPv6 address. First, it is converted to EUI-64, forming the address 00:30:48:ff:fe:2a:19:89. Next, the *u* bit is inverted, forming the IID value 02:30:48:ff:fe:2a:19:89. To complete the link-local IPv6 address, we use the reserved link-local prefix fe80::/10 (see Section 2.5). Together, these form the complete address, fe80::230:48ff:fe2a:1989. The presence of /64 is the standard length used for identifying the subnetwork/host portion of an IPv6 address derived from an IID as required by [RFC4291].

Another interesting example is from a Windows system with IPv6. In this case, we see a special *tunnel endpoint*, which is used to carry IPv6 traffic through networks that otherwise support only IPv4:

```
c:\> ipconfig /all
...
Tunnel adapter Automatic Tunneling Pseudo-Interface:

   Connection-specific DNS Suffix  . : foo
   Description . . . . . . . . . . . : Automatic Tunneling
                                       Pseudo-Interface

   Physical Address. . . . . . . . . : 0A-99-8D-87
   Dhcp Enabled. . . . . . . . . . . : No
   IP Address. . . . . . . . . . . . : fe80::5efe:10.153.141.135%2
   Default Gateway . . . . . . . . . :
   DNS Servers . . . . . . . . . . . : fec0:0:0:ffff::1%2
                                       fec0:0:0:ffff::2%2
                                       fec0:0:0:ffff::3%2
   NetBIOS over Tcpip. . . . . . . . : Disabled
...
```

In this case, we can see a special tunneling interface called ISATAP [RFC5214]. The so-called physical address is really the hexadecimal encoding of an IPv4 address: 0A-99-8D-87 is the same as 10.153.141.135. Here, the OUI used (00–00-5E) is the one assigned to the IANA [IANA]. It is used in combination with the hex value fe, indicating an embedded IPv4 address. This combination is then combined with the standard link-local prefix fe80::/10 to give the address fe80::5efe:10.153.141.135. The %2 appended to the end of the address is called a *zone ID* in Windows and indicates the interface index number on the computer corresponding to the IPv6 address. IPv6 addresses are often created by a process of automatic configuration, a process we discuss in more detail in Chapter 6.

2.4 CIDR and Aggregation

In the early 1990s, after the adoption of subnet addressing to ease one form of growing pains, the Internet started facing a serious set of scaling problems. Three particular issues were considered so important as to require immediate attention:

1. By 1994, over half of all class B addresses had already been allocated. It was expected that the class B address space would be exhausted by about 1995.

2. The 32-bit IPv4 address was thought to be inadequate to handle the size of the Internet anticipated by the early 2000s.

3. The number of entries in the global routing table (one per network number), about 65,000 in 1995, was growing. As more and more class A, B, and C routing entries appeared, routing performance would suffer.

These three issues were attacked by a group in the IETF called ROAD (for ROuting and ADdressing), starting in 1992. They considered problems 1 and 3 to be of immediate concern, and problem 2 as requiring a long-term solution. The short-term solution they proposed was to effectively remove the class breakdown of IP addresses and also promote the ability to aggregate hierarchically assigned IP addresses. These measures would help problems 1 and 3. IPv6 was envisioned to deal with problem 2.

2.4.1 Prefixes

In order to help relieve the pressure on the availability of IPv4 addresses (especially class B addresses), the classful addressing scheme was generalized using a scheme similar to VLSM, and the Internet routing system was extended to support *Classless Inter-Domain Routing* (CIDR) [RFC4632]. This provided a way to conveniently allocate contiguous address ranges that contained more than 255 hosts but fewer than 65,536. That is, something other than single class B or multiple class C network numbers could be allocated to sites. Using CIDR, any address range is not predefined as being part of a class but instead requires a mask similar to a subnet mask, sometimes called a *CIDR mask*. CIDR masks are not limited to a site but are instead visible to the global routing system. Thus, the core Internet routers must be able to interpret and process masks in addition to network numbers. This combination of numbers, called a network *prefix*, is used for both IPv4 and IPv6 address management.

Eliminating the predefined separation of network and host number within an IP address makes finer-grain allocation of IP address ranges possible. As with classful addressing, dividing the address spaces into chunks is most easily achieved by grouping numerically contiguous addresses for use as a type or for some particular special purpose. Such groupings are now commonly expressed using a prefix of the address space. An n-bit prefix is a predefined value for the first n bits of an address. The value of n (the length of the prefix) is typically expressed as an integer in the range 0–32 for IPv4 and 0–128 for IPv6. It is generally appended to the base IP address following a / character. Table 2-6 gives some examples of prefixes and their corresponding IPv4 or IPv6 address ranges.

In the table, the bits defined and fixed by the prefix are enclosed in a box. The remaining bits may be set to any combination of 0s and 1s, thereby covering the possible address range. Clearly, a smaller prefix length corresponds to a larger number of possible addresses. In addition, the earlier classful addressing approach is easily generalized by this scheme. For example, the class C network number 192.125.3.0 can be written as the prefix 192.125.3.0/24 or 192.125.3/24. Classful A and B network numbers can be expressed using /8 and /16 prefix lengths, respectively.

Table 2-6 Examples of prefixes and their corresponding IPv4 or IPv6 address range

Prefix	Prefix (Binary)	Address Range
0.0.0.0/0	00000000 00000000 00000000 00000000	0.0.0.0–255.255.255.255
128.0.0.0/1	10000000 00000000 00000000 00000000	128.0.0.0–255.255.255.255
128.0.0.0/24	10000000 00000000 00000000 00000000	128.0.0.0–128.0.0.255
198.128.128.192/27	11000110 10000000 10000000 11000000	198.128.128.192–198.128.128.223
165.195.130.107/32	10100101 11000011 10000010 01101011	165.195.130.107
2001:db8::/32	0010000000000001 0000110110111000 0000000000000000 0000000000000000 0000000000000000 0000000000000000 0000000000000000 0000000000000000	2001:db8::–2001:db8:ffff:ffff

2.4.2 Aggregation

Removing the classful structure of IP addresses made it possible to allocate IP address blocks in a wider variety of sizes. Doing so, however, did not address the third concern from the list of problems; it did not help to reduce the number of routing table entries. A routing table entry tells a router where to send traffic. Essentially, the router inspects the destination IP address in an arriving datagram, finds a matching routing table entry, and from the entry extracts the "next hop" for the datagram. This is somewhat like driving to a particular address in a car and in every intersection along the way finding a sign indicating what direction to take to get to the next intersection on the way to the destination. If you consider the number of signs that would have to be present at every intersection for every possible destination neighborhood, you get some sense of the problem facing the Internet in the early 1990s.

At the time, few techniques were known to dramatically reduce the number of routing table entries while maintaining shortest-path routes to all destinations in the Internet. The best-known approach was published in a study of *hierarchical routing* [KK77] in the late 1970s by Kleinrock and Kamoun. They observed that if the network topology were arranged as a tree[1] and addresses were assigned in a way that was "sensitive" to this topology, very small routing tables could be used while still maintaining shortest-path routes to all destinations. Consider Figure 2-8.

In this figure, circles represent routers and lines represent network links between them. The left-hand and right-hand sides of the diagram show tree-shaped networks. The difference between them is the way addresses have been assigned to the routers. In the left-hand (a) side, addresses are essentially random—there is no direct relationship between the addresses and the location of

---

1. In graph theory, a tree is a connected graph with no cycles. For a network of routers and links, this means that there is only one simple (nonduplicative) path between any two routers.

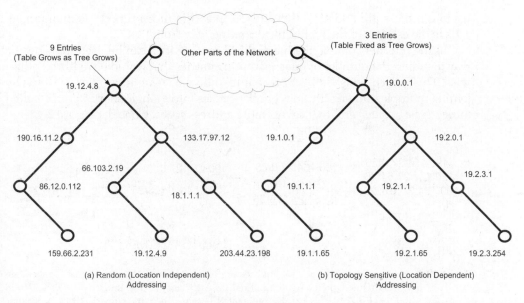

Figure 2-8 In a network with a tree topology, network addresses can be assigned in a special way so as to limit the amount of routing information ("state") that needs to be stored in a router. If addresses are not assigned in this way (left side), shortest-path routes cannot be guaranteed without storing an amount of state proportional to the number of nodes to be reached. While assigning addresses in a way that is sensitive to the tree topology saves state, if the network topology changes, a reassignment of addresses is generally required.

the routers in the tree. On the right-hand (b) side of the diagram, the addresses are assigned based upon where the router is located in the tree. If we consider the number of entries each top router requires, we see that there is a significant difference.

The root (top) of the tree on the left is the router labeled 19.12.4.8. In order to know a next hop for every possible destination, it needs an entry for all the routers "below" it in the tree: 190.16.11.2, 86.12.0.112, 159.66.2.231, 133.17.97.12, 66.103.2.19, 18.1.1.1, 19.12.4.9, and 203.44.23.198. For any other destination, it simply routes to the cloud labeled "Other Parts of the Network." This results in a total of nine entries. In contrast, the root of the right-hand tree is labeled 19.0.0.1 and requires only three entries in its routing table. Note that all of the routers on the left side of the right tree begin with the prefix 19.1 and all to the right begin with 19.2. Thus, the table in router 19.0.0.1 need only show 19.1.0.1 as the next hop for any destination starting with 19.1, whereas 19.2.0.1 is the next hop for any destination starting with 19.2. Any other destination goes to the cloud labeled "Other Parts of the Network." This results in a total of three entries. Note that this behavior is recursive—any router in the (b) side of the tree never requires more entries than the number of links it has. This is a direct result of the special method used to assign the addresses. Even if more routers are added to the (b)-side tree, this nice property is maintained. This is the essence of the hierarchical routing idea from [KK77].

In the Internet context, the hierarchical routing idea can be used in a specific way to reduce the number of Internet routing entries that would be required otherwise. This is accomplished by a procedure known as *route aggregation*. It works by joining multiple numerically adjacent IP prefixes into a single shorter prefix (called an *aggregate* or *summary*) that covers more address space. Consider Figure 2-9.

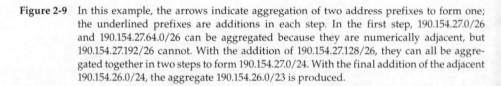

Figure 2-9   In this example, the arrows indicate aggregation of two address prefixes to form one; the underlined prefixes are additions in each step. In the first step, 190.154.27.0/26 and 190.154.27.64.0/26 can be aggregated because they are numerically adjacent, but 190.154.27.192/26 cannot. With the addition of 190.154.27.128/26, they can all be aggregated together in two steps to form 190.154.27.0/24. With the final addition of the adjacent 190.154.26.0/24, the aggregate 190.154.26.0/23 is produced.

We start with three address prefixes on the left in Figure 2-9. The first two, 190.154.27.0/26 and 190.154.27.64/26, are numerically adjacent and can therefore be combined (aggregated). The arrows indicate where aggregation takes place. The prefix 190.154.27.192/26 cannot be aggregated in the first step because it is not numerically adjacent. When a new prefix, 190.154.27.128/26, is added (underlined), the 190.154.27.192/26 and 190.154.27.128/26 prefixes may be aggregated, forming the 190.154.27.128/25 prefix. This aggregate is now adjacent to the 190.154.27.0/25 aggregate, so they can be aggregated further to form 190.154.27.0/24. When the prefix 190.154.26.0/24 (underlined) is added, the two class C prefixes can be aggregated to form 190.154.26.0/23. In this way, the original three prefixes and the two that were added can be aggregated into a single prefix.

2.5   Special-Use Addresses

Both the IPv4 and IPv6 address spaces include a few address ranges that are used for special purposes (and are therefore not used in assigning unicast addresses). For IPv4, these addresses are given in Table 2-7 [RFC5735].

Table 2-7   IPv4 special-use addresses (defined January 2010)

Prefix	Special Use	Reference
0.0.0.0/8	Hosts on the local network. May be used only as a source IP address.	[RFC1122]
10.0.0.0/8	Address for private networks (intranets). Such addresses never appear on the public Internet.	[RFC1918]
127.0.0.0/8	Internet host loopback addresses (same computer). Typically only 127.0.0.1 is used.	[RFC1122]
169.254.0.0/16	"Link-local" addresses—used only on a single link and generally assigned automatically. See Chapter 6.	[RFC3927]
172.16.0.0/12	Address for private networks (intranets). Such addresses never appear on the public Internet.	[RFC1918]
192.0.0.0/24	IETF protocol assignments (IANA reserved).	[RFC5736]
192.0.2.0/24	TEST-NET-1 addresses approved for use in documentation. Such addresses never appear on the public Internet.	[RFC5737]
192.88.99.0/24	Used for 6to4 relays (anycast addresses).	[RFC3068]
192.168.0.0/16	Address for private networks (intranets). Such addresses never appear on the public Internet.	[RFC1918]
198.18.0.0/15	Used for benchmarks and performance testing.	[RFC2544]
198.51.100.0/24	TEST-NET-2. Approved for use in documentation.	[RFC5737]
203.0.113.0/24	TEST-NET-3. Approved for use in documentation.	[RFC5737]
224.0.0.0/4	IPv4 multicast addresses (formerly class D); used only as destination addresses.	[RFC5771]
240.0.0.0/4	Reserved space (formerly class E), except 255.255.255.255.	[RFC1112]
255.255.255.255/32	Local network (limited) broadcast address.	[RFC0919] [RFC0922]

In IPv6, a number of address ranges and individual addresses are used for specific purposes. They are listed in Table 2-8 [RFC5156].

For both IPv4 and IPv6, address ranges not designated as special, multicast, or reserved are available to be assigned for unicast use. Some unicast address space (prefixes 10/8, 172.16/12, and 192.168/16 for IPv4 and fc00::/7 for IPv6) is reserved for building private networks. Addresses from these ranges can be used by cooperating hosts and routers within a site or organization, but not across the global Internet. Thus, these addresses are sometimes called *nonroutable* addresses. That is, they will not be routed by the public Internet.

The management of private, nonroutable address space is entirely a local decision. The IPv4 private addresses are very common in home networks and for the internal networks of moderately sized and large enterprises. They are frequently used in combination with *network address translation* (NAT), which rewrites IP addresses inside IP datagrams as they enter the Internet. We discuss NAT in detail in Chapter 7.

Table 2-8   IPv6 special-use addresses (defined April 2008)

Prefix	Special Use	Reference
::/0	Default route entry. Not used for addressing.	[RFC5156]
::/128	The unspecified address; may be used as a source IP address.	[RFC4291]
::1/128	The IPv6 host loopback address; not used in datagrams sent outside the local host.	[RFC4291]
::ffff:0:0/96	IPv4-mapped addresses. Such addresses never appear in packet headers. For internal host use only.	[RFC4291]
::{ipv4-address}/96	IPv4-compatible addresses. Deprecated; not to be used.	[RFC4291]
2001::/32	Teredo addresses.	[RFC4380]
2001:10::/28	Overlay Routable Cryptographic Hash Identifiers. Such addresses never appear on the public Internet.	[RFC4843]
2001:db8::/32	Address range used for documentation and for examples. Such addresses never appear on the public Internet.	[RFC3849]
2002::/16	6to4 addresses of 6to4 tunnel relays.	[RFC3056]
3ffe::/16	Used by 6bone experiments. Deprecated; not to be used.	[RFC3701]
5f00::/16	Used by 6bone experiments. Deprecated; not to be used.	[RFC3701]
fc00::/7	Unique, local unicast addresses; not used on the global Internet.	[RFC4193]
fe80::/10	Link-local unicast addresses.	[RFC4291]
ff00::/8	IPv6 multicast addresses; used only as destination addresses.	[RFC4291]

2.5.1   Addressing IPv4/IPv6 Translators

In some networks, it may be attractive to perform translation between IPv4 and IPv6 [RFC6127]. A framework for this has been developed for unicast translations [RFC6144], and one is currently under development for multicast translations [IDv-4v6mc]. One of the basic functions is to provide automated, algorithmic translation of addresses. Using the "well-known" IPv6 prefix 64:ff9b::/96 or another assigned prefix, [RFC6052] specifies how this is accomplished for unicast addresses.

The scheme makes use of a specialized address format called an *IPv4-embedded IPv6 address*. This type of address contains an IPv4 address inside an IPv6 address. It can be encoded using one of six formats, based on the length of the IPv6 prefix, which is required to be one of the following: 32, 40, 48, 56, 64, or 96. The formats available are shown in Figure 2-10.

In the figure, the prefix is either the well-known prefix or a prefix unique to the organization deploying translators. Bits 64–71 must be set to 0 to maintain compatibility with identifiers specified in [RFC4291]. The suffix bits are reserved and should be set to 0. The method to produce an IPv4-embedded IPv6 address is then simple: concatenate the IPv6 prefix with the 32-bit IPv4 address, ensuring that the bits 63–71 are set to 0 (inserting if necessary). Append the suffix as 0 bits until a 128-bit address is produced. IPv4-embedded IPv6 addresses using

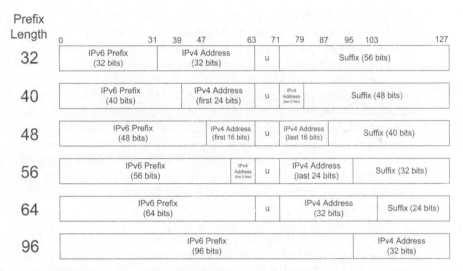

Figure 2-10   IPv4 addresses can be embedded within IPv6 addresses, forming an IPv4-embedded IPv6 address. Six different formats are available, depending on the IPv6 prefix length in use. The well-known prefix 64:ff9b::/96 can be used for automatic translation between IPv4 and IPv6 unicast addresses.

the 96-bit prefix option may be expressed using the convention for IPv6-mapped addresses mentioned previously (Section 2.2(3) of [RFC4291]). For example, embedding the IPv4 address 198.51.100.16 with the well-known prefix produces the address 64:ff9b::198.51.100.16.

2.5.2   Multicast Addresses

Multicast addressing is supported by IPv4 and IPv6. An IP multicast address (also called *group* or *group address*) identifies a group of host interfaces, rather than a single one. Generally speaking, the group could span the entire Internet. The portion of the network that a single group covers is known as the group's *scope* [RFC2365]. Common scopes include *node-local* (same computer), *link-local* (same subnet), *site-local* (applicable to some site), *global* (entire Internet), and *administrative*. Administrative scoped addresses may be used in an area of the network that has been manually configured into routers. A site administrator may configure routers as *admin-scope boundaries*, meaning that multicast traffic of the associated group is not forwarded past the router. Note that the site-local and administrative scopes are available for use only with multicast addressing.

Under software control, the protocol stack in each Internet host is able to join or leave a multicast group. When a host sends something to a group, it creates a datagram using one of its own (unicast) IP addresses as the source address and a multicast IP address as the destination. All hosts in scope that have joined the group should receive any datagrams sent to the group. The sender is not generally aware of the hosts receiving the datagram unless they explicitly reply. Indeed, the sender does not even know in general how *many* hosts are receiving its datagrams.

The original multicast service model, described so far, has become known as *any-source multicast* (ASM). In this model, any sender may send to any group; a receiver joins the group by specifying only the group address. A newer approach, called *source-specific multicast* (SSM) [RFC3569][RFC4607], uses only a single sender per group (also see the errata to [RFC4607]). In this case, when joining a group, a host specifies the address of a *channel*, which comprises both a group address *and* a source IP address. SSM was developed to avoid some of the complexities in deploying the ASM model. Although neither form of multicast is widely available throughout the Internet, it seems that SSM is now the more likely candidate for adoption.

Understanding and implementing wide area multicasting has been an ongoing effort within the Internet community for more than a decade, and a large number of protocols have been developed to support it. Full details of how global Internet multicasting works are therefore beyond the scope of this text, but the interested reader is directed to [IMR02]. Details of how local IP multicast operates are given in Chapter 9. For now, we shall discuss the format and meaning of IPv4 and IPv6 multicast addresses.

2.5.3 IPv4 Multicast Addresses

For IPv4, the class D space (224.0.0.0–239.255.255.255) has been reserved for supporting multicast. With 28 bits free, this provides for the possibility of $2^{28} =$ 268,435,456 host groups (each host group is an IP address). This address space is divided into major sections based on the way they are allocated and handled with respect to routing [IP4MA]. Those major sections are presented in Table 2-9.

The blocks of addresses up to 224.255.255.255 are allocated for the exclusive use of certain application protocols or organizations. These are allocated as the result of action by the IANA or by the IETF. The local network control block is limited to the local network of the sender; datagrams sent to those addresses are never forwarded by multicast routers. The All Hosts group (224.0.0.1) is one group in this block. The internetwork control block is similar to the local network control range but is intended for control traffic that needs to be routed off the local link. An example from this block is the *Network Time Protocol* (NTP) multicast group (224.0.1.1) [RFC5905].

The first ad hoc block was constructed to hold addresses that did not fall into either the local or internetwork control blocks. Most of the allocations in this range are for commercial services, some of which do not (or never will) require global address allocations; they may eventually be returned in favor of GLOP[2] addressing (see the next paragraphs). The SDP/SAP block contains addresses used by

---

2. GLOP is not an acronym but instead simply a name for a portion of address space.

Table 2-9   Major sections of IPv4 class D address space used for supporting multicast

Range (Inclusive)	Special Use	Reference
224.0.0.0–224.0.0.255	Local network control; not forwarded	[RFC5771]
224.0.1.0–224.0.1.255	Internetwork control; forwarded normally	[RFC5771]
224.0.2.0–224.0.255.255	Ad hoc block I	[RFC5771]
224.1.0.0–224.1.255.255	Reserved	[RFC5771]
224.2.0.0–224.2.255.255	SDP/SAP	[RFC4566]
224.3.0.0–224.4.255.255	Ad hoc block II	[RFC5771]
224.5.0.0–224.255.255.255	Reserved	[IP4MA]
225.0.0.0–231.255.255.255	Reserved	[IP4MA]
232.0.0.0–232.255.255.255	Source-specific multicast (SSM)	[RFC4607] [RFC4608]
233.0.0.0–233.251.255.255	GLOP	[RFC3180]
233.252.0.0–233.255.255.255	Ad hoc block III (233.252.0.0/24 is reserved for documentation)	[RFC5771]
234.0.0.0–234.255.255.255	Unicast-prefix-based IPv4 multicast addresses	[RFC6034]
235.0.0.0–238.255.255.255	Reserved	[IP4MA]
239.0.0.0–239.255.255.255	Administrative scope	[RFC2365]

applications such as the session directory tool (SDR) [H96] that send multicast session announcements using the *Session Announcement Protocol* (SAP) [RFC2974]. Originally a component of SAP, the newer *Session Description Protocol* (SDP) [RFC4566] is now used not only with IP multicast but also with other mechanisms to describe multimedia sessions.

The other major address blocks were created somewhat later in the evolution of IP multicast. The SSM block is used by applications employing SSM in combination with their own unicast source IP address in forming SSM channels, as described previously. In the GLOP block, multicast addresses are based on the *autonomous system* (AS) number of the host on which the application allocating the address resides. AS numbers are used by Internet-wide routing protocols among ISPs in order to aggregate routes and apply routing policies. Each such AS has a unique AS number. Originally, AS numbers were 16 bits but have now been extended to 32 bits [RFC4893]. GLOP addresses are generated by placing a 16-bit AS number in the second and third bytes of the IPv4 multicast address, leaving room for 1 byte to represent the possible multicast addresses (i.e., up to 256 addresses). Thus, it is possible to map back and forth between a 16-bit AS number and the GLOP multicast address range associated with an AS number. Although this computation is simple, several online calculators have been developed to do it, too.[3]

---

3. For example, http://gigapop.uoregon.edu/glop/.

The most recent of the IPv4 multicast address allocation mechanisms associates a number of multicast addresses with an IPv4 unicast address prefix. This is called *unicast-prefix-based* multicast addressing (UBM) and is described in [RFC6034]. It is based on a similar structure developed earlier for IPv6 that we discuss in Section 2.5.4. The UBM IPv4 address range is 234.0.0.0 through 234.255.255.255. A unicast address allocation with a /24 or shorter prefix may make use of UBM addresses. Allocations with fewer addresses (i.e., a /25 or longer prefix) must use some other mechanism. UBM addresses are constructed as a concatenation of the 234/8 prefix, the allocated unicast prefix, and the multicast group ID. Figure 2-11 shows the format.

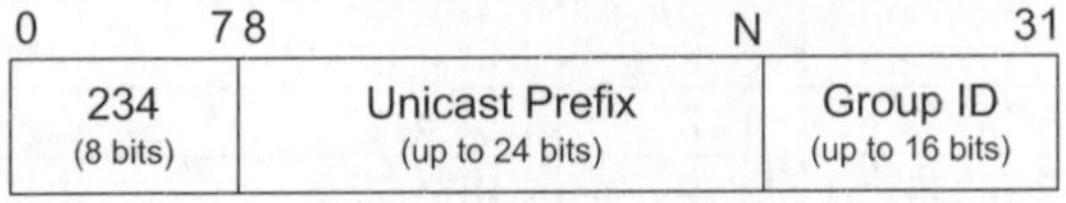

0 7 8	N 31
234 (8 bits)	Unicast Prefix (up to 24 bits)	Group ID (up to 16 bits)

Figure 2-11   The IPv4 UBM address format. For unicast address allocations of /24 or shorter, associated multicast addresses are allocated based on a concatenation of the prefix 234/8, the assigned unicast prefix, and the multicast group ID. Allocations with shorter unicast prefixes therefore contain more unicast and multicast addresses.

To determine the set of UBM addresses associated with a unicast allocation, the allocated prefix is simply prepended with the 234/8 prefix. For example, the unicast IPv4 address prefix 192.0.2.0/24 has a single associated UBM address, 234.192.0.2. It is also possible to determine the owner of a multicast address by simply "left-shifting" the multicast address by 8 bit positions. We know that the multicast address range 234.128.32.0/24 is allocated to UC Berkeley, for example, because the corresponding unicast IPv4 address space 128.32.0.0/16 (the "left-shifted" version of 234.128.32.0) is owned by UC Berkeley (as can be determined using a WHOIS query; see Section 2.6.1.1).

UBM addresses may offer advantages over the other types of multicast address allocations. For example, they do not carry the 16-bit restriction for AS numbers used by GLOP addressing. In addition, they are allocated as a consequence of already-existing unicast address space allocations. Thus, sites wishing to use multicast addresses already know which addresses they can use without further coordination. Finally, UBM addresses are allocated at a finer granularity than GLOP addresses, which correspond to AS number allocations. In today's Internet, a single AS number may be associated with multiple sites, frustrating the simple mapping between address and owner supported by UBM.

The administratively scoped address block can be used to limit the distribution of multicast traffic to a particular collection of routers and hosts. These are the multicast analogs of private unicast IP addresses. Such addresses should not be used for distributing multicast into the Internet, as most of them are blocked at enterprise boundaries. Large sites sometimes subdivide administratively scoped multicast addresses to cover specific useful scopes (e.g., work group, division, and geographical area).

2.5.4 IPv6 Multicast Addresses

For IPv6, which is considerably more aggressive in its use of multicast, the prefix ff00::/8 has been reserved for multicast addresses, and 112 bits are available for holding the group number, providing for the possibility of

$$2^{112} = 5,192,296,858,534,827,628,530,496,329,220,096$$

groups. Its general format is as shown in Figure 2-12.

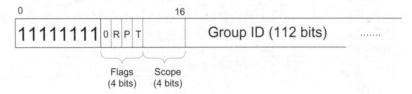

Figure 2-12   The base IPv6 multicast address format includes 4 *flag* bits (*0*, reserved; *R*, contains rendezvous point; *P*, uses unicast prefix; *T*, is transient). The 4-bit *Scope* value indicates the scope of the multicast (global, local, etc.). The *Group ID* is encoded in the low-order 112 bits. If the *P* or *R* bit is set, an alternative format is used.

The second byte of the IPv6 multicast address includes a 4-bit *Flags* field and a 4-bit *Scope ID* field in the second nibble. The *Scope* field is used to indicate a limit on the distribution of datagrams addressed to certain multicast addresses. The hexadecimal values 0, 3, and f are reserved. The hex values 6, 7, and 9 through d are unassigned. The values are given in Table 2-10, which is based on Section 2.7 of [RFC4291].

Table 2-10   Values of the IPv6 *Scope* field

Value	Scope
0	Reserved
1	Interface-/machine-local
2	Link-/subnet-local
3	Reserved
4	Admin
5	Site-local
6–7	Unassigned
8	Organizational-local
9–d	Unassigned
e	Global
f	Reserved

Many IPv6 multicast addresses allocated by the IANA for permanent use intentionally span multiple scopes. Each of these is defined with a certain offset relative to every scope (such addresses are called *scope-relative* or *variable-scope* for this reason). For example, the variable-scope multicast address ff0x::101 is reserved for NTP servers by [IP6MA]. The x indicates variable scope; Table 2-11 shows some of the addresses defined by this reservation.

Table 2-11   Example permanent variable-scope IPv6 multicast address reservations for NTP (101)

Address	Meaning
ff01::101	All NTP servers on the same machine
ff02::101	All NTP servers on the same link/subnet
ff04::101	All NTP servers within some administratively defined scope
ff05::101	All NTP servers at the same site
ff08::101	All NTP servers at the same organization
ff0e::101	All NTP servers in the Internet

In IPv6, the multicast address format given in Figure 2-12 is used when the P and R bit fields are set to 0. When P is set to 1, two alternative methods exist for multicast addresses that do not require global agreement on a per-group basis. These are described in [RFC3306] and [RFC4489]. In the first, called *unicast-prefix-based* IPv6 multicast address assignment, a unicast prefix allocation provided by an ISP or address allocation authority also effectively allocates a collection of multicast addresses, thereby limiting the amount of global coordination required for avoiding duplicates. With the second method, *link-scoped* IPv6 multicast, interface identifiers are used, and multicast addresses are based on a host's IID. To understand how these various formats work, we need to first understand the use of the bit fields in the IPv6 multicast address in more detail. They are defined in Table 2-12.

Table 2-12   IPv6 multicast address flags

Bit Field (Flag)	Meaning	Reference
R	Rendezvous point flag (0, regular; 1, RP address included)	[RFC3956]
P	Prefix flag (0, regular; 1, address based on unicast prefix)	[RFC3306]
T	Transient flag (0, permanently assigned; 1, transient)	[RFC4291]

The T bit field, when set, indicates that the included group address is temporary or dynamically allocated; it is not one of the standard addresses defined in [IP6MA]. When the P bit field is set to 1, the T bit must also be set to 1. When this happens, a special format of IPv6 multicast addresses based on unicast address prefixes is enabled, as shown in Figure 2-13.

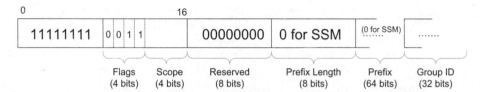

Figure 2-13   IPv6 multicast addresses can be created based upon unicast IPv6 address assignments [RFC3306]. When this is done, the *P* bit field is set to 1, and the unicast prefix is carried in the address, along with a 32-bit group ID. This form of multicast address allocation eases the need for global address allocation agreements.

We can see here how using unicast-prefix-based addressing changes the format of the multicast address to include space for a unicast prefix and its length, plus a smaller (32-bit) group ID. The purpose of this scheme is to provide a way of allocating globally unique IPv6 multicast addresses without requiring a new global mechanism for doing so. Because IPv6 unicast addresses are already allocated globally in units of prefixes (see Section 2.6), it is possible to use bits of this prefix in multicast addresses, thereby leveraging the existing method of unicast address allocation for multicast use. For example, an organization receiving a unicast prefix allocation of 3ffe:ffff:1::/48 would also consequently receive a unicast-based multicast prefix allocation of ff3x:30:3ffe:ffff:1::/96, where x is any valid scope. SSM is also supported using this format by setting the prefix length and prefix fields to 0, effectively requiring the prefix ff3x::/32 (where x is any valid scope value) for use in all such IPv6 SSM multicast addresses.

To create unique multicast addresses of link-local scope, a method based on IIDs can be used [RFC4489], which is preferred to unicast-prefix-based allocation when only link-local scope is required. In this case, another form of IPv6 multicast address structure is used (see Figure 2-14).

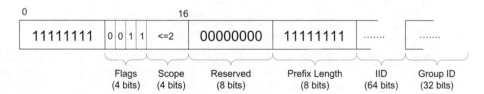

Figure 2-14   The IPv6 link-scoped multicast address format. Applicable only to link- (or smaller) scoped addresses, the multicast address can be formed by combining an IPv6 interface ID and a group ID. The mapping is straightforward, and all such addresses use prefixes of the form ff3x:0011/32, where x is the scope ID and is less than 3.

The address format shown in Figure 2-14 is very similar to the format in Figure 2-13, except that the *Prefix Length* field is set to 255, and instead of a prefix being carried in the subsequent field, an IPv6 IID is instead. The advantage of this structure over the previous one is that no prefix need be supplied in forming the multicast address. In ad hoc networks where no routers may be available, an individual machine can form unique multicast addresses based on its own IID without having to engage in a complex agreement protocol. As stated before, this format works only for link- or node-local multicast scoping, however. When larger scopes are required, either unicast-prefix-based addressing or permanent multicast addresses are used. As an example of this format, a host with IID 02-11-22-33-44-55-66-77 would use multicast addresses of the form ff3x:0011:0211:2233:4455:6677:gggg:gggg, where x is a scope value of 2 or less and gggg:gggg is the hexadecimal notation for a 32-bit multicast group ID.

The bit field we have yet to discuss is the *R* bit field. It is used when unicast-prefix-based multicast addressing is used (the *P* bit is set) along with a multicast routing protocol that requires knowledge of a rendezvous point.

Note

A *rendezvous point* (RP) is the IP address of a router set up to handle multicast routing for one or more multicast groups. RPs are used by the PIM-SM protocol [RFC4601] to help senders and receivers participating in the same multicast group to find each other. One of the problems encountered in deploying Internet-wide multicast has been locating rendezvous points. This scheme overloads the IPv6 multicast address to include an RP address. Therefore, it is simple to find an RP from a group address by just selecting the appropriate subset of bits.

When the *P* bit is set, the modified format for a multicast address shown in Figure 2-15 is used.

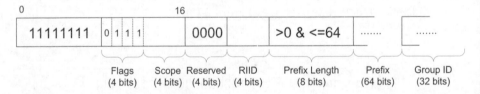

Figure 2-15   The unicast IPv6 address of an RP can be embedded inside an IPv6 multicast address [RFC3956]. Doing so makes it straightforward to find an RP associated with an address for routing purposes. An RP is used by the multicast routing system in order to coordinate multicast senders with receivers when they are not on the same subnetwork.

The format shown in Figure 2-15 is similar to the one shown in Figure 2-13, but SSM is not used (so the prefix length cannot be zero). In addition, a new 4-bit field called the *RIID* is introduced. To form the IPv6 address of an RP based on a multicast address of the form in Figure 2-15, the number of bits indicated in the *Prefix Length* field are extracted from the *Prefix* field and placed as the upper bits in a fresh IPv6 address. Then, the contents of the *RIID* field are used as the low-order 4 bits of the RP address. The rest is filled with zeros. As an example, consider a multicast address ff75:940:2001:db8:dead:beef:f00d:face. In this case, the scope is 5 (site-local), the *RIID* field has the value 9, and the prefix length is 0x40 = 64 bits. The prefix itself is therefore 2001:db8:dead:beef, so the RP address is 2001:db8:dead:beef::9. More examples are given in [RFC3956].

As with IPv4, there are a number of reserved IPv6 multicast addresses. These addresses are grouped by scope, except for the variable-scope addresses mentioned before. Table 2-13 gives a list of the major reservations from the IPv6 multicast space. Consult [IP6MA] for additional information.

Table 2-13   Reserved addresses within the IPv6 multicast address space

Address	Scope	Special Use	Reference
ff01::1	Node	All nodes	[RFC4291]
ff01::2	Node	All routers	[RFC4291]
ff01::fb	Node	mDNSv6	[IDChes]
ff02::1	Link	All nodes	[RFC4291]
ff02::2	Link	All routers	[RFC4291]
ff02::4	Link	DVMRP routers	[RFC1075]
ff02::5	Link	OSPFIGP	[RFC2328]
ff02::6	Link	OSPFIGP designated routers	[RFC2328]
ff02::9	Link	RIPng routers	[RFC2080]
ff02::a	Link	EIGRP routers	[EIGRP]
ff02::d	Link	PIM routers	[RFC5059]
ff02::16	Link	MLDv2-capable routers	[RFC3810]
ff02::6a	Link	All snoopers	[RFC4286]
ff02::6d	Link	LL-MANET-routers	[RFC5498]
ff02::fb	Link	mDNSv6	[IDChes]
ff02::1:2	Link	All DHCP agents	[RFC3315]
ff02::1:3	Link	LLMNR	[RFC4795]
ff02::1:ffxx:xxxx	Link	Solicited-node address range	[RFC4291]
ff05::2	Site	All routers	[RFC4291]
ff05::fb	Site	mDNSv6	[IDChes]
ff05::1:3	Site	All DHCP servers	[RFC3315]
ff0x::	Variable	Reserved	[RFC4291]
ff0x::fb	Variable	mDNSv6	[IDChes]
ff0x::101	Variable	NTP	[RFC5905]
ff0x::133	Variable	Aggregate Server Access Protocol	[RFC5352]
ff0x::18c	Variable	All ACs address (CAPWAP)	[RFC5415]
ff3x::/32	(Special)	SSM block	[RFC4607]

2.5.5   Anycast Addresses

An *anycast* address is a unicast IPv4 or IPv6 address that identifies a different host depending on where in the network it is used. This is accomplished by configuring Internet routers to advertise the same unicast routes from multiple locations in the Internet. Thus, an anycast address refers not to a single host in the Internet, but to the "most appropriate" or "closest" single host that is responding to the anycast address. Anycast addressing is used most frequently for finding a computer that provides a common service [RFC4786]. For example, a datagram sent to an anycast address could be used to find a DNS server (see Chapter 11), a 6to4 gateway that encapsulates IPv6 traffic in IPv4 tunnels [RFC3068], or RPs for multicast routing [RFC4610].

2.6   Allocation

IP address space is *allocated*, usually in large chunks, by a collection of hierarchically organized *authorities*. The authorities are generally organizations that allocate address space to various owners—usually ISPs or other smaller authorities. Authorities are most often involved in allocating portions of the global unicast address space, but other types of addresses (multicast and special-use) are also sometimes allocated. The authorities can make allocations to users for an undetermined amount of time, or for a limited time (e.g., for running experiments). The top of the hierarchy is the IANA [IANA], which has wide-ranging responsibility for allocating IP addresses and other types of numbers used in the Internet protocols.

2.6.1   Unicast

For unicast IPv4 and IPv6 address space, the IANA delegates much of its allocation authority to a few *regional Internet registries* (RIRs). The RIRs coordinate with each other through an organization formed in 2003 called the Number Resource Organization (NRO) [NRO]. At the time of writing (mid-2011), the set of RIRs includes those shown in Table 2-14, all of which participate in the NRO. Note in addition that, as of early 2011, all the remaining unicast IPv4 address space held by IANA for allocation had been handed over to these RIRs.

These entities typically deal with relatively large address blocks [IP4AS] [IP6AS]. They allocate address space to smaller registries operating in countries (e.g., Australia and Singapore) and to large ISPs. ISPs, in turn, provide address space to their customers and themselves. When users sign up for Internet service, they are ordinarily provided a (typically small) fraction or range of their ISP's address space in the form of an address prefix. These address ranges are owned and managed by the customer's ISP and are called *provider-aggregatable* (PA) addresses because they consist of one or more prefixes that can be aggregated with other prefixes the ISP owns. Such addresses are also sometimes called *non-portable* addresses. Switching providers typically requires customers to change the

Table 2-14   Regional Internet registries that participate in the NRO

RIR Name	Area of Responsibility	Reference
AfriNIC—African Network Information Center	Africa	http://www.afrinic.net
APNIC—Asia Pacific Network Information Center	Asia/Pacific Area	http://www.apnic.net
ARIN—American Registry for Internet Numbers	North America	http://www.arin.net
LACNIC—Regional Latin America and Caribbean IP Address Registry	Latin America and some Caribbean islands	http://lacnic.net/en/index.html
RIPE NCC—Réseaux IP Européens	Europe, Middle East, Central Asia	http://www.ripe.net

IP prefixes on all computers and routers they have that are attached to the Internet (an often unpleasant operation called *renumbering*).

An alternative type of address space is called *provider-independent* (PI) address space. Addresses allocated from PI space are allocated to the user directly and may be used with any ISP. However, because such addresses are owned by the customer, they are not numerically adjacent to the ISP's own addresses and are therefore not aggregatable. An ISP being asked to provide routing for a customer's PI addresses may require additional payment for service or simply not agree to support such a configuration. In some sense, an ISP that agrees to provide routing for a customer's PI addresses is taking on an extra cost relative to other customers by having to increase the size of its routing tables. On the other hand, many sites prefer to use PI addresses, and might be willing to pay extra for them, because it helps to avoid the need to renumber when switching ISPs (avoiding what has become known as *provider lock*).

2.6.1.1 Examples

It is possible to use the Internet WHOIS service to determine how address space has been allocated. For example, we can form a query for information about the IPv4 address 72.1.140.203 by accessing the corresponding URL http://whois.arin.net/rest/ip/72.1.140.203.txt:

```
NetRange:       72.1.140.192 - 72.1.140.223
CIDR:           72.1.140.192/27
OriginAS:
NetName:        SPEK-SEA5-PART-1
NetHandle:      NET-72-1-140-192-1
Parent:         NET-72-1-128-0-1
NetType:        Reassigned
RegDate:        2005-06-29
Updated:        2005-06-29
Ref:            http://whois.arin.net/rest/net/NET-72-1-140-192-1
```

Here we see that the address 72.1.140.203 is really part of the network called SPEK-SEA5-PART-1, which has been allocated the address range 72.1.140.192/27. Furthermore, we can see that SPEK-SEA5-PART-1's address range is a portion of the PA address space called NET-72-1-128-0-1. We can formulate a query for information about this network by visiting the URL http://whois.arin.net/rest/net/NET-72-1-128-0-1.txt:

```
NetRange:       72.1.128.0 - 72.1.191.255
CIDR:           72.1.128.0/18
OriginAS:
NetName:        SPEAKEASY-6
NetHandle.      NET-72-1-128-0-1
Parent:         NET-72-0-0-0-0
NetType:        Direct Allocation
RegDate:        2004-09-09
Updated:        2009-05-19
Ref:            http://whois.arin.net/rest/net/NET-72-1-128-0-1
```

This record indicates that the address range 72.1.128.0/18 (called by the "handle" or name NET-72-1-128-0-1) has been directly allocated out of the address range 72.0.0.0/8 managed by ARIN. More details on data formats and the various methods ARIN supports for WHOIS queries can be found at [WRWS].

We can look at a different type of result using one of the other RIRs. For example, if we search for information regarding the IPv4 address 193.5.93.80 using the Web query interface at http://www.ripe.net/whois, we obtain the following result:

```
% This is the RIPE Database query service.
% The objects are in RPSL format.
%
% The RIPE Database is subject to Terms and Conditions.
% See http://www.ripe.net/db/support/db-terms-conditions.pdf
%
% Note: This output has been filtered.
%       To receive output for a database update, use the "-B" flag.
% Information related to '193.5.88.0 - 193.5.95.255'
inetnum:        193.5.88.0 - 193.5.95.255
netname:        WIPONET
descr:          World Intellectual Property Organization
descr:          UN Specialized Agency
descr:          Geneva
country:        CH
admin-c:        AM4504-RIPE
tech-c:         AM4504-RIPE
status:         ASSIGNED PI
mnt-by:         CH-UNISOURCE-MNT
mnt-by:         DE-COLT-MNT
source:         RIPE # Filtered
```

Here, we can see that the address 193.5.93.80 is a portion of the 193.5.88.0/21 block allocated to WIPO. Note that the status of this block is ASSIGNED PI, meaning that this particular block of addresses is of the provider-independent variety. The reference to RPSL indicates that the database records are in the *Routing Policy Specification Language* [RFC2622][RFC4012], used by ISPs to express their routing policies. Such information allows network operators to configure routers to help minimize Internet routing instabilities.

2.6.2 Multicast

In IPv4 and IPv6, multicast addresses (i.e., group addresses) can be described based on their scope, the way they are determined (statically, dynamically by agreement, or algorithmically), and whether they are used for ASM or SSM. Guidelines have been constructed for allocation of these groups ([RFC5771] for IPv4; [RFC3307] for IPv6) and the overall architecture is detailed in [RFC6308]. The groups that are not of global scope (e.g., administratively scoped addresses and IPv6 link-scoped multicast addresses) can be reused in various parts of the Internet and are either configured by a network administrator out of an administratively scoped address block or selected automatically by end hosts. Globally scoped addresses that are statically allocated are generally fixed and may be hard-coded into applications. This type of address space is limited, especially in IPv4, so such addresses are really intended for uses applicable to any Internet site. Algorithmically determined globally scoped addresses can be created based on AS numbers, as in GLOP, or an associated unicast prefix allocation. Note that SSM can use globally scoped addresses (i.e., from the SSM block), administratively scoped addresses, or unicast-prefix-based IPv6 addresses where the prefix is effectively zero.

As we can see from the relatively large number of protocols and the complexity of the various multicast address formats, multicast address management is a formidable issue (not to mention global multicast routing [RFC5110]). From a typical user's point of view, multicasting is used rarely and may be of limited concern. From a programmer's point of view, it may be worthwhile to support multicast in application designs, and some insight has been provided into how to do so [RFC3170]. For network administrators faced with implementing multicast, some interaction with the service provider is likely necessary. In addition, some guidelines for multicast address allocation have been developed by vendors [CGEMA].

2.7 Unicast Address Assignment

Once a site has been allocated a range of unicast IP addresses, typically from its ISP, the site or network administrator must determine how to assign addresses in the address range to each network interface and how to set up the subnet structure. If the site has only a single physical network segment (e.g., most private homes), this process is relatively straightforward. For larger enterprises, especially those receiving service from multiple ISPs and that use multiple physical network segments distributed over a large geographical area, this process can be complicated. We shall begin to see how this works by looking at the case where a home user uses a private address range and a single IPv4 address provided by an ISP. This is a common scenario today. We then move on to provide some introductory guidance for more complicated situations.

2.7.1   Single Provider/No Network/Single Address

The simplest type of Internet service that can be obtained today is to receive a single IP address (typically IPv4 only in the United States) from an ISP to be used with a single computer. For services such as DSL, the single address might be assigned as the end of a point-to-point link and might be temporary. For example, if a user's computer connects to the Internet over DSL, it might be assigned the address 63.204.134.177 on a particular day. Any running program on the computer may send and receive Internet traffic, and any such traffic will carry the source IPv4 address 63.204.134.177. Even a host this simple has other active IP addresses as well. These include the local "loopback" address (127.0.0.1) and some multicast addresses, including, at a minimum, the All Hosts multicast address (224.0.0.1). If the host is running IPv6, at a minimum it is using the All Nodes IPv6 multicast address (ff02::1), any IPv6 addresses it has been assigned by the ISP, the IPv6 loopback address (::1), and a link-local address for each network interface configured for IPv6 use.

To see a host's active multicast addresses (groups) on Linux, we can use the `ifconfig` and `netstat` commands to see the IP addresses and groups in use:

```
Linux% ifconfig ppp0
ppp0      Link encap:Point-to-Point Protocol
          inet addr:71.141.244.213
          P-t-P:71.141.255.254  Mask:255.255.255.255
          UP POINTOPOINT RUNNING NOARP MULTICAST  MTU:1492  Metric:1
          RX packets:33134 errors:0 dropped:0 overruns:0 frame:0
          TX packets:41031 errors:0 dropped:0 overruns:0 carrier:0
          collisions:0 txqueuelen:3
          RX bytes:17748984 (16.9 MiB)  TX bytes:9272209 (8.8 MiB)


Linux% netstat -gn
IPv6/IPv4 Group Memberships
Interface       RefCnt Group
--------------- ------ --------------------
lo              1      224.0.0.1
ppp0            1      224.0.0.251
ppp0            1      224.0.0.1
lo              1      ff02::1
```

Here we see that the point-to-point link associated with the device ppp0 has been assigned the IPv4 address 71.141.244.213; no IPv6 address has been assigned. The host system does have IPv6 enabled, however, so when we inspect its group memberships we see that it is subscribed to the IPv6 All Nodes multicast group on its local loopback (lo) interface. We can also see that the IPv4 All Hosts group is in use, in addition to the mDNS (multicast DNS) service [IDChes]. The mDNS protocol uses the static IPv4 multicast address 224.0.0.251.

2.7.2 Single Provider/Single Network/Single Address

Many Internet users who own more than one computer find that having only a single computer attached to the Internet is not an ideal situation. As a result, they have home LAN or WLAN networks and use either a router or a computer acting as a router to provide connectivity to the Internet. Such configurations are very similar to the single-computer case, except the router forwards packets from the home network to the ISP and also performs NAT (see Chapter 7; also called *Internet Connection Sharing* (ICS) in Windows) by rewriting the IP addresses in packets being exchanged with the customer's ISP. From the ISP's point of view, only a single IP address has been used. Today, much of this activity is automated, so the need for manual address configuration is minimal. The routers provide automatic address assignment to the home clients using DHCP. They also handle address assignment for the link set up with the ISP if necessary. Details of DHCP operation and host configuration are given in Chapter 6.

2.7.3 Single Provider/Multiple Networks/Multiple Addresses

Many organizations find that the allocation of a single unicast address, especially if it is only temporarily assigned, is insufficient for their Internet access needs. In particular, organizations intending to run Internet servers (such as Web sites) generally wish to have an IP address that does not change over time. These sites also often have multiple LANs; some of them are internal (separated from the Internet by firewalls and NAT devices), and others may be external (providing services to the Internet). For such networks, there is typically a site or network administrator who must decide how many IP addresses the site requires, how to structure subnets at the site, and which subnets should be internal and which external. The arrangement shown in Figure 2-16 is typical for small and medium-size enterprises.

In this figure, a site has been allocated the prefix 128.32.2.64/26, providing up to 64 (minus 2) routable IPv4 addresses. The "DMZ" network ("demilitarized zone" network, outside the primary firewall; see Chapter 7) is used to attach servers that can be accessed by users on the Internet. Such computers typically provide Web access, login servers, and other services. These servers are assigned IP addresses from a small subset of the prefix range; many sites have only a few public servers. The remaining addresses from the site prefix are given to the NAT router as the basis for a "NAT pool" (see Chapter 7). This router can rewrite datagrams entering and leaving the internal network using any of the addresses in its pool. The network setup in Figure 2-16 is convenient for two primary reasons.

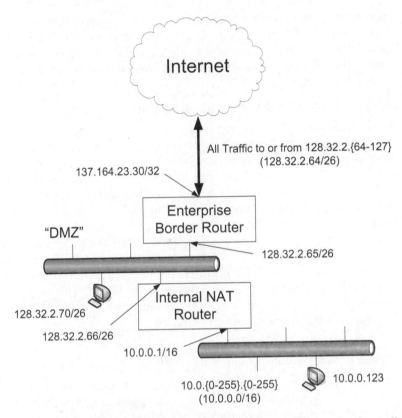

Figure 2-16 A typical small to medium-size enterprise network. The site has been allocated 64 public (routable) IPv4 addresses in the range 128.32.2.64/26. A "DMZ" network holds servers that are visible to the Internet. The internal router provides Internet access for computers internal to the enterprise using NAT.

First, the separation of the internal network from the DMZ helps protect internal computers from damage should the DMZ servers be compromised. In addition, this setup partitions the IP address assignment. Once the border router, DMZ, and internal NAT router have been set up, any address structure can be used internally, where many (private) IP addresses are available. Of course, this example is only one way of setting up small enterprise networks, and other factors such as cost might ultimately drive the way routers, networks, and IP addresses are deployed for any particular small or medium-size enterprise.

2.7.4   Multiple Providers/Multiple Networks/Multiple Addresses (Multihoming)

Some organizations that depend on Internet access for their continued operations attach to the Internet using more than one provider (called *multihoming*) in order to provide for redundancy in case of failure, or for other reasons. Because of CIDR, organizations with a single ISP tend to have PA IP addresses associated with that ISP. If they obtain a second ISP, the question arises as to what IP addresses should be used in each of the hosts. Some guidance has been developed for operating with multiple ISPs, or when transitioning from one to another (which raises some similar concerns). For IPv4, [RFC4116] discusses how either PI or PA addresses can be used for multihoming. Consider the situation shown in Figure 2-17.

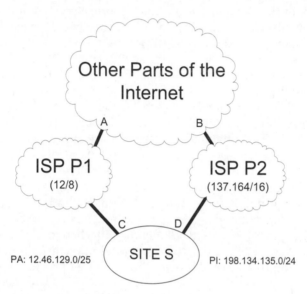

Figure 2-17 Provider-aggregatable and provider-independent IPv4 addresses used in a hypothetical multihomed enterprise. Site operators tend to prefer using PI space if it is available. ISPs prefer PA space because it promotes prefix aggregation and reduces routing table size.

Here, a (somewhat) fictitious site S has two ISPs, P1 and P2. If it uses PA address space from P1's block (12.46.129.0/25), it advertises this prefix at points C and D to P1 and P2, respectively. The prefix can be aggregated by P1 into its 12/8 block in advertisements to the rest of the Internet at point A, but P2 is not able to aggregate it at point B because it is not numerically adjacent to its own prefix (137.164/16). In addition, from the point of view of some host in the other parts of the Internet, traffic for 12.46.129.0/25 tends to go through ISP P2 rather than ISP P1 because the prefix for site S is longer ("more specific") than when it goes through P1. This is a consequence of the way the *longest matching prefix* algorithm works for Internet routing (see Chapter 5 for more details). In essence, a host in the other parts of the Internet could reach the address 12.46.129.1 via either a matching prefix 12.0.0.0/8 at point A or the prefix 12.46.129.0/25 at point B. Because each prefix matches (i.e., contains a common set of prefix bits with the destination address 12.46.129.1), the one with the larger or longer mask (larger number of matching bits) is preferred, which in this case is P2. Thus, P2 is in the position of being unable to aggregate the prefix from S and also winds up carrying most of S's traffic.

If site S decides to use PI space instead of PA space, the situation is more symmetric. However, no aggregation is possible. In this case, the PI prefix 198.134.135.0/24 is advertised to P1 and P2 at points C and D, respectively, but neither ISP is able to aggregate it because it is not numerically adjacent to either of the ISPs' address blocks. Thus, both ISPs advertise the identical prefix 198.134.135.0/24 at points A and B. In this fashion the "natural" shortest-path computations in Internet routing can take place, and site S can be reached by whichever ISP is closer to the host sending to it. In addition, if site S decides to switch ISPs, it does not have to change its assigned addresses. Unfortunately, the inability to aggregate such addresses can be a concern for future scalability of the Internet, so PI space is in relatively short supply.

Multihoming for IPv6 has been the subject of study within the IETF for some time, resulting in the *Multi6* architecture [RFC4177] and the *Shim6* protocol [RFC5533]. Multi6 outlines a number of approaches that have been proposed for handling the issue. Broadly, the options mentioned include using a routing approach equivalent to IPv4 multihoming mentioned previously, using the capabilities of *Mobile IPv6* [RFC6275], and creating a new method that splits the identification of nodes away from their locators. Today, IP addresses serve as both *identifiers* (essentially a form of name) and *locators* (an address understood by the routing system) for a network interface attached to the Internet. Providing a separation would allow the network protocol implementation to function even if the underlying IP address changes. Protocols that provide this separation are sometimes called *identifier/locator separating* or *id/loc split* protocols.

Shim6 introduces a "shim" network-layer protocol that separates the "upper-layer protocol identifier" used by the transport protocols from the IP address. Multihoming is achieved by selecting which IP address (locator) to use based on dynamic network conditions and without requiring PI address allocations. Communicating hosts (peers) agree on which locators to use and when to switch between them. Separation of identifiers from locators is the subject of several other efforts, including the experimental *Host Identity Protocol* (HIP) [RFC4423], which identifies hosts using cryptographic host identifiers. Such identifiers are effectively the public keys of public/private key pairs associated with hosts, so HIP traffic can be authenticated as having come from a particular host. Security issues are discussed in more detail in Chapter 18.

2.8   Attacks Involving IP Addresses

Given that IP addresses are essentially numbers, few network attacks involve only them. Generally, attacks can be carried out when sending "spoofed" datagrams (see Chapter 5) or with other related activities. That said, IP addresses are now being used to help identify individuals suspected of undesirable activities (e.g., copyright infringement in peer-to-peer networks or distribution of illegal materials). Doing this can be misleading for several reasons. For example, in many circumstances IP addresses are only temporary and are reassigned to different users at different times. Therefore, any errors in accurate timekeeping can easily cause databases that map IP addresses to users to be incorrect. Furthermore, access controls are not widely and securely deployed; it is often possible to attach to the Internet through some public access point or some unintentionally open wireless router in someone's home or office. In such circumstances, the unsuspecting home or business owner may be targeted based on IP address even though that person was not the originator of traffic on the network. This can also happen when compromised hosts are used to form botnets. Such collections of computers (and routers) can now be leased on what has effectively become an Internet-based black market for carrying out attacks, serving illicit content, and other misdeeds [RFC4948].

2.9 Summary

The IP address is used to identify and locate network interfaces on devices throughout the Internet system (unicast addresses). It may also be used for identifying more than one such interface (multicast, broadcast, or anycast addresses). Each interface has a minimum of one 32-bit IPv4 address (when IPv4 is being used) and usually has several 128-bit addresses if using IPv6. Unicast addresses are allocated in blocks by a hierarchically structured set of administrative entities. Prefixes allocated by such entities represent a chunk of unicast IP address space typically given to ISPs that in turn provide addresses to their users. Such prefixes are usually a subrange of the ISP's address block (called provider-aggregatable or PA addresses) but may instead be owned by the user (called provider-independent or PI addresses). Numerically adjacent address prefixes (PA addresses) can be aggregated to save routing table space and improve scalability of the Internet. This approach arose when the Internet's "classful" network structure consisting of class A, B, and C network numbers was abandoned in favor of classless inter-domain routing (CIDR). CIDR allows for different sizes of address blocks to be assigned to organizations with different needs for address space; essentially, CIDR enables more efficient allocation of address space. Anycast addresses are unicast addresses that refer to different hosts depending on where the sender is located; such addresses are often used for discovering network services that may be present in multiple locations.

    IPv6 unicast addresses differ somewhat from IPv4 addresses. Most important, IPv6 addresses have a scope concept, for both unicast and multicast addresses, that specifically indicates where an address is valid. Typical scopes include node-local, link-local, and global. Link-local addresses are often created based on a standard prefix in combination with an IID that can be based on addresses provided by lower-layer protocols (such as hardware/MAC addresses) or random values. This approach aids in autoconfiguration of IPv6 addresses.

Both IPv4 and IPv6 support addressing formats that refer to more than one network interface at a time. Broadcast and multicast addresses are supported in IPv4, but only multicast addresses are supported in IPv6. Broadcast allows for one-to-all communication, whereas multicast allows for one-to-many communication. Senders send to multicast groups (IP addresses) that act somewhat like television channels; the sender has no direct knowledge of the recipients of its traffic or how many receivers there are on a channel. Global multicast in the Internet has evolved over more than a decade and involves many protocols—some for routing, some for address allocation and coordination, and some for signaling that a host wishes to join or leave a group. There are also many types and uses of IP multicast addresses, both in IPv4 and (especially) in IPv6. Variants of the IPv6 multicast address format provide ways for allocating groups based on unicast prefixes, embedding routing information (RP addresses) in groups, and creating multicast addresses based on IIDs.

The development and deployment of CIDR was arguably the last fundamental change made to the Internet's core routing system. CIDR was successful in handling the pressure to have more flexibility in allocating address space and for promoting routing scalability through aggregation. In addition, IPv6 was pursued at the time (early 1990s) with much energy, based on the belief that a much larger number of addresses would be required soon. Unforeseen at the time, the widespread use of NAT (see Chapter 7) has since significantly delayed adoption of IPv6 by not requiring every host attached to the Internet to have a unique address. Instead, large networks using private address space are now commonplace. Ultimately, however, the number of available routable IP addresses will eventually dwindle to zero, so some change will be required. In February 2011 the last five /8 IPv4 address prefixes were allocated from the IANA, one to each of the five RIRs. On April 15, 2011, APNIC exhausted all of its allocatable prefixes. The remaining prefixes held by various RIRs are expected to remain unallocated for only a few years at most. A current snapshot of IPv4 address utilization can be found at [IP4R].

2.10 References

[CGEMA] Cisco Systems, "Guidelines for Enterprise IP Multicast Address Allocation," 2004, http://www.cisco.com/warp/public/cc/techno/tity/prodlit/ipmlt_wp.pdf

[EIGRP] B. Albrightson, J. J. Garcia-Luna-Aceves, and J. Boyle, "EIGRP—A Fast Routing Protocol Based on Distance Vectors," *Proc. Infocom*, 2004.

[EUI64] Institute for Electrical and Electronics Engineers, "Guidelines for 64-Bit Global Identifier (EUI-64) Registration Authority," Mar. 1997, http://standards.ieee.org/regauth/oui/tutorials/EUI64.html

[H96] M. Handley, "The SDR Session Directory: An Mbone Conference Scheduling and Booking System," Department of Computer Science, University College London, Apr. 1996, http://cobweb.ecn.purdue.edu/~ace/mbone/mbone/sdr/intro.html

[IANA] Internet Assigned Numbers Authority, http://www.iana.org

[IDChes] S. Cheshire and M. Krochmal, "Multicast DNS," Internet draft-cheshire-dnsext-multicastdns, work in progress, Oct. 2010.

[IDv4v6mc] S. Venaas, X. Li, and C. Bao, "Framework for IPv4/IPv6 Multicast Translation," Internet draft-venaas-behave-v4v6mc-framework, work in progress, Dec. 2010.

[IEEERA] IEEE Registration Authority, http://standards.ieee.org/regauth

[IMR02] B. Edwards, L. Giuliano, and B. Wright, *Interdomain Multicast Routing: Practical Juniper Networks and Cisco Systems Solutions* (Addison-Wesley, 2002).

[IP4AS] http://www.iana.org/assignments/ipv4-address-space

[IP4MA] http://www.iana.org/assignments/multicast-addresses

[IP4R] IPv4 Address Report, http://www.potaroo.net/tools/ipv4

[IP6AS] http://www.iana.org/assignments/ipv6-address-space

[IP6MA] http://www.iana.org/assignments/ipv6-multicast-addresses

[KK77] L. Kleinrock and F. Kamoun, "Hierarchical Routing for Large Networks, Performance Evaluation and Optimization," *Computer Networks*, 1(3), 1977.

[NRO] Number Resource Organization, http://www.nro.net

[RFC0919] J. C. Mogul, "Broadcasting Internet Datagrams," Internet RFC 0919/BCP 0005, Oct. 1984.

[RFC0922] J. C. Mogul, "Broadcasting Internet Datagrams in the Presence of Subnets," Internet RFC 0922/STD 0005, Oct. 1984.

[RFC0950] J. C. Mogul and J. Postel, "Internet Standard Subnetting Procedure," Internet RFC 0950/STD 0005, Aug. 1985.

[RFC1075] D. Waitzman, C. Partridge, and S. E. Deering, "Distance Vector Multicast Routing Protocol," Internet RFC 1075 (experimental), Nov. 1988.

[RFC1112] S. E. Deering, "Host Extensions for IP Multicasting," Internet RFC 1112/STD 0005, Aug. 1989.

[RFC1122] R. Braden, ed., "Requirements for Internet Hosts—Communication Layers," Internet RFC 1122/STD 0003, Oct. 1989.

[RFC1812] F. Baker, ed., "Requirements for IP Version 4 Routers," Internet RFC 1812/STD 0004, June 1995.

[RFC1918] Y. Rekhter, B. Moskowitz, D. Karrenberg, G. J. de Groot, and E. Lear, "Address Allocation for Private Internets," Internet RFC 1918/BCP 0005, Feb. 1996.

[RFC2080] G. Malkin and R. Minnear, "RIPng for IPv6," Internet RFC 2080, Jan. 1997.

[RFC2328] J. Moy, "OSPF Version 2," Internet RFC 2328/STD 0054, Apr. 1988.

[RFC2365] D. Meyer, "Administratively Scoped IP Multicast," Internet RFC 2365/BCP 0023, July 1998.

[RFC2544] S. Bradner and J. McQuaid, "Benchmarking Methodology for Network Interconnect Devices," Internet RFC 2544 (informational), Mar. 1999.

[RFC2622] C. Alaettinoglu, C. Villamizar, E. Gerich, D. Kessens, D. Meyer, T. Bates, D. Karrenberg, and M. Terpstra, "Routing Policy Specification Language (RPSL)," Internet RFC 2622, June 1999.

[RFC2644] D. Senie, "Changing the Default for Directed Broadcasts in Routers," Internet RFC 2644/BCP 0034, Aug. 1999.

[RFC2974] M. Handley, C. Perkins, and E. Whelan, "Session Announcement Protocol," Internet RFC 2974 (experimental), Oct. 2000.

[RFC3056] B. Carpenter and K. Moore, "Connection of IPv6 Domains via IPv4 Clouds," Internet RFC 3056, Feb. 2001.

[RFC3068] C. Huitema, "An Anycast Prefix for 6to4 Relay Routers," Internet RFC 3068, June 2001.

[RFC3170] B. Quinn and K. Almeroth, "IP Multicast Applications: Challenges and Solutions," Internet RFC 3170 (informational), Sept. 2001.

[RFC3180] D. Meyer and P. Lothberg, "GLOP Addressing in 233/8," Internet RFC 3180/BCP 0053, Sept. 2001.

[RFC3306] B. Haberman and D. Thaler, "Unicast-Prefix-Based IPv6 Multicast Addresses," Internet RFC 3306, Aug. 2002.

[RFC3307] B. Haberman, "Allocation Guidelines for IPv6 Multicast Addresses," Internet RFC 3307, Aug. 2002.

[RFC3315] R. Droms, ed., J. Bound, B. Volz, T. Lemon, C. Perkins, and M. Carney, "Dynamic Host Configuration Protocol for IPv6 (DHCPv6)," Internet RFC 3315, July 2003.

[RFC3569] S. Bhattacharyya, ed., "An Overview of Source-Specific Multicast (SSM)," Internet RFC 3569 (informational), July 2003.

[RFC3701] R. Fink and R. Hinden, "6bone (IPv6 Testing Address Allocation) Phaseout," Internet RFC 3701 (informational), Mar. 2004.

[RFC3810] R. Vida and L. Costa, eds., "Multicast Listener Discovery Version 2 (MLDv2) for IPv6," Internet RFC 3810, June 2004.

[RFC3849] G. Huston, A. Lord, and P. Smith, "IPv6 Address Prefix Reserved for Documentation," Internet RFC 3849 (informational), July 2004.

[RFC3879] C. Huitema and B. Carpenter, "Deprecating Site Local Addresses," Internet RFC 3879, Sept. 2004.

[RFC3927] S. Cheshire, B. Aboba, and E. Guttman, "Dynamic Configuration of IPv4 Link-Local Addresses," Internet RFC 3927, May 2005.

[RFC3956] P. Savola and B. Haberman, "Embedding the Rendezvous Point (RP) Address in an IPv6 Multicast Address," Internet RFC 3956, Nov. 2004.

[RFC4012] L. Blunk, J. Damas, F. Parent, and A. Robachevsky, "Routing Policy Specification Language Next Generation (RPSLng)," Internet RFC 4012, Mar. 2005.

[RFC4116] J. Abley, K. Lindqvist, E. Davies, B. Black, and V. Gill, "IPv4 Multihoming Practices and Limitations," Internet RFC 4116 (informational), July 2005.

[RFC4177] G. Huston, "Architectural Approaches to Multi-homing for IPv6," Internet RFC 4177 (informational), Sept. 2005.

[RFC4193] R. Hinden and B. Haberman, "Unique Local IPv6 Unicast Addresses," Oct. 2005.

[RFC4286] B. Haberman and J. Martin, "Multicast Router Discovery," Internet RFC 4286, Dec. 2005.

[RFC4291] R. Hinden and S. Deering, "IP Version 6 Addressing Architecture," Internet RFC 4291, Feb. 2006.

[RFC4380] C. Huitema, "Teredo: Tunneling IPv6 over UDP through Network Address Translations (NATs)," Internet RFC 4380, Feb. 2006.

[RFC4423] R. Moskowitz and P. Nikander, "Host Identity Protocol (HIP) Architecture," Internet RFC 4423 (informational), May 2006.

[RFC4489] J.-S. Park, M.-K. Shin, and H.-J. Kim, "A Method for Generating Link-Scoped IPv6 Multicast Addresses," Internet RFC 4489, Apr. 2006.

[RFC4566] M. Handley, V. Jacobson, and C. Perkins, "SDP: Session Description Protocol," Internet RFC 4566, July 2006.

[RFC4601] B. Fenner, M. Handley, H. Holbrook, and I. Kouvelas, "Protocol Independent Multicast-Sparse Mode (PIM-SM): Protocol Specification (Revised)," Internet RFC 4601, Aug. 2006.

[RFC4607] H. Holbrook and B. Cain, "Source-Specific Multicast for IP," Internet RFC 4607, Aug. 2006.

[RFC4608] D. Meyer, R. Rockell, and G. Shepherd, "Source-Specific Protocol Independent Multicast in 232/8," Internet RFC 4608/BCP 0120, Aug. 2006.

[RFC4610] D. Farinacci and Y. Cai, "Anycast-RP Using Protocol Independent Multicast (PIM)," Internet RFC 4610, Aug. 2006.

[RFC4632] V. Fuller and T. Li, "Classless Inter-domain Routing (CIDR): The Internet Address Assignment and Aggregation Plan," Internet RFC 4632/BCP 0122, Aug. 2006.

[RFC4786] J. Abley and K. Lindqvist, "Operation of Anycast Services," Internet RFC 4786/BCP 0126, Dec. 2006.

[RFC4795] B. Aboba, D. Thaler, and L. Esibov, "Link-Local Multicast Name Resolution (LLMNR)," Internet RFC 4795 (informational), Jan. 2007.

[RFC4843] P. Nikander, J. Laganier, and F. Dupont, "An IPv6 Prefix for Overlay Routable Cryptographic Hash Identifiers (ORCHID)," Internet RFC 4843 (experimental), Apr. 2007.

[RFC4893] Q. Vohra and E. Chen, "BGP Support for Four-Octet AS Number Space," Internet RFC 4893, May 2007.

[RFC4948] L. Andersson, E. Davies, and L. Zhang, eds., "Report from the IAB Workshop on Unwanted Traffic March 9–10, 2006," Internet RFC 4948 (informational), Aug. 2007.

[RFC5059] N. Bhaskar, A. Gall, J. Lingard, and S. Venaas, "Bootstrap Router (BSR) Mechanism for Protocol Independent Multicast (PIM)," Internet RFC 5059, Jan. 2008.

[RFC5110] P. Savola, "Overview of the Internet Multicast Routing Architecture," Internet RFC 5110 (informational), Jan. 2008.

[RFC5156] M. Blanchet, "Special-Use IPv6 Addresses," Internet RFC 5156 (informational), Apr. 2008.

[RFC5214] F. Templin, T. Gleeson, and D. Thaler, "Intra-Site Automatic Tunnel Addressing Protocol (ISATAP)," Internet RFC 5214 (informational), Mar. 2008.

[RFC5352] R. Stewart, Q. Xie, M. Stillman, and M. Tuexen, "Aggregate Server Access Protocol (ASAP)," Internet RFC 5352 (experimental), Sept. 2008.

[RFC5415] P. Calhoun, M. Montemurro, and D. Stanley, eds., "Control and Provisioning of Wireless Access Points (CAPWAP) Protocol Specification," Internet RFC 5415, Mar. 2009.

[RFC5498] I. Chakeres, "IANA Allocations for Mobile Ad Hoc Network (MANET) Protocols," Internet RFC 5498, Mar. 2009.

[RFC5533] E. Nordmark and M. Bagnulo, "Shim6: Level 3 Multihoming Shim Protocol for IPv6," Internet RFC 5533, June 2009.

[RFC5735] M. Cotton and L. Vegoda, "Special Use IPv4 Addresses," Internet RFC 5735/BCP 0153, Jan. 2010.

[RFC5736] G. Huston, M. Cotton, and L. Vegoda, "IANA IPv4 Special Purpose Address Registry," Internet RFC 5736 (informational), Jan. 2010.

[RFC5737] J. Arkko, M. Cotton, and L. Vegoda, "IPv4 Address Blocks Reserved for Documentation," Internet RFC 5737 (informational), Jan. 2010.

[RFC5771] M. Cotton, L. Vegoda, and D. Meyer, "IANA Guidelines for IPv4 Multicast Address Assignments," Internet RFC 5771/BCP 0051, Mar. 2010.

[RFC5952] S. Kawamura and M. Kawashima, "A Recommendation for IPv6 Address Text Representation," Internet RFC 5952, Aug. 2010.

[RFC5905] D. Mills, J. Martin, ed., J. Burbank, and W. Kasch, "Network Time Protocol Version 4: Protocol and Algorithms Specification," Internet RFC 5905, June 2010.

[RFC6034] D. Thaler, "Unicast-Prefix-Based IPv4 Multicast Addresses," Internet RFC 6034, Oct. 2010.

[RFC6052] C. Bao, C. Huitema, M. Bagnulo, M. Boucadair, and X. Li, "IPv6 Addressing of IPv4/IPv6 Translators," Internet RFC 6052, Oct. 2010.

[RFC6217] J. Arkko and M. Townsley, "IPv4 Run-Out and IPv4-IPv6 Co-Existence Scenarios," Internet RFC 6127 (experimental), May 2011.

[RFC6144] F. Baker, X. Li, C. Bao, and K. Yin, "Framework for IPv4/IPv6 Translation," Internet RFC 6144 (informational), Apr. 2011.

[RFC6164] M. Kohno, B. Nitzan, R. Bush, Y. Matsuzaki, L. Colitti, and T. Narten, "Using 127-Bit IPv6 Prefixes on Inter-Router Links," Internet RFC 6164, Apr. 2011.

[RFC6275] C. Perkins, ed., D. Johnson, and J. Arkko, "Mobility Support in IPv6," Internet RFC 3775, July 2011.

[RFC6308] P. Savola, "Overview of the Internet Multicast Addressing Architecture," Internet RFC 6308 (informational), June 2011.

[WRWS] http://www.arin.net/resources/whoisrws

3

Link Layer

3.1 Introduction

In Chapter 1, we saw that the purpose of the link layer in the TCP/IP protocol suite is to send and receive IP datagrams for the IP module. It is also used to carry a few other protocols that help support IP, such as ARP (see Chapter 4). TCP/IP supports many different link layers, depending on the type of networking hardware being used: wired LANs such as Ethernet, *metropolitan area networks* (MANs) such as cable TV and DSL connections available through service providers, and wired voice networks such as telephone lines with modems, as well as the more recent wireless networks such as Wi-Fi (wireless LAN) and various wireless data services based on cellular technlology such as HSPA, EV-DO, LTE, and WiMAX. In this chapter we shall look at some of the details involved in using the Ethernet and Wi-Fi link layers, how the *Point-to-Point Protocol* (PPP) is used, and how link-layer protocols can be carried inside other (link- or higher-layer) protocols, a technique known as tunneling. Covering the details of every link technology available today would require a separate text, so we instead focus on some of the most commonly used link-layer protocols and how they are used by TCP/IP.

Most link-layer technologies have an associated protocol format that describes how the corresponding PDUs must be constructed in order to be carried by the network hardware. When referring to link-layer PDUs, we usually use the term *frame*, so as to distinguish the PDU format from those at higher layers such as packets or segments, terms used to describe network- and transport-layer PDUs, respectively. Frame formats usually support a variable-length frame size ranging from a few bytes to a few kilobytes. The upper bound of the range is called the *maximum transmission unit* (MTU), a characteristic of the link layer that we shall encounter numerous times in the remaining chapters. Some network technologies, such as modems and serial lines, do not impose their own maximum frame size, so they can be configured by the user.

3.2   Ethernet and the IEEE 802 LAN/MAN Standards

The term *Ethernet* generally refers to a set of standards first published in 1980 and revised in 1982 by Digital Equipment Corp., Intel Corp., and Xerox Corp. The first common form of Ethernet is now sometimes called "10Mb/s Ethernet" or "shared Ethernet," and it was adopted (with minor changes) by the IEEE as standard number 802.3. Such networks were usually arranged like the network shown in Figure 3-1.

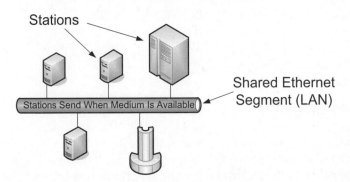

Figure 3-1 A basic shared Ethernet network consists of one or more stations (e.g., workstations, supercomputers) attached to a shared cable segment. Link-layer PDUs (frames) can be sent from one station to one or more others when the medium is determined to be free. If multiple stations send at the same time, possibly because of signal propagation delays, a collision occurs. Collisions can be detected, and they cause sending stations to wait a random amount of time before retrying. This common scheme is called carrier sense, multiple access with collision detection.

Because multiple stations share the same network, this standard includes a distributed algorithm implemented in each Ethernet network interface that controls when a station gets to send data it has. The particular method, known as *carrier sense, multiple access with collision detection* (CSMA/CD), mediates which computers can access the shared medium (cable) without any other special agreement or synchronization. This relative simplicity helped to promote the low cost and resulting popularity of Ethernet technology.

With CSMA/CD, a station (e.g., computer) first looks for a signal currently being sent on the network and sends its own frame when the network is free. This is the "carrier sense" portion of the protocol. If some other station happens to send at the same time, the resulting overlapping electrical signal is detected as a collision. In this case, each station waits a random amount of time before trying again. The amount of time is selected by drawing from a uniform probability distribution that doubles in length each time a subsequent collision is detected.

Eventually, each station gets its chance to send or times out trying after some number of attempts (16 in the case of conventional Ethernet). With CSMA/CD, only one frame is traveling on the network at any given time. Access methods such as CSMA/CD are more formally called *Media Access Control* (MAC) protocols. There are many types of MAC protocols; some are based on having each station try to use the network independently (contention-based protocols like CSMA/CD), and others are based on prearranged coordination (e.g., by allocating time slots for each station to send).

Since the development of 10Mb/s Ethernet, faster computers and infrastructure have driven the need for ever-increasing speeds in LANs. Given the popularity of Ethernet, significant innovation and effort have managed to increase its speed from 10Mb/s to 100Mb/s to 1000Mb/s to 10Gb/s, and now to even more. The 10Gb/s form is becoming popular in larger data centers and large enterprises, and speeds as high as 100Gb/s have been demonstrated. The very first (research) Ethernet ran at 3Mb/s, but the DIX (Digital, Intel, Xerox) standard ran at 10Mb/s over a shared physical cable or set of cable segments interconnected by electrical repeaters. By the early 1990s, the shared cable had largely been replaced by twisted-pair wiring (resembling telephone wires and often called "10BASE-T"). With the development of 100Mb/s (also called "fast Ethernet," the most popular version of which is known as "100BASE-TX"), contention-based MAC protocols have become less popular. Instead, the wiring between each LAN station is often not shared but instead provides a dedicated electrical path in a star topology. This can be accomplished with Ethernet *switches*, as shown in Figure 3-2.

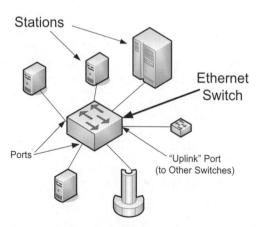

Figure 3-2   A switched Ethernet network consists of one or more stations, each of which is attached to a switch port using a dedicated wiring path. In most cases where switched Ethernet is used, the network operates in a full-duplex fashion and the CSMA/CD algorithm is not required. Switches may be cascaded to form larger Ethernet LANs by interconnecting switch ports, sometimes called "uplink" ports.

At present, switches are commonly used, providing each Ethernet station with the ability to send and receive data simultaneously (called "full-duplex Ethernet"). Although half-duplex (one direction at a time) operation is still supported even by 1000Mb/s Ethernet (1000BASE-T), it is rarely used relative to full-duplex Ethernet. We shall discuss how switches process PDUs in more detail later.

One of the most popular technologies used to access the Internet today is wireless networking, the most common for wireless local area networks (WLANs) being an IEEE standard known as Wireless Fidelity or *Wi-Fi*, and sometimes called "wireless Ethernet" or 802.11. Although this standard is distinct from the 802 wired Ethernet standards, the frame format and general interface are largely borrowed from 802.3, and all are part of the set of IEEE 802 LAN standards. Thus, most of the capabilities used by TCP/IP for Ethernet networks are also used for Wi-Fi networks. We shall explore each of these in more detail. First, however, it is useful to get a bigger picture of all of the IEEE 802 standards that are relevant for setting up home and enterprise networks. We also include references to those IEEE standards governing MAN standards, including IEEE 802.16 (WiMAX) and the standard for media-independent handoffs in cellular networks (IEEE 802.21).

3.2.1   The IEEE 802 LAN/MAN Standards

The original Ethernet frame format and operation were described by industry agreement, mentioned earlier. This format was known as the DIX format or Ethernet II format. This type of Ethernet network, with slight modification, was later standardized by the IEEE as a form of CSMA/CD network, called 802.3. In the world of IEEE standards, standards with the prefix 802 define the operations of LANs and MANs. The most popular 802 standards today include 802.3 (essentially Ethernet) and 802.11 (WLAN/Wi-Fi). These standards have evolved over time and have changed names as freestanding amendments (e.g., 802.11g) are ultimately incorporated in revised standards. Table 3-1 shows a fairly complete list of the IEEE 802 LAN and MAN standards relevant to supporting the TCP/IP protocols, as of mid-2011.

Table 3-1   LAN and MAN IEEE 802 standards relevant to the TCP/IP protocols (2011)

Name	Description	Official Reference
802.1ak	Multiple Registration Protocol (MRP)	[802.1AK-2007]
802.1AE	MAC Security (MACSec)	[802.1AE-2006]
802.1AX	Link Aggregation (formerly 802.3ad)	[802.1AX-2008]
802.1d	MAC Bridges	[802.1D-2004]
802.1p	Traffic classes/priority/QoS	[802.1D-2004]
802.1q	Virtual Bridged LANs/Corrections to MRP	[802.1Q-2005/Cor1-2008]
802.1s	Multiple Spanning Tree Protocol (MSTP)	[802.1Q-2005]

Table 3-1 LAN and MAN IEEE 802 standards relevant to the TCP/IP protocols (2011) (*continued*)

Name	Description	Official Reference
802.1w	Rapid Spanning Tree Protocol (RSTP)	[802.1D-2004]
802.1X	Port-Based Network Access Control (PNAC)	[802.1X-2010]
802.2	Logical Link Control (LLC)	[802.2-1998]
802.3	Baseline Ethernet and 10Mb/s Ethernet	[802.3-2008] (Section One)
802.3u	100Mb/s Ethernet ("Fast Ethernet")	[802.3-2008] (Section Two)
802.3x	Full-duplex operation and flow control	[802.3-2008]
802.3z/802.3ab	1000Mb/s Ethernet ("Gigabit Ethernet")	[802.3-2008] (Section Three)
802.3ae	10Gb/s Ethernet ("Ten-Gigabit Ethernet")	[802.3-2008] (Section Four)
802.3ad	Link Aggregation	[802.1AX-2008]
802.3af	Power over Ethernet (PoE) (to 15.4W)	[802.3-2008] (Section Two)
802.3ah	Access Ethernet ("Ethernet in the First Mile (EFM)")	[802.3-2008] (Section Five)
802.3as	Frame format extensions (to 2000 bytes)	[802.3-2008]
802.3at	Power over Ethernet enhancements ("PoE+", to 30W)	[802.3at-2009]
802.3ba	40/100Gb/s Ethernet	[802.3ba-2010]
802.11a	54Mb/s Wireless LAN at 5GHz	[802.11-2007]
802.11b	11Mb/s Wireless LAN at 2.4GHz	[802.11-2007]
802.11e	QoS enhancement for 802.11	[802.11-2007]
802.11g	54Mb/s Wireless LAN at 2.4GHz	[802.11-2007]
802.11h	Spectrum/power management extensions	[802.11-2007]
802.11i	Security enhancements/replaces WEP	[802.11-2007]
802.11j	4.9–5.0GHz operation in Japan	[802.11-2007]
802.11n	6.5–600Mb/s Wireless LAN at 2.4 and 5GHz using optional MIMO and 40MHz channels	[802.11n-2009]
802.11s (draft)	Mesh networking, congestion control	Under development
802.11y	54Mb/s wireless LAN at 3.7GHz (licensed)	[802.11y-2008]
802.16	Broadband Wireless Access Systems (WiMAX)	[802.16-2009]
802.16d	Fixed Wireless MAN Standard (WiMAX)	[802.16-2009]
802.16e	Fixed/Mobile Wireless MAN Standard (WiMAX)	[802.16-2009]
802.16h	Improved Coexistence Mechanisms	[802.16h-2010]
802.16j	Multihop Relays in 802.16	[802.16j-2009]
802.16k	Bridging of 802.16	[802.16k-2007]
802.21	Media Independent Handovers	[802.21-2008]

Other than the specific types of LAN networks defined by the 802.3, 802.11, and 802.16 standards, there are some related standards that apply across all of the IEEE standard LAN technologies. Common to all three of these is the 802.2 standard that defines the *Logical Link Control* (LLC) frame header common among many of the 802 networks' frame formats. In IEEE terminology, LLC and MAC are "sublayers" of the link layer, where the LLC (mostly frame format) is generally common to each type of network and the MAC layer may be somewhat different. While the original Ethernet made use of CSMA/CD, for example, WLANs often make use of CSMA/CA (CA is "collision avoidance").

Note

Unfortunately the combination of 802.2 and 802.3 defined a different frame format from Ethernet II until 802.3x finally rectified the situation. It has been incorporated into [802.3-2008]. In the TCP/IP world, the encapsulation of IP datagrams is defined in [RFC0894] and [RFC2464] for Ethernet networks, although the older LLC/SNAP encapsulation remains published as [RFC1042]. While this is no longer much of an issue, it was once a source of concern, and similar issues occasionally arise [RFC4840].

The frame format has remained essentially the same until fairly recently. To get an understanding of the details of the format and how it has evolved, we now turn our focus to these details.

3.2.2   The Ethernet Frame Format

All Ethernet (802.3) frames are based on a common format. Since its original specification, the frame format has evolved to support additional functions. Figure 3-3 shows the current layout of an Ethernet frame and how it relates to a relatively new term introduced by IEEE, the IEEE *packet* (a somewhat unfortunate term given its uses in other standards).

The Ethernet frame begins with a *Preamble* area used by the receiving interface's circuitry to determine when a frame is arriving and to determine the amount of time between encoded bits (called *clock recovery*). Because Ethernet is an asynchronous LAN (i.e., precisely synchronized clocks are not maintained in each Ethernet interface card), the space between encoded bits may differ somewhat from one interface card to the next. The preamble is a recognizable pattern (0xAA typically), which the receiver can use to "recover the clock" by the time the *start frame delimiter* (SFD) is found. The SFD has the fixed value 0xAB.

Note

The original Ethernet encoded bits using a *Manchester Phase Encoding* (MPE) with two voltage levels. With MPE, bits are encoded as voltage transitions rather than absolute values. For example, the bit 0 is encoded as a transition from -0.85 to +0.85V, and a 1 bit is encoded as a +0.85 to -0.85V transition (0V indicates that the shared wire is idle). The 10Mb/s Ethernet specification required network hardware to use an oscillator running at 20MHz, because MPE requires two clock cycles per bit. The bytes 0xAA (10101010 in binary) present in the Ethernet pre-amble would be a square wave between +0.85 and -0.85V with a frequency of 10MHz. Manchester encoding was replaced with different encodings in other Eth-ernet standards to improve efficiency.

This basic frame format includes 48-bit (6-byte) *Destination* (*DST*) and *Source* (*SRC*) *Address* fields. These addresses are sometimes known by other names such as "MAC address," "link-layer address," "802 address," "hardware address," or "physical address." The destination address in an Ethernet frame is also allowed to address more than one station (called "broadcast" or "multicast"; see Chapter 9). The broadcast capability is used by the ARP protocol (see Chapter 4) and multicast capability is used by the ICMPv6 protocol (see Chapter 8) to convert between network-layer and link-layer addresses.

Following the source address is a *Type* field that doubles as a *Length* field. Ordinarily, it identifies the type of data that follows the header. Popular values used with TCP/IP networks include IPv4 (0x0800), IPv6 (0x86DD), and ARP (0x0806). The value 0x8100 indicates a Q-tagged frame (i.e., one that can carry a "virtual LAN" or VLAN ID according to the 802.1q standard). The size of a basic Ethernet frame is 1518 bytes, but the more recent standard extended this size to 2000 bytes.

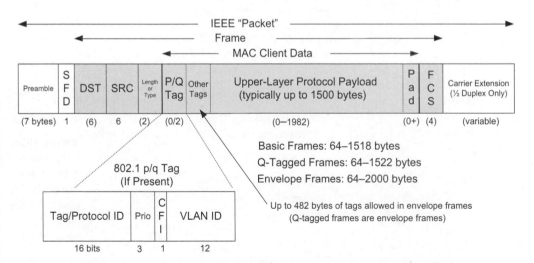

Figure 3-3   The Ethernet (IEEE 802.3) frame format contains source and destination addresses, an overloaded *Length/Type* field, a field for data, and a frame check sequence (a CRC32). Additions to the basic frame format provide for a tag containing a VLAN ID and priority information (802.1p/q) and more recently for an extensible number of tags. The preamble and SFD are used for synchronizing receivers. When half-duplex operation is used with Ethernet running at 100Mb/s or more, additional bits may be appended to short frames as a carrier extension to ensure that the collision detection circuitry operates properly.

Note

The original IEEE (802.3) specification treats the *Length/Type* field as a *Length* field instead of a *Type* field. The field is thereby *overloaded* (used for more than one purpose). The trick is to look at the value of the field. Today, if the value in the field is greater than or equal to 1536, the field must contain a type value, which is assigned by standards to have values exceeding 1536. If the value of the field is 1500 or less, the field indicates the length. The full list of types is given by [ETHERTYPES].

Following the *Destination* and *Source Address* fields, [802.3-2008] provides for a variable number of *tags* that contain various protocol fields defined by other IEEE standards. The most common of these are the tags used by 802.1p and 802.1q, which provide for virtual LANs and some *quality-of-service* (QoS) indicators. These are discussed in Section 3.2.3.

Note

The current [802.3-2008] standard incorporates the frame format modifications of 802.3 as that provides for a maximum of 482 bytes for holding "tags" to be carried with each Ethernet frame. These larger frames, called *envelope frames*, may be up to 2000 bytes in length. Frames containing 802.1p/q tags, called *Q-tagged frames*, are also envelope frames. However, not all envelope frames are necessarily Q-tagged frames.

Following the fields discussed so far is the data area or *payload* portion of the frame. This is the area where higher-layer PDUs such as IP datagrams are placed. Traditionally, the payload area for Ethernet has always been 1500 bytes, representing the MTU for Ethernet. Most systems today use the 1500-byte MTU size for Ethernet, although it is generally possible to configure a smaller value if this is desired. The payload sometimes is *padded* (appended) with 0 bytes to ensure that the overall frame meets the minimum length requirements we discuss in Section 3.2.2.2.

3.2.2.1 Frame Check Sequence/Cyclic Redundancy Check (CRC)

The final field of the Ethernet frame format follows the payload area and provides an integrity check on the frame. The *Cyclic Redundancy Check* (CRC) field at the end includes 32 bits and is sometimes known as the IEEE/ANSI standard CRC32 [802.3-2008]. To use an n-bit CRC for detection of data transmission in error, the message to be checked is first appended with n 0 bits, forming the *augmented message*. Then, the augmented message is divided (using modulo-2 division) by an (n + 1)-bit value called the *generator polynomial*, which acts as the divisor. The value placed in the CRC field of the message is the one's complement of the remainder of this division (the quotient is discarded). Generator polynomials are standardized for a number of different values of n. For Ethernet, which uses $n = 32$, the CRC32 generator polynomial is the 33-bit binary number 100000100110000010001110110 110111. To get a feeling for how the remainder is computed using long (mod-2) binary division, we can examine a simpler case using CRC4. The ITU has standardized the value 10011 for the CRC4 generator polynomial in a standard called G.704 [G704]. If we wish to send the 16-bit message 1001111000101111, we first begin with the long (mod-2) binary division shown in Figure 3-4.

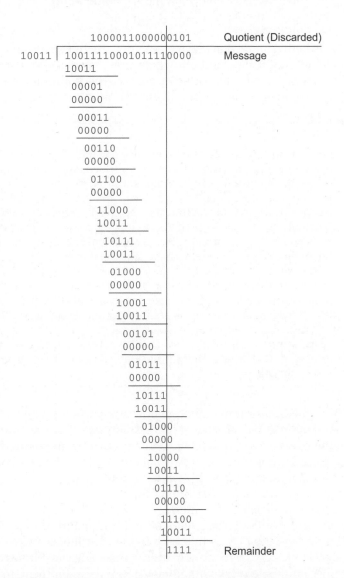

Figure 3-4   Long (mod-2) binary division demonstrating the computation of a CRC4

In this figure, we see that the remainder after division is the 4-bit value 1111. Ordinarily, the one's complement of this value (0000) would be placed in a *CRC* or *Frame Check Sequence* (*FCS*) field in the frame. Upon receipt, the receiver performs the same division and checks whether the value in the *FCS* field matches the computed remainder. If the two do not match, the frame was likely damaged in transit and is usually discarded. The CRC family of functions can be used to provide a strong indicator of corrupted messages because any change in the bit pattern is highly likely to cause a change in the remainder term.

3.2.2.2 Frame Sizes

There is both a minimum and a maximum size of Ethernet frames. The minimum is 64 bytes, requiring a minimum data area (payload) length of 48 bytes (no tags). In cases where the payload is smaller, pad bytes (value 0) are appended to the end of the payload portion to ensure that the minimum length is enforced.

Note

The minimum was important for the original 10Mb/s Ethernet using CSMA/CD. In order for a transmitting station to know which frame encountered a collision, a limit of 2500m (five 500m cable segments with four repeaters) was placed upon the length of an Ethernet network. Given that the propagation rate for electrons in copper is about .77c or 231M m/s, and given the transmission time of 64 bytes to be (64 * 8/10,000,000) = 51.2μs at 10Mb/s, a minimum-size frame could consume about 11,000m of cable. With a maximum of 2500m of cable, the maximum round-trip distance from one station to another is 5000m. The designers of Ethernet included a factor of 2 overdesign in fixing the minimum frame size, so in all compliant cases (and many noncompliant cases), the last bit of an outgoing frame would still be in the process of being transmitted after the time required for its signal to arrive at a maximally distant receiver and return. If a collision is detected, the transmitting station thus knows with certainty which frame collided—the one it is currently transmitting. In this case, the station sends a *jamming signal* (high voltage) to alert other stations, which then initiate a random binary exponential backoff procedure.

The maximum frame size of conventional Ethernet is 1518 bytes (including the 4-byte CRC and 14-byte header). This value represents a sort of trade-off: if a frame contains an error (detected on receipt by an incorrect CRC), only 1.5KB need to be retransmitted to repair the problem. On the other hand, the size limits the MTU to not more than 1500 bytes. In order to send a larger message, multiple frames are required (e.g., 64KB, a common larger size used with TCP/IP networks, would require at least 44 frames).

The unfortunate consequence of requiring multiple Ethernet frames to hold a larger upper-layer PDU is that each frame contributes a fixed overhead (14 bytes header, 4 bytes CRC). To make matters worse, Ethernet frames cannot be squished together on the network without any space between them, in order to allow the

Ethernet hardware receiver circuits to properly recover data from the network and to provide the opportunity for other stations to interleave their traffic with the existing Ethernet traffic. The Ethernet II specification, in addition to specifying a 7-byte preamble and 1-byte SFD that precedes any Ethernet frame, also specifies an *inter-packet gap* (IPG) of 12 byte times (9.6μs at 10Mb/s, 960ns at 100Mb/s, 96ns at 1000Mb/s, and 9.6ns at 10,000Mb/s). Thus, the per-frame efficiency for Ethernet II is at most 1500/(12 + 8 + 14 + 1500 + 4) = 0.975293, or about 98%. One way to improve efficiency when moving large amounts of data across an Ethernet would be to make the frame size larger. This has been accomplished using Ethernet *jumbo frames* [JF], a nonstandard extension to Ethernet (in 1000Mb/s Ethernet switches primarily) that typically allows the frame size to be as large as 9000 bytes. Some environments make use of so-called *super jumbo frames*, which are usually understood to carry more than 9000 bytes. Care should be taken when using jumbo frames, as these larger frames are not interoperable with the smaller 1518-byte frame size used by most legacy Ethernet equipment.

3.2.3   802.1p/q: Virtual LANs and QoS Tagging

With the growing use of switched Ethernet, it has become possible to interconnect every computer at a site on the same Ethernet LAN. The advantage of doing this is that any host can directly communicate with any other host, using IP and other network-layer protocols, and requiring little or no administrator configuration. In addition, broadcast and multicast traffic (see Chapter 9) is distributed to all hosts that may wish to receive it without having to set up special multicast routing protocols. While these represent some of the advantages of placing many stations on the same Ethernet, having broadcast traffic go to every computer can create an undesirable amount of network traffic when many hosts use broadcast, and there may be some security reasons to disallow complete any-to-any station communication.

To address some of these problems with running large, multiuse switched networks, IEEE extended the 802 LAN standards with a capability called *virtual LANs* (VLANs) in a standard known as 802.1q [802.1Q-2005]. Compliant Ethernet switches isolate traffic among hosts to common VLANs. Note that because of this isolation, two hosts attached to the same switch but operating on different VLANs require a router between them for traffic to flow. Combination switch/router devices have been created to address this need, and ultimately the performance of routers has been improved to match the performance of VLAN switching. Thus, the appeal of VLANs has diminished somewhat, in favor of modern high-performance routers. Nonetheless, they are still used, remain popular in some environments, and are important to understand.

Several methods are used to specify the station-to-VLAN mapping. Assigning VLANs by port is a simple and common method, whereby the switch port to which the station is attached is assigned a particular VLAN, so any station so attached becomes a member of the associated VLAN. Other options include MAC-address-based VLANs that use tables within Ethernet switches to map a station's

MAC address to a corresponding VLAN. This can become difficult to manage if stations change their MAC addresses (which they do sometimes, thanks to the behavior of some users). IP addresses can also be used as a basis for assigning VLANs.

When stations in different VLANs are attached to the same switch, the switch ensures that traffic does not leak from one VLAN to another, irrespective of the types of Ethernet interfaces being used by the stations. When multiple VLANs must span multiple switches (*trunking*), it becomes necessary to label Ethernet frames with the VLAN to which they belong before they are sent to another switch. Support for this capability uses a tag called the *VLAN tag* (or header), which holds 12 bits of *VLAN identifier* (providing for 4096 VLANs, although VLAN 0 and VLAN 4095 are reserved). It also contains 3 bits of priority for supporting QoS, defined in the 802.1p standard, as indicated in Figure 3-3. In many cases, the administrator must configure the ports of the switch to be used to send 802.1p/q frames by enabling trunking on the appropriate ports. To make this job somewhat easier, some switches support a *native VLAN* option on trunked ports, meaning that untagged frames are by default associated with the native VLAN. Trunking ports are used to interconnect VLAN-capable switches, and other ports are typically used to attach stations. Some switches also support proprietary methods for VLAN trunking (e.g., the Cisco *Inter-Switch Link* (ISL) protocol).

802.1p specifies a mechanism to express a QoS identifier on each frame. The 802.1p header includes a 3-bit-wide *Priority* field indicating a QoS level. This standard is an extension of the 802.1q VLAN standard. The two standards work together and share bits in the same header. With the 3 available bits, eight classes of service are defined. Class 0, the lowest priority, is for conventional, best-effort traffic. Class 7 is the highest priority and might be used for critical routing or network management functions. The standards specify how priorities are encoded in packets but leave the policy that governs which packets should receive which class, and the underlying mechanisms implementing prioritized services, to be defined by the implementer. Thus, the way traffic of one priority class is handled relative to another is implementation- or vendor-defined. Note that 802.1p can be used independently of VLANs if the *VLAN ID* field in the 802.1p/q header is set to 0.

The Linux command for manipulating 802.1p/q information is called vconfig. It can be used to add and remove virtual interfaces associating VLAN IDs to physical interfaces. It can also be used to set 802.1p priorities, change the way virtual interfaces are identified, and influence the mapping between packets tagged with certain VLAN IDs and how they are prioritized during protocol processing in the operating system. The following commands add a virtual interface to interface eth1 with VLAN ID 2, remove it, change the way such virtual interfaces are named, and add a new interface:

```
Linux# vconfig add eth1 2
Added VLAN with VID == 2 to IF -:eth1:-
Linux# ifconfig eth1.2
```

```
eth1.2 Link encap:Ethernet HWaddr 00:04:5A:9F:9E:80
          BROADCAST MULTICAST MTU:1500 Metric:1
          RX packets:0 errors:0 dropped:0 overruns:0 frame:0
          TX packets:0 errors:0 dropped:0 overruns:0 carrier:0
          collisions:0 txqueuelen:0
          RX bytes:0 (0.0 b) TX bytes:0 (0.0 b)
Linux# vconfig rem eth1.2
Removed VLAN -:eth1.2:-
Linux# vconfig set_name_type VLAN_PLUS_VID
Set name-type for VLAN subsystem. Should be visible in
          /proc/net/vlan/config
Linux# vconfig add eth1 2
Added VLAN with VID == 2 to IF -:eth1:-
Linux# ifconfig vlan0002
vlan0002 Link encap:Ethernet HWaddr 00:04:5A:9F:9E:80
          BROADCAST MULTICAST MTU:1500 Metric:1
          RX packets:0 errors:0 dropped:0 overruns:0 frame:0
          TX packets:0 errors:0 dropped:0 overruns:0 carrier:0
          collisions:0 txqueuelen:0
          RX bytes:0 (0.0 b) TX bytes:0 (0.0 b)
```

Here we can see that the default method of naming virtual interfaces in Linux
is based on concatenating the associated physical interface with the VLAN ID. For
example, VLAN ID 2 associated with the interface eth1 is called eth1.2. This
example also shows how an alternative naming method can be used, whereby the
VLANs are enumerated by the names vlan<n> where <n> is the identifier of the
VLAN. Once this is set up, frames sent on the VLAN device are tagged with the
VLAN ID, as expected. We can see this using Wireshark, as shown in Figure 3-5.

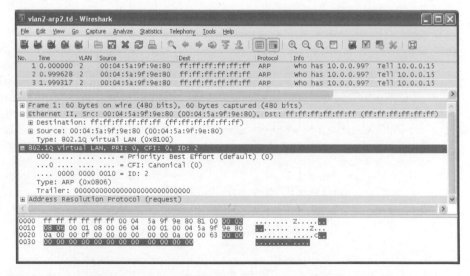

Figure 3-5   Frames tagged with the VLAN ID as shown in Wireshark. The default columns and settings have been changed to display the VLAN ID and raw Ethernet addresses.

This figure shows an ARP packet (see Chapter 4) carried on VLAN 2. We can see that the frame size is 60 bytes (not including CRC). The frame is encapsulated using the Ethernet II encapsulation with type 0x8100, indicating a VLAN. Other than the VLAN header, which indicates that this frame belongs to VLAN 2 and has priority 0, this frame is unremarkable. All the other fields are as we would expect with a regular ARP packet.

3.2.4 802.1AX: Link Aggregation (Formerly 802.3ad)

Some systems equipped with multiple network interfaces are capable of *bonding* or *link aggregation*. With link aggregation, two or more interfaces are treated as one in order to achieve greater reliability through redundancy or greater performance by splitting (striping) data across multiple interfaces. The IEEE Amendment 802.1AX [802.1AX-2008] defines the most common method for performing link aggregation and the *Link Aggregation Control Protocol* (LACP) to manage such links. LACP uses IEEE 802 frames of a particular format (called LACPDUs).

Using link aggregation on Ethernet switches that support it can be a cost-effective alternative to investing in switches with high-speed network ports. If more than one port can be aggregated to provide adequate bandwidth, higher-speed ports may not be required. Link aggregation may be supported not only on network switches but across multiple *network interface cards* (NICs) on a host computer. Often, aggregated ports must be of the same type, operating in the same mode (i.e., half- or full-duplex).

Linux has the capability to implement link aggregation (bonding) across different types of devices using the following commands:

```
Linux# modprobe bonding
Linux# ifconfig bond0 10.0.0.111 netmask 255.255.255.128
Linux# ifenslave bond0 eth0 wlan0
```

This set of commands first loads the bonding driver, which is a special type of device driver supporting link aggregation. The second command creates the bond0 interface with the IPv4 address information provided. Although providing the IP-related information is not critical for creating an aggregated interface, it is typical. Once the ifenslave command executes, the bonding device, bond0, is labeled with the MASTER flag, and the eth0 and wlan0 devices are labeled with the SLAVE flag:

```
bond0 Link encap:Ethernet HWaddr 00:11:A3:00:2C:2A
          inet addr:10.0.0.111 Bcast:10.0.0.127 Mask:255.255.255.128
          inet6 addr: fe80::211:a3ff:fe00:2c2a/64 Scope:Link
          UP BROADCAST RUNNING MASTER MULTICAST MTU:1500 Metric:1
          RX packets:2146 errors:0 dropped:0 overruns:0 frame:0
          TX packets:985 errors:0 dropped:0 overruns:0 carrier:0
          collisions:18 txqueuelen:0
          RX bytes:281939 (275.3 KiB) TX bytes:141391 (138.0 KiB)
```

```
eth0 Link encap:Ethernet HWaddr 00:11:A3:00:2C:2A
          UP BROADCAST RUNNING SLAVE MULTICAST MTU:1500 Metric:1
          RX packets:1882 errors:0 dropped:0 overruns:0 frame:0
          TX packets:961 errors:0 dropped:0 overruns:0 carrier:0
          collisions:18 txqueuelen:1000
          RX bytes:244231 (238.5 KiB) TX bytes:136561 (133.3 KiB)
          Interrupt:20 Base address:0x6c00
wlan0 Link encap:Ethernet HWaddr 00:11:A3:00:2C:2A
          UP BROADCAST SLAVE MULTICAST MTU:1500 Metric:1
          RX packets:269 errors:0 dropped:0 overruns:0 frame:0
          TX packets:24 errors:0 dropped:0 overruns:0 carrier:0
          collisions:0 txqueuelen:1000
          RX bytes:38579 (37.6 KiB) TX bytes:4830 (4.7 KiB)
```

In this example, we have bonded together a wired Ethernet interface with a Wi-Fi interface. The master device, bond0, is assigned the IPv4 address information we would typically assign to either of the individual interfaces, and it receives the first slave's MAC address by default. When IPv4 traffic is sent out of the bond0 virtual interface, there are a number of possibilities as to which of the slave interfaces will carry it. In Linux, the options are selected using arguments provided when the bonding driver is loaded. For example, a mode option determines whether round-robin delivery is used between the interfaces, one interface acts as a backup to the other, the interface is selected based on performing an XOR of the MAC source and destination addresses, frames are copied to all interfaces, 802.3ad standard link aggregation is performed, or more advance load-balancing options are used. The second mode is used for high-availability systems that can fail over to a redundant network infrastructure if one link has ceased functioning (detectable by MII monitoring; see [BOND] for more details). The third mode is intended to choose the slave interface based on the traffic flow. With enough different destinations, traffic between the two stations is pinned to one interface. This can be useful when trying to minimize reordering while also trying to load-balance traffic across multiple slave interfaces. The fourth mode is for fault tolerance. The fifth mode is for use with 802.3ad-capable switches, to enable dynamic aggregation over homogeneous links.

The LACP protocol is designed to make the job of setting up link aggregation simpler by avoiding manual configuration. Typically the LACP "actor" (client) and "partner" (server) send LACPDUs every second once enabled. LACP automatically determines which member links can be aggregated into a *link aggregation group* (LAG) and aggregates them. This is accomplished by sending a collection of information (MAC address, port priority, port number, and key) across the link. A receiving station can compare the values it sees from other ports and perform the aggregation if they match. Details of LACP are covered in [802.1AX-2008].

3.3   Full Duplex, Power Save, Autonegotiation, and 802.1X Flow Control

When Ethernet was first developed, it operated only in half-duplex mode using a shared cable. That is, data could be sent only one way at one time, so only one station was sending a frame at any given point in time. With the development of switched Ethernet, the network was no longer a single piece of shared wire, but instead many sets of links. As a result, multiple pairs of stations could exchange data simultaneously. In addition, Ethernet was modified to operate in full duplex, effectively disabling the collision detection circuitry. This also allowed the physical length of the Ethernet to be extended, because the timing constraints associated with half-duplex operation and collision detection were removed.

In Linux, the ethtool program can be used to query whether full duplex is supported and whether it is being used. This tool can also display and set many other interesting properties of an Ethernet interface:

```
Linux# ethtool eth0
Settings for eth0:
        Supported ports: [ TP MII ]
        Supported link modes: 10baseT/Half 10baseT/Full
        100baseT/Half 100baseT/Full
        Supports auto-negotiation: Yes
        Advertised link modes: 10baseT/Half 10baseT/Full
        100baseT/Half 100baseT/Full
        Advertised auto-negotiation: Yes
        Speed: 10Mb/s
        Duplex: Half
        Port: MII
        PHYAD: 24
        Transceiver: internal
        Auto-negotiation: on
        Current message level: 0x00000001 (1)
        Link detected: yes
Linux# ethtool eth1
Settings for eth1:
        Supported ports: [ TP ]
        Supported link modes: 10baseT/Half 10baseT/Full
                              100baseT/Half 100baseT/Full
                              1000baseT/Full
        Supports auto-negotiation: Yes
        Advertised link modes: 10baseT/Half 10baseT/Full
                               100baseT/Half 100baseT/Full
                               1000baseT/Full
        Advertised auto-negotiation: Yes
        Speed: 100Mb/s
        Duplex: Full
        Port: Twisted Pair
        PHYAD: 0
        Transceiver: internal
        Auto-negotiation: on
```

```
Supports Wake-on: umbg
Wake-on: g
Current message level: 0x00000007 (7)
Link detected: yes
```

In this example, the first Ethernet interface (`eth0`) is attached to a half-duplex 10Mb/s network. We can see that it is capable of *autonegotiation*, which is a mechanism originating with 802.3u to enable interfaces to exchange information such as speed and capabilities such as half- or full-duplex operation. Autonegotiation information is exchanged at the physical layer using signals sent when data is not being transmitted or received. We can see that the second Ethernet interface (`eth1`) also supports autonegotiation and has set its rate to 100Mb/s and operation mode to full duplex. The other values (`Port`, `PHYAD`, `Transceiver`) identify the physical port type, its address, and whether the physical-layer circuitry is internal or external to the NIC. The current message-level value is used to configure log messages associated with operating modes of the interface; its behavior is specific to the driver being used. We discuss the wake-on values after the following example.

In Windows, details such as these are available by navigating to Control Panel | Network Connections and then right-clicking on the interface of interest, selecting Properties, and then clicking the Configure box and selecting the Advanced tab. This brings up a menu similar to the one shown in Figure 3-6 (this particular example is from an Ethernet interface on a Windows 7 machine).

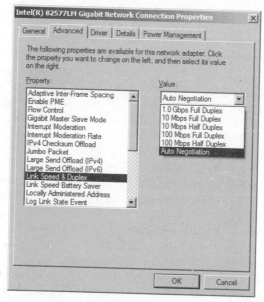

Figure 3-6   Advanced tab of network interface properties in Windows (7). This control allows the user to supply operating parameters to the network device driver.

In Figure 3-6, we can see the special features that can be configured using the adapter's device driver. For this particular adapter and driver, 802.1p/q tags can be enabled or disabled, as can flow control and wake-up capabilities (see Section 3.3.2). The speed and duplex can be set by hand, or to the more typical autonegotiation option.

3.3.1   Duplex Mismatch

Historically, there have been some interoperability problems using autonegotiation, especially when a computer and its associated switch port are configured using different duplex configurations or when autonegotiation is disabled at one end of the link but not the other. In this case, a so-called *duplex mismatch* can occur. Perhaps surprisingly, when this happens the connection does not completely fail but instead may suffer significant performance degradation. When the network has moderate to heavy traffic in both directions (e.g., during a large data transfer), a half-duplex interface can detect incoming traffic as a collision, triggering the exponential backoff function of the CSMA/CD Ethernet MAC. At the same time, the data triggering the collision is lost and may require higher-layer protocols such as TCP to retransmit. Thus, the performance degradation may be noticed only when there is sufficient traffic for the half-duplex interface to be receiving data at the same time it is sending, a situation that does not generally occur under light load. Some researchers have attempted to build analysis tools to detect this unfortunate situation [SC05].

3.3.2   Wake-on LAN (WoL), Power Saving, and Magic Packets

In both the Linux and Windows examples, we saw some indication of power management capabilities. In Windows the *Wake-Up Capabilities* and in Linux the *Wake-On* options are used to bring the network interface and/or host computer out of a lower-power (sleep) state based on the arrival of certain kinds of packets. The kinds of packets used to trigger the change to full-power state can be configured. In Linux, the Wake-On values are zero or more bits indicating whether receiving the following types of frames trigger a wake-up from a low-power state: any physical-layer (PHY) activity (p), unicast frames destined for the station (u), multicast frames (m), broadcast frames (b), ARP frames (a), magic packet frames (g), and magic packet frames including a password. These can be configured using options to ethtool. For example, the following command can be used:

```
Linux# ethtool -s eth0 wol umgb
```

This command configures the eth0 device to signal a wake-up if any of the frames corresponding to the types u, m, g, or b is received. Windows provides a similar capability, but the standard user interface allows only magic packet frames and a predefined subset of the u, m, b, and a frame types. Magic packets contain a special repeated pattern of the byte value 0xFF. Often, such frames are sent as a form of UDP packet (see Chapter 10) encapsulated in a broadcast Ethernet frame. Several tools are available to generate them, including wol [WOL]:

```
Linux# wol 00:08:74:93:C8:3C
Waking up 00:08:74:93:C8:3C...
```

The result of this command is to construct a magic packet, which we can view using Wireshark (see Figure 3-7).

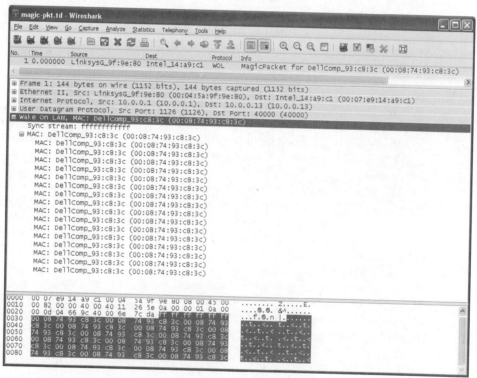

Figure 3-7 A magic packet frame in Wireshark begins with 6 0xFF bytes and then repeats the MAC address 16 times.

The packet shown in Figure 3-7 is mostly a conventional UDP packet, although the port numbers (1126 and 40000) are arbitrary. The most unusual part of the packet is the data area. It contains an initial 6 bytes with the value 0xFF. The rest of the data area includes the destination MAC address 00:08:74:93:C8:3C repeated 16 times. This data payload pattern defines the magic packet.

3.3.3   Link-Layer Flow Control

Operating an extended Ethernet LAN in full-duplex mode and across segments of different speeds may require the switches to buffer (store) frames for some period of time. This happens, for example, when multiple stations send to the same destination (called output port contention). If the aggregate traffic rate headed for a station exceeds the station's link rate, frames start to be stored in the intermediate switches. If this situation persists for a long time, frames may be dropped.

One way to mitigate this situation is to apply *flow control* to senders (i.e., slow them down). Some Ethernet switches (and interfaces) implement flow control by sending special signal frames between switches and NICs. Flow control signals to the sender that it must slow down its transmission rate, although the specification leaves the details of this to the implementation. Ethernet uses an implementation of flow control called *PAUSE messages* (also called *PAUSE frames*), specified by 802.3x [802.3-2008].

PAUSE messages are contained in MAC control frames, identified by the Ethernet *Length/Type* field having the value 0x8808 and using the MAC control opcode of 0x0001. A receiving station seeing this is advised to slow its rate. PAUSE frames are always sent to the MAC address 01:80:C2:00:00:01 and are used only on full-duplex links. They include a *hold-off* time value (specified in *quantas* equal to 512 bit times), indicating how long the sender should pause before continuing to transmit.

The MAC control frame is a frame format using the regular encapsulation from Figure 3-3, but with a 2-byte opcode immediately following the *Length/Type* field. PAUSE frames are essentially the only type of frames that uses MAC control frames. They include a 2-byte quantity encoding the hold-off time. Implementation of the "entire" MAC control layer (basically, just 802.3x flow control) is optional.

Using Ethernet-layer flow control may have a significant negative side effect, and for this reason it is typically not used. When multiple stations are sending through a switch (see the next section) that is becoming overloaded, the switch may naturally send PAUSE frames to all hosts. Unfortunately, the utilization of the switch's memory may not be symmetric with respect to the sending hosts, so some may be penalized (flow-controlled) even though they were not responsible for much of the traffic passing through the switch.

3.4   Bridges and Switches

The IEEE 802.1d standard specifies the operation of bridges, and thus switches, which are essentially high-performance bridges. A bridge or switch is used to join multiple physical link-layer networks (e.g., a pair of physical Ethernet segments) or groups of stations. The most basic setup involves connecting two switches to form an extended LAN, as shown in Figure 3-8.

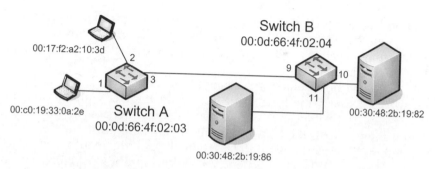

Figure 3-8 A simple extended Ethernet LAN with two switches. Each switch port has a number for reference, and each station (including each switch) has its own MAC address.

Switches A and B in the figure have been interconnected to form an extended LAN. In this particular example, client systems are connected to A and servers to B, and ports are numbered for reference. Note that every network element, including each switch, has its own MAC address. Nonlocal MAC addresses are "learned" by each bridge over time so that eventually every switch knows the port upon which every station can be reached. These lists are stored in tables (called *filtering databases*) within each switch on a per-port (and possibly per-VLAN) basis. As an example, after each switch has learned the location of every station, these databases would contain the information shown in Figure 3-9.

Station	Port
00:17:f2:a2:10:3d	2
00:c0:19:33:0a:2e	1
00:0d:66:4f:02:03	
00:0d:66:4f:02:04	3
00:30:48:2b:19:82	3
00:30:48:2b:19:86	3

Switch A's Database

Station	Port
00:17:f2:a2:10:3d	9
00:c0:19:33:0a:2e	9
00:0d:66:4f:02:03	9
00:0d:66:4f:02:04	
00:30:48:2b:19:82	10
00:30:48:2b:19:86	11

Switch B's Database

Figure 3-9 Filtering databases on switches A and B from Figure 3-8 are created over time ("learned") by observing the source address on frames seen on switch ports.

When a switch (bridge) is first turned on, its database is empty, so it does not know the location of any stations except itself. Whenever it receives a frame destined for a station other than itself, it makes a copy for each of the ports other than the one on which the frame arrived and sends a copy of the frame out of each one. If switches (bridges) never learned the location of stations, every frame would be delivered across every network segment, leading to unwanted overhead. The learning capability reduces overhead significantly and is a standard feature of switches and bridges.

Today, most operating systems support the capability to bridge between network interfaces, meaning that a standard computer with multiple interfaces can be used as a bridge. In Windows, for example, interfaces may be bridged together by navigating to the Network Connections menu from the Control Panel, highlighting the interfaces to bridge, right-clicking the mouse, and selecting Bridge Connections. When this is done, a new icon appears that represents the bridging function itself. Most of the normal network properties associated with the interfaces are gone and instead appear on the bridge device (see Figure 3-10).

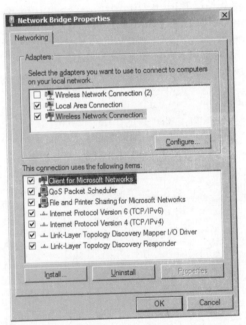

Figure 3-10   In Windows, the bridge device is created by highlighting the network interfaces to be bridged, right-clicking, and selecting the Bridge Network Interfaces function. Once the bridge is established, further modifications are made to the bridge device.

Figure 3-10 shows the Properties panels for the network bridge virtual device on Windows 7. The bridge device's properties include a list of the underlying devices being bridged and the set of services running on the bridge (e.g., the Microsoft Networks client, File and Printer Sharing, etc.). Linux works in a similar way, using command-line arguments. We use the topology shown in Figure 3-11 for this example.

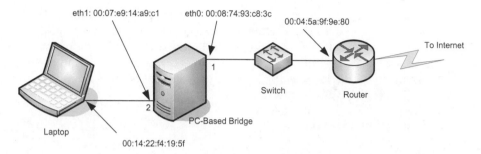

Figure 3-11 In this simple topology, a Linux-based PC is configured to operate as a bridge between the two Ethernet segments it interconnects. As a learning bridge, it accumulates tables of which port should be used to reach the various other systems on the extended LAN.

The simple network in Figure 3-11 uses a Linux-based PC with two Ethernet ports as a bridge. Attached to port 2 is a single station, and the rest of the network is attached to port 1. The following commands enable the bridge:

```
Linux# brctl addbr br0
Linux# brctl addif br0 eth0
Linux# brctl addif br0 eth1
Linux# ifconfig eth0 up
Linux# ifconfig eth1 up
Linux# ifconfig br0 up
```

This series of commands creates a bridge device br0 and adds the interfaces eth0 and eth1 to the bridge. Interfaces can be removed using the brctl delif command. Once the interfaces are established, the brctl showmacs command can be used to inspect the filter databases (called *forwarding databases* or *fdb*s in Linux terminology):

```
Linux# brctl show
bridge name bridge id           STP enabled interfaces
br0          8000.0007e914a9c1 no           eth0 eth1

Linux# brctl showmacs br0
port no mac addr is local? ageing timer
  1 00:04:5a:9f:9e:80 no 0.79
  2 00:07:e9:14:a9:c1 yes 0.00
  1 00:08:74:93:c8:3c yes 0.00
  2 00:14:22:f4:19:5f no 0.81
  1 00:17:f2:e7:6d:91 no 2.53
  1 00:90:f8:00:90:b7 no 17.13
```

The output of this command reveals one other detail about bridges. Because stations may move around, have their network cards replaced, have their MAC address changed, or other things, once the bridge discovers that a MAC address is reachable via a certain port, this information cannot be assumed to be correct forever. To deal with this issue, each time an address is learned, a timer is started (commonly defaulted to 5 minutes). In Linux, a fixed amount of time associated with the bridge is applied to each learned entry. If the address in the entry is not seen again within the specified "ageing" time, the entry is removed, as indicated here:

```
Linux# brctl setageing br0 1
Linux# brctl showmacs br0
port no mac addr is local? ageing timer
  1 00:04:5a:9f:9e:80 no 0.76
  2 00:07:e9:14:a9:c1 yes 0.00
  1 00:08:74:93:c8:3c yes 0.00
  2 00:14:22:f4:19:5f no 0.78
  1 00:17:f2:e7:6d:91 no 0.00
```

Here, we have set the ageing value unusually low for demonstration purposes. When an entry is removed because of aging, subsequent frames for the removed destination are once again sent out of every port except the receiving one (called *flooding*), and the entry is placed anew into the filtering database. The use of filtering databases and learning is really a performance optimization—if the tables are empty, the network experiences more overhead but still functions. Next we turn our attention to the case where more than two bridges are interconnected with redundant links. In this situation, flooding of frames could lead to a sort of flooding catastrophe with frames looping forever. Obviously, we require a way of dealing with this problem.

3.4.1 Spanning Tree Protocol (STP)

Bridges may operate in isolation, or in combination with other bridges. When more than two bridges are in use (or in general when switch ports are cross-connected), the possibility exists for a cascading, looping set of frames to be formed. Consider the network shown in Figure 3-12.

Assume that the switches in Figure 3-12 have just been turned on and their filtering databases are empty. When station S sends a frame, switch B replicates the frame on ports 7, 8, and 9. So far, the initial frame has been "amplified" three times. These frames are received by switches A, D, and C. Switch A produces copies of the frame on ports 2 and 3. Switches D and C produce more copies on ports 20, 22 and 13, 14, respectively. The amplification factor has grown to 6, with copies of the frames traveling in both directions among switches A, C, and D. Once these frames arrive, the forwarding databases begin to oscillate as the bridge attempts to figure out which port is really the one through which station S should be reached. Obviously, this situation is intolerable. If it were allowed to occur, bridges used in such configurations would be useless. Fortunately, there is a protocol that is used to avoid this situation called the *Spanning Tree Protocol* (STP). We describe STP in

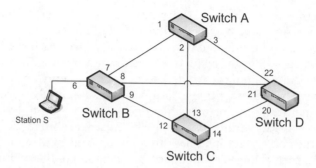

Figure 3-12 An extended Ethernet network with four switches and multiple redundant links. If simple flooding were used in forwarding frames through this network, a catastrophe would occur because of excess multiplying traffic (a so-called broadcast storm). This type of situation requires the use of the STP.

some detail to explain why some approach to duplicate suppression is needed for bridges and switches. In the current standard [802.1D-2004], conventional STP is replaced with the *Rapid Spanning Tree Protocol* (RSTP), which we describe after the conventional STP preliminaries.

STP works by disabling certain ports at each bridge so that topological loops are avoided (i.e., no duplicate paths between bridges are permitted), yet the topology is not partitioned—all stations can be reached. Mathematically, a spanning tree is a collection of all of the nodes and some of the edges of a graph such that there is a path or route from any node to any other node (*spanning* the graph), but there are no loops (the edge set forms a *tree*). There can be many spanning trees on a graph. STP finds one of them for the graph formed by bridges as nodes and links as edges. Figure 3-13 illustrates the idea.

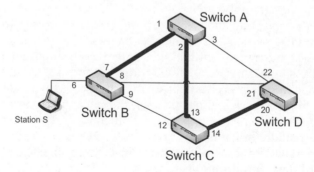

Figure 3-13 Using STP, the B-A, A-C, and C-D links have become active on the spanning tree. Ports 6, 7, 1, 2, 13, 14, and 20 are in the forwarding state; all other ports are blocked (i.e., not forwarding). This keeps frames from looping and avoids broadcast storms. If a configuration change occurs or a switch fails, the blocked ports are changed to the forwarding state and the bridges compute a new spanning tree.

In this figure, the dark lines represent the links in the network selected by STP for forwarding frames. None of the other links are used—ports 8, 9, 12, 21, 22, and 3 are *blocked*. With STP, the various problems raised earlier do not occur, as frames are created only as the result of another frame arriving. There is no amplification. Furthermore, looping is avoided because there is only one path between any two stations. The spanning tree is formed and maintained by bridges using a distributed algorithm running in each bridge.

As with forwarding databases, STP must deal with the situation where bridges are turned off and on, interface cards are replaced, or MAC addresses are changed. Clearly, such changes could affect the operation of the spanning tree, so the STP adapts to these changes. The adaptation is implemented using an exchange of special frames called *Bridge Protocol Data Units* (BPDUs). These frames are used for forming and maintaining the spanning tree. The tree is "grown" from a bridge elected by the others and known as the "root bridge."

As mentioned previously, there are many possible spanning trees for a given network. Determining which one might be the best to use for forwarding frames depends on a set of *costs* that can be associated with each link and the location of the root bridge. Costs are simply integers that are (recommended to be) inversely proportional to the link speeds. For example, a 10Mb/s link has a recommended cost of 100, and 100Mb/s and 1000Mb/s links have recommended cost values of 19 and 4, respectively. STP operates by computing least-cost paths to the root bridge using these costs. If multiple links must be traversed, the corresponding cost is simply the sum of the link costs.

3.4.1.1 Port States and Roles

To understand the basic operation of STP, we need to understand the operation of the state machine for each port at each bridge, as well as the contents of BPDUs. Each port in each bridge may be in one of five states: blocking, listening, learning, forwarding, and disabled. The relationship among them can be seen in the state transition diagram shown in Figure 3-14.

The normal transitions for ports on the spanning tree are indicated in Figure 3-14 by solid arrows, and the smaller arrows with dashed lines indicate changes due to administrative configuration. After initialization, a port enters the blocking state. In this state, it does not learn addresses, forward frames, or transmit BPDUs, but it does monitor received BPDUs in case it needs to be included in the future on a path to the root bridge, in which case the port transitions to the listening state. In the listening state, the port is now permitted to send as well as receive BPDUs but not learn addresses or forward data. After a typical forwarding delay timeout of 15s, a port enters the learning state. Here it is permitted to do all procedures except forward data. It waits another forwarding delay before entering the forwarding state and commencing to forward frames.

Related to the port state machine, each port is said to have a *role*. This terminology becomes more important with RSTP (see Section 3.4.1.6). A port may have the role of *root port*, *designated port*, *alternate port*, or *backup port*. Root ports are those

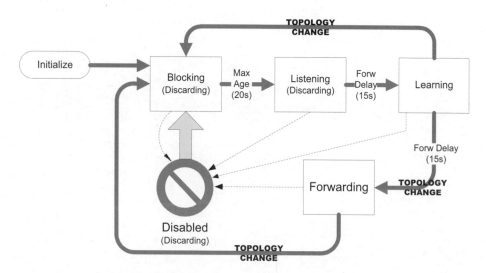

Figure 3-14 Ports transition among four major states in normal STP operation. In the blocking state, frames are not forwarded, but a topology change or timeout may cause a transition to the listening state. The forwarding state is the normal state for active switch ports carrying data traffic. The state names in parentheses indicate the port states according to the RSTP.

ports at the end of an edge on the spanning tree headed toward the root. Designated ports are ports in the forwarding state acting as the port on the least-cost path to the root from the attached segment. Alternate ports are other ports on an attached segment that could also reach the root but at higher cost. They are not in the forwarding state. A backup port is a port connected to the same segment as a designated port *on the same bridge*. Thus, backup ports could easily take over for a failing designated port without disrupting any of the rest of the spanning tree topology but do not offer an alternate path to the root should the entire bridge fail.

3.4.1.2 BPDU Structure

To determine the links in the spanning tree, STP uses BPDUs that adhere to the format shown in Figure 3-15.

The format shown in Figure 3-15 applies to both the original STP as well as the newer RSTP (see Section 3.4.1.6). BPDUs are always sent to the group address 01:80:C2:00:00:00 (see Chapter 9 for details of link-layer group and Internet multicast addressing) and are not forwarded through a bridge without modification. In the figure, the *DST, SRC*, and *L/T* (*Length/Type*) fields are part of the conventional Ethernet (802.3) header of the frame carrying the example BPDU. The 3-byte *LLC/SNAP* header is defined by 802.1 and for BPDUs is set to the constant 0x424203. Not all BPDUs are encapsulated using LLC/SNAP, but this is a common option.

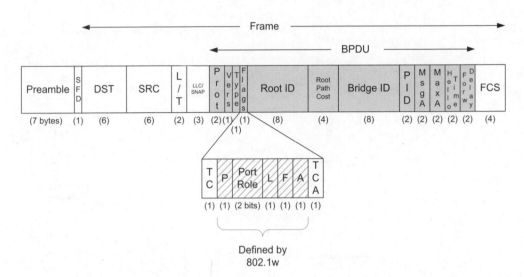

Figure 3-15 BPDUs are carried in the payload area of 802 frames and exchanged between bridges to establish the spanning tree. Important fields include the source, root node, cost to root, and topology change indication. With 802.1w and [802.1D-2004] (including Rapid STP or RSTP), additional fields indicate the state of the ports.

The *Protocol* (*Prot*) field gives the protocol ID number, set to 0. The *Version* (*Vers*) field is set to 0 or 2, depending on whether STP or RSTP is in use. The *Type* field is assigned similarly. The *Flags* field contains *Topology Change* (*TC*) and *Topology Change Acknowledgment* (*TCA*) bits, defined by the original 802.1d standard. Additional bits are defined for *Proposal* (*P*), *Port Role* (00, unknown; 01, alternate; 10, root; 11, designated), *Learning* (*L*), *Forwarding* (*F*), and *Agreement* (*A*). These are discussed in the context of RSTP in Section 3.4.1.6. The *Root ID* field gives the identifier of the root bridge in the eyes of the sender of the frame, whose MAC address is given in the *Bridge ID* field. Both of these ID fields are encoded in a special way that includes a 2-byte *Priority* field immediately preceding the MAC address. The priority values can be manipulated by management software in order to force the spanning tree to be rooted at any particular bridge (Cisco, for example, uses a default value of 0x8000 in its Catalyst switches).

The root path cost is the computed cost to reach the bridge specified in the *Root ID* field. The *PID* field is the port identifier and gives the number of the port from which the frame was sent appended to a 1-byte configurable *Priority* field (default 0x80). The *Message A* (*MsgA*) field gives the message age (see the next paragraph). The *Maximum Age* (*MaxA*) field gives the maximum age before timeout (default: 20s). The *Hello Time* field gives the time between periodic transmissions of configuration frames. The *Forward Delay* (*Forw Delay*) field gives the time spent in the learning and listening states. All of the age and time fields are given in units of 1/256s.

The *Message Age* field is not a fixed value like the other time-related fields. When the root bridge sends a BPDU, it sets this field to 0. Any bridge receiving the frame emits frames on its non-root ports with the *Message Age* field incremented by 1. In essence, the field acts as a hop count, giving the number of bridges by which the BPDU has been processed before being received. When a BPDU is received on a port, the information it contains is kept in memory and participates in the STP algorithm until it is timed out, which happens at time (*MaxA* – *MsgA*). Should this time pass on a root port without receipt of another BPDU, the root bridge is declared "dead" and the bridge starts the root bridge election process over again.

3.4.1.3 Building the Spanning Tree

The first job of STP is to elect the root bridge. The root bridge is discovered as the bridge in the network (or VLAN) with the smallest identifier (priority combined with MAC address). When a bridge initializes, it assumes itself to be the root bridge and sends configuration BPDUs with the *Root ID* field matching its own bridge ID, but if it detects a bridge with a smaller ID, it ceases sending its own frames and instead adopts the frame it received containing the smaller ID to be the basis for further BPDUs it sends. The port where the BPDU with the smaller root ID was received is then marked as the root port (i.e., the port on the path to the root bridge). The remaining ports are placed in either blocked or forwarding states.

3.4.1.4 Topology Changes

The next important job of STP is to handle topology changes. Although we could conceivably use the basic database aging mechanism described earlier to adapt to changing topologies, this is a poor approach because the aging timers can take a long time (5 minutes) to delete incorrect entries. Instead, STP incorporates a way to detect topology changes and inform the network about them quickly. In STP, a topology change occurs when a port has entered the blocking or forwarding states. When a bridge detects a connectivity change (e.g., a link goes down), the bridge notifies its parent bridges on the tree to the root by sending *topology change notification* (TCN) BPDUs out of its root port. The next bridge on the tree to the root acknowledges the TCN BPDUs to the notifying bridge and also forwards them on toward the root. Once informed of the topology change, the root bridge sets the *TC* bit field in subsequent periodic configuration messages. Such messages are relayed by every bridge in the network and are received by ports in either the blocking or forwarding states. The setting of this bit field allows bridges to reduce their aging time to that of the forward delay timer, on the order of seconds instead of the 5 minutes normally recommended for the aging time. This allows database entries that may now be incorrect to be purged and relearned more quickly, yet it also allows stations that are actively communicating to not have their entries deleted erroneously.

3.4.1.5 Example

In Linux, the bridge function disables STP by default, on the assumption that topologies are relatively simple in most cases where a regular computer is being used as a bridge. To enable STP on the example bridge we are using so far, we can do the following:

```
Linux# brctl stp br0 on
```

The consequences of executing this command can be inspected as follows:

```
Linux# brctl showstp br0

br0

  bridge id              8000.0007e914a9c1
  designated root        8000.0007e914a9c1
  root port              0              path cost             0
  max age                19.99          bridge max age        19.99
  hello time             1.99           bridge hello time     1.99
  forward delay          14.99          bridge forward delay  14.99
  ageing time            0.99
  hello timer            1.26           tcn timer             0.00
  topology change timer  3.37           gc timer              3.26

  flags                  TOPOLOGY_CHANGE TOPOLOGY_CHANGE_DETECTED

eth0 (0)
  port id                0000           state              forwarding
  designated root        8000.0007e914a9c1  path cost          100
  designated bridge      8000.0007e914a9c1  message age timer   0.00
  designated port        8001           forward delay timer 0.00

  designated cost        0              hold timer           0.26

  flags

eth1 (0)
  port id                0000           state              forwarding
  designated root        8000.0007e914a9c1  path cost          19
  designated bridge      8000.0007e914a9c1  message age timer   0.00
  designated port        8002           forward delay timer 0.00
  designated cost        0              hold timer           0.26

  flags
```

Here we can see the STP setup for a simple bridged network. The bridge device, br0, holds information for the bridge as a whole. This includes the bridge ID (8000.0007e914a9c1), derived from the smallest MAC address on the PC-based bridge (port 1) of Figure 3-11. The major configuration parameters (e.g., hello time, topology change timer, etc.) are given in seconds. The flags values indicate a recent topology change, which is expected given the fact that the network was recently connected. The rest of the output describes per-port information for eth0 (bridge port 1) and `eth0` (bridge port 2). Note that the path cost for `eth0` is about ten times greater than the cost of `eth1`. This is consistent with the observation that `eth0` is a 10Mb/s Ethernet network and `eth1` is a full-duplex 100Mb/s network.

We can use Wireshark to look at a BPDU. In Figure 3-16 we see the contents of a 52-byte BPDU. The length of 52 bytes (less than the Ethernet minimum of 64 bytes because the Linux capture facility removed the padding) is derived from the *Length/Type* field of the Ethernet header by adding 14, in this case giving the length of 52. The destination address is the group address, 01:80:C2:00:00:00, as expected. The payload length is 38 bytes, the value contained in the *Length* field. The *SNAP/LLC* field contains the constant 0x424243, and the encapsulated frame is a spanning tree (version 0) frame. The rest of the protocol fields indicate that the station 00:07:e9:14:a9:c1 believes it is the root of the spanning tree, using priority 32768 (a low priority), and the BPDU has been sent from port 2 with priority 0x80. It also indicates a maximum age of 20s, a hello time of 2s, and a forwarding delay of 15s.

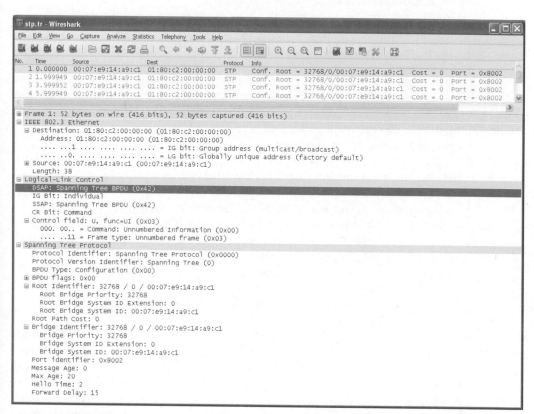

Figure 3-16   Wireshark showing a BPDU. The Ethernet destination is a group address for bridges (01:80:c2:00:00:00).

3.4.1.6 Rapid Spanning Tree Protocol (RSTP) (Formerly 802.1w)

One of the perceived problems with conventional STP is that a change in topology is detected only by the failure to receive a BPDU in a certain amount of time. If the timeout is large, the convergence time (time to reestablish data flow along the spanning tree) could be larger than desired. The IEEE 802.1w standard (now part of [802.1D-2004]) specifies enhancements to the conventional STP and adopts the new name *Rapid Spanning Tree Protocol* (RSTP). The main improvement in RSTP over STP is to monitor the status of each port and upon indication of failure to *immediately* trigger a topology change indication. In addition, RSTP uses all 6 bits in the *Flag* field of the BPDU format to support agreements between bridges that avoid some of the need for timers to initiate protocol operations. It reduces the normal STP five port states to three (discarding, learning, and forwarding, as indicated by the state names in parentheses in Figure 3-14). The discarding state in RSTP absorbs the disabled, blocking, and listening states in conventional STP. RSTP also creates a new port role called an *alternate port*, which acts as an immediate backup should a root port cease to operate.

RSTP uses only one type of BPDU, so there are no special topology change BPDUs, for example. RSTP BPDUs, as they are called, use version and type number 2 instead of 0. In RSTP, any switch detecting a topology change sends BPDUs indicating a topology change, and any switch receiving them clears its filtering databases immediately. This change can significantly affect the protocol's convergence time. Instead of waiting for the topology change to migrate to the root bridge and back followed by the forwarding delay wait time, entries are cleared immediately. Overall, convergence time can be cut from tens of seconds down to a fraction of a second in most cases.

RSTP makes a distinction between *edge ports* (those attached only to end stations) and normal spanning tree ports and also between point-to-point links and shared links. Edge ports and ports on point-to-point links do not ordinarily form loops, so they are permitted to skip the listening and learning states and move directly to the forwarding state. Of course, the assumption of being an edge port could be violated if, for example, two ports were cross-connected, but this is handled by reclassifying ports as spanning tree ports if they ever carry any form of BPDUs (simple end stations do not normally generate BPDUs). Point-to-point links are inferred from the operating mode of the interface; if the interface is running in full-duplex mode, the link is classified as a point-to-point link.

In regular STP, BPDUs are ordinarily relayed from a notifying or root bridge. In RSTP, BPDUs are sent periodically by all bridges as "keepalives" to determine if connections to neighbors are operating properly. This is what most higher-layer routing protocols do also. If a bridge fails to receive an updated BPDU within three times the hello interval, the bridge concludes that it has lost its connection with its neighbor. Note that in RSTP, topology changes are not induced as a result of edge ports being connected or disconnected as they are in regular STP. When a topology change is detected, the notifying bridge sends BPDUs with the *TC* bit field set, not only to the root but also to all other bridges. Doing so allows the entire network to be notified of the topology change much faster than with conventional STP. When a bridge receives these messages, it flushes all table entries except those associated with edge ports and restarts the learning process.

Many of RSTP's features were developed by Cisco Systems and other companies that had for some time provided proprietary enhancements to regular STP in their products. The IEEE committee incorporated many of these enhancements into the updated 802.1d standard, which covers both types of STP, so extended LANs can run regular STP on some segments and RSTP on others (although the RSTP benefits are lost). RSTP has been extended to include VLANs [802.1Q-2005]—a protocol called the *Multiple Spanning Tree Protocol* (MSTP). This protocol retains the RSTP (and hence STP) BPDU format, so backward compatibility is possible, but it also supports the formation of multiple spanning trees (one for each VLAN).

3.4.2 802.1ak: Multiple Registration Protocol (MRP)

The *Multiple Registration Protocol* (MRP) provides a general method for registering attributes among stations in a bridged LAN environment. [802.1ak-2007] defines two particular "applications" of MRP called MVRP (for registering VLANs) and MMRP (for registering group MAC addresses). MRP replaces the earlier GARP framework; MVRP and MMRP replace the older GVRP and GMRP protocols, respectively. All were originally defined by 802.1q.

With MVRP, once an end station is configured as a member of a VLAN, this information is communicated to its attached switch, which in turn propagates the fact of the station's participation in the VLAN to other switches. This allows switches to augment their filtering tables based on station VLAN IDs and allows changes of VLAN topology without necessarily triggering a recalculation of the existing spanning tree via STP. Avoiding STP recalculation was one of the reasons for migrating from GVRP to MVRP.

MMRP is a method for stations to register their interest in group MAC addresses (multicast addresses). This information may be used by switches to establish the ports through which multicast traffic must be delivered. Without such a facility, switches would have to broadcast all multicast traffic, potentially leading to unwanted overhead. MMRP is a layer 2 protocol with similarities to IGMP and MLD, layer 3 protocols, and the "IGMP/MLD snooping" capability supported in many switches. We discuss IGMP, MLD and snooping in Chapter 9.

3.5 Wireless LANs—IEEE 802.11(Wi-Fi)

One of the most popular technologies being used to access the Internet today is *wireless fidelity* (Wi-Fi), also known by its IEEE standard name 802.11, effectively a wireless version of Ethernet. Wi-Fi has developed to become an inexpensive, highly convenient way to provide connectivity and performance levels acceptable for most applications. Wi-Fi networks are easy to set up, and most portable computers and smartphones now include the necessary hardware to access Wi-Fi infrastructure. Many coffee shops, airports, hotels, and other facilities include Wi-Fi "hot spots," and Wi-Fi is even seeing considerable advancement in developing countries where other infrastructure may be difficult to obtain. The architecture of an IEEE 802.11 network is shown in Figure 3-17.

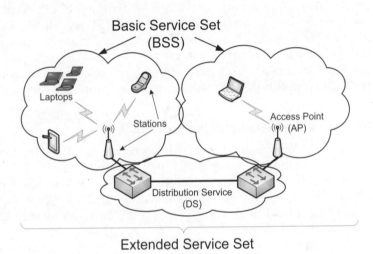

Figure 3-17   The IEEE 802.11 terminology for a wireless LAN. Access points (APs) can be connected using a distribution service (DS, a wireless or wired backbone) to form an extended WLAN (called an ESS). Stations include both APs and mobile devices communicating together that form a basic service set (BSS). Typically, an ESS has an assigned ESSID that functions as a name for the network.

The network in Figure 3-17 includes a number of *stations* (STAs). Typically stations are organized with a subset operating also as *access points* (APs). An AP and its associated stations are called a *basic service set* (BSS). The APs are generally connected to each other using a wired *distribution service* (called a DS, basically a "backbone"), forming an *extended service set* (ESS). This setup is commonly termed *infrastructure mode*. The 802.11 standard also provides for an *ad hoc mode*. In this configuration there is no AP or DS; instead, direct station-to-station (peer-to-peer) communication takes place. In IEEE terminology, the STAs participating in an ad hoc network form an *independent basic service set* (IBSS). A WLAN formed from a collection of BSSs and/or IBSSs is called a *service set*, identified by a *service set identifier* (SSID). An *extended service set identifier* (ESSID) is an SSID that names a collection of connected BSSs and is essentially a name for the LAN that can be up to 32 characters long. Such names are ordinarily assigned to Wi-Fi APs when a WLAN is first installed.

3.5.1   802.11 Frames

There is one common overall frame format for 802.11 networks but multiple types of frames. Not all the fields are present in every type of frame. Figure 3-18 shows the format of the common frame and a (maximal-size) data frame.

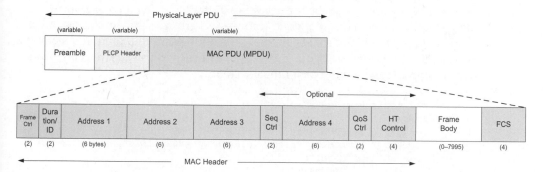

Figure 3-18   The 802.11 basic data frame format (as of [802.11n-2009]). The MPDU format resembles that of Ethernet but has additional fields depending on the type of DS being used among access points, whether the frame is headed to the DS or from it, and if frames are being aggregated. The *QoS Control* field is used for special performance features, and the *HT Control* field is used for control of 802.11n's "high-throughput" features.

The frame shown in Figure 3-18 includes a preamble for synchronization, which depends on the particular variant of 802.11 being used. Next, the *Physical Layer Convergence Procedure* (PLCP) header provides information about the specific physical layer in a somewhat PHY-independent way. The PLCP portion of the frame is generally transmitted at a lower data rate than the rest of the frame. This serves two purposes: to improve the probability of correct delivery (lower speeds tend to have better error resistance) and to provide compatibility with and protection from interference from legacy equipment that may operate in the same area at slower rates. The *MAC PDU* (MPDU) corresponds to a frame similar to Ethernet, but with some additional fields.

At the head of the MPDU is the *Frame Control Word*, which includes a 2-bit *Type* field identifying the frame type. There are three types of frames: *management frames*, *control frames*, and *data frames*. Each of these can have various subtypes, depending on the type. The full table of types and subtypes is given in [802.11n-2009, Table 7-1]. The contents of the remaining fields, if present, are determined by the frame type, which we discuss individually.

3.5.1.1 Management Frames

Management frames are used for creating, maintaining, and ending associations between stations and access points. They are also used to determine whether encryption is being used, what the name (SSID or ESSID) of the network is, what transmission rates are supported, and a common time base. These frames are used to provide the information necessary when a Wi-Fi interface "scans" for nearby access points.

Scanning is the procedure by which a station discovers available networks and related configuration information. This involves switching to each available frequency and passively listening for traffic to identify available access points. Stations may also actively probe for networks by transmitting a particular management frame ("probe request") while scanning. There are some limitations on such probe requests to ensure that 802.11 traffic is not transmitted on a frequency that is being used for non-802.11 purposes (e.g., medical services). Here is an example of initiating a scan by hand on a Linux system:

```
Linux# iwlist wlan0 scan
wlan0 Scan completed :
          Cell 01 - Address: 00:02:6F:20:B5:84
                    ESSID:"Grizzly-5354-Aries-802.11b/g"
                    Mode:Master
                    Channel:4
                     Frequency:2.427 GHz (Channel 4)
                    Quality=5/100 Signal level=47/100
                    Encryption key:on
                    IE: WPA Version 1
                        Group Cipher : TKIP
                        Pairwise Ciphers (2) : CCMP TKIP
                        Authentication Suites (1) : PSK
                    Bit Rates:1 Mb/s; 2 Mb/s; 5.5 Mb/s; 11 Mb/s;
                          6 Mb/s; 12 Mb/s; 24 Mb/s; 36 Mb/s; 9 Mb/s;
                          18 Mb/s; 48 Mb/s; 54 Mb/s
                    Extra:tsf=0000009d832ff037
```

Here we see the result of a hand-initiated scan using wireless interface wlan0. An AP with MAC address 00:02:6F:20:B5:84 is acting as a master (i.e., is acting as an AP in infrastructure mode). It is broadcasting the ESSID "Grizzly-5354-Aries-802.11b/g" on channel 4 (2.427GHz). (See Section 3.5.4 on channels and frequencies for more details on channel selection.) The quality and signal level give indications of how well the scanning station is receiving a signal from the AP, although the meaning of these values varies among manufacturers. WPA encryption is being used on this link (see Section 3.5.5), and bit rates from 1Mb/s to 54Mb/s are available. The tsf (*time sync function*) value indicates the AP's notion of time, which is used for synchronizing various features such as power-saving mode (see Section 3.5.2).

When an AP broadcasts its SSID, any station may attempt to establish an association with the AP. When an association is established, most Wi-Fi networks today also set up the necessary configuration information to provide Internet access to the station (see Chapter 6). However, an AP's operator may wish to control which stations make use of the network. Some operators intentionally make this more difficult by having the AP not broadcast its SSID, as a security measure.

This approach provides little security, as the SSID may be guessed. More robust security is provided by link encryption and passwords, which we discuss in Section 3.5.5.

3.5.1.2 Control Frames: RTS/CTS and ACKs

Control frames are used to handle a form of flow control as well as acknowledgments for frames. Flow control helps ensure that a receiver can slow down a sender that is too fast. Acknowledgments help a sender know what frames have been received correctly. These concepts also apply to TCP at the transport layer (see Chapter 15). 802.11 networks support optional *request-to-send* (RTS)/*clear-to-send* (CTS) moderation of transmission for flow control. When these are enabled, prior to sending a data frame a station transmits an RTS frame, and when the recipient is willing to receive additional traffic, it responds with a CTS. After the RTS/CTS exchange, the station has a window of time (identified in the CTS frame) to transmit data frames that are acknowledged when successfully received. Such transmission coordination schemes are common in wireless networks and mimic the flow control signaling that has been used on wired serial lines for years (sometimes called hardware flow control).

The RTS/CTS exchange helps to avoid the *hidden terminal problem* by instructing each station when it is permitted to transmit, so as to avoid simultaneous transmissions from stations that cannot hear each other. Because RTS and CTS frames are short, they do not use the channel for long. An AP generally initiates an RTS/CTS exchange for a packet if the size of the packet is large enough. Typically, an AP has a configuration option called the *packet size threshold* (or similar). Frames larger than the threshold cause an RTS to be sent prior to transmission of the data. Most vendors use a default setting for this value of approximately 500 bytes if RTS/CTS exchanges are desired. In Linux, the RTS/CTS threshold can be set in the following way:

```
Linux# iwconfig wlan0 rts 250
wlan0 IEEE 802.11g ESSID:"Grizzly-5354-Aries-802.11b/g"
        Mode:Managed
        Frequency:2.427 GH
        Access Point: 00:02:6F:20:B5:84
        Bit Rate=24 Mb/s Tx-Power=0 dBm
        Retry min limit:7 RTS thr=250 B Fragment thr=2346 B
        Encryption key:xxxx- ... -xxxx [3]
        Link Quality=100/100 Signal level=46/100
        Rx invalid nwid:0 Rx invalid crypt:0 Rx invalid frag:0
        Tx excessive retries:0 Invalid misc:0 Missed beacon:0
```

The iwconfig command can be used to set many variables, including the RTS and fragmentation thresholds (see Section 3.5.1.3). It can also be used to determine statistics such as the number of frame errors due to wrong network ID (ESSID) or wrong encryption key. It also gives the number of excessive retries (i.e., the number of retransmission attempts), a rough indicator of the reliability of the link that is popular for guiding routing decisions in wireless networks [ETX]. In WLANs with limited coverage, where hidden terminal problems are unlikely to occur, it may be preferable to disable RTS/CTS by adjusting the stations' RTS thresholds to be a high value (1500 or larger). This avoids the overhead imposed by requiring RTS/CTS exchanges for each packet.

In wired Ethernet networks, the absence of a collision indicates that a frame has been received correctly with high probability. In wireless networks, there is a wider range of reasons a frame may not be delivered correctly, such as insufficient signal or interference. To help address this potential problem, 802.11 extends the 802.3 retransmission scheme with a retransmission/acknowledgment (ACK) scheme. An acknowledgment is expected to be received within a certain amount of time for each unicast frame sent (802.11a/b/g) or each group of frames sent (802.11n or 802.11e with "block ACKs"). Multicast and broadcast frames do not have associated ACKs to avoid "ACK implosion" (see Chapter 9). Failure to receive an ACK within the specified time results in retransmission of the frame(s).

With retransmissions, it is possible to have duplicate frames formed within the network. The *Retry* bit field in the *Frame Control Word* is set when any frame represents a retransmission of a previously transmitted frame. A receiving station can use this to help eliminate duplicate frames. Stations are expected to keep a small cache of entries indicating addresses and sequence/fragment numbers seen recently. When a received frame matches an entry, the frame is discarded.

The amount of time necessary to send a frame and receive an ACK for it relates to the distance of the link and the *slot time* (a basic unit of time related to the 802.11 MAC protocol; see Section 3.5.3). The time to wait for an ACK (as well as the slot time) can be configured in most systems, although the method for doing so varies. In most cases such as home or office use, the default values are adequate. When using Wi-Fi over long distances, these values may require adjusting (see, for example, [MWLD]).

3.5.1.3 Data Frames, Fragmentation, and Aggregation

Most frames seen on a busy network are data frames, which do what one would expect—carry data. Typically, there is a one-to-one relationship between 802.11 frames and the link-layer (LLC) frames made available to higher-layer protocols such as IP. However, 802.11 supports frame *fragmentation*, which can divide frames into multiple fragments. With the 802.11n specification, it also supports frame *aggregation*, which can be used to send multiple frames together with less overhead.

When fragmentation is used, each fragment has its own MAC header and trailing CRC and is handled independently of other fragments. For example, fragments to different destinations can be interleaved. Fragmentation can help improve performance when the channel has significant interference. Unless block ACKs are used, each fragment is sent individually, producing one ACK per fragment by the receiver. Because fragments are smaller than full-size frames, if a retransmission needs to be invoked, a smaller amount of data will need to be repaired.

Fragmentation is applied only to frames with a unicast (non-broadcast or multicast) destination address. To enable this capability, the *Sequence Control* field contains a *fragment number* (4 bits) and a *sequence number* (12 bits). If a frame is fragmented, all fragments contain a common sequence number value, and each adjacent fragment has a fragment number differing by 1. A total of 15 fragments for the same frame is possible, given the 4-bit-wide field. The *More Frag* field in the *Frame Control Word* indicates that further fragments are yet to come. Terminal fragments have this bit set to 0. A destination *defragments* the original frame from fragments it receives by assembling the fragments in order based on fragment number order within the frame sequence number. Provided that all fragments constituting a sequence number have been received and the last fragment has a *More Frag* field of 0, the frame is reconstructed and passed to higher-layer protocols for processing.

Fragmentation is not often used because it does require some tuning. If used without tuning, it can worsen performance slightly. When smaller frames are used, the chance of having a bit error (see the next paragraph) can be reduced. The fragment size can usually be set from 256 bytes to 2KB as a threshold (only those frames that exceed the threshold in size are fragmented). Many APs default to not using fragmentation by setting the threshold high (such as 2437 bytes on a Linksys-brand AP).

The reason fragmentation can be useful is a fairly simple exercise in probability. If the bit error rate (BER) is P, the probability of a bit being successfully delivered is $(1 - P)$ and the probability that N bits are successfully delivered is $(1 - P)^N$. As N grows, this value shrinks. Thus, if we can shorten a frame, we can in principle improve its error-free delivery probability. Of course, if we divide a frame of size N bits into K fragments, we have to send at least $\lceil N/K \rceil$ fragments. As a concrete example, assume that we wish to send a 1500-byte (12,000-bit) frame. If we assume $P = 10^{-4}$ (a relatively high BER), the probability of successful delivery without fragmentation would be $(1 - 10^{-4})^{12,000} = .301$. So we have only about a 30% chance of such a frame being delivered without errors the first time, and on average we would have to send the frame three or four times for it to be received successfully.

If we use fragmentation for the same example and set the fragmentation threshold to 500, we produce three fragments of about 4000 bits each. The probability of one such fragment being delivered without error is about $(1 - 10^{-4})^{4000} = .670$. Thus, each fragment has about a 67% chance of being delivered successfully. Of course, we have to have three of them delivered successfully to reconstruct the whole frame. The probabilities of 3, 2, 1, and 0 fragments being delivered successfully are $(.67)^3 = 0.30$, $3(.67)^2(.33) = 0.44$, $3(0.67)(.33)^2 = .22$, and $(.33)^3 = .04$, respectively. So, although the chances that all three are delivered successfully without retries are about the same as for the nonfragmented frame being delivered successfully, the chances that two or three fragments are delivered successfully are fairly good. If this should happen, at most a single fragment would have to be retransmitted, which would take significantly less time (about a third) than sending the original 1500-byte unfragmented frame. Of course, each fragment consumes some overhead, so if the BER is effectively 0, fragmentation only decreases performance by creating more frames to handle.

One of the enhancements provided by 802.11n is the support of frame aggregation, in two forms. One form, called the *aggregated MAC service data unit* (A-MSDU), allows for multiple complete 802.3 (Ethernet) frames to be aggregated within an 802.11 frame. The other form, called the *aggregated MAC protocol data unit* (A-MPDU), allows multiple MPDUs with the same source, destination, and QoS settings to be aggregated by being sent in short succession. The two aggregation types are depicted in Figure 3-19.

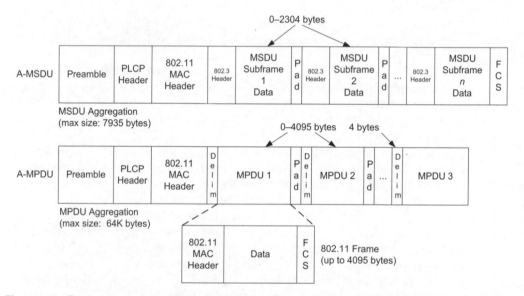

Figure 3-19 Frame aggregation in 802.11n includes A-MSDU and A-MPDU. A-MSDU aggregates frames using a single FCS. A-MPDU aggregation uses a 4-byte delimiter between each aggregated 802.11 frame. Each A-MPDU subframe has its own FCS and can be individually acknowledged using block ACKs and retransmitted if necessary.

For a single aggregate, the A-MSDU approach is technically more efficient. Each 802.3 header is ordinarily 14 bytes, which is relatively small compared to an 802.11 MAC header that could be as long as 36 bytes. Thus, with only a single 802.11 MAC header for multiple 802.3 frames, a savings of up to 22 bytes per extra aggregated frame could be achieved. An A-MSDU may be up to 7935 bytes, which can hold over 100 small (e.g., 50-byte) packets, but only a few (5) larger (1500-byte) data packets. The A-MSDU is covered by a single FCS. This larger size of an A-MSDU frame increases the chances it will be delivered with errors, and because there is only a single FCS for the entire aggregate, the entire frame would have to be retransmitted on error.

A-MPDU aggregation is a different form of aggregation whereby multiple (up to 64) 802.11 frames, each with its own 802.11 MAC header and FCS and up to 4095 bytes each, are sent together. A-MPDUs may carry up to 64KB of data—enough for more than 1000 small packets and about 40 larger (1.5KB) packets. Because each constituent frame (subframe) carries its own FCS, it is possible to selectively retransmit only those subframes received with errors. This is made possible by the *block acknowledgment* facility in 802.11n (originating in 802.11e), which is a form of extended ACK that provides feedback to a transmitter indicating which particular A-MPDU subframes were delivered successfully. This capability is similar in purpose, but not in its details, to the selective acknowledgments we will see in TCP (see Chapter 14). So, although the type of aggregation offered by A-MSDUs may be more efficient for error-free networks carrying large numbers of small packets, in practice it may not perform as well as A-MPDU aggregation [S08].

3.5.2 Power Save Mode and the Time Sync Function (TSF)

The 802.11 specification provides a way for stations to enter a limited power state, called *power save mode* (PSM). PSM is designed to save power by allowing an STA's radio receive circuitry to be powered down some of the time. Without PSM, the receiver circuitry would always be running, draining power. When in PSM, an STA's outgoing frames have a bit set in the *Frame Control Word*. A cooperative AP noticing this bit being set buffers any frames for the station until the station requests them. APs ordinarily send out beacon frames (a type of management frame) indicating various things like SSID, channel, and authentication information. When supporting stations that use PSM, APs can also indicate the presence of buffered frames to a station by setting an indication in the *Frame Control Word* of frames it sends. When stations enter PSM, they do so until the next AP beacon time, when they wake up and determine if there are pending frames stored at the AP for them.

PSM should be used with care and understanding. Although it may extend battery life, the NIC is not the only module drawing power in most wireless devices. Other parts of the system such as the screen and hard drive can be significant consumers of power, so overall battery life may not be extended much. Furthermore, using PSM can affect throughput performance significantly as idle periods are added between frame transmissions and time is spent switching modes [SHK07].

The ability to awaken an STA to check for pending frames at exactly the correct time (i.e., when an AP is about to send a beacon frame) depends on a common sense of time at the AP and the PSM stations it serves. Wi-Fi synchronizes time using the *time synchronization function* (TSF). Each station maintains a 64-bit counter reference time (in microseconds) that is synchronized with other stations in the network. Synchronization is maintained to within 4μs plus the maximum propagation delay of the PHY (for PHYs of rate 1Mb/s or more). This is accomplished by having any station that receives a TSF update (basically, a copy of the 64-bit counter sent from another station) check to see if the provided value is larger than its own. If so, the receiving station updates its own notion of time to be the larger value. This approach ensures that clocks always move forward, but it also raises some concern that, given stations with slightly differing clock rates, the slower ones will tend to be synced to the fastest one.

With the incorporation of 802.11e (QoS) features into 802.11, the basic PSM of 802.11 has been extended to include the ability to schedule periodic batch processing of buffered frames. The frequency is expressed in terms of the number of beacon frames. The capability, called *automatic power save delivery* (APSD), uses some of the subfields of the QoS control word. APSD may be especially useful for small power-constrained devices, as they need not necessarily awaken at each beacon interval as they do in conventional 802.11 PSM. Instead, they may elect to power down their radio transceiver circuitry for longer periods of their own choosing. 802.11n also extends the basic PSM by allowing an STA equipped with multiple radio circuits operating together (see MIMO, Section 3.5.4.2) to power down all but one of the circuits until a frame is ready. This is called *spatial multiplexing* power save mode. The specification also includes an enhancement to APSD called *Power Save Multi-Poll* (PSMP) that provides a way to schedule transmissions of frames in both directions (e.g., to and from AP) at the same time.

3.5.3   802.11 Media Access Control

In wireless networks, it is much more challenging to detect a "collision" than in wired networks such as 802.3 LANs. In essence, the medium is effectively simplex, and multiple simultaneous transmitters must be avoided, by coordinating transmissions in either a centralized or a distributed manner. The 802.11 standard has three approaches to control sharing of the wireless medium, called the *point coordination function* (PCF), the *distributed coordinating function* (DCF), and the *hybrid coordination function* (HCF). HCF was brought into the 802.11 specification [802.11-2007] with the addition of QoS support in 802.11e and is also used by 802.11n. Implementation of the DCF is mandatory for any type of station or AP, but implementation of the PCF is optional and not widespread (so we shall not discuss it in detail). HCF is found in relatively new QoS-capable Wi-Fi equipment, such as 802.11n APs and earlier APs that support 802.11e. We turn our attention to DCF for now and describe HCF in the context of QoS next.

DCF is a form of CSMA/CA for contention-based access to the medium. It is used for both infrastructure and ad hoc operation. With CSMA/CA, stations listen to see if the medium is free and, if so, may have an opportunity to transmit. If not, they avoid sending for a random amount of time before checking again to see if the medium is free. This behavior is similar to how a station sensing a collision backs off when using CSMA/CD on wired LANs. Channel arbitration in 802.11 is based on CSMA/CA with enhancements to provide priority access to certain stations or frame types.

802.11 carrier sense is performed in both a physical and a virtual way. Generally, stations wait for a period of time when ready to send (called the *distributed inter-frame space* or DIFS) to allow higher-priority stations to access the channel. If the channel becomes busy during the DIFS period, a station starts the waiting period again. When the medium appears idle, a would-be transmitter initiates the collision avoidance/backoff procedure described in Section 3.5.3.3. This procedure is also initiated after a successful (unsuccessful) transmission is indicated by the receipt (lack of receipt) of an ACK. In the case of unsuccessful transmission, the backoff procedure is initiated with different timing (using the *extended inter-frame space* or EIFS). We now discuss the implementation of DCF in more detail, including the virtual and physical carrier sense mechanisms.

3.5.3.1 Virtual Carrier Sense, RTS/CTS, and the Network Allocation Vector (NAV)

In the 802.11 MAC protocol, a *virtual carrier sense* mechanism operates by observing the *Duration* field present in each MAC frame. This is accomplished by a station listening to traffic not destined for it. The *Duration* field is present in both RTS and CTS frames optionally exchanged prior to transmission, as well as conventional data frames, and provides an estimate of how long the medium will be busy carrying the frame.

The transmitter sets the *Duration* field based on the frame length, transmit rate, and PHY characteristics (e.g., rate, etc.). Each station keeps a local counter called the *Network Allocation Vector* (NAV) that estimates how long the medium will be busy carrying the current frame, and consequently how long it will need to wait before attempting its next transmission. A station overhearing traffic with a *Duration* field greater than its NAV updates its NAV to the new value. Because the *Duration* field is present in both RTS and CTS frames, if used, any station in range of either the sender or the receiver is able to ascertain the *Duration* field value. The NAV is maintained in time units and decremented based on a local clock. The medium is considered busy when the local NAV is nonzero. It is reset to 0 upon receipt of an ACK.

3.5.3.2 Physical Carrier Sense (CCA)

Each 802.11 PHY specification (e.g., for different frequencies and radio technology) is required to provide a function for assessing whether the channel is clear based upon energy and waveform recognition (usually recognition of a well-formed PLCP). This function is called *clear channel assessment* (CCA) and its implementation is PHY-dependent. The CCA capability represents the physical carrier sense capability for the 802.11 MAC to understand whether the medium is currently busy. It is used in conjunction with the NAV to determine when a station must *defer* (wait) prior to transmission.

3.5.3.3 DCF Collision Avoidance/Backoff Procedure

Upon determining that the channel is likely to be free (i.e., because the NAV duration has been met and CCA does not indicate a busy channel), a station defers access prior to transmission. Because many stations may have been waiting for the channel to become free, each station computes and waits for a *backoff time* prior to sending. The backoff time is equal to the product of a random number and the *slot time* (unless the station attempting to transmit already has a nonzero backoff time, in which case it is not recomputed). The slot time is PHY-dependent but is generally a few tens of microseconds. The random number is drawn from a uniform distribution over the interval [0, CW], where the *contention window* (CW) is an integer containing a number of time slots to wait, with limits *aCWmin* ≤ CW ≤ *aCWmax* defined by the PHY. The set of CW values increases by powers of 2 (minus 1) beginning with the PHY-specific constant *aCWmin* value and continuing up to and including the constant *aCWmax* value for each successive transmission attempt. This is similar in effect to Ethernet's backoff procedure initiated during a collision detection event.

In a wireless environment, collision *detection* is not practical because it is difficult for a transmitter and receiver to operate simultaneously in the same piece of equipment and hear any transmissions other than its own, so collision *avoidance* is used instead. In addition, ACKs are generated in response to unicast frames to determine whether a frame has been delivered successfully. A station receiving a correct frame begins transmitting an ACK after waiting a small period of time (called the *Short Interframe Space* or SIFS), without regard to the busy/idle state of the medium. This should not cause a problem because the SIFS value is always smaller than DIFS, so in effect stations generating ACKs get priority access to the channel to complete their transactions. The source station waits a certain amount of time without receiving an ACK frame before concluding that a transmission has failed. Upon failure, the backoff procedure discussed previously is initiated and the frame is retried. The same procedure is initiated if a CTS is not received in response to an earlier RTS within a certain (different) amount of time (a constant called *CTStimeout*).

3.5.3.4 HCF and 802.11e/n QoS

Clauses 5, 6, 7, and 9 of the 802.11 standard [802.11-2007] are based in part on the work of the 802.11e group within IEEE, and the terms 802.11e, Wi-Fi QoS, and WMM (for Wi-Fi Multimedia) are often used. They cover the *QoS facility*—changes to the 802.11 MAC-layer and system interfaces in support of multimedia applications such as voice over IP (VoIP) and streaming video. Whether the QoS facility is really necessary or not often depends on the congestion level of the network and the types of applications to be supported. If utilization of the network tends to be low, the QoS MAC support may be unnecessary, although some of the other 802.11e capabilities may still be useful (e.g., block ACKs and APSD). In situations where utilization and congestion are high and there is a need to support a low-jitter delivery capability for services such as VoIP, QoS support may be desirable. These specifications are relatively new, so QoS-capable Wi-Fi equipment is likely to be more expensive and complex than non-QoS equipment.

The QoS facility introduces new terminology such as *QoS stations* (QSTAs), *QoS access points* (QAPs), and the *QoS BSS* (QBSS, a BSS supporting QoS). In general, any of the devices supporting QoS capabilities also support conventional non-QoS operation. 802.11n "high-throughput" stations (called HT STAs) are also QSTAs. A new form of coordination function, the *hybrid coordination function* (HCF), supports both contention-based and controlled channel access, although the controlled channel variant is seldom used. Within the HCF, there are two specified channel access methods that can operate together: *HFCA-controlled channel access* (HCCA) and the more popular *enhanced DCF channel access* (EDCA), corresponding to reservation-based and contention-based access, respectively. There is also some support for *admission control*, which may deny connectivity entirely under high load.

EDCA builds upon the basic DCF access. With EDCA, there are eight *user priorities* (UPs) that are mapped to four *access categories* (ACs). The user priorities use the same structure as 802.1d priority tags and are numbered 1 through 7, with 7 being the highest priority. (There is also a 0 priority between 2 and 3.) The four ACs are nominally intended for background, best-effort, video, and audio traffic. Priorities 1 and 2 are intended for the background AC, priorities 0 and 3 are for the best-effort AC, 4 and 5 are for the video AC, and 6 and 7 are for the voice AC. For each AC, a variant of DCF contends for channel access credits called *transmit opportunities* (TXOPs), using alternative MAC parameters that tend to favor the higher-priority traffic. In EDCA, many of the various MAC parameters from DCF (e.g., DIFS, *aCWmin*, *aCWmax*) become adjustable as configuration parameters. These values are communicated to QSTAs using management frames.

HCCA builds loosely upon PCF and uses polling-controlled channel access. It is designed for synchronous-style access control and takes precedence ahead of the contention-based access of EDCA. A *hybrid coordinator* (HC) is located within an AP and has priority to allocate channel accesses. Prior to transmission, a station can issue a *traffic specification* (TSPEC) for its traffic and use UP values between 8 and 15. The HC can allocate reserved TXOPs to such requests to be used during short-duration controlled access phases of frame exchange that take place before EDCA-based frame transmission. The HC can also deny TXOPs to TSPECs based on admission control policies set by the network administrator. The HCF exploits the virtual carrier sense mechanism discussed earlier with DCF to keep contention-based stations from interfering with contention-free access. Note that a single network comprising QSTAs and conventional stations can have both HCF and DCF running simultaneously by alternating between the two, but ad hoc networks do not support the HC and thus do not handle TSPECs and do not perform admission control. Such networks might still run HCF, but TXOPs are gained through EDCA-based contention.

3.5.4 Physical-Layer Details: Rates, Channels, and Frequencies

The [802.11-2007] standard now includes the following earlier amendments: 802.11a, 802.11b, 802.11d, 802.11g, 802.11h, 802.11i, 802.11j, and 802.11e. The 802.11n standard was adopted as an amendment to 802.11 in 2009 [802.11n-2009]. Most of these amendments provide additional modulation, coding, and operating frequencies for 802.11 networks, but 802.11n also adds multiple data streams and a method for aggregating multiple frames (see Section 3.5.1.3). We will avoid detailed discussion of the physical layer, but to appreciate the breadth of options, Table 3-2 includes those parts of the 802.11 standard that describe this layer in particular.

Table 3-2   Parts of the 802.11 standard that describe the physical layer

Standard (Clause)	Speeds (Mb/s)	Frequency Range; Modulation	Channel Set
802.11a (Clause 17)	6, 9, 12, 18, 24, 36, 48, 54	5.16–5.35 and 5.725–5.825GHz; OFDM	34–165 (varies by country) 20MHz/10MHz/5MHz channel width options
802.11b (Clause 18)	1, 2, 5.5, 11	2.401–2.495GHz; DSSS	1–14 (varies by country)
802.11g (Clause 19)	1, 2, 5.5, 6, 9, 11, 12, 18, 24, 36, 48, 54 (plus 22, 33)	2.401–2.495GHz; OFDM	1–14 (varies by country)
802.11n	6.5–600 with many options (up to 4 MIMO streams)	2.4 and 5GHz modes with 20MHz- or 40MHz-wide channels; OFDM	1–13 (2.4GHz band); 36–196 (5GHz band) (varies by country)
802.11y	(Same as 802.11-2007)	3.650–3.700GHz (licensed); OFDM	1–25, 36–64, 100–161 (varies by country)

The first column gives the original standard name and its present location in [802.11-2007], plus details for the 802.11n and 802.11y amendments. It is important to note from this table that 802.11b/g operate in the 2.4GHz *Industrial, Scientific, and Medical* (ISM) band, 802.11a operates only in the higher 5GHz *Unlicensed National Information Infrastructure* (U-NII) band, and 802.11n can operate in both. The 802.11y amendment provides for licensed use in the 3.65–3.70GHz band within the United States. An important practical consequence of the data in this table is that 802.11b/g equipment does not interoperate or interfere with 802.11a equipment, but 802.11n equipment may interfere with either if not deployed carefully.

3.5.4.1 Channels and Frequencies

Regulatory bodies (e.g., the Federal Communications Commission in the United States) divide the electromagnetic spectrum into frequency ranges allocated for various uses across the world. For each range and use, a license may or may not be required, depending on local policy. In 802.11, there are sets of channels that may be used in various ways at various power levels depending on the regulatory domain or country. Wi-Fi channels are numbered in 5MHz units starting at some base center frequency. For example, channel 36 with a base center frequency of 5.00GHz gives the frequency 5000 + 36 * 5 = 5180MHz, the center frequency of channel 36. Although channel center frequencies are 5MHz apart from each other, channels may be *wider* than 5MHz (up to 40MHz for 802.11n). Consequently, some channels within channel sets of the same band usually overlap. Practically speaking, this means that transmissions on one channel might interfere with transmissions on nearby channels.

Figure 3-20 presents the channel-to-frequency mapping for the 802.11b/g channels in the 2.4GHz ISM band. Each channel is 22MHz wide. Not all channels are available for legal use in every country. For example, channel 14 is authorized at present for use only in Japan, and channels 12 and 13 are authorized for use in Europe, while the United States permits channels 1 through 11 to be used. Other countries may be more restrictive (see Annex J of the 802.11 standard and amendments). Note that policies and licensing requirements may change over time.

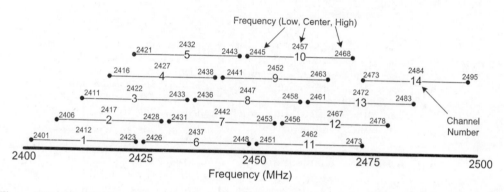

Figure 3-20   The 802.11b and 802.11g standards use a frequency band between about 2.4GHz and 2.5GHz. This band is divided into fourteen 22MHz-wide overlapping channels, of which some subset is generally available for legal use depending on the country of operation. It is advisable to assign nonoverlapping channels, such as 1, 6, and 11 in the United States, to multiple base stations operating in the same area. Only a single 40MHz 802.11n channel may be used in this band without overlap.

As shown in Figure 3-20, the effect of overlapping channels is now clear. A transmitter on channel 1, for example, overlaps with channels 2, 3, 4, and 5 but not higher channels. This becomes important when selecting which channels to assign for use in environments where multiple access points are to be used and even more important when multiple access points serving multiple different networks in the same area are to be used. One common approach in the United States is to assign up to three APs in an area using nonoverlapping channels 1, 6, and 11, as channel 11 is the highest-frequency channel authorized for unlicensed use in the United States. In cases where other WLANs may be operating in the same bands, it is worth considering jointly planning channel settings with all the affected WLAN administrators.

As shown in Figure 3-21, 802.11a/n/y share a somewhat more complicated channel set but offer a larger number of nonoverlapping channels to use (i.e., 12 unlicensed 20MHz channels in the United States).

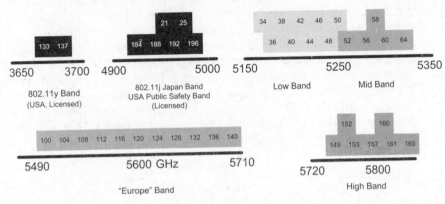

Figure 3-21   Many of the approved 802.11 channel numbers and center frequencies for 20MHz channels. The most common range for unlicensed use involves the U-NII bands, all above 5GHz. The lower band is approved for use in most countries. The "Europe" band is approved for use in most European countries, and the high band is approved for use in the United States and China. Channels are typically 20MHz wide for 802.11a/y but may be 40MHz wide for 802.11n. Narrower channels and some channels available in Japan are also available (not shown).

In Figure 3-21, the channels are numbered in 5MHz increments, but different channel widths are available: 5MHz, 10MHz, 20MHz, and 40MHz. The 40MHz channel width is an option with 802.11n (see Section 3.5.4.2), along with several proprietary Wi-Fi systems that aggregate two 20MHz channels (called channel bonding).

For typical Wi-Fi networks, an AP has its operating channel assigned during installation, and client stations change channels in order to associate with the AP. When operating in ad hoc mode, there is no controlling AP, so a station is typically hand-configured with the operating channel. The sets of channels available and operating power may be constrained by the regulatory environment, the hardware capabilities, and possibly the supporting driver software.

3.5.4.2 802.11 Higher Throughput/802.11n

In late 2009, the IEEE standardized 802.11n [802.11n-2009] as an amendment to [802.11-2007]. It makes a number of important changes to 802.11. To support higher throughput, it incorporates support for *multiple input, multiple output* (MIMO) management of multiple simultaneously operating data streams carried on multiple antennas, called *spatial streams*. Up to four such spatial streams are supported on a given channel. 802.11n channels may be 40MHz wide (using two adjacent 20MHz channels), twice as wide as conventional channels in 802.11a/b/g/y. Thus, there is an immediate possibility of having up to eight times the maximum data rate of

802.11a/g (54Mb/s), for a total of 432Mb/s. However, 802.11n also improves the single-stream performance by using a more efficient modulation scheme (802.11n uses MIMO- orthogonal frequency division multiplexing (OFDM) with up to 52 data subcarriers per 20MHz channel and 108 per 40MHz channel, instead of 48 in 802.11a and 802.11g), plus a more efficient forward error-correcting code (rate 5/6 instead of 3/4), bringing the per-stream performance to 65Mb/s (20MHz channel) or 135Mb/s (40MHz channel). By also reducing the *guard interval* (GI, a forced idle time between symbols) duration to 400ns from the legacy 800ns, the maximum per-stream performance is raised to about 72.2Mb/s (20MHz channel) and 150Mb/s (40MHz channel). With four spatial streams operating in concert perfectly, this provides a maximum of about 600Mb/s.

Some 77 combinations of modulation and coding options are supported by 802.11n, including 8 options for a single stream, 24 using the same or *equal modulation* (EQM) on all streams, and 43 using *unequal modulation* (UEQM) on multiple streams. Table 3-3 gives some of the combinations for modulation and coding scheme according to the first 33 values of the *modulation and coding scheme* (MCS) value. Higher values (33–76) include combinations for two channels (values 33–38), three channels (39–52), and four channels (53–76). MCS value 32 is a special combination where the signals in the two halves of the 40MHz channel

Table 3-3   MCS values for 802.11n include combinations of equal and unequal modulation, different FEC coding rates, up to four spatial streams using 20MHz- or 40MHz-wide channels, and an 800ns or 400ns GI. The 77 combinations provide data rates from 6Mb/s to 600Mb/s.

MCS Value	Modulation Type	FEC Code Rate	Spatial Streams	Rates (Mb/s) (20MHz) [800/400ns]	Rates (Mb/s) (40MHz) [800/400ns]
0	BPSK	1/2	1	6.5/7.2	13.5/15
1	QPSK	1/2	1	13/14.4	27/30
2	QPSK	3/4	1	19.5/21.7	40.5/45
3	16-QAM	1/2	1	26/28.9	54/60
4	16-QAM	3/4	1	39/43.3	81/90
5	64-QAM	2/3	1	52/57.8	108/120
6	64-QAM	3/4	1	58.5/65	121.5/135
7	64-QAM	5/6	1	65/72.2	135/150
8	BPSK	1/2	2	13/14.4	27/30
...	...	...	...	...	...
15	64-QAM	5/6	2	130/144.4	270/300
16	BPSK	1/2	3	19.5/21.7	40.5/45
...	...	...	...	...	...
31	64-QAM	5/6	4	260/288.9	540/600
32	BPSK	1/2	1	N/A	6/6.7
...	...	...	...	...	...
76	64x3/16x1-QAM	3/4	4	214.5/238.3	445.5/495

contain the same information. Each data rate column gives two values, one using the legacy 800ns GI and one giving the greater data rate available using the shorter 400ns GI. The underlined values, 6Mb/s and 600Mb/s, represent the smallest and largest throughput rates, respectively.

Table 3-3 shows the various combinations of coding, including *binary phase shift keying* (BPSK), *quadrature phase shift keying* (QPSK), and various levels of *quadrature amplitude modulation* (16- and 64-QAM), available with 802.11n. These modulation schemes provide an increasing data rate for a given channel bandwidth. However, the more high-performance and complex a modulation scheme, the more vulnerable it tends to be to noise and interference. *Forward error correction* (FEC) includes a set of methods whereby redundant bits are introduced at the sender that can be used to detect and repair bit errors introduced during delivery. For FEC, the *code rate* is the ratio of the effective useful data rate to the rate imposed on the underlying communication channel. For example, a ½ code rate would deliver 1 useful bit for every 2 bits sent.

802.11n may operate in one of three modes. In 802.11n-only environments, the optional so-called *greenfield mode*, the PLCP contains special bit arrangements ("training sequences") known only to 802.11n equipment and does not interoperate with legacy equipment. To maintain compatibility, 802.11n has two other interoperable modes. However, both of these impose a performance penalty to native 802.11n equipment. One mode, called *non-HT mode*, essentially disables all 802.11n features but remains compatible with legacy equipment. This is not a very interesting mode, so we shall not discuss it further. However, a required mode called *HT-mixed mode* supports both 802.11n and legacy operation, depending on which stations are communicating. The information required to convey an AP's 802.11n capability to HT STAs yet protect legacy STAs is provided in the PLCP, which is augmented to contain both HT and legacy information and is transmitted at a slower rate than in greenfield mode so that it can be processed by legacy equipment. HT protection also requires an HT AP to use self-directed CTS frames (or RTS/CTS frame exchanges) at the legacy rate to inform legacy stations when it will use shared channels. Even though RTS/CTS frames are short, the requirement to send them at the legacy rate (6Mb/s) can significantly reduce an 802.11n WLAN's performance.

When deploying an 802.11n AP, care should be taken to set up appropriate channel assignments. When using 40MHz channels, 802.11n APs should be operated in the U-NII bands above 5GHz as there is simply not enough useful spectrum to use these wider channels in the 2.4GHz ISM band. An optional BSS feature called *phased coexistence operation* (PCO) allows an AP to periodically switch between 20MHz and 40MHz channel widths, which can provide better coexistence between 802.11n APs operating near legacy equipment at the cost of some additional throughput. Finally, it is worth mentioning that 802.11n APs generally require more power than conventional APs. This higher power level exceeds the basic 15W provided by 802.3af *power-over-Ethernet* (PoE) system wiring, meaning that PoE+ (802.3at, capable of 30W) should be used unless some other form of power such as a direct external power supply is available.

3.5.5 Wi-Fi Security

There has been considerable evolution in the security model for 802.11 networks. In its early days, 802.11 used an encryption method known as *wired equivalent privacy* (WEP). WEP was later shown to be so weak that some replacement was required. Industry responded with *Wi-Fi protected access* (WPA), which replaced the way keys are used with encrypted blocks (see Chapter 18 for the basics of cryptography). In WPA, a scheme called the *Temporal Key Integrity Protocol* (TKIP) ensures, among other things, that each frame is encrypted with a different encryption key. It also includes a message integrity check, called *Michael*, that fixed one of the major weaknesses in WEP. WPA was created as a placeholder that could be used on fielded WEP-capable equipment by way of a firmware upgrade while the IEEE 802.11i standards group worked on a stronger standard that was ultimately absorbed into Clause 8 of [802.11-2007] and dubbed "WPA2" by industry. Both WEP and WPA use the RC4 encryption algorithm [S96]. WPA2 uses the *Advanced Encryption Standard* (AES) algorithm [AES01].

The encryption techniques we just discussed are aimed at providing privacy between the station and AP, assuming the station has legitimate authorization to be accessing the network. In WEP, and small-scale environments that use WPA or WPA2, authorization is typically implemented by pre-placing a shared key or password in each station as well as in the AP during configuration. A user knowing the key is assumed to have legitimate access to the network. These keys are also frequently used to initialize the encryption keys used to ensure privacy. Using such *pre-shared keys* (PSKs) has limitations. For example, an administrator may have considerable trouble in providing keys only to authorized users. If a user becomes de-authorized, the PSK has to be replaced and all legitimate users informed. This approach does not scale to environments with many users. As a result, WPA and later standards support a *port-based network access control* standard called 802.1X [802.1X-2010]. It provides a way to carry the *Extensible Authentication Protocol* (EAP) [RFC3748] in IEEE 802 LANs (called EAPOL), including 802.3 and 802.11 [RFC4017]. EAP, in turn, can be used to carry many other standard and non-standard authentication protocols. It can also be used to establish keys, including WEP keys. Details of these protocols are given in Chapter 18, but we shall also see the use of EAP when we discuss PPP in Section 3.6.

With the completion of the IEEE 802.11i group's work, the RC4/TKIP combination in WPA was extended with a new algorithm called CCMP as part of WPA2. CCMP is based on using the *counter mode* (CCM [RFC3610]) of the AES for confidentiality with *cipher block chaining message authentication code* (CBC-MAC; note the "other" use of the term MAC here) for authentication and integrity. All AES processing is performed using a 128-bit block size and 128-bit keys. CCMP and TKIP form the basis for a Wi-Fi security architecture named the *Robust Security Network* (RSN), which supports *Robust Security Network Access* (RSNA). Earlier methods, such as WEP, are called *pre-RSNA methods*. RSNA compliance requires support for CCMP (TKIP is optional), and 802.11n does away with TKIP entirely. Table 3-4 provides a summary of this somewhat complicated situation.

Table 3-4 Wi-Fi security has evolved from WEP, which was found to be insecure, to WPA, to the now-standard WPA2 collection of algorithms.

Name/Standard	Cipher	Key Stream Management	Authentication
WEP (pre-RSNA)	RC4	(WEP)	PSK, (802.1X/EAP)
WPA	RC4	TKIP	PSK, 802.1X/EAP
WPA2/802.11(i)	CCMP	CCMP, (TKIP)	PSK, 802.1X/EAP

In all cases, both pre-shared keys as well as 802.1X can be used for authentication and initial keying. The major attraction of using 802.1X/EAP is that a managed authentication server can be used to provide access control decisions on a per-user basis to an AP. For this reason, authentication using 802.1X is sometimes referred to as "Enterprise" (e.g., WPA-Enterprise). EAP itself can encapsulate various specific authentication protocols, which we discuss in more detail in Chapter 18.

3.5.6 Wi-Fi Mesh (802.11s)

The IEEE is working on the 802.11s standard, which covers Wi-Fi *mesh* operation. With mesh operation, wireless stations can act as data-forwarding agents (like APs). The standard is not yet complete as of writing (mid-2011). The draft version of 802.11s defines the *Hybrid Wireless Routing Protocol* (HWRP), based in part on the IETF standards for *Ad-Hoc On-Demand Distance Vector* (AODV) routing [RFC3561] and the *Optimized Link State Routing* (OLSR) protocol [RFC3626]. *Mesh stations* (mesh STAs) are a type of QoS STA and may participate in HWRP or other routing protocols, but compliant nodes must include an implementation of HWRP and the associated *airtime link metric*. Mesh nodes coordinate using EDCA or may use an optional coordinating function called *mesh deterministic access*. *Mesh points* (MPs) are those nodes that form mesh links with neighbors. Those that also include AP functionality are called *mesh APs* (MAPs). Conventional 802.11 stations can use either APs or MAPs to access the rest of the wireless LAN.

The 802.11s draft specifies a new optional form of security for RSNA called *Simultaneous Authentication of Equals* (SAE) authentication [SAE]. This security protocol is a bit different from others because it does not require lockstep operation between a specially designated initiator and responder. Instead, stations are treated as equals, and any station that first recognizes another may initiate a security exchange (or this may happen simultaneously as two stations initiate an association).

3.6   Point-to-Point Protocol (PPP)

PPP stands for the *Point-to-Point Protocol* [RFC1661][RFC1662][RFC2153]. It is a popular method for carrying IP datagrams over serial links—from low-speed dial-up modems to high-speed optical links [RFC2615]. It is widely deployed by some DSL service providers, which also use it for assigning Internet system parameters (e.g., initial IP address and domain name server; see Chapter 6).

PPP should be considered more of a collection of protocols than a single protocol. It supports a basic method to establish a link, called the *Link Control Protocol* (LCP), as well as a family of NCPs, used to establish network-layer links for various kinds of protocols, including IPv4 and IPv6 and possibly non-IP protocols, after LCP has established the basic link. A number of related standards cover control of compression and encryption for PPP, and a number of authentication methods can be employed when a link is brought up.

3.6.1   Link Control Protocol (LCP)

The LCP portion of PPP is used to establish and maintain a low-level two-party communication path over a point-to-point link. PPP's operation therefore need be concerned only with two ends of a single link; it does not need to handle the problem of mediating access to a shared resource like the MAC-layer protocols of Ethernet and Wi-Fi.

PPP generally, and LCP more specifically, imposes minimal requirements on the underlying point-to-point link. The link must support bidirectional operation (LCP uses acknowledgments) and operate either asynchronously or synchronously. Typically, LCP establishes a link using a simple bit-level framing format based on the *High-Level Data Link Control* (HDLC) protocol. HDLC was already a well-established framing format by the time PPP was designed [ISO3309] [ISO4335]. IBM modified it to form *Synchronous Data Link Control* (SDLC), a protocol used as the link layer in its proprietary *System Network Architecture* (SNA) protocol suite. HDLC was also used as the basis for the LLC standard in 802.2 and ultimately for PPP as well. The format is shown in Figure 3-22.

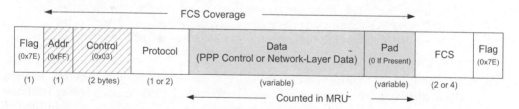

Figure 3-22   The PPP basic frame format was borrowed from HDLC. It provides a protocol identifier, payload area, and 2- or 4-byte FCS. Other fields may or may not be present, depending on compression options.

The PPP frame format, in the common case when HDLC-like framing is used as shown in Figure 3-22, is surrounded by two 1-byte *Flag* fields containing the fixed value 0x7E. These fields are used by the two stations on the ends of the point-to-point link for finding the beginning and end of the frame. A small problem arises if the value 0x7E itself occurs inside the frame. This is handled in one of two ways, depending on whether PPP is operating over an asynchronous or a synchronous link. For asynchronous links, PPP uses *character stuffing* (also called *byte stuffing*). If the flag character appears elsewhere in the frame, it is replaced with the 2-byte sequence 0x7D5E (0x7D is known as the "PPP escape character"). If the escape character itself appears in the frame, it is replaced with the 2-byte sequence 0x7D5D. Thus, the receiver replaces 0x7D5E with 0x7E and 0x7D5D with 0x7D upon receipt. On synchronous links (e.g., T1 lines, T3 lines), PPP uses *bit stuffing*. Noting that the flag character has the bit pattern 01111110 (a contiguous sequence of six 1 bits), bit stuffing arranges for a 0 bit to be inserted after any contiguous string of five 1 bits appearing in a place other than the flag character itself. Doing so implies that bytes may be sent as more than 8 bits, but this is generally OK, as low layers of the serial processing hardware are able to "unstuff" the bit stream, restoring it to its prestuffed pattern.

After the first *Flag* field, PPP adopts the HDLC *Address* (*Addr*) and *Control* fields. In HDLC, the *Address* field would specify which station is being addressed, but because PPP is concerned only with a single destination, this field is always defined to have the value 0xFF (all stations). The *Control* field in HDLC is used to indicate frame sequencing and retransmission behavior. As these link-layer reliability functions are not ordinarily implemented by PPP, the *Control* field is set to the fixed value 0x03. Because both the *Address* and *Control* fields are fixed constants in PPP, they are often omitted during transmission with an option called *Address and Control Field Compression* (ACFC), which essentially eliminates the two fields.

Note

There has been considerable debate over the years as to how much reliability link-layer networks should provide, if any. With Ethernet, up to 16 retransmission attempts are made before giving up. Typically, PPP is configured to do no retransmission, although there do exist specifications for adding retransmission [RFC1663]. The trade-off can be subtle and is dependent on the types of traffic to be carried. A detailed discussion of the considerations is contained in [RFC3366].

The *Protocol* field of the PPP frame indicates the type of data being carried. Many different types of protocols can be carried in a PPP frame. The official list and the assigned number used in the *Protocol* field are given by the "Point-to-Point Protocol Field Assignments" document [PPPn]. In conforming to the HDLC specification, any protocol numbers are assigned such that the least significant bit of the most significant byte equals 0 and the least significant bit of the least significant byte equals 1. Values in the (hexadecimal) range 0x0000–0x3FFF identify network-layer protocols, and values in the 0x8000–0xBFFF range identify data belonging to an associated NCP. Protocol values in the range 0x4000–0x7FFF are used for "low-volume" protocols with no associated NCP. Protocol values in the range 0xC000–0XEFFF identify control protocols such as LCP. In some circumstances the *Protocol* field can be compressed to a single byte, if the *Protocol Field Compression* (PFC) option is negotiated successfully during link establishment. This is applicable to protocols with protocol numbers in the range 0x0000–0x00FF, which includes most of the popular network-layer protocols. Note, however, that LCP packets always use the 2-byte uncompressed format.

The final portion of the PPP frame contains a 16-bit FCS (a CRC16, with generator polynomial 10001000000100001) covering the entire frame except the *FCS* field itself and *Flag* bytes. Note that the FCS value covers the frame before any byte or bit stuffing has been performed. With an LCP option (see Section 3.6.1.2), the CRC can be extended from 16 to 32 bits. This case uses the same CRC32 polynomial mentioned previously for Ethernet.

3.6.1.1 LCP Operation

LCP has a simple encapsulation beyond the basic PPP packet. It is illustrated in Figure 3-23.

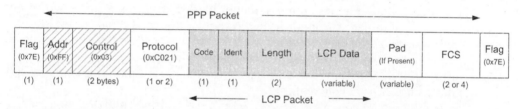

Figure 3-23   The LCP packet is a fairly general format capable of identifying the type of encapsulated data and its length. LCP frames are used primarily in establishing a PPP link, but this basic format also forms the basis of many of the various network control protocols.

The PPP *Protocol* field value for LCP is always 0xC021, which is not eliminated using PFC, so as to minimize ambiguity. The *Ident* field is a sequence number provided by the sender of LCP request frames and is incremented for each subsequent message. When forming a reply (ACK, NACK, or REJECT response), this field is constructed by copying the value included in the request to the response packet. In this fashion, the requesting side can identify replies to the appropriate request by matching identifiers. The *Code* field gives the type of operation being either requested or responded to: configure-request (0x01), configure-ACK (0x02), configure-NACK (0x03), configure-REJECT (0x04), terminate-request (0x05), terminate-ACK (0x06), code-REJECT (0x07), protocol-REJECT (0x08), echo-request (0x09), echo-reply (0x0A), discard-request (0x0B), identification (0x0C), and time-remaining (0x0D). Generally, ACK messages indicate acceptance of a set of options, and NACK messages indicate a partial rejection with suggested alternatives. A REJECT message rejects one or more options entirely. A rejected code indicates that one of the field values contained in a previous packet is unknown. The *Length* field gives the length of the LCP packet in bytes and is not permitted to exceed the link's *maximum received unit* (MRU), a form of maximum advised frame limit we shall discuss later. Note that the *Length* field is part of the LCP protocol; the PPP protocol in general does not provide such a field.

The main job of LCP is to bring up a point-to-point link to a minimal level. *Configure* messages cause each end of the link to start the basic configuration procedure and establish agreed-upon options. *Termination* messages are used to clear a link when complete. LCP also provides some additional features mentioned previously. *Echo Request/Reply* messages may be exchanged anytime a link is active by LCP in order to verify operation of the peer. The *Discard Request* message can be used for performance measurement; it instructs the peer to discard the packet without responding. The *Identification* and *Time-Remaining* messages are used for administrative purposes: to know the type of the peer system and to indicate the amount of time allowed for the link to remain established (e.g., for administrative or security reasons).

Historically, one common problem with point-to-point links occurs if a remote station is in *loopback mode* or is said to be "looped." Telephone company wide area data circuits are sometimes put into loopback mode for testing—data sent at one side is simply returned from the other. Although this may be useful for line testing, it is not at all helpful for data communication, so LCP includes ways to send a *magic number* (an arbitrary number selected by the sender) to see if it is immediately returned in the same message type. If so, the line is detected as being looped, and maintenance is likely required.

To get a better feeling for how PPP links are established and options are negotiated, Figure 3-24 illustrates a simplified packet exchange timeline as well as a simplified state machine (implemented at both ends of the link).

The link is considered to be established once the underlying protocol layer has indicated that an association has become active (e.g., carrier detected for modems). Link quality testing, which involves an exchange of link quality reports and acknowledgments (see Section 3.6.1.2), may also be accomplished during this period. If the link requires authentication, which is common, for example, when dialing in to an ISP, a number of additional exchanges may be required to establish the authenticity of one or both parties attached to the link. The link is terminated once the underlying protocol or hardware has indicated that the association has stopped (e.g., carrier lost) or after having sent a link termination request and received a termination ACK from the peer.

3.6.1.2 LCP Options

Several *options* can be negotiated by LCP as it establishes a link for use by one or more NCPs. We shall discuss two of the more common ones. The *Asynchronous Control Character Map* (ACCM) or simply "asyncmap" option defines which control characters (i.e., ASCII characters in the range 0x00–0x1F) need to be "escaped" as PPP operates. Escaping a character means that the true value of the character is

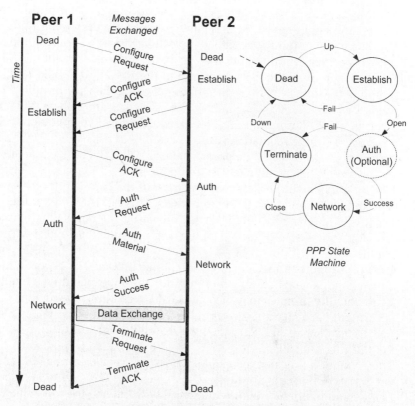

Figure 3-24 LCP is used to establish a PPP link and agree upon options by each peer. The typical exchange involves a pair of configure requests and ACKs that contain the option list, an authentication exchange, data exchange (not pictured), and a termination exchange. Because PPP is such a general-purpose protocol with many parts, many other types of operations may occur between the establishment of a link and its termination.

not sent, but instead the PPP escape character (0x7D) is stuffed in front of a value formed by XORing the original control character with the value 0x20. For example, the XOFF character (0x13) would be sent as (0x7D33). ACCM is used in cases where control characters may affect the operation of the underlying hardware. For example, if software flow control using XON/XOFF characters is enabled and the XOFF character is passed through the link unescaped, the data transfer ceases until the hardware observes an XON character. The asyncmap option is generally specified as a 32-bit hexadecimal number where a 1 bit in the nth least significant bit position indicates that the control character with value n should be escaped. Thus, the asyncmap 0xffffffff would escape all control characters, 0x00000000 would escape none of them, and 0x000A0000 would escape XON (value 0x11) and XOFF (value 0x13). Although the value 0xffffffff is the specified default, many links today can operate safely with the asyncmap set to 0x00000000.

Because PPP lacks a *Length* field and serial lines do not typically provide framing, no immediate hard limit is set on the length of a PPP frame, in theory. In practice, some maximum frame size is typically given by specifying the MRU. When a host specifies an MRU option (type 0x01), the peer is requested to never send frames longer than the value provided in the MRU option. The MRU value is the length of the data field in bytes; it does not count the various other PPP overhead fields (i.e., *Protocol, FCS, Flag* fields). Typical values are 1500 or 1492 but may be as large as 65,535. A minimum of 1280 is required for IPv6 operations. The standard requires PPP implementations to accept frames as large as 1500 bytes, so the MRU serves more as advice to the peer in choosing the packet size than as a hard limit on the size. When small packets are interleaved with larger packets on the same PPP link, the larger packets may use most of the bandwidth of a low-bandwidth link, to the detriment of the small packets. This can lead to jitter (delay variance), negatively affecting interactive applications such as remote login and VoIP. Configuring a smaller MRU (or MTU) can help mitigate this issue at the cost of higher overhead.

PPP supports a mechanism to exchange link quality reporting information. During option negotiation, a configuration message including a request for a particular quality protocol may be included. Sixteen bits of the option are reserved to specify the particular protocol, but the most common is a PPP standard involving *Link Quality Reports* (LQRs) [RFC1989], using the value 0xC025 in the PPP *Protocol* field. If this is enabled, the peer is asked to provide LQRs at some periodic rate. The maximum time between LQRs requested is encoded as a 32-bit number present in the configuration option and expressed in 1/100s units. Peers may generate LQRs more frequently than requested. LQRs include the following information: a magic number, the number of packets and bytes sent and received, the number of incoming packets with errors and the number of discarded packets, and the total number of LQRs exchanged. A typical implementation allows the user to configure how often LQRs are requested from the peer. Some also provide a way to terminate the link if the quality history fails to meet some configured threshold. LQRs may be requested after the PPP link has reached the Establish state. Each LQR is given a sequence number, so it is possible to determine trends over time, even in the face of reordering of LQRs.

Many PPP implementations support a *callback* capability. In a typical callback setup, a PPP dial-up callback client calls in to a PPP callback server, authentication information is provided, and the server disconnects and calls the client back. This may be useful in situations where call toll charges are asymmetric or for some level of security. The protocol used to negotiate callback is an LCP option with value 0x0D [RFC1570]. If agreed upon, the *Callback Control Protocol* (CBCP) completes the negotiation.

Some compression and encryption algorithms used with PPP require a certain minimum number of bytes, called the *block size*, when operating. When data is not otherwise long enough, padding may be added to cause the length to become an even multiple of the block size. If present, padding is included beyond the data area and prior to the PPP *FCS* field. A padding method known as *self-describing padding* [RFC1570] alters the value of padding to be nonzero. Instead, each byte gets the value of its offset in the pad area. Thus, the first byte of pad would have the value 0x01, and the final byte contains the number of pad bytes that were added. At most, 255 bytes of padding are supported. The self-describing padding option (type 10) indicates to a peer the ability to understand this form of padding and includes the *maximum pad value* (MPV), which is the largest pad value allowed for this association. Recall that the basic PPP frame lacks an explicit *Length* field, so a receiver can use self-describing padding to determine how many pad bytes should be trimmed from the received data area.

To lessen the impact of the fixed costs of sending a header on every frame, a method has been introduced to multiplex multiple distinct payloads of potentially different protocols into the same PPP frame, an approach called *PPPMux* [RFC3153]. The primary PPP header *Protocol* field is set to *multiplexed frame* (0x0059), and then each payload block is inserted into the frame. This is accomplished by introducing a 1- to 4-byte subframe header in front of each payload block. It includes 1 bit (called PFF) indicating whether a *Protocol* field is included in the subframe header and another 1-bit field (called *LXT*) indicating whether the following *Length* field is 1 or 2 bytes. Beyond this, if present, is the 1- or 2-byte *Protocol ID* using the same values and same compression approach as with the outer PPP header. A 0 value for PFF (meaning no *PID* field is present) is possible when the subframe matches the default PID established when the configuration state is set up using the *PPPMux Control Protocol* (PPPMuxCP).

The PPP frame format in Figure 3-19 indicates that the ordinary PPP/HDLC FCS can be either 16 or 32 bits. While the default is 16, 32-bit FCS values can be enabled with the 32-bit FCS option. Other LCP options include the use of PFC and ACFC, and selection of an authentication algorithm.

Internationalization [RFC2484] provides a way to convey the language and character set to be used. The character set is one of the standard values from the "charset registry" [IANA-CHARSET], and the language value is chosen from the list in [RFC5646][RFC4647].

3.6.2   Multilink PPP (MP)

A special option to PPP called *multilink PPP* (MP) [RFC1990] can be used to aggregate multiple point-to-point links to act as one. This idea is similar to link aggregation, discussed earlier, and has been used for aggregating multiple circuit-switched channels together (e.g., ISDN B channels). MP includes a special LCP option to indicate multilink support as well as a negotiation protocol to fragment and recombine fragmented PPP frames across multiple links. An aggregated link, called a *bundle*, operates as a complete virtual link and can contain its own configuration information. The bundle comprises a number of *member links*. Each member link may also have its own set of options.

The obvious method to implement MP would be to simply alternate packets across the member links. This approach, called the *bank teller's algorithm*, may lead to reordering of packets, which can have undesirable performance impacts on other protocols. (Although TCP/IP, for example, can function properly with reordered packets, it may not function as well as it could without reordering.) Instead, MP places a 2- or 4-byte *sequencing header* in each packet, and the remote MP receiver is tasked with reconstructing the proper order. The data frame appears as shown in Figure 3-25.

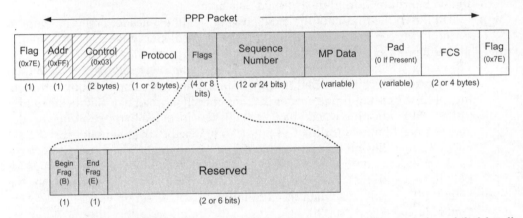

Figure 3-25   An MP fragment contains a sequencing header that allows the remote end of a multilink bundle to reorder fragments. Two formats of this header are supported: a short header (2 bytes) and a long header (4 bytes).

In Figure 3-25 we see an MP fragment with the begin (*B*) and end (*E*) fragment bit fields and *Sequence Number* field. Note that there is both a long format, in which 4 bytes are used for the fragmentation information, and a short format, in which only 2 bytes are used. The format being used is selected during option negotiation using the LCP *short sequence number* option (type 18). If a frame is not fragmented but is carried in this format, both the *B* and *E* bits are set, indicating that the fragment is the first and last (i.e., it is the whole frame). Otherwise, the first fragment has the *BE* bit combination set to 10 and the final fragment has the *BE* bits set to 01, and all fragments in between have them set to 00. The sequence number then gives the packet number offset relative to the first fragment.

Use of MP is requested by including an LCP option called the *multilink maximum received reconstructed unit* (MRRU, type 18) that can act as a sort of larger MRU applying to the bundle. Frames larger than any of the member link MRUs may still be permitted across the MP link, up to the limit advertised in this value.

Because an MP bundle may span multiple member links, a method is needed to identify member links as belonging to the same bundle. Member links in the same bundle are identified by the LCP *endpoint discriminator* option (type 19). The endpoint discriminator could be a phone number, a number derived from an IP or MAC address, or some administrative string. Other than being common to each member link, there are few restrictions on the form of this option.

The basic method of establishing MP as defined in [RFC1990] expects that member links are going to be used symmetrically—about the same number of fragments will be allocated to each of a fixed number of links. In order to achieve more sophisticated allocations than this, the *Bandwidth Allocation Protocol* (BAP) and *Bandwidth Allocation Control Protocol* (BACP) are specified in [RFC2125]. BAP can be used to dynamically add or remove links from a bundle, and BACP can be used to exchange information regarding how links should be added or removed using BAP. This capability can be used to help implement *bandwidth on demand* (BOD). In networks where some fixed resource needs to be allocated in order to meet an application's need for bandwidth (e.g., by dialing some number of telephone connections), BOD typically involves monitoring traffic and creating new connections when usage is high and shutting down connections when usage is low. This is useful, for example, in cases where some monetary charge is associated with the number of connections being used.

BAP/BACP makes use of a new *link discriminator* LCP option (LCP option type 23). This option contains a 16-bit numeric value that is required to be different for each member link of a bundle. It is used by BAP to identify which links are to be added or removed. BACP is negotiated once per bundle during the network phase of a PPP link. Its main purpose is to identify a *favored peer*. That is, if more than one bundle is being set up simultaneously among multiple peers, the favored peer is preferentially allocated member links.

BAP includes three packet types: request, response, and indication. Requests are to add a link to a bundle or to request the peer to delete a link from a bundle. Indications convey the results of attempted additions back to the original requester and are acknowledged. Responses are either ACKs or NACKs for these requests. More details can be found in [RFC2125].

3.6.3 Compression Control Protocol (CCP)

Historically, PPP has been the protocol of choice when using relatively slow dial-up modems. As a consequence, a number of methods have been developed to compress data sent over PPP links. This type of compression is distinct both from the types of compression supported in modem hardware (e.g., V.42bis, V.44) and also from protocol *header compression*, which we discuss later. Today, several compression options are available. To choose among them for each direction on a PPP link, LCP can negotiate an option to enable the *Compression Control Protocol* (CCP) [RFC1962]. CCP acts like an NCP (see Section 3.6.5) but handles the details of configuring compression once the compression option is indicated in the LCP link establishment exchange.

In behaving like an NCP, CCP can be negotiated only once the link has entered the Network state. It uses the same packet exchange procedures and formats as

LCP, except the *Protocol* field is set to 0x80FD, there are some special options, and in addition to the common *Code* field values (1–7) two new operations are defined: reset-request (0x0e) and reset-ACK (0x0f). If an error is detected in a compressed frame, a reset request can be used to cause the peer to reset compression state (e.g., dictionaries, state variables, state machines, etc.). After resetting, the peer responds with a reset-ACK.

One or more compressed packets may be carried within the information portion of a PPP frame (i.e., the portion including the LCP data and possibly pad portions). Compressed frames carry the *Protocol* field value of 0x00FD, but the mechanism used to indicate the presence of multiple compressed datagrams is dependent on the particular compression algorithm used (see Section 3.6.6). When used in conjunction with MP, CCP may be used either on the bundle or on some combination of the member links. If used only on member links, the *Protocol* field is set to 0x00FB (individual link compressed datagram).

CCP can enable one of about a dozen compression algorithms [PPPn]. Most of the algorithms are not official standards-track IETF documents, although they may be described in informational RFCs (e.g., [RFC1977] describes the BSD compression scheme, and [RFC2118] describes the *Microsoft Point-to-Point Compression Protocol* (MPPC)). If compression is being used, PPP frames are reconstructed before further processing, so higher-layer PPP operations are not generally concerned with the details of the compressed frames.

3.6.4 PPP Authentication

Before a PPP link becomes operational in the Network state, it is often necessary to establish the identity of the peer(s) of the link using some *authentication* (identity verification) mechanism. The basic PPP specification has a default of no authentication, so the authentication exchange of Figure 3-24 would not be used in such cases. More often, however, some form of authentication is required, and a number of protocols have evolved over the years to deal with this situation. In this chapter we discuss them only from a high-level point of view and leave the details for the chapter on security (Chapter 18). Other than no authentication, the simplest and least secure authentication scheme is called the *Password Authentication Protocol* (PAP). This protocol is very simple—one peer requests the other to send a password, and the password is so provided. As the password is sent unencrypted over the PPP link, any eavesdropper on the line can simply capture the password and use it later. Because of this significant vulnerability, PAP is not recommended for authentication. PAP packets are encoded as LCP packets with the *Protocol* field value set to 0xC023.

A somewhat more secure approach to authentication is provided by the *Challenge-Handshake Authentication Protocol* (CHAP) [RFC1994]. Using CHAP, a random value is sent from one peer (called the authenticator) to the other. A response is formed by using a special *one-way* (i.e., not easily invertible) function to combine the random value with a shared secret key (usually derived from a password) to produce a number that is sent in response. Upon receiving this response, the authenticator can determine with a very high degree of confidence that its peer possesses the correct secret key. This protocol never sends the key or password over the link in a clear (unencrypted) form, so any eavesdropper is unable to learn the secret. Because a different random value is used each time, the result of the function changes for each challenge/response, so the values an eavesdropper may be able to capture cannot be reused (played back) to impersonate the peer. However, CHAP is vulnerable to a "man in the middle" form of attack (see Chapter 18).

EAP [RFC3748] is an authentication framework available for many different network types. It also supports many (about 40) different authentication methods, ranging from simple passwords such as PAP and CHAP to more elaborate types of authentication (e.g., smart cards, biometrics). EAP defines a message format for carrying a variety of specific types of authentication formats, but additional specifications are needed to define how EAP messages are carried over particular types of links.

When EAP is used with PPP, the basic authentication method discussed so far is altered. Instead of negotiating a specific authentication method early in the link establishment (at LCP link establishment), the authentication operation may be postponed until the Auth state (just before the Network state). This allows for a greater richness in the types of information that can be used to influence access control decisions by *remote access servers* (RASs). When there is a standard protocol for carrying a variety of authentication mechanisms, a network access server may not need to process the contents of EAP messages at all but can instead depend on some other infrastructure authentication server (e.g., a RADIUS server [RFC2865]) to determine access control decisions. This is currently the design of choice for enterprise networks and ISPs.

3.6.5 Network Control Protocols (NCPs)

Although many different NCPs can be used on a PPP link (even simultaneously), we shall focus on the NCPs supporting IPv4 and IPv6. For IPv4, the NCP is called the *IP Control Protocol* (IPCP) [RFC1332]. For IPv6, the NCP is *IPV6CP* [RFC5072]. Once LCP has completed its link establishment and authentication, each end of the link is in the Network state and may proceed to negotiate a network-layer association using zero or more NCPs (one, such as IPCP, is typical).

IPCP, the standard NCP for IPv4, can be used to establish IPv4 connectivity over a link and configure *Van Jacobson header compression* (VJ compression) [RFC1144]. IPCP packets may be exchanged after the PPP state machine has reached the Network state. IPCP packets use the same packet exchange mechanism and packet format as LCP, except the *Protocol* field is set to 0x8021, and the *Code* field is limited to the range 0–7. These values of the *Code* field correspond to the message types: vendor-specific (see [RFC2153]), configure-request, configure-ACK, configure-REJECT, terminate-request, terminate-ACK, and code-REJECT. IPCP can negotiate a number of options, including an IP compression protocol (2), the IPv4 address

(3), and Mobile IPv4 [RFC2290] (4). Other options are available for learning the location of primary and secondary domain name servers (see Chapter 11).

IPV6CP uses the same packet exchange and format as LCP, except it has two different options: interface-identifier and IPv6-compression-protocol. The interface identifier option is used to convey a 64-bit IID value (see Chapter 2) used as the basis for forming a link-local IPv6 address. Because it is used only on the local link, it does not require global uniqueness. This is accomplished using a standard link-local prefix for the higher-order bits of the IPv6 address and allowing the lower-order bits to be a function of the interface identifier. This mimics IPv6 auto-configuration (see Chapter 6).

3.6.6   Header Compression

PPP dial-up lines have historically been comparatively slow (54,000 bits/s or less), and many small packets are often used with TCP/IP (e.g., for TCP's acknowledgments; see Chapter 15). Most of these packets contain a TCP and IP header that changes little from one packet to another on the same TCP connection. Other higher-layer protocols behave similarly. Thus, it is useful to have a way of compressing the headers of these higher-layer protocols (or eliminating them) so that fewer bytes need to be carried over relatively slow point-to-point links. The methods employed to compress or eliminate headers have evolved over time. We discuss them in chronological order, beginning with VJ compression, mentioned earlier.

In VJ compression, portions of the higher-layer (TCP and IP) headers are replaced with a small, 1-byte connection identifier. [RFC1144] discusses the origin of this approach, using an older point-to-point protocol called CSLIP (Compressed Serial Line IP). A typical IPv4 header is 20 bytes, and a TCP header without options is another 20. Together, a common combined TCP/IPv4 header is thus 40 bytes, and many of the fields do not change from packet to packet. Furthermore, many of the fields that do change from packet to packet change only slightly or in a limited way. When the nonchanging values are sent over a link once (or a small number of times) and kept in a table, a small index can be used as a replacement for the constants in subsequent packets. The limited changing values are then encoded differentially (i.e., only the amount of change is sent). As a result, the entire 40-byte header can usually be compressed to an effective 3 or 4 bytes. This can significantly improve TCP/IP performance over slow links.

The next step in the evolution of header compression is simply called *IP header compression* [RFC2507][RFC3544]. It provides a way to compress the headers of multiple packets using both TCP or UDP transport-layer protocols and either IPv4 or IPv6 network-layer protocols. The techniques are a logical extension and generalization of the VJ compression technique that applies to more protocols, and to links other than PPP links. [RFC2507] points out the necessity of some strong error detection mechanism in the underlying link layer because erroneous packets can be constructed at the egress of a link if compressed header values are damaged in transit. This is important to recognize when header compression is used on links that may not have as strong an FCS computation as PPP.

The most recent step in the evolution of header compression is known as *Robust Header Compression* (ROHC) [RFC5225]. It further generalizes IP header compression to cover more transport protocols and allows more than one form of header compression to operate simultaneously. Like the IP header compression mentioned previously, it can be used over various types of links, including PPP.

3.6.7 Example

We now look at the debugging output of a PPP server interacting with a client over a dial-in modem. The dialing-in client is an IPv6-capable Microsoft Windows Vista machine, and the server is Linux. The Vista machine is configured to negotiate multilink capability even on single links (Properties | Options | PPP Settings), for demonstration purposes, and the server is configured to require an encryption protocol negotiated using CCP (see `MPPE` in the following listing):

```
data dev=ttyS0, pid=28280, caller='none', conn='38400',
    name='',cmd='/usr/sbin/pppd', user='/AutoPPP/'
pppd 2.4.4 started by a_ppp, uid 0
using channel 54
Using interface ppp0
ppp0 <--> /dev/ttyS0
sent [LCP ConfReq id=0x1 <asyncmap 0x0> <auth eap>
    <magic 0xa5ccc449><pcomp> <accomp>]
rcvd [LCP ConfNak id=0x1 <auth chap MS-v2>]
sent [LCP ConfReq id=0x2 <asyncmap 0x0> <auth chap MS-v2>
    <magic 0xa5ccc449><pcomp> <accomp>]
rcvd [LCP ConfAck id=0x2 <asyncmap 0x0> <auth chap MS-v2>
    <magic 0xa5ccc449><pcomp> <accomp>]
rcvd [LCP ConfReq id=0x2 <asyncmap 0x0> <magic 0xa531e06>
    <pcomp> <accomp><callback CBCP> <mrru 1614>
    <endpoint [local:12.92.67.ef.2f.fe.44.6e.84.f8.
               c9.3f.5f.8c.5c.41.00.00.00.00]>]
sent [LCP ConfRej id=0x2 <callback CBCP> <mrru 1614>]
rcvd [LCP ConfReq id=0x3 <asyncmap 0x0> <magic 0xa531e06>
    <pcomp> <accomp>
    <endpoint [local:12.92.67.ef.2f.fe.44.6e.84.f8.
               c9.3f.5f.8c.5c.41.00.00.00.00]>]
sent [LCP ConfAck id=0x3 <asyncmap 0x0> <magic 0xa531e06>
    <pcomp> <accomp>
    <endpoint [local:12.92.67.ef.2f.fe.44.6e.84.f8.
               c9.3f.5f.8c.5c.41.00.00.00.00]>]
sent [CHAP Challenge id=0x1a <4d53c52b8e7dcfe7a9ea438b2b4daf55>,
     name = "dialer"]
rcvd [LCP Ident id=0x4 magic=0xa531e06 "MSRASV5.20"]
rcvd [LCP Ident id=0x5 magic=0xa531e06 "MSRAS-0-VISTA"]
rcvd [CHAP Response id=0x1a
    <4b5dc95ed4e1788b959025de0233d4fc0000000
     00000000033a555d2a77bd1fa692f2a0af707cd 4f0c0072c379c82e0f00>,
    name = "dialer"]
sent [CHAP Success id=0x1a
    "S=7E0B6B513215C87520BEF6725EF8A9945C28E918M=Access granted"]
```

```
sent [CCP ConfReq id=0x1 <mppe +H -M +S +L -D -C>]
rcvd [IPV6CP ConfReq id=0x6 <addr fe80::0000:0000:dead:beef>]
sent [IPV6CP TermAck id=0x6]
rcvd [CCP ConfReq id=0x7 <mppe -H -M -S -L -D +C>]
sent [CCP ConfNak id=0x7 <mppe +H -M +S +L -D -C>]
rcvd [IPCP ConfReq id=0x8 <compress VJ 0f 01> <addr 0.0.0.0>
      <ms-dns1 0.0.0.0> <ms-wins 0.0.0.0> <ms-dns3 0.0.0.0>
      <ms-wins 0.0.0.0>]
sent [IPCP TermAck id=0x8]
rcvd [CCP ConfNak id=0x1 <mppe -H -M +S -L -D -C>]
sent [CCP ConfReq id=0x2 <mppe -H -M +S -L -D -C>]
rcvd [CCP ConfReq id=0x9 <mppe -H -M +S -L -D -C>]
sent [CCP ConfAck id=0x9 <mppe -H -M +S -L -D -C>]
rcvd [CCP ConfAck id=0x2 <mppe -H -M +S -L -D -C>]
MPPE 128-bit stateful compression enabled
sent [IPCP ConfReq id=0x1 <compress VJ 0f 01> <addr 192.168.0.1>]
sent [IPV6CP ConfReq id=0x1 <addr fe80::0206:5bff:fedd:c5c3>]
rcvd [IPCP ConfAck id=0x1 <compress VJ 0f 01> <addr 192.168.0.1>]
rcvd [IPV6CP ConfAck id=0x1 <addr fe80::0206:5bff:fedd:c5c3>]
rcvd [IPCP ConfReq id=0xa <compress VJ 0f 01>
      <addr 0.0.0.0> <ms-dns1 0.0.0.0>
      <ms-wins 0.0.0.0> <ms-dns3 0.0.0.0> <ms-wins 0.0.0.0>]
sent [IPCP ConfRej id=0xa <ms-wins 0.0.0.0> <ms-wins 0.0.0.0>]
rcvd [IPV6CP ConfReq id=0xb <addr fe80::0000:0000:dead:beef>]
sent [IPV6CP ConfAck id=0xb <addr fe80::0000:0000:dead:beef>]
rcvd [IPCP ConfAck id=0x1 <compress VJ 0f 01> <addr 192.168.0.1>]
rcvd [IPV6CP ConfAck id=0x1 <addr fe80::0206:5bff:fedd:c5c3>]
local LL address fe80::0206:5bff:fedd:c5c3
remote LL address fe80::0000:0000:dead:beef
rcvd [IPCP ConfReq id=0xc <compress VJ 0f 01>
      <addr 0.0.0.0> <ms-dns1 0.0.0.0> <ms-dns3 0.0.0.0>]
sent [IPCP ConfNak id=0xc <addr 192.168.0.2> <ms-dns1 192.168.0.1>
      <ms-dns3 192.168.0.1>]
sent [IPCP ConfAck id=0xd <compress VJ 0f 01> <addr 192.168.0.2>
      <ms-dns1 192.168.0.1> <ms-dns3 192.168.0.1>]
local IP address 192.168.0.1
remote IP address 192.168.0.2
... data ...
```

Here we can see a somewhat involved PPP exchange, as viewed from the server. The PPP server process creates a (virtual) network interface called ppp0, which is awaiting an incoming connection on the dial-up modem attached to serial port ttyS0. Once the incoming connection arrives, the server requests an asyncmap of 0x0, EAP authentication, PFC, and ACFC. The client refuses EAP authentication and instead suggests MS-CHAP-v2 (ConfNak) [RFC2759]. The server then tries again, this time using MS-CHAP-v2, which is then accepted and acknowledged (ConfAck). Next, the incoming request includes CBCP; an MRRU of 1614 bytes, which is associated with MP support; and an endpoint ID. The server rejects the request for CBCP and multilink operation (ConfRej). The endpoint discriminator is once again sent by the client, this time without the MRRU, and is accepted and acknowledged. Next, the server sends a CHAP challenge with the name dialer. Before a response to the challenge arrives, two incoming identity messages arrive, indicating that the peer is identified by the strings MSRASV5.20 and MSRAS-0-VISTA. Finally, the CHAP response arrives and is validated as correct, and an acknowledgment indicates that access is granted. PPP then moves on to the Network state.

Once in the Network state, the CCP, IPCP, and IPV6CP NCPs are exchanged. CCP attempts to negotiate *Microsoft Point-to-Point Encryption* (MPPE) [RFC3078]. MPPE is somewhat of an anomaly, as it is really an encryption protocol, and rather than compressing the packet it actually expands it by 4 bytes. It does, however, provide a relatively simple means of establishing encryption early in the negotiation process. The options +H -M +S +L -D -C indicate whether MPPE stateless operation is desired (H), what cryptographic key strength is available (secure, S; medium, M; or low, L), an obsolete D bit, and whether a separate, proprietary compression protocol called MPPC [RFC2118] is desired (C). Eventually the two peers agree on stateful mode using strong 128-bit keying (-H, +S). Note that during the middle of this negotiation, the client attempts to send an IPCP request, but the server responds with an unsolicited TermAck (a message defined within LCP that ICPC adopts). This is used to indicate to the peer that the server is "in need of renegotiation" [RFC1661].

After the successful negotiation of MPPE, the server requests the use of VJ header compression and provides its IPv4 and IPv6 addresses, 192.168.0.1 and fe80::0206:5bff:fedd:c5c3. This IPv6 address is derived from the server's Ethernet MAC address 00:06:5B:DD:C5:C3. The client initially suggests its IPv4 address and name servers to be 0.0.0.0 using IPCP, but this is rejected. The client then requests to use fe80::0000:0000:dead:beef as its IPv6 address, which is accepted and acknowledged. Finally, the client ACKs both the IPv4 and IPv6 addresses of the server, and the IPv6 addresses have been established. Next, the client again requests IPv4 and server addresses of 0.0.0.0, which is rejected in favor of 192.168.0.1. These are accepted and acknowledged.

As we can see from this exchange, the PPP negotiation is both flexible and tedious. There are many options that can be attempted, rejected, and renegotiated. While this may not be a big problem on a link with low delay, imagine how long this exchange could take if each message took a few seconds (or longer) to reach its destination, as might occur over a satellite link, for example. Link establishment would be a visibly long procedure for the user.

3.7 Loopback

Although it may seem surprising, in many cases clients may wish to communicate with servers on the same computer using Internet protocols such as TCP/IP. To enable this, most implementations support a network-layer *loopback* capability that typically takes the form of a virtual loopback network interface. It acts like a real network interface but is really a special piece of software provided by the operating system to enable TCP/IP and other communications on the same host computer. IPv4 addresses starting with 127 are reserved for this, as is the IPv6 address ::1 (see Chapter 2 for IPv4 and IPv6 addressing conventions). Traditionally, UNIX-like systems including Linux assign the IPv4 address of 127.0.0.1 (::1 for IPv6) to the loopback interface and assign it the name localhost. An IP datagram sent to the loopback interface must not appear on any network. Although we could imagine the transport layer detecting that the other end is a loopback address and short-circuiting some of the transport-layer logic and all of the network-layer logic, most implementations perform complete processing of the data in the transport layer and network layer and loop the IP datagram back up in the network stack only when the datagram leaves the bottom of the network layer. This can be useful for performance measurement, for example, because the amount of time required to execute the stack software can be measured without any hardware overheads. In Linux, the loopback interface is called lo.

```
Linux% ifconfig lo
lo Link encap:Local Loopback
          inet addr:127.0.0.1 Mask:255.0.0.0
          inet6 addr: ::1/128 Scope:Host
          UP LOOPBACK RUNNING MTU:16436 Metric:1
          RX packets:458511 errors:0 dropped:0 overruns:0 frame:0
          TX packets:458511 errors:0 dropped:0 overruns:0 carrier:0
          collisions:0 txqueuelen:0
          RX bytes:266049199 (253.7 MiB)
          TX bytes:266049199 (253.7 MiB)
```

Here we see that the local loopback interface has the IPv4 address 127.0.0.1 and a subnet mask of 255.0.0.0 (corresponding to class A network number 127 in classful addressing). The IPv6 address ::1 has a 128-bit-long prefix, so it represents only a single address. The interface has an MTU of 16KB (this can be configured to a much larger size, up to 2GB). A significant amount of traffic, nearly half a million packets, has passed through the interface without error since the machine was initialized two months earlier. We would not expect to see errors on the local loopback device, given that it never really sends packets on any network.

In Windows, the Microsoft Loopback Adapter is not installed by default, even though IP loopback is still supported. This adapter can be used for testing various network configurations even when a physical network interface is not available. To install it under Windows XP, select Start | Control Panel | Add Hardware | Select Network Adapters from list | Select Microsoft as manufacturer | Select Microsoft Loopback Adapter. For Windows Vista or Windows 7, run the program hdwwiz from the command prompt and add the Microsoft Loopback Adapter manually. Once this is performed, the ipconfig command reveals the following (this example is from Windows Vista):

```
C:\> ipconfig /all
...
Ethernet adapter Local Area Connection 2:
   Connection-specific DNS Suffix . :
   Description . . . . . . . . . . . : Microsoft Loopback Adapter
   Physical Address. . . . . . . . . : 02-00-4C-4F-4F-50
   DHCP Enabled. . . . . . . . . . . : Yes
   Autoconfiguration Enabled . . . . : Yes
   Link-local IPv6 Address . . . . . :
           fe80::9c0d:77a:52b8:39f0%18(Preferred)
   Autoconfiguration IPv4 Address. . : 169.254.57.240(Preferred)
   Subnet Mask . . . . . . . . . . . : 255.255.0.0
   Default Gateway . . . . . . . . . :
   DHCPv6 IAID . . . . . . . . . . . : 302121036
   DNS Servers . . . . . . . . . . . : fec0:0:0:ffff::1%1
           fec0:0:0:ffff::2%1
           fec0:0:0:ffff::3%1
   NetBIOS over Tcpip. . . . . . . . : Enabled
```

Here we can see that the interface has been created, has been assigned both
IPv4 and IPv6 addresses, and appears as a sort of virtual Ethernet device. Now the
machine has several loopback addresses:

```
C:\> ping 127.1.2.3
Pinging 127.1.2.3 with 32 bytes of data:
Reply from 127.1.2.3: bytes=32 time<1ms TTL=128
Reply from 127.1.2.3: bytes=32 time<1ms TTL=128
Reply from 127.1.2.3: bytes=32 time<1ms TTL=128
Reply from 127.1.2.3: bytes=32 time<1ms TTL=128
Ping statistics for 127.1.2.3:
       Packets: Sent = 4, Received = 4, Lost = 0 (0% loss),
Approximate round trip times in milli-seconds:
       Minimum = 0ms, Maximum = 0ms, Average = 0ms


C:\> ping ::1
Pinging ::1 from ::1 with 32 bytes of data:
Reply from ::1: time<1ms
Reply from ::1: time<1ms
Reply from ::1: time<1ms
Reply from ::1: time<1ms
Ping statistics for ::1:
       Packets: Sent = 4, Received = 4, Lost = 0 (0% loss),
Approximate round trip times in milli-seconds:

       Minimum = 0ms, Maximum = 0ms, Average = 0ms

C:\> ping 169.254.57.240
Pinging 169.254.57.240127.1.2.3 with 32 bytes of data:
Reply from 169.254.57.240: bytes=32 time<1ms TTL=128
Reply from 169.254.57.240: bytes=32 time<1ms TTL=128
Reply from 169.254.57.240: bytes=32 time<1ms TTL=128
```

```
Reply from 169.254.57.240: bytes=32 time<1ms TTL=128
Ping statistics for 169.254.57.240:
Packets: Sent = 4, Received = 4, Lost = 0 (0% loss),
Approximate round trip times in milli-seconds:
     Minimum = 0ms, Maximum = 0ms, Average = 0ms
```

Here we can see that in IPv4, any destination address starting with 127 is looped back. For IPv6, however, only the single address ::1 is defined for loopback operation. We can also see how the loopback adapter with address 169.254.57.240 returned data immediately. One subtlety to which we will return in Chapter 9 is whether multicast or broadcast datagrams should be copied back to the sending computer (over the loopback interface). This choice can be made by each individual application.

3.8   MTU and Path MTU

As we can see from Figure 3-3, there is a limit on the size of the frame available for carrying the PDUs of higher-layer protocols in many link-layer networks such as Ethernet. This usually limits the number of payload bytes to about 1500 for Ethernet and often the same amount for PPP in order to maintain compatibility with Ethernet. This characteristic of the link layer is called the *maximum transmission unit* (MTU). Most packet networks (like Ethernet) have a fixed upper limit. Most stream-type networks (serial links) have a configurable limit that is then used by framing protocols such as PPP. If IP has a datagram to send, and the datagram is larger than the link layer's MTU, IP performs *fragmentation*, breaking the datagram up into smaller pieces (fragments), so that each fragment is smaller than the MTU. We discuss IP fragmentation in Chapters 5 and 10.

When two hosts on the same network are communicating with each other, it is the MTU of the local link interconnecting them that has a direct effect on the size of datagrams that are used during the conversation. When two hosts communicate across multiple networks, each link can have a different MTU. The minimum MTU across the network path comprising all of the links is called the *path MTU*.

The path MTU between any two hosts need not be constant over time. It depends on the path being used at any time, which can change if the routers or links in the network fail. Also, paths are often not *symmetric* (i.e., the path from host A to B may not be the reverse of the path from B to A); hence the path MTU need not be the same in the two directions.

[RFC1191] specifies the *path MTU discovery* (PMTUD) mechanism for IPv4, and [RFC1981] describes it for IPv6. A complementary approach that avoids some of the issues with these mechanisms is described in [RFC4821]. PMTU discovery is used to determine the path MTU at a point in time and is required of IPv6 implementations. In later chapters we shall see how this mechanism operates after we have described ICMP and IP fragmentation. We shall also see what effect it can have on transport performance when we discuss TCP and UDP.

3.9   Tunneling Basics

In some cases it is useful to establish a virtual link between one computer and another across the Internet or other network. VPNs, for example, offer this type of service. The method most commonly used to implement these types of services is called *tunneling*. Tunneling, generally speaking, is the idea of carrying lower-layer traffic in higher-layer (or equal-layer) packets. For example, IPv4 can be carried in an IPv4 or IPv6 packet; Ethernet can be carried in a UDP or IPv4 or IPv6 packet, and so on. Tunneling turns the idea of strict layering of protocols on its head and allows for the formation of *overlay networks* (i.e., networks where the "links" are really virtual links implemented in some other protocol instead of physical connections). It is a very powerful and useful technique. Here we discuss the basics of some of the tunneling options.

There is a great variety of methods for tunneling packets of one protocol and/or layer over another. Three of the more common protocols used to establish tunnels include *Generic Routing Encapsulation* (GRE) [RFC2784], the Microsoft proprietary *Point-to-Point Tunneling Protocol* (PPTP) [RFC2637], and the *Layer 2 Tunneling Protocol* (L2TP) [RFC3931]. Others include the earlier nonstandard IP-in-IP tunneling protocol [RFC1853]. GRE and LT2P were developed to standardize and replace IP-in-IP and PPTP, respectively, but all of these approaches are still in use. We shall focus on GRE and PPTP, with more emphasis on PPTP, as it is more visible to individual users even though it is not an IETF standard. L2TP is often used with security at the IP layer (IPsec; see Chapter 18) because L2TP by itself does not provide security. Because GRE and PPTP are closely related, we now look at the GRE header in Figure 3-26, in both its original standard and revised standard forms.

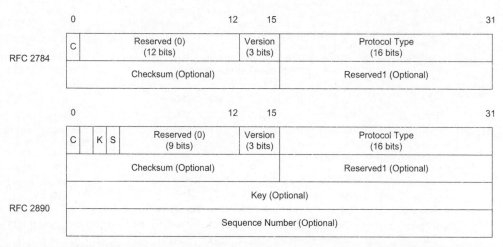

Figure 3-26   The basic GRE header is only 4 bytes but includes the option of a 16-bit checksum (of a type common to many Internet protocols). The header was later extended to include an identifier (*Key* field) common to multiple packets in a flow, and a *Sequence Number*, to help in resequencing packets that get out of order.

As can be seen from the headers in Figure 3-26, the baseline GRE specification [RFC2784] is rather simple and provides only a minimal encapsulation for other packets. The first bit field (C) indicates whether a checksum is present. If it is, the *Checksum* field contains the same type of checksum found in many Internet-related protocols (see Section 5.2.2). If the *Checksum* field is present, the *Reserved1* field is also present and is set to 0. [RFC2890] extends the basic format to include optional *Key* and *Sequence Number* fields, present if the *K* and *S* bit fields from Figure 3-26 are set to 1, respectively. If present, the *Key* field is arranged to be a common value in multiple packets, indicating that they belong to the same flow of packets. The *Sequence Number* field is used in order to reorder packets if they should become out of sequence (e.g., by going through different links).

Although GRE forms the basis for and is used by PPTP, the two protocols serve somewhat different purposes. GRE tunnels are typically used within the network infrastructure to carry traffic between ISPs or within an enterprise intranet to serve branch offices and are not necessarily encrypted, although GRE tunnels can be combined with IPsec. PPTP, conversely, is most often used between users and their ISPs or corporate intranets and is encrypted (e.g., using MPPE). PPTP essentially combines GRE with PPP, so GRE can provide the virtual point-to-point link upon which PPP operates. GRE carries its traffic using IPv4 or IPv6 and as such is a layer 3 tunneling technology. PPTP is more often used to carry layer 2 frames (such as Ethernet) so as to emulate a direct LAN (link-layer) connection. This can be used for remote access to corporate networks, for example. PPTP uses a non-standard variation on the standard GRE header (see Figure 3-27).

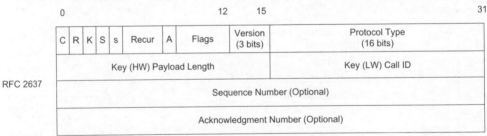

Figure 3-27   The PPTP header is based on an older, nonstandard GRE header. It includes a sequence number, a cumulative packet acknowledgment number, and some identification information. Most of the fields in the first word are set to 0.

We can see a number of differences in Figure 3-27 from the standard GRE header, including the extra *R*, *s*, and *A* bit fields, additional *Flags* field, and *Recur* field. Most of these are simply set to 0 and not used (their assignment is based on an older, nonstandard version of GRE). The *K*, *S*, and *A* bit fields indicate that the *Key*, *Sequence Number*, and *Acknowledgment Number* fields are present. If present, the value of the *Sequence Number* field holds the largest packet number seen by the peer.

We now turn to the establishment of a PPTP session. We shall conclude later with a brief discussion of some of PPTP's other capabilities. The following example is similar to the PPP link establishment example given earlier, except now instead of using a dial-up link, PPTP is providing the "raw" link to PPP. Once again, the client is Windows Vista, and the server is Linux. This output comes from the /var/log/messages file when the debug option is enabled:

```
pptpd: MGR: Manager process started
pptpd: MGR: Maximum of 100 connections available
pptpd: MGR: Launching /usr/sbin/pptpctrl to handle client
pptpd: CTRL: local address = 192.168.0.1
pptpd: CTRL: remote address = 192.168.1.1
pptpd: CTRL: pppd options file = /etc/ppp/options.pptpd
pptpd: CTRL: Client 71.141.227.30 control connection started
pptpd: CTRL: Received PPTP Control Message (type: 1)
pptpd: CTRL: Made a START CTRL CONN RPLY packet
pptpd: CTRL: I wrote 156 bytes to the client.
pptpd: CTRL: Sent packet to client
pptpd: CTRL: Received PPTP Control Message (type: 7)

pptpd: CTRL: Set parameters to 100000000 maxbps, 64 window size
pptpd: CTRL: Made a OUT CALL RPLY packet
pptpd: CTRL: Starting call (launching pppd, opening GRE)
pptpd: CTRL: pty_fd = 6
pptpd: CTRL: tty_fd = 7
pptpd: CTRL (PPPD Launcher): program binary = /usr/sbin/pppd
pptpd: CTRL (PPPD Launcher): local address = 192.168.0.1
pptpd: CTRL (PPPD Launcher): remote address = 192.168.1.1
pppd: pppd 2.4.4 started by root, uid 0
pppd: using channel 60
pptpd: CTRL: I wrote 32 bytes to the client.
pptpd: CTRL: Sent packet to client
pppd: Using interface ppp0
pppd: Connect: ppp0 <--> /dev/pts/1
pppd: sent [LCP ConfReq id=0x1 <asyncmap 0x0> <auth chap MS-v2>
          <magic 0x4e2ca200> <pcomp> <accomp>]
pptpd: CTRL: Received PPTP Control Message (type: 15)
pptpd: CTRL: Got a SET LINK INFO packet with standard ACCMs
pptpd: GRE: accepting packet #0
pppd: rcvd [LCP ConfReq id=0x0 <mru 1400> <magic 0x5e565505>
          <pcomp> <accomp>]
pppd: sent [LCP ConfAck id=0x0 <mru 1400> <magic 0x5e565505>
          <pcomp> <accomp>]
pppd: sent [LCP ConfReq id=0x1 <asyncmap 0x0> <auth chap MS-v2>
          <magic 0x4e2ca200> <pcomp> <accomp>]
pptpd: GRE: accepting packet #1
pppd: rcvd [LCP ConfAck id=0x1 <asyncmap 0x0> <auth chap MS-v2>
          <magic 0x4e2ca200> <pcomp> <accomp>]
pppd: sent [CHAP Challenge id=0x3
          <eb88bfff67d1c239ef73e98ca32646a5>, name = "dialer"]
pptpd: CTRL: Received PPTP Control Message (type: 15)
pptpd: CTRL: Ignored a SET LINK INFO packet with real ACCMs!
```

```
pptpd: GRE: accepting packet #2
pppd: rcvd [CHAP Response id=0x3<276f3678f0f03fa57f64b3c367529565000000
            00000000000fa2b2ae0ad8db9d986f8e222a0217a620638a24
            3179160900>, name = "dialer"]
pppd: sent [CHAP Success id=0x3
            "S=C551119E0E1AAB68E86DED09A32D0346D7002E05
            M=Accessgranted"]
pppd: sent [CCP ConfReq id=0x1 <mppe +H -M +S +L -D -C>]
pptpd: GRE: accepting packet #3
pppd: rcvd [IPV6CP ConfReq id=0x1 <addr fe80::1cfc:fddd:8e2c:e118>]
pppd: sent [IPV6CP TermAck id=0x1]
pptpd: GRE: accepting packet #4
pppd: rcvd [CCP ConfReq id=0x2 <mppe +H -M -S -L -D -C>]
pppd: sent [CCP ConfNak id=0x2 <mppe +H -M +S +L -D -C>]
pptpd: GRE: accepting packet #5
pptpd: GRE: accepting packet #6
pppd: rcvd [IPCP ConfReq id=0x3 <addr 0.0.0.0> <ms-dns1 0.0.0.0>
            <ms-wins 0.0.0.0> <ms-dns3 0.0.0.0> <ms-wins 0.0.0.0>]
pptpd: GRE: accepting packet #7
pppd: sent [IPCP TermAck id=0x3]
pppd: rcvd [CCP ConfNak id=0x1 <mppe +H -M +S -L -D -C>]
pppd: sent [CCP ConfReq id=0x2 <mppe +H -M +S -L -D -C>]
pppd: rcvd [CCP ConfReq id=0x4 <mppe +H -M +S -L -D -C>]
pppd: sent [CCP ConfAck id=0x4 <mppe +H -M +S -L -D -C>]
pptpd: GRE: accepting packet #8
pppd: rcvd [CCP ConfAck id=0x2 <mppe +H -M +S -L -D -C>]
pppd: MPPE 128-bit stateless compression enabled
pppd: sent [IPCP ConfReq id=0x1 <addr 192.168.0.1>]
pppd: sent [IPV6CP ConfReq id=0x1 <addr fe80::0206:5bff:fedd:c5c3>]
pptpd: GRE: accepting packet #9
pppd: rcvd [IPCP ConfAck id=0x1 <addr 192.168.0.1>]
pptpd: GRE: accepting packet #10
pppd: rcvd [IPV6CP ConfAck id=0x1 <addr fe80::0206:5bff:fedd:c5c3>]
pptpd: GRE: accepting packet #11
pppd: rcvd [IPCP ConfReq id=0x5 <addr 0.0.0.0>
            <ms-dns1 0.0.0.0> <ms-wins 0.0.0.0>
            <ms-dns3 0.0.0.0> <ms-wins 0.0.0.0>]
pppd: sent [IPCP ConfRej id=0x5 <ms-wins 0.0.0.0> <ms-wins 0.0.0.0>]
pptpd: GRE: accepting packet #12
pppd: rcvd [IPV6CP ConfReq id=0x6 <addr fe80::1cfc:fddd:8e2c:e118>]
pppd: sent [IPV6CP ConfAck id=0x6 <addr fe80::1cfc:fddd:8e2c:e118>]
pppd: local LL address fe80::0206:5bff:fedd:c5c3
pppd: remote LL address fe80::1cfc:fddd:8e2c:e118
pptpd: GRE: accepting packet #13
pppd: rcvd [IPCP ConfReq id=0x7 <addr 0.0.0.0>
            <ms-dns1 0.0.0.0> <ms-dns3 0.0.0.0>]
pppd: sent [IPCP ConfNak id=0x7 <addr 192.168.1.1>
            <ms-dns1 192.168.0.1> <ms-dns3 192.168.0.1>]
pptpd: GRE: accepting packet #14
pppd: rcvd [IPCP ConfReq id=0x8 <addr 192.168.1.1>
            <ms-dns1 192.168.0.1> <ms-dns3 192.168.0.1>]
pppd: sent [IPCP ConfAck id=0x8 <addr 192.168.1.1>
            <ms-dns1 192.168.0.1> <ms-dns3 192.168.0.1>]
```

```
pppd: local IP address 192.168.0.1
pppd: remote IP address 192.168.1.1
pptpd: GRE: accepting packet #15
pptpd: CTRL: Sending ECHO REQ id 1
pptpd: CTRL: Made a ECHO REQ packet
pptpd: CTRL: I wrote 16 bytes to the client.
pptpd: CTRL: Sent packet to client
```

This output looks similar to the PPP example we examined earlier, except this one has output from both the `pppd` process as well as a `pptpd` process. These processes work together to establish PPTP sessions at the server. The setup begins with `pptpd` receiving a type 1 control message, indicating that the client wishes to establish a control connection. PPTP uses a separate control and data stream, so first the control stream is set up. After responding to this request, the server receives a type 7 control message indicating an outgoing call request from the peer. The maximum speed (in bits per second) is set to a large value of 100,000,000, which effectively means it is unbounded. The *window* is set to 64, a concept we typically encounter in transport protocols such as TCP (see Chapter 15). Here the window is used for flow control. That is, PPTP uses its sequence numbers and acknowledgment numbers to determine how many frames reach the destination successfully. If too few frames are successfully delivered, the sender slows down. To determine the amount of time to wait for an acknowledgment for frames it sends, PPTP uses an adaptive timeout mechanism based on estimating the round-trip time of the link. We shall see this type of calculation again when we study TCP.

Soon after the window is set, the `pppd` application begins to run and process the PPP data as we saw before in the dial-up example. The only real difference between the two is that `pptpd` relays packets to the `pppd` process as they arrive and depart, and a few special PPTP messages (such as `set link info` and `echo request`) are processed by `pptpd` itself. This example illustrates how the PPTP protocol really acts as a GRE tunneling agent for PPP packets. This is convenient because an existing PPP implementation (here, `pppd`) can be used as is to process the encapsulated PPP packets. Note that while GRE is itself ordinarily encapsulated in IPv4 packets, similar functionality is available using IPv6 to tunnel packets [RFC2473].

3.9.1 Unidirectional Links

An interesting issue arises when the link to be used operates in only one direction. Such links are called *unidirectional links* (UDLs), and many of the protocols described so far do not operate properly in such circumstances because they require exchanges of information (e.g., PPP's configuration messages). To deal with this situation, a standard has been created whereby tunneling over a second Internet interface can be combined with operation of the UDL [RFC3077]. The typical situation where this arises is an Internet connection that uses a satellite for downstream traffic (headed to the user) and a dial-up modem link for upstream traffic. This setup can be useful in cases where the satellite-connected user's usage is dominated by downloading as opposed to uploading and was commonly used in early satellite Internet installations. It operates by encapsulating link-layer upstream traffic in IP packets using a GRE encapsulation.

To establish and maintain tunnels automatically at the receiver, [RFC3077] specifies a *Dynamic Tunnel Configuration Protocol* (DTCP). DTCP involves sending multicast *Hello messages* on the downlink so that any interested receiver can learn about the existence of the UDL and its MAC and IP addresses. In addition, Hello messages indicate a list of tunnel endpoints within the network that can be reached by the user's secondary interface. After the user selects which tunnel endpoint to use, DTCP arranges for return traffic to be encapsulated with the same MAC type as the UDL in GRE tunnels. The service provider arranges to receive these GRE-encapsulated layer 2 frames (frequently Ethernet), extract them from the tunnel, and forward them appropriately. Thus, although the upstream side of the UDLs (provider's side) requires manual tunnel configuration, the downstream side, which includes many more users, has automatically configured tunnels. Note that this approach to handling UDLs essentially "hides" the link asymmetry from the upper-layer protocols. As a consequence, the performance (latency, bandwidth) of the "two" directions of the link may be highly asymmetric and may adversely affect higher-layer protocols [RFC3449].

As the satellite example helps to illustrate, one significant issue with tunnels is the amount of effort required to configure them, which has traditionally been done by hand. Typically, tunnel configuration involves selecting the endpoints of a tunnel and configuring the devices located at the tunnel endpoints with an IP address of the peer, and perhaps also providing protocol selection and authentication information. A number of techniques have arisen to help in configuring or using tunnels automatically. One such approach specified for transitioning from IPv4 to IPv6 is called *6to4* [RFC3056]. In 6to4, IPv6 packets are tunneled over an IPv4 network using the encapsulation specified in [RFC3056]. A problem with this approach occurs when corresponding hosts are located behind network address translators (see Chapter 7). This is common today, especially for home users. Dealing with the IPv6 transition using automatically configured tunnels is specified in an approach called *Teredo* [RFC4380]. Teredo tunnels IPv6 packets over UDP/IPv4 packets. Because this approach requires some background in IPv4 and IPv6, as well as UDP, we postpone any detailed discussion of such tunnel autoconfiguration options to Chapter 10.

3.10 Attacks on the Link Layer

Attacking layers below TCP/IP in order to affect the operations of TCP/IP networks has been a popular approach because much of the link-layer information is not shared by the higher layers and can therefore be somewhat difficult to detect and mitigate. Nevertheless, many such attacks are now well understood, and we mention a few of them here to better understand how problems at the link layer can affect higher-layer operations.

In conventional wired Ethernet, interfaces can be placed in *promiscuous mode*, which allows them to receive traffic even if it is not destined for them. In the early days of Ethernet, when the medium was literally a shared cable, this capability allowed anyone with a computer attached to the Ethernet cable to "sniff" anybody else's frames and inspect their contents. As many higher-layer protocols at the time included sensitive information such as passwords, it was nearly trivial to intercept a person's password by merely looking at the ASCII decode of a packet trace. Two factors have affected this approach substantially: the deployment of switches and the deployment of encryption in higher-layer protocols. With switches, the only traffic that is provided on a switch port to which an end station is attached is traffic destined for the station itself (or others for which it is bridging) and broadcast/multicast traffic. As this type of traffic rarely contains information such as passwords, the attack is largely thwarted. Much more effective, however, is simply the use of encryption at higher layers, which is now common. In this case, sniffing packets leads to little benefit as the contents are essentially impossible to read.

Another type of attack targets the operation of switches. Recall that switches hold tables of stations on a per-port basis. If these tables are able to be filled quickly (e.g., by quickly masquerading as a large number of stations), it is conceivable that the switch might be forced into discarding legitimate entries, leading to service interruption for legitimate stations. A related but probably worse attack can be mounted using the STP. In this case, an attacking station can masquerade as a switch with a low-cost path to the root bridge and cause traffic to be directed toward it.

With Wi-Fi networks, some of the eavesdropping and masquerading issues present in wired Ethernet networks are exacerbated, as any station can enter a monitoring mode and sniff packets from the air (although placing an 802.11 interface into monitoring mode tends to be more challenging than placing an Ethernet interface into promiscuous mode, as doing so depends on an appropriate device driver). Some of the earliest "attacks" (which may not really have been attacks, depending on the relevant legal framework) involved simply roaming about while scanning, looking for access points providing Internet connectivity (i.e., *war driving*). Although many access points use encryption to limit access to authorized users, others are either open or use so-called *capturing portals* that direct a would-be user to a registration Web page and then filter access based on MAC address. Capturing portal systems have been subverted by observing a station as it registers and "hijacking" the connection as it is formed by impersonating the legitimate registering user.

A more sophisticated set of attacks on Wi-Fi involves attacking the cryptographic protection, especially the WEP encryption used on many early access points. Attacks on WEP [BHL06] were sufficiently devastating so as to prod the IEEE into revising the standard. The more recent WPA2 encryption framework (and WPA, to a lesser extent) is known to be significantly stronger, and WEP is no longer recommended for use.

PPP links can be attacked in a number of ways if the attacker can gain access to the channel between the two peers. For very simple authentication mechanisms (e.g., PAP), sniffing can be used to capture the password in order to facilitate illegitimate subsequent use. Depending on the type of higher-layer traffic being carried over the PPP link (e.g., routing traffic), additional unwanted behaviors can be induced.

In terms of attacks, tunneling can play the role of both target and tool. In terms of a target, tunnels pass through a network (often the Internet) and thus are subject to being intercepted and analyzed. The configured tunnel endpoints can also be attacked, either by attempting to establish more tunnels than the endpoint can support (a DoS attack) or by attacking the configuration itself. If the configuration is compromised, it may be possible to open an unauthorized tunnel to an endpoint. At this point the tunnel becomes a tool rather than a target, and protocols such as L2TP can provide a convenient protocol-independent method of gaining access to private internal networks at the link layer. In one GRE-related attack, for example, traffic is simply inserted in a nonencrypted tunnel, where it appears at the tunnel endpoint and is injected to the attached "private" network as though it were sent locally.

3.11 Summary

In this chapter we examined the lowest layer in the Internet protocol suite with which we are concerned—the link layer. We looked at the evolution of Ethernet, in terms of both its increases in speed from 10Mb/s to 10Gb/s and beyond, as well as its evolution of capabilities, including VLANs, priorities, link aggregation, and frame formats. We saw how switches provide improved performance over bridges by implementing a direct electrical path between multiple independent sets of stations, and how full-duplex operation has largely replaced the earlier half-duplex operation. We also looked at the IEEE 802.11 wireless LAN "Wi-Fi" standard in some detail, noting its similarities and differences with respect to Ethernet. It has become one of the most popular IEEE standards and provides license-free network access across the two primary bands of 2.4GHz and 5GHz. We also looked at the evolution of the security methods for Wi-Fi, with the evolution from the relatively weak WEP to the more formidable WPA and WPA2 frameworks. Moving beyond IEEE standards, we discussed point-to-point links and the PPP protocol. PPP can encapsulate essentially any kind of packets used for TCP/IP and non-TCP/IP networks using an HDLC-like frame format, and it is used on links ranging from low-speed dial-up modems to high-speed fiber-optic lines. It is a whole suite of protocols itself, including methods for compression, encryption, authentication, and link aggregation. Because it supports only two parties, it does not have to deal with controlling access to a shared medium like the MAC protocols of Ethernet or Wi-Fi.

The loopback interface is provided by most implementations. Access to this interface is either through the special loopback address, normally 127.0.0.1 (::1 for IPv6), or by sending IP datagrams to one of a host's own IP addresses. Loopback data has been completely processed by the transport layer and by IP when it loops around to go up the protocol stack. We described an important feature of many link layers, the MTU, and the related concept of a path MTU.

We also discussed the use of tunneling, which involves carrying lower-layer protocols in higher-layer (or equal-layer) packets. This technique allows for the formation of overlay networks, using tunnels over the Internet as links in another level of network infrastructure. This technique has become very popular, both for experimentation with new capabilities (e.g., running an IPv6 network overlay on an IPv4 internet) and for operational use (e.g., with VPNs).

We concluded the chapter with a brief discussion of the types of attacks involving the link layer—as either target or tool. Many attacks simply involve intercepting traffic for analysis (e.g., looking for passwords), but more sophisticated attacks involve masquerading as endpoints or modifying traffic in transit. Other attacks involve compromising control information such as tunnel endpoints or the STP to direct traffic to otherwise unintended locations. Access to the link layer also provides an attacker with a general way to perform DoS attacks. Perhaps the best-known variant of this is jamming communication signals, an endeavor undertaken by certain parties since nearly the advent of radio.

This chapter has covered only some of the common link technologies used with TCP/IP today. One reason for the success of TCP/IP is its ability to work on top of almost any link technology. In essence, IP requires only that there exists some path between sender and receiver(s) across a cascade of intermediate links. Although this is a relatively modest requirement, some research is aimed at stretching this even farther—to cases where there may never be an end-to-end path between sender and receiver(s) at any single point in time [RFC4838].

3.12 References

[802.11-2007] "IEEE Standard for Local and Metropolitan Area Networks, Part 11: Wireless LAN Medium Access Control (MAC) and Physical Layer (PHY) Specifications," June 2007.

[802.11n-2009] "IEEE Standard for Local and Metropolitan Area Networks, Part 11: Wireless LAN Medium Access Control (MAC) and Physical Layer (PHY) Specifications Amendment 5: Enhancements for Higher Throughput," Oct. 2009.

[802.11y-2008] "IEEE Standard for Local and Metropolitan Area Networks, Part 11: Wireless LAN Medium Access Control (MAC) and Physical Layer (PHY) Specifications Amendment 3: 3650-3700 MHz Operation in USA," Nov. 2009.

[802.16-2009] "IEEE Standard for Local and Metropolitan Area Networks, Part 16: Air Interface for Fixed Broadband Wireless Access Systems," May 2009.

[802.16h-2010] "IEEE Standard for Local and Metropolitan Area Networks, Part 16: Air Interface for Fixed Broadband Wireless Access Systems Amendment 2: Improved Coexistence Mechanisms for License-Exempt Operation," July 2010.

[802.16j-2009] "IEEE Standard for Local and Metropolitan Area Networks, Part 16: Air Interface for Fixed Broadband Wireless Access Systems Amendment 1: Multihop Relay Specification," June 2009.

[802.16k-2007] "IEEE Standard for Local and Metropolitan Area Networks, Part 16: Air Interface for Fixed Broadband Wireless Access Systems Amendment 5: Bridging of IEEE 802.16," Aug. 2010.

[802.1AK-2007] "IEEE Standard for Local and Metropolitan Area Networks, Virtual Bridged Local Area Networks Amendment 7: Multiple Registration Protocol," June 2007.

[802.1AE-2006] "IEEE Standard for Local and Metropolitan Area Networks Media Access Control (MAC) Security," Aug. 2006.

[802.1ak-2007] "IEEE Standard for Local and Metropolitan Area Networks—Virtual Bridged Local Area Networks—Amendment 7: Multiple Registration Protocol," June 2007.

[802.1AX-2008] "IEEE Standard for Local and Metropolitan Area Networks—Link Aggregation," Nov. 2008.

[802.1D-2004] "IEEE Standard for Local and Metropolitan Area Networks Media Access Control (MAC) Bridges," June 2004.

[802.1Q-2005] IEEE Standard for Local and Metropolitan Area Networks Virtual Bridged Local Area Networks," May 2006.

[802.1X-2010] "IEEE Standard for Local and Metropolitan Area Networks Port-Based Network Access Control," Feb. 2010.

[802.2-1998] "IEEE Standard for Local and Metropolitan Area Networks Logical Link Control" (also ISO/IEC 8802-2:1998), May 1998.

[802.21-2008] "IEEE Standard for Local and Metropolitan Area Networks, Part 21: Media Independent Handover Services," Jan. 2009.

[802.3-2008] "IEEE Standard for Local and Metropolitan Area Networks, Part 3: Carrier Sense Multiple Access with Collision Detection (CSMA/CD) Access Method and Physical Layer Specifications," Dec. 2008.

[802.3at-2009] "IEEE Standard for Local and Metropolitan Area Networks—Specific Requirements, Part 3: Carrier Sense Multiple Access with Collision Detection (CSMA/CD) Access Method and Physical Layer Specifications Amendment 3: Date Terminal Equipment (DTE) Power via the Media Dependent Interface (MDI) Enhancements," Oct. 2009.

[802.3ba-2010] "IEEE Standard for Local and Metropolitan Area Networks, Part 3: Carrier Sense Multiple Access with Collision Detection (CSMA/CD) Access Method and Physical Layer Specifications, Amendment 4: Media Access Control Parameters, Physical Layers, and Management Parameters for 40Gb/s and 100Gb/s Operation," June 2010.

[802.11n-2009] "IEEE Standard for Local and Metropolitan Area Networks, Part 11: Wireless LAN Medium Access Control (MAC) and Physical Layer (PHY) Specifications, Amendment 5: Enhancements for Higher Throughput," Oct. 2009.

[AES01] U.S. National Institute of Standards and Technology, FIPS PUB 197, "Advanced Encryption Standard," Nov. 2001.

[BHL06] A. Bittau, M. Handley, and J. Lackey, "The Final Nail in WEP's Coffin," *Proc. IEEE Symposium on Security and Privacy*, May 2006.

[BOND] http://bonding.sourceforge.net

[ETHERTYPES] http://www.iana.org/assignments/ethernet-numbers

[ETX] D. De Couto, D. Aguayo, J. Bicket, and R. Morris, "A High-Throughput Path Metric for Multi-Hop Wireless Routing," *Proc. Mobicom*, Sep. 2003.

[G704] ITU, "General Aspects of Digital Transmission Systems: Synchronous Frame Structures Used at 1544, 6312, 2048k, 8488, and 44736 kbit/s Hierarchical Levels," ITU-T Recommendation G.704, July 1995.

[IANA-CHARSET] "Character Sets," http://www.iana.org/assignments/character-sets

[ISO3309] International Organization for Standardization, "Information Processing Systems—Data Communication High-Level Data Link Control Procedure—Frame Structure," IS 3309, 1984.

[ISO4335] International Organization for Standardization, "Information Processing Systems—Data Communication High-Level Data Link Control Procedure—Elements of Procedure," IS 4335, 1987.

[JF] M. Mathis, "Raising the Internet MTU," http://www.psc.edu/~mathis/MTU

[MWLD] "Long Distance Links with MadWiFi," http://madwifi-project.org/wiki/UserDocs/LongDistance

[PPPn] http://www.iana.org/assignments/ppp-numbers

[RFC0894] C. Hornig, "A Standard for the Transmission of IP Datagrams over Ethernet Networks," Internet RFC 0894/STD 0041, Apr. 1984.

[RFC1042] J. Postel and J. Reynolds, "Standard for the Transmission of IP Datagrams over IEEE 802 Networks," Internet RFC 1042/STD 0043, Feb. 1988.

[RFC1144] V. Jacobson, "Compressing TCP/IP Headers for Low-Speed Serial Links," Internet RFC 1144, Feb. 1990.

[RFC1191] J. Mogul and S. Deering, "Path MTU Discovery," Internet RFC 1191, Nov. 1990.

[RFC1332] G. McGregor, "The PPP Internet Protocol Control Protocol," Internet RFC 1332, May 1992.

[RFC1570] W. Simpson, ed., "PPP LCP Extensions," Internet RFC 1570, Jan. 1994.

[RFC1661] W. Simpson, "The Point-to-Point Protocol (PPP)," Internet RFC 1661/ STD 0051, July 1994.

[RFC1662] W. Simpson, ed., "PPP in HDLC-like Framing," Internet RFC 1662/ STD 0051, July 1994.

[RFC1663] D. Rand, "PPP Reliable Transmission," Internet RFC 1663, July 1994.

[RFC1853] W. Simpson, "IP in IP Tunneling," Internet RFC 1853 (informational), Oct. 1995.

[RFC1962] D. Rand, "The PPP Compression Protocol (CCP)," Internet RFC 1962, June 1996.

[RFC1977] V. Schryver, "PPP BSD Compression Protocol," Internet RFC 1977 (informational), Aug. 1996.

[RFC1981] J. McCann and S. Deering, "Path MTU Discovery for IP Version 6," Internet RFC 1981, Aug. 1996.

[RFC1989] W. Simpson, "PPP Link Quality Monitoring," Internet RFC 1989, Aug. 1996.

[RFC1990] K. Sklower, B. Lloyd, G. McGregor, D. Carr, and T. Coradetti, "The PPP Multilink Protocol (MP)," Internet RFC 1990, Aug. 1996.

[RFC1994] W. Simpson, "PPP Challenge Handshake Authentication Protocol (CHAP)," Internet RFC 1994, Aug. 1996.

[RFC2118] G. Pall, "Microsoft Point-to-Point (MPPC) Protocol," Internet RFC 2118 (informational), Mar. 1997.

[RFC2125] C. Richards and K. Smith, "The PPP Bandwidth Allocation Protocol (BAP)/The PPP Bandwidth Allocation Control Protocol (BACP)," Internet RFC 2125, Mar. 1997.

[RFC2153] W. Simpson, "PPP Vendor Extensions," Internet RFC 2153 (informational), May 1997.

[RFC2290] J. Solomon and S. Glass, "Mobile-IPv4 Configuration Option for PPP IPCP," Internet RFC 2290, Feb. 1998.

[RFC2464] M. Crawford, "Transmission of IPv6 Packets over Ethernet Networks," Internet RFC 2464, Dec. 1988.

[RFC2473] A. Conta and S. Deering, "Generic Packet Tuneling in IPv6 Specification," Internet RFC 2473, Dec. 1998.

[RFC2484] G. Zorn, "PPP LCP Internationalization Configuration Option," Internet RFC 2484, Jan. 1999.

[RFC2507] M. Degermark, B. Nordgren, and S. Pink, "IP Header Compression," Internet RFC 2507, Feb. 1999.

[RFC2615] A. Malis and W. Simpson, "PPP over SONET/SDH," Internet RFC 2615, June 1999.

[RFC2637] K. Hamzeh, G. Pall, W. Verthein, J. Taarud, W. Little, and G. Zorn, "Point-to-Point Tunneling Protocol (PPTP)," Internet RFC 2637 (informational), July 1999.

[RFC2759] G. Zorn, "Microsoft PPP CHAP Extensions, Version 2," Internet RFC 2759 (informational), Jan. 2000.

[RFC2784] D. Farinacci, T. Li, S. Hanks, D. Meyer, and P. Traina, "Generic Routing Encapsulation (GRE)," Internet RFC 2784, Mar. 2000.

[RFC2865] C. Rigney, S. Willens, A. Rubens, and W. Simpson, "Remote Authentication Dial In User Service (RADIUS)," Internet RFC 2865, June 2000.

[RFC2890] G. Dommety, "Key and Sequence Number Extensions to GRE," Internet RFC 2890, Sept. 2000.

[RFC3056] B. Carpenter and K. Moore, "Connection of IPv6 Domains via IPv4 Clouds," Internet RFC 3056, Feb. 2001.

[RFC3077] E. Duros, W. Dabbous, H. Izumiyama, N. Fujii, and Y. Zhang, "A Link-Layer Tunneling Mechanism for Unidirectional Links," Internet RFC 3077, Mar. 2001.

[RFC3078] G. Pall and G. Zorn, "Microsoft Point-to-Point Encryption (MPPE) Protocol," Internet RFC 3078 (informational), Mar. 2001.

[RFC3153] R. Pazhyannur, I. Ali, and C. Fox, "PPP Multiplexing," Internet RFC 3153, Aug. 2001.

[RFC3366] G. Fairhurst and L. Wood, "Advice to Link Designers on Link Automatic Repeat reQuest (ARQ)," Internet RFC 3366/BCP 0062, Aug. 2002.

[RFC3449] H. Balakrishnan, V. Padmanabhan, G. Fairhurst, and M. Sooriyabandara, "TCP Performance Implications of Network Path Asymmetry," Internet RFC 3449/BCP 0069, Dec. 2002.

[RFC3544] T. Koren, S. Casner, and C. Bormann, "IP Header Compression over PPP," Internet RFC 3544, July 2003.

[RFC3561] C. Perkins, E. Belding-Royer, and S. Das, "Ad Hoc On-Demand Distance Vector (AODV) Routing," Internet RFC 3561 (experimental), July 2003.

[RFC3610] D. Whiting, R. Housley, and N. Ferguson, "Counter with CBC-MAC (CCM)," Internet RFC 3610 (informational), Sept. 2003.

[RFC3626] T. Clausen and P. Jacquet, eds., "Optimized Link State Routing Protocol (OLSR)," Internet RFC 3626 (experimental), Oct. 2003.

[RFC3748] B. Aboba et al., "Extensible Authentication Protocol (EAP)," Internet RFC 3748, June 2004.

[RFC3931] J. Lau, M. Townsley, and I. Goyret, eds., "Layer Two Tunneling Protocol—Version 3 (L2TPv3)," Internet RFC 3931, Mar. 2005.

[RFC4017] D. Stanley, J. Walker, and B. Aboba, "Extensible Authentication Protocol (EAP) Method Requirements for Wireless LANs," Internet RFC 4017 (informational), Mar. 2005.

[RFC4380] C. Huitema, "Teredo: Tunneling IPv6 over UDP through Network Address Translations (NATs)," Internet RFC 4380, Feb. 2006.

[RFC4647] A. Phillips and M. Davis, "Matching of Language Tags," Internet RFC 4647/BCP 0047, Sept. 2006.

[RFC4821] M. Mathis and J. Heffner, "Packetization Layer Path MTU Discovery," Internet RFC 4821, Mar. 2007.

[RFC4838] V. Cerf et al., "Delay-Tolerant Networking Architecture," Internet RFC 4838 (informational), Apr. 2007.

[RFC4840] B. Aboba, ed., E. Davies, and D. Thaler, "Multiple Encapsulation Methods Considered Harmful," Internet RFC 4840 (informational), Apr. 2007.

[RFC5072] S. Varada, ed., D. Haskins, and E. Allen, "IP Version 6 over PPP," Internet RFC 5072, Sept. 2007.

[RFC5225] G. Pelletier and K. Sandlund, "RObust Header Compression Version 2 (ROHCv2): Profiles for RTP, UDP, IP, ESP, and UDP-Lite," Internet RFC 5225, Apr. 2008.

[RFC5646] A. Phillips and M. Davis, eds., "Tags for Identifying Languages," Internet RFC 5646/BCP 0047, Sept. 2009.

[S08] D. Skordoulis et al., "IEEE 802.11n MAC Frame Aggregation Mechanisms for Next-Generation High-Throughput WLANs," *IEEE Wireless Communications*, Feb. 2008.

[S96] B. Schneier, *Applied Cryptography, Second Edition* (John Wiley & Sons, 1996).

[SAE] D. Harkins, "Simultaneous Authentication of Equals: A Secure, Password-Based Key Exchange for Mesh Networks," *Proc. SENSORCOMM*, Aug. 2008.

[SC05] S. Shalunov and R. Carlson, "Detecting Duplex Mismatch on Ethernet," *Proc. Passive and Active Measurement Workshop*, Mar. 2005.

[SHK07] C. Sengul, A. Harris, and R. Kravets, "Reconsidering Power Management," Invited Paper, *Proc. IEEE Broadnets*, 2007.

[WOL] http://wake-on-lan.sourceforge.net

4

ARP: Address Resolution Protocol

4.1 Introduction

We have seen that the IP protocol is designed to provide interoperability of packet switching across a large variety of physical network types. Doing so requires, among other things, converting between the addresses used by the network-layer software and those interpreted by the underlying network hardware. Generally, network interface hardware has one primary hardware address (e.g., a 48-bit value for an Ethernet or 802.11 wireless interface). Frames exchanged by the hardware must be addressed to the correct interface using the correct hardware addresses; otherwise, no data can be transferred. But a conventional IPv4 network works with its own addresses: 32-bit IPv4 addresses. Knowing a host's IP address is insufficient for the system to send a frame to that host efficiently on networks where hardware addresses are used. The operating system software (i.e., the Ethernet driver) must know the destination's hardware address to send data directly. For TCP/IP networks, the *Address Resolution Protocol* (ARP) [RFC0826] provides a dynamic mapping between IPv4 addresses and the hardware addresses used by various network technologies. ARP is used with IPv4 only; IPv6 uses the Neighbor Discovery Protocol, which is incorporated into ICMPv6 (see Chapter 8).

It is important to note here that the network-layer and link-layer addresses are assigned by different authorities. For network hardware, the primary address is defined by the manufacturer of the device and is stored in permanent memory within the device, so it does not change. Thus, any protocol suite designed to operate with that particular hardware technology must make use of its particular types of addresses. This allows network-layer protocols of different protocol suites to operate *at the same time*. On the other hand, the IP address assigned to a network interface is installed by the user or network administrator and selected by that person to meet his or her needs. The IP addresses assigned to a portable device may, for example, be changed when it is moved. IP addresses are typically derived from a pool of addresses maintained near the network attachment point and are installed when systems are turned on or configured (see Chapter 6). When an Ethernet frame containing an IP datagram is sent from one host on a LAN to another, it is the 48-bit Ethernet address that determines to which interface(s) the frame is destined.

Address resolution is the process of discovering the mapping from one address to another. For the TCP/IP protocol suite using IPv4, this is accomplished by running the ARP. ARP is a generic protocol, in the sense that it is designed to support mapping between a wide variety of address types. In practice, however, it is almost always used to map between 32-bit IPv4 addresses and Ethernet-style 48-bit MAC addresses. This case, the one specified in [RFC0826], is also the one of interest to us. For this chapter, we shall use the terms Ethernet address and MAC address interchangeably.

ARP provides a dynamic mapping from a network-layer address to a corresponding hardware address. We use the term dynamic because it happens automatically and adapts to changes over time without requiring reconfiguration by a system administrator. That is, if a host were to have its network interface card changed, thereby changing its hardware address (but retaining its assigned IP address), ARP would continue to operate properly after some delay. ARP operation is normally not a concern of either the application user or the system administrator.

Note

A related protocol that provides the reverse mapping from ARP, called RARP, was used by systems lacking a disk drive (normally diskless workstations or X terminals). It is rarely used today and requires manual configuration by the system administrator. See [RFC0903] for details.

4.2   An Example

Whenever we use Internet services, such as opening a Web page with a browser, our local computer must determine how to contact the server in which we are interested. The most basic decision it makes is whether that service is local (part of the same IP subnetwork) or remote. If it is remote, a router is required to reach the destination. ARP operates only when reaching those systems on the same IP subnet. For this example, then, let us assume that we use a Web browser to contact the following URL:

```
http://10.0.0.1
```

Note that this URL contains an IPv4 address rather than the more common domain or host name. The reason for using the address here is to underscore the fact that our demonstration of ARP is most relevant to systems sharing the same IPv4 prefix (see Chapter 2). Here, we use a URL containing an address identifying a local Web server and explore how *direct delivery* operates. Such local servers are becoming more common as embedded devices such as printers and VoIP adapters include built-in Web servers for configuration.

4.2.1 Direct Delivery and ARP

In this section, we enumerate the steps taken in direct delivery, focusing on the operation of ARP. Direct delivery takes place when an IP datagram is sent to an IP address with the same IP prefix as the sender's. It plays an important role in the general method of forwarding of IP datagrams (see Chapter 5). The following list captures the basic operation of direct delivery with IPv4, using the previous example:

1. The application, in this case a Web browser, calls a special function to parse the URL to see if it contains a host name. Here it does not, so the application uses the 32-bit IPv4 address 10.0.0.1.

2. The application asks the TCP protocol to establish a connection with 10.0.0.1.

3. TCP attempts to send a connection request segment to the remote host by sending an IPv4 datagram to 10.0.0.1. (We shall see the details of how this is done in Chapter 15.)

4. Because we are assuming that the address 10.0.0.1 is using the same network prefix as our sending host, the datagram can be sent directly to that address without going through a router.

5. Assuming that Ethernet-compatible addressing is being used on the IPv4 subnet, the sending host must convert the 32-bit IPv4 destination address into a 48-bit Ethernet-style address. Using the terminology from [RFC0826], a translation is required from the *logical* Internet address to its corresponding *physical* hardware address. This is the function of ARP. ARP works in its normal form only for *broadcast networks*, where the link layer is able to deliver a single message to all attached network devices. This is an important requirement imposed by the operation of ARP. On non-broadcast networks (sometimes called NBMA for *non-broadcast multiple access*), other, more complex mapping protocols may be required [RFC2332].

6. ARP sends an Ethernet frame called an *ARP request* to every host on the shared link-layer segment. This is called a *link-layer broadcast*. We show the *broadcast domain* in Figure 4-1 with a crosshatched box. The ARP request contains the IPv4 address of the destination host (10.0.0.1) and seeks an answer to the following question: "If you are configured with IPv4 address 10.0.0.1 as one of your own, please respond to me with your MAC address."

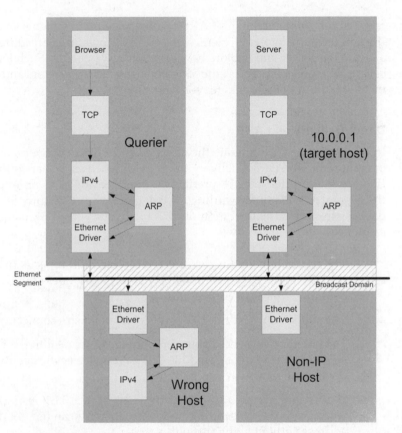

Figure 4-1   Ethernet hosts in the same broadcast domain. ARP queries are sent using link-layer broadcast frames that are received by all hosts. The single host with the assigned address responds directly to the requesting host. Non-IP hosts must actively discard ARP queries.

7. With ARP, all systems in the same broadcast domain receive ARP requests. This includes systems that may not be running the IPv4 or IPv6 protocols at all but does not include systems on different VLANs, if they are supported (see Chapter 3 for details on VLANs). Provided there exists an attached system using the IPv4 address specified in the request, it alone responds with an *ARP reply*. This reply contains the IPv4 address (for matching with the request) and the corresponding MAC address. The reply does not ordinarily use broadcast but is directed only to the sender. The host receiving the ARP request also learns of the sender's IPv4-to-MAC address mapping at this time and records it in memory for later use (see Section 4.3).

8. The ARP reply is then received by the original sender of the request, and the datagram that forced the ARP request/reply to be exchanged can now be sent.

9. The sender now sends the datagram directly to the destination host by encapsulating it in an Ethernet frame and using the Ethernet address learned by the ARP exchange as the destination Ethernet address. Because the Ethernet address refers only to the correct destination host, no other hosts or routers receive the datagram. Thus, when only direct delivery is used, no router is required.

ARP is used in multi-access link-layer networks running IPv4, where each host has its own primary hardware address. Point-to-point links such as PPP (see Chapter 3) do not use ARP. When these links are established (normally by action of the user or a system boot), the system is told of the addresses in use at each end of the link. Because hardware addresses are not involved, there is no need for address resolution or ARP.

4.3 ARP Cache

Essential to the efficient operation of ARP is the maintenance of an *ARP cache* (or table) on each host and router. This cache maintains the recent mappings from network-layer addresses to hardware addresses for each interface that uses address resolution. When IPv4 addresses are mapped to hardware addresses, the normal expiration time of an entry in the cache is 20 minutes from the time the entry was created, as described in [RFC1122].

We can examine the ARP cache with the `arp` command on Linux or in Windows. The –a option displays all entries in the cache for either system. Running `arp` on Linux yields the following type of output:

```
Linux% arp
Address              HWtype  HWaddress          Flags Mask Iface
gw.home              ether   00:0D:66:4F:60:00  C          eth1
printer.home         ether   00:0A:95:87:38:6A  C          eth1

Linux% arp -a
printer.home (10.0.0.4) at     00:0A:95:87:38:6A [ether] on eth1
gw.home (10.0.0.1) at 00:0D:66:4F:60:00 [ether] on eth1
```

Running `arp` on Windows provides output similar to the following:

```
c:\> arp -a

Interface: 10.0.0.56 --- 0x2
  Internet Address      Physical Address      Type
  10.0.0.1              00-0d-66-4f-60-00     dynamic
  10.0.0.4              00-0a-95-87-38-6a     dynamic
```

Here we see the IPv4-to-hardware addressing cache. In the first (Linux) case, each mapping is given by a five-element entry: the host name (corresponding to an IP address), hardware address type, hardware address, flags, and local network interface for which this mapping is active. The `Flags` column contains a symbol: `C`, `M`, or `P`. C-type entries have been learned dynamically by the ARP protocol. M-type entries are entered by hand (by `arp -s`; see Section 4.9), and P-type entries mean "publish." That is, for any `P` entry, the host responds to incoming ARP requests with an ARP response. This option is used for configuring proxy ARP (see Section 4.7). The second Linux example displays similar information using the "BSD style." Here, both the host's name and address are given, along with the address type (here, `[ether]` indicates an Ethernet type of address) and on which interface the mappings are active.

The Windows `arp` program displays the IPv4 address of the interface, and its interface number in hexadecimal (`0x2` here). The Windows version also indicates whether the address was entered by hand or learned by ARP. In this example, both entries are dynamic, meaning they were learned by ARP (they would say `static` if entered by hand). Note that the 48-bit MAC addresses are displayed as six hexadecimal numbers separated by colons in Linux and dashes in Windows. Traditionally, UNIX systems have always used colons, whereas the IEEE standards and other operating systems tend to use dashes. We discuss additional features and other options of the `arp` command in Section 4.9.

4.4   ARP Frame Format

Figure 4-2 shows the common format of an ARP request and reply packet, when used on an Ethernet network to resolve an IPv4 address. (As mentioned previously, ARP is general enough to be used with addresses other than IPv4 addresses, although this is very rare.) The first 14 bytes constitute the standard Ethernet header, assuming no 802.1p/q or other tags, and the remaining portion is defined by the ARP protocol. The first 8 bytes of the ARP frame are generic, and the remaining portion in this example applies specifically when mapping IPv4 addresses to 48-bit Ethernet-style addresses.

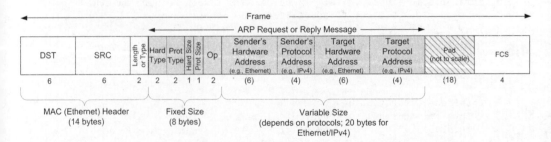

Figure 4-2   ARP frame format as used when mapping IPv4 addresses to 48-bit MAC (Ethernet) addresses

In the Ethernet header of the ARP frame shown in Figure 4-2, the first two fields contain the destination and source Ethernet addresses. For ARP requests, the special Ethernet destination address of ff:ff:ff:ff:ff:ff (all 1 bits) means the broadcast address—all Ethernet interfaces in the same broadcast domain receive these frames. The 2-byte Ethernet frame *Length* or *Type* field is required to be 0x0806 for ARP (requests or replies).

The first four fields following the *Length/Type* field specify the types and sizes of the final four fields. The values are maintained by the IANA [RFC5494]. The adjectives *hardware* and *protocol* are used to describe the fields in the ARP packets. For example, an ARP request asks for the hardware address (an Ethernet address in this case) corresponding to a protocol address (an IPv4 address in this case). These adjectives are rarely used outside the ARP context. Rather, the more common terminology for the hardware address is *MAC*, *physical*, or *link-layer* address (or *Ethernet* address when the network in use is based on the IEEE 802.3/Ethernet series of specifications). The *Hard Type* field specifies the type of hardware address. Its value is 1 for Ethernet. The *Prot Type* field specifies the type of protocol address being mapped. Its value is 0x0800 for IPv4 addresses. This is purposely the same value as the *Type* field of an Ethernet frame containing an IPv4 datagram. The next two 1-byte fields, *Hard Size* and *Prot Size*, specify the sizes, in bytes, of the hardware addresses and the protocol addresses. For an ARP request or reply for an IPv4 address on an Ethernet they are 6 and 4, respectively. The *Op* field specifies whether the operation is an ARP request (a value of 1), ARP reply (2), RARP request (3), or RARP reply (4). This field is required because the *Length/Type* field is the same for an ARP request and an ARP reply.

The next four fields that follow are the *Sender's Hardware Address* (an Ethernet MAC address in this example), the *Sender's Protocol Address* (an IPv4 address), the *Target Hardware* (MAC/Ethernet) *Address*, and the *Target Protocol* (IPv4) *Address*. Notice that there is some duplication of information: the sender's hardware address is available both in the Ethernet header and in the ARP message. For an ARP request, all the fields are filled in except the *Target Hardware Address* (which is set to 0). When a system receives an ARP request directed to it, it fills in its hardware address, swaps the two sender addresses with the two target addresses, sets the *Op* field to 2, and sends the reply.

4.5   ARP Examples

In this section we will use the `tcpdump` command to see what really happens with ARP when we execute normal TCP/IP utilities such as Telnet. Telnet is a simple application that can establish a TCP/IP connection between two systems.

4.5.1   Normal Example

To see the operation of ARP, we will execute the `telnet` command, connecting to a Web server on host `10.0.0.3` using TCP port 80 (called `www`).

```
C:\> arp -a                    Verify that the ARP cache is empty
No ARP Entries Found
C:\> telnet 10.0.0.3 www       Connect to the Web server [port 80]
Connecting to 10.0.0.3...
Escape character is '^]'.
```

Type Control + right bracket to get the Telnet client prompt.

```
Welcome to Microsoft Telnet Client
Escape Character is 'CTRL+]'
Microsoft Telnet> quit
```

The quit directive exits the program.

While this is happening, we run the tcpdump command on another system that can observe the traffic exchanged. We use the -e option, which displays the MAC addresses (which in our examples are 48-bit Ethernet addresses).

The following listing contains the output from tcpdump. We have deleted the final four lines of the output that correspond to the termination of the connection (we cover such details in Chapter 13); they are not relevant to the discussion here. Note that different versions of tcpdump on different systems may provide slightly different output details.

```
Linux#  tcpdump -e
1       0.0 0:0:c0:6f:2d:40 ff:ff:ff:ff:ff:ff arp 60:
        arp who-has 10.0.0.3 tell 10.0.0.56
2       0.002174 (0.0022)0:0:c0:c2:9b:26 0:0:c0:6f:2d:40 arp 60:
        arp reply 10.0.0.3 is-at 0:0:c0:c2:9b:26

3       0.002831 (0.0007)0:0:c0:6f:2d:40 0:0:c0:c2:9b:26 ip 60:
        10.0.0.56.1030 > 10.0.0.3.www: S 596459521:596459521(0)
        win 4096 <mss 1024> [tos 0x10]
4       0.007834 (0.0050)0:0:c0:c2:9b:26 0:0:c0:6f:2d:40 ip 60:
        10.0.0.3.www > 10.0.0.56.1030: S 3562228225:3562228225(0)
        ack 596459522 win 4096 <mss 1024>
5       0.009615 (0.0018)0:0:c0:6f:2d:40 0:0:c0:c2:9b:26 ip 60:
        10.0.0.56.1030 > 10.0.0.3.discard: . ack 1 win 4096 [tos 0x10]
```

In packet 1 the hardware address of the source is 0:0:c0:6f:2d:40. The destination hardware address is ff:ff:ff:ff:ff:ff, which is the Ethernet broadcast address. All Ethernet interfaces in the same broadcast domain (all those on the same LAN or VLAN, whether or not they are running TCP/IP) receive the frame and process it, as shown in Figure 4-1. The next output field in packet 1, arp, means that the *Frame Type* field is 0x0806, specifying either an ARP request or an ARP reply. The value 60 printed after the words arp and ip in each of the five packets is the length of the Ethernet frame. The size of an ARP request or ARP reply is always 42 bytes (28 bytes for the ARP message, 14 bytes for the Ethernet header). Each frame has been padded to the Ethernet minimum: 60 bytes of data plus a 4-byte CRC (see Chapter 3).

The next part of packet 1, arp who-has, identifies the frame as an ARP request with the IPv4 address of 10.0.0.3 as the target address and the IPv4 address of 10.0.0.56 as the sender's address. tcpdump prints the host names corresponding to the IP addresses by default, but here they are not displayed (because no reverse DNS mappings for them are set up; Chapter 11 explains details of DNS). We will use the -n option later to see the IP addresses in the ARP request, whether or not DNS mappings are available.

From packet 2 we see that while the ARP request is broadcast, the destination address of the ARP reply is the (unicast) MAC address 0:0:c0:6f:2d:40. The ARP reply is thus sent directly to the requesting host; it is not ordinarily broadcast (see Section 4.8 for some cases where this rule is altered). tcpdump prints the ARP reply for this frame, along with the IPv4 address and hardware address of the responder. Line 3 is the first TCP segment requesting that a connection be established. Its destination hardware address is the destination host (10.0.0.3). We shall cover the details of this segment in Chapter 13.

For each packet, the number printed after the packet number is the relative time (in seconds) when the packet was received by tcpdump. Each packet other than the first also contains the time difference (in seconds) from the previous time, in parentheses. We can see in the output that the time between sending the ARP request and receiving the ARP reply is about 2.2ms. The first TCP segment is sent 0.7ms after this. The overhead involved in using ARP for dynamic address resolution in this example is less than 3ms. Note that if the ARP entry for host 10.0.0.3 was valid in the ARP cache at 10.0.0.56, the initial ARP exchange would not have occurred, and the initial TCP segment could have been sent immediately using the destination's Ethernet address.

A subtle point about the tcpdump output is that we do not see an ARP request from 10.0.0.3 before it sends its first TCP segment to 10.0.0.56 (line 4). While it is possible that 10.0.0.3 already has an entry for 10.0.0.56 in its ARP cache, normally when a system receives an ARP request addressed to it, in addition to sending the ARP reply, it also saves the requestor's hardware address and IPv4 address in its own ARP cache. This is an optimization based on the logical assumption that if the requestor is about to send it a datagram, the receiver of the datagram will probably send a reply.

4.5.2 ARP Request to a Nonexistent Host

What happens if the host specified in an ARP request is down or nonexistent? To see this, we attempt to access a nonexistent local IPv4 address—the prefix corresponds to that of the local subnet, but there is no host with the specified address. We will use the IPv4 address 10.0.0.99 in this example.

```
Linux% date ; telnet 10.0.0.99 ; date
Fri Jan 29 14:46:33 PST 2010
Trying 10.0.0.99...
telnet: connect to address 10.0.0.99: No route to host
```

```
Fri Jan 29 14:46:36 PST 2010          3s after previous date

Linux% arp -a
? (10.0.0.99) at <incomplete> on eth0
```

Here is the output from `tcpdump`:

```
Linux# tcpdump -n arp
1 21:12:07.440845 arp who-has 10.0.0.99 tell 10.0.0.56
2 21:12:08.436842 arp who-has 10.0.0.99 tell 10.0.0.56
3 21:12:09.436836 arp who-has 10.0.0.99 tell 10.0.0.56
```

This time we did not specify the –e option because we already know that the ARP requests are sent using broadcast addressing. The frequency of the ARP request is very close to one per second, the maximum suggested by [RFC1122]. Testing on a Windows system (not illustrated) reveals a different behavior. Rather than three requests spaced 1s apart, the spacing varies based on the application and the other protocols being used. For ICMP and UDP (see Chapters 8 and 10, respectively), a spacing of approximately 5s is used, whereas for TCP 10s is used. For TCP, the 10s interval allows two ARP requests to be sent without responses before TCP gives up trying to establish a connection.

4.6   ARP Cache Timeout

A timeout is normally associated with each entry in the ARP cache. (Later we shall see that the `arp` command enables the administrator to place an entry into the cache that will never time out.) Most implementations have a timeout of 20 minutes for a completed entry and 3 minutes for an incomplete entry. (We saw an incomplete entry in our previous example where we forced an ARP to a nonexistent host.) These implementations normally restart the 20-minute timeout for an entry each time the entry is used. [RFC1122], the Host Requirements RFC, says that this timeout should occur even if the entry is in use, but many implementations do not do this—they restart the timeout each time the entry is referenced.

Note that this is one of our first examples of *soft state*. Soft state is information that is discarded if not refreshed before some timeout is reached. Many Internet protocols use soft state because it helps to initiate automatic reconfiguration if network conditions change. The cost of soft state is that some protocol must *refresh* the state to avoid expiration. "Soft state refreshes" are often incorporated in a protocol design to keep the soft state active.

4.7   Proxy ARP

Proxy ARP [RFC1027] lets a system (generally a specially configured router) answer ARP requests for a different host. This fools the sender of the ARP request into thinking that the responding system is the destination host, when in fact the destination host may be elsewhere (or may not exist). Proxy ARP is not commonly used and is generally to be avoided if possible.

Proxy ARP has also been called *promiscuous ARP* or the *ARP hack*. These names are from a historical use of proxy ARP: to hide two physical networks from each other. In this case both physical networks can use the same IP prefix as long as a router in the middle is configured as a proxy ARP agent to respond to ARP requests on one network for a host on the other network. This technique can be used to "hide" one group of hosts from another. In the past, there were two common reasons for doing this: some systems were unable to handle subnetting, and some used an older broadcast address (a host ID of all 0 bits, instead of the current standard of a host ID with all 1 bits).

Linux supports a feature called *auto-proxy ARP*. It can be enabled by writing the character 1 into the file /proc/sys/net/ipv4/conf/*/proxy_arp, or by using the sysctl command. This supports the ability of using proxy ARP without having to manually enter ARP entries for every possible IPv4 address that is being proxied. Doing so allows a range of addresses, instead of each individual address, to be automatically proxied.

4.8   Gratuitous ARP and Address Conflict Detection (ACD)

Another feature of ARP is called *gratuitous ARP*. It occurs when a host sends an ARP request looking for its *own* address. This is usually done when the interface is configured "up" at bootstrap time. Here is an example trace taken on a Linux machine showing our Windows host booting up:

```
Linux#        tcpdump -e -n arp
1             0.0 0:0:c0:6f:2d:40 ff:ff:ff:ff:ff:ff arp 60:
              arp who-has 10.0.0.56 tell 10.0.0.56
```

(We specified the -n flag for tcpdump to always print numeric dotted-decimal addresses instead of host names.) In terms of the fields in the ARP request, the *Sender's Protocol Address* and the *Target Protocol Address* are identical: 10.0.0.56. Also, the *Source Address* field in the Ethernet header, 0:0:c0:6f:2d:40 as shown by tcpdump, equals the sender's hardware address. Gratuitous ARP achieves two goals:

1. It lets a host determine if another host is already configured with the same IPv4 address. The host sending the gratuitous ARP is not expecting a reply to its request. If a reply is received, however, the error message "Duplicate IP address sent from Ethernet address . . ." is usually displayed. This is a warning to the system administrator and user that one of the systems in the same broadcast domain (e.g., LAN or VLAN) is misconfigured.

2. If the host sending the gratuitous ARP has just changed its hardware address (perhaps the host was shut down, the interface card was replaced, and then the host was rebooted), this frame causes any other host receiving the broadcast that has an entry in its cache for the old hardware address to update its ARP cache entry accordingly. As mentioned before, if a host receives an ARP request from an IPv4 address that is already in the receiver's cache, that cache entry is updated with the sender's hardware address from the ARP request. This is done for any ARP request received by the host; gratuitous ARP happens to take advantage of this behavior.

Although gratuitous ARP provides some indication that multiple stations may be attempting to use the same IPv4 address, it really provides no mechanism to react to the situation (other than by printing a message that is ideally acted upon by a system administrator). To deal with this issue, [RFC5227] describes *IPv4 Address Conflict Detection* (ACD). ACD defines *ARP probe* and *ARP announcement* packets. An ARP probe is an ARP request packet in which the *Sender's Protocol* (IPv4) *Address* field is set to 0. Probes are used to see if a candidate IPv4 address is being used by any other systems in the broadcast domain. Setting the *Sender's Protocol Address* field to 0 avoids cache pollution should the candidate IPv4 address already be in use by another host, a difference from the way gratuitous ARP works. An ARP announcement is identical to an ARP probe, except both the *Sender's Protocol Address* and the *Target Protocol Address* fields are filled in with the candidate IPv4 address. It is used to announce the sender's intention to use the candidate IPv4 address as its own.

To perform ACD, a host sends an ARP probe when an interface is brought up or out of sleep, or when a new link is established (e.g., when an association with a new wireless network is made). It first waits a random amount of time (in the range 0–1s, distributed uniformly) before sending up to three probe packets. The delay is used to avoid power-on congestion when multiple systems powered on simultaneously would otherwise attempt to perform ACD at once, leading to a network traffic spike. The probes are spaced randomly, with between 1 and 2s of delay (distributed uniformly) placed between.

While sending its probes, a requesting station may receive ARP requests or replies. A reply to its probe indicates that a different station is already using the candidate IP address. A request containing the same candidate IPv4 address in the *Target Protocol Address* field sent from a different system indicates that the other system is simultaneously attempting to acquire the candidate IPv4 address. In either case, the system should indicate an address conflict message and pursue some alternative address. For example, this is the recommended behavior when being assigned an address using DHCP (see Chapter 6). [RFC5227] places a limit of ten conflicts when trying to acquire an address before the requesting host enters a rate-limiting phase when it is permitted to perform ACD only once every 60s until successful.

If a requesting host does not discover a conflict according to the procedure just described, it sends two ARP announcements spaced 2s apart to indicate to systems in the broadcast domain the IPv4 address it is now using. In the announcements, both the *Sender's Protocol Address* and the *Target Protocol Address* fields are set to the address being claimed. The purpose of sending these announcements is to ensure that any preexisting cached address mappings are updated to reflect the sender's current use of the address.

ACD is considered to be an ongoing process, and in this way it differs from gratuitous ARP. Once a host has announced an address it is using, it continues inspecting incoming ARP traffic (requests and replies) to see if its address appears in the *Sender's Protocol Address* field. If so, some other system believes it is rightfully using the same address. In this case, [RFC5227] provides three possible resolution mechanisms: cease using the address, keep the address but send a "defensive" ARP announcement and cease using it if the conflict continues, or continue to use the address despite the conflict. The last option is recommended only for systems that truly require a fixed, stable address (e.g., an embedded device such as a printer or router).

[RFC5227] also suggests the potential benefit of having some ARP replies be sent using link-layer broadcast. Although this has not traditionally been the way ARP works, there can be some benefit in doing so, at the expense of requiring all stations on the same segment to process all ARP traffic. Broadcast replies allow ACD to occur more quickly because all stations will notice the reply and invalidate their caches during a conflict.

4.9   The arp Command

We have used the arp command with the −a flag on Windows and Linux to display all the entries in the ARP cache (on Linux we get similar information without using −a). The superuser or administrator can specify the −d option to delete an entry from the ARP cache. (This was used before running a few of the examples, to force an ARP exchange to be performed.)

Entries can also be added using the −s option. It requires an IPv4 address (or host name that can be converted to an IPv4 address using DNS) and an Ethernet address. The IPv4 address and the Ethernet address are added to the cache as an entry. This entry is made semipermanent (i.e., it does not time out from the cache, but it disappears when the system is rebooted).

The Linux version of arp provides a few more features than the Windows version. When the temp keyword is supplied at the end of the command line when adding an entry using −s, the entry is considered to be temporary and times out in the same way that other ARP entries do. The keyword pub at the end of a command line, also used with the −s option, causes the system to act as an ARP responder for that entry. The system answers ARP requests for the IPv4 address, replying with the specified Ethernet address. If the advertised address is one of the system's own, the system is acting as a proxy ARP agent (see Section 4.7) for the specified IPv4 address. If `arp -s` is used to enable proxy ARP, Linux responds for the address specified even if the file `/proc/sys/net/ipv4/conf/*/proxy_arp` contains 0.

4.10 Using ARP to Set an Embedded Device's IPv4 Address

As more embedded devices are made compatible with Ethernet and the TCP/IP protocols, it is increasingly common to find network-attached devices that have no direct way to enter their network configuration information (e.g., they have no keyboard, so entering an IP address for them to use is not possible). These devices are typically configured in one of two ways. First, DHCP can be used to automatically assign an address and other information (see Chapter 6). Another way is to use ARP to set an IPv4 address, although this method is less common.

Using ARP to configure an embedded device's IPv4 address was not the original intent of the protocol, so it is not entirely automatic. The basic idea is to manually establish an ARP mapping for the device (using the `arp -s` command), then send an IP packet to the address. Because the ARP entry is already present, no ARP request/reply is generated. Instead, the hardware address can be used immediately. Of course, the Ethernet (MAC) address of the device must be known. It is typically printed on the device itself and sometimes doubles as the manufacturer's device serial number. When the device receives a packet destined for its hardware address, whatever destination address is contained in the datagram is used to assign its initial IPv4 address. After that, the device can be fully configured using other means (e.g., by an embedded Web server).

4.11 Attacks Involving ARP

There have been a series of attacks involving ARP. The most straightforward is to use the proxy ARP facility to masquerade as some host, responding to ARP requests for it. If the victim host is not present, this is straightforward and may not be detected. It is considerably more difficult if the host is still running, as more than one response may be generated per ARP request, which is easily detected.

A more subtle attack has been launched against ARP that involves cases where a machine is attached to more than one network, and ARP entries from one interface "leak" over into the ARP table of the other, because of a bug in the ARP software. This can be exploited to improperly direct traffic onto the wrong network segment. Linux provides a way to affect this behavior directly, by modifying the file `/proc/sys/net/ipv4/conf/*/arp_filter`. If the value 1 is written into this file, then when an incoming ARP request arrives over an interface, an IP forwarding check is made. The IP address of the requestor is looked up to determine which interface would be used to send IP datagrams back to it. If the interface used by the arriving ARP request is different from the interface that would be used to return an IP datagram to the requestor, the ARP response is suppressed (and the triggering ARP request is dropped).

A somewhat more damaging attack on ARP involves the handling of static entries. As discussed previously, static entries may be used to avoid the ARP request/reply when seeking the Ethernet (MAC) address corresponding to a particular IP address. Such static entries have been used in an attempt to enhance security. The idea is that static entries placed in the ARP cache for important hosts would soon detect any hosts masquerading with that IP address. Unfortunately, most implementations of ARP have traditionally replaced even static cache entries with entries provided by ARP replies. The consequence of this is that a machine receiving an ARP reply (even if did not send an ARP request) would be coaxed into replacing its static entries with those provided by an attacker.

4.12 Summary

ARP is a basic protocol in almost every TCP/IP implementation, but it normally does its work without the application or user being aware of it. ARP is used to determine the hardware addresses corresponding to the IPv4 addresses in use on the locally reachable IPv4 subnet. It is invoked when forwarding datagrams destined for the same subnet as the sending host's and is also used to reach a router when the destination of a datagram is not on the subnet (the details of this are explained in Chapter 5). The ARP cache is fundamental to its operation, and we have used the `arp` command to examine and manipulate the cache. Each entry in the cache has a timer that is used to remove both incomplete and completed entries. The `arp` command displays and modifies entries in the ARP cache.

We followed through the normal operation of ARP along with specialized versions: proxy ARP (when a router answers ARP requests for hosts accessible on another of the router's interfaces) and gratuitous ARP (sending an ARP request for your own IP address, normally when bootstrapping). We also discussed address conflict detection for IPv4, which uses a continually operating gratuitous ARP-like exchange to avoid address duplication within the same broadcast domain. Finally, we discussed a number of attacks that involve ARP. Most of these involve impersonating hosts by fabricating ARP responses for them. This can lead to problems with higher-layer protocols if they do not implement strong security (see Chapter 18).

4.13 References

[RFC0826] D. Plummer, "Ethernet Address Resolution Protocol: Or Converting Network Protocol Addresses to 48.bit Ethernet Address for Transmission on Ethernet Hardware," Internet RFC 0826/STD 0037, Nov. 1982.

[RFC0903] R. Finlayson, T. Mann, J. C. Mogul, and M. Theimer, "A Reverse Address Resolution Protocol," Internet RFC 0903/STD 0038, June 1984.

[RFC1027] S. Carl-Mitchell and J. S. Quarterman, "Using ARP to Implement Transparent Subnet Gateways," Internet RFC 1027, Oct. 1987.

[RFC1122] R. Braden, ed., "Requirements for Internet Hosts," Internet RFC 1122/STD 0003, Oct. 1989.

[RFC2332] J. Luciani, D. Katz, D. Piscitello, B. Cole, and N. Doraswamy, "NBMA Next Hop Resolution Protocol (NHRP)," Internet RFC 2332, Apr. 1998.

[RFC5227] S. Cheshire, "IPv4 Address Conflict Detection," Internet RFC 5227, July 2008.

[RFC5494] J. Arkko and C. Pignataro, "IANA Allocation Guidelines for the Address Resolution Protocol (ARP)," Internet RFC 5494, Apr. 2009.

5

The Internet Protocol (IP)

5.1   Introduction

IP is the workhorse protocol of the TCP/IP protocol suite. All TCP, UDP, ICMP, and IGMP data gets transmitted as IP datagrams. IP provides a best-effort, connection-less datagram delivery service. By "best-effort" we mean there are no guarantees that an IP datagram gets to its destination successfully. Although IP does not simply drop all traffic unnecessarily, it provides no guarantees as to the fate of the packets it attempts to deliver. When something goes wrong, such as a router temporarily running out of buffers, IP has a simple error-handling algorithm: throw away some data (usually the last datagram that arrived). Any required reliability must be provided by the upper layers (e.g., TCP). IPv4 and IPv6 both use this basic best-effort delivery model.

The term *connectionless* means that IP does not maintain any connection state information about related datagrams within the network elements (i.e., within the routers); each datagram is handled independently from all other others. This also means that IP datagrams can be delivered out of order. If a source sends two consecutive datagrams (first A, then B) to the same destination, each is routed independently and can take different paths, and B may arrive before A. Other things can happen to IP datagrams as well: they may be duplicated in transit, and they may have their data altered as the result of errors. Again, some protocol above IP (usually TCP) has to handle all of these potential problems in order to provide an error-free delivery abstraction for applications.

In this chapter we take a look at the fields in the IPv4 (see Figure 5-1) and IPv6 (see Figure 5-2) headers and describe how IP forwarding works. The official specification for IPv4 is given in [RFC0791]. A series of RFCs describe IPv6, starting with [RFC2460].

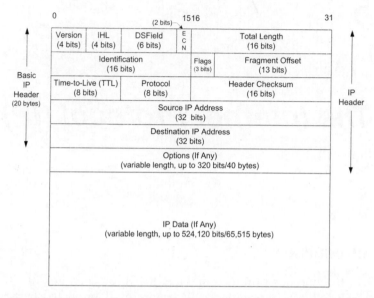

Figure 5-1 The IPv4 datagram. The header is of variable size, limited to fifteen 32-bit words (60 bytes) by the 4-bit *IHL* field. A typical IPv4 header contains 20 bytes (no options). The source and destination addresses are 32 bits long. Most of the second 32-bit word is used for the IPv4 fragmentation function. A header checksum helps ensure that the fields in the header are delivered correctly to the proper destination but does not protect the data.

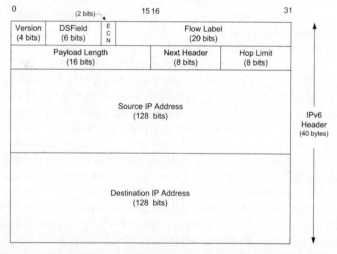

Figure 5-2 The IPv6 header is of fixed size (40 bytes) and contains 128-bit source and destination addresses. The *Next Header* field is used to indicate the presence and types of additional extension headers that follow the IPv6 header, forming a daisy chain of headers that may include special extensions or processing directives. Application data follows the header chain, usually immediately following a transport-layer header.

5.2   IPv4 and IPv6 Headers

Figure 5-1 shows the format of an IPv4 datagram. The normal size of the IPv4 header is 20 bytes, unless *options* are present (which is rare). The IPv6 header is twice as large but never has any options. It may have *extension headers*, which provide similar capabilities, as we shall see later. In our pictures of headers and datagrams, the most significant bit is numbered 0 at the left, and the least significant bit of a 32-bit value is numbered 31 on the right.

The 4 bytes in a 32-bit value are transmitted in the following order: bits 0–7 first, then bits 8–15, then 16–23, and bits 24–31 last. This is called *big endian* byte ordering, which is the byte ordering required for all binary integers in the TCP/IP headers as they traverse a network. It is also called *network byte order.* Computer CPUs that store binary integers in other formats, such as the little endian format used by most PCs, must convert the header values into network byte order for transmission and back again for reception.

5.2.1   IP Header Fields

The first field (only 4 bits or one nibble wide) is the *Version* field. It contains the version number of the IP datagram: 4 for IPv4 and 6 for IPv6. The headers for both IPv4 and IPv6 share the location of the *Version* field but no others. Thus, the two protocols are not directly interoperable—a host or router must handle either IPv4 or IPv6 (or both, called *dual stack*) separately. Although other versions of IP have been proposed and developed, only versions 4 and 6 have any significant amount of use. The IANA keeps an official registry of these version numbers [IV].

The *Internet Header Length (IHL)* field is the number of 32-bit words in the IPv4 header, including any options. Because this is also a 4-bit field, the IPv4 header is limited to a maximum of fifteen 32-bit words or 60 bytes. Later we shall see how this limitation makes some of the options, such as the Record Route option, nearly useless today. The normal value of this field (when no options are present) is 5. There is no such field in IPv6 because the header length is fixed at 40 bytes.

Following the header length, the original specification of IPv4 [RFC0791] specified a *Type of Service (ToS)* byte, and IPv6 [RFC2460] specified the equivalent *Traffic Class* byte. Use of these never became widespread, so eventually this 8-bit field was split into two smaller parts and redefined by a set of RFCs ([RFC3260] [RFC3168][RFC2474] and others). The first 6 bits are now called the *Differentiated Services Field (DS Field)*, and the last 2 bits are the *Explicit Congestion Notification (ECN)* field or indicator bits. These RFCs now apply to both IPv4 and IPv6. These fields are used for special processing of the datagram when it is forwarded. We discuss them in more detail in Section 5.2.3.

The *Total Length* field is the total length of the IPv4 datagram in bytes. Using this field and the *IHL* field, we know where the data portion of the datagram starts, and its length. Because this is a 16-bit field, the maximum size of an IPv4 datagram (including header) is 65,535 bytes. The *Total Length* field is required in the header because some lower-layer protocols that carry IPv4 datagrams do not (accurately) convey the size of encapsulated datagrams on their own. Ethernet, for example, pads small frames to be a minimum length (64 bytes). Even though the minimum Ethernet payload size is 46 bytes (see Chapter 3), an IPv4 datagram can be smaller (as few as 20 bytes). If the *Total Length* field were not provided, the IPv4 implementation would not know how much of a 46-byte Ethernet frame was really an IP datagram, as opposed to padding, leading to possible confusion.

Although it is possible to send a 65,535-byte IP datagram, most link layers (such as Ethernet) are not able to carry one this large without fragmenting it (chopping it up) into smaller pieces. Furthermore, a host is not required to be able to receive an IPv4 datagram larger than 576 bytes. (In IPv6 a host must be able to process a datagram at least as large as the MTU of the link to which it is attached, and the minimum link MTU is 1280 bytes.) Many applications that use the UDP protocol (see Chapter 10) for data transport (e.g., DNS, DHCP, etc.) use a limited data size of 512 bytes to avoid the 576-byte IPv4 limit. TCP chooses its own datagram size based on additional information (see Chapter 15).

When an IPv4 datagram is fragmented into multiple smaller fragments, each of which itself is an independent IP datagram, the *Total Length* field reflects the length of the particular fragment. Fragmentation is described in detail along with UDP in Chapter 10. In IPv6, fragmentation is not supported by the header, and the length is instead given by the *Payload Length* field. This field measures the length of the IPv6 datagram *not* including the length of the header; extension headers, however, are included in the *Payload Length* field. As with IPv4, the 16-bit size of the field limits its maximum value to 65,535. With IPv6, however, it is the *payload* length that is limited to 64KB, not the entire datagram. In addition, IPv6 supports a *jumbogram* option (see Section 5.3.1.2) that provides for the possibility, at least theoretically, of single packets with payloads as large as 4GB (4,294,967,295 bytes)!

The *Identification* field helps indentify each datagram sent by an IPv4 host. To ensure that the fragments of one datagram are not confused with those of another, the sending host normally increments an internal counter by 1 each time a datagram is sent (from one of its IP addresses) and copies the value of the counter into the IPv4 *Identification* field. This field is most important for implementing fragmentation, so we explore it further in Chapter 10, where we also discuss the *Flags* and *Fragment Offset* fields. In IPv6, this field shows up in the Fragmentation extension header, as we discuss in Section 5.3.3.

The *Time-to-Live* field, or *TTL*, sets an upper limit on the number of routers through which a datagram can pass. It is initialized by the sender to some value (64 is recommended [RFC1122], although 128 or 255 is not uncommon) and decremented by 1 by every router that forwards the datagram. When this field reaches 0, the datagram is thrown away, and the sender is notified with an ICMP message (see Chapter 8). This prevents packets from getting caught in the network forever should an unwanted routing loop occur.

Note

The *TTL* field was originally specified to be the maximum lifetime of an IP datagram in seconds, but routers were also always required to decrement the value by at least 1. Because virtually no routers today hold on to a datagram longer than 1s under normal operation, the earlier rule is now ignored or forgotten, and in IPv6 the field has been renamed to its de facto use: *Hop Limit.*

The *Protocol* field in the IPv4 header contains a number indicating the type of data found in the payload portion of the datagram. The most common values are 17 (for UDP) and 6 (for TCP). This provides a demultiplexing feature so that the IP protocol can be used to carry payloads of more than one protocol type. Although this field originally specified the transport-layer protocol the datagram is encapsulating, it is now understood to identify the encapsulated protocol, which may or not be a transport protocol. For example, other encapsulations are possible, such as IPv4-in-IPv4 (value 4). The official list of the possible values of the *Protocol* field is given in the assigned numbers page [AN]. The *Next Header* field in the IPv6 header generalizes the *Protocol* field from IPv4. It is used to indicate the type of header following the IPv6 header. This field may contain any values defined for the IPv4 *Protocol* field, or any of the values associated with the IPv6 extension headers described in Section 5.3.

The *Header Checksum* field is calculated *over the IPv4 header only*. This is important to understand because it means that the payload of the IPv4 datagram (e.g., TCP or UDP data) is not checked for correctness by the IP protocol. To help ensure that the payload portion of an IP datagram has been correctly delivered, other protocols must cover any important data that follows the header with their own data-integrity-checking mechanisms. We shall see that almost all protocols encapsulated in IP (ICMP, IGMP, UDP, and TCP) have a checksum in their own headers to cover their header and data and also to cover certain parts of the IP header they deem important (a form of "layering violation"). Perhaps surprisingly, the IPv6 header does not have any checksum field.

Note

Omitting the checksum field from the IPv6 header was a somewhat controversial decision. The reasoning behind this action is roughly as follows: Higher-layer protocols requiring correctness in the IP header are required to compute their own checksums over the data they believe to be important. A consequence of errors in the IP header is that the data is delivered to the wrong destination, is indicated to have come from the wrong source, or is otherwise mangled during delivery. Because bit errors are relatively rare (thanks to fiber-optic delivery of Internet traffic) and stronger mechanisms are available to ensure correctness of the other fields (higher-layer checksums or other checks), it was decided to eliminate the field from the IPv6 header.

The algorithm used in computing a checksum is also used by most of the other Internet-related protocols that use checksums and is sometimes known as the *Internet checksum*. Note that when an IPv4 datagram passes through a router, its header checksum must change as a result of decrementing the *TTL* field. We discuss the methods for computing the checksum in more detail in Section 5.2.2.

Every IP datagram contains the *Source IP Address* of the sender of the datagram and the *Destination IP Address* of where the datagram is destined. These are 32-bit values for IPv4 and 128-bit values for IPv6, and they usually identify a single interface on a computer, although multicast and broadcast addresses (see Chapter 2) violate this rule. While a 32-bit address can accommodate a seemingly large number of Internet entities (4.5 billion), there is widespread agreement that this number is inadequate, a primary motivation for moving to IPv6. The 128-bit address of IPv6 can accommodate a huge number of Internet entities. As was restated in [H05], IPv6 has 3.4×10^{38} (340 undecillion) addresses. Quoting from [H05] and others: "The optimistic estimate would allow for 3,911,873,538,269,506,102 addresses per square meter of the surface of the planet Earth." It certainly seems as if this should last a very, very long time indeed.

5.2.2   The Internet Checksum

The Internet checksum is a 16-bit mathematical sum used to determine, with reasonably high probability, whether a received message or portion of a message matches the one sent. Note that the Internet checksum algorithm is not the same as the common *cyclic redundancy check* (CRC) [PB61], which offers stronger protection.

To compute the IPv4 header checksum for an outgoing datagram, the value of the datagram's *Checksum* field is first set to 0. Then, the 16-bit one's complement sum of the header is calculated (the entire header is considered a sequence of 16-bit words). The 16-bit one's complement of this sum is then stored in the *Checksum* field to make the datagram ready for transmission. One's complement addition can be implemented by "end-round-carry addition": when a carry bit is produced using conventional (two's complement) addition, the carry is added back in as a 1 value. Figure 5-3 presents an example, where the message contents are represented in hexadecimal.

When an IPv4 datagram is received, a checksum is computed across the whole header, including the value of the *Checksum* field itself. Assuming there are no errors, the computed checksum value is always 0 (a one's complement of the value FFFF). Note that for any nontrivial packet or header, the value of the *Checksum* field in the packet can never be FFFF. If it were, the sum (prior to the final one's complement operation at the sender) would have to have been 0. No sum can ever be 0 using one's complement addition unless all the bytes are 0—something that never happens with any legitimate IPv4 header. When the header is found to be bad (the computed checksum is nonzero), the IPv4 implementation discards the received datagram. No error message is generated. It is up to the higher layers to somehow detect the missing datagram and retransmit if necessary.

Sending

Message:	E3 4F 23 96 44 27 99 F3 [00 00] ◄── Checksum Field = 0000
Two's Complement Sum:	1E4FF
One's Complement Sum:	E4FF+1 = E500
One's Complement:	~(E500) = ~(1110 0101 0000 0000) = 0001 1010 1111 1111 = 1AFF (the checksum)

Receiving

Message + Checksum =	E34F + 2396 + 4427 + 99F3 + 1AFF = E500 + 1AFF = FFFF
	~(Message + Checksum) = 0000

Figure 5-3   The Internet checksum is the one's complement of a one's complement 16-bit sum of the data being checksummed (zero padding is used if the number of bytes being summed is odd). If the data being summed includes a *Checksum* field, the field is first set to 0 prior to the checksum operation and then filled in with the computed checksum. To check whether an incoming block of data that contains a *Checksum* field (header, payload, etc.) is valid, the same type of checksum is computed over the whole block (including the *Checksum* field). Because the *Checksum* field is essentially the inverse of the checksum of the rest of the data, computing the checksum on correctly received data should produce a value of 0.

5.2.2.1 Mathematics of the Internet Checksum

For the mathematically inclined, the set of 16-bit hexadecimal values V = {0001, . . . , FFFF} and the one's complement sum operation + together form an Abelian group. For the combination of a set and an operator to be a group, several properties need to be obeyed: closure, associativity, existence of an identity element, and existence of inverses. To be an Abelian (commutative) group, commutativity must also be obeyed. If we look closely, we see that all of these properties are indeed obeyed:

- For any X,Y in V, (X + Y) is in V   [closure]

- For any X,Y,Z in V, X + (Y + Z) = (X + Y) + Z   [associativity]

- For any X in V, e + X = X + e = X where e = FFFF   [identity]

- For any X in V, there is an X′ in V such that X + X′ = e   [inverse]

- For any X,Y in V, (X + Y) = (Y + X)   [commutativity]

What is interesting about the set V and the group <V,+> is that we have deleted the number 0000 from consideration. If we put the number 0000 in the set V, then <V,+> is not a group any longer. To see this, we first observe that 0000 and FFFF appear to perform the role of zero (additive identity) using the + operation. For example, AB12 + 0000 = AB12 = AB12 + FFFF. However, in a group there can be only one identity element. If we have some element 12AB, and assume the identity element is 0000, then we need some inverse X' so that $(12AB + X') = 0000$, but we see that no such value of X' exists in V that satisfies the criteria. Therefore, we need to exclude 0000 from consideration as the identity element in <V,+> by removing it from the set V to make this structure a true group. For an introduction to abstract algebra, the reader may wish to consult a detailed text on the subject, such as the popular book by Pinter [P90].

5.2.3 *DS Field* **and** *ECN* **(Formerly Called the** *ToS Byte* **or IPv6** *Traffic Class***)**

The third and fourth fields of the IPv4 header (second and third fields of the IPv6 header) are the *Differentiated Services* (called *DS Field*) and *ECN* fields. Differentiated Services (called *DiffServ*) is a framework and set of standards aimed at supporting differentiated classes of service (i.e., beyond just best-effort) on the Internet [RFC2474][RFC2475][RFC3260]. IP datagrams that are marked in certain ways (by having some of these bits set according to predefined patterns) may be forwarded differently (e.g., with higher priority) than other datagrams. Doing so can lead to increased or decreased queuing delay in the network and other special effects (possibly with associated special fees imposed by an ISP). A number is placed in the *DS Field* termed the *Differentiated Services Code Point* (DSCP). A "code point" refers to a particular predefined arrangement of bits with agreed-upon meaning. Typically, datagrams have a DSCP assigned to them when they are given to the network infrastructure that remains unmodified during delivery. However, policies (such as how many high-priority packets are allowed to be sent in a period of time) may cause a DSCP in a datagram to be changed during delivery.

The pair of *ECN* bits in the header is used for marking a datagram with a *congestion indicator* when passing through a router that has a significant amount of internally queued traffic. Both bits are set by persistently congested ECN-aware routers when forwarding packets. The use case envisioned for this function is that when a marked packet is received at the destination, some protocol (such as TCP) will notice that the packet is marked and indicate this fact back to the sender, which would then slow down, thereby easing congestion before a router is forced to drop traffic because of overload. This mechanism is one of several aimed at avoiding or dealing with network congestion, which we explore in more detail in Chapter 16. Although the *DS Field* and *ECN* field are not obviously closely related, the space for them was carved out of the previously defined IPv4 *Type of Service* and IPv6 *Traffic Class* fields. For this reason, they are often discussed together, and the terms "ToS byte" and "Traffic Class byte" are still in widespread use.

Although the original uses for the ToS and Traffic Class bytes are not widely supported, the structure of the *DS Field* has been arranged to provide some backward compatibility with them. To get a clear understanding of how this has been accomplished, we first review the original structure of the *Type of Service* field [RFC0791] as shown in Figure 5-4.

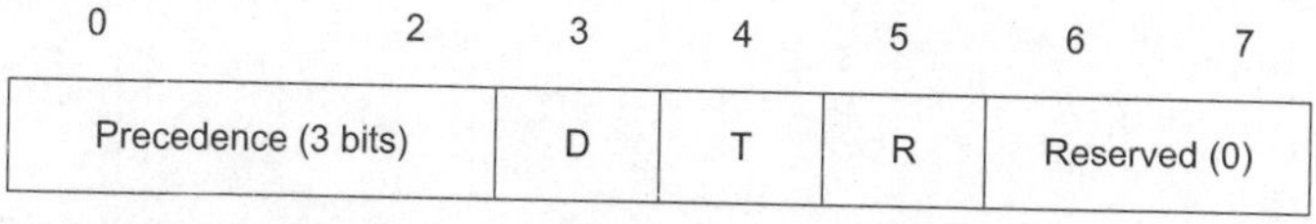

0	2	3	4	5	6	7
Precedence (3 bits)		D	T	R	Reserved (0)	

Figure 5-4 The original IPv4 *Type of Service* and IPv6 *Traffic Class* field structures. The *Precedence* subfield was used to indicate which packets should receive higher priority (larger values mean higher priority). The *D, T,* and *R* subfields refer to delay, throughput, and reliability. A value of 1 in these fields corresponds to a desire for low delay, high throughput, and high reliability, respectively.

The D, T, and R subfields are for indicating that the datagram should receive good treatment with respect to delay, throughput, and reliability. A value of 1 indicates better treatment (low delay, high throughput, high reliability, respectively). The precedence values range from 000 (routine) to 111 (network control) with increasing priority (see Table 5-1). They are based on a call preemption scheme called *Multilevel Precedence and Preemption* (MLPP) dating back to the U.S. Department of Defense's AUTOVON telephone system [A92], in which lower-precedence calls could be preempted by higher-precedence calls. These terms are still in use and are being incorporated into VoIP systems.

Table 5-1 The original IPv4 *Type of Service* and IPv6 *Traffic Class* precedence subfield values

Value	Precedence Name
000	Routine
001	Priority
010	Immediate
011	Flash
100	Flash Override
101	Critical
110	Internetwork Control
111	Network Control

In defining the *DS Field*, the precedence values have been taken into account [RFC2474] so as to provide a limited form of backward compatibility. Referring to Figure 5-5, the 6-bit *DS Field* holds the DSCP, providing support for 64 distinct code points. The particular value of the DSCP tells a router the forwarding treatment or special handling the datagram should receive. The various forwarding treatments are expressed as *per-hop behavior* (PHB), so the DSCP value effectively tells a router which PHB to apply to the datagram. The default value for the DSCP is generally 0, which corresponds to routine, best-effort Internet traffic. The 64 possible DSCP values are broadly divided into a set of pools for various uses, as given in [DSCPREG] and shown in Table 5-2.

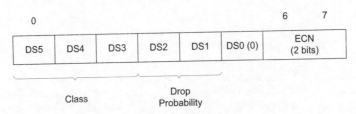

Figure 5-5   The *DS Field* contains the DSCP in 6 bits (5 bits are currently standardized to indicate the forwarding treatment the datagram should receive when forwarded by a compliant router). The following 2 bits are used for ECN and may be turned on in the datagram when it passes through a persistently congested router. When such datagrams arrive at their destinations, the congestion indication is sent back to the source in a later datagram to inform the source that its datagrams are passing through one or more congested routers.

Table 5-2   The DSCP values are divided into three pools: standardized, experimental/local use (EXP/LU), and experimental/local use that is eventually intended for standardization (*).

Pool	Code Point Prefix	Policy
1	xxxxx0	Standards
2	xxxx11	EXP/LU
3	xxxx01	EXP/LU(*)

The arrangement provides for some experimentation and local use by researchers and operators. DSCPs ending in 0 are subject to standardized use, and those ending in 1 are for experimental/local use (EXP/LU). Those ending in 01 are intended initially for experimentation or local use but with eventual intent toward standardization.

Referring to Figure 5-5, the *class* portion of the *DS Field* contains the first 3 bits and is based on the earlier definition of the *Precedence* subfield of the *Type of Service* field. Generally, a router is to first segregate traffic into different classes. Traffic within a common class may have different drop probabilities, allowing the router to decide what traffic to drop first if it is forced to discard traffic. The 3-bit class selector provides for eight defined code points (called the *class selector code points*) that correspond to PHBs with a specified minimum set of features providing similar functionality to the earlier IP precedence capability. These are called *class selector compliant PHBs*. They are intended to support partial backward compatibility with the original definition given for the IP *Precedence* subfield given in [RFC0791]. Code points of the form xxx000 always map to such PHBs, although other values may also map to the same PHBs.

Table 5-3 indicates the class selector DSCP values with their corresponding terms for the IP *Precedence* field from [RFC0791]. The *Assured Forwarding* (AF) group provides forwarding of IP packets in a fixed number of independent AF classes, effectively generalizing the precedence concept. Traffic from one class is forwarded separately from other classes. Within a traffic class, a datagram is assigned a *drop precedence*. Datagrams of higher drop precedence in a class are handled preferentially (i.e., are forwarded with higher priority) over those with lower drop precedence in the same class. Combining the traffic class and drop precedence, the name *AFij* corresponds to assured forwarding class *i* with drop precedence *j*. For example, a datagram marked with AF32 is in traffic class 3 with drop precedence 2.

Table 5-3   The *DS Field* values are designed to be somewhat compatible with the IP *Precedence* subfield specified for the *Type of Service* and IPv6 *Traffic Class* field. AF and EF provide enhanced services beyond simple best-effort.

Name	Value	Reference	Description
CS0	000000	[RFC2474]	Class selector (best-effort/routine)
CS1	001000	[RFC2474]	Class selector (priority)
CS2	010000	[RFC2474]	Class selector (immediate)
CS3	011000	[RFC2474]	Class selector (flash)
CS4	100000	[RFC2474]	Class selector (flash override)
CS5	101000	[RFC2474]	Class selector (CRITIC/ECP)
CS6	110000	[RFC2474]	Class selector (internetwork control)
CS7	111000	[RFC2474]	Class selector (control)
AF11	001010	[RFC2597]	Assured Forwarding (class 1,dp 1)
AF12	001100	[RFC2597]	Assured Forwarding (1,2)
AF13	001110	[RFC2597]	Assured Forwarding (1,3)
AF21	010010	[RFC2597]	Assured Forwarding (2,1)
AF22	010100	[RFC2597]	Assured Forwarding (2,2)
AF23	010110	[RFC2597]	Assured Forwarding (2,3)
AF31	011010	[RFC2597]	Assured Forwarding (3,1)
AF32	011100	[RFC2597]	Assured Forwarding (3,2)
AF33	011110	[RFC2597]	Assured Forwarding (3,3)
AF41	100010	[RFC2597]	Assured Forwarding (4,1)
AF42	100100	[RFC2597]	Assured Forwarding (4,2)
AF43	100110	[RFC2597]	Assured Forwarding (4,3)
EF PHB	101110	[RFC3246]	Expedited Forwarding
VOICE-ADMIT	101100	[RFC5865]	Capacity-Admitted Traffic

The *Expedited Forwarding* (EF) service provides the appearance of an uncongested network—that is, EF traffic should receive relatively low delay, jitter, and loss. Intuitively, this requires the rate of EF traffic going out of a router to be at least as large as the rate coming in. Consequently, EF traffic will only ever have to wait in a router queue behind other EF traffic.

Delivering differentiated services in the Internet has been an ongoing effort for over a decade. Although much of the standardization effort in terms of mechanisms took place in the late 1990s, only in the twenty-first century are some of its capabilities being realized and implemented. Some guidance on how to configure systems to take advantage of these capabilities is given in [RFC4594]. The complexity of differentiated services is due, in part, to the linkage between differentiated services and the presumed differentiated pricing structure and consequent issues of fairness that would go along with it. Such economic relationships can be complex and are outside the scope of the present discussion. For more information on this and related topics, please see [MB97] and [W03].

5.2.4   IP Options

IP supports a number of options that may be selected on a per-datagram basis. Most of these options were introduced in [RFC0791] at the time IPv4 was being designed, when the Internet was considerably smaller and when threats from malicious users were less of a concern. As a consequence, many of the options are no longer practical or desirable because of the limited size of the IPv4 header or concerns regarding security. With IPv6, most of the options have been removed or altered and are not an integral part of the basic IPv6 header. Instead, they are placed after the IPv6 header in one or more extension headers. An IP router that receives a datagram containing options is usually supposed to perform special processing on the datagram. In some cases IPv6 routers process extension headers, but many headers are designed to be processed only by end hosts. In some routers, datagrams with options or extensions are not forwarded as fast as ordinary datagrams. We briefly discuss the IPv4 options as background and then look at how IPv6 implements extension headers and options. Table 5-4 shows most of the IPv4 options that have been standardized over the years.

Table 5-4 gives the reserved IPv4 options for which descriptive RFCs can be found. The complete list is periodically updated and is available online [IPPA-RAM]. The options area always ends on a 32-bit boundary. Pad bytes with a value of 0 are added if necessary. This ensures that the IPv4 header is always a multiple of 32 bits (as required by the *IHL* field). The "Number" column in Table 5-4 is the number of the option. The "Value" column indicates the number placed inside the option *Type* field to indicate the presence of the option. These values from the two columns are not necessarily the same because the *Type* field has additional structure. In particular, the first (high-order) bit indicates whether the option should be copied into fragments if the associated datagram is fragmented. The next 2 bits indicate the option's *class*. Currently, all options in Table 5-4 use option class 0 (control) except Timestamp and Traceroute, which are both class 2 (debugging and measurement). Classes 1 and 3 are reserved.

Most of the standardized options are rarely or never used in the Internet today. Options such as Source and Record Route, for example, require IPv4 addresses to be placed inside the IPv4 header. Because there is only limited space in the header

Table 5-4   Options, if present, are carried in IPv4 packets immediately after the basic IPv4 header. Options are identified by an 8-bit option *Type* field. This field is subdivided into three subfields: *Copy* (1 bit), *Class* (2 bits), and *Number* (5 bits). Options 0 and 1 are a single byte long, and most others are variable in length. Variable options consist of 1 byte of type identifier, 1 byte of length, and the option itself.

Name	Number	Value	Length	Description	Reference	Comments
End of List	0	0	1	Indicates no more options.	[RFC0791]	If required
No Op	1	1	1	Indicates no operation to perform (used for padding).	[RFC0791]	If required
Source Routing	3 9	131 137	Variable	Sender lists router "way-points" for packet to traverse when forwarded. Loose means other routers can be included between waypoints (3,131). Strict means all waypoints have to be traversed exactly in order (9,137).	[RFC0791]	Rare, often filtered
Security and Handling Labels	2 5	130 133	11	Specifies how to include security labels and handling restrictions with IP datagrams in U.S. military environments.	[RFC1108]	Historic
Record Route	7	7	Variable	Records the route taken by a packet in its header.	[RFC0791]	Rare
Timestamp	4	68	Variable	Records the time of day at a packet's source and destination.	[RFC0791]	Rare
Stream ID	8	136	4	Carries the 16-bit SATNET stream identifier.	[RFC0791]	Historic
EIP	17	145	Variable	Extended Internet Protocol (an experiment in the early 1990s)	[RFC1385]	Historic
Traceroute	18	82	Variable	Adds a route-tracing option and ICMP message (an experiment in the early 1990s).	[RFC1393]	Historic
Router Alert	20	148	4	Indicates that a router needs to interpret the contents of the datagram.	[RFC2113] [RFC5350]	Occasional
Quick-Start	25	25	8	Indicates fast transport protocol start (experimental).	[RFC4782]	Rare

(60 bytes total, of which 20 are devoted to the basic IPv4 header), these options are not very useful in today's IPv4 Internet where the number of router hops in an average Internet path is about 15 [LFS07]. In addition, the options are primarily for diagnostic purposes and make the construction of firewalls more cumbersome and risky. Thus, IPv4 options are typically disallowed or stripped at the perimeter of enterprise networks by firewalls (see Chapter 7).

Within enterprise networks, where the average path length is smaller and protection from malicious users may be less of a concern, options can still be useful. In addition, the Router Alert option represents somewhat of an exception to the problems with the other options for use on the Internet. Because it is designed primarily as a performance optimization and does not change fundamental router behavior, it is permitted more often than the other options. As suggested previously, some router implementations have a highly optimized internal pathway for forwarding IP traffic containing no options. The Router Alert option informs routers that a packet requires processing beyond the conventional forwarding algorithms. The experimental Quick-Start option at the end of the table is applicable to both IPv4 and IPv6, and we describe it in the next section when discussing IPv6 extension headers and options.

5.3   IPv6 Extension Headers

In IPv6, special functions such as those provided by options in IPv4 can be enabled by adding extension headers that follow the IPv6 header. The routing and time-stamp functions from IPv4 are supported this way, as well as some other functions such as fragmentation and extra-large packets that were deemed to be rarely used for most IPv6 traffic (but still desired) and thereby did not justify allocating bits in the IPv6 header to support them. With this arrangement, the IPv6 header is fixed at 40 bytes, and extension headers are added only when needed. In choosing the IPv6 header to be of a fixed size, and requiring that extension headers be processed only by end hosts (with one exception), the designers of IPv6 have made the design and construction of high-performance routers easier because the demands on packet processing at routers can be simpler than with IPv4. In practice, packet-processing performance is governed by many factors, including the complexity of the protocol, the capabilities of the hardware and software in the router, and traffic load.

Extension headers, along with headers of higher-layer protocols such as TCP or UDP, are chained together with the IPv6 header to form a cascade of headers (see Figure 5-6). The *Next Header* field in each header indicates the type of the subsequent header, which could be an IPv6 extension header or some other type. The value of 59 indicates the end of the header chain. The possible values for the *Next Header* field are available at [IP6PARAM], and most are provided in Table 5-5.

As we can see from Table 5-5, the IPv6 extension header mechanism distinguishes some functions (e.g., routing and fragmentation) from options. The order

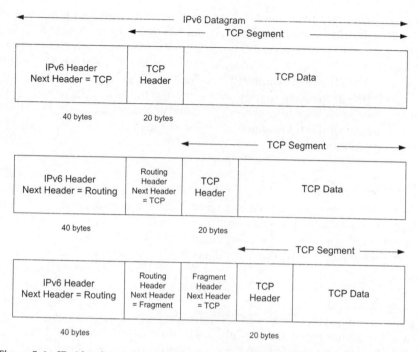

Figure 5-6   IPv6 headers form a chain using the *Next Header* field. Headers in the chain may be IPv6 extension headers or transport headers. The IPv6 header appears at the beginning of the datagram and is always 40 bytes long.

Table 5-5   The values for the IPv6 *Next Header* field may indicate extensions or headers for other protocols. The same values are used with the IPv4 *Protocol* field, where appropriate.

Header Type	Order	Value	References
IPv6 header	1	41	[RFC2460][RFC2473]
Hop-by-Hop Options (HOPOPT)	2	0	[RFC2460]; must immediately follow IPv6 header
Destination Options	3,8	60	[RFC2460]
Routing	4	43	[RFC2460][RFC5095]
Fragment	5	44	[RFC2460]
Encapsulating Security Payload (ESP)	7	50	(See Chapter 18)
Authentication (AH)	6	51	(See Chapter 18)
Mobility (MIPv6)	9	135	[RFC6275]
(None—no next header)	Last	59	[RFC2460]
ICMPv6	Last	58	(See Chapter 8)
UDP	Last	17	(See Chapter 10)
TCP	Last	6	(See Chapters 13–17)
Various other upper-layer protocols	Last	—	See [AN] for complete list

of the extension headers is given as a recommendation, except for the location of the Hop-by-Hop Options, which is mandatory, so an IPv6 implementation must be prepared to process extension headers in the order in which they are received. Only the Destination Options header can be used twice—the first time for options pertaining to the destination IPv6 address contained in the IPv6 header and the second time (position 8) for options pertaining to the final destination of the datagram. In some cases (e.g., when the Routing header is used), the *Destination IP Address* field in the IPv6 header changes as the datagram is forwarded to its ultimate destination.

5.3.1   IPv6 Options

As we have seen, IPv6 provides a more flexible and extensible way of incorporating extensions and options as compared to IPv4. Those options from IPv4 that ceased to be useful because of space limitations in the IPv4 header appear in IPv6 as variable-length extension headers or options encoded in special extension headers that can accommodate today's much larger Internet. Options, if present, are grouped into either *Hop-by-Hop Options* (those relevant to every router along a datagram's path) or *Destination Options* (those relevant only to the recipient). Hop-by-Hop Options (called HOPOPTs) are the only ones that need to be processed by every router a packet encounters. The format for encoding options within the Hop-by-Hop and Destination Options extension headers is common.

The Hop-by-Hop and Destination Options headers are capable of holding more than one option. Each of these options is encoded as *type-length-value* (TLV) sets, according to the format shown in Figure 5-7.

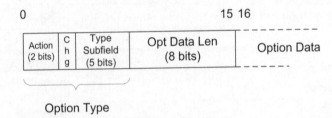

Figure 5-7   Hop-by-hop and Destination Options are encoded as TLV sets. The first byte gives the option type, including subfields indicating how an IPv6 node should behave if the option is not recognized, and whether the option data might change as the datagram is forwarded. The *Opt Data Len* field gives the size of the option data in bytes.

The TLV structure shown in Figure 5-7 includes 2 bytes followed by a variable-length number of data bytes. The first byte indicates the type of the option and includes three subfields. The first subfield gives the action to be taken by an IPv6 node attempting to process the option that does not recognize the 5-bit option *Type* subfield. Its possible values are presented in Table 5-6.

Table 5-6   The 2 high-order bits in an IPv6 TLV option type indicate whether an IPv6 node should forward or drop the datagram if the option is not recognized, and whether a message indicating the datagram's fate should be sent back to the sender.

Value	Action
00	Skip option, continue processing
01	Discard the datagram (silently)
10	Discard the datagram and send an ICMPv6 Parameter Problem message to the source address
11	Same as 10, but send the ICMPv6 message only if the offending packet's destination was not multicast

If an unknown option were included in a datagram destined for a multicast destination, a large number of nodes could conceivably generate traffic back to the source. This can be avoided by use of the 11-bit pattern for the *Action* subfield. The flexibility of the *Action* subfield is useful in the development of new options. A newly specified option can be carried in datagrams and simply ignored by those routers that do not understand it, helping to promote incremental deployment of new options. The *Change* bit field (*Chg* in Figure 5-7) is set to 1 when the option data may be modified as the datagram is forwarded. The options shown in Table 5-7 have been defined for IPv6.

Table 5-7   Options in IPv6 are carried in either Hop-by-Hop (H) or Destination (D) Options extension headers. The option *Type* field contains the value from the "Type" column with the *Action* and *Change* subfields denoted in binary. The "Length" column contains the value of the *Opt Data Len* byte from Figure 5-7. The Pad1 option is the only one lacking this byte.

Option Name	Header	Action	Change	Type	Length	References
Pad1	HD	00	0	0	N/A	[RFC2460]
PadN	HD	00	0	1	var	[RFC2460]
Jumbo Payload	H	11	0	194	4	[RFC2675]
Tunnel Encapsulation Limit	D	00	0	4	4	[RFC2473]
Router Alert	H	00	0	5	4	[RFC2711]
Quick-Start	H	00	1	6	8	[RFC4782]
CALIPSO	H	00	0	7	8+	[RFC5570]
Home Address	D	11	0	201	16	[RFC6275]

5.3.1.1 Pad1 and PadN

IPv6 options are aligned to 8-byte offsets, so options that are naturally smaller are padded with 0 bytes to round out their lengths to the nearest 8 bytes. Two padding options are available to support this, called Pad1 and PadN. The Pad1 option (type 0) is the only option that lacks *Length* and *Value* fields. It is simply 1 byte long and contains the value 0. The PadN option (type 1) inserts 2 or more bytes of padding into the options area of the header using the format of Figure 5-7. For n bytes of padding, the *Opt Data Len* field contains the value (n - 2).

5.3.1.2 IPv6 Jumbo Payload

In some TCP/IP networks, such as those used to interconnect supercomputers, the normal 64KB limit on the IP datagram size can lead to unwanted overhead when moving large amounts of data. The IPv6 Jumbo Payload option specifies an IPv6 datagram with payload size larger than 65,535 bytes, called a *jumbogram*. This option need not be implemented by nodes attached to links with MTU sizes below 64KB. The Jumbo Payload option provides a 32-bit field for holding the payload size for datagrams with payloads of sizes between 65,535 and 4,294,967,295 bytes.

When a jumbogram is formed for transmission, its normal *Payload Length* field is set to 0. As we shall see later, the TCP protocol makes use of the *Payload Length* field in order to compute its checksum using the Internet checksum algorithm described previously. When the Jumbo Payload option is used, TCP must be careful to use the length value from the option instead of the regular *Length* field in the base header. Although this procedure is not difficult, larger payloads can lead to an increased chance of undetected error [RFC2675].

5.3.1.3 Tunnel Encapsulation Limit

Tunneling refers to the encapsulation of one protocol in another that does not conform to traditional layering (see Chapters 1 and 3). For example, IP datagrams may be encapsulated inside the payload portion of another IP datagram. Tunneling can be used to form virtual overlay networks, in which one network (e.g., the Internet) acts as a well-connected link layer for another layer of IP [TWEF03]. Tunnels can be nested in the sense that datagrams that are in a tunnel may themselves be placed in a tunnel, in a recursive fashion.

When sending an IP datagram, a sender does not ordinarily have much control over how many tunnel levels are ultimately used for encapsulation. Using this option, however, a sender can specify this limit. A router intending to encapsulate an IPv6 datagram into a tunnel first checks for the presence and value of the Tunnel Encapsulation Limit option. If the limit value is 0, the datagram is discarded and an ICMPv6 Parameter Problem message (see Chapter 8) is sent to the source of the datagram (i.e., the previous tunnel entry point). If the limit is nonzero, the tunnel encapsulation is permitted, but the newly formed (encapsulating) IPv6 datagram must include a Tunnel Encapsulation Limit option whose value is 1 less than the option value in the arriving datagram. In effect, the encapsulation limit acts like the IPv4 *TTL* or IPv6 *Hop Limit* field, but for levels of tunnel encapsulation instead of forwarding hops.

5.3.1.4 Router Alert

The Router Alert option indicates that the datagram contains information that needs to be processed by a router. It is used for the same purpose as the IPv4 Router Alert option. [RTAOPTS] gives the current set of values for the option.

5.3.1.5 Quick-Start

The Quick-Start (QS) option is used in conjunction with the experimental Quick-Start procedure for TCP/IP specified in [RFC4782]. It is applicable to both IPv4 and IPv6 but at present is suggested only for private networks and not the global Internet. The option includes a value encoding the sender's desired transmission rate in bits per second, a QS TTL value, and some additional information. Routers along the path may agree that supporting the desired rate is acceptable, in which case they decrement the QS TTL and leave the rate request unchanged when forwarding the containing datagram. When they disagree (i.e., wish to support a lower rate), they can reduce the number to an acceptable rate. Routers that do not recognize the QS option do not decrement the QS TTL. A receiver provides feedback to the sender, including the difference between the received datagram's IPv4 *TTL* or IPv6 *Hop Limit* field and its QS TTL, along with the resulting rate that may have been adjusted by the routers along the forward path. This information is used by the sender to determine its sending rate (which, for example, may exceed the rate TCP it would otherwise use). Comparison of the TTL values is used to ensure that every router along the path participates in the QS negotiation; if any routers are found to be decrementing the IPv4 *TTL* (or IPv6 *Hop Limit*) field and not modifying the QS TTL value, QS is not enabled.

5.3.1.6 CALIPSO

This option is used for supporting the *Common Architecture Label IPv6 Security Option* (CALIPSO) [RFC5570] in certain private networks. It provides a method to label datagrams with a security-level indicator, along with some additional information. In particular, it is intended for use in multilevel secure networking environments (e.g., government, military, and banking) where the security level of all data must be indicated by some form of label.

5.3.1.7 Home Address

This option holds the "home" address of the IPv6 node sending the datagram when IPv6 mobility options are in use. Mobile IP (see Section 5.5) specifies a set of procedures for handling IP nodes that may change their point of network attachment without losing their higher-layer network connections. It has a concept of a node's "home," which is derived from the address prefix of its typical location. When roaming away from home, the node is generally assigned a different IP address. This option allows the node to provide its normal home address in addition to its (presumably temporarily assigned) new address while traveling. The home address can be used by other IPv6 nodes when communicating with the mobile node. If the Home Address option is present, the Destination Options header containing it must appear after a Routing header and before the Fragment, Authentication, and ESP headers (see Chapter 18), if any of them is also present. We discuss this option in more detail in the context of Mobile IP.

5.3.2 Routing Header

The IPv6 Routing header provides a mechanism for the sender of an IPv6 datagram to control, at least in part, the path the datagram takes through the network. At present, two different versions of the routing extension header have been specified, called type 0 (RH0) and type 2 (RH2), respectively. RH0 has been deprecated because of security concerns [RFC5095], and RH2 is defined in conjunction with Mobile IP. To best understand the Routing header, we begin by discussing RH0 and then investigate why it has been deprecated and how it differs from RH2. RH0 specifies one or more IPv6 nodes to be "visited" as the datagram is forwarded. The header is shown in Figure 5-8.

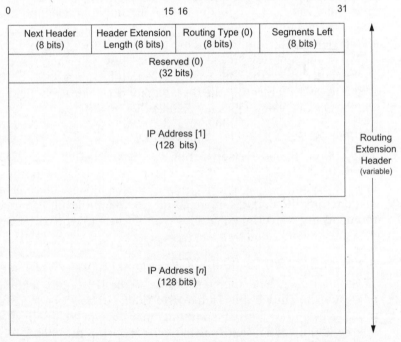

Figure 5-8   The now-deprecated Routing header type 0 (RH0) generalizes the IPv4 loose and strict Source Route and Record Route options. It is constructed by the sender to include IPv6 node addresses that act as waypoints when the datagram is forwarded. Each address can be specified as a loose or strict address. A strict address must be reached by a single IPv6 hop, whereas a loose address may contain one or more other hops in between. The IPv6 *Destination IP Address* field in the base header is modified to contain the next waypoint address as the datagram is forwarded.

The IPv6 Routing header shown in Figure 5-8 generalizes the loose Source and Record Route options from IPv4. It also supports the possibility of routing on identifiers other than IPv6 addresses, although this feature is not standardized and is not discussed further here. For standardized routing on IPv6 addresses, RH0 allows the sender to specify a vector of IPv6 addresses for nodes to be visited.

The header contains an 8-bit *Routing Type* identifier and an 8-bit *Segments Left* field. The type identifier for IPv6 addresses is 0 for RH0 and 2 for RH2. The *Segments Left* field indicates how many route segments remain to be processed—that is, the number of explicitly listed intermediate nodes still to be visited before reaching the final destination. The block of addresses starts with a 32-bit reserved field set by the sender to 0 and ignored by receivers. The addresses are nonmulticast IPv6 addresses to be visited as the datagram is forwarded.

A Routing header is not processed until it reaches the node whose address is contained in the *Destination IP Address* field of the IPv6 header. At this time, the *Segments Left* field is used to determine the next hop address from the address vector, and this address is swapped with the *Destination IP Address* field in the IPv6 header. Thus, as the datagram is forwarded, the *Segments Left* field grows smaller, and the list of addresses in the header reflects the node addresses that forwarded the datagram. The forwarding procedure is better understood with an example (see Figure 5-9).

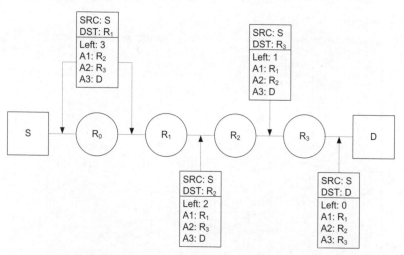

Figure 5-9   Using an IPv6 Routing header (RH0), the sender (S) is able to direct the datagram through the intermediate nodes R_2 and R_3. The other nodes traversed are determined by the normal IPv6 routing. Note that the destination address in the IPv6 header is updated at each hop specified in the Routing header.

In Figure 5-9 we can see how the Routing header is processed by intermediate nodes. The sender (S) constructs the datagram with destination address R_1 and a Routing header (type 0) containing the addresses R_2, R_3, and D. The final destination of the datagram is the last address in the list (D). The *Segments Left* field (labeled "Left" in Figure 5-9) starts at 3. The datagram is forwarded toward R_1 automatically by S and R_0. Because R_0's address is not present in the datagram, no modifications of the Routing header or addresses are performed by R_0. Upon reaching R_1, the destination address from the base header is swapped with the first address listed in the Routing header and the *Segments Left* field is decremented.

As the datagram is forwarded, the process of swapping the destination address with the next address from the address list in the Routing header repeats until the last destination listed in the Routing header is reached.

We can arrange to include a Routing header with a simple command-line option to the `ping6` command in Windows XP (Windows Vista and later include only the `ping` command, which incorporates IPv6 support):

```
C:\> ping6 -r -s 2001:db8::100 2001:db8::1
```

This command arranges to use the source address 2001:db8::100 when sending a ping request to 2001:db8::1. The `-r` option arranges for a Routing header (RH0) to be included. We can see the outgoing request using Wireshark (see Figure 5-10).

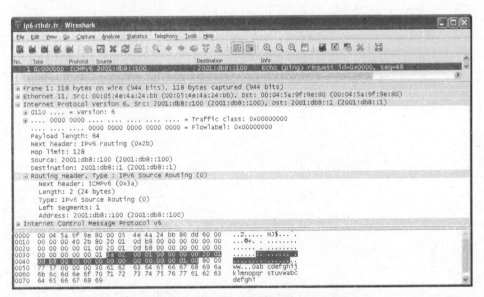

Figure 5-10   The ping request appears as an ICMPv6 Echo Request in Wireshark. The IPv6 header includes a *Next Header* field indicating that the packet contains a type 0 Routing header, followed by an ICMPv6 header. The number of segments in the RH0 left to be processed is one (2001:db8::100).

The `ping` message appears as an ICMPv6 Echo Request packet (see Chapter 8). By following the *Next Header* field values, we can see that the base header is followed by a Routing header. In the Routing header, we can see that the type is 0 (indicating an RH0), and there is one segment (hop) left to process. The hop is specified by the first slot in the address list (number 0): 2001:db8::100.

As mentioned previously, RH0 has been deprecated by [RFC5095] because of a security concern that allows RH0 to be used to increase the effectiveness of DoS attacks. The problem is that RH0 allows the same address to be specified in multiple locations within the Routing header. This can lead to traffic being forwarded many times between two or more hosts or routers along a particular path. The potentially high traffic loads that can be created along particular paths in the network can cause disruption to other traffic flows competing for bandwidth across the same path. Consequently, RH0 has been deprecated and only RH2 remains as the sole Routing header supported by IPv6. RH2 is equivalent to RH0 except it has room for only a single address and uses a different value in the *Routing Type* field.

5.3.3   Fragment Header

The Fragment header is used by an IPv6 source when sending a datagram larger than the path MTU of the datagram's intended destination. Path MTU and how it is determined are discussed in more detail in Chapter 13, but 1280 bytes is a network-wide link-layer minimum MTU for IPv6 (see section 5 of [RFC2460]). In IPv4, any host or router can fragment a datagram if it is too large for the MTU on the next hop, and fields within the second 32-bit word of the IPv4 header indicate the fragmentation information. In IPv6, only the sender of the datagram is permitted to perform fragmentation, and in such cases a Fragment header is added.

The Fragment header includes the same information as is found in the IPv4 header, but the *Identification* field is 32 bits instead of the 16 that are used for IPv4. The larger field provides the ability for more fragmented packets to be outstanding in the network simultaneously. The Fragment header uses the format shown in Figure 5-11.

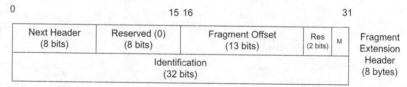

Figure 5-11   The IPv6 Fragment header contains a 32-bit *Identification* field (twice as large as the *Identification* field in IPv4). The *M* bit field indicates whether the fragment is the last of an original datagram. As with IPv4, the *Fragment Offset* field gives the offset of the payload into the original datagram in 8-byte units.

Referring to Figure 5-11, the *Reserved* field and 2-bit *Res* field are both zero and ignored by receivers. The *Fragment Offset* field indicates where the data that follows the Fragment header is located, as a positive offset in 8-byte units, relative to the "fragmentable part" (see the next paragraph) of the original IPv6 datagram. The *M* bit field, if set to 1, indicates that more fragments are contained in the datagram. A value of 0 indicates that the fragment contains the last bytes of the original datagram.

The datagram serving as input to the fragmentation process is called the "original packet" and consists of two parts: the "unfragmentable part" and the "fragmentable part." The unfragmentable part includes the IPv6 header and any included extension headers required to be processed by intermediate nodes to the destination (i.e., all headers up to and including the Routing header, otherwise the Hop-by-Hop Options extension header if only it is present). The fragmentable part constitutes the remainder of the datagram (i.e., Destination Options header, upper-layer headers, and payload data).

When the original packet is fragmented, multiple fragment packets are produced, each of which contains a copy of the unfragmentable part of the original packet, but for which each IPv6 header has the *Payload Length* field altered to reflect the size of the fragment packet it describes. Following the unfragmentable part, each new fragment packet contains a Fragment header with an appropriately assigned *Fragment Offset* field (e.g., the first fragment contains offset 0) and a copy of the original packet's *Identification* field. The last fragment has its *M* (*More Fragments*) bit field set to 0.

The following example illustrates the way an IPv6 source might fragment a datagram. In the example shown in Figure 5-12, a payload of 3960 bytes is fragmented such that no fragment's total packet size exceeds 1500 bytes (a typical MTU for Ethernet), yet the fragment data sizes still are arranged to be multiples of 8 bytes.

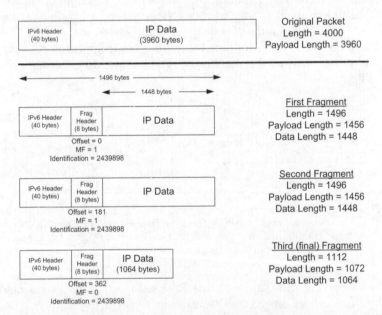

Figure 5-12   An example of IPv6 fragmentation where a 3960-byte payload is split into three fragment packets of size 1448 bytes or less. Each fragment contains a Fragment header with the identical *Identification* field. All but the last fragment have the *More Fragments* field (*M*) set to 1. The offset is given in 8-byte units—the last fragment, for example, contains data beginning at offset (362 * 8) = 2896 bytes from the beginning of the original packet's data. The scheme is similar to fragmentation in IPv4.

In Figure 5-12 we see how the larger original packet has been fragmented into three smaller packets, each containing a Fragment header. The IPv6 header's *Payload Length* field is modified to reflect the size of the data and newly formed Fragment header. The Fragment header in each fragment contains a common *Identification* field , and the sender ensures that no distinct original packets are assigned the same field value within the expected lifetime of a datagram on the network.

The *Offset* field in the Fragment header is given in 8-byte units, so fragmentation is performed at 8-byte boundaries, which is why the first and second fragments contain 1448 data bytes instead of 1452. Thus, all but the last fragment (possibly) is a multiple of 8 bytes. The receiver must ensure that all fragments of an original datagram have been received before performing *reassembly*. The reassembly procedure aggregates the fragments, forming the original datagram. As with fragmentation in IPv4 (see Chapter 10), fragments may arrive out of order at the receiver but are reassembled in order to form a datagram that is given to other protocols for processing.

We can see the construction of an IPv6 fragment using this command on Windows 7:

```
C:\> ping -l 3952 ff01::2
```

Figure 5-13 shows the Wireshark output of the activity on the network as it runs.

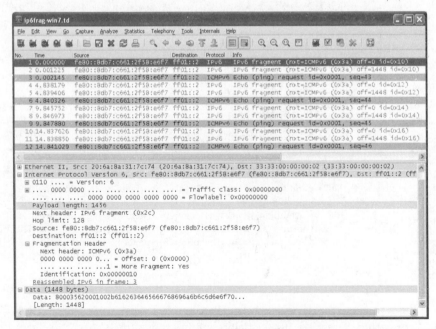

Figure 5-13   The ping program generates ICMPv6 packets (see Chapter 8) containing 3960 IPv6 payload bytes in this example. These packets are fragmented to produce three packet fragments, each of which is small enough to fit in the Ethernet MTU size of 1500 bytes.

In Figure 5-13 we see the fragments constituting four ICMPv6 Echo Request messages sent to the IPv6 multicast address ff01::2. Each request requires fragmentation because the –l 3952 option indicates that 3952 data bytes are to be carried in the data area of each ICMPv6 message (leading to an IPv6 payload length of 3960 bytes due to the 8-byte ICMPv6 header). The IPv6 source address is link-local. To determine the target's link-layer multicast address, a mapping procedure specific to IPv6 is performed, described in Chapter 9. The ICMPv6 Echo Request (generated by the ping program) spans several fragments, which Wireshark reassembles to display once it has processed all the constituent fragments. Figure 5-14 shows the second fragment in more detail.

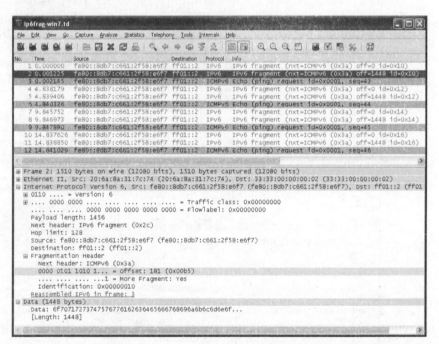

Figure 5-14   The second fragment of an ICMPv6 Echo Request contains 1448 IPv6 payload bytes including the 8-byte Fragment header. The presence of the Fragment header indicates that the overall datagram was fragmented at the source, and the *Offset* field of 181 indicates that this fragment contains data starting at byte offset 1448. The *More Fragments* bit field being set indicates that other fragments are needed to reassemble the datagram. All fragments from the same original datagram contain the same *Identification* field (2 in this case).

In Figure 5-14 we see the IPv6 header, with payload length 1448 bytes, as expected. The *Next Header* field contains the value 44 (0x2c) we saw in Table 5-5, indicating that a Fragment header follows the IPv6 header. The Fragment header indicates that the following header is for ICMPv6, meaning there are no more extension headers. Also, the *Offset* field is 181, meaning this fragment contains data at byte offset 1448 in the original datagram. We know it is not the last fragment because the *More Fragments* field is set (displayed as **Yes** by Wireshark). Figure 5-15 shows the final fragment of the initial ICMPv6 Echo Request datagram.

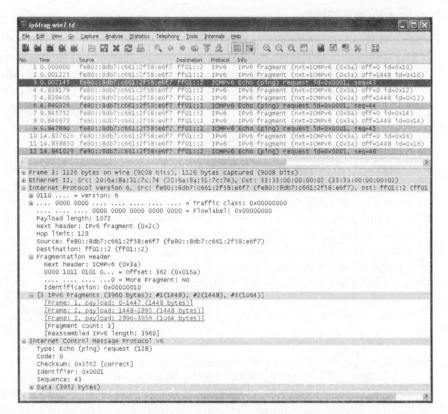

Figure 5-15   The last fragment of the first ICMPv6 Echo Request datagram has an offset of 362 * 8 = 2896 and payload length of 1072 bytes (1064 bytes of the original datagram's payload plus 8 bytes of Fragment header). The *More Fragments* bit field being set to 0 indicates that this is the last fragment, and the original datagram's total payload length is 2896 + 1064 = 3960 bytes (3956 bytes of ICMP data plus 8 bytes for the ICMPv6 header; see Chapter 8).

In Figure 5-15 we see that the *Offset* field has the value 362, but this is in 8-byte units, meaning that the byte offset relative to the original datagram is 362 * 8 = 2896. The *Total Length* field has the value 1072, which includes 8 bytes for the Fragment header. Wireshark computes the fragmentation pattern for us, indicating that the first and second fragments contained the first and second sets of 1448 bytes, and the final fragment contained 1064. All in all, the fragmentation process added 40*2 + 8*3 = 104 bytes to be carried by the network layer (two additional

IPv6 headers plus an 8-byte Fragment header for each fragment). If we add link-layer overhead, the total comes to 104 + (2*18) = 140 bytes. (Each new Ethernet frame includes a 14-byte header and a 4-byte CRC.)

5.4   IP Forwarding

Conceptually, IP forwarding is simple, especially for a host. If the destination is directly connected to the host (e.g., a point-to-point link) or on a shared network (e.g., Ethernet), the IP datagram is sent directly to the destination—a router is not required or used. Otherwise, the host sends the datagram to a single router (called the *default* router) and lets the router deliver the datagram to its destination. This simple scheme handles most host configurations.

In this section we investigate the details of this simple situation and also how IP forwarding works when the situation is not as simple. We begin by noting that most hosts today can be configured to be routers as well as hosts, and many home networks use an Internet-connected PC to act as a router (and also a firewall, as we discuss in Chapter 7). What differentiates a host from a router to IP is how IP datagrams are handled: a host never forwards datagrams it does not originate, whereas routers do.

In our general scheme, the IP protocol can receive a datagram either from another protocol on the same machine (TCP, UDP, etc.) or from a network interface. The IP layer has some information in memory, usually called a *routing table* or *forwarding table*, which it searches each time it receives a datagram to send. When a datagram is received from a network interface, IP first checks if the destination IP address is one of its own IP addresses (i.e., one of the IP addresses associated with one of its network interfaces) or some other address for which it should receive traffic such as an IP broadcast or multicast address. If so, the datagram is delivered to the protocol module specified by the *Protocol* field in the IPv4 header or *Next Header* field in the IPv6 header. If the datagram is not destined for one of the IP addresses being used locally by the IP module, then (1) if the IP layer was configured to act as a router, the datagram is forwarded (that is, handled as an outgoing datagram as described in Section 5.4.2); or (2) the datagram is silently discarded. Under some circumstances (e.g., no route is known in case 1), an ICMP message may be sent back to the source indicating an error condition.

5.4.1   Forwarding Table

The IP protocol standards do not dictate the precise data required to be in a forwarding table, as this choice is left up to the implementer of the IP protocol. Nevertheless, several key pieces of information are generally required to implement the forwarding table for IP, and we shall discuss these now. Each entry in the routing or forwarding table contains the following information fields, at least conceptually:

- **Destination**: This contains a 32-bit field (or 128-bit field for IPv6) used for matching the result of a masking operation (see the next bulleted item). The destination can be as simple as zero, for a "default route" covering all destinations, or as long as the full length of an IP address, in the case of a "host route" that describes only a single destination.

- **Mask:** This contains a 32-bit field (128-bit field for IPv6) applied as a bitwise AND mask to the destination IP address of a datagram being looked up in the forwarding table. The masked result is compared with the set of destinations in the forwarding table entries.

- **Next-hop**: This contains the 32-bit IPv4 address or 128-bit IPv6 address of the next IP entity (router or host) to which the datagram should be sent. The next-hop entity is typically on a network shared with the system performing the forwarding lookup, meaning the two share the same network prefix (see Chapter 2).

- **Interface**: This contains an identifier used by the IP layer to reference the network interface that should be used to send the datagram to its next hop. For example, it could refer to a host's 802.11 wireless interface, a wired Ethernet interface, or a PPP interface associated with a serial port. If the forwarding system is also the sender of the IP datagram, this field is used in selecting which source IP address to use on the outgoing datagram (see Section 5.6.2.1).

IP forwarding is performed on a *hop-by-hop* basis. As we can see from this forwarding table information, the routers and hosts do not contain the complete forwarding path to any destination (except, of course, those destinations that are directly connected to the host or router). IP forwarding provides the IP address of only the next-hop entity to which the datagram is sent. It is assumed that the next hop is really "closer" to the destination than the forwarding system is, and that the next-hop router is directly connected to (i.e., shares a common network prefix with) the forwarding system. It is also generally assumed that no "loops" are constructed between the next hops so that a datagram does not circulate around the network until its TTL or hop limit expires. The job of ensuring correctness of the routing table is given to one or more routing protocols. Many different *routing protocols* are available to do this job, including RIP, OSPF, BGP, and IS-IS, to name a few (see, for example, [DC05] for more detail on routing protocols).

5.4.2 IP Forwarding Actions

When the IP layer in a host or router needs to send an IP datagram to a next-hop router or host, it first examines the destination IP address (D) in the datagram. Using the value D, the following *longest prefix match* algorithm is executed on the forwarding table:

1. Search the table for all entries for which the following property holds: $(D \wedge m_j) = d_j$, where m_j is the value of the mask field associated with the forwarding entry e_j having index j, and d_j is the value of the destination field associated with e_j. This means that the destination IP address D is bitwise ANDed with the mask in each forwarding table entry (m_j), and the result is compared against the destination in the same forwarding table entry (d_j). If the property holds, the entry (e_j here) is a "match" for the destination IP address. When a match happens, the algorithm notes the entry index (j here) and how many bits in the mask m_j were set to 1. The more bits set to 1, the "better" the match.

2. The best matching entry e_k (i.e., the one with the largest number of 1 bits in its mask m_k) is selected, and its next-hop field n_k is used as the next-hop IP address in forwarding the datagram.

If no matches in the forwarding table are found, the datagram is undeliverable. If the undeliverable datagram was generated locally (on this host), a "host unreachable" error is normally returned to the application that generated the datagram. On a router, an ICMP message is normally sent back to the host that sent the datagram.

In some circumstances, more than one entry may match an equal number of 1 bits. This can happen, for example, when more than one default route is available (e.g., when attached to more than one ISP, called multihoming). The end-system behavior in such cases is not set by standards and is instead specific to the operating system's protocol implementation. A common behavior is for the system to simply choose the first match. More sophisticated systems may attempt to *load-balance* or split traffic across the multiple routes. Studies suggest that multihoming can be beneficial not only for large enterprises, but also for residential users [THL06].

5.4.3   Examples

To get a solid understanding of how IP forwarding works both in the simple local environment (e.g., same LAN) and in the somewhat more complicated multihop (global Internet) environment, we look at two cases. The first case, where all systems are using the same network prefix, is called *direct delivery*, and the other case is called *indirect delivery* (see Figure 5-16).

5.4.3.1 Direct Delivery

First consider a simple example. Our Windows XP host (with IPv4 address S and MAC address S̲), which we will just call S, has an IP datagram to send to our Linux host (IPv4 address D, MAC address D̲), which we will call D. These systems are interconnected using a switch. Both hosts are on the same Ethernet (see inside front cover). Figure 5-16 (top) shows the delivery of the datagram. When the IP layer in S receives a datagram to send from one of the upper layers such as TCP or UDP, it searches its forwarding table. We would expect the forwarding table on S to contain the information shown in Table 5-8.

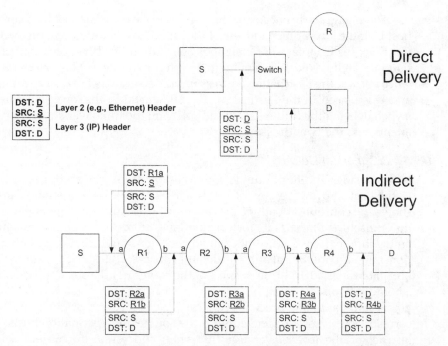

Figure 5-16   Direct delivery does not require the presence of a router—IP datagrams are encapsulated in a link-layer frame that directly identifies the source and destination. Indirect delivery involves a router—data is forwarded to the router using the router's link-layer address as the destination link-layer address. The router's IP address does not appear in the IP datagram (unless the router itself is the source or destination, or when source routing is used).

In Table 5-8, the destination IPv4 address D (10.0.0.9) matches both the first and second forwarding table entries. Because it matches the second entry better (25 bits instead of none), the "gateway" or next-hop address is 10.0.0.100, the address S. Thus, the gateway portion of the entry contains the address of the sending host's own network interface (no router is referenced), indicating that direct delivery is to be used to send the datagram.

Table 5-8   The (unicast) IPv4 forwarding table at host S contains only two entries. Host S is configured with IPv4 address and subnet mask 10.0.0.100/25. Datagrams destined for addresses in the range 10.0.0.1 through 10.0.0.126 use the second forwarding table entry and are sent using direct delivery. All other datagrams use the first entry and are given to router R with IPv4 address 10.0.0.1.

Destination	Mask	Gateway (Next Hop)	Interface
0.0.0.0	0.0.0.0	10.0.0.1	10.0.0.100
10.0.0.0	255.255.255.128	10.0.0.100	10.0.0.100

The datagram is encapsulated in a lower-layer frame destined for the target host D. If the lower-layer address of the target host is unknown, the ARP protocol (for IPv4; see Chapter 4) or Neighbor Solicitation (for IPv6; see Chapter 8) operation may be invoked at this point to determine the correct lower-layer address, $\underline{D}$. Once known, the destination address in the datagram is D's IPv4 address (10.0.0.9), and $\underline{D}$ is placed in the *Destination IP Address* field in the lower-layer header. The switch delivers the frame to D based solely on the link-layer address $\underline{D}$; it pays no attention to the IP addresses.

5.4.3.2 Indirect Delivery

Now consider another example. Our Windows host has an IP datagram to send to the host `ftp.uu.net`, whose IPv4 address is 192.48.96.9. Figure 5-16 (bottom) shows the conceptual path of the datagram through four routers. First, the Windows machine searches its forwarding table but does not find a matching prefix on the local network. It uses its default route entry (which matches every destination, but with no 1 bits at all). The default entry indicates that the appropriate next-hop gateway is 10.0.0.1 (the "a side" of the router R1). This is a typical scenario for a home network.

Recall that in the direct delivery case, the source and destination IP addresses correspond to those associated with the source and destination hosts. The same is true for the lower-layer (e.g., Ethernet) addresses. In indirect delivery, the IP addresses correspond to the source and destination hosts as before, but the lower-layer addresses do not. Instead, the lower-layer addresses determine which machines receive the frame containing the datagram on a per-hop basis. In this example, the lower-layer address needed is the Ethernet address of the next-hop router R1's a-side interface, the lower-layer address corresponding to IPv4 address 10.0.0.1. This is accomplished by ARP (or a Neighbor Solicitation request if this example were using IPv6) on the network interconnecting S and R1. Once R1 responds with its a-side lower-layer address, S sends the datagram to R1. Delivery from S to R1 takes place based on processing only the lower-layer headers (more specifically, the lower-layer destination address). Upon receipt of the datagram, R1 checks its forwarding table. The information in Table 5-9 would be typical.

Table 5-9   The forwarding table at R1 indicates that address translation should be performed for traffic. The router has a private address on one side (10.0.0.1) and a public address on the other (70.231.132.85). Address translation is used to make datagrams originating on the 10.0.0.0/25 network appear to the Internet as though they had been sent from 70.231.132.85.

Destination	Mask	Gateway (Next Hop)	Interface	Note
0.0.0.0	0.0.0.0	70.231.159.254	70.231.132.85	NAT
10.0.0.0	255.255.255.128	10.0.0.100	10.0.0.1	NAT

When R1 receives the datagram, it realizes that the datagram's destination IP address is not one of its own, so it forwards the datagram. Its forwarding table is searched and the default entry is used. The default entry in this case has a next hop within the ISP servicing the network, 70.231.159.254 (this is R2's a-side interface). This address happens to be within SBC's DSL network called by the somewhat cumbersome name adsl-70-231-159-254.dsl.snfc21.sbcglobal.net. Because this router is in the global Internet and the Windows machine's source address is the private address 10.0.0.100, R1 performs *Network Address Translation* (NAT) on the datagram to make it routable on the Internet. The NAT operation results in the datagram having the new source address 70.231.132.85, which corresponds to R1's b-side interface. Networks that do not use private addressing (e.g., ISPs and larger enterprises) avoid the last step and the original source address remains unchanged. NAT is described in more detail in Chapter 7.

When router R2 (inside the ISP) receives the datagram, it goes through the same steps that the local router R1 did (except for the NAT operation). If the datagram is not destined for one of its own IP addresses, the datagram is forwarded. In this case, the router usually has not only a default route but several others, depending on its connectivity to the rest of the Internet and its own local policies.

Note that IPv6 forwarding varies only slightly from conventional IPv4 forwarding. Aside from the larger addresses, IPv6 uses a slightly different mechanism (Neighbor Solicitation messages) to ascertain the lower-layer address of its next hop. It is described in more detail in Chapter 8, as it is part of ICMPv6. In addition, IPv6 has both link-local addresses and global addresses (see Chapter 2). While global addresses behave like regular IP addresses, link-local addresses can be used only on the same link. In addition, because all the link-local addresses share the same IPv6 prefix (fe80::/10), a multihomed host may require user input to determine which interface to use when sending a datagram destined for a link-local destination.

To illustrate the use of link-local addresses, we start with our Windows XP machine, assuming IPv6 is enabled and operational:

```
C:\> ping6 fe80::204:5aff:fe9f:9e80

Pinging fe80::204:5aff:fe9f:9e80 with 32 bytes of data:

No route to destination.
  Specify correct scope-id or use -s to specify source address.
  ...

C:\> ping6 fe80::204:5aff:fe9f:9e80%6

Pinging fe80::204:5aff:fe9f:9e80%6
from fe80::205:4eff:fe4a:24bb%6 with 32 bytes of data:

Reply from fe80::204:5aff:fe9f:9e80%6: bytes=32 time=1ms
Reply from fe80::204:5aff:fe9f:9e80%6: bytes=32 time=1ms
```

```
Reply from fe80::204:5aff:fe9f:9e80%6: bytes=32 time=1ms
Reply from fe80::204:5aff:fe9f:9e80%6: bytes=32 time=1ms

Ping statistics for fe80::204:5aff:fe9f:9e80%6:
    Packets: Sent = 4, Received = 4, Lost = 0 (0% loss),
Approximate round trip times in milli-seconds:
    Minimum = 1ms, Maximum = 1ms, Average = 1ms
```

Here we see that failing to specify which interface to use for outbound link-local traffic results in an error. In Windows XP, we can specify either a scope ID or a source address. In this example we specify the scope ID as an interface number using the %6 extension to the destination address. This informs the system to use interface number 6 as the correct interface when sending the ping traffic.

To see the path taken to an IP destination, we can use the traceroute program (called tracert on Windows, which has a slightly different set of options) with the -n option to not convert IP addresses to names:

```
Linux% traceroute -n ftp.uu.net
traceroute to ftp.uu.net (192.48.96.9), 30 hops max, 38 byte packets
 1  70.231.159.254   9.285 ms   8.404 ms   8.887 ms
 2  206.171.134.131  8.412 ms   8.764 ms   8.661 ms
 3  216.102.176.226  8.502 ms   8.995 ms   8.644 ms
 4  151.164.190.185  8.705 ms   8.673 ms   9.014 ms
 5  151.164.92.181   9.149 ms   9.057 ms   9.537 ms
 6  151.164.240.134  9.680 ms   10.389 ms  11.003 ms
 7  151.164.41.10    11.605 ms  37.699 ms  11.374 ms
 8  12.122.79.97     13.449 ms  12.804 ms  13.126 ms
 9  12.122.85.134    15.114 ms  15.020 ms  13.654 ms
     MPLS Label=32307 CoS=5 TTL=1 S=0
10  12.123.12.18     16.011 ms  13.555 ms  13.167 ms
11  192.205.33.198   15.594 ms  15.497 ms  16.093 ms
12  152.63.57.102    15.103 ms  14.769 ms  15.128 ms
13  152.63.34.133    77.501 ms  77.593 ms  76.974 ms
14  152.63.38.1      77.906 ms  78.101 ms  78.398 ms
15  207.18.173.162   81.146 ms  81.281 ms  80.918 ms
16  198.5.240.36     77.988 ms  78.007 ms  77.947 ms
17  198.5.241.101    81.912 ms  82.231 ms  83.115 ms
```

This program lists each of the IP hops traversed while sending a series of datagrams to the destination ftp.uu.net (192.48.96.9). The traceroute program uses a combination of UDP datagrams (with increasing TTL over time) and ICMP messages (used to detect each hop when the UDP datagrams expire) to accomplish its task. Three UDP packets are sent at each TTL value, providing three round-trip-time measurements to each hop. Traditionally, traceroute has carried only IP information, but here we also see the following line:

```
MPLS Label=32307 CoS=5 TTL=1 S=0
```

This indicates that *Multiprotocol Label Switching* (MPLS) [RFC3031] is being used on the path, and the label ID is 32307, class of service is 5, TTL is 1, and the message is not the bottom of the MPLS label stack (S = 0; see [RFC4950]). MPLS is a form of link-layer network capable of carrying multiple network-layer protocols. Its interaction with ICMP is described in [RFC4950], and its handling of IPv4 packets containing options is described in [RFC6178]. Many network operators use it for traffic engineering purposes (i.e., controlling where network traffic flows through their networks).

5.4.4   Discussion

In the examples we have just seen there are a few key points that should be kept in mind regarding the operation of IP unicast forwarding:

1. Most of the hosts and routers in this example used a default route consisting of a single forwarding table entry of this form: mask 0, destination 0, next hop <some IP address>. Indeed, most hosts and most routers at the edge of the Internet can use a default route for everything other than destinations on local networks because there is only one interface available that provides connectivity to the rest of the Internet.

2. The source and destination IP addresses in the datagram never change once in the regular Internet. This is always the case unless either source routing is used, or when other functions (such as NAT, as in the example) are encountered along the data path. Forwarding decisions at the IP layer are based on the destination address.

3. A different lower-layer header is used on each link that uses addressing, and the lower-layer destination address (if present) always contains the lower-layer address of the next hop. Therefore, lower-layer headers routinely change as the datagram is moved along each hop toward its destination. In our example, both Ethernet LANs encapsulated a link-layer header containing the next hop's Ethernet address, but the DSL link did not. Lower-layer addresses are normally obtained using ARP (see Chapter 4) for IPv4 and ICMPv6 Neighbor Discovery for IPv6 (see Chapter 8).

5.5   Mobile IP

So far we have discussed the conventional ways that IP datagrams are forwarded through the Internet, as well as private networks that use IP. One assumption of the model is that a host's IP address shares a prefix with its nearby hosts and routers. If such a host should move its point of network attachment, yet remain connected to the network at the link layer, all of its upper-layer (e.g., TCP) connections would fail because either its IP address would have to be changed or routing would not deliver packets to the (moved) host properly. A multiyear (actually, multidecade!) effort known as *Mobile IP* addresses this issue. (Other protocols have also been suggested; see [RFC6301].) Although there are versions of Mobile IP for both IPv4 [RFC5944] (MIPv4) and IPv6 [RFC6275], we focus on Mobile IPv6 (called MIPv6) because it is more flexible and somewhat easier to explain. Also, it currently appears more likely to be deployed in the quickly growing smartphone market. Note that we do not discuss MIPv6 comprehensively; it is sufficiently complex to merit a book on its own (e.g., [RC05]). Nonetheless, we will cover its basic concepts and principles.

Mobile IP is based on the idea that a host has a "home" network but may visit other networks from time to time. While at home, ordinary forwarding is performed, according to the algorithms discussed in this chapter. When away from home, the host keeps the IP address it would ordinarily use at home, but some special routing and forwarding tricks are used to make the host appear to the network, and to the other systems with which it communicates, as though it is attached to its home network. The scheme depends on a special type of router called a "home agent" that helps provide routing for mobile nodes.

Most of the complexity in MIPv6 involves signaling messages and how they are secured. These messages use various forms of the Mobility extension header (*Next Header* field value 135 in Table 5-5, often just called the *mobility header*), so Mobile IP is, in effect, a special protocol of its own. The IANA maintains a registry of the various header types (17 are reserved currently), along with many other parameters associated with MIPv6 [MP]. We shall focus on the basic messages specified in [RFC6275]. Other messages are used to implement "fast handovers" [RFC5568], changing of the home agent [RFC5142], and experiments [RFC5096]. To understand MIPv6, we begin by introducing the basic model for IP mobility and the associated terminology.

5.5.1   The Basic Model: Bidirectional Tunneling

Figure 5-17 shows the entities involved in making MIPv6 work. Much of the terminology also applies to MIPv4 [RFC5944]. A host that might move is called a *mobile node* (MN), and the hosts with which it is communicating are called *correspondent nodes* (CNs). The MN is given an IP address chosen from the network prefix used in its home network. This address is known as its *home address* (HoA). When it travels to a visited network, it is given an additional address, called its *care-of address* (CoA). In the basic model, whenever a CN communicates with an MN, the traffic is routed through the MN's *home agent* (HA). HAs are a special type of router deployed in the network infrastructure like other important systems (e.g., routers and Web servers). The association between an MN's HoA and its CoA is called a *binding* for the MN.

The basic model (see Figure 5-17) works in cases where an MN's CNs do not engage in the MIPv6 protocol. This model is also used for network mobility (called "NEMO" [RFC3963]), when an entire network is mobile. When the MN (or mobile

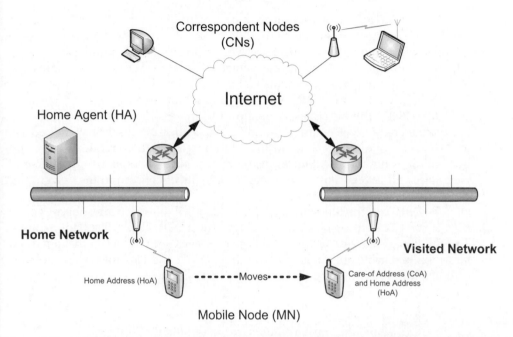

Figure 5-17 Mobile IP supports the ability of nodes to change their point of network attachment and keep network connections operating. The mobile node's home agent helps to forward traffic for mobiles it serves and also plays a role in route optimization, which can substantially improve routing performance by allowing mobile and correspondent nodes to communicate directly.

network router) attaches to a new point in the network, it receives its CoA and sends a *binding update* message to its HA. The HA responds with a *binding acknowledgment*. Assuming that all goes well, traffic between the MN and CNs is thereafter routed through the MN's HA using a two-way form of IPv6 packet tunneling [RFC2473] called *bidirectional tunneling*. These messages are ordinarily protected using IPsec with the *Encapsulating Security Payload* (ESP) (see Chapter 18). Doing so ensures that an HA is not fooled into accepting a binding update from a fake MN.

5.5.2 Route Optimization (RO)

Bidirectional tunneling makes MIPv6 work in a relatively simple way, and with CNs that are not Mobile-IP-aware, but the routing can be extremely inefficient, especially if the MN and CNs are near each other but far away from the MN's HA. To improve upon the inefficient routing that may occur in basic MIPv6, a process called *route optimization* (RO) can be used, provided it is supported by the various nodes involved. As we shall see, the methods used to ensure that RO is secure and useful are somewhat complicated. We shall sketch only its basic operations. For a more detailed discussion, see [RFC6275] and [RFC4866]. For a discussion of the design rationale behind RO security, see [RFC4225].

When used, RO involves a *correspondent registration* whereby an MN notifies its CNs of its current CoA to allow routing to take place without help from the HA. RO operates in two parts: one part involves establishing and maintaining the registration bindings; another involves the method used to exchange datagrams once all bindings are in place. To establish a binding with its CNs, an MN must prove to each CN that it is the proper MN. This is accomplished by a *Return Routability Procedure* (RRP). The messages that support RRP are not protected using IPsec as are the messages between an MN and its HA. Expecting IPsec to work between an MN and any CN was believed to be too unreliable (IPv6 requires IPsec support but does not require its use). Although the RRP is not as strong as IPsec, it is simpler and covers most of the security threats of concern to the designers of Mobile IP.

The RRP uses the following *mobility messages*, all of which are subtypes of the IPv6 Mobility extension header: Home Test Init (HoTI), Home Test (HoT), Care-of Test Init (CoTI), Care-of Test (CoT). These messages verify to a CN that a particular MN is reachable both at its home address (HoTI and HoT messages) and at its care-of addresses (CoTI and CoT messages). The protocol is shown in Figure 5-18.

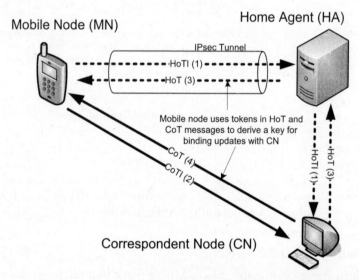

Figure 5-18   The return routability check procedure used in sending binding updates from an MN to a CN in order to enable route optimization. The check aims to demonstrate to a CN that an MN is reachable at both its home address and its care-of address. In this figure, messages routed indirectly are indicated with dashed arrows. The numbers indicate the ordering of messages, although the HoTI and CoTI messages can be sent by an MN in parallel.

To understand the RRP, we take the simplest case of a single MN, its HA, and a CN as shown in Figure 5-18. The MN begins by sending both a HoTI and CoTI message to the CN. The HoTI message is forwarded through the HA on its way to the CN. The CN receives both messages in some order and responds with a HoT and CoT message to each, respectively. The HoT message is sent to the MN via the HA. Inside these messages are random bit strings called *tokens*, which the MN uses to form a cryptographic key (see Chapter 18 for a discussion of the basics of cryptography and keys). The key is then used to form authenticated binding updates that are sent to the CN. If successful, the route can be optimized and data can flow directly between an MN and a CN, as shown in Figure 5-19.

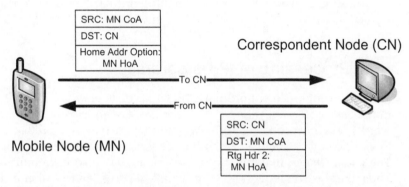

Figure 5-19   Once a binding is established between an MN and a CN, data flows directly between them. The direction from MN to CN uses an IPv6 Home Address Destination option. The reverse direction uses a type 2 Routing header (RH2).

Once a binding has been established successfully, data may flow directly between an MN and its CNs without the inefficiency of bidirectional tunneling. This is accomplished using an IPv6 Destination option for traffic moving from the MN to a CN and a type 2 Routing header (RH2) for traffic headed in the reverse direction, as detailed in Figure 5-19. The packets from MN to CN include a *Source IP Address* field of the MN's CoA, which avoids problems associated with ingress filtering [RFC2827] that might cause packets containing the MN's HoA in the *Source IP Address* field to be dropped. The MN's HoA, contained in the Home Address option, is not processed by routers, so it passes through to the CN without modification. On the return path, packets are destined for the MN's CoA. After successfully receiving a returning packet, the MN processes the extension headers and replaces the destination IP address with the HoA contained in the RH2. The resulting packet is delivered to the rest of the MN's protocol stack, so applications "believe" they are using the MN's HoA instead of its CoA for establishing connections and other actions.

5.5.3   Discussion

There are a number of issues with Mobile IP. It is designed to address a certain type of mobility in which a node's IP address may change while the underlying link layer remains more or less connected. This type of usage is not common for portable computers, which tend to shut down or be put to sleep when being moved from place to place. The usage model requiring Mobile IP (and MIPv6 in particular) is more likely to be a large number of smartphones that use IP. Such devices may be running real-time applications (e.g., VoIP) that have latency requirements. Consequently, several approaches are being explored to reduce the amount of time required to execute binding updates. These include fast handovers [RFC5568], a modification to MIPv6 called Hierarchical MIPv6 (HMIPv6) [RFC5380], and a modification in which the mobile signaling ordinarily required of an MN is performed by a proxy (called proxy MIPv6 or PMIPv6 [RFC5213]).

5.6   Host Processing of IP Datagrams

Although routers do not ordinarily have to consider which IP addresses to place in the *Source IP Address* and *Destination IP Address* fields of the packets they forward, hosts must consider both. Applications such as Web browsers may attempt to make connections to a named host or server that can have multiple addresses. The client system making such connections may also have multiple addresses. Thus, there is some question as to which address (and version of IP) should be used when sending a datagram. A more subtle point we shall explore is whether to accept traffic destined for a local IP address if it arrives on the wrong interface (i.e., one that is not configured with the destination address present in a received datagram).

5.6.1   Host Models

Although it may appear to be a straightforward decision to determine whether a received unicast datagram matches one of a host's IP addresses and should be processed, this decision depends on the *host model* of the receiving system [RFC1122] and is most relevant for multihomed hosts. There are two host models, the *strong host model* and the *weak host model*. In the strong host model, a datagram is accepted for delivery to the local protocol stack only if the IP address contained in the *Destination IP Address* field matches one of those configured on the interface upon which the datagram arrived. In systems implementing the weak host model, the opposite is true—a datagram carrying a destination address matching any of the local addresses may arrive on any interface and is processed by the receiving protocol stack, irrespective of the network interface upon which it arrived. Host models also apply to sending behavior. That is, a host using the strong host model sends datagrams from a particular interface only if one of the interface's configured addresses matches the *Source IP Address* field in the datagram being sent.

Figure 5-20 illustrates a case where the host model becomes important. In this example, two hosts (A and B) are connected through the global Internet but also through a local network. If host A is set up to conform to the strong host model, packets it receives destined for 203.0.113.1 from the Internet or destined for 192.0.2.1 from the local network are dropped. This situation can arise, for example, if host B is configured to obey the weak host model. It may choose to send packets to 192.0.2.1 using the local network (e.g., because doing so may be cheaper or faster). This situation seems unfortunate, as A receives what appear to be perfectly legitimate packets, yet drops them merely because it is operating according to the strong host model. So a reasonable question would be: Why is it ever a good idea to use the strong host model?

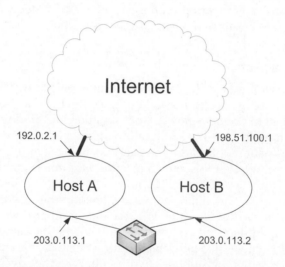

Figure 5-20 Hosts may be connected by more than one interface. In such cases, they must decide which addresses to use for the *Source IP Address* and *Destination IP Address* fields of the packets they exchange. The addresses used result from a combination of each host's forwarding table, application of an address selection algorithm [RFC 3484], and whether hosts are operating using a weak or strong host model.

The attraction of using the strong host model relates to a security concern. Referring to Figure 5-20, consider a malicious user on the Internet who injects a packet destined for the address 203.0.113.2. This packet could also include a forged ("spoofed") source IP address (e.g., 203.0.113.1). If the Internet cooperates in routing such a packet to B, applications running on B may be tricked into believing they have received local traffic originating from A. This can have significant negative consequences if such applications make access control decisions based on the source IP address.

The host model, for both sending and receiving behavior, can be configured in some operating systems. In Windows (Vista and later), strong host behavior is the default for sending and receiving for IPv4 and IPv6. In Linux, the IP behavior defaults to the weak host model. BSD (including Mac OS X) uses the strong host model. In Windows, the following commands can be used to configure weak host receive and send behavior, respectively:

```
C:\> netsh interface ipvX set interface <ifname> weakhostreceive=Yabled
```

```
C:\> netsh interface ipvX set interface <ifname> weakhostsend=Yabled
```

For these commands, `<ifname>` is replaced with the appropriate interface name; X is replaced with either 4 or 6, depending on which version of IP is being configured; and Y is replaced with either en or dis, depending on whether weak behavior is to be enabled or disabled, respectively.

5.6.2   Address Selection

When a host sends an IP datagram, it must decide which of its IP addresses to place in the *Source IP Address* field of the outgoing datagram, and which destination address to use for a particular destination host if multiple addresses for it are known. In some cases the source address is already known because it is provided by an application or because the packet is being sent in response to a previously received packet on the same connection (see, for example, Chapter 13 for how addresses are managed with TCP).

In modern IP implementations, the IP addresses used in the *Source IP Address* and *Destination IP Address* fields of the datagram are selected using a set of procedures called *source address selection* and *destination address selection*. Historically, most Internet hosts had only one IP address for external communication, so selecting the addresses was not terribly difficult. With the advent of multiple addresses per interface and the use of IPv6 in which simultaneous use of addresses with multiple scopes is normal, some procedure must be used. The situation is further complicated when communication is to take place between two hosts that implement both IPv4 and IPv6 ("dual-stack" hosts; see [RFC4213]). Failure to select the correct addresses can lead to asymmetric routing, unwanted filtering, or discarding of packets. Fixing such problems can be a challenge.

[RFC3484] gives the rules for selecting IPv6 default addresses; IPv4-only hosts do not ordinarily have such complex issues. In general, applications can invoke special API operations to override the default behavior, as suggested previously. Even then, tricky deployment situations may still arise [RFC5220]. The default rules in [RFC3484] are to prefer source/destination address pairs where the addresses are of the same scope, to prefer smaller over larger scopes, to avoid the use of temporary addresses when other addresses are available, and to otherwise prefer pairs with the longest common prefix. Global addresses are preferred over temporary addresses when available. The specification also includes a method of providing "administrative override" to the default rules, but this is deployment-specific and we do not discuss it further.

The selection of default addresses is controlled by a *policy table*, present (at least conceptually) in each host. It is a longest-matching-prefix lookup table, similar to a forwarding table used with IP routing. For an address A, a lookup in this table produces a *precedence value* for A, P(A), and a *label* for A, L(A). A higher precedence value indicates greater preference. The labels are used for grouping of similar address types. For example if L(S) = L(D), the algorithm prefers to use the pair (S,D) as a source/destination pair. If no other policy is specified, [RFC3484] suggests that the policy values from Table 5-10 be used.

Table 5-10   The default host policy table, according to [RFC3484]. Higher precedence values indicate a greater preference.

Prefix	Precedence P()	Label L()
::1/128	50	0
::/0	40	1
2002::/16	30	2
::/96	20	3
::ffff:0:0/96	10	4

This table, or one configured at a site based upon administrative configuration parameters, is used to drive the address selection algorithm. The function CPL(A,B) or "common prefix length" is the length, in bits, of the longest common prefix between IPv6 addresses A and B, starting from the left-most significant bit. The function S(A) is the scope of IPv6 address A mapped to a numeric value with larger scopes mapping to larger values. If A is link-scoped and B is global scope, then S(A) < S(B). The function M(A) maps an IPv4 address A to an IPv4-mapped IPv6 address. Because the scope properties of IPv4 addresses are based on the value of the address itself, the following relations need to be defined: S(M(169.254.x.x)) = S(M(127.x.x.x)) < S(M(private address space)) < S(M(any other address)). The notation $\Lambda(A)$ is the *lifecycle* of the address (see Chapter 6). $\Lambda(A) < \Lambda(B)$ if A is a *deprecated* address (i.e., one whose use is discouraged) and B is a *preferred* address (i.e., an address preferred for active use). Finally, H(A) is true if A is a home address and C(A) is true if A is a care-of address. These last two terms are used only in the context of Mobile IP.

5.6.2.1 The Source Address Selection Algorithm

The source address selection algorithm defines a *candidate set* CS(D) of potential source addresses based on a particular destination address D. There is a restriction that anycast, multicast, and the unspecified address are never in CS(D) for any D. We shall use the notation R(A) to indicate the *rank* of address A in the set CS(D). A higher rank (i.e., greater value of R(A)) for A versus B in CS(D), denoted R(A) > R(B), means that A is preferred to B for use as a source address for reaching the machine with address D. The notation R(A) *> R(B) means to assign A a higher rank than B in CS(D). The notation I(D) indicates the interface selected (i.e., by the forwarding longest matching prefix algorithm described previously) to reach destination D. The notation @(i) is the set of addresses assigned to interface i. The notation T(A) is the Boolean true if A is a temporary address (see Chapter 6) and false otherwise.

The following rules are applied to establish a partial ordering between addresses A and B in CS(D) for destination D:

1. Prefer same address: if A = D, R(A) *> R(B); if B = D, R(B) *> R(A).

2. Prefer appropriate scope: if S(A) < S(B) and S(A) < S(D), R(B) *> R(A) else R(A) *> R(B); if S(B) < S(A) and S(B) < S(D), R(A) *> R(B) else R(B) *> R(A).

3. Avoid deprecated addresses: if S(A) = S(B), { if Λ(A) < Λ(B), R(B) *> R(A) else R(A) *> R(B) }.

4. Prefer home address: if H(A) and C(A) and ¬(C(B) and H(B)), R(A) *> R(B); if H(B) and C(B) and ¬(C(A) and H(A)), R(B) *> R(A); if (H(A) and ¬C(A)) and (¬H(B) and C(B)), R(A) *> R(B); if (H(B) and ¬C(B)) and (¬H(A) and C(A)), R(B) *> R(A).

5. Prefer outgoing interface: if A ∈ @(I(D)) and B ∈ @(I(D)), R(A) *> R(B); if B ∈ @(I(D)) and A ∈ @(I(D)), R(B) *> R(A).

6. Prefer matching label: if L(A) = L(D) and L(B) ≠ L(D), R(A) *> R(B); if L(B) = L(D) and L(A) ≠ L(D), R(B) *> R(A).

7. Prefer nontemporary addresses: if T(B) and ¬T(A), R(A) *> R(B); if T(A) and ¬T(B), R(B) *> R(A).

8. Use longest matching prefix: if CPL(A,D) > CPL(B,D), R(A) *> R(B); if CPL(B,D) > CPL(A,D), R(B) *> R(A).

The partial ordering rules can be used to form a total ordering of all the candidate addresses in CS(D). The one with the largest rank is the selected source address for destination D, denoted Q(D), and is used by the destination address selection algorithm. If Q(D) = Ø (null), no source could be determined for destination D.

5.6.2.2 The Destination Address Selection Algorithm

We now turn to the problem of default destination address selection. It is specified in a way similar to source address selection. Recall that Q(D) is the source address selected in the preceding example to reach the destination D. Let U(B) be the Boolean true if destination B is not reachable and E(A) indicate that destination A is reached using some "encapsulating transport" (e.g., tunneled routing). Using the same structure as before on pairwise elements A and B of the set SD(S), we have the following rules:

1. Avoid unusable destinations: if U(B) or Q(B) = Ø, R(A) *> R(B); if U(A) or Q(A) = Ø, R(B) *> R(A).

2. Prefer matching scope: if S(A) = S(Q(A)) and S(B) ≠ S(Q(B)), R(A) *> R(B); if S(B) = S(Q(B)) and S(A) ≠ S(Q(A)), R(B)*>R(A).

3. Avoid deprecated addresses: if Λ (Q(A)) < Λ (Q(B)), R(B) *> R(A); if Λ (Q(B)) < Λ (Q(A)), R(A) *> R(B).

4. Prefer home address: if H(Q(A)) and C(Q(A)) and ¬(C(Q(B)) and H(Q(B))), R(A) *> R(B); if (Q(B)) and C(Q(B)) and ¬(C(Q(A)) and H(Q(A))), R(B) *> R(A); if (H(Q(A)) and ¬C(Q(A))) and (¬H(Q(B)) and C(Q(B))), R(A) *> R(B); if (H(Q(B)) and ¬C(Q(B))) and (¬H(Q(A)) and C(Q(A))), R(B) *> R(A).

5. Prefer matching label: if L(Q(A)) = L(A) and L(Q(B)) ≠ L(B), R(A) *> R(B); if L(Q(A)) ≠ L(A) and L(Q(B)) = L(B), R(B) *> R(A).

6. Prefer higher precedence: if P(A) > P(B), R(A) *> R(B); if P(A) < P(B), R(B) *> R(A).

7. Prefer native transport: if E(A) and ¬E(B), R(B) *> R(A); if E(B) and ¬E(A), R(A) *> R(B).

8. Prefer smaller scope: if S(A) < S(B), R(A) *> R(B) else R(B) *> R(A).

9. Use longest matching prefix: if CPL(A, Q(A)) > CPL(B, Q(B)), R(A) *> R(B); if CPL(A, Q(A)) < CPL (B, Q(B)), R(B) *> R(A).

10. Otherwise, leave rank order unchanged.

As with source address selection, these rules form a partial ordering between two elements of the set of possible destinations in the set of destinations SD(S) for source S. The highest-rank address gives the output for the destination address selection algorithm. As mentioned previously, some issues have been raised regarding operation of this algorithm (e.g., step 9 of the destination address selection can lead to problems with DNS round-robin; see Chapter 11). As a result, an update to [RFC3484] is being considered [RFC3484-revise]. Importantly, this revision addresses how so-called *Unique Local IPv6 Unicast Addresses* (ULAs) [RFC4193] are treated by the address selection algorithms. ULAs are globally scoped IPv6 addresses that are constrained to be used only within a common (private) network.

5.7   Attacks Involving IP

There have been a number of attacks on the IP protocol over the years, based primarily on the operation of options, or by exploiting bugs in specialized code (such as fragment reassembly). Simple attacks involve trying to get a router to crash or perform poorly because one or more of the IP header fields is not valid (e.g., bad header length or version number). Typically, routers in the Internet today ignore or strip IP options, and the bugs in basic packet processing have been fixed. Thus, these types of simple attacks are not a big concern. Attacks involving fragmentation can be addressed using other means [RFC1858][RFC3128].

Without authentication or encryption (or when it is disabled for IPv6), IP spoofing attacks are possible. Some of the earliest attacks involved fabricating the source IP address. Because early access control mechanisms depended on the source IP address, many such systems were circumvented. Spoofing would sometimes be combined with various combinations of source routing options. Under some circumstances, a remote attacker's computer would appear to be a host on the local network (or even the same computer) requesting some sort of service. Although the spoofing of IP addresses is still a concern today, there are several approaches to limit its damage, including ingress filtering [RFC2827][RFC3704], whereby an ISP checks the source addresses of its customers' traffic to ensure that datagrams contain source addresses from an assigned IP prefix.

As IPv6 and Mobile IP are relatively new, at least compared to IPv4, all of their vulnerabilities have undoubtedly not yet been discovered. With the newer and more flexible types of options headers, an attacker could have considerable influence on the processing of an IPv6 packet. For example, the Routing header (type 0) was discovered to have such severe security problems that its use has been deprecated entirely. Other possibilities include spoofing the source address and/or Routing header entries to make packets appear as if they have come from other places. These attacks are avoided by configuring packet-filtering firewalls to take into account the contents of Routing headers. It is worth noting that simply filtering out all packets containing extension headers and options in IPv6 would severely restrict its use. In particular, disabling extension headers would prevent Mobile IPv6 from functioning.

5.8   Summary

In this chapter we started with a description of the IPv4 and IPv6 headers, discussing some of the related functions such as the Internet checksum and fragmentation. We saw how IPv6 increases the size of addresses, improves upon IP's method of including options in packets by use of the extension headers, and removes several of the noncritical fields from the IPv4 header. With the addition of this functionality, the IP header increases in size by only a factor of 2 even though the size of the addresses has increased fourfold. The IPv4 and IPv6 headers are not directly compatible and share only the 4-bit *Version* field in common. Because of this, some level of translation is required to interconnect IPv4 and IPv6 nodes. Dual-stack hosts implement both IPv4 and IPv6 but must choose which protocol to use and when.

Since its inception, IP has included a header field to indicate a type of traffic or service class associated with each datagram. This mechanism has been redefined over the years in hopes of providing mechanisms to support differentiated services on the Internet. If it is widely implemented, the Internet could potentially offer improved performance for some traffic or users versus others in a standard way. To what extent this happens will be based in part on working out the business models surrounding the differentiated services capability.

IP forwarding describes the way IP datagrams are transported through single and multihop networks. IP forwarding is performed on a hop-by-hop basis unless special processing takes place. The destination IP address never changes as the datagram proceeds through all the hops, but the link-layer encapsulation and destination link-layer address change on each hop. Forwarding tables and the longest prefix match algorithm are used by hosts and routers to determine the best matching forwarding entry and determine the next hops along a forwarding path. In many circumstances, very simple tables consisting of only a default route, which matches all possible destinations equally, are adequate.

Using a special set of protocols for security and signaling, Mobile IP establishes secure bindings between a mobile node's home address and care-of address. These bindings may be used to communicate with a mobile node even when it is not at home. The basic function involves tunneling traffic through a cooperating home agent, but this may lead to very inefficient routing. A number of additional features support a route optimization feature that allows a mobile node to talk directly with other remote nodes and vice versa. This requires a mobile node's correspondent hosts to support MIPv6 as well as route optimization, which is an optional feature. Ongoing work aims at reducing the latency involved in the route optimization binding update procedure.

We also looked at how the host model, strong or weak, affects how IP datagrams are processed. In the strong model, each interface is permitted to receive or send only datagrams that use addresses associated with the interface, whereas the weak model is less restrictive. The weak host model permits communication in some cases where it would not otherwise be possible but may be more vulnerable to certain kinds of attacks. The host model also relates to how a host chooses which addresses to use when communicating. Early on, most hosts had only one IP address so the decision was fairly straightforward. With IPv6, in which a host may have several addresses, and for multihomed hosts using several network interfaces, the decision is less straightforward yet nonetheless may have an important impact on routing. A set of address selection algorithms, for both source and destination addresses, was presented. These algorithms tend to prefer limited-scope, permanent addresses.

We discussed some of the attacks targeted against the IP protocol. Such attacks have often involved spoofing addresses, including options to alter routing behavior, and attempts to exploit bugs in the implementation of IP, especially with respect to fragmentation. The protocol implementation bugs have been fixed in modern operating systems, and in most cases options are disabled at the edge routers of enterprises. Although spoofing remains somewhat of a concern, procedures such as ingress filtering help to eliminate this problem as well.

5.9   References

[A92] P. Mersky, "Autovon: The DoD Phone Company," http://www.chips.navy.mil/archives/92_oct/file3.htm

[AN] http://www.iana.org/assignments/protocol-numbers

[DC05] J. Doyle and J. Carroll, *Routing TCP/IP, Volume 1, Second Edition* (Cisco Press, 2005).

[DSCPREG] http://www.iana.org/assignments/dscp-registry/dscp-registry.xml

[H05] G. Huston, "Just How Big Is IPv6?—or Where Did All Those Addresses Go?" *The ISP Column*, July 2005, http://cidr-report.org/papers/isoc/2005-07/ipv6size.html

[IP6PARAM] http://www.iana.org/assignments/ipv6-parameters

[IPPARAM] http://www.iana.org/assignments/ip-parameters

[IV] http://www.iana.org/assignments/version-numbers

[LFS07] J. Leguay, T. Friedman, and K. Salamatian, "Describing and Simulating Internet Routes," *Computer Networks*, 51(8), June 2007.

[MB97] L. McKnight and J. Bailey, eds., *Internet Economics* (MIT Press, 1997).

[MP] http://www.iana.org/assignments/mobility-parameters

[P90] C. Pinter, *A Book of Abstract Algebra, Second Edition* (Dover, 2010; reprint of 1990 edition).

[PB61] W. Peterson and D. Brown, "Cyclic Codes for Error Detection," *Proc. IRE*, 49(228), Jan. 1961.

[RC05] S. Raab and M. Chandra, *Mobile IP Technology and Applications* (Cisco Press, 2005).

[RFC0791] J. Postel, "Internet Protocol," Internet RFC 0791/STD 0005, Sept. 1981.

[RFC1108] S. Kent, "U.S. Department of Defense Security Options for the Internet Protocol," Internet RFC 1108 (historical), Nov. 1991.

[RFC1122] R. Braden, ed., "Requirements for Internet Hosts—Communication Layers," Internet RFC 1122/STD 0003, Oct. 1989.

[RFC1385] Z. Wang, "EIP: The Extended Internet Protocol," Internet RFC 1385 (informational), Nov. 1992.

[RFC1393] G. Malkin, "Traceroute Using an IP Option," Internet RFC 1393 (experimental), Jan. 1993.

[RFC1858] G. Ziemba, D. Reed, and P. Traina, "Security Consideration for IP Fragment Filtering," Internet RFC 1858 (informational), Oct. 1995.

[RFC2113] D. Katz, "IP Router Alert Option," Internet RFC 2113, Feb. 1997.

[RFC2460] S. Deering and R. Hinden, "Internet Protocol, Version 6 (IPv6)," Internet RFC 2460, Dec. 1998.

[RFC2473] A. Conta and S. Deering, "Generic Packet Tunneling in IPv6 Specification," Internet RFC 2473, Dec. 1998.

[RFC2474] K. Nichols, S. Blake, F. Baker, and D. Black, "Definition of the Differentiated Services Field (DS Field) in the IPv4 and IPv6 Headers," Internet RFC 2474, Dec. 1998.

[RFC2475] S. Blake, D. Black, M. Carlson, E. Davies, Z. Wang, and W. Weiss, "An Architecture for Differentiated Services," Internet RFC 2475 (informational), Dec. 1998.

[RFC2597] J. Heinanen, F. Baker, W. Weiss, and J. Wroclawski, "Assured Forwarding PHB Group," Internet RFC 2597, June 1999.

[RFC2675] D. Borman, S. Deering, and R. Hinden, "IPv6 Jumbograms," Internet RFC 2675, Aug. 1999.

[RFC2711] C. Partridge and A. Jackson, "IPv6 Router Alert Option," Internet RFC 2711, Oct. 1999.

[RFC2827] P. Ferguson and D. Senie, "Network Ingress Filtering: Defeating Denial of Service Attacks Which Employ IP Source Address Spoofing," Internet RFC 2827/BCP 0038, May 2000.

[RFC3031] E. Rosen, A. Viswanathan, and R. Callon, "Multiprotocol Label Switching Architecture," Internet RFC 3031, Jan. 2001.

[RFC3128] I. Miller, "Protection Against a Variant of the Tiny Fragment Attack," Internet RFC 3128 (informational), June 2001.

[RFC3168] K. Ramakrishnan, S. Floyd, and D. Black, "The Addition of Explicit Congestion Notification (ECN) to IP," Internet RFC 3168, Sept. 2001.

[RFC3246] B. Davie, A. Charny, J. C. R. Bennett, K. Benson, J. Y. Le Boudec, W. Courtney, S. Davari, V. Firoiu, and D. Stiliadis, "An Expedited Forwarding PHB (Per-Hop Behavior)," Internet RFC 3246, Mar. 2002.

[RFC3260] D. Grossman, "New Terminology and Clarifications for Diffserv," Internet RFC 3260 (informational), Apr. 2002.

[RFC3484] R. Draves, "Default Address Selection for Internet Protocol Version 6 (IPv6)," Internet RFC 3484, Feb. 2003.

[RFC3484-revise] A. Matsumoto, J. Kato, T. Fujisaki, and T. Chown, "Update to RFC 3484 Default Address Selection for IPv6," Internet draft-ietf-6man-rfc3484-revise, work in progress, July 2011.

[RFC3704] F. Baker and P. Savola, "Ingress Filtering for Multihomed Hosts," Internet RFC 3704/BCP 0084, May 2004.

[RFC3963] V. Devarapalli, R. Wakikawa, A. Petrescu, and P. Thubert, "Network Mobility (NEMO) Basic Support Protocol," Internet RFC 3963, Jan. 2005.

[RFC4193] R. Hinden and B. Haberman, "Unique Local IPv6 Unicast Addresses," Internet RFC 4193, Oct. 2005.

[RFC4213] E. Nordmark and R. Gilligan, "Basic Transition Mechanisms for IPv6 Hosts and Routers," Internet RFC 4213, Oct. 2005.

[RFC4225] P. Nikander, J. Arkko, T. Aura, G. Montenegro, and E. Nordmark, "Mobile IP Version 6 Route Optimization Security Design Background," Internet RFC 4225 (informational), Dec. 2005.

[RFC4594] J. Babiarz, K. Chan, and F. Baker, "Configuration Guidelines for Diffserv Service Classes," Internet RFC 4594 (informational), Aug. 2006.

[RFC4782] S. Floyd, M. Allman, A. Jain, and P. Sarolahti, "Quick-Start for TCP and IP," Internet RFC 4782 (experimental), Jan. 2007.

[RFC4866] J. Arkko, C. Vogt, and W. Haddad, "Enhanced Route Optimization for Mobile IPv6," Internet RFC 4866, May 2007.

[RFC4950] R. Bonica, D. Gan, D. Tappan, and C. Pignataro, "ICMP Extensions for Multiprotocol Label Switching," Internet RFC 4950, Aug. 2007.

[RFC5095] J. Abley, P. Savola, and G. Neville-Neil, "Deprecation of Type 0 Routing Headers in IPv6," Internet RFC 5095, Dec. 2007.

[RFC5096] V. Devarapalli, "Mobile IPv6 Experimental Messages," Internet RFC 5094, Dec. 2007.

[RFC5142] B. Haley, V. Devarapalli, H. Deng, and J. Kempf, "Mobility Header Home Agent Switch Message," Internet RFC 5142, Jan. 2008.

[RFC5213] S. Gundavelli, ed., K. Leung, V. Devarapalli, K. Chowdhury, and B. Patil, "Proxy Mobile IPv6," Internet RFC 5213, Aug. 2008.

[RFC5220] A. Matsumoto, T. Fujisaki, R. Hiromi, and K. Kanayama, "Problem Statement for Default Address Selection in Multi-Prefix Environments:

Operationa. Issues of RFC 3484 Default Rules," Internet RFC 5220 (informational), July 2008.

[RFC5350] J. Manner and A. McDonald, "IANA Considerations for the IPv4 and IPv6 Router Alert Options," Internet RFC 5350, Sept. 2008.

[RFC5380] H. Soliman, C. Castelluccia, K. ElMalki, and L. Bellier, "Hierarchical Mobile IPv6 (HMIPv6) Mobility Management," Internet RFC 5380, Oct. 2008.

[RFC5568] R. Koodli, ed., "Mobile IPv6 Fast Handovers," Internet RFC 5568, July 2009.

[RFC5570] M. StJohns, R. Atkinson, and G. Thomas, "Common Architecture Label IPv6 Security Option (CALIPSO)," Internet RFC 5570 (informational), July 2009.

[RFC5865] F. Baker, J. Polk, and M. Dolly, "A Differentiated Services Code Point (DSCP) for Capacity-Admitted Traffic," Internet RFC 5865, May 2010.

[RFC5944] C. Perkins, ed., "IP Mobility Support for IPv4, Revised," Internet RFC 5944, Nov. 2010.

[RFC6178] D. Smith, J. Mullooly, W. Jaeger, and T. Scholl, "Label Edge Router Forwarding of IPv4 Option Packets," Internet RFC 6178, Mar. 2011.

[RFC6275] C. Perkins, ed., D. Johnson, and J. Arkko, "Mobility Support in IPv6," Internet RFC 6275, June 2011.

[RFC6301] Z. Zhu, R. Rakikawa, and L. Zhang, "A Survey of Mobility Support in the Internet," Internet RFC 6301 (informational), July 2011.

[RTAOPTS] http://www.iana.org/assignments/ipv6-routeralert-values

[THL06] N. Thompson, G. He, and H. Luo, "Flow Scheduling for End-Host Multihoming," *Proc. IEEE INFOCOM*, Apr. 2006.

[TWEF03] J. Touch, Y. Wang, L. Eggert, and G. Flinn, "A Virtual Internet Architecture," *Proc. ACM SIGCOMM Future Directions in Network Architecture Workshop*, Mar. 2003.

[W03] T. Wu, "Network Neutrality, Broadband Discrimination," *Journal of Telecommunications and High Technology Law*, 2, 2003 (revised 2005).

6

System Configuration: DHCP and Autoconfiguration

6.1 Introduction

To make use of the TCP/IP protocol suite, each host and router requires a certain amount of configuration information. Configuration information is used to assign local names to systems, and identifiers (such as IP addresses) to interfaces. It is also used to either provide or make use of various network services, such as the *Domain Name System* (DNS) and Mobile IP home agents. Over the years there have been many ways of providing and obtaining this information, but fundamentally there are three approaches: type in the information by hand, have a system obtain it using a network service, or use some sort of algorithm to automatically determine it. We shall explore each of these options and see how they are used with both IPv4 and IPv6. Understanding how configuration works is important, because it is one of the issues that every system administrator and nearly every end user must deal with to some extent.

Recall from Chapter 2 that every interface to be used with TCP/IP networking requires an IP address, subnet mask, and broadcast address (for IPv4). The broadcast address can ordinarily be determined using the address and mask. With this minimal information, it is generally possible to carry out communication with other systems on the same subnetwork. To engage in communication beyond the local subnet, called indirect delivery in Chapter 5, a system requires a routing or forwarding table that indicates what router(s) are to be used for reaching various destinations. To be able to use services such as the Web and e-mail, the DNS (see Chapter 11) is used to map user-friendly domain names to the IP addresses required by the lower-protocol layers. Because the DNS is a distributed service, any system making use of it must know how to reach at least one DNS server. All in all, having an IP address, subnet mask, and the IP address of a DNS server and router are the "bare essentials" to get a system running on the Internet that is capable of using or providing popular services such as Web and e-mail. To use Mobile IP, a system also needs to know how to find a home agent.

In this chapter we will focus primarily on the protocols and procedures used to establish the bare essentials in Internet client hosts: the *Dynamic Host Configuration Protocol* (DHCP) and *stateless address autoconfiguration* in IPv4 and IPv6. We will also discuss how some ISPs use PPP with Ethernet for configuration of client systems. Servers and routers are more often configured by hand, usually by typing the relevant configuration information into a file or graphical user interface. There are several reasons for this distinction. First, client hosts are moved around more often than servers and routers, meaning they should have mechanisms for flexibly reassigning their configuration information. Second, server hosts and routers are expected to be "always available" and relatively autonomous. As such, having their configuration information not depend on other network services can lead to greater confidence in their reliability. Third, there are often far more clients in an organization than servers or routers, so it is simpler and less error-prone to use a centralized service to dynamically assign configuration information to client hosts. Fourth, the operators of clients often have less system administration experience than server and router administrators, so it is once again less error-prone to have most clients configured by a centralized service administered by an experienced staff.

Beyond the bare essentials, there are numerous other bits of configuration information a host or router may require, depending on the types of services it uses or provides. These may include the locations of home agents, multicast routers, VPN gateways, and *Session Initiation Protocol* (SIP)/VoIP gateways. Some of these services have standardized mechanisms and supporting protocols to obtain the relevant configuration information; others do not and instead require the user to type in the necessary information.

6.2   Dynamic Host Configuration Protocol (DHCP)

DHCP [RFC2131] is a popular client/server protocol used to assign configuration information to hosts (and, less frequently, to routers). DHCP is very widely used, in both enterprises and home networks. Even the most basic home router devices support embedded DHCP servers. DHCP clients are incorporated into all common client operating systems and a large number of embedded devices such as network printers and VoIP phones. Such devices usually use DHCP to acquire their IP address, subnet mask, router IP address, and DNS server IP address. Information pertaining to other services (e.g., SIP servers used with VoIP) may also be conveyed using DHCP. DHCP was originally conceived for use with IPv4, so references to it or its relationship with IP in this chapter will refer to IPv4 unless otherwise specified. IPv6 can also use a version of DHCP called DHCPv6 [RFC3315], which we discuss in Section 6.2.5, but IPv6 also supports its own automatic processes to determine configuration information. In a hybrid configuration, IPv6 automatic configuration can be combined with the use of DHCPv6.

The design of DHCP is based on an earlier protocol called the *Internet Bootstrap Protocol* (BOOTP) [RFC0951][RFC1542], which is now effectively obsolete. BOOTP provides limited configuration information to clients and does not have a mechanism to support changing that information after it has been provided. DHCP extends the BOOTP model with the concept of *leases* [GC89] and can provide all information required for a host to operate. Leases allow clients to use the configuration information for an agreed-upon amount of time. A client may request to renew the lease and continue operations, subject to agreement from the DHCP server. BOOTP and DHCP are backward-compatible in the sense that BOOTP-only clients can make use of DHCP servers and DHCP clients can make use of BOOTP-only servers. BOOTP, and therefore DHCP as well, is carried using UDP/IP (see Chapter 10). Clients use port 68 and servers use port 67.

DHCP comprises two major parts: address management and delivery of configuration data. Address management handles the dynamic allocation of IP addresses and provides address leases to clients. Configuration data delivery includes the DHCP protocol's message formats and state machines. A DHCP server can be configured to provide three levels of address allocation: automatic allocation, dynamic allocation, and manual allocation. The differences among the three have to do with whether the addresses assigned are based on the identity of the client and whether such addresses are subject to being revoked or changed. The most commonly used method is dynamic allocation, whereby a client is given a revocable IP address from a *pool* (usually a predefined range) of addresses configured at the server. In automatic allocation, the same method is used but the address is never revoked. In manual allocation, the DHCP protocol is used to convey the address, but the address is fixed for the requesting client (i.e., it is not part of an allocatable pool maintained by the server). In this last mode, DHCP acts like BOOTP. We shall focus on dynamic allocation, as it is the most interesting and common case.

6.2.1 Address Pools and Leases

In dynamic allocation, a DHCP client requests the allocation of an IP address. The server responds with one address selected from a pool of available addresses. Typically, the pool is a contiguous range of IP addresses allocated specifically for DHCP's use. The address given to the client is allocated for only a specific amount of time, called the *lease duration*. The client is permitted to use the IP address until the lease expires, although it may request extension of the lease as required. In most situations, clients are able to renew leases they wish to extend.

The lease duration is an important configuration parameter of a DHCP server. Lease durations can range from a few minutes to days or more ("infinite" is possible but not recommended for anything but simple networks). Determining the best value to use for leases is a trade-off between the number of expected clients, the size of the address pool, and the desire for the stability of addresses. Longer lease durations tend to deplete the available address pool faster but provide greater stability in addresses and somewhat reduced network overhead (because there are fewer requests to renew leases). Shorter leases tend to keep the pool available for other clients, with a consequent potential decrease in stability and increase in network traffic load. Common defaults include 12 to 24 hours, depending on the particular DHCP server being used. Microsoft, for example, recommends 8 days for small networks and 16 to 24 days for larger networks. Clients begin trying to renew leases after half of the lease duration has passed.

When making a DHCP request, a client is able to provide information to the server. This information can include the name of the client, its requested lease duration, a copy of the address it is already using or last used, and other parameters. When the server receives such a request, it can make use of whatever information the client has provided (including the requesting MAC address) in addition to other exogenous information (e.g., the time of day, the interface on which the request was received) to determine what address and configuration information to provide in response. In providing a lease to a client, a server stores the lease information in persistent memory, typically in nonvolatile memory or on disk. If the DHCP server restarts and all goes well, leases are maintained intact.

6.2.2 DHCP and BOOTP Message Format

DHCP extends BOOTP, DHCP's predecessor. Compatibility is maintained between the protocols by defining the DHCP message format as an extension to BOOTP's in such a way that BOOTP clients can be served by DHCP servers, and BOOTP *relay agents* (see Section 6.2.6) can be used to support DHCP use, even on networks where DHCP servers do not reside. The message format includes a fixed-length initial portion and a variable-length tail portion (see Figure 6-1).

The message format of Figure 6-1 is defined by BOOTP and DHCP in several RFCs ([RFC0951][RFC1542][RFC2131]). The *Op* (*Operation*) field identifies the message as either a request (1) or a reply (2). The *HW Type* (*htype*) field is assigned based on values used with ARP (see Chapter 4) and defined in the corresponding IANA ARP parameters page [IARP], with the value 1 (Ethernet) being very common. The *HW Len* (*hlen*) field gives the number of bytes used to hold the hardware (MAC) address and is commonly 6 for Ethernet-like networks. The *Hops* field is used to store the number of relays through which the message has traveled. The sender of the message sets this value to 0, and it is incremented at each relay. The *Transaction ID* is a (random) number chosen by the client and copied into responses by the server. It is used to match replies with requests.

The *Secs* field is set by the client with the number of seconds that have elapsed since the first attempt to establish or renew an address. The *Flags* field currently contains only a single defined bit called the broadcast flag. Clients may set this bit in requests if they are unable or unwilling to process incoming unicast IP datagrams but can process incoming broadcast datagrams (e.g., because they do not

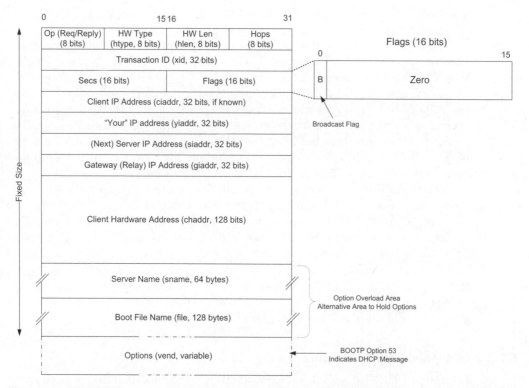

Figure 6-1 The BOOTP message format, including field names from [RFC0951], [RFC1542], and [RFC2131]. The BOOTP message format is used to hold DHCP messages by appropriate assignment of options. In this way, BOOTP relay agents can process DHCP messages, and BOOTP clients can use DHCP servers. The *Server Name* and *Boot File Name* fields can be used to carry DHCP options if necessary.

yet have an IP address). Setting the bit informs the server and relays that broadcast addressing should be used for replies.

Note

There has been some difficulty in Windows environments regarding the use of the broadcast flag. Windows XP and Windows 7 DHCP clients do not set the flag, but Windows Vista clients do. Some DHCP servers in use do not process the flag properly, leading to apparent difficulties in supporting Vista clients, even though the Vista implementation is RFC-compliant. See [MKB928233] for more information.

The next four fields are various IP addresses. The *Client IP Address* (*ciaddr*) field includes a current IP address of the requestor, if known, and is 0 otherwise. The *"Your" IP Address* (*yiaddr*) field is filled in by a server when providing an address to a requesting client. The *Next Server IP Address* (*siaddr*) field gives the IP address of the next server to use for the client's bootstrap process (e.g., if the client needs to download an operating system image that may be accomplished from a server other than the DHCP server). The *Gateway (or Relay) IP Address* (*giaddr*) field is filled in by a DHCP or BOOTP relay with its address when forwarding DHCP (BOOTP) messages. The *Client Hardware Address* (*chaddr*) field holds a unique identifier of the client and can be used in various ways by the server, including arranging for the same IP address to be given each time a particular client makes an address request. This field has traditionally held the client's MAC address, which has been used as an identifier. Nowadays, the Client Identifier, an option described in Sections 6.2.3 and 6.2.4, is preferred for this use.

The remaining fields include the *Server Name* (*sname*) and *Boot File Name* (*file*) fields. These fields are not always filled in, but if they are, they contain 64 or 128 bytes, respectively, of ASCII characters indicating the name of the server or path to the boot file. Such strings are null-terminated, as in the C programming language. They can also be used instead to hold DHCP options if space is tight (see Section 6.2.3). The final field, originally known as the *Vendor Extensions* field in BOOTP and fixed in length, is now known as the *Options* field and is variable in length. As we shall see, options are used extensively with DHCP and are required to distinguish DHCP messages from legacy BOOTP messages.

6.2.3   DHCP and BOOTP Options

Given that DHCP extends BOOTP, any fields needed by DHCP that were not present when BOOTP was designed are carried as options. Options take a standard format beginning with an 8-bit tag indicating the option type. For some options, a fixed number of bytes following the tag contain the option value. All others consist of the tag followed by 1 byte containing the length of the option value (not including the tag or length), followed by a variable number of bytes containing the option value itself.

A large number of options are available with DHCP, some of which are also supported by BOOTP. The current list is given by the BOOTP/DHCP parameters page [IBDP]. The first 77 options, including the most common ones, are specified in [RFC2132]. Common options include Pad (0), Subnet Mask (1), Router Address (3), Domain Name Server (6), Domain Name (15), Requested IP Address (50), Address Lease Time (51), DHCP Message Type (53), Server Identifier (54), Parameter Request List (55), DHCP Error Message (56), Lease Renewal Time (58), Lease Rebinding Time (59), Client Identifier (61), Domain Search List (119), and End (255).

The DHCP Message Type option (53) is a 1-byte-long option that is always used with DHCP messages and has the following possible values: DHCPDISCOVER (1), DHCPOFFER (2), DHCPREQUEST (3), DHCPDECLINE (4), DHCPACK (5), DHCPNAK (6), DHCPRELEASE (7), DHCPINFORM (8), DHCPFORCERENEW (9) [RFC3203], DHCPLEASEQUERY (10), DHCPLEASEUNASSIGNED (11),

DHCPLEASEUNKNOWN (12), and DHCPLEASEACTIVE (13). The last four values are defined by [RFC4388].

Options may be carried in the *Options* field of a DHCP message, as well as in the *Server Name* and *Boot File Name* fields mentioned previously. When options are carried in either of these latter two places, called *option overloading*, a special Overload option (52) is included to indicate which fields have been appropriated for holding options. For options whose lengths exceed 255 bytes, a special *long options* mechanism has been defined [RFC3396]. In essence, if the same option is repeated multiple times in the same message, the contents are concatenated in the order in which they appear in the message, and the result is processed as a single option. If a long option also uses option overloading, the order of processing is last to first: *Options* field, *Boot File Name* field, and then *Server Name* field.

Options tend to either provide relatively simple configuration information or be used in supporting some other agreement protocol. For example, [RFC2132] specifies options for most of the traditional configuration information a TCP/IP node requires (addressing information, server addresses, Boolean assignments of configuration information such as enabling IP forwarding, initial TTL values). Subsequent specifications describe simple configuration information for NetWare [RFC2241][RFC2242], user classes [RFC3004], FQDN [RFC4702], Internet Storage Name Service server (iSNS, used in storage networks) [RFC4174], Broadcast and Multicast Service controller (BCMCS, used with 3G cellular networks) [RFC4280], time zone [RFC4833], autoconfiguration [RFC2563], subnet selection [RFC3011], name service selection (see Chapter 11) [RFC2937], and servers for the *Protocol for Carrying Authentication for Network Access* (PANA) (see Chapter 18) [RFC5192]. Those options defined for use in support of other protocols and functions are described later, starting with Section 6.2.7.

6.2.4   DHCP Protocol Operation

DHCP messages are essentially BOOTP messages with a special set of options. When a new client attaches to a network, it first discovers what DHCP servers are available and what addresses they are offering. It then decides which server to use and which address it desires and requests it from the offering server (while informing all the servers of its choice). Unless the server has given away the address in the meantime, it responds by acknowledging the address allocation to the requesting client. The time sequence of events between a typical client and server is depicted in Figure 6-2.

Requesting clients set the BOOTP *Op* field to BOOTREQUEST and the first 4 bytes of the *Options* field to the decimal values 99, 130, 83, and 99, respectively (the *magic cookie* value from [RFC2132]). Messages from client to server are sent as UDP/IP datagrams containing a BOOTP BOOTREQUEST operation and an appropriate DHCP message type (usually DHCPDISCOVER or DHCPREQUEST). Such messages are sent from address 0.0.0.0 (port 68) to the limited broadcast address 255.255.255.255 (port 67). Messages traveling in the other direction (from server to

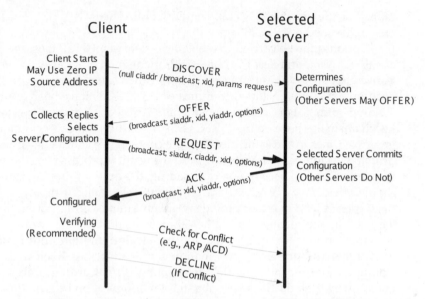

Figure 6-2   A typical DHCP exchange. A client discovers a set of servers and addresses they are offering using broadcast messages, requests the address it desires, and receives an acknowledgment from the selected server. The transaction ID (xid) allows requests and responses to be matched up, and the server ID (an option) indicates which server is providing and committing the provided address binding with the client. If the client already knows the address it desires, the protocol can be simplified to include use of only the REQUEST and ACK messages.

client) are sent from the IP address of the server and port 67 to the IP local broadcast address and port 68 (see Chapter 10 for details on UDP).

In a typical exchange, a client first broadcasts a DHCPDISCOVER message. Each server receiving the request, either directly or through a relay, may respond with a DHCPOFFER message, including an offered IP address in the *"Your" IP Address* field. Other configuration options (e.g., IP address of DNS server, subnet mask) are often included. The offer message includes the *lease time* (T), which provides the upper bound on the amount of time the address can be used if it is not renewed. The message also contains the *renewal time* (T1), which is the amount of time before the client should attempt to renew its lease with the server from which it acquired its lease, and the *rebinding time* (T2), which bounds the time in which it should attempt to renew its address with any DHCP server. By default, T1 = (T/2) and T2 = (7T/8).

After receiving one or more DHCPOFFER messages from one or more servers, the client determines which offer it will accept and broadcasts a DHCPREQUEST message including the Server Identifier option. The Requested IP Address option is set to the address received in the selected DHCPOFFER message. Multiple servers may receive the broadcast DHCPREQUEST message, but only the server identified within the DHCPREQUEST message acts by committing the address binding to persistent storage; the others clear any state regarding the request. After handling the binding, the selected server responds with a DHCPACK message, indicating to the client that the address binding can now be used. In the case where the server cannot allocate the address contained in the DHCPREQUEST message (e.g., it has been allocated in some other way or is not available), the server responds with a DHCPNAK message.

Once the client receives the DHCPACK message and other associated configuration information, it may probe the network to ensure that the address provided is not in use (e.g., by sending an ARP request for the address to perform ACD, described in Chapter 4). Should the client determine that the address is already in use, the client ceases using the address and sends a DHCPDECLINE message to the server to indicate that the address cannot be used. After a recommended 10s delay, the client is able to retry. If a client elects to relinquish its address before its lease expires, it sends a DHCPRELEASE message.

In circumstances where a client already has an IP address and wishes only to renew its lease, the initial DHCPDISCOVER/DHCPOFFER messages can be skipped. Instead, the protocol begins with the client requesting the address it is currently using with a DHCPREQUEST message. At this point, the protocol works as already described: the server will likely grant the request (with a DHC-PACK) or deny the request by issuing a DHCPNAK. Another circumstance arises when a client already has an address, does not need to renew it, but requires other (non-address) configuration information. In this case, it can use a DHCPINFORM message in place of a DHCPREQUEST message to indicate its use of an existing address and desire to obtain additional information. Such messages elicit a DHC-PACK message from the server, which includes the requested additional configuration information.

6.2.4.1 Example

To see DHCP in action, we now inspect the packets exchanged when a Microsoft Vista laptop attaches to a wireless LAN supported by a Linux-based DHCP server (Windows 7 systems are nearly identical). The client was recently associated with a different wireless network, using a different IP prefix, and is now being connected to the new network. Because it remembers the address it had from the previous network, the client first tries to continue using that address using a DHCPREQUEST message (see Figure 6-3).

Note

There is now an agreed-upon procedure for *detecting network attachment* (DNA), specified in [RFC4436] for IPv4 and [RFC6059] for IPv6. These specifications do not contain new protocols but instead suggest how unicast ARP (for IPv4) and a combination of unicast and multicast Neighbor Solicitation/Router Discovery messages (for IPv6; see Chapter 8) can be used to reduce the latency of acquiring configuration information when a host switches network links. As these specifications are relatively new (especially for IPv6), not all systems implement them.

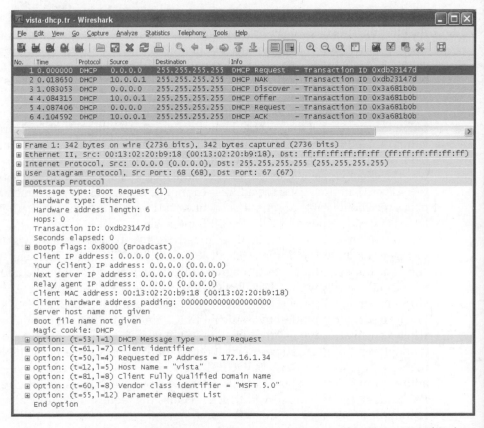

Figure 6-3   A client has switched networks and attempts to request its old address, 172.16.1.34, from a DHCP server on the new network using a DHCPREQUEST message.

In Figure 6-3 we can see a DHCP request sent in a link-layer broadcast frame (destination ff:ff:ff:ff:ff:ff) using the unspecified source IP address 0.0.0.0 and the limited broadcast destination address 255.255.255.255. Because the client does not yet know if the address it is requesting will be successfully allocated and does not know the network prefix used on the network to which it is attaching, it has little alternative to using these addresses. The message is a UDP/IP datagram sent from the BOOTP client port 68 (`bootpc`) to the server port 67 (`bootps`). As DHCP is really part of BOOTP, the protocol is the Bootstrap Protocol and the message type is a BOOTREQUEST (1), with hardware type set to 1 (Ethernet) and address length of 6 bytes. The transaction ID is 0xdb23147d, a random number chosen by the client. The BOOTP broadcast flag is set in this message, meaning responses should be sent using broadcast addressing. The requested address of 172.16.1.34 is contained in one of several options. We shall have a closer look at the types of options that appear in DHCP messages beginning in Section 6.2.9.

The nearby DHCP server receives the client's DHCPREQUEST message including the requested IP address of 172.16.1.34. However, the server is unable to allocate the address because 172.16.1.34 is not in use on the current network. Consequently, the server refuses the client's request by sending a DHCPNAK message (see Figure 6-4).

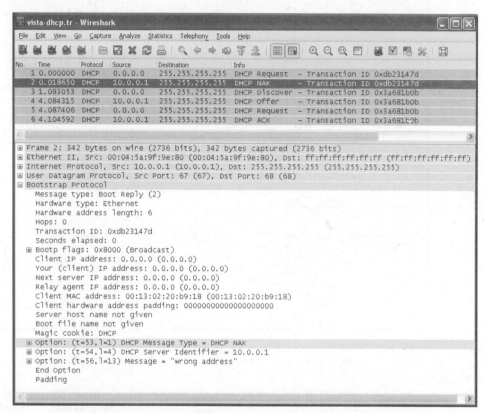

Figure 6-4 A DHCPNAK message is sent by the DHCP server, indicating that the client should not attempt to use IP address 172.16.1.34. The transaction ID allows the client to know that the message corresponds to its address request.

The DHCPNAK message shown in Figure 6-4 is sent as a broadcast BOOTP reply from the server. It includes the message type of DHCPNAK, a transaction ID matching the client's request, a Server Identifier option containing 10.0.0.1, a copy of the client's identifier (MAC address in this case), and a textual string indicating the form of error, "`wrong address`". At this point the client ceases trying to use its old address of 172.16.1.34 and instead starts over, looking for whatever servers and addresses it can find, using a DHCPDISCOVER message (see Figure 6-5).

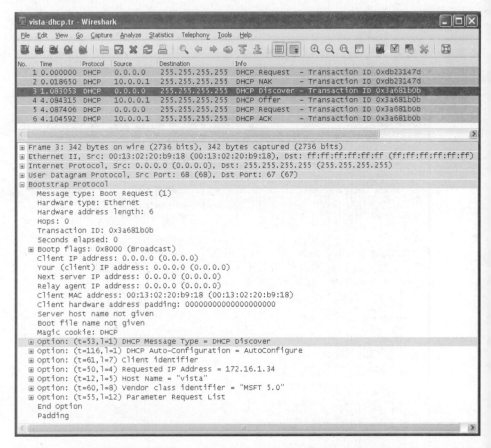

Figure 6-5   The DHCPDISCOVER message indicates that the client is retrying its attempt to obtain an address after the previous failure of its DHCPREQUEST message.

The DHCPDISCOVER message sent by the client and shown in Figure 6-5 is similar to the DHCPREQUEST message, including the requested IP address it used before (it does not have any other address to request), but it contains a richer list of options and a new transaction ID (0x3a681b0b). Most of the rest of the primary BOOTP fields are left empty and set to 0, except the client MAC address, which appears in the *Client Hardware Address* (*chaddr*) field. Note that this address matches the Ethernet frame source MAC address, as expected, because the packet was not forwarded through a BOOTP relay agent. The rest of the DISCOVER message contains eight options, most of which are expanded in the screen shot in Figure 6-6 so that the various option subtypes can be seen.

Figure 6-6 details the options included in the BOOTP request message. The first option indicates that the message is a DHCPDISCOVER message. The second option indicates a client's desire to know whether to use *address autoconfiguration* [RFC2563] (described in Section 6.3). If it is unable to obtain an address using DHCP, it is permitted to determine one itself if allowed to do so by the DHCP server.

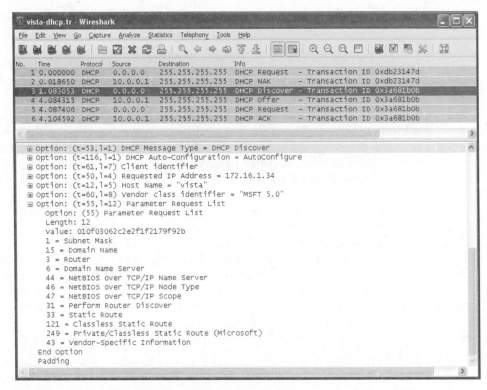

Figure 6-6 The DHCPDISCOVER message may contain a rich list of parameter requests, indicating what configuration information the client seeks.

The next option indicates that the Client Identifier (ID) option is set to 0100130220B918 (not shown). The DHCP server can use the client ID to determine if there is any special configuration information to be given to the particular requesting client. Most operating systems now allow the user to specify the client ID for the DHCP client to use when obtaining an address. Generally, however, it is better to allow the client ID to be chosen automatically, as the use of the same client ID by multiple clients can lead to DHCP problems. The automatically selected client ID is generally based on the MAC address of the client. In the case of Windows, it is the MAC address with a 1-byte hardware type identifier prepended to it (in this case, the value of the byte is 1, indicating Ethernet).

Note

There has been a move to use client identifiers that are not based on MAC addresses. This is motivated by the desire to have a persistent identifier for a client for use with IPv4 or IPv6 that remains consistent even if the system's network interface hardware changes (which usually causes its MAC address to change). [RFC4361] specifies node-specific identifiers for IPv4, using a scheme originally defined for IPv6. It involves using a DHCP Unique Identifier (DUID) in combination with an Identity Association Identifier (IAID) as specified for DHCPv6 [RFC3315] (also see Sections 6.2.5.3 and 6.2.5.4), but with conventional DHCPv4. It also deprecates the use of the *Client Hardware Address* (*chaddr*) field in DHCP messages. However, it is not yet widely deployed.

The next (Requested IP Address) option indicates that the client is requesting IP address 172.16.1.34. This is the IP address it was using when associated with the previous wireless network. As mentioned before, this address is not available on the new network because a different network prefix is being used.

Other options indicate a configured host name of "vista," a vendor class ID of "MSFT 5.0" (for Microsoft Windows 2000 and later systems), and a parameter request list. The Parameter Request List option provides an indication to the DHCP server of what sort of configuration information the client is requesting. It consists of a string of bytes in which each byte indicates a particular option number. Here we can see that it includes conventional Internet information (subnet mask, domain name, DNS server, default router) but also a number of other options common to Microsoft systems (i.e., NetBIOS options). It also includes an indication that the client is interested in knowing whether to perform ICMP Router Discovery (see Chapter 8) and whether any static forwarding table entries should be placed in the client's forwarding table when starting up (see Chapter 5).

Note

The reason there are three different types of static route parameters listed is a consequence of the history of addressing. Before the full adoption of subnet masks and network prefixes, the network portion of an address was known by inspection of the address alone ("classful addressing"), and this is the form of route used with the Static Route (33) parameter. With the adoption of classless routes, DHCP was updated to hold a mask that could be applied, resulting in the so-called Classless Static Route (CSR) parameter (121) defined in [RFC3442]. Microsoft's variant (using code 249) is similar.

The last parameter request (43) is for vendor-specific information. It is ordinarily used in conjunction with the Vendor-Class Identifier option (60), to allow clients to receive nonstandard information, although another proposal combines the vendor's identity with the vendor-specific information [RFC3925], providing a method to determine the vendor given any vendor-specific information, even for a single client. In the case of Microsoft systems, vendor-specific information is used for selecting the use of NetBIOS, indicating whether a DHCP lease should be released on shutdown, and how the metric (preference) of a default route in the forwarding table should be processed. It is also used by Microsoft's *Network Access Protection* (NAP) system [MS-DHCPN]. Mac OS systems use vendor-specific information in supporting Apple's NetBoot service and *Boot Server Discovery Protocol* (BSDP) [F07].

Upon receipt of the DHCPDISCOVER message, a DHCP server responds with an offer of an IP address, lease, and additional configuration information contained in a DHCPOFFER message. In the example shown in Figure 6-7, there is only one DHCP server (which is also a router and DNS server).

Figure 6-7   The DHCPOFFER sent from the DHCP server at 10.0.0.1 is offering IP address 10.0.0.57 for up to 12 hours. Additional information includes the address of a DNS server, domain name, default router IP address, subnet mask, and broadcast address. In this example, the system with IP address 10.0.0.1 is the default router, DHCP server, and DNS server.

In the DHCPOFFER message shown in Figure 6-7 we again see that the message format includes a BOOTP portion as well as a set of options that relate to its DHCP address handling. The BOOTP message type is BOOTREPLY. The client IP address provided by the server is 10.0.0.57, located in the *"Your"* [client] *IP Address* field. Note that this address does *not* match the requested value of 172.16.1.34 contained in the DHCPDISCOVER message, as the 172.16/12 prefix is not in use on the local network.

Additional information contained in the set of options includes the server's IP address (10.0.0.1), the lease time of the offered IP address (12 hours), and the T1 (renewal) and T2 (rebinding) timeouts of 6 and 10.5 hours, respectively. In addition, the server provides the subnet mask for the client to use (255.255.255.128), the proper broadcast address (10.0.0.127), the default router and DNS server (all 10.0.0.1, the same as the DHCP server in this case), and a default domain name of "home". The domain name home is not standardized in any way and would not be used outside of a private network. This example is a home network, so by the author's convention the names of machines used on it have the form <name>.home. Once the client has collected a DHCPOFFER message and decided to attempt leasing the IP address 10.0.0.57 it has been offered, it continues with a second DHCPREQUEST message (see Figure 6-8).

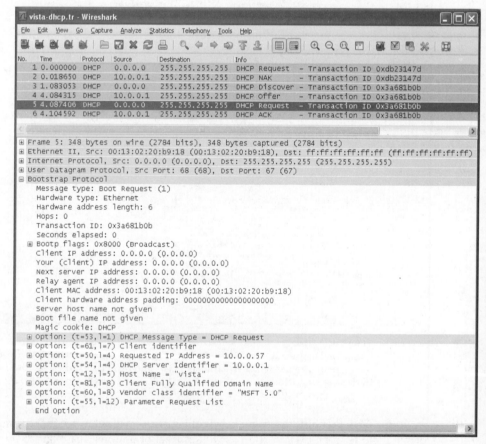

Figure 6-8   The second DHCPREQUEST indicates that the client wishes to be assigned the IP address 10.0.0.57. The message is sent to the broadcast address and includes the address 10.0.0.1 in the Server ID option. This allows any other servers that may receive the broadcast to know which DHCP server and address the client has selected.

The second DHCPREQUEST message, shown in Figure 6-8, is similar to the DHCPDISCOVER message, except the requested IP address is now set to 10.0.0.57, the DHCP message type is set to DHCPREQUEST, the DHCP autoconfiguration option is not present, and the Server Identifier option is now filled in with the address of the server (10.0.0.1). Note that this message, like the DHCPDISCOVER message, is sent using broadcast, so any server or client present on the local network receives it. The Server Identifier option field is used to keep unselected servers from committing the address binding. When the selected server receives the DHCPREQUEST and commits the binding, it ordinarily responds with a DHCPACK message, as we see in Figure 6-9.

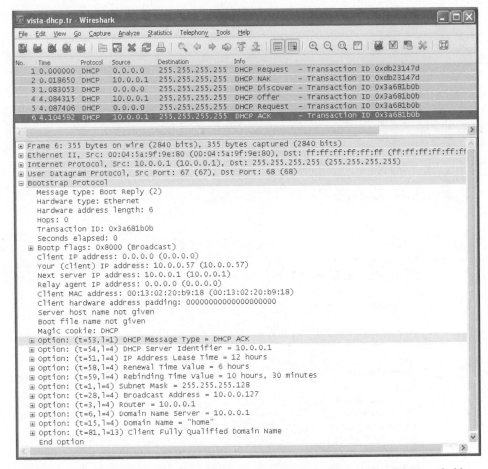

Figure 6-9   The DHCPACK message verifies to the client (and other servers) the allocation of address 10.0.0.57 for up to 12 hours.

The DHCPACK message shown in Figure 6-9 is very similar to the DHCPOFFER message we have seen before. However, now the client's FQDN option is included as well. In this case (not shown), it is set to vista.home. At this point, the client is free to use the address 10.0.0.57, as far as the DHCP server is concerned. It is still advised to use techniques such as ACD, described in Chapter 4, to ensure that its address is not used by some other host.

The DHCP messages exchanged in this example are typical of a system when it boots or is attached to a new network. It is also possible to induce a system to perform the release or acquisition of DHCP configuration information by hand. For example, in Windows the following command will release the data acquired using DHCP:

```
C:\> ipconfig /release
```

and the following command will acquire it:

```
C:\> ipconfig /renew
```

In Linux, the following commands can be used to achieve the same results:

```
Linux# dhclient -r
```

to release a DHCP lease, and

```
Linux# dhclient
```

to renew one.

The type of information acquired by DHCP and assigned to the local system can be ascertained with a variant of the ipconfig command on Windows. Here is an excerpt from its output:

```
C:\> ipconfig /all
...
Wireless LAN adapter Wireless Network Connection:

        Connection-specific DNS Suffix  . : home
        Description . . . . . . . . . . . : Intel(R) PRO/Wireless 3945ABG
                                            Network Connection
        Physical Address. . . . . . . . . : 00-13-02-20-B9-18
        DHCP Enabled. . . . . . . . . . . : Yes
        Autoconfiguration Enabled . . . . : Yes
        IPv4 Address. . . . . . . . . . . : 10.0.0.57(Preferred)
        Subnet Mask . . . . . . . . . . . : 255.255.255.128
        Lease Obtained. . . . . . . . . . : Sunday, December 21, 2008
                                            11:31:48 PM
        Lease Expires . . . . . . . . . . : Monday, December 22, 2008
                                            11:31:40 AM
        Default Gateway . . . . . . . . . : 10.0.0.1
```

```
DHCP Server . . . . . . . . . . . : 10.0.0.1
DNS Servers . . . . . . . . . . . : 10.0.0.1
NetBIOS over Tcpip. . . . . . . . : Enabled
Connection-specific DNS Suffix Search List :home
```

This command is very useful to see what configuration information has been assigned to a host using DHCP or other means.

6.2.4.2 The DHCP State Machine

The DHCP protocol operates a state machine at the clients and servers. The states dictate which types of messages the protocol is expecting to process next. The client state machine is illustrated in Figure 6-10. Transitions between states (arrows) occur because of messages that are received and sent or when timers expire.

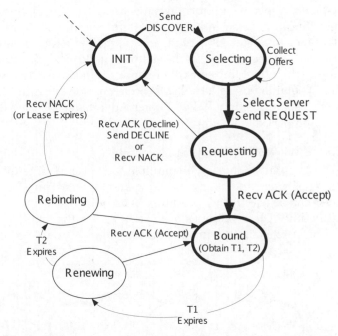

Figure 6-10   The DHCP client state machine. The boldface states and transitions are typical for a client first acquiring a leased address. The dashed line and INIT state are where the protocol begins.

As shown in Figure 6-10, a client begins in the INIT state when it has no information and broadcasts the DHCPDISCOVER message. In the Selecting state, it collects DHCPOFFER messages until it decides which address and server it wishes to use. Once its selection has been made, it responds with a DHCPREQUEST message and enters the Requesting state. At this point it may receive ACKs for other addresses it does not want. If it finds no address it wants, it sends a DHCPDECLINE and reverts to the INIT state. More likely, however, it receives a DHCPACK message for an address it wants, accepts it, obtains the timeout values T1 and T2, and enters the Bound state, where it is able to use the address until expiration. Upon the first timer expiration (timer T1), the client enters the Renewing state and attempts to reestablish its lease. This succeeds if a fresh DHCPACK is received (returning the client to the Bound state). If not, T2 ultimately expires, causing the client to attempt to reacquire an address from any server. If the lease time finally expires, the client must give up the leased address and becomes disconnected if it has no alternative address or network connection to use.

6.2.5 DHCPv6

Although the IPv4 and IPv6 DHCP protocols achieve conceptually similar goals, their respective protocol designs and deployment options differ. DHCPv6 [RFC3315] can be used in either a "stateful" mode, in which it works much like DHCPv4, or in a "stateless" mode in conjunction with stateless address autoconfiguration (see Section 6.3). In the stateless mode, IPv6 clients are assumed to self-configure their IPv6 addresses but require additional information (e.g., DNS server address) obtained using DHCPv6. Another option exists for deriving the location of a DNS server using ICMPv6 Router Advertisement messages (see Chapters 8 and 11 and [RFC6106]).

6.2.5.1 IPv6 Address Lifecycle

IPv6 hosts usually operate with multiple addresses per interface, and each address has a set of timers indicating how long and for what purposes the corresponding address can be used. In IPv6, addresses are assigned with a *preferred* lifetime and *valid* lifetime. These lifetimes are used to form timeouts that move an address from one state to another in an address's state machine (see Figure 6-11).

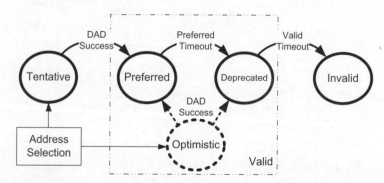

Figure 6-11   The lifecycle of an IPv6 address. Tentative addresses are used only for DAD until verified as unique. After that, they become preferred and can be used without restriction until an associated timeout changes their state to deprecated. Deprecated addresses are not to be used for initiating new connections and may not be used at all after the associated valid timeout expires.

Figure 6-11 shows the lifecycle of an IPv6 address. An address is in the preferred state when it is available for general use and is available as either a source or destination IPv6 address. A preferred address becomes deprecated when its preferred timeout occurs. When it becomes deprecated, it may still be used for existing transport (e.g., TCP) connections but is not to be used for initiating new connections.

When an address is first selected for use, it enters a *tentative* or *optimistic* state. When in the tentative state, it may be used only for the IPv6 Neighbor Discovery protocol (see Chapter 8). It is not used as a source or destination address for any other purposes. While in this state the address is being checked for duplication, to see if any other nodes on the same network are already using the address. The procedure for doing this is called *duplicate address detection* (DAD) and is described in more detail in Section 6.3.2.1. An alternative to conventional DAD is called *optimistic DAD* [RFC4429], whereby a selected address is used for a limited set of purposes until DAD completes. Because an optimistic use of an address is really just a special set of rules for DAD, it is not a truly complete state itself. Optimistic addresses are treated as deprecated for most purposes. In particular, an address may be both optimistic and deprecated simultaneously, depending on the preferred and valid lifetimes.

6.2.5.2 DHCPv6 Message Format

DHCPv6 messages are encapsulated as UDP/IPv6 datagrams, with client port 546 and server port 547 (see Chapter 10). Messages are sent using a host's link-scoped source address to either relay agents or servers. There are two message formats, one used directly between a client and a server, and another when a relay is used (see Figure 6-12).

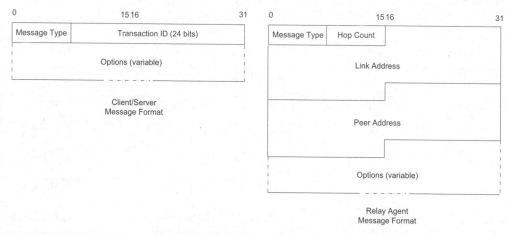

Figure 6-12   The basic DHCPv6 message format (left) and relay agent message format (right). Most interesting information in DHCPv6 is carried in options.

The primary DHCPv6 message format is given in Figure 6-12 on the left and an extended version, which includes the *Link Address* and *Peer Address* fields, is given on the right. The format on the right is used between a DHCPv6 relay agent and a DHCPv6 server. The *Link Address* field gives the global IPv6 address used by the server to identify the link on which the client is located. The *Peer Address* field contains the address of the relay agent or client from which the message to be relayed was received. Note that relaying may be chained, so a relay may be relaying a message received from another relay. Relaying, for DHCPv4 and DHCPv6, is described in Section 6.2.6.

The message type for messages in the format on the left include typical DHCP-style messages (REQUEST, REPLY, etc.), whereas the message types for messages in the format on the right include RELAY-FORW and RELAY-REPL, to indicate a message forwarded from a relay or destined to a relay, respectively. The *Options* field for the format on the right always includes a Relay Message option, which includes the complete message being forwarded by the relay. Other options may also be included.

One of the differences between DHCPv4 and DHCPv6 is how DHCPv6 uses IPv6 multicast addressing. Clients send requests to the All DHCP Relay Agents and Servers multicast address (ff02::1:2). Source addresses are of link-local scope. In IPv6, there is no legacy BOOTP message format. The message semantics, however, are similar. Table 6-1 gives the types of DHCPv6 messages, their values, defining RFCs, and the roughly equivalent message and defining RFC for DHCPv4.

Table 6-1 DHCPv6 message types, values, and defining standards. The approximately equivalent message types for DHCPv4 are given to the right.

DHCPv6 Message	DHCPv6 Value	Reference	DHCPv4 Message	Reference
SOLICIT	1	[RFC3315]	DISCOVER	[RFC2132]
ADVERTISE	2	[RFC3315]	OFFER	[RFC2132]
REQUEST	3	[RFC3315]	REQUEST	[RFC2132]
CONFIRM	4	[RFC3315]	REQUEST	[RFC2132]
RENEW	5	[RFC3315]	REQUEST	[RFC2132]
REBIND	6	[RFC3315]	DISCOVER	[RFC2132]
REPLY	7	[RFC3315]	ACK/NAK	[RFC2132]
RELEASE	8	[RFC3315]	RELEASE	[RFC2132]
DECLINE	9	[RFC3315]	DECLINE	[RFC2132]

Table 6-1   DHCPv6 message types, values, and defining standards. The approximately equivalent message types for DHCPv4 are given to the right (*continued*).

DHCPv6 Message	DHCPv6 Value	Reference	DHCPv4 Message	Reference
RECONFIGURE	10	[RFC3315]	FORCERENEW	[RFC3203]
INFORMATION-REQUEST	11	[RFC3315]	INFORM	[RFC2132]
RELAY-FORW	12	[RFC3315]	N/A	
RELAY-REPL	13	[RFC3315]	N/A	
LEASEQUERY	14	[RFC5007]	LEASEQUERY	[RFC4388]
LEASEQUERY-REPLY	15	[RFC5007]	LEASE{UNASSIGNED, UNKNOWN,ACTIVE}	[RFC4388]
LEASEQUERY-DONE	16	[RFC5460]	LEASEQUERYDONE	[ID4LQ]
LEASEQUERY-DATA	17	[RFC5460]	N/A	N/A
N/A	N/A	N/A	BULKLEASEQUERY	[ID4LQ]

In DHCPv6, most interesting information, including addresses, lease times, location of services, and client and server identifiers, is carried in options. Two of the more important concepts used with these options are called the *Identity Association* (IA) and the *DHCP Unique Identifier* (DUID). We discuss them next.

6.2.5.3 Identity Association (IA)

An *Identity Association* (IA) is an identifier used between a DHCP client and server to refer to a collection of addresses. Each IA comprises an *IA identifier* (IAID) and associated configuration information. Each client interface that requests a DHCPv6-assigned address requires at least one IA. Each IA can be associated with only a single interface. The client chooses the IAID to uniquely identify each IA, and this value is then shared with the server.

The configuration information associated with an IA includes one or more addresses and associated lease information (T1, T2, and total lease duration values). Each address in an IA has both a preferred and a valid lifetime [RFC4862], which define the address's lifecycle. The types of addresses requested may be regular addresses or *temporary* addresses [RFC4941]. Temporary addresses are derived in part from random numbers to help improve privacy by frustrating the tracking of IPv6 hosts based on IPv6 addresses. Temporary addresses are ordinarily assigned at the same time nontemporary addresses are assigned but are regenerated using a different random number more frequently.

When responding to a request, a server assigns one or more addresses to a client's IA based on a set of address *assignment policies* determined by the server's administrator. Generally, such policies depend on the link on which the request arrived, standard information about the client (see DUID in Section 6.2.5.4), and other information supplied by the client in DHCP options. The formats of the IA option for nontemporary and temporary addresses are as shown in Figure 6-13.

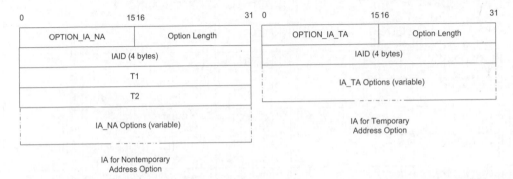

Figure 6-13   The format for a DHCPv6 IA for nontemporary addresses (left) and temporary addresses (right). Each option may include additional options describing particular IPv6 addresses and corresponding leases.

The main difference between a nontemporary and a temporary address IA option, as shown in Figure 6-13, is the inclusion of the T1 and T2 values in the nontemporary case. These values are expected, as they are also the values used in DHCPv4. For temporary addresses, the lack of T1 and T2 is made possible because the lifetimes are generally determined based upon the T1 and T2 values assigned to a nontemporary address that has been acquired previously. Details of temporary addresses are given in [RFC4941].

6.2.5.4 DHCP Unique Identifier (DUID)

A *DHCP Unique Identifier* (DUID) identifies a single DHCPv6 client or server and is designed to be persistent over time. It is used by servers to identify clients for the selection of addresses (as part of IAs) and configuration information, and by clients to identify the server in which they are interested. DUIDs are variable in length and are treated as opaque values by both clients and servers for most purposes.

DUIDs are supposed to be globally unique yet easy to generate. To satisfy these concerns simultaneously, [RFC3315] defines three different types of possible DUIDs but also mentions that these are not the only three types that might ever be created. The three types of DUIDs are as follows:

1. DUID-LLT: a DUID based on link-layer address plus time

2. DUID-EN: a DUID based on enterprise number and vendor assignment

3. DUID-LL: a DUID based on link-layer address only

The standard format for encoding a DUID begins with a 2-byte identifier indicating which type of DUID is being expressed. The current list is maintained by the IANA [ID6PARAM]. This is followed by a 16-bit hardware type derived from [RFC0826] in the cases of DUID-LLT and DUID-LL, and a 32-bit Private Enterprise Number in the case of DUID-EN.

Note

A *Private Enterprise Number* (PEN) is a 32-bit value given out by the IANA to an enterprise. It is usually used in conjunction with the SNMP protocol for network management purposes. About 38,000 of them have been assigned as of mid-2011. The current list is available from the IANA [IEPARAM].

The first form of DUID, DUID-LLT, is the recommended form. Following the hardware type, it includes a 32-bit timestamp containing the number of seconds since midnight (UTC), January 1, 2000 (mod 2^{32}). This rolls over (returns to zero) in the year 2136. The last portion is a variable-length link-layer address. The link-layer address can be selected from any of the host's interfaces, and the same DUID should be used, once selected, for traffic on any interface. This form of DUID is required to be stable even if the network interface from which the DUID was derived is removed. Thus, it requires the host system to maintain stable storage. The DUID-LL form is very similar but is recommended for systems lacking stable storage (but having a stable link-layer address). The RFC says that a DUID-LL must not be used by clients or servers that cannot determine if the link-layer address they are using is associated with a removable interface.

6.2.5.5 Protocol Operation

The DHCPv6 protocol operates much like its DHCPv4 counterpart. Whether or not a client initiates the use of DHCP is dependent on configuration options carried in an ICMPv6 Router Advertisement message the host receives (see Chapter 8). Router advertisements include two important bit fields. The M field is the *Managed Address Configuration* flag and indicates that IPv6 addresses can be obtained using DHCPv6. The O field is the *Other Configuration* flag and indicates that information other than IPv6 addresses is available using DHCPv6. Both fields, along with several others, are specified in [RFC5175]. Any combination of the M and O bit fields is possible, although having M on and O off is probably the least useful combination. If both are off, DHCPv6 is not used, and address assignment takes place using stateless address autoconfiguration, described in Section 6.3. Having M off and O on indicates that clients should use stateless DHCPv6 and obtain their addresses using stateless address autoconfiguration. The DHCPv6 protocol operates using the messages defined in Table 6-1 and illustrated in Figure 6-14.

Typically, a client starting out first determines what link-local address to use and performs an ICMPv6 Router Discovery operation (see Chapter 8) to determine if there is a router on the attached network. A router advertisement includes the M and O bit fields mentioned previously. If DHCPv6 is in use, at least the M bit field

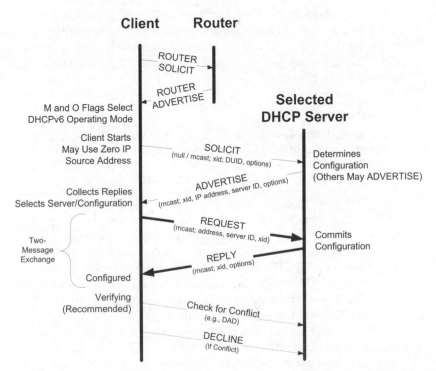

Figure 6-14   Basic operation of DHCPv6. A client determines whether or not to use DHCPv6 from information carried in ICMPv6 router advertisements. If used, DHCPv6 operations are similar to those in DHCPv4 but differ significantly in the details.

is set and the client multicasts (see Chapter 9) the DHCPSOLICIT message to find DHCPv6 servers. A response comes in the form of one or more DHCPADVERTISE messages, indicating the presence of at least one DHCPv6 server. These messages constitute two of the so-called *four-message exchange* operations of DHCPv6.

In cases where the location of a DHCPv6 server is already known or an address need not be allocated (e.g., stateless DHCPv6 or the Rapid Commit option is being used—see Section 6.2.9), the four-message exchange can be shortened to become a two-message exchange, in which case only the REQUEST and REPLY messages are used. A DHCPv6 server commits a binding formed from the combination of a DUID, IA type (temporary, nontemporary, or prefix—see Section 6.2.5.3), and IAID. The IAID is a 32-bit number chosen by the client. Each binding can have one or more leases, and one or more bindings can be manipulated using a single DHCPv6 transaction.

6.2.5.6 Extended Example

Figure 6-15 shows an example of a Windows Vista (Service Pack 1) machine attaching to a wireless network. Its IPv4 stack has been disabled. It begins by assigning its link-local address and checking to see if that address is already being used.

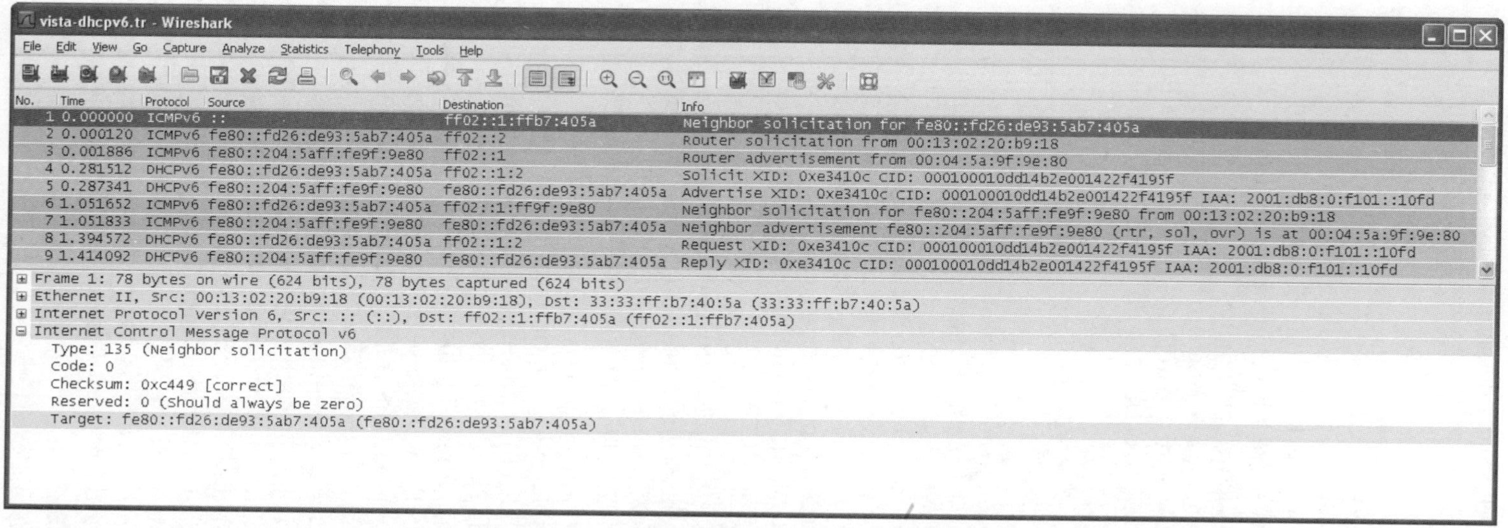

Figure 6-15 DAD for the client system's link-local address is a Neighbor Solicitation for its own IPv6 address.

In Figure 6-15 we see the ICMPv6 Neighbor Solicitation (DAD) for the client's optimistic address fe80::fd26:de93:5ab7:405a. (DAD is described in more detail when we discuss stateless address autoconfiguration in Section 6.3.2.1.) The packet is sent to the corresponding solicited-node address ff02::1:ffb7:405a. It optimistically assumes that this address is not otherwise in use on the link, so it continues on immediately with a Router Solicitation (RS) (see Figure 6-16).

The RS shown in Figure 6-16 is sent to the All Routers multicast address ff02::2. It induces each router on the network to respond with a Router Advertisement (RA), which carries the important M and O bits the client requires to determine what to do next.

Note

This example shows a router solicitation being sent from an optimistic address including a source link-layer address option (SLLAO), in violation of [RFC4429]. The problem here is potential pollution of neighbor caches in any listening IPv6 routers. They will process the option and establish a mapping in their neighbor caches between the tentative address and the link-layer address that may be a duplicate. However, this is very unlikely and is probably not of significant concern. Nonetheless, a pending "optimistic" option [IDDN], if standardized, will allow a router solicitation to include an SLLAO that avoids this issue.

The RA in Figure 6-17 indicates the presence of a router, including its SLLAO of 00:04:5a:9f:9e:80, which will be useful to the client for encapsulating subsequent link-layer frames destined for the router. The *Flags* field indicates that the M and O bit fields are both enabled (set to 1), so the client should proceed with DHCPv6, both for obtaining its addresses as well as for obtaining other configuration information. This is accomplished by soliciting a DHCPv6 server (see Figure 6-18).

The DHCPv6 SOLICIT message shown in Figure 6-18 includes a transaction ID (as in DHCPv4), an elapsed time (0, not shown), and the DUID consisting of a time and 6-byte MAC address. In this example, the MAC address 00:14:22:f4:19:5f is the MAC address of the wired Ethernet interface on this client, which is *not* the interface being used to send the SOLICIT message. Recall that for DUID-LL and DUID-TLL types of DUIDs the link-layer information should be the same across interfaces. The IA is for a nontemporary address, and the client has selected the IAID 09001302. The time values are left at 0 in the request, meaning that the client is not expressing a particular desire; they will be determined by the server.

The next option is the FQDN option specified by [RFC4704]. It is used to carry the FQDN of the client but also to affect how DHCPv6 and DNS interact (see Section 6.4 on DHCP and DNS interaction). This option is used to enable dynamic updates to FQDN-to-IPv6 address mapping by client or server. (The reverse is generally handled by the server.) The first portion of this option contains three

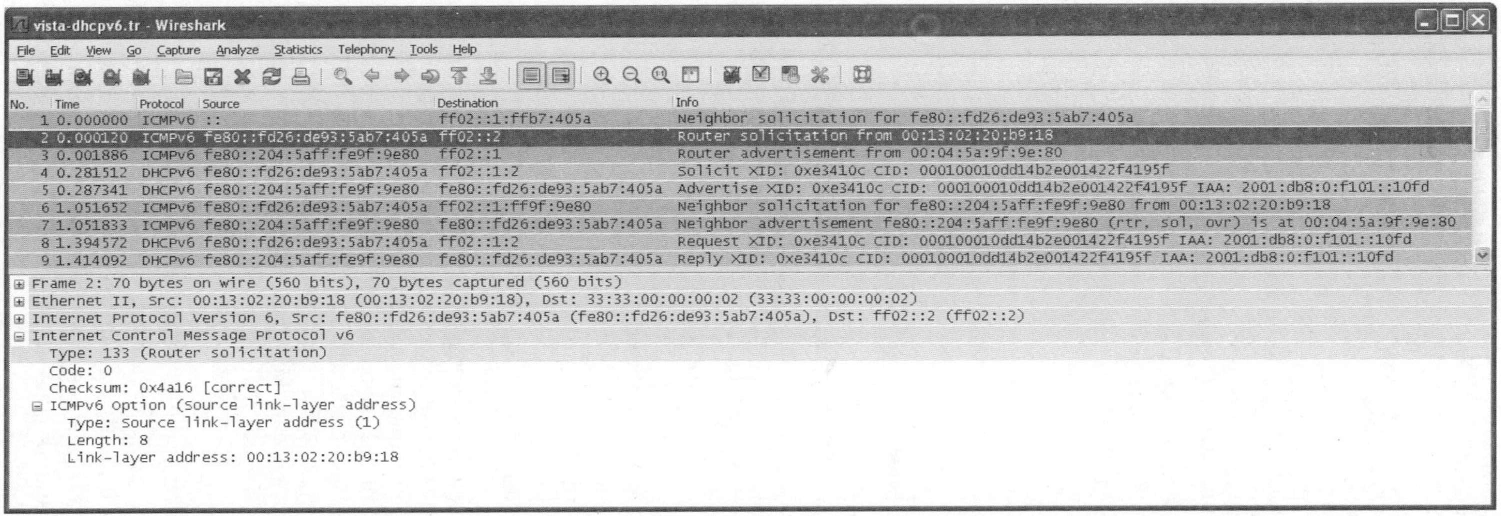

File Edit View Go Capture Analyze Statistics Telephony Tools Help

No.   Time   Protocol Source   Destination   Info
1 0.000000   ICMPv6   ::   ff02::1:ffb7:405a   Neighbor solicitation for fe80::fd26:de93:5ab7:405a
2 0.000120   ICMPv6   fe80::fd26:de93:5ab7:405a   ff02::2   Router solicitation from 00:13:02:20:b9:18
3 0.001886   ICMPv6   fe80::204:5aff:fe9f:9e80   ff02::1   Router advertisement from 00:04:5a:9f:9e:80
4 0.281512   DHCPv6   fe80::fd26:de93:5ab7:405a   ff02::1:2   Solicit XID: 0xe3410c CID: 0001000100d14b2e00142f4195f
5 0.287341   DHCPv6   fe80::204:5aff:fe9f:9e80   fe80::fd26:de93:5ab7:405a Advertise XID: 0xe3410c CID: 0001000100d14b2e00142f4195f IAA: 2001:db8:0:f101::10fd
6 1.051652   ICMPv6   fe80::204:5aff:fe9f:9e80   ff02::1:ff9f:9e80   Neighbor solicitation for fe80::204:5aff:fe9f:9e80 from 00:13:02:20:b9:18
7 1.051833   ICMPv6   fe80::204:5aff:fe9f:9e80   fe80::fd26:de93:5ab7:405a Neighbor advertisement fe80::204:5aff:fe9f:9e80 (rtr, sol, ovr) is at 00:04:5a:9f:9e:80
8 1.394572   DHCPv6   fe80::fd26:de93:5ab7:405a   ff02::1:2   Request XID: 0xe3410c CID: 0001000100d14b2e00142f4195f IAA: 2001:db8:0:f101::10fd
9 1.414092   DHCPv6   fe80::204:5aff:fe9f:9e80   fe80::fd26:de93:5ab7:405a Reply XID: 0xe3410c CID: 0001000100d14b2e00142f4195f IAA: 2001:db8:0:f101::10fd

⊞ Frame 2: 70 bytes on wire (560 bits), 70 bytes captured (560 bits)
⊞ Ethernet II, Src: 00:13:02:20:b9:18 (00:13:02:20:b9:18), Dst: 33:33:00:00:00:02 (33:33:00:00:00:02)
⊞ Internet Protocol Version 6, Src: fe80::fd26:de93:5ab7:405a (fe80::fd26:de93:5ab7:405a), Dst: ff02::2 (ff02::2)
⊟ Internet Control Message Protocol v6
     Type: 133 (Router solicitation)
     Code: 0
     Checksum: 0x4a16 [correct]
  ⊟ ICMPv6 option (Source link-layer address)
       Type: Source link-layer address (1)
       Length: 8
       Link-layer address: 00:13:02:20:b9:18

Figure 6-16 The Router Solicitation induces a nearby router to provide a Router Advertisement. The solicitation message is sent to the All Routers address (ff02::2).

261

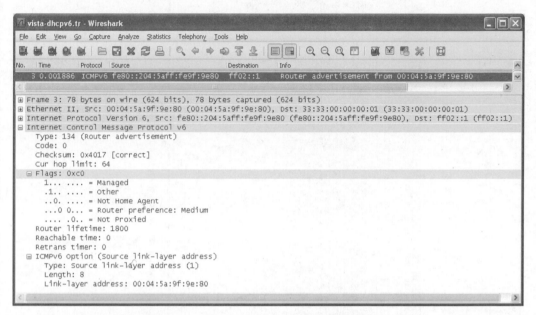

Figure 6-17   A Router Advertisement indicates that addresses are managed (available by assignment using DHCPv6) and that other information (e.g., DNS server) is also available using DHCPv6. This network uses stateful DHCPv6. IPv6 Router Advertisement messages use ICMPv6 (see Chapter 8).

bit fields: *N* (server should not perform update), *O* (client request overridden by server), and *S* (server should perform update). The second portion of the option contains a domain name, which may be fully qualified or not.

Note

The Wireshark tool indicates that the FQDN name record in Figure 6-18 is malformed and speculates that the packet may have been generated by a MS Vista client, which indeed it was. The reason the field is malformed is because the original specification for this option allowed a simple domain name encoding using ASCII characters. This method has been deprecated by [RFC4704], and the two encodings are not directly compatible. Microsoft provides a "hotfix" to address this issue for Vista systems. Microsoft Windows 7 systems exhibit behavior compliant with [RFC4704].

Other information in the solicitation message includes the identification of the vendor class and requested option list. In this case, the vendor class data includes the string "MSFT 5.0", which can be used by a DHCPv6 server to determine what types of processing the client is capable of doing. In response to the client's solicitation, the server responds with an ADVERTISE message (see Figure 6-19).

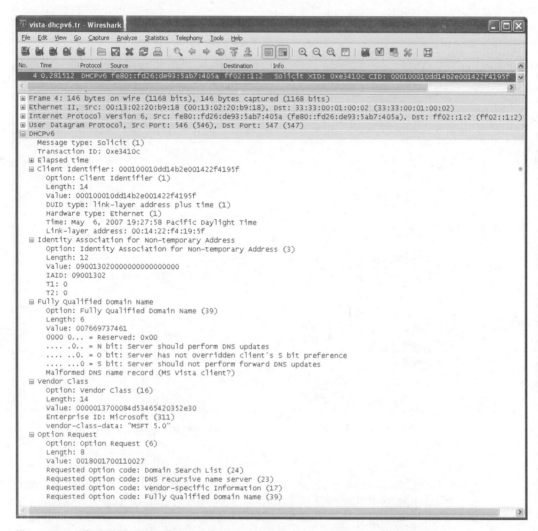

Figure 6-18   The DHCPv6 SOLICIT message requests the location of one or more DHCPv6 servers and includes information identifying the client and the options in which it is interested.

The ADVERTISE message shown in Figure 6-19 provides a wealth of information to the client. The Client Identifier option echoes the client's configuration information. The Server Identifier option gives the time plus a link-layer address of 10:00:00:00:09:20 to identify the server. The IA has the value IAID 09001302 (provided by the client) and includes the global address 2001:db8:0:f101::10fd with preferred lifetime and valid lifetime of 130 and 200s, respectively (fairly short timeouts). The status code of 0 indicates success. Also provided with the DHCPv6

Figure 6-19 The DHCPv6 ADVERTISE message includes an address and lease, plus DNS server IPv6 address and domain search list.

advertisement is the DNS Recursive Name Server option [RFC3646] indicating a server address of 2001:db8:0:f101::1 and a Domain Search List option containing the string home. Note that the server does not include an FQDN option, as it does not implement that option.

The next two packets are a conventional Neighbor Solicitation and Neighbor Advertisement messages between the client and the router, which we do not detail further. That exchange is followed by the client's request for a commitment of the global nontemporary address 2001:db8:0:f101::10fd (see Figure 6-20).

The REQUEST message shown in Figure 6-20 is very similar to the SOLICIT message but includes the information carried in the ADVERTISE message from the server (address, T1, and T2 values). The transaction ID remains the same for all of the DHCPv6 messages we have seen. The exchange is completed with the REPLY message, which is identical to the ADVERTISE message except for the different message type and therefore is not detailed.

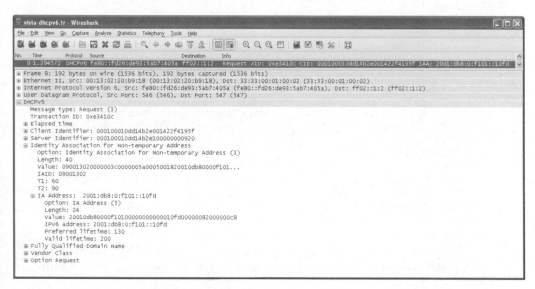

Figure 6-20 The DHCPv6 REQUEST message is similar to a SOLICIT message but includes information learned from the server's ADVERTISE message.

The DHCPv6 messages exchanged in this example are typical of a system when it boots or is attached to a new network. As with DHCPv4, it is possible to induce a system to perform the release or acquisition of this information by hand. For example, in Windows the following command will release the data acquired using DHCPv6:

```
C:\> ipconfig /release6
```

and the following command will acquire it:

```
C:\> ipconfig /renew6
```

The type of information acquired by DHCP and assigned to the local interface can be ascertained with another variant of this command that we have seen before. Here is an excerpt of its output:

```
C:\> ipconfig /all
...
Wireless LAN adapter Wireless Network Connection:

        Connection-specific DNS Suffix  . : home
        Description . . . . . . . . . . . : Intel(R) PRO/Wireless 3945ABG
                                            Network Connection
        Physical Address. . . . . . . . . : 00-13-02-20-B9-18
        DHCP Enabled. . . . . . . . . . . : Yes
```

```
Autoconfiguration Enabled . . . . : Yes
IPv6 Address. . . . . . . . . . . : 2001:db8:0:f101::12cd(Preferred)
Lease Obtained. . . . . . . . . . : Sunday, December 21, 2008
                                    11:30:45 PM
Lease Expires . . . . . . . . . . : Sunday, December 21, 2008
                                    11:37:04 PM
Link-local IPv6 Address . . . . . :
                              fe80::fd26:de93:5ab7:405a%9(Preferred)
Default Gateway . . . . . . . . . : fe80::204:5aff:fe9f:9e80%9
DHCPv6 IAID . . . . . . . . . . . : 150999810
DHCPv6 Client DUID. . . . . . . . :
                        00-01-00-01-0D-D1-4B-2E-00-14-22-F4-19-5F
DNS Servers . . . . . . . . . . . : 2001:db8:0:f101::1
NetBIOS over Tcpip. . . . . . . . : Disabled
Connection-specific DNS Suffix Search List :
                              home
```

Here we can see the link-layer address of the system (00:13:02:20:b9:18). Note how this address was never used as a basis for forming the IPv6 addresses in this example.

6.2.5.7 DHCPv6 Prefix Delegation (DHCPv6-PD and 6rd)

Although the discussion so far has revolved around configuring hosts, DHCPv6 can also be used to configure routers. This works by having one router *delegate* a range of address space to another router. The range of addresses is described by an IPv6 address prefix. The prefix is carried in a DHCP Prefix option, defined by [RFC3633]. This is used in situations where the delegating router, which now acts as a DHCPv6 server as well, does not require detailed topology information about the network to which the prefix is being delegated. Such a situation can arise, for example, when an ISP gives out a range of IP addresses to be used and potentially reassigned by a customer. In such a circumstance, the ISP may choose to delegate a prefix to the customer's premises equipment using DHCPv6-PD.

With prefix delegation, a new form of IA called an IA_PD is defined. Each IA_PD consists of an IAID and associated configuration information and is similar to an IA for addresses, as discussed previously. DHCPv6-PD is useful not only for prefix delegation for fixed routers, but is also suggested to be used when routers (and their attached subnets) can be mobile [RFC6276].

A special form of PD (6rd, described in [RFC5569]) has been created for supporting IPv6 rapid deployment by service providers. The OPTION_6RD (212) option [RFC5969] holds the IPv6 6rd prefix that is used in assigning IPv6 addresses at a customer's site based on the customer's assigned IPv4 address. IPv6 addresses are algorithmically assigned by taking the service provider's provisioned 6rd prefix as the first n bits, with n being recommended as less than 32. A customer's assigned unicast IPv4 address is then appended as the next 32 (or fewer) bits, resulting in an IPv6 6rd delegated prefix that is handled identically to DHCPv6-PD and is recommended to be 64 bits or shorter in length to allow automatic address configuration (see Section 6.4) to operate without problems.

The OPTION_6RD option is variable in length and includes the following values: the IPv4 mask length, 6rd prefix length, 6rd prefix, and a list of 6rd relay addresses (IPv4 addresses of relays that provide 6rd). The IPv4 mask length gives the number of bits from the IPv4 address to use in assigning IPv6 addresses (counted from the left).

6.2.6 Using DHCP with Relays

In most simple networks, a single DHCP server is made available directly to clients on the same LAN. However, in more complicated enterprises it may be necessary or convenient to relay DHCP traffic through one or more DHCP *relay agents*, as illustrated in Figure 6-21.

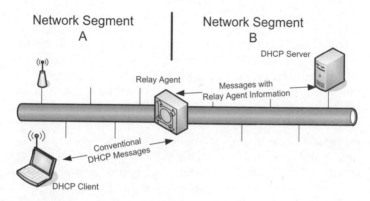

Figure 6-21   A DHCP relay agent extends the operation of DHCP beyond a single network segment. Information carried only between relays and DHCPv4 servers can be carried in the Relay Agent Information option. Relaying in DHCPv6 works in a similar fashion but with a different set of options.

A relay agent is used to extend the operation of DHCP across multiple network segments. In Figure 6-21 the relay between network segments A and B forwards DHCP messages and may annotate the messages with additional information using options or by filling in empty fields. Note that in ordinary circumstances, a relay does not participate in all DHCP traffic exchanged between a client and a server. Rather, it relays only those messages that are broadcast (or multicast in IPv6). Such messages are usually exchanged when a client is obtaining its address for the first time. Once a client has acquired an IP address and the server's IP address using the Server Identification option, it can carry out a unicast conversation with the server that does not involve the relay. Note that relay agents have traditionally been layer 3 devices and tend to incorporate routing capabilities. After discussing the basics of layer 3 relays, we will look briefly at alternatives that operate (mostly) at layer 2.

6.2.6.1 Relay Agent Information Option

In the original concept of a BOOTP or DHCP relay [RFC2131], a relay agent served the purpose only of relaying a message from one subnet to another that would otherwise not be passed on by a router. This allowed systems that could not yet perform indirect delivery to acquire an address from a centralized location. This is sensible for a network operating in an enterprise under one administrative authority, but in cases where DHCP is used at a subscriber's premises and the DHCP infrastructure is provided elsewhere (e.g., an ISP), more information may be required. There are a number of possible reasons. For example, the ISP may not trust the subscriber completely, or billing and logging may be associated with other information not available in the basic DHCP protocol. It has therefore become useful to include extra information in the messages that pass between the relay and the server. The Relay Agent Information option (for DHCPv4, abbreviated RAIO) [RFC3046] provides ways to include such information for IPv4 networks. IPv6 works somewhat differently, and we cover it in the following section.

The RAIO for DHCPv4 specified in [RFC3046] is really a meta-option, in the sense that it specifies a framework in which a number of suboptions can be defined. Many such suboptions have been defined, including several that are used by ISPs to identify from which user, circuit, or network a request is coming. In many cases we shall see that a suboption of the DHCPv4 information option has a corresponding IPv6 option.

Because some of the information conveyed between a relay and a server may be important to secure, the DHCP Authentication suboption of the RAIO has been defined in [RFC4030]. It provides a method to ensure data integrity of the messages exchanged between relay and server. The approach is very similar to the DHCP deferred authentication method (see Section 6.2.7), except the SHA-1 algorithm is used instead of the MD5 algorithm (see Chapter 18).

6.2.6.2 Relay Agent Remote-ID Suboption and IPv6 Remote-ID Option

One common requirement placed upon a relay is to identify the client making a DHCP request with information beyond what the client itself provides. A suboption of the Relay Agent Information option, called the Remote-ID suboption, provides a way to identify the requesting DHCP client using a number of naming approaches that are locally interpreted (e.g., caller ID, user name, modem ID, remote IP address of a point-to-point link). The DHCPv6 Relay Agent Remote-ID option [RFC4649] provides the same capability but also includes an extra field, the enterprise number, which indicates the vendor associated with the identifying information. This format of the Remote-ID information is then specified in a vendor-specific way based on the enterprise number. A common method is to use a DUID for the remote ID.

6.2.6.3 Server Identifier Override

In some cases a relay may wish to interpose itself for processing between a DHCP client and server. This can be accomplished with a special Server Identifier

Override suboption [RFC5107]. The suboption is a variant of the RAIO mentioned previously.

Ordinarily, a relay forwards SOLICIT messages and may append options to these messages as they pass from client to server. Relays are necessary in this circumstance because the client is likely to not yet have an acceptable IP address and only sends its messages to the local subnet using broadcast or multicast addressing. Once a client receives and selects its address, it can talk directly to the DHCP server based upon the server's identity carried in the Server Identifier option. In effect, this cuts the relay out of subsequent transactions between client and server.

It is often useful to allow the relay to include a variety of options (e.g., RAIO carrying a circuit ID) for other types of messages, such as REQUEST, in addition to SOLICIT. This option includes a 4-byte value specifying the IPv4 address to use in the Server Identifier option present in DHCPREPLY messages formed by servers. The Server Identifier Override option is supposed to be used in conjunction with the Relay Agents Flag suboption [RFC5010]. This suboption of the RAIO is a set of flags that carry information from relay to server. So far, only one such flag is defined: whether the destination address on the initial message from the client used broadcast or unicast addressing. The server may make different address allocation decisions based upon the setting of this flag.

6.2.6.4 Lease Query and Bulk Lease Query

In some environments it is useful to allow a third-party system (such as a relay or access concentrator) to learn the address bindings for a particular DHCP client. This facility is provided by DHCP *leasequery* ([RFC4388][RFC6148] for DHCPv4 and [RFC5007] for DHCPv6). In the case of DHCPv6, it can also provide lease information for delegated prefixes. In Figure 6-21, the relay agent may "glean" information from DHCP packets that pass through it in order to influence what information is provided to the DHCP server. Such information may be kept by the relay but may be lost upon relay failure. The DHCPLEASEQUERY message allows such an agent to reacquire this type of information on demand, usually when relaying traffic for which it has lost a binding. The DHCPLEASEQUERY message supports four types of queries for DHCPv4: IPv4 address, MAC address, Client Identifier, and Remote ID. For DHCPv6, it supports two: IPv6 address and Client Identifier (DUID).

DHCPv4 servers may respond to lease queries with one of the following types of messages: DHCPLEASEUNASSIGNED, DHCPLEASEACTIVE, or DHCPLEASEUNKNOWN. The first message indicates that the responding server is authoritative for the queried value but no current associated lease is assigned. The second form indicates that a lease is active, and the lease parameters (including T1 and T2) are provided. There is no particular presumed use for this information; it is made available to the requestor for whatever purposes it desires. DHCPv6 servers respond with a LEASEQUERY-REPLY message that contains a Client Data option. This option, in turn, includes a collection of the following options: Client ID, IPv6 Address, IPv6 Prefix, and Client Last Transaction Time.

The last value is the time (in seconds) since the server last communicated with the client in question. A LEASEQUERY-REPLY message may also contain the following two options: Relay Data and Client Link. The first includes the data last sent from a relay about the associated query, and the second indicates the link on which the subject client has one or more address bindings. Once again, this information is used for whatever purposes the requestor desires.

An extension to lease query called *Bulk Leasequery* (BL) [RFC5460][ID4LQ] allows multiple bindings to be queried simultaneously, uses TCP/IP rather than UDP/IP, and supports a wider range of query types. BL is designed as a special service for obtaining binding information and is not really part of conventional DHCP. Thus, clients wishing to obtain conventional configuration information do not use BL. One particular use of BL is when DHCP is being used for prefix delegation. In this case, it is common for a router to be acting as a DHCP-PD client. It obtains a prefix and then provides an address from the address range represented by the prefix as an assignment to conventional DHCP clients. However, if such a router fails or reboots, it may lose the prefix information and have a difficult time recovering because the conventional lease query mechanism requires an identifier for the binding in order to form the query. BL helps this situation, and others, by generalizing the set of possible query types.

BL provides several extensions to basic lease query. First, it uses TCP/IP (port 547 for IPv6 and port 67 for IPv4) instead of UDP/IP. This change allows for large amounts of query information to be returned for a single query, as may be necessary when retrieving a large number of delegated prefixes. BL also provides a Relay Identifier option to allow queries to identify the querier more easily. A BL query can then be based on relay identifier, link address (network segment), or relay ID.

The Relay ID DHCPv6 option and Relay ID DHCPv4 suboption [ID4RI] may include a DUID that identifies the relay agent. Relays can insert this option in messages they forward, and the server can use it to associate bindings it receives with the particular relay providing them. BL supports queries by address and DUID specified in [RFC5007] and [RFC4388] but also queries by relay ID, link address, and remote ID. These newer queries are supported only on TCP/IP-based servers that support BL. Conversely, BL servers support only LEASEQUERY messages, not the full set of ordinary DHCP messages.

BL extends the basic lease query mechanism with the LEASEQUERY-DATA and LEASEQUERY-DONE messages. When responding successfully to a query, a server first includes a LEASEQUERY-REPLY message. If additional information is available, it includes a set of LEASEQUERY-DATA messages, one per binding, and completes the set with a LEASEQUERY-DONE message. All messages pertaining to the same group of bindings share a common transaction ID, the same one provided in the initial LEASEQUERY-REQUEST message.

6.2.6.5 Layer 2 Relay Agents

In some network environments, there are layer 2 devices (e.g., switches, bridges) that are located near end systems that relay and process DHCP requests. These layer 2 devices do not have a full TCP/IP implementation stack and are not address-able using IP. As a result, they cannot act as conventional relay agents. To deal with this issue, [IDL2RA] and [RFC6221] specify how layer 2 *"lightweight" DHCP relay agents* (LDRAs) should behave, for IPv4 and IPv6, respectively. When referring to relay behaviors, interfaces are labeled as client-facing or network-facing, and as either trusted or untrusted. Network-facing interfaces are topologically closer to DHCP servers, and trusted interfaces are those where it is assumed that arriving packets are not spoofed.

The primary issue for IPv4 LDRAs is how to handle the DHCP *giaddr* field and insert a RAIO when the LDRA itself has no IP layer information. The approach recommended by [IDL2RA] is to have LDRAs insert the RAIO into DHCP requests received from clients but not fill in the *giaddr* field. The resulting DHCP message is sent in a broadcast fashion to one or more DHCP servers, as well as any other receiving LDRAs. Such messages are flooded (i.e., sent on all interfaces except the one upon which the message was received) unless received on an untrusted interface. LDRAs receiving such a message already including a RAIO do not add another such option but perform flooding. Responses (e.g., DHCPOFFER mes-sages) sent using broadcast may be intercepted by the LDRA, which in turn strips the RAIO and uses its information to forward the response to the original request-ing client. Many LDRAs also intercept unicast DHCP traffic. In these cases, the RAIO is also created or stripped as necessary. Note that compatible DHCP serv-ers must support the ability to process and return DHCP messages containing RAIOs without a valid *giaddr* field, whether such messages are sent using unicast or broadcast.

IPv6 LDRAs process DHCPv6 traffic by creating RELAY-FORW and RELAY-REPL messages. ADVERTISE, REPLY, RECONFIGURE, and RELAY-REPL mes-sages received on client-facing interfaces are discarded. In addition, RELAY-FORW messages received on untrusted client-facing interfaces are also discarded as a security precaution. RELAY-FORW messages are built containing options that identify the client-facing interface (i.e., *Link-Address* field, *Peer-Address* field, and Interface-ID option). The *Link-Address* field is set to 0, the *Peer-Address* field is set to the client's IP address, and the Interface-ID option is set to a value configured in the LDRA. When receiving a RELAY-REPL message containing a *Link-Address* field with value 0, the LDRA decapsulates the included message and sends it to toward the client on the interface specified in the received Interface-ID option (provided by the server). RELAY-FORW messages received on client-facing inter-faces are modified by incrementing the hop count. Messages other than RELAY-REPL messages received on network-facing interfaces are dropped.

6.2.7 DHCP Authentication

While we ordinarily discuss various security vulnerabilities at the end of each chapter (as we do in this one), for DHCP it is worth mentioning them here. It should be apparent that if the smooth operation of DHCP is interfered with, hosts are likely to be configured with erroneous information and significant disruption could result. Unfortunately, as we have discussed so far, DHCP has no provision for security, so it is possible for unauthorized DHCP clients or servers to be set up, either intentionally or accidentally, that could cause havoc with an otherwise functioning network.

In an attempt to mitigate these problems, a method to authenticate DHCP messages is specified in [RFC3118]. It defines a DHCP option, the Authentication option, with the format shown in Figure 6-22.

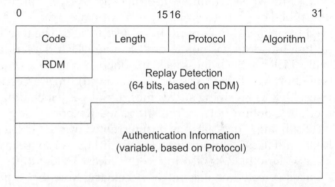

Figure 6-22   The DHCP Authentication option includes replay detection and can use various methods for authentication. Specified back in 2001, this option is not widely used today.

The purpose of the Authentication option is to help determine whether a DHCP message has come from an authorized sender. The *Code* field is set to 90, and the *Length* field gives the number of bytes in the option (not including the *Code* or *Length* fields). If the *Protocol* and *Algorithm* fields have the value 0, the *Authentication Information* field holds a simple shared *configuration token*. As long as the configuration token matches at the client and server, the message is accepted. This could be used, for example, to hold a password or similar text string, but such traffic could be intercepted by an attacker, so this method is not very secure. It might help to fend off accidental DHCP problems, however.

A somewhat more secure method involves so-called *deferred authentication*, indicated if the *Protocol* and *Algorithm* fields are set to 1. In this case, the client's DHCPDISCOVER or DHCPINFORM message includes an Authentication option, and the server responds with authentication information included in its DHCPOFFER or DHCPACK message. The authentication information includes a message authentication code (MAC; see Chapter 18), which provides authentication of the sender and an integrity check on the message contents. Assuming that the server and client have a shared secret, the MAC can be used to ensure that the client is trusted by the server and vice versa. It can also be used to ensure that the DHCP messages exchanged between them have not been modified or replayed from an earlier DHCP exchange. The replay detection method (RDM) is determined by the value of the *RDM* field. For RDM set to 0, the *Replay Detection* field contains a monotonically increasing value (e.g., timestamp). Received messages are checked to ensure that this value always increases. If the value does not increase, it is likely that an earlier DHCP message is simply being replayed (captured, stored, and played back later). It is conceivable that the value in the *Replay Detection* field could fail to advance in a situation where packets are reordered, but this is highly unlikely in a LAN (where DHCP is most prevalent) because only a single routing path is ordinarily used between the DHCP client and server.

There are (at least) two reasons why DHCP authentication has not seen widespread use. First, the approach requires shared keys to be distributed between a DHCP server and each client requiring authentication. Second, the Authentication option was specified after DHCP was already in relatively widespread use. Nonetheless, [RFC4030] builds upon this specification to help secure DHCP messages passed through relay agents (see Section 6.2.6).

6.2.8 Reconfigure Extension

In ordinary operation, a DHCP client initiates the renewal of address bindings. [RFC3203] defines the *reconfigure extension* and associated DHCPFORCERENEW message. This extension allows a server to cause a single client to change to the Renewing state and attempt to renew its lease by an otherwise ordinary operation (i.e., DHCPREQUEST). A server that does not wish to renew the lease for the requested address may respond with a DHCPNAK, causing the client to restart in the INIT state. The client would then begin again using a DHCPDISCOVER message.

The purpose of this extension is to cause the client to reestablish an address or to cause it to lose its address as the result of some significant change of state within the network. This could happen, for example, if the network is being administratively taken down or renumbered. Because this message is such an obvious candidate for a DoS attack, it must be authenticated using DHCP authentication. Because DHCP authentication is not in widespread use, neither is the reconfigure extension.

6.2.9 Rapid Commit

The DHCP *Rapid Commit* option [RFC4039] allows a DHCP server to respond to the DHCPDISCOVER message with a DHCPACK, effectively skipping the DHCPREQUEST message and ultimately using a two-message exchange instead of a four-message exchange. The motivation for this option is to quickly configure hosts that may change their point of network attachment frequently (i.e., mobile hosts). When only a single DHCP server is available and addresses are plentiful, this option should be of no significant concern.

To use rapid commit, a client includes the option in a DHCPDISCOVER message; it is not permitted to include it in any other message. Similarly, a server uses this option only in DHCPACK messages. When a server responds with this option, the receiving client knows that the returned address may be used immediately. If it should determine later that the address is already in use by another system (e.g., via ARP), the client sends a DHCPDECLINE message and abandons the address. It may also voluntarily relinquish the address it has received using a DHCPRELEASE message.

6.2.10 Location Information (LCI and LoST)

In some cases, it is useful for a host being configured to become aware of its location in the world. Such information may be encoded using, for example, latitude, longitude, and altitude. An IETF effort known as Geoconf ("Geographic configuration") resulted in [RFC6225], which specifies how to provide such geospatial *Location Configuration Information* (LCI) to clients using the GeoConf (123) and GeoLoc (144) DHCP options. Geospatial LCI includes not only the value of the latitude, longitude, and altitude coordinates, but also resolution indicators for each. LCI can be used for a number of purposes, including emergency services. If a caller using an IP phone requests emergency assistance, LCI can be used to indicate where the emergency is taking place.

Although the physical location information just mentioned is useful to locate a particular individual or system, sometimes it is important to know the *civic location* of an entity. The civic location expresses location in terms of geopolitical institutions such as country, city, district, street, and other such parameters. Civic location information can be provided using DHCP in the same way a physical location can, using the same LCI structure as is used with geospatial LCI. [RFC4776] defines the GEOCONF_CIVIC (99) option for carrying civic location LCI. This form of LCI is trickier than the geospatial information because the geopolitical method for naming locations varies by country. An additional complexity arises because such names may also require languages and character sets beyond the English and ASCII language and characters ordinarily used with DHCP. There is also a concern regarding the privacy of location in general, not just with respect to DHCP. The IETF is undertaking this issue in a framework called "Geopriv." See, for example, [RFC3693] for more information.

An alternative high-layer protocol known as the *HTTP-Enabled Location Delivery* (HELD) protocol [RFC5985] may also be used to provide location information. Instead of encoding the LCI directly in DHCP messages, DHCP options OPTION_V4_ACCESS_DOMAIN (213) and OPTION_V6_ACCESS_DOMAIN (57) provide the FQDN of a HELD server for IPv4 and IPv6, respectively [RFC5986].

Once a host knows its location, it may need to contact services associated with the location (e.g., the location of the nearest hospital). The IETF *Location-to-Service Translation* (LoST) framework [RFC5222] accomplishes this using an application-layer protocol accessed using a location-dependent URI. The DHCP options

OPTION_V4_LOST (137) and OPTION_V6_LOST (51) provide for variable-length encodings of an FQDN specifying the name of a LoST server for DHCPv4 and DHCPv6, respectively [RFC5223]. The encoding is in the same format used by DNS for encoding domain names (see Chapter 11).

6.2.11 Mobility and Handoff Information (MoS and ANDSF)

In response to the increased use of mobile computers and smartphones accessing the Internet with cellular technology, frameworks and related DHCP options have been specified to convey information about the cellular configuration and hand-overs between different wireless networks. At present, there are two sets of DHCP options relating to this information: IEEE 802.21 *Mobility Services* (MoS) Discovery and *Access Network Discovery and Selection Function* (ANDSF). The latter framework is being standardized by the 3rd Generation Partnership Project (3GPP), one of the organizations responsible for creating cellular data communications standards.

The IEEE 802.21 standard [802.21-2008] specifies a framework for *media-independent handoff* (MIH) services between various network types, including those defined by IEEE (802.3, 802.11, 802.16), those defined by 3GPP, and those defined by 3GPP2. A design of such a framework in the IETF context is provided in [RFC5677]. MoS provides three types of services known as information services, command services, and event services. Roughly speaking, these services provide information about available networks, functions for controlling link parameters, and notification of link status changes. The MoS Discovery DHCP options [RFC5678] provide a means for a mobile node to acquire the addresses or domain names of servers providing each of these services using either DHCPv4 or DHCPv6. For IPv4, the OPTION-IPv4_Address-MoS option (139) contains a vector of suboptions containing IP addresses for servers providing each of the services. A suboption of the OPTION-IPv4_FQDN-MoS option (140) provides a vector of FQDNs for servers for each of the services. Similar options, OPTION-IPv6_Address-MoS (54) and OPTION-IPv6_FQDN (55), provide equivalent capabilities for IPv6.

Based upon 3GPP's ANDSF specification, [RFC6153] defines DHCPv4 and DHCPv6 options for carrying ANDSF information. In particular, it defines options for mobile devices to discover the address of an ANDSF server. ANDSF servers are configured by cellular infrastructure operators and may hold information such as the availability and access policies of multiple transport networks (e.g., simultaneous use of 3G and Wi-Fi).

The ANDSF IPv4 Address Option (142) contains a vector of IPv4 addresses for ANDSF servers. The addresses are provided in preference order (first is most preferred). The ANDSF IPv6 Address Option (143) contains a vector of IPv6 addresses for ANDSF servers. To request ANDSF information using DHCPv4, the mobile node includes an ANDSF IPv4 Address option in the Parameter Request List. To request ANDSF information using DHCPv6, the client includes an ANDSF IPv6 Address option in the Option Request Option (ORO) (see Section 22.7 of [RFC3315]).

6.2.12 DHCP Snooping

DHCP "snooping" is a capability that some switch vendors offer in their products that inspects the contents of DHCP messages and ensures that only those addresses listed on an access control list are able to exchange DHCP traffic. This can help to protect against two potential problems. First, a "rogue" DHCP server is limited in the damage it can do because other hosts are not able to hear its DHCP address offers. Also, the technique can limit the allocation of addresses to a particular set of MAC addresses. While this provides some protection, MAC addresses can be changed in a system fairly easily using operating system commands, so this technique offers only limited protection.

6.3   Stateless Address Autoconfiguration (SLAAC)

While most routers have their addresses configured manually, hosts can be assigned addresses manually, using an assignment protocol like DHCP, or automatically using some sort of algorithm. There are two forms of automatic assignment, depending on what type of address is being formed. For addresses that are to be used only on a single link (link-local addresses), a host need only find some appropriate address not already in use on the link. For addresses that are to be used for global connectivity, however, some portion of the address must generally be managed. There are mechanisms in both IPv4 and IPv6 for link-local address autoconfiguration, whereby a host determines its address(es) largely without help. This is called *stateless address autoconfiguration* (SLAAC).

6.3.1 Dynamic Configuration of IPv4 Link-Local Addresses

In cases where a host without a manually configured address attaches to a network lacking a DHCP server, IP-based communication is unable to take place unless the host somehow generates an IP address to use. [RFC3927] describes a mechanism whereby a host can automatically generate its own IPv4 address from the link-local range 169.254.1.1 through 169.254.254.254 using the 16-bit subnet mask 255.255.0.0 (see [RFC5735]). This method is known as dynamic link-local address configuration or *Automatic Private IP Addressing* (APIPA). In essence, a host selects a random address in the range to use and checks to see if that address is already in use by some other system on the subnetwork. This check is implemented using IPv4 ACD (see Chapter 4).

6.3.2 IPv6 SLAAC for Link-Local Addresses

The goal of IPv6 SLAAC is to allow nodes to automatically (and autonomously) self-assign link-local IPv6 addresses. IPv6 SLAAC is described in [RFC4862]. It involves three major steps: obtaining a link-local address, obtaining a global address using stateless autoconfiguration, and detecting whether the link-local address is already in use on the link. Stateless autoconfiguration can be used without routers, in which case only link-local addresses are assigned. When routers are present, a global address is formed using a combination of the prefix advertised by a router and locally generated information. SLAAC can also be used in conjunction with DHCPv6 (or manual address assignment) to allow a host to obtain information in addition to its address (called "stateless" DHCPv6). Hosts that perform SLAAC can be used on the same network as those configured using stateful or stateless DHCPv6. Generally, stateful DHCPv6 is used when finer control is required in assigning address to hosts, but it is expected that stateless DHCPv6 in combination with SLAAC will be the most common deployment option.

In IPv6, tentative (or optimistic) link-local addresses are selected using procedures specified in [RFC4291] and [RFC4941]. They apply only to multicast-capable networks and are assigned infinite preferred and valid lifetimes once established. To form the numeric address, a unique number is appended to the well-known link-local prefix fe80::0 (of appropriate length). This is accomplished by setting the right-most N bits of the address to be equal to the (N-bit-long) number, the left-most bits equal to the 10-bit link-local prefix 1111111010, and the rest to 0. The resulting address is placed into the tentative (or optimistic) state and checked for duplicates (see the next section).

6.3.2.1 IPv6 Duplicate Address Detection (DAD)

IPv6 DAD uses ICMPv6 Neighbor Solicitation and Neighbor Advertisement messages (see Chapter 8) to determine if a particular (tentative or optimistic) IPv6 address is already in use on the attached link. For purposes of this discussion, we refer only to tentative addresses, but it is understood that DAD applies to optimistic addresses as well. DAD is specified in [RFC4862] and is recommended to be used every time an IPv6 address is assigned to an interface manually, using autoconfiguration, or using DHCPv6. If a duplicate address is discovered, the procedure causes the tentative address to not be used. If DAD succeeds, the tentative address transitions to the preferred state and can be used without restriction.

DAD is performed as follows: A node first joins the All Nodes multicast address and the Solicited-Node multicast address of the tentative address (see Chapter 9). To check for use of an address duplicate, a node sends one or more ICMPv6 Neighbor Solicitation messages. The source and destination IPv6 addresses of these messages are the unspecified address and Solicited-Node address of the target address being checked, respectively. The *Target Address* field is set to the address being checked (the tentative address). If a Neighbor Advertisement message is received in response, DAD has failed, and the address being checked is abandoned.

Note

As a consequence of joining multicast groups, MLD messages are sent (see Chapter 9), but their transmission is delayed by a random interval according to [RFC4862] to avoid congesting the network when many nodes simultaneously join the All Hosts group (e.g., after a restoration of power). For DAD, these MLD messages are used to inform MLD-snooping switches to forward multicast traffic as necessary.

When an address has not yet successfully completed DAD, any received neighbor solicitations for it are treated in a special way, as this is indicative of some other host's intention to use the same address. If such messages are received, they are dropped, the current tentative address is abandoned, and DAD fails.

If DAD fails, by receiving a similar neighbor solicitation from another node or a neighbor advertisement for the target address, the address is not assigned to an interface and does not become a preferred address. If the address is a link-local address being configured based on an interface identifier derived from a local MAC address, it is unlikely that the same procedure will ultimately produce a nonconflicting address, so the use of this address is abandoned and administrator input is required. If the address is based on a different form of interface identifier, IPv6 operations may be retried using another address based on an alternative tentative address.

6.3.2.2 IPv6 SLAAC for Global Addresses

Once a node has acquired a link-local address, it is likely to require one or more global addresses as well. Global addresses are formed using a process similar to that for link-local SLAAC but using a prefix provided by a router. Such prefixes are carried in the Prefix option of a router advertisement (see Chapter 8), and a flag indicates whether the prefix should be used in forming global addresses with SLAAC. If so, the prefix is combined with an interface identifier (e.g., the same one used in forming a link-local address if the privacy extension is not being used) to form a global address. The preferred and valid lifetimes of such addresses are also determined by information present in the Prefix option.

6.3.2.3 Example

The trace in Figure 6-23 shows the series of events an IPv6 (Windows Vista/SP1) host uses when allocating its addresses with SLAAC. The system first selects a link-local address based on the link-local prefix of fe80::/64 and a random number. This method is designed to enhance the privacy of a user by making the address of the host system change over time [RFC4941]. The other common method involves using the bits of the MAC address in forming the link-local address. It performs DAD on this address (fe80::fd26:de93:5ab7:405a) to look for conflicts.

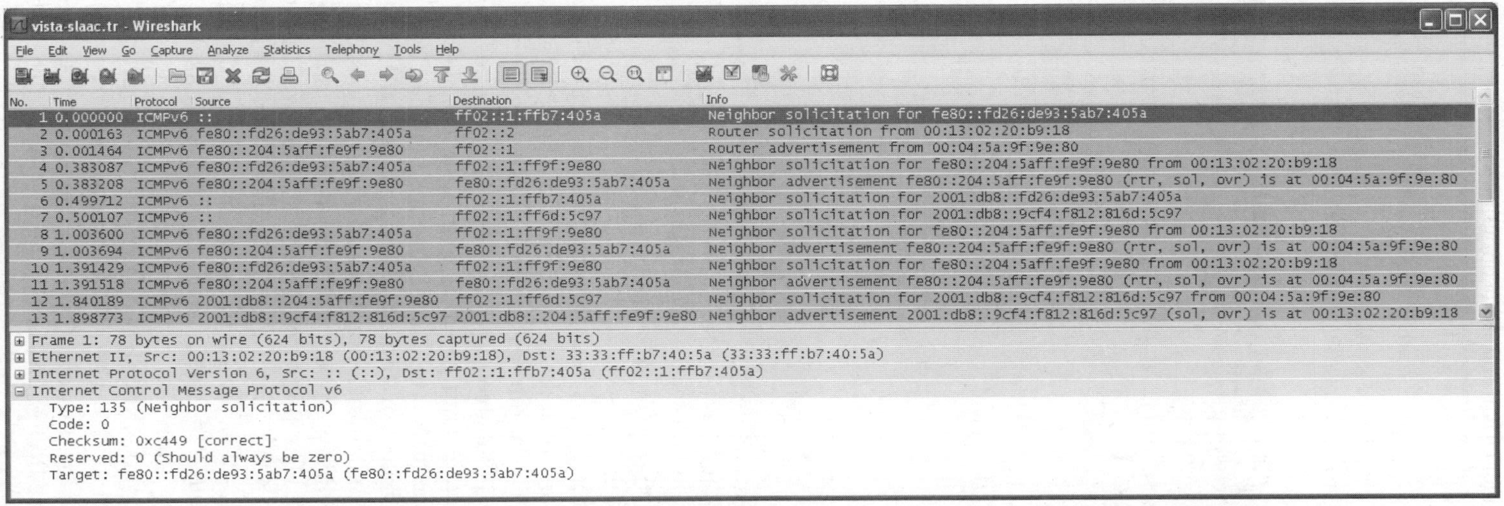

Figure 6-23 During SLAAC, a host begins by performing DAD on the tentative link-local address it wishes to use by sending an ICMPv6 Neighbor Solicitation message for this address from the unspecified address.

Figure 6-23 shows the operation of DAD, which involves the host sending an NS to see if its selected link-local address is in use. It then quickly performs an RS to determine how to proceed (see Figure 6-24).

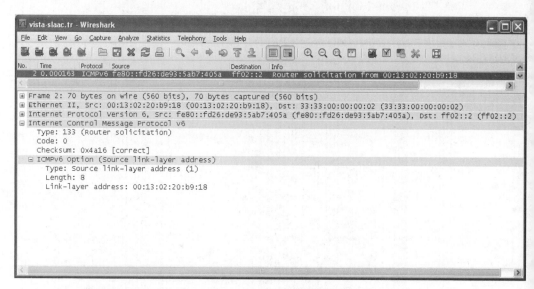

Figure 6-24   The ICMPv6 RS message induces a nearby router to supply configuration information such as the global network prefix in use on the attached network.

The Router Solicitation message shown in Figure 6-24 is sent to the All Routers multicast address (ff02::2) using the autoconfigured link-local IPv6 address as a source address. The response is given in an RA sent to the All Systems multicast address (ff02::1), so that all attached systems can see (see Figure 6-25).

The RA shown in Figure 6-25 is sent from fe80::204:5aff:fe9f:9e80, the link-local address of the router, to the All Systems multicast address ff02::1. The *Flags* field in the RA, which may contain several configuration options and extensions [RFC5175], is set to 0, indicating that addresses are not "managed" on this link by DHCPv6. The Prefix option indicates that the global prefix 2001:db8::/64 is in use on the link. The prefix length of 64 is not carried but is instead defined according to [RFC4291]. The *Flags* field value of 0xc0 associated with the Prefix option indicates that the prefix is on-link (can be use in conjunction with a router) and the auto flag is set, meaning that the prefix can be used by the host to configure other addresses automatically. It also includes the Recursive DNS Server (RDNSS) option [RFC6106], which indicates that a DNS server is available at the address 2001::db8::1. The SLLAO indicates that the router's MAC address is 00:04:5a:9f:9e:80. This information is made available for any node to populate its neighbor cache (the IPv6 equivalent of the IPv4 ARP cache; Neighbor Discovery is discussed in Chapter 8).

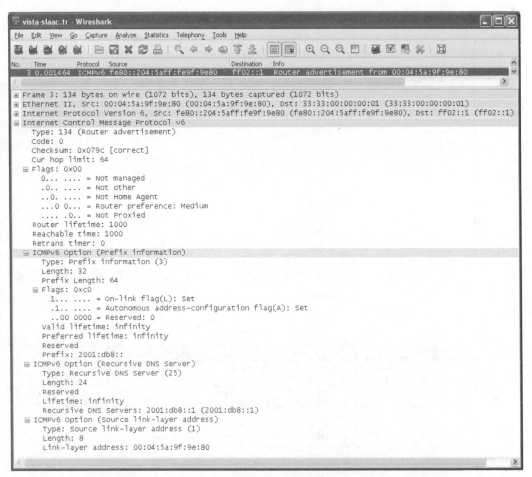

Figure 6-25   An ICMPv6 RA message provides the location and availability of a default router plus the global address prefix in use on the network. It also includes the location of a DNS server and indicates whether the router sending the advertisement can also act as a Mobile IPv6 home agent (no in this case). The client may use some or all of this information in configuring its operation.

After an exchange of Neighbor Solicitation and Neighbor Advertisement messages between the client and the router, the client performs another DAD operation on the new (global) address it selects (see Figure 6-26).

The address 2001:db8::fd26:de93:5ab7:405a has been chosen by the client based on the prefix 2001::db8 carried in the router advertisement it received earlier. The low-order bits of this address are based on the same random number as was used to configure its link-local address. As such, the Solicited-Node multicast address ff02::1:ffb7:405a is the same for DAD for both addresses. After this address has been tested for duplication, the client allocates another address and applies DAD to it (see Figure 6-27).

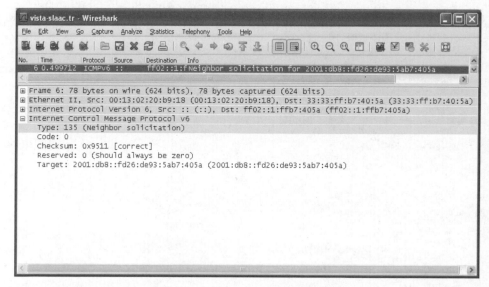

Figure 6-26   DAD for the global address derived from the prefix 2001:db8::/64 is sent to the same Solicited-Node multicast address as the first packet.

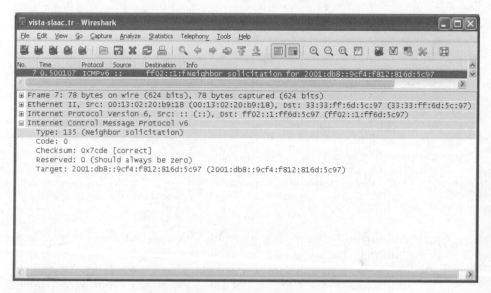

Figure 6-27   DAD for the address 2001:db8::9cf4:f812:816d:5c97.

The DAD operation in Figure 6-27 is for the address 2001:db8::9cf4:f812:816d:5c97. This address is a temporary IPv6 address, generated using a different random number for its lower-order bits for privacy reasons. The difference between the two global addresses here is that the temporary address has a shorter lifetime. Lifetimes are computed as the lower (smaller) of the following two values: the lifetimes included in the Prefix Information option received in the RA and a local pair of defaults. In the case of Windows Vista, the default valid lifetime is one week and the default preferred lifetime is one day. Once this message has completed, the client has performed SLAAC for its link-local address, plus two global addresses. This is enough addressing information to perform local or global communication. The temporary address will change periodically to help enhance privacy. In cases where privacy protection is not desired, the following command can be employed to disable this feature in Windows:

```
C:\> netsh interface ipv6 set privacy state=disabled
```

In Linux, temporary addresses can be enabled using this set of commands:

```
Linux# sysctl -w net.ipv6.conf.all.use_tempaddr=2
```

```
Linux# sysctl -w net.ipv6.conf.default.use_tempaddr=2
```

and disabled using these commands:

```
Linux# sysctl -w net.ipv6.conf.all.use_tempaddr=0
```

```
Linux# sysctl -w net.ipv6.conf.default.use_tempaddr=0
```

6.3.2.4 Stateless DHCP

We have mentioned that DHCPv6 can be used in a "stateless" mode where the DHCPv6 server does not assign addresses (or keep any per-client state) but does provide other configuration information. Stateless DHCPv6 is specified in [RFC3736] and combines SLAAC with DHCPv6. It is believed that this combination is an attractive deployment option because network administrators need not be directly concerned with address pools as they have been when deploying DHCPv4.

In a stateless DHCPv6 deployment, nodes are assumed to have obtained their addresses using some method other than DHCPv6. Thus, the DHCPv6 server does not need to handle any of the address management messages specified in Table 6-1. In addition, it does not need to handle any of the options required for establishing IA bindings. This simplifies the server software and server configuration considerably. The operation of relay agents is unchanged.

Stateless DHCPv6 clients use the DHCPv6 INFORMATION-REQUEST message to request information that is provided in REPLY messages from servers. The INFORMATION-REQUEST message includes an Option Request option listing the options about which the client wishes to know more. The INFORMATION-REQUEST may include a Client Identifier option, which allows answers to be customized for particular clients.

To be a compliant stateless DHCPv6 server, a system must implement the following messages: INFORMATION-REQUEST, REPLY, RELAY-FORW, and RELAY-REPL. It also must implement the following options: Option Request, Status Code, Server Identifier, Client Message, Server Message, Interface-ID. The last three are used when relay agents are involved. To be a *useful* stateless DHCPv6 server, several other options will likely be necessary: DNS Server, DNS Search List, and possibly SIP Servers. Other potentially useful, but not required, options include Preference, Elapsed Time, User Class, Vendor Class, Vendor-Specific Information, Client Identifier, and Authentication.

6.3.2.5 The Utility of Address Autoconfiguration

The utility of address autoconfiguration for IP is typically limited because routers that may be on the same network as the client are configured with particular IP address ranges in use that differ from the addresses a client is likely to autoconfigure. This is especially true for the IPv4 (APIPA) case, as the private link-local prefix 169.254/16 is very unlikely to be used by a router. Therefore, the consequence of self-assigning an IP address is that local subnet access may work, but Internet routing and name services (DNS) are likely to fail. When DNS fails, much of the common Internet "experience" fails with it. Thus, it is often more useful to have a client fail to get an IP address (which is relatively easily detected) than to allow it to obtain one that cannot really be used effectively.

Note

There are name services other than conventional DNS that may be of use for link-local addressing, including Bonjour/ZeroConf (Apple), LLMNR, and NetBIOS (Microsoft). Because these have evolved over time from different vendors, and are not established IETF standards, the exact behavior involved when mapping names to addresses in the local environment varies considerably. See Chapter 11 for more details on local alternatives to DNS.

The use of APIPA can be disabled, which prevents a system from self-assigning an IP address. In Windows, this is accomplished by creating the following registry key (the key is a single line but is wrapped here for illustration):

```
HKLM\SYSTEM\CurrentControlSet\Services\Tcpip\Parameters\
IPAutoconfigurationEnabled
```

This REG_DWORD value may be set to 0 to disable APIPA for all network interfaces. In Linux, the file /etc/sysconfig/network can be modified to include the following directive:

```
NOZEROCONF=yes
```

This disables the use of APIPA for all network interfaces. It is also possible to disable APIPA for specific interfaces by modifying the per-interface configuration files (e.g., /etc/sysconfig/network-scripts/ifcfg-eth0 for the first Ethernet device).

In the case of IPv6 SLAAC, it is relatively easy to obtain a global IPv6 address, but the relationship between a name and its address is not secured, leading to a potential set of unpleasant consequences (see Chapters 11 and 18). Thus, it may still be desirable to avoid SLAAC in deployments for the time being. To disable SLAAC for IPv6 global addresses, there are two methods. First, the Router Advertisement messages provided by the local router can be arranged to turn off the "auto" flag in the Prefix option (or configure it to not provide a Prefix option, as illustrated in the preceding example). In addition, a local configuration setting causes a client to avoid autoconfiguration of global addresses.

To disable SLAAC in a Linux client, the following command may be given:

```
Linux# sysctl -w net.ipv6.conf.all.autoconf=0
```

To do so on a Mac OS or FreeBSD system, at least for link-local addresses, the following command should be used:

```
FreeBSD# sysctl -w net.inet6.ip6.auto_linklocal=0
```

And, finally, for Windows:

```
C:\> netsh
netsh> interface ipv6
netsh interface ipv6> set interface {ifname} managedaddress=disabled
```

where {ifname} should be replaced with the appropriate interface name (in this example, "Wireless Network Connection"). Note that the behavior of these configuration commands sometimes changes over time. Please check the operating system documentation for the current method if these changes do not perform as expected.

6.4 DHCP and DNS Interaction

One of the important parts of the configuration information a DHCP client typically receives when obtaining an IP address is the IP address of a DNS server. This allows the client system to convert DNS names to the IPv4 and/or IPv6 addresses required by the protocol implementation to make transport-layer connections. Without a DNS server or other way to map names to addresses, most users would find the system nearly useless for accessing the Internet. If the local DNS is working properly, it should be able to provide address mappings for the Internet as a whole, but also for local private networks (like .home mentioned earlier), if properly configured.

Because DNS mappings for local private networks are cumbersome to manage by hand, it is convenient to couple the act of providing a DHCP-assigned address with a method for updating the DNS mappings corresponding to that address. This can be done either using a combined DHCP/DNS server or with *dynamic DNS* (see Chapter 11).

A combined DNS/DHCP server (such as the Linux `dnsmasq` package) is a server program that can be configured to give out IP address leases and other information but that also reads the Client Identifier or Domain Name present in a DHCPREQUEST and updates an internal DNS database with the name-to-address binding before responding with the DHCPACK. In doing so, any subsequent DNS requests initiated either by the DHCP client or by other systems interacting with the same DNS server are able to convert between the name of the client and its freshly assigned IP address.

6.5 PPP over Ethernet (PPPoE)

For most LANs and some WAN connections, DHCP provides the most common method for configuring client systems. For WAN connections such as DSL, another method based on PPP is often used instead. This method involves carrying PPP on Ethernet and is called *PPP over Ethernet* (PPPoE). PPPoE is used in cases where the WAN connection device (e.g., DSL modem) acts as a switch or bridge instead of a router. PPP is preferred as a basis for establishing connectivity by some ISPs because it may provide finer-grain configuration control and audit logs than other configuration options such as DHCP. To provide Internet connectivity, some device such as a user's PC must implement the IP routing and addressing functions. Figure 6-28 shows the typical use case.

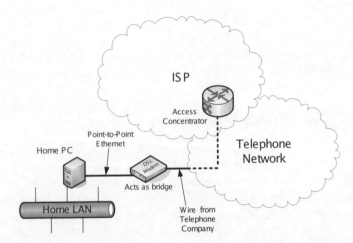

Figure 6-28   A simplified view of DSL service using PPPoE as provided to a customer. The home PC implements the PPPoE protocol and authenticates the subscriber with the ISP. It may also act as a router, DHCP server, DNS server, and/or NAT device for the home LAN.

The figure shows an ISP providing services to many customers using DSL. DSL provides a point-to-point digital link that can operate simultaneously with a conventional analog telephone line (called *plain old telephone service* or POTS). This simultaneous use of the customer's physical phone wires is accomplished using frequency division multiplexing—the DSL information is carried on higher frequencies than POTS. A filter is required when attaching conventional telephone handsets to avoid interference from the higher DSL frequencies. The DSL modem effectively provides a bridged service to a PPP port on the ISP's *access concentrator* (AC), which interconnects the customer's modem line and the ISP's networking equipment. The modem and AC also support the PPPoE protocol, which the user has elected in this example to configure on a home PC attached to the DSL modem using a point-to-point Ethernet network (i.e., an Ethernet LAN using only a single cable).

Once the DSL modem has successfully established a low-layer link with the ISP, the PC can begin the PPPoE exchange, as defined in the informational document [RFC2516] and shown in Figure 6-29.

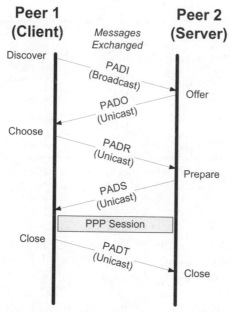

Figure 6-29 The PPPoE message exchange starts in a Discovery stage and establishes a PPP Session stage. Each message is a PAD message. PADI requests responses from PPPoE servers. PADO offers connectivity. PADR expresses the client's selection among multiple possible servers. PADS provides an acknowledgment to the client from the selected server. After the PAD exchanges, a PPP session begins. The PPP session can be terminated by either side sending a PADT message or when the underlying link fails or is shut down.

The protocol includes a Discovery phase and a PPP Session phase. The Discovery phase involves the exchange of several *PPPoE Active Discovery* (PAD) messages: PADI (Initiation), PADO (Offer), PADR (Request), PADS (Session Confirmation). Once the exchange is complete, an Ethernet-encapsulated PPP session proceeds and ultimately concludes with either side sending a PADT (Termination) message. The session also concludes if the underlying connection is broken. PPPoE messages use the format shown in Figure 6-30 and are encapsulated in the Ethernet payload area.

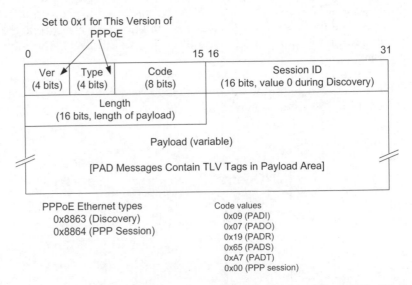

Figure 6-30   PPPoE messages are carried in the payload area of Ethernet frames. The Ethernet *Type* field is set to 0x8863 during the Discovery phase and 0x8864 when carrying PPP session data. For PAD messages, a TLV scheme is used for carrying configuration information, similar to DHCP options. The PPPoE *Session ID* is chosen by the server and conveyed in the PADS message.

In Figure 6-30, the PPPoE *Ver* and *Type* fields are both 4 bits long and contain the value 0x1 for the current version of PPPoE. The *Code* field contains an indication of the PPPoE message type, as shown in the lower right part of Figure 6-30. The *Session ID* field contains the value 0x0000 for PADI, PADO, and PADR messages and contains a unique 16-bit number in subsequent messages. The same value is maintained during the PPP Session phase. PAD messages contain one or more *tags*, which are TLVs arranged as a 16-bit *TAG_TYPE* field followed by a 16-bit *TAG_LENGTH* field and a variable amount of tag value data. The values and meanings of the *TAG_TYPE* field are given in Table 6-2.

Table 6-2 PPPoE TAG_TYPE values, name, and purpose. PAD messages may contain one or more tags.

Value	Name	Purpose
0x0000	End-of-List	Indicates that no further tags are present. TAG_LENGTH must be 0.
0x0101	Service-Name	Contains a UTF-8-encoded service name (for ISP use).
0x0102	AC-Name	Contains a UTF-8-encoded string identifying the access concentrator.
0x0103	Host-Uniq	Binary data used by client to match messages; not interpreted by AC.
0x0104	AC-Cookie	Binary data used by AC for DoS protection; echoed by client.
0x0105	Vendor-Specific	Not recommended; see [RFC2516] for details.
0x0110	Relay-Session-ID	May be added by a relay relaying PAD traffic.
0x0201	Service-Name-Error	The requested Service-Name tag cannot be honored by AC.
0x0202	AC-System-Error	The AC experienced an error in performing a requested action.
0x0203	Generic-Error	Contains a UTF-8 string describing an unrecoverable error.

To see PPPoE in action, we can monitor the exchange between a home system such as the home PC from Figure 6-28 and an access concentrator. The Discovery phase and first PPP session packet are shown in Figure 6-31.

Figure 6-31 shows the expected exchange of PADI, PADO, PADR, and PADS messages. Each contains the Host-Uniq tag with value 9c3a0000. Messages coming from the concentrator also include the value 90084090400368-rback37.snfcca in the AC-Name tag. The PADS message can be seen in more detail in Figure 6-32.

In Figure 6-32, the PADS message indicates the establishment of a PPP session for the client and the use of the session ID 0xecbd. The AC-Name tag is also maintained to indicate the originating AC. The Discovery phase is now complete, and a regular PPP session (see Chapter 3) can commence. Figure 6-33 shows the first PPP session packet.

The figure indicates the beginning of the PPP Session phase within the PPPoE exchange. The PPP session begins with link configuration (PPP LCP) by the client sending a Configuration Request (see Chapter 3). It indicates that the client wishes to use the Password Authentication Protocol, a relatively insecure method, for authenticating itself to the AC. Once the authentication exchange is complete and various link parameters are exchanged (e.g., MRU), IPCP is used to obtain and configure the assigned IP address. Note that additional configuration information (e.g., IP addresses of the ISP's DNS servers) may need to be obtained separately and, depending on the ISP's configuration, configured by hand.

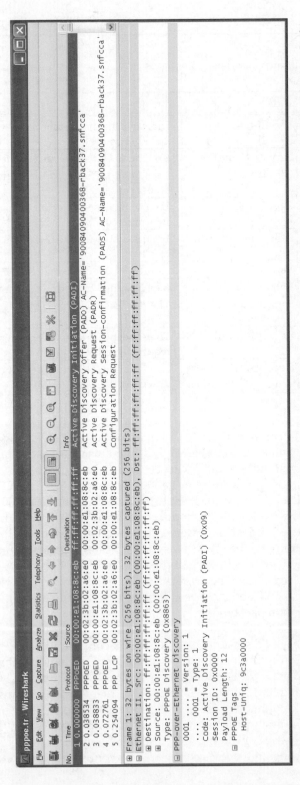

Figure 6-31 The PPPoE exchange begins with a PADI message sent to the Ethernet broadcast address. Subsequent messages use unicast addressing. In this exchange, only the Host-Uniq and AC-Name tags are used. The PPP session begins with the fifth packet, which begins a PPP link configuration exchange that ultimately assigns the system's IPv4 address using the IPCP (see Chapter 3).

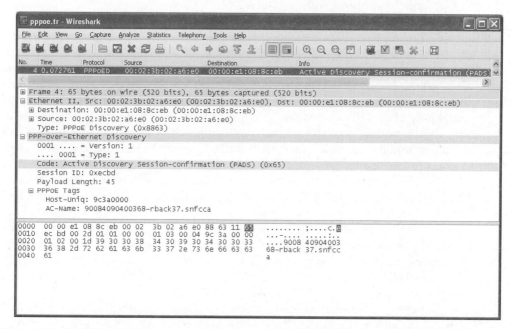

Figure 6-32   The PPPoE PADS message confirms the association between the client and the access concentrator. This message also defines the session ID as 0xecbd, which is used in subsequent PPP session packets.

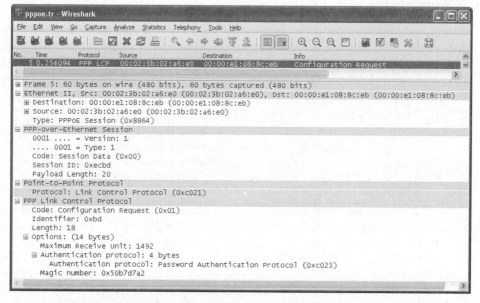

Figure 6-33   The first PPP message of the PPPoE session is a Configuration Request. The Ethernet type has changed to 0x8864 to indicate an active PPP session, and the *Session ID* is set to 0xecbd. In this case, the PPP client wishes to authenticate using the (relatively insecure) Password Authentication Protocol.

6.6   Attacks Involving System Configuration

A wide variety of attacks can be mounted relating to system and network configuration. They range from deploying unauthorized clients or unauthorized servers that interfere with DHCP to various forms of DoS attacks that involve resource exhaustion, such as requesting all possible IP addresses a server may have to give out. Many of these problems are widespread because the older IPv4-based protocols used for address configuration were designed for networks where trust was assumed, and the newer ones have seen little deployment to date. (Secured deployments are even rarer.) Therefore, none of these attacks are directly addressed by typical DHCP deployments, although link-layer authentication (e.g., WPA2 as used with Wi-Fi networks) helps to limit the number of unauthorized clients that are able to attach to a particular network.

An effort is under way within the IETF to provide security for IPv6 Neighbor Discovery, which, when or if it is deployed, would directly impact the security of operating networks using SLAAC. The trust and threat assumptions are outlined in [RFC3756] from 2004, and the *Secure Neighbor Discovery* (SEND) protocol is defined in [RFC3971]. SEND applies IPsec (see Chapter 18) to Neighbor Discovery packets, in combination with cryptographically generated addresses (CGAs) [RFC3972]. Such addresses are derived from a keyed hash function, so they can be generated only by a system holding the appropriate key material.

6.7   Summary

A basic set of configuration information is required for a host or router to operate on the Internet or on a private network using Internet protocols. At a minimum, routers typically require the assignment of addressing information, whereas hosts require addresses, a next-hop router, and the location of a DNS server. DHCP is available for both IPv4 as well as IPv6, but the two are not directly interoperable. DHCP allows appropriately configured servers to lease one or more addresses to requesting clients for a defined period of time. Clients renew their leases if they require ongoing use. DHCP can also be used by the client to acquire additional information, such as the subnet mask, default routers, vendor-specific configuration information, DNS server, home agents, and default domain name. DHCP can be used through relay agents when a client and server are located on different networks. Several extensions to DHCP allow for additional information to be carried between a relay agent and server when this is used. DHCPv6 can also be used to delegate a range of IPv6 address space to a router.

With IPv6, a host typically uses multiple addresses. An IPv6 client is able to generate its link-local address autonomously by combining a special link-local IPv6 prefix with other local information such as bits derived from one of its MAC addresses or from a random number to help promote privacy. To obtain a global address, it can obtain a global address prefix from either ICMP Router

Advertisement messages or from a DHCPv6 server. DHCPv6 servers may operate in a "stateful" mode, in which they lease IPv6 addresses to requesting clients, or a "stateless" mode, in which they provide configuration information other than the addresses.

PPPoE carries PPP messages over Ethernet to establish Internet connectivity with ISPs, especially those ISPs that provide service using DSL. When using PPPoE, a user usually has a DSL modem with an Ethernet port acting as a bridge or switch. PPPoE first exchanges a set of Discovery messages to determine the identity of an access controller and establish a PPP session. After the Discovery phase is successfully completed, PPP traffic, which can be encapsulated in Ethernet and carry various protocols such as IP, may continue until the PPPoE association is terminated, either intentionally or as a result of disconnection of the underlying link. When PPPoE is used, the PPP protocol's configuration capabilities such as IPCP (discussed in Chapter 3) are ultimately responsible for assigning the IP address to the client system.

DHCP and the ICMPv6 router advertisements used with IPv6 stateless autoconfiguration are ordinarily deployed without security mechanisms being applied to them. Because of this, they are susceptible to a number of attacks, including network access by unauthorized clients, operation of rogue DHCP servers that give out bogus addresses and cause various forms of denial of service, and resource exhaustion attacks in which a client may request more addresses than are available. Most of these attacks can be mitigated by security mechanisms that have been added to DHCP such as DHCP authentication and the relatively recent SEND protocol. However, these are not commonly found in operation today.

6.8   References

[802.21-2008] "IEEE Standard for Local and Metropolitan Area Networks—Part 21: Media Independent Handover Services," Nov. 2008.

[F07] R. Faas, "Hands On: Configuring Apple's NetBoot Service, Part 1," *Computerworld*, Sept. 2007.

[GC89] C. Gray and D. Cheriton, "Leases: An Efficient Fault-Tolerant Mechanism for Distributed File Cache Consistency," *Proc. ACM Symposium on Operating System Principles (SOSP)*, 1989.

[IARP] http://www.iana.org/assignments/arp-parameters

[IBDP] http://www.iana.org/assignments/bootp-dhcp-parameters

[ID4LQ] K. Kinnear, B. Volz, M. Stapp, D. Rao, B. Joshi, N. Russell, and P. Kurapati, "Bulk DHCPv4 Lease Query," Internet draft-ietf-dhc-dhcpv4-bulk-leasequery, work in progress, Apr. 2011.

[ID4RI] B. Joshi, R. Rao, and M. Stapp, "The DHCPv4 Relay Agent Identifier Sub-option," Internet draft-ietf-dhc-relay-id-suboption, work in progress, June 2011.

[ID6PARAM] http://www.iana.org/assignments/dhcpv6-parameters

[IDDN] G. Daley, E. Nordmark, and N. Moore, "Tentative Options for Link-Layer Addresses in IPv6 Neighbor Discovery," Internet draft-ietf-dna-tentative (expired), work in progress, Oct. 2009.

[IDL2RA] B. Joshi and P. Kurapati, "Layer 2 Relay Agent Information," Internet draft-ietf-dhc-l2ra, work in progress, Apr. 2011.

[IEPARAM] http://www.iana.org/assignments/enterprise-numbers

[MKB928233] Microsoft Knowledge Base Article 928233 at http://support.microsoft.com

[MS-DHCPN] Microsoft Corporation, "[MS-DHCPN]: Dynamic Host Configuration Protocol (DHCP) Extensions for Network Access Protection (NAP)," http://msdn.microsoft.com/en-us/library/cc227316.aspx, Oct. 2008.

[RFC0826] D. Plummer, "Ethernet Address Resolution Protocol: Or Converting Network Protocol Addresses to 48.bit Ethernet Address for Transmission on Ethernet Hardware," Internet RFC 0826/STD 0037, Nov. 1982.

[RFC0951] W. J. Croft and J. Gilmore, "Bootstrap Protocol," Internet RFC 0951, Sept. 1985.

[RFC1542] W. Wimer, "Clarifications and Extensions for the Bootstrap Protocol," Internet RFC 1542, Oct. 1993.

[RFC2131] R. Droms, "Dynamic Host Configuration Protocol," Internet RFC 2131, Mar. 1997.

[RFC2132] S. Alexander and R. Droms, "DHCP Options and BOOTP Vendor Extensions," Internet RFC 2132, Mar. 1997.

[RFC2241] D. Provan, "DHCP Options for Novell Directory Services," Internet RFC 2241, Nov. 1997.

[RFC2242] R. Droms and K. Fong, "NetWare/IP Domain Name and Information," Internet RFC 2242, Nov. 1997.

[RFC2516] L. Mamakos, K. Lidl, J. Evarts, D. Carrel, D. Simone, and R. Wheeler, "A Method for Transmitting PPP over Ethernet (PPPoE)," Internet RFC 2516 (informational), Feb. 1999.

[RFC2563] R. Troll, "DHCP Option to Disable Stateless Auto-Configuration in IPv4 Clients," Internet RFC 2563, May 1999.

[RFC2937] C. Smith, "The Name Service Search Option for DHCP," Internet RFC 2937, Sept. 2000.

[RFC3004] G. Stump, R. Droms, Y. Gu, R. Vyaghrapuri, A. Demirtjis, B. Beser, and J. Privat, "The User Class Option for DHCP," Internet RFC 3004, Nov. 2000.

[RFC3011] G. Waters, "The IPv4 Subnet Selection Option for DHCP," Internet RFC 3011, Nov. 2000.

[RFC3046] M. Patrick, "DHCP Relay Agent Information Option," Internet RFC 3046, Jan. 2001.

[RFC3118] R. Droms and W. Arbaugh, eds., "Authentication of DHCP Messages," Internet RFC 3118, June 2001.

[RFC3203] Y. T'Joens, C. Hublet, and P. De Schrijver, "DHCP Reconfigure Extension," Internet RFC 3203, Dec. 2001.

[RFC3315] R. Droms, ed., J. Bound, B. Volz, T. Lemon, C. Perkins, and M. Carney, "Dynamic Host Configuration Protocol for IPv6 (DHCPv6)," Internet RFC 3315, July 2003.

[RFC3396] T. Lemon and S. Cheshire, "Encoding Long Options in the Dynamic Host Configuration Protocol (DHCPv4)," Internet RFC 3396, Nov. 2002.

[RFC3442] T. Lemon, S. Cheshire, and B. Volz, "The Classless Static Route Option for Dynamic Host Configuration Protocol (DHCP) Version 4," Internet RFC 3442, Dec. 2002.

[RFC3633] O. Troan and R. Droms, "IPv6 Prefix Options for Dynamic Host Configuration Protocol (DHCP) Version 6," Internet RFC 3633, Dec. 2003.

[RFC3646] R. Droms, ed., "DNS Configuration Options for Dynamic Host Configuration Protocol for IPv6 (DHCPv6)," Internet RFC 3646, Dec. 2003.

[RFC3693] J. Cuellar, J. Morris, D. Mulligan, J. Peterson, and J. Polk, "Geopriv Requirements," Internet RFC 3693 (informational), Feb. 2004.

[RFC3736] R. Droms, "Stateless Dynamic Host Configuration Protocol (DHCP) Service for IPv6," Internet RFC 3736, Apr. 2004.

[RFC3756] P. Nikander, ed., J. Kempf, and E. Nordmark, "IPv6 Neighbor Discovery (ND) Trust Models and Threats," Internet RFC 3756 (informational), May 2004.

[RFC3925] J. Littlefield, "Vendor-Identifying Vendor Options for Dynamic Host Configuration Protocol Version 4 (DHCPv4)," Internet RFC 3925, Oct. 2004.

[RFC3927] S. Cheshire, B. Aboba, and E. Guttman, "Dynamic Configuration of IPv6 Link-Local Addresses," Internet RFC 3927, May 2005.

[RFC3971] J. Arkko, ed., J. Kempf, B. Zill, and P. Nikander, "SEcure Neighbor Dicovery (SEND)," Internet RFC 3971, Mar. 2005.

[RFC3972] T. Aura, "Cryptographically Generated Addresses (CGA)," Internet RFC 3972, Mar. 2005.

[RFC4030] M. Stapp and T. Lemon, "The Authentication Suboption for the Dynamic Host Configuration Protocol (DHCP) Relay Agent Option," Internet RFC 4030, Mar. 2005.

[RFC4039] S. Park, P. Kim, and B. Volz, "Rapid Commit Option for the Dynamic Host Configuration Protocol Version 4 (DHCPv4)," Internet RFC 4039, Mar. 2005.

[RFC4174] C. Monia, J. Tseng, and K. Gibbons, "The IPv4 Dynamic Host Configuration Protocol (DHCP) Option for the Internet Storage Name Service," Internet RFC 4174, Sept. 2005.

[RFC4280] K. Chowdhury, P. Yegani, and L. Madour, "Dynamic Host Configuration Protocol (DHCP) Options for Broadcast and Multicast Control Servers," Internet RFC 4280, Nov. 2005.

[RFC4291] R. Hinden and S. Deering, "IP Version 6 Addressing Architecture," Internet RFC 4291, Feb. 2006.

[RFC4361] T. Lemon and B. Sommerfield, "Node-Specific Client Identifiers for Dynamic Host Configuration Protocol Version Four (DHCPv4)," Internet RFC 4361, Feb. 2006.

[RFC4388] R. Woundy and K. Kinnear, "Dynamic Host Configuration Protocol (DHCP) Leasequery," Internet RFC 4388, Feb. 2006.

[RFC4429] N. Moore, "Optimistic Duplicate Address Detection (DAD) for IPv6," Internet RFC 4429, Apr. 2006.

[RFC4436] B. Aboba, J. Carlson, and S. Cheshire, "Detecting Network Attachment in IPv4 (DNAv4)," Internet RFC 4436, Mar. 2006.

[RFC4649] B. Volz, "Dynamic Host Configuration Protocol (DHCPv6) Relay Agent Remote-ID Option," Internet RFC 4649, Aug. 2006.

[RFC4702] M. Stapp, B. Volz, and Y. Rekhter, "The Dynamic Host Configuration Protocol (DHCP) Client Fully Qualified Domain Name (FQDN) Option," Internet RFC 4702, Oct. 2006.

[RFC4704] B. Volz, "The Dynamic Host Configuration Protocol for IPv6 (IPv6) Client Fully Qualified Domain Name (FQDN) Option," Internet RFC 4704, Oct. 2006.

[RFC4776] H. Schulzrinne, "Dynamic Host Configuration Protocol (DHCPv4 and DHCPv6) Option for Civic Addresses Configuration Information," Internet RFC 4776, Nov. 2006.

[RFC4833] E. Lear and P. Eggert, "Timezone Options for DHCP," Internet RFC 4833, Apr. 2007.

[RFC4862] S. Thomson, T. Narten, and T. Jinmei, "IPv6 Stateless Address Auto-configuration," Internet RFC 4862, Sept. 2007.

[RFC4941] T. Narten, R. Draves, and S. Krishnan, "Privacy Extensions for State-less Address Autoconfiguration in IPv6," Internet RFC 4941, Sept. 2007.

[RFC5007] J. Brzozowski, K. Kinnear, B. Volz, and S. Zeng, "DHCPv6 Lease-query," Internet RFC 5007, Sept. 2007.

[RFC5010] K. Kinnear, M. Normoyle, and M. Stapp, "The Dynamic Host Configuration Protocol Version 4 (DHCPv4) Relay Agent Flags Suboption," Internet RFC 5010, Sept. 2007.

[RFC5107] R. Johnson, J. Kumarasamy, K. Kinnear, and M. Stapp, "DHCP Server Identifier Override Suboption," Internet RFC 5107, Feb. 2008.

[RFC5175] B. Haberman, ed., and R. Hinden, "IPv6 Router Advertisement Flags Option," Internet RFC 5175, Mar. 2008.

[RFC5192] L. Morand, A. Yegin, S. Kumar, and S. Madanapalli, "DHCP Options for Protocol for Carrying Authentication for Network Access (PANA) Authentication Agents," Internet RFC 5192, May 2008.

[RFC5222] T. Hardie, A. Newton, H. Schulzrinne, and H. Tschofenig, "LoST: A Location-to-Service Translation Protocol," Internet RFC 5222, Aug. 2008.

[RFC5223] H. Schulzrinne, J. Polk, and H. Tschofenig, "Discovering Location-to-Service Translation (LoST) Servers Using the Dynamic Host Configuration Protocol (DHCP)," Internet RFC 5223, Aug. 2008.

[RFC5460] M. Stapp, "DHCPv6 Bulk Leasequery," Internet RFC 5460, Feb. 2009.

[RFC5569] R. Despres, "IPv6 Rapid Deployment on IPv4 Infrastructures (6rd)," Internet RFC 5569 (informational), Jan. 2010.

[RFC5677] T. Melia, ed., G. Bajko, S. Das, N. Golmie, and JC. Zuniga, "IEEE 802.21 Mobility Services Framework Design (MSFD)," Internet RFC 5677, Dec. 2009.

[RFC5678] G. Bajko and S. Das, "Dynamic Host Configuration Protocol (DHCPv4 and DHCPv6) Options for IEEE 802.21 Mobility Services (MoS) Discovery," Internet RFC 5678, Dec. 2009.

[RFC5735] M. Cotton and L. Vegoda, "Special-Use IPv4 Addresses," Internet RFC 5735/BCP 0153, Jan. 2010.

[RFC5969] W. Townsley and O. Troan, "IPv6 Rapid Deployment on IPv4 Infrastructures (6rd)—Protocol Specification," Internet RFC 5969, Aug. 2010.

[RFC5985] M. Barnes, ed., "HTTP-Enabled Location Delivery (HELD)," Internet RFC 5985, Sept. 2010.

[RFC5986] M. Thomson and J. Winterbottom, "Discovering the Local Location Information Server (LIS)," Internet RFC 5986, Sept. 2010.

[RFC6059] S. Krishnan and G. Daley, "Simple Procedures for Detecting Network Attachment in IPv6," Internet RFC 6059, Nov. 2010.

[RFC6106] J. Jeong, S. Park, L. Beloeil, and S. Madanapalli, "IPv6 Router Advertisement Options for DNS Configuration," Internet RFC 6106, Nov. 2010.

[RFC6148] P. Kurapati, R. Desetti, and B. Joshi, "DHCPv4 Lease Query by Relay Agent Remote ID," Internet RFC 6148, Feb. 2011.

[RFC6153] S. Das and G. Bajko, "DHCPv4 and DHCPv6 Options for Access Network Discovery and Selection Function (ANDSF) Discovery," Internet RFC 6153, Feb. 2011.

[RFC6221] D. Miles, ed., S. Ooghe, W. Dec, S. Krishnan, and A. Kavanagh, "Lightweight DHCPv6 Relay Agent," Internet RFC 6221, May 2011.

[RFC6225] J. Polk, M. Linsner, M. Thomson, and B. Aboba, ed., "Dynamic Host Configuration Protocol Options for Coordinate-Based Location Configuration Information," Internet RFC 6225, Mar. 2011.

[RFC6276] R. Droms, P. Thubert, F. Dupont, W. Haddad, and C. Bernardos, "DHCPv6 Prefix Delegation for Network Mobility (NEMO)," Internet RFC 6276, July 2011.

7

Firewalls and Network Address Translation (NAT)

7.1   Introduction

During the early years of the Internet and its protocols, most network designers and developers were from universities or other entities engaged in research. These researchers were generally friendly and cooperative, and the Internet system was not especially resilient to attack, but not many people were interested in attacking it, either. By the late 1980s and especially the early to mid-1990s the Internet had gained the interest of the mass population and ultimately people interested in compromising its security. Successful attacks became commonplace, and many problems were caused by bugs or unplanned protocol operations in the software implementations of Internet hosts. Because some sites had a large number of end systems with various versions of operating system software, it became very difficult for system administrators to ensure that all the various bugs in these end systems had been fixed. Furthermore, for obsolete systems, this task was all but impossible. Fixing the problem would have required a way to control the Internet traffic to which the end hosts were exposed. Today, this is provided by a *firewall*— a type of router that restricts the types of traffic it forwards.

As firewalls were being deployed to protect enterprises, another problem was becoming important: the number of available IPv4 addresses was diminishing, with a threat of exhaustion. Something would have to be done with the way addresses were allocated and used. One of the most important mechanisms developed to deal with this, aside from IPv6, is called *Network Address Translation* (NAT). With NAT, Internet addresses need not be globally unique, and as a consequence they can be reused in different parts of the Internet, called *address realms*. Allowing the same addresses to be reused in multiple realms greatly eased the problem of address exhaustion. As we shall see, NAT can also be synergistically combined with firewalls to produce combination devices that have become the most popular types of routers used to connect end users, including home net-works and small enterprises, to the Internet. We shall now explore both firewalls and NATs in further detail.

7.2   Firewalls

Given the enormous management problems associated with trying to keep end system software up-to-date and bug-free, the focus of resisting attacks expanded from securing end systems to restricting the Internet traffic allowed to flow to end systems by filtering out some traffic using firewalls. Today, firewalls are common, and several different types have evolved.

The two major types of firewalls commonly used include *proxy firewalls* and *packet-filtering firewalls*. The main difference between them is the layer in the pro-tocol stack at which they operate, and consequently the way IP addresses and port numbers are used. The packet-filtering firewall is an Internet router that drops datagrams that (fail to) meet specific criteria. The proxy firewall operates as a multihomed server host from the viewpoint of an Internet client. That is, it is the endpoint of TCP and UDP transport associations; it does not typically route IP datagrams at the IP protocol layer.

7.2.1   Packet-Filtering Firewalls

Packet-filtering firewalls act as Internet routers and *filter* (drop) some traffic. They can generally be configured to discard or forward packets whose headers meet (or fail to meet) certain criteria, called *filters*. Simple filters include range compari-sons on various parts of the network-layer or transport-layer headers. The most popular filters involve undesired IP addresses or options, types of ICMP mes-sages, and various UDP or TCP services, based on the port numbers contained in each packet. As we shall see, the simplest packet-filtering firewalls are stateless, whereas the more sophisticated ones are stateful. Stateless packet-filtering fire-walls treat each datagram individually, whereas stateful firewalls are able associ-ate packets with either previously observed packets or packets that arrive in the future to make inferences about datagrams or streams—either those belonging to a single transport association or those IP fragments that constitute an IP datagram (see Chapter 10). IP fragmentation can significantly complicate a firewall's job, and stateless packet-filtering firewalls are easily confused by fragments.

A typical packet-filtering firewall is shown in Figure 7-1. Here, the firewall is an Internet router with three network interfaces: an "inside," an "outside," and a third "DMZ" interface. The DMZ subnet provides access to an extranet or DMZ where servers are deployed for Internet users to access. Network administrators install filters or *access control lists* (ACLs, basically policy lists indicating what types of packets to discard or forward) in the firewall. Typically, these filters con-servatively block traffic from the outside that may be harmful and liberally allow traffic to travel from inside to outside.

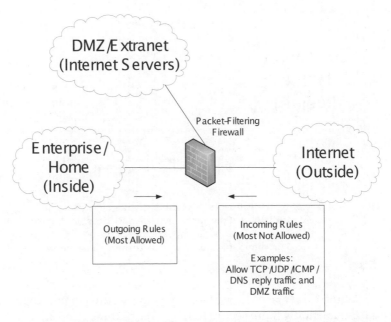

Figure 7-1   A typical packet-filtering firewall configuration. The firewall acts as an IP router between an "inside" and an "outside" network, and sometimes a third "DMZ" or extranet network, allowing only certain traffic to pass through it. A common configuration allows all traffic to pass from inside to outside but only a small subset of traffic to pass in the reverse direction. When a DMZ is used, only certain services are permitted to be accessed from the Internet.

7.2.2   Proxy Firewalls

Packet-filtering firewalls act as routers that selectively drop packets. Other types of firewalls, called *proxy firewalls*, are not really Internet routers in the true sense. Instead, they are essentially hosts running one or more *application-layer gateways* (ALGs)—hosts with more than one network interface that relay traffic of certain types between one connection/association and another at the application layer. They do not typically perform IP forwarding as routers do, although more sophisticated proxy firewalls are now available that combine various functions.

Figure 7-2 illustrates a proxy firewall. For this type of firewall, clients on the inside of the firewall are usually configured in a special way to associate (or connect) with the proxy instead of the actual end host providing the desired service. (Applications capable of operating with proxy firewalls this way include configuration options for it.) These firewalls act as multihomed hosts, and their IP forwarding capability, if present, is typically disabled. As with packet-filtering firewalls, a common configuration is to have an "outside" interface assigned a globally routable IP address and for its "inner" interface to be configured with a private IP address. Thus, proxy firewalls support the use of private address realms.

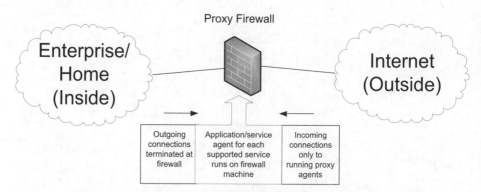

Figure 7-2   The proxy firewall acts as a multihomed Internet host, terminating TCP connections and UDP associations at the application layer. It does not act as a conventional IP router but rather as an ALG. Individual applications or proxies for each service supported must be enabled for communication to take place through the proxy firewall.

While this type of firewall can be quite secure (some people believe this type is fundamentally more secure than packet-filtering firewalls), this security comes at a cost of brittleness and lack of flexibility. In particular, because this style of firewall must contain a proxy for each transport-layer service, any new services to be used must have a corresponding proxy installed and operated for connectivity to take place through the proxy. In addition, each client must typically be configured to find the proxy (e.g., using the Web Proxy Auto-Discovery Protocol, or WPAD [XIDAD], although there are some alternatives—so-called capturing proxies that catch all traffic of a certain type regardless of destination address). With respect to deployment, these firewalls work well in environments where all types of network services being accessed are known with certainty in advance, but they may require significant intervention from network operators to support additional services.

The two most common forms of proxy firewalls are *HTTP proxy firewalls* [RFC2616] and *SOCKS firewalls* [RFC1928]. The first type, also called *Web proxies*, work only for the HTTP and HTTPS (Web) protocols, but because these protocols are so popular, such proxies are commonly used. These proxies act as Web servers for internal clients and as Web clients when accessing external Web sites. Such proxies often also operate as *Web caches*. These caches save copies of Web pages so that subsequent accesses can be served directly from the cache instead of from the originating Internet Web server. Doing so can reduce latency to display Web pages and improve the experience of users accessing the Web. Some Web proxies are also used as *content filters*, which attempt to block access to certain Web sites based on a "blacklist" of prohibited sites. Conversely, a number of so-called *tunneling proxy servers* are available on the Internet. These servers (e.g., psiphon, CGIProxy) essentially perform the opposite function—to allow users to avoid being blocked by content filters.

The SOCKS protocol is more generic than HTTP for proxy access and is applicable to more services than just the Web. Two versions of SOCKS are currently in use: version 4 and version 5. Version 4 provides the basic support for proxy traversal, and version 5 adds strong authentication, UDP traversal, and IPv6 addressing. To use a SOCKS proxy, an application must be written to use SOCKS (it must be "socksified") and configured to know about the location of the proxy and which version of SOCKS to use. Once this is accomplished, the client uses the SOCKS protocol to request the proxy to perform network connections and, optionally, DNS lookups.

7.3   Network Address Translation (NAT)

NAT is essentially a mechanism for allowing the same sets of IP addresses to be reused in different parts of the Internet. The primary motivation for the creation of NAT was the limited and diminishing availability of IP address space. The most common use case for a NAT is when a site with a single Internet connection is assigned a small range of IP addresses (perhaps only a single address), but there are multiple computers requiring Internet access. When all incoming and outgoing traffic passes through a single NAT device that partitions the inside (private) address realm from the global Internet address realm, all the internal systems can be provided Internet connectivity as clients using locally assigned, private IP addresses. Allowing privately addressed systems to offer services on the Internet, however, is somewhat more complicated. We discuss this case in Section 7.3.4.

NAT was introduced to solve two problems: address depletion and concerns regarding the scalability of routing. At the time of its introduction (early 1990s), NAT was suggested as a stopgap, temporary measure to be used until the deployment of some protocol with a larger number of addresses (ultimately, IPv6) became widespread. Routing scalability was being tackled with the development of Classless Inter-Domain Routing (CIDR; see Chapter 2). NAT is popular because it reduces the need for globally routable Internet addresses but also because it offers some degree of natural firewall capability and requires little configuration. Perhaps ironically, the development and eventual widespread use of NAT has contributed to significantly slow the adoption of IPv6. Among its other benefits, IPv6 was intended to make NAT unnecessary [RFC4864].

Despite its popularity, NAT has several drawbacks. The most obvious is that offering Internet-accessible services from the private side of a NAT requires special configuration because privately addressed systems are not directly reachable from the Internet. In addition, for a NAT to work properly, every packet in both directions of a connection or association must pass through the same NAT. This is because the NAT must actively rewrite the addressing information in each packet in order for communication between a privately addressed system and a conventionally addressed Internet host to work. In many ways, NATs run counter to a fundamental tenet of the Internet protocols: the "smart edge" and "dumb middle." To do their job, NATs require connection state on a *per-association* (or *per-connection*) basis and must operate across multiple protocol layers, unlike conventional routers. Modifying an address at the IP layer also requires modifying checksums at the transport layer (see Chapters 10 and 13 regarding the pseudo-header checksum to see why).

NAT poses problems for some application protocols, especially those that send IP addressing information inside the application-layer payload. The *File Transfer Protocol* (FTP) [RFC0959] and SIP [RFC5411] are among the best-known protocols of this type. They require a special application-layer gateway function that rewrites the application content in order to work unmodified with NAT or other NAT traversal methods that allow the applications to determine how to work with the specific NAT they are using. A more complete list of considerations regarding NAT appears in [RFC3027]. Despite their numerous problems, NATs are very widely used, and most network routers (including essentially all low-end home routers) support it. Today, NATs are so prevalent that application designers are encouraged to make their applications "NAT-friendly" [RFC3235]. It is worth mentioning that despite its shortcomings, NAT supports the basic protocols (e.g., e-mail, Web browsing) that are needed by millions of client systems accessing the Internet every day.

A NAT works by rewriting the identifying information in packets transiting through a router. Most commonly this happens for two directions of a data transfer. In its most basic form, NAT involves rewriting the source IP address of packets as they are forwarded in one direction and the destination IP addresses of packets traveling in the reverse direction (see Figure 7-3). This allows the source IP address in outgoing packets to become one of the NAT router's Internet-facing interfaces instead of the originating host's. Thus, to a host on the Internet, packets coming from any of the hosts on the privately addressed side of the NAT appear to be coming from a globally routable IP address of the NAT router.

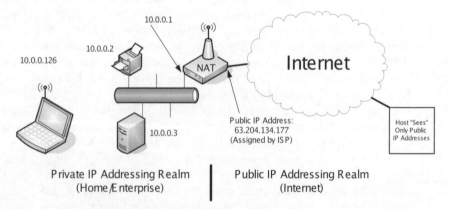

Figure 7-3   A NAT isolates private addresses and the systems using them from the Internet. Packets with private addresses are not routed by the Internet directly but instead must be translated as they enter and leave the private network through the NAT router. Internet hosts see traffic as coming from a public IP address of the NAT.

Most NATs perform both *translation* and *packet filtering*, and the packet-filtering criteria depend on the dynamics of the NAT state. The choice of packet-filtering policy may have a different granularity—for example, the treatment of unsolicited packets (those not associated with packets originating from behind the NAT) received by the NAT may depend on source and destination IP address and/or source and destination port number. The behavior may vary between NATs or in some cases vary over time through the same NAT. This presents challenges for applications that must operate behind a wide variety of NATs.

7.3.1 Traditional NAT: Basic NAT and NAPT

The precise behavior of a NAT remained unspecified for many years. Nonetheless, a taxonomy of NAT types has emerged, based largely on observing how different implementations of the NAT idea behave. The so-called *traditional NAT* includes both *basic NAT* and *Network Address Port Translation* (NAPT) [RFC3022]. Basic NAT performs rewriting of IP addresses only. In essence, a private address is rewritten to be a public address, often from a pool or range of public addresses supplied by an ISP. This type of NAT is not the most popular because it does not help to dramatically reduce the need for IP addresses—the number of globally routable addresses must equal or exceed the number of internal hosts that wish to access the Internet simultaneously. A much more popular approach, NAPT involves using the transport-layer identifiers (i.e., ports for TCP and UDP, query identifiers for ICMP) to differentiate which host on the private side of the NAT is associated with a particular packet (see Figure 7-4). This allows a large number of internal hosts (i.e., multiple thousands) to access the Internet simultaneously using a limited number of public addresses, often only a single one. We shall ordinarily use the term NAT to include both traditional NAT and NAPT unless the distinction is important in a particular context.

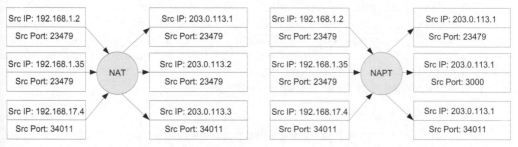

Figure 7-4   A basic IPv4 NAT (left) rewrites IP addresses from a pool of addresses and leaves port numbers unchanged. NAPT (right), also known as IP masquerading, usually rewrites address to a single address. NAPT must sometimes rewrite port numbers in order to avoid collisions. In this case, the second instance of port number 23479 was rewritten to use port number 3000 so that returning traffic for 192.168.1.2 could be distinguished from the traffic returning to 192.168.1.35.

The addresses used in a private addressing realm "behind" or "inside" a NAT are not enforced by anyone other than the local network administrator. Thus, it is possible for a private realm to make use of global address space. In principle, this is acceptable. However, when such global addresses are owned and being used by another entity on the Internet, local systems in the private realm would most likely be unable to reach the public systems using the same addresses because the close proximity of the local systems would effectively "mask" the visibility of the farther-away systems using the same addresses. To avoid this undesirable situation, there are three IPv4 address ranges reserved for use with private addressing realms [RFC1918]: 10.0.0.0/8, 172.16.0.0/12, and 192.168.0.0/16. These address ranges are often used as default values for address pools in embedded DHCP servers (see Chapter 6).

As suggested earlier, a NAT provides some degree of security similar to that of a firewall. By default, all systems on the private side of the NAT cannot be reached from the Internet. In most NAT deployments, the internal systems use private addresses. Consequently, communications between hosts in the private addressing realm and those in the public realm can be facilitated only with participation from the NAT, according to its usage policies and behavior. While a large variety of policies may be used in practice, a common policy allows almost all outgoing and returning traffic (associated with outgoing traffic) to pass through the NAT but blocks almost all incoming new connection requests. This behavior inhibits "probing" attacks that attempt to ascertain which IP addresses have active hosts available to exploit. In addition, a NAT (especially a NAPT) "hides" the number and configuration of internal addresses from the outside. Some users feel this topology information is proprietary and should remain confidential. NAT helps by providing so-called topology hiding.

As we shall now explore, NATs are tailored to the protocols and applications that they need to support, so it is difficult to discuss NAT behavior without also mentioning the particular protocol(s) it is being asked to handle. Thus, we now turn to how NAT behaves with each major transport protocol and how it may be used in mixed IPv4/IPv6 environments. Many of the behavioral specifics for NATs have been the subject of the IETF Behavior Engineering for Hindrance Avoidance (BEHAVE) working group. BEHAVE has produced a number of documents, starting in 2007, that clarify consistent behaviors for NATs. These documents are useful for application writers and NAT developers so that a consistent expectation can be established as to how NATs should operate.

7.3.1.1 NAT and TCP

Recall from Chapter 1 that the primary transport-layer protocol for the Internet, TCP, uses an IP address and port number to identify each end of a connection. A connection is identified by the combination of two ends; each unique TCP connection is identified by two IP addresses and two port numbers. When a TCP connection starts, an "active opener" or client usually sends a synchronization (SYN) packet to a "passive opener" or server. The server responds with its own

SYN packet, which also includes an acknowledgment (ACK) of the client's SYN. The client then responds with an ACK to the server. This "three-way handshake" establishes the connection. A similar exchange with finish (FIN) packets is used to gracefully close a connection. The connection can also be forcefully closed right away using a reset (RST) packet. (See Chapter 13 for more detail on TCP connections.) The behavioral requirements for traditional NAT with TCP are defined in [RFC5382] and relate primarily to the TCP three-way handshake.

Referring to the example home network in Figure 7-3, consider a TCP connection initiated by the wireless client at 10.0.0.126 destined for the Web server on the host www.isoc.org (IPv4 address 212.110.167.157). Using the following notation to indicate IPv4 addresses and port numbers—(source IP:source port; destination IP:destination port)—the packet initiating the connection on the private segment might be addressed as (10.0.0.126:9200; 212.110.167.157:80). The NAT/ firewall device, acting as the default router for the client, receives the first packet. The NAT notices that the incoming packet is a new connection (because the SYN bit in the TCP header is turned on; see Chapter 13). If policy permits (which it typically does because this is an outgoing connection), the source IP address is modified in the packet to reflect the routable IP address of the NAT router's external interface. Thus, when the NAT forwards this packet, the addressing is (63.204.134.177:9200; 212.110.167.157:80). In addition to forwarding the packet, the NAT creates internal state to remember the fact that a new connection is being handled by the NAT (called a *NAT session*). At a minimum, this state includes an entry (called a *NAT mapping*) containing the source port number and IP address of the client. This becomes useful when the Internet server replies. The server replies to the endpoint (63.204.134.177:9200), the external NAT address, using the port number chosen initially by the client. This behavior is called *port preservation*. By matching the destination port number on the received datagram against the appropriate NAT mapping, the NAT is able to ascertain the internal IP address of the client that made the initial request. In our example, this address is 10.0.0.126, so the NAT rewrites the response packet from (212.110.167.157:80; 63.204.134.177:9200) to (212.110.167.157:80; 10.0.0.126:9200) and forwards it. The client then receives a response to its request and for most purposes is now connected to the server.

This example conveys how a basic NAT session is established in the normal case, but not how the session is cleared. Session state is removed if FINs are exchanged, but not all TCP connections are cleared gracefully. Sometimes a computer is simply turned off, which can leave stale NAT mappings in the NAT's memory. Thus, a NAT must also remove mappings thought to have "gone dead" because of a lack of traffic (or if an RST segment indicates some other form of problem).

Most NATs include a simplified version of the TCP connection establishment procedures and can distinguish between connection success and failure. In particular, when an outgoing SYN segment is observed, a *connection timer* is activated, and if no ACK is seen before the timer expires, the session state is cleared. If an ACK does arrive, the timer is canceled and a *session timer* is created, with a considerably longer timeout (e.g., hours instead of minutes). When this happens, the NAT may send an additional packet to the internal endpoint, just to double-check if the session is indeed dead (called *probing*). If it receives an ACK, the NAT realizes that the connection is still active, resets the session timer, and does not delete the session. If it receives either no response (after a *close timer* has expired) or an RST segment, the connection has gone dead, and the state is cleared.

[RFC5382], a product of the BEHAVE working group, notes that a TCP connection can be configured to send "keepalive" packets (see Chapter 17), and the default rate is one packet every 2 hours, if enabled. Otherwise, a TCP connection can remain established indefinitely. While a connection is being set up or cleared, however, the maximum idle time is 4 minutes. Consequently, [RFC5382] requires (REQ-5) that a NAT wait at least 2 hours and 4 minutes before concluding that an established connection is dead and at least 4 minutes before concluding that a partially opened or closed connection is dead.

One of the tricky problems for a TCP NAT is handling peer-to-peer applications operating on hosts residing on the private sides of multiple NATs [RFC5128]. Some of these applications use a *simultaneous open* whereby each end of the connection acts as a client and sends SYN packets more or less simultaneously. TCP is able to handle this case by responding with SYN + ACK packets that complete the connection faster than with the three-way handshake, but many existing NATs do not handle it properly. [RFC5382] addresses this by requiring (REQ-2) that a NAT handle all valid TCP packet exchanges, and simultaneous opens in particular. Some peer-to-peer applications (e.g., network games) use this behavior. In addition, [RFC5382] specifies that an inbound SYN for a connection about which the NAT knows nothing should be silently discarded. This can occur when a simultaneous open is attempted but the external host's SYN arrives at the NAT before the internal host's SYN. Although this may seem unlikely, it can happen as a result of clock skew, for example. If the incoming external SYN is dropped, the internal SYN has time to establish a NAT mapping for the same connection represented by the external SYN. If no internal SYN is forthcoming in 6s, the NAT may signal an error to the external host.

7.3.1.2 NAT and UDP

The NAT behavioral requirements for unicast UDP are defined in [RFC4787]. Most of the same issues arise when performing NAT on a collection of UDP datagrams as arise when performing NAT on TCP. UDP is somewhat different, however, because there are no connection establishment and clearing procedures as there are in TCP. More specifically, there are no indicators such as the SYN, FIN, and RST bits to indicate that a session is being created or destroyed. Furthermore, the participants in an association may not be completely clear. UDP does not use a 4-tuple to identify a connection like TCP; instead, it can rely on only the two endpoint address/port number combinations. To handle these issues, UDP NATs use a *mapping timer* to clear NAT state if a binding has not been used "recently." There is considerable variation in the values used for this timer to determine what "recently" means, but [RFC4787] requires the timer to be at least 2 minutes and recommends that it be 5 minutes. A related consideration is when the timer should be considered refreshed. Timers can be refreshed when packets travel from the inside to the outside of the NAT (NAT outbound refresh behavior) or vice versa (NAT inbound refresh behavior). [RFC4787] requires NAT outbound refresh behavior to be true. Inbound behavior may or may not be true.

As we discussed in Chapter 5 (and will see again in Chapter 10), UDP and IP packets can be fragmented. Fragmentation allows for a single IP packet to span multiple chunks (fragments), each of which is treated as an independent datagram. However, because of the layering of UDP above IP, an IP fragment other than the first one does not contain the port number information needed by NAPT to operate properly. This also applies to TCP and ICMP. Thus, in general, fragments cannot be handled properly by simple NATs or NAPTs.

7.3.1.3 NAT and Other Transport Protocols (DCCP, SCTP)

Although TCP and UDP are by far the most widely used Internet transport protocols, there are two other protocols for which NAT behaviors have been defined or are being defined. The *Datagram Congestion Control Protocol* (DCCP) [RFC4340] provides a congestion-controlled datagram service. [RFC5597] gives NAT behavioral requirements with respect to DCCP, and [RFC5596] gives a modification to DCCP to support a TCP-like simultaneous open procedure for use with DCCP. The *Stream Control Transmission Protocol* (SCTP) [RFC4960] provides a reliable messaging service that can accommodate hosts with multiple addresses. Considerations for NAT with SCTP are given in [HBA09] and [IDSNAT].

7.3.1.4 NAT and ICMP

ICMP, the Internet Control Message Protocol, is detailed in Chapter 8. It provides status information about IP packets and can also be used for making certain measurements and gathering information about the state of the network. The NAT behavioral requirements for ICMP are defined in [RFC5508]. There are two issues involved when NAT is used for ICMP. ICMP has two categories of messages: informational and error. Error messages generally contain a (partial or full) copy of the IP packet that induced the error condition. They are sent from the point where an error was detected, often in the middle of the network, to the original sender. Ordinarily, this presents no difficulty, but when an ICMP error message passes through a NAT, the IP addresses in the included "offending datagram" need to be rewritten by the NAT in order for them to make sense to the end client (called *ICMP fix-up*). For informational messages, the same issues arise, but in this case most message types are of a query/response or client/server nature and include a *Query ID* field that is handled much like port numbers for TCP or UDP. Thus, a NAT handling these types of messages can recognize outgoing informational requests and set a timer in anticipation of a returning response.

7.3.1.5 NAT and Tunneled Packets

In some cases, tunneled packets (see Chapter 3) are to be sent through a NAT. When this happens, not only must a NAT rewrite the IP header, but it may also have to rewrite the headers or payloads of other packets that are encapsulated in them. One example of this is the Generic Routing Encapsulation (GRE) header used with the Point-to-Point Tunneling Protocol (PPTP; see Chapter 3). When the GRE header is passed through a NAT, its *Call-ID* field could conflict with the NAT's (or with other hosts' tunneled connections). If the NAT fails to handle this mapping appropriately, communication is not possible. As we might imagine, additional levels of encapsulation serve only to complicate a NAT's job further.

7.3.1.6 NAT and Multicast

So far we have discussed only unicast IP traffic with NATs. NATs can be configured to support multicast traffic (see Chapter 9), although this is rare. [RFC5135] gives the requirements for handling multicast traffic through NATs. In effect, to support multicast traffic a NAT is augmented with an IGMP proxy (see [RFC4605] and Chapter 9). In addition, the destination IP addresses and port numbers of packets traveling from a host on the outside to the inside of NAT are *not* modified. For traffic flowing from inside to outside, the source addresses and port numbers may be modified according to the same behaviors as with unicast UDP.

7.3.1.7 NAT and IPv6

Given the tremendous popularity of NAT for IPv4, it is natural to wonder whether NAT will be used with IPv6. At present, this is a contentious issue [RFC5902]. To many protocol designers, NAT arose as a necessary but undesirable "wart" that has added a tremendous amount of complexity to the design of every other protocol. Consequently, there is staunch resistance to supporting the use of NAT with IPv6 based on the idea that saving address space is unnecessary with IPv6 and that other desirable NAT features (e.g., firewall-like functionality, topology hiding, and privacy) can be better achieved using *Local Network Protection* (LNP) [RFC4864]. LNP represents a collection of techniques with IPv6 that match or exceed the properties of NATs.

Aside from its packet-filtering properties, NAT supports the coexistence of multiple address realms and thereby helps to avoid the problem of a site having to change its IP addresses when it switches ISPs. For example, [RFC4193] defines *Unique Local IPv6 Unicast Addresses* (ULAs) that could conceivably be used with an experimental version of IPv6-to-IPv6 prefix translation called *NPTv6* [RFC6296]. It uses an algorithm instead of a table to translate IPv6 addresses to (different) IPv6 addresses (e.g., in different realms) based on their prefix and as a result does not require keeping per-connection state as with conventional NAT. In addition, the algorithm modifies addresses in such a way that the resulting checksum computation for common transport protocols (TCP, UDP) remains the same. This significantly reduces the complexity of NAT because it does not have to modify the data in a packet beyond the network layer and does not require access to transport layer port numbers in order to operate properly. However, applications that require access to a NAT's external address must still use a NAT traversal method or depend on an ALG. In addition, NPTv6 does not by itself offer the packet-filtering capabilities of a firewall, so additional deployment considerations must be made.

7.3.2   Address and Port Translation Behavior

There has been considerable variation in the way NATs operate. Most of the details relate to the specifics of the address and port mappings. One of the primary goals of the BEHAVE working group in IETF was to clarify the common behaviors and set guidelines as to which are the most appropriate. To better understand the issues involved, we begin with a generic NAT mapping example (see Figure 7-5).

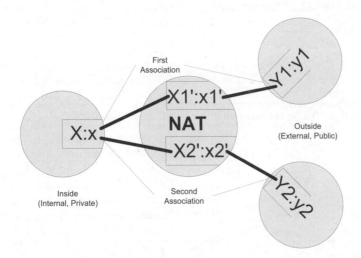

Figure 7-5   A NAT's address and port behavior is characterized by what its mappings depend on. The inside host uses IP address:port $X:x$ to contact $Y1:y1$ and then $Y2:y2$. The address and port used by the NAT for these associations are $X1':x1'$ and $X2':x2'$, respectively. If $X1':x1'$ equals $X2':x2'$ for any $Y1:y1$ or $Y2:y2$, the NAT has endpoint-independent mappings. If $X1':x1'$ equals $X2':x2'$ if and only if $Y1$ equals $Y2$, the NAT has address-dependent mappings. If $X1':x1'$ equals $X2':x2'$ if and only if $Y1:y1$ equals $Y2:y2$, the NAT has address- and port-dependent mappings. A NAT with multiple external addresses (i.e., where $X1'$ may not equal $X2'$) has an address pooling behavior of arbitrary if the outside address is chosen without regard to inside or outside address. Alternatively, it may have a pooling behavior of paired, in which case the same $X1$ is used for any association with $Y1$.

In Figure 7-5, we use the notation $X:x$ to indicate that a host in the private addressing realm (inside host) uses IP address X with port number x (for ICMP, the query ID is used instead of the port number). The IP address X is ordinarily chosen from the private IPv4 address space defined in [RFC1918]. To reach the remote address/port combination $Y:y$, the NAT establishes a mapping using an external (usually a public, globally routable) address $X1'$ and port number $x1'$. Assuming that the internal host contacts $Y1:y1$ followed by $Y2:y2$, the NAT establishes mappings $X1':x1'$ and $X2':x2'$, respectively. In most cases, $X1'$ equals $X2'$ because most sites use only a single globally routable IP address. The mapping is said to be *reused* if $x1'$ equals $x2'$. If $x1'$ and $x2'$ equal x, the NAT implements port preservation, mentioned earlier. In some cases, port preservation is not possible, so the NAT must deal with port collisions as suggested by Figure 7-4.

Table 7-1 and Figure 7-5 summarize the various NAT port and address behaviors based on definitions from [RFC4787]. Table 7-1 also gives filtering behaviors that use similar terminology and that we discuss in Section 7.3.3. For all common transports, including TCP and UDP, the required NAT address- and port-handling behavior is endpoint-independent (a similar behavior is recommended for ICMP). The purpose of this requirement is to help applications that attempt to determine the external addresses used for their traffic to work more reliably. We discuss this in more detail in Section 7.4 when we discuss NAT traversal.

Table 7-1   A NAT's overall behavior is defined by both its translation and filtering behaviors. Each of these may be independent of host address, dependent on address, or dependent on both address and port number.

Behavior Name	Translation Behavior	Filtering Behavior
Endpoint-independent	$X1':x1' = X2':x2'$ for all $Y2:y2$ (required)	Allows any packets for $X1:x1$ as long as any $X1':x1'$ exists (recommended for greatest transparency)
Address-dependent	$X1':x1' = X2':x2'$ iff $Y1 = Y2$	Allows packets for $X1:x1$ from $Y1:y1$ as long as $X1$ has previously contacted $Y1$ (recommended for more stringent filtering)
Address- and port-dependent	$X1':x1' = X2':x2'$ iff $Y1:y1 = Y2:y2$	Allows packets for $X1:x1$ from $Y1:y1$ as long as $X1$ has previously contacted $Y1:y1$

As stated previously, a NAT may have several external addresses available to use. The set of addresses is typically called the *NAT pool* or *NAT address pool*. Most moderate to large-scale NATs use address pools. Note that NAT address pools are distinct from the DHCP address pools discussed in Chapter 6, although a single device may need to handle both NAT and DHCP address pools. One question in such environments is that when a single host behind the NAT opens multiple simultaneous connections, is each assigned the same external IP address (called address *pairing*) or not? A NAT's *IP address pooling behavior* is said to be *arbitrary* if there is no restriction on which external address is used for any association. It is said to be *paired* if it implements address pairing. Pairing is the recommended NAT behavior for all transports. If pairing is not used, the communication peer of an internal host may erroneously conclude that it is communicating with different hosts. For NATs with only a single external address, this is obviously not a problem.

A very brittle type of NAT overloads not only addresses but also ports (called *port overloading*). In this case, the traffic of multiple internal hosts may be rewritten to the same external IP address *and port number*. This is a dangerous prospect because if multiple hosts associate with a service on the same external host, it is no longer possible to determine the appropriate destination for traffic returning from the external host. For TCP, this is a consequence of all four elements of the connection identifier (source and destination address and port numbers) being identical in the external network among the various connections. Such behavior is now disallowed.

Some NATs implement a special feature called *port parity*. Such NATs attempt to preserve the "parity" (evenness or oddness) of port numbers. Thus, if $x1$ is even, $x1'$ is even and vice versa. Although not as strong as port preservation, such behavior is sometimes useful for specific application protocols that use special port numberings (e.g., the *Real-Time Protocol*, abbreviated RTP, has traditionally used multiple ports, but there are proposed methods for avoiding this issue [RFC5761]). Port parity preservation is a recommended NAT feature but not a requirement. It is also expected to become less important over time as more sophisticated NAT traversal methods become widespread.

7.3.3 Filtering Behavior

When a NAT creates a binding for a TCP connection, UDP association, or various forms of ICMP traffic, not only does it establish the address and port mappings, but it must also determine its filtering behavior for the returning traffic if it acts as a firewall, which is the common case. The type of filtering a NAT performs, although logically distinct from its address- and port-handling behavior, is often related. In particular, the same terminology is used: endpoint-independent, address-dependent, and address- and port-dependent.

A NAT's filtering behavior is usually related to whether it has established an address mapping. Clearly, a NAT lacking any form of address mapping is unable to forward any traffic it receives from the outside to the inside because it would not know which internal destination to use. For the most common case of outgoing traffic, when a binding is established, filtering is disabled for relevant return traffic. For NATs with endpoint-independent behavior, as soon as any mapping is established for an internal host, any incoming traffic is permitted, regardless of source. For address-dependent filtering behavior, traffic destined for $X1{:}x1$ is permitted from $Y1{:}y1$ only if $Y1$ had been previously contacted by $X1{:}x1$. For those NATs with address- and port-dependent filtering behavior, traffic destined for $X1{:}x1$ is permitted from $Y1{:}y1$ only if $Y1{:}y1$ had been previously contacted by $X1{:}x1$. The difference between the last two is that the last form takes the port number $y1$ into account.

7.3.4   Servers behind NATs

One of the most obvious problems with NATs is that a system wishing to provide a service from behind a NAT is not directly reachable from the outside. Consider the example in Figure 7-3 once again. If the host with address 10.0.0.3 is to provide a service to the Internet, it cannot be reached without participation from the NAT, for at least two reasons. First, the NAT is acting as the Internet router, so it must agree to forward the incoming traffic destined for 10.0.0.3. Second, and more important, the IP address 10.0.0.3 is not routable through the Internet and cannot be used to identify the server by hosts in the Internet. Instead, the external address of the NAT must be used to find the server, and the NAT must arrange to properly rewrite and forward the appropriate traffic to the server so that it can operate. This process is most often called *port forwarding* or *port mapping*.

With port forwarding, incoming traffic to a NAT is forwarded to a specific configured destination behind the NAT. By employing NAT with port forwarding, it is possible to allow servers to provide services to the Internet even though they may be assigned private, nonroutable addresses. Port forwarding typically requires static configuration of the NAT with the address of the server and the associated port number whose traffic should be forwarded. The port forwarding directive acts like an always-present static NAT mapping. If the server's IP address is changed, the NAT must be updated with the new addressing information. Port forwarding also has the limitation that it has only one set of port numbers for each of its (IP address, transport protocol) combinations. Thus, if the NAT has only a single external IP address, it can forward only a single port of the same transport protocol to at most one internal machine (e.g., it could not support two independent Web servers on the inside being remotely accessible using TCP port 80 from the outside).

7.3.5   Hairpinning and NAT Loopback

An interesting issue arises when a client wishes to reach a server and both reside on the same, private side of the same NAT. NATs that support this scenario implement so-called *hairpinning* or *NAT loopback*. Referring to Figure 7-6, assume that host $X1$ attempts to establish a connection to host $X2$. If $X1$ knows the private addressing information, $X2{:}x2$, there is no problem because the connection can be made directly. However, in some cases $X1$ knows only the public address information, $X2'{:}x2'$. In these cases, $X1$ attempts to contact $X2$ using the NAT with destination $X2'{:}x2'$. The hairpinning process takes place when the NAT notices the existence of the mapping between $X2'{:}x2'$ and $X2{:}x2$ and forwards the packet to $X2{:}x2$ residing on the private side of the NAT. At this point a question arises as to which source address is contained in the packet heading to $X2{:}x2$—$X1{:}x1$ or $X1'{:}x1'$?

If the NAT presents the hairpinned packet to $X2$ with source addressing information $X1'{:}x1'$, the NAT is said to have "external source IP address and port" hairpinning behavior. This behavior is required for TCP NAT [RFC5382]. The

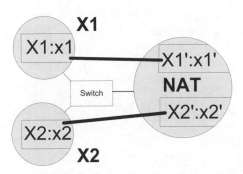

Figure 7-6   A NAT that implements hairpinning or NAT loopback allows a client to reach a server on the same side of the NAT using the server's external IP address and port numbers. That is, *X1* can reach *X2:x2* using the addressing information *X2':x2'*.

justification for requiring this behavior is for applications that identify their peers using globally routable addresses. In our example, *X2* may be expecting an incoming connection from *X1'* (e.g., because of coordination from a third-party system).

7.3.6   NAT Editors

Together, packets using the UDP and TCP transport protocols account for most of the IP traffic carried on the Internet. These transport protocols, by themselves, can be supported by NAT without additional complexity because their formats are well understood. When application-layer protocols used in conjunction with them carry transport-layer or lower-layer information such as IP addresses, the NAT problem becomes considerably more complicated. The most common example is FTP [RFC0959]. In normal operation, it communicates transport- and network-layer endpoint information (an IP address and port number) so that additional connections can be made when bulk data is to be transferred. This requires a NAT to rewrite not only the IP addresses and port numbers in the IP and TCP portions of a datagram, but also some of the application payload itself. NATs with this capability are sometimes called *NAT editors*. If a NAT changes the size of a packet's application payload, considerable work may be required. For example, TCP numbers every byte in the data transfer using sequence numbers (see Chapter 15), so if the size of a packet is changed, the sequence numbers also require modification. PPTP [RFC2637] also requires a NAT editor for transparent operation (see Chapter 3).

7.3.7   Service Provider NAT (SPNAT) and Service Provider IPv6 Transition

A relatively recent development involves the idea of moving NATs from the customer premises into the ISP. This is sometimes called *service provider NAT* (SPNAT), *carrier-grade NAT* (CGN), or *large-scale NAT* (LSN) and is intended to further mitigate the IPv4 address depletion problem. With SPNAT, it is conceivable that many ISP customers could share a single global IPv4 address. In effect, this moves the point of aggregation from the edge of the customer to the edge of the ISP. In its basic form, there is no functional difference between conventional NAT and SPNAT; the difference is really in the proposed domain of use. However, moving the NAT function from customer to ISP raises security concerns and brings into question whether individual end users are able to deploy Internet servers and control firewall policy [MBCB08]. A study from 2009 found that a significant number of users accept incoming connections, largely because of peer-to-peer programs [ANM09].

SPNAT can help with the IPv4 address depletion problem, but IPv6 is viewed as the ultimate solution. For a number of reasons already discussed, however, IPv6 deployment has lagged expectations. Originally, a scheme known as dual-stack (see [RFC4213]), whereby each system uses both IPv6 and IPv4 addresses, was intended to support transition to IPv6, but this approach was anticipated to be temporary and rendered unnecessary long before the depletion of IPv4 addresses. An arguably more pragmatic approach is now being undertaken that combines tunneling, address translation, and dual-stack systems in various configurations. We'll discuss some of these in Section 7.6 after exploring the methods that have been developed for dealing with existing NATs.

7.4   NAT Traversal

As an alternative to the complexity of placing ALGs and NAT editors in NAT devices, an application may attempt to perform its own *NAT traversal*. Usually this involves the application trying to ascertain the external IP address and port numbers that will be used when its traffic passes through a NAT and modifying its protocol operations accordingly. If an application is distributed across the network (e.g., has multiple clients and servers, some of which are not behind NATs), the servers can be used to shuttle (copy) data between the clients that connect from behind NATs or enable such clients to discover each other's NAT bindings and possibly facilitate direct communication. Using a server to copy data between clients is usually a last-resort option because of the overheads involved and potential for abuse. Consequently, most approaches attempt to provide for some method that allows direct communication.

Direct methods have been popular for peer-to-peer file sharing, games, and communication applications. However, such techniques are often confined to a particular application, meaning that each new distributed application requiring NAT traversal tends to implement its own method(s). This can lead to redundancy and interoperability problems, ultimately increasing users' frustration and cost. To combat this situation, a standard approach for handling NAT traversal has been established, and it depends on a collection of several distinct, subordinate protocols that we discuss in the following sections. For now, we begin with one of the more robust yet nonstandard approaches used by distributed applications. We then move on to standardized frameworks for NAT traversal.

7.4.1   Pinholes and Hole Punching

As discussed previously, a NAT typically includes both traffic rewriting and filtering capabilities. When a NAT mapping is established, traffic for a particular application is usually permitted to traverse the NAT in both directions. Such mappings are narrow; they usually apply only to a single application for its duration of execution. These types of mappings are called *pinholes*, because they are designed to permit only a certain temporary traffic flow (e.g., a pair of IP address and port number combinations). Pinholes are usually established and removed dynamically as a consequence of communication between programs.

A method that attempts to allow two or more systems, each behind a NAT, to communicate directly using pinholes is called *hole punching*. It is described for UDP in Section 3.3 of [RFC5128] and for TCP in Section 3.4. To punch a hole, a client contacts a known server using an outgoing connection that establishes a mapping in its local NAT. When another client contacts the same server, the server has connections to each of the clients and knows their external addressing information. It then exchanges the client external addressing information between the clients. Once this information is known, a client can attempt a direct connection to the other client(s). The popular Skype peer-to-peer application uses this approach (and some others).

Referring to Figure 7-7, assume client A contacts server S1 followed by client B. S1 will have learned A's and B's external addressing information: IPv4 addresses 192.0.2.201 and 203.0.113.100, respectively. By sending B's information to A and vice versa, A can attempt to contact B directly at its external address (and vice versa). Whether this will work depends on the type of NATs that have been deployed. NAT state for the (A,S1) connection lives in N1 and NAT state for (B,S1) lives in both N2 and N3. If all NATs are endpoint-independent, this is sufficient for direct connections to be possible. Any other type of NAT will not accept traffic from other than S1 and will thus prohibit direct communication. Said another way, this approach fails if both hosts are behind NATs with address-dependent or address- and port-dependent mapping behavior.

7.4.2   UNilateral Self-Address Fixing (UNSAF)

Applications employ a number of methods to determine the addresses their traffic will use when passed through a NAT. This is called *fixing* (learning and maintaining) the addressing information. There are indirect and direct methods for address fixing. The indirect methods involve inferring a NATs behavior by exchanging traffic through the NAT. The direct methods involve a direct conversation between the application and the NAT itself using one or more special protocols (that are not currently IETF standards). Considerable effort within IETF has gone into development of the indirect methods, and they are widely supported in certain applications, with VoIP applications being the most popular. Some of the direct methods are now supported by some NATs. These methods also provide for

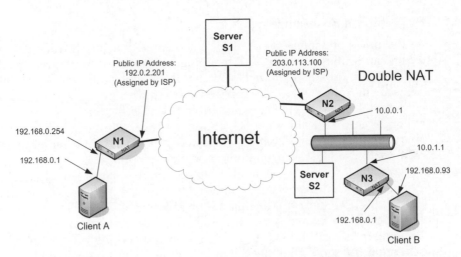

Figure 7-7   Applications running on clients behind a NAT may require help from a server to engage in direct communication. In hole punching, a server, often specialized for a specific application, provides rendezvous information among clients that first establish NAT state and then perform direct communication, if possible. Some applications attempt to "fix" (determine and maintain) the addresses (and port numbers) their traffic will be assigned when passing through a NAT using standard generic protocols. These methods may encounter troubles in certain situations such as environments with multiple levels of NAT. In this example, client A's external address visible at S1 is 192.0.2.201 and client B's is 203.0.113.100. At S2, however, B's external address is 10.0.1.1.

basic configuration of NATs, so we discuss them later in the context of NAT setup and configuration.

An application attempting to fix its address without help from the NAT performs the address fixing in a so-called unilateral fashion. Applications that do so are said to perform *UNilateral Self-Address Fixing* (UNSAF) [RFC3424]. As the name suggests, such methods are considered to be undesirable in the long run but a necessary evil for the time being. UNSAF involves a set of heuristics and is not guaranteed to work in all cases, especially because NAT behaviors vary significantly based on vendor and particular circumstance. The BEHAVE documents mentioned earlier are aimed at specifying more consistent NAT behavior. If widely adopted, UNSAF methods will work more reliably.

In most cases of interest, UNSAF methods operate in a client/server fashion similar to hole punching, but with added generality. Figure 7-7 illustrates some of the hazards that can arise in this situation. One issue is the lack of a single "outside" address realm for every NAT. In this example, there are two levels of NAT between client B and server S1. This situation can cause complications. For example, if an application on B wishes to obtain its "outside" address by using UNSAF with a server, it receives different answers depending on whether it contacts server S1 or S2. Finally, because UNSAF uses servers that are distinct from the NATs, there is always the possibility that the NAT behavior reported will change over time or become inconsistent with what the UNSAF approach reports.

Given the various problems with NATs and UNSAF, the IAB, an elected group of architectural advisers within the IETF, has indicated that UNSAF protocol proposals must include responses to the concerns in their specifications:

1. Define a limited-scope problem that the "short-term" UNSAF proposal addresses.

2. Define an exit strategy/transition plan.

3. Discuss what design decisions make the approach "brittle."

4. Identify requirements for longer-term, sound technical solutions.

5. Discuss any noted practical issues or experiences known.

This is an unusual list of requirements imposed on a protocol specification, but it results from long-standing interoperability problems between different NATs and NAT traversal techniques. Despite all the aforementioned problems, UNSAF methods are commonly used, partly because a wide range of NATs are found in operation today with little consistent behavior. We now look at how these methods are used as building blocks to form robust, general-purpose NAT traversal techniques to maximize the chances that communication among systems behind NATs, even between systems across multiple NATs such as the one illustrated in Figure 7-7, will be possible.

7.4.3   Session Traversal Utilities for NAT (STUN)

One of the primary workhorses for UNSAF and NAT traversal is called *Session Traversal Utilities for NAT* (STUN) [RFC5389]. STUN has evolved from a previous version called *Simple Tunneling of UDP through NATs*, now known as "classic STUN." Classic STUN has been used with VoIP/SIP applications for some time but has been revised to be a tool that can be used by other protocols for performing NAT traversal. Applications requiring a complete solution for NAT traversal are recommended to begin with other mechanisms we discuss in Section 7.4.5 (e.g., ICE and SIP-Outbound). These frameworks may make use of STUN in one or more particular ways called STUN *usages*. Usages may extend the set of basic STUN operations, message types, or error codes defined in [RFC5389].

STUN is a relatively simple client/server protocol that is able to ascertain the external IP address and port numbers being used on a NAT in most circumstances. It can also keep NAT bindings current by using keepalive messages. It requires a cooperating server on the "other" side of a NAT to be effective, and several public STUN servers are configured with globally reachable IP addresses and are available for use on the Internet. The main job of a STUN server is to echo back STUN requests sent to it in a way that allows the client addressing information to be fixed. As with UNSAF methods in general, the approach is not foolproof. However, the attraction of STUN is that it does not require modification of network routers, application protocols, or servers. It requires only that clients implement the STUN request protocol, and that at least one STUN server be available in an appropriate location. STUN was envisioned as a "temporary" measure (as were many standard protocols now in widespread use a decade or more after their creation) until a more sophisticated direct protocol was developed and implemented, or NATs became obsolete because of the adoption of IPv6.

STUN operates using UDP, TCP, or TCP with *Transport Layer Security* (TLS; see Chapter 18). STUN usage specifications define which transport protocols are supported for the particular usage. It uses port 3478 for UDP and TCP, and 3479 for TCP/TLS. The STUN base protocol has two types of transactions: *request/response transactions* and *indication transactions*. Indications do not require a response and can be generated by either the client or the server. All messages include a type, length, magic cookie with value 0x2112A442, and a random 96-bit transaction ID used for matching requests with responses or for debugging. Each message begins with two 0 bits and may contain zero or more *attributes*. STUN message types are defined in the context of *methods* that support a particular STUN usage. The various STUN parameters, including method and attribute numbers, are maintained by the IANA [ISP]. Attributes have their own types and can vary in length. The basic STUN header, most often located immediately following a UDP transport header in an IP packet, is shown in Figure 7-8.

The basic STUN header is 20 bytes in length (see Figure 7-8), and the *Message Length* field provides for an entire STUN message length of $2^{16} - 1$ bytes (the 20-byte header length is not included in the *Message Length* field), although messages are always padded to a multiple of 4 bytes so this field always has its 2 low-order bits set to 0. STUN messages sent over UDP/IP are supposed to form IP datagrams less than the path MTU, if known, to avoid fragmentation (see Chapter 10). If not known, the entire datagram length (including IP and UDP headers and any options) should be less than 576 bytes (IPv4) or 1280 bytes (IPv6). STUN has no provision for cases where a response might exceed the path MTU in the reverse direction, so servers should arrange to use messages of appropriate size.

STUN messages carried over UDP/IP are not reliable, so STUN applications are required to implement their own reliability. This is accomplished by resending messages thought to be lost. The retransmission interval is based on the estimated time to send and receive a message from the peer called the *round-trip time* (RTT). RTT computation and setting retransmission timers will be a major consideration when we discuss TCP (see Chapter 14). STUN uses a similar approach, but with minor modifications to the standard TCP values. See [RFC5389] for more details. Reliability issues for STUN over TCP/IP or TCP-with-TLS/IP are handled by TCP. Multiple pending STUN transactions can be supported over TCP-based connections.

STUN attributes are encoded in a TLV arrangement, a technique used by several other Internet protocols. The type and length portions of a TLV are each 16

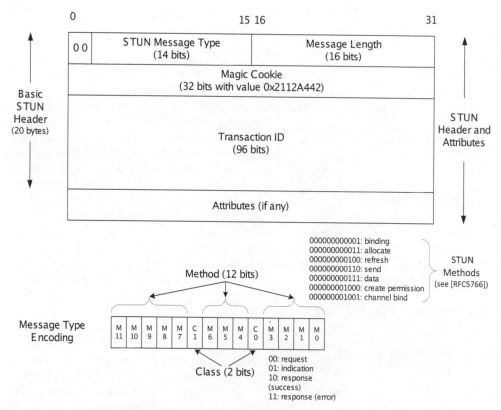

Figure 7-8 STUN messages always begin with two 0 bits and are usually encapsulated in UDP, although TCP is also allowed. The *Message Type* field gives both the method (e.g., binding) as well as class (request, response, error, or success). The *Transaction ID* is a random 96-bit number used to match requests with responses, or for debugging in the case of indications. Each STUN message can hold zero or more attributes, depending on the particular usage of STUN.

bits, and the value portion is variable-length (up to 64KB, if supported), but padded to the next multiple of 4 bytes (padding bits may be any value). The same attribute type may appear more than once in the same STUN message, although only the first is necessarily processed by a receiver. Attributes with type numbers below 0x8000 are called *comprehension-required* attributes, and the others are called *comprehension-optional* attributes. If a STUN agent receives a message containing comprehension-required attributes it does not know how to process, it generates an error. Most of the attributes defined to date are comprehension-required [ISP].

[RFC5389] defines a single STUN method called *binding*, which can be used in either request/response or indication transactions for address fixing and keeping NAT bindings current. It also defines 11 attributes, given in Table 7-2.

Table 7-2   STUN, defined in [RFC5389] and sometimes called STUN2, replaces classic STUN. These 11 attributes may be used by a STUN2-compliant client or server.

Name	Value	Purpose/Use
MAPPED-ADDRESS	0x0001	Contains an address family indicator and the reflexive transport address (IPv4 or IPv6)
USERNAME	0x0006	User name and password; used for message integrity checks (up to 513 bytes)
MESSAGE-INTEGRITY	0x0008	Message authentication code value on the STUN message (see Chapter 18 and [RFC5389])
ERROR-CODE	0x0009	Contains 3-bit error class, 8-bit error code value, and variable-length textual description of error
UNKNOWN-ATTRIBUTES	0x000A	Used with error messages to indicate the unknown attributes (one 16-bit value per attribute)
REALM	0x0014	Indicates the authentication "realm" name for long-term credentials
NONCE	0x0015	Nonrepeated value optionally carried in requests and responses (see Chapter 18) to prevent replay attacks
XOR-MAPPED-ADDRESS	0x0020	XORed version of MAPPED-ADDRESS
SOFTWARE	0x8022	Textual description of the software that sent the message (e.g., manufacturer and version number)
ALTERNATE-SERVER	0x8023	Provides an alternate IP address for a client to use; encoded as with MAPPED-ADDRESS
FINGERPRINT	0x8028	CRC-32 of message XORed with 0x5354554E; must be last attribute if used (optional)

Referring to Figure 7-5, a STUN client with addressing information $X:x$ is often interested in determining $X1':x1'$, called the *reflexive transport address* or *mapped address*. A STUN server at $Y1:y1$ includes the reflexive transport address in a MAPPED-ADDRESS attribute in a STUN message returned to the client. The MAPPED-ADDRESS attribute holds an 8-bit *Address Family* field, a 16-bit *Port Number* field, and either a 32-bit or 128-bit *Address* field, depending on whether IPv4 or IPv6 is indicated by the *Address Family* field (0x01 for IPv4; 0x02 for IPv6). This attribute is included to remain backward-compatible with classic STUN. The more important attribute is the XOR-MAPPED-ADDRESS attribute, which holds exactly the same value as the MAPPED-ADDRESS attribute, but XORed with the magic cookie value (for IPv4) or a concatenation with the magic cookie and transaction ID values (for IPv6). The reason for using XORed values in this way is to detect and bypass generic ALGs that look through packets and rewrite whatever IP addresses they find. Such ALGs are very brittle because they may rewrite information that protocols such as STUN require. Experience has shown that XORing IP addresses in the packet payload is usually sufficient to bypass such ALGs.

A STUN client, including most VoIP devices and "softphone" applications such as pjsua [PJSUA], is initially configured with the IP address(es) or names of one or more STUN servers. It is desirable to use STUN servers that are likely to "see" the same IP addresses as the peer to which the application ultimately wishes to talk, although that may be difficult to determine. Using STUN servers located on the public Internet (e.g., `stun.ekiga.net`, `stun.xten.com`, `numb.viagenie.ca`) is usually adequate. Some servers may be discovered using DNS Service (SRV) records (see Chapter 11). An example STUN binding request is given in Figure 7-9.

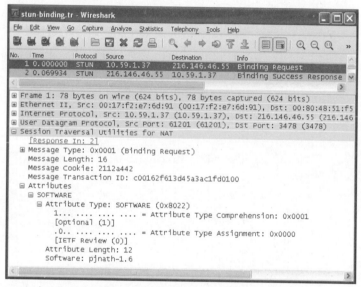

Figure 7-9   A STUN binding request. The request contains a 96-bit transaction ID and the SOFT-WARE attribute that identifies the client making the request. The attribute contains 10 characters, but this value is rounded up to the next multiple of 4, giving an attribute value of 12. The message length of 16 also includes the 4 bytes used to include the attribute's type and length (the STUN header is not included).

The sample STUN binding request in Figure 7-9 is initiated from a client. The transaction ID has been selected randomly, and the request is sent to numb .viagenie.ca (with IPv4 addresses 216.146.46.55 and 216.146.46.59), which is both a STUN and a TURN server (see Section 7.4.4). The request contains the SOFTWARE attribute that identifies the client application. In this case, the request was initiated by `pjnath-1.6`. This is the "PJSIP NAT helper" application included with pjsua. The message length includes 4 bytes for the attribute type and length, plus 12 bytes used to hold the attribute. The length of `pjnath-1.6` is only 10 bytes, but attribute lengths are always rounded up to the nearest 4-byte multiple. After passing through a NAT, the response is given as shown in Figure 7-10.

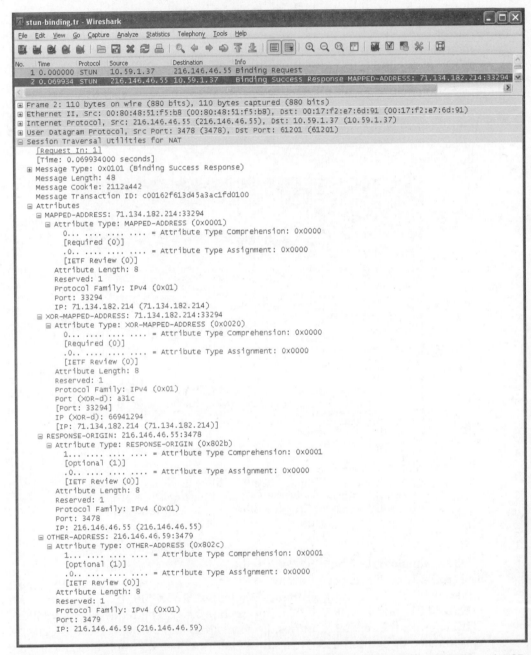

Figure 7-10 A STUN binding response containing four attributes. The MAPPED-ADDRESS and XOR-MAPPED-ADDRESS attributes contain the server-reflexive addressing information. The other attributes are used with an experimental NAT behavior discovery mechanism [RFC5780].

The binding response shown in Figure 7-10 gives useful information to the client, encoded as a collection of attributes. The MAPPED-ADDRESS and XOR-MAPPED address attributes indicate that the STUN server determined the server-reflexive address of 71.134.182.214:33294. The RESPONSE-ORIGIN and OTHER-ADDRESS attributes are used by an experimental facility for discovering NAT behavior [RFC5780]. The first gives the communication endpoint used to send the STUN message (216.146.46.55:3478, which matches the sending IPv4 address and UDP port number). The second attribute indicates which source IPv4 address and port number (216.146.45.59:3479) would have been used if the client requested "change address" or "change port" behavior. This latter attribute is equivalent to the now-deprecated CHANGED-ADDRESS attribute in classic STUN. If a change address or port is specified in a request, a cooperating STUN server attempts to use a different address when responding to the client, if possible.

STUN can be used to perform address fixing as well as a number of other functions called *mechanisms*, including DNS discovery, a method to redirect to an alternate server, and message integrity exchanges. Mechanisms are selected in the context of a particular STUN usage, so in general they are considered optional STUN features. One of the more important mechanisms provides authentication and message integrity. It has two forms: the *short-term credential mechanism* and the *long-term credential mechanism*.

Short-term credentials are intended to last for a single session; the particular duration is defined by the STUN usage. Long-term credentials last across sessions; they correspond to a login ID or account. Short-term credentials are often used in particular message exchanges, and long-term credentials are used when some particular resource is to be allocated (e.g., with TURN; see Section 7.4.4). Passwords are never sent in the clear where they could be intercepted.

The short-term credential mechanism uses the USERNAME and MESSAGE-INTEGRITY attributes. Both are required on any request. The USERNAME gives an indication of which credentials are required and allows the message sender to use the appropriate shared password in forming an integrity check on the message (a MAC computed on the message contents; see Chapter 18). When using short-term credentials, it is assumed that some form of credential information (e.g., user name and password) has been exchanged earlier. The credential is used for forming an integrity check on STUN messages that is encoded in the MESSAGE-INTEGRITY attribute. The ability to form a valid MESSAGE-INTEGRITY attribute value is an indication that the sender holds a current ("fresh") copy of the appropriate credential.

The long-term credential mechanism ensures freshness in a different way, using a *digest challenge*. When using this mechanism, a client initially makes a request without any authentication material. The server rejects the request but provides a REALM attribute in response. This can be used by the client to determine which credential is needed to provide adequate authentication, as the client may have credentials for various services (e.g., multiple VoIP accounts). Along with the REALM, the server provides a never-reused NONCE value, which the client uses in forming a subsequent request. This mechanism also uses a MESSAGE-INTEGRITY attribute, but its integrity function is computed by including the NONCE value. Thus, it is difficult for an eavesdropper that overheard a previous long-term credential exchange to simply replay a validated request (i.e., because the NONCE value is different). The use of NONCE values in authentication and related concerns are discussed in more detail in Chapter 18. The long-term credential mechanism cannot be used to protect STUN indications, as these transactions do not operate as request/response pairs.

7.4.4   Traversal Using Relays around NAT (TURN)

Traversal Using Relays around NAT (TURN) [RFC5766] provides a way for two or more systems to communicate even if they are located behind relatively uncooperative NATs. As a last-resort method to support communication in such circumstances, it involves a relay server that shuttles data between systems that could otherwise not communicate. Using extensions to STUN and some TURN-specific messages, it supports communication even when most other approaches have failed, provided a common server that is not behind a NAT can be reached by each client. If all NATs were compliant with the BEHAVE specifications, TURN would not be necessary. Direct communication methods (i.e., that do not use TURN) are almost always preferable to using TURN servers.

Referring to Figure 7-11, a TURN client behind a NAT contacts a TURN server, usually on the public Internet, and indicates the other systems (called *peers*) with which it wishes to communicate. Finding the server's address and the appropriate protocol to use for communication is accomplished using a special DNS NAPTR record (see Chapter 11 and [RFC5928]) or by manual configuration. The client obtains address and port information, called the *relayed transport address*, from the server, which are the address and port number used by the TURN server to communicate with the peers. The client also obtains its own server-reflexive transport address. Peers also have server-reflexive transport addresses that represent their external addresses. These addresses are needed by the client and server to perform the "plumbing" necessary to interconnect the client and its peers. The method used to exchange this addressing information is not defined within the scope of TURN. Instead, this information must be exchanged using some other mechanism (e.g., ICE; see Section 7.4.5) in order for TURN servers to be used effectively.

The client uses TURN commands to create and maintain *allocations* on the server. An allocation resembles a multiway NAT binding and includes the (unique) relayed transport address that each peer can use to reach the client. Server/peer data is sent using straightforward TURN messages traditionally carried in UDP/IPv4. Enhancements support TCP [RFC6062] and IPv6 (and also relaying between IPv4 and IPv6) [RFC6156]. Server/client data is encapsulated with an indication of corresponding peer(s) that sent or should receive the associated data. The client/server connection has been specified for UDP/IPv4, TCP/IPv4, and TCP/IPv4

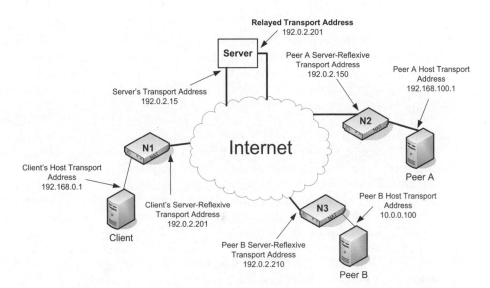

Figure 7-11 Based on [RFC5766], a TURN server helps clients behind "bad" NATs to communicate by relaying traffic. Traffic flowing between client and server may use TCP, UDP, or TCP with TLS. Traffic between the server and one or more peers uses UDP. Relaying is a last-resort measure for communication; direct methods are preferred if available.

with TLS. Establishing an allocation requires the client to be authenticated, usually using the STUN long-term credential mechanism.

TURN supports two methods for copying data between a client and its peers. The first encodes data using STUN methods called Send and Data, defined in [RFC5766], which are STUN indicators and therefore not authenticated. The other uses a TURN-specific concept called *channels*. Channels are communication paths between a client and a peer that have less overhead than the Send and Data methods. Messages carried over channels use a smaller, 4-byte header that is incompatible with the larger STUN-formatted messages ordinarily used by TURN. Up to 16K channels can be associated with an allocation. Channels were developed to help some applications such as VoIP that prefer to use relatively small packets to reduce latency and overhead.

In operation, the client makes a request to obtain an allocation using a TURN-defined STUN Allocate method. If successful, the server responds with a success indicator and the allocated relayed transport address. A request might be denied if the client fails to provide adequate authentication to the server. The client must now send refresh messages to keep the allocation alive. Allocations expire in 10 minutes if not refreshed, unless the client included an alternate lifetime value, encoded as a STUN LIFETIME attribute, in the allocation request. Allocations may be deleted by requesting an allocation with zero lifetime. When an allocation expires, so do all of its associated channels.

Allocations are represented using a "5-tuple." At the client, the 5-tuple includes the client's host transport address and port number, server transport address and port number, and the transport protocol used to communicate with the server. At the server, the same 5-tuple is used, except the client's host transport address and port are replaced with its server-reflexive address and port. An allocation may have zero or more associated *permissions*, to limit the patterns of connectivity that are permitted through the TURN server. Each permission includes an IP address restriction such that only packets with the matching source address received at the TURN server have their data payloads forwarded to the corresponding client. Permissions are deleted if not refreshed within 5 minutes.

TURN enhances STUN with six methods, nine attributes, and six error response codes. These can be partitioned roughly into support for establishing and maintaining allocations, authentication, and manipulating channels. The six methods and their method numbers are as follows: Allocate (3), Refresh (4), Send (6), Data (7), CreatePermission (8), and ChannelBind (9). The first two establish and keep allocations alive. Send and Data use STUN messages to encapsulate data from client to server and vice versa, respectively. CreatePermission establishes or refreshes a permission, and ChannelBind associates a particular peer with a 16-bit channel number. The error messages indicate problems with TURN features such as authentication failure or running out of resources (e.g., channel numbers). The nine STUN attribute names, values, and purposes defined by TURN are given in Table 7-3.

Table 7-3   STUN attributes defined by TURN

Name	Value	Purpose/Use
CHANNEL-NUMBER	0x000C	Indicates what channel associated data belongs to
LIFETIME	0x000D	Requested allocation timeout (seconds)
XOR-PEER-ADDRESS	0x0012	A peer's address and port, using XORed encoding
DATA	0x0013	Holds data for a Send or Data indication
XOR-RELAYED-ADDRESS	0x0016	Server's address and port allocated for a client
EVEN-PORT	0x0018	Requests that the relayed transport addressing information use an even port; optionally requests allocation of the next port in sequence
REQUESTED-TRANSPORT	0x0019	Used in a client to request that a specific transport be used in forming the transport address; values are drawn from the IPv4 *Protocol* or IPv6 *Next Hop* header field values
DONT-FRAGMENT	0x001A	Requests that the server set the "don't fragment" bit in the IPv4 header in packets sent to peers
RESERVATION-TOKEN	0x0022	Unique identifier for a relayed transport address held by the server; the value is provided to the client as a reference

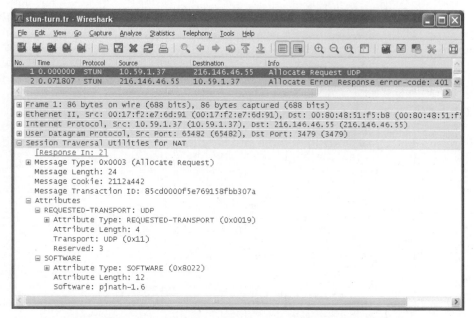

Figure 7-12 A TURN allocation request is a STUN message using message type 0x0003. This request also includes the REQUESTED-TRANSPORT and SOFTWARE attributes. It does not include authentication information. According to STUN long-term credentials, this request will fail.

A TURN request takes the form of a STUN message whose message type is an allocation request. Figure 7-12 shows an example. According to the STUN long-term credential mechanism, the initial allocation request shown in Figure 7-12 did not include authentication information, so it is rejected by the server. The rejection is indicated by an allocation error response, shown in Figure 7-13.

The error message in Figure 7-13 provides the REALM attribute (viagenie.ca) and the NONCE value the client requires to form its next request. The message also includes the MESSAGE-INTEGRITY attribute so the client can check that the message has not been modified and the requested REALM and NONCE are correct. A subsequent request includes the USERNAME, NONCE, and MESSAGE-INTEGRITY attributes. See Figure 7-14.

After receiving the request including long-term credentials, as shown in Figure 7-14, the server computes its own version of the message integrity value and compares the result against the MESSAGE-INTEGRITY attribute value. If they match, this is sufficient information for the TURN server to conclude that the client must hold the appropriate password. It then permits the allocation and indicates the result to the client (see Figure 7-15).

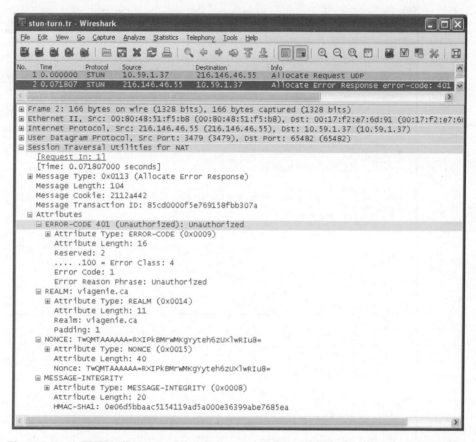

Figure 7-13   A TURN allocation error response includes the ERROR-CODE attribute with value 401 (Unauthorized). The message is integrity-protected and includes the REALM and NONCE attributes required by the client in forming another, authenticated allocation request.

The allocation request is successful, as shown in Figure 7-15, and the relayed transport address is 216.146.46.55:49261 (note that Wireshark performs the XOR operation to display the decoded address). At this point, the client can proceed to use the TURN server for relaying to peers. Once this is finished, the allocation can be removed. About 4s later, packets 5 and 6 in Figure 7-15 indicate the client's request to remove the allocation. The request is expressed as a refresh with lifetime set to 0. The server responds with a success indicator and removes the allocation. Note that the BANDWIDTH attribute has been included in the allocation and refresh success indicators. This attribute, defined by a draft version of [RFC5766] but ultimately deprecated, was intended to hold the peak bandwidth, in kilobytes per second, permitted on the allocation. This attribute may be redefined in the future.

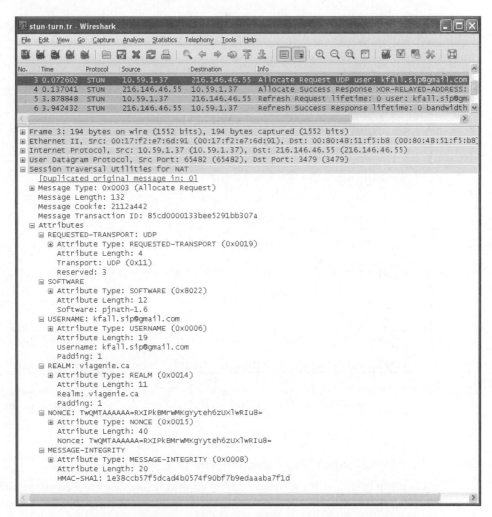

Figure 7-14 A second TURN allocation request includes the USERNAME, REALM, NONCE, and MESSAGE-INTEGRITY attributes. These are used by the server to verify integrity of the message and the identity of the client. If successful, the server authenticates the request and performs the allocation.

As suggested previously, TURN has the disadvantage that traffic must be relayed through the TURN server, and this can lead to inefficient routing (i.e., the TURN server may be far away from a client and peer that are proximal). In addition, certain other traffic contents are not passed through from peer to client using TURN. This includes ICMP values (see Chapter 8), *TTL* (*Hop Limit*) field values, and IP *DS Field* values. Also, a requesting TURN client must implement the STUN long-term credential mechanism and have some form of login credential or account assigned by the TURN server operator. This helps to avoid uncontrolled use of open TURN servers but creates somewhat greater configuration complexity.

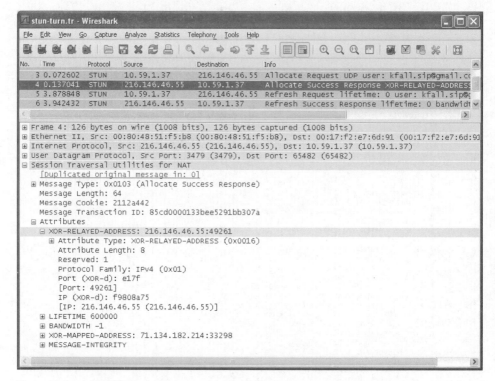

Figure 7-15   A TURN allocation success response. The message is integrity-protected and includes the XOR-RELAYED-ADDRESS attribute, identifying the port and address allocated by the TURN server. The allocation is deleted if not refreshed.

7.4.5   Interactive Connectivity Establishment (ICE)

Given the large variety of NATs deployed and the various mechanisms that may be necessary to traverse them, a generic facility called *Interactive Connectivity Establishment* (ICE) [RFC5245] has been developed to help UDP-based applications hosted behind a NAT establish connectivity. ICE is a set of heuristics by which an application can perform UNSAF in a relatively predictable fashion. In its operation, ICE makes use of other protocols such as TURN and STUN. A proposal extends the use of ICE to TCP-based applications [IDTI].

ICE works with and extends "offer/answer" protocols, such as the Session Description Protocol (SDP) used with unicast SIP connection establishment [RFC3264]. These protocols involve an offer of service with an accompanying set of service parameters followed by an answer that also includes a set of selected options. It is increasingly common to find ICE clients incorporated into VoIP applications that use SDP/SIP for establishing communications. However, in such circumstances, ICE is used for establishing NAT traversal for media streams (such as the audio or video portion of a call carried using RTP [RFC3550] or SRTP

[RFC3711]), while another mechanism, called *SIP Outbound* [RFC5626], handles the SIP signaling information such as who is being called. Although in practice ICE has been used primarily with SIP/SDP-based applications, it can also be used as a generic NAT traversal mechanism for other applications. One such example is the use of ICE (over UDP) with *Jingle* [XEP-0176], defined as an extension to the core *Extensible Messaging and Presence Protocol* (XMPP) [RFC6120].

Ordinarily, ICE works to establish communication between two SDP entities (called *agents*) by first determining a set of *candidate transport addresses* that each agent might use for communicating with the other. Referring to Figure 7-11, these addresses could be host transport, server-reflexive, or relayed addresses. ICE may make use of both STUN and TURN to determine the candidate transport addresses. ICE then orders these addresses according to a priority assignment algorithm. The algorithm arranges for addresses that provide direct connectivity to receive greater priority than those that require data relaying. ICE then provides the set of prioritized addresses to its peer agent, which engages in a similar behavior. Ultimately, two agents agree on the best set of usable address pairs and indicate the selected results to the other peer. Determination of which candidate transport addresses are available is accomplished using a sequence of *checks* encoded as STUN messages. ICE has several optimizations to decrease the latency of agreeing on the selected candidate, which are beyond the scope of this discussion.

ICE begins by attempting to discover all available candidate addresses. Addresses may be locally assigned transport addresses (multiple if the agent is multihomed), server-reflexive addresses, or relayed addresses determined by TURN. After assigning each address a priority, an agent sends the prioritized list to its peer using SDP. The peer performs the same operation, resulting in each agent having two prioritized lists. Each agent then forms an identical set of prioritized *candidate pairs* by pairing up the two lists. A set of checks are performed on the candidate pairs in a particular order to determine which addresses will ultimately be selected. Generally, the priority ordering prefers candidate pairs with fewer NATs or relays. The candidate pair ultimately selected is determined by a *controlling agent* assigned by ICE. The controlling agent *nominates* which valid candidate pairs are to be used, according to its order of preference. The controlling agent may try all pairs and subsequently make its choice (called *regular nomination*) or may use the first viable pair (called *aggressive nomination*). A nomination is expressed as a flag in a STUN message referring to a particular pair; aggressive nomination is performed by setting the nominate flag in every request.

Checks are sent as STUN binding request messages exchanged between the two agents using the addressing information being checked. Checks are initiated by timer, or scheduled as a result of an incoming check from a peer (called a *triggered check*). Responses arrive in the form of STUN binding responses that contain addressing information. In some circumstances this may reveal a new server-reflexive address to the agent (e.g., because a different NAT is used between agents from the one that was used when the candidate addresses were first determined using STUN or TURN servers). Should this happen, the agent gains a new address called a *peer-reflexive candidate*, which ICE adds to the set of candidate addresses. ICE checks are integrity-checked using STUN's short-term credential mechanism and use the STUN FINGERPRINT attribute. When TURN is used, the ICE client uses TURN permissions to limit the TURN binding to the remote candidate address of interest.

ICE incorporates the concept of different implementations. *Lite* implementations are designed for deployment in systems that do not employ NAT. They do not ever act as a controlling agent unless interacting with another Lite implementation. They also do not perform the checks mentioned earlier as do *full* implementations. The type of an ICE implementation is indicated in the STUN messages it sends. All ICE implementations must comply with STUN [RFC5389], but Lite implementations will only ever act as STUN servers. ICE extends STUN with the attributes described in Table 7-4.

Table 7-4   STUN attributes defined by ICE

Name	Value	Purpose/Use
PRIORITY	0x0024	Computed priority of associated candidate address
USE-CANDIDATE	0x0025	Indicates selection of candidate by controlling agent
ICE-CONTROLLED	0x8029	Indicates sender of message is controlled agent
ICE-CONTROLLING	0x802A	Indicates sender of message is controlling agent

A check is a STUN binding request containing the PRIORITY attribute. The value is equal to the value assigned by the algorithm described in Section 4.1.2 of [RFC5245]. The ICE-CONTROLLING and ICE-CONTROLLED attributes are included in STUN requests when the sender is the controlling or controlled agent, respectively. A controlling agent may also include a USE-CANDIDATE attribute. If present, this attribute indicates which candidate the controlling agent wishes to select for subsequent use.

7.5   Configuring Packet-Filtering Firewalls and NATs

Although NATs frequently require little configuration (unless port forwarding is being used), firewalls usually do, and sometimes they require extensive configuration. In most home networks the same device is providing NAT, IP routing, and firewall capabilities and may require some configuration. Although the configuration is logically separate for each of these, they are sometimes merged, either in configuration files, command-line interfaces, Web page controls, or other network management tools.

7.5.1 Firewall Rules

A packet-filtering firewall must be given a set of instructions indicating criteria for selecting traffic to be dropped or forwarded. Nowadays when configuring a router, the network administrator usually configures a set of one or more ACLs. Each ACL consists of a list of *rules*, and each rule typically contains *pattern-matching criteria* and an *action*. The matching criteria generally allow the rule to express the values of packet fields at either the network or transport layer (e.g., source and destination IP addresses, port numbers, ICMP type field, etc.) and a *direction* specification. The direction pattern matches traffic in a direction-dependent manner and allows for a different set of rules to apply for incoming versus outgoing traffic. Many firewalls also allow the rules to be applied at a certain point in the order of processing within the firewall. Examples of this include the ability to specify an ACL to be checked prior to or after the IP routing decision process. In some circumstances (especially when more than one interface is used), this flexibility becomes important.

When a packet arrives, the matching criteria in the appropriate ACL are consulted in order. For most firewalls, the first matching rule is acted upon. Typical actions include a specification to block or forward the traffic and may also adjust a counter or write a log entry. Some firewalls may include additional features as well, such as having some packets directed to applications or other hosts. Each firewall vendor usually has its own method for specifying rules, although Cisco Systems' ACL format has emerged as a popular format supported by many vendors of enterprise-class routers. ACLs for home users are typically configured using a simple Web interface.

One of the popular systems for building firewalls is included with modern versions of Linux and is called `iptables`, built using a network filtering capability called NetFilter [NFWEB]. It is the evolution of an earlier facility called `ipchains` and provides stateless and stateful packet-filtering support as well as NAT and NAPT. We shall examine how it works to get a better understanding of the types of capabilities a firewall and modern NAT provide.

`iptables` includes the concepts of filter *tables* and filter *chains*. A table contains several predefined chains and may contain zero or more user-defined chains. Three predefined tables are named as follows: `filter`, `nat`, and `mangle`. The default `filter` table is for basic packet filtering and contains the predefined chains INPUT, FORWARD, and OUTPUT. These actions correspond to packets destined for programs running on the firewall router itself, those passing through it while being routed, and those originating at the firewall machine. The `nat` table contains the chains PREROUTING, OUTPUT, and POSTROUTING. The `mangle` table has all five chains. It is used for arbitrary rewriting of packets.

Each filter chain is a list of rules, and each rule has matching criteria and an action. The action (called a *target*) may be to execute a special user-defined chain or to perform one of the following predefined actions: ACCEPT, DROP, QUEUE, and RETURN. A packet matching a rule with one of these targets is immediately acted on. ACCEPT (DROP) means the packet is forwarded (dropped). QUEUE means the packet is delivered to a user program for arbitrary processing, and RETURN means that processing continues in a previously invoked chain, which forms a sort of packet filter chain subroutine call.

The design of a complete firewall configuration can be fairly complex and is specific to the needs of particular users and the types of services they require, so we will not attempt to give one here. Instead, the following examples illustrate only a small number of the possible uses for `iptables`. The following gives an example Linux firewall configuration file. It is invoked by a shell such as `bash`:

```
EXTIF="ext0"
INTIF="eth0"
LOOPBACK_INTERFACE="lo"
ALL="0.0.0.0/0"                     # matches all

# set default filter table policies to drop
iptables -P INPUT DROP
iptables -P OUTPUT DROP
iptables -P FORWARD DROP

# all local traffic OK
iptables -A INPUT -i $LOOPBACK_INTERFACE -j ACCEPT
iptables -A OUTPUT -i $LOOPBACK_INTERFACE -j ACCEPT

# accept incoming DHCP requests on internal interface
iptables -A INPUT -i $INTIF -p udp -s 0.0.0.0 \
     --sport 67 -d 255.255.255.255 --dport 68 -j ACCEPT

# drop unusual/suspect TCP traffic with no flags set
iptables -A INPUT -p tcp --tcp-flags ALL NONE -j DROP
```

This example illustrates some of the flexibility one can employ in setting up a filter criteria list. Initially, the chains are given a default policy (-P option), which affects packets that fail to match any rules. Next, traffic to or from the local computer (which is delivered using the *pseudo interface* lo) is given to the ACCEPT target (i.e., it is allowed) for the INPUT and OUTPUT chains in the default `filter` table. The -j option indicates "jump" to a particular processing target. Next, incoming UDP broadcast traffic originating from IPv4 address 0.0.0.0 and destined for local/subnet broadcast using the DHCP port numbers (67, 68) is allowed in via the internal interface. Next, the *Flags* fields of incoming TCP segments (see Chapter 13) is ANDed with all 1s (ALL) and compared against zero (NONE). A match occurs only if all the *Flags* fields are 0, which is not a very useful TCP segment (ordinarily all TCP segments after the first one contain a valid ACK bit, and the first one contains a SYN).

While syntax illustrated by this example is specific to the `iptables` facility, its capabilities are not. Most filtering firewalls are capable of performing similar types of checks and actions.

7.5.2   NAT Rules

In most simple routers, NAT can be configured in conjunction with firewall rules. In basic Windows systems, NAT is called *Internet Connection Sharing* (ICS), and in Linux it is called *IP masquerading*. On Windows XP, for example, ICS has a number of special characteristics. It assigns the "internal" IPv4 address as 192.168.0.1 to the machine running ICS and starts a DHCP server and DNS server. Other computers are assigned addresses in the 192.168.0/24 subnet, with the ICS machine as DNS server. Therefore, ICS should not be enabled on networks where these services are already being provided by another computer or router, or where the addresses might conflict. A registry setting can be used to change the default address range.

Enabling ICS for an Internet connection on Windows XP can be accomplished by using the Network Setup Wizard, or by changing the Advanced properties on an already-operating Internet connection (under Settings | Network Connections). At this point, the user may also decide to allow other users to control or disable the shared Internet connection. This facility, known as *Internet Gateway Device Discovery and Control* (IGDDC), uses the Universal Plug and Play framework, described in Section 7.5.3, for controlling a local Internet gateway from a client. The functions supported include connect and disconnect, along with reading various status messages. The Windows firewall facility, which works in conjunction with ICS, supports the creation of *service definitions*. Service definitions are equivalent to port forwarding, as defined previously. To enable it, the Advanced property tab on the Internet connection is selected and a new service may be added (or an existing one edited). The user is then given the opportunity to fill in the appropriate TCP and UDP port numbers, both at the external interface and at the internal server machine. It thus works as a way to configure NAPT for incoming connections.

As with Windows, Linux combines the masquerade capability with its firewall implementation. The following script configures masquerading in a simple manner. Note that this script is only for illustration and is not recommended for production use.

```
EXTIF="ext0"
echo "Default FORWARD policy: DROP"
iptables -P FORWARD DROP

echo "Enabling NAT on $EXTIF for hosts 192.168.0.0/24"
iptables -t nat -A POSTROUTING -o $EXTIF -s 192.168.0.0/24 \
    -j MASQUERADE

echo "FORWARD policy: DROP unknown traffic"
iptables -A INPUT -i $EXTIF -m state --state NEW,INVALID -j DROP
iptables -A FORWARD -i $EXTIF -m state --state NEW,INVALID -j DROP
```

Here, the default policy for the FORWARDING chain in the `filter` table is set to DROP. The next item arranges for hosts with IPv4 addresses assigned from the 192.168.0.0/24 subnet to have their addresses rewritten for any IPv4 traffic (via

NAT, implemented by the nat table and -t nat options) after routing has determined the external interface to be the appropriate one. Because of the stateful way that NAT works, it is now possible to adjust the filter table's rules to allow only traffic associated with a connection known to NAT. The last two lines adjust the INPUT and FORWARD chains so that any incoming traffic that is either invalid or unknown (NEW) is dropped. The special operators NEW and INVALID are defined within the iptables command.

7.5.3   Direct Interaction with NATs and Firewalls: UPnP, NAT-PMP, and PCP

In many cases, a client system wishes to or needs to interact directly with its firewall. For example, a firewall may need to be configured or reconfigured for different services by allowing traffic destined for a particular port to not be dropped (establishing a "pinhole"). In cases where a proxy firewall is in use, each client must be informed of the proxy's identity. Otherwise, communication beyond the firewall is not possible. A number of protocols have been developed for supporting communication between clients and firewalls. The two most prevalent ones are called *Universal Plug and Play* (UPnP) and the *NAT Port Mapping Protocol* (NAT-PMP). The standards for UPnP are developed by an industry group called the UPnP Forum [UPNP]. NAT-PMP is currently an expired draft document within the IETF [XIDPMP]. NAT-PMP is supported by most Mac OS X systems. UPnP has native support on Windows systems and can be added to Mac OS and Linux systems. UPnP is also used in support of consumer electronics device discovery protocols for home networks being developed by the Digital Living Network Alliance (DLNA) [DLNA].

With UPnP, controlled devices are configured with IP addresses based first upon DHCP and using dynamic link-local address configuration (see Chapter 6) if DHCP is not available. Next, the *Simple Service Discovery Protocol* (SSDP) [XIDS] announces the presence of the device to control points (e.g., client computers) and allows the control points to query the devices for additional information. SSDP uses two variants of HTTP with UDP instead of the more standard TCP. They are called HTTPU and HTTPMU [XIDMU], and the latter uses multicast addressing (IPv4 address 239.255.255.250, port 1900). For SSDP carried on IPv6, the following addresses are used: ff01::c (node-local), ff02::c (link-local), ff05::c (site-local), ff08::c (organization-local), and ff0e::c (global).

Subsequent control and event notification ("eventing") is controlled by the *General Event Notification Architecture* (GENA), which uses the *Simple Object Access Protocol* (SOAP). SOAP supports a client/server *remote procedure call* (RPC) mechanism and uses messages encoded in the *Extensible Markup Language* (XML), which is commonly used for Web pages. UPnP is used for a wide variety of consumer electronic devices, including audio and video playback and storage devices. NAT/firewall devices are controlled using the *Internet Gateway Device* (IGD) protocol [IGD]. IGD supports a variety of capabilities, including the ability to learn NAT mappings and configure port forwarding. The interested reader may obtain a simple IGD client useful for experimentation from the MiniUPnP Project HomePage [UPNPC]. A second version of UPnP IGD [IGD2] adds general IPv6 support to UPnP.

While UPnP is a broad framework that includes NAT control and several other unrelated specifications, NAT-PMP provides an alternative specifically targeted at programmatic communications with NAT devices. NAT-PMP is part of Apple's set of Bonjour specifications for zero configuration networking. NAT-PMP does not use a discovery process, as the device being managed is usually a system's default gateway as learned by DHCP. NAT-PMP uses UDP port 5351. NAT-PMP supports a simple request/response protocol for learning a NAT's outside address and configuring port mappings. It also supports a basic eventing mechanism that notifies listeners when a NAT outside address changes. This is accomplished using a UDP multicast message sent to address 224.0.0.1 (the All Hosts address) when the outside address changes. NAT-PMP uses UDP port 5350 for client/server interactions and 5351 for multicast event notification. The idea of NAT-PMP can be extended for use with SPNAT, as proposed by the *Port Control Protocol* (PCP) [IDPCP].

7.6   NAT for IPv4/IPv6 Coexistence and Transition

With the depletion of the last top-level unicast IPv4 address prefixes in early in 2011, the embracing of IPv6 is beginning to accelerate. It was thought that hosts could be equipped with dual-stack functionality (i.e., each implements a complete IPv4 and IPv6 stack) [RFC4213] and network services would transition over to IPv6-only operation. It is now understood that IPv4 and IPv6 are likely to coexist for an extended period of time, perhaps indefinitely, and that for various economic reasons network infrastructure may operate using either IPv4 or IPv6 or both. Assuming that this is true, there will be an ongoing need to support communications between IPv4 and IPv6 systems, whether they are dual-stack or not. The two major approaches that have been used to support combinations of IPv4 and IPv6 are tunneling and translation. The tunneling approaches include Teredo (see Chapter 10), Dual-Stack Lite (DS-Lite), and IPv6 Rapid Deployment (6rd). Although DS-Lite involves SPNAT as part of its architecture, a purer translation approach is given by the framework described in [RFC6144], which uses the IPv4-embedded IPv6 addresses we saw in Chapter 2. We will discuss both DS-Lite and the translation framework in more detail in this section.

7.6.1   Dual-Stack Lite (DS-Lite)

DS-Lite [RFC6333] is an approach to make transition to IPv6 (and support for legacy IPv4 users) easier for service providers that wish to run IPv6 internally. In essence, it allows providers to focus on deploying an operational IPv6 core network yet provide IPv4 and IPv6 connectivity to their customers using a small number of IPv4 addresses. The approach combines IPv4-in-IPv6 "softwire" tunneling [RFC5571] with SPNAT. Figure 7-16 shows the type of deployment envisioned.

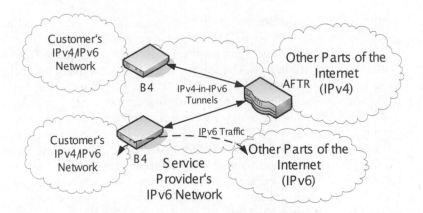

Figure 7-16   DS-Lite allows service providers to support IPv4 and IPv6 customer networks using an IPv6-only infrastructure. IPv4 address usage is minimized by using SPNAT at the provider's edge.

In Figure 7-16, each customer network operates with any combination of IPv4 and IPv6. The service provider's network is assumed to be managed using only IPv6. Customer access to the IPv6 Internet is provided using conventional IPv6 routing. For IPv4 access, each customer uses a special "before" gateway (labeled "B4" in Figure 7-16). A B4 element provides basic IPv4 services (e.g., DHCP service, a DNS proxy, etc.) but also encapsulates the customer's IPv4 traffic in multi-point-to-point tunnels terminated at the "after" element (labeled "AFTR" in Figure 7-16). The AFTR element performs decapsulation of traffic headed to the IPv4 Internet and encapsulation in the reverse direction. AFTR also performs NAT and acts as a form of SPNAT. More specifically, the AFTR may use the identity of the customer's tunnel endpoint for disambiguating traffic returning to the AFTR from the IPv4 Internet. This allows multiple customers to use the same IPv4 address space. A B4 element can learn the name of its corresponding AFTR element using a DHCPv6 option called AFTR-Name [RFC6334].

It is instructive to recall the discussion of IPv6 rapid deployment (6rd) from Chapter 6. Whereas DS-Lite provides IPv4 access to customers over a service provider's IPv6 network, 6rd aims to provide IPv6 access to customers over a service provider's IPv4 network. In essence, they take opposite approaches with similar architectural components. However, with 6rd, mapping from an IPv6 address to the address of the corresponding IPv4 tunnel endpoint (and vice versa) is computed in a stateless fashion using an address-mapping algorithm. Stateless address translation is also used in the framework for full protocol translation between IPv4 and IPv6, which we discuss next.

7.6.2   IPv4/IPv6 Translation Using NATs and ALGs

The biggest disadvantage of using tunneling techniques for supporting IPv4/IPv6 coexistence is that network services running on hosts using one address family cannot be reached directly by the hosts using the other. Thus, an IPv6-only host can communicate only with other IPv6-capable systems. This is an undesirable situation because many valuable services offered on the legacy IPv4 Internet would remain unavailable to new systems that may support only IPv6. To address this concern, a significant effort was undertaken between 2008 and 2010 to develop a framework to provide direct translation between IPv4 and IPv6. This effort was informed by poor experiences with NAT-PT [RFC2766], which was ultimately determined to be too brittle and unscalable for ongoing use and was deprecated [RFC4966].

The IPv4/IPv6 translation framework is given in [RFC6144]. The basic translation architecture involves both stateful and stateless methods to convert between IPv4 and IPv6 addresses, translations for DNS (see Chapter 11), and the definition of any additional behaviors or ALGs in cases where they are necessary (including for ICMP and FTP). In this section, we will discuss the basics of the stateless and stateful address translation for IP based on [RFC6145], [RFC6146], and the addressing from [RFC6052] we discussed in Chapter 2. Other protocol-specific translation issues will be covered in subsequent chapters.

7.6.2.1 IPv4-Converted and IPv4-Translatable Addresses

In Chapter 2, we discussed the structure of IPv4-embedded IPv6 addresses. Such addresses are IPv6 addresses that can be used as input to a function that produces a corresponding IPv4 address. The function is also easily inverted. There are two important types of IPv4-embedded IPv6 addresses, called *IPv4-converted addresses* and *IPv4-translatable addresses*. Each type of address mentioned is a subset of the other types. That is, if we treat each address category as a set, then (IPv4-translatable) ⊂ (IPv4-converted) ⊂ (IPv4-embedded) ⊂ (IPv6). IPv4-translatable addresses are IPv6 addresses for which an IPv4 address can be determined in a stateless fashion (see Section 7.6.2.2).

Algorithmic translation between IPv4 and IPv6 addresses involves the use of a prefix, as described in Chapter 2. The prefix may be either the Well-Known Prefix (WKP) 64:ff9b::/96 or another Network-Specific Prefix that is ordinarily owned by a service provider and used specifically with its translators. The WKP is used only in representing ordinary globally routable IPv4 addresses; private addresses [RFC1918] are not to be used with the WKP. In addition, the WKP is not to be used for creating IPv4-translatable addresses. Such addresses are intended to be defined within the scope of a provider's network, so it is not appropriate to use them at a global scope.

The WKP is interesting because it is *checksum-neutral* with respect to the Internet checksum. Recall the Internet checksum calculation from Chapter 5. If we treat the prefix 64:ff9b::/96 as being composed of the hexadecimal values 0064, ff9b, 0000, 0000, 0000, 0000, 0000, 0000, the sum of these values is ffff, which is equal to 0 in one's complement. Consequently, when an IPv4 address has the WKP prepended, the associated Internet checksums in packets created as a result of translation (e.g., in the IPv4 header, TCP, or UDP checksum) are unaffected. Naturally, an appropriately chosen Network-Specific Prefix can also be checksum-neutral.

In the following two subsections, we will use the notation To4(A6, P) to represent the IPv4 address derived from IPv6 address A6 in conjunction with prefix P. P is either the WKP or some Network-Specific Prefix. We will use the notation To6(A4, P) to represent the IPv6 address derived from IPv4 address A4 in conjunction with prefix P. Note that, with a few special exceptions, A6 = To6(To4(A6,P),P) and A4 = To4(To6(A4,P),P).

7.6.2.2 Stateless Translation

Stateless IP/ICMP Translation (SIIT) refers to a method of translating between IPv4 and IPv6 packets without using state tables [RFC6145]. The translation is performed without table lookups and uses IPv4-translatable addresses along with a defined scheme to translate IP headers. For the most part, IPv4 options are not translated (they are ignored), nor are IPv6 extension headers (except the Fragment header). The exception is an unexpired IPv4 Source Route option. If such an option is present, the packet is dropped and a corresponding ICMP error message (Destination Unreachable, Source Route Failed; see Chapter 8) is generated. Table 7-5 describes how the IPv6 header fields are assigned when translating an IPv4 datagram to IPv6.

Table 7-5   Methods for creating an IPv6 header when translating IPv4 to IPv6

IPv6 Field	Assignment Method
Version	Set to 6.
DS Field/ECN	Copied from same values in IPv4 header
Flow Label	Set to 0.
Payload Length	Set to IPv4 *Total Length* minus length of the IPv4 header (including options).
Next Header	Set to IPv4 *Protocol* field (or 58 if the *Protocol* field had value 1). Set to value 44 to indicate a Fragment header if the IPv6 datagram being created is a fragment or DF bit not set.
Hop Limit	Set to the IPv4 *TTL* field minus 1 (if this value is 0, the packet is discarded and an ICMP Time Exceeded message is generated; see Chapter 8).
Source IP Address	Set to To6(IPv4 Source IP Address, P).
Destination IP Address	Set to To6(IPv4 Destination IP Address, P).

During the translation process, the IPv4 header is stripped and replaced with an IPv6 header. If the arriving IPv4 datagram is too large to fit in the MTU for the next link and the *DF* bit field in its header is not set, multiple IPv6 fragment packets may be produced, each containing a Fragment header. This also occurs when the arriving IPv4 datagram is a fragment. [RFC6145] recommends a Fragment header be included in the resulting IPv6 datagram whenever the arriving IPv4 datagram's *DF* bit field has value zero, whether or not the translator needs to perform fragmentation or the arriving datagram is a fragment. This allows the IPv6 receiver to know that the IPv4 sender was likely not using PMTUD. When a Fragment header is included, its fields are set according to the methods listed in Table 7-6.

Table 7-6 Methods for assigning fields of the Fragment header, if used, during IPv4-to-IPv6 translation

Fragment Header Field	Assignment Method
Next Header	Set to the IPv4 *Protocol* field.
Fragment Offset	Copied from the IPv4 *Fragment Offset* field.
More Fragments Bit	Copied from the IPv4 *More Fragments* (M) bit field.
Identification	The low-order 16 bits are set from the IPv4 *Identification* field. The high-order 16 bits are set to 0.

The reverse direction (IPv6-to-IPv4 translation) involves creating an IPv4 datagram with header field values based on fields in the arriving IPv6 header. Obviously the much larger IPv6 address space does not allow an IPv4-only host to access every host on the IPv6 Internet. Table 7-7 gives the methods used to assign the fields in the outgoing IPv4 datagram's header when an unfragmented IPv6 datagram arrives.

Table 7-7 Methods for creating an IPv4 header when translating unfragmented IPv6 to IPv4

IPv4 Header Field	Assignment Method
Version	Set to 4.
IHL	Set to 5 (no IPv4 options).
DS Field/ECN	Copied from same values in IPv6 header.
Total Length	The value of the IPv6 *Payload Length* field plus 20.
Identification	Set to 0 (with option to set to some other predetermined value).
Flags	*More Fragments* (M) is set to 0. *Don't Fragment* (DF) is set to 1.
Fragment Offset	Set to 0.
TTL	The value of the IPv6 *Hop Limit* field minus 1 (must be at least 1).
Protocol	Copied from the first IPv6 *Next Header* field that does not refer to a Fragment header, HOPOPT, IPv6-Route, or IPv6-Opts. Value 58 is changed to 1 to support ICMP (see Chapter 8).
Header Checksum	Computed for the newly created IPv4 header.
Source IP Address	To4(IPv6 Source IP Address, P).
Destination IP Address	To4(IPv6 Destination IP Address, P).

If the arriving IPv6 datagram includes a Fragment header, the outgoing IPv4 datagram uses field values based on assignment methods modified from those in Table 7-7. Table 7-8 gives this case.

Table 7-8   Methods for creating an IPv4 header when translating fragmented IPv6 to IPv4

IPv4 Header Field	Assignment Method
Total Length	The value of the IPv6 *Payload Length* field minus 8 plus 20.
Identification	Copied from the low-order 16 bits in the *Identification* field of the IPv6 Fragment header.
Flags	*More Fragments* (*M*) copied from the *M* bit field in the IPv6 Fragment header. *Don't Fragment* (*DF*) is set to 0 to allow fragmentation in the IPv4 network.
Fragment Offset	Copied from the *Fragment Offset* field of the IPv6 Fragment header.

In the case of fragmented IPv6 datagrams, the translator produces fragmented IPv4 datagrams. Note that in IPv6 the *Identification* field is larger, so there is a possibility that certain fragments could fail to be reassembled properly if multiple distinct IPv6 datagrams from the same host are fragmented in such a way that the *Identification* field values they use share a common lower-order 16 bits. However, this situation is no more risky than having the conventional IPv4 *Identification* field wrap. Furthermore, integrity checks at higher layers make this issue nothing much to worry about.

7.6.2.3 Stateful Translation

In stateful translation, *NAT64* [RFC6146] is used to support IPv6-only clients communicating with IPv4 servers. This is expected to be important during the period when many important services continue to be offered using only IPv4. The translation method for headers is nearly identical to the methods described for stateless translation in Section 7.6.2.2. As a NAT, NAT64 complies with BEHAVE specifications and supports only endpoint-independent mappings, along with both endpoint-independent and address-dependent filtering. Thus, it is compatible with the NAT traversal techniques (e.g., ICE, STUN, TURN) we discussed previously. Lacking these additional protocols, NAT64 supports dynamic translation only for IPv6 hosts initiating communications with IPv4 hosts.

NAT64 works much like conventional NAT (NAPT) across address families, except translations in the IPv4-to-IPv6 direction are simpler than in the reverse direction. A NAT64 device is assigned an IPv6 prefix, which can be used to form a valid IPv6 address directly from an IPv4 address using the mechanism described in Chapter 2 and [RFC6052]. Because of the comparative scarcity of the IPv4 address space, translations in the IPv6-to-IPv4 direction make use of a pool of IPv4 addresses that are ordinarily managed dynamically. This requires NAT64 to support NAPT functionality, whereby multiple distinct IPv6 addresses may map to the same IPv4 address. NAT64 currently defines methods for translation of TCP, UDP, and ICMP messages initiated by IPv6 nodes. (In the case of ICMP queries and responses, the ICMP *Identifier* field is used instead of the transport-layer port number; see Chapter 8.)

NAT64 handles fragments differently from its stateful counterpart. For arriving TCP or UDP fragments where the transport checksum is nonzero (see Chapter 10), the NAT64 may either queue the fragments and translate them together or translate them individually. A NAT64 must handle fragments, even those arriving out of order. A NAT64 may be configured with a time limit (at least 2s) bounding the time during which fragments will be cached. Otherwise, the NAT could be subject to a DoS attack resulting from the exhaustion of packet buffers holding fragments.

7.7 Attacks Involving Firewalls and NATs

Given that the primary purpose of deploying firewalls is to reduce the exposure to attacks, it is not surprising that firewalls have fewer obvious shortcomings than end hosts or routers. That said, they are not without their faults. The most common types of firewall problems result from incomplete or incorrect configuration. Configuring firewalls is not a trivial task, especially for large enterprises where many services may be employed on a daily basis. Other forms of attacks exploit the weaknesses of some firewalls, including the inability of many of them (especially older ones) to deal with IP fragments.

One type of problem arises when a NAT/firewall can be hijacked from outside to provide a masquerading capability for an attacker. If the firewall is configured with NAT enabled, traffic arriving at its external interface may be rewritten so as to appear to have come from the NAT device, thereby hiding an attacker's actual address. What is worse, this is "normal" behavior from the NAT's point of view; it just happens to be getting its input packets from outside rather than inside. This has been a particular problem with `ipchains`-based NAT/firewall rules on Linux. The simplest configuration for setting up masquerading:

```
Linux# ipchains -P FORWARD MASQUERADE
```

allows this attack to take place and is therefore *not* recommended. As we can see, it sets the default forwarding policy to `masquerade`, which potentially applies to any IP forwarding.

Another type of problem that can arise with firewall and NAT rules is that they may be stale. In particular, they may contain port forwarding entries or other so-called holes that allow traffic through for services that are no longer used. A related problem is that some routers keep more than one copy of the firewall rules in memory, and the router must be specifically instructed when to enable which rules. Finally, another common configuration problem is that many routers *merge* new firewall rules with the existing set when new ones are added. This can potentially lead to undesired results if the operator is unaware of this behavior.

The problem with fragments is related to how IP fragments are constructed. When an IP datagram is fragmented (see Chapter 10), the transport header, which contains the port numbers, appears only in the first fragment and in none of the others. This is a direct result of the layering and encapsulation of the TCP/IP protocol architecture. Unfortunately for a firewall, receiving a fragment other than the first provides little information about the transport layer or service to which the packet relates. The only obvious way to make this association is to find the first fragment (if there ever was one), and this obviously requires a stateful firewall capability, which might be subject to resources exhaustion attacks. Even stateful firewalls could fall short: if the first fragment arrives after subsequent fragments, the firewall may not be smart enough to perform reassembly prior to its filtering operation. In some cases, the firewall simply drops fragments it cannot fully identify, which could pose problems for legitimate traffic that happens to use large datagrams.

7.8   Summary

Firewalls provide a mechanism for network administrators to restrict the flow of information that may be harmful to end systems. The two major types of firewalls are packet-filtering firewalls and proxy firewalls. Packet-filtering firewalls may be further separated into the stateful and stateless varieties, and they usually act as IP routers. The stateful variety is more sophisticated and supports successful operation of a wider variety of application-layer protocols (and might do more sophisticated logging or filtering across multiple packets in a packet stream). Proxy firewalls usually act as a form of application-layer gateway. For these firewalls, each application-layer service must have its own proxy handler on the firewall, but this does allow handlers to make modifications even to the data portion of the transiting traffic. Protocols such as SOCKS support proxy firewalls in a standardized way.

Network Address Translation (NAT) is a mechanism whereby a relatively large number of end hosts can share one or more globally routable IP address(es). NAT is used extensively for this purpose but can also be used in conjunction with firewall rules to form a NAT/firewall combination. In this popular configuration, computers "behind" the NAT are allowed to send traffic out to the global Internet, but only traffic returning in response to the outgoing traffic is ordinarily admitted back. This presents a small problem for implementing services behind a NAT that is handled by port forwarding, which allows the NAT to pass on incoming traffic for a service to end hosts inside the NAT. NAT is also being proposed for helping the transition from IPv4 to IPv6 by translating addresses between the two realms. In addition, NAT is being considered for use within ISPs to further allay IPv4 address depletion concerns. If this happens on a large scale, it may become (even more) difficult for ordinary users to offer Internet services from their home networks.

Some applications use a set of heuristics in order to determine what addresses are used on the outside of the NATs they are behind. Many of these operate unilaterally, without direct help from the NAT. Such applications are said to use UNSAF (pronounced "unsafe") methods and may not be completely reliable. A set of documents (developed by the IETF BEHAVE working group) specifies the proper behavior of NATs for different protocols, but not all NATs implement these specifications. Consequently, NAT traversal techniques may need to be employed to ensure that connectivity can take place.

NAT traversal involves determining a set of addresses and port numbers that can be used to support communications even when one or more NATs must be used. STUN is the primary workhorse protocol for determining addresses. TURN is a particular STUN usage that relays traffic through a specially configured TURN server, usually located in the Internet. Deciding which addresses or relays to use can be accomplished using a complete NAT traversal protocol such as ICE. ICE determines all possible addresses that can be used between a pair of communicating endpoints using local information, plus addresses determined using STUN and TURN. It then selects the "best" addresses for subsequent communication. Mechanisms such as ICE have received the most attention for supporting VoIP services that use the SIP protocol for signaling.

Firewalls and NATs may require configuration. The basic settings are adequate for many home users, but firewalls may require modifications to allow certain services to work. In addition, if a user behind a NAT wishes to offer an Internet service, port forwarding will likely have to be configured on the NAT device. Some applications support configuration by performing direct communication with a NAT using protocols such as UPnP and NAT-PMP. When supported and enabled, these allow a NAT to have its port forwarding and binding data accessed and modified by the application automatically, without user intervention. For a home user to run a Web server behind a dynamically provisioned NAT (i.e., one with an Internet-facing IP address that changes), additional services such as dynamic DNS (see Chapter 11) may also be important.

7.9   References

[ANM09] S. Alcock, R. Nelson, and D. Miles, "Investigating the Impact of Service Provider NAT on Residential Broadband Users," University of Waikato, unpublished technical report, 2009.

[DLNA] http://www.dlna.org

[HBA09] D. Hayes, J. But, and G. Armitage, "Issues with Network Address Translation for SCTP," *Computer Communications Review*, Jan. 2009.

[IDPCP] D. Wing, ed., S. Cheshire, M. Boucadair, R. Penno, and P. Selkirk, "Port Control Protocol (PCP)," Internet draft-ietf-pcp-base, work in progress, July 2011.

[IDSNAT] R. Stewart, M. Tuexen, and I. Ruengeler, "Stream Control Transmission Protocol (SCTP) Network Address Translation," Internet draft-ietf-behave-sctpnat, work in progress, June 2011.

[IDTI] J. Rosenberg, A. Keranen, B. Lowekamp, and A. Roach, "TCP Candidates with Interactive Connectivity Establishment (ICE)," Internet draft-ietf-mmusic-ice-tcp, work in progress, Sep. 2011.

[IGD] UPnP Forum, "Internet Gateway Devices (IGD) Standardized Device Control Protocol V 1.0," Nov. 2001.

[IGD2] UPnP Forum, "IDG:2 Improvements over IGD:1," Mar. 2009.

[ISP] http://www.iana.org/assignments/stun-parameters

[MBCB08] O. Maennel, R. Bush, L. Cittadini, and S. Bellovin, "A Better Approach to Carrier-Grade-NAT," Columbia University Technical Report CUCS-041-08, Sept. 2008.

[NFWEB] http://netfilter.org

[PJSUA] http://www.pjsip.org/pjsua.htm

[RFC0959] J. Postel and J. Reynolds, "File Transfer Protocol," Internet RFC 0959/STD 0009, Oct. 1985.

[RFC1918] Y. Rekhter, B. Moskowitz, D. Karrenberg, G. J. de Groot, and E. Lear, "Address Allocation for Private Internets," Internet RFC 1918BCP 0005, Feb. 1996.

[RFC1928] M. Leech, M. Ganis, Y. Lee, R. Kuris, D. Koblas, and L. Jones, "SOCKS Protocol Version 5," Internet RFC 1928, Mar. 1996.

[RFC2616] R. Fielding, J. Gettys, J. Mogul, H. Frystyk, L. Masinter, P. Leach, and T. Berners-Lee, "Hypertext Transfer Protocol—HTTP/1.1," Internet RFC 2616, June 1999.

[RFC2637] K. Hamzeh, G. Pall, W. Verthein, J. Taarud, W. Little, and G. Zorn, "Point-to-Point Tunneling Protocol (PPTP)," Internet RFC 2637 (informational), July 1999.

[RFC2766] G. Tsirtsis and P. Srisuresh, "Network Address Translation—Protocol Translation (NAT-PT)," Internet RFC 2766 (obsoleted by [RFC4966]), Feb. 2000.

[RFC3022] P. Srisuresh and K. Egevang, "Traditional IP Network Address Translator (Traditional NAT)," Internet RFC 3022 (informational), Jan. 2001.

[RFC3027] M. Holdrege and P. Srisuresh, "Protocol Complications with the IP Network Address Translator," Internet RFC 3027 (informational), Jan. 2001.

[RFC3235] D. Senie, "Network Address Translator (NAT)-Friendly Application Design Guidelines," Internet RFC 3235 (informational), Jan. 2002.

[RFC3264] J. Rosenberg and H. Schulzrinne, "An Offer/Answer Model with Session Description Protocol (SDP)," Internet RFC 3264, June 2002.

[RFC3424] L. Daigle, ed., and IAB, "IAB Considerations for UNilateral Self-Address Fixing (UNSAF) across Network Address Translation," Internet RFC 3424 (informational), Nov. 2002.

[RFC3550] H. Schulzrinne, S. Casner, R. Frederick, and V. Jacobson, "RTP: A Transport Protocol for Real-Time Applications," Internet RFC 3550/STD 0064, July 2003.

[RFC3711] M. Baugher, D. McGrew, M. Naslund, E. Carrara, and K. Norrman, "The Secure Real-Time Transport Protocol (SRTP)," Internet RFC 3711, Mar. 2004.

[RFC4193] R. Hinden and B. Haberman, "Unique Local IPv6 Unicast Addresses," Internet RFC 4193, Oct. 2005.

[RFC4213] E. Nordmark and R. Gilligan, "Basic Transition Mechanisms for IPv6 Hosts and Routers," Internet RFC 4213, Oct. 2005.

[RFC4340] E. Kohler, M. Handley, and S. Floyd, "Datagram Congestion Control Protocol (DCCP)," Internet RFC 4340, Mar. 2006.

[RFC4605] B. Fenner, H. He, B. Haberman, and H. Sandick, "Internet Group Management Protocol (IGMP)/Multicast Listener Discovery (MLD)-Based Multicast Forwarding (IGMP/MLD Proxying)," Internet RFC 4605, Aug. 2006.

[RFC4787] F. Audet, ed., and C. Jennings, "Network Address Translation (NAT) Behavioral Requirements for Unicast UDP," Internet RFC 4787/BCP 0127, Jan. 2007.

[RFC4864] G. Van de Velde, T. Hain, R. Droms, B. Carpenter, and E. Klein, "Local Network Protection for IPv6," Internet RFC 4864 (informational), May 2007.

[RFC4960] R. Stewart, ed., "Stream Control Transmission Protocol," Internet RFC 4960, Sept. 2007.

[RFC4966] C. Aoun and E. Davies, "Reasons to Move the Network Address Translator-Protocol Translator (NAT-PT) to Historic Status," Internet RFC 4966 (informational), July 2007.

[RFC5128] P. Srisuresh, B. Ford, and D. Kegel, "State of Peer-to-Peer (P2P) Communication across Network Address Translators (NATs)," Internet RFC 5128 (informational), Mar. 2008.

[RFC5135] D. Wing and T. Eckert, "IP Multicast Requirements for a Network Address Translator (NAT) and a Network Address Port Translator (NAPT)," Internet RFC 5135/BCP 0135, Feb. 2008.

[RFC5245] J. Rosenberg, "Interactive Connectivity Establishment (ICE): A Protocol for Network Address Translator (NAT) Traversal for Offer/Answer Protocols," Internet RFC 5245, Apr. 2010.

[RFC5382] S. Guha, ed., K. Biswas, B. Ford, S. Sivakumar, and P. Srisuresh, "NAT Behavioral Requirements for TCP," Internet RFC 5382/BCP 0142, Oct. 2008.

[RFC5389] J. Rosenberg, R. Mahy, P. Matthews, and D. Wing, "Session Traversal Utilities for NAT (STUN)," Internet RFC 5389, Oct. 2008.

[RFC5411] J. Rosenberg, "A Hitchhiker's Guide to the Session Initiation Protocol (SIP)," Internet RFC 5411 (informational), Feb. 2009.

[RFC5508] P. Srisuresh, B. Ford, S. Sivakumar, and S. Guha, "NAT Behavioral Requirements for ICMP," Internet RFC 5508/BCP 0148, Apr. 2009.

[RFC5571] B. Storer, C. Pignataro, ed., M. Dos Santos, B. Stevant, ed., L. Toutain, and J. Tremblay, "Softwire Hub and Spoke Deployment Framework with Layer Two Tunneling Protocol Version 2 (L2TPv2)," Internet RFC 5571, June 2009.

[RFC5596] G. Fairhurst, "Datagram Congestion Control Protocol (DCCP) Simultaneous-Open Technique to Facilitate NAT/Middlebox Traversal," Internet RFC 5596, Sept. 2009.

[RFC5597] R. Denis-Courmont, "Network Address Translation (NAT) Behavioral Requirements for the Datagram Congestion Control Protocol," Internet RFC 5597/BCP 0150, Sept. 2009.

[RFC5626] C. Jennings, R. Mahy, and F. Audet, eds., "Managing Client-Initiated Connections in the Session Initiation Protocol (SIP)," Internet RFC 5626, Oct. 2009.

[RFC5761] C. Perkins and M. Westerlund, "Multiplexing RTP Data and Control Packets on a Single Port," Internet RFC 5761, Apr. 2010.

[RFC5766] R. Mahy, P. Matthews, and J. Rosenberg, "Traversal Using Relays around NAT (TURN): Relay Extensions to Session Traversal Utilities for NAT (STUN)," Internet RFC 5766, Apr. 2010.

[RFC5780] D. MacDonald and B. Lowekamp, "NAT Behavior Discovery Using Session Traversal Utilities for NAT (STUN)," Internet RFC 5780 (experimental), May 2010.

[RFC5902] D. Thaler, L. Zhang, and G. Lebovitz, "IAB Thoughts on IPv6 Network Address Translation," Internet RFC 5902 (informational), July 2010.

[RFC5928] M. Petit-Huguenin, "Traversal Using Relays around NAT (TURN) Resolution Mechanism," Internet RFC 5928, Aug. 2010.

[RFC6052] C. Bao, C. Huitema, M. Bagnulo, M. Boucadair, and X. Li, "IPv6 Addressing of IPv4/IPv6 Translators," Internet RFC 6052, Oct. 2010.

[RFC6062] S. Perreault, ed., and J. Rosenberg, "Traversal Using Relays around NAT (TURN) Extensions for TCP Allocations," Internet RFC 6062, Nov. 2010.

[RFC6120] P. Saint-Andre, "Extensible Messaging and Presence Protocol (XMPP): Core," Internet RFC 6120, Mar. 2011.

[RFC6144] F. Baker, X. Li, C. Bao, and K. Yin, "Framework for IPv4/IPv6 Translation," Internet RFC 6144 (informational), Apr. 2011.

[RFC6145] X. Li, C. Bao, and F. Baker, "IP/ICMP Translation Algorithm," Internet RFC 6145, Apr. 2011.

[RFC6146] M. Bagnulo, P. Matthews, and I. van Beijnum, "Stateful NAT64: Network Address and Protocol Translation from IPv6 Clients to IPv4 Servers," Internet RFC 6146, Apr. 2011.

[RFC6156] G. Camarillo, O. Novo, and S. Perreault, ed., "Traversal Using Relays around NAT (TURN) Extension for IPv6," Internet RFC 6156, Apr. 2011.

[RFC6296] M. Wasserman and F. Baker, "IPv6-to-IPv6 Network Prefix Translation," Internet RFC 6296 (experimental), June 2011.

[RFC6333] A. Durand, R. Droms, J. Woodyatt, and Y. Lee, "Dual-Stack Lite Broadband Deployments Following IPv4 Exhaustion," Internet RFC 6333, Aug. 2011.

[RFC6334] D. Hankins and T. Mrugalski, "Dynamic Host Configuration Protocol for IPv6 (DHCPv6) Option for Dual-Stack Lite," Internet RFC 6334, Aug. 2011.

[UPNP] http://www.upnp.org

[UPNPC] http://miniupnp.free.fr

[XEP-0176] J. Beda, S. Ludwig, P. Saint-Andre, J. Hildebrand, S. Egan, and R. McQueen, "XEP-0176: Jingle ICE-UDP Transport Method," XMPP Standards Foundation, June 2009, http://xmpp.org/extensions/xep-0176.html

[XIDAD] P. Gauthier, J. Cohen, M. Dunsmuir, and C. Perkins, "Web Proxy Auto-Discovery Protocol," Internet draft-ietf-wrec-wpad-01, work in progress (expired), June 1999.

[XIDMU] Y. Goland, "Multicast and Unicast UDP HTTP Messages," Internet draft-goland-http-udp-01.txt, work in progress (expired), Nov. 1999.

[XIDPMP] S. Cheshire, M. Krochmal, and K. Sekar, "NAT Port Mapping Protocol (NAT-PMP)," Internet draft-cheshire-nat-pmp-03.txt, work in progress (expired), Apr. 2008.

[XIDS] Y. Goland, T. Cai, P. Leach, Y. Gu, and S. Albright, "Simple Service Discovery Protocol/1.0 Operating without an Arbiter," Internet draft-cai-ssdp-v1-03.txt, work in progress (expired), Oct. 1999.

8

ICMPv4 and ICMPv6: Internet Control Message Protocol

8.1   Introduction

The IP protocol alone provides no direct way for an end system to learn the fate of IP packets that fail to make it to their destinations. In addition, IP provides no direct way of obtaining diagnostic information (e.g., which routers are used along a path or a method to estimate the round-trip time). To address these deficiencies, a special protocol called the *Internet Control Message Protocol* (ICMP) [RFC0792] [RFC4443] is used in conjunction with IP to provide diagnostics and control information related to the configuration of the IP protocol layer and the disposition of IP packets. ICMP is often considered part of the IP layer itself, and it is required to be present with any IP implementation. It uses the IP protocol for transport. So, precisely, it is neither a network nor a transport protocol but lies somewhere between the two.

ICMP provides for the delivery of error and control messages that may require attention. ICMP messages are usually acted on by the IP layer itself, by higher-layer transport protocols (e.g., TCP or UDP), and in some cases by user applications. Note that ICMP does not provide reliability for IP. Rather, it indicates certain classes of failures and configuration information. The most common cause of packet drops (buffer overrun at a router) does not elicit any ICMP information. Other protocols, such as TCP, handle such situations.

Because of the ability of ICMP to affect the operation of important system functions and obtain configuration information, hackers have used ICMP messages in a large number of attacks. As a result of concerns about such attacks, network administrators often arrange to block ICMP messages with firewalls, especially at border routers. If ICMP is blocked, however, a number of common diagnostic utilities (e.g., ping, traceroute) do not work properly [RFC4890].

When discussing ICMP, we shall use the term ICMP to refer to ICMP in general, and the terms ICMPv4 and ICMPv6 to refer specifically to the versions of ICMP used with IPv4 and IPv6, respectively. As we shall see, ICMPv6 plays a far more important role in the operation of IPv6 than ICMPv4 does for IPv4.

[RFC0792] contains the official base specification of ICMPv4, which is refined and clarified in [RFC1122] and [RFC1812]. [RFC4443] provides the base specification for ICMPv6. [RFC4884] provides a method to add extension objects to certain ICMP messages. This facility is used for holding *Multiprotocol Label Switching* (MPLS) information [RFC4950] and for indicating which interface and next hop a router would use in forwarding a particular datagram [RFC5837]. [RFC5508] gives standard behavioral characteristics of ICMP through NATs (also discussed in Chapter 7). In IPv6, ICMPv6 is used for several purposes beyond simple error reporting and signaling. It is used for *Neighbor Discovery* (ND) [RFC4861], which plays the same role as ARP does for IPv4 (see Chapter 4). It also includes the *Router Discovery* function used for configuring hosts (see Chapter 6) and multicast address management (see Chapter 9). Finally, it is also used to help manage handoffs in Mobile IPv6.

8.1.1 Encapsulation in IPv4 and IPv6

ICMP messages are encapsulated for transmission within IP datagrams, as shown in Figure 8-1.

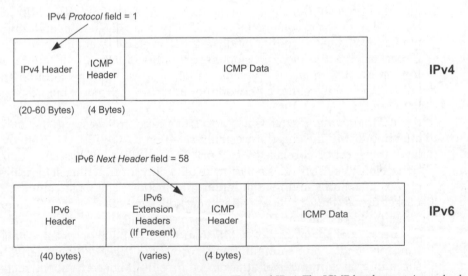

Figure 8-1   Encapsulation of ICMP messages in IPv4 and IPv6. The ICMP header contains a checksum covering the ICMP data area. In ICMPv6, the checksum also covers the *Source* and *Destination IPv6 Address*, *Length*, and *Next Header* fields in the IPv6 header.

In IPv4, a *Protocol* field value of 1 indicates that the datagram caries ICMPv4. In IPv6, the ICMPv6 message may begin after zero or more extension headers. The last extension header before the ICMPv6 header includes a *Next Header* field with value 58. ICMP messages may be fragmented like other IP datagrams (see Chapter 10), although this is not common.

Figure 8-2 shows the format of both ICMPv4 and ICMPv6 messages. The first 4 bytes have the same format for all messages, but the remainder differ from one message to the next.

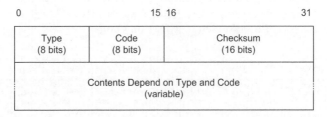

Figure 8-2   All ICMP messages begin with 8-bit *Type* and *Code* fields, followed by a 16-bit *Checksum* that covers the entire message. The type and code values are different for ICMPv4 and ICMPv6.

In ICMPv4, 42 different values are reserved for the *Type* field [ICMPTYPES], which identify the particular message. Only about 8 of these are in regular use, however. We will show the exact format of each commonly used message throughout the chapter. Many types of ICMP messages also use different values of the *Code* field to further specify the meaning of the message. The *Checksum* field covers the entire ICMPv4 message; in ICMPv6 it also covers a *pseudo-header* derived from portions of the IPv6 header (see Section 8.1 of [RFC2460]). The algorithm used for computing the checksum is the same as that used for the IP header checksum defined in Chapter 5. Note that this is our first example of an *end-to-end* checksum. It is carried all the way from the sender of the ICMP message to the final recipient. In contrast, the IPv4 header checksum discussed in Chapter 5 is changed at every router hop. If an ICMP implementation receives an ICMP message with a bad checksum, the message is discarded; there is no ICMP message to indicate a bad checksum in a received ICMP message. Recall that the IP layer has no protection on the payload portion of the datagram. If ICMP did not include a checksum, the contents of the ICMP message might not be correct, leading to incorrect system behavior.

8.2   ICMP Messages

We now look at ICMP messages in general and the most commonly used ones in more detail. ICMP messages are grouped into two major categories: those messages relating to problems with delivering IP datagrams (called *error mes-sages*), and those related to information gathering and configuration (called *query* or *informational messages*).

8.2.1   ICMPv4 Messages

For ICMPv4, the informational messages include Echo Request and Echo Reply (types 8 and 0, respectively), and Router Advertisement and Router Solicitation (types 9 and 10, respectively, together called Router Discovery). The most common error message types are Destination Unreachable (type 3), Redirect (type 5), Time Exceeded (type 11), and Parameter Problem (type 12). Table 8-1 lists the message types defined for standard ICMPv4 messages.

Table 8-1   The standard ICMPv4 message types, as determined by the *Type* field*

Type	Official Name	Reference	E/I	Use/Comment
0 (*)	Echo Reply	[RFC0792]	I	Echo (ping) reply; returns data
3 (*)(+)	Destination Unreachable	[RFC0792]	E	Unreachable host/protocol
4	Source Quench	[RFC0792]	E	Indicates congestion (deprecated)
5 (*)	Redirect	[RFC0792]	E	Indicates alternate router should be used
8 (*)	Echo	[RFC0792]	I	Echo (ping) request (data optional)
9	Router Advertisement	[RFC1256]	I	Indicates router addresses/preferences
10	Router Solicitation	[RFC1256]	I	Requests Router Advertisement
11 (*)(+)	Time Exceeded	[RFC0792]	E	Resource exhausted (e.g., IPv4 TTL)
12 (*)(+)	Parameter Problem	[RFC0792]	E	Malformed packet or header

*Types marked with asterisks (*) are the most common. Those marked with a plus (+) may contain [RFC4884] extension objects. In the fourth column, *E* is for error messages and *I* indicates query/informational messages.

For the commonly used messages (those with the asterisks next to the type number in Table 8-1), the code numbers shown in Table 8-2 are used. Some mes-sages are capable of carrying extended information [RFC4884] (those marked in Table 8-1 with the plus sign).

The official list of message types is maintained by IANA [ICMPTYPES]. Many of these message types were defined by the original ICMPv4 specifica-tion [RFC0792] in 1981, prior to any significant experience using them. Additional experience and the development of other protocols (e.g., DHCP) have resulted in many of the messages defined then to cease being used. When IPv6 (and ICMPv6) was designed, this fact was understood, so a somewhat more rational arrange-ment of types and codes has been defined for ICMPv6.

Table 8-2 Common ICMPv4 message types that use code numbers in addition to 0. Although all of these message types are relatively common, only a few of the codes are commonly used.

Type	Code	Official Name	Use/Comment
3	0	Net Unreachable	No route (at all) to destination
3 (*)	1	Host Unreachable	Known but unreachable host
3	2	Protocol Unreachable	Unknown (transport) protocol
3 (*)	3	Port Unreachable	Unknown/unused (transport) port
3 (*)	4	Fragmentation Needed and Don't Fragment Was Set (PTB message)	Needed fragmentation prohibited by *DF* bit; used by PMTUD [RFC1191]
3	5	Source Route Failed	Intermediary hop not reachable
3	6	Destination Network Unknown	Deprecated [RFC1812]
3	7	Destination Host Unknown	Destination does not exist
3	8	Source Host Isolated	Deprecated [RFC1812]
3	9	Communication with Destination Network Administratively Prohibited	Deprecated [RFC1812]
3	10	Communication with Destination Host Administratively Prohibited	Deprecated [RFC1812]
3	11	Destination Network Unreachable for Type of Service	Type of service not available (net)
3	12	Destination Host Unreachable for Type of Service	Type of service not available (host)
3	13	Communication Administratively Prohibited	Communication prohibited by filtering policy
3	14	Host Precedence Violation	Precedence disallowed for src/dest/port
3	15	Precedence Cutoff in Effect	Below minimum ToS [RFC1812]
5	0	Redirect Datagram for the Network (or Subnet)	Indicates alternate router
5 (*)	1	Redirect Datagram for the Host	Indicates alternate router (host)
5	2	Redirect Datagram for the Type of Service and Network	Indicates alternate router (ToS/net)
5	3	Redirect Datagram for the Type of Service and Host	Indicates alternate router (ToS/host)
9	0	Normal Router Advertisement	Router's address and configuration information
9	16	Does Not Route Common Traffic	With Mobile IP [RFC5944], router does not route ordinary packets
11 (*)	0	Time to Live Exceeded in Transit	Hop limit/TTL exceeded
11	1	Fragment Reassembly Time Exceeded	Not all fragments of datagram arrived before reassembly timer expired
12 (*)	0	Pointer Indicates the Error	Byte offset (pointer) indicates first problem field
12	1	Missing a Required Option	Deprecated/historic
12	2	Bad Length	Packet had invalid *Total Length* field

8.2.2 ICMPv6 Messages

Table 8-3 shows the message types defined for ICMPv6. Note that ICMPv6 is responsible not only for error and informational messages but also for a great deal of IPv6 router and host configuration.

Table 8-3   In ICMPv6, error messages have message types from 0 to 127. Informational messages have message types from 128 to 255. The plus (+) notation indicates that the message may contain an extension structure. Reserved, unassigned, experimental, and deprecated values are not shown.

Type	Official Name	Reference	Description
1 (+)	Destination Unreachable	[RFC4443]	Unreachable host, port, protocol
2	Packet Too Big (PTB)	[RFC4443]	Fragmentation required
3 (+)	Time Exceeded	[RFC4443]	Hop limit exhausted or reassembly timed out
4	Parameter Problem	[RFC4443]	Malformed packet or header
100,101	Reserved for private experimentation	[RFC4443]	Reserved for experiments
127	Reserved for expansion of ICMPv6 error messages	[RFC4443]	Hold for more error messages
128	Echo Request	[RFC4443]	ping request; may contain data
129	Echo Reply	[RFC4443]	ping response; returns data
130	Multicast Listener Query	[RFC2710]	Queries multicast subscribers (v1)
131	Multicast Listener Report	[RFC2710]	Multicast subscriber report (v1)
132	Multicast Listener Done	[RFC2710]	Multicast unsubscribe message (v1)
133	Router Solicitation (RS)	[RFC4861]	IPv6 RS with Mobile IPv6 options
134	Router Advertisement (RA)	[RFC4861]	IPv6 RA with Mobile IPv6 options
135	Neighbor Solicitation (NS)	[RFC4861]	IPv6 Neighbor Discovery (Solicit)
136	Neighbor Advertisement (NA)	[RFC4861]	IPv6 Neighbor Discovery (Advertisement)
137	Redirect Message	[RFC4861]	Use alternative next-hop router
141	Inverse Neighbor Discovery Solicitation Message	[RFC3122]	Inverse Neighbor Discovery request: requests IPv6 addresses given link-layer address
142	Inverse Neighbor Discovery Advertisement Message	[RFC3122]	Inverse Neighbor Discovery response: reports IPv6 addresses given link-layer address
143	Version 2 Multicast Listener Report	[RFC3810]	Multicast subscriber report (v2)

Table 8-3   In ICMPv6, error messages have message types from 0 to 127. Informational messages have message types from 128 to 255. The plus (+) notation indicates that the message may contain an extension structure. Reserved, unassigned, experimental, and deprecated values are not shown. (*continued*)

Type	Official Name	Reference	Description
144	Home Agent Address Discovery Request Message	[RFC6275]	Requests Mobile IPv6 HA address; send by mobile node
145	Home Agent Address Discovery Reply Message	[RFC6275]	Contains MIPv6 HA address; sent by eligible HA on home network
146	Mobile Prefix Solicitation	[RFC6275]	Request home prefix while away
147	Mobile Prefix Advertisement	[RFC6275]	Provides prefix from HA to mobile
148	Certification Path Solicitation Message	[RFC3971]	Secure Neighbor Discovery (SEND) request for a certification path
149	Certification Path Advertisement Message	[RFC3971]	SEND response to certification path request
151	Multicast Router Advertisement	[RFC4286]	Provides address of multicast router
152	Multicast Router Solicitation	[RFC4286]	Requests address of multicast router
153	Multicast Router Termination	[RFC4286]	Done using multicast router
154	FMIPv6 Messages	[RFC5568]	MIPv6 fast handover messages
200,201	Reserved for private experimentation	[RFC4443]	Reserved for experiments
255	Reserved for expansion of ICMPv6 informational messages	[RFC4443]	Hold for more informational messages

Immediately apparent in this list is the separation between the first set of message types and the second set (i.e., those messages with types below 128 and those at or above). In ICMPv6, as in ICMPv4, messages are grouped into the informational and error classes. In ICMPv6, however, all the error messages have a 0 in the high-order bit of the *Type* field. Thus, ICMPv6 types 0 through 127 are all errors, and types 128 through 255 are all informational. Many of the informational messages are request/reply pairs.

In comparing the common ICMPv4 messages with the ICMPv6 standard messages, we conclude that some of the effort in designing ICMPv6 was to eliminate the unused messages from the original specification while retaining the useful ones. Following this approach, ICMPv6 also makes use of the *Code* field, primarily to refine the meanings of certain error messages. In Table 8-4 we list those standard ICMPv6 message types (i.e., Destination Unreachable, Time Exceeded, and Parameter Problem) for which more than the code value 0 has been defined.

Table 8-4   ICMPv6 standard message types with codes in addition to 0 assigned

Type	Code	Name	Use/Comment
1	0	No Route to Destination	Route not present
1	1	Administratively Prohibited	Policy (e.g., firewall) prohibited
1	2	Beyond Scope of Source Address	Destination scope exceeds source's
1	3	Address Unreachable	Used if codes 0–2 are not appropriate
1	4	Port Unreachable	No transport entity listening on port
1	5	Source Address Failed Policy	Ingress/egress policy violation
1	6	Reject Route to Destination	Specific reject route to destination
3	0	Hop Limit Exceeded in Transit	*Hop Limit* field decremented to 0
3	1	Reassembly Time Exceeded	Unable to reassemble in limited time
4	0	Erroneous Header Field Found	General header processing error
4	1	Unrecognized Next Header	Unknown *Next Header* field value
4	2	Unrecognized IPv6 Option	Unknown Hop-by-Hop or Destination option

In addition to the *Type* and *Code* fields that define basic functions in ICMPv6, a large number of standard options are also supported, some of which are required. This distinguishes ICMPv6 from ICMPv4 (ICMPv4 does not have options). Currently, standard ICMPv6 options are defined for use only with the ICMPv6 ND messages (types 135 and 136) using the *Option Format* field discussed in [RFC4861]. We discuss these options when exploring ND in more detail in Section 8.5.

8.2.3   Processing of ICMP Messages

In ICMP, the processing of incoming messages varies from system to system. Generally speaking, the incoming informational requests are handled automatically by the operating system, and the error messages are delivered to user processes or to a transport protocol such as TCP [RFC5461]. The processes may choose to act on them or ignore them. Exceptions to this general rule include the Redirect message and the Destination Unreachable—Fragmentation Required messages. The former results in an automatic update to the host's routing table, whereas the latter is used in the path MTU discovery (PMTUD) mechanism, which is generally implemented by the transport-layer protocols such as TCP. In ICMPv6 the handling of messages has been tightened somewhat. The following rules are applied when processing incoming ICMPv6 messages [RFC4443]:

1. Unknown ICMPv6 error messages must be passed to the upper-layer process that produced the datagram causing the error (if possible).

2. Unknown ICMPv6 informational messages are dropped.

3. ICMPv6 error messages include as much of the original ("offending") IPv6 datagram that caused the error as will fit without making the error message datagram exceed the minimum IPv6 MTU (1280 bytes).

4. When processing ICMPv6 error messages, the upper-layer protocol type is extracted from the *original* or "offending" packet (contained in the body of the ICMPv6 error message) and used to select the appropriate upper-layer process. If this is not possible, the error message is silently dropped after any IPv6-layer processing.

5. There are special rules for handling errors (see Section 8.3).

6. An IPv6 node must limit the rate of ICMPv6 error messages it sends. There are a variety of ways of implementing the rate-limiting function, including the token bucket approach mentioned in Section 8.3.

8.3   ICMP Error Messages

The distinction between the error and informational classes of ICMP messages mentioned in the previous section is important because certain restrictions are placed on the generation of ICMPv4 error messages by [RFC1812] and on the generation of ICMPv6 error messages by [RFC4443] that do not apply to queries. In particular, an ICMP error message is not to be sent in response to any of the following messages: another ICMP error message, datagrams with bad headers (e.g., bad checksum), IP-layer broadcast/multicast datagrams, datagrams encapsulated in link-layer broadcast or multicast frames, datagrams with an invalid or network zero source address, or any fragment other than the first. The reason for imposing these restrictions on the generation of ICMP errors is to limit the creation of so-called *broadcast storms*, a scenario in which the generation of a small number of messages creates an unwanted traffic cascade (e.g., by generating error responses in response to error responses, indefinitely). These rules can be summarized as follows:

An ICMPv4 error message is never generated in response to

- An ICMPv4 error message. (An ICMPv4 error message may, however, be generated in response to an ICMPv4 query message.)

- A datagram destined for an IPv4 broadcast address or an IPv4 multicast address (formerly known as a class D address).

- A datagram sent as a link-layer broadcast.

- A fragment other than the first.

- A datagram whose source address does not define a single host. This means that the source address cannot be a zero address, a loopback address, a broadcast address, or a multicast address.

ICMPv6 is similar. An ICMPv6 error message is never generated in response to

- An ICMPv6 error message
- An ICMPv6 Redirect message
- A packet destined for an IPv6 multicast address, with two exceptions:
  - The Packet Too Big (PTB) message
  - The Parameter Problem message (code 2)
- A packet sent as a link-layer multicast (with the exceptions noted previously)
- A packet sent as a link-layer broadcast (with the exceptions noted previously)
- A packet whose source address does not uniquely identify a single node. This means that the source address cannot be an unspecified address, an IPv6 multicast address, or any address known by the sender to be an anycast address.

In addition to the rules governing the conditions under which ICMP messages are generated, there is also a rule that limits the overall ICMP traffic level from a single sender. In [RFC4443], a recommendation for rate-limiting ICMP messages is to use a *token bucket*. With a token bucket, a "bucket" holds a maximum number (B) of "tokens," each of which allows a certain number of messages to be sent. The bucket is periodically filled with new tokens (at rate N) and drained by 1 for each message sent. Thus, a token bucket (or *token bucket filter*, as it is often called) is characterized by the parameters (B, N). For small or midsize devices, [RFC4443] provides an example token bucket using the parameters (10, 10). Token buckets are a common mechanism used in protocol implementations to limit bandwidth utilization, and in many cases B and N are in byte units rather than message units.

When an ICMP error message is sent, it contains a copy of the full IP header from the "offending" or "original" datagram (i.e., the IP header of the datagram that caused the error to be generated, including any IP options), plus any other data from the original datagram's IP payload area such that the generated IP/ICMP datagram's size does not exceed a specific value. For IPv4 this value is 576 bytes, and for IPv6 it is the IPv6 minimum MTU, which is at least 1280 bytes. Including a portion of the payload from the original IP datagram lets the receiving ICMP module associate the message with one particular protocol (e.g., TCP or UDP) from the *Protocol* or *Next Header* field in the IP header and one particular user process (from the TCP or UDP port numbers that are in the TCP or UDP header contained in the first 8 bytes of the IP datagram payload area).

Before the publication of [RFC1812], the ICMP specification required only the first 8 bytes of the offending IP datagram to be included (because this is enough to determine the port number for UDP and TCP; see Chapters 10 and 12), but as more complex protocol layerings have become popular (such as IP being encapsulated in IP), additional information is now needed for the effective diagnosis of problems. In addition, several error messages may include *extensions*. We begin by briefly discussing the extension method, and then we discuss each of the more important ICMP error messages.

8.3.1 Extended ICMP and Multipart Messages

[RFC4884] specifies a method for extending the utility of ICMP messages by allowing an *extension data structure* to be appended to them. The extension structure includes an extension header and extension objects that may contain a variable amount of data, as illustrated in Figure 8-3.

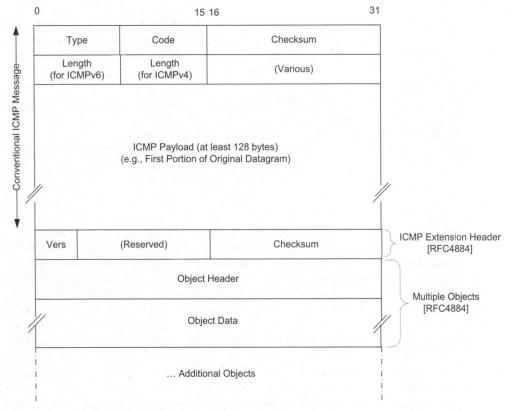

Figure 8-3   Extended ICMPv4 and ICMPv6 messages include a 32-bit extension header and zero or more associated objects. Each object includes a fixed-size header and a variable-length data area. For compatibility, the primary ICMP payload area is at least 128 bytes.

The *Length* field is repurposed from the sixth byte of the ICMPv4 header and the fifth byte of the ICMPv6 header. (These bytes had previously been reserved with value 0.) In ICMPv4, it indicates the offending datagram size in 32-bit word units. For ICMPv6, it is in 64-bit units. These datagram portions are padded with zeros as necessary to be 32-bit- and 64-bit-aligned, respectively. When extensions are used, the ICMP payload area containing the original datagram must be at least 128 bytes long.

The extension structure may be used with ICMPv4 Destination Unreachable, Time Exceeded, and Parameter Problem messages as well as ICMPv6 Destination Unreachable and Time Exceeded messages. We will look at each of these in some detail in the following sections.

8.3.2   Destination Unreachable (ICMPv4 Type 3, ICMPv6 Type 1) and Packet Too Big (ICMPv6 Type 2)

We now look more closely at one of the more common ICMP message types, Destination Unreachable. Messages of this type are used to indicate that a datagram could not be delivered all the way to its destination because of either a problem in transit or the lack of a receiver interested in receiving it. Although 16 different codes are defined for this message in ICMPv4, only 4 are commonly used. These include Host Unreachable (code 1), Port Unreachable (code 3), Fragmentation Required/ Don't-Fragment Specified (code 4), and Communication Administratively Prohibited (code 13). In ICMPv6, the Destination Unreachable message is type 1 with seven possible code values. In ICMPv6, as compared with IPv4, the Fragmentation Required message has been replaced by an entirely different type (type 2), but the usage is very similar to the corresponding ICMP Destination Unreachable message, so we discuss it here. In ICMPv6 this is called the Packet Too Big (PTB) message. We will use the simpler ICMPv6 PTB terminology from here onward to refer to either the ICMPv4 (type 3, code 4) message or the ICMPv6 (type 2, code 0) message.

The formats for all of the Destination Unreachable messages specified for ICMPv4 and ICMPv6 are shown in Figure 8-4. For Destination Unreachable messages, the *Type* field is 3 for ICMPv4 and 1 for ICMPv6. The *Code* field indicates the particular item or reason for the reachability failure. We now look at each of these messages in detail.

8.3.2.1 ICMPv4 Host Unreachable (Code 1) and ICMPv6 Address Unreachable (Code 3)

This form of the Destination Unreachable message is generated by a router or host when it is required to send an IP datagram to a host using direct delivery (see Chapter 5) but for some reason cannot reach the destination. This situation may arise, for example, because the last-hop router is attempting to send an ARP request to a host that is either missing or down. This situation is explored in Chapter 4, which describes ARP. For ICMPv6, which uses a somewhat different mechanism for detecting unresponsive hosts, this message can be the result of a failure in the ND process (see Section 8.5).

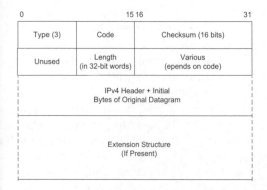

Figure 8-4   The ICMP Destination Unreachable messages in ICMPv4 (left) and ICMPv6 (right). The *Length* field, present in extended ICMP implementations that conform to [RFC4884], gives the number of words used to hold the original datagram measured in 4-byte units (IPv4) or 8-byte units (IPv6). An optional extension structure may be included. The ICMP field labeled *various* is used to hold the next-hop MTU when the code value is 4, which is used by PMTUD. ICMPv6 uses a different ICMPv6 PTB message (ICMPv6 type 2) for this purpose.

8.3.2.2 ICMPv6 No Route to Destination (Code 0)

This message refines the Host Unreachable message from ICMPv4 to differentiate those hosts not reachable because of failure of direct delivery and those that cannot be reached because no route is present. This message is generated only in cases where an arriving datagram must be forwarded without using direct delivery, but where no route entry exists to indicate what router to use as a next hop. As we have seen, IP routers must contain a valid next-hop forwarding entry for the destination in any packets they receive if they are going to successfully perform forwarding.

8.3.2.3 ICMPv4 Communication Administratively Prohibited (Code 13) and ICMPv6 Communication with Destination Administratively Prohibited (Code 1)

In ICMPv4 and ICMPv6, these Destination Unreachable messages provide the ability to indicate that an *administrative prohibition* is preventing successful communication with the destination. This is typically the result of a firewall (see Chapter 7) that intentionally drops traffic that fails to comply with some operational policy enforced by the router that sent the ICMP error. In many cases, the fact that there is a special policy to drop traffic should not be advertised, so it is generally possible to disable the generation of these messages by either silently discarding incoming packets or generating some other ICMP error message instead.

8.3.2.4 ICMPv4 Port Unreachable (Code 3) and ICMPv6 Port Unreachable (Code 4)

The Port Unreachable message is generated when an incoming datagram is destined for an application that is not ready to receive it. This occurs most commonly in conjunction with UDP (see Chapter 10), when a message is sent to a port number that is not in use by any server process. If UDP receives a datagram and the destination port does not correspond to a port that some process has in use, UDP responds with an ICMP Port Unreachable message.

We can illustrate the operation of ICMPv4 Port Unreachable messages using the *Trivial File Transfer Protocol* (TFTP) [RFC1350] client on Windows or Linux while watching the packet exchange using `tcpdump`. The well-known UDP port for the TFTP service is 69. However, while the TFTP client is available on many systems, most systems do not run TFTP servers. Therefore, it is easy to see what happens when we try to access a nonexistent server. In the example shown in Listing 8-1, we execute the TFTP client, called `tftp`, on a Windows machine and attempt to fetch a file from a Linux machine. The –s option for `tcpdump` causes 1500 bytes to be captured per packet; the –i eth1 option tells `tcpdump` to monitor traffic on the Ethernet interface named eth1; the –vv option causes additional descriptive output to be included; and the expression `icmp or port tftp` causes traffic matching either the TFTP port (69) or the ICMPv4 protocol to be included in the output.

Listing 8-1   TFTP client demonstrating an application timeout and ICMP rate limiting

```
C:\> tftp 10.0.0.1 get /foo     try to fetch file "/foo" from 10.0.0.1
Timeout occurred               timeout occurred after about 9 seconds

Linux# tcpdump -s 1500 -i eth1 -vv icmp or port tftp

1 09:45:48.974812 IP (tos 0x0, ttl 128, id 9914, offset 0,
              flags [none], length: 44)

                 10.0.0.54.3871 > 10.0.0.1.tftp: [udp sum ok]  16
                 RRQ "/foo" netascii

2 09:45:48.974812 IP (tos 0xc0, ttl 255, id 43734, offset 0, flags
              [none], length: 72)
              10.0.0.1 > 10.0.0.54: icmp 52:
                 10.0.0.1 udp port tftp unreachable
                 for IP (tos 0x0, ttl 128, id 9914, offset 0,
                 flags [none], length: 44)
                    10.0.0.54.3871 > 10.0.0.1.tftp: [udp sum ok]  16
                    RRQ "/foo" netascii

3 09:45:49.014812 IP (tos 0x0, ttl 128, id 9915, offset 0,
              flags [none], length: 44)

                 10.0.0.54.3871 > 10.0.0.1.tftp: [udp sum ok]  16
                 RRQ "/foo" netascii

4 09:45:49.014812 IP (tos 0xc0, ttl 255, id 43735, offset 0, flags
              [none], length: 72)
              10.0.0.1 > 10.0.0.54: icmp 52:
                 10.0.0.1 udp port tftp unreachable
                 for IP (tos 0x0, ttl 128, id 9915, offset 0,
```

```
            flags [none], length: 44)
               10.0.0.54.3871 > 10.0.0.1.tftp: [udp sum ok]  16
               RRQ "/foo" netascii

 5 09:45:49.014812 IP (tos 0x0, ttl 128, id 9916, offset 0,
            flags [none], length: 44)

            10.0.0.54.3871 > 10.0.0.1.tftp: [udp sum ok]  16
            RRQ "/foo" netascii

 6 09:45:49.014812 IP (tos 0xc0, ttl 255, id 43736, offset 0, flags
            [none], length: 72)
            10.0.0.1 > 10.0.0.54: icmp 52:
            10.0.0.1 udp port tftp unreachable
            for IP (tos  0x0, ttl 128, id 9916, offset 0,
            flags [none], length: 44)
               10.0.0.54.3871 > 10.0.0.1.tftp: [udp sum ok]  16
               RRQ "/foo" netascii

 7 09:45:49.024812 IP (tos 0x0, ttl 128, id 9917, offset 0,
            flags [none], length: 44)

            10.0.0.54.3871 > 10.0.0.1.tftp: [udp sum ok]  16
            RRQ "/foo" netascii

 8 09:45:49.024812 IP (tos 0xc0, ttl 255, id 43737, offset 0,
            flags [none], length: 72)
            10.0.0.1 > 10.0.0.54: icmp 52:
            10.0.0.1 udp port tftp unreachable
            for IP (tos 0x0, ttl 128, id 9917, offset 0,
            flags [none], length: 44)
               10.0.0.54.3871 > 10.0.0.1.tftp: [udp sum ok]  16
               RRQ "/foo" netascii

 9 09:45:49.024812 IP (tos 0x0, ttl 128, id 9918, offset 0,
            flags [none], length: 44)

            10.0.0.54.3871 > 10.0.0.1.tftp: [udp sum ok]  16
            RRQ "/foo" netascii

10 09:45:49.024812 IP (tos 0xc0, ttl 255, id 43738, offset 0,
            flags [none], length: 72)
            10.0.0.1 > 10.0.0.54: icmp 52:
            10.0.0.1 udp port tftp unreachable
               for IP (tos 0x0, ttl 128, id 9918, offset 0,
               flags [none], length: 44)
                  10.0.0.54.3871 > 10.0.0.1.tftp: [udp sum ok]  16
                  RRQ "/foo" netascii

11 09:45:49.034812 IP (tos 0x0, ttl 128, id 9919, offset 0,
            flags [none], length: 44)
               10.0.0.54.3871 > 10.0.0.1.tftp: [udp sum ok]  16
               RRQ "/foo" netascii
```

```
12 09:45:49.034812 IP (tos 0xc0, ttl 255, id 43739, offset 0,
               flags [none], length: 72)
               10.0.0.1 > 10.0.0.54: icmp 52:
               10.0.0.1 udp port tftp unreachable
                  for IP (tos 0x0, ttl 128, id 9919, offset 0,
                  flags [none], length: 44)
                     10.0.0.54.3871 > 10.0.0.1.tftp: [udp sum ok]  16
                     RRQ "/foo" netascii

13 09:45:49.034812 IP (tos 0x0, ttl 128, id 9920, offset 0,
               flags [none], length: 44)
               10.0.0.54.3871 > 10.0.0.1.tftp: [udp sum ok]  16
               RRQ "/foo" netascii

14 09:45:57.054812 IP (tos 0x0, ttl 128, id 22856, offset 0,
               flags [none], length: 44)
               10.0.0.54.3871 > 10.0.0.1.tftp: [udp sum ok]  16
               RRQ "/foo" netascii

15 09:45:57.054812 IP (tos 0xc0, ttl 255, id 43740, offset 0,
               flags [none], length: 72)
               10.0.0.1 > 10.0.0.54: icmp 52:
                  10.0.0.1 udp port tftp unreachable
                  for IP (tos 0x0, ttl 128, id 22856, offset 0,
                  flags [none], length: 44)
                     10.0.0.54.3871 > 10.0.0.1.tftp: [udp sum ok]  16
                     RRQ "/foo" netascii

16 09:45:57.064812 IP (tos 0x0, ttl 128, id 22906, offset 0,
               flags [none], length: 51)
               10.0.0.54.3871 > 10.0.0.1.tftp: [udp sum ok]
                  23 ERROR EUNDEF timeout on receive"

17 09:45:57.064812 IP (tos 0xc0, ttl 255, id 43741, offset 0,
               flags [none], length: 79)
               10.0.0.1 > 10.0.0.54: icmp 59:
                  10.0.0.1 udp port tftp unreachable
                  for IP  (tos  0x0, ttl 128, id 22906, offset 0,
                  flags [none], length: 51)
                     10.0.0.54.3871 > 10.0.0.1.tftp: [udp sum ok]
                        23 ERROR EUNDEF timeout on receive"
```

Here we see a set of seven requests grouped very close to each other in time. The initial request (identified as RRQ for file /foo) comes from UDP port 3871, destined for the TFTP service (port 69). An ICMPv4 Port Unreachable message is immediately returned (packet 2), but the TFTP client appears to ignore the message, sending another UDP datagram right away. This continues immediately six more times. After waiting about another 8s, the client tries one last time and finally gives up.

Note that the ICMPv4 messages are sent without any port number designation, and each 16-byte TFTP packet is from a specific port (3871) and to a specific port (TFTP, equal to 69). The number 16 at the end of each TFTP read request (RRQ) line is the length of the data in the UDP datagram. In this example, 16 is the sum of the TFTP's 2-byte opcode, the 5-byte null-terminated name /foo, and the 9-byte null-terminated string netascii. The full ICMPv4 Unreachable message is depicted in Figure 8-5. It is 52 bytes long (not including the IPv4 header): 4 bytes for the basic ICMPv4 header, followed by 4 unused bytes (see Figure 8-5; this implementation does not use [RFC4884] extensions), the 20-byte offending IPv4 header, 8 bytes for the UDP header, and finally the remaining 16 bytes from the original tftp application request (4 + 4 + 20 + 8 + 16 = 52).

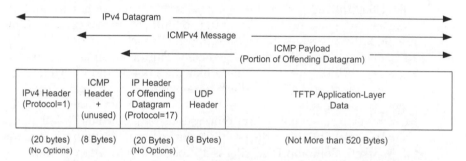

Figure 8-5   An ICMPv4 Destination Unreachable – Port Unreachable error message contains as much of the offending IPv4 datagram as possible such that the overall IPv4 datagram does not exceed 576 bytes. In this example, there is enough room to include the entire TFTP request message.

As mentioned previously, one reason ICMP includes the offending IP header in error messages is that doing so helps ICMP know how to interpret the bytes that follow encapsulated IP header (the UDP header in this example). Because a copy of the offending UDP header is included in the returned ICMP message, the source and destination port numbers can be learned. It is this destination port number (tftp, 69) that caused the ICMP Port Unreachable message to be generated. The source port number (3871) can be used by the system receiving the ICMP error to associate the error with a particular user process (the TFTP client in this example, although we saw that this client does not make much use of the indication).

Note that after the seventh request (packet 13), no error is returned for some time. The reason for this is that the Linux-based server performs *rate limiting*. That is, it limits the number of ICMP messages of the same type that can be generated in a period of time, as suggested by [RFC1812]. If we look at the elapsed time between the initial error message (packet 2, with timestamp 48.974812) and the final message before the 8s gap (packet 12, with timestamp 49.034812), we compute that 60ms have elapsed. If we count the number of ICMP messages over this time, we conclude that (6 messages/.06s) = 100 messages/s is the rate limit. This can be verified by inspecting the values of the ICMPv4 rate mask and rate limit in Linux:

```
Linux% sysctl -a | grep icmp_rate
net.ipv4.icmp_ratemask = 6168
net.ipv4.icmp_ratelimit = 100
```

Here we see that several ICMPv4 messages are to be rate-limited, and that the rate limit for all of them is 100 (measured in messages per second). The `ratemask` variable indicates which messages have the limit applied to them, by turning on the kth bit in the mask if the message with code number k is to be limited, starting from 0. In this case, codes 3, 4, 11, and 12 are being limited (because 6168 = 0x1818 = 0001100000011000, where bits 3, 4, 11, and 12 from the right are turned on). If we were to set the rate limit to 0 (meaning no limit), we would find that Linux returns nine ICMPv4 messages, one corresponding to each `tftp` request packet, and the `tftp` client times out almost immediately. This behavior also occurs when trying to access a Windows XP machine, which does not perform ICMP rate limiting.

Why does the TFTP client keep retransmitting its request when the error messages are being returned? A detail of network programming is revealed here. Most systems do not notify user processes using UDP that ICMP that messages for them have arrived unless the process calls a special function (i.e., `connect` on the UDP socket). Common TFTP clients do not call this function, so they never receive the ICMP error notification. Without hearing any response regarding the fate of its TFTP protocol requests, the TFTP client tries again and again to retrieve its file. This is an example of a poor request and retry mechanism. Although TFTP does have extensions for adjusting this behavior (see [RFC2349]), we shall see later (in Chapter 16) that a more sophisticated transport protocol such as TCP has a much better algorithm.

8.3.2.5 ICMPv4 PTB (Code 4)

If an IPv4 router receives a datagram that it intends to forward, and if the datagram does not fit into the MTU in use on the selected outgoing network interface, the datagram must be fragmented (see Chapter 10). If the arriving datagram has the *Don't Fragment* bit field set in its IP header, however, it is not forwarded but instead is dropped, and this ICMPv4 Destination Unreachable (PTB) message is generated. Because the router sending this message knows the MTU of the next hop, it is able to include the MTU value in the error message it generates.

This message was originally intended to be used for network diagnostics but has since been used for path MTU discovery. PMTUD is used to determine an appropriate packet size to use when communicating with a particular host, on the assumption that avoiding packet fragmentation is desirable. It is used most commonly with TCP, and we cover it in more detail in Chapter 14.

8.3.2.6 ICMPv6 PTB (Type 2, Code 0)

In ICMPv6, a special message and type code combination is used to indicate that a packet is too large for the MTU of the next hop (see Figure 8-6).

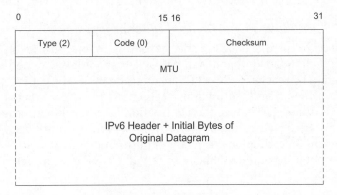

0   15 16   31

Type (2)	Code (0)	Checksum
MTU		

IPv6 Header + Initial Bytes of
Original Datagram

Figure 8-6   The ICMPv6 Packet Too Big message (type 2) works like the corresponding ICMPv4 Destination Unreachable message. The ICMPv6 variant includes 32 bits to hold the next-hop MTU.

This message is not a Destination Unreachable message. Recall that in IPv6, packet fragmentation is performed only by the sender of a datagram and that MTU discovery is always supposed to be used. Thus, this message is used primarily by the IPv6 PMTUD mechanism, but also in the (rare) circumstances that a packet arrives that is too large to be carried over the next hop. Because routes may change after the operation of PMTUD and after a packet is injected into the network, it is always possible that a packet arriving at a router is too large for the outgoing MTU. As is the case with modern implementations of ICMPv4 Destination Unreachable code 4 (PTB) messages, the suggested MTU size of the packet, based on the MTU of the egress link of the router generating the ICMP message, is carried in the indication.

8.3.2.7 ICMPv6 Beyond Scope of Source Address (Code 2)

As we saw in Chapter 2, IPv6 uses addresses of different scopes. Thus, it is possible to construct a packet with source and destination addresses of different scopes. Furthermore, it is possible that the destination address may not be reachable within the same scope. For example, a packet with a source address using link-local scope may be destined for a globally scoped destination that requires traversal of more than one router. Because the source address is of insufficient scope, the packet is dropped by a router, and this form of ICMPv6 error is produced to indicate the problem.

8.3.2.8 ICMPv6 Source Address Failed Ingress/Egress Policy (Code 5)

Code 5 is a more refined version of code 1, to be used when a particular ingress or egress filtering policy is the reason for prohibiting the successful delivery of a datagram. This might be used, for example, when a host attempts to send traffic using a source IPv6 address from an unexpected network prefix [RFC3704].

8.3.2.9 ICMPv6 Reject Route to Destination (Code 6)

A *reject* or *blocking route* is a special routing or forwarding table entry (see Chapter 5), which indicates that matching packets should be dropped and an ICMPv6 Destination Unreachable Reject Route message should be generated. (A similar type of entry called a *blackhole route* also causes matching packets to be dropped, but usually without generating the Destination Unreachable message.) Such routes may be installed in a router's forwarding table to prevent leakage of packets sent to unwanted destinations. Unwanted destinations may include *martian* routes (prefixes not used on the public Internet) and *bogons* (valid prefixes not yet allocated).

8.3.3   Redirect (ICMPv4 Type 5, ICMPv6 Type 137)

If a router receives a datagram from a host and can determine that it is not the correct next hop for the host to have used to deliver the datagram to its destination, the router sends a Redirect message to the host and sends the datagram on to the correct router (or host). That is, if it can determine that there is a better next hop than itself for the given datagram, it redirects the host to update its forwarding table so that future traffic for the same destination will be directed toward the new node. This facility provides a crude form of routing protocol by indicating to the IP forwarding function where to send its packets. The process of IP forwarding is discussed in detail in Chapter 5.

In Figure 8-7, a network segment has a host and two routers, R1 and R2. When the host sends a datagram incorrectly through router R2, R2 responds by sending the Redirect message to the host, while forwarding the datagram to R1. Although hosts may be configured to update their forwarding tables based on ICMP redirects, routers are discouraged from doing so under the assumption that routers should already know the best next-hop nodes for all reachable destinations because they are using dynamic routing protocols.

The ICMP Redirect message includes the IP address of the router (or destination host, if it is reachable using direct delivery) a host should use as a next hop for the destination specified in the ICMP error message (see Figure 8-8). Originally the redirect facility supported a distinction between a redirect for a *host* and a redirect for a *network*, but once classless addressing was used (CIDR; see Chapter 2), the network redirect form effectively vanished. Thus, when a host receives a host redirect, it is effective only for that single IP destination address. A host that consistently chooses the wrong router can wind up with a forwarding table entry for every destination it contacts outside its local subnet, each of which has been added as the result of receiving a Redirect message from its configured default router. The format of the ICMPv4 Redirect message is shown in Figure 8-8.

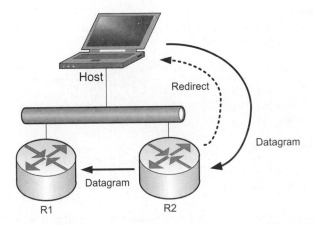

Figure 8-7 The host incorrectly sends a datagram via R2 toward its destination. R2 realizes the host's mistake and sends the datagram to the proper router, R1. It also informs the host of the error by sending an ICMP Redirect message. The host is expected to adjust its forwarding tables so that future datagrams to the same destination go through R1 without bothering R2.

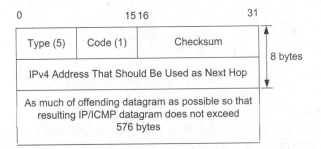

Figure 8-8 The ICMPv4 Redirect message includes the IPv4 address of the correct router to use as a next hop for the datagram included in the payload portion of the message. A host typically checks the IPv4 source address of the incoming Redirect message to verify that it is coming from the default router it is currently using.

We can examine the behavior of a Redirect message by changing our host to use an incorrect router (another host on the same network) as its default next hop. As an example, we first change our default route and then attempt to contact a remote server. Our system will mistakenly attempt to forward its outgoing packets to the specified host:

```
C:\> netstat -rn
Network Dest    Netmask       Gateway       Interface      Metric
0.0.0.0         0.0.0.0       10.212.2.1    10.212.2.88    1
```

```
C:\> route delete 0.0.0.0                               delete default
C:\> route add 0.0.0.0 mask 0.0.0.0 10.212.2.112        add new
C:\> ping ds1.eecs.berkeley.edu                         sends thru 10.212.2.112
Pinging ds1.eecs.berkeley.edu [169.229.60.105] with 32 bytes of data:

Reply from 169.229.60.105: bytes=32 time=1ms TTL=250
Reply from 169.229.60.105: bytes=32 time=5ms TTL=250
Reply from 169.229.60.105: bytes=32 time=1ms TTL=250
Reply from 169.229.60.105: bytes=32 time=1ms TTL=250

Ping statistics for 169.229.60.105:
    Packets: Sent = 4, Received = 4, Lost = 0 (0% loss),
Approximate round trip times in milli-seconds:
    Minimum = 1ms, Maximum = 5ms, Average = 2ms
```

While this is taking place, we can run tcpdump to observe the activities (some lines have been wrapped for clarity):

```
Linux# tcpdump host 10.212.2.88

1 20:27:00.759340 IP 10.212.2.88 > ds1.eecs.berkeley.edu: icmp 40:
                  echo request seq 15616
2 20:27:00.759445 IP 10.212.2.112 > 10.212.2.88: icmp 68:
                  redirect ds1.eecs.berkeley.edu to host 10.212.2.1
3 20:27:00.759468 IP 10.212.2.88 > ds1.eecs.berkeley.edu: icmp 40:
                  echo request seq 15616
...
```

Here our host (10.212.2.88) sends an ICMPv4 Echo Request (ping) message to the host ds1.eecs.berkeley.edu. After the name is resolved by DNS (see Chapter 11) to the IPv4 address 169.229.60.105, the Request message is sent to the first hop, 10.212.2.112, rather than the correct default router, 10.212.2.1. Because the system with IPv4 address 10.212.2.112 is properly configured, it understands that the original sending host should have used the router 10.212.2.1. As expected, it responds with an ICMPv4 Redirect message toward the host, indicating that in the future, any traffic destined for ds1.eecs.berkeley.edu should go through the router 10.212.2.1.

In ICMPv6, the Redirect message (type 137) contains the target address and the destination address (see Figure 8-9), and it is defined in conjunction with the ND process (see Section 8.5). The *Target Address* field contains the correct node's link-local IPv6 address that should be used for the next hop. The *Destination Address* is the destination IPv6 address in the datagram that evoked the redirect. In the particular situation where the destination is an on-link neighbor to the host receiving the redirect, the *Target Address* and *Destination Address* fields are identical. This provides a method for informing a host that another host is on the same link, even if the two hosts do not share a common address prefix [RFC5942].

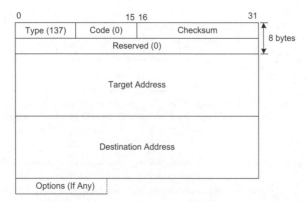

Figure 8-9   The ICMPv6 Redirect message. The target address indicates the IPv6 address of a better next-hop router for the node identified by the destination address. This message can also be used to indicate that the destination address is an on-link neighbor to the node sending the message that induced the error message. In this case, the destination and target addresses are the same.

As with other ND messages in ICMPv6, this message can include options. The types of options include the Target Link-Layer Address option and the Redirected Header option. The Target Link-Layer Address option is required in cases where the Redirect message is used on a *non-broadcast multiple access* (NBMA) network, because in such cases there may be no other efficient way for the host receiving the Redirect message to determine the link-layer address for the new next hop. The Redirected Header option holds a portion of the IPv6 packet that caused the Redirect message to be generated. We discuss the format of these options and others in Section 8.5 when exploring IPv6 Neighbor Discovery.

8.3.4   ICMP Time Exceeded (ICMPv4 Type 11, ICMPv6 Type 3)

Every IPv4 datagram has a *Time-to-Live* (*TTL*) field in its IPv4 header, and every IPv6 datagram has a *Hop Limit* field in its header (see Chapter 5). As originally conceived, the 8-bit *TTL* field was to hold the number of seconds a datagram was allowed to remain active in the network before being forcibly discarded (a good thing if forwarding loops are present). Because of an additional rule that said that any router must decrement the *TTL* field by at least 1, combined with the fact that datagram forwarding times grew to be small fractions of a second, the *TTL* field has been used in practice as a limitation on the number of hops an IPv4 datagram is allowed to take before it is discarded by a router. This usage was formalized and ultimately adopted in IPv6. ICMP Time Exceeded (code 0) messages are generated when a router discards a datagram because the *TTL* or *Hop Limit* field is too low (i.e., arrives with value 0 or 1 and must be forwarded). This message is important for the proper operation of the `traceroute` tool (called `tracert` on Windows). Its format, for both ICMPv4 and ICMPv6, is given in Figure 8-10.

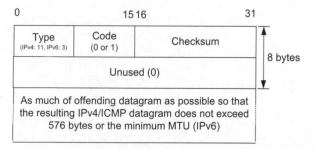

Figure 8-10   The ICMP Time Exceeded message format for ICMPv4 and ICMPv6. The message is standardized for both the TTL or hop count being exceeded (code 0) or the time for reassembling fragments exceeding some preconfigured threshold (code 1).

Another less common variant of this message is when a fragmented IP datagram only partially arrives at its destination (i.e., all its fragments do not arrive after a period of time). In such cases, a variant of the ICMP Time Exceeded message (code 1) is used to inform the sender that its overall datagram has been discarded. Recall that if any fragment of a datagram is dropped, the entire datagram is lost.

8.3.4.1 Example: The `traceroute` Tool

The `traceroute` tool is used to determine the routers used along a path from a sender to a destination. We shall discuss the operation of the IPv4 version. The approach involves sending datagrams first with an IPv4 *TTL* field set to 1 and allowing the expiring datagrams to induce routers along the path to send ICMPv4 Time Exceeded (code 0) messages. Each round, the sending TTL value is increased by 1, causing the routers that are one hop farther to expire the datagrams and generate ICMP messages. These messages are sent from the router's primary IPv4 address "facing" the sender. Figure 8-11 shows how this approach works.

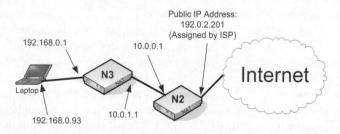

Figure 8-11   The `traceroute` tool can be used to determine the routing path, assuming it does not fluctuate too quickly. When using `traceroute`, routers are typically identified by the IP addresses assigned to the interfaces "facing" or nearest to the host performing the trace.

In this example, `traceroute` is used to send UDP datagrams (see Chapter 10) from the laptop to the host `www.eecs.berkeley.edu` (an Internet host with IPv4 address `128.32.244.172`, not shown in Figure 8-11). This is accomplished using the following command:

```
Linux% traceroute -m 2 www.cs.berkeley.edu
traceroute to web2.eecs.berkeley.edu (128.32.244.172), 2 hops max,
52 byte packets
 1   gw (192.168.0.1)  3.213 ms  0.839 ms  0.920 ms
 2   10.0.0.1 (10.0.0.1)  1.524 ms  1.221 ms  9.176 ms
```

The —m option instructs `traceroute` to perform only two rounds: one using TTL = 1 and one using TTL = 2. Each line gives the information found at the corresponding TTL. For example, line 1 indicates that one hop away a router with IPv4 address `192.168.0.1` was found and that three independent round-trip-time measurements (`3.213`, `0.839`, and `0.920`ms) were taken. The difference between the first and subsequent times relates to additional work that is involved in the first measurement (i.e., an ARP transaction). Figures 8-12 and 8-13 show Wireshark packet captures indicating how the outgoing datagrams and returning ICMPv4 messages are structured.

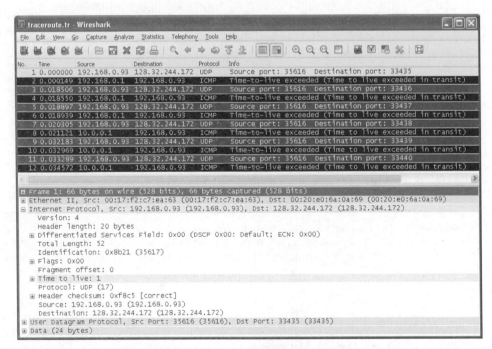

Figure 8-12 traceroute using IPv4 begins by sending a UDP/IPv4 datagram with TTL = 1 to destination port number 33435. Each TTL value is tried three times before being incremented by 1 and retried. Each expiring datagram causes the router at the appropriate hop distance to send an ICMPv4 Time Exceeded message back to the source. The message's source address is that of the router "facing" the sender.

Looking at Figure 8-12, we can see that `traceroute` sends six datagrams, and that each datagram is sent to a destination port number in sequence, starting with 33435. If we look more closely, we can see that the first three datagrams are sent with TTL = 1 and the second set of three are sent with TTL = 2. Figure 8-12 shows the first one. Each datagram causes an ICMPv4 Time Exceeded (code 0) message to be sent. The first three are sent from router N3 (IPv4 address 192.168.0.1), and the next three are sent from router N2 (IPv4 address 10.0.0.1). Figure 8-13 shows the last ICMP message in more detail.

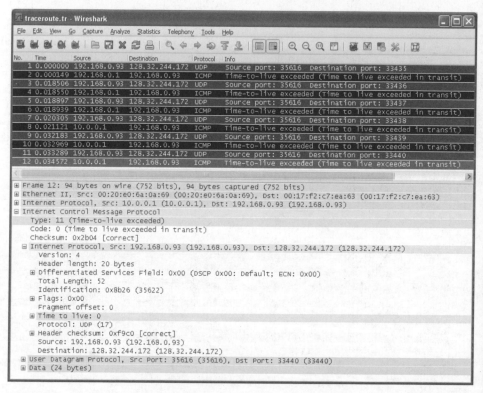

Figure 8-13   The final ICMPv4 Time Exceeded message of the trace is sent by N2 (IPv4 address 10.0.0.1). It includes a copy of the original datagram that caused the Time Exceeded message to be generated. The TTL of the inner IPv4 header is 0 because N2 decremented it from 1.

This is the final Time Exceeded message of the trace. It contains the original IPv4 datagram (packet 11), as seen by N2 upon receipt. This datagram arrives with TTL = 1, but after being decremented is too small for N2 to perform additional forwarding to 128.32.244.172. Consequently, N2 sends a Time Exceeded message back to the source of the original datagram.

8.3.5 Parameter Problem (ICMPv4 Type 12, ICMPv6 Type 4)

ICMP Parameter Problem messages are generated by a host or router receiving an IP datagram containing some problem in its IP header that cannot be repaired. When a datagram cannot be handled and no other ICMP message adequately describes the problem, this message acts as a sort of "catchall" error condition indicator. In both ICMPv4 and ICMPv6, if there is an error in the header such that some field is out of acceptable range, a special ICMP error message *Pointer* field indicates the byte offset of the field where the error was found, relative to the beginning of the offending IP header. With ICMPv4, for example, a value of 1 in the *Pointer* field indicates a bad IPv4 *DS Field* or *ECN* field (together, these fields used to be called the IPv4 *Type of Service* or *ToS Byte* which has since been redefined and renamed; see Chapter 5). The format of the ICMPv4 Parameter Problem message is shown in Figure 8-14.

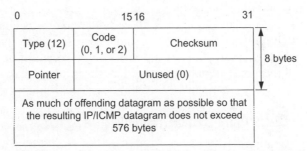

Figure 8-14 The ICMPv4 Parameter Problem message is used when no other message applies. The *Pointer* field indicates the byte index of the problematic value in the offending IPv4 header. Code 0 is most common. Code 1 was formerly used to indicate that a required option was missing but is now historic. Code 2 indicates that the offending IPv4 datagram has a bad *IHL* or *Total Length* field.

Code 0 is the most common variant of the ICMPv4 Parameter Problem messages and is used when there is almost any problem with the IPv4 header, although problems with the header or datagram *Total Length* fields may instead generate code 2 messages. Code 1 was once used to indicate missing options such as security labels on packets but is now historic. Code 2, a more recently defined code, indicates a bad length in the *IHL* or *Total Length* fields (see Chapter 5). The ICMPv6 version of this error message is shown in Figure 8-15.

In ICMPv6, the treatment of this error has been refined somewhat, relative to the ICMPv4 version, into three cases: erroneous header field encountered (code 0), unrecognized *Next Header* type encountered (code 1), and unrecognized IPv6 option encountered (code 2). As with the corresponding error message in ICMPv4, the ICMPv6 parameter problem *Pointer* field gives the byte offset into the offending IPv6 header that caused the problem. For example, a *Pointer* field of 40 would indicate a problem with the first IPv6 extension header.

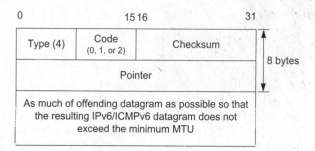

Figure 8-15   The ICMPv6 Parameter Problem message. The *Pointer* field gives the byte offset into the original datagram where an error was encountered. Code 0 indicates a bad header field. Code 1 indicates an unrecognized *Next Header* type, and Code 2 indicates that an unknown IPv6 option was encountered.

The erroneous header (code 0) error occurs when a field in one of the IPv6 headers contains an illegal value. A code 1 error occurs when an IPv6 *Next Header* (header chaining) field contains a value corresponding to a header type that the IPv6 implementation does not support. Finally, code 2 is used when an IPv6 header option is received but not recognized by the implementation.

8.4   ICMP Query/Informational Messages

Although ICMP defines a number of query messages such as Address Mask Request/Reply (types 17/18), Timestamp Request/Reply (types 13/14), and Information Request/Reply (types 15/16), these functions have been replaced by other, more purpose-specific protocols (including DHCP; see Chapter 6). The only remaining popular ICMP query/informational messages are the Echo Request/Response messages, more commonly called `ping`, and the Router Discovery messages. Even the Router Discovery mechanism is not in wide use with IPv4, but its analog (part of Neighbor Discovery) in IPv6 is fundamental. In addition, ICMPv6 has been extended to support Mobile IPv6 and the discovery of multicast-capable routers. In this section, we investigate the Echo Request/Reply functions and the messages used for basic router and Multicast Listener Discovery (also see Chapters 6 and 9). In the subsequent section, we explore the operation of Neighbor Discovery in IPv6.

8.4.1   Echo Request/Reply (`ping`) (ICMPv4 Types 0/8, ICMPv6 Types 129/128)

One of the most commonly used ICMP message pairs is Echo Request and Echo Response (or Reply). In ICMPv4 these are types 8 and 0, respectively, and in ICMPv6 they are types 128 and 129, respectively. ICMP Echo Request messages may be of nearly arbitrary size (limited by the ultimate size of the encapsulating

IP datagram). With ICMP Echo Reply messages, the ICMP implementation is required to return any data received back to the sender, even if multiple IP fragments are involved. The ICMP Echo Request/Response message format is shown in Figure 8-16.

As with other ICMP query/informational messages, the server must echo the *Identifier* and *Sequence Number* fields back in the reply.

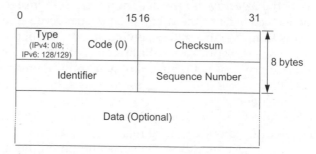

Figure 8-16   Format of the ICMPv4 and ICMPv6 Echo Request and Echo Reply messages. Any optional data included in a request must be returned in a reply. NATs use the *Identifier* field to match requests with replies, as discussed in Chapter 7.

These messages are sent by the `ping` program, which is commonly used to quickly determine if a computer is reachable on the Internet. At one time, if you could "ping" a host, you could almost certainly reach it by other means (remote login, other services, etc.). With firewalls in common use, however, this is now far from certain.

Note

The name *ping* is taken from the sonar operation to locate objects. The `ping` program was written by Mike Muuss, who maintained an amusing Web page describing its history [PING].

Implementations of `ping` set the *Identifier* field in the ICMP message to some number that the sending host can use to demultiplex returned responses. In UNIX-based systems, for example, the process ID of the sending process is typically placed in the *Identifier* field. This allows the `ping` application to identify the returned responses if there are multiple instances of `ping` running at the same time on the same host, because the ICMP protocol does not have the benefit of transport-layer port numbers. This field is often known as the *Query Identifier* field when referring to firewall behavior (see Chapter 7).

When a new instance of the `ping` program is run, the *Sequence Number* field starts with the value 0 and is increased by 1 every time a new Echo Request message is sent. ping prints the sequence number of each returned packet, allowing the user to see if packets are missing, reordered, or duplicated. Recall that IP (and consequently ICMP) is a *best-effort* datagram delivery service, so any of these three conditions can occur. ICMP does, however, include a data checksum not provided by IP.

The ping program also typically includes a copy of the local time in the optional data area of outgoing echo requests. This time, along with the rest of the contents of the data area, is returned in an Echo Response message. The ping program notes the current time when a response is received and subtracts the time in the reply from the current time, giving an estimate of the RTT to reach the host that was "pinged." Because only the original sender's notion of the current time is used, this feature does not require any synchronization between the clocks at the sender and receiver. A similar approach is used by the traceroute tool for its RTT measurements.

Early versions of the ping program operated by sending an Echo Request message once per second, printing each returning echo reply. Newer implementations, however, have increased the variability in output formats and behaviors. On Windows, the default is to send four echo requests, one per second, print some statistics, and exit; the -t option is required to allow the Windows ping application to continue until stopped by the user. On Linux, the behavior is the traditional one—the default is to run until interrupted by the user, sending an echo request each second and printing any responses. Many other variants of ping have been developed over the years, and there are several other standard options. With some versions of the application, a large packet can be constructed to contain special data patterns. This has been used to look for data-dependent errors in network communications equipment.

In the following example, we send an ICMPv4 Echo Request to the subnet broadcast address. This particular version of the ping application (Linux) requires us to specify the -b flag to indicate that it is indeed our intention (and it gives us a warning regarding this, because it can generate a substantial volume of network traffic) to use the broadcast address:

```
Linux% ping -b 10.0.0.127
WARNING: pinging broadcast address
PING 10.0.0.127 (10.0.0.127) from 10.0.0.1 : 56(84) bytes of data.
64 bytes from 10.0.0.1: icmp_seq=0 ttl=255 time=1.290 msec
64 bytes from 10.0.0.6: icmp_seq=0 ttl=64 time=1.853 msec (DUP!)
64 bytes from 10.0.0.47: icmp_seq=0 ttl=64 time=2.311 msec (DUP!)
64 bytes from 10.0.0.1: icmp_seq=1 ttl=255 time=382 usec
64 bytes from 10.0.0.6: icmp_seq=1 ttl=64 time=1.587 msec (DUP!)
64 bytes from 10.0.0.47: icmp_seq=1 ttl=64 time=2.406 msec (DUP!)
64 bytes from 10.0.0.1: icmp_seq=2 ttl=255 time=380 usec
64 bytes from 10.0.0.6: icmp_seq=2 ttl=64 time=1.573 msec (DUP!)
64 bytes from 10.0.0.47: icmp_seq=2 ttl=64 time=2.394 msec (DUP!)
64 bytes from 10.0.0.1: icmp_seq=3 ttl=255 time=389 usec
64 bytes from 10.0.0.6: icmp_seq=3 ttl=64 time=1.583 msec (DUP!)
64 bytes from 10.0.0.47: icmp_seq=3 ttl=64 time=2.403 msec (DUP!)
```

```
--- 10.0.0.127 ping statistics ---
4 packets transmitted, 4 packets received,
+8 duplicates, 0% packet loss
round-trip min/avg/max/mdev = 0.380/1.545/2.406/0.765 ms
```

Here, 4 outgoing Echo Request messages are sent and we see 12 responses. This behavior is typical of using the broadcast address: all receiving nodes are compelled to respond. We therefore see the sequence numbers 0, 1, 2, and 3, but for each one we see 3 responses. The (DUP!) notation indicates that an Echo Reply has been received containing a *Sequence Number* field identical to a previously received one. Observe that the TTL values are different (255 and 64), suggesting that different kinds of computers are responding.

Note that this procedure (sending echo requests to the IPv4 broadcast address) can be used to quickly populate the local system's ARP table (see Chapter 4). Those systems responding to the Echo Request message form an Echo Reply message directed at the sender of the request. When the reply is destined for a system on the same subnet, an ARP request is issued looking for the link-layer address of the originator of the request. In so doing, ARP is exchanged between every responder and the request sender. This causes the sender of the Echo Request message to learn the link-layer addresses of all the responders. In this example, even if the local system had no link-layer address mappings for the addresses 10.0.0.1, 10.0.0.6, and 10.0.0.47, they would all be present in the ARP table after the broadcast. Note that returning Echo Reply messages to requests sent to the broadcast address is optional. By default, Linux systems return such replies and Windows XP systems do not.

8.4.2 Router Discovery: Router Solicitation and Advertisement (ICMPv4 Types 9, 10)

In Chapter 6, we looked at how DHCP can be used for a host to acquire an IP address and learn about the existence of nearby routers. An alternative option we mentioned for learning about routers is called *Router Discovery* (RD). Although specified for configuring both IPv4 and IPv6 hosts, it is not widely used with IPv4 because of widespread preference for DHCP. However, it is now specified for use in conjunction with Mobile IP, so we provide a brief description. The IPv6 version forms part of the IPv6 SLAAC function (see Chapter 6) and is logically part of IPv6 ND. Therefore, we shall return to discussing it in the broader context of ND in Section 8.5.

Router Discovery for IPv4 is accomplished using a pair of ICMPv4 informational messages [RFC1256]: Router Solicitation (RS, type 10) and Router Advertisement (RA, type 9). The advertisements are sent by routers in two ways. First, they are periodically multicast on the local network (using TTL = 1) to the All Hosts multicast address (224.0.0.1), and they are also provided to hosts on demand that ask for them using RS messages. RS messages are sent using multicast to the All Routers multicast address (224.0.0.2). The primary purpose of Router Discovery is for a host to learn about all the routers on its local subnetwork, so that it can choose a default route among them. It is also used to discover the presence of routers that are willing to act as Mobile IP home agents. See Chapter 9 for details on local network multicast. Figure 8-17 shows the ICMPv4 RA message format, which includes a list of the IPv4 addresses that can be used by a host as a default router.

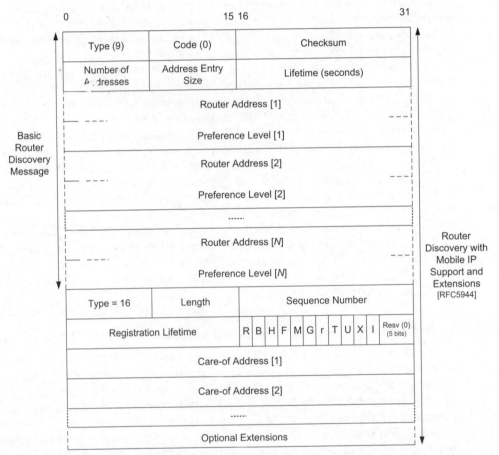

Figure 8-17 The ICMPv4 Router Advertisement message includes a list of IPv4 addresses of routers that can be used as default next hops. The preference level lets network operators arrange for some ordering of preferences to be applied with respect to the list (higher is more preferred). Mobile IPv4 [RFC5944] augments RA messages with extensions in order to advertise MIPv4 mobility agents and the prefix lengths of the advertised router addresses.

In Figure 8-17, the *Number of Addresses* field gives the number of router address blocks in the message. Each block contains an IPv4 address and accompanying *preference level*. The *Address Entry Size* field gives the number of 32-bit words per block (two in this case). The *Lifetime* field gives the number of seconds for which the list of addresses should be considered valid. The preference level is a 32-bit signed two's-complement integer for which higher values indicate greater preference. The default preference level is 0; the special value 0x80000000 indicates an address that should not be used as a valid default router.

RA messages are also used by Mobile IP [RFC5944] for a node to locate a mobility (i.e., home and/or foreign) agent. Figure 8-17 depicts a Router Advertisement message including a Mobility Agent Advertisement extension. This extension follows the conventional RA information and includes a *Type* field with value 16 and a *Length* field giving the number of bytes in the extension area (not including the *Type* and *Length* fields). Its value is equal to (6 + 4K), assuming that K care-of addresses are included. The *Sequence Number* field gives the number of such extensions produced by the agent since initialization. The registration gives the maximum number of seconds during which the sending agent is willing to accept MIPv4 registrations (0xFFFF indicates infinity). There are a number of *Flags* bit fields with the following meanings: R (registration required for MIP services), B (agent is too busy to accept new registrations), H (agent is willing to act as home agent), F (agent is willing to act as foreign agent), M (the minimum encapsulation format [RFC2004] is supported), G (the agent supports GRE tunnels for encapsulated datagrams), r (reserved zero), T (reverse tunneling [RFC3024] is supported), U (UDP tunneling [RFC3519] is supported), X (registration revocation [RFC3543] is supported), and I (foreign agent supports regional registration [RFC4857]).

In addition to the Mobility Agent Advertisement extension, one other extension has been designed to help mobile nodes. The Prefix-Lengths extension may follow a Mobility Agent Advertisement extension and indicates the prefix length of each corresponding router address provided in the base router advertisement. The format is shown in Figure 8-18.

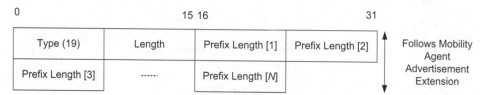

Figure 8-18 The ICMPv4 optional RA Prefix-Lengths extension gives the number of significant prefix bits for each of the N router addresses present in the basic Router Advertisement portion of the message. This extension follows the Mobility Agent Advertisement extension, if present.

In Figure 8-18, the *Length* field is set equal to N, the *Number of Addresses* field from the basic RA message. Each 8-bit *Prefix Length* field gives the number of bits in the corresponding *Router Address* field (see Figure 8-17) in use on the local subnetwork. This extension can be used by a mobile node to help determine whether it has moved from one network to another. Using algorithm 2 of [RFC5944], a mobile node may cache the set of prefixes available on a particular link. A move can be detected if the set of network prefixes has changed.

8.4.3   Home Agent Address Discovery Request/Reply (ICMPv6 Types 144/145)

[RFC6275] defines four ICMPv6 messages used in support of MIPv6. Two of the ICMPv6 messages are used for dynamic home agent address discovery, and the other two are used for renumbering and mobile configuration. The Home Agent Address Discovery Request message is used by an MIPv6 node when visiting a new network to dynamically discover a home agent (see Figure 8-19).

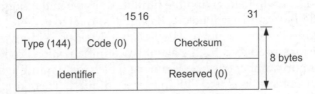

Figure 8-19   The MIPv6 Home Agent Address Discovery Request message contains an identifier that is returned in the response. It is sent to the Home Agents anycast address for the mobile node's home prefix.

The message is sent to the MIPv6 Home Agents anycast address for its home prefix. The IPv6 source address is typically the care-of address—the address a mobile node has acquired on the network it is currently visiting (see Chapter 5). A Home Agent Address Discovery Response message (see Figure 8-20) is sent by a node willing to act as a home agent for the given node and its home prefix.

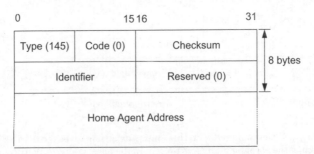

Figure 8-20   The MIPv6 Home Agent Address Discovery Reply message contains the identifier from the corresponding request and one or more addresses of a home agent willing to forward packets for the mobile node.

The home agent address is provided directly to the mobile node's unicast address, which is most likely a care-of address. These messages are intended to handle cases where a mobile node's HA has changed while transitioning between networks. After reestablishing an appropriate HA, the mobile may initiate MIPv6 binding updates (see Chapter 5).

8.4.4 Mobile Prefix Solicitation/Advertisement (ICMPv6 Types 146/147)

The Mobile Prefix Solicitation message (see Figure 8-21) is used to solicit a routing prefix update from an HA when a node's home address is about to become invalid. The mobile includes a Home Address option (IPv6 Destination Options; see Chapter 5) and protects the solicitation using IPsec (see Chapter 18).

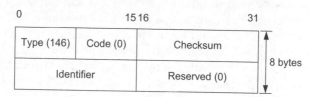

Figure 8-21 The MIPv6 Mobile Prefix Solicitation message is sent by a mobile node when away to request a home agent to provide a mobile prefix advertisement.

The solicitation message includes a random value in the *Identifier* field, used to match requests with replies. It is similar to a Router Solicitation message but is sent to a mobile node's HA instead of to the local subnetwork. In the advertisement form of this message (see Figure 8-22), the encapsulating IPv6 datagram must include a type 2 routing header (see Chapter 5). The *Identifier* field contains a copy of the identifier provided in the solicitation message. The M (*Managed Address*) field indicates that hosts should use stateful address configuration and avoid autoconfiguration. The O (*Other*) field indicates that information other than the address is provided by a stateful configuration method. The advertisement then contains one or more Prefix Information options.

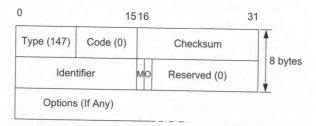

Figure 8-22 The MIPv6 Mobile Prefix Advertisement message. The *Identifier* field matches the corresponding field in the solicitation. The M (*Managed*) flag indicates that the address is provided by a stateful configuration mechanism. The O (*Other*) flag indicates that other information beyond the address is supplied by stateful mechanisms.

The Mobile Prefix Advertisement message is designed to inform a traveling mobile node that its home prefix has changed. This message is normally secured using IPsec (see Chapter 18) in order to help a mobile node protect itself from spoofed prefix advertisements. The Prefix Information option, which uses the format described in [RFC4861], contains the prefix(es) the mobile node should use for configuring its home address(es).

8.4.5   Mobile IPv6 Fast Handover Messages (ICMPv6 Type 154)

A variant of MIPv6 defines *fast handovers* [RFC5568] for MIPv6 (called FMIPv6). It specifies methods for improving the IP-layer handoff latency when a mobile node moves from one network access point (AP) to another. This is accomplished by predicting the routers and addressing information that will be used prior to the handoff taking place. The protocol involves the discovery of so-called *proxy routers*, which behave like routers a mobile is likely to encounter after it is handed off to a new network. There are corresponding ICMPv6 Proxy Router Solicitation and Advertisement messages (called RtSolPr and PrRtAdv, respectively). The basic format of the RtSolPr and PrRtAdv messages is given in Figure 8-23.

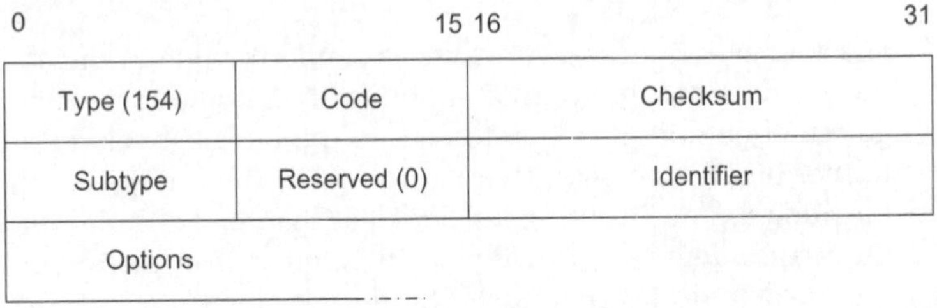

0	15 16	31
Type (154)	Code	Checksum
Subtype	Reserved (0)	Identifier
Options		

Figure 8-23   The common ICMPv6 message type used for FMIPv6 messages. The *Code* and *Subtype* fields give further information. Solicitation messages use code 0 and subtype 2 and may include the sender's link-layer address and the link-layer address of its preferred next access point (if known) as options. Advertisements use codes 0–5 and subtype 3. The different code values indicate the presence of various options, whether the advertisement was solicited, if the prefix or router information has changed, and the handling of DHCP.

A mobile node may have some information available regarding the addresses or identifiers of APs it will use in the future (e.g., by "scanning" for 802.11 networks). A RtSolPr message uses code 0 and subtype 2 and must contain at least one option, the New Access Point Link-Layer Address option. This is used to indicate which AP the mobile is requesting information about. The RtSolPr message may also contain a Link-Layer Address option identifying the source, if known. These options use the IPv6 ND option format, so we shall defer discussion of them until we look at ND in detail.

8.4.6   Multicast Listener Query/Report/Done (ICMPv6 Types 130/131/132)

Multicast Listener Discovery (MLD) [RFC2710][RFC3590] provides management of multicast addresses on links using IPv6. It is similar to the IGMP protocol used by IPv4, described in Chapter 9. That chapter deals with the operation of IGMP and the use of this ICMPv6 message in detail; here we describe the message formats that constitute MLD (version 1), including the Multicast Listener Query, Report, and Done messages. The basic format is given in Figure 8-24. These messages are sent with an IPv6 *Hop Limit* field value of 1 and the Router Alert Hop-by-Hop IPv6 option.

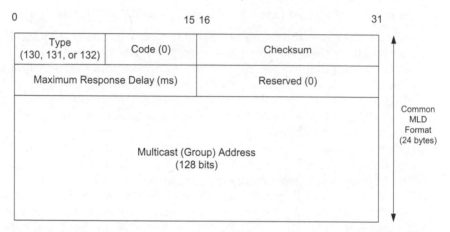

Figure 8-24   ICMPv6 MLD version 1 messages are all of this form. Queries (type 130) are either general or multicast-address-specific. General queries ask hosts to report which multicast addresses they have in use, and address-specific queries are used to determine if a specific address is (still) in use. The maximum response time gives the maximum number of milliseconds a host may delay sending a report in response to a query. The destination multicast address is 0 for general queries and the multicast address in question for specific reports. For Report (type 131) and Done messages (type 132), it includes the address related to the report or what address is no longer of interest, respectively.

The main purpose of MLD is for multicast routers to learn the multicast addresses used by the hosts on each link to which they are mutually attached. MLDv2 (described in the next section) extends this capability by allowing hosts to specify particular hosts from which they wish to (or not to) receive traffic. Two forms of MLD queries are sent by multicast routers: *general* queries and *multicast-address-specific* queries. Generally, routers send the query messages and hosts respond with reports, either in response to the queries, or unsolicited if a host's multicast address membership changes.

The *Maximum Response Time* field, nonzero only in queries, gives the maximum number of milliseconds a host may delay sending a report in response to a query. Because the multicast router need only know that *at least one* host is interested in traffic destined for a particular multicast address (because link-layer multicast support allows the router to not have to replicate the message for each destination), nodes may intentionally and randomly delay their reports, suppressing them entirely if they notice that another neighbor has responded already. This field provides an upper bound on how long this delay may be. The *Multicast Address* field is 0 for general queries and the address for which the router is interested in reports otherwise. For MLD Report messages (type 131) and MLD Done messages (type 132) it includes the address related to the report or what address is no longer of interest, respectively.

8.4.7   Version 2 Multicast Listener Discovery (MLDv2) (ICMPv6 Type 143)

[RFC3810] defines extensions to the MLD facility described in [RFC2710]. In particular, it defines a way for a multicast listener to specify a desire to hear from only one specific set of senders (or, alternatively, to exclude one specific set). It is therefore useful in supporting source-specific multicast (SSM; see Chapter 9 and [RFC4604] [RFC4607]). It is basically a translation of the IGMPv3 protocol used with IPv4 for use with IPv6, which uses ICMPv6 for most multicast address management. Therefore, we will describe the message format here, but the detailed operation of multicast address dynamics is covered in Chapter 9. MLDv2 extends the MLD Query message with additional information pertaining to specific sources (see Figure 8-25). The first 24 bytes of the message are identical to the common MLD format.

The *Maximum Response Code* field specifies the maximum time allowed before sending an MLD Response message. The value of this field is special and therefore is interpreted slightly differently than in MLDv1: if it is less than 32,768, the maximum response delay is set equal to the value (in milliseconds) as in MLDv1. If the value is equal to or greater than 32,769, the field encodes a floating-point number using the format shown in Figure 8-26.

In this case, the maximum response delay is set equal to ((*mant* | 0x1000) << (*exp* + 3)) ms. The reason for this seemingly complex encoding strategy is to allow small and large values of the response delay to be encoded in this field and retain some compatibility with MLDv1. In particular, it allows for carefully adjusting the leave latency and affecting the report burstiness (see Chapter 9).

The *Multicast Address* field is set to 0 for a general query. For a multicast-address-specific query or multicast-address- and source-specific query it is set to the multicast address being queried. The *S* field indicates whether router-side processing should be suppressed. When set, it indicates to any receiving multicast router that it must suppress the normal timer updates computed when hearing a query. It does not indicate that querier election or normal "host-side" processing should be suppressed if the router is itself a multicast listener.

The *QRV* (*Querier Robustness Variable*) field, if set, contains a value of no more than 7. If the sender's internal QRV value exceeds 7, this field is set to 0. Robustness variables, described in Chapter 9, are used to fine-tune the rate of MLD updates based on an expectation of packet loss on a subnetwork. The *QQIC* (*Querier's Query Interval Code*) field encodes the query interval and is shown in Figure 8-27.

The query interval, measured in seconds, is computed from the QQIC field as follows: if QQIC < 128, then QQI = QQIC; otherwise, QQI = ((*mant* | 0x10) << (*exp* + 3)).

The *Number of Sources* (*N*) field indicates the number of source addresses present in the query. This field contains 0 for a general query or for a multicast-address-specific query. It is nonzero for multicast-address- and source-specific query messages.

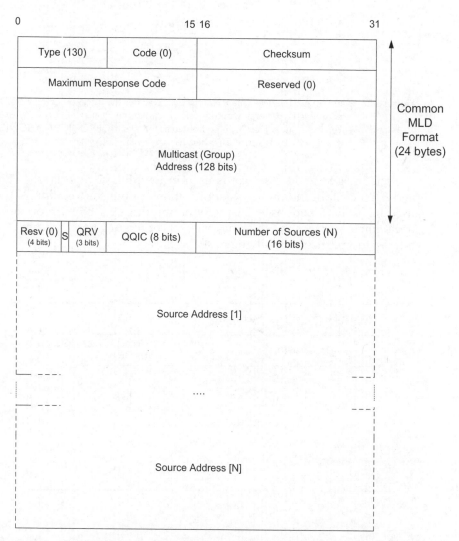

Figure 8-25   The MLDv2 Query message format, which is compatible with the MLD version 1 message common format. The major difference is the capability to limit or exclude specific multicast sources from the host's list of interests.

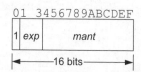

Figure 8-26   Floating-point format used with MLDv2 Query messages when the *Maximum Response Code* value is at least 32,768. In these cases, the delay is set to $((mant \mid 0x1000) << (exp + 3))$ms.

Figure 8-27   The MLDv2 *Querier's Query Interval Code* encodes the interval between MLDv2 queries. The (unencoded) version of this value is called the *Querier's Query Interval* and is measured in seconds. The *QQI* is computed as follows: QQI = QQIC (if QQIC < 128) and QQI = ((*mant* | 0x10) << (*exp* + 3)) otherwise.

The multicast address records used in the MLDv2 reports (see Figures 8-28 and 8-29) contain indicators of modifications to the source address filter being used by an IPv6 node (see Chapter 9 on multicast for more information on the operation of such filters, which describe sets of sending hosts that are or are not of interest to a particular receiving host).

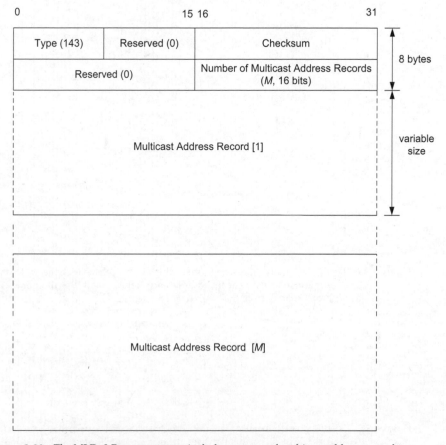

Figure 8-28   The MLDv2 Report message includes a vector of multicast address records.

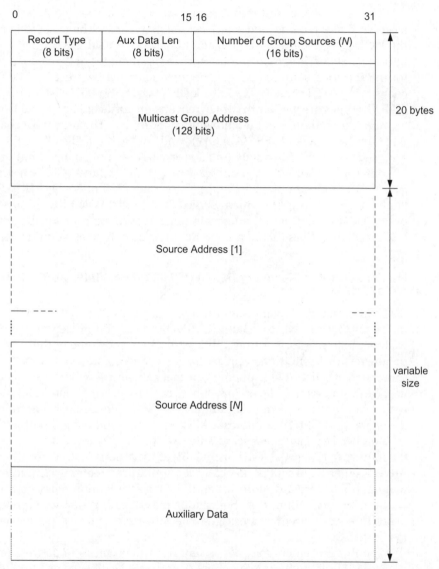

Figure 8-29   A multicast address (group) record. Multiple such records may be present in an MLDv2 Report message. The *Record Type* field is one of the following: MODE_IS_INCLUDE, MODE_IS_EXCLUDE, CHANGE_TO_INCLUDE_MODE, CHANGE_TO_EXCLUDE_MODE, ALLOW_NEW_SOURCES, or BLOCK_OLD_SOURCES. LW-MLDv2 simplifies MLDv2 by removing the EXCLUDE modes. The *Aux Data Len* field contains the amount of auxiliary data present in the record, in 32-bit-word units. For MLDv2, as specified in [RFC3810], this field must contain the value 0, indicating no auxiliary data.

The record types fall into three primary categories: *current state* records, *filter mode change* records, and *source list change* records. The first category includes the MODE_IS_INCLUDE (IS_IN) and MODE_IS_EXCLUDE (IS_EX) types, which indicate that the filter mode for the address is "include" or "exclude," respectively, for the specified sources (at least one of which must be present). The filter mode change types CHANGE_TO_INCLUDE (TO_IN) or CHANGE_TO_EXCLUDE (TO_EX) types are similar to the current state records but are sent when there is a change and need not include a nonempty source list. The source list change types, ALLOW_NEW_SOURCES (ALLOW) and BLOCK_OLD_SOURCES (BLOCK), are used when the filter state (include/exclude) is not changed but only the list of sources is modified. A modification to MLDv2 (and IGMPv3) removes the EXCLUDE modes in order to simplify the operation of MLDv2 [RFC5790]. This "lightweight" approach, called LW-MLDv2 (and LW-IGMPv3), uses the same previously defined message formats but removes support for the seldom-used EXCLUDE directives that require multicast routers to keep additional state.

8.4.8 Multicast Router Discovery (MRD) (IGMP Types 48/49/50, ICMPv6 Types 151/152/153)

[RFC4286] describes *Multicast Router Discovery* (MRD), a method defining special messages that can be used with ICMPv6 and IGMP to discover the presence of routers capable of forwarding multicast packets and some of their configuration parameters. It is envisioned primarily for use in conjunction with "IGMP/MLD snooping." IGMP/MLD snooping is a mechanism by which systems other than hosts and routers (e.g., layer 2 switches) can also learn about the location of network layer multicast routers and interested hosts. We discuss it in more detail in the context of IGMP in Chapter 9. MRD messages are always sent with the IPv4 *TTL* or IPv6 *Hop Limit* field set to 1 with a Router Alert option and may be one of the following types: Advertisement (151), Solicitation (152), or Termination (153). Advertisements are sent periodically at a configured interval to indicate a router's willingness to forward multicast traffic. The Termination message indicates the cessation of such willingness. Solicitation messages may be used to induce routers to produce Advertisement messages. The Advertisement message format is shown in Figure 8-30.

The Advertisement message is sent from the router's IP address (a link-local address for IPv6) to the All Snoopers IP address: 224.0.0.106 for IPv4 and the link-local multicast address ff02::6a for IPv6. A receiver is able to learn the router's advertising interval and MLD parameters (QQI and QRV, described in more detail in Chapter 9). Note that the QQI value is the query interval (in seconds), and not the QQIC (encoded version of the QQI value) as previously described for MLDv2 queries.

The formats of Solicitation and Termination messages are nearly the same (see Figure 8-31), differing only in the value of the *Type* field.

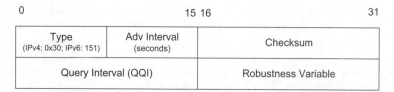

Figure 8-30 The MRD Advertisement message (ICMPv6 type 151; IGMP type 48) contains the advertisement interval (in seconds) indicating how often unsolicited advertisements are sent, the sender's query interval (QQI), and the robustness variable as defined by MLD. The IP address of the sender is used to indicate to a receiver the router that is able to forward multicast traffic. The message is sent to the All Snoopers multicast address (IPv4, 224.0.0.106; IPv6, ff02::6a).

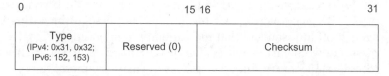

Figure 8-31 The ICMPv6 MRD Solicitation (ICMPv6 type 152; IGMP type 49) and Termination (ICMPv6 type 153; IGMP type 50) messages use a common format. MRD messages set the IPv6 *Hop Limit* field or IPv4 *TTL* field to 1 and include the Router Alert option. Solicitations are sent to the All Routers multicast address (IPv4, 224.0.0.2; IPv6, ff02::2).

Figure 8-31 shows the (nearly) common format used for Solicitation and Termination messages. The Solicitation message induces a multicast router to send an Advertisement message on demand. Such messages are sent to the All Routers address: 224.0.0.2 for IPv4 and the link-local multicast address ff02::2 for IPv6. Termination messages are sent to the All Snoopers IP address to indicate that the sending router is no longer willing to forward multicast traffic.

8.5   Neighbor Discovery in IPv6

The Neighbor Discovery Protocol in IPv6 (sometimes abbreviated as NDP or ND) [RFC4861] brings together the Router Discovery and Redirect mechanisms of ICMPv4 with the address-mapping capabilities provided by ARP. It is also specified for use in supporting Mobile IPv6. In contrast to ARP and IPv4, which generally use broadcast addressing (except for Router Discovery), ICMPv6 makes extensive use of multicast addressing, at both the network and link layers. (Recall from Chapters 2 and 5 that IPv6 does not even have broadcast addresses.)

ND is designed to allow nodes (routers and hosts) on the same link or segment to find each other, determine if they have bidirectional connectivity, and determine if a neighbor has become inoperative or unavailable. It also supports stateless address autoconfiguration (see Chapter 6). All of the ND functionality is provided by ICMPv6 at or above the network layer, making it largely independent of the particular link-layer technology employed underneath. However, ND does prefer to make use of link-layer multicast capabilities (see Chapter 9), and for this reason operation on non-broadcast- and non-multicast-capable link layers (called non-broadcast multiple access or NBMA links) may differ somewhat.

The two main parts of ND are Neighbor Solicitation/Advertisement (NS/NA), which provides the ARP-like function of mapping between network- and link-layer addresses, and Router Solicitation/Advertisement (RS/RA), which provides the functions of router discovery, Mobile IP agent discovery, and redirects, as well as some support for autoconfiguration. A secure variant of ND called SEND [RFC3971] adds authentication and special forms of addressing, primarily by introducing additional ND options.

ND messages are ICMPv6 messages sent using an IPv6 *Hop Limit* field value of 255. Receivers verify that incoming ND messages have this value to protect against off-link senders that may attempt to spoof local ICMPv6 messages (such messages would arrive with values less than 255). ND has a rich set of options that messages may carry. First we discuss the primary message types and then detail the available options.

8.5.1   ICMPv6 Router Solicitation and Advertisement (ICMPv6 Types 133, 134)

Router Advertisement (RA) messages indicate the presence and capabilities of a nearby router. They are sent periodically by routers, or in response to a Router Solicitation (RS) message. The RS message (see Figure 8-32) is used to induce on-link routers to send RA messages. RS messages are sent to the All Routers multicast address, ff02::2. A Source Link-Layer Address option is supposed to be included if the sender of the message is using an IPv6 address other than the unspecified address (used during autoconfiguration). It is the only valid option for such messages as of [RFC4861].

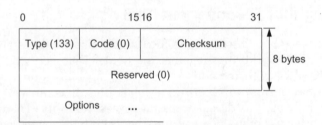

Figure 8-32   The ICMPv6 Router Solicitation message is very simple but ordinarily contains a Source Link-Layer Address option (unlike its ICMPv4 counterpart). It may also contain an MTU option if an unusual MTU value is in use on the link.

The Router Advertisement (RA) message (see Figure 8-33) is sent by routers to the All Nodes multicast address (ff02::1) or the unicast address of the requesting host, if the advertisement is sent in response to a solicitation. RA messages inform local hosts and other routers of configuration details relevant to the local link.

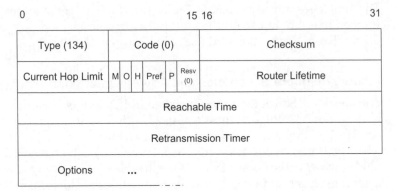

Figure 8-33   An ICMPv6 Router Advertisement message is sent to the All Nodes multicast address (ff02::1). Receiving nodes check to make sure that the *Hop Limit* field is 255, ensuring that the packet has not been forwarded through a router. The message includes three flags: *M* (*Managed* address configuration), *O* (*Other* stateful configuration), and *H* (*Home Agent*).

The *Current Hop Limit* field specifies the default hop limit hosts are supposed to use for sending IPv6 datagrams. A value of 0 indicates that the sending router does not care. The next byte contains a number of bit fields, as summarized and extended in [RFC5175]. The *M* (*Managed*) field indicates that the local assignment of IPv6 addresses is handled by stateful configuration, and that hosts should avoid using stateless autoconfiguration. The *O* (*Other*) field indicates that other stateful information (that is, other than IPv6 addresses) uses a stateful configuration mechanism (see Chapter 6). The *H* (*Home Agent*) field indicates that the sending router is willing to act as a home agent for Mobile IPv6 nodes. The *Pref* (*Preference*) field gives the level of preference for the sender of the message to be used as a default router as follows: 01, high; 00, medium (default); 11, low; 10, reserved (not used). More details about this field are given in [RFC4191]. The *P* (*Proxy*) flag is used in conjunction with the experimental *ND proxy* facility [RFC4389]. It provides a proxy-ARP-like capability (see Chapter 4) for IPv6.

The *Router Lifetime* field indicates the amount of time during which the sending router can be used as a default next hop, in seconds. If it is set to 0, the sending router should never be used as a default router. This field applies only to the use of the sending router as a default router; it does not affect other options carried in the same message. The *Reachable Time* field gives the number of milliseconds in which a node is to assume that another is reachable, assuming mutual communications have taken place. This is used by the *Neighbor Unreachability Detection* mechanism (see Section 8.5.4). The *Retransmission Timer* field dictates the time, in milliseconds, during which hosts delay sending successive ND messages.

This message usually includes the Source Link-Layer option (if applicable) and should include an MTU option if variable-length MTUs are used on the link. The router should also include Prefix Information options that indicate which IPv6 prefixes are in use on the local link. Chapter 6 includes an example of how RS and RA messages are used (e.g., see Figures 6-24 and 6-25).

8.5.2   ICMPv6 Neighbor Solicitation and Advertisement (IMCPv6 Types 135, 136)

The Neighbor Solicitation (NS) message in ICMPv6 (see Figure 8-34) effectively replaces the ARP Request messages used with IPv4. Its primary purpose is to convert IPv6 addresses to link-layer addresses. However, it is also used for detecting whether nearby nodes can be reached, and if they can be reached bidirectionally (that is, whether the nodes can talk to each other). When used to determine address mappings, it is sent to the Solicited-Node multicast address corresponding to the IPv6 address contained in the *Target Address* field (prefix f02::1:f/104, combined with the low-order 24 bits of the solicited IPv6 address). For more details on how Solicited-Node multicast addressing is used, see Chapter 9. When this message is used to determine connectivity to a neighbor, it is sent to that neighbor's IPv6 unicast address instead of the Solicited-Node address.

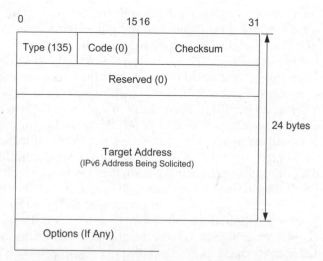

Figure 8-34   The ICMPv6 Neighbor Solicitation message is similar to the RS message but contains a target IPv6 address. These messages are sent to Solicited-Node multicast addresses to provide ARP-like functionality and to unicast addresses to test reachability to other nodes. NS messages contain a Source Link-Layer Address option on links that use lower-layer addressing.

The NS message contains the IPv6 address for which the sender is trying to learn the link-layer address. The message may contain the Source Link-Layer Address option. This option must be included in networks that use link-layer addressing when the solicitation is sent to a multicast address and should be included for unicast solicitations. If the sender of the message is using the unspecified address as its source address (e.g., during duplicate address detection), this option is not to be included.

The ICMPv6 Neighbor Advertisement (NA) message (see Figure 8-35) serves the purpose of the ARP Response message in IPv4 in addition to helping with neighbor unreachability detection (see Section 8.5.4). It is either sent as a response to an NS message or sent asynchronously when a node's IPv6 address changes. It is sent either to the unicast address of the soliciting node, or to the All Nodes multicast address if the soliciting node used the unspecified address as its source address.

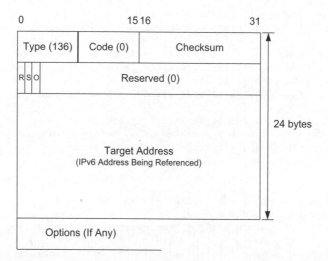

Figure 8-35 The ICMPv6 Neighbor Advertisement message contains the following flags: *R* indicates that the sender is a router, *S* indicates that the advertisement is a response to a solicitation, and *O* indicates that the message contents should override other cached address mappings. The *Target Address* field contains the IPv6 address of the sender of the message (generally, the unicast address of the solicited node from the ND solicitation). A Target Link-Layer Address option is included to enable ARP-like functionality for IPv6.

The *R* (*Router*) field indicates that the sender of the message is a router. This could change, for example, if a router ceases being a router and becomes only a host instead. The *S* (*Solicited*) field indicates that the advertisement is in response to a solicitation received earlier. This field is used to verify that bidirectional connectivity between neighbors has been achieved. The *O* (*Override*) field indicates that information in the advertisement should override any previously cached information the receiver of the message has. It is not supposed to be set for solicited advertisements, for anycast addresses, or in solicited proxy advertisements. It is supposed to be set in other (solicited or unsolicited) advertisements.

For solicited advertisements, the *Target Address* field is the IPv6 address being looked up. For unsolicited advertisements, it is the IPv6 address that corresponds to a link-layer address that has changed. This message must contain the Target Link-Layer Address option on networks that support link-layer addressing when the advertisement was solicited via a multicast address. We will now look at a simple example.

8.5.2.1 Example

Here we see the results of using ICMPv6 Echo Request/Reply, in conjunction with NDP. The sender is a Windows XP system with IPv6 enabled, and a packet trace is captured on a nearby Linux system. Some lines have been wrapped for clarity.

```
C:\> ping6 -s fe80::210:18ff:fe00:100b fe80::211:11ff:fe6f:c603

Pinging fe80::211:11ff:fe6f:c603
from fe80::210:18ff:fe00:100b with 32 bytes of data:

Reply from fe80::211:11ff:fe6f:c603: bytes=32 time<1ms
Reply from fe80::211:11ff:fe6f:c603: bytes=32 time<1ms
Reply from fe80::211:11ff:fe6f:c603: bytes=32 time<1ms
Reply from fe80::211:11ff:fe6f:c603: bytes=32 time<1ms

Ping statistics for fe80::211:11ff:fe6f:c603:
    Packets: Sent = 4, Received = 4, Lost = 0 (0% loss),
Approximate round trip times in milli-seconds:
    Minimum = 0ms, Maximum = 0ms, Average = 0ms


Linux# tcpdump -i eth0 -s1500 -vv -p ip6
tcpdump: listening on eth0,
        link-type EN10MB (Ethernet), capture size 1500 bytes

1 21:22:01.389656 fe80::211:11ff:fe6f:c603 > ff02::1:ff00:100b:
                [icmp6 sum ok] icmp6: neighbor sol: who has
                                fe80::210:18ff:fe00:100b
                                (src lladdr: 00:11:11:6f:c6:03)
                                (len 32, hlim 255)
2 21:22:01.389845 fe80::210:18ff:fe00:100b > fe80::211:11ff:fe6f:c603:
                [icmp6 sum ok] icmp6: neighbor adv: tgt is
                                fe80::210:18ff:fe00:100b(SO)
                                (tgt lladdr:  00:10:18:00:10:0b)
                                (len 32, hlim 255)

3 21:22:02.390713 fe80::210:18ff:fe00:100b > fe80::211:11ff:fe6f:c603:
                [icmp6 sum ok] icmp6: echo request seq 18
                                (len 40, hlim 128)
4 21:22:02.390780 fe80::211:11ff:fe6f:c603 > fe80::210:18ff:fe00:100b:
                [icmp6 sum ok] icmp6: echo reply seq 18
                                (len 40, hlim 64)
... continues ...
```

The ping6 program is available on Windows XP and Linux. (Later versions of Windows incorporate the IPv6 functionality into the regular ping program.) The —s option tells it which source address to use. Recall that with IPv6 a host may have multiple addresses from which to choose, and here we have chosen one of its link-local addresses, fe80::211:11ff:fe6f:c603. The trace shows the NS/NA exchange and an ICMP Echo Request/Reply pair. Observe that all of the ND messages use IPv6 *Hop-Limit* field values of 255, and the ICMPv6 Echo Request and Echo Reply messages use a value of 128 or 64.

The NS message is sent to the multicast address ff02::1:ff00:100b, which is the Solicited-Node multicast address corresponding to the IPv6 address being solicited (fe80::210:18ff:fe00:100b). We see that the soliciting node also includes its own link-layer address, 00:11:11:6f:c6:03, in a Source Link-Layer Address option.

The NA response message is sent using link-layer (and IP-layer) unicast addressing back to the soliciting node. The *Target Address* field contains the value requested in the solicitation: fe80::210:18ff:fe00:100b. In addition, we see that the *S* and *O* flag fields are set, indicating that the advertisement is in response to the earlier solicitation provided, and that the information being provided should override any other information the soliciting node may have cached. The *R* flag field is unset, indicating that the responding host is not acting as a router. Finally, the solicited node includes the most important information in a Target Link-Layer Address option: the solicited node's link-layer address of 00:10:18:00:10:0b.

8.5.3 ICMPv6 Inverse Neighbor Discovery Solicitation/Advertisement (ICMPv6 Types 141/142)

The *Inverse Neighbor Discovery* (IND) facility in IPv6 [RFC3122] originated from a need to determine IPv6 addresses given link-layer addresses on Frame Relay networks. It resembles reverse ARP, a protocol once used with IPv4 networks primarily for supporting diskless computers. Its main function is to ascertain the network-layer address(es) corresponding to a known link-layer address. Figure 8-36 shows the basic format of IND Solicitation and Advertisement messages.

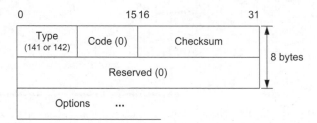

Figure 8-36   The ICMPv6 IND Solicitation (type 141) and Advertisement (type 142) messages have the same basic format. They are used to map known link-layer addresses to IPv6 addresses in environments where this is useful.

The IND Solicitation message is sent to the All Nodes multicast address at the IPv6 layer but is encapsulated in a unicast link-layer address (the one being looked up). It must contain both a Source Link-Layer Address option and a Destination Link-Layer Address option. It may also contain a Source/Target Address List option and/or an MTU option.

8.5.4   Neighbor Unreachability Detection (NUD)

One of the important features of ND is to detect when reachability between two systems on the same link has become lost or asymmetric (i.e., is not available in both directions). This is accomplished using the *Neighbor Unreachability Detection* (NUD) algorithm. It is used to manage the *neighbor cache* present on each node. The neighbor cache is analogous to the ARP cache described in Chapter 4; it is a (conceptual) data structure that holds the IPv6-to-link-layer-address mapping information required to perform direct delivery of IPv6 datagrams to on-link neighbors as well as information regarding the state of the mapping. Figure 8-37 shows how it maintains entries in the neighbor cache.

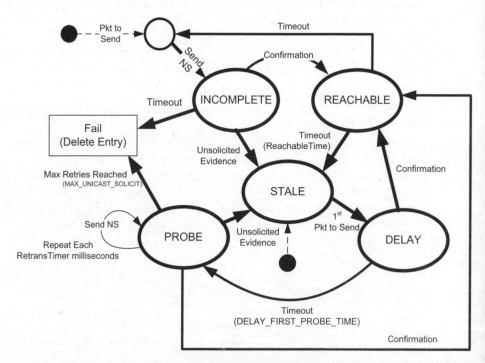

Figure 8-37   Neighbor Unreachability Detection helps maintain the neighbor cache consisting of several neighbor entries. Each entry is in one of five states at any given time. Confirmations of reachability are accomplished by receiving Neighbor Advertisement messages or using other higher-layer protocol information, if available. Unsolicited evidence includes unsolicited Neighbor and Router Advertisement messages.

Each mapping may be in one of five states: INCOMPLETE, REACHABLE, STALE, DELAY, or PROBE. The transition diagram in Figure 8-37 shows the initial states to be either INCOMPLETE or STALE. When an IPv6 node has a unicast datagram to send to a destination, it checks its *destination cache* to see if an entry corresponding to the destination is present. If so, and the destination is on-link, the neighbor cache is consulted to see if the neighbor's state is REACHABLE. If so, the datagram is sent using direct delivery (see Chapter 5). If no neighbor cache entry is present but the destination appears to be on-link, NUD enters the INCOMPLETE state and sends an NS message. Successful receipt of a solicited NA message provides confirmation that the node is reachable, and the entry enters the REACHABLE state. The STALE state corresponds to apparently valid entries that have not yet been confirmed. This state is entered when either an entry has not been updated for some time when it was previously REACHABLE, or when unsolicited information is received (e.g., a node has changed its address and sent an unsolicited NA message). These cases suggest that reachability is possible, but confirmation in the form of a valid NA is still required.

The other states, DELAY and PROBE, are temporary states. DELAY is used when a packet is sent but ND has no current evidence to suggest that reachability is possible. The state gives upper-layer protocols an opportunity to provide additional evidence. If after DELAY_FIRST_PROBE_TIME seconds (the constant 5) no evidence is received, the state changes to PROBE. In the PROBE state, ND sends periodic NS messages (every RetransTimer milliseconds, with constant default value RETRANS_TIMER equal to 1000). If no evidence has been received after sending MAX_UNICAST_SOLICIT NS messages (default 3), the entry is supposed to be deleted.

8.5.5 Secure Neighbor Discovery (SEND)

SEND [RFC3971] is a special set of enhancements aimed at providing additional security for ND messages. This is to help resist various spoofing attacks in which one host or router might masquerade as another (see Section 8.6, Chapter 18, and [RFC3756] for additional details). It specifically aims to protect against nodes masquerading as others when responding to NS messages. SEND does not use IPsec (see Chapter 18) but instead its own special mechanism. This mechanism is also used for securing FMIPv6 handoffs [RFC5269].

SEND operates in a framework with a set of assumptions. First, each SEND-capable router has a *certificate*, or cryptographic credential, that it can use to prove its identity to a host. Next, each host is also equipped with a *trust anchor*—configuration information enabling the credential to be verified. Finally, each node generates a public/private key pair when configuring the IPv6 addresses it will use. Details of credentials, trust anchors, key pairs, and other associated security techniques are given in Chapter 18.

8.5.5.1 Cryptographically Generated Addresses (CGAs)

Perhaps its most interesting feature, SEND uses an entirely different type of IPv6 address called a *cryptographically generated address* (CGA) [RFC3972][RFC4581]

[RFC4982]. This type of address is based on a node's public key information, thereby linking the address to the node's credential. Consequently, a node or address owner in possession of the corresponding private key is able to prove it is the authorized user of a particular CGA. CGAs also encode the subnet prefix with which they are associated so they cannot be moved trivially from one subnet to another. This approach is quite different from how addresses are typically assigned.

An IPv6 CGA is generated by ORing a 64-bit subnet prefix with a specially constructed interface identifier. The CGA interface identifier is computed using a *secure hash function* (a hash function believed difficult to invert; see Chapter 18) called *Hash1* with inputs derived from the node's public key and a special CGA parameters data structure. These parameters are also used as input to another secure hash function, *Hash2*, which provides a *hash extension* technique that effectively extends the number of bits of output for the hash function, increasing its security (i.e., strength against an adversary producing a different input resulting in the same hash value) [A03][RFC6273]. The CGA technique allows for the address owner's public key to be self-generated, so this approach can be used without an accompanying *public key infrastructure* (PKI) or other trusted third party.

The CGA parameters data structure is shown in Figure 8-38. The *Modifier* field is initialized with a random value, and the *Collision Count* field is initialized to 0. The structure includes an *Extension Fields* area that can be adapted for future uses [RFC4581].

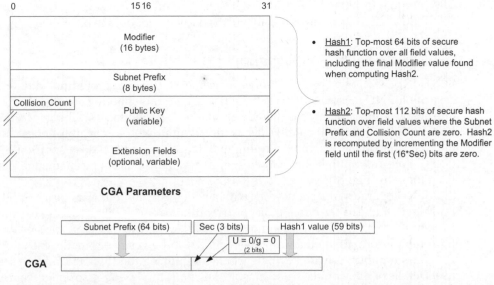

Figure 8-38   The SEND method for computing CGAs. The CGA parameters data structure is used as input to two cryptographic hash functions, Hash1 and Hash2. The Hash2 value must have (16*Sec) initial 0 bits, where Sec is a 3-bit parameter. The *Modifier* is changed until Hash2 computes appropriately. The resulting values are used to compute Hash1, which is combined with Sec and the subnet prefix to produce the CGA.

A 3-bit unsigned parameter called Sec influences how resistant the approach is to mathematical compromise, which secure hash function is used [RFC4982], and how computationally expensive the computations are (they are exponential in the Sec value). The IANA maintains a registry for Sec values [SI]. The Hash1 and Hash2 functions operate on the same CGA parameter block in conjunction with the Sec value. The address owner begins by picking a random value for the *Modifier* field, treating the subnet prefix field as 0, and computing the Hash2 value. The result is required to have (16*Sec) initial 0 bits, so the input is modified by incrementing the modifier value by 1 and recomputing Hash2 until the condition is satisfied. This computation has time complexity $O(2^{16*Sec})$ and therefore becomes much more expensive as Sec increases. However, this computation is required only when the address is initially established.

Once the proper modifier has been found, 59 bits of the Hash1 value are used in forming the low-order 59 bits of the interface identifier. The top 3 bits constitute the 3-bit Sec value, and bits 6–7 (from the left) contain two 0 bits (corresponding to the *u* and *g* address bits described in Chapter 2). If the address is found to be in conflict (e.g., using duplicate address detection, described in Chapter 6), the *Collision Count* field is incremented and Hash1 is recomputed. The collision count value is not permitted to grow beyond 2. Given that address collisions are unlikely to begin with, multiple such collisions should be considered evidence of a configuration error or attack. Once all the necessary calculations are complete, the complete CGA can be formed by concatenating the subnet prefix, Sec value, and Hash1 value. Note that if the subnet prefix changes, only Hash1 needs to be recomputed as the modifier value can remain the same. (The reader interested in alternatives to CGAs should consult [RFC5535], which describes *hash-based addresses*, or HBAs. HBAs are used for multihomed hosts using multiple prefixes in a somewhat different context and with a different form of cryptography that is less computationally expensive, although HBA-CGA-compatible options have also been defined.)

At this point we have seen how a CGA is generated but not how it is used for security. Note that anyone can generate a CGA given a subnet prefix, Sec value, and their own (or someone else's) public key. To ensure that a CGA is well formed and is using an appropriate subnet prefix, it must be verified, a process called *CGA verification*. A verifier requires knowledge of the CGA and CGA parameters. The verification process involves ensuring all of the following: the collision count is not greater than 2, the CGA's subnet prefix matches that in the CGA parameters, Hash1 computed on the CGA parameters matches the interface identifier portion of the CGA (where the first 3 bits and bits 6 and 7 are "don't cares"), and the value of Hash2 computed on the CGA parameters with the *Subnet Prefix* and *Collision Count* fields set to 0 has (16*Sec) initial 0 bits. If all of these checks are successful, the CGA is a legitimate one for the corresponding subnet prefix. This computation involves at most two hash functions; it is far simpler than the address generation process.

To verify that a CGA is being used by its authorized address owner, called *signature verification*, the owner forms a typed message and attaches a CGA signature that can be computed only with knowledge of the private key corresponding to the public key used with the CGA. A verifier forms a data block by concatenating a special 128-bit type tag with the message. The CGA ownership is verified using an RSA signature (RSASSA-PKCS1-v1_5 [RFC3447]) with the public key (extracted from the CGA parameters), data block, and signature as parameters. Generally, a CGA and its user are considered valid only if both the CGA verification and signature verification processes have completed successfully.

The handling of CGAs and verification is accomplished using two ICMPv6 messages and six options defined in [RFC3971]. The RFC also defines two IANA-managed registries for holding *Name Type* fields in the Trust Anchor option and the *Cert Type* field in the Certificate option (see Section 8.5.6.13). [RFC3972] defines the CGA Message Type registry, with the 128-bit value 0x086FCA5E10B200C99C8 CE00164277C08 given in [RFC3971] (other values are defined for uses other than SEND). A registry for Sec values is defined by [RFC4982] but at present provides only for values 0, 1, and 2, which correspond to use of the SHA-1 secure hash function using 0, 16, or 32 initial 0 bits for the Hash2 function, respectively. An extension format defined in [RFC4581] supports TLV encodings that can be used for future standard extensions, but only one has been defined to date [RFC5535]. We will now describe the two ICMPv6 messages used with SEND and defer discussion of the options until we cover all of the ICMPv6 options in the next section.

8.5.5.2 Certification Path Solicitation/Advertisement (ICMPv6 Types 148/149)

SEND defines Solicitation and Advertisement messages to help hosts determine certificates constituting a certification path. This is used for a host to verify the authenticity of router advertisements. Figure 8-39 shows the Solicitation message.

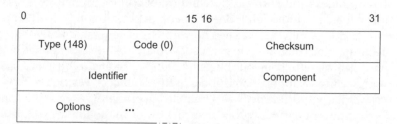

Figure 8-39   The Certification Path Solicitation message. The sender requests a particular certificate by position index, provided as the value of the *Component* field. The value 65535 indicates that all certificates in the path rooted at the identity given within an attached Trust Anchor option are desired.

The Certification Path Solicitation message contains a random *Identifier* field used for matching solicitations with advertisements. The value of the *Component* field provides an index to the point in the certification path in which the requestor is interested. This value is set to all 1s (value 65535) if certificates for the entire path are desired. The messages may contain a Trust Anchor option (see Section 8.5.6.12). Certificates and certification paths are described in more detail in Chapter 18.

The Certification Path Advertisement message, shown in Figure 8-40, provides a method to express one component (certificate) in a multicomponent advertisement. These messages are sent in response to a solicitation, or periodically by a SEND-capable router. When sent in response to a solicitation, the destination IPv6 address is the Solicited-Node multicast address of the receiver.

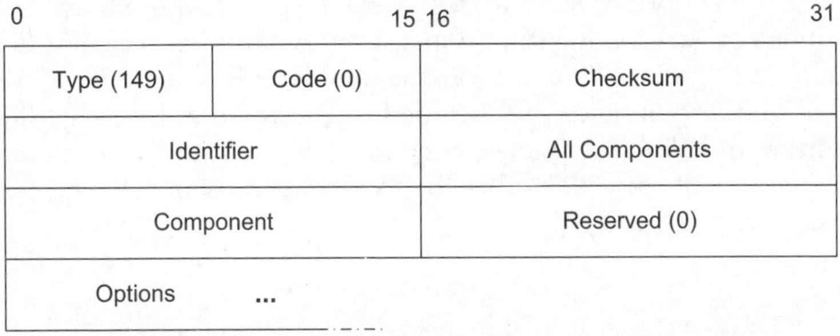

0	15 16	31
Type (149)	Code (0)	Checksum
Identifier		All Components
Component		Reserved (0)
Options ...		

Figure 8-40   The Certification Path Advertisement message. The sender requests a particular certificate by position index, provided as the value of the *Component* field. The value 65535 indicates all certificates in the path rooted at an identity given within an attached Trust Anchor option.

The *Identifier* field holds the value received in a corresponding Solicitation message. It is set to 0 for unsolicited Advertisement messages that are sent to the All Nodes multicast address. The *All Components* field indicates the total number of components in the entire certification path, including the trust anchor. Note that a single advertisement message is recommended to avoid fragmentation, so such messages contain only a single component. The *Component* field gives the index in the certification path of the associated certificate (provided in an attached Certificate option). The recommended order for sending advertisements for an N-component certification path is $(N - 1, N - 2, \ldots, 0)$. Component N need not be sent as it is already present from the trust anchor.

8.5.6   ICMPv6 Neighbor Discovery (ND) Options

As with many of the protocols of the IPv6 family, a set of standard protocol headers are defined, and one or more options may also be included. ND messages may contain zero or more options, and some options can occur more than once. However, with certain messages some of the options are mandatory. The general format for ND options is given in Figure 8-41.

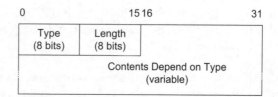

Figure 8-41   ND options are variable-length and begin with a common TLV arrangement. The *Length* field gives the total length of the option in 8-byte units (including the *Type* and *Length* fields).

All ND options start with an 8-bit *Type* and an 8-bit *Length* field, supporting options of variable length, up to 255 bytes. Options are padded to 8-byte boundaries, and the *Length* field gives the total length of the option in 8-byte units. The *Type* and *Length* fields are included in the value of the *Length* field, which has a minimum value of 1. Table 8-5 gives a list of 25 standard options that have been defined as of mid-2011 (plus the experimental values). The official list may be found in [ICMP6TYPES].

Table 8-5   IPv6 ND option types, defining reference, use, and description

Type	Name	Reference	Use/Comment
1	Source Link-Layer Address	[RFC4861]	Sender's link-layer address; used with NS, RS, and RA messages
2	Target Link-Layer Address	[RFC4861]	Target's link-layer address; used with NA and Redirect messages
3	Prefix Information	[RFC4861] [RFC6275]	An IPv6 prefix or address; used with RA messages
4	Redirected Header	[RFC4861]	Portion of original IPv6 datagram; used with Redirect messages
5	MTU	[RFC4861]	Recommended MTU; used with RA messages, IND Advertisement messages
6	NMBA Shortcut Limit	[RFC2491]	Hop limit for "shortcut attempt"; used with NS messages
7	Advertisement Interval	[RFC6275]	Sending interval of unsolicited RA messages; used with RA messages
8	Home Agent Information	[RFC6275]	Preference and lifetime to be an MIPv6 HA; used with RA messages (*H* bit on)
9	Source Address List	[RFC3122]	Host's addresses; used with IND messages
10	Target Address List	[RFC3122]	Target addresses; used with IND messages
11	CGA	[RFC3971]	Crypto-based address; used with secure Neighbor Discovery (SEND) messages
12	RSA Signature	[RFC3971]	Credential for host signature (SEND)

Table 8-5   IPv6 ND option types, defining reference, use, and description (*continued*)

Type	Name	Reference	Use/Comment
13	Timestamp	[RFC3971]	Anti-replay timestamp (SEND)
14	Nonce	[RFC3971]	Anti-replay random number (SEND)
15	Trust Anchor	[RFC3971]	Indicates credential type (SEND)
16	Certificate	[RFC3971]	Encodes a certificate (SEND)
17	IP Address/Prefix	[RFC5568]	Care-of or NAR addresses; used with FMIPv6 PrRtAdv messages
19	Link-Layer Address	[RFC5568]	Desired next access point or mobile node's address; used with FMIPv6 RtSolPr or PrRtAdv messages
20	Neighbor Advertisement ACK	[RFC5568]	Tells mobile about next valid CoA; used with RA messages
24	Route Information	[RFC4191]	Route prefix/preferred router list
25	Recursive DNS Server	[RFC6106]	IP address of DNS server; added to RA messages
26	RA Flags Extension	[RFC5175]	Expands space for RA flags
27	Handover Key Request	[RFC5269]	FMIPv6—request key using SEND
28	Handover Key Reply	[RFC5269]	FMIPv6—key reply using SEND
31	DNS Search List	[RFC6106]	DNS domain search names; added to RA messages
253, 254	Experimental	[RFC4727]	[RFC3692]-style experiments 1/2

8.5.6.1 Source/Target Link-Layer Address Option (Types 1, 2)

The Source Link-Layer Address option (type 1; see Figure 8-42) is supposed to be included in ICMPv6 RS messages, NS messages, and RA messages whenever used on a network supporting link-layer addressing. It specifies a link-layer address associated with the message. More than one of these options may be included for nodes with more than one address.

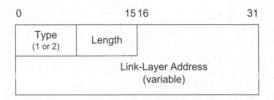

Figure 8-42   The Source (type 1) and Target (type 2) Link-Layer Address options. The *Length* field gives the length of the entire option, including the address, in units of 8 bytes (e.g., an IEEE Ethernet-type address would have the value of 1 in the *Length* field).

The Target Link-Layer Address option (type 2), which uses a similar format, must be provided in an NA message when responding to multicast solicitations. This option is also typically included in Redirect messages (discussed previously) and must be included in such messages when operating on an NBMA network.

8.5.6.2 Prefix Information Option (Type 3)

The Prefix Information option (PIO), provided on RA messages and Mobile Prefix Advertisement messages, indicates the IPv6 address prefixes and (in some cases) complete IPv6 addresses of individual nodes present on the link (see Figure 8-43). In cases where multiple prefixes or addresses are reported, multiple copies of this option may be included in a single message. A router is supposed to include a PIO for each prefix it uses. An R bit field set to 1 indicates that the *Prefix* field contains the *entire* global IPv6 address of the sending router, rather than just its prefix with the remaining bits of the prefix field being 0 or its link-local address (present in the *Source IP Address* field of the containing IPv6 datagram). This is useful for Mobile IPv6 home agent discovery, and home agents sending router advertisements must include this option with the R bit field set for at least one prefix.

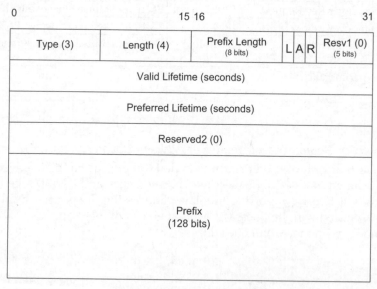

Figure 8-43   The Prefix Information option contains an IPv6 address prefix in use on the local network. It is used to provide hosts with prefixes for address autoconfiguration if the *A* bit field is set. The *L* bit field indicates that the prefix is acceptable for use in on-link determination. The *R* bit field is used to indicate that the included prefix is the entire global IPv6 address of the sending router.

The *Prefix Length* field gives the number of bits (up to 128) in the *Prefix* field that should be considered valid for use in configuration. The *L* bit field is the "on-link" flag and indicates that the provided prefix is eligible to be used for on-link determination (see the next paragraph). If it is not set, it makes no statement one way or another about its use in on-link determination. The *A* bit field is the "autonomous autoconfiguration" flag and indicates that the provided prefix may be used for autoconfiguration (see Chapter 6). The *Valid Lifetime* and *Preferred Lifetime* fields indicate the number of seconds in which the prefix can be used for on-link determination and automatic address autoconfiguration, respectively. A value of 0xFFFFFFFF for either field indicates infinity.

In IPv6, nodes that are "on-link" correspond to those that can be reached using direct delivery (Chapter 5). In IPv4, nodes are assumed to be on-link if they share a common prefix, determined using a combination of their own IPv4 address and assigned subnet mask. Although this arrangement can be achieved using IPv6, it is not necessary, and on-link status is not assumed without confirmation. Instead, the *L* bit field indicates to a host or router which prefixes or list of individual hosts is present on-link [RFC5942]. Other mechanisms can also serve this purpose (e.g., DHCPv6, manual configuration, or ICMPv6 Redirect messages). A node is considered off-link unless there is confirming information to indicate that it is on-link.

8.5.6.3 Redirected Header Option (Type 4)

The Redirected Header option is used to include a copy of (or part of) the original ("offending") IPv6 datagram that caused a Redirect message to be generated. The option format is given in Figure 8-44. The option is ignored if it appears in any other type of message.

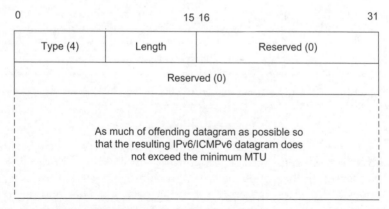

Figure 8-44   The Redirected Header option marks the beginning of a partial (or complete) copy of the offending IPv6 datagram. In any case, the message is limited to at most the minimum IPv6 MTU (currently 1280 bytes).

8.5.6.4 MTU Option (Type 5)

The MTU option is provided on RA messages and ignored otherwise (see Figure 8-45). It provides the MTU to be used by hosts, assuming that a configurable MTU size is supported.

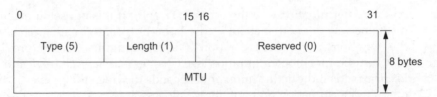

Figure 8-45   The MTU option includes the MTU to be used on the local link. This option is used with RA messages and is most useful if a nonstandard or unknown MTU is to be used.

The MTU option is important, for example, when bridging two or more heterogeneous link-layer technologies that have different MTUs. Without this option (and assuming bridges do not generate ICMPv6 PTB messages), hosts may not be able to communicate reliably with other hosts on the bridged link-layer network. Note that this message reserves 32 bits to hold the MTU, supporting very large MTUs.

8.5.6.5 Advertisement Interval Option (Type 7)

This option may be included in RA messages and is ignored otherwise. It specifies the maximum interval between unsolicited multicast router advertisements (see Figure 8-46).

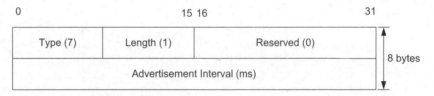

Figure 8-46   The Advertisement Interval gives the number of milliseconds between unsolicited multicast Router Advertisement messages.

The Advertisement Interval option gives the time between periodic router advertisement messages. The *Advertisement Interval* field defines the maximum number of milliseconds between transmissions of RA messages sent by the sender of this message on the arriving network. The sending router may send advertisements more frequently than the option indicates, but not less frequently. This option is used by Mobile IPv6 nodes in its movement detection algorithms [RFC6275].

8.5.6.6 Home Agent Information Option (Type 8)

This option may be included in RA messages being sent from routers willing to act as Mobile IPv6 home agents [RFC6275] (i.e., those that set the *H* bit field in their

RA messages) and is ignored otherwise. The option is not allowed to be included if the *H* bit field is not set. In cases where solicited RA messages are used such that multiple addresses are carried in separate messages and the *R* bit field is set, this option must be included with each of them and each must contain the same value. Figure 8-47 shows the Home Agent Information option format.

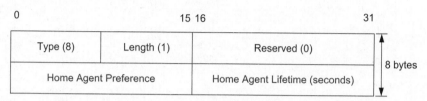

Figure 8-47   The Home Agent Information option indicates the preference and amount of time in which the sender of the option is willing to be considered a home agent for Mobile IPv6. Larger values of the *Home Agent Preference* field indicate a more desirable home agent. The *Home Agent Lifetime* field gives the number of seconds during which the sender is willing to be an HA.

The *Home Agent Preference* field is a 16-bit unsigned integer used to help a mobile node order the addresses provided to it via Home Agent Address Discovery Reply messages. Larger values indicate a greater degree of preference for using the sending router as a home agent. If this option is *not* included in a Router Advertisement message where the *H* bit field (home agent) is set, the preference value of the originating router must be considered to be 0 (lowest preference).

The *Home Agent Lifetime* field, also a 16-bit unsigned integer, specifies the number of seconds in which the sender of the message should be considered eligible to act as a home agent (with the corresponding preference described previously). The default value of this field is equal to the *Lifetime* field of the containing RA message. The maximum value of this field (65,535) corresponds to 18.2 hours, and the minimum value is 1 (0 is not allowed). If both the *Home Agent Lifetime* and the *Home Agent Preference* fields contain only default values, the entire option is not supposed to be included in the RA message.

8.5.6.7 Source/Target Address List Options (Types 9, 10)

These options may be included with an IND message [RFC3122]. The format is given in Figure 8-48. The Source Address List option (type 9) contains a list of the IPv6 addresses identified by the Source Link-Layer Address option. The Target Address List option (type 10) contains a list of the IPv6 addresses identified by the Destination Link-Layer Address option. The number of addresses included in the option is equal to (*Length* – 1)/2, where the *Length* field value contains the size of the option in 8-byte units.

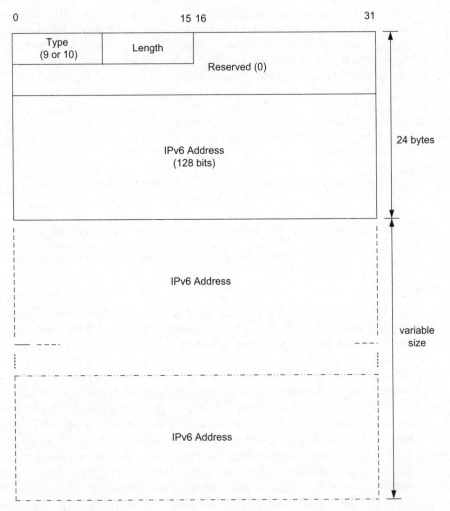

Figure 8-48 The Source (type 9) and Target (type 10) Address List options. These are used in supporting IND and provide a list of a node's IPv6 addresses. Only the addresses used on the interface used to send the message should be included.

8.5.6.8 CGA Option (Type 11)

The CGA option is used with SEND [RFC3971] to carry the CGA parameters necessary for a verifier to perform CGA validation and signature validation. Its format is given in Figure 8-49.

The *CGA Parameters* area is composed of the same fields depicted in Figure 8-38. See [RFC3971] for more details.

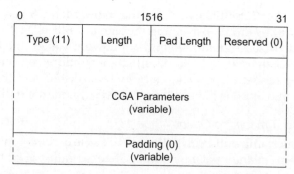

Figure 8-49 The CGA option used with SEND. The option encodes the CGA parameters shown in Figure 8-38.

8.5.6.9 RSA Signature Option (Type 12)

The RSA Signature option is used with SEND [RFC3971] to carry an RSA signature (see Chapter 18) that a verifier can use, in conjunction with CGA parameters, to determine if a sending system has possession of the private key associated with a CGA's public key. Its format is given in Figure 8-50.

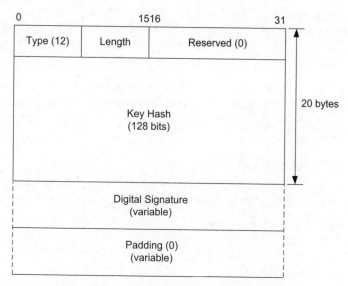

Figure 8-50 The RSA Signature option used with SEND. The signature is encoded in the PKCS#1 v 1.5 (see Chapter 18) format and is used to verify that the sender possesses the matching private key and is consequently the correct owner of the CGA.

The *Key Hash* field contains the high-order 128 bits of a SHA-1 hash of the public key used in constructing the signature. The *Digital Signature* field contains a standardized signature over the following values: the CGA Message Type tag for SEND, the source IP and destination IP addresses, the first 32-bit word of the ICMPv6 header (*Type, Code,* and *Checksum* fields), and the ND protocol message header and options (not including the RSA signature option).

8.5.6.10 Timestamp Option (Type 13)

The Timestamp option gives the current time of day known to the sending system. This helps counter potential replay attacks against SEND [RFC3971]. Its format is given in Figure 8-51.

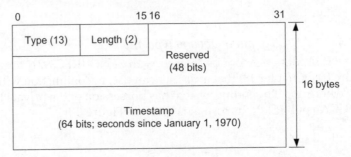

Figure 8-51   The Timestamp option used with SEND. The value encodes the number of seconds that have elapsed since January 1, 1970. It is used to guard against replay attacks.

The *Timestamp* field contains the number of seconds since January 1, 1970, 00:00 UTC. The format is fixed-point. The high-order 48 bits encode the number of complete seconds. The remaining bits indicate the number of (1/64K) fractions of a second.

8.5.6.11 Nonce Option (Type 14)

The Nonce option holds a recently generated random number. This helps counter potential replay attacks against SEND [RFC3971]. Its format is given in Figure 8-52.

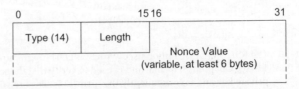

Figure 8-52   The Nonce option used with SEND. The value encodes a random number used in pairs of SEND messages. It is used to guard against replay attacks.

The nonce value is a random number selected by the sender. The length of the number must be at least 6 bytes. Details on using nonces to combat replay attacks are given in Chapter 18.

8.5.6.12 Trust Anchor Option (Type 15)

The Trust Anchor option includes the name (root) of a certification path (see Chapter 18). This is used with SEND for a host to verify the authenticity of RA messages. Its format is given in Figure 8-53.

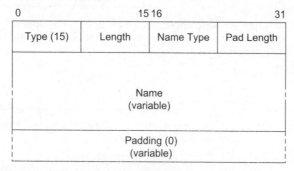

Figure 8-53   The Trust Anchor option used with SEND. The trust anchor is the name of the root of a certificate chain. Subordinate certificates may be validated against the trust anchor. Certificate chains are used in SEND for a host to validate router advertisements.

The *Name Type* field indicates the type of name used. Currently, two values have been defined: 1, DER X.502 names; 2, fully qualified domain name (FQDN). More than one Trust Anchor option may be included. The *Name* field gives the name of the trust anchor in the format specified by the *Name Type* field. The trust anchor is the root of trust for a certificate chain that the sender of the message is willing to accept (see Chapter 18).

8.5.6.13 Certificate Option (Type 16)

The Certificate option holds a single certificate used with SEND [RFC3971] in providing a certification path. Its format is given in Figure 8-54.

The *Cert Type* field indicates the type of certificate used. Currently, one value has been defined: 1, X.509v3 certificate. Certificates and how they are managed are discussed in more detail in Chapter 18.

8.5.6.14 IP Address/Prefix Option (Type 17)

The IP Address/Prefix option is used with FMIPv6 messages (ICMPv6 type 154) [RFC5568]. Its format is given in Figure 8-55.

The *Option-Code* field value indicates which type of address is encoded: 1, old care-of address; 2, new care-of address; 3, new access router's (NAR's) IPv6

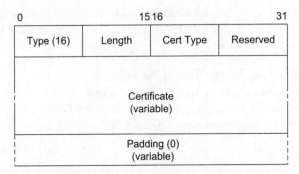

Figure 8-54   The Certificate option used with SEND. The option holds a cryptographic certificate comprising one component of a certification path. This is used to validate router advertisements.

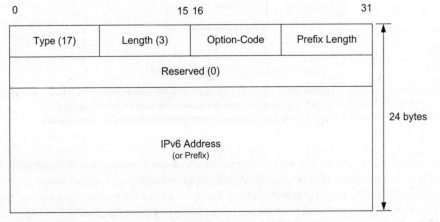

Figure 8-55   The IP Address/Prefix option used with FMIPv6. The option holds a prefix or IPv6 address of the next access router or care-of address used by a mobile node.

address; 4, NAR's prefix (in PrRtAdv). The *Prefix Length* field gives the number of valid leading bits in the *IPv6 Address* field. The *IPv6 Address* field encodes the IPv6 address identified in the *Option-Code* field.

8.5.6.15 Link-Layer Address (LLA) Option (Type 19)

The Link-Layer Address (LLA) option is used with FMIPv6 messages (ICMPv6 type 154) [RFC5568]. Its format is given in Figure 8-56.

The *Option-Code* field value indicates how the associated *Link-Layer Address* field value is to be interpreted: 0, wildcard—resolution requested for all nearby APs; 1, address of the new AP; 2, address of the mobile node; 3, address of the new access router; 4, address of the source of the RtSolPr/PrRtAdv message; 5, address is current for the router; 6, no prefix information available for the AP

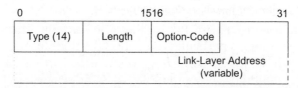

Figure 8-56   The Link-Layer Address option used with FMIPv6. The option-code value indicates what entity is associated with the address (i.e., any AP, particular AP, NAR, sender of RtSolPr or PrRtAdv message, router), if prefix information is available, and if fast handovers are supported by the AP indicated in the LLA.

corresponding to the address; 7, no fast handovers available for the AP addressed. The *Link-Layer Address* field contains the address identified by the *Option-Code* field.

8.5.6.16 Neighbor Advertisement ACK (NAACK) Option (Type 20)

This option is used with FMIPv6 messages (ICMPv6 type 154) [RFC5568]. Its format is given in Figure 8-57.

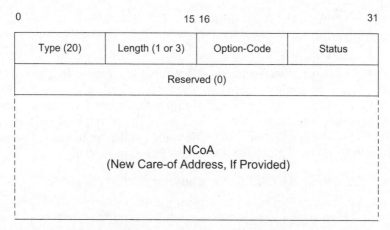

Figure 8-57   The Neighbor Advertisement Acknowledgment option used with FMIPv6. When a mobile node moves from a previous access router to a new access router and proposes to use a particular new care-of address, the new router indicates the acceptability of the proposed address.

The *Option-Code* value is 0. The *Status* field indicates the disposition of the unsolicited neighbor advertisement. The following values are defined: 1, new care-of address (NCoA) is invalid (perform address configuration); 2, NCoA is invalid (use NCoA supplied in IP Address option); 3, NCoA is invalid (use NAR's address as NCoA); 4, previous care-of address (PCoA) supplied (do not send binding update); 128, link-layer address unrecognized.

8.5.6.17 Route Information Option (Type 24)

This option is used with RA messages to indicate which off-link prefixes are reachable through a particular router [RFC4191]. Its format is given in Figure 8-58.

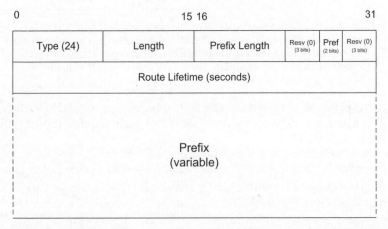

Figure 8-58   The Route Information option indicates the preference for using a particular router to reach a particular off-link prefix. It is most useful in cases where multiple default routers are available and perform differently in reaching the same destinations.

The *Prefix Length* field gives the number of valid leading bits in the *Prefix* field. The *Pref* field indicates whether the router associated with the included prefix should be preferred over others. If this field contains the value 2, the option must be ignored. The *Route Lifetime* field gives the number of seconds for which the prefix is to be considered valid. The value of all 1s indicates infinity. The variable-length *Prefix* field gives the IPv6 prefix being described.

8.5.6.18 Recursive DNS Server Option (RDNSS) (Type 25)

The Recursive DNS Server (RDNSS) option, defined in [RFC6106], can be used with RA messages to enhance stateless autoconfiguration by providing the IPv6 address of one or more DNS servers (see Chapters 6 and 11). Multiple RDNSS options may be included with an RA message. The format is given in Figure 8-59.

The *Lifetime* field gives the amount of time in seconds during which the list of DNS server addresses should be considered valid. The all-1s value indicates an infinite lifetime. If different lifetimes are required, multiple distinct RDNSS options may be included in the same RA message.

8.5.6.19 Router Advertisement Flags Extension Option (EFO) (Type 26)

This option extends the *Flags* field used in RA messages [RFC5175]. It is also sometimes called the *Expanded Flags option* (EFO). Its format is given in Figure 8-60.

The *Length* field is currently defined to be 1 until the subsequent bits are allocated.

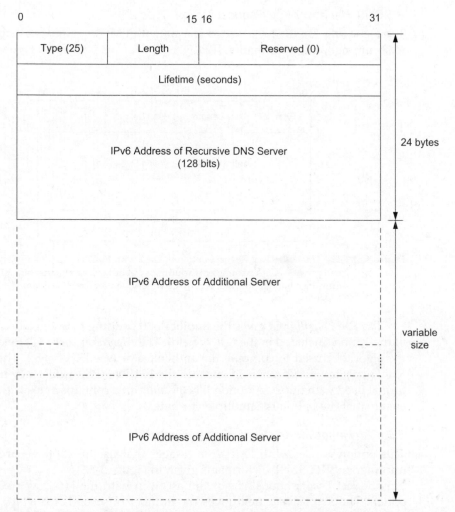

Figure 8-59 The Recursive DNS Server option indicates the IPv6 address(es) of one or more DNS servers capable of performing recursive lookups (see Chapter 11).

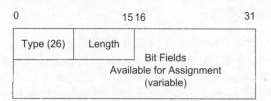

Figure 8-60 The Router Advertisement Expanded Flags option provides an arbitrary amount of additional space for defining future RA flags.

8.5.6.20 Handover Key Request Option (Type 27)

The Handover Key Request option is used with FMIPv6 messages that use SEND to secure signaling information [RFC5269]. Its format is given in Figure 8-61.

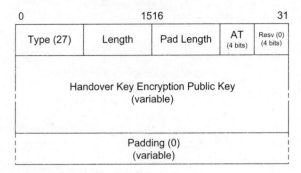

Figure 8-61   The Handover Key Request option is used with FMIPv6 signaling secured by SEND and provides CGA parameters including a public key. A router uses this information in forming a handoff key that is provided encrypted for a mobile node.

The *Pad Length* field gives the number of 0 padding bytes included at the end of the option (included in the *Length* field). The *Algorithm Type* (*AT*) field identifies the algorithm used to compute the authenticator (see [RFC5568]). The *Handover Key Encryption Public Key* field encodes the FMIPv6 CGA public key in the same format used with the CGA option. The *Padding* area contains bytes with value 0 to ensure that the option is a multiple of 8 bytes.

8.5.6.21 Handover Key Reply Option (Type 28)

This option is used with FMIPv6 messages that use SEND to secure signaling information [RFC5269]. Its format is given in Figure 8-62.

The *Pad Length* and *AT* fields are as given with the Handover Key Request option. The *Key Lifetime* field gives the number of seconds for which the handover key is valid (the default is HK-LIFETIME or 43,200s). The *Encrypted Handover Key* field holds a symmetric key (see Chapter 18) encrypted using the mobile node's handover key encryption key. The encoding format is RSAES-PKCS1-v1_5 [RFC3447]. The *Padding* field contains bytes with value 0 to ensure that the option is a multiple of 8 bytes.

8.5.6.22 DNS Search List Option (DNSSL) (Type 31)

The DNS Search List (DNSSL) option [RFC6106] is used to indicate a list of domain name extensions to be added to DNS queries a host might issue. Search lists are part of the DNS configuration information that may be provided to a host when it is initialized (see Chapter 6). The format of the DNSSL option is shown in Figure 8-63.

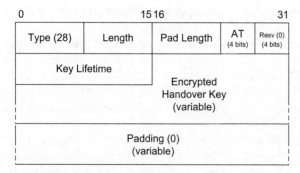

Figure 8-62 The Handover Key Reply option is used with FMIPv6 signaling secured by SEND and provides a symmetric handoff key encrypted using the mobile node's public key. Only the correct mobile node possessing the corresponding private key can decrypt the option to recover the key.

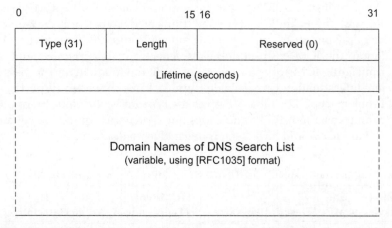

Figure 8-63 The DNS Search List option provides a list of default domain name extensions used when configuring a host's DNS parameters. The encoding format is the same one used for encoding DNS names (see Chapter 11).

The *Lifetime* field indicates how many seconds from the time the message is sent that the domain search list should be considered valid. The domain name search list includes a list of (uncompressed) domain name extensions used as a form of default for forming FQDNs from partial strings (see Chapter 11).

8.5.6.23 Experimental Values (Types 253, 254)

These values are used only for experimentation, as described in [RFC3692].

8.6 Translating ICMPv4 and ICMPv6

In Chapter 7 we discussed a framework for IPv4/IPv6 translation based on [RFC6144] and [RFC6145] and discussed how IP headers are translated. The methods used to translate ICMPv4 to ICMPv6 and vice versa are also described in [RFC6145]. When translating ICMP, both the IP and ICMP headers are translated (i.e., modified and replaced). In addition, ICMP error messages, which contain an internal offending packet header and data, have the internal (offending) datagram's headers translated. Aside from mapping the appropriate type and code numbers, there are additional concerns regarding fragmentation, MTU sizes, and checksum computations. Recall that ICMPv6 uses a pseudo-header checksum covering information at the network layer, whereas the ICMPv4 checksum is computed only over ICMPv4 information.

8.6.1 Translating ICMPv4 to ICMPv6

When translating ICMPv4 informational messages to ICMPv6, only the Echo Request and Echo Reply types are translated. To perform the translation, the type values (8 and 0) are translated to values 128 and 129, respectively. After this translation, the ICMPv6 pseudo-header checksum is computed and applied. When translating ICMPv4 error messages, only the following error messages are translated: Destination Unreachable (type 3), Time Exceeded (type 11), and Parameter Problem (type 12). Table 8-6 gives the type and code value mappings used to perform translation. Types and codes not shown are not translated, and the arriving packet that would have been translated is instead dropped.

Table 8-6   Type and code mappings used to translate ICMPv4 error messages to ICMPv6

ICMPv4 Type/Code	ICMPv4 Descriptive Name	ICMPv6 Type/Code	ICMPv6 Descriptive Name (Note)
3/0	Destination Unreachable—Network	1/0	Destination Unreachable—No Route
3/1	Destination Unreachable—Host	1/0	Destination Unreachable—No Route
3/2	Destination Unreachable—Protocol	4/1	Parameter Problem—Unrecognized Next Header (set *Pointer* to indicate *Next Header*)
3/3	Destination Unreachable—Port	1/4	Destination Unreachable—Port
3/4	Destination Unreachable—Fragmentation Required (PTB)	2/0	PTB (adjust MTU field to reflect size of larger IPv6 header)
3/5	Destination Unreachable—Source Route Failed	1/0	Destination Unreachable—No Route (unlikely to occur)
3/{6,7}	Destination Unreachable—Destination Network/Host Unknown	1/0	Destination Unreachable—No Route

Table 8-6   Type and code mappings used to translate ICMPv4 error messages to ICMPv6 (*continued*)

ICMPv4 Type/Code	ICMPv4 Descriptive Name	ICMPv6 Type/Code	ICMPv6 Descriptive Name (Note)
3/8	Destination Unreachable— Source Host Isolated	1/0	Destination Unreachable—No Route
3/{9,10}	Destination Unreachable— Destination Network/Host Administratively Prohibited	1/1	Destination Unreachable— Communication with Destination Administratively Prohibited
3/{11,12}	Destination Unreachable—ToS Unavailable	1/0	Destination Unreachable—No Route
3/13	Destination Unreachable— Administratively Prohibited	1/1	Destination Unreachable— Communication with Destination Administratively Prohibited
3/14	Destination Unreachable— Host Precedence Violation	N/A	(Drop)
3/15	Destination Unreachable— Precedence Cutoff in Effect	1/1	Destination Unreachable— Communication with Destination Administratively Prohibited
11/{0,1}	Time Exceeded—TTL, Fragment Reassembly	3/{0,1}	Time Exceeded (code remains unchanged)
12/0	Parameter Problem—Pointer Contains Byte Offset of Error	4/0	Parameter Problem—Erroneous Header Field Encountered (update *Pointer* as in Table 8-7)
12/1	Parameter Problem—Missing Option	N/A	(Drop)
12/2	Parameter Problem—Bad Length	4/0	Parameter Problem—Erroneous Header Field Encountered (update *Pointer* as in Table 8-7)

As shown in Table 8-6, for Parameter Problem messages where the *Pointer* field gives the byte offset of the problem, an additional mapping is used to form the appropriate value for the IPv6 *Pointer* field. Table 8-7 gives this mapping.

In addition to performing the header translations, the offending datagram carried in an ICMPv4 error message is also translated according to the rules for IPv4/IPv6 translation. Note that this implies the resulting ICMPv6 datagram may be of a significantly different size from what it would be if the internal translation were not performed. The *Total Length* field in the base IPv6 header is updated to reflect any such effects. Note that only a single level of such inner translation is supported. If one or more additional internal headers are discovered, the packet being translated is discarded. Generally, packets other than ICMP messages failing translation result in an ICMPv4 Destination Unreachable—Communication Administratively Prohibited (code 13) message being sent to the sender of the failed packet.

Table 8-7 *Pointer* field mappings used when translating ICMPv4 Parameter Problem messages to ICMPv6

IPv4 Pointer Value	IPv4 Header Field	IPv6 Pointer Value	IPv6 Header Field
0	Version/IHL	0	Version/DS Field/ECN (Traffic Class)
1	DS Field/ECN (ToS)	1	DS Field/ECN (Traffic Class)/Flow Label
2, 3	Total Length	4	Payload Length
4, 5	Identification	N/A	
6	Flags/Fragment Offset	N/A	
7	Fragment Offset	N/A	
8	Time to Live	7	Hop Limit
9	Protocol	6	Next Header
10,11	Header Checksum	N/A	
12–15	Source IP Address	8	Source IP Address
16–19	Destination IP Address	24	Destination IP Address

Note that as with other IPv4 traffic being translated to IPv6 (see Chapter 7), packets arriving with the *DF* bit field not set result in one or more IPv6 packets with Fragment headers included and resulting fragments not exceeding the IPv6 minimum MTU. This is to deal with the issue that IPv4 routers are permitted to fragment IPv4 traffic (including ICMPv4 traffic) but IPv6 routers are not. ICMPv4 PTB messages may need to be translated to ICMPv6 PTB messages that contain an MTU less than the IPv6 minimum link MTU of 1280 bytes. A properly operating IPv6 stack processes all such messages and sends subsequent datagrams to the same destination equipped with Fragment headers.

8.6.2   Translating ICMPv6 to ICMPv4

Among ICMPv6 informational messages, Echo Request (type 128) and Echo Reply (type 129) messages are translated to ICMPv4 Echo Request (type 8) and Echo Reply (type 0) messages, respectively. The checksum is updated to take into account the type value changes and the lack of the pseudo-header computation. Other informational messages are discarded. Table 8-8 shows how error messages are translated, giving the incoming (ICMPv6) and outgoing (ICMPv4) type and code numbers.

Once again, the *Pointer* field used with the Parameter Problem message requires special handling. Table 8-9 provides this mapping for the ICMPv6-to-ICMPv4 case.

Note that the ICMPv4 checksum does not use a pseudo-header, so when performing a header translation, the resulting checksum must be updated appropriately if a non-checksum-neutral address translation is performed. In addition, the internal IPv6 datagram may contain addresses that are not IPv4-translatable addresses, resulting in a need for stateful translation (see Chapter 7).

Table 8-8   Type and code mappings used to translate ICMPv6 error messages to ICMPv4

ICMPv6 Type/Code	ICMPv6 Descriptive Name	ICMPv4 Type/Code	ICMPv4 Descriptive Name (Note)
1/0	Destination Unreachable—No Route	3/1	Destination Unreachable—Host
1/1	Destination Unreachable—Communication with Destination Administratively Prohibited	3/10	Destination Unreachable—Destination Host Administratively Prohibited
1/2	Destination Unreachable—Beyond Scope of Source Address	3/1	Destination Unreachable—Host
1/3	Destination Unreachable—Address	3/1	Destination Unreachable—Host
1/4	Destination Unreachable—Port	3/3	Destination Unreachable—Port
2/0	PTB (adjust MTU field to reflect size of larger IPv6 header)	3/4	Destination Unreachable—Fragmentation Required (PTB)
3/{0, 1}	Time Exceeded—Hop Limit, Fragment Reassembly	11/{0,1}	Time Exceeded—TTL, Fragment Reassembly (code value is unchanged)
4/0	Parameter Problem—Erroneous Header Field Encountered	12/0	Parameter Problem—Pointer Contains Byte Offset of Error (update *Pointer* as in Table 8-7)
4/1	Parameter Problem—Unrecognized Next Header	3/2	Destination Unreachable—Protocol (set *Pointer* to indicate *Protocol* field)
4/2	Parameter Problem—Unrecognized IPv6 Option Encountered	N/A	(Drop)

Table 8-9   *Pointer* field mappings used when translating ICMPv6 Parameter Problem messages to ICMPv4

IPv6 Pointer Value	IPv6 Header Field	IPv4 Pointer Value	IPv4 Header Field
0	*Version/DS Field/ECN (Traffic Class)*	0	*Version/IHL/DS Field/ECN (ToS)*
1	*DS Field/ECN (Traffic Class)/Flow Label*	1	*DS Field/ECN (ToS)*
2, 3	*Flow Label*	N/A	
4, 5	*Payload Length*	N/A	*Total Length*
6	*Next Header*	9	*Protocol*
7	*Hop Limit*	8	*Time to Live*
8–23	*Source IP Address*	12	*Source IP Address*
24–39	*Destination IP Address*	16	*Destination IP Address*

When handling differences in packet sizes, recall that there is no *Don't Fragment* indication in IPv6 datagrams ("don't fragment" is implicitly always true), and routers cannot perform fragmentation. As a result, IPv6 packets arriving at the translator that do not fit in the MTU of the IPv4 interface used to reach the next hop are discarded and an appropriate ICMPv6 PTB message is sent back to the IPv6 source of the offending datagram.

8.7   Attacks Involving ICMP

The types of attacks involving ICMP fall primarily into three categories: *floods*, *bombs*, and *information disclosure*. In essence, floods cause a large amount of traffic to be generated, leading to an effective DoS attack on one or more computers. The bomb class (sometimes called *nuke* class) refers to sending specially constructed messages that cause IP or ICMP processing to crash or hang. Information disclosure attacks do not typically cause harm by themselves but can be used to inform the approaches used by other attack methods to avoid wasting time or avoid being detected. ICMP attacks against TCP have been documented separately [RFC5927].

One of the early attacks involving ICMP is called the *smurf* attack. This amounts to using ICMPv4 with a broadcast destination address to induce a large number of computers to respond. If this is done rapidly, it can result in a DoS attack because the victim computer is too busy processing the ICMP traffic to do anything else. Generally this attack is mounted by setting the source IP address to the intended victim's address. Thus, when the broadcast ICMP message is received by several computers, all of them respond simultaneously to the source address in the ICMP message (i.e., the victim's). This attack is easily handled by disallowing incoming directed broadcast traffic at the firewall perimeter.

With ICMPv4 Echo Request/Reply (`ping`) messages, it is possible to construct packet fragments in such a way that when they are reassembled, they form an IPv4 datagram that is too large (larger than the maximum of 64KB). This has been used to cause some systems to crash and therefore represents another form of DoS attack. It is sometimes called the *ping of death* attack. A somewhat related attack involves changing the *Fragment Offset* fields in IPv4 headers so as to induce errors in the IPv4 fragment reassembly routes. This is known as the *teardrop* attack.

Another unanticipated situation that has been taken advantage of is the assumption that an ICMP message would have distinct source and destination addresses. In the *land* attack, an ICMP message containing a source and destination IP address equal to the victim's is sent to the victim. Some implementations react in unfortunate ways when receiving such a message.

The ICMP redirect capability can be used to cause an end system to use an incorrect system as a next-hop router. Although a number of checks are made on incoming ICMP Redirect messages in hopes of ensuring that they really originated with the current default router, these together fail to ensure that the message is authentic. With this attack, a man-in-the-middle (see Chapter 18) can be inserted along the flow of traffic, which is then recorded and analyzed. In addition, it could be modified to cause unwanted actions. It can achieve similar results to the ARP poisoning attack (see Chapter 4). In addition, it has been used to cause a victim to believe that *itself* is the preferred gateway to a destination. This causes an infinite loop and a consequential lockup of the victim computer.

The ICMP Router Advertisement and Router Solicitation messages can be used to create an attack that somewhat resembles the redirect attack. In particular, these messages can be used to induce victim systems to change their default routes to point to a compromised machine. In addition, passively receiving these messages can enable an attacker to learn about the topology of the local network environment. Note that the problem of such "rogue RAs," whether malicious or accidental, has been considered in more detail separately [RFC6104].

ICMP can be used as a communication channel among invading programs that wish to coordinate. In the *TFN* (*Tribe Flood Network*) attack, ICMP is used to coordinate among a group of collaborating viruses after they have compromised computers.

The set of ICMP Destination Unreachable messages can be used to cause denial of service to currently existing connections (e.g., TCP connections). In some implementations, receiving a Host Unreachable, Port Unreachable, or Protocol Unreachable message from an IP address causes all transport-layer connections currently associated with that address to be closed. These attacks are sometimes called *smack* or *bloop* attacks.

The ICMP Timestamp Request/Reply message (which is not used anymore in normal operations) can be used, if enabled, to learn the time of day according to some host. Because many approaches to security are based on using cryptography with random keys, if the source and state of randomness were to be known, an external actor could predict the sequence of pseudo-random numbers (that is why they are only *pseudo*-random) used for creating cryptographic keys, possibly allowing a third party to guess otherwise secret values and hijack connections (see Chapter 13 on TCP and Chapter 18's discussion of random numbers). Because many random numbers are based on the current time of day, revealing a host's precise notion of the time could be a problem.

Yet another attack involves modification of the PTB message. Recall that this message contains a field indicating the recommended MTU. This is used by transport protocols such as TCP to pick their packet size. If an attacker modifies this value, it can force an endpoint TCP to run with very small packets (resulting in poor performance).

Most of these attacks have been made ineffective by modifying the ICMP implementations present in popular operating systems. However, without cryptography, spoofing or masquerading attacks are still possible, in general. Protocols that use cryptographic methods (e.g., SEND) offer an enhanced level of security but may be considerably more complicated to deploy and analyze when problems arise.

8.8   Summary

In this chapter we have looked at the Internet Control Message Protocol (ICMPv4 and ICMPv6), a required part of every IP implementation. ICMP messages are carried in IP datagrams and are the first messages we have discussed that carry an end-to-end checksum (a pseudo-header checksum in the case of ICMPv6). ICMP messages may be broadly divided into error and informational message types. Generally speaking, ICMP error messages are not generated in response to problematic ICMP error messages to avoid message flooding. For IP, ICMP provides a limited information and error-reporting capability. However, the important Echo Request/Reply and Time Exceeded messages are necessary to support the popular ping and traceroute tools. Other (less visible) uses include the Destination Unreachable, PTB, and Redirect messages that are necessary for proper operation of path MTU discovery and efficient router selection.

We looked at the ICMP Destination Unreachable, Redirect, and Echo Request/ Reply messages in some detail. We also saw the fairly common ICMP Port Unreachable error message. This let us examine the information returned in an ICMP error: the IP header and as much of the IP datagram that caused the error as possible without causing the error message to become fragmented. This information is required by the receiver of the ICMP error, to know more about the cause of the error and to help direct the error message to the appropriate process or protocol implementation. There is an extension facility that can be applied to certain ICMP messages to carry additional information (e.g., MPLS tags or next-hop router information).

ICMPv6 is a far more complex and important protocol to IPv6 as compared to ICMPv4 for IPv4. It is critical for the basic configuration and operation of IPv6 systems. ICMPv6 includes most of the useful ICMPv4 messages (e.g., Destination Unreachable, Time Exceeded, Fragmentation Required, Echo Request/Reply) but also handles ND (like ARP in IPv4), allows IPv6 nodes to discover their on-link hosts and default routers, and provides discovery services and dynamic configuration for MIPv6 nodes. ICMPv6 is also used for managing multicast group memberships, whereas this is accomplished using the IGMP protocol for IPv4. We shall examine both in Chapter 9. ICMPv6 defines a rich set of options used with ND, some of which are required. Because ICMPv6 is used for so many host configuration messages that could be subject to attack, there is a secure variant (SEND) that allows addresses to be verified using cryptographically generated addresses (CGAs). CGAs are interesting in their own right and are used in protocols other than SEND.

8.9   References

[A03] T. Aura, "Cryptographically Generated Addresses (CGA)," *Proc. 6th Information Security Conference (ISC)*, Oct. 2003.

[ICMP6TYPES] http://www.iana.org/assignments/icmpv6-parameters

[ICMPTYPES] http://www.iana.org/assignments/icmp-parameters

[PING] http://ftp.arl.army.mil/~mike/ping.html

[RFC0792] J. Postel, "Internet Control Message Protocol," Internet RFC 0792/STD 0005, Sept. 1981.

[RFC1122] R. Braden, ed., "Requirements for Internet Hosts—Communication Layers," Internet RFC 1122/STD 0003, Oct. 1989.

[RFC1191] J. C. Mogul and S. E. Deering, "Path MTU Discovery," Internet RFC 1191, Nov. 1990.

[RFC1256] S. Deering, ed., "ICMP Router Discovery Messages," Internet RFC 1256, Sept. 1991.

[RFC1350] K. Sollins, "The TFTP Protocol (Revision 2)," Internet RFC 1350/STD 0033, July 1992.

[RFC1812] F. Baker, ed., "Requirements for IP Version 4 Routers," Internet RFC 1812, June 1995.

[RFC2004] C. Perkins, "Minimal Encapsulation within IP," Internet RFC 2004, Oct. 1996.

[RFC2349] G. Malkin and A. Harkin, "TFTP Timeout Interval and Transfer Size Options," Internet RFC 2349, May 1998.

[RFC2460] S. Deering and R. Hinden, "Internet Protocol, Version 6 (IPv6) Specification," Internet RFC 2460, Dec. 1998.

[RFC2491] G. Armitage, P. Schulter, M. Jork, and G. Harter, "IPv6 over Non-Broadcast Multiple Access (NBMA) Networks," Internet RFC 2491, Jan. 1999.

[RFC2710] S. Deering, W. Fenner, and B. Haberman, "Multicast Listener Discovery (MLD) for IPv6," Internet RFC 2710, Oct. 1999.

[RFC3024], G. Montenegro, ed., "Reverse Tunneling for Mobile IP, Revised," Internet RFC 3024, Jan. 2001.

[RFC3122] A. Conta, "Extensions to IPv6 Neighbor Discovery for Inverse Discovery Specification," Internet RFC 3122, June 2001.

[RFC3447] J. Jonsson and B. Kaliski, "Public-Key Cryptography Standards (PKCS) #1: RSA Cryptography Specifications Version 2.1," Internet RFC 3447 (informational), Feb. 2003.

[RFC3519] H. Levkowetz and S. Vaarala, "Mobile IP Traversal of Network Address Translation (NAT) Devices," Internet RFC 3519, Apr. 2003.

[RFC3543] S. Glass and M. Chandra, "Registration Revocation in Mobile IPv4," Internet RFC 3543, Aug. 2003.

[RFC3590] B. Haberman, "Source Address Selection for the Multicast Listener Discovery (MLD) Protocol," Internet RFC 3590, Sept. 2003.

[RFC3692] T. Narten, "Assigning Experimental and Testing Numbers Considered Useful," Internet RFC 3692/BCP 0082, Jan. 2004.

[RFC3704] F. Baker and P. Savola, "Ingress Filtering for Multihomed Networks," Internet RFC 3704/BCP 0084, Mar. 2004.

[RFC3756] P. Nikander, ed., J. Kempf, and E. Nordmark, "IPv6 Neighbor Discovery (ND) Trust Models and Threats," Internet RFC 3756 (informational), May 2004.

[RFC3810] R. Vida and L. Costa, eds., "Multicast Listener Discovery Version 2 (MLDv2) for IPv6," Internet RFC 3810, June 2004.

[RFC3971] J. Arkko, ed., J. Kempf, B. Zill, and P. Nikander, "SEcure Neighbor Discovery (SEND)," Internet RFC 3971, Mar. 2005.

[RFC3972] T. Aura, "Cryptographically Generated Addresses (CGA)," Internet RFC 4972, Mar. 2005.

[RFC4191] R. Draves and D. Thaler, "Default Router Preferences and More-Specific Routes," Internet RFC 4191, Nov. 2005.

[RFC4286] B. Haberman and J. Martin, "Multicast Router Discovery," Internet RFC 4286, Dec. 2005.

[RFC4389] D. Thaler, M. Talwar, and C. Patel, "Neighbor Discovery Proxies (ND Proxy)," Internet RFC 4389 (experimental), Apr. 2006.

[RFC4443] A. Conta, S. Deering, and M. Gupta, ed.; "Internet Control Message Protocol (ICMPv6) for the Internet Protocol Version 6 (IPv6) Specification," Internet RFC 4443, Mar. 2006.

[RFC4581] M. Bagnulo and J. Arkko, "Cryptographically Generated Addresses (CGA) Extension Field Format," Internet RFC 4581, Oct. 2006.

[RFC4604] H. Holbrook, B. Cain, and B. Haberman, "Using Internet Group Management Protocol Version 3 (IGMPv3) and Multicast Listener Discovery Protocol Version 2 (MLDv2) for Source-Specific Multicast," Internet RFC 4604, Aug. 2006.

[RFC4607] H. Holbrook and B. Cain, "Source-Specific Multicast for IP," Internet RFC 4607, Aug. 2006.

[RFC4727] B. Fenner, "Experimental Values in IPv4, IPv6, ICMPv4, ICMPv6, UDP, and TCP Headers," Internet RFC 4727, Nov. 2006.

[RFC4857] E. Fogelstroem, A. Jonsson, and C. Perkins, "Mobile IPv4 Regional Registration," Internet RFC 4857 (experimental), June 2007.

[RFC4861] T. Narten, E. Nordmark, W. Simpson, and H. Soliman, "Neighbor Discovery for IP Version 6 (IPv6)," Internet RFC 4861, Sept. 2007.

[RFC4884] R. Bonica, D. Gan, D. Tappan, and C. Pignataro, "Extended ICMP to Support Multi-Part Messages," Internet RFC 4884, Apr. 2007.

[RFC4890] E. Davies and J. Mohacsi, "Recommendations for Filtering ICMPv6 Messages in Firewalls," Internet RFC 4890 (informational), May 2007.

[RFC4950] R. Bonica, D. Gan, D. Tappan, and C. Pignataro, "ICMP Extensions for Multiprotocol Label Switching," Internet RFC 4950, Aug. 2007.

[RFC4982] M. Bagnulo and J. Arkko, "Support for Multiple Hash Algorithms in Cryptographically Generated Addresses (CGAs)," Internet RFC 4982, July 2007.

[RFC5175] B. Haberman, ed., and R. Hinden, "IPv6 Router Advertisement Flags Option," Internet RFC 5175, Mar. 2008.

[RFC5269] J. Kempf and R. Koodli, "Distributing a Symmetric Fast Mobile IPv6 (FMIPv6) Handover Key Using SEcure Neighbor Discovery (SEND)," Internet RFC 5269, June 2008.

[RFC5461] F. Gont, "TCP's Reaction to Soft Errors," Internet RFC 5461 (informational), Feb. 2009.

[RFC5508] P. Srisuresh, B. Ford, S. Sivakumar, and S. Guha, "NAT Behavioral Requirements for ICMP," Internet RFC 5508/BCP 0148, Apr. 2009.

[RFC5535] M. Bagnulo, "Hash-Based Addresses (HBA)," Internet RFC 5535, June 2009.

[RFC5568] R. Koodli, ed., "Mobile IPv6 Fast Handovers," Internet RFC 5568, July 2009.

[RFC5790] H. Liu, W. Cao, and H. Asaeda, "Lightweight Internet Group Management Protocol Version 3 (IGMPv3) and Multicast Listener Discovery Version 2 (MLDv2) Protocols," Internet RFC 5790, Feb. 2010.

[RFC5837] A. Atlas, ed., R. Bonica, ed., C. Pignataro, ed., N. Shen, and JR. Rivers, "Extending ICMP for Interface and Next-Hop Identification," Internet RFC 5837, Apr. 2010.

[RFC5927] F. Gont, "ICMP Attacks against TCP," Internet RFC 5927 (informational), July 2010.

[RFC5942] H. Singh, W. Beebee, and E. Nordmark, "IPv6 Subnet Model: The Relationship between Links and Subnet Prefixes," Internet RFC 5942, July 2010.

[RFC5944] C. Perkins, ed., "IP Mobility Support for IPv4, Revised," Internet RFC 5944, Nov. 2010.

[RFC6104] T. Chown and S. Venaas, "Rogue IPv6 Advertisement Problem Statement," Internet RFC 6104 (informational), Feb. 2011.

[RFC6106] J. Jeong, S. Park, L. Beloeil, and S. Madanapalli, "IPv6 Router Advertisement Options for DNS Configuration," Internet RFC 6106, Nov. 2010.

[RFC6144] F. Baker, X. Li, C. Bao, and K. Yin, "Framework for IPv4/IPv6 Translation," Internet RFC 6144 (informational), Apr. 2011.

[RFC6145] X. Li, C. Bao, and F. Baker, "IP/ICMP Translation Algorithm," Internet RFC 6145, Apr. 2011.

[RFC6273] A. Kubec, S. Krishnan, and S. Jiang, "The Secure Neighbor Discovery (SEND) Hash Threat Analysis," Internet RFC 6273 (informational), June 2011.

[RFC6275] C. Perkins, D. Johnson, and J. Arkko, "Mobility Support in IPv6," Internet RFC 6275, June 2011.

[SI] http://www.iana.org/assignments/cga-message-types

9

Broadcasting and Local Multicasting (IGMP and MLD)

9.1 Introduction

We mentioned in Chapter 2 that there are four kinds of IP addresses: *unicast, anycast, multicast,* and *broadcast*. IPv4 may use all of them, and IPv6 uses any except the last form. In this chapter we discuss broadcasting and multicasting in more detail, including how link-layer addressing can be used to send multicast or broadcast traffic efficiently from one computer to several others. We also examine the *Internet Group Management Protocol* (IGMP) [RFC3376] and the IPv6 Multicast Listener Discovery (MLD) [RFC3810] protocols, which are used to inform IPv4 and IPv6 multicast routers which multicast addresses are in use on a subnetwork. One topic we do not cover in this chapter (or this book) is how multicast routing is implemented in wide area networks such as the global Internet. At the present time, multicast is used more in enterprise and local networks than in the wide area. While the protocols we discuss in this chapter are prerequisites for a complete understanding of wide area multicasting, the wide area routing protocols are comparatively complex and would unnecessarily complicate the explanation of the important local area case. The reader interested in exploring these issues is referred to [EGW02].

Broadcasting and multicasting provide two services for an application: delivery of packets to multiple destinations, and solicitation/discovery of servers by clients.

- **Delivery to multiple destinations**

  There are many applications that deliver information to multiple recipients: interactive conferencing and dissemination of mail or news to multiple recipients, for example. Without broadcasting or multicasting, these types of services tend to use TCP today (delivering a separate copy to each destination, which can be very inefficient).

- **Solicitation of servers by clients**

    Using broadcasting or multicasting, an application can send a request for a server without knowing any particular server's IP address. This capability is very useful during configuration when little is known about the local networking environment. A laptop, for example, might need to get its initial IP address and find its nearest router using DHCP (see Chapter 6).

Although both broadcasting and multicasting can provide these important capabilities, multicasting is generally preferable to broadcasting because multicasting involves only those systems that support or use a particular service or protocol, and broadcasting does not. Thus, a broadcast request affects *all* hosts that are reachable within the scope of the broadcast, whereas multicast affects only those hosts that are likely to be interested in the request. These concepts will become clearer as we explore the details of broadcasting and multicasting. For now, keep in mind that there is a trade-off between the higher overhead and simplicity of broadcast and the improved efficiency but greater complexity associated with multicast.

Broadcasting has been supported by the IPv4 protocol since its inception, and multicast was added with the publication of [RFC1112]. IPv6 supports multicasting but does *not* support broadcasting. Generally, only user applications that use the UDP transport protocol (Chapter 10) take advantage of broadcasting and multicasting, where it makes sense for an application to send a single message to multiple recipients. TCP is a connection-oriented protocol that implies a connection between two hosts (specified by IP addresses) and one process on each host (specified by port numbers). TCP can use unicast and anycast addresses (recall that anycast addresses behave like unicast addresses), but not broadcast or multicast addresses.

Note

Broadcasting and multicasting are also used by important system processes such as routing protocols, ARP, ND in IPv6, and others. Although IP multicasting support was once an "add-on," requiring users to patch their systems to make use of it, modern operating systems include the capability by default. Multicasting is an important but arguably optional feature in IPv4, but it is mandatory in IPv6 because of its use in ND (see Chapter 8), a service critical even to unicast communication.

9.2   Broadcasting

Broadcasting refers to sending a message to all possible receivers in a network. In principle, this is simple: a router simply forwards a copy of any message it receives out of every interface other than the one on which the message arrived. Things are slightly more complicated when multiple hosts are attached to the same local area network. In this case, features of the link layer may be used to make broadcasting somewhat more efficient.

Consider a set of hosts on a network such as an Ethernet that supports broadcasting at the link layer. Each Ethernet frame contains the source and destination MAC addresses (48-bit values). Normally, each IP packet is destined for a single host, so unicast addressing is used and the destination's unique MAC address is determined using ARP or IPv6 ND. When a frame is sent to a unicast destination in this way, communication between any two hosts does not bother any of the remaining hosts on the network. For switched Ethernet networks, these are the types of addresses found in the station caches in switches and bridges (see Chapter 3). There are times, however, when a host wants to send a frame to every other host on the network (or VLAN)—this is called a *broadcast*. We saw this with ARP in Chapter 4.

9.2.1 Using Broadcast Addresses

On an Ethernet or similar network, a multicast MAC address has the low-order bit of the high-order byte turned on. In hexadecimal this looks like 01:00:00:00:00:00. We may consider the Ethernet broadcast address ff:ff:ff:ff:ff:ff as a special case of the Ethernet multicast address. From Chapter 2 recall that in IPv4, each subnet has a local subnet-directed broadcast address formed by placing all 1 bits in the host portion of the address, and the special address 255.255.255.255 corresponds to a local network (also called "limited") broadcast.

9.2.1.1 Example

In Linux, the IPv4 subnet-directed broadcast address associated with each interface can be found or set with the `ifconfig` command. We can see it displayed as follows:

```
Linux% ifconfig eth0
eth0      Link encap:Ethernet  HWaddr 00:08:74:93:C8:3C
          inet addr:10.0.0.13  Bcast:10.0.0.127  Mask:255.255.255.128
          inet6 addr: 2001:5c0:9ae2:0:208:74ff:fe93:c83c/64
                    Scope:Global
          inet6 addr: fe80::208:74ff:fe93:c83c/64
                    Scope:Link
          UP BROADCAST RUNNING MULTICAST  MTU:1500  Metric:1
          RX packets:426469 errors:0 dropped:0 overruns:1 frame:0
          TX packets:779338 errors:0 dropped:0 overruns:0 carrier:0
          collisions:298048 txqueuelen:1000
          RX bytes:44414543 (42.3 MiB)  TX bytes:1094425223 (1.0 GiB)
          Interrupt:19 Base address:0xec00
```

Here, the address 10.0.0.127 is the (subnet-directed) broadcast address used on the network to which device eth0 is attached. This address is formed by taking the network prefix (10.0.0.0/25) and combining it with $32 - 25 = 7$ bits of 1s in the host portion of the address: 10.0.0.0 OR 0.0.0.127 = `10.0.0.127`. A simple utility called `ipcalc` is available on some systems to perform this calculation.

To see how simple broadcasting works, we can send an ICMPv4 Echo Request message using the `ping` program to the broadcast address of `10.0.0.127` indicated by the output of the `ifconfig` command:

```
Linux# ping -b 10.0.0.127
WARNING: pinging broadcast address
PING 10.0.0.127 (10.0.0.127) 56(84) bytes of data.
64 bytes from 10.0.0.6: icmp_seq=1 ttl=64 time=1.05 ms
64 bytes from 10.0.0.113: icmp_seq=1 ttl=64 time=1.55 ms (DUP!)
64 bytes from 10.0.0.120: icmp_seq=1 ttl=64 time=3.09 ms (DUP!)

--- 10.0.0.127 ping statistics ---
1 packets transmitted, 1 received, +2 duplicates,
0% packet loss, time 0ms
```

We mentioned in Chapter 8 that in this type of broadcast, all the hosts on the local LAN (or VLAN) are affected. Here we receive replies from three other hosts on the network, and the `ping` program notes that more responses were received than the number of requests sent (the `DUP!` indication). To see the addresses being used, we can investigate the action using Wireshark (see Figure 9-1).

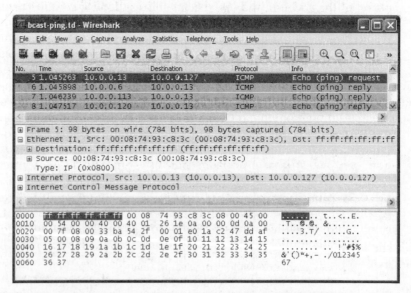

Figure 9-1   An ICMPv4 Echo Request message sent to the directed broadcast address on the local subnetwork is encapsulated in a link-layer broadcast frame with a destination address of all 1s.

The Echo Request message is sent to the address 10.0.0.127. The IPv4 implementation determines this to be the subnet-directed broadcast address by consulting information in the local routing table and interface configuration information, and it sends the datagram using the link-layer broadcast address ff:ff:ff:ff:ff:ff, so no ARP request is needed to determine the MAC addresses for each destination. In fact, the sender is unaware of what hosts will respond until they do. It knows only that 10.0.0.127 is a broadcast address and that it should therefore use a broadcast link-layer destination address when sending. The source addresses at both the IP and link layers are entirely conventional unicast; multicast addresses are used only as destination addresses.

In this particular example, notice that each of the responses generated is directed at 10.0.0.13, the unicast address of the original sender, and that each response includes the IPv4 address of the responder: 10.0.0.6, 10.0.0.113, and 10.0.0.120. This is a simple example of a more general principle: broadcast addressing (and multicast addressing, as we shall see shortly) can be used to discover systems or services that are otherwise unknown. In this example, the outgoing broadcast `ping` request discovered three hosts that are willing to respond to broadcast Echo Request messages.

9.2.2 Sending Broadcast Datagrams

Generally speaking, applications using broadcast use the UDP protocol (or ICMPv4 protocol) and invoke an ordinary set of API calls to send traffic. The only exception is that when invoking the API calls, a special flag (SO_BROADCAST) is used in some operating systems to indicate that the application really does intend to send broadcast datagrams. For example, in Linux, failing to use the −b flag when attempting to do a broadcast `ping` causes the following output:

```
Linux% ping 10.0.0.127
Do you want to ping broadcast? Then −b
```

This error is caused because the SO_BROADCAST flag is provided through the API only when the −b option is provided in the command line. This helps to avoid accidentally generating broadcast traffic that could temporarily congest a network.

To determine which interfaces are used for broadcasting, the IPv4 forwarding table (called "routing table" here) is consulted. The following is an example of a Windows Vista routing table (later versions of Windows use an identical format) showing the interface list and broadcast-related routing information (other information has been removed for clarity):

```
C:\> netstat -rn
===========================================================================
Interface List
 10 ...02 00 4c 4f 4f 50 ...... Microsoft Loopback Adapter
  9 ...00 13 02 20 b9 18 ...... Intel(R) PRO/Wireless 3945ABG Network
                                Connection
```

```
   8 ...00 14 22 f4 19 5f ...... Broadcom 440x 10/100 Integrated
                                 Controller
   1 ........................ Software Loopback Interface 1
  12 ...00 00 00 00 00 00 00 e0  Microsoft ISATAP Adapter
  13 ...00 00 00 00 00 00 00 e0  Microsoft ISATAP Adapter #2
  11 ...00 00 00 00 00 00 00 e0  isatap.
                                 {2523E0D6-A8E2-42F1-8188-6AA108FEA1EA}
===========================================================================

IPv4 Route Table
===========================================================================
Active Routes:
Network Destination  Netmask           Gateway     Interface       Metric
0.0.0.0              0.0.0.0           10.0.0.1    10.0.0.57       25
10.0.0.127           255.255.255.255   On-link     10.0.0.57       281
127.255.255.255      255.255.255.255   On-link     127.0.0.1       306
169.254.255.255      255.255.255.255   On-link     169.254.57.240  286
255.255.255.255      255.255.255.255   On-link     127.0.0.1       306
255.255.255.255      255.255.255.255   On-link     169.254.57.240  286
255.255.255.255      255.255.255.255   On-link     10.0.0.57       281
```

The first portion of this output shows seven different network interfaces that may be used for carrying network traffic. The first is the virtual loopback interface, the next is a Wi-Fi wireless interface, the third is a wired Ethernet interface (that is disconnected), the fourth is another loopback interface, and the next three are used as part of the nonstandard *Intra-Site Automatic Tunnel Addressing Protocol* (ISATAP) [RFC5214][RFC5579]. ISATAP is used in supporting IPv6 hosts separated by an IPv4 network.

Moving on to the routing table, we see that there are seven entries that could be used to determine where broadcast traffic should be sent. The first entry is the default route (mask 0.0.0.0), so it matches any destination. This could be used by broadcasts directed beyond the local network, if such a facility were enabled. This type of directed broadcast, which travels beyond the local network, is usually disabled by routers to avoid a number of security problems, as suggested by [RFC2644].

The next three entries are the directed subnet broadcast addresses associated with the three interfaces having IPv4 addresses 10.0.0.57, 127.0.0.1, and 169.254.57.240, respectively. The last two are software loopback interfaces. These entries show how Windows expresses a directed subnet broadcast route as the network prefix combined with all 1s bits in the host part as the destination, and a /32 or 255.255.255.255 subnet mask. The Gateway column indicates On-link, so traffic is delivered using direct delivery (see Chapter 5) on the interface identified in the Interface column. In these cases, there is not more than one match for each subnet-directed broadcast address, so the Metric column is not consulted.

The last three entries are routing entries for the limited broadcast address, 255.255.255.255. In some ways, this address acts like a multicast address because it is not directly associated with the addresses in use on any directly attached network. Thus, it is not immediately obvious which interface(s) should be used for sending traffic destined for the limited broadcast address. Unfortunately, Section 3.3.6 of the Host Requirements RFC [RFC1122] provides little guidance:

> There has been discussion on whether a datagram addressed to the Limited Broadcast address ought to be sent from all the interfaces of a multihomed host. This specification takes no stand on the issue.

As a consequence, the way outgoing traffic to the limited broadcast address is handled is operating-system-specific. Most systems pick a single broadcast-capable interface to use for sending such traffic. Linux and FreeBSD behave this way. FreeBSD actually converts the limited broadcast address into a subnet-directed broadcast address of the "primary" (first configured) interface, although an application can disable this behavior using the IP_ONESBCAST API option. Windows, for example, has behaved differently in different versions. Up to Windows 2000, limited broadcasts were forwarded over multiple interfaces. With Windows XP and later, the default behavior is to send over a single interface. In this example, there are multiple possible matching routes for such traffic, so the entry with the lowest metric (interface 10.0.0.57) is used.

9.3   Multicasting

To reduce the amount of overhead involved in broadcasting, it is possible to send traffic only to those receivers that are interested in it. This is called *multicasting*. Fundamentally, this is accomplished by either having the sender indicate the receivers, or instead having the receivers independently indicate their interest. The network then becomes responsible for sending traffic only to intended/interested recipients. Implementing multicast is considerably more challenging than broadcast because *multicast state* (information) must be maintained by hosts and routers as to what traffic is of interest to what receivers. In the TCP/IP model of multicasting, receivers indicate their interest in what traffic they wish to receive by specifying a multicast address and optional list of sources. This information is maintained as *soft state* (see Chapter 4) within hosts and routers, meaning that it must be updated regularly or it will time out and be deleted. When this happens, delivery of multicast traffic either ceases or reverts to broadcast.

The inefficiencies of broadcast apply not only to wide area networks, where they can be extremely severe, but also to local area and enterprise networks. Every host that can be reached on the same LAN or VLAN must process broadcast packets. IP multicasting provides a more efficient way to carry out the same types of tasks. If IP multicasting is used properly, only those hosts involved or interested in the communication need to process the associated packets, traffic is carried only on those links where it will be used, and only one copy of any multicast datagram is carried on any such link. To make multicasting work, applications that wish to be involved in a communication require a mechanism to notify their protocol implementations of their desires. The host software can then arrange to receive packets matching the applications' criteria.

IP multicasting originated using a design based on the way group addressing works in link-layer networks such as Ethernet. In this approach, each station selects the group address for which it is willing to accept traffic, irrespective of the sender. This approach is also sometimes called any-source multicast (ASM) because of the insensitivity to the identity of the sender. As IP multicasting has evolved, an alternative form that is sensitive to the identity of the sender called source-specific multicast (SSM) [RFC4607] has been developed that allows end stations to explicitly include or exclude traffic sent to a multicast group from a particular set of senders. The SSM service model is easier to implement than ASM, primarily because in wide area multicasting it is easier to determine the location of a single source than the locations of many sources. In the local area, however, much of the machinery involved in supporting either ASM or SSM is identical, so we treat them together and explain the few differences when they are important. We begin by investigating how IP multicast traffic makes use of MAC-layer multicast addresses on multicast-capable IEEE LAN technology.

9.3.1   Converting IP Multicast Addresses to 802 MAC/Ethernet Addresses

When using unicast addresses on Ethernet-like networks, ARP (see Chapter 4) is usually used to determine a local destination's MAC address given its IPv4 address. In IPv6, ND serves a similar role (see Chapter 8). When we looked at broadcasting earlier, we noticed that there is a single well-known broadcast MAC address that can always be used to reach all stations on a LAN or VLAN. What destination MAC address should be placed in a link-layer frame when we wish to send multicast traffic? Ideally, we would not have to use a protocol message to determine the appropriate MAC address but could instead simply map an IP multicast address directly to some corresponding MAC address. To see how this is done, we shall focus on IEEE 802 networks, especially Ethernet and Wi-Fi. These networks represent the most common types of networks where IP multicasting is used. We will first discuss how the mapping works with IPv4, and then move on to the slightly different method used with IPv6.

To carry IP multicast efficiently on a link-layer network, there should be a one-to-one mapping between packets and addresses at the IP layer and frames at the link layer. The IANA owns the IEEE Organizationally Unique Identifier (abbreviated OUI, or more informally Ethernet address prefix) 00:00:5e. With it, IANA is given the right to use group (multicast) MAC addresses starting with 01:00:5e as well as unicast addresses starting with 00:00:5e. This prefix is used as the high-order 24 bits of the Ethernet address, meaning that this block includes unicast addresses in the range 00:00:5e:00:00:00 through 00:00:5e:ff:ff:ff and group addresses in the range 01:00:5e:00:00:00 through 01:00:5e:ff:ff:ff. Other organizations besides IANA own address blocks as well, but only IANA devotes some of its space to support of IP multicasting.

The IANA allocates half of its group block to identifying IPv4 multicast traffic on IEEE 802 LANs. This means that the Ethernet addresses corresponding to IPv4 multicasting are in the range 01:00:5e:00:00:00 through 01:00:5e:7f:ff:ff.

Note

Our notation here uses the Internet standard bit order as the bits appear in memory. This is what most programmers and system administrators deal with. The IEEE documentation uses the transmission order of the bits.

The mapping of IPv4 addresses to their corresponding IEEE 802-style link-layer addresses can be seen in Figure 9-2.

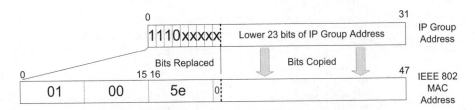

Example: 224.0.1.17 → 01:00:5e:01:11

Figure 9-2   The IPv4-to-IEEE-802 MAC multicast address mapping uses the lower-order 23 bits of the IPv4 group address as the suffix of a MAC address starting with 01:00:5e. Because only 23 of the 28 group address bits are used, 32 groups are mapped to the same MAC-layer address.

Recall from Chapter 2 that all IPv4 multicast addresses are contained within the address space from 224.0.0.0 to 239.255.255.255 (formerly known as class D address space). All such addresses share a common 4-bit sequence of 1110 in the high-order bits. Thus, there are $32 - 4 = 28$ bits available to encode the entire space of $2^{28} = 268{,}435{,}456$ multicast IPv4 addresses (also called group IDs). For IPv4, the IANA policy of allocating half of its group addresses for use in supporting IPv4 multicast means that all 268,435,456 IPv4 multicast group IDs need to be mapped into a link-layer address space containing only $2^{23} = 8{,}388{,}608$ unique entries. The mapping therefore is *nonunique*. That is, more than one IPv4 group ID is mapped to the same MAC-layer group address. Specifically, $2^{28}/2^{23} = 2^5 = 32$ distinct IPv4 multicast group IDs are mapped to each group address. For example, both the multicast addresses 224.128.64.32 (hexadecimal e0.80.40.20) and 224.0.64.32 (hexadecimal e0.00.40.20) are mapped into the Ethernet address 01:00:5e:00:40:20.

For IPv6, the 16-bit OUI hexadecimal prefix is 33:33. This means that the last 32 bits of the IPv6 address can be used to form the link-layer address. Thus, any address ending with the same 32 bits maps to the same MAC address (see Figure 9-3). Given that all IPv6 multicast addresses begin with ff, and the subsequent 8 bits are used for flags and scope information, this leaves $128 - 16 = 112$ bits for representing 2^{112} groups. Thus, with the 32 bits of MAC-layer address available to encode these groups, there can be as many as $2^{112}/2^{32} = 2^{80}$ groups that map to the same MAC address!

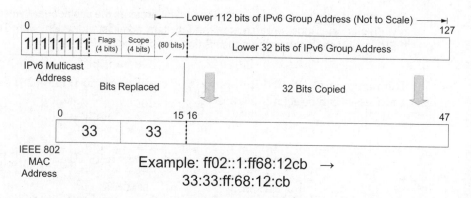

Figure 9-3   The IPv6-to-IEEE-802 MAC multicast address mapping uses the low-order 32 bits of the IPv6 multicast address as the suffix of a MAC address starting with 33:33. Because only 32 of the 112 multicast address bits are used, 2^{80} groups are mapped to the same MAC-layer address.

9.3.2 Examples

In a previous example, we used a subnet broadcast address to determine all the hosts on the local subnet that would respond to a broadcast ICMPv4 Echo Request message. Here, because we can use multicast addressing to determine hosts that offer a particular service, we can send an ICMPv4 echo request to those hosts that respond to the *Multicast DNS* (mDNS [CK11]) address 224.0.0.251:

```
Linux% ping 224.0.0.251
PING 224.0.0.251 (224.0.0.251) 56(84) bytes of data.
64 bytes from 10.0.0.2: icmp_seq=1 ttl=60 time=1.10 ms
64 bytes from 10.0.0.11: icmp_seq=1 ttl=60 time=1.60 ms (DUP!)
64 bytes from 10.0.0.120: icmp_seq=1 ttl=64 time=2.59 ms (DUP!)
--- 224.0.0.251 ping statistics ---
1 packets transmitted, 1 received, +2 duplicates,
0% packet loss, time 0ms
rtt min/avg/max/mdev = 1.109/1.767/2.590/0.615 ms
```

Here, hosts 10.0.0.2, 10.0.0.11, and 10.0.0.120 all respond, indicating that they are subscribed to the mDNS group. Notice that these hosts are not the same ones that responded when we used the broadcast address of 10.0.0.127. This is not so surprising, as not all hosts support the mDNS protocol.

Note

Multicast DNS (mDNS) is a service designed to support zero configuration (effortless system and device configuration). mDNS has been supported on Apple systems where it is part of Bonjour. Microsoft has promoted an alternative protocol that includes similar features known as Link Local Multicast Name Resolution (LLMNR) [RFC4795]. Neither protocol is currently an Internet standard within the IETF, but at present mDNS enjoys a longer history than LLMNR. See Chapter 11 for more details.

For IPv6, we can perform a similar operation using an ICMPv6 Echo Request message:

```
Linux% ping6 -I eth0 ff02::fb
PING ff02::fb(ff02::fb) from fe80::208:74ff:fe93:c83c eth0:
    56 data bytes
64 bytes from fe80::217:f2ff:fee7:6d91: icmp_seq=1 ttl=64 time=2.76 ms

--- ff02::fb ping statistics ---
1 packets transmitted, 1 received, 0% packet loss, time 0ms
rtt min/avg/max/mdev = 2.768/2.768/2.768/0.000 ms
```

Note that in this case, we provide the outgoing interface as input to the ping6 program. This allows the program to select the appropriate outgoing IPv6 address in Windows XP. As we can see in Figure 9-4, the address selected is a link-local address associated with the eth0 device.

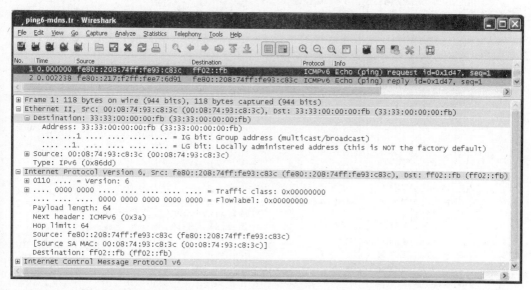

Figure 9-4   An ICMPv6 Echo Request message is sent from a link-local unicast address associated with the eth0 network interface to the multicast address ff02::fb. The reply includes the sender's IPv6 link-local IPv6 address.

The packets are identified as ICMPv6 Echo Request/Reply messages with the *Identifier* field set to 0x1d47 and *Sequence Number* field set to 1. The source IPv6 addresses are link-local in all cases. The destination address of the request is the multicast address ff02::fb, which is mapped to the MAC address 33:33:00:00:00:fb. The Echo Reply message is sent directly to the link-local IPv6 unicast address of the sender, fe80::208:74ff:fe93:c83c, from the responder's link-local unicast address, fe80::217:f2ff:fee7:6d91. Note that the sender of the Echo Reply message arranges to use a source IPv6 address of the same scope (see the discussion on source address selection in Chapter 5, and compare Figure 9-4 with Figure 5-16).

9.3.3 Sending Multicast Datagrams

When sending any IP packet, a decision must be made as to which source address and interface to use. This is especially true for IPv6, where having multiple addresses per interface is considered normal. To help determine this, we can look at the forwarding table present in the host. In either Windows or Linux, the net-stat command can be used. Here are the IPv4 and IPv6 routing tables as output on Windows Vista (later versions use an identical format):

```
C:\> netstat -rn
... interface list ...

IPv4 Route Table
===========================================================================
Active Routes:
Network Destination   Netmask            Gateway     Interface        Metric
0.0.0.0               0.0.0.0            10.0.0.1    10.0.0.57        25
224.0.0.0             240.0.0.0          On-link     127.0.0.1        306
224.0.0.0             240.0.0.0          On-link     169.254.57.240   286
224.0.0.0             240.0.0.0          On-link     10.0.0.57        281
255.255.255.255       255.255.255.255    On-link     127.0.0.1        306
255.255.255.255       255.255.255.255    On-link     169.254.57.240   286
255.255.255.255       255.255.255.255    On-link     10.0.0.57        281
===========================================================================
Persistent Routes:
  None

IPv6 Route Table
===========================================================================
Active Routes:
 If Metric Network Destination      Gateway
  9    281 ::/0                     fe80::204:5aff:fe9f:9e80
  1    306 ff00::/8                 On-link
 10    286 ff00::/8                 On-link
  9    281 ff00::/8                 On-link
===========================================================================
Persistent Routes:
  None
```

From this table we can see that a default route for IPv4 traffic goes to 10.0.0.1 using interface 10.0.0.57. Although this does match multicast traffic, there are other entries that are more specific. The entries listed as 224.0.0.0/4 (subnet mask 240.0.0.0) indicate that three different interfaces can carry outgoing multicast traffic. The interface with the lowest metric (10.0.0.57, with metric 281) is the most preferred, so it is used unless an application specifies otherwise. For IPv6, all multicast addresses begin with ff, and there are no broadcast addresses, so interfaces 1, 9, and 10 can all be used. Interface 9 (which happens to be the same interface used for IPv4 and the default for IPv6 unicast traffic) has the lowest metric. Additional information indicating which interfaces have which IP addresses can be determined using the Windows command ipconfig /all.

The output on Linux is separate for different protocol families (such as IPv4 and IPv6). It is generated by different arguments to the netstat command, to indicate which version of IP (or other) protocol is of interest. For IPv4, there is nothing to show, as there is no special entry for multicast; a conventional default route handles the multicast traffic. For IPv6, however, we can see the following:

```
Linux% netstat -rn -A inet6
Kernel IPv6 routing table
Destination   Next Hop           Flags Metric Ref   Use  Iface
ff00::/8      ::                 U     256    0     0    eth0
```

In this case, there is no direct "next hop," so the unspecified address (::) is listed in the table, but we can see that the outgoing interface is eth0. The Flags column contains only U, indicating that the route is usable, but the lack of a G flag indicates that it is an on-link route, not requiring forwarding to a router.

9.3.4 Receiving Multicast Datagrams

Fundamental to multicasting is the concept of a process *joining* or *leaving* one or more multicast groups on a given interface on a host. (We use the term *process* to mean a program being executed by the operating system, often on behalf of a user.) Membership in a multicast group on a given interface is dynamic—it changes over time as processes join and leave groups. In addition to joining or leaving groups, additional methods are needed if a process wishes to specify sources it cares to hear from or exclude. These are required parts of any API on a host that supports multicasting. We use the qualifier "interface" because membership in a group is associated with an interface. A process can join the same group on multiple interfaces, multiple groups on the same interface, or any combination thereof.

9.3.4.1 Example

It is possible to determine what multicast groups are in use on each interface using an operating-system-specific command. In Windows, the commands are part of the netsh package. For IPv6, this works as follows (for IPv4, replace ipv6 with ip):

```
C:\> netsh interface ipv6 show joins
Interface 1:  Loopback Pseudo-Interface 1
Scope          References    Last  Address
-------        ----------    ----- ------------------------------------------
0                      1     Yes   ff02::c


Interface 8:  Local Area Connection
Scope          References    Las   Address
-------        ----------    ----- ------------------------------------------
0                      0     Yes   ff01::1
0                      0     Yes   ff02::1
0                      1     Yes   ff02::c
0                      1     Yes   ff02::1:3
0                      1     Yes   ff02::1:ffdc:fc85
```

Here we can see how IPv6 uses several multicast addresses per interface. The first interface is a loopback, local interface. The only multicast group used on it is the link-local scoped Simple Service Discovery Protocol (SSDP) multicast address, which we saw in Chapter 7.

Note

SSDP is described in an (expired) Internet draft [GCLG99] authored by Microsoft and Hewlett-Packard. SSDP also operates on IPv4, using address 239.255.255.250 and UDP port 1900.

On the other network interface, the addresses ff01::1 (node-local All Nodes address) and ff02::1 (link-local All Nodes address) show joins for all nodes, and ff02::c shows the use of SSDP. The next address, ff02::1:3, is for support of LLMNR, a local multicast name resolution system mentioned previously and discussed in more detail in Chapter 11. Finally, the address ff02::1:ffdc:fc85 is the Solicited-Node multicast address for this node, used by IPv6 ND. Recall that in IPv6, determining a neighbor's MAC address is accomplished using multicast ICMPv6 ND messages, as opposed to the ARP mechanism used in IPv4.

On Linux, the `netstat` command displays the IP group memberships:

```
Linux% netstat -gn
IPv6/IPv4 Group Memberships
Interface          RefCnt Group
-----------------  ------ --------------------
lo                 1      224.0.0.1
eth1               1      224.0.0.1
lo                 1      ff02::1
eth1               1      ff02::1:ff2a:1988
eth1               1      ff02::1
```

The output from this command includes the join information for multiple interfaces and for both IPv4 and IPv6. In this case, we see 224.0.0.1 (All Hosts) on both the Ethernet interface (eth1) as well as the local loopback interface (lo).

We can also see the link-local scope All Nodes bindings for each interface. Finally, the Solicited-Node address is `ff02::1:ff2a:1988`.

Note

With IP multicasting, a process may send to a multicast group without joining it. More commonly, processes do join the multicast groups with which they are interacting, and on one or more specific interfaces. There is a special option in the socket API (IP_MULTICAST_LOOP) to alter the way multicast traffic is handled among processes on the same host that are members of the same group on the same interface. In UNIX, this option applies to the send path, meaning that if the option is enabled, other processes on the same host receive the multicast datagrams, even if they have the option disabled. Conversely, on Windows, the option applies on the receive path, meaning that any processes enabling the option receive multicast traffic from other applications on the same host even if they have the option disabled.

9.3.5   Host Address Filtering

To understand how the operating system processes received multicast datagrams for multicast groups that programs have joined, recall from Chapter 3 that *filtering* takes place on each host's network interface card (NIC), each time a frame is presented to it (e.g., by a bridge or switch) for possible reception. Figure 9-5 indicates how this occurs.

In a typical switched Ethernet environment, broadcast and multicast frames are replicated on all segments within a VLAN, along a spanning tree formed among the switches. Such frames are delivered to the NIC on each host which checks the correctness of the frame (using the CRC) and makes a decision about whether to receive the frame and deliver it to the device driver and network stack. Normally the NIC receives only those frames whose destination address is either the hardware address of the interface or the broadcast address. However, when multicast frames are involved, the situation is somewhat more complicated.

NICs tend to come in two varieties. One type performs filtering based on the hash values of the multicast hardware addresses in which the host software has expressed interest, which means that some unwanted frames can always get through because of hash collisions. The other type listens for a finite table of multicast addresses, meaning that if the host needs to receive frames destined for more multicast addresses than can fit in the table, the NIC is put into a "multicast-promiscuous" mode, in which case all multicast traffic is given to the host software. Hence, both types of interfaces require that the device driver or higher-layer software perform checking that the received frame is really wanted. Even if the interface performs perfect multicast filtering (based on the 48-bit hardware address), because the mapping from a multicast IPv4 or IPv6 address to a 48-bit hardware address is not unique, filtering is still required. Despite this imperfect address mapping and hardware filtering, multicasting is still more efficient than broadcasting.

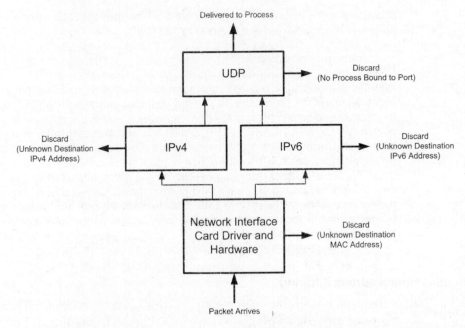

Figure 9-5   Each layer implements filtering on some portion of the received message. MAC address filtering can take place in either software or hardware. Cheaper NICs tend to impose a larger processing burden on software because they perform fewer functions in hardware.

For NICs that support a multi-entry address table, the destination address on each received frame is compared against this table, and if the address is found in the table, the frame is received and processed by the device driver. The entries of this table are managed by the device driver software in combination with other layers of the protocol stack (such as the IPv4 and IPv6 implementations). Another method of implementing this type of filtering is to apply a hash function to the destination address, forming an index into a (smaller) binary vector. When the indexed entry in the vector contains a 1 bit, the corresponding address is deemed to be acceptable and the frame is processed further. This approach can save memory on the NIC, but because of collisions in the hash function, some frames may be considered admissible when they should not be. This is not a fatal problem, however, because higher layers of the stack also perform filtering, and no frames are ever discarded when they should not have been (i.e., there are no false negatives, but there may be false positives).

Note

The specific capabilities of an NIC vary based on manufacturer. As an example, the Intel 82583V Ethernet controller includes a 16-entry exact match table (unicast or multicast), a 4096-bit hash filter for multicast destinations, and support for

both promiscuous reception and promiscuous multicast reception in addition to
filtering based on up to 4096 VLAN tags.

Once the NIC hardware has verified a frame as acceptable (i.e., the CRC is correct, any VLAN tags match, and the destination MAC address matches an address entry in one or more of the NIC's tables), the frame is passed to the device driver, where additional filtering is performed. First, the frame type must specify a protocol that is supported (e.g., IPv4, IPv6, ARP, etc.). Second, additional multicast filtering may be performed to check whether the host belongs to the addressed multicast group (indicated by the destination IP address). This is necessary for NICs that may generate false positives.

The device driver then passes the frame to the next layer, such as IP, if the frame type specifies an IP datagram. IP performs more filtering, based on the source and destination IP addresses, and passes the datagram up to the next layer (such as TCP or UDP) if all is well. Each time UDP receives a datagram from IP, it performs filtering based on the destination port number, and sometimes the source port number, too. If no process is currently using the destination port number, the datagram is discarded and an ICMPv4 or ICMPv6 Port Unreachable message is normally generated. (TCP performs similar filtering based on its port numbers.) If the UDP datagram has a checksum error, UDP silently discards it.

One of the primary motivations behind the development of the multicast addressing features was to avoid the overhead of broadcasting. Consider an application that is designed to use UDP broadcasts. If there are 50 hosts on the network (or VLAN), but only 20 are participating in the application, every time one of the 20 sends a UDP broadcast, the other 30 nonparticipating hosts have to process the broadcast, all the way up through the UDP layer, before the UDP datagram is discarded. The UDP datagram is discarded by these 30 hosts because the destination port number is not in use. The intent of multicasting is to reduce this load on hosts with no interest in the application. With multicasting, a host specifically joins one or more multicast groups. If possible, the NIC is told which multicast groups the host belongs to, and only those multicast frames associated with the IP-layer multicast groups are allowed through the filter in the NIC. All of this machinery offers less overhead imposed on the host, in exchange for additional complexity in managing multicast addresses and group memberships.

9.4   The Internet Group Management Protocol (IGMP) and Multicast Listener Discovery Protocol (MLD)

So far we have discussed how multicast datagrams are transmitted, filtered, and received from a host's perspective. When multicast datagrams are to be forwarded over a wide area network or within an enterprise across multiple subnets, we require that *multicast routing* be enabled by one or more multicast routers. This complicates the situation considerably, because multicast routers require knowledge about which hosts are interested in what multicast groups, in order to arrange for multicast traffic to be delivered appropriately. They also execute a special procedure called the *Reverse Path Forwarding* (RPF) check. This procedure performs a routing lookup on the source address of an arriving multicast datagram. Only if the outgoing interface for routing matches the interface on which the datagram arrived is the datagram forwarded. The RPF check is important for avoiding multicast loops. Multicast routing is largely separate from conventional unicast routing provided by IP routers. However, some capabilities of multicast routing are required for the IPv6 ND protocol (see Chapter 8) to operate properly.

Two major protocols are used to allow multicast routers to learn the groups in which nearby hosts are interested: the *Internet Group Management Protocol* (IGMP) used by IPv4 and the *Multicast Listener Discovery* (MLD) protocol used by IPv6. Both are used by hosts and routers that support multicasting, and the protocols are very similar. These protocols let the multicast routers on a LAN (VLAN) know which hosts currently belong to which multicast groups. This information is required by the routers so that they know which multicast datagrams to forward on to which interfaces. In most cases, a multicast router only requires knowledge that *at least one* listening host is reachable by a particular interface, as link-layer multicast addressing (assuming it is supported) permits the multicast router to send link-layer multicast frames that will be received by all interested listeners. This allows a multicast router to do its job without keeping track of every individual host on each interface that might be interested in multicast traffic for a particular group.

IGMP has evolved over time, and [RFC3376] defines version 3 (the most current one at the time of writing). MLD has evolved in parallel, and its current version (2) is defined in [RFC3810]. IGMPv3 and/or MLDv2 are required for supporting SSM. See [RFC4604] for more details on how these protocols are restricted when using only a single source per multicast group.

Version 1 of IGMP was the first commonly used version of IGMP. Version 2 added the ability to leave groups more quickly (also supported by MLDv1). IGMPv3 and MLDv2 add the ability to select the sources of multicast traffic and are required for deployment of SSM. While IGMP is a separate protocol used with IPv4, MLD is really part of ICMPv6 (see Chapter 8).

Figure 9-6 indicates how IGMP (MLD) is used by an IPv4 (IPv6) multicast-enabled router. Such routers are interested in ascertaining which multicast groups are of interest on each of its attached interfaces. These routers require this information in order to avoid simply broadcasting all traffic out of every interface.

In Figure 9-6, we can see how IGMP (MLD) queries are sent by multicast routers. These are sent to the All Hosts multicast address, 224.0.0.1 (IGMP), or the All Nodes link-scope multicast address, ff02::1 (MLD), and processed by every host implementing IP multicast (see the exception in Section 9.4.2 for "specific" queries). Membership report messages are sent by group members (hosts) in response to the queries but may also be sent in an unsolicited way from hosts that wish to inform multicast routers that their group membership(s) and/or interest in particular sources has changed. IGMPv3 reports are sent to the IGMPv3-capable

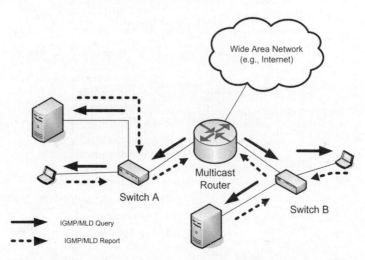

Figure 9-6   Multicast routers send IGMP (MLD) requests to each attached subnet periodically to determine which groups and sources are of interest to the attached hosts. Hosts respond with reports indicating which groups and sources are of interest. Hosts may also send unsolicited reports if membership changes occur.

multicast router address 224.0.0.22. MLDv2 reports are sent to the corresponding MLDv2 Listeners IPv6 multicast address ff02::16. Note that multicast routers themselves may also act as members when they join multicast groups.

Note

In IGMPv1 and IGMPv2, after receiving a query, hosts do not respond immediately but instead may wait a small random amount of time to see if any other host responds for the same group. If so, a host's response is suppressed (not sent). This is accomplished by having reports sent to the multicast address of the group in question. Appendix A of [RFC3376] indicates why this operation was removed in IGMPv3. In short, multicast routers may wish to track individual hosts' subscriptions, suppression does not work well in bridged LANs using IGMP snooping (see Section 9.4.7), handling suppression complicates the protocol implementation, and IGMPv3 reports contain information on multiple groups, making successful suppression less likely. Note that both IGMPv3 and MLDv2 require backward compatibility with earlier versions of themselves and revert to using older-version protocol messages of older hosts or routers detected on the same subnet.

The encapsulations for IGMP and MLD are shown in Figure 9-7. Like ICMP, IGMP is considered part of the IP layer. Also like ICMP, IGMP messages are transmitted in IPv4 datagrams. Unlike other protocols that we have seen, IGMP uses a fixed TTL of 1, so packets are limited to the local subnetwork. IGMP packets also use the IPv4 Router Alert option and use the 6-bit value 0x30 in the *DS Field*

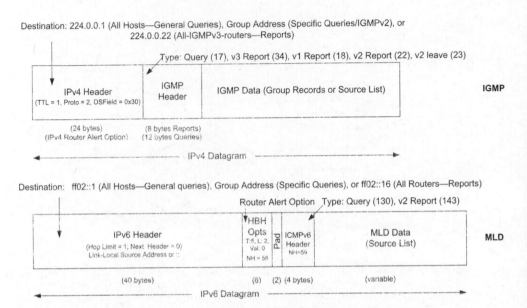

Figure 9-7   IGMP is encapsulated as a separate protocol in IPv4. MLD is a type of ICMPv6 message.

to represent Internetwork Control (CS6, see Chapter 5). In IPv6, MLD is part of ICMPv6, but the functionality of MLD is nearly identical to that of IGMP, so we describe it here (we described its message formats briefly when describing ICMPv6 in Chapter 8). Its encapsulation makes use of an IPv6 Hop-by-Hop extension header to hold the Router Alert option. In many cases, the list of sources is empty.

IGMP and MLD define two sets of protocol processing rules: those performed by hosts that are group members and those performed by multicast routers. Generally speaking, the job of the member hosts (which we will call "group members") is to spontaneously report changes in interest in multicast groups and sources and to respond to periodic queries. Multicast routers send queries to ascertain whether any interest is present on an attached link for any groups, or for a specific multicast group and source. Routers also interact with wide area multicast protocols (such as PIM-SM and BIDIR-PIM) to bring the desired traffic to the interested hosts or prohibit traffic from flowing to uninterested hosts. For more details on these protocols, please see [RFC4601] and [RFC5015].

9.4.1   IGMP and MLD Processing by Group Members ("Group Member Part")

The group members' portion of IGMP and MLD is designed to allow hosts to specify what groups they are interested in and whether traffic sent from particular sources should be accepted or filtered out. This is accomplished by sending reports to one or more multicast routers (and participating hosts) attached to the same subnet. Reports may be sent as a result of receiving a query, or spontaneously (unsolicited) because of a local change in reception state (e.g., an application joins or leaves a group). IGMP reports take the form shown in Figure 9-8.

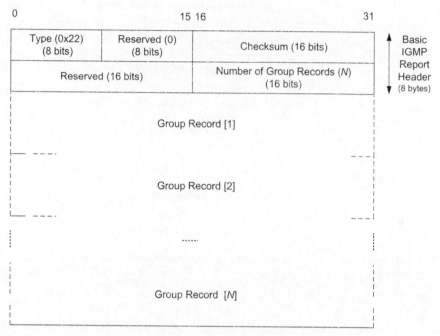

Figure 9-8   The IGMPv3 membership report contains group records for N groups. Each group record indicates a multicast address and optional list of sources.

Report messages are fairly simple. They contain a vector of *group records*, each of which provides information about a particular multicast group, including the address of the subject group, and an optional list of sources used for establishing *filters* (see Figure 9-9).

Each group record contains a type, the address of the subject group, and a list of source addresses to either include or exclude. There is also support for including auxiliary data, but this feature is not used by IGMPv3. Table 9-1 reveals the significant flexibility that can be achieved using IGMPv3 report record types. MLD uses the same values. A list of sources is said to refer to *include* mode or *exclude* mode. In include mode, the sources in the list are the only sources from which traffic should be accepted. In exclude mode, the sources in the list are the ones to be filtered out (all others are allowed). Leaving a group can be expressed as using an include mode filter with no sources, and a simple join of a group (i.e., for any source) can be expressed as using the exclude mode filter with no sources. Note that when using SSM, types 0x02 and 0x04 are not used, as only a single source is assumed for any group.

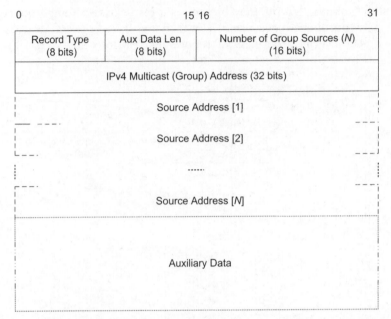

Figure 9-9   An IGMPv3 group record includes a multicast address (group) and an optional list of sources. Groups of sources are either allowed as senders (include mode) or filtered out (exclude mode). Previous versions of IGMP reports did not include a list of sources.

Table 9-1   Type values for IGMP and MLD source lists indicate the filtering mode (include or exclude) and whether the source list has changed

Type	Name and Meaning	When Sent
0x01	MODE_IS_INCLUDE (IS_IN): traffic sent from any of the associated source addresses is not to be filtered.	In response to a query from a multicast router
0x02	MODE_IS_EXCLUDE (IS_EX): traffic sent from any of the associated source addresses should be filtered.	In response to a query from a multicast router
0x03	CHANGE_TO_INCLUDE_MODE (TO_IN): a change from exclude mode; traffic sent from any of the associated source addresses should now not be filtered.	In response to a local action changing the filter mode from exclude to include
0x04	CHANGE_TO_EXCLUDE_MODE (TO_EX): a change from include mode; traffic sent from any of the associated source addresses should now be filtered.	In response to a local action changing the filter mode from include to exclude
0x05	ALLOW_NEW_SOURCES (ALLOW): a change in source list; traffic sent from any of the associated source addresses should now not be filtered.	In response to a local action changing the source list to allow new sources
0x06	BLOCK_OLD_SOURCES (BLOCK): a change in source list; traffic sent from any of the associated source addresses should now be filtered.	In response to a local action changing the source list to disallow previously allowed sources

The first two message types (0x01, 0x02) are known as *current-state records* and are used to report the current filter state in response to a query. The next two (0x03, 0x04) are known as *filter-mode-change records*, which indicate a change from include to exclude mode or vice versa. The last two (0x05, 0x06) are known as *source-list-change records* and indicate a change to the sources being handled in either exclude or include mode. The last four types are also described more generally as *state-change records* or *state-change reports*. These are sent as a result of some local state change such as a new application being started or stopped, or a running application changing its group/source interests. Note that IGMP and MLD queries/reports themselves are never filtered. MLD reports use a structure similar to IGMP reports but accommodate larger addresses and use an ICMPv6 type code of 143 (see Chapter 8).

When receiving a query, group members do not respond immediately. Instead, they set a random (bounded) timer to determine when to respond. During this delay interval, processes may alter their group/source interests. Any such modifications can be processed together before a timer expires to trigger the report. In this way, once the timer does expire, the status of multiple groups can more likely be merged into a single report, saving overhead.

The source address used for IGMP is the primary or preferred IPv4 address of the sending interface. For MLD, the source address is a link-local IPv6 address. One complication arises when a host is booting and attempting to determine its own IPv6 address. During this time, it selects a potential IPv6 address to use and executes the duplicate address detection (DAD) procedure (see Chapter 6) to determine if any other systems are already using this address. Because DAD involves multicast, some source address must be assigned to outgoing MLD messages. This is addressed by [RFC3590], which allows the unspecified address (::) to be used as the source IPv6 address for MLD traffic during configuration.

9.4.2   IGMP and MLD Processing by Multicast Routers ("Multicast Router Part")

In IGMP and MLD, the job of the multicast router is to determine, for each multicast group, interface, and source list, whether at least one group member is present to receive corresponding traffic. This is accomplished by sending queries and building state describing the existence of such members based on the reports they send. This state is soft state, meaning that it is cleared after a certain amount of time if not refreshed. To build this state, multicast routers send IGMPv3 queries of the form depicted in Figure 9-10.

The IGMP query message is very similar to the ICMPv6 MLD query we discussed in Chapter 8. In this case, the group (multicast) address is 32 bits in length and the *Max Resp Code* field is 8 bits instead of 16. The *Max Resp Code* field encodes the maximum amount of time the receiver of the query should delay before sending a report, encoded in 100ms units for values below 128. For values above 127, the field is encoded as shown in Figure 9-11.

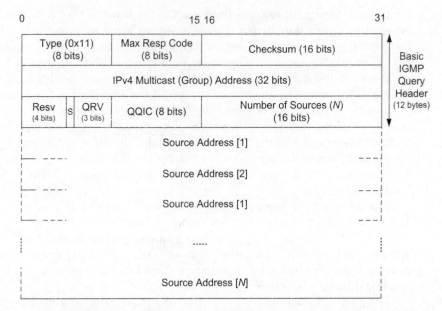

Figure 9-10 The IGMPv3 query includes the multicast group address and optional list of sources. General queries use a group address of 0 and are sent to the All Hosts multicast address, 224.0.0.1. The *QRV* value encodes the maximum number of retransmissions the sender will use, and the *QQIC* field encodes the periodic query interval. Specific queries are used before terminating traffic flow for a group or source/group combination. In this case (and all cases with IGMPv2 or IGMPv1), the query is sent to the address of the subject group.

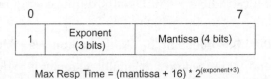

Max Resp Time = (mantissa + 16) * $2^{(exponent+3)}$

Figure 9-11 The *Max Resp Code* field encodes the maximum time to delay responses in 100ms units. For values above 127, an exponential value can be used to accommodate larger values.

This encoding provides for a possible range of $(16)(8) = 128$ to $(31)(1024) = 31,744$ (i.e., about 13s to 53 minutes). Using smaller values for the *Max Resp Code* field allows for tuning the *leave latency* (the elapsed time from when the last group member leaves to the time corresponding traffic ceases to be forwarded). Larger values of this field reduce the traffic load of the IGMP messages generated by members by increasing the likelihood of longer periods for reporting.

The remaining fields in a query include an Internet-style checksum across the whole message, the address of the subject group, a list of sources, and the *S*, *QRV*, and *QQIC* fields we defined in Chapter 8 with MLD. In cases where the multicast router wishes to know about interest in all multicast groups, the *Group Address* field is set to 0 (such queries are called "general queries"). The *S* and *QRV* fields are used for fault tolerance and retransmission of reports and are discussed in Section 9.4.5. The *QQIC* field is the *Querier's Query Interval Code*. This value is the query sending period, in units of seconds and encoded using the same method as the *Max Resp Code* field (i.e., a range from 0 to 31,744).

There are three variants of the query message that can be sent by a multicast router: *general query*, *group-specific query*, and *group-and-source-specific query*. The first form is used by the multicast router to update information regarding any multicast group, and for such queries the group list is empty. Group-specific queries are similar to general queries but are specific to the identified group. The last type is essentially a group-specific query with a set of sources included. The specific queries are sent to the destination IP address of the subject group, as opposed to general queries that are sent to the All Systems multicast address (for IPv4) or the link-scope All Nodes multicast address for IPv6 (ff02::1).

The specific queries are sent in response to state-change reports in order to verify that it is appropriate for the router to take some action (e.g., to ensure that no interest remains in a particular group before constructing a filter). When receiving either filter-mode-change records or source-list-change records, the multicast router arranges to add new traffic sources and may be able to filter out traffic from certain sources. In cases where the multicast router is prepared to begin filtering out traffic that was flowing previously, it uses the group-specific query and group-and-source-specific query first. If these queries elicit no reports, the router is free to begin filtering out the corresponding traffic. Because such changes can significantly affect the flow of multicast traffic, state-change reports and specific queries are retransmitted (see Section 9.4.5).

9.4.3 Examples

Figure 9-12 shows a packet trace containing a combination of IGMPv2, IGMPv3, MLDv1, and MLDv2 protocols, all working on the same subnet. The trace is 16 packets in length (the first 10 are shown in Figure 9-12) and begins with an MLD query from fe80::204:5aff:fe9f:9e80, the link-local IPv6 address of the querier. Recall that MLD and MLDv2 use the same query format. This same system also acts as an IGMP querier using the IPv4 source address 10.0.0.1.

In Figure 9-12, the MLD query (packet 1) is sent by the querier using its link-local IPv6 address fe80::204:5aff:fe9f:9e80 to the multicast address ff02::1 (All Nodes). The MAC-layer addresses are 00:04:5a:9f:9e:80 and 33:33:00:00:00:01, respectively. Here we can see how an IPv6 link-local unicast address relates to the corresponding MAC address, and also how the All Nodes address is mapped to the MAC address using prefix 33:33, as we discussed earlier. The IPv6 *Hop Limit* field is set to 1, as MLD messages are applicable only to the local link. The IPv6 *Payload Length* field indicates 36 bytes, which includes 8 bytes holding the MLD

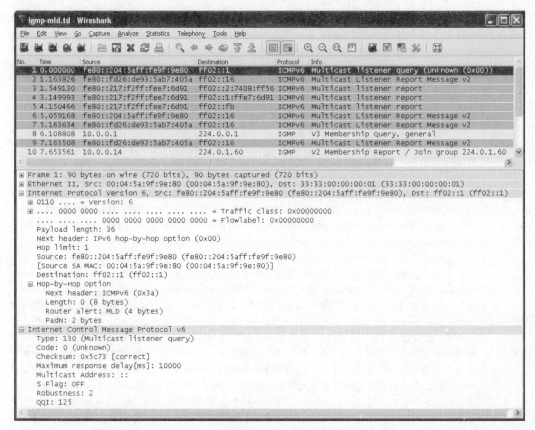

Figure 9-12   IGMPv2, IGMPv3, MLDv1, and MLDv2, all working on the same subnet. The highlighted packet is an MLD query.

form of Router Alert (a Hop-by-Hop option), 4 bytes of ICMPv6 header information, and 24 bytes to hold the MLD data itself. The *Type*, *Code*, *Checksum*, and *Max Response* fields of the MLD message together require 8 bytes of the 24; 16 more are used to hold the *Multicast Address* field (set to 0/unknown or the unspecified address to refer to all groups). The *S* bit field, *QRV*, and *QQIC* fields together use 2 more bytes, and the last 2 hold the number of sources identified, which in this case is 0. In this example, we see default values for all MLD information: 10s for the maximum response delay, QRV = 2, and 125s for the query interval. The next message (packet 2, Figure 9-13) is the response for the query.

Figure 9-13 is an MLDv2 report indicating interest in the multicast address ff02::c (the link-local multicast address for SSDP). Interest is indicated in such reports using an exclude mode report containing an empty source list. The next few packets of the trace show the use of MLDv1 (still used by some systems).

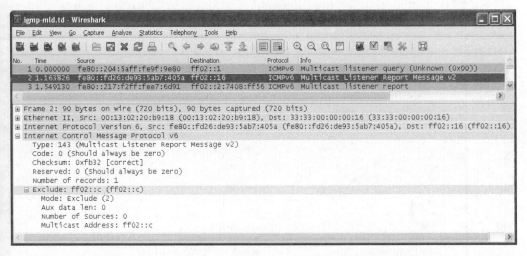

Figure 9-13   An MLDv2 listener report message expresses interest in the group ff02::c (the link-local scope multicast address for SSDP) by using an exclude-type message with no sources.

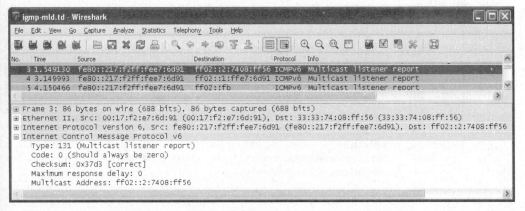

Figure 9-14   The MLDv1 report message expresses an interest in the multicast address ff02::2:7408:ff56, which is also the destination IPv6 address.

Packets 3 through 5 in Figure 9-14 are all MLDv1 reports. Only packet 3 is shown here, as the others are similar (they differ only in their respective destination IPv6 addresses). As with MLDv2, each report uses the same structure for the IPv6 base and extension headers, but the destination address of the report is the multicast address of interest, ff02::2:7408:ff56. Note that at the MAC layer, this destination address is mapped to 33:33:74:08:ff:56. The next portion of the trace, starting with packet 6 in Figure 9-15, shows how MLDv2 can report multiple interests.

Figure 9-15   This MLDv2 report expresses interest in five multicast groups. Each multicast address record reports interest in a single group by indicating that no sources are to be excluded (i.e., mode is exclude with no associated sources).

Packet 6 in Figure 9-15 is the first MLDv2 report indicating interest in more than one multicast address. In this case, it is from fe80::204:5aff:fe9f:9e80 (the MLD querier) and contains information for five groups: ff02::16 (all MLDv2-capable routers), ff02::1:ff00:0 (first solicited-node address), ff02::2 (All Routers), ff02::202 (ONC RPC, a form of remote procedure call), and ff02::1:ff9f:9e80 (its own solicited-node group). Packet 7 (not detailed) is an MLDv2 report indicating that host fe80::fd26:de93:5ab7:405a has interest in address ff02::1:ffb7:405a, its solicited-node address. We now move on to the non-IPv6 traffic in the trace as shown in Figure 9-16.

Packet 8 in Figure 9-16 is the first IPv4 packet of the trace, and it is an IGMPv3 general query from the querier 10.0.0.1. The packet is sent to the All Nodes address, 224.0.0.1, and this multicast address is mapped to the link-layer address

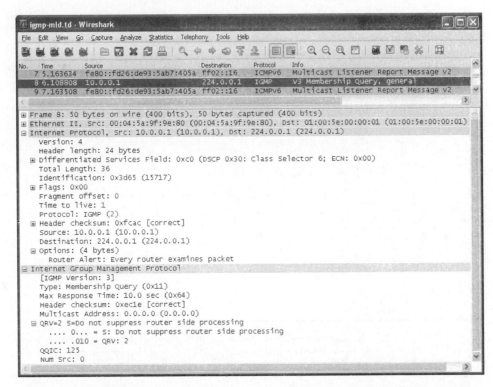

Figure 9-16 An IGMPv3 general membership query is sent to the All Nodes multicast address, 224.0.0.1. Its IPv4 header contains a DSCP value of 0x30 (class selector 6) and the IPv4 Router Alert option.

01:00:5e:00:00:01. The TTL is set to 1, as IGMP messages are not forwarded through routers. The IPv4 header is 24 bytes, which is 4 bytes larger than a basic IPv4 header in order to hold the 4-byte Router Alert option. This particular packet is an IGMPv3 membership query, with the default maximum response time of 10s and query interval of 125s. The multicast address (group) identified is 0.0.0.0, so this is a general query requesting knowledge about all multicast groups in use. Packet 9 (not detailed but similar to packets 7 and 2) is an interspersed MLDv2 response, indicating interest in the multicast address ff02::1:3 (LLMNR). The last seven packets are shown in Figure 9-17.

Packet 10 in Figure 9-17 is an IGMPv2 membership report sent from 10.0.0.14 (a network-attached printer) to 224.0.1.60, which is a discovery service used for equipment manufactured by Hewlett-Packard. As with MLDv1, IGMPv2 messages are sent to the IP address of the group being referenced. Such messages have TTL = 1, include the Router Alert option, and are 32 bytes in length (24 bytes of IPv4 header plus 8 bytes of IGMP report information).

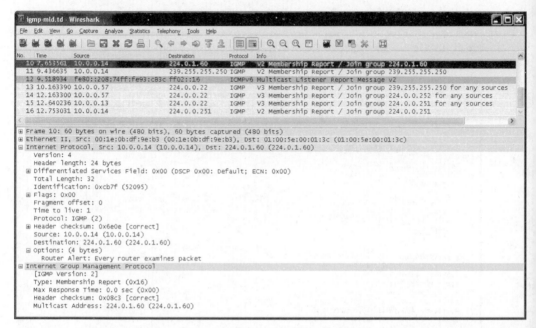

Figure 9-17   Packet 10 is detailed along with the last seven packets, which are a mix of IGMPv2 and IGMPv3 membership reports (except packet 12). IGMPv2 reports do not contain source-specific information.

The remaining packets are not detailed as they are similar to other packets we have already seen in detail. Packet 11 reports that the same system, 10.0.0.14, wishes to join the group 239.255.255.250 (part of UPnP). Packet 12 is an MLDv2 report indicating that the host fe80::208:74ff:fe93:c83c is interested in the multicast addresses ff02::202 (ONC RPC) and ff02::1:ff93:f83c (its solicited-node address). Packets 13 and 14 are IGMPv3 reports indicating that the host with IPv4 address 10.0.0.57 has interest in groups 239.255.255.250 and 224.0.0.252 (LLMNR), respectively. The last two packets indicate that hosts 10.0.0.13 and 10.0.0.14 wish to join group 224.0.0.251 (mDNS; see Chapter 11). They are IGMPv3 and IGMPv2 reports, respectively.

9.4.4   Lightweight IGMPv3 and MLDv2

As we have seen, hosts maintain filter state about what multicast groups their applications and system software are interested in. With IGMPv3 or MLDv2 they also maintain a list of sources that are excluded or included. Multicast routers maintain similar state in order to know what traffic needs to be forwarded on to a link for receipt by interested hosts. The reverse is also true: a multicast router can forgo forwarding multicast traffic sent from a host that is in every receiver's exclude list. Practical experience has shown, however, that applications rarely need to block specific sources, and support for this function is somewhat complicated.

However, hosts often wish to include a specific source associated with a group, especially when SSM is in use. As a consequence, simplified versions of IGMPv3 and MLDv2, called *Lightweight IGMPv3* (LW-IGMPv3) and *Lightweight MLDv2* (LW-MLDv2), respectively, have been defined in [RFC5790].

LW-IGMPv3 and LW-MLDv2 are subsets of their progenitors. They support both ASM and SSM and use a message format compatible with IGMPv3 and MLDv2, but they lack the specific source-blocking function. Instead, the only exclude mode supported is the case with no sources listed, which corresponds to a conventional group join in all versions of IGMP or MLD (e.g., as with Figure 9-13). For a multicast router, this means that the only state required is to keep track of which groups are of interest, and possibly which sources are of interest. It does not need to keep track of any individual sources that are not desired.

Table 9-2 shows the modifications in message types used in the lightweight variants of IGMPv3 and MLDv2. In this table, the empty set notation ({}) indicates a null source address list. For example, TO_EX({}) indicates a message of type 0x04 indicating a change to EXCLUDE mode with no associated sources. The notation (*, G) indicates group G associated with any sources, and the notation (S, G) indicates group G associated with specific source S.

Table 9-2   Comparison of operations of full versions of IGMPv3 and MLDv2 and their "lightweight" counterparts, LW-IGMPv3 and LW-MLDv2

Full	Lightweight	When Sent
IS_EX({})	TO_EX({})	Query response for (*, G) join
IS_EX(S)	N/A	Query response for EXCLUDE (S, G) join
IS_IN(S)	ALLOW(S)	Query response for INCLUDE (S, G) join
ALLOW(S)	ALLOW(S)	INCLUDE (S, G) join
BLOCK(S)	BLOCK(S)	INCLUDE (S, G) leave
TO_IN(S)	TO_IN(S)	Change to INCLUDE (S, G) join
TO_IN({})	TO_IN({})	(*, G) leave
TO_EX(S)	N/A	Change to EXCLUDE (S, G) join
TO_EX({})	TO_EX({})	(*, G) join

Compare the values in Table 9-2 with those in Table 9-1. Notably, the non-null EXCLUDE modes are not used and the state indicator types have been removed. In addition, the current-state records (IS_EX and IS_EN) have been removed for compliant hosts. Lightweight multicast routers are still supposed to be able to receive such messages but may treat them as though they always contain a null source list.

9.4.5   IGMP and MLD Robustness

There are two main concerns with the robustness and reliability of the IGMP and MLD protocols. Failures of IGMP or MLD, or multicast more generally, can lead to either the distribution of unwanted multicast traffic or the inability to deliver desired multicast traffic. The types of failures handled by IGMP and MLD include the failure of a multicast router and the loss of protocol messages.

The potential failure of a multicast router is handled by allowing more than one multicast router to operate on the same link. As mentioned previously, in this configuration the router with the lowest IP address is elected the "querier." The querier is responsible for sending general and specific queries to determine the current state of hosts on the subnet. Other (non-querier) routers monitor the protocol messages, because they are also group members or multicast-promiscuous listeners, and a different router is able to step in as the querier should the current querier fail. To make this work properly, all the multicast routers attached to the same link need to coordinate their queries, responses, and some of their configuration information (primarily timers).

The first type of coordination that multiple multicast routers accomplish is *querier election*. Each multicast router can hear the others' queries. When a multicast router starts, it believes itself to be the querier and sends a general query to determine what groups are active on a subnet. When a router receives a multicast query from another router, it compares the source IP address with its own. If the source IP address in the received query is smaller than its own, the receiving router enters a standby mode. As a result, the router with the lowest IP address is deemed the winner and becomes the single querier responsible for sending queries to its attached subnet. Routers that are standing by set timers, and if they do not see more queries within a specified period of time (called the *other-querier-present* timer), they become queriers again.

The querying multicast router sends periodic general queries to determine which groups and hosts are of interest to the hosts on the same subnet. The rate at which these queries are sent is determined by the querier's *query interval*, a configurable timer parameter. When more than one multicast router operates on the same subnet, the interval of the current querier is adopted by all other routers. In this way, if the current querier fails, a switch to an alternative multicast router does not perturb the periodic query rate.

A multicast router that has reason to believe a group (or source) is no longer of interest sends specific queries prior to discontinuing the forwarding of the corresponding multicast traffic (or informing the multicast routing protocol). These queries are sent with a different interval (called the *Last Member Query Time* or LMQT) from that of general queries. The LMQT is typically lower (shorter) than the query interval and governs the leave latency. A complication can arise when multiple multicast routers operate on the same subnet, hosts wish to leave groups (or drop sources), and protocol messages are lost.

To help guard against lost protocol messages, some messages are retransmitted up to a small number of times (determined by the querier robustness variable or QRV). The QRV value is encoded in the *QRV* field included in queries, and nonquerying routers adopt the querier's QRV as their own. Once again, this helps to keep consistency if a change of querier occurs. The types of messages protected with retransmission include state-change reports and specific queries. Other messages (current-state reports) do not typically result in a change of forwarding state but instead only involve refreshing soft state by adjusting timers, so they are not protected using retransmission. When retransmissions do occur, the retransmission interval of reports is chosen at random uniformly between 0 and a configurable parameter called the *Unsolicited Report Interval*, and the retransmission interval for queries is periodic (with the interval based on the LMQT). Links that are expected to be more prone to loss (e.g., wireless links) may require increasing the robustness variable to increase robustness to packet loss at the expense of generating additional traffic.

To help keep multicast routers synchronized when handling specific queries, the *S* bit field in the query message indicates that router-side (timer) processing should be suppressed. When a specific query is sent by the querier, a number (QRV) of retransmissions are scheduled. In the first query sent, the *S* bit field is clear. Upon transmission or receipt of such queries, a multicast router lowers its timer for subsequent retransmissions to the LMQT. At this point, it is possible for an interested host to provide a report indicating its continued interest in a group or source. If no messages are lost, the report causes each multicast router to reset its timer to its ordinary value and continue without change. However, the scheduled retransmissions are not abandoned. Instead, retransmissions of the specific query are sent with the *S* bit field set, which causes receiving routers to *not* lower their timers to the LMQT.

The reason for keeping query retransmissions even after the receipt of a report expressing interest is so that the timeouts for groups across all multicast routers can be made consistent. The purpose of the *S* bit field, then, is to allow specific queries to be (re)sent, but to avoid lowering the timer to LMQT because a legitimate report expressing interest may have been received, even if it or the initial query was missed by the non-querier router(s). Without this capability, retransmitted specific queries would cause non-querier routers to lower their timers incorrectly (because a legitimate report indicating interest had already been received).

9.4.6 IGMP and MLD Counters and Variables

IGMP and MLD are soft-state protocols that also deal with failures of routers, loss of protocol messages, and interoperability with earlier protocol versions. Much of the machinery to enable these capabilities is based on timers that trigger state changes and protocol actions. Table 9-3 provides a summary of all of the configuration parameters and state variables used by IGMP and MLD.

In Table 9-3, it is clear that MLD and IGMP share most of their timers and configuration parameters, although in some cases the terminology is different. Some values, those indicated as "cannot be changed," are set as a function of other values and are not independently changeable.

Table 9-3   Parameters and timer values for IGMP and MLD. Most values can be altered as configuration parameters in an implementation.

Name and Meaning	Default Value (Restrictions)
Robustness Variable (RV)—arranges for up to RV - 1 retransmissions for some state-change reports/queries.	2 (must not be 0; should not be 1)
Query Interval (QI)—time between general queries sent by the current querier.	125s
Query Response Interval (QRI)—the maximum response time to wait for generation of reports. This value is encoded to form the *Max Response* field.	10s
Group Membership Interval (GMI) in IGMP and Multicast Address Listening Interval (MALI) in MLD—the amount of time that must pass without seeing a report for a multicast router to declare that there is no remaining interest in a group or source/group combination.	RV * QI + QRI (cannot be changed)
Other Querier Present Interval in IGMP and Other Querier Present Timeout in MLD—the amount of time that must pass without seeing a general request for a non-querier multicast router to declare that there is no longer an active querier.	RV * QI + (0.5) * QRI (cannot be changed)
Startup Query Interval—the interval between general queries used by a querier just starting up.	(0.25) * QI
Startup Query Count—the number of general queries sent by a querier just starting up.	RV
Last Member Query Interval (LMQI) in IGMP and Last Listener Query Interval (LLQI) in MLD—the maximum response time to wait for generation of reports responding to specific queries. This value is encoded to form the *Max Response* field in specific queries.	1s
Last Member Query Count in IGMP and Last Listener Query Count in MLD—the number of specific queries to send without receiving a response to declare that there is no longer an interested host.	RV
Unsolicited Report Interval—the time between retransmissions of a host's initial state-change report.	1s
Older Version Querier Present Timeout—the amount of time a host waits without receiving an IGMPv1 or IGMPv2 request message to revert back to IGMPv3.	RV * QI + QRI (cannot be changed)
Older Host Present Interval in IGMP and Older Version Host Present Timeout in MLD—the amount of time a querier waits without receiving an IGMPv1 or IGMPv2 report message to revert back to IGMPv3.	RV * QI + QRI (cannot be changed)

9.4.7   IGMP and MLD Snooping

IGMP and MLD manage the flow of IP multicast traffic among routers. To optimize traffic flow even further, it is possible for layer 2 switches (that would not ordinarily process layer 3 IGMP or MLD messages) to become aware of whether certain multicast traffic flows are of interest or not by looking at layer 3 information. This capability is indicated by a switch feature known as *IGMP (MLD) snooping* [RFC4541] and is supported by many switch vendors. Without IGMP snooping, switches typically send link-layer multicast traffic by broadcasting it along all the branches of the spanning tree formed among switches. This can be wasteful for the reasons we described earlier. IGMP (MLD)-aware (sometimes called *IGS* for IGMP snooping) switches monitor IGMP (MLD) traffic between hosts and multicast routers and are able to keep track of which ports require which particular multicast flows in much the same way as a multicast router does. Doing so can substantially affect the amount of unwanted multicast traffic being carried through a switched network.

There are a few details that complicate the straightforward implementation of IGMP/MLD snooping. In IGMPv3 and MLDv2, reports are generated in response to queries. However, in earlier versions of these protocols, a report generated by one host and heard by others that are group members on the same link cause the additional members to suppress their reports. This can lead to a problem if IGS switches were to forward reports to all attached interfaces, as hosts on some LAN (VLAN) segments with group members may not be noticed. Thus, IGS switches supporting earlier versions of IGMP and MLD avoid broadcasting reports out of all interfaces. Instead, they forward reports only to the nearest multicast router. Determining the location of multicast routers is made easier if Multicast Router Discovery (MRD) is used (see Chapter 8).

Another issue of concern when implementing snooping relates to the difference in message formats between IGMP and MLD. Because MLD is encapsulated as part of ICMPv6 instead of its own separate protocol, MLD-snooping switches must process ICMPv6 information and be careful to separate the MLD messages from the others. In particular, other ICMPv6 traffic must be allowed to flow freely for the various other functions for which ICMPv6 is used (see Chapter 8).

Other nonstandard proprietary protocols have been implemented to further optimize IP multicast traffic carried through layer 2 devices. For example, Cisco has proposed the *Router-port Group Management Protocol* (RGMP) [RFC3488]. In RGMP, a mechanism is employed so that not only do hosts report their groups and sources of interest (as in IGMP/MLD), but multicast routers also do the same. This information is used to optimize layer 2 forwarding of multicast traffic among multicast routers (not just hosts).

9.5   Attacks Involving IGMP and MLD

Because IGMP and MLD are signaling protocols that control the flow of multicast traffic, attacks using these protocols primarily are either DoS attacks or resource utilization attacks. There have also been attacks that exploit buggy implementation of the protocols, to either disable hosts or cause them to execute code provided by an attacker.

A simple DoS attack can be mounted by sending IGMP or MLD to subscribe to a large number of high-bandwidth multicast groups. Doing so can cause bandwidth exhaustion, leading to a denial of service. A more complex attack can be mounted by generating requests using a relatively low IP address. In this case, the attacker is elected to be the querier for the link and can advertise its own robustness variable, query interval, and maximum response time that will be adopted by the other multicast routers. If the maximum response time is very small, hosts are induced to send reports rapidly, using CPU resources.

Several attacks have been carried out by exploiting implementation bugs. Fragmented IGMP packets have been used to induce crashes in certain operating systems. More recently, specially crafted IGMP or MLD packets using SSM information have been used to induce remote code execution bugs. Overall, the impact of IGMP or MLD vulnerabilities tends to be somewhat less than with other protocols, as multicast tends to be supported only in the local area. As a result, remote attackers lacking on-link access to the target LAN are likely to be limited.

9.6 Summary

Broadcasting, generically, means sending traffic to all nodes on a network. In the context of TCP/IP, broadcasting means sending a packet to all hosts in a network or subnetwork, typically the locally attached network. Multicasting refers to sending traffic to only a subset of nodes in a network. In TCP/IP, multicasting means sending a packet to a subset of the interested hosts in the network. The method for selecting the subset is dependent on the scope of the multicast traffic and the interest of receivers. In many applications multicasting is better than broadcasting, since multicasting imposes less overhead on hosts that are not participating in the communication. Broadcasting is supported in IPv4 but not in IPv6. Broadcasting and multicasting can be used to avoid having to send the same content to multiple destinations by repeatedly using unicast connections. It can also be used to discover servers that are otherwise unknown. Multicasting is a more complex capability than broadcasting, as state must be maintained to determine which hosts are interested in which groups.

In IPv4 there are two types of broadcast addresses: limited (255.255.255.255) and directed. The directed broadcast address is based on the network prefix and its length and is formed by creating a 32-bit address whose initial bits are equal to the network prefix and whose low-order bits are set to 1. It is usually preferable to use directed broadcasts instead of the limited broadcast address. Selection of which interfaces are used to send outgoing broadcast traffic is operating-system-dependent. A typical case is to use one primary interface for limited broadcast traffic and use the information present in the host's forwarding table to select the interface for outgoing directed broadcasts and multicasts.

Multicasting in IP supports a model whereby processes interested in receiving multicast packets subscribe to a particular group (using an IP address) on a set of interfaces. Transmitting multicast IPv4 traffic on multicast-capable IEEE link-layer networks (such as Ethernet) involves combining the low-order 23 bits of the group address with the prefix 01:00:5e to form a MAC-layer destination address used for link-layer multicasting. Transmitting IPv6 multicast traffic involves combining the lower-order 32 bits of the group address with the 16-bit prefix 33:33 to form a MAC-layer destination address. These mappings are nonunique, meaning that more than one IPv4 or IPv6 group address uses the same MAC-layer address. As a consequence, host software performs filtering of incoming traffic to remove traffic for unwanted groups.

The IGMP and MLD protocols are used with IPv4 and IPv6, respectively, in supporting multicast packet delivery. Multicast routers send query messages to nearby hosts in order to determine which hosts are interested in which groups, and (for IGMPv3 and MLDv2) which senders are of interest to these groups. Hosts respond by sending reports indicating the groups of interest. MLD is part of the ICMPv6 protocol, whereas IGMP is an independent protocol layered above IPv4 (like ICMP). Some switches are equipped to "snoop" IGMP and MLD traffic in order to avoid sending multicast IP traffic along spanning tree branches where there are no interested receiving hosts. IGMP and MLD have a "robustness variable" that can be set to enable retransmissions of important messages on networks prone to loss.

Because IGMP and MLD are both signaling protocols that control the flow of other traffic, attacks against them tend to cause extra resource consumption, possibly leading to denial of service. Other forms of attacks that exploit implementation bugs have also been seen and have been used to cause execution of unwanted code provided by an attacker. As MLD (and MLDv2) are relatively new in terms of deployment, it is likely that additional exploits will ultimately be found, but these protocols are limited in operation to a single link.

9.7 References

[CK11] S. Cheshire and M. Krochmal, "Multicast DNS," Internet draft-cheshire-dnsext-multicastdns, work in progress, Feb. 2011.

[EGW02] B. Edwards, L. Giuliano, and B. Wright, *Interdomain Multicast Routing: Practical Juniper Networks and Cisco Systems Solutions* (Addison-Wesley, 2002).

[GCLG99] Y. Goland, T. Cai, P. Leach, and Y. Gu, "Simple Service Discovery Protocol/1.0 Operating without an Arbiter," Internet draft-cai-ssdp-v1-03.txt (expired), Oct. 1999.

[RFC1112] S. Deering, "Host Extensions for IP Multicasting," Internet RFC 1112/STD 0005, Aug. 1989.

[RFC1122] R. Braden, ed., "Requirements for Internet Hosts," Internet RFC 1122/STD 0003, Oct. 1989.

[RFC2644] D. Senie, "Changing the Default for Directed Broadcasts in Routers," Internet RFC 2644/BCP 0034, Aug. 1999.

[RFC3376] B. Cain, S. Deering, I. Kouvelas, B. Fenner, and A. Thyagarajan, "Internet Group Management Protocol, Version 3," Internet RFC 3376, Oct. 2002.

[RFC3488] I. Wu and T. Eckert, "Cisco Systems Router-port Group Management Protocol (RGMP)," Internet RFC 3488 (informational), Feb. 2003.

[RFC3590] B. Haberman, "Source Address Selection for the Multicast Listener Discovery (MLD) Protocol," Internet RFC 3590, Sept. 2003.

[RFC3810] R. Vida and L. Costa, eds., "Multicast Listener Discovery Version 2 (MLDv2) for IPv6," Internet RFC 3810, June 2004.

[RFC4541] M. Christensen and K. Kimball, "Considerations for Internet Group Management Protocol (IGMP) and Multicast Listener Discovery (MLD) Snooping Switches," Internet RFC 4541 (informational), May 2006.

[RFC4601] B. Fenner, M. Handley, H. Holbrook, and I. Kouvelas, "Protocol Independent Multicast—Sparse Mode (PIM-SM): Protocol Specification (Revised)," Internet RFC 4601, Aug. 2006.

[RFC4604] H. Holbrook, B. Cain, and B. Haberman, "Using Internet Group Management Protocol Version 3 (IGMPv3) and Multicast Listener Discovery Protocol Version 2 (MLDv2) for Source-Specific Multicast," Internet RFC 4604, Aug. 2006.

[RFC4607] H. Holbrook and B. Cain, "Source-Specific Multicast for IP," Internet RFC 4607, Aug. 2006.

[RFC4795] B. Aboba, D. Thaler, and L. Esibov, "Link-Local Multicast Name Resolution (LLMNR)," Internet RFC 4795 (informational), Jan. 2007.

[RFC5015] M. Handley, I. Kouvelas, T. Speakman, and L. Vicisano, "Bidirectional Protocol Independent Multicast (BIDIR-PIM)," Internet RFC 5015, Oct. 2007.

[RFC5214] F. Templin, T. Gleeson, and D. Thaler, "Intra-Site Automatic Tunnel Addressing Protocol (ISATAP)," Internet RFC 5214 (informational), Mar. 2008.

[RFC5579] F. Templin, ed., "Transmission of IPv4 Packets over Intra-Site Automatic Tunnel Addressing Protocol (ISATAP) Interfaces," Internet RFC 5579 (informational), Feb. 2010.

[RFC5790] H. Liu, W. Cao, and H. Asaeda, "Lightweight Internet Group Management Protocol Version 3 (IGMPv3) and Multicast Listener Discovery Version 2 (MLDv2) Protocols," Internet RFC 5790, Feb. 2010.

10

User Datagram Protocol (UDP) and IP Fragmentation

10.1 Introduction

UDP is a simple, datagram-oriented, transport-layer protocol that preserves message boundaries. It does not provide error correction, sequencing, duplicate elimination, flow control, or congestion control. It can provide error detection, and it includes the first true *end-to-end* checksum at the transport layer that we have encountered. This protocol provides minimal functionality itself, so applications using it have a great deal of control over how packets are sent and processed. Applications wishing to ensure that their data is reliably delivered or sequenced must implement these protections themselves. Generally, each UDP output operation requested by an application produces exactly one UDP datagram, which causes one IP datagram to be sent. This is in contrast to a stream-oriented protocol such as TCP (see Chapter 15), where the amount of data written by an application may have little relationship to what actually gets sent in a single IP datagram or what is consumed at the receiver.

[RFC0768] is the official specification of UDP, and it has remained as a standard without significant revisions for more than 30 years. As mentioned, UDP provides no error correction: it sends the datagrams that the application writes to the IP layer, but there is no guarantee that they ever reach their destination. In addition, there is no protocol mechanism to prevent high-rate UDP traffic from negatively impacting other network users. Given this lack of reliability and protection, we might be tempted to conclude that there are no benefits to using UDP at all. This is not true, however. Because of its connectionless character, it has less overhead than other transport protocols. In addition, broadcast and multicast operations (see Chapter 9) are much more straightforward using a connectionless transport such as UDP. Finally, the ability of an application to choose its own unit of retransmission can be an important consideration (see [CT90], for example).

473

Figure 10-1 shows the encapsulation of a UDP datagram as a single IPv4 datagram. The IPv6 encapsulation is similar, but other details differ slightly and we discuss them in Section 10.5. The IPv4 *Protocol* field has the value 17 to indicate UDP. IPv6 uses the same value in the *Next Header* field. Later in this chapter we will examine what happens when the size of the UDP datagram exceeds the MTU size and the datagram must be fragmented into more than one IP-layer packet.

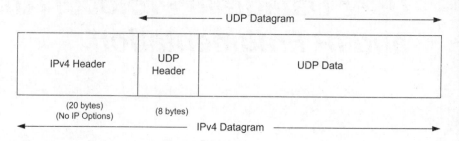

Figure 10-1   Encapsulation of a UDP datagram in a single IPv4 datagram (the typical case with no IPv4 options). The IPv6 encapsulation is similar; the UDP header follows the header chain.

10.2 UDP Header

Figure 10-2 shows a UDP datagram, including the payload and UDP header (which is always 8 bytes in size).

Port numbers act as *mailboxes* and help a protocol implementation identify the sending and receiving processes (see Chapter 1). They are purely *abstract*—they do not correspond to any physical entity on a host. In UDP, port numbers are positive 16-bit numbers, and the source port number is optional; it may be set to 0 if the sender of the datagram never requires a reply. Transport protocols such as TCP, UDP, and SCTP [RFC4960] use the destination port number to help demultiplex incoming data from IP. Because IP demultiplexes the incoming IP datagram to a particular transport protocol based on the value of the *Protocol* field in the IPv4 header or *Next Header* field in the IPv6 header, this means that the port numbers can be made independent among the transport protocols. That is, TCP port numbers are used only by TCP, and the UDP port numbers only by UDP, and so on. A straightforward consequence of this separation is that two completely distinct servers can use the same port number and IP address, as long as they use different transport protocols.

Note

Despite this independence, if a well-known service is provided (or can conceivably be provided) by both TCP and UDP, the port number is normally allocated to be the same for both transport protocols. This is purely for convenience and is not required by the protocols. See [IPORT] for details on how port numbers are formally assigned.

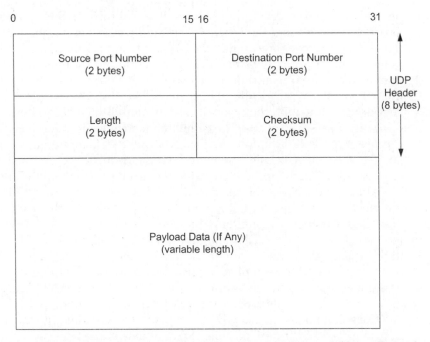

0   15 16   31

| Source Port Number (2 bytes) | Destination Port Number (2 bytes) |
| Length (2 bytes) | Checksum (2 bytes) |

UDP Header (8 bytes)

Payload Data (If Any) (variable length)

Figure 10-2   The UDP header and payload (data) area. The *Checksum* field is end-to-end and is computed over the UDP pseudo-header, which includes the *Source* and *Destination IP Address* fields from the IP header. Thus, any modification made to those fields (e.g., by NAT) requires a modification to the UDP checksum.

Referring to Figure 10-2, the UDP *Length* field is the length of the UDP header and the UDP data in bytes. The minimum value for this field is 8 except when UDP is used with IPv6 jumbograms (see Section 10.5). Sending a UDP datagram with 0 bytes of data is acceptable, although rare. Note that the UDP *Length* field is redundant; the IPv4 header contains the datagram's total length (see Chapter 5), and the IPv6 header contains the payload length. The length of a UDP/IPv4 datagram is then the total length of the IPv4 datagram minus the length of the IPv4 header. A UDP/IPv6 datagram's length is the value of the *Payload Length* field contained in the IPv6 header minus the lengths of any extension headers (unless jumbograms are being used). In either case, the UDP *Length* field should match the length computed from the IP-layer information.

10.3 UDP Checksum

The UDP checksum is the first end-to-end transport-layer checksum we have encountered (ICMP has an end-to-end checksum but is not a true transport protocol). It covers the UDP header, the UDP data, and a pseudo-header (defined later in this section). It is computed at the initial sender and checked at the final destination.

It is not modified in transit (except when it passes through a NAT, as described in Chapter 7). Recall that the checksum in the IPv4 header covers only the header (i.e., it does not cover any data in the IP packet) and is recomputed at each IP hop (required because the IPv4 *TTL* field is decremented by routers when the datagram is forwarded). Transport protocols (e.g., TCP, UDP) use checksums to cover their headers *and* data. With UDP, the checksum is optional (although strongly suggested), while with the others it is mandatory. When UDP is used with IPv6, computation and use of the checksum are mandatory because there is no header checksum at the IP layer. To provide error-free data to applications, a transport-layer protocol such as UDP must always compute a checksum or use some other error detection mechanism before delivering the data to a receiving application.

Although the basics for calculating the UDP checksum are similar to what we described in Chapter 5 for the general Internet checksum (the one's complement of the one's complement sum of 16-bit words), there are two small special details. First, the length of the UDP datagram can be an odd number of bytes, whereas the checksum algorithm adds 16-bit words (always an even number of bytes). The procedure for UDP is to append a (virtual) pad byte of 0 to the end of odd-length datagrams, just for the checksum computation and verification. This pad byte is not actually transmitted and is thus called "virtual" here.

The second detail is that UDP (as well as TCP) computes its checksum over a 12-byte *pseudo-header* derived (solely) from fields in the IPv4 header or a 40-byte pseudo-header derived from fields in the IPv6 header. This pseudo-header is also virtual and is used only for purposes of the checksum computation (at both the sender and the receiver). It is never actually transmitted. This pseudo-header includes the source and destination addresses and *Protocol* or *Next Header* field (which should contain the value 17) from the IP header. Its purpose is to let the UDP layer verify that the data has arrived at the correct destination (i.e., that IP has not accepted a misaddressed datagram, and that IP has not given UDP a datagram that is for another transport protocol). Figure 10-3 shows what is covered when computing the UDP checksum, including the pseudo-header along with the UDP header and payload.

Note

The careful reader will note that this causes a so-called *layering violation*. That is, the UDP protocol (transport layer) is directly processing bits "owned" by IP (network layer). While true, it is of only minor consequence to protocol implementations, which in general have IP-layer information readily available when data is passed to (or from) UDP. It is of far greater concern for NATs (see Chapter 7), especially if UDP datagrams are fragmented.

Figure 10-3 shows a datagram with an odd data length, requiring a pad byte for the checksum computation. Note that the length of the UDP datagram appears twice in the checksum computation. If the value of the calculated checksum

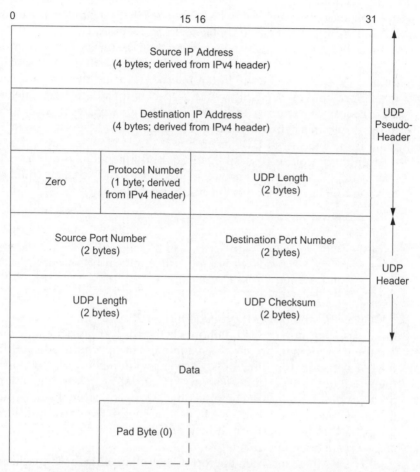

Figure 10-3   Fields used in computing the checksum for UDP/IPv4 datagrams, including the pseudo-header, the UDP header, and data. If the data is not an even number of bytes, it is padded with one 0 byte for purposes of computing the checksum. The pseudo-header and any pad bytes are not transmitted with the datagram.

happens to be 0x0000, it is stored in the header as all 1 bits (0xFFFF), which is equivalent in one's complement arithmetic (see Chapter 5). Upon receipt, a *Checksum* field value of 0x0000 indicates that the sender did not compute a checksum. If the sender *did* compute a checksum and the receiver detects a checksum error, the UDP datagram is silently discarded. No error message is generated, although some statistical counts may be updated. (This is what happens if an IPv4 header checksum error is detected.)

Despite UDP checksums being optional in the original UDP specification, they are currently required to be enabled on hosts by default [RFC1122]. During the 1980s some computer vendors turned off UDP checksums by default to speed up their implementation of Sun's Network File System (NFS), which uses UDP. While this might not cause problems in many cases because of the presence of layer 2 CRC protection (which is stronger than the Internet checksum; see Chapter 3), it is considered bad form (and a violation of the RFCs) to disable checksums by default. Early experience in the Internet revealed that when datagrams pass through routers, all bets are off with respect to their correctness. Believe it or not, there have been routers with software and hardware bugs that have modified bits in the datagrams being forwarded. These errors are undetectable in a UDP datagram if the end-to-end UDP checksum is disabled. Also realize that some older data-link protocols (e.g., serial line IP, or SLIP) do not have any form of data-link checksum, thereby leaving open the possibility that IP packets could be undetectably modified unless another checksum is employed.

Note

[RFC1122] requires that UDP checksums be enabled by default. It also states that an implementation must verify a received checksum if the sender calculated one (i.e., if the received checksum is not 0).

Given the structure of the pseudo-header, it is clear that when a UDP/IPv4 datagram passes through a NAT, not only is the IP-layer header checksum modified, but the UDP pseudo-header checksum must be appropriately modified because the IP-layer addressing and/or UDP-layer port numbers may have changed. NATs therefore routinely perform "layering violations" by modifying multiple layers of protocol within packets at the same time. Of course, given that the pseudo-header is itself a layering violation, a NAT has little choice. The particular rules that apply when UDP traffic is processed by a NAT are given in [RFC4787]. We also discussed them briefly in Chapter 7.

Recently there has been interest in relaxation of the UDP checksum for applications that are partially insensitive to errors (multimedia applications being the typical case). The discussion relates to whether having a *partial checksum* is a valuable concept. A partial checksum covers only a portion of the payload specified by the application. We discuss this in Section 10.6 in the context of UDP-Lite.

10.4 Examples

We will use the sock program [SOCK] to generate some UDP datagrams that we can watch with tcpdump. In the first example, we are running a server on the discard port (9) on the destination machine. In the second example, we have disabled the server, and the client is informed of this fact as illustrated here. Very few UDP-based services are made available in typical machine configurations because of security concerns, so the second part of the example is not unusual.

```
Linux% sock -v -u -i 10.0.0.3 discard
connected on 10.0.0.5.46274 to 10.0.0.3
wrote 1024 bytes
...                                              (1023 more times)

Linux% sock -v -u -i 10.0.0.3 discard
connected on 10.0.0.5.46294 to 10.0.0.3
wrote 1 bytes
write returned -1, expected 1024: Connection refused
```

When we execute the sock program, we specify the verbose mode, -v, to see the ephemeral port numbers, specify UDP -u instead of the default TCP, and use the -i option to send data instead of trying to read and write standard input and output. The default number of datagrams (1024) is sent to the destination host with IP address 10.0.0.3. In this case we have arranged a server to process incoming datagrams to the discard port. To capture the traffic sent, we use the following command on a host with access to the traffic stream:

```
Linux# tcpdump -n -p -s 1500 -vvv host 10.0.0.3 and \( udp or icmp \)
```

This command captures any UDP or ICMP traffic between the two machines (and possibly additional traffic not illustrated). The -s 1500 option directs tcpdump to collect packets up to 1500 bytes in length (longer than the 1024 bytes we are sending, in this case), and the –vvv option indicates verbose printing. The –n option tells tcpdump to not convert IP addresses to machine names, and the –p option avoids placing the default network interface into promiscuous mode. The resulting tcpdump output is illustrated in Listing 10-1 (some lines have been wrapped for clarity).

Listing 10-1   tcpdump output showing packets from the first sock command (server running)

```
1 22:52:53.102838 10.0.0.5.46274 > 10.0.0.3.9:
                   [udp sum ok] udp 1024 (DF) (ttl 64, id 24462, len 1052)
2 22:52:53.102964 10.0.0.5.46274 > 10.0.0.3.9:
                   [udp sum ok] udp 1024 (DF) (ttl 64, id 24463, len 1052)
3 22:52:53.103091 10.0.0.5.46274 > 10.0.0.3.9:
                   [udp sum ok] udp 1024 (DF) (ttl 64, id 24464, len 1052)
4 22:52:53.103215 10.0.0.5.46274 > 10.0.0.3.9:
                   [udp sum ok] udp 1024 (DF) (ttl 64, id 24465, len 1052)
... repeated 1020 times ...
```

This output shows four 1052-byte UDP/IPv4 datagrams (1024 bytes of UDP payload plus 8 bytes of UDP header and the 20-byte IPv4 header) sent from IPv4 address 10.0.0.5 and port 46274 to port 9 (the discard port), with an inter-packet time of about 100µs. In addition, we may observe that UDP checksums are enabled and are valid (checked by tcpdump), that the *Don't Fragment* (*DF*) bit field is turned on, the IPv4 *TTL* field is 64, and the IPv4 *Identification* field is different (and increasing by 1) for each datagram. No ICMP traffic is generated, and it would appear that all data was successfully delivered to the destination machine; although because there are no acknowledgments, we do not know with certainty. We shall see in Chapter 13 that the other major transport protocol, TCP, normally uses a handshake with the other end before the first byte of data can be sent and uses subsequent acknowledgments to know what data has been successfully transferred to the receiver.

The second time we run the sock program with the same arguments, but this time we send our datagrams to the discard service after the server has been disabled. Listing 10-2 shows the trace for this example (some lines have been wrapped for clarity).

Listing 10-2 tcpdump output showing ICMP Destination Unreachable (Port Unreachable) message from host (server disabled)

```
1 22:55:07.223094 10.0.0.5.46294 > 10.0.0.3.9:
                 [udp sum ok] udp 1024 (DF) (ttl 64, id 37874, len 1052)

2 22:55:07.223134 10.0.0.3 > 10.0.0.5: icmp:
                 10.0.0.3 udp port 9 unreachable for
                      10.0.0.5.46294 > 10.0.0.3.9:
                            udp 1024 (DF) (ttl 64, id 37874, len 1052)
                 [tos 0xc0] (ttl 255, id 63302, len 576)
```

In this example we see somewhat different behavior. Here, only a single UDP datagram is sent, and an ICMP message is returned in response. Although all other parameters are the same, no server is running to receive the incoming datagrams. In this case, the underlying UDP implementation causes an ICMPv4 Destination Unreachable (Port Unreachable) message (see Chapter 8) to be generated and returned to the sender. This message includes a copy of the first 556 bytes of the original ("offending") datagram. If the ICMP message is not discarded by the intervening network (accidentally or on purpose by firewalls), the sending application (if it is still running when the ICMP message arrives) can learn of the absence of the receiver and print an error, as indicated in the listing at the beginning of this section (i.e., the write returned –1 message). Note that the returning ICMP error message contains enough information for the sending host to ascertain which port was not reachable. Finally, note that the source UDP port number changes each time the program is run. First it was 46274 and then it was 46294. We mentioned in Chapter 1 that the ephemeral port numbers used by clients are suggested to be in the range 49152 through 65535, so here we observe noncompliant behavior.

Note

For Linux, the local port parameter range can be easily modified by changing the contents of the file /proc/sys/net/ipv4/ip_local_port_range. In Windows Vista and later, the netsh command can be used to set the dynamic port range [KB929851]. See [IPORT] for current port numbers.

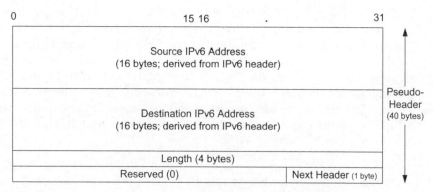

Figure 10-4   The UDP (and TCP) pseudo-header used with IPv6 ([RFC2460]). The pseudo-header includes the source and destination IPv6 addresses and a larger 32-bit *Length* field value. The pseudo-header checksum is required when UDP is used with IPv6 because the IPv6 header lacks a checksum. The *Next Header* field is copied from the last IPv6 header of the chain.

10.5   UDP and IPv6

Given its simplicity, UDP requires only small changes when operating over IPv6 instead of IPv4. The most obvious differences are the 128-bit addresses used by IPv6 and the corresponding effect on the construction of the pseudo-header. A related but more subtle distinction is that in IPv6, no IP-layer header checksum is present. Thus, if UDP were to operate with checksums disabled, there would be *no end-to-end check whatsoever* on the correctness of the IP-layer addressing information. For this reason, when UDP is used with IPv6, a pseudo-header checksum, common to both UDP and TCP, is required (by Section 8 of [RFC2460]). The construction of the pseudo-header is given in Figure 10-4. Note that the *Length* field has expanded from its IPv4 counterpart to 32 bits. Recall from earlier that this field is redundant for UDP, but we shall see in Chapter 13 that it is not redundant when used with TCP (either TCP/IPv4 or TCP/IPv6) and has thus been retained for use with both UDP/IPv6 and TCP/IPv6.

Expanding the discussion regarding the IPv6 packet length, two aspects of IPv6's packet size can affect UDP. First, in IPv6, the minimum MTU size is 1280 bytes (as opposed to the 576 bytes required by IPv4 as the minimum size required to be supported by all hosts). Second, IPv6 supports *jumbograms* (packets larger than 65,535 bytes). If we inspect the IPv6 header and option set (see Chapter 5), we can observe that with jumbograms, 32 bits are available to hold the payload length. This implies that a single UDP/IPv6 datagram could be very large indeed. As described in [RFC2675], this poses a problem for the UDP *Length* field in the UDP header, which is only 16 bits long. As such, when encapsulated in IPv6, a UDP/IPv6 datagram exceeding 65,535 bytes has its UDP *Length* field value set to 0. Note that the size of the *Length* field in the pseudo-header is still large enough

(32 bits). Computing the value of this field for IPv6 jumbograms involves taking the total length of the UDP header plus data. Checking this field when receiving a packet involves computing the size of the UDP datagram (header plus data) by subtracting the size of all IPv6 extension headers from the value found in the Jumbo Payload option, which gives the length of the IPv6 payload (i.e., the total datagram length minus the 40-byte IPv6 header). In the "unexpected" case where the *Length* field in the UDP header is 0 but no Jumbo Payload option is present, the UDP length can be inferred based on the nonzero IPv6 *Payload Length* field (see Section 4 of [RFC2675]).

10.5.1 Teredo: Tunneling IPv6 through IPv4 Networks

Although it was once thought that a worldwide transition to IPv6 might happen quickly, this has not materialized exactly as forecast. Consequently, a number of (theoretically temporary) *transition mechanisms* [RFC4213][RFC5969] have been proposed to ease the transition burden. One such mechanism is called *6to4* [RFC3056], whereby IPv6 packets used by hosts are encapsulated in IPv4 packets that may be delivered over an IPv4-only infrastructure. One problem with 6to4 is that it suffers from the same types of NAT traversal problems as other applications on the Internet. It is also known to have scaling problems that make its continued use unattractive [RFC6343]. Although methods we have seen such as ICE (see Chapter 7) could conceivably be used for handling this issue, a special protocol called *Teredo* (originally called "shipworm" but renamed based on the Latin name for a common genus of shipworm to avoid confusion with computer worms) has been devised especially to address this problem [RFC4380][RFC5991][RFC6081]. It is popular because of its widespread availability in modern versions of Microsoft Windows.

Teredo (also called *Teredo tunneling*) transports IPv6 datagrams in the payload area of UDP/IPv4 datagrams for systems that have no other IPv6 connectivity options. An example scenario is given in Figure 10-5. Teredo *clients* are IPv4/IPv6 hosts that implement a Teredo tunneling interface. Such interfaces are assigned special Teredo addresses using the 2001::/32 IPv6 prefix after having successfully engaged in a "qualification" procedure, described in the next paragraph. Teredo *servers*, which serve a general purpose similar to STUN servers (Chapter 7), are used to help establish direct tunnels of Teredo-encapsulated IPv6 packets through NATs. Teredo *relays* serve a purpose similar to TURN servers and consequently may take significant processing resources if used by many clients. Note that servers must include all of the capabilities of relays, but not vice versa. Using Teredo relays is a "last-resort" option for IPv6 connectivity. Nodes cease to perform Teredo tunneling if they discover that they have any other IPv6 connectivity option (e.g., direct or using 6to4).

Referring to Figure 10-5, a Teredo client is initially configured with the name or IPv4 address and UDP port number (usually 3544) of a Teredo server. Teredo was initially developed by Microsoft, and a Teredo server is available using the

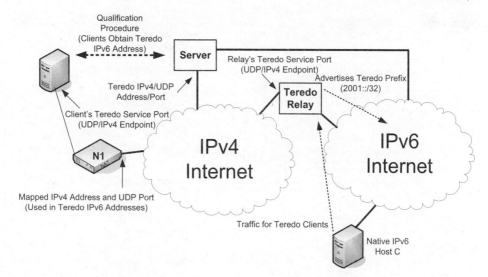

Figure 10-5   Teredo, an IPv6 transition mechanism, encapsulates IPv6 datagrams and optional trailers within the payload area of UDP/IPv4 datagrams to carry IPv6 traffic across IPv4-
only infrastructures. The server helps clients obtain an IPv6 address and determine
their mapped addresses and port numbers. Relays, if required, can forward traffic
between Teredo, 6to4, and native IPv6 clients.

name `teredo.ipv6.microsoft.com`. When ready to obtain an address, it starts
the *qualification procedure*. The client begins by sending an ICMPv6 RS packet (see
Chapter 8) from one of its link-local IPv6 addresses using its Teredo service port,
the agent responsible for encapsulating and decapsulating IPv6 traffic within
UDP/IPv4. The encapsulation format is the Origin Indication format, one of two
shown in Figure 10-6.

Successful responses are ICMPv6 RA messages that use the Origin Indication Encapsulation format from Figure 10-6. The RA contains a Prefix Information
option with a valid Teredo prefix (see Chapter 2). The Origin Indication provides
the client with knowledge of its own mapped address and port information. The
source address of the RA is a valid link-local IPv6 address of the server. The destination is the client's link-local IPv6 address used as the source of the RS message.
Assuming that all goes well, the client is now "qualified" and can build its Teredo
IPv6 address based on the prefix and origin information provided by the server.
The Teredo address is an IPv6 address constructed from various parameters using
the format of Figure 10-7.

A Teredo address (see Figure 10-7) contains the Teredo prefix (2001::/32), the
IPv4 address of the Teredo server, a 16-bit *Flags* field detailed in the next paragraph, followed by the mapped port number and mapped IPv4 address. The last
two values are the addressing information of the client as seen from the Teredo
server and are usually determined by the client's outermost NAT. The actual

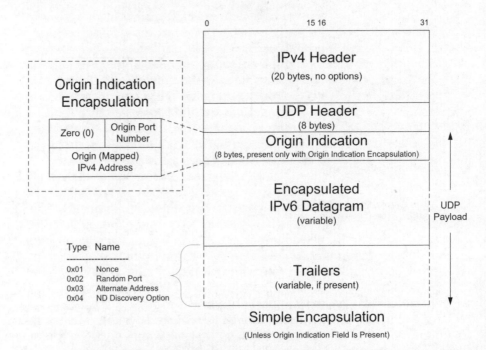

Figure 10-6   The Simple Encapsulation and Origin Indication Encapsulation formats used by Teredo. The Origin Indication Encapsulation carries UDP address and port number information between the UDP header and encapsulated IPv6 datagram. This information is used to inform Teredo clients about their mapped addresses and port numbers when creating a Teredo address. Addresses and port numbers are "obfuscated" by inverting each bit present to fend off NATs that attempt to rewrite this information. Zero or more trailers may be present, encoded as TLV triples. They are used to implement a number of Teredo extensions (e.g., support for symmetric NATs).

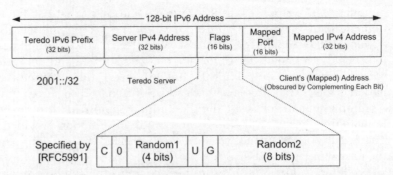

Figure 10-7   Teredo clients use IPv6 addresses from the 2001::/32 Teredo prefix. The subsequent bits contain the Teredo server's IPv4 address, 16 flag bits that identify the type of NAT encountered and random bits to help thwart address-guessing attacks, and 16 bits containing the client's mapped port number and the client's mapped 32-bit IPv4 address. The last two values are "obfuscated."

address and port number information is bitwise-inverted to cause indiscriminate NATs to not rewrite them.

The 16-bit *Flags* field has been used to indicate the type of NAT discovered during the qualification process. Some NATs (formerly called symmetric NATs—the types of NATs that have either address-dependent mapping or address- and port-dependent mapping along with either address-dependent or address- and port-dependent filtering behavior) work with Teredo only when extensions are supported (see later in this section), but the most common types for household networks (including "cone NATs"—NATs with endpoint-independent mapping and endpoint-independent filtering behavior) work without such extensions. Originally, the *C* (cone NAT) bit field was used to indicate if a cone NAT was encountered and to arrange appropriate support, but this usage is now deprecated and the field should be set to 0 (clients ignore the field; servers inspect it to look for legacy clients). The next bit field is set to 0. The *U* (*Universal*) and *G* (*Group*) bit fields are available for future use but are also currently set to 0. The *Random1* and *Random2* field values are chosen as random numbers according to [RFC5991] to make Teredo addresses harder to guess (a security measure intended to reduce random probes by potential attackers).

Once a qualified client builds its Teredo address, it can send IPv6 traffic. For details on what happens when qualification fails or a secure qualification is to be used, see [RFC4380]. In general, a Teredo client may wish to communicate with another client on the same link, another client within the IPv4 Internet, or with a host on the IPv6 Internet. In each case, Teredo provides some UDP/IPv4-based alternative to IPv6 ND. For clients on the same link, Teredo uses an IPv4 multicast discovery protocol that operates using the multicast address 224.0.0.253. Special Teredo "bubble" packets (those with no data payload) are used to determine if a destination is on the same link. Such bubbles appear as minimum-size Teredo packets using the Simple Encapsulation format of Figure 10-6. They contain an IPv6 header with the *Destination IP Address* field set to the target of the communication. The IPv6 packet contains an IPv6 header with no payload or additional extensions (the *Next Header* field is set to 0x3b, indicating none). For clients within the IPv4 Internet, recall that the Teredo IPv6 address contains the IPv4-mapped address and port number. Thus, it is straightforward for one client to send a Teredo-encapsulated packet to another's NAT. For NATs that are restrictive, Teredo uses bubble packets to perform hole punching and establish UDP NAT mappings (see Chapter 7 and [RFC6081]).

When a qualified client has a packet to send to an IPv6 host (i.e., one that does not use a Teredo address), it first determines whether it already knows a Teredo relay for the destination. If so, the packet is sent using Simple Encapsulation. If not, the client formats an ICMPv6 Echo Request containing a large (e.g., 64-bit) random number and sends it to the IPv6 destination by way of the Teredo server. The server forwards this packet to the destination IPv6 host. The receiving host sees an incoming IPv6 datagram with the source address equal to the Teredo address of the client. It forms an Echo Reply, which is routed to the nearest Teredo relay. The relay then forwards the reply back to the client. The receiving client observes the IPv4 address of the relay and updates a cache to indicate that subsequent packets destined for the IPv6 host should use the relay address it just determined.

As of [RFC6081], Teredo can support a number of optional extensions, several of which help to support Teredo operation with symmetric NATs. The extensions are protocol behavior modifications and include the following: Symmetric NAT Support (SNS), UPnP-Enabled Symmetric NAT (UP), Port-Preserving Symmetric NAT (PP), Sequential Port-Symmetric NAT (SP), Hairpinning (HP), and Server Load Reduction (SLR). The extensions can be used independently, except that both the UP and PP extensions depend on the SNS extension. The various NAT types that can be supported with various extension combinations are given in a table (see Section 3 of [RFC6081]).

To implement the extensions, one or more *trailers* may be present in a Teredo message. Trailers are encoded as an ordered list of TLV combinations, using the same basic format as for ICMPv6 ND options (Figure 8-41), which contain an 8-bit *Type* field and an 8-bit *Length* field. The two highest-order bits of the *Type* field encode what processing should be performed if the host does not recognize the trailer type. The bit pattern 01 indicates that the host should discard the packet; all others indicate that the unknown trailer should be skipped and others should be processed in order. The official list of trailer type values is maintained by the IANA [TTYPES]. The trailers currently defined are listed here in Table 10-1.

Table 10-1   Teredo trailers are carried after the IPv6 payload encapsulated in a UDP/IPv4 datagram. Each trailer has a type value, name, and associated explanation. In some cases, the length value is a constant.

Type	Length	Name	Use	Notes
0x00	Reserved	(Unassigned)	(Unassigned)	(Unassigned)
0x01	0x04	Nonce	SNS, UP, PP, SP, HP	32-bit nonce for protection against replays (see Chapter 18)
0x02	Reserved	(Unassigned)	(Unassigned)	(Unassigned)
0x03	[8, 26]	Alternate Address	HP	Additional addresses/ports usable by Teredo clients behind the same NAT
0x04	0x04	ND Option	SLR	Allows NAT refresh using direct bubbles (that carry NS messages)
0x05	0x02	Random Port	PP	Sender's predicted mapped port

The Nonce trailer contains a 32-bit random value that is unique for each message. It is a security measure to guard against replay attacks (see Chapter 18) and is used with either HP or SNS (IPv4 address, port) pairs. Each pair is 6 bytes long, and the trailer can hold from one to four such pairs. These pairs identify

UDP/IPv4 endpoints that other Teredo clients on the same side of a NAT can use to contact the sender, and they are used with the HP extension.

The ND Option trailer includes 1 byte that indicates either TeredoDiscovery-Solicitation (0x00) or TeredoDiscoveryAdvertisement (0x01). In the first case, the receiver is requested to respond with a direct bubble (i.e., sent directly between Teredo clients) containing the second form of message. The TeredoDiscoveryAd-vertisement type is the response. This trailer is used in supporting the SLR exten-sion, which effectively allows NS/NA messages carried in direct bubbles to be used for refreshing NAT state instead of indirect bubbles, which require process-ing by servers. Finally, the Random Port trailer contains a 16-bit UDP port number, which is the sender's best guess as to its mapped port number. This is used by the PP extension (see Section 6.3 of [RFC6081]).

10.6 UDP-Lite

Some applications are tolerant of bit errors that may be introduced in the data they send and receive. Often, these types of applications wish to use UDP in order to avoid connection setup overhead or to use broadcast or multicast addressing, but UDP uses a checksum that covers either the entire payload or none of it (i.e., when no checksum is computed by the sender). A protocol called *UDP-Lite* or *UDPLite* [RFC3828] addresses this issue by modifying the conventional UDP protocol to provide partial checksums. Such checksums cover only a portion of the payload in each UDP datagram. UDP-Lite has its own IPv4 *Protocol* and IPv6 *Next Header* field value (136), so it effectively counts as a separate transport protocol. UDP-Lite modifies the UDP header by replacing the (redundant) *Length* field with a *Check-sum Coverage* field (see Figure 10-8).

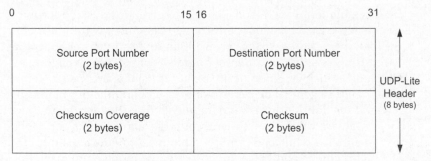

Figure 10-8   UDP-Lite includes a *Checksum Coverage* field that gives the number of bytes (starting with the first byte of the UDP-Lite header) covered by the checksum. The minimum value is 0, indicating that the whole datagram is covered. Values 1 through 7 are invalid, as the header is always covered. UDP-Lite uses a different IPv4 protocol number (136) from UDP (17). IPv6 uses the same values in the *Next Header* field.

The *Checksum Coverage* field in Figure 10-8 is the number of bytes (starting from the first byte of the UDP-Lite header) covered by the checksum. Except for the special value 0, the minimum value is 8, because the UDP-Lite header itself is always required to be covered by the checksum. The value 0 indicates that the entire payload is covered by the checksum, as with conventional UDP. There is a slight issue with IPv6 jumbograms because of the limited space used to hold the *Checksum Coverage* field. For such datagrams, the number of bytes covered can be at most 64KB or the entire datagram (i.e., when the *Checksum Coverage* field has value 0). Special socket API options are used for applications to specify the use of UDP-Lite (IPPROTO_UDPLITE) and the amount of checksum coverage requested (using the SOL_UDPLITE, UDPLITE_SEND_CSCOV, and UDPLITE_RECV_CSCOV options to `setsockopt`).

10.7 IP Fragmentation

As we described in Chapter 3, link-layer framing normally imposes an upper limit on the maximum size of a frame that can be transmitted. To keep the IP datagram abstraction consistent and isolated from link-layer details, IP employs *fragmentation* and *reassembly*. Whenever the IP layer receives an IP datagram to send, it determines which local interface the datagram is to be sent over next (via a forwarding table lookup; see Chapter 5) and what MTU is required. IP compares the outgoing interface's MTU with the datagram size and performs fragmentation if the datagram is too large. Fragmentation in IPv4 can take place at the original sending host and at any intermediate routers along the end-to-end path. Note that datagram fragments can themselves be fragmented. Fragmentation in IPv6 is somewhat different because only the source is permitted to perform fragmentation. We saw an example of IPv6 fragmentation in Chapter 5.

When an IP datagram is fragmented, it is not reassembled until it reaches its final destination. Two reasons have been given for this, the second more compelling than the first. First, not performing reassembly within the network alleviates the forwarding software (or hardware) in routers from implementing this feature. Second, it is possible for different fragments of the same datagram to follow different paths to their common destination. If this happens, no single router along the path would in general be capable of reassembling the original datagram because it would see only a subset of the fragments. The first argument is not terribly convincing at face value given the current performance levels of routers, but it is even less convincing when one considers that most routers must ultimately be capable of functioning as end hosts anyhow (e.g., when being managed or configured). The second argument remains compelling.

10.7.1 Example: UDP/IPv4 Fragmentation

An application using UDP may need to worry about the size of the resulting IP datagram it creates if it wishes to avoid IP-layer fragmentation. In particular, if the size of the resulting datagram exceeds the link's MTU, the IP datagram is split across multiple IP packets, which can lead to performance issues because *if any fragment is lost, the entire datagram is lost*. Figure 10-9 illustrates the situation when a 3020-byte UDP/IPv4 datagram is split into multiple IPv4 packets.

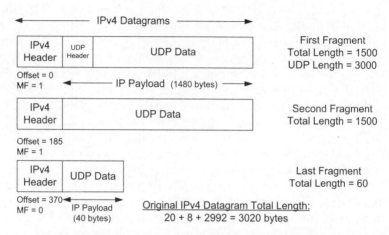

Figure 10-9   A single UDP datagram with 2992 UDP payload bytes is fragmented into three UDP/IPv4 packets (no options). The UDP header that contains the source and destination port numbers appears only in the first fragment (a complicating factor for firewalls and NATs). Fragmentation is controlled by the *Identification, Fragment Offset*, and *More Fragments (MF)* fields in the IPv4 header.

In Figure 10-9, we conclude that the original UDP datagram included 2992 bytes of application (UDP payload) data and 8 bytes of UDP header, resulting in an IPv4 *Total Length* field value of 3020 bytes (recall that this size includes a 20-byte IPv4 header as well). When this datagram was fragmented into three packets, 40 extra bytes were created (20 bytes for each of the newly created IPv4 fragment headers). Thus, the total number of bytes sent is 3060, an increase in IP-layer overhead of about 1.3%. The *Identification* field value (set by the original sender) is copied to each fragment and is used to group them together when they arrive. The *Fragment Offset* field gives the offset of the first byte of the fragment payload byte in the original IPv4 datagram (in 8-byte units). Clearly, the first fragment always has offset 0. Here, we observe the second fragment with offset 185 (185 * 8 = 1480). The size of 1480 is the size of the first fragment less the size of the IPv4 header. A similar analysis applies to the third fragment. Finally, the *MF* bit field indicates whether more fragments in the datagram should be expected and is 0 only in the final fragment. When the fragment with MF = 0 is received, the reassembly process can ascertain the length of the original datagram, as a sum of the *Fragment Offset* field value (times 8) and the IPv4 *Total Length* field value (minus the IPv4 header length). Because each *Offset* field is relative to the original datagram, the reassembly process can handle fragments that arrive out of order. When a datagram is fragmented, the *Total Length* field in the IPv4 header of each fragment is changed to be the total size of that fragment.

Although IP fragmentation looks transparent, there is one feature mentioned earlier that makes it less than desirable: if one fragment is lost, the entire datagram is lost. To understand why this happens, realize that IP itself has no error correction mechanism of its own. Mechanisms such as timeout and retransmission are left as the responsibility of the higher layers. (TCP performs timeout and retransmission; UDP does not. Some UDP-based *applications* perform timeout and retransmission themselves, but this happens at a layer above UDP.) When a fragment of a TCP segment is lost, TCP retransmits the entire TCP segment, which corresponds to an entire IP datagram. There is no way to resend only one fragment of a datagram. Indeed, if the fragmentation was done by an intermediate router, and not the originating system, there is no way for the originating system to know how the datagram was fragmented. For this reason, fragmentation is often avoided. [KM87] provides arguments for avoiding fragmentation.

Using UDP, it is easy to generate IP fragmentation. (We shall see later that TCP tries to avoid fragmentation and that it is nearly impossible for an application to force TCP to send segments large enough to require fragmentation.) We can use our sock program and increase the size of the datagram until fragmentation occurs. On an Ethernet, the maximum amount of data in a frame is ordinarily 1500 bytes (see Chapter 3), which leaves at most 1472 bytes for application data to avoid fragmentation, assuming 20 bytes for the IPv4 header and 8 bytes for the UDP header.[1] We will run our sock program with data sizes of 1471, 1472, 1473, and 1474 bytes. We expect the last two to cause fragmentation:

```
Linux% sock -u -i -n1 -w1471 10.0.0.3 discard
Linux% sock -u -i -n1 -w1472 10.0.0.3 discard
Linux% sock -u -i -n1 -w1473 10.0.0.3 discard
Linux% sock -u -i -n1 -w1474 10.0.0.3 discard
```

Listing 10-3 illustrates the tcpdump output (some lines are wrapped for clarity).

Listing 10-3   UDP fragmentation on a 1500-byte MTU Ethernet link

```
1 23:42:43.562452 10.0.0.5.46530 > 10.0.0.3.9:
                udp 1471 (DF) (ttl 64, id 61350, len 1499)
2 23:42:50.267424 10.0.0.5.46531 > 10.0.0.3.9:
                udp 1472 (DF) (ttl 64, id 62020, len 1500)
3 23:42:57.814555 10.0.0.5 > 10.0.0.3:
                udp (frag 37671:1@1480) (ttl 64, len 21)
4 23:42:57.814715 10.0.0.5.46532 > 10.0.0.3.9:
                udp 1473 (frag 37671:1480@0+) (ttl 64, len 1500)
```

---

1. Recall the assumption that no options are used. For IPv4 datagrams with options, the header exceeds 20 bytes, up to a maximum of 60 bytes.

```
5 23:43:04.368677 10.0.0.5 > 10.0.0.3:
                 udp (frag 37672:2@1480) (ttl 64, len 22)
6 23:43:04.368838 10.0.0.5.46535 > 10.0.0.3.9:
                 udp 1474 (frag 37672:1480@0+) (ttl 64, len 1500)
```

The first two UDP datagrams (packets 1 and 2) fit into 1500-byte Ethernet frames (using the typical "DIX" or "Ethernet" encapsulation) and are not fragmented. In the third case, the length of the IPv4 datagram corresponding to the application write of 1473 bytes is 1501, which must be fragmented (packets 3 and 4). Similarly, the datagram generated by the write of 1474 bytes is 1502 bytes long and is also fragmented (packets 5 and 6).

When it captures a fragmented datagram, tcpdump prints additional information. First, the outputs frag 37671 (packets 3 and 4) and frag 37672 (packets 5 and 6) specify the value of the *Identification* field in the IPv4 header. The next number in the fragmentation information (between the colon and the @ sign in packets 4 and 6) is the IPv4 packet size, excluding the IPv4 header. The first fragment of both datagrams contains 1480 bytes of data: 8 bytes for the UDP header and 1472 bytes of user data. (The 20-byte option-free IPv4 header makes the packet exactly 1500 bytes.) The second fragment of the first fragmented datagram (packet 3) contains 1 byte of data (the remaining byte of user data). The second fragment of the second fragmented datagram (packet 5) contains the remaining 2 bytes of user data. Fragmentation requires that the data portion of the generated fragments (that is, everything excluding the IPv4 header) be a multiple of 8 bytes for all fragments other than the final one. In this example, 1480 is a multiple of 8. (Constrast this case with the IPv6 fragmentation example in Chapter 5, where the 1500-byte Ethernet MTU was not able to be fully utilized.)

The number following the @ is the offset of the data in the fragment from the start of the datagram. The first fragment of each new fragmented datagram starts with offset 0 (packets 4 and 6), and the second fragment of both datagrams starts at byte offset 1480 (packets 3 and 5). The + sign following an offset value means that there are more fragments composing this datagram, corresponding to the *MF* bit field being set to 1 in the 3-bit *Flags* field in the IPv4 header.

One observation that may be surprising is that the fragments with larger offsets are delivered *prior* to the first fragments. In effect, the sender has intentionally reordered the fragments. Upon reflection, we realize that this behavior can be beneficial. If the last fragment is delivered first, the receiving host is able to ascertain the maximum amount of buffer space it will require in order to reassemble the entire datagram. Given that the reassembly process is robust to reordering anyhow, this presents no major problem. On the other hand, there are techniques that would like to take advantage of higher-layer information available in the first fragment (including UDP port numbers) that is not present in the later fragments [KEWG96].

Finally, note that packets 3 and 5 (fragments other than the first) omit the source and destination UDP port numbers. In order for tcpdump to print the port numbers associated with fragments other than the first, it would have to reassemble fragmented datagrams to recover the port numbers that appear only in the UDP header located in the first fragments (which it does not do).

10.7.2 Reassembly Timeout

The IP layer must start a timer when any fragment of a datagram first arrives. If this were not done, fragments that never arrive (as we see in Listing 10-4) could eventually cause the receiver to run out of buffers and can constitute a form of attack opportunity. The example in the listing was created with a special program that constructs and sends only the first two fragments of an ICMPv4 Echo Request message separated by a delay but then never sends any additional fragments. Listing 10-4 illustrates the response (some lines have been wrapped for clarity).

Listing 10-4   Timeout during IPv4 fragment reassembly

```
1 17:35:59.609387 10.0.0.5 > 10.0.0.3:
      icmp: echo request (frag 28519:380@0+) (ttl 255, len 400)
2 17:36:19.617272 10.0.0.5 > 10.0.0.3:
      icmp (frag 28519:380@376+) (ttl 255, len 400)
3 17:36:29.602373 10.0.0.3 > 10.0.0.5:
      icmp: ip reassembly time exceeded for 10.0.0.5 > 10.0.0.3:
         icmp: echo request (frag 28519:380@0+) (ttl 255, len 400)
         [tos 0xc0](ttl 64, id 38816, len 424)
```

Here we see that the first fragment (in both time and sequence space) is sent, with total length 400. A second fragment is sent 20s later, but no final fragment is ever sent. Thirty seconds after receiving the first fragment, the target machine responds with an ICMPv4 Time Exceeded (code 1) message, telling the sender that the datagram has been discarded by including a copy of the first fragment. A normal timeout value is 30 or 60s. As we can see, the timer starts when any of the fragments is received and is not reset when new fragments arrive. Thus, the timer places a sort of bound on the maximum span of time by which fragments of the same datagram can be separated.

Note

Historically, most Berkeley-UNIX-derived IP implementations simply never generated this error. While these implementations *did* set a timer, and *did* discard all fragments when the timer expired, the ICMP error was never generated. Another detail one sometimes encounters is that an implementation is not required to generate the ICMP error unless the *first* fragment has been received (i.e., the one with the 0 *Fragment Offset* field). The reason is that the receiver of the ICMP error cannot tell which user process sent the datagram that was discarded, because the transport-layer header is not available. It is assumed that higher-layer protocols will eventually time out and retransmit if necessary.

10.8 Path MTU Discovery with UDP

Let us examine the interaction between an application using UDP and the path MTU discovery mechanism (PMTUD) [RFC1191]. For a protocol such as UDP, in which the calling application is generally in control of the outgoing datagram size, it is useful if there is some way to determine an appropriate datagram size if fragmentation is to be avoided. Conventional PMTUD uses ICMP PTB messages (see Chapter 8) in determining the largest packet size along a routing path that can be used without inducing fragmentation. These messages are typically processed below the UDP layer and are not directly visible to an application, so either an API call is used for the application to learn the best current estimate of the path MTU size for each destination with which it has communicated, or the IP layer can perform PMTUD independently without the application knowing. The IP layer often caches PMTUD information on a per-destination basis and times it out if it is not refreshed.

10.8.1 Example

In the following example, we use the `sock` program to create a UDP datagram that produces a 1501-byte IPv4 datagram. Both our host system and the attached LAN support an MTU larger than 1500 bytes, but the outgoing link to the Internet at the router does not. The command attempts to send three UDP messages to the `echo` service (UDP port 7) in quick succession.

```
Linux% sock -u -i -n 3 -w1473 www.cs.berkeley.edu echo
```

Listing 10-6 illustrates the corresponding packet trace we can see using `tcp-dump` at the sender (some lines are wrapped for clarity).

Listing 10-6 `tcpdump` output illustrating ICMP PTB message. The suggested MTU is included.

```
1 14:42:18.359366 IP (tos 0x0, ttl 64, id 18331, offset 0, flags [DF],
      proto UDP (17), length 1501)
      12.46.129.28.33954 > 128.32.244.172.7: UDP, length 1473

2 14:42:18.359384 IP (tos 0x0, ttl 64, id 18332, offset 0, flags [DF],
      proto UDP (17), length 1501)
      12.46.129.28.33954 > 128.32.244.172.7: UDP, length 1473

3 14:42:18.359402 IP (tos 0x0, ttl 64, id 18333, offset 0, flags [DF],
      proto UDP (17), length 1501)
      12.46.129.28.33954 > 128.32.244.172.7: UDP, length 1473

4 14:42:18.360156 IP (tos 0x0, ttl 255, id 23457, offset 0,
      flags [none],  proto ICMP (1), length 56)
      12.46.129.1 > 12.46.129.28: ICMP
      128.32.244.172 unreachable - need to frag (mtu 1500), length 36
```

```
IP (tos 0x0, ttl 63, id 18331, offset 0, flags [DF],
proto UDP (17), length 1501)
12.46.129.28.33954 > 128.32.244.172.7: UDP, length 1473
```

In Listing 10-6 we see three UDP datagrams of 1473 UDP (application) payload bytes each. Each produces a 1501-byte (unfragmented) IPv4 datagram. Each of these datagrams has the IPv4 *DF* bit field turned on (the default on this system), so when one of them reaches a router (IPv4 address 12.46.129.1), an ICMPv4 PTB message is produced, which includes the suggested next-hop MTU of 1500 bytes. We may also observe that the ICMPv4 messages produced contain the UDP/IPv4 headers (and first 8 data bytes) from our discarded ("offending") datagrams. In this example, our sock program sent its datagrams so quickly (in under a millisecond) that it completed its execution before any of the ICMP messages were returned and processed.

Note

The 1500-byte MTU is now a common minimum MTU among ISPs. Some ISPs that incorporate PPPoE for address assignment and management use smaller, 1492-byte MTUs. The PPPoE header (see Chapter 3) comprises 6 bytes, and the following PPP header is 2, leaving 1500 – 6 – 2 = 1492 bytes for the encapsulated datagram.

If we use another destination host (one about which we have no path MTU history), and we add additional delay between writes, we can observe different behavior. Using the sock command with the –p 2 option, which adds 2s of delay between each send, we use the following two (identical) commands:

```
Linux% sock -u -i -n 3 -w1473 -p 2 www.wisc.edu echo
write returned -1, expected 1473: Message too long
Linux% sock -u -i -n 3 -w1473 -p 2 www.wisc.edu echo
```

The tcpdump output, using an alternative version of tcpdump, for these commands is given in Listing 10-7 (some lines are wrapped for clarity).

Listing 10-7   Illustration of successful Path MTU discovery on 3000-byte MTU link adapting to 1500-byte path MTU

```
1 17:22:16.331023 IP (tos 0x0, ttl  64, id 58648, offset 0, flags [DF],
    proto: UDP (17), length: 1501)
    12.46.129.28.33955 > 144.92.9.185.7: UDP, length 1473

2 17:22:16.331581 IP (tos 0x0, ttl 255, id 38518, offset 0,
    flags [none], proto: ICMP (1), length: 56)
    12.46.129.1 > 12.46.129.28: ICMP
    144.92.9.185 unreachable - need to frag (mtu 1500), length 36
```

```
      IP (tos 0x0, ttl  63, id 58648, offset 0, flags [DF],
      proto: UDP (17), length: 1501)
      12.46.129.28.33955 > 144.92.9.185.7: UDP, length 1473

3 17:22:24.284866 IP (tos 0x0, ttl 64, id 53776, offset 0, flags [+],
      proto: UDP (17), length: 1500)
      12.46.129.28.33955 > 144.92.9.185.7: UDP, length 1473

4 17:22:24.284873 IP (tos 0x0, ttl 64, id 53776, offset 1480,
      flags [none], proto: UDP (17), length: 21)
      12.46.129.28 > 144.92.9.185: udp

5 17:22:26.293554 IP (tos 0x0, ttl  64, id 53777, offset 0, flags [+],
      proto: UDP (17), length: 1500)
      12.46.129.28.33955 > 144.92.9.185.7: UDP, length 1473

6 17:22:26.293559 IP (tos 0x0, ttl  64, id 53777, offset 1480,
      flags [none], proto: UDP (17), length: 21)
      12.46.129.28 > 144.92.9.185: udp

7 17:22:28.301469 IP (tos 0x0, ttl  64, id 53778, offset 0, flags [+],
      proto: UDP (17), length: 1500)
      12.46.129.28.33955 > 144.92.9.185.7: UDP, length 1473

8 17:22:28.301474 IP (tos 0x0, ttl  64, id 53778, offset 1480,
      flags [none], proto: UDP (17), length: 21)
      12.46.129.28 > 144.92.9.185: udp
```

In Listing 10-7 we can see that the first time we ran our program it resulted in an error due to the ICMPv4 PTB message. The extra time provided within and between runs provides an opportunity for the PTB message to reach the sending host and for the error condition to be delivered back to the sender for processing. Interestingly, when we run the program a second time, the path MTU has been discovered to be 1500 bytes and the system is able to send the program's three datagrams using fragmentation (packets 3, 5, and 7 indicate the first fragments of the three datagrams). After 15 minutes (not illustrated), the path MTU information is considered stale, the datagram is sent unfragmented, another ICMPv4 PTB message is returned, and the process repeats.

Note

[RFC1191] recommends a PMTU value determined using PMTUD to be considered stale after 10 minutes. Path MTU discovery can sometimes cause problems because firewalls and filtering gateways may drop ICMP traffic indiscriminately, which can harm the PMTU discovery algorithm. Because of this, it is possible to disable PMTU discovery on a system-wide or finer-granularity basis. On Linux, the file /proc/sys/net/ipv4/ip_no_pmtu_disc can have a 1 written to it to disable the feature. On Windows, it involves editing the registry entry HKEY_LOCAL_MACHINE\System\CurrentControlSet\Services\Tcpip\Parameters\

EnablePMTUDiscovery to include the value 0. An alternative to conventional PMTUD that does not use ICMP has also been developed [RFC4821]; we will discuss it in the context of TCP in Chapter 15.

10.9 Interaction between IP Fragmentation and ARP/ND

Using UDP, we can see the relationship between induced IP fragmentation and typical implementations of ARP. Recall that ARP is used to map IP-layer addresses to corresponding MAC-layer addresses on the same IPv4 subnet (see Chapter 4). The questions with which we are concerned include, When multiple fragments are to be sent, how many ARP messages should be generated, and how many of the fragments are held until a pending ARP request/response is completed? (Similar questions apply with IPv6 ND.) Returning to our host and LAN using a 1500-byte MTU, we use the following two commands to see the answer:

```
Linux% sock -u -i -n1 -w8192 10.0.0.20 echo
Linux% sock -u -i -n1 -w8192 10.0.0.3 echo
```

These arguments cause our sock program to generate a single UDP datagram with 8192 bytes of user data. We expect this to generate six fragments on an Ethernet using a 1500-byte MTU size. We also make sure that the ARP cache is empty before running the program, so that an ARP request and reply must be exchanged before any fragments are sent (see Listing 10-8; some lines are wrapped for clarity).

Listing 10-8   ARP and fragmentation on Ethernet with 1500-byte MTU

```
1 15:45:49.063561 arp who-has 10.0.0.20 tell 10.0.0.5
2 15:45:50.059523 arp who-has 10.0.0.20 tell 10.0.0.5
3 15:45:51.059505 arp who-has 10.0.0.20 tell 10.0.0.5
---
4 15:46:08.555725 arp who-has 10.0.0.3 tell 10.0.0.5
5 15:46:08.555973 arp reply 10.0.0.3 is-at 0:0:c0:c2:9b:26
6 15:46:08.555992 10.0.0.5 > 10.0.0.3:
    udp (frag 27358:1480@2960+) (ttl 64, len 1500)
7 15:46:08.555998 10.0.0.5 > 10.0.0.3:
    udp (frag 27358:1480@1480+) (ttl 64, len 1500)
8 15:46:08.556004 10.0.0.5.32808 > 10.0.0.3.7:
    udp 8192 (frag 27358:1480@0+) (ttl 64, len 1500)
```

For this experiment, we happen to know that there is no running host assigned address 10.0.0.20, so we should expect no reply. In the first part of Listing 10-8 (packets 1–3), we observe three ARP requests spaced approximately 1s apart. No host responds after three requests are sent, so the ARP requestor gives up. In the next case, an ARP response is received in about 250μs, and a fragment is sent about 20μs thereafter. After this, the remaining fragments are sent very closely together, within about 6µs of each other. Recall that in this system (Linux), the last fragment is sent first.

Note

Historically, the interaction between fragmentation and ARP has been problematic. For example, in some cases an ARP request was sent for each fragment, and in many cases only one of the fragments was queued pending the ARP response (thus losing the datagram, as all but one of its fragments were discarded). The first problem was addressed in [RFC1122], which requires an implementation to prevent this type of ARP flooding. The recommended maximum rate is one per second. The second problem is also discussed in [RFC1122], but this states only that the link layer "SHOULD save (rather than discard) at least one (the latest) packet of each set of packets destined to the same unresolved IP address, and transmit the saved packet when the address has been resolved." This approach can lead to unnecessary packet loss and has been addressed in individual implementations by providing a larger queue for packets while their ARP requests are pending.

10.10 Maximum UDP Datagram Size

Theoretically, the maximum size of an IPv4 datagram is 65,535 bytes, imposed by the 16-bit *Total Length* field in the IPv4 header (see Chapter 5). With an optionless IPv4 header of 20 bytes and a UDP header of 8 bytes, this leaves a maximum of 65,507 bytes of user data in a UDP datagram. For IPv6, the 16-bit *Payload Length* field permits an effective UDP payload of 65,527 bytes (8 of the 65,535 IPv6 payload bytes are used for the UDP header), assuming jumbograms are not being used. There are two main reasons why a full-size datagram of these sizes may not be delivered end-to-end, however. First, the system's local protocol implementation may have some limitation. Second, the receiving application may not be prepared to handle such large datagrams.

10.10.1 Implementation Limitations

Protocol implementations provide an API to applications that pick some default buffer size for sending and receiving. Some implementations provide defaults that are less than the maximum IP datagram size, and some actually do not support sending datagrams larger than a few tens of kilobytes (although this problem is not common).

The sockets API [UNP3] provides a set of functions that an application can call to set or query the size of the receive and send buffers. For a UDP socket, this size is directly related to the maximum size of UDP datagram the application can read or write. Typical default values are 8192 bytes or 65,535 bytes, but these can generally be made larger by invoking the `setsockopt()` API call.

We mentioned in Chapter 5 that a host is required to provide enough buffering to receive at least a 576-byte IPv4 datagram on reassembly. Many UDP applications are designed to restrict their application data size to 512 bytes or less (resulting in IPv4 datagrams under 576 bytes), to stay below this limit. Examples employing such limitations to their UDP datagram size include the DNS (see Chapter 11) and DHCP (see Chapter 6).

10.10.2 Datagram Truncation

Just because UDP/IP is capable of sending and receiving a datagram of a given (large) size does not mean the receiving application is prepared to read that size. UDP programming interfaces allow the application to specify the maximum number of bytes to return each time a network read operation completes. What happens if the received datagram exceeds the size specified?

In most cases, the answer to this question is that the API *truncates* the datagram, discarding any excess data in the datagram beyond the number of bytes specified by the receiving application. However, the exact behavior varies from implementation to implementation. Some systems provide the unconsumed portion of the datagram in subsequent read operations, and others inform the caller of how much data was truncated (or, in yet other cases, that *some* data was truncated, but not exactly how much).

Note

In Linux, the MSG_TRUNC option may be given to the sockets API to discover how much data was truncated. On HP-UX, MSG_TRUNC is instead a flag set when a read call returns that some data was truncated. The sockets API under SVR4 (including Solaris 2.x) does *not* truncate the datagram. Any excess data is returned in subsequent reads. The application is not notified that multiple reads are being fulfilled from a single UDP datagram.

When we discuss TCP we shall see that it provides a continuous stream of bytes to the application, without any message boundaries. Thus, an application consumes however much data it requests, provided sufficient data is available (if not, it usually waits).

10.11 UDP Server Design

There are some characteristics of UDP that affect the design and implementation of networking application software wishing to use it [RFC5405]. Servers typically interact with the operating system, and most need a way to handle multiple clients at the same time. Client design and implementation are usually simpler, and therefore we will not discuss them here.

In the typical client/server scenario, a client starts, immediately communicates with a single server, and is done. Servers, on the other hand, start and then go to sleep, waiting for a client's request to arrive. They awaken when a client's datagram arrives, which usually requires the server to evaluate the request and possibly perform further processing. Our interest here is not in the programming aspects of clients and servers ([UNP3] covers all those details) but in the protocol features of UDP that affect the design and implementation of a server using UDP. (We examine the details of TCP server design in Chapter 13.) Although some of the features we describe depend slightly on the implementation of UDP being used, the features are common to most implementations.

10.11.1 IP Addresses and UDP Port Numbers

What arrives at a UDP server from a client is a UDP datagram. The IP header contains the source and destination IP addresses, and the UDP header contains the source and destination UDP port numbers. When an application receives a UDP message, the IP and UDP headers have been stripped off; the application must be told by the operating system in some other way who sent the message (the source IP address and port number), if it intends to furnish a reply. This feature allows a UDP server to handle multiple clients.

Some servers need to know *to whom* the datagram was sent, that is, the destination IP address. While it may seem obvious that such information would immediately be known by a server without looking into the received datagram, this is not always the case. For example, because of multihoming, IP address aliasing, and ordinary IPv6 usage with multiple scopes, a host may have multiple IP addresses, and a single server may receive incoming datagrams using any of them (this is in fact the common case). Any server wishing to perform its tasks differently depending on the destination IP address selected by the client would require access to the destination IP address information. In addition, some services may respond differently if the destination address is broadcast or multicast (e.g., the Host Requirements RFC [RFC1122] states that a TFTP server should ignore received datagrams that are sent to a broadcast address).

Note

A DNS server is one type of server that is sensitive to the destination IP address. It can use this information to arrange a particular sorting order on the address mappings it returns. This behavior of DNS is described in more detail in Chapter 11.

The lesson here is that even though an API may deliver all the data contained in a transport-layer datagram, additional information from the various layers (typically addressing information) may be required for a server to operate most effectively. This issue is not unique to UDP, of course, but because it is the first transport-layer protocol we study, it is worthwhile to point out now.

UDP servers designed for use with both IPv4 and IPv6 must consider the fact that these two types of addresses have significantly different lengths and require different data structures. In addition, the interoperability mechanism of encoding IPv4 addresses in IPv6 addresses may allow the use of IPv6 sockets to handle both IPv4 and IPv6 addressing. See [UNP3] for more details.

10.11.2 Restricting Local IP Addresses

Most UDP servers *wildcard* their local IP address when they bind a UDP endpoint. This means that an incoming UDP datagram destined for the server's port is accepted on any local IP address (any IP address in use on the local machine, including the local loopback address). For example, we can start an IPv4 UDP server on port 7777:

```
Linux% sock -u -s 7777
```

We can then use the `netstat` command to see the state of the endpoint (see Listing 10-9).

Listing 10-9   `netstat` listing of IPv4 UDP servers using wildcarded address bindings

```
Linux% netstat -l --udp -n
Active Internet connections (only servers)
Proto Recv-Q Send-Q Local Address          Foreign Address
udp        0      0 *:7777                 0.0.0.0:*
```

We have deleted several lines of output other than the one in which we are interested. The -l flag reports on all listening sockets (servers). The --udp flag provides data relating only to the UDP protocol. The -n flag prints IP addresses rather than fully expanded host names.

Note

While not all systems provide exactly these (Linux) flags for `netstat`, most provide the `netstat` command with some combination of flags to obtain similar results. On BSD, the -l and -p udp flags are supported. On Windows, the -n, -a, and -p udp flags can be used.

The local address is printed as *:7777, where the asterisk means that the local IP address has been wildcarded. When the server creates its endpoint, it can specify one of the host's local IP addresses, including a broadcast address, as the local IP address for the endpoint. In such cases, incoming UDP datagrams are then passed to this endpoint only if the destination IP address matches the specified local address. With our `sock` program, if we specify an IP address before the port number, that IP address becomes the local IP address for the endpoint. For example, the command

```
Linux% sock -u -s 127.0.0.1 7777
```

restricts the server to accepting only datagrams arriving on the local loopback interface (127.0.0.1), which can be generated only on the same host. The netstat output in Listing 10-10 shows this case.

Listing 10-10   netstat listing of UDP IPv4 server bound to only the local loopback interface

```
Active Internet connections (only servers)
Proto Recv-Q Send-Q Local Address          Foreign Address
udp        0      0 127.0.0.1:7777         0.0.0.0:*
```

If we try to send this server a datagram from a host on the same Ethernet, an ICMPv4 Port Unreachable message is returned, and the sending application receives an error. The server never sees the datagram.

```
Linux% sock -u -v 10.0.0.3 6666
connected on 10.0.0.5.50997 to 10.0.0.3.6666
123
error: Connection refused
```

10.11.3 Using Multiple Addresses

It is possible to start different servers on the same port number, each with a different local IP address. Normally, however, the system must be told by the application that it is OK to reuse the same port number in this way.

Note

With the sockets API, the SO_REUSEADDR socket option must be specified. This is done in our sock program by specifying the –A option.

Even if we have only one true network interface, we can establish additional IP addresses for it to use. Here, our host has a native IPv4 address of 10.0.0.30, but we will give it two additional addresses:

```
Linux# ip addr add 10.0.2.13 scope host dev eth0
Linux# ip addr add 10.0.2.14 scope host dev eth0
```

Now our host has four unicast IPv4 addresses: its native address, the two we have just added, plus its local loopback address. We can start three different instances of the UDP on the same port using our sock program on the same UDP port (8888):

```
Linux% sock -u -s -A 10.0.2.13 8888
Linux% sock -u -s -A 10.0.2.14 8888
Linux% sock -u -s -A 8888
```

The servers must be started with the −A flag, telling the system that it is OK to reuse the same addressing information. The netstat output in Listing 10-11 shows the addresses and port numbers on which the servers are listening.

Listing 10-11   Restricted and wildcarded UDP servers on the same UDP port

```
Active Internet connections (only servers)
Proto Recv-Q Send-Q Local Address       Foreign Address
udp        0      0 10.0.2.13:8888       0.0.0.0:*
udp        0      0 0.0.0.0:8888         0.0.0.0:*
udp        0      0 10.0.2.14:8888       0.0.0.0:*
```

In this scenario, the only IPv4 datagrams that will go to the server with the wildcarded local address are those destined for 10.0.0.30, the directed broadcast address (e.g., 10.255.255.255), the limited broadcast address (255.255.255.255), or the local loopback address (127.0.0.1), because the restricted servers cover all other possibilities.

There is a priority implied when an endpoint with a wildcard address exists. An endpoint with a specific IP address that matches the destination IP address is always chosen over a wildcard. The wildcard endpoint is used only when a specific match is not found.

10.11.4 Restricting Foreign IP Address

In all the netstat output that we showed earlier, the foreign IP address (i.e., the one not local to the host where the server is running) and foreign port number are shown as 0.0.0.0:*, meaning that the endpoint will accept an incoming UDP datagram from any IPv4 address and any port number. However, there is an option to restrict the foreign address. This means that the endpoint receives UDP datagrams only from that specific IPv4 address and port number. Note that this restriction can be added once a server has heard from a client, in order to filter out additional traffic from other clients. Our sock program uses the −f option to specify the foreign IPv4 address and port number:

```
Linux% sock -u -s -f 10.0.0.14.4444 5555
```

This sets the foreign IPv4 address to 10.0.0.14 and the foreign port number to 4444. The server's port is 5555. If we run netstat, we see that the local address has also been set, even though we did not specify it explicitly (see Listing 10-12).

Listing 10-12   Restricting the foreign address causes assignment of a local address.

```
Linux% netstat   --udp -n
Active Internet connections (w/o servers)
Proto Recv-Q Send-Q Local Address   Foreign Address    State
udp        0      0 10.0.0.30:5555 10.0.0.14:4444      ESTABLISHED
```

This is a typical side effect of specifying the foreign IP address and foreign port: if the local address has not been chosen when the foreign address is specified, the local address is chosen automatically. Its value becomes the IP address of the interface chosen by IP routing to reach the specified foreign IP address. Indeed, in this example the primary IPv4 address for the Ethernet that is connected to the foreign address is 10.0.0.30. Note that as a consequence of the endpoints being determined and the foreign address restricted, the `state` column now indicates that the association is ESTABLISHED.

Table 10-2 summarizes the three types of address bindings that a UDP server can establish.

Table 10-2 Types of address bindings for a UDP server

Local Address	Foreign Address	Description
local_IP.local_port	*foreign_IP.foreign_port*	Restricted to one client
local_IP.local_port	**.* (wildcard)*	Restricted to one local IP address and port (but for any client)
*.local_port	**.* (wildcard)*	Restricted to local port only

In all cases, *local_port* is the server's port and *local_IP* must be one of the locally assigned IP addresses. The ordering of the three rows in the table is the order that the UDP module applies when trying to determine which local endpoint receives an incoming datagram. The most specific binding (the first row) is tried first, and the least specific (the last row with both IP addresses wildcarded) is tried last.

10.11.5 Using Multiple Servers per Port

Although it is not specified in the RFCs, by default most implementations allow only one application endpoint at a time to be associated with any one (local IP address, UDP port number) pair for a given *address family* (i.e., IPv4 or IPv6). When a UDP datagram arrives at a host destined for its IP address and an active port number, one copy is delivered to that single endpoint (e.g., a listening application). The IP address of the endpoint can be the wildcard, as shown earlier, but only a single application can receive datagrams for the address(es) specified. If we then try to start another server with the same wildcarded local address and the same port using the same address family, it does not work:

```
Linux% sock -u -s 12.46.129.3 8888 &
Linux% sock -u -s 12.46.129.3 8888
can't bind local address: Address already in use
```

In support of multicasting (see Chapter 9), multiple endpoints can be allowed to use the same (local IP address, UDP port number) pair, although the application normally must tell the API that this is OK (i.e., our −A flag to specify the SO_REUSEADDR socket option illustrated previously).

Note

4.4BSD requires the application to set a different socket option (SO_REUSEPORT) to allow multiple endpoints to share the same port. Furthermore, each endpoint must specify this option, including the first one to use the port.

When a UDP datagram arrives whose destination IP address is a broadcast or multicast address, and there are multiple endpoints at the destination IP address and port number, one copy of the incoming datagram is passed to each endpoint. (The endpoint's local IP address can be the wildcard, which matches any destination IP address.) But if a UDP datagram arrives whose destination IP address is a *unicast* address (i.e., an ordinary address), only a single copy of the datagram is delivered to *one* of the endpoints. Which endpoint gets the unicast datagram is implementation-dependent, but this policy helps to allow multithreaded and multiprocess servers to operate without being invoked multiple times on the same incoming request.

10.11.6 Spanning Address Families: IPv4 and IPv6

It is possible to write servers that span not only protocols (such as servers that respond to both TCP and UDP) but also across address families. That is, we may write a UDP server that responds to incoming requests for IPv4 as well as for IPv6. While this may seem entirely straightforward (IPv6 addresses are just additional IP addresses on the same host that happen to be 128 bits long), there is a subtlety related to the sharing of the port space. On some systems, the port space between IPv6 and IPv4 for UDP (and TCP) is *shared*. This means that if a service binds to a UDP port using IPv4, it is also allocated the same port in the IPv6 port space (and vice versa), preventing other services from using it (unless the SO_REUSEADDR socket option is used, as mentioned before). Furthermore, because IPv6 addresses can encode IPv4 addresses in an interoperable way (see Chapter 2), wildcard bindings in IPv6 may receive incoming IPv4 traffic.

Note

The situation is implementation-specific. In Linux, all port space is shared, and any wildcard IPv6 binding implies a corresponding IPv4 binding. In FreeBSD, the IPV6_V6ONLY socket option may be used to ensure that bindings are present only in the IPv6 space. Programmers should consult the socket interface for IPv6 for whichever operating environment they are supporting. C language bindings are described in [RFC3493].

10.11.7 Lack of Flow and Congestion Control

Most UDP servers are *iterative* servers. This means that a single server thread (or process) handles all the client requests on a single UDP port (e.g., the server's well-known port). Normally there is a limited-size input queue associated with each UDP port that an application is using. This means that requests arriving at about the same time from different clients are automatically queued by UDP. The received UDP datagrams are passed to the application (when it asks for the next one) in the order in which they were received (i.e., FCFS—first come, first served).

It is possible, however, for this queue to overflow, causing the UDP implementation to discard incoming datagrams. This can happen even if only one client is being served because UDP provides no *flow control* (that is, no way for the server to tell the client to slow down). Because UDP is a connectionless protocol with no reliability mechanism of its own, applications are not told when the UDP input queue overflows. The excess datagrams are just discarded by UDP.

Another concern arises from the fact that queues are also present in the IP routers between the sender and the receiver—in the middle of the network. When these queues become full, traffic may be discarded in a fashion similar to that of the UDP input queue. When this happens, the network is said to be *congested*. Congestion is undesirable because it affects all network users with traffic that traverses the point where congestion is occurring, as opposed to the UDP input case mentioned previously, where only a single application server was affected. UDP poses a special concern for congestion because it has no way of being informed that it should slow down its sending rate if the network is being driven into congestion. (It also has no mechanism for slowing down, even if it were told to do so.) Thus, it is said to lack *congestion control*. Congestion control is a complex subject and still an active area of research. We will return to considerations of congestion control when we discuss TCP (see Chapter 16).

10.12 Translating UDP/IPv4 and UDP/IPv6 Datagrams

In Chapter 7 we discussed a framework for translating IP datagrams from IPv4 to IPv6 and vice versa. Chapter 8 described how this framework applies to ICMP. When UDP passes through a translator, the translation takes place as described in Chapter 7, except there are issues specific to the UDP checksum. For UDP/IPv4 datagrams, the UDP header's *Checksum* field is allowed to be 0 (uncomputed), whereas in UDP/IPv6 this is not allowed. Consequently, complete datagrams arriving with a zero checksum being translated from IPv4 to IPv6 result in either a UDP/IPv6 datagram with a fully computed pseudo-header checksum being generated, or with the arriving packet being dropped. The translator is supposed to provide a configuration option to select which is desired, as the overhead of generating such checksums may be objectionable. Packets containing a nonzero checksum being translated in either direction require the checksum to be updated if a non-checksum-neutral address mapping is used (see Chapter 7).

Fragmented datagrams present another challenge. For stateless translators, a fragmented UDP/IPv4 datagram with a zero checksum cannot be translated, as the appropriate UDP/IPv6 checksum cannot be computed. Such datagrams are dropped. Stateful translators (i.e., NAT64) can reassemble a number of fragments and compute the required checksum. Fragmented UDP/IP datagrams with computed checksums are handled as ordinary fragments in either direction, as specified in Chapter 7. Large UDP/IPv4 datagrams that require fragmentation to fit within the IPv6 minimum MTU after translation are also handled as conventional IPv4 datagrams (i.e., they are fragmented as needed).

10.13 UDP in the Internet

If we attempt to characterize the amount of UDP traffic in the Internet, we find that useful, publicly available data is somewhat hard to come by, and that the breakdown of traffic load by protocol varies from site to site. That said, studies such as [FKMC03] find that UDP accounts for between 10% and 40% of Internet traffic observed, and that as peer-to-peer applications gain in popularity, the use of UDP is also on the rise [Z09], although TCP traffic still dominates in terms of packets and bytes.

In [SMC02], fragmentation of Internet traffic is found to be most common with UDP (68.3% of the fragmented traffic is UDP), although very little traffic overall is fragmented (about 0.3% of packets, 0.8% of bytes). The authors report that the most common type of traffic that is fragmented is UDP-based multimedia traffic (53%; Microsoft's Media Player is responsible for about half of this) and encapsulated/tunneled traffic such as that present in VPN tunnels (about 22%). Furthermore, about 10% of the fragmentation is *reverse-order* (we said this earlier in the examples where the last IP fragment was sent prior to the first), and the most commonly seen fragment size is 1500 bytes (79%), followed by 1484 bytes (18%) and 1492 bytes (1%).

Note

The 1500-byte MTU is related to the native usable payload size for Ethernet. The 1484 size was produced by Digital Equipment Corporation's GigaSwitch (now defunct), which represented significant portions of the topology measured at the time.

The causes of fragmentation appear to derive from two factors: careless encapsulation and lack of path MTU discovery and adaptation for applications that like to use large messages. The former case relates to multiple levels of encapsulation across many protocol layers that add additional headers, forcing IP packets that initially fit into 1500-byte MTUs (the most common size) to no longer fit (e.g., application traffic carried over VPN tunnels). The second factor arises for applications that use larger packets (e.g., video applications) that end up being fragmented. A curious (and unfortunate) finding in the [SMC02] study is that numerous UDP packets with the IPv4 *DF* bit field turned on (presumably trying to perform PMTU discovery) are encapsulated in UDP packets that do not (thereby defeating the attempt and leaving the responsible application ignorant of the fact).

10.14 Attacks Involving UDP and IP Fragmentation

Most attacks involving UDP relate to exhaustion of some shared resource (buffers, link capacity, etc.) or exploitation of bugs in protocol implementations causing system crashes or other undesired behavior. Both fall into the broad category of DoS attacks: the successful attacker is able to cause services to be made unavailable to legitimate users. The most straightforward DoS attack with UDP is simply generating massive amounts of traffic as fast as possible. Because UDP does not regulate its sending traffic rate, this can negatively impact the performance of other applications sharing the same network path. This can happen even without malicious intent.

A more sophisticated form of DoS attack frequently associated with UDP is a *magnification* attack. This type of attack generally involves an attacker sending a small amount of traffic that induces other systems to generate much more. In the so-called *fraggle* attack, a malicious UDP sender forges the IP source address to be that of a victim and sets the destination address to a form of broadcast (e.g., the directed broadcast address). UDP packets are sent to a service that generates traffic in response to an incoming datagram. When the servers implementing these services respond, they direct their messages to the IP address contained in the *Source IP Address* field of the arriving UDP packet. In this case, the source address is that of the victim, and so the victim host is subject to being overloaded by the multiple UDP traffic responders. Variants of this magnification attack are numerous, including inducing a character-generating service to be coupled to the echo service, thereby causing traffic to be "ping-ponged" forever. This attack is closely related to the ICMP smurf attack (see Chapter 8).

Several attacks involving IP fragmentation have appeared. IP fragmentation processing is somewhat more complex than UDP processing, so it is not so surprising that bugs in its implementation have been found and exploited. One form of attack involves sending fragments that contain no data whatsoever. This attack exploited a bug in IPv4 reassembly code and caused some systems to crash. Another attack on the IPv4 reassembly layer is the *teardrop* attack, which involves carefully constructing a series of fragments with overlapping *Fragment Offset* fields that crash or otherwise badly affect some systems. A variant of this involves overlapping fragment offsets that overwrite the UDP header from an earlier fragment. Overlapping fragments are now prohibited with IPv6 [RFC5722]. Finally, the also-related *ping of death* attack (typically constructed with ICMPv4 Echo Request but also applicable to UDP) operates by creating an IPv4 datagram that on reassembly exceeds the maximum limit. This is fairly straightforward because the *Fragment Offset* field can be set to a value as high as 8191, which represents a byte offset of 65,528 bytes. Any such fragment with length exceeding 7 bytes would—if not prevented from doing so—result in a reconstructed datagram exceeding the maximum size of 65,535 bytes. Mitigation techniques for some forms of fragment attacks are given in [RFC3128].

10.15 Summary

UDP is a simple protocol. Its official specification, [RFC0768], requires only three pages (including references!). The services it provides to a user process, above and beyond IP, are port numbers and a checksum. It provides no flow control, no congestion control, and no error correction. It does provide error detection (optional for UDP/IPv4 but mandatory for UDP/IPv6) and preservation of message boundaries. We used UDP to examine the Internet checksum and to see how IP fragmentation is performed. We also looked at other aspects of UDP: how it is used with path MTU discovery, how it impacts server design, and its presence in the Internet.

UDP is most commonly used when the overhead of connection establishment is to be avoided, when multipoint delivery (multicasting, broadcasting) is used, or when the comparatively "heavyweight" reliability semantics of TCP (such as sequencing, flow control, and retransmission) are not desired. It has enjoyed a growing level of use because of multimedia and peer-to-peer applications and is the primary protocol for supporting VoIP [RFC3550][RFC3261]. It is also a convenient method for encapsulating traffic that must transition a NAT without introducing much extra overhead (only 8 bytes for the UDP header). We have seen this use for supporting an IPv6 transition mechanism (Teredo) and for aiding NAT traversal with STUN (see Chapter 7), and we will see it again in Chapter 18 where it is used for IPsec NAT traversal. One of UDP's other major uses is for supporting the DNS. We explore this important application next, in Chapter 11.

10.16 References

[CT90] D. Clark and D. Tennenhouse, "Architectural Considerations for a New Generation of Protocols," *Proc. ACM SIGCOMM*, 1990.

[FKMC03] M. Fomenkov, K. Keys, D. Moore, and k claffy, "Longitudinal Study of Internet Traffic in 1998–2003," CAIDA Report, available from http://www.caida.org, 2003.

[IPORT] http://www.iana.org/assignments/port-numbers

[KB929851] Microsoft Support Article ID 929851, "The Default Dynamic Port Range for TCP/IP Has Changed in Windows Vista and in Windows Server 2008," Nov. 19, 2009 (rev. 6.2).

[KEWG96] F. Kaashoek, D. Engler, D. Wallach, and G. Ganger, "Server Operating Systems," *Proc. SIGOPS European Workshop*, 1996.

[KM87] C. Kent and J. Mogul, "Fragmentation Considered Harmful," DEC WRL Technical Report 87/3, 1987.

[RFC0768] J. Postel, "User Datagram Protocol," Internet RFC 0768/STD 0006, Aug. 1980.

[RFC1122] R. Braden, ed., "Requirements for Internet Hosts—Communication Layers," Internet RFC 1122/STD 0003, Oct. 1989.

[RFC1191] J. C. Mogul and S. E. Deering, "Path MTU Discovery," Internet RFC 1191, Nov. 1990.

[RFC2460] S. Deering and R. Hinden, "Internet Protocol, Version 6 (IPv6) Specification," Internet RFC 2460, Dec. 1998.

[RFC2675] D. Borman, S. Deering, and R. Hinden, "IPv6 Jumbograms," Internet RFC 2675, Aug. 1999.

[RFC3056] B. Carpenter and K. Moore, " Connection of IPv6 Domains via IPv4 Clouds," Internet RFC 3056, Feb. 2001.

[RFC3128] I. Miller, "Protection against a Variant of the Tiny Fragment Attack (RFC 1858)," Internet RFC 3128 (informational), June 2001.

[RFC3261] J. Rosenberg, H. Schulzrinne, G. Camarillo, A. Johnston, J. Peterson, R. Sparks, M. Handley, and E. Schooler, "SIP: Session Initiation Protocol," Internet RFC 3261, June 2002.

[RFC3493] R. Gilligan, S. Thomson, J. Bound, J. McCann, and W. Stevens, "Basic Socket Interface Extensions for IPv6," Internet RFC 3493 (informational), Feb. 2003.

[RFC3550] H. Schulzrinne, S. Casner, R. Frederick, and V. Jacobson, "RTP: A Transport Protocol for Real-Time Applications," Internet RFC 3550/STD 0064, July 2003.

[RFC3828] L-A. Larzon, M. Degermark, S. Pink, L-E. Jonsson, ed., and G. Fairhurst, ed., "The Lightweight User Datagram Protocol (UDP-Lite)," Internet RFC 3828, July 2004.

[RFC4213] E. Nordmark and R. Gilligan, "Basic Transition Mechanisms for IPv6 Hosts and Routers," Internet RFC 4213, Oct. 2005.

[RFC4380] C. Huitema, "Teredo: Tunneling IPv6 over UDP through Network Address Translations (NATs)," Internet RFC 4380, Feb. 2006.

[RFC4787] F. Audet, ed., and C. Jennings, "Network Address Translation (NAT) Behavioral Requirements for Unicast UDP," Internet RFC 4787/BCP 0127, Jan. 2007.

[RFC4821] M. Mathis and J. Heffner, "Packetization Layer Path MTU Discovery," Internet RFC 4821, Mar. 2007.

[RFC4960] R. Stewart, ed., "Stream Control Transmission Protocol," Internet RFC 4960, Sept. 2007.

[RFC5405] L. Eggert and G. Fairhurst, "Unicast UDP Usage Guidelines for Application Designers," Internet RFC 5405/BCP 0145, Nov. 2008.

[RFC5722] S. Krishnan, "Handling of Overlapping IPv6 Fragments," Internet RFC 5722, Dec. 2009.

[RFC5969] W. Townsley and O. Troan, "IPv6 Rapid Deployment on IPv4 Infrastructures (6rd)—Protocol Specification," Internet RFC 5969, Aug. 2010.

[RFC5991] D. Thaler, S. Krishnan, and J. Hoagland, "Teredo Security Updates," Internet RFC 5991, Sept. 2010.

[RFC6081] D. Thaler, "Teredo Extensions," Internet RFC 6081, Jan. 2011.

[RFC6343] B. Carpenter, "Advisory Guidelines for 6to4 Deployment," Internet RFC 6343 (informational), Aug. 2011.

[SMC02] C. Shannon, D. Moore, and k claffy, "Beyond Folklore: Observations on Fragmented Traffic," *IEEE/ACM Transactions on Networking*, 10(6), Dec. 2002.

[SOCK] http://www.icir.org/christian/sock.html

[TTYPES] http://www.iana.org/assignments/trailer-types

[UNP3] W. Stevens, B. Fenner, and A. Rudoff, *UNIX Network Programming, Volume 1, Third Edition* (Addison-Wesley, 2004).

[Z09] M. Zhang et al., "Analysis of UDP Traffic Usage on Internet Backbone Links," *Proc. 9th Annual International Symposium on Applications and the Internet*, 2009.

11

Name Resolution and the Domain Name System (DNS)

11.1 Introduction

The protocols we have studied so far operate using IP addresses to identify the hosts that participate in a distributed application. These addresses (especially IPv6 addresses) are cumbersome for humans to use and remember, so the Internet supports the use of *host names* to identify hosts, both clients and servers. In order to be used by protocols such as TCP and IP, host names are converted into IP addresses using a process known as *name resolution*. There are different forms of name resolution in the Internet, but the most prevalent and important one uses a distributed database system known as the *Domain Name System* (DNS) [MD88]. DNS runs as an application on the Internet, using IPv4 or IPv6 (or both). For scalability, DNS names are hierarchical, as are the servers that support name resolution.

DNS is a distributed client/server networked database that is used by TCP/IP applications to map between host names and IP addresses (and vice versa), to provide electronic mail routing information, service naming, and other capabilities. We use the term distributed because no single site on the Internet knows all of the information. Each site (university department, campus, company, or department within a company, for example) maintains its own database of information and runs a server program that other systems across the Internet (clients) can query. The DNS provides the protocol that allows clients and servers to communicate with each other and also a protocol for allowing servers to exchange information.

From an application's point of view, access to the DNS is through an application library called a *resolver*. In general, an application must convert a host name to an IPv4 and/or IPv6 address before it can ask TCP to open a connection or send a unicast datagram using UDP. The TCP and IP protocol implementations know nothing about the DNS; they operate only with the addresses.

In this chapter we will take a look at how the names in DNS are set up, how resolvers and servers communicate using the Internet protocols (mainly UDP), and some of the other resolution mechanisms that are used in Internet environments. We do not cover all of the administrative details of running a name server or all of the options available with resolvers and servers. Such information is available from various other sources, including Albitz and Liu's *DNS and BIND* text [AL06] and in [RFC6168]. We discuss the details of DNS security (DNSSEC) in Chapter 18.

11.2   The DNS Name Space

The set of all names used with DNS constitutes the DNS *name space*. This space is partitioned hierarchically and is case insensitive, similar to computer file system folders (directories) and files. The current DNS name space is a tree of domains with an unnamed root at the top. The top echelons of the tree are the so-called top-level domains (TLDs), which include *generic TLDs* (gTLDs), *country-code TLDs* (ccTLDs), and *internationalized country-code TLDs* (IDN ccTLDs), plus a special *infrastructure TLD* called, for historical reasons, *ARPA* [RFC3172]. These form the top levels of a naming tree with the form shown in Figure 11-1.

There are five commonly used groups of TLDs, and one group of specialized domains being used for *internationalized domain names* (IDNs).[1] The history of IDNs, one piece of the "internationalization" or "i18n" of the Internet, is long and somewhat complicated. Across the world, there are multiple languages, and each uses one or more written scripts. While the Unicode standard [U11] aims to capture the entire set of characters, many characters look the same but have different Unicode values. Furthermore, characters written as text may flow from right to left, left to right, or (when combining certain texts with others) in both directions. Couple these (and other) somewhat technical concerns with concerns regarding equity and international law and politics, and a considerable hurdle results. The interested reader may wish to consult the IAB's review of IDNs [RFC4690], published in 2006, for more information. Current information is available from [IIDN].

The gTLDs are grouped into categories: *generic, generic-restricted,* and *sponsored.* The generic gTLDs (*generic* appears twice) are open for unrestricted use. The others (generic-restricted and sponsored) are limited to various sorts of uses or are constrained as to what entity may assign names from the domain. For example, EDU is used for educational institutions, MIL and GOV are used for military and government institutions of the United States, and INT is used for international organizations (such as NATO). Table 11-1 provides a summary of the 22 gTLDs from [GTLD] as of mid-2011. There is a "new gTLD" program in the works that may significantly expand the current set, possibly to several hundred or even thousand. This program and policies relating to TLD management in general are maintained by the Internet Corporation for Assigned Names and Numbers (ICANN) [ICANN].

---

1. Figure 11-1 also shows 11 test IDN domains, which are still available.

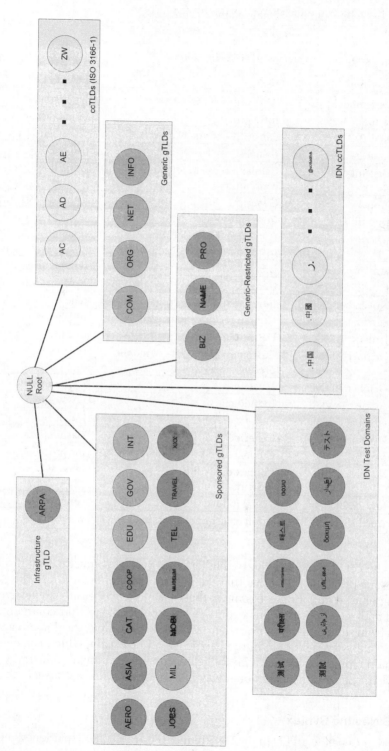

Figure 11-1   The DNS name space forms a hierarchy with an unnamed root at the top. The top-level domains (TLDs) include generic TLDs (gTLDs), country-code TLDs (ccTLDs), internationalized TLDs (IDN ccTLDs), and a special infrastructure TLD called *ARPA*.

Table 11-1   The generic top-level domains (gTLDs), circa 2011

TLD	First Use (est.)	Use	Example
AERO	December 21, 2001	Air-transport industry	www.sita.aero
ARPA	January 1, 1985	Infrastructure	18.in-addr.arpa
ASIA	May 2, 2007	Pan-Asia and Asia Pacific	www.seo.asia
BIZ	June 26, 2001	Business uses	neustar.biz
CAT	December 19, 2005	Catalan linguistic/cultural community	www.domini.cat
COM	January 1, 1985	Generic	icanhascheezburger.com
COOP	December 15, 2001	Cooperative associations	www.ems.coop
EDU	January 1, 1985	Post-secondary educational institutions recognized by U.S.A.	hpu.edu
GOV	January 1, 1985	U.S. government	whitehouse.gov
INFO	June 25, 2001	Generic	germany.info
INT	November 3, 1988	International treaty organizations	nato.int
JOBS	September 8, 2005	Human resource managers	intel.jobs
MIL	January 1, 1985	U.S. military	dtic.mil
MOBI	October 30, 2005	Customers/providers of mobile products/services	flowers.mobi
MUSEUM	October 30, 2001	Museums	icom.museum
NAME	August 16, 2001	Individuals	www.name
NET	January 1, 1985	Generic	ja.net
ORG	December 9, 2002	Generic	slashdot.org
PRO	May 6, 2002	Credentialed professionals/entities	nic.pro
TEL	March 1, 2007	Contact data for businesses/individuals	telnic.tel
TRAVEL	July 27, 2005	Travel industry	cancun.travel
XXX	April 15, 2011	Adult entertainment industry	whois.nic.xxx

The ccTLDs include the two-letter country codes specified by the ISO 3166 standard [ISO3166], plus five that are not: uk, su, ac, eu, and tp (the last one is being phased out). Because some of these two-letter codes are suggestive of other uses and meanings, various countries have been able to find commercial windfalls from selling names within their ccTLDs. For example, the domain name cnn.tv is really a registration in the Pacific island of Tuvalu, which has been selling domain names associated with the television entertainment industry. Creating a name in such an unconventional way is sometimes called a *domain hack*.

11.2.1 DNS Naming Syntax

The names below a TLD in the DNS name tree are further partitioned into groups known as *subdomains*. This is very common practice, especially for the ccTLDs. For example, most educational sites in England use the suffix .ac.uk, whereas names for most for-profit companies there end in the suffix .co.uk. In the United States, city government Web sites tend to use the subdomain ci.*city*.*state*.us where *state* is the two-letter abbreviation for the name of the state and *city* is the name of the city. For example, the site www.ci.manhattan-beach.ca.us is the site of Manhattan Beach, California's, city government in the United States.

The example names we have seen so far are known as fully qualified domain names (FQDNs). They are sometimes written more formally with a trailing period (e.g., mit.edu.). This trailing period indicates that the name is complete; no additional information should be added to the name when performing a name resolution. In contrast to the FQDN, an *unqualified domain name*, which is used in combination with a default domain or domain search list set during system configuration, has one or more strings appended to the end. When a system is configured (see Chapter 6), it is typically assigned a default domain extension and search list using DHCP (or, less commonly, the RDNSS and DNSSL RA options). For example, the default domain cs.berkeley.edu might be configured in systems at the computer science department at UC Berkeley. If a user on one of these machines types in the name vangogh, the local resolver software converts this name to the FQDN vangogh.cs.berkeley.edu. before invoking a resolver to determine vangogh's IP address.

A domain name consists of a sequence of *labels* separated by periods. The name represents a location in the name hierarchy, where the period is the hierarchy delimiter and descending down the tree takes place from right to left in the name. For example, the FQDN

```
www.net.in.tum.de.
```

contains a host name label (www) in a four-level-deep domain (net.in.tum.de). Starting from the root, and working from right to left in the name, the TLD is de (the ccTLD for Germany), tum is shorthand for Technische Universität München, in is shorthand for *informatik* (German for "computer science"), and finally net is shorthand for the networks group within the computer science department. Labels are case-insensitive for matching purposes, so the name ACME.COM is equivalent to acme.com or AcMe.cOm [RFC4343]. Each label can be up to 63 characters long, and an entire FQDN is limited to at most 255 (1-byte) characters. For example, this domain name:

```
thelongestdomainnameintheworldandthensomeandthensomemoreandmore.com
```

was allegedly submitted as a potential world record for the longest name, with a label of length 63, but was judged to have been of insufficient merit to justify a place in the Guinness World Records.

The hierarchical structure of the DNS name space allows different administrative authorities to manage different parts of the name space. For example, creating a new DNS name of the form `elevator.cs.berkeley.edu` would likely require dealing with the owner of the `cs.berkeley.edu` subdomain only. The `berkeley` `.edu` and `edu` portions of the name space would not require alteration, so the owners of those would not need to be bothered. This feature of DNS is one key aspect of its *scalability*. That is, no single entity is required to administer all the changes for the entire DNS name space. Indeed, creating a hierarchical structure for names was one of the first responses in the Internet community to the pressures of scaling and a major motivator for the structure used today. The original Internet naming scheme was flat (i.e., no hierarchy), and a single entity was responsible for assigning, maintaining, and distributing the list of nonconflicting names. Over time, as more names were required and more changes were being made, this approach became unworkable [MD88].

11.3 Name Servers and Zones

Management responsibility for portions of the DNS name space is assigned to individuals or organizations. A person given responsibility for managing part of the active DNS name space (one or more domains) is supposed to arrange for at least two *name servers* or *DNS servers* to hold information about the name space so that users of the Internet can perform queries on the names. The collection of servers forms the DNS (service) itself, a distributed system whose primary job is to provide name-to-address mappings. However, it can also provide a wide array of additional information.

The unit of administrative delegation, in the language of DNS servers, is called a *zone*. A zone is a subtree of the DNS name space that can be administered separately from other zones. Every domain name exists within some zone, even the TLDs that exist in the *root zone*. Whenever a new record is added to a zone, the DNS administrator for the zone allocates a name and additional information (usually an IP address) for the new entry and enters these into the name server's database. At a small campus, for example, one person could do this each time a new server is added to the network, but in a large enterprise the responsibility would have to be delegated (probably by departments or other organizational units), as one person likely could not keep up with the work.

A DNS server can contain information for more than one zone. At any hierarchical change point in a domain name (i.e., wherever a period appears), a different zone and containing server may be accessed to provide information for the name. This is called a *delegation*. A common delegation approach uses a zone for implementing a second-level domain name, such as `berkeley.edu`. In this domain, there may be individual hosts (e.g., `www.berkeley.edu`) or other domains (e.g., `cs.berkeley.edu`). Each zone has a designated owner or responsible party who is given authority to manage the names, addresses, and subordinate zones within the zone. Often this person manages not only the contents of the zone but also the name servers that contain the zone's database(s).

Zone information is supposed to exist in at least two places, implying that there should be at least two servers containing information for each zone. This is for redundancy; if one server is not functioning properly, at least one other server is available. All of these servers contain identical information about a zone. Typically, among the servers, a *primary* server contains the zone database in a disk file, and one or more *secondary* servers obtain copies of the database in its entirety from the primary using a process called a *zone transfer*. DNS has a special protocol for performing zone transfers, but copies of a zone's contents can also be obtained using other means (e.g., the `rsync` utility [RSYNC]).

11.4 Caching

Name servers contain information such as name-to-IP-address mappings that may be obtained from three sources. The name server obtains the information directly from the zone database, as the result of a zone transfer (e.g., for a slave server), or from another server in the course of processing a resolution. In the first case, the server is said to contain *authoritative* information about the zone and may be called an *authoritative server* for the zone. Such servers are identified by name within the zone information.

Most name servers (except some of the root and TLD servers) also *cache* zone information they learn, up to a time limit called the *time to live* (TTL). They use this cached information to answer queries. Doing so can greatly decrease the amount of DNS message traffic that would otherwise be carried on the Internet [J02]. When answering a query, a server indicates whether the information it is returning has been derived from its cache or from its authoritative copy of the zone. When cached information is returned, it is common for a server to also include the domain names of the name servers that can be contacted to retrieve authoritative information about the corresponding zone.

As we shall see, each DNS record (e.g., name-to-IP-address mapping) has its own TTL that controls how long it can be cached. These values are set and altered by the zone administrator when necessary. The TTL dictates how long a mapping can be cached anywhere within DNS, so if a zone changes, there still may exist cached data within the network, potentially leading to incorrect DNS resolution behavior until expiry of the TTL. For this reason, some zone administrators, anticipating a change to the zone contents, first reduce the TTL before implementing the change. Doing so reduces the window for incorrect cached data to be present in the network.

It is worth mentioning that caching is applied both for successful resolutions and for unsuccessful resolutions (called *negative caching*). If a request for a particular domain name fails to return a record, this fact is also cached. Doing so can help to reduce Internet traffic when errant applications repeatedly make requests for names that do not exist. Negative caching was changed from optional to mandatory by [RFC2308].

In some network configurations (e.g., those using older UNIX-compatible systems), the cache is maintained in a nearby name server, not in the resolvers resident in the clients. Placing the cache in the server allows any hosts on the LAN that use the nearby server to benefit from the server's cache but implies a small delay in accessing the cache over the local network. In Windows and more recent systems (e.g., Linux), the client can maintain a cache, and it is made available to all applications running on the same system. In Windows, this happens by default, and in Linux, it is a service that can be enabled or disabled.

On Windows, the local system's cache parameters may be modified by editing the following registry entry:

```
HKLM\SYSTEM\CurrentControlSet\Services\DNSCache\Parameters
```

The DWORD value `MaxNegativeCacheTtl` gives the maximum number of seconds that a negative DNS result remains in the resolver cache. The DWORD value `MaxCacheTtl` gives the maximum number of seconds that a DNS record may remain in the resolver cache. If this value is less than the TTL of a received DNS record, the lesser value controls how long the record remains in cache. These two registry keys do not exist by default, so they must be created in order to be used.

In Linux and other systems that support it, the *Name Service Caching Daemon* (NSCD) provides a client-side caching capability. It is controlled by the `/etc/nscd.conf` file that can indicate which types of resolutions (for DNS and some other services) are cached, along with some cache parameters such as TTL settings. In addition, the file `/etc/nsswitch.conf` controls how name resolution for applications takes place. Among other things, it can control whether local files, the DNS protocol (see Section 11.5), and/or NSCD is employed for mappings.

11.5 The DNS Protocol

The DNS protocol consists of two main parts: a query/response protocol used for performing queries against the DNS for particular names, and another protocol for name servers to exchange database records (zone transfers). It also has a way to notify secondary servers that the zone database has evolved and a zone transfer is necessary (DNS Notify), and a way to dynamically update the zone (dynamic updates). By far, the most typical usage is a simple query/response to look up the IPv4 address that corresponds to a domain name.

Most often, DNS name resolution is the process of mapping a domain name to an IPv4 address, although IPv6 addresses mappings work in essentially the same way. DNS query/response operations are supported over the distributed DNS infrastructure consisting of servers deployed locally at each site or ISP, and a special set of *root servers*. There is also a special set of *generic top-level domain servers* used for scaling some of the larger gTLDs, including COM and NET. As of mid-2011, there are 13 root servers named by the letters *A* through *M* (see [ROOTS] for more information about them); 9 of them have IPv6 addresses. There are also 13 gTLD servers, also labeled *A* through *M*; 2 of them have IPv6 addresses. By contacting a root server and possibly a gTLD server, the name server for any TLD in the Internet can be discovered. These servers are mutually coordinated to provide the same information. Some of them are not a single physical server but instead a group of servers (over 50 for the *J* root server) that use the same IP address (i.e., using IP anycast addressing; see Chapter 2).

A full resolution that is unable to benefit from preexisting cached entries takes place among several entities, as shown in Figure 11-2.

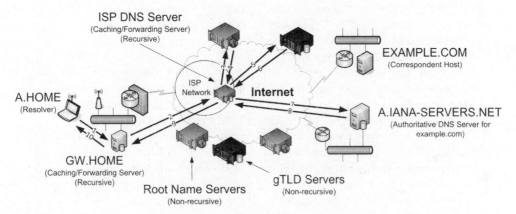

Figure 11-2 A typical recursive DNS query for EXAMPLE.COM from A.HOME involves up to ten messages. The local recursive server (GW.HOME here) uses a DNS server provided by its ISP. That server, in turn, uses an Internet root name server and a gTLD server (for COM and NET TLDs) to find the name server for the EXAMPLE.COM domain. That name server (A.IANA-SERVERS.NET here) provides the required IP address for the host EXAMPLE.COM. All of the recursive servers cache any information learned for later use.

Here, we have a laptop called A.HOME residing nearby the DNS server GW.HOME. The domain HOME is private, so it is not known to the Internet—only locally at the user's residence. When a user on A.HOME wishes to connect to the host EXAMPLE.COM (e.g., because a Web browser has been instructed to access the page http://EXAMPLE.COM), A.HOME must determine the IP address for the server EXAMPLE.COM. Assuming it does not know this address already (it might if it has accessed the host recently), the resolver software on A.HOME first makes a request to its local name server, GW.HOME. This is a request to convert the name EXAMPLE.COM into an address and constitutes message 1 (labeled on an arrow in Figure 11-2).

Note

If the A.HOME system is configured with a default domain search list, there may be additional queries. For example, if .HOME is a default search domain used by A.HOME, the first DNS query may be for the name EXAMPLE.COM.HOME, which will fail at the GW.HOME name server, which is authoritative for .HOME. A subsequent query will typically remove the default extension, resulting in a query for EXAMPLE.COM.

If GW.HOME does not already know the IP address for EXAMPLE.COM or the name servers for either the EXAMPLE.COM domain or the COM TLD, it forwards the request to another DNS server (called *recursion*). In this case, a request (message 2) goes to an ISP-provided DNS server. Assuming that this server also does not know the required address or other information, it contacts one of the root name servers (message 3). The root servers are not recursive, so they do not process the request further but instead return the information required to contact a name server for the COM TLD. For example, it might return the name A.GTLD-SERVERS .NET and one or more of its IP addresses (message 4). With this information, the ISP-provided server contacts the gTLD server (message 5) and discovers the name and IP addresses of the name servers for the domain EXAMPLE.COM (message 6). In this case, one of the servers is A.IANA-SERVERS.NET.

Given the correct server for the domain, the ISP-provided server contacts the appropriate server (message 7), which responds with the requested IP address (message 8). At this point, the ISP-provided server can respond to GW.HOME with the required information (message 9). GW.HOME is now able to complete the initial query and responds to the client with the desired IPv4 and/or IPv6 address(es) (message 10).

From the perspective of A.HOME, the local name server was able to perform the request. However, what really happened is a *recursive query*, where the GW.HOME and ISP-provided servers in turn made additional DNS requests to satisfy A.HOME's query. In general, most name servers perform recursive queries such as this. The notable exceptions are the root servers and other TLD servers that do not perform recursive queries. These servers are a relatively precious resource, so encumbering them with recursive queries for every machine that performs a DNS query would lead to poor global Internet performance.

11.5.1   DNS Message Format

There is one basic DNS message format [RFC6195]. It is used for all DNS operations (queries, responses, zone transfers, notifications, and dynamic updates), as illustrated in Figure 11-3.

The basic DNS message begins with a fixed 12-byte header followed by four variable-length *sections*: questions (or queries), answers, authority records, and additional records. All but the first section contain one or more *resource records*

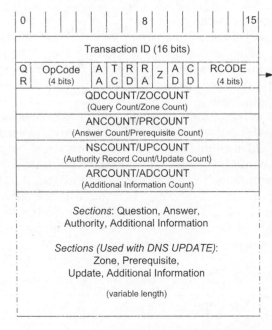

							8							15

Figure 11-3   The DNS message format has a fixed 12-byte header. The entire message is usually carried in a UDP/IPv4 datagram and limited to 512 bytes. DNS UPDATE (DNS with dynamic updates) uses the field names *ZOCOUNT*, *PRCOUNT*, *UPCOUNT*, and *ADCOUNT*. A special extension format (called EDNS0) allows messages to be larger than 512 bytes, which is required for DNSSEC (see Chapter 18).

(RRs), which we discuss in detail in Section 11.5.6. (The question section contains a data item that is very close in structure to an RR.) RRs can be cached; questions are not.

In the fixed-length header, the *Transaction ID* field is set by the client and returned by the server. It lets the client match responses to requests. The second 16-bit word includes a number of flags and other subfields. Beginning from the left-most bit, *QR* is a 1-bit field: 0 means the message is a query; 1 means it is a response. The next is the *OpCode*, a 4-bit field. The normal value is 0 (a standard query) for requests and responses. Other values are: 4 (notify), and 5 (update). Other values (1–3) are deprecated or never seen in operational use. Next is the *AA* bit field that indicates an "authoritative answer" (as opposed to a cached answer). *TC* is a 1-bit field that means "truncated." With UDP, this flag being set means that the total size of the reply exceeded 512 bytes, and only the first 512 bytes of the reply were returned.

RD is a bit field that means "recursion desired." It can be set in a query and is then returned in the response. It tells the server to perform a recursive query. If the bit is not set, and the requested name server does not have an authoritative answer, the requested name server returns a list of other name servers to contact for the answer. At this point, the overall query may be continued by contacting the list of other name servers. This is called an *iterative query*. *RA* is a bit field that means "recursion available." This bit is set in the response if the server supports recursion. Root servers generally do *not* support recursion, thereby forcing clients to perform iterative queries to complete name resolution. The *Z* bit field must be 0 for now but is reserved for future use.

The *AD* bit field is set to true if the contained information is *authenticated*, and the *CD* bit is set to true if security checking is disabled (see Chapter 18). The *Response Code* (or *RCODE*) field is a 4-bit field with the return code whose possible values are given in [DNSPARAM]. The common values include 0 (no error) and 3 (name error or "nonexistent domain," written as NXDOMAIN). A list of the first 11 error codes is given in Table 11-2 (values 11 through 15 are unassigned). Additional types are defined using a special extension (see Section 11.5.2). A name error is returned only from an authoritative name server and means that the domain name specified in the query does not exist.

Table 11-2   The first ten error types used with the *RCODE* field

Value	Name	Reference	Description and Purpose
0	NoError	[RFC1035]	No error
1	FormErr	[RFC1035]	Format error; query cannot be interpreted
2	ServFail	[RFC1035]	Server failure; error in processing at server
3	NXDomain	[RFC1035]	Nonexistent domain; unknown domain referenced
4	NotImp	[RFC1035]	Not implemented; request not supported in server
5	Refused	[RFC1035]	Refused; server unwilling to provide answer
6	YXDomain	[RFC2136]	Name exists but should not (used with updates)
7	YXRRSet	[RFC2136]	RRSet exists but should not (used with updates)
8	NXRRSet	[RFC2136]	RRSet does not exist but should (used with updates)
9	NotAuth	[RFC2136]	Server not authorized for zone (used with updates)
10	NotZone	[RFC2136]	Name not contained in zone (used with updates)

The next four fields are 16 bits in size and specify the number of entries in the question, answer, authority, and additional information sections that complete the DNS message. For a query, the number of questions is normally 1 and the other three counts are 0. For a reply, the number of answers is at least 1. Questions have a name, type, and class. (Class supports non-Internet records, but we ignore this for our purposes. The type identifies the type of object being looked up.) All of the other sections contain zero or more RRs. RRs contain a name, type, and class information, but also the TTL value that controls how long the data can be cached. We shall discuss the most important RR types in detail once we have a look at how DNS encodes names and selects which transport protocol to use when carrying DNS messages.

11.5.1.1 Names and Labels

The variable-length sections at the end of a DNS message contain a collection of questions, answers, authority information (names of name servers that contain authoritative information for certain data), and additional information that may be useful to reduce the number of necessary queries. Each question and each RR begins with a *name* (called the domain name or owning name) to which it refers. Each name consists of a sequence of *labels*. There are two categories of label types: *data labels* and *compression labels*. Data labels contain characters that constitute a label; compression labels act as pointers to other labels. Compression labels help to save space in a DNS message when multiple copies of the same string of characters are present across multiple labels.

11.5.1.2 Data Labels

Each data label begins with a 1-byte count that specifies the number of bytes that immediately follow. The name is terminated with a byte containing the value 0, which is a label with a length of 0 (the label of the root). For example, the encoding of the name www.pearson.com would be as shown in Figure 11-4.

Figure 11-4 DNS names are encoded as a sequence of labels. This example encodes the name www. pearson.com, which (technically) has four labels. The end of the name is identified by a 0-length label of the nameless root.

For data labels, each label *Length* byte must be in the range of 0 to 63, as labels are limited to 63 bytes. No padding is used for labels, so the total name length could be odd. Although these labels are sometimes called "text" labels, they are capable of containing non-ASCII values. This use, however, is uncommon and not recommended. Indeed, even the internationalized domain names, which can encode Unicode characters [RFC5890][RFC5891], use a curious encoding syntax called "punycode" [RFC3492] that expresses Unicode characters using the ASCII character set. To be completely safe, it is recommended to follow the requirements in [RFC1035], which suggest that labels "start with a letter, end with a letter or digit, and have as interior characters only letters, digits and hyphen."

11.5.1.3 Compression Labels

In many cases, a DNS response carries information in the answer, authority, and additional information sections relating to the same domain name. If data labels were used, the same characters would be repeated in the DNS message when referring to the same name. To avoid this redundancy and save space, a compression scheme is used. Anywhere the label portion of a domain name can occur, the single preceding count byte (which is normally between 0 and 63) instead has its 2 high-order bits turned on, and the remaining bits are combined with the bits in the subsequent byte to form a 14-bit pointer (offset) in the DNS message. The offset gives the number of bytes from the beginning of the DNS message where a data label (called the *compression target*) is to be found that should be substituted for the compression label. Compression labels are thus able to point to a location up to 16,383 bytes from the beginning. Figure 11-5 illustrates how we might encode the domain names `usc.edu` and `ucla.edu` using compression labels.

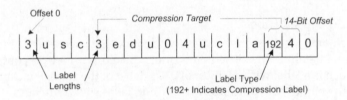

Figure 11-5   A compression label can reference other labels to save space. This is accomplished by setting the 2 high-order bits of the byte preceding the label contents. This signals that the following 14 bits are used in providing an offset for the replacement label. In this example, `usc.edu` and `ucla.edu` share the `edu` label.

In Figure 11-5 we see how the common label `edu` can be shared by the two domain names. Assuming the names start at offset 0, data labels are used to encode `usc.edu` as described previously. The next name is `ucla.edu`, and the label `ucla` is encoded using a data label. However, the label `edu` may be reused from the encoding of `usc.edu`. This is accomplished by setting the 2 high-order bits of the label *Type* byte to 1 and encoding the offset of `edu` in the remaining 14 bits. Because the first occurrence of `edu` is at offset 4, we only need to set the first byte to 192 (6 bits of 0) and the next byte to 4. The example in Figure 11-5 shows a savings of only 4 bytes, but it is clear how compression of larger common labels can result in more substantial savings.

11.5.2 The DNS Extension Format (EDNS0)

The basic DNS message format described so far can be restrictive in a number of ways. It has fixed-length fields, a total length limitation of 512 bytes when used with UDP (not including UDP or IP headers), and limited space (the 4-bit *RCODE* field) for indicating error types. An extension mechanism called *EDNS0* (because there could be future extensions beyond the index 0) is specified in [RFC2671]. While its use is not ubiquitous at present, it is necessary for supporting DNS security (DNSSEC; see Chapter 18), so it is likely to receive more widespread deployment over time.

EDNS0 specifies a particular type of RR (called an *OPT pseudo-RR* or *meta-RR*) that is added to the additional data section of a request or response to indicate the use of EDNS0. At most one such record may be present in any DNS message. We will discuss the particular format of an OPT pseudo-RR when we discuss the other RR types in Section 11.5.6. For now, the important thing to note is that if a UDP DNS message includes an OPT RR, it is permitted to exceed the 512-byte length limitation and may contain an expanded set of error codes.

EDNS0 also defines an extended label type (extending beyond the data labels and compression labels mentioned earlier). Extended labels have their first 2 bits in the label *Type/Length* byte set to 01, corresponding to values between 64 and 127 (inclusive). An experimental binary labeling scheme (type 65) was used at one time but is now not recommended. The value 127 is reserved for future use, and values above 127 are unallocated.

11.5.3 UDP or TCP

The well-known port number for DNS is 53, for both UDP and TCP. The most common format uses the UDP/IPv4 datagram structure shown in Figure 11-6.

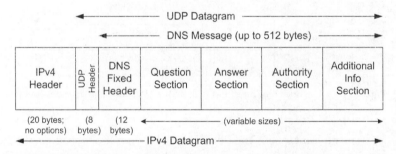

Figure 11-6   DNS messages are typically encapsulated in a UDP/IPv4 datagram and are limited to 512 bytes in size unless TCP and/or EDNS0 is used. Each section (except the question section) contains a set of resource records.

When a resolver issues a query and the response comes back with the *TC* bit field set ("truncated"), the size of the true response exceeded 512 bytes, so only the first 512 bytes are returned by the server. The resolver may issue the request again, using TCP, which now must be a supported configuration [RFC5966]. This allows more than 512 bytes to be returned because TCP breaks up large messages into multiple segments.

When a secondary name server for a zone starts up, it normally performs a zone transfer from the primary name server for the zone. Zone transfers can also be initiated by a timer or as a result of a DNS NOTIFY message (see Section 11.5.8.3). Full zone transfers use TCP as they can be large. Incremental zone transfers, where only the updated entries are transferred, may use UDP at first but switch to TCP if the response is too large, just like a conventional query.

When UDP is used, both the resolver and the server application software must perform their own timeout and retransmission. A recommendation for how to do this is given in [RFC1536]. It suggests starting with a timeout of at least 4s, and that subsequent timeouts result in an exponential increase of the timeout (a bit like TCP's algorithms; see Chapter 14). Linux and UNIX-like systems allow a change to be made to the retransmission timeout parameters by altering the contents of the /etc/resolv.conf file (by setting the timeout and attempts options).

11.5.4 Question (Query) and Zone Section Format

The question or query section of a DNS message lists the question(s) being referenced. The format of each question in the question section is shown in Figure 11-7. There is normally just one, although the protocol can support more. The same structure is also used for the zone section in dynamic updates (see Section 11.5.7), but with different names.

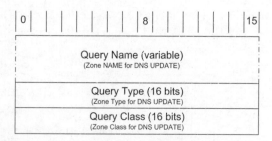

Figure 11-7 The query (or question) section of a DNS message does not contain a TTL because it is not cached.

The *Query Name* is the domain name being looked up, using the encoding for labels we described before. Each question has a *Query Type* and *Query Class*. The class value is 1, 254, or 255, indicating the Internet class, no class, or all classes, respectively, for all cases in which we are interested (other values are not typically used for TCP/IP networks). The *Query Type* field holds a value indicating the type of query being performed using the values from Table 11-2. The most common query type is A (or AAAA if IPv6 DNS resolution is enabled), which means that an IP address is desired for the query name. It is also possible to create a query of type ANY, which returns all RRs of any type in the same class that match the query name.

11.5.5 Answer, Authority, and Additional Information Section Formats

The final three sections in the DNS message, the answer, authority, and additional information sections, contain sets of RRs. RRs in these sections can, for the most part, have *wildcard* domain names as owning names. These are domain names in which the asterisk label—a data label containing only the asterisk character

[RFC4592]—appears first (i.e., leftmost). Each resource record has the form shown in Figure 11-8.

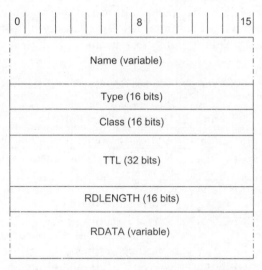

Figure 11-8   The format of a DNS resource record. For DNS in the Internet, the *Class* field always contains the value 1. The *TTL* field gives the maximum amount of time the RR can be cached (in seconds).

The *Name* field (sometimes called the "owning name," "owner," or "record owner's name") is the domain name to which the following resource data corresponds. It is in the same format we described earlier for names and labels. The *Type* field specifies one of the RR type codes (see Section 11.5.6). These are the same as the query type values we described earlier. The *Class* field is 1 for Internet data. The *TTL* field is the number of seconds for which the RR can be cached. The *Resource Data Length* (*RDLENGTH*) field specifies the number of bytes contained in the *Resource Data* (*RDATA*) field. The format of this data depends on the type. For example, A records (type 1) have a 32-bit IPv4 address in the RDATA area. We discuss other RR types later.

[RFC2181] defines the term *Resource Record Set* (RRSet) to be a set of resource records that share the same name, class, and type but not the same data. This occurs, for example, when a host has more than one address record for its name (e.g., because it has more than one IP address). TTLs for RRs in the same RRSet must be equal.

11.5.6 Resource Record Types

Although DNS is most commonly used to determine the IP address(es) that correspond to a particular name, it can also be used for the opposite purpose and for a number of other things. It can be used with both IPv4 and IPv6 and can even provide a distributed database function for other than Internet data (other classes, in DNS terminology [RFC6195]). The wide range of capabilities provided by DNS is largely attributable to its ability to have different types of resource records.

There are many types of resource records (see [DNSPARAMS] for the complete list), and a single name may have multiple matching RRs. Table 11-3 provides a listing of the most common RR types used with conventional DNS (i.e., DNS without the DNSSEC security extensions).

Table 11-3   The popular resource record and query types used in DNS protocol messages. Additional records (not shown) are used when DNS security (DNSSEC) is employed.

Value	RR Type	Reference	Description and Purpose
1	A	[RFC1035]	Address record for IPv4 (32-bit IPv4 address)
2	NS	[RFC1035]	Name server; provides name of authoritative name server for zone
5	CNAME	[RFC1035]	Canonical name; maps one name to another (to provide a form of name aliasing)
6	SOA	[RFC1035]	Start of authority; provides authoritative information for the zone (name servers, e-mail address of contact, serial number, zone transfer timers)
12	PTR	[RFC1035]	Pointer; provides address to (canonical) name mapping; used with `in-addr.arpa` and `ip6.arpa` domains for IPv4 and IPv6 reverse queries
15	MX	[RFC1035]	Mail exchanger; provides name of e-mail handling host for a domain
16	TXT	[RFC1035] [RFC1464]	Text; provides a variety of information (e.g., used with SPF anti-spam scheme to identify authorized e-mail servers)
28	AAAA	[RFC3596]	Address record for IPv6 (128-bit IPv6 address)
33	SRV	[RFC2782]	Server selection; transport endpoints of a generic service
35	NAPTR	[RFC3403]	Name authority pointer; supports alternative name spaces
41	OPT	[RFC2671]	Pseudo-RR; supports larger datagrams, labels, return codes in EDNS0
251	IXFR	[RFC1995]	Incremental zone transfer
252	AXFR	[RFC1035] [RFC5936]	Full zone transfer; carried over TCP
255	(ANY)	[RFC1035]	Request for all (any) records

Resource records are used for many purposes but can be divided into three broad categories: data types, query types, and meta types. Data types are used to convey information stored in the DNS such as IP addresses and the names of authoritative name servers. Query types use the same values as data types, with a few additional values (e.g., AXFR, IXFR, and *). They can be used in the question section we described previously. Meta types designate transient data associated with a particular single DNS message. The OPT RR is the only meta type we discuss in this chapter (all others are covered in Chapter 18). The most common data-type RRs include A, NS, SOA, MX, CNAME, PTR, TXT, AAAA, SRV, and NAPTR. The NS records are used to relate the DNS name space to the servers that perform resolution, and they contain the names of authoritative name servers for a zone. The A and AAAA records are used to provide an IPv4 or IPv6 address, respectively, given a particular name. The CNAME record provides a way to have an alias for another domain name. SRV and NAPTR records help applications to discover the location of servers supporting particular services, and to use alternative naming schemes (beyond DNS) to access such services. We shall explore each of these record types in the following sections.

11.5.6.1 Address (A, AAAA) and Name Server (NS) Records

Arguably, the most important records within DNS are the address (A, AAAA) and name server (NS) records. The A records contain 32-bit IPv4 addresses, and AAAA (called "quad-A") records contain IPv6 addresses. An NS record contains the name of an authoritative DNS server that contains information for a particular zone. Because the name of a DNS server alone is not sufficient to perform a query, the IP address(es) of these servers is also typically provided as a so-called glue record in the additional information section of DNS responses. Indeed, such glue records are required to avoid loops whenever the names of the authoritative name servers use the same domain name for which they are authoritative. (Consider how ns1. example.com would be resolved if the name server for example.com was ns1. example.com.) We can see the structure of A, AAAA, and NS records using the dig tool provided on most Linux/UNIX-like systems. Here, we make a request for records of any type associated with the domain name rfc-editor.org:

```
Linux% dig +nostats -t ANY rfc-editor.org

; <<>> DiG 9.6.0-P1 <<>> +nostats -t ANY rfc-editor.org
;; global options: +cmd
;; Got answer:
;; ->>HEADER<<- opcode: QUERY, status: NOERROR, id: 53052
;; flags: qr rd ra; QUERY: 1, ANSWER: 12, AUTHORITY: 0, ADDITIONAL: 2

;; QUESTION SECTION:
;rfc-editor.org.    IN ANY

;; ANSWER SECTION:
...
rfc-editor.org.   1654 IN AAAA 2001:1890:1112:1::2f
rfc-editor.org.   1654 IN A 64.170.98.47
rfc-editor.org.   1654 IN NS ns0.ietf.org.
rfc-editor.org.   1654 IN NS ns1.hkg1.afilias-nst.info.
...
;; ADDITIONAL SECTION:
ns0.ietf.org.      756   IN    A     64.170.98.2
ns0.ietf.org.      756   IN    AAAA  2001:1890:1112:1::14
```

In the command's output, the first two lines indicate the version of the dig program being used and the options provided to it, plus implied options (+cmd means that this information itself should be printed). The next portion indicates data in the DNS reply message: the QUERY opcode, NOERROR status indicating no errors were encountered, and a transaction ID of 53052. In the *OpCode* field, QUERY is used for both queries and responses. Next, the flags line indicates that the message is a query response (qr flag) and not a query and that recursion was desired in the original query (rd flag) and is provided by the responding server (ra flag). The message contains a section with one query, and 12 resource records in the answer section (only 4 are shown). There are no RRs in the authority section, meaning that this response is likely from a caching server (the RRs are not authoritative). Different results might be obtained by interacting with different servers. The additional information section contains IPv4 and IPv6 addresses for one of the authoritative servers, should we wish to contact it. The question section contains a copy of our original query: type ANY for domain name rfc-editor.org.

Among the four RRs in the answer section shown, we find one A type, one AAAA type, and two NS types. From this information we can see that the domain name rfc-editor.org is a host with IPv4 address 64.170.98.47 and IPv6 address 2001:1890:1112:1::2f. It is also a subdomain, as indicated by the presence of the NS records. We can quickly guess and verify that there is at least one host in this subdomain using the following command:

```
Linux% host ftp.rfc-editor.org
ftp.rfc-editor.org has address 64.170.98.47
```

This example indicates a few interesting aspects of A, AAAA, and NS records. First, it is possible for a single domain name to have records of each of these types (and more). This is fairly common for IPv6-capable servers that are the "well-known" servers for a particular organization. We can also see that each record has a TTL value, and they differ considerably, except for those in the same RRSet. The TTL for the records in the answer section is 1654s (about half an hour), and the TTL for records in the additional information section is 756s (about 12 minutes). Note that the TTL value of a cached record is never more than the TTL of the same record retrieved from the authoritative source. TTLs for cached records "decay" until the record is retrieved again from an authoritative server. As a result, retrieving a cached record multiple times from the same server usually shows a decreasing TTL value.

11.5.6.2 Example

Now that we have seen the DNS message format, transport protocol options, and RR types for basic queries and responses, let us see an example. We start with a simple case to see the communication between a resolver on a client, a local name server, and a remote name server managed by an ISP. This scenario demonstrates the importance of caching in DNS. The topology is shown in Figure 11-9.

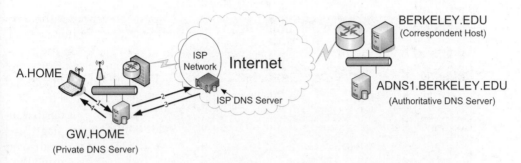

Figure 11-9   A simple DNS query/response example. The local DNS server (GW.HOME) provides recursion to the client (A.HOME), and uses the DNS server provided at the ISP when requested data is not present in the cache.

On our Windows client (A.HOME) we begin with a command that removes any DNS data cached by the resolver libraries. We then perform a query for the address (A record type) of the domain name berkeley.edu:

```
C:\> ipconfig /flushdns
Windows IP Configuration

Successfully flushed the DNS Resolver Cache.

C:\> nslookup
Default Server:  gw
Address:   10.0.0.1

> set type=a
> berkeley.edu.
Server:  gw
Address:   10.0.0.1

Non-authoritative answer:
Name:     berkeley.edu
Address:   169.229.131.81
```

The first command is specific to Windows and removes data cached by the client's resolver software. The nslookup program, available on both Windows and Linux/UNIX-based systems, provides a basic way to query the DNS for specific data. Upon execution, it indicates which name server it is using for resolution (here the server is gw at the address 10.0.0.1). Using the set command, we arrange to query for A records, and then query for the name berkeley.edu.. Once again, nslookup indicates which server it uses for the resolution. It then also gives us an indication that the answer is nonauthoritative (i.e., it is being provided by a caching server) and the requested address is 169.229.131.81.

To see what happens with the DNS protocol at the packet level, we use Wireshark and have a look at the first packet in detail, as shown in Figure 11-10.

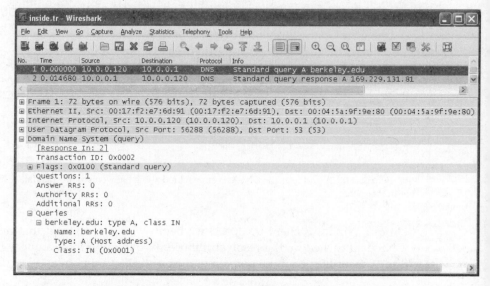

Figure 11-10 A UDP/IPv4 datagram containing a DNS standard query for the IPv4 address associated with `berkeley.edu`..

There are two messages in the trace: a standard query and a standard query response. In the first message (the query), the source IPv4 address is 10.0.0.120 (a DHCP-assigned address at the client; see Chapter 6), and the destination is 10.0.0.1 (the DNS server). The query is a UDP/IPv4 datagram with source port 56288 (an ephemeral port) and destination port 53 (the well-known DNS port). In terms of its full encapsulation, the request is an Ethernet frame containing 72 bytes. This size can be derived by summing the following parts: Ethernet header (14 bytes), IPv4 header (20 bytes), UDP header (8 bytes), DNS fixed header (12 bytes), query type (2 bytes), query class (2 bytes), plus the data labels for `berkeley` (9 bytes) and `edu` (4 bytes), plus the trailing 0 byte.

Turning to the details of the DNS header, the transaction ID is 0x0002 and forms the first 2 bytes of the DNS header, located at the start of the UDP payload. Only a single flag (recursion requested, the default) is set, so this message is a query. The message contains a standard query with one question. The other sections are empty. The question itself is for the name `berkeley.edu` and is seeking information of type A (address records) in the IN (Internet) class. After receiving this message, the name server process running on 10.0.0.1, unable to directly respond because it does not know the address, forwards the query to the next (upstream) name server it is configured to use. In this particular case, that name server is at the address 206.13.28.12 (see Figure 11-11).

In Figure 11-11 we see a query similar to the one sent by the client, but in this case the source IPv4 address is 70.231.136.162 (the ISP-side IPv4 address of `GW.HOME`). The destination address is 206.13.28.12, the IPv4 address of the ISP-provided DNS server, and the source port is an ephemeral port on the local DNS server (60961).

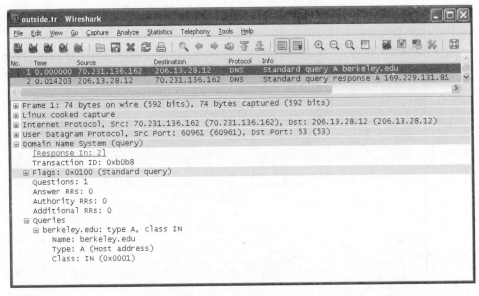

Figure 11-11 A DNS request generated at GW.HOME being sent to the ISP name server as a consequence of recursion.

The transaction ID is generated anew and set to 0xb0b8. Note that Wireshark indicates that the response to the query is contained in packet number 2.

Packet 2 in Figure 11-12 is the first DNS response we have seen. First, we note that the UDP source port number is 53, but the destination port is the ephemeral port number 60961. The transaction ID matches the query (0xb0b8), but the *Flags* field now contains the value 0x8180 (response, recursion requested, and recursion available are all set). The question section contains a copy of the question for which answers are being provided and typically matches the original query sent by the client exactly (e.g., case is preserved). There is one RR in the answer section. It is of type A (address), has a TTL of 10 minutes and a data length of 4 bytes (the size of an IPv4 address), and the value is 169.229.131.81, the IPv4 address we requested for berkeley.edu. Note that the authority flag is *not* set, and the authority section of the reply is empty. This response is based upon cached data; it is not authoritative for the domain. At this point, the local name server also caches the value (but only for up to 10 minutes as specified by the TTL in the RR it received) and responds to the requesting client (see Figure 11-13).

The response in Figure 11-13, packet 2, is much like the one from 206.13.28.12, except it is now sent from 10.0.0.1 to our original client at 10.0.0.120, and the transaction ID matches the one in the original DNS request. Note also that from the client's point of view the entire round-trip time of the transaction was about 14.7ms, but we know that most of that time (14.2ms) was taken up in the transaction between the local name server (GW.HOME) and the ISP's name server (206.13.28.12).

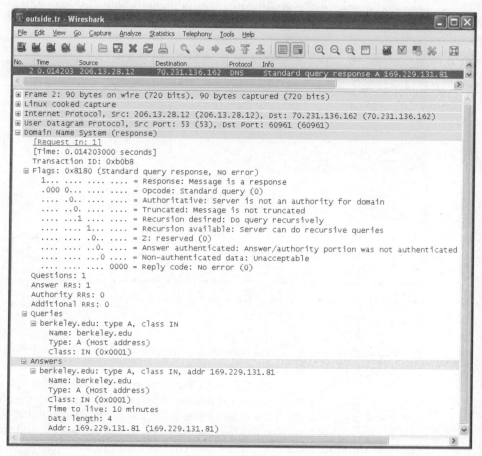

Figure 11-12   A standard DNS response sent from the ISP's DNS server back to GW.HOME.

11.5.6.3 Canonical Name (CNAME) Records

The CNAME record stands for *canonical name* record and is used to introduce an alias for a single domain name into the DNS naming system. For example, the name www.berkeley.edu may have a CNAME record that maps to some other machine (e.g., www.w3.berkeley.edu), so that if the Web server is located at a different computer, a relatively simple change to the DNS database may be all that is required for the rest of the world to find the new system. It is now common practice to use CNAME records to establish aliases for common services. As a result, names such as www.berkeley.edu, ftp.sun.com, mail.berkeley.edu, and www.ucsd.edu are all CNAME entries in the DNS that refer to other RRs.

Within a CNAME RR, the RDATA section contains the "canonical name" associated with the domain name (alias). Such names use the same type of encoding as other names (e.g., data labels and compression labels). When a CNAME RR is present for a particular name, no other data is permitted [RFC1912] (unless DNSSEC

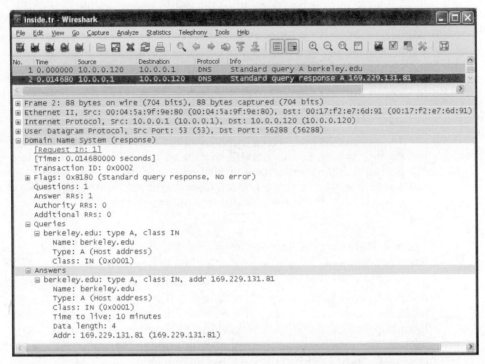

Figure 11-13 A response generated by GW.HOME and destined for the client. This message completes the recursive DNS transaction.

is in use; see Chapter 18). Domain names of CNAME RRs may not be used in all places that regular domain names can (e.g., as the target of an NS RR). Also, the canonical name may itself be a CNAME (called *CNAME chaining*), but this is usually discouraged, as it can cause DNS resolvers to make more queries than would otherwise be necessary. Nonetheless, there are certain services that make use of this feature. For example, the high-volume site www.whitehouse.gov (at the time of writing) uses a *content delivery network* (CDN)[2] provided by the Akamai Corporation. When we look up this domain name, we find the following:

```
Linux% host -t any www.whitehouse.gov
www.whitehouse.gov is an alias for www.whitehouse.gov.edgesuite.net.
Linux% host -t any www.whitehouse.gov.edgesuite.net
www.whitehouse.gov.edgesuite.net is an alias for a1128.h.akamai.net.
Linux% host -t any a1128.h.akamai.net
a1128.h.akamai.net has address 92.123.65.42
a1128.h.akamai.net has address 92.123.65.51
```

2. A content delivery network typically includes a number of synchronized content caches located in particular topological locations in the network. CDNs attempt to minimize latency for consumers accessing content in exchange for payment from content providers.

Thus, CNAME chains can be used with DNS. However, because of their potential performance impact, such chains are often limited by resolvers to a few "links" (such as five). Long chains are likely the result of an error in execution or a misunderstanding, as it is hard to imagine why they should be necessary under normal circumstances.

Note

There is a standard resource record called DNAME (type 39) [RFC2672][IDDN]. DNAME records act like CNAME records but for an entire zone. For example, all names of the form NAME.example.com could be mapped to NAME.newexample.com using a single DNAME resource record. However, DNAME records do not apply to the top-level record itself (example.com here).

11.5.6.4 Reverse DNS Queries: PTR (Pointer) Records

Although the most critical function of DNS is to provide mappings from names to IP addresses, there are many circumstances where the reverse mapping is required. For example, a server receiving an incoming TCP/IP connection request is able to ascertain the source IP address of the connection from the incoming IP datagram, but the name(s) corresponding to the address are not carried in the connection itself; such name(s) must be looked up in some other way. Fortunately, a clever use of the DNS can provide this capability.

The PTR RR type is used in response to reverse DNS queries, which are typically necessary when converting an IP address to a name. This uses the special in-addr.arpa (ip6.arpa for IPv6) domain, in a special way. Consider an IPv4 address such as 128.32.112.208. In the classful address structure (see Chapter 2), this address is taken from the 128.32 class B address space. To determine the name corresponding to this address, the address is first reversed, and then the special domain is added. In this example, a query for a PTR record using the name

```
208.112.32.128.in-addr.arpa.
```

would be used. In effect, this is a query for the "host" 208 in the "domain" 112.32.128.in-addr.arpa.. We shall see more examples of reverse DNS queries later in this section.

Note

The regular DNS name space, which usually uses NS, A, and AAAA records, is not automatically linked with the "reverse" name space supported by PTR records. Thus it is possible (and even relatively common) to have an existing forward resolution that does not have a corresponding reverse mapping set up (or has a different one). Some services check to see that both directions are set up with equivalent mappings and may deny service under such circumstances.

Recall that IPv4 addresses are typically written in the "dotted-decimal" format and IPv6 addresses are written in the hex format (e.g., 169.229.131.81 and 2001:503:a83e::2:30, respectively). These addresses can be thought of as names existing in a left-to-right hierarchy. For example, the address 169.229.131.81 has the top-down hierarchy (reading left to right) 169, 229, 131, 81. By reversing the dotted-decimal IPv4 address and treating it as a DNS name, we can employ DNS to perform the mapping from IP address to name(s). So, the name 81.131.229.169 would effectively be the reversal of the IPv4 address 169.229.131.81. For IPv6, the scheme is similar, but any suppressed zeros are expanded, and each hexadecimal digit becomes a character. For example, the reversal of 2001:503:a83e::2:30 would be 0.3.0.0.2.0.0.0.0.0.0.0.0.0.0.0.0.0.0.0.e.3.8.a.3.0.5.0.1.0.0.2. Fortunately, users rarely have to type in these names directly.

As mentioned previously, the special domains .in-addr.arpa (for IPv4) and .ip6.arpa (for IPv6) are used in conjunction with the PTR ("pointer") RR type in support of these types of names and reverse DNS lookups. For example, consider the following commands:

```
C:\> nslookup
Default Server:  gw
Address:  10.0.0.1
> server c.in-addr-servers.arpa
Default Server:  c.in-addr-servers.arpa
Address:  196.216.169.10
> set type=ptr
> 81.131.229.169.in-addr.arpa.
Server:  c.in-addr-servers.arpa
Address:  196.216.169.10

169.in-addr.arpa   nameserver = w.arin.net
169.in-addr.arpa   nameserver = t.arin.net
169.in-addr.arpa   nameserver = dill.arin.net
169.in-addr.arpa   nameserver = x.arin.net
169.in-addr.arpa   nameserver = z.arin.net
169.in-addr.arpa   nameserver = y.arin.net
169.in-addr.arpa   nameserver = u.arin.net
169.in-addr.arpa   nameserver = v.arin.net
```

This example shows how the .in-addr.arpa domain is set up. According to [RFC5855], the in-addr-servers.arpa and ip6-servers.arpa domains are used in forming the domain names associated with the servers that provide reverse DNS mappings for IPv4 and IPv6, respectively. As of 2011, there are five such servers for each version of IP: X.in-addr-servers.arpa and X.ip6-servers.arpa, where X is any letter a through f (inclusive).

Although the ten servers we have mentioned contain authoritative data for reverse mappings, they do not contain the information we are looking for. In our example, the first server contacted instead told us to contact one of the eight name servers maintained by ARIN, the American Registry for Internet Numbers, which is authoritative for IPv4 addresses that start with 169. If we in turn contact one

of these servers, we find that a PTR query for 81.131.229.169.in-addr.arpa.
gives the following response:

```
> server w.arin.net
Default Server: w.arin.net
Address: 72.52.71. 2
Default Server: w.arin.net
Address: 2001:470:1a::2
> 81.131.229.169.in-addr.arpa.
Server:  w.arin.net
Address: 72.52.71.2

229.169.in-addr.arpa nameserver = adns1.berkeley.edu.
229.169.in-addr.arpa nameserver = phloem.uoregon.edu.
229.169.in-addr.arpa nameserver = aodns1.berkeley.edu.
229.169.in-addr.arpa nameserver = adns2.berkeley.edu.
```

Here we can surmise that the network prefix 169.229/16 is owned by an educational institution called Berkeley, that the campus maintains three name servers covering its in-addr.arpa space, and that the University of Oregon also provides a copy. Continuing by contacting one of these servers, we find our answer (this time using the Linux version of nslookup with slightly different output):

```
Linux% nslookup
> set type=ptr
> server adns1.berkeley.edu
Default Server:  adns1.berkeley.edu
Address:  128.32.136.3#53
Default Server:  adns1.berkeley.edu
Address:  2607:f140:ffff:fffe::3#53
> 81.131.229.169.in-addr.arpa.
Server:  adns1.berkeley.edu
Address: 128.32.136.3#53

81.131.229.169.in-addr.arpa      name = webfarm.Berkeley.EDU
```

Here we obtain the result we were looking for, that the IPv4 address 169.229.131.81 has the name webfarm.Berkeley.EDU. The DNS server uses port 53, as indicated by the #53 following the IP addresses. This output makes it obvious that accessing the DNS with UDP/IPv4 (as opposed to UDP/IPv6) can still provide mappings for IPv6 addresses using "quad-A" (AAAA) DNS records because we can see that the IPv6 address of the server is 2607:f140:ffff:fffe::3.

If there were not a separate branch of the DNS tree for handling the address-to-name translation, there would be essentially no way to do the reverse translation other than starting at the root of the tree and trying every top-level domain. This is clearly an unreasonable option, given the current size of the Internet. The in-addr.arpa solution is effective and fairly efficient, although the reversed bytes of the IPv4/IPv6 address and the special domains can be confusing.

Fortunately, as mentioned before, users can typically avoid having to type or refer to them. Even application writers do not typically have to manipulate addresses to perform reverse queries, as library functions (such as the C library function `getnameinfo()`) perform this task.

It is worth mentioning here that PTR queries have become a significant concern for the global DNS servers. Consider a home network using one of the private address prefixes such as 10.0.0.0/8 (IPv4) or fc00:/7 (IPv6). When a system receives an incoming connection request from another system on the same privately addressed subnet, it may wish to resolve the source address to a name and does so by performing a PTR query. If the query is not answered by the local DNS server, it will likely propagate to the global Internet. For this reason (and a few others), [RFC6303] specifies that local name servers—especially those operating in networks using private IP addressing that are attached to the Internet—provide PTR mappings for the private address space defined in [RFC1918] for IPv4 and [RFC4193] for IPv6 (i.e., in IN-ADDR.ARPA and D.F.IP6.ARPA, respectively).

11.5.6.5 *Classless* in-addr.arpa *Delegation*

When organizations join the Internet and obtain authority to fill in a portion of the DNS name space, they often also obtain authority for a portion of the `in-addr.arpa` name space corresponding to their IPv4 addresses on the Internet. In the case of UC Berkeley, authority includes the network prefix 169.229/16, which, using older terminology, is "class B" network number 169.229. Thus, UC Berkeley would be expected to populate a portion of the DNS tree with PTR records using names ending in `229.169.in-addr.arpa`. This works fine for cases where the address prefix assigned to the organization is one of the older class A, B, or C styles where the number of bits is an integral multiple of 8. However, many organizations today are given prefix lengths of greater than 24 bits or greater than 16 bits (but less than 24). In these cases, the address range is not easily written as a simple reversal of the IP address. Instead, some method of conveying the network prefix length must be included as well.

The standard method for implementing this, given by [RFC2317], is to append the length of the prefix to the reversed octets and use it as the first label in the domain name. For example, assume that a site is assigned the prefix 12.17.136.128/25, a prefix that includes 128 addresses. According to [RFC2317], two types of records should be provided. First, for each name of the form *X*.`136.17.12.in-addr.arpa` (where *X* is at least 128 and not more than 255), a CNAME RR is created, likely maintained by a site's ISP, according to the following pattern:

```
128.136.17.12.in-addr.arpa. canonical name =
                            128.128/25.136.17.12.in-addr.arpa.
129.136.17.12.in-addr.arpa. canonical name =
                            129.128/25.136.17.12.in-addr.arpa.
...
255.136.17.12.in-addr.arpa. canonical name =
                            255.128/25.136.17.12.in-addr.arpa.
```

Here we can see how the network prefix is encoded, with the / notation associated with the second label in the domain name (for this example). These entries are typically placed by an ISP and allow for delegations on non-byte-aligned address ranges. In this example, the customer is now able to provide mappings for the zone 128.128/25.136.17.12.in-addr.arpa. We can trace the delegation as follows:

```
C:\> nslookup
Default Server:  gw
Address:  10.0.0.1
> server f.in-addr-servers.arpa
Default Server:  f.in-addr-servers.arpa
Addresses:  193.0.9.1
> set type=ptr
> 129.128/25.136.17.12.in-addr.arpa.
Server:  f.in-addr-servers.arpa
Address:  193.0.9.1
12.in-addr.arpa nameserver = dbru.br.ns.els-gms.att.net
12.in-addr.arpa nameserver = cbru.br.ns.els-gms.att.net
12.in-addr.arpa nameserver = cmtu.mt.ns.els-gms.att.net
12.in-addr.arpa nameserver = dmtu.mt.ns.els-gms.att.net
> server dbru.br.ns.els-gms.att.net.
Default Server:  dbru.br.ns.els-gms.att.net
Address:  199.191.128.106

> 129.128/25.136.17.12.in-addr.arpa.
128/25.136.17.12.in-addr.arpa    nameserver = ns2.intel-research.net
128/25.136.17.12.in-addr.arpa    nameserver= ns1.intel-research.net

> server ns1.intel-research.net.
Server:  ns1.intel-research.net
Address:  12.155.161.131
> 129.128/25.136.17.12.in-addr.arpa.

129.128/25.136.17.12.in-addr.arpa
                    name = dmz.slouter.seattle.intel-research.net
128/25.136.17.12.in-addr.arpa
            nameserver = bldmzsvr.berkeley.intel-research.net
128/25.136.17.12.in-addr.arpa
            nameserver = sldmzsvr.intel-research.net
bldmzsvr.berkeley.intel-research.net internet address = 12.155.161.131
sldmzsvr.intel-research.net internet address = 12.17.136.131
```

In this example, we wish to find out the name for the host associated with IPv4 address 12.17.136.129. We have already seen that it has a CNAME RR pointing to the canonical name 129.128/25.136.17.12.in-addr.arpa.. We instruct our resolver to use one of the root servers (F) and arrange for the query type to be for a PTR RR. At this point we request a resolution for 129.128/25.136.17.12.in-addr.arpa.. The root name server does not have this information, and it does not perform recursion, so it returns the name of the authoritative servers for the domain

`12.in-addr.arpa.`. Picking one of them (`DBRU`), we again try to resolve our question. This time we find two name servers (`ns1` and `ns2`). Picking one of these, we are able to resolve the PTR request. It resolves to the name `dmz.slouter.seattle.intel-research.net`.

11.5.6.6 Authority (SOA) Records

In DNS, each zone has an authority record, using an RR type called *start of authority* (SOA). These records provide authoritative links between portions of the DNS name space and the servers that provide the zone information allowing various queries to be performed for addresses and other information. The SOA RR is used to identify the name of the host providing the official permanent database, the responsible party's e-mail address (where "." is used instead of @), zone update parameters, and the default TTL. The default TTL is applied to RRs in the zone that are not otherwise assigned an explicit per-RR TTL.

The zone update parameters include a serial number, refresh time, retry time, and expire time. The serial number is increased (by at least 1), usually by the network administrator, anytime there is a change to the zone contents. It is used by secondary servers to determine if they should initiate a zone transfer (when they do not have a copy of the zone contents with largest serial number). The refresh time tells secondary servers how long to wait before checking the SOA record from the primary and its version number to determine if a zone transfer is required. The retry and expire times are used in the case of zone transfer failure. The retry value gives the time (in seconds) a secondary will wait before retrying. The expire time is an upper bound (in seconds) that a secondary server will keep retrying zone transfers before giving up. If it gives up, such a server ceases to respond to queries for the zone. In general, a zone can contain a mix of IPv4 and IPv6 data and can be accessed using either version of IP. In this example, we use IPv6 (using `nslookup` on an IPv6-only Windows host):

```
C:\> nslookup
Default Server:  gw
Address:    fe80::204:5aff:fe9f:9e80

> set type=soa
> berkeley.edu.
Server:  gw
Address:    fe80::204:5aff:fe9f:9e80

Non-authoritative answer:
berkeley.edu
        primary name server = ns-master1.berkeley.edu
        responsible mail addr = hostmaster.berkeley.edu
        serial  = 2009050116
        refresh = 10800 (3 hours)
        retry   = 1800 (30 mins)
        expire  = 3600000 (41 days 16 hours)
        default TTL = 300 (5 mins)
```

```
> server adns1.berkeley.edu.
Default Server:  adns1.berkeley.edu
Addresses:  2607:f140:ffff:fffe::3
            128.32.136.3

> berkeley.edu.
Server:  adns1.berkeley.edu
Addresses:  2607:f140:ffff:fffe::3
            128.32.136.3

berkeley.edu
        primary name server = ns-master1.berkeley.edu
        responsible mail addr = hostmaster.berkeley.edu
        serial  = 2009050116
        refresh = 10800 (3 hours)
        retry   = 1800 (30 mins)
        expire  = 3600000 (41 days 16 hours)
        default TTL = 300 (5 mins)
berkeley.edu       nameserver = ns.v6.berkeley.edu
berkeley.edu       nameserver = aodns1.berkeley.edu
berkeley.edu       nameserver = adns2.berkeley.edu
berkeley.edu       nameserver = phloem.uoregon.edu
berkeley.edu       nameserver = adns1.berkeley.edu
berkeley.edu       nameserver = ucb-ns.NYU.edu
ns.v6.berkeley.edu      internet address = 128.32.136.6
ns.v6.berkeley.edu      AAAA IPv6 address = 2607:f140:ffff:fffe::6
adns1.berkeley.edu      internet address = 128.32.136.3
adns1.berkeley.edu      AAAA IPv6 address = 2607:f140:ffff:fffe::3
adns2.berkeley.edu      internet address = 128.32.136.14
adns2.berkeley.edu      AAAA IPv6 address = 2607:f140:ffff:fffe::e
aodns1.berkeley.edu     internet address = 192.35.225.133
aodns1.berkeley.edu     AAAA IPv6 address =
                            2607:f010:3f8:8000:214:4fff:fe45:e6a2
phloem.uoregon.edu      internet address = 128.223.32.35
phloem.uoregon.edu      AAAA IPv6 address = 2001:468:d01:20::80df:2023
```

Here we can see that not only did we receive the SOA record, but we also received a list of six authoritative name servers, and the IPv4/IPv6 addresses (glue records) for five of them (the address for the NYU server is not given, as glue records for NYU.edu would be in a different zone supported by a different server). As this is one of the more interesting responses we have seen, let us look at the packet contents corresponding to the request sent to the authoritative name server, adns1.berkeley.edu (see Figure 11-14).

This trace contains two packets, and we have chosen to display the reply, which is the more interesting of the two. A query for an SOA RR was sent to the host 2607:f140:ffff:fffe::3 (adns1.Berkeley.EDU) from the local system's globally scoped IPv6 address 2001:5c0:1101:ed00:5571:5f81:e0a6:4978. The response is carried in an IPv6 datagram with 491 bytes total length (the *Payload Length* field is 451). This particular packet contains the IPv6 header (40 bytes), UDP header (8 bytes), plus the DNS message (443 bytes). The DNS message includes one question, one answer, six authority RRs, and ten additional RRs.

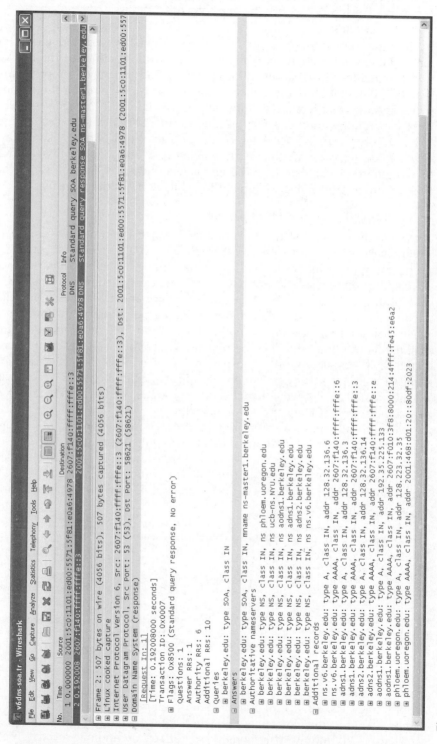

Figure 11-14 Response to a DNS query for an SOA record using IPv6. The response includes IPv4 and IPv6 addresses for the zone.

The question section contains the labels `berkeley` and `edu` and is 18 bytes long. The answer section contains the relevant information for the `berkeley.edu` domain described earlier and is able to take advantage of compression labels thanks to the contents of the question section. The total length for this section is 58 bytes. The authority section contains six NS records identifying name servers. This information takes another 135 bytes. The additional information section includes five A records and five AAAA records for a total of 220 bytes. The size of the *RDATA* field for each AAAA record is 16 bytes, so although the IPv6 address can be written in textual form with the `::` convention to save space, it is not encoded this way in the packet. Instead, the full 128 bits of the address are used.

11.5.6.7 Mail Exchanger (MX) Records

An MX record provides the name of a *mail exchanger*—a host willing to engage in the *Simple Mail Transfer Protocol* (SMTP) [RFC5321] to receive incoming e-mail on behalf of users associated with a domain name. When the Internet was still developing, some sites did not have permanent connections but instead would dial up and connect to hosts that did have permanent Internet connections. In such scenarios, the e-mail destination might be disconnected from the network when e-mail was in transit, so another host would hold on to the mail until the destination was attached. This was one motivation for the inclusion of MX records in the DNS—to allow sending hosts to deliver e-mail to an intermediary ("relay server") even if the true destination was not available. Today, MX records are still used, and mail agents prefer to deliver e-mail to the host(s) listed in an MX record associated with a particular domain name.

MX records include a *preference* value, so that more than one MX record may be present for a particular domain name. The preference value allows a sending agent to sort the hosts in preference order (smaller is more preferable) in deciding which host to use as an e-mail destination. For example, we can use the `host` command again to query the DNS for MX records associated with the domain name `cs.ucla.edu`:

```
Linux% host -t MX cs.ucla.edu ns3.dns.ucla.edu
Using domain server:
Name: ns3.dns.ucla.edu
Address: 2607:f600:8001:1::ff:fe01:35#53
Aliases:

cs.ucla.edu mail is handled by 13 Pelican.cs.ucla.edu.
cs.ucla.edu mail is handled by 3 Moa.cs.ucla.edu.
cs.ucla.edu mail is handled by 13 Mailman.cs.ucla.edu.
```

Here we can see that an e-mail addressed to `person@cs.ucla.edu` is handled by one of three mail servers configured in the DNS. All of these mail servers are part of the `cs.ucla.edu` domain, but in general mail servers do not have to be named with the same domain as the e-mail they are handling. These three servers can be grouped into two parts: one with preference 3 and one set with preference

13. The server with the smaller preference number is preferred, so the sender first tries `Moa.cs.ucla.edu`. If that fails, it tries either `Pelican` or `Mailman`, selected at random.

It is possible that none of the MX record target hosts is reachable. This is an error condition. It is also possible that there are no MX records present, but there are CNAME, A, or AAAA records for the domain name. If there is a CNAME record, the target of the CNAME is used in place of the original domain name. If there are A or AAAA records, the mail agent may connect to these addresses. Each is considered to have a preference of zero (called *implicit MX*). MX record targets must be domain names that resolve to A or AAAA records; they cannot point to CNAMEs [RFC5321].

11.5.6.8 Fighting Spam: The Sender Policy Framework (SPF) and Text (TXT) Records

For outgoing e-mail, MX records allow the DNS to help determine the names of mail relays and servers for a domain. More recently, the DNS has been leveraged by receiving mail agents to determine which relaying or sending mail servers are authorized to send mail from a particular domain name. This is used to help combat spam (unwanted e-mail) that is sent by a rogue mail agent pretending to be an authorized mail sender.

E-mail received by a mail server is rejected, stored, or forwarded to another mail server. Rejection can happen for a number of reasons, such as a protocol error or lack of available storage space at the receiver. It can also be rejected because the sending mail client does not appear to be the proper one for sending e-mail. This capability is supported by the *Sender Policy Framework* (SPF) and documented in [RFC4408], an experimental RFC. There is another framework known as *Sender ID* [RFC4406] that incorporates SPF's functions. It is also experimental but less widely deployed.

Version 1 of SPF uses DNS TXT or SPF (type 99) resource records. Records are set up and published in the DNS by a domain's owner to indicate which servers are authorized to send mail originating from the domain. Although the SPF record type is a more "proper" place to carry SPF-related information in some sense, some DNS client implementations do not process SPF records properly, so to avoid this complication TXT records are used. TXT records hold simple strings associated with a domain name. Historically they have held strings useful for human consumption, to aid in debugging or identifying the owner or location of a domain. Today, they are usually processed by programs such as the SPF application.

SPF supports a rich syntax to express criteria used to match against details about an incoming mail message and the connection in which it is carried. For example, UC Berkeley uses the following SPF entry (some lines have been wrapped for clarity):

```
Linux% host -t txt berkeley.edu
berkeley.edu descriptive text
        "v=spf1 ip4:169.229.218.128/25 ip6:2607:F140:0:1000::/64
        include:outboundmail.convio.net ~all"
```

In this example, the information being provided is for SPF version 1 (indicated by the `v=spf1` string in the version section) and uses a TXT RR. When a receiving mail agent receives e-mail purportedly coming from the domain `berkeley.edu`, it performs a DNS query for records of type TXT against the `berkeley.edu` domain. The value of the text record contains the matching criteria (called *mechanisms*) and other information (called *modifiers*). Preceding each mechanism is a *qualifier* that determines the consequence of a matching mechanism. Processing of SPF records takes place using a function called `check_host()`. The function evaluates various mechanisms and completes when the first matching mechanism is encountered. Ultimately, `check_host()` provides a return value that is one of the following: None, Neutral, Pass, Fail, SoftFail, TempError, PermError. The None and Neutral return values indicate that no information was available or that information was available but that no result is asserted. These are handled identically. Pass indicates a match, as described in the next paragraph. Fail indicates that the sending host is not authorized to send mail from the domain. SoftFail is somewhat ambiguous but is to be treated "somewhere between a 'Fail' and a 'Neutral,'" according to [RFC4408]. The TempError return indicates some transient failure (e.g., communication failure) that is likely to abate. The PermError return indicates that there was a problem in the SPF configuration, usually due to a malformed TXT or SPF record for the domain.

Reading from left to right in the example, the string `v=spf1` is a modifier indicating that the SPF version is 1. The `ip4` mechanism specifies that the SMTP sender has an IPv4 address from the prefix `169.229.218.128/25`. The `ip6` mechanism specifies any sending host with IPv6 address prefix `2607:F140:0:1000::/64`. Finally, the `include` mechanism incorporates, by reference, the TXT records with `outboundmail.convio.net`:

```
Linux% host -t txt outboundmail.convio.net
outboundmail.convio.net descriptive text
        "v=spf1 +ip4:66.45.103.0/25 +ip4:69.48.252.128/25
        +ip4:209.163.168.192/26 ~all"
outboundmail.convio.net descriptive text
        "spf2.0/pra
        +ip4:66.45.103.0/25 +ip4:69.48.252.128/25
        +ip4:209.163.168.192/26 ~all"
```

Note that these TXT records are used for both SPF and for Sender ID (which uses the value of `spf2.0/pra` in the version section). The first record is used by SPF. The + qualifier indicates that a match results in a Pass indication. Any mechanism missing a qualifier is assumed to have the + qualifier. Other possible qualifiers include − (Fail), ~ (Soft Fail), and ? (Neutral). If none of the matching mechanisms produces a Pass result, the final mechanism (`all`) matches any condition. The tilde character (~) before the `all` criterion indicates that a SoftFail return should be generated if `all` is the only matching mechanism. The exact way a soft failure is handled is dependent on the receiving e-mail software. Note that even with SPF support, validation is provided only on the sending domain and system, and not on the sending user. In Chapter 18 we will look at DKIM, which provides SPF-like capabilities but uses cryptography for authentication.

11.5.6.9 Option (OPT) Pseudo-Records

In conjunction with EDNS0, described previously, a special *OPT pseudo-RR* has been defined [RFC2671]. It is "pseudo" in the sense that it pertains only to the contents of a single DNS message and is not conventional DNS RR data. Consequently, OPT RRs are not cached, forwarded, or persistently stored, and they may appear only once (or not at all) in a DNS message. If one is present in a DNS message, it is found in the additional information section.

An OPT RR contains a 10-byte fixed portion followed by a variable portion. The fixed portion includes 16 bits indicating the RR type (41), 16 bits indicating the UDP payload size, 32 bits constituting an extended *RCODE* field and flags area, and 16 bits giving the size of the variable portion in bytes. These fields are located in the same relative positions as the *Name*, *Type*, *Class*, *TTL*, and *RDLEN* fields, respectively, in a conventional RR (see Figure 11-8). OPT RRs use a null domain name in the *Name* field (0 bytes). The extended *RCODE* and *Flags* area (32 bits, corresponding to the *TTL* field in Figure 11-8) is subdivided into an 8-bit area to hold an extra 8 high-order bits augmenting the *RCODE* field in Figure 11-3, and an 8-bit *Version* field (currently set to 0 to indicate EDNS0). The remaining 16 bits are not yet defined and must be 0. The additional 8 bits provide an extended set of possible DNS error types, and these values are given in Table 11-4. (Note that value 16 is defined by two distinct RFCs.)

Table 11-4 Extended *RCODE* values. Most are used to support security extensions.

Value	Name	Reference	Description and Purpose
16	BADVERS	[RFC2671]	Bad EDNS version
16	BADSIG	[RFC2845]	Bad TSIG signature (see Chapter 18)
17	BADKEY	[RFC2845]	Bad TSIG key (see Chapter 18)
18	BADTIME	[RFC2845]	Bad TSIG signature (time problem; see Chapter 18)
19	BADMODE	[RFC2930]	Bad TKEY mode (see Chapter 18)
20	BADNAME	[RFC2930]	Duplicate key name (see Chapter 18)
21	BADALG	[RFC2930]	Algorithm not supported (see Chapter 18)

As we have mentioned, OPT RRs contain a variable-length *RDATA* field. This field is used to hold an extensible list of attribute-value pairs. The current set of attributes, meanings, and defining RFCs is maintained by the IANA [DNSPARAMS]. One such option, called NSID (EDNS option code 3) [RFC5001], indicates a special identifying value for a responding DNS server. The format of this value is not defined by standard but is instead configurable by the system administrator of the DNS server. This capability may be useful in circumstances where an any-cast address is used to identify a group of servers. The NSID is able to identify a specific responding server using a value other than the sending IP address. We shall see more examples of OPT RRs and EDNS0 usage when we look at DNSSEC in Chapter 18.

11.5.6.10 Service (SRV) Records

[RFC2782] defines the *service* (SRV) resource record. SRV RRs generalize the MX record format to describe the host, protocols, and port numbers used to contact a particular service. An SRV RR is ordinarily structured as follows:

```
_Service._Proto.Name TTL IN  SRV     Prio    Weight    Port    Target
```

The *Service* identifier is the official name of a service. The *Proto* identifier is the transport protocol used to access the service, usually TCP or UDP. The TTL value is a conventional RR TTL, and IN and SRV indicate the Internet class and SRV RR type, respectively. The *Prio* value is a 16-bit unsigned value and works like the priority value in MX records (lower numbers represent higher priorities). The *Weight* value is used to choose an RR among several whose priority values are equal. The idea is that the weight is to be used as a weighted probability to select the particular entry for load balancing, so larger weights indicate a greater probability of selection. The *Port* is the TCP or UDP (or other transport protocol's) port number. The *Target* is the domain name of the target host where the service is being provided. The *Name* identifier is the containing domain in which a particular service is to be found. One of the purposes of SRV records is to identify when multiple individual servers in a domain support the same service.

For example, if a client would like to determine the host and port where the ldap service is available using the TCP protocol in the domain example.com, it would perform a query for SRV records using the domain name _ldap._tcp .example.com. Here is a real-world example:

```
Linux% host -t srv _ldap._tcp.openldap.org
_ldap._tcp.openldap.org has SRV record 0 0 389 www.openldap.org.
```

In this example, we are looking for a server providing the *Lightweight Directory Access Protocol* (LDAP) [RFC4510] service over TCP within the domain openldap.org. We find that it can be accessed at the server www.openldap.org using TCP port 389 (the default LDAP port). The *Priority* and *Weight* values are 0, as there are no alternative servers.

[RFC2782] did not specify a new IANA registry for SRV *Service* and *Proto* values. So, by default, the names correspond to the names maintained in IANA's "Service Name and Transport Protocol Port Number" registry [ISPR], and the *Proto* values are either _tcp or _udp. There are a few exceptions, however. [RFC5509] establishes conventions for SIP-based presence and instant messaging using the following SRV `Service` and `Proto` names: `_im._sip` and `_pres._sip`. [RFC6186] defines the following SRV `Service` names for e-mail user agents to easily discover the contact information for IMAPS, SMTP, IMAP, and POP3 servers (the first two are ordinarily preferred when setting up an e-mail client): `_submission`, `_imap`, `_imaps`, `_pop3`, `_pop3s`. Although [RFC6186] doesn't require these names to use TCP as the corresponding `Proto` value, this is currently the only real option. For example, a user configuring a new *mail user agent* (MUA, essentially an e-mail program) might specify only the domain `example.com`. The MUA implementation would then likely perform DNS queries for at least `_submission._tcp.example.com` and `_imaps._tcp.example.com`.

11.5.6.11 Name Authority Pointer (NAPTR) Records

The *Name Authority Pointer* (NAPTR) RR type is used when DNS supports a *Dynamic Delegation Discovery System* (DDDS) [RFC3401]. A DDDS is a general, abstract algorithm for applying dynamically retrieved string transformation rules to strings provided by applications and using the results, most often, for locating resources. Each DDDS application customizes the operation of the general DDDS rules for its particular use case. A DDDS includes a rules database and a set of algorithms for forming strings that are used with the database to produce output strings. DNS is one such database [RFC3403], and with it the NAPTR resource record type is used to hold the transformation rules. One such DDDS application has been defined for use with DNS to handle multinational telephone numbers and convert them to a standard *Uniform Resource Identifier* (URI) format [RFC3986] using ENUM (see Section 11.5.6.12).

In a DDDS, an *algorithm* [RFC3402] directs how an *application-unique string* (AUS) is processed by rules contained in a database. The result can be either a *terminal string* (complete output) or another (nonterminal) string used to retrieve another rule that is applied to the AUS. In all, the collection forms a powerful string rewriting system that can be used to encode nearly anything that has a sufficiently regular syntax. The essence of this algorithm is captured in Figure 11-15.

The process illustrated in Figure 11-15 starts by applying the first Well-Known Rule to the AUS, which is uniquely identified for each application. The result forms a key used to retrieve another rule from a database. Rules are string-rewriting patterns and flags that are applied to the AUS, but never to the result of a rewritten string. The particular way this works is dependent on the application, but usually the rules are regular expression substitutions, similar to those used with the UNIX `sed` program [DR97]. When using the DNS as a database for supporting a DDDS [RFC3403], the case in which we are interested, the keys are domain names and the rules are stored in NAPTR resource records. Each NAPTR RR contains the following fields: *Order, Preference, Flags, Services, Regular Expression* (sometimes abbreviated *Regexp*), and *Replacement*.

The *Order* field is a 16-bit unsigned integer specifying which NAPTR record to use before others (lower numbers are preferred to higher ones), as the DNS architecture does not guarantee the ordering of any particular set of resource records.

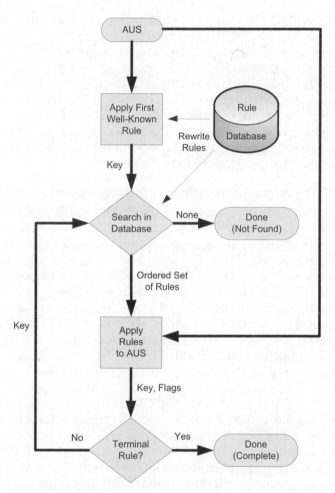

Figure 11-15   Abstract operation of the DDDS algorithm. Non-terminal records are permitted to form loops. Each iteration involves a string rewrite operation on the application's unique string.

The *Preference* field is used to influence the order of records containing the same order number. The *Order* field is supposed to place a mandatory ordering on RRs, whereas the preference number is advisory. The *Flags* field contains an unordered list of single characters from the set A–Z and 0–9 (case-insensitive). The particular application using NAPTR records (e.g., ENUM, described in the next section) defines the interpretation of the *Flags* field. The *Services* field is defined by the application to indicate which type of service is being described. The *Regular Expression* field contains a substitution expression that is applied to the AUS to form the identity of another server to use for another NAPTR lookup (non-terminal case) or the output string (terminal case). The *Replacement* field (which exists only when the *Regular Expression* does not) indicates the next server to query for NAPTR records. It is encoded as a separate FQDN (no name compression is used within the DNS message). The uses for these two final (mutually exclusive) fields are very similar for historical reasons in the development of the NAPTR RR.

To get a better sense of how NAPTR processing works with applications, we will have a brief look at the ENUM and SIP DDDS applications, the URI/URN DDDS applications, and alternatives for regular NAPTR records called S-NAPTR and U-NAPTR. Specifying a DDDS entails specifying the application's AUS, first Well-Known Rule, expected output, valid databases, flags, and service parameters.

11.5.6.12 ENUM and SIP

In the ENUM DDDS [R06][RFC6116][RFC6117][RFC5483], which is used to map phone numbers to URI information, the AUS is an E.164-format telephone number (up to 15 digits starting with the + character). The initial + character differentiates E.164 numbers acceptable for use with the ENUM DDS from numbers in other name spaces. The first Well-Known Rule starts by removing any dashes or other non-digit characters in the AUS. The DDDS database is the DNS, where keys are domain names created from the AUS (which now consists only of digits) as follows: dot (.) characters are inserted between each digit and the result is reversed. Then, the suffix .e164.arpa is added. For example, the E.164 number +1–415–555–1212 would be tranformed to the key 2.1.2.1.5.5.5.5.1.4.1.e164.arpa. The resulting domain name is used to query for NAPTR records.

The final output, possibly after multiple loops of the DDDS algorithm shown in Figure 11-15, is an absolute (not relative) URI. The only flag defined is the *U* flag, indicating a terminal rule that produces a URI. The lack of any flag indicates a non-terminal rule, sometimes called a *non-terminal NAPTR* (NTN). The service parameters, encoded in the *Service* field of the NAPTR record, are of the form E2U+Service, which derives from the string E2U (an indicator for E.164 to URI) plus a Service name subfield providing information about particular services associated with the number. Together, they form an *enumservice* identifier, and such services are registered with the IANA [ENUM][RFC6117]. Many have been created, including enumservices for fax, instant messaging, and presence indicators.

To see how this all works, we can construct a query for the number +420738511111 at the University of Ostrava in the Czech Republic (lines are wrapped for clarity):

```
Linux% host -t naptr 1.1.1.1.1.5.8.3.7.0.2.4.e164.arpa
1.1.1.1.1.5.8.3.7.0.2.4.e164.arpa has NAPTR record
        50 50 "u" "E2U+sip" "!^\\+(.*)$!sip:\\1@osu.cz!" .
1.1.1.1.1.5.8.3.7.0.2.4.e164.arpa has NAPTR record
        100 50 "u" "E2U+sip""!^\\+(.*)$!sip:\\1@cesnet.cz!" .
1.1.1.1.1.5.8.3.7.0.2.4.e164.arpa has NAPTR record
        200 50 "u" "E2U+h323" "!^\\+(.*)$!h323:\\1@gklext.cesnet.cz!" .
```

Here we see the contents of three NAPTR records in the ENUM DDDS application, two for the SIP service and one for the H.323 service, used for Internet telephony. The order numbers are 50 and 100 for the SIP entries and 200 for the H.323 entry, showing how it is possible using ENUM and NAPTR records to have multiple services associated with a single telephone number, and how the provider of the NAPTR records can indicate a preferred ordering of more than one gateway providing the same service.

Note

SIP is an IETF-specified protocol used for signaling and is especially popular for facilitating the connection of multimedia clients and servers. H.323 is an ITU-specified protocol for multimedia conferencing and communication, including a signaling sub-protocol. It is widely implemented in teleconferencing equipment. In this example and those that follow, the host program produces output that can be used as input to a zone file for a DNS server such as BIND. As a consequence, the output shows extra escape "\" characters (which appear as "\\") that are not present in the actual DNS responses provided by the server.

To better understand how a NAPTR record's rules are applied to the AUS, we will look at the second SIP record from the preceding example. After the DNS query is performed and the NAPTR RR is received, the string appearing between the first and second ! characters is used as a regular expression match and replacement. Thus, the string +420738511111 is matched against the regular expression ^\+(.*)$. According to the matching rules for regular expressions, the match is successful, so the string rewrite rule becomes sip:\1@cesnet.cz . The special variable \1 is replaced with the substring matching the first regular expression contained in parenthesis characters, (), which in this case is everything in the AUS except for the initial + character. In summary, the AUS +420738511111 is transformed into the URI sip:420738511111@cesnet.cz.

Once this URI is formed, the natural next step is for the driving application to contact a SIP server. However, SIP can itself be carried over different transport protocols, so the next step uses another DDDS that is tailored for SIP [RFC3263]. In this application, NAPTR records contain targets that identify the domain that should be used to perform SRV record queries. Continuing with the preceding example:

```
Linux% host -t naptr cesnet.cz
cesnet.cz has NAPTR record 200 50 "s" "SIP+D2T" "" _sip._tcp.cesnet.cz.
cesnet.cz has NAPTR record 100 50 "s" "SIP+D2U" "" _sip._udp.cesnet.cz.
```

Here we see the use of the s flag in the NAPTR, indicating that an SRV record is the result. The *Regexp* field is not used, so the result is a simple domain name substitution, given by the string in the *Replacement* field. The *Service* field is of the form SIP+D2*x* or SIPS+D2*x* where SIP and SIPS indicate the use of the SIP protocol and SIP protocol with security (TLS; see Chapter 18), respectively, and *x* is the single-letter identifier of the transport protocol: U for UDP, T for TCP, and S for SCTP [RFC4960]. In this example, the application would first attempt to look up and use the SRV record corresponding to SIP/UDP and would resort to SIP/TCP if that fails because the UDP entry has a lower preference value.

11.5.6.13 URI/URN Resolution

Although ENUM may be the most mature use of NAPTR records in the DNS, there are also DDDS applications defined for resolving URIs [RFC3404] and for persistent, location-independent URIs called *Uniform Resource Names* (URNs) [RFC2141]. All URIs (including URNs) consist of a scheme name followed by a substring compliant with semantics that are specific to the scheme. The current list of official schemes is maintained by the IANA [URI]. The URI and URN applications are so similar that it is worth considering them together. For the URI/URN DDDS application, then, the AUS is the URI or URN for which an authoritative "resolution" server is being located. The first Well-Known Rule for the URI application is simply the scheme name. For URNs, it is the name space identifier (the substring that appears after the `urn:` scheme identifier and before the next colon character). For example, `http://www.pearson.com` is a URI using the scheme (key) `http`, and the URN `urn:foo:foospace` would use `foo` as the first key. Four possible flags are currently defined: *S*, *A*, *U*, and *P*. The first three are terminal and indicate that the result is the domain name to use for fetching an SRV record, an IP address, or a URI, respectively. The *P* flag indicates that processing of the DDDS algorithm is to be discontinued and some application-specific processing (defined elsewhere) begins. All such flags are mutually exclusive. As with ENUM, the lack of any flag indicates an NTN.

Support for the URI/URN DDDS is still evolving. If we take a current (2011) look into the DNS, we can see how some of the schemes have been populated into the `uri.arpa` TLD:

```
Linux% host -t naptr http.uri.arpa
http.uri.arpa has NAPTR record 0 0 "" "" "!^http://([^:/?#]*).*$!\\1!i" .
Linux% host -t naptr ftp.uri.arpa
ftp.uri.arpa has NAPTR record 0 0 "" "" "!^ftp://([^:/?#]*).*$!\\1!i" .

Linux% host -t naptr mailto.uri.arpa
mailto.uri.arpa has NAPTR record 0 0 "" "" "!^mailto:(.*)@(.*)$!\\2!i" .
Linux% host -t naptr urn.uri.arpa
urn.uri.arpa has NAPTR record 0 0 "" "" "/urn:([^:]+)/\\1/i" .
```

The first three of these NAPTR records contain rewrite rules and no flags. Thus, they essentially indicate that the application should extract the domain name from the corresponding URI and continue the DDDS algorithm. The trailing i flag after the last ! character indicates that case checking is to be performed in an insensitive way. For example, `mAiLto:person@example.com` is rewritten to be just `example.com`. The fourth record is used to extract the URN name space ID and continue processing. For URNs, there are a small number (two at present) of NAPTR records in the DNS set up in `urn.arpa`:

```
Linux% host -t naptr pin.urn.arpa
pin.urn.arpa has NAPTR record 100 100 "" "" "" pin.verisignlabs.com.
Linux% host -t naptr uci.urn.arpa
uci.urn.arpa has NAPTR record 100 100 "" "" "" uci.or.kr.
```

These URN name spaces appear to be receiving little attention at present, and it is still unclear to what extent URNs will be widely used, as there are now competing methods for expressing and locating objects using persistent identifiers (e.g., see [P10]). Nevertheless, more than 40 URN name spaces have been defined [URN], so there continues to be community interest in establishing name spaces, even though few have corresponding global, active NAPTR records.

11.5.6.14 S-NAPTR and U-NAPTR

A common issue arises when an application wishes to determine the particular host, protocol, and port number to use for reaching a service within a domain. For example, a mail-reading application running on a user's computer in the example.com domain may need to find a server offering the IMAP service. A convention has arisen to simply prepend the service name to the domain (e.g., imap.example.com). Using CNAME, A, or AAAA records is somewhat inflexible, because these record types do not convey any indication of which transport protocol or port number to use. SRV records go further by providing another layer of indirection, but their targets may contain only domain names for which an A or AAAA record is subsequently retrieved. Using NAPTR records instead provides more flexibility through an additional layer of indirection and allows for other target record types (such as SRV records) to be used.

The NAPTR structure and rewrite capabilities have caused concern for some implementers and operators given the complexity of the regular expressions. In an effort to simplify the situation yet still provide a method beyond basic SRV records for locating services, *straightforward NAPTR* (S-NAPTR) [RFC3958] specifies a DDDS application for mapping domain "labels" that contain a service name using certain simplifying restrictions on the contents of the NAPTR records.

For S-NAPTR, the AUS is a domain label for which an authoritative server for a particular service is sought. The first Well-Known Rule is the identity function. The expected output is the information necessary to contact a particular application service within a domain (e.g., protocol, host, port). Only *S* and *A* terminal flags are permitted, which indicate an SRV RR or a domain name (which is to be used to form a subsequent request for an A or AAAA RR), respectively. The service parameters are taken from a set maintained in an IANA registry [SNP], and the *Regexp* field is not used. Only the *Replacement* field is active. S-NAPTR is used in conjunction with the *Internet Registry Information Service* (IRIS) [RFC3981], an XML-based text application protocol for exchanging information pertaining to domain name and other registration information whose database is contained within the iris.arpa portion of the DNS name space; for example:

```
Linux% host -t naptr areg.iris.arpa
reg.iris.arpa NAPTR
        100 10 "" "AREG1:iris.xpc:iris.lwz" "" areg.nro.net.
```

This example uses S-NAPTR (no regular expression) to indicate that in order to perform an ISIS query for AREG1-type data (see [RFC4698]), a subsequent NAPTR query should be initiated to areg.nro.net.

Experience and further consideration of S-NAPTR led to the development of *URI-enabled NAPTR* (U-NAPTR) [RFC4848], which relaxes some of the restrictions of S-NAPTR but maintains all of its other features and registries. Most important, an additional *U* flag is permitted, which enables the NAPTR record target to be a URI and thus allows the use of regular expressions. This is similar to the fully generic version of NAPTR, except U-NAPTR regular expressions are restricted to the following form: !.*!<URI>!. That is, the entire AUS is replaced with a URI. U-NAPTR is being used in conjunction with the *Location-to-Service Translation protocol* (LoST) [RFC5222], which can be used to determine the correct service given a point of network attachment and geographical location. Such information is useful in public safety applications where geography dictates the particular jurisdiction and responsible parties that should provide emergency services.

11.5.7 Dynamic Updates (DNS UPDATE)

It is possible to dynamically update a zone, called *DNS UPDATE*, using a protocol defined in [RFC2136]. It supports the ability to specify *prerequisites* in conjunction with an update request. Prerequisites are evaluated at the server; if they are not true, the update is not performed and an error message is returned.

DNS UPDATE is accomplished by sending *dynamic update* DNS messages to an authoritative DNS server for a zone. The structure of such messages is the same as for a conventional DNS message, except the header fields and sections have different names (see Figure 11-3). The sections indicate the zone being updated, prerequisites that require various RRs to be present (or not) for the update to take effect, and the *update information*. In an update, the header mirrors the format for a query, but the *Opcode* field is set to Update (5). The header fields *ZOCOUNT, PRCOUNT, UPCOUNT*, and *ADCOUNT* contain counts of the following: zones to be updated (this will have the value 1), prerequisites to consider, updates to be made, and additional information records, respectively. [RFC2136] also defines a collection of RCODE values carried in DNS response messages capable of indicating conditions relating to problems with the prerequisites or server (values 6–10 in Table 11-2).

The zone section of an update message (see Figure 11-7) indicates the zone's name, a type, and a class. The type value will be 6 to indicate the presence of an SOA record, which identifies the zone. The class value will be 1 (Internet) for any update message with which we are concerned. All records being updated must be in the same zone.

The prerequisite section of an update message contains one or more prerequisites, expressed using the format for RRs we discussed previously in Section 11.5.5. There are five types of prerequisites: *RRSet exists* (value-dependent and value-independent varieties), *RRSet does not exist, name is in use,* and *name is not in use.* Recall that an RRSet is a group of RRs from the same zone sharing a common name, class, and type. To express the semantics of a prerequisite, a combination of an RR's class, type, and RDATA values are set according to Table 11-5.

The *RRSet exists* type means that at least one RRSet exists in the zone specified in the zone section that matches the name and type of the corresponding RR in

Table 11-5 *RR Class* and *Type* fields used in prerequisite section to indicate prerequisite type

Prerequisite Type (Semantics)	Class Setting	Type Setting	RDATA Setting
RRSet exists (value-independent)	ANY	Same as zone's type	Empty
RRSet exists (value-dependent)	Same as zone's class	Type being checked	RRSet being checked
RRSet does not exist	NONE	Type being checked	Empty
Name is in use	ANY	ANY	Empty
Name is not in use	NONE	ANY	Empty

the prerequisite section. In the value-dependent case, the prerequisite is true only if the matching RRs also contain matching RDATA values. The *RRSet does not exist* type means that no RRSet in the zone specified in the zone section matches the name and type of the RR in the Prerequisites section. The last two cases (*Name is in use* and *Name is not in use*) refer only to the domain name; the type value is not used. The values for NONE and ANY as DNS classes are 254 and 255, respectively.

Following the Prerequisite section, the Update section contains RRs to be added or deleted from the zone specified in the zone section. There are four types of updates, encoded as an RR with various combinations of values in the *Class*, *Type*, and *RDATA* fields, as indicated in Table 11-6.

Table 11-6 *RR Class* and *Type* fields used in Update section to indicate update type

Use	Class Setting	Type Setting	RDATA
Add RR to RRSet	Same as zone's class	Type of RR being added	RDATA of RR being added
Delete RRSet	ANY	Type of RRSet to delete	Empty (TTL and RDLENGTH also zero)
Delete all RRSets from a name	ANY	ANY	Empty (TTL and RDLENGTH also zero)
Delete RR from RRSet	NONE	Type of RR being deleted	Matching RDATA to delete

The update section contains a collection of RRs that are processed provided no errors have occurred due to prerequisites or server problems. Each RR encodes an addition or deletion operation. Modifications can be performed as a deletion followed by an addition. To see an example of DNS UPDATE, we can induce a Windows machine to perform a dynamic DNS update using the following command:

```
C:\> ipconfig /registerdns
```

Windows clients issue updates for their computer name and domain name by default, but this behavior can also be enabled for IPv4 on a per-DNS-suffix basis by checking the box labeled "Use this connection's DNS suffix in DNS registration" under the DNS section of the Advanced TCP/IP Settings, found on the General tab of the Internet Protocol (TCP/IP) Properties menu associated with each interface enabled for TCP/IP. For IPv6, the same procedure is used, but on the IPv6 Properties menu. In the example shown in Figure 11-16, we can see how the machine named vista updates the local zone dyn.home as it issues the DNS update message shown.

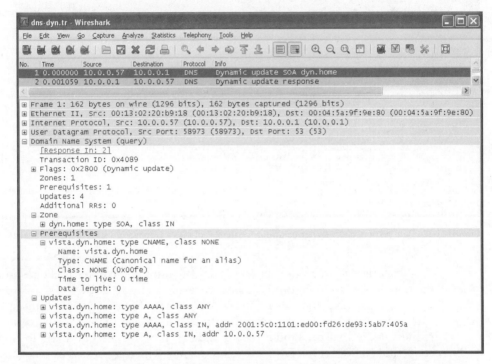

Figure 11-16   A DNS dynamic update contains an SOA record in the zone section and RRs in the update section. This case includes new IPv4 and IPv6 addresses for the host vista.dyn.home.

Figure 11-16 shows how a dynamic update is encoded. The DNS server at 10.0.0.1 (running BIND9 [AL06] in this example) is configured to allow dynamic updates. The zone section contains an SOA record identifying the zone to be updated (vista.dyn.home). The prerequisite section contains an RR with a zero-length RDATA section and 0 TTL value. The RR corresponds to the type of pre-requisite in the third row of Table 11-5 (*RRset does not exist*) because its type is not ANY (it is CNAME) and its class is set to NONE (254).

In this particular case, the addresses 10.0.0.57 and 2001:5c0:1101:ed00:fd26: de93:5ab7:405a are to be associated with the name vista.dyn.home. This is accomplished by first deleting the AAAA and A RRSets (corresponding to row 2 in Table 11-6), and then adding the AAAA and A RRSets (corresponding to row 1 in Table 11-6) for the desired addresses.

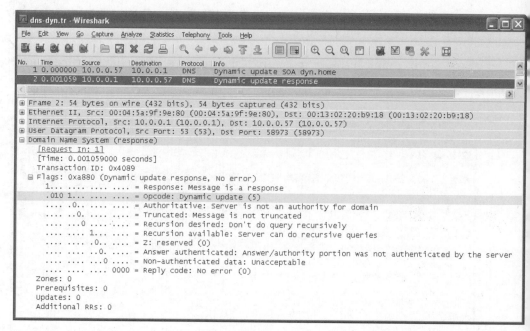

Figure 11-17   The response to a dynamic update request includes a transaction ID and status flag set.

Responses to DNS updates are straightforward and compact. The response for the update shown in Figure 11-16 is illustrated in Figure 11-17.

The *Flags* field indicates a successful update (no error). The transaction ID (0x4089) is used to ensure that the update response matches a corresponding request. Note that on Linux, the `nsupdate` program can be used to update a cooperative DNS server. DNS servers cooperate with a requested update only if an authentication and access control procedure indicates that the request is acceptable. This can be as simple as nothing or listing the IP addresses of clients at the server, neither of which is very secure, or using somewhat more complex and secure methods that provide *transaction authentication* (see TSIG and SIG(0) in Chapter 18).

11.5.8   Zone Transfers and DNS NOTIFY

A zone transfer is used to copy a set of RRs for a zone from one server to another (generally from the master server to slave servers). The purpose of doing so is to keep multiple servers in sync with respect to a zone's contents. Multiple servers provide resiliency to failure, in case a server should go down. Performance can also be improved as multiple servers can be used to share the processing load for incoming queries. Finally, the latency of a DNS query/response can potentially be reduced if servers are placed in locations close to clients (i.e., where the network latency between resolver and server is small).

As originally specified, zone transfers are initiated after *polling*, where slaves periodically contact masters to see if a zone transfer is necessary by comparing the zones' version numbers. A later method says if a zone transfer needs to be initiated using an asynchronous update mechanism when the zone contents change. This is called *DNS NOTIFY*. Once a zone transfer is initiated, either the entire zone is transferred (using DNS AXFR messages) [RFC5936], or an *incremental zone transfer* option may be used (using DNS IXFR messages) [RFC1995]. The general scheme operates according to the illustration in Figure 11-18.

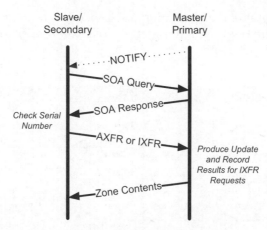

Figure 11-18   A DNS zone transfer copies the contents of zones between servers. An optional notification can cause a slave to request a full or incremental zone transfer.

We will now have a closer look at each of the options, including full and incremental zone transfers, plus DNS Notify.

11.5.8.1 Full Zone Transfers (AXFR Messages)

Full zone transfers are controlled by the zone transfer parameters carried in a zone's SOA record: primary name server, serial number, and the refresh, retry, and expire intervals. When configured, a slave server attempts to contact the primary server to see if a zone transfer is necessary. Contacts are attempted periodically, according to the refresh interval. They are also attempted when a server first starts. If a contact is not successful (no response from the server), retries are attempted periodically according to the retry interval (generally shorter than the refresh interval). The entire zone contents are flushed if not refreshed within the expire interval, effectively incapacitating the server for the zone.

An All Zone Transfer (AXFR) DNS message (a standard query containing type AXFR in the Question section) is used to request a complete zone transfer using TCP. To see such a message, we may arrange for a request to be initiated using the host program in our local network:

```
Linux% host -l home.
Using domain server:
Name: 10.0.0.1
Address: 10.0.0.1#53
Aliases:

home name server gw.home.
ap.home has address 10.0.0.6
gw.home has address 10.0.0.1
...
```

The –l flag asks the host program to perform a full zone transfer from a local DNS server. The program initiates a TCP-based query/response dialogue, illustrated in Figure 11-19.

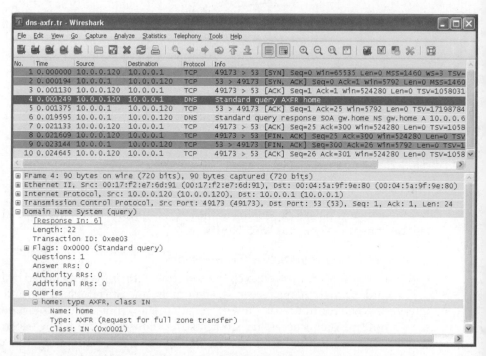

Figure 11-19   A DNS request for a full zone transfer uses the AXFR record type and TCP as a transport protocol.

In Figure 11-19 we can see how the zone transfer takes place using TCP. The first three TCP segments are part of the standard TCP connection establishment process (see Chapter 13). The fourth (decoded) packet is the request. It is a normal DNS standard, with type AXFR and class IN (Internet). The query is for the domain name home. The response to this query is contained in message 6, following the TCP ACK (see Figure 11-20).

Figure 11-20   The successful response for a full zone transfer request includes all of the records for the zone. The transaction takes place using TCP, as the zone contents may be large and a reliable copy is required.

In Figure 11-20 we can see how the entire zone is carried in the response. After receiving the response, the client's TCP ACKs the data and initiates a TCP connection close. The connection is closed gracefully using the FIN-ACK handshake (packets 8–10). See Chapter 13 for more details on the standard TCP connection establishment and clearing.

Although it used to be possible to perform such zone transfers with virtually any DNS server, they are now typically restricted to the authoritative servers in a zone (e.g., those listed in NS records for the zone). The reason for this restriction is privacy and security—knowledge of the hosts within the zone might help an attacker target particular services or hosts.

11.5.8.2 Incremental Zone Transfers (IXFR Messages)

To improve the efficiency of zone transfers, [RFC1995] defines the use of *incremental* zone transfers. Using incremental zone transfers and the IXFR message type, only the changes in a zone are provided. To execute an incremental zone transfer, the client (e.g., slave server) must provide its current serial number for the zone. In the following example, we can emulate a requesting server by providing the serial number and using the `dig` program:

```
Linux% dig +short @10.0.0.1 -t ixfr=1997022700 home.
gw.home. hostmaster.gw.home. 1997022700 10800 15 604800 10800
```

The command line indicates that output from the command should be short, 10.0.0.1 is the address of the DNS server to use, and an incremental zone transfer starting with serial number 1997022700 should be performed. This example creates an exchange similar to the one illustrated in Figures 11-19 and 11-20 for AXFR, except in this case the serial number of the request matches the current serial number (see Figure 11-21).

Figure 11-21   An incremental zone transfer request (IXFR record type) carried on TCP. The serial number is used to determine which records, if any, have changed since an earlier zone transfer took place.

Figure 11-22 shows how the IXFR request includes a mostly empty SOA RR in the authority section. The SOA record includes the serial number specified (1997022700). The response (packet 6) contains no real information because this serial number matches the current one at the server.

Figure 11-22 The response to an IXFR request when the serial number is current contains only an SOA record and no additional information.

The response in Figure 11-22 contains only the SOA RR in the answer section. Unlike the one contained in the query, this one is filled in with the complete SOA fields (e.g., mailbox, zone transfer parameters). However, there are no additional answers because the current serial number for the zone matches that of the request. Thus, the requesting client is assumed to be up-to-date and not in need of any additional information or a zone transfer.

11.5.8.3 DNS NOTIFY

As mentioned previously, polling has traditionally been used to determine the need for zone transfers, meaning that the slave servers would check with a master periodically (the "refresh" interval) to see if the zone had been updated (indicated by a different serial number), in which case a zone transfer would be initiated. This is a somewhat wasteful process because many useless polls may occur before the zone is updated. To improve the situation, [RFC1996] developed the *DNS NOTIFY* mechanism. DNS NOTIFY allows a server with modified zone contents to notify slave servers that an update has been made and a zone transfer should be initiated. More specifically, if enabled, a notification message is sent to a set of interested servers if the SOA RR for a zone changes (e.g., if the serial number increases). This allows zone transfers to be initiated easily when required. Using a local (home) name server, we can see how this works (see Figure 11-23).

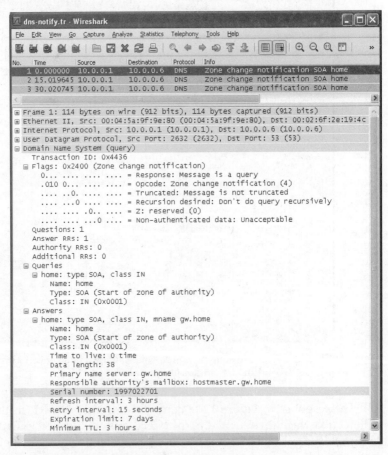

Figure 11-23   A DNS NOTIFY indicating an update to the zone file. There are two retransmissions spaced 15s apart (contrary to the method suggested in the standard).

This example illustrates the simple DNS NOTIFY message sent to a host in the server's *notify set* of servers that should be informed of a zone change. The message is a UDP/IPv4 DNS query message with the *Flags* field indicating a zone change notification. The query section contains the type and class for an SOA record, and the answer section contains the current SOA RR for the zone (with TTL 0), including the serial number. This provides sufficient information for a notified server to determine that a zone transfer may be necessary. Note that a single server may receive notifications from multiple other servers as they update their zone information. This does not present a problem for the protocol's operation.

The DNS NOTIFY mechanism defaults to using UDP, an unreliable protocol. In this particular example, the notify set contains only the address 10.0.0.11, which does not run a DNS server. Consequently, the message is resent every 15s hoping for a response that never arrives.

Note

The time between retransmissions and the total number of retransmissions to attempt are suggested by [RFC1996] to be 60s and five retransmissions, respectively. It also suggests that a timer backoff method (additive or exponential) be used. Here we can see that the BIND9 implementation fails to respect these suggestions, as the two retransmissions are 15s apart.

Responses are simply DNS response messages with no useful information except the transaction ID; they are used only to complete the protocol and cancel retransmissions at the sending server.

11.6   Sort Lists, Round-Robin, and Split DNS

So far we have discussed how domain names are set up, the types of resource records DNS supports, and the DNS protocol used to fetch and update a zone. One subtle point to consider is what data is returned and in what order in response to a DNS query. A DNS server could return all matching data to any client in whatever order the server finds most convenient. However, special configuration options and behaviors are available in most DNS server software to achieve certain operational, privacy, or performance goals. Consider the topology shown in Figure 11-24.

The type of topology shown in Figure 11-24 is typical of a small enterprise. There is a private network and a public network including a DNS server. In addition, there is a pair of hosts on the DMZ (A and B), one on the internal network (C) and one on the Internet (R). A multihomed host (M) spans the DMZ and internal networks. M therefore has two IP addresses drawn from two different network prefixes.

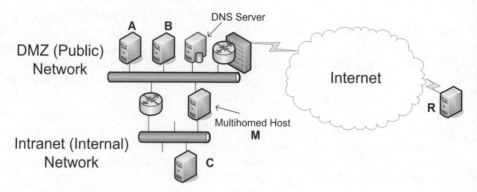

Figure 11-24   In a small enterprise topology, DNS may be configured to return different addresses depending on the requesting IP address.

A host wishing to contact M performs a DNS lookup that returns two addresses—one associated with the internal network and one with the DMZ. Naturally, it would be more efficient if A, B, and R reached M via the DMZ and C reached M via the internal network. This generally happens if the DNS server orders its returned address records based on the source IP address of the request. (It could also use the destination IP address, especially if M uses multiple IP addresses from different subnets on the same network interface.) If the requesting system uses a source IP address with the same network prefix as the source of a returning address record, the DNS server places the set of such matching records early in the returned message. This behavior encourages the client to find the "closest" IP address for a particular server it is attempting to contact, because most simple applications attempt to contact the first address found among the returned address records. The precise behavior can usually be controlled using a so-called `sortlist` or `rrset-order` directive (options used in configuration files for resolvers and servers). Such sorting behavior may also happen automatically if performed by the DNS server software by default.

A somewhat related situation arises when one service is offered using more than one server such that the incoming connections are load-balanced (i.e., divided among the servers). In the preceding example, imagine that a service is offered on both A and B. Such a service may be identified by the URL `http://www.example` `.com`. Requesting clients (like R) perform a DNS query on the domain name `www.example.com`, and the DNS server eventually returns a set of address records. To achieve load balancing, the DNS server may be configured to use *DNS round-robin*, which means that the server permutes the order of the returned address records. Doing so encourages each new client to access the service on a different server from the previous client. While this helps to balance load, it is far from perfect. When records are cached, the desired effect may not occur because of reuse of existing cached address records. In addition, this scheme may balance the number of connections well across servers, but not the load. Different connections can have radically different processing requirements, so the true processing load is likely to remain unbalanced unless the particular service always has the same processing requirements.

A final consideration regarding the data returned by a DNS server is support for privacy. In this example, we may wish to arrange for hosts within the enterprise to be able to retrieve resource records for every computer in the network, while we limit the set of systems that remain visible to R. A technique for implementing this goal is called *split DNS*. In split DNS, the set of resource records returned in response to a query is dependent on the identity of the client and possibly query destination address. Most often, the client is identified by IP address or address prefix. With split DNS, we could arrange for any host in the enterprise (i.e., those sharing a set of prefixes) to be provided with the entire DNS database, whereas those outside are given visibility only to A and B, where the main Web service is offered.

11.7 Open DNS Servers and DynDNS

Many home users are assigned a single IPv4 address by their ISP, and this address may change over time as the user's computer or home gateway connects, disconnects, and reconnects to the Internet. Consequently, it is often difficult for the user to establish a DNS entry that allows for running services that are visible from the Internet. A number of so-called open *Dynamic DNS* (DDNS) servers are available that support a special update protocol called the *DNS Update API* [DYNDNS], whereby a user may update an entry in a provider's DNS server given a preregistration or account. This scheme does *not* use the [RFC2136] DNS UPDATE protocol described earlier but is instead a separate application-layer protocol.

To use the service, a DDNS client program (e.g., `inadyn` or `ddclient` on Linux and `DynDNS Updater` for Windows) runs on the client system, which could also be a user's home router. Most often, these programs are configured with login information used to access a remote DDNS service. When the service is invoked, the client program contacts the server, provides the current global IP address of its host (the one assigned by an ISP, often a NAT mapped address), and goes quiescent. After that, it periodically renews the information with the server. Doing so allows the server to clear the information if an update is not received within a certain time interval. Such services include those provided at the following Web sites (as of 2011): `http://www.dyndns.com/services/dns/dyndns`, `http://freedns .afraid.org`, and `http://www.no-ip.com/services/managed_dns/free_ dynamic_dns.html`.

11.8 Transparency and Extensibility

The DNS is one of the most ubiquitous services on the Internet and has been an attractive service to consider as a basis for adding new capabilities through extensions. There are, for example, numerous record types such as TXT, SRV, and even A (e.g., see [RFC5782]) that could be used for encoding data useful for various future services. [RFC5507] considers various methods for extending the DNS, ultimately concluding that creation and implementation of new RR types is the most attractive approach. Thanks to an earlier specification [RFC3597], there is a standard method for handling unknown RR types as opaque data. That is, they are not interpreted unless recognized; the processing is *transparent*. This allows for new RR types to be carried along without causing negative impact on the processing of existing RR types.

One complication with preserving transparency is the encoding of embedded domain names and compression. For known RR types, embedded domain names are permitted to have their cases altered in order to achieve compression with compression labels. Owner domain names (the "keys" of queries) are always subject to compression. For unknown RR types, however, embedded domain names are not permitted to use compression labels. In addition, future RR types that contain embedded domain names are likewise prohibited (see Section 4 of [RFC3597]). Unknown types can still be compared (e.g., for dynamic updates) in a bitwise fashion. This implies that any embedded domain names are compared in a case-*sensitive* manner [RFC4343], contrary to most other DNS operations. This same situation appears for embedded domain names used with TXT records.

A different issue arises regarding transparency when new forms of servers and proxies are introduced that process DNS traffic. It is now relatively common practice to include a *DNS proxy* colocated inside a home gateway or firewall. A typical proxy handles incoming DNS requests from a user's home network and forwards the request to an ISP-provided name server. It also receives returned information and may or may not cache the results. Historically, some proxies have tried to do more than merely relay requests and replies, and this has caused some problems with DNS interoperability. [RFC5625] specifies the proper operation of a DNS proxy, essentially requiring DNS RRs to be uninterpreted and merely relayed by the proxy. In cases where packet truncation cannot be avoided, any such proxy must set the *TC* bit field to indicate that some DNS data was removed. Furthermore, any such proxies should be prepared to handle TCP requests, as this is the conventional fallback mechanism when a previous UDP-based request was truncated and is required by [RFC5966].

11.9   Translating DNS from IPv4 to IPv6 (DNS64)

In Chapter 7 we described a framework for translating IP datagrams back and forth between IPv4 and IPv6. Translators supporting such capabilities are envisioned to be deployed with a related capability that translates between DNS A and AAAA records [RFC6147], allowing IPv6-only clients to access DNS information that appears in A records (e.g., in the IPv4 Internet). The capability is called DNS64, and one of its proposed deployment scenarios (called "DNS64 in DNS recursive-resolver mode") is illustrated in Figure 11-25.

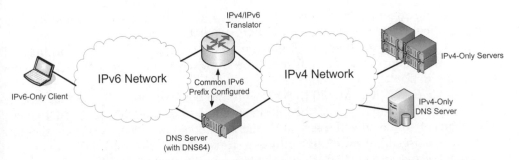

Figure 11-25   DNS64 translates A records to AAAA records and works together with an IPv4/IPv6 translator to allow IPv6-only clients to access services in IPv4 networks.

As shown in Figure 11-25, DNS64 is used in conjunction with an IPv4/IPv6 translator (see Chapter 7). Each device is configured with one or more common IPv6 prefixes used in creating IPv4-embedded addresses. Each prefix may be a Network-Specific Prefix (e.g., that is owned by an operator) or the Well-Known Prefix (64:ff9b::/96). The DNS64 device acts as a caching DNS server. IPv6-only clients use it as the primary DNS server and are able to request AAAA records for domain names. DNS64 converts such requests to requests for both A and AAAA records on its IPv4 side. If no AAAA records are returned, DNS64 provides *synthetic* AAAA records by forming an IPv4-embedded address based on the configured prefix and the contents of each A record it retrieves. DNS64 also responds to PTR queries for any of the IPv6 prefixes it uses for synthesizing AAAA RRs.

To implement AAA RR synthesis in a DNS64 device, only the answer section of a DNS message is effectively altered. Other sections remain as they appear when retrieved on the IPv4 side. In cases of CNAME or DNAME chains, the chain is followed recursively until an A or AAAA record is found and the elements of the chain are included in the response. In addition, DNS64 may be configured so as to avoid synthesis for particular excluded IPv6 or IPv4 address ranges. This prevents certain anomalous behavior (e.g., forming IPv4-embedded addresses based on special-use IPv4 addresses). Note that DNS64 has subtle interactions with DNSSEC; these issues are covered in Chapter 18.

11.10 LLMNR and mDNS

The ordinary DNS system requires a set of DNS servers to be configured to provide mappings between names and addresses, and possibly other information. Sometimes this is too much overhead when only a few local hosts wish to communicate. In cases where a DNS server is not available (e.g., a quickly formed ad hoc network of clients that connect only to each other), a special local version of DNS called *Link-Local Multicast Name Resolution* (LLMRR) [RFC4795] may be available. It is a (nonstandard) protocol based on DNS developed by Microsoft and used in local environments to help discover devices on a local area network, such as printers and file servers. It is supported in Windows Vista, Server 2008, and 7. It uses UDP port 5355 with the IPv4 multicast address 224.0.0.252 and IPv6 address ff02::1:3. The servers also use TCP on port 5355 from whatever unicast IP address they respond from.

Multicast DNS (mDNS) [IDMDNS] is another form of local DNS-like capability developed by Apple. When it is combined with the DNS Service Discovery protocol, Apple calls the resulting framework Bonjour. mDNS uses DNS messages carried over local multicast addresses. It uses UDP with port 5353. It specifies that the special TLD `.local` is to be treated with special semantics. The `.local` TLD is link-local in scope. Any DNS queries for domain names in this TLD are sent to the mDNS IPv4 address 224.0.0.251 or the IPv6 address ff02::fb. Queries for other domains may optionally be sent to these multicast addresses. Allowing link-local servers to respond to mappings for global names can raise significant security concerns. To combat this problem, DNSSEC can be employed (see Chapter 18). mDNS supports autonomous assignment of names in the `.local` pseudo-TLD, although this pseudo-TLD has not been officially reserved for this purpose [RFC2606]. Thus, hosts on small networks such as home LANs can be assigned convenient names such as `printer.local`, `fileserver.local`, `cameral.local`, `kevinlaptop.local`, and the like. A mechanism in mDNS is used to detect and resolve conflicts.

11.11 LDAP

So far we have discussed DNS and local name services that resemble DNS. To support richer queries and data manipulations, there is a more general directory service we mentioned earlier called LDAP [RFC4510]. LDAP (now LDAPv3) is an application protocol for the Internet that provides access to general directories (e.g., "white pages") in accordance with the X.500 (1993) [X500] data and service models. It provides the ability to search, modify, add, compare, and remove entries based on user-selected patterns. An LDAP directory is a tree of directory entries, where each entry consists of a set of attributes. As TCP/IP has become more popular, LDAP has evolved from its roots to work in conjunction with DNS. For example, a query about directory entries matching the chancellor's office at MIT could be formed using the LDAP search tool `ldapsearch` (Microsoft has a comparable tool called `ldp` available as a support tool from its Web site), which works as follows:

```
Linux% ldapsearch -x -h ldap.mit.edu -b "dc=mit,dc=edu" \
"(ou=*Chancellor*)"
# extended LDIF
#
# LDAPv3
# base <dc=mit,dc=edu> with scope sub
```

```
# filter: (ou=*Chancellor*)
# requesting: ALL
#
.....
```

The command line indicates that the server `ldap.mit.edu` should be contacted without using any special authentication protocol (-x option). While a complete discussion of LDAP is well beyond the scope of this chapter (and book!), the partial output shows how the `dc` (domain component) attribute is used to link LDAP data with the DNS. Each `dc` component holds one DNS label, and together they can be used to encode an entire domain name, which is used as the "base" portion for the LDAP query. Using this convention, it is not especially difficult to form valid LDAP queries. In this case, it is for the organizational unit (ou) containing the word `Chancellor`. Note that wildcards can be used.

LDAP servers are used most often within enterprises to hold directory information such as location, telephone number, and organizational unit. Microsoft's Active Directory product includes LDAP capabilities and is used extensively for managing user accounts, services, and access rights in large enterprises using Windows. Some LDAP servers (such as MIT's and those of many other universities) are also available through the public Internet.

11.12 Attacks on the DNS

The DNS is a critical component of the Internet and has been the object of several attacks and countermeasures over the years [RFC3833]. Relatively recently, a global effort called DNS Security (DNSSEC) has made substantial progress in adding strong authentication to DNS operations. We defer the detailed discussion of how DNSSEC works to Chapter 18, where we also cover the necessary cryptography background. We now explore some of the attacks that have been waged against the DNS.

There have been two main forms of attacks against the DNS. The first form involves a DoS attack where the DNS is rendered inoperative because of overloading of important DNS servers, such as the root or TLD servers. The second form alters the contents of resource records or masquerades as an official DNS server but responds with bogus resource records, thereby causing hosts to contact the incorrect IP address when attempting to connect to another machine (e.g., a Web site such as a bank).

The first major DoS attack on DNS took place in early 2001. The attack involved generating many requests for the MX records of AOL.COM. The attacker generated DNS requests for an MX record using forged source IP addresses. The request is a relatively small packet, whereas the response is larger (by about a factor of 20), so this type of attack is called an *amplification* attack because the amount of bandwidth consumed as the result of the attack is greater than the amount used in generating the attack by a significant factor. The responses are directed at the

IP address contained in the request packets, so the attacker could essentially cause the response traffic to be directed wherever (s)he intended. The attack is documented in detail in a CERT incident note [CIN].

A form of attack involving modification of the data within DNS was reported in late 2008 [CKB] and is now known as the *Kaminsky Attack*. It involves *cache poisoning*, where the cached contents of a DNS server are replaced with erroneous or forged data and ultimately served to the resolvers on end hosts. In one variant, an attacker responds to a caching server's query for an A record with an NS record for the domain using a particular host domain name. The host's IP address (chosen by the attacker) is also provided in the additional information section of the DNS response. The host domain name may or may not share the same subdomains as the original DNS request. The main risk associated with this form of attack is that clients that depend on proper DNS name-to-address resolution may be directed to fake servers. If such servers are intentionally configured to mimic the original host (e.g., masquerading as a bank's Web server), users may unwittingly trust the masquerading server and divulge sensitive information. Mitigation techniques for this and other related attacks are given by [RFC5452]. One approach not described in [RFC5452] called *DNS-0x20* [D08] involves encoding a nonce in the 0x20 bit position of each character in the Query Name part of a question section that is echoed back in the corresponding area of each response. This is made possible because, although domain names are compared in a case-insensitive way, servers tend to return an exact copy of the Query Name when forming responses. If the case of the owner's name is intentionally mixed up in the query, an unsolicited response will have difficulty reproducing the nonce, and can more readily be identified (and ignored).

11.13 Summary

The DNS is an essential part of the Internet, and DNS technology is widely used in private networks as well. The DNS name space is worldwide in scope and is divided into a hierarchy starting with top-level domains (TLDs). Domain names can be represented in multiple languages and scripts using internationalized domain names (IDNs). Applications use resolvers to contact one or more DNS servers to perform lookup tasks against a zone database, such as converting a host name to an IP address and vice versa. Resolvers then contact a local name server, and this server may act recursively to contact one of the root servers or other servers to fulfill the request. Most DNS servers, and some resolvers, cache information learned in order to provide it to subsequent clients for some period of time called the time to live (TTL). Queries and responses use a special DNS protocol that works with either TCP or UDP. The protocol also works with either IPv4 or IPv6, or any mixture of the two.

All DNS queries and responses have the same basic message format that includes questions, answers, authority information, and additional information.

Resource records are used to hold most DNS information, and there are many such types: addresses, mail exchange points, pointers to names, among others. In the Internet, most DNS messages are carried using UDP/IPv4 and are limited to 512 bytes in length, but a special extension option (EDNS0) provides for longer messages and is required to support DNS security (DNSSEC), which we discuss in detail in Chapter 18.

DNS supports some special features such as zone transfers and dynamic updates. Zone transfers (complete or incremental) are used to allow redundant slave servers to synchronize the zone contents with a master server, primarily for redundancy. Dynamic updates allow zone contents to be modified by an application using an online protocol. There are really two forms of this capability, one standardized by [RFC2136] and used in enterprises and a nonstandard but very popular dynamic DNS capability that allows users assigned temporary IP addresses (e.g., on cable or DSL) to obtain a DNS entry so that services they provide can be found by name throughout the world.

DNS has been the subject of numerous attacks, ranging from DoS attacks that leave the DNS with limited capability, to cache poisoning attacks that can be used to make malicious servers appear to be legitimate. Various techniques have arisen to combat this problem, including cryptographic techniques (covered in Chapter 18) and modifications to DNS servers to be less accepting of unsolicited DNS responses.

11.14 References

[AL06] P. Albitz and C. Liu, *DNS and BIND, Fifth Edition* (O'Reilly Media, Inc., 2006).

[CIN] http://www.cert.org/incident_notes/IN-2000-04.html

[CKB] http://www.kb.cert.org/vuls/id/800113

[D08] D. Dagon et al., "Increased DNS Forgery Resistance Through 0x20-bit Encoding," *Proc. ACM CCS*, Oct. 2008.

[DNSPARAM] http://www.iana.org/assignments/dns-parameters

[DR97] D. Dougherty and A. Robbins, *sed & awk, Second Edition* (O'Reilly Media, 1997).

[DYNDNS] http://www.dyndns.com/about/technology

[ENUM] http://www.iana.org/assignments/enum-services

[GTLD] http://www.iana.org/domains/root/db

[ICANN] http://www.icann.org/en/tlds

[IDDN] S. Rose and W. Wijngaards, "Update to DNAME Redirection in the DNS," Internet draft-ietf-dnsext-rfc2672bis-dname, work in progress, July 2011.

[IDMDNS] S. Cheshire and M. Krochmal, "Multicast DNS," Internet draft-cheshire-dnsext-multicastdns, work in progress, Feb. 2011.

[IIDN] http://www.icann.org/en/topics/idn

[ISO3166] International Organization for Standardization, "International Standard for Country Codes," ISO 3166-1, 2006.

[ISPR] http://www.iana.org/assignments/service-names-port-numbers

[J02] J. Jung et al., "DNS Performance and the Effectiveness of Caching," *IEEE/ACM Transactions on Networking*, 10(5), Oct. 2002.

[MD88] P. Mockapetris and K. Dunlap, "Development of the Domain Name System," *Proc. ACM SIGCOMM*, Aug. 1988.

[P10] N. Paskin, "Digital Object Identifier (DOI©) System," *Encyclopedia of Library and Information Sciences, Third Edition* (Taylor and Francis, 2010).

[R06] H. Rice, "ENUM—The Mapping of Telephone Numbers to the Internet," *The Telecommunications Review*, 17, Aug. 2006.

[RFC1035] P. Mockapetris, "Domain Names—Implementation and Specification," Internet RFC 1035/STD 0013, Nov. 1987.

[RFC1464] R. Rosenbaum, "Using the Domain Name System to Store Arbitrary String Attributes," Internet RFC 1464 (experimental), May 1993.

[RFC1536] A. Kumar et al., "Common DNS Implementation Errors and Suggested Fixes," Internet RFC 1536 (informational), Oct. 1993.

[RFC1912] D. Barr, "Common DNS Operational and Configuration Errors," Internet RFC 1912 (informational), Feb. 1996.

[RFC1918] Y. Rekhter, B. Moskowitz, D. Karrenberg, G. J. de Groot, and E. Lear, "Address Allocation for Private Internets," RFC 1918/BCP 0005, Feb. 1996.

[RFC1995] M. Ohta, "Incremental Zone Transfer in DNS," Internet RFC 1995, Aug. 1996.

[RFC1996] P. Vixie, "A Mechanism for Prompt Notification of Zone Changes (DNS NOTIFY)," Internet RFC 1996, Aug. 1996.

[RFC2136] P. Vixie, ed., S. Thomson, Y. Rekhter, and J. Bound, "Dynamic Updates in the Domain Name System (DNS UPDATE)," Internet RFC 2136, Apr. 1997.

[RFC2141] R. Moats, "URN Syntax," Internet RFC 2141, May 1997.

[RFC2181] R. Elz and R. Bush, "Clarifications to the DNS Specification," Internet RFC 2181, July 1997.

[RFC2308] M. Andrews, "Negative Caching of DNS Queries (DNS NCACHE)," Internet RFC 2308, Mar. 1998.

[RFC2317] H. Eidnes, G. de Groot, and P. Vixie, "Classless IN-ADDR.ARPA Delegation," Internet RFC 2317/BCP 0020, Mar. 1998.

[RFC2606] D. Eastlake 3rd and A. Panitz, "Reserved Top Level DNS Names," Internet RFC 2606/BCP 0032, June 1999.

[RFC2671] P. Vixie, "Extension Mechanisms for DNS (EDNS0)," Internet RFC 2671, Aug. 1999.

[RFC2672] M. Crawford, "Non-Terminal DNS Name Redirection," Internet RFC 2672, Aug. 1999.

[RFC2782] A. Gulbrandsen, P. Vixie, and L. Esibov, "A DNS RR for Specifying the Location of Services (DNS SRV)," Internet RFC 2782, Feb. 2000.

[RFC2845] P. Vixie, O. Gudmundsson, D. Eastlake 3rd, and B. Wellington, "Secret Key Transaction Authentication for DNS (TSIG)," Internet RFC 2845, May 2000.

[RFC2930] D. Eastlake 3rd, "Secret Key Establishment for DNS (TKEY RR)," Internet RFC 2930, Sept. 2000.

[RFC3172] G. Huston, ed., "Management Guidelines and Operational Requirements for the Address and Routing Parameter Area Domain (arpa)," Internet RFC 3172/BCP 0052, Sept. 2001.

[RFC3263] J. Rosenberg and H. Schulzrinne, "Session Initiation Protocol (SIP): Locating SIP Servers," Internet RFC 3263, June 2002.

[RFC3401] M. Mealling, "Dynamic Delegation Discovery System (DDDS)—Part One: The Comprehensive DDDS," Internet RFC 3401 (informational), Oct. 2002.

[RFC3402] M. Mealling, "Dynamic Delegation Discovery System (DDDS)—Part Two: The Algorithm," Internet RFC 3402, Oct. 2002.

[RFC3403] M. Mealling, "Dynamic Delegation Discovery System (DDDS)—Part Three: The Domain Name System (DNS) Database," Internet RFC 3403, Oct. 2002.

[RFC3404] M. Mealling, "Dynamic Delegation Discovery System (DDDS)—Part Four: The Uniform Resource Identifiers (URI) Resolution Application," Internet RFC 3404, Oct. 2002.

[RFC3492] A. Costello, "Punycode: A Bootstring Encoding of Unicode for Internationalized Domain Names in Applications (IDNA)," Internet RFC 3492, Mar. 2003.

[RFC3596] S. Thomson, C. Huitema, V. Ksinant, and M. Souissi, "DNS Extensions to Support IP Version 6," Internet RFC 3596, Oct. 2003.

[RFC3597] A. Gustafsson, "Handling of Unknown DNS Resource Record (RR) Types," Internet RFC 3597, Sept. 2003.

[RFC3833] D. Atkins and R. Austein, "Threat Analysis of the Domain Name System (DNS)," Internet RFC 3833 (informational), Aug. 2004.

[RFC3958] L. Daigle and A. Newton, "Domain-Based Application Service Location Using SRV RRs and the Dynamic Delegation Discovery Service (DDDS)," Internet RFC 3958, Jan. 2005.

[RFC3981] A. Newton and M. Sanz, "IRIS: The Internet Registry Information Service (IRIS) Core Protocol," Internet RFC 3981, Jan. 2005.

[RFC3986] T. Berners-Lee, R. Fielding, and L. Masinter, "Uniform Resource Identifier (URI): Generic Syntax," Internet RFC 3986/STD 0066, Jan. 2005.

[RFC4193] R. Hinden and B. Haberman, "Unique Local IPv6 Unicast Addresses," Internet RFC 4193, Oct. 2005.

[RFC4343] D. Eastlake 3rd, "Domain Name System (DNS) Case Insensitivity Clarification," Internet RFC 4343, Jan. 2006.

[RFC4406] J. Lyon and M. Wong, "Sender ID: Authenticating E-Mail," Internet RFC 4406 (experimental), Apr. 2006.

[RFC4592] E. Lewis, "The Role of Wildcards in the Domain Name System," Internet RFC 4592, July 2006.

[RFC4408] M. Wong and W. Schlitt, "Sender Policy Framework (SPF) for Authorizing Use of Domains in E-Mail, Version 1," Internet RFC 4408 (experimental), Apr. 2006.

[RFC4510] K. Zeilenga, ed., "Lightweight Directory Access Protocol (LDAP): Technical Specification Road Map," Internet RFC 4510, June 2006.

[RFC4690] J. Klensin, P. Falstrom, and C. Karp, "Review and Recommendations for Internationalized Domain Names (IDNs)," Internet RFC 4690 (informational), Sept. 2006.

[RFC4698] E. Gunduz, A. Newton, and S. Kerr, "IRIS: An Address Registry (areg) Type for the Internet Registry Information Service," Internet RFC 4698, Oct. 2006.

[RFC4795] B . Aboba, D. Thaler, and L. Esibov, "Link-Local Multicast Name Resolution (LLMNR)," Internet RFC 4795 (informational), Jan. 2007.

[RFC4848] L. Daigle, "Domain-Based Application Service Location Using URIs and the Dynamic Delegation Discovery Service (DDDS)," Internet RFC 4848, Apr. 2007.

[RFC4960] R. Stewart, ed., "Stream Control Transmission Protocol," Internet RFC 4960, Sept. 2007.

[RFC5001] R. Austein, "DNS Name Server Identifier (NSID) Option," Internet RFC 5001, Aug. 2007.

[RFC5222] T. Hardie et al., "LoST: A Location-to-Service Translation Protocol," Internet RFC 5222, Aug. 2008.

[RFC5321] J. Klensin, "Simple Mail Transfer Protocol," Internet RFC 5321, Oct. 2008.

[RFC5452] A. Hubert and R. van Mook, "Measures for Making DNS More Resilient against Forged Answers," Internet RFC 5452, Jan. 2009.

[RFC5483] L. Conroy and K. Fujiwara, "ENUM Implementation Issues and Experiences," Internet RFC 5483 (informational), Mar. 2009.

[RFC5507] P. Falstrom, R. Austein, and P. Koch, eds., "Design Choices When Expanding the DNS," Internet RFC 5507 (informational), Apr. 2009.

[RFC5509] S. Loreto, "Internet Assigned Numbers Authority (IANA) Registration of Instant Messaging and Presence DNS SRV RRs for the Session Initiation Protocol (SIP)," Internet RFC 5509, Apr. 2009.

[RFC5625] R. Bellis, "DNS Proxy Implementation Guidelines," Internet RFC 5625/BCP 0152, Aug. 2009.

[RFC5782] J. Levine, "DNS Blacklists and Whitelists," Internet RFC 5782 (informational), Feb. 2010.

[RFC5855] J. Abley and T. Manderson, "Nameservers for IPv4 and IPv6 Reverse Zones," Internet RFC 5855/BCP 0155, May 2010.

[RFC5890] J. Klensin, "Internationalized Domain Names for Applications (IDNA): Definitions and Document Framework," Internet RFC 5890, Aug. 2010.

[RFC5891] J. Klensin, "Internationalized Domain Names in Applications (IDNA): Protocol," Internet RFC 5891, Aug. 2010.

[RFC5936] E. Lewis and A. Hoenes, ed., "DNS Zone Transfer Protocol (AXFR)," Internet RFC 5936, June 2010.

[RFC5966] R. Bellis, "DNS Transport over TCP—Implementation Requirements," Internet RFC 5966, Aug. 2010.

[RFC6116] S. Bradner, L. Conroy, and K. Fujiwara, "The E.164 to Uniform Resource Identifiers (URI) Dynamic Delegation Discovery System (DDDS) Application (ENUM)," Internet RFC 6116, Mar. 2011.

[RFC6117] B. Hoeneisen, A. Mayrhofer, and J. Livingood, "IANA Registration of Enumservices: Guide, Template, and IANA Considerations," Internet RFC 6117, Mar. 2011.

[RFC6147] M. Bagnulo, A. Sullivan, P. Matthews, and I. van Beijnum, "DNS64: DNS Extensions for Network Address Translation from IPv6 Clients to IPv4 Servers," Internet RFC 6147, Apr. 2011.

[RFC6168] W. Hardaker, "Requirements for Management of Name Servers for the DNS," Internet RFC 6168 (informational), May 2011.

[RFC6186] C. Daboo, "Use of SRV Records for Locating Email Submission/Access Services," Internet RFC 6186, Mar. 2011.

[RFC6195] D. Eastlake 3rd, "Domain Name System (DNS) IANA Considerations," Internet RFC 6195/BCP 0042, Mar. 2011.

[RFC6303] M. Andrews, "Locally Served DNS Zones," Internet RFC 6303/BCP 0163, July 2011.

[ROOTS] http://www.root-servers.org

[RSYNC] http://rsync.samba.org

[SNP] http://www.iana.org/assignments/s-naptr-parameters

[U11] The Unicode Consortium, *The Unicode Standard, Version 6.0.0* (The Unicode Consortium, 2011).

[URI] http://www.iana.org/assignments/uri-schemes

[URN] http://www.iana.org/assignments/urn-namespaces

[X500] International Telecommunication Union—Telecommunication Standardization Sector, "The Directory—Overview of Concepts, Models and Services," ITU-T X.500, 1993.

12

TCP: The Transmission Control Protocol (Preliminaries)

12.1 Introduction

So far we have been discussing protocols that do not include their own mechanisms for delivering data reliably. They may *detect* that erroneous data has been received, using a mathematical function such as a checksum or CRC, but they do not try very hard to repair errors. With IP and UDP, no error repair is done at all. With Ethernet and other protocols based on it, the protocol provides some number of retries and then gives up if it cannot succeed.

The problem of communicating in environments where the communication medium may lose or alter the messages being delivered has been studied for years. Some of the most important theoretical work on the topic was developed by Claude Shannon in 1948 [S48]. This work, which popularized the term bit and became the foundation of the field of *information theory*, helps us understand the fundamental limits on the amount of information that can be moved across an information channel that is *lossy* (that may delete or alter bits). Information theory is closely related to the field of *coding theory*, which provides ways of encoding information so that it is as resilient as possible to errors in the communications channel. Using *error-correcting codes* (basically, adding redundant bits so that the real information can be retrieved even if some bits are damaged) to correct communications problems is one very important method for handling errors. Another is to simply "try sending again" until the information is finally received. This approach, called *Automatic Repeat Request* (ARQ), forms the basis for many communications protocols, including TCP.

12.1.1   ARQ and Retransmission

If we consider not only a single communication channel but the multihop cascade of several, we realize that not only may we have the types of errors mentioned so far (packet bit errors), but there may be others. These problems might arise at an intermediate router and are the types of problems we brought up when discussing IP: packet reordering, packet duplication, and packet erasures (drops). An error-correcting protocol designed for use over a multihop communications channel (such as IP) must cope with all of these problems. Let us now explore the protocol mechanisms that can be brought to bear on them. After we discuss these in the abstract, we shall explore how they are used by TCP in the Internet.

A straightforward method of dealing with packet drops (and bit errors) is to resend the packet until it is received properly. This requires a way to determine (1) whether the receiver has received the packet and (2) whether the packet it received was the same one the sender sent. The method for a receiver to signal to a sender that it has received a packet is called an *acknowledgment*, or ACK. In its most basic form, the sender sends a packet and awaits an ACK. When the receiver receives the packet, it sends the ACK. When the sender receives the ACK, it sends another packet, and the process continues. Interesting questions to ask here are (1) How long should the sender wait for an ACK? (2) What if the ACK is lost? (3) What if the packet was received but had errors in it?

As we shall see, the first question turns out to be deep. Deciding how long to wait relates to how long the sender should *expect* to wait for an ACK. Determining this may be difficult; we postpone the discussion of techniques for it until we discuss TCP in detail later (see Chapter 14). The answer to question 2 is easier: if an ACK is dropped, the sender cannot readily distinguish this case from the case in which the original packet is dropped, so it simply sends the packet again. Of course, the receiver may receive two or more copies in that case, so it must be prepared to handle that situation (see the next paragraph). As for the third question, we appeal to the codes mentioned in Section 12.1. It is generally much easier to use codes to *detect* errors in a large packet (with high probability) using only a few bits than it is to correct them. Simpler codes are typically not capable of correcting errors but are capable of detecting them. That is why checksums and CRCs are so popular. In order to detect errors in a packet, then, we use a form of checksum. When a receiver receives a packet containing an error, it refrains from sending an ACK. Eventually, the sender resends the packet, which ideally arrives undamaged.

Even with the simple scenario presented so far, there is the possibility that the receiver might receive *duplicate* copies of the packet being transferred. This problem is addressed using a *sequence number*. Basically, every unique packet gets a new sequence number when it is sent at the source, and this sequence number is carried along in the packet itself. The receiver can use this number to determine whether it has already seen the packet and if so, discard it.

The protocol described so far is reliable but not very efficient. Consider what happens when the time to deliver even a small packet from sender to receiver (the delay or latency) is large (e.g., a second or two, which is not unusual for satellite links) and there are several packets to send. The sender is able to inject a single packet into the communications path but then must stop until it hears the ACK. This protocol is therefore called "stop and wait." Its throughput performance (data sent on the network per unit time) is proportional to M/R where M is the packet size and R is the round-trip time (RTT), assuming no packets are lost or irreparably damaged in transit. For a fixed-size packet, as R goes up, the throughput goes down. If packets are lost or damaged, the situation is even worse: the "goodput" (useful amount of data transferred per unit time) can be considerably less than the throughput.

For a network that doesn't damage or drop many packets, the cause for low throughput is usually that the network is not being kept busy. The situation is similar to using an assembly line where new work cannot enter the line until a complete product emerges. Most of the line goes idle. If we take this comparison one step further, it seems obvious that we would do better if we could have more than one work unit in the line at a time. It is the same for network communication—if we could have more than one packet in the network, we would keep it "more busy," leading to higher throughput.

Allowing more than one packet to be in the network at a time complicates matters considerably. Now the sender must decide not only when to inject a packet into the network, but also how many. It also must figure out how to keep the timers when waiting for ACKs, and it must keep a copy of each packet not yet acknowledged in case retransmissions are necessary. The receiver needs to have a more sophisticated ACK mechanism: one that can distinguish which packets have been received and which have not. The receiver may need a more sophisticated buffering (packet storage) mechanism—one that allows it to hold "out-of-sequence" packets (those packets that have arrived earlier than those expected because of loss or reordering), unless it simply wants to throw away such packets, which is very inefficient. There are other issues that may not be so obvious. What if the receiver is slower than the sender? If the sender simply injects many packets at a very high rate, the receiver might just drop them because of processing or memory limitations. The same question can be asked about the routers in the middle. What if the network infrastructure cannot handle the rate of data the sender and receiver wish to use?

12.1.2 Windows of Packets and Sliding Windows

To handle all of these problems, we begin with the assumption that each unique packet has a sequence number, as described earlier. We define a *window* of packets as the collection of packets (or their sequence numbers) that have been injected by the sender but not yet completely acknowledged (i.e., the sender has not received an ACK for them). We refer to the *window size* as the number of packets in the window. The term *window* comes from the idea that if you lined up all the packets sent during a communication session in a long row but had only a small aperture through which to view them, you would see only a subset of them—like peering through a window. The sender's window (and the line of other packets) can be graphically depicted as shown in Figure 12-1.

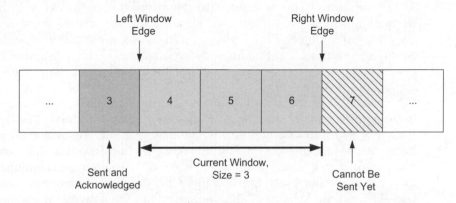

Figure 12-1   The sender's window, showing which packets are eligible to be sent (or have already been sent), which are not yet eligible, and which have already been sent and acknowledged. In this example, the window size is fixed at three packets.

This figure shows the current window of three packets, for a total window size of 3. Packet number 3 has already been sent and acknowledged, so the copy of it that the sender was keeping can now be released. Packet 7 is ready at the sender but not yet able to be sent because it is not yet "in" the window. If we now imagine that data starts to flow from the sender to the receiver and ACKs start to flow in the reverse direction, the sender might next receive an ACK for packet 4. When this happens, the window "slides" to the right by one packet, meaning that the copy of packet 4 can be released and packet 7 can be sent. This movement of the window gives rise to another name for this type of protocol, a *sliding window* protocol.

The sliding window approach can be used to combat many of the problems described so far. Typically, this window structure is kept at both the sender and the receiver. At the sender, it keeps track of what packets can be released, what packets are awaiting ACKs, and what packets cannot yet be sent. At the receiver, it keeps track of what packets have already been received and acknowledged, what packets are expected (and how much memory has been allocated to hold them), and which packets, even if received, will not be kept because of limited memory. Although the window structure is convenient for keeping track of data as it flows between sender and receiver, it does not provide guidance as to how large the window should be, or what happens if the receiver or network cannot handle the sender's data rate. We shall now see how these are related.

12.1.3 Variable Windows: Flow Control and Congestion Control

To handle the problem that arises when a receiver is too slow relative to a sender, we introduce a way to force the sender to slow down when the receiver cannot keep up. This is called *flow control* and is usually handled in one of two ways. One way, called *rate-based* flow control, gives the sender a certain data rate allocation and ensures that data is never allowed to be sent at a rate that exceeds the allocation. This type of flow control is most appropriate for streaming applications and can be used with broadcast and multicast delivery (see Chapter 9).

The other predominant form of flow control is called *window-based* flow control and is the most popular approach when sliding windows are being used. In this approach, the window size is not fixed but is instead allowed to vary over time. To achieve flow control using this technique, there must be a method for the receiver to signal the sender how large a window to use. This is typically called a *window advertisement*, or simply a *window update*. This value is used by the sender (i.e., the receiver of the window advertisement) to adjust its window size. Logically, a window update is separate from the ACKs we discussed previously, but in practice the window update and ACK are carried in a single packet, meaning that the sender tends to adjust the size of its window at the same time it slides it to the right.

If we consider the effect of changing the window size at the sender, it becomes clear how this achieves flow control. The sender is allowed to inject W packets into the network before it hears an ACK for any of them. If the sender and receiver are sufficiently fast, and the network loses no packets and has an infinite capacity, this means that the transfer rate is proportional to (SW/R) bits/s, where W is the window size, S is the packet size in bits, and R is the RTT. When the window advertisement from the receiver clamps the value of W at the sender, the sender's overall rate can be limited so as to not overwhelm the receiver. This approach works fine for protecting the receiver, but what about the network in between? We may have routers with limited memory between the sender and the receiver that have to contend with slow network links. When this happens, it is possible for the sender's rate to exceed a router's ability to keep up, leading to packet loss. This is addressed with a special form of flow control called *congestion control*.

Congestion control involves the sender slowing down so as to not overwhelm the network between itself and the receiver. Recall that in our discussion of flow control, we used a window advertisement to signal the sender to slow down for the receiver. This is called *explicit* signaling, because there is a protocol field specifically used to inform the sender about what is happening. Another option might be for the sender to *guess* that it needs to slow down. Such an approach would involve *implicit* signaling—that is, it would involve deciding to slow down based on some other evidence.

The problem of congestion control in datagram-style networks, and more generally *queuing theory* to which it is closely related, has remained a major research topic for years, and it is unlikely to ever be solved completely for all circumstances. It is also not practical to discuss all the options and methods of performing flow control here. The interested reader is referred to [J90], [K97], and [K75]. In Chapter 16 we will explore the particular congestion control technique used with TCP in more detail, along with a number of variants that have arisen over the years.

12.1.4 Setting the Retransmission Timeout

One of the most important performance issues the designer of a retransmission-based reliable protocol faces is how long to wait before concluding that a packet has been lost and should be resent. Stated another way, What should the retransmission timeout be? Intuitively, the amount of time the sender should wait before resending a packet is about the sum of the following times: the time to send the packet, the time for the receiver to process it and send an ACK, the time for the ACK to travel back to the sender, and the time for the sender to process the ACK. Unfortunately, in practice, none of these times are known with certainty. To make matters worse, any or all of them vary over time as additional load is added to or removed from the end hosts or routers.

Because it is not practical for the user to tell the protocol implementation what the values of all the times are (or to keep them up-to-date) for all circumstances, a better strategy is to have the protocol implementation try to estimate them. This is called *round-trip-time estimation* and is a statistical process. Basically, the true RTT is likely to be close to the sample mean of a collection of samples of RTTs. Note that this average naturally changes over time (it is not stationary), as the paths taken through the network may change.

Once some estimate of the RTT is made, the question of setting the actual timeout value, used to trigger retransmissions, remains. If we recall the definition of a mean, it can never be the extreme value of a set of samples (unless they are all the same). So, it would not be sensible to set the retransmission timer to be exactly equal to the mean estimator, as it is likely that many actual RTTs will be larger, thereby inducing unwanted retransmissions. Clearly, the timeout should be set to something larger than the mean, but exactly what this relationship is (or even if the mean should be directly used) is not yet clear. Setting the timeout too large is also undesirable, as this leads back to letting the network go idle, reducing throughput. We shall defer further exploration of this topic to Chapter 14, where we explore how TCP, in particular, approaches this problem.

12.2 Introduction to TCP

Given the background we now have regarding the issues affecting reliable delivery in general, let us see how they play out in TCP and what type of service it provides to Internet applications. We also look at the fields in the TCP header, noticing how many of the concepts we have seen so far (e.g., ACKs, window advertisements) are captured in the header description. In the chapters that follow, we examine all of these header fields in more detail.

Our description of TCP starts in this chapter and continues in the next five chapters. Chapter 13 describes how a TCP connection is established and terminated. Chapter 14 details how TCP estimates the per-connection RTT and how the retransmission timeout is set based on this estimate. Chapter 15 looks at the normal transfer of data, starting with "interactive" applications (such as chat). It then covers window management and flow control, which apply to both interactive and "bulk" data flow applications (such as file transfer), along with TCP's *urgent mechanism*, which allows a sender to mark certain data in the data stream as special. Chapter 16 takes a look at congestion control algorithms in TCP that help to reduce packet loss when the network is very busy. It also discusses some modifications that have been proposed to increase throughput on fast networks or improve resiliency on lossy (e.g., wireless) networks. Finally, Chapter 17 shows how TCP keeps connections active even when no data is flowing.

The original specification for TCP is [RFC0793], although some errors in that RFC are corrected in the Host Requirements RFC, [RFC1122]. Since then, specifications for TCP have been revised and extended to include clarified and improved congestion control behavior [RFC5681][RFC3782][RFC3517][RFC3390][RFC3168], retransmission timeouts [RFC6298][RFC5682][RFC4015], operation with NATs [RFC5382], acknowledgment behavior [RFC2883], security [RFC6056][RFC5927][RFC5926], connection management [RFC5482], and urgent mechanism implementation guidelines [RFC6093]. There have also been a rich variety of experimental modifications covering retransmission behaviors [RFC5827][RFC3708], congestion detection and control [RFC5690][RFC5562][RFC4782][RFC3649][RFC2861], and other features. Finally, there is an effort to explore how TCP might take advantage of multiple simultaneous network-layer paths [RFC6182].

12.2.1 The TCP Service Model

Even though TCP and UDP use the same network layer (IPv4 or IPv6), TCP provides a totally different service to the application layer from what UDP does. TCP provides a *connection-oriented*, reliable, byte stream service. The term *connection-oriented* means that the two applications using TCP must establish a TCP connection by contacting each other before they can exchange data. The typical analogy is dialing a telephone number, waiting for the other party to answer the phone and saying "Hello," and then saying "Who's calling?" There are exactly two endpoints communicating with each other on a TCP connection; concepts such as broadcasting and multicasting (see Chapter 9) are not applicable to TCP.

TCP provides a byte stream abstraction to applications that use it. The consequence of this design decision is that no record markers or message boundaries are automatically inserted by TCP (see Chapter 1). A record marker corresponds to an indication of an application's write extent. If the application on one end writes 10 bytes, followed by a write of 20 bytes, followed by a write of 50 bytes, the application at the other end of the connection cannot tell what size the individual writes were. For example, the other end may read the 80 bytes in four reads of 20 bytes at a time or in some other way. One end puts a stream of bytes into TCP, and the identical stream of bytes appears at the other end. Each endpoint individually chooses its read and write sizes.

TCP does not interpret the contents of the bytes in the byte stream at all. It has no idea if the data bytes being exchanged are binary data, ASCII characters, EBCDIC characters, or something else. The interpretation of this byte stream is up to the applications on each end of the connection. TCP does, however, support the urgent mechanism mentioned before, although it is no longer recommended for use.

12.2.2 Reliability in TCP

TCP provides reliability using specific variations on the techniques just described. Because it provides a byte stream interface, TCP must convert a sending application's stream of bytes into a set of packets that IP can carry. This is called *packetization*. These packets contain sequence numbers, which in TCP actually represent the byte offsets of the first byte in each packet in the overall data stream rather than packet numbers. This allows packets to be of variable size during a transfer and may also allow them to be combined, called *repacketization*. The application data is broken into what TCP considers the best-size chunks to send, typically fitting each segment into a single IP-layer datagram that will not be fragmented. This is different from UDP, where each write by the application usually generates a UDP datagram of that size (plus headers). The chunk passed by TCP to IP is called a *segment* (see Figure 12-2). In Chapter 15 we shall see how TCP decides what size a segment should be.

TCP maintains a mandatory checksum on its header, any associated application data, and fields from the IP header. This is an end-to-end pseudo-header checksum whose purpose is to detect any bit errors introduced in transit. If a segment arrives with an invalid checksum, TCP discards it without sending any acknowledgment for the discarded packet. The receiving TCP might acknowledge a *previous* (already acknowledged) segment, however, to help the sender with its congestion control computations (see Chapter 16). The TCP checksum uses the same mathematical function as is used by other Internet protocols (UDP, ICMP, etc.). For large data transfers, there is some concern that this checksum is not really strong enough [SP00], so careful applications should apply their own error protection methods (e.g., stronger checksums or CRCs) or use a middleware layer to achieve the same result (e.g., see [RFC5044]).

When TCP sends a group of segments, it normally sets a single retransmission timer, waiting for the other end to acknowledge reception. TCP does not set a different retransmission timer for every segment. Rather, it sets a timer when it sends a window of data and updates the timeout as ACKs arrive. If an acknowledgment is not received in time, a segment is retransmitted. In Chapter 14 we will look at TCP's adaptive timeout and retransmission strategy in more detail.

When TCP receives data from the other end of the connection, it sends an acknowledgment. This acknowledgment may not be sent immediately but is normally delayed a fraction of a second. The ACKs used by TCP are *cumulative* in the sense that an ACK indicating byte number N implies that all bytes up to number N

(but not including it) have already been received successfully. This provides some robustness against ACK loss—if an ACK is lost, it is very likely that a subsequent ACK is sufficient to ACK the previous segments.

TCP provides a *full-duplex* service to the application layer. This means that data can be flowing in each direction, independent of the other direction. Therefore, each end of a connection must maintain a sequence number of the data flowing in each direction. Once a connection is established, every TCP segment that contains data flowing in one direction of the connection also includes an ACK for segments flowing in the opposite direction. Each segment also contains a window advertisement for implementing flow control in the opposite direction. Thus, when a TCP segment arrives on a connection, the window may slide forward, the window size may change, and new data may have arrived. As we shall see in Chapter 13, a fully active TCP connection is bidirectional and symmetric; data can flow equally well in either direction.

Using sequence numbers, a receiving TCP discards duplicate segments and reorders segments that arrive out of order. Recall that any of these anomalies can happen because TCP uses IP to deliver its segments, and IP does not provide duplicate elimination or guarantee correct ordering. Because it is a byte stream protocol, however, TCP never delivers data to the receiving *application* out of order. Thus, the receiving TCP may be forced to hold on to data with larger sequence numbers before giving it to an application until a missing lower-sequence-numbered segment (a "hole") is filled in.

We will now begin to look at some of the details of TCP. In this chapter we will only introduce the encapsulation and header structure for TCP. Other details appear in the next five chapters. TCP can be used with IPv4 or IPv6, and the pseudo-header checksum it uses (similar to UDP's) is mandatory for use with either IPv4 or IPv6.

12.3 TCP Header and Encapsulation

TCP is encapsulated in IP datagrams as shown in Figure 12-2.

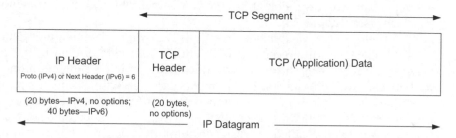

Figure 12-2   The TCP header appears immediately following the IP header or last IPv6 extension header and is often 20 bytes long (with no TCP options). With options, the TCP header can be as large as 60 bytes. Common options include Maximum Segment Size, Timestamps, Window Scaling, and Selective ACKs.

The header itself is considerably more complicated than the header we saw for UDP in Chapter 10. This is not very surprising, as TCP is a significantly more complicated protocol that must keep each end of the connection informed (synchronized) about the current state. It is shown in Figure 12-3.

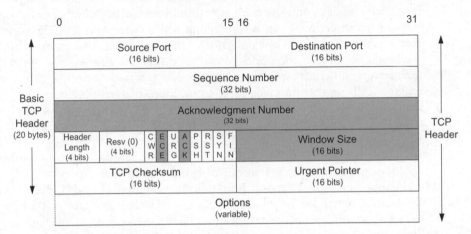

Figure 12-3   The TCP header. Its normal size is 20 bytes, unless options are present. The *Header Length* field gives the size of the header in 32-bit words (minimum value is 5). The shaded fields (*Acknowledgment Number, Window Size*, plus *ECE* and *ACK* bits) refer to the data flowing in the opposite direction relative to the sender of this segment.

Each TCP header contains the source and destination port number. These two values, along with the source and destination IP addresses in the IP header, uniquely identify each connection. The combination of an IP address and a port number is sometimes called an *endpoint* or *socket* in the TCP literature. The latter term appeared in [RFC0793] and was ultimately adopted as the name of the Berkeley-derived programming interface for network communications (now frequently called "Berkeley sockets"). It is a *pair* of sockets or endpoints (the 4-tuple consisting of the client IP address, client port number, server IP address, and server port number) that uniquely identifies each TCP connection. This fact will become important when we look at how a TCP server can communicate with multiple clients (see Chapter 13).

The *Sequence Number* field identifies the byte in the stream of data from the sending TCP to the receiving TCP that the first byte of data in the containing segment represents. If we consider the stream of bytes flowing in one direction between two applications, TCP numbers each *byte* with a sequence number. This sequence number is a 32-bit unsigned number that wraps back around to 0 after reaching $(2^{32}) - 1$. Because every byte exchanged is numbered, the *Acknowledgment Number* field (also called the *ACK Number* or *ACK* field for short) contains the next sequence number that the sender of the acknowledgment expects to receive. This is therefore the sequence number of the last successfully received byte of data plus 1. This field is valid only if the *ACK* bit field (described later in this section) is on, which it usually is for all but initial and closing segments. Sending an ACK costs nothing more than sending any other TCP segment because the 32-bit *ACK Number* field is *always* part of the header, as is the *ACK* bit field.

When a new connection is being established, the *SYN* bit field is turned on in the first segment sent from client to server. Such segments are called *SYN segments*, or simply *SYNs*. The *Sequence Number* field then contains the first sequence number to be used on that direction of the connection for subsequent sequence numbers and in returning ACK numbers (recall that connections are all bidirectional). Note that this number is *not* 0 or 1 but instead is another number, often randomly chosen, called the *initial sequence number* (ISN). The reason for the ISN not being 0 or 1 is a security measure and will be discussed in Chapter 13. The sequence number of the first byte of data sent on this direction of the connection is the ISN plus 1 because the *SYN* bit field *consumes* one sequence number. As we shall see later, consuming a sequence number also implies reliable delivery using retransmission. Thus, SYNs and application bytes (and FINs, which we will see later) are reliably delivered. ACKs, which do not consume sequence numbers, are not.

TCP can be described as "a sliding window protocol with cumulative positive acknowledgments." The *ACK Number* field is constructed to indicate the largest byte received in order at the receiver (plus 1). For example, if bytes 1–1024 are received OK, and the next segment contains bytes 2049–3072, the receiver cannot use the regular *ACK Number* field to signal the sender that it received this new segment. Modern TCPs, however, have a *selective acknowledgment* (SACK) option that allows the receiver to indicate to the sender out-of-order data it has received correctly. When paired with a TCP sender capable of *selective repeat*, a significant performance benefit may be realized [FF96]. In Chapter 14 we will see how TCP uses *duplicate acknowledgments* (multiple segments with the same *ACK* field) to help with its congestion control and error control procedures.

The *Header Length* field gives the length of the header in 32-bit words. This is required because the length of the *Options* field is variable. With a 4-bit field, TCP is limited to a 60-byte header. Without options, however, the size is 20 bytes.

Currently eight bit fields are defined for the TCP header, although some older implementations understand only the last six of them.[1] One or more of them can be turned on at the same time. We briefly mention their use here and discuss each of them in more detail in later chapters.

1. *CWR*—Congestion Window Reduced (the sender reduced its sending rate); see Chapter 16.

2. *ECE*—ECN Echo (the sender received an earlier congestion notification); see Chapter 16.

3. *URG*—Urgent (the *Urgent Pointer* field is valid—rarely used); see Chapter 15.

---

1. Note that [RFC3540], an experimental RFC, also defines the least significant of the Resv bits as a nonce sum (NS). See Section 16.12.

4. *ACK*—Acknowledgment (the *Acknowledgment Number* field is valid— always on after a connection is established); see Chapters 13 and 15.

5. *PSH*—Push (the receiver should pass this data to the application as soon as possible—not reliably implemented or used); see Chapter 15.

6. *RST*—Reset the connection (connection abort, usually because of an error); see Chapter 13.

7. *SYN*—Synchronize sequence numbers to initiate a connection; see Chapter 13.

8. *FIN*—The sender of the segment is finished sending data to its peer; see Chapter 13.

TCP's flow control is provided by each end advertising a window size using the *Window Size* field. This is the number of bytes, starting with the one specified by the ACK number, that the receiver is willing to accept. This is a 16-bit field, limiting the window to 65,535 bytes, and thereby limiting TCP's throughput performance. In Chapter 15 we will look at the Window Scale option that allows this value to be scaled, providing much larger windows and improved performance for high-speed and long-delay networks.

The *TCP Checksum* field covers the TCP header and data and some fields in the IP header, using a pseudo-header computation similar to the one used with ICMPv6 and UDP that we discussed in Chapters 8 and 10. It is mandatory for this field to be calculated and stored by the sender, and then verified by the receiver. The TCP checksum is calculated with the same algorithm as the IP, ICMP, and UDP ("Internet") checksums.

The *Urgent Pointer* field is valid only if the *URG* bit field is set. This "pointer" is a positive offset that must be added to the *Sequence Number* field of the segment to yield the sequence number of the *last* byte of urgent data. TCP's urgent mechanism is a way for the sender to provide specially marked data to the other end.

The most common *Option* field is the Maximum Segment Size option, called the MSS. Each end of a connection normally specifies this option on the first segment it sends (the ones with the *SYN* bit field set to establish the connection). The MSS option specifies the maximum-size segment that the sender of the option is willing to receive in the reverse direction. We describe the MSS option in more detail in Chapter 13 and some of the other TCP options in Chapters 14 and 15. Other common options we investigate include SACK, Timestamp, and Window Scale.

In Figure 12-2 we note that the data portion of the TCP segment is optional. We will see in Chapter 13 that when a connection is established, and when a connection is terminated, segments are exchanged that contain only the TCP header (with or without options) but no data. A header without any data is also used to acknowledge received data, if there is no data to be transmitted in that direction (called a *pure ACK*), and to notify the communication peer of a change in the window size (called a *window update*). There are also some cases resulting from timeouts when a segment can be sent without any data.

12.4 Summary

The problem of providing reliable communications over lossy communication channels has been studied for years. The two primary methods for dealing with errors include error-correcting codes and data retransmission. The protocols using retransmissions must also handle data loss, usually by setting a timer, and must also arrange some way for the receiver to signal the sender what it has received. Deciding how long to wait for an ACK can be tricky, as the appropriate time may change as network routing or load on the end systems varies. Modern protocols estimate the round-trip time and set the retransmission timer based on some function of these measurements.

Except for setting the retransmission timer, retransmission protocols are simple when only one packet may be in the network at one time, but they perform poorly for networks where the delay is high. To be more efficient, multiple packets must be injected into the network before an ACK is received. This approach is more efficient but also more complex. A typical approach to managing the complexity is to use sliding windows, whereby packets are marked with sequence numbers, and the window size bounds the number of such packets. When the window size varies based on either feedback from the receiver or other signals (such as dropped packets), both flow control and congestion control can be achieved.

TCP provides a reliable, connection-oriented, byte stream, transport-layer service built using many of these techniques. We looked briefly at all of the fields in the TCP header, noting that most of them are directly related to these abstract concepts in reliable delivery. We will examine them in detail in the chapters that follow. TCP packetizes the application data into segments, sets a timeout anytime it sends data, acknowledges data received by the other end, reorders out-of-order data, discards duplicate data, provides end-to-end flow control, and calculates and verifies a mandatory end-to-end checksum. It is the most widely used protocol on the Internet. It is used by most of the popular applications, such as HTTP, SSH/TLS, NetBIOS (NBT—NetBIOS over TCP), Telnet, FTP, and electronic mail (SMTP). Many distributed file-sharing applications (e.g., BitTorrent, Shareaza) also use TCP.

12.5 References

[FF96] K. Fall and S. Floyd, "Simulation-Based Comparisons of Tahoe, Reno and SACK TCP," *ACM Computer Communications Review*, July 1996.

[J90] R. Jain, "Congestion Control in Computer Networks: Issues and Trends," *IEEE Network Magazine*, May 1990.

[K75] L. Kleinrock, *Queuing Systems, Volume 1: Theory* (Wiley-Interscience, 1975).

[K97] S. Keshav, *An Engineering Approach to Computer Networking* (Addison-Wesley, 1997). (Note: A second edition is being developed.)

[RFC0793] J. Postel, "Transmission Control Protocol," Internet RFC 0793/STD 0007, Sept. 1981.

[RFC1122] R. Braden, ed., "Requirements for Internet Hosts—Communication Layers," Internet RFC 1122/STD 0003, Oct. 1989.

[RFC2861] M. Handley, J. Padhye, and S. Floyd, "TCP Congestion Window Validation," Internet RFC 2861 (experimental), June 2000.

[RFC2883] S. Floyd, J. Mahdavi, M. Mathis, and M. Podolsky, "An Extension to the Selective Acknowledgement (SACK) Option for TCP," Internet RFC 2883, July 2000.

[RFC3168] K. Ramakrishnan, S. Floyd, and D. Black, "The Addition of Explicit Congestion Notification (ECN) to IP," Internet RFC 3168, Sept. 2001.

[RFC3390] M. Allman, S. Floyd, and C. Partridge, "Increasing TCP's Initial Window," Internet RFC 3390, Oct. 2002.

[RFC3517] E. Blanton, M. Allman, K. Fall, and L. Wang, "A Conservative Selective Acknowledgment (SACK)-Based Loss Recovery Algorithm for TCP," Internet RFC 3517, Apr. 2003.

[RFC3540] N. Spring, D. Wetherall, and D. Ely, "Robust Explicit Congestion Notification (ECN) Signaling with Nonces," Internet RFC 3540 (experimental), June 2003.

[RFC3649] S. Floyd, "HighSpeed TCP for Large Congestion Windows," Internet RFC 3649 (experimental), Dec. 2003.

[RFC3708] E. Blanton and M. Allman, "Using TCP Duplicate Selective Acknowledgement (DSACKs) and Stream Control Transmission Protocol (SCTP) Duplicate Transmission Sequence Numbers (TSNs) to Detect Spurious Retransmissions," Internet RFC 3708 (experimental), Feb. 2004.

[RFC3782] S. Floyd, T. Henderson, and A. Gurtov, "The NewReno Modification to TCP's Fast Recovery Algorithm," Internet RFC 3782, Apr. 2004.

[RFC4015] R. Ludwig and A. Gurtov, "The Eifel Response Algorithm for TCP," Internet RFC 4015, Feb. 2005.

[RFC4782] S. Floyd, M. Allman, A. Jain, and P. Sarolahti, "Quick-Start for TCP and IP," Internet RFC 4782 (experimental), Jan. 2007.

[RFC5044] P. Culley, U. Elzur, R. Recio, S. Bailey, and J. Carrier, "Marker PDU Aligned Framing for TCP Specification," Internet RFC 5044, Oct. 2007.

[RFC5382] S. Guha, ed., K. Biswas, B. Ford, S. Sivakumar, and P. Srisuresh, "NAT Behavioral Requirements for TCP," Internet RFC 5382/BCP 0142, Oct. 2008.

[RFC5482] L. Eggert and F. Gont, "TCP User Timeout Option," Internet RFC 5482, Mar. 2009.

[RFC5562] A. Kuzmanovic, A. Mondal, S. Floyd, and K. Ramakrishnan, "Adding Explicit Congestion Notification (ECN) Capability to TCP's SYN/ACK Packets," Internet RFC 5562 (experimental), June 2009.

[RFC5681] M. Allman, V. Paxson, and E. Blanton, "TCP Congestion Control," Internet RFC 5681, Sept. 2009.

[RFC5682] P. Sarolahti, M. Kojo, K. Yamamoto, and M. Hata, "Forward RTO-Recovery (F-RTO): An Algorithm for Detecting Spurious Retransmission Time-outs with TCP," Internet RFC 5682, Sept. 2009.

[RFC5690] S. Floyd, A. Arcia, D. Ros, and J. Iyengar, "Adding Acknowledgement Congestion Control to TCP," Internet RFC 5690 (informational), Feb. 2010.

[RFC5827] M. Allman, K. Avrachenkov, U. Ayesta, J. Blanton, and P. Hurtig, "Early Retransmit for TCP and Stream Control Transmission Protocol (SCTP)," Internet RFC 5827 (experimental), May 2010.

[RFC5926] G. Lebovitz and E. Rescorla, "Cryptographic Algorithms for the TCP Authentication Option (TCP-AO)," Internet RFC 5926, June 2010.

[RFC5927] F. Gont, "ICMP Attacks against TCP," Internet RFC 5927 (experimental), July 2010.

[RFC6056] M. Larsen and F. Gont, "Recommendations for Transport-Protocol Port Randomization," Internet RFC 6056/BCP 0156, Jan. 2011.

[RFC6093] F. Gont and A. Yourtchenko, "On the Implementation of the TCP Urgent Mechanism," Internet RFC 6093, Jan. 2011.

[RFC6182] A. Ford, C. Raiciu, M. Handley, S. Barre, and J. Iyengar, "Architectural Guidelines for Multipath TCP Development," Internet RFC 6182 (informational), Mar. 2011.

[RFC6298] V. Paxson, M. Allman, J. Chu, and M. Sargent, "Computing TCP's Retransmission Timer," Internet RFC 6298, June 2011.

[S48] C. Shannon, "A Mathematical Theory of Communication," *Bell System Technical Journal*, July/Oct. 1948.

[SP00] J. Stone and C. Partridge, "When the CRC and TCP Checksum Disagree," *Proc. ACM SIGCOMM*, Aug./Sept. 2000.

13

TCP Connection Management

13.1 Introduction

TCP is a unicast *connection-oriented* protocol. Before either end can send data to the other, a connection must be established between them. In this chapter, we take a detailed look at what a TCP connection is, how it is established, and how it is terminated. Recall that TCP's service model is a byte stream. TCP detects and repairs essentially all the data transfer problems that may be introduced by packet loss, duplication, or errors at the IP layer (or below).

Because of its management of *connection state* (information about the connection kept by both endpoints), TCP is a considerably more complicated protocol than UDP (see Chapter 10). UDP is a *connectionless* protocol that involves no connection establishment or termination. One of the major differences we shall see between the two is the amount of detail required to handle the various TCP states properly: when connections are created, terminated normally, and reset without warning. In other chapters we will look at what happens once the connection is established and data is transferred.

During connection establishment, several *options* can be exchanged between the two endpoints regarding the parameters of the connection. Some options are allowed to be sent only when the connection is established, and others can be sent later. Recall from Chapter 12 that the TCP header has a limited space for holding options (40 bytes).

13.2 TCP Connection Establishment and Termination

A TCP *connection* is defined to be a 4-tuple consisting of two IP addresses and two port numbers. More precisely, it is a pair of *endpoints* or *sockets* where each endpoint is identified by an (IP address, port number) pair.

A connection typically goes through three phases: setup, data transfer (called *established*), and teardown (closing). As we will see, some of the difficulty in creating a robust TCP implementation is handling all of the transitions between and among these phases correctly. A typical TCP connection establishment and close (without any data transfer) is shown in Figure 13-1.

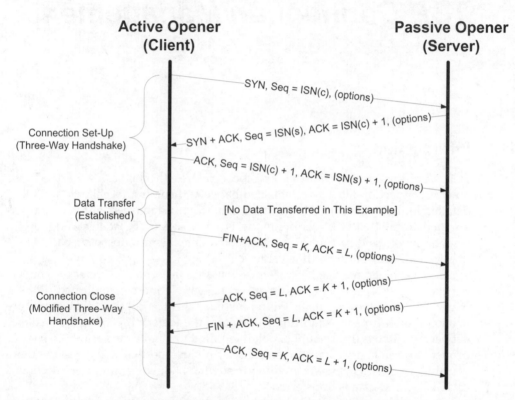

Figure 13-1   A normal TCP connection establishment and termination. Usually, the client initiates a three-way handshake to exchange initial sequence numbers carried on SYN segments for the client and server (ISN(c) and ISN(s), respectively). The connection terminates after each side has sent a FIN and received an acknowledgment for it.

The figure shows a timeline of what happens during connection establishment. To establish a TCP connection, the following events usually take place:

1. The *active opener* (normally called the client) sends a SYN segment (i.e., a TCP/IP packet with the *SYN* bit field turned on in the TCP header) specifying the port number of the peer to which it wants to connect and the client's

initial sequence number or ISN(c) (see Section 13.2.3). It typically sends one or more options at this point (see Section 13.3). This is segment 1.

2. The server responds with its own SYN segment containing its initial sequence number (ISN(s)). This is segment 2. The server also acknowledges the client's SYN by ACKing ISN(c) plus 1. A SYN consumes one sequence number and is retransmitted if lost.

3. The client must acknowledge this SYN from the server by ACKing ISN(s) plus 1. This is segment 3.

These three segments complete the connection establishment. This is often called the *three-way handshake*. Its main purposes are to let each end of the connection know that a connection is starting and the special details that are carried as options, and to exchange the ISNs.

The side that sends the first SYN is said to perform an *active open*. As mentioned, this is typically a client. The other side, which receives this SYN and sends the next SYN, performs a *passive open*. It is most commonly called the server. (In Section 13.2.2 we describe a supported but unusual *simultaneous open* when both sides can do an active open at the same time and become both clients and servers.)

Note

TCP supports the capability of carrying application data on SYN segments. This is rarely used, however, because the Berkeley sockets API does not support it.

Figure 13-1 also shows how a TCP connection is closed (also called cleared or terminated). Either end can initiate a close operation, and simultaneous closes are also supported but are rare. Traditionally, it was most common for the client to initiate a close (as shown in Figure 13-1). However, other servers (e.g., Web servers) initiate a close after they have completed a request. Usually a close operation starts with an application indicating its desire to terminate its connection (e.g., using the `close()` system call). The closing TCP initiates the close operation by sending a FIN segment (i.e., a TCP segment with the *FIN* bit field set). The complete close operation occurs after both sides have completed the close:

1. The *active closer* sends a FIN segment specifying the current sequence number the receiver expects to see (*K* in Figure 13-1). The FIN also includes an ACK for the last data sent in the other direction (labeled *L* in Figure 13-1).

2. The *passive closer* responds by ACKing value *K* + 1 to indicate its successful receipt of the active closer's FIN. At this point, the application is notified that the other end of its connection has performed a close. Typically this results in the application initiating its own close operation. The passive closer then effectively becomes another active closer and sends its own FIN. The sequence number is equal to *L*.

3. To complete the close, the final segment contains an ACK for the last FIN. Note that if a FIN is lost, it is retransmitted until an ACK for it is received.

While it takes three segments to establish a connection, it takes four to terminate one. It is also possible for the connection to be in a half-open state (see Section 13.6.3), although this is not common. This reason is that TCP's data communications model is bidirectional, meaning it is possible to have only one of the two directions operating. The *half-close* operation in TCP closes only a single direction of the data flow. Two half-close operations together close the entire connection. The rule is that either end can send a FIN when it is done sending data. When a TCP receives a FIN, it must notify the application that the other end has terminated that direction of data flow. The sending of a FIN is normally the result of the application issuing a close operation, which typically causes both directions to close.

The seven segments we have seen are baseline overheads for any TCP connection that is established and cleared "gracefully." (There are more abrupt ways to tear down a TCP connection using special reset segments, which we cover later.) When a small amount of data needs to be exchanged, it is now apparent why some applications prefer to use UDP because of its ability to send and receive data without establishing connections. However, such applications are then faced with handling their own error repair features, congestion management, and flow control.

13.2.1 TCP Half-Close

As we have mentioned, TCP supports a half-close operation. Few applications require this capability, so it is not common. To use this feature, the API must provide a way for the application to say, essentially, "I am done sending data, so send a FIN to the other end, but I still want to receive data from the other end, until it sends me a FIN." The Berkeley sockets API supports half-close, if the application calls the shutdown() function instead of calling the more typical close() function. Most applications, however, terminate both directions of the connection by calling close. Figure 13-2 shows an example of a half-close being used. We show the client on the left side initiating the half-close, but either end can do this.

The first two segments are the same as for a regular close: a FIN by the initiator, followed by an ACK of the FIN by the recipient. The operation then differs from Figure 13-1, because the side that receives the half-close can still send data. We show only one data segment, followed by an ACK, but any number of data segments can be sent. (We talk more about the exchange of data segments and acknowledgments in Chapter 15.) When the end that received the half-close is done sending data, it closes its end of the connection, causing a FIN to be sent, and this delivers an end-of-file indication to the application that initiated the half-close. When this second FIN is acknowledged, the connection is completely closed.

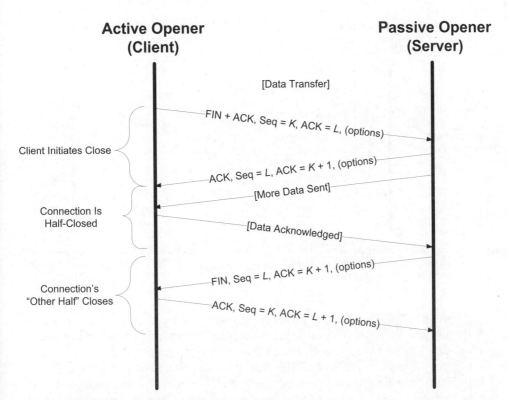

Figure 13-2   With the TCP half-close operation, one direction of the connection can terminate while the other continues until it is closed. Few applications use this feature.

13.2.2 Simultaneous Open and Close

It is possible, although highly improbable unless specifically arranged, for two applications to perform an active open to each other at the same time. Each end must have transmitted a SYN before receiving a SYN from the other side; the SYNs must pass each other on the network. This scenario also requires each end to have an IP address and port number that are known to the other end, which is rare (except for the firewall "hole-punching" techniques we saw in Chapter 7). If this happens, it is called a *simultaneous open*.

For example, a simultaneous open occurs when an application on host A using local port 7777 performs an active open to port 8888 on host B, while at the same time an application on host B using local port 8888 performs an active open to port 7777 on host A. This is *not* the same as connecting a client on host A to a server on host B, while at the same time having a client on host B connect to a conventional server on host A. In that case, both servers perform passive opens, not active opens, and the clients assign themselves different ephemeral port numbers. This results in two distinct TCP connections. Figure 13-3 shows the segments exchanged during a simultaneous open.

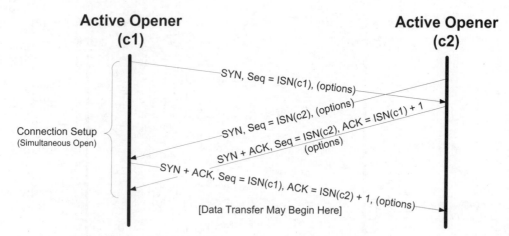

Figure 13-3   Segments exchanged during simultaneous open. One additional segment is required compared to the ordinary connection establishment procedure. The *SYN* bit field is on in each segment until an ACK for it is received.

A simultaneous open requires the exchange of four segments, one more than the normal three-way handshake. Also note that we do not call either end a client or a server, because both ends act as client and server. A *simultaneous close* is not very different. We said earlier that one side (often, but not always, the client) performs the active close, causing the first FIN to be sent. In a simultaneous close, both do. Figure 13-4 shows the segments exchanged during a simultaneous close.

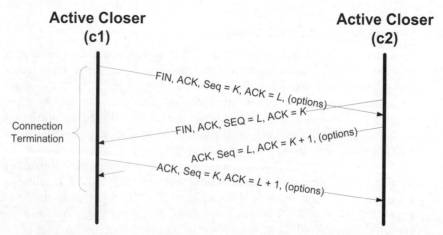

Figure 13-4   Segments exchanged during simultaneous close work like a conventional close, but the segment ordering is interleaved.

With a simultaneous close the same number of segments are exchanged as in the normal close. The only real difference is that the segment sequence is interleaved instead of sequential. Later we will see that simultaneous open and close operations use particular states in the TCP implementation that are not commonly exercised.

13.2.3 Initial Sequence Number (ISN)

When a connection is open, any segment with the appropriate two IP addresses and port numbers is accepted as valid provided the sequence number is valid (i.e., within the window) and the checksum is OK. This brings up the question of whether it might be possible to have TCP segments being routed through the network that could show up later and disrupt a connection. This concern is addressed by careful selection of the ISN, which we now investigate.

Before each end sends its SYN to establish the connection, it chooses an ISN for that connection. The ISN should change over time, so that each connection has a different one. [RFC0793] specifies that the ISN should be viewed as a 32-bit counter that increments by 1 every 4μs. The purpose of doing this is to arrange for the sequence numbers for segments on one connection to not overlap with sequence numbers on a another (new) identical connection. In particular, new sequence numbers must not be allowed to overlap between different *instantiations* (or *incarnations*) of the *same* connection.

The idea of different instantiations of the same connection becomes clear when we recall that a TCP connection is identified by a pair of endpoints, creating a 4-tuple of two address/port pairs. If a connection had one of its segments delayed for a long period of time and closed, but then opened again with the same 4-tuple, it is conceivable that the delayed segment could reenter the new connection's data stream as valid data. This would be most troublesome. By taking steps to avoid overlap in sequence numbers between connection instantiations, we can try to minimize this risk. It does suggest, however, that an application with a very great need for data integrity should employ its own CRCs or checksums at the application layer to ensure that its own data has been transferred without error. This is generally good practice in any case, and it is commonly done for large files.

As we shall see, knowing the connection 4-tuple as well as the currently active window of sequence numbers is all that is required to form a TCP segment that is considered valid to a communicating TCP endpoint. This represents a form of vulnerability for TCP: anyone can forge a TCP segment and, if the sequence numbers, IP addresses, and port numbers are chosen appropriately, can interrupt a TCP connection [RFC5961]. One way of repelling this is to make the initial sequence number (or ephemeral port number [RFC6056]) relatively hard to guess. Another is encryption (see Chapter 18).

In modern systems, the ISN is typically selected in a semirandom way. An interesting discussion of the subtleties of doing this properly is contained in CERT Advisory CA-2001-09 [CERTISN]. Linux goes through a fairly elaborate process to select its ISNs. It uses a clock-based scheme but starts the clock at a random offset for each connection. The random offset is chosen as a cryptographically hashed function on the connection identifier (4-tuple). A secret input to the hash function changes every 5 minutes. Of the 32 bits in the ISN, the top-most 8 bits are a sequence number of the secret, and the remaining bits are generated by the hash. This produces an ISN that is difficult to guess, but also one that increases over time. Windows reportedly uses a similar scheme based on RC4 [S96].

13.2.4 Example

Now that we have a basic idea of how a TCP connection is established and cleared, let us look at the packet-level details. To do so we make a TCP connection to a nearby Web server running on the machine with IPv4 address 10.0.0.2. The client is the Telnet application on Windows:

```
C:\> telnet 10.0.0.2 80
Welcome to Microsoft Telnet Client
Escape Character is 'CTRL+]'
... wait about 4.4 seconds ...
Microsoft Telnet> quit
```

The telnet command establishes a TCP connection with the host having IPv4 address 10.0.0.2 on the port corresponding to the http or Web service (port 80). When the Telnet program connects to a port other than 23 (the well-known port for the Telnet protocol [RFC0854]), it does not engage in the application protocol. Instead, it merely copies bytes from its input to its TCP connection and vice versa. When a Web server receives the incoming connection request, the first thing it does is await a request for a Web page. In this case, we do not provide one, so the server does not produce any data. This is ideal for us, because for now we are interested only in the connection establishment and termination packet exchange. Figure 13-5 shows the Wireshark output for the segments generated by this command.

In the figure, we can see that the client begins with a SYN segment containing an ISN of 685506836 and window advertisement of 65535. This segment also contains several options we discuss in Section 13.3. The second segment is both a SYN from the server and an ACK for the client. The sequence number (server's ISN) is 1479690171 and the ACK number is 685506837, 1 more than the client's ISN. This indicates successful receipt of the client's ISN. This segment also includes a window advertisement indicating that the server is willing to accept up to 64,240 bytes. Completion of the three-way handshake takes place with segment 3, which contains ACK number 1479690172. Remember that ACK numbers are cumulative and always indicate the sequence number the sender of the ACK expects to see *next* (not the one that it last received).

After a pause of about 4.4s, the Telnet application is instructed to close the connection. This results in the client's TCP sending the FIN in segment 4. The sequence number of the FIN is 685506837, which is ACKed in segment 5 (with

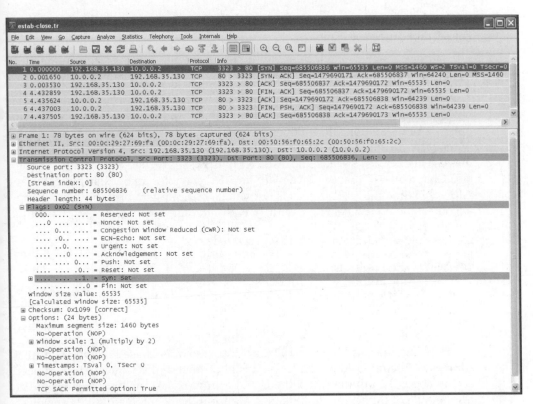

Figure 13-5 A TCP connection between 192.168.35.130 and 10.0.0.2 is established and cleared without sending any data. The *PSH* (*Push*) bit indicates that segment 6 is sending all data from its buffer (which is none).

ACK number 685506838). Shortly thereafter the server sends its own FIN with sequence number 1479690172. This segment also (redundantly) ACKs the client's FIN once again. Note that the *PSH* bit field is on. This has no real effect on the closing of the connection but usually indicates that the server has no additional data to send. The final segment ACKs the server's FIN by including ACK number 1479690173.

Note

[RFC1025] calls a segment with the maximum number of features enabled (e.g., flags and options) a "Kamikaze" packet. Other colorful terms include "nastygram," "Christmas tree packet," and "lamp test segment."

One thing we can see in Figure 13-5 is that the SYN segments contain one or more options. These take up additional space in the TCP header. For example, the length of the first TCP header is 44 bytes, 24 bytes greater than the minimum size. TCP has several supported options, which we detail after we see what happens when a connection cannot be established.

13.2.5 Timeout of Connection Establishment

There are several circumstances in which a connection cannot be established. One obvious case is when the server host is down. To simulate this scenario, we issue our `telnet` command to a nonexistent host in the same subnet. If we do this without modifying the ARP table, the client exits with a "No route to host" error message, generated because no ARP reply is ever returned for the ARP request (see Chapter 4). If, however, we place an ARP entry for a nonexistent host in the ARP table first, the ARP request is not sent, and the system immediately attempts to contact the nonexistent host with TCP/IP. First, the commands:

```
Linux# arp -s 192.168.10.180 00:00:1a:1b:1c:1d
Linux% date; telnet 192.168.10.180 80; date
Tue June   7 21:16:34 PDT 2009
Trying 192.168.10.180...
telnet: connect to address 192.168.10.180: Connection timed out
Tue June   7 21:19:43 PDT 2009
Linux%
```

Here the MAC address `00:00:1a:1b:1c:1d` was chosen simply as a MAC address not being used on the LAN; it is of no special consequence. The timeout occurs about 3.2 minutes after the initial command. Because there is no host to respond, all of the segments generated are from the client. Listing 13-1 shows the output using Wireshark in packet summary (text) mode.

Listing 13-1   Wireshark output for connection establishment that times out

No.	Time	Source	Destination	Protocol	Info
1	0.000000	192.168.10.144	192.168.10.180	TCP	32787 > http
2	2.997928	192.168.10.144	192.168.10.180	TCP	32787 > http
3	8.997962	192.168.10.144	192.168.10.180	TCP	32787 > http
4	20.997942	192.168.10.144	192.168.10.180	TCP	32787 > http
5	44.997936	192.168.10.144	192.168.10.180	TCP	32787 > http
6	92.997937	192.168.10.144	192.168.10.180	TCP	32787 > http

The interesting point in this output is how frequently the client's TCP sends a SYN to try to establish the connection. The second segment is sent 3s after the first, the third is sent 6s after the second, the fourth is sent 12s after the third, and so on. This behavior is called *exponential backoff*, and we saw something like it before when we discussed the behavior of Ethernet's CSMA/CD media access control protocol (see Chapter 3). In that case, it was a little different, however, because here each backoff is deterministically (i.e., always) twice the previous backoff, whereas in Ethernet, the *maximum* backoff is doubled and the actual backoff is chosen randomly.

The number of times to retry an initial SYN can be configured on some systems and usually has a fairly small value such as 5. In Linux, the system configuration variable `net.ipv4.tcp_syn_retries` gives the maximum number of times to attempt to resend a SYN segment during an active open. A corresponding value called `net.ipv4.tcp_synack_retries` gives the maximum number of times to attempt to resend a SYN + ACK segment when responding to a peer's active open request. It can also be used on an individual connection basis by setting the Linux-specific TCP_SYNCNT socket option. Its default value is five retries, as we see here. The exponential backoff timing between these retransmissions is part of TCP's congestion management response. We shall examine it in detail when we discuss Karn's algorithm (see Chapter 16).

13.2.6 Connections and Translators

In Chapter 7 we discussed how conventional NAT translates the addresses and port numbers used by protocols such as TCP and UDP. We also examined how IP packets can be translated between IPv6 and IPv4. When NAT is used with TCP, the pseudo-header checksum usually requires adjustment (except in cases where a checksum-neutral address modifier is used). This is also true for other protocols that use pseudo-header checksums, because the computation involves information at the transport layer as well as the network layer.

When a TCP connection is first established, a NAT (or NAT64) can ascertain this fact because of the presence of the *SYN* bit field in a segment. It can also determine when a connection has become fully established by looking for subsequent SYN + ACK and ACK segments containing the appropriate sequence numbers. The same applies for the termination of a connection. By implementing a portion of the TCP state machine in a NAT (see, for example, Sections 3.5.2.1 and 3.5.2.2 of [RFC6146]), the connection can be tracked, including the current states, sequence numbers in each direction, and corresponding ACK numbers. Such state tracking is typical for NAT implementations.

Further complications arise when a NAT acts as an editor and rewrites contents in the transport protocol's data payload. For TCP, this may involve removing or adding bytes to the data stream, and consequently affecting the sequence numbers (and segment) lengths. Doing so also necessarily affects the checksum, but it also affects the data sequence. If data is inserted or removed from the data stream by the NAT, these values can be adjusted appropriately. Doing so is somewhat fragile because if the NAT state becomes desynchronized with the state in the end hosts, the connection will not operate properly.

13.3 TCP Options

The TCP header can contain options (see Figure 12-3). The only options defined in the original TCP specification are the *End of Option List* (EOL), the *No Operation* (NOP), and the *Maximum Segment Size* (MSS) options. Since then, several options have been

Table 13-1   The TCP option values. Up to 40 bytes are available to hold options.

Kind	Length	Name	Reference	Description and Purpose
0	1	EOL	[RFC0793]	End of Option List
1	1	NOP	[RFC0793]	No Operation (used for padding)
2	4	MSS	[RFC0793]	Maximum Segment Size
3	3	WSOPT	[RFC1323]	Window Scaling Factor (left-shift amount on window)
4	2	SACK-Permitted	[RFC2018]	Sender supports SACK options
5	Var.	SACK	[RFC2018]	SACK block (out-of-order data received)
8	10	TSOPT	[RFC1323]	Timestamps option
28	4	UTO	[RFC5482]	User Timeout (abort after idle time)
29	Var.	TCP-AO	[RFC5925]	Authentication option (using various algorithms)
253	Var.	Experimental	[RFC4727]	Reserved for experimental use
254	Var.	Experimental	[RFC4727]	Reserved for experimental use

defined. The entire list is maintained by the IANA [TPARAMS]; Table 13-1 gives the current options of interest (i.e., those with standards-track RFC descriptions).

Every option begins with a 1-byte *kind* that specifies the type of option. Options that are not understood are simply ignored, according to [RFC1122]. The options with a *kind* value of 0 and 1 occupy a single byte. The other options have a *len* byte that follows the *kind* byte. The length is the total length, including the *kind* and *len* bytes. The reason for the NOP option is to allow the sender to pad fields to a multiple of 4 bytes, if it needs to. Remember that the TCP header's length is always required to be a multiple of 32 bits because the TCP *Header Length* field uses that unit. The EOL option indicates the end of the list and that no further processing of the options list is to be performed. Now we will have a look at the other options.

13.3.1 Maximum Segment Size (MSS) Option

The maximum segment size (MSS) is the largest segment that a TCP is willing to receive from its peer and, consequently, the largest size its peer should ever use when sending. The MSS value counts only TCP data bytes and does not include the sizes of any associated TCP or IP header [RFC0879]. When a connection is established, each end usually announces its MSS in an MSS option carried with its SYN segment. The option allows for 16 bits to be used to specify the MSS value. If no MSS option is provided, a default value of 536 bytes is used. Recall the rule that requires any host to be capable of processing IPv4 datagrams at least as large as 576. With minimum-size IPv4 and TCP headers, a TCP using a sending MSS size of 536 bytes produces an IPv4 datagram of size 20 + 20 + 536 = 576 bytes.

The MSS values in Figure 13-5 are all 1460, which is typical for IPv4. The resulting IPv4 datagram is normally 40 bytes larger (1500 bytes total, the typical

MTU size for Ethernet and path MTU for the Internet): 20 bytes for the TCP header and 20 bytes for the IPv4 header. When IPv6 is used, the MSS is usually 1440, 20 bytes less because of the larger IPv6 header. The special MSS value of 65535 can be used with IPv6 jumbograms to indicate an effective MSS of infinity [RFC2675]. In this case the SMSS will be determined as the PMTU minus 60 bytes (40 bytes for the IPv6 header and 20 bytes for the TCP header). Note that the MSS option is not a negotiation between one TCP and its peer; it is a limit. When one TCP gives its MSS option to the other, it is indicating its unwillingness to accept any segments larger than that size for the duration of the connection.

13.3.2 Selective Acknowledgment (SACK) Options

In Chapter 12 we introduced the concept of a sliding window, and we described how TCP handles its sequence numbers and acknowledgments. Because it uses cumulative ACKs, TCP is never able to acknowledge data it has received correctly but that is not contiguous, in terms of sequence numbers, with data it has received previously. In such cases, the TCP receiver is said to have *holes* in its received data queue. A receiving TCP prevents applications from consuming data beyond a hole because of the byte stream abstraction it provides.

If a TCP sender were able to learn of the existence of holes (and out-of-sequence data blocks beyond holes in the sequence space) at the receiver, it could better select which particular TCP segments to retransmit when segments are lost or otherwise missing at the receiver. The TCP selective acknowledgment (SACK) options [RFC2018][RFC2883] provide this capability. The scheme works effectively, however, only if the TCP sender logic is able to make effective use of the SACK information it receives from a SACK-capable receiver.

A TCP learns that its peer is capable of advertising SACK information by receiving the SACK-Permitted option in a SYN (or SYN + ACK) segment. Once this has taken place, the TCP receiving out-of-sequence data may provide a SACK option that describes the out-of-sequence data to help its peer perform retransmissions more efficiently. SACK information contained in a SACK option consists of a range of sequence numbers representing data blocks the receiver has successfully received. Each range is called a *SACK block* and is represented by a pair of 32-bit sequence numbers. Thus, a SACK option containing n SACK blocks is $(8n + 2)$ bytes long. Two bytes are used to hold the kind and length of the SACK option.

Because of the limited amount of space available in the option space of a TCP header, the maximum number of SACK blocks available to be sent in a single segment is three (assuming the Timestamps option is also used, described in Section 13.3.4, which is typical for modern TCP implementations). Although the SACK-Permitted option is only ever sent in a SYN segment, the SACK blocks themselves may be sent in any segment once the sender has sent the SACK-Permitted option. Because the operation of SACK is most easily (and importantly) related to the error and congestion control operations of TCP, we discuss it in further detail when we cover these topics in Chapters 14 and 16.

13.3.3 Window Scale (WSCALE or WSOPT) Option

The *Window Scale* option (denoted WSCALE or WSOPT) [RFC1323] effectively increases the capacity of the TCP *Window Advertisement* field from 16 to about 30 bits. Instead of changing the field size, however, the header still holds a 16-bit value, and an option is defined that applies a *scaling factor* to the 16-bit value. This factor effectively left-shifts the window field value by the scale factor. This, in effect, multiplies the window value by the value 2^s, where s is the scale factor. The 1-byte shift count is between 0 and 14 (inclusive). A shift count of 0 indicates no scaling. The maximum scale value of 14 provides for a maximum window of 1,073,725,440 bytes (65,535 × 2^{14}), close to 1,073,741,823 (2^{30} –1), effectively 1GB. TCP then mai.ains the "real" window size internally as a 32-bit value.

This option can appear only in a SYN segment, so the scale factor is fixed in each direction when the connection is established. To enable window scaling, both ends must send the option in their SYN segments. The end doing the active open sends the option in its SYN, but the end doing the passive open can send the option only if the received SYN specifies the option. The scale factor can be different in each direction. If the end doing the active open sends a nonzero scale factor but does not receive a Window Scale option from the other end, it sets its send and receive scale values to 0. This lets systems that do not understand the option interoperate with systems that do.

Assume we are using the Window Scale option, with a shift count of S for sending and a shift count of R for receiving. Then every 16-bit advertised window that we receive from the other end is left-shifted by R bits to obtain the real advertised window size. Every time we send a window advertisement to the other end, we take our real 32-bit window size and right-shift it S bits, placing the resulting 16-bit value in the TCP header.

The shift count is automatically chosen by TCP, based on the size of the receive buffer. The size of this buffer is set by the system, but the capability is normally provided for the application to change it. The Window Scale option is most relevant when TCP is used to provide bulk data transfer over networks with large-bandwidth-delay products (i.e., those with a product of round-trip time and bandwidth being relatively large). Thus, we shall discuss the importance and use of this option more in Chapter 16.

13.3.4 Timestamps Option and Protection against Wrapped Sequence Numbers (PAWS)

The *Timestamps* option (sometimes called the *Timestamp* option and written as TSOPT or TSopt) lets the sender place two 4-byte timestamp values in every segment. The receiver reflects these values in the acknowledgment, allowing the sender to calculate an estimate of the connection's RTT for each ACK received. (We must say "each ACK received" and not "each segment" because TCP often acknowledges multiple segments per ACK; we will see this in Chapter 15.) When using the Timestamps option, the sender places a 32-bit value in the Timestamp

Value field (called TSV or TSval) in the first part of the TSOPT, and the receiver echoes this back unchanged in the second *Timestamp Echo Retry* field (called TSER or TSecr). TCP headers containing this option increase by 10 bytes (8 bytes for the two timestamp values and 2 to indicate the option value and length).

The timestamp is a monotonically increasing value. Because the receiver simply echoes what it receives, it does not care what the timestamp units or values actually are. This option does not require any form of clock synchronization between the two hosts. [RFC1323] recommends that the sender increment the timestamp value by at least 1 every second. Figure 13-6 shows the Timestamps option, as displayed by Wireshark.

Figure 13-6   A TCP connection with the Timestamps, Window Scaling, and MSS options being used. The TCP header is 44 bytes long. The initial SYN (packet 1) starts with the *TSV* set to 81813090. The second packet, highlighted, echoes this value back to the active opener and includes its own value of 349742014.

Here, both ends participate by generating and echoing back the other's timestamps. The first segment (client's SYN) uses an initial timestamp value of 81813090. This value is placed in the TSV. The second portion, TSER, has a value of 0 on the first segment because the client does not know the server's timestamp value yet.

The main reason for wishing to calculate a good estimate of the connection's RTT is to set the retransmission timeout, which tells TCP when it should try resending a segment that is likely lost. In Chapter 12 we discussed the need to set this timeout based on some function of the RTT. With the Timestamps option, we can get relatively fine-grain measurements of the RTT. Prior to the creation of the Timestamps option, most TCPs would perform just one RTT sample per window of data. With the Timestamps option, more samples can be taken, leading to the potential of a better RTT estimate (see [RFC1323] and [RFC6298]).

Because the Timestamps option is most relevant to the setting of the retransmission timer, we discuss its use for that purpose in more detail when we discuss retransmission in Chapter 14. We say "for that purpose" because although the Timestamps option allows for more frequent RTT samples, it also provides a way for the receiver to avoid receiving old segments and considering them as valid. This is called *Protection Against Wrapped Sequence Numbers* (PAWS), and it is described in [RFC1323] along with the Timestamps option. We'll now take a look at how it works.

Consider a TCP connection using the Window Scale option with the largest possible window, about 1GB (2^{30}). Also assume that the Timestamps option is being used and that the timestamp value assigned by the sender increments by 1 for each window that is sent. (This is conservative. Normally the timestamp increments faster than this.) Table 13-2 shows the possible data flow between the two hosts when transferring 6GB. To avoid lots of ten-digit numbers, we use the notation G to mean a multiple of 1,073,741,824. We also use the notation from `tcpdump` that $J:K$ means byte J through and including byte $K - 1$.

Table 13-2   The TCP Timestamps option can disambiguate segments with the same sequence numbers by providing an extra 32 bits of effective sequence number space.

Time	Bytes Sent	Send Seq. No.	Send Timestamp	Receive
A	0G:1G	0G:1G	1	OK
B	1G:2G	1G:2G	2	OK, but one segment lost and retransmitted
C	2G:3G	2G:3G	3	OK
D	3G:4G	3G:4G	4	OK
E	4G:5G	0G:1G	5	OK
F	5G:6G	1G:2G	6	OK, but retransmitted segment reappears

The 32-bit *Sequence Number* field wraps between times D and E. We assume that one segment gets lost at time B and is retransmitted. We also assume that this lost segment reappears at time F. This assumes that the time difference between the segment getting lost and reappearing is less than the maximum time a segment can live in the network (called the MSL; see Section 13.5.2); otherwise the segment would have been discarded by some router when its TTL expired. As we mentioned earlier, it is only with relatively high-speed connections that this problem appears, where old segments can reappear and contain sequence numbers currently being transmitted.

We can also see from Table 13-2 that using the Timestamps option prevents this problem. The receiver considers the timestamp as a 32-bit extension of the sequence number. Because the lost segment that reappears at time F has a timestamp of 2, which is less than the most recent valid timestamp (5 or 6), it is discarded by the PAWS algorithm. The PAWS algorithm does not require any form of time synchronization between the sender and the receiver. All the receiver needs is for the timestamp values to be monotonically increasing, and to increase by at least 1 per window of data.

13.3.5 User Timeout (UTO) Option

The *User Timeout* (UTO) option is a relatively new TCP capability described in [RFC5482]. The UTO value (also called USER_TIMEOUT) specifies the amount of time a TCP sender is willing to wait for an ACK of outstanding data before concluding that the remote end has failed. USER_TIMEOUT has traditionally been a local configuration parameter for TCP [RFC0793]. The UTO option allows one TCP to signal its USER_TIMEOUT value to its connection peer. This allows the receiving TCP to adjust its behavior (e.g., to tolerate a longer period of disrupted connectivity prior to aborting a connection). NAT devices could also interpret such information to help set their connection activity timers.

UTO option values are advisory; just because one end of a connection might wish to use a large or small UTO value does not mean that the other end needs to comply. [RFC1122] refines the definition of USER_TIMEOUT and suggests that a TCP reaching a threshold of three (R1) retransmissions should notify the requesting application, and that after 100s (R2) the connection should be closed. Some implementations have an API function to change R1 and R2. Because long UTOs might lead to resource exhaustion concerns and short UTOs might result in some connections being torn down early (a type of DoS attack), upper and lower limits are placed on the possible UTO values. The way to set USER_TIMEOUT, then, is as follows:

```
USER_TIMEOUT = min(U_LIMIT, max(ADV_UTO, REMOTE_UTO, L_LIMIT))
```

where ADV_UTO is the UTO option advertised to the remote TCP, REMOTE_UTO is the peer's advertised UTO option value, U_LIMIT is the local system's upper UTO limit, and L_LIMIT is the local system's UTO lower limit. Note that this formula does not guarantee that each end of the same connection will arrive at the same USER_TIMEOUT value. In all cases the L_LIMIT value must be greater than the associated connection's retransmission timeout (RTO) value (see Chapter 14), and it is recommended to be set to 100s to retain compatibility with [RFC1122].

UTO options are included on SYN segments when a connection is established, on the first non-SYN segments, and whenever the USER_TIMEOUT value is changed. The option value is expressed as a 15-bit value in units of seconds or minutes following a bit field ("granularity") that indicates that the value is in minutes (1) or seconds (0). As a relatively new option, it is not yet widely deployed.

13.3.6 Authentication Option (TCP-AO)

There is an option used to enhance the security of TCP connections. It is designed to enhance and replace an earlier mechanism called TCP-MD5 [RFC2385]. Called the *TCP Authentication Option* (TCP-AO) [RFC5925], it uses a cryptographic hash algorithm (see Chapter 18), in combination with a secret value known to each end of a TCP connection, to authenticate each segment. TCP-AO improves upon TCP-MD5 by supporting a variety of cryptographic algorithms and identifying changing of keys using in-band signaling. It does not provide a comprehensive key management solution, however. That is, each end still has to have a way to establish a shared set of keys prior to operation.

When sending, the TCP derives a traffic key from the shared secret key and computes the hash value according to a particular cryptographic algorithm [RFC5926]. A receiver, equipped with the same secret key, is likewise able to derive the traffic key and use it to ensure that an arriving segment has not been modified in transit (with high probability). This option is intended as a strong countermeasure to a variety of TCP spoofing attacks (see Section 13.8). However, because it requires creation and distribution of a shared key (and is a relatively new option), it is not yet widely deployed.

13.4 Path MTU Discovery with TCP

In Chapter 3, we described the concept of the path MTU. It is the minimum MTU on any network segment that is currently in the path between two hosts. Knowing the path MTU can help protocols such as TCP avoid fragmentation. In Chapter 10, we looked at how discovery of the path MTU (PMTUD) is accomplished based on ICMP messages, but in that case UDP is not usually able to adapt its datagram size because the application specifies the size (i.e., not the transport protocol). TCP, in providing the byte stream abstraction it implements, determines what segment size to use and as a result has a much greater degree of control over the size of IP datagrams that are ultimately generated.

In this section we will examine how PMTUD is used by TCP. Our discussion will apply to both TCP/IPv4 and TCP/IPv6. More details are provided by [RFC1191] and [RFC1981], respectively. A method that avoids the use of ICMP, called *Packetization Layer Path MTU Discovery* (PLPMTUD), can also be used by TCP [RFC4821] or by other transport protocols. We shall use the ICMPv6 Packet Too Big (PTB) terminology to refer to either ICMPv4 Destination Unreachable (Fragmentation Required) or ICMPv6 Packet Too Big messages.

TCP's regular PMTUD process operates as follows: When a connection is established, TCP uses the minimum of the MTU of the outgoing interface, or the MSS announced by the other end, as the basis for selecting its send maximum segment size (SMSS). PMTUD does not allow TCP to exceed the MSS announced by the other end. If the other end does not specify an MSS, the sender assumes a default of 536 bytes, but this situation is now rare. It is also possible for an implementation to save path MTU information on a per-destination basis to help in selecting its segment size. Note that the path MTU in each direction of a connection could be different.

Once the initial SMSS is chosen, all IPv4 datagrams sent by TCP on that connection have the IPv4 *DF* bit field set. For TCP/IPv6, this is not necessary because there is no *DF* bit field; all datagrams are assumed to have it set implicitly. If a PTB is received, TCP decreases the segment size and retransmits using a different segment size. If the PTB contains the suggested next-hop MTU, the segment size can be set to the next-hop MTU minus the sizes of the IPv4 (or IPv6) and TCP headers. If the next-hop MTU value is not present (e.g., an older ICMP error was returned that lacks this information), the sender may try a variety of values (e.g., binary search for a usable value). This also affects TCP's congestion control management (see Chapter 16). For PLPMTUD the situation is similar, except PTB messages are not used. Instead, the protocol performing PMTUD must be able to detect message discards quickly and perform its own datagram size adjustments.

Because routes can change dynamically, when some time has passed since the last decrease of the segment size, a larger value (up to the initial SMSS) can be tried. Guidance in [RFC1191] and [RFC1981] recommends that this time interval be about 10 minutes.

There are a number of problems with PMTUD when it operates in an Internet environment with firewalls that block PTB messages [RFC2923]. Of the various operational problems with PMTUD, *black holes* have been the most problematic, although the situation is improving (in [LS10], 80% of systems studied were able to properly process PTB messages). PMTUD black holes arise when a TCP implementation that depends on the delivery of ICMP messages to adjust its segment size never receives them. This could be for several reasons, including a firewall or NAT configuration that prohibits such ICMP messages from being forwarded. The consequence is a TCP connection that cannot proceed once it starts to use larger packets. It can be difficult to diagnose because only large packets cannot be forwarded. The smaller ones (such as SYN and SYN + ACK packets used to establish the connection) generally succeed. Some TCP implementations have "black hole detection," which amounts to trying a smaller segment size when a segment is retransmitted several times.

13.4.1 Example

We can see the correct behavior of PMTUD when an intermediate router has an MTU less than either of the endpoints' MSS. To create this situation, we begin with a router (a Linux host with local address 10.0.0.1) that has a PPPoE interface to a

DSL service provider. The PPPoE link uses an MTU of 1492 (1500 bytes for Ethernet, minus 6 bytes of PPPoE overhead, minus another 2 bytes of PPP overhead; see Chapter 3). Figure 13-7 is an illustration of the topology.

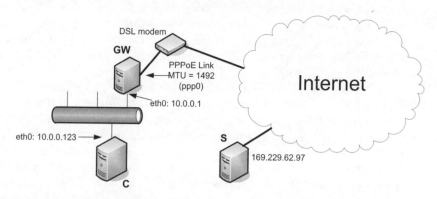

Figure 13-7 The PPPoE encapsulation drops the path MTU of most TCP connections to 1492 bytes from what might otherwise have been 1500 bytes (the typical MTU for Ethernet). To demonstrate TCP's use of PMTUD, we set the MTU even smaller (288 bytes).

In order to induce this behavior specifically, we can reduce the MTU size on the PPPoE link from 1492 to, say, 288 bytes. On the GW machine, the following command accomplishes this task:

```
Linux(GW)# ifconfig ppp0 mtu 288
```

In addition, we need to tell the client system (C) that small segments are allowed:

```
Linux(C)# sysctl -w net.ipv4.route.min_pmtu=68
```

If we did not perform this second operation, Linux would clamp its minimum path MTU at the default value of 552 bytes, which helps avoid certain small MTU attacks (see Section 13.8). The consequence of doing so in our example here is that any packets larger than 288 bytes would be fragmented. To avoid this, and to demonstrate PMTUD more effectively, we remove this minimum. We then start a file transfer from machine C (address 10.0.0.123) to the server S on the Internet (address 169.229.62.97). Listing 13-2 shows a tcpdump packet trace from this exchange. Several lines have been wrapped and extraneous fields have been removed for clarity.

Listing 13-2 The path MTU discovery mechanism finds an appropriate segment size to use when transiting the network where the middle link has a smaller MTU than the endpoints.

```
1 20:20:21.992721 IP (tos 0x0, ttl 45, id 43565, offset 0, flags [DF],
                proto 6, length: 588)
                169.229.62.97.22 > 10.0.0.123.1027: P [tcp sum ok]
                41:577(536) ack 23
```

2 20:20:21.993727 IP (tos 0x0, ttl 64, id 57659, offset 0, flags [DF],
        proto 6, length: 588)
        10.0.0.123.1027 > 169.229.62.97.22: P [tcp sum ok]
        23:559(536) ack 577

3 20:20:21.994093 IP (tos 0xc0, ttl 64, id 57547, offset 0, flags
        [none], proto 1, length: 576)
        10.0.0.1 > 10.0.0.123: icmp 556:
        169.229.62.97 unreachable - need to frag (mtu 288) for
          IP (tos 0x0, ttl 63, id 57659, offset 0, flags [DF],
          proto 6, length: 588)
            10.0.0.123.1027 > 169.229.62.97.22:
            P 23:559(536) ack 577

4 20:20:21.994884 IP (tos 0x0, ttl 64, id 57660, offset 0, flags [DF],
        proto 6, length: 288)
        10.0.0.123.1027 > 169.229.62.97.22: . [tcp sum ok]
        23:259(236) ack 577

...

5 20:20:22.488856 IP (tos 0x0, ttl 45, id 6712, offset 0, flags [DF],
        proto 6, length: 836)
        169.229.62.97.22 > 10.0.0.123.1027: P [tcp sum ok]
        857:1641(784)ack 855

...

6 20:20:29.672947 IP (tos 0x8, ttl 64, id 57679, offset 0, flags [DF],
        proto 6, length: 1452)
        10.0.0.123.1027 > 169.229.62.97.22: . [tcp sum ok]
        1431:2831(1400) ack 2105

7 20:20:29.674123 IP (tos 0xc8, ttl 64, id 57548, offset 0, flags
        [none], proto 1, length: 576)
        10.0.0.1 > 10.0.0.123: icmp 556:
        169.229.62.97 unreachable - need to frag (mtu 288) for
          IP (tos 0x8, ttl 63, id 57679, offset 0, flags [DF],
          proto 6, length: 1452)
            10.0.0.123.1027 > 169.229.62.97.22: .
            1431:2831(1400) ack 2105

8 20:20:29.673751 IP (tos 0x8, ttl 64, id 57680, offset 0, flags [DF],
        proto 6, length: 1452)
        10.0.0.123.1027 > 169.229.62.97.22: . [tcp sum ok]
        2831:4231(1400) ack 2105

9 20:20:29.675180 IP (tos 0xc8, ttl 64, id 57549, offset 0, flags
        [none], proto 1, length: 576)
        10.0.0.1 > 10.0.0.123: icmp 556:
        169.229.62.97 unreachable - need to frag (mtu 288) for
          IP (tos 0x8, ttl 63, id 57680, offset 0, flags [DF],
          proto 6, length: 1452)
            10.0.0.123.1027 > 169.229.62.97.22: .
            2831:4231(1400) ack 2105

```
10 20:20:29.674932 IP (tos 0x8, ttl  64, id 57681, offset 0, flags
          [DF], proto 6, length: 288)
          10.0.0.123.1027 > 169.229.62.97.22: . [tcp sum ok]
          1431:1667(236) ack 2105

11 20:20:29.675143 IP (tos 0x8, ttl  64, id 57682, offset 0, flags
          [DF], proto 6, length: 288)
          10.0.0.123.1027 > 169.229.62.97.22: . [tcp sum ok]
          1667:1903(236) ack 2105
```

In the `tcpdump` output, the connection has already been set up and MSS options have been exchanged. All packets on the connection have the *DF* bit field set, so both ends are performing PMTUD. The remote side's first packet is 588 bytes long, which transitions the router successfully in one piece, despite our configuration of the MTU on the PPPoE links being 288 bytes. The reason for this is asymmetry in the MTU configuration. Although the local end of the PPPoE link is using a maximum *transmission* unit of 288 bytes, the other end is using a larger size SMSS, presumably 1492 bytes. This leaves us in the situation where our outgoing packets need to be small (288 bytes or less), and packets traveling in the reverse direction can be larger.

When the local end attempts to send a larger packet of size 588 bytes with the *DF* bit field turned on, a PTB message is generated by the router (10.0.0.1), indicating that the appropriate MTU for the next-hop link is 288 bytes. The TCP responds by sending its next packet with size 288 bytes, as instructed. To then send the rest of the sequence numbers it attempted to send in its 588-byte packet, it sends two additional packets, of sizes 288 and 116. We see a similar pattern of sizes repeats during the course of the file transfer.

The PMTU discovery process is one of the only ways TCP explicitly attempts to adapt its segment size after a connection has started, at least when large amounts of data are transferred. The size of a segment can affect the overall throughput performance, as can the window size. We discuss how these affect overall performance in Chapter 15.

13.5 TCP State Transitions

We have described numerous rules regarding the initiation and termination of a TCP connection, and we have seen which types of segments are sent during different phases of a connection. The rules that determine what TCP does are determined by what state TCP is in. The current state is changed based on various stimuli, such as segments that are transmitted or received, timers that expire, application reads or writes, or information from other layers. These rules can be summarized in TCP's state transition diagram.

13.5.1 TCP State Transition Diagram

TCP's state transition diagram is shown in Figure 13-8. States are indicated by ovals and transitions between states by arrows. Each endpoint of a connection transitions through the states. Some transitions are triggered by the receipt of a segment with certain control bit fields set (e.g., *SYN*, *ACK*, *FIN*). Some transitions

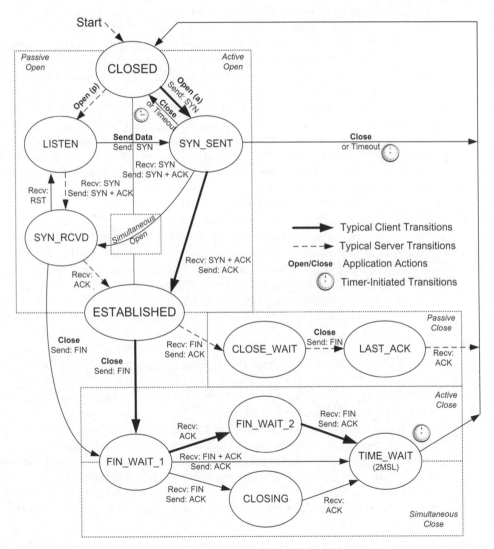

Figure 13-8   The TCP state transition diagram (also called finite state machine). Arrows represent transitions between states due to segment transmission, segment reception, or timers expiring. The bold arrows indicate typical client behavior, and the dashed arrows indicate typical server behavior. The boldface directives (e.g., open, close) are actions performed by applications.

also cause a segment with particular control bit fields set to be sent. Other transitions may be triggered by application actions or by timers expiring. Each of these cases is indicated in the diagram as a textual annotation near the associated transition arrow. When initialized, TCP starts in the CLOSED state. Usually an immediate transition takes it to either the SYN_SENT or LISTEN state, depending on whether the TCP is asked to perform an active or passive open, respectively.

Note in this diagram that only a subset of the state transitions is "typical." We have marked the normal client transitions with a darker solid arrow, and the normal server transitions with a dashed arrow. The two transitions leading to the ESTABLISHED state correspond to opening a connection, and the two transitions leading from the ESTABLISHED state are for the termination of a connection. The ESTABLISHED state is where data transfer can occur between the two ends in both directions. Chapters 14–17 describe what happens in this state.

We have labeled the FIN_WAIT_1, FIN_WAIT_2, and TIME_WAIT states as being (at least partially) in a box called "Active Close." These are the set of states entered when the local application initiates a close request. Two other states (CLOSE_WAIT and LAST_ACK) are collected in a dashed box with the label "Passive Close." These states correspond to waiting for a peer to acknowledge a FIN segment and perform its close. Simultaneous close, which is a form of double active close, uses the CLOSING state.

The names of the 11 states (CLOSED, LISTEN, SYN_SENT, etc.) in this figure are based on the names output by the `netstat` command in UNIX, Linux, and Windows, which are themselves based on the names originally used in [RFC0793]. The state CLOSED is not really an "official" state but has been added as a useful starting point and ending point for the diagram.

The state transition from LISTEN to SYN_SENT is legal in the TCP protocol but is not supported by Berkeley sockets and is rarely seen. The transition from SYN_RCVD back to LISTEN is valid only if the SYN_RCVD state was entered from the LISTEN state (the normal scenario), not from the SYN_SENT state (a simultaneous open). This means that if we perform a passive open (enter LISTEN), receive a SYN, send a SYN with an ACK (enter SYN_RCVD), and then receive a reset instead of an ACK, the endpoint returns to the LISTEN state and waits for another connection request to arrive.

Figure 13-9 shows the normal TCP connection establishment and termination, detailing the different states through which the client and server pass. It is a simpler version of Figure 13-1 showing the relevant states but not the options or ISN details. We assume in Figure 13-9 that the client on the left side does an active open and the server on the right side does a passive open. Although we show the client doing the active close, as we mentioned earlier, either side can do the active close.

13.5.2 TIME_WAIT (2MSL Wait) State

The TIME_WAIT state is also called the 2MSL wait state. It is a state in which TCP waits for a time equal to twice the *Maximum Segment Lifetime* (MSL), sometimes called *timed wait*. Every implementation must choose a value for the MSL. It is

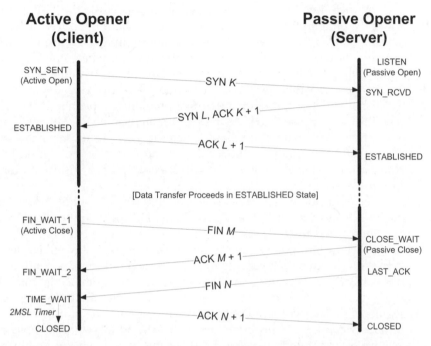

Figure 13-9   TCP states corresponding to normal connection establishment and termination

the maximum amount of time any segment can exist in the network before being discarded. We know that this time limit is bounded, because TCP segments are transmitted as IP datagrams, and the IP datagram has the *TTL* field or *Hop Limit* field that limits its effective lifetime (see Chapter 5). [RFC0793] specifies the MSL as 2 minutes. Common implementation values, however, are 30s, 1 minute, or 2 minutes. In most cases, the value can be modified. On Linux, the value `net.ipv4. tcp_fin_timeout` holds the 2MSL wait timeout value (in seconds). On Windows, the following registry key:

`HKLM\SYSTEM\CurrentControlSet\Services\Tcpip\Parameters\TcpTimedWaitDelay`

holds the timeout. It is permitted to be in the range of 30 to 300s. For IPv6, replace the term `Tcpip` with `Tcpip6`.

Given the MSL value for an implementation, the rule is: When TCP performs an active close and sends the final ACK, that connection must stay in the TIME_ WAIT state for twice the MSL. This lets TCP resend the final ACK in case it is lost. The final ACK is resent not because the TCP retransmits ACKs (they do not consume sequence numbers and are not retransmitted by TCP), but because the other side will retransmit its FIN (which does consume a sequence number). Indeed, TCP will always retransmit FINs until it receives a final ACK.

Another effect of this 2MSL wait state is that while the TCP implementation waits, the endpoints defining that connection (client IP address, client port number, server IP address, and server port number) cannot be reused. That connection can be reused only when the 2MSL wait is over, or when a new connection uses an ISN that exceeds the highest sequence number used on the previous instantiation of the connection [RFC1122], or if the use of the Timestamps option allows the disambiguation of segments from a previous connection instantiation to not otherwise be confused [RFC6191]. Unfortunately, some implementations impose a more stringent constraint. In these systems, a local port number cannot be reused while that port number is the local port number of *any* endpoint that is in the 2MSL wait state on the system. We will see examples of this constraint in Listings 13-3 and 13-4.

Most implementations and APIs provide a way to bypass this restriction. With the Berkeley sockets API, the SO_REUSEADDR socket option enables the bypass operation. It lets the caller assign itself a local port number even if that port number is part of some connection in the 2MSL wait state. We will see, however, that even with this bypass mechanism for one socket (address, port number pair), the rules of TCP still (should) prevent this port number from being reused by another instantiation of the same connection that is in the 2MSL wait state. Any delayed segments that arrive for a connection while it is in the 2MSL wait state are discarded. Because the connection defined by the address/port 4-tuple in the 2MSL wait state cannot be reused during this time period, when a valid connection is finally established, we know that delayed segments from an earlier instantiation of this connection cannot be misinterpreted as being part of the new connection.

For interactive applications, it is normally the client that does the active close and enters the TIME_WAIT state. The server usually does the passive close and does not go through the TIME_WAIT state. The implication is that if we terminate a client, and restart the same client immediately, that new client cannot reuse the same local port number. This is not ordinarily a problem, because clients normally use ephemeral ports assigned by the operating system and do not care what the assigned port number is. (Recall, it is actually a recommended practice for them to be randomized for security reasons [RFC6056].) This is important to know because a client that makes a large number of connections quickly (especially to the same server) could conceivably have to delay while other connections terminate if ephemeral ports are in short supply.

With servers, however, the situation is different. They almost always use well-known ports. If we terminate a server process that has a connection established and immediately try to restart it, the server cannot assign its assigned port number to its endpoint (it gets an "Address already in use" binding error), because that port number is part of a connection that is in a 2MSL wait state. It may take from 1 to 4 minutes for the server to be able to restart, depending on the local system's value for the MSL. We can see this scenario using our sock program. In Listing 13-3 we start the server, connect to it from a client, and then terminate the server.

Listing 13-3   A TCP connection must complete a 2MSL delay in the TIME_WAIT state before a port
number can be reused by another process.

```
Linux% sock -v -s 6666
(now a client on another computer connects to this server)
connection on 192.168.10.144.6666 from 192.168.10.140.2623
(server stopped by typing interrupt character)
(now server is restarted)
Linux% sock -v -s 6666
can't bind local address: Address already in use

Linux% netstat -n -t
Active Internet connections (w/o servers)
Proto Recv-Q Send-Q  Local Address        Foreign Address       State
tcp    0      0       192.168.10.144:6666 192.168.10.140:2623 TIME_WAIT

(wait one minute and restart server again)
Linux% sock -v -s 6666
```

When we try to restart the server, the program outputs an error message indicating that it cannot bind its port number because the address is already in use. This really means that the address and port number combination is already in use; it is in a 2MSL wait state because of the previous connection. This is the more stringent restriction on port number reuse mentioned before. The output from the `netstat` command shows that the connection is in the TIME_WAIT state. Although clients do not typically experience as many issues with 2MSL wait states as servers do, we can demonstrate the same issue by having the client specify its own port number, as shown in Listing 13-4.

Listing 13-4   A client cannot reuse a port number while it is still being used by another connection
in the 2MSL wait state.

```
(start server in one window)
Linux% sock -s -v 6666

(connect to it from another window)
Linux% sock -v 127.0.0.1 6666

(server identifies incoming connection)
connection on 127.0.0.1.6666 from 127.0.0.1.2091

(client identifies connection establishment, and is interrupted)
connected on 127.0.0.1.2091 to 127.0.0.1.6666

^C

(server identifies connection has terminated and exits)
connection closed by peer
Linux%
```

(client is restarted, specifying same port number as before)
```
Linux% sock -b 2091 -v 127.0.0.1 6666
bind() error: Address already in use
```

(wait 30 seconds and try again)
```
Linux% sock -b 2091 -v 192.168.10.144 6666
connect() error: Connection refused
```

The first time we execute the client we specify the –v option to see what the local (ephemeral) port number assigned to the client is (2091). The second time we execute the client we specify the –b option, telling the client to assign itself 2091 as its local port number instead of being given another ephemeral port number by the operating system. As we expect, the client cannot do this, because port 2091 is part of a connection that is in a 2MSL wait state. Once the wait is over (1 minute on this Linux machine), the client attempts to connect again, but the server exited when the connection was interrupted the first time, so it is refused. We shall see how TCP reset segments are used to signal this connection refused condition in Section 13.6.

We mentioned earlier that most systems provide a way of overriding the default behavior, which allows processes to bind to ports even if those ports are part of connections in the 2MSL wait state. Now we try the same scenario as before, but using the –A option to sock, which enables the bypass mechanism:

```
Linux% sock -A -v -s 6666
Linux% sock -A -v -s 6666
```

In this example, we start the server with the –A option, which enables the SO_REUSEADDR socket option that we mentioned. By doing this, we allow the server to bind to its port even though it is part of a connection in the 2MSL wait state. If we try to use the client right away with the same port, however, the following happens:

```
Linux% sock -b 32840 -v 127.0.0.1 6666
bind() error: Address already in use
```

Once again, the endpoint 127.0.0.1.32840 is in use, so the client fails. If, however, we also use the –A option for the client, we can force the connection to work:

```
Linux% sock -A -b 32840 -v 127.0.0.1 6666
Connected on 127.0.0.1.32840 to 127.0.0.1.6666
TCP_MAXSEG = 16383
```

Here we see that even though the same connection (4-tuple) is being used again before the 2MSL wait state expires, the use of the –A option has forced the connection to be allowed. Of course, this is all taking place on the same computer, so the operating system is able to ascertain what processes represent what ends of the connections in the 2MSL wait state and (potentially, at least) keep them separate. What if we try the same thing again but establish the connection from another host? Here we test this idea:

(start server on first machine)
```
Linux% sock -v -s 6666
```

(connect to it from second - Windows - machine)
```
C:\> sock -A -v 10.0.0.1 6666
```

(server identifies incoming connection)
```
connection on 10.0.0.1.6666 from 10.0.0.3.2172
```

(client identifies connection establishment, and is interrupted)
```
connected on 10.0.0.3.2172 to 10.0.0.1.6666
^C
C:\>
```

(server identifies connection has terminated and exits)

```
connection closed by peer
Linux%
```

(client is restarted, specifying same port number as before)

```
C:\> sock -A -b 2091 -v 10.0.0.1 6666
connect() error: Address already in use
C:\> sock -A -b 2091 -v 10.0.0.1 6666
connect() error: Address already in use
```

(wait 30 seconds and try again)

```
C:\> sock -A -b 2091 -v 10.0.0.1 6666
connect() error: Connection refused
```

This example is similar to the previous one, except the client and server are on different machines. We observe that irrespective of the -A flag on the client, the 2MSL wait time is induced. Here the 2MSL wait lasts for 30s. After that, the client attempts to contact the server, which has already exited.

One interesting thing happens if we switch the client and server machines. We will now use Windows as the server and Linux as the client and repeat the experiment:

(start server on Windows machine)
```
C:\> sock -v -s 6666
```

(connect to it from second - Linux - machine)
```
Linux% sock -A -v 192.168.10.145 6666
```

(server identifies incoming connection)
```
connection on 192.168.10.145.6666 from 192.168.10.145.32843
```

(client identifies connection establishment, and is interrupted)
```
connected on 192.168.10.144.32843 to 192.168.10.145.6666
^C
Linux%
```

(server identifies connection has terminated and exits)

```
connection closed by peer
c:\>
```

(client is restarted, specifying same port number as before)

```
Linux% sock -A -b 32843 -v 192.168.10.144 6666
bind() error: Connection refused
```

At this point we would expect local port 32843 to be unavailable, but because of the way –A works on Linux, we are allowed to make use of it. This is a violation of the original TCP specification, but it is allowed by [RFC1122] and [RFC6191], as mentioned before. These specifications allow a new connection request to arrive and be accepted for a connection that is in the TIME_WAIT state, if there is a strong reason to believe that segments on the new connection will not be confused with segments on the previous instantiation of the connection based on a combination of the sequence numbers and timestamps. [RFC1337] and the appendix of [RFC1323] show some of the pitfalls related to this rule.

13.5.3 Quiet Time Concept

The 2MSL wait provides protection against delayed segments from an earlier instantiation of a connection being interpreted as part of a new connection that uses the same local and foreign IP addresses and port numbers. But this works only if a host with connections in the 2MSL wait does not crash.

What if a host with connections in the TIME_WAIT state crashes, reboots within the MSL, and immediately establishes new connections using the same local and foreign IP addresses and port numbers corresponding to the local connections that were in the TIME_WAIT state before the crash? In this scenario, delayed segments from the connections that existed before the crash can be misinterpreted as belonging to the new connections created after the reboot. This can happen regardless of how the initial sequence number is chosen after the reboot.

To protect against this scenario, [RFC0793] states that TCP should wait an amount of time equal to the MSL before creating any new connections after a reboot or crash. This is called the *quiet time*. Few implementations abide by this because most hosts take longer than the MSL to reboot after a crash. Also, if applications use their own checksums or encryption, errors such as these are easily detected.

13.5.4 FIN_WAIT_2 State

In the FIN_WAIT_2 state, TCP has sent a FIN and the other end has acknowledged it. Unless a half-close is being performed, the TCP must wait for the application on the other end to recognize that it has received an end-of-file notification and close its end of the connection, which causes a FIN to be sent. Only when the application performs this close (and its FIN is received) does the active closing TCP move from the FIN_WAIT_2 to the TIME_WAIT state. This means that one end of the connection can remain in this state forever. The other end is still in the CLOSE_WAIT state and can remain there forever, until the application decides to issue its close.

Many implementations prevent this infinite wait in the FIN_WAIT_2 state as follows: If the application that does the active close does a complete close, not a half-close indicating that it expects to receive data, a timer is set. If the connection is idle when the timer expires, TCP moves the connection into the CLOSED state. In Linux, the variable `net.ipv4.tcp_fin_timeout` can be adjusted to control the number of seconds to which the timer is set. Its default value is 60s.

13.5.5 Simultaneous Open and Close Transitions

We have seen the normal uses for the SYN_SENT and SYN_RCVD states that correspond to sending and receiving SYN segments, respectively. As illustrated in Figure 13-3, TCP was purposely designed to handle simultaneous opens that result in a single connection. When a simultaneous open occurs, the state transitions differ from those shown in Figure 13-9. Both ends send a SYN at about the same time, entering the SYN_SENT state. When each end receives its peer's SYN segments, the state changes to SYN_RCVD, and each end resends a SYN and acknowledges the received SYN. When each end receives the SYN plus the ACK, the state changes to ESTABLISHED.

For a simultaneous close, in terms of Figure 13-6, both ends go from ESTAB-LISHED to FIN_WAIT_1 when the application issues the close. This causes both FINs to be sent, and they probably pass each other somewhere in the network. When its peer's FIN arrives, each end transitions from FIN_WAIT_1 to the CLOS-ING state, and each endpoint sends its final ACK. Upon receiving a final ACK, each endpoint's state changes to TIME_WAIT, and the 2MSL wait is initiated.

13.6 Reset Segments

We mentioned the *RST* bit field in the TCP header in Chapter 12. A segment having this bit set to "on" is called a "reset segment" or simply a "reset." In general, a reset is sent by TCP whenever a segment arrives that does not appear to be correct for the referenced connection. (We use the term *referenced connection* to mean the connection specified by the 4-tuple in the TCP and IP headers of the reset.) Resets ordinarily result in a fast teardown of a TCP connection. We can construct scenarios to demonstrate the use of reset segments.

13.6.1 Connection Request to Nonexistent Port

A common case for generating a reset segment is when a connection request arrives and no process is listening on the destination port. We saw this previously when we encountered the "connection refused" error messages. These are common with TCP. In the case of UDP, we saw in Chapter 10 that an ICMP Destination Unreachable (Port Unreachable) message is generated when a datagram arrives for a destination port that is not in use. TCP uses a reset segment instead.

An example of this is trivial to generate—we use the Telnet client and specify a port number that is not in use on the destination. This destination can just as well be the local computer:

```
Linux% telnet localhost 9999
Trying 127.0.0.1...
telnet: connect to address 127.0.0.1: Connection refused
```

This error message is output by the Telnet client immediately. Listing 13-5 shows the packet exchange corresponding to this command.

Listing 13-5   Reset generated by attempt to open connection to nonexistent port

```
1 22:15:16.348064 127.0.0.1.32803 > 127.0.0.1.9999:
       S [tcp sum ok] 3357881819:3357881819(0) win 32767
       <mss 16396,sackOK,timestamp 16945235 0,nop,wscale 0>
       (DF) [tos 0x10]  (ttl 64, id 42376, len 60)
2 22:15:16.348105 127.0.0.1.9999 > 127.0.0.1.32803:
       R [tcp sum ok] 0:0(0) ack 3357881820 win 0
       (DF) [tos 0x10]  (ttl 64, id 0, len 40)
```

The values we need to examine in Listing 13-5 are the *Sequence Number* field and *ACK Number* field in the reset (second) segment. Because the *ACK* bit field was not on in the arriving SYN segment, the sequence number of the reset is set to 0 and the ACK number is set to the incoming ISN plus the number of data bytes in the segment. Although there is no data in the arriving segment, the SYN bit logically occupies 1 byte of sequence number space; therefore, in this example the ACK number in the reset segment is set to the ISN, plus the data length (0), plus 1 for the SYN bit.

For a reset segment to be accepted by a TCP, the *ACK* bit field must be set and the *ACK Number* field must be within the valid window (see Chapter 12). This helps to prevent a simple attack in which anyone able to generate a reset matching the appropriate connection (4-tuple) could disrupt a connection [RFC5961].

13.6.2 **Aborting a Connection**

We saw in Figure 13-1 that the normal way to terminate a connection is for one side to send a FIN. This is sometimes called an *orderly release* because the FIN is sent after all previously queued data has been sent, and there is normally no loss of data. But it is also possible to abort a connection by sending a reset instead of a FIN at any time. This is sometimes called an *abortive release*.

Aborting a connection provides two features to the application: (1) any queued data is thrown away and a reset segment is sent immediately, and (2) the receiver of the reset can tell that the other end did an abort instead of a normal close. The API being used by the application must provide a way to generate the abort instead of a normal close.

The sockets API provides this capability by using the "linger on close" socket option (SO_LINGER) with a 0 linger value. Essentially this means "Linger for no time in making sure data gets to the other side, then abort." In the following example, we show what happens when a remote command that generates a large amount of output is canceled by the user:

```
Linux% ssh linux cat /usr/share/dict/words
Aarhus
Aaron
Ababa
aback
abaft
abandon
abandoned
abandoning
abandonment
abandons
... continues ...
^C
Killed by signal 2.
```

Here the user has decided to abort the output of this command. The words file has 45,427 words in it, so this command was probably some sort of mistake. When the user types the interrupt character, the system indicates that the process (here, the ssh program) has been killed by signal number 2. This signal is called SIGINT and usually terminates a program when it is delivered. Listing 13-6 shows the tcpdump output for this example. (We have deleted many of the intermediate packets, because they add nothing to the discussion.)

Listing 13-6   Aborting a connection with a reset (RST) instead of a FIN

```
Linux# tcpdump -vvv -s 1500 tcp

 1 22:33:06.386747 192.168.10.140.2788 > 192.168.10.144.ssh:
          S [tcp sum ok] 1520364313:1520364313(0) win 65535
          <mss 1460,nop,nop,sackOK>
          (DF) (ttl 128, id 43922, len 48)
```

```
2 22:33:06.386855 192.168.10.144.ssh > 192.168.10.140.2788:
            S [tcp sum ok] 181637276:181637276(0) ack 1520364314
            win 5840
            <mss 1460,nop,nop,sackOK>
            (DF) (ttl 64, id 0, len 48)

3 22:33:06.387676 192.168.10.140.2788 > 192.168.10.144.ssh:
            . [tcp sum ok] 1:1(0) ack 1 win 65535
            (DF) (ttl 128, id 43923, len 40)
```

(... ssh encrypted authentication exchange and bulk data transfer ...)

```
4 22:33:13.648247 192.168.10.140.2788 > 192.168.10.144.ssh:
            R [tcp sum ok] 1343:1343(0) ack 132929 win 0
            (DF) (ttl 128, id 44004, len 40)
```

Segments 1–3 show the normal connection establishment. When the interrupt character is hit, the connection is aborted. The reset segment contains a sequence number and acknowledgment number. Also notice that the reset segment elicits no response from the other end—it is not acknowledged at all. The receiver of the reset aborts the connection and advises the application that the connection was reset. This often results in the error indication "Connection reset by peer" or a similar message.

13.6.3 Half-Open Connections

A TCP connection is said to be *half-open* if one end has closed or aborted the connection without the knowledge of the other end. This can happen anytime one of the peers crashes. As long as there is no attempt to transfer data across a half-open connection, the end that is still up does not detect that the other end has crashed.

Another common cause of a half-open connection is when one host is powered off instead of shut down properly. This happens, for example, when PCs are being used to run remote login clients and are switched off at the end of the day. If there was no data transfer going on when the power was cut, the server will never know that the client disappeared (it would still think the connection is in the ESTABLISHED state). When the user comes in the next morning, powers on the PC, and starts a new session, a new occurrence of the server is started on the server host. This can lead to many half-open TCP connections on the server host. (In Chapter 17 we will see a way for one end of a TCP connection to discover that the other end has disappeared using TCP's keepalive option.)

We can easily create a half-open connection. In this case, we do so on the client rather than the server. We will execute the Telnet client on 10.0.0.1, connecting to the Sun RPC Service (sunrpc, port 111) server at 10.0.0.7 (see Listing 13-7). We type one line of input and watch it go across with tcpdump, and then we disconnect the Ethernet cable on the server's host and reboot the server host. This simulates the server host crashing. (We disconnect the Ethernet cable before rebooting the server to prevent it from sending a FIN out of the open connections, which some TCPs do when they are shut down.) After the server has rebooted, we reconnect the cable and try to send another line from the client to the server. After rebooting, the server's TCP has lost all memory of the connections that existed before, so it knows nothing about the connection that the data segment references. The rule of TCP is that the receiver responds with a reset.

Listing 13-7   The server host is disconnected and rebooted, leaving a half-open connection at the client. When it receives additional data on the connection it now knows nothing about, the server responds with a reset segment, closing the connection at both ends.

```
Linux% telnet 10.0.0.7 sunrpc
Trying 10.0.0.7...
Connected to 10.0.0.7.
Escape character is '^]'.
foo
(Ethernet cable disconnected and server rebooted)
bar
Connection closed by remote host
```

Listing 13-8 shows the `tcpdump` output for this example.

Listing 13-8   Reset in response to data segment on a half-open connection

```
1 23:15:48.804142 IP (tos 0x10, ttl  64, id 20095, offset 0,
       flags [DF], proto 6, length: 60)
       10.0.0.1.1310 > 10.0.0.7.sunrpc:
       S [tcp sum ok] 2365970104:2365970104(0) win 5840
       <mss 1460,sackOK,timestamp 3849492679 0,nop,wscale 2>

2 23:15:48.804742 IP (tos 0x0, ttl  64, id 0, offset 0, flags [DF],
       proto 6, length: 60)
       10.0.0.7.sunrpc > 10.0.0.1.1310:
       S [tcp sum ok] 2093796387:2093796387(0) ack 2365970105 win 5792
       <mss 1460,sackOK,timestamp 654784 3849492679,nop,wscale 0>

3 23:15:48.805028 IP (tos 0x10, ttl  64, id 20097, offset 0,
       flags [DF], proto 6, length: 52)
       10.0.0.1.1310 > 10.0.0.7.sunrpc:
       . [tcp sum ok] 1:1(0) ack 1 win 1460
       <nop,nop,timestamp 3849492680 654784>

4 23:15:51.999394 IP (tos 0x10, ttl  64, id 20099, offset 0,
       flags [DF], proto 6, length: 57)
               10.0.0.1.1310 > 10.0.0.7.sunrpc:
       P [tcp sum ok] 1:6(5) ack 1 win 1460
       <nop,nop,timestamp 3849495875 654784>

5 23:15:51.999874 IP (tos 0x0, ttl  64, id 12773, offset 0,
       flags [DF], proto 6, length: 52)
               10.0.0.7.sunrpc > 10.0.0.1.1310:
       . [tcp sum ok] 1:1(0) ack 6 win 5792
       <nop,nop,timestamp 656421 3849495875>
```

```
 6 23:17:19.419611 arp who-has 10.0.0.7 (Broadcast) tell 0.0.0.0
 7 23:17:20.419142 arp who-has 10.0.0.7 (Broadcast) tell 0.0.0.0
 8 23:17:21.427458 arp reply 10.0.0.7 is-at 00:e0:00:88:ad:d6

 9 23:17:21.921745 arp who-has 10.0.0.1 tell 10.0.0.7
10 23:17:21.921892 arp reply 10.0.0.1 is-at 00:04:5a:9f:9e:80

11 23:17:23.437114 arp who-has 10.0.0.7 (Broadcast) tell 10.0.0.7

12 23:17:34.804196 arp who-has 10.0.0.7 tell 10.0.0.1
13 23:17:34.804650 arp reply 10.0.0.7 is-at 00:e0:00:88:ad:d6

14 23:17:43.684786 IP (tos 0x10, ttl  64, id 20101, offset 0,
       flags [DF], proto 6, length: 57)
       10.0.0.1.1310 > 10.0.0.7.sunrpc:
       P [tcp sum ok] 6:11(5) ack 1 win 1460
       <nop,nop,timestamp 3849607577 656421>

15 23:17:43.685277 IP (tos 0x10, ttl  64, id 0, offset 0,
       flags [DF], proto 6, length: 40)
       10.0.0.7.sunrpc > 10.0.0.1.1310:
       R [tcp sum ok] 2093796388:2093796388(0) win 0
```

Segments 1–3 are the normal connection establishment. Segment 4 sends the line "foo" to the sunrpc server (the 5 bytes required include a carriage return and newline character), and segment 5 is the acknowledgment.

At this point we disconnect the Ethernet cable from the server (address 10.0.0.7), reboot, and reconnect the cable. This takes about 90s. We then type the next line of input to the client ("bar"), and when we type the return key the line is sent to the server (the first TCP segment after the ARP traffic in Listing 13-9). This elicits a reset response from the server, which no longer has any knowledge of the existence of the connection.

Note that when the host reboots, it uses gratuitous ARP (see Chapter 4) in order to determine if its IPv4 address is already in use on the segment, and to supply it to others. It also requests the MAC address for IPv4 address 10.0.0.1 because that is its default router to the Internet.

13.6.4 TIME-WAIT Assassination (TWA)

As mentioned previously, the TIME_WAIT state is intended to allow any datagrams lingering from a closed connection to be discarded. During this period, the waiting TCP usually has little to do; it merely holds the state until the 2MSL timer expires. If, however, it receives certain segments from the connection during this period, or more specifically an RST segment, it can become desynchronized. This is called *TIME-WAIT Assassination* (TWA) [RFC1337]. Consider the exchange of packets shown in Figure 13-10.

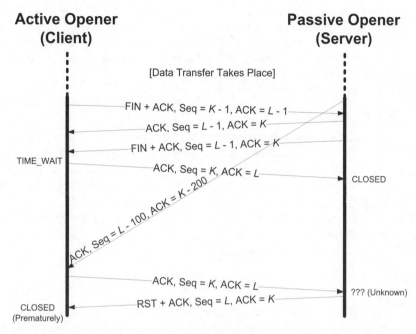

Figure 13-10   An RST segment can "assassinate" the TIME_WAIT state and force the connection to
close prematurely. Various methods exist to resist this problem, including ignoring
RST segments when in the TIME_WAIT state.

In the example shown in Figure 13-10, the server has completed its role in the
connection and cleared any state. The client remains in the TIME_WAIT state.
When the FIN exchange completes, the client's next sequence number is K and
the server's is L. The late-arriving segment is sent from the server to the client
using sequence number $L - 100$ and containing ACK number $K - 200$. When the client receives this segment, it determines that both the sequence number and ACK
values are "old." When receiving such old segments, TCP responds by sending an
ACK with the most current sequence number and ACK values (K and L, respectively). However, when the server receives this segment, it has no information
whatsoever about the connection and therefore replies with an RST segment. This
is no problem for the server, but it causes the client to prematurely transition from
TIME_WAIT to CLOSED. Most systems avoid this problem by simply not reacting
to reset segments while in the TIME_WAIT state.

13.7 TCP Server Operation

We said in Chapter 1 that most TCP servers are concurrent. When a new connection request arrives at a server, the server accepts the connection and invokes

a new process or thread to handle the new client. Depending on the operating system, various other resources may be allocated to invoke the new server. We are interested in the interaction of TCP with concurrent servers. In particular, we wish to become familiar with how TCP servers use port numbers and how multiple concurrent clients are handled.

13.7.1 TCP Port Numbers

We can see how TCP handles port numbers by watching any TCP server. We shall watch the secure shell server (called `sshd`) using the `netstat` command on a dual-stack IPv4/IPv6-capable host. The `sshd` application implements the *Secure Shell Protocol* [RFC4254], which provides an encrypted and authenticated remote terminal capability. The following output is on a system with no active secure shell connections. (We have deleted all of the output lines except the one associated with the server.)

```
Linux% netstat -a -n -t
Active Internet connections (servers and established)
Proto Recv-Q Send-Q    Local Address     Foreign Address    State
tcp      0      0          :::22                 :::*      LISTEN
```

The `-a` option reports on all network endpoints, including those in either listening or non-listening state. The `-n` flag prints IP addresses as dotted-decimal (or hex) numbers, instead of trying to use the DNS to convert the address to a name, and prints numeric port numbers (e.g., 22) instead of service names (e.g., `ssh`). The `-t` option selects only TCP endpoints.

The local address (which really means local endpoint) is output as `:::22`, which is the IPv6-oriented way of referring to the all-zeros address, also called the *wildcard* address, along with port number 22. This means that an incoming connection request (i.e., a SYN) to port 22 will be accepted on any local interface. If the host were multihomed (this one is), we could specify a single IP address for the local IP address (one of the host's IP addresses), and only connections received on that interface would be accepted. (We will see an example of this later in this section.) Port 22 is the well-known port number reserved for the Secure Shell Protocol. Other port numbers are maintained by the IANA [ITP].

The foreign address is output as `:::*`, which means both a wildcard address and port number (i.e., it represents a wildcard endpoint). Here, the foreign IP address and foreign port number are not known yet, because the local endpoint is in the LISTEN state, waiting for a connection to arrive. We now start a secure shell client on the host 10.0.0.3 that connects to this server. Here are the relevant lines from the `netstat` output (the Recv-Q and Send-Q columns, which contain only values of zero, have been removed for clarity):

```
Linux% netstat -a -n -t
Active Internet connections (servers and established)
```

```
Proto        Local Address      Foreign Address   State
tcp                  :::22                 :::*    LISTEN
tcp      ::ffff:10.0.0.1:22 ::ffff:10.0.0.3:16137 ESTABLISHED
```

The second line for port 22 is the ESTABLISHED connection. All four elements of the local and foreign endpoints are filled in for this connection: the local IP address and port number, and the foreign IP address and port number. The local IP address corresponds to the interface on which the connection request arrived (the Ethernet interface, identified by its IPv4-mapped IPv6 address, ::ffff:10.0.0.1).

The local endpoint in the LISTEN state is left alone. This is the endpoint that the concurrent server uses to accept future connection requests. It is the TCP module in the operating system that creates the new endpoint in the ESTABLISHED state, when the incoming connection request arrives and is accepted. Also notice that the port number for the ESTABLISHED connection does not change: it is 22, the same as the LISTEN endpoint.

We now initiate another client request from the same system (10.0.0.3) to this server. Here is the relevant netstat output:

```
Linux% netstat -a -n -t
Active Internet connections (servers and established)
Proto        Local Address      Foreign Address   State
tcp                  :::22                 :::*    LISTEN
tcp      ::ffff:10.0.0.1:22 ::ffff:10.0.0.3:16140 ESTABLISHED
tcp      ::ffff:10.0.0.1:22 ::ffff:10.0.0.3:16137 ESTABLISHED
```

We now have two ESTABLISHED connections from the same host to the same server. Both have a local port number on the server of 22. This is not a problem for TCP because the foreign port numbers are different. They must be different because each of the secure shell clients uses an ephemeral port, and the definition of an ephemeral port is one that is not currently in use on that host (10.0.0.3).

This example reiterates, yet again, that TCP demultiplexes incoming segments using all four values that constitute the local and foreign endpoints: destination IP address, destination port number, source IP address, and source port number. TCP cannot determine which process gets an incoming segment by looking at the destination port number only. Also, the only one of the three endpoints at port 22 that will receive incoming connection requests is the one in the LISTEN state. The endpoints in the ESTABLISHED state cannot receive SYN segments, and the endpoint in the LISTEN state cannot receive data segments. The host operating system ensures this. (If it did not, TCP could become quite confused and not work properly.)

Next we initiate a third client connection, from the IP address 169.229.62.97 that is across the DSL PPPoE link from the server 10.0.0.1, and not on the same Ethernet. (The output below has the Proto column removed, which contains only tcp, for clarity.)

```
Linux% netstat -a -n -t
Active Internet connections (servers and established)
Send-Q              Local Address           Foreign Address    State
     0                     :::22                       :::*     LISTEN
     0          ::ffff:10.0.0.1:22      ::ffff:10.0.0.3:16140  ESTABLISHED
     0          ::ffff:10.0.0.1:22      ::ffff:10.0.0.3:16137  ESTABLISHED
   928 ::ffff:67.125.227.195:22 ::ffff:169.229.62.97:1473     ESTABLISHED
```

The local IP address of the third ESTABLISHED connection now corresponds to the interface address of the PPPoE link on the multihomed host (67.125.227.195). Note that the Send-Q status is not 0 but is instead 928 bytes. This means that the server host has sent 928 bytes on the connection for which it has not yet heard an acknowledgment.

13.7.2 Restricting Local IP Addresses

We can see what happens when the server does not wildcard the local IP address but instead sets it to one particular local address. If we run our sock program as a server and provide it with a particcular IP address, that address becomes the local address of the listening endpoint. For example:

```
Linux% sock -s 10.0.0.1 8888
```

This restricts this server to using connections that arrive only on the local IPv4 address 10.0.0.1. The netstat output reflects this:

```
Linux% netstat -a -n -t
Active Internet connections (servers and established)
Proto Recv-Q Send-Q   Local Address   Foreign Address    State
tcp        0      0    10.0.0.1:8888        0.0.0.0:*     LISTEN
```

One thing that is especially interesting about this example is that our sock program is binding only to the local IPv4 address 10.0.0.1, so our netstat output looks significantly different. In our previous example, the wildcard address and port number indications were across both versions of IP. In this case, however, we are bound to a particular address, port, and address family (IPv4 only). If we now connect to this server from the local network, from the host 10.0.0.3, it works fine:

```
Linux% netstat -a -n -t
Active Internet connections (servers and established)
Proto Recv-Q Send-Q   Local Address   Foreign Address    State
tcp        0      0    10.0.0.1:8888        0.0.0.0:*     LISTEN
tcp        0      0    10.0.0.1:8888     10.0.0.3:16153   ESTABLISHED
```

If we instead try to connect to this server from a host using a destination address other than 10.0.0.1 (even including the local address 127.0.0.1), the connection request is not accepted by the TCP module. If we watch with `tcp-dump`, the SYN elicits an RST segment, as we show in Listing 13-9.

Listing 13-9   Rejection of a connection request based on local IP address of server

```
1 22:29:19.905593 IP 127.0.0.1.1292 > 127.0.0.1.8888:
    S 591843787:591843787(0) win 32767
    <mss 16396,sackOK,timestamp 3587463952 0,nop,wscale 2>
2 22:29:19.906095 IP 127.0.0.1.8888 > 127.0.0.1.1292:
    R 0:0(0) ack 591843788 win 0
```

The server application never sees the connection request—the rejection is done by the operating system's TCP module, based on the local address specified by the application and the destination address contained in the arriving SYN segment. We see that the capability of restricting local IP addresses is quite strict.

13.7.3 Restricting Foreign Endpoints

In Chapter 10, we saw that a UDP server can normally specify the foreign IP address and foreign port number, in addition to specifying the local IP address and local port number. The abstract interface functions for TCP given in [RFC0793] allow a server doing a passive open to have either a fully specified foreign endpoint (to wait for a particular client to issue an active open) or an unspecified foreign endpoint (to wait for any client).

Unfortunately, the ordinary Berkeley sockets API does not provide a way to do this. The server must leave the client's endpoint unspecified, wait for the connection to arrive, and then examine the IP address and port number of the client. Table 13-3 summarizes the three types of address bindings that a TCP server can establish.

Table 13-3   Address and port number binding options available to a TCP server

Local Address	Foreign Address	Restricted to	Comment
`local_IP.lport`	`foraddr.foreign_port`	One client	Not usually supported
`local_IP.lport`	`*.*`	One local endpoint	Unusual (used by DNS servers)
`*.local_port`	`*.*`	One local port	Most common; multiple address families (IPv4/IPv6) may be supported

In all cases, `local_port` is the server's assigned port and `local_IP` must be a unicast IP address used by the local system. The ordering of the three rows in the table is the order that the TCP module applies when trying to determine which local endpoint receives an incoming connection request. The most specific binding (the first row, if supported) is tried first, and the least specific (the last row with both IP addresses wildcarded) is tried last. For systems supporting IPv4 and IPv6 ("dual-stack"), the port space may be combined. In essence, this means that writing a server that binds to a port using IPv6 addressing is also bound to the same port in IPv4.

13.7.4 Incoming Connection Queue

A concurrent server invokes a new process or thread to handle each client, so the listening server should always be ready to handle the next incoming connection request. That is the underlying reason for using concurrent servers. But there is still a chance that multiple connection requests will arrive while the listening server is creating a new process, or while the operating system is busy running other higher-priority processes, or worse yet, that the server is being attacked with bogus connection requests that are never allowed to be established. How does TCP handle these scenarios?

To fully explore this question, we must first understand that new connections may be in one of two distinct states before they are made available to an application. The first case is connections that have not yet completed but for which a SYN has been received (these are in the SYN_RCVD state). The second case is connections that have already completed the three-way handshake and are in the ESTABLISHED state but have not yet been accepted by the application. Internally the operating system ordinarily has two distinct connection queues, one for each of these cases.

An application has limited control over the sizing of these queues. Traditionally, using the Berkeley sockets API, an application had only indirect control of the sum of the sizes of these two queues. In modern Linux kernels this behavior has been changed to be the number of connections in the second case (ESTABLISHED connections). The application can therefore limit the number of fully formed connections waiting for it to handle. In Linux, then, the following rules apply:

1. When a connection request arrives (i.e., the SYN segment), the system-wide parameter net.ipv4.tcp_max_syn_backlog is checked (default 1000). If the number of connections in the SYN_RCVD state would exceed this threshold, the incoming connection is rejected.

2. Each listening endpoint has a fixed-length queue of connections that have been completely accepted by TCP (i.e., the three-way handshake is complete) but not yet accepted by the application. The application specifies a limit to this queue, commonly called the *backlog*. This backlog must be between 0 and a system-specific maximum called net.core.somaxconn, inclusive (default 128).

Keep in mind that this backlog value specifies only the maximum number of queued connections for *one* listening endpoint, all of which have already been accepted by TCP and are waiting to be accepted by the application.

This backlog has no effect whatsoever on the maximum number of established connections allowed by the system, or on the number of clients that a concurrent server can handle concurrently.

3. If there is room on this listening endpoint's queue for this new connection, the TCP module ACKs the SYN and completes the connection. The server application with the listening endpoint does not see this new connection until the third segment of the three-way handshake is received. Also, the client may think the server is ready to receive data when the client's active open completes successfully, before the server application has been notified of the new connection. If this happens, the server's TCP just queues the incoming data.

4. If there is not enough room on the queue for the new connection, the TCP delays responding to the SYN, to give the application a chance to catch up. Linux is somewhat unique in this behavior—it persists in not ignoring incoming connections if it possibly can. If the net.ipv4.tcp_abort_on_ overflow system control variable is set, new incoming connections are reset with a reset segment.

Sending reset segments on overflow is not generally advisable and is not turned on by default. The client has attempted to contact the server, and if it receives a reset during the SYN exchange, it may falsely conclude that no server is present (instead of concluding that there is a server present but it is busy). Being too busy is really a form of "soft" or temporary error rather than a hard error. Normally, when the queue is full, the application or the operating system is busy, preventing the application from servicing incoming connections. This condition could change in a short while. But if the server's TCP responded with a reset, the client's active open would abort (which is what we saw happen if the server was not started). Without the reset, if the listening server does not get around to accepting some of the already-accepted connections that have filled its queue to the limit, the client's active open eventually times out, according to normal TCP mechanisms. In the case of Linux, the connecting clients are just slowed for a significant period of time—they will neither time out nor be reset.

We can see what happens when the incoming connection queue becomes full using our sock program. We invoke it with a new option (-O) that tells it to pause after creating the listening endpoint, before accepting any connection requests. If we then invoke multiple clients during this pause period, the server's queue of accepted connections should fill, and we can see what happens with tcpdump.

```
Linux% sock -s -v -q1 -O30000 6666
```

The -q1 option sets the backlog of the listening endpoint to 1. The -O30000 option causes the program to sleep for 30,000s (basically a long time, about 8 hours) before accepting any client connections. If we now try to connect to this server continually, the first four connections are completed immediately. After that, two connections are completed every 9s. Other operating systems vary considerably in how this is handled. In Solaris 8 and FreeBSD 4.7, for example, two connections are handled immediately and the third times out; subsequent connections time out as well.

Listing 13-10 shows the tcpdump output of a Linux client connecting to a FreeBSD server running the sock program with the arguments just given. (We have marked the client port numbers in bold when the TCP connection is established—when the three-way handshake completes.)

Listing 13-10   The FreeBSD server accepts two connections immediately. Subsequent connections receive no response and eventually time out at the client.

```
1 21:28:47.399872 IP (tos 0x0, ttl  64, id 46646, offset 0,
       flags [DF], proto 6, length: 60)
       63.203.76.212.2461 > 169.229.62.97.6666:
       S [tcp sum ok] 2998137201:2998137201(0) win 5808
       <mss 1452,sackOK,timestamp 4102309703 0,nop,wscale 2>

2 21:28:47.413770 IP (tos 0x0, ttl  47, id 6876, offset 0,
       flags [DF], proto 6, length: 60)
       169.229.62.97.6666 > 63.203.76.212.2461:
       S [tcp sum ok] 5583769:5583769(0) ack 2998137202 win 1460
       <mss 1412,nop,wscale 0,nop,nop,timestamp 219082980 4102309703>

3 21:28:47.414058 IP (tos 0x0, ttl  64, id 46648, offset 0,
       flags [DF], proto 6, length: 52)
       63.203.76.212.2461 > 169.229.62.97.6666:
       . [tcp sum ok] 1:1(0) ack 1 win 1452
       <nop,nop,timestamp 4102309717 219082980>

4 21:28:47.423673 IP (tos 0x0, ttl  64, id 19651, offset 0,
       flags [DF], proto 6, length: 60)
       63.203.76.212.2462 > 169.229.62.97.6666:
       S [tcp sum ok] 2996964252:2996964252(0) win 5808
       <mss 1452,sackOK,timestamp 4102309727 0,nop,wscale 2>

5 21:28:47.436897 IP (tos 0x0, ttl  47, id 26581, offset 0,
       flags [DF], proto 6, length: 60)
       169.229.62.97.6666 > 63.203.76.212.2462:
       S [tcp sum ok] 3761536245:3761536245(0) ack 2996964253 win 1460
       <mss 1412,nop,wscale 0,nop,nop,timestamp 219082983 4102309727>

6 21:28:47.437186 IP (tos 0x0, ttl  64, id 19653, offset 0,
       flags [DF], proto 6, length: 52)
       63.203.76.212.2462 > 169.229.62.97.6666:
       . [tcp sum ok] 1:1(0) ack 1 win 1452
       <nop,nop,timestamp 4102309741 219082983>

7 21:28:47.446198 IP (tos 0x0, ttl  64, id 24292, offset 0,
       flags [DF], proto 6, length: 60)
```

```
       63.203.76.212.2463 > 169.229.62.97.6666:
       S [tcp sum ok] 2991331729:2991331729(0) win 5808
       <mss 1452,sackOK,timestamp 4102309749 0,nop,wscale 2>

 8 21:28:50.445771 IP (tos 0x0, ttl  64, id 24294, offset 0,
       flags [DF], proto 6, length: 60)
       63.203.76.212.2463 > 169.229.62.97.6666:
       S [tcp sum ok] 2991331729:2991331729(0) win 5808
       <mss 1452,sackOK,timestamp 4102312750 0,nop,wscale 2>

 9 21:28:56.444900 IP (tos 0x0, ttl  64, id 24296, offset 0,
       flags [DF], proto 6, length: 60)
       63.203.76.212.2463 > 169.229.62.97.6666:
       S [tcp sum ok] 2991331729:2991331729(0) win 5808
       <mss 1452,sackOK,timestamp 4102318750 0,nop,wscale 2>

10 21:29:08.443031 IP (tos 0x0, ttl  64, id 24298, offset 0,
       flags [DF], proto 6, length: 60) 6
       3.203.76.212.2463 > 169.229.62.97.6666:
       S [tcp sum ok] 2991331729:2991331729(0) win 5808
       <mss 1452,sackOK,timestamp 4102330750 0,nop,wscale 2>

11 21:29:32.439406 IP (tos 0x0, ttl  64, id 24300, offset 0,
       flags [DF], proto 6, length: 60)
       63.203.76.212.2463 > 169.229.62.97.6666:
       S [tcp sum ok] 2991331729:2991331729(0) win 5808
       <mss 1452,sackOK,timestamp 4102354750 0,nop,wscale 2>

12 21:30:20.432118 IP (tos 0x0, ttl  64, id 24302, offset 0,
       flags [DF], proto 6, length: 60)
       63.203.76.212.2463 > 169.229.62.97.6666:
       S [tcp sum ok] 2991331729:2991331729(0) win 5808
       <mss 1452,sackOK,timestamp 4102402750 0,nop,wscale 2>
```

The first client's connection request from port 2461 is accepted by TCP (segments 1–3). The second client's connection request from port 2462 is also accepted by TCP (segments 4–6). The server application is still asleep and has not accepted either connection yet. Everything has been done by the TCP module in the operating system. Also, the two clients have returned successfully from their active opens, because the three-way handshakes are complete.

We try to start a third whose SYN appears as segment 7 (port 2463), but the server-side TCP ignores the SYNs because the queue for this listening endpoint is full. The client retransmits its SYN in segments 8–12 using binary exponential backoff. In FreeBSD and Solaris, TCP ignores the incoming SYN when the queue is full.

Recall that TCP accepts an incoming connection request (i.e., a SYN) if there is room on the listener's queue, without giving the application a chance to see where it is from (the source IP address and source port number). This is not required by TCP; it is just the common implementation technique (i.e., the way Berkeley sockets work). If an alternative to the Berkeley sockets API were used (e.g., TLI/ XTI), the application could be provided a way to learn when a connection request arrives and then allow the application to choose whether to accept the connection or not. Even though TLI provided this capability in theory, it never fully caught on, so we are effectively left with the TCP interface provided by Berkeley sockets.

So with Berkeley sockets, be aware that with TCP, when the application is told that a connection has just arrived, TCP's three-way handshake is *already over*. This behavior also means that a TCP server has no way to cause a client's active open to fail. When a new client connection is passed to the server application, TCP's three-way handshake is over, and the client's active open has completed successfully. If the server then looks at the client's IP address and port number and decides it does not want to service this client, all the server can do is either close the connection (causing a FIN to be sent) or reset the connection (causing an RST to be sent). In either case the client thought everything was OK when its active open completed and may have already sent a request to the server. Other transport-layer protocols may be implemented that provide this separation to the application between arrival and acceptance (i.e., the OSI transport layer), but not TCP.

13.8 Attacks Involving TCP Connection Management

A *SYN flood* is a TCP DoS attack whereby one or more malicious clients generate a series of TCP connection attempts (SYN segments) and send them at a server, often with a "spoofed" (e.g., random) source IP address. The server allocates some amount of connection resources to each partial connection. Because the connections are never established, the server may start to deny service to future legitimate requests because its memory is exhausted holding state for many half-open connections.

This attack is somewhat difficult to repel, because it is not always easy to distinguish between legitimate connection attempts and SYN floods. One mechanism invented to deal with this issue is called *SYN cookies* [RFC4987]. The main insight with SYN cookies is that most of the information that would be stored for a connection when a SYN arrives could be encoded inside the *Sequence Number* field supplied with the SYN + ACK. The target machine using SYN cookies need not allocate any storage for the incoming connection request—it allocates real memory only once the SYN + ACK segment has itself been acknowledged (and the initial sequence number is returned). In that case, all the vital connection parameters can be recovered and the connection can be placed in the ESTABLISHED state.

Producing SYN cookies involves a careful selection process of the TCP ISN at servers. Essentially, the server must encode any essential state in the *Sequence Number* field in its SYN + ACK that is returned in the *ACK Number* field from a legitimate client. There are several ways of doing this, but we will mention the technique adopted by Linux.

A server receiving an incoming SYN causes its ISN (supplied to the client in the SYN + ACK segment) to be set to a value constructed in the following way: the top 5 bits are (t mod 32) where t is a 32-bit counter that increases by 1 every 64s, the next 3 bits are an encoding of the server's MSS (one of eight possibilities), and the remaining 24 bits are a server-selected cryptographic hash of the connection 4-tuple and t value. (See Chapter 18 for a detailed explanation of cryptographic hashes.)

When SYN cookies are used, the server always responds with a SYN + ACK (as with any typical TCP connection establishment), and the server is able to rebuild its queue of arriving SYNs when it receives a legitimate ACK where the value for t still produces the same output from the cryptographic hash. There are at least two pitfalls of this approach. First, the scheme prohibits the use of arbitrary-size segments because of the encoding of the MSS. Second, and much less serious, connection establishment cycles that are very long (longer than 64s) do not work properly because the counter would wrap. For these reasons, this function is not enabled by default.

Another type of degradation attack on TCP involves PMTUD. In this case, an attacker fabricates an ICMP PTB message containing a very small MTU value (e.g., 68 bytes). This forces the victim TCP to attempt to fit its data into very small packets, greatly reducing its performance. This problem can be addressed in several ways. The most brute-force way would be to simply disable PMTUD for the host. Other options would be to disable PMTUD in cases where an ICMP PTB message with next-hop MTU under 576 bytes is received. Another option, implemented by Linux and mentioned briefly earlier, is to insist that the minimum packet size (for large packets used by TCP) always be fixed at some value, and larger packets simply not have the IPv4 *DF* bit field turned on. This approach is similar, although perhaps somewhat more attractive, than completely disabling PMTUD.

Another type of attack involves disrupting an existing TCP connection and possibly taking it over (called *hijacking*). These forms of attacks usually involve a first step of "desynchronizing" the two TCP endpoints so that if they were to talk to each other, they would be using invalid sequence numbers. They are particular examples of *sequence number attacks* [RFC1948]. They can be accomplished in at least two ways: by causing invalid state transitions during connection establishment (similar to TWA; see Section 13.6.4), and by generating extra data while in the ESTABLISHED state. Once the two ends can no longer communicate (but believe they have an open connection), an attacker can introduce traffic into the connection, which is considered (by TCP at least) as valid.

A collection of attacks generally called *spoofing attacks* involve TCP segments that have been specially tailored by an attacker to disrupt or alter the behavior of an existing TCP connection. A variety of these attacks and their mitigation techniques are discussed in [RFC4953]. An attacker can generate a spoofed reset segment and send it to an existing TCP endpoint. Provided the connection 4-tuple and checksum are correct, and the sequence number is in range, the reset generally results in a connection abort at either endpoint. This is of growing concern because as networks become faster, a wider range of sequence numbers are considered "in window" to maintain performance (see Chapter 15). Other types of segments (SYNs, even ACKs) can also be spoofed (and combined with flooding attacks), causing myriad problems. Mitigation techniques include authenticating each segment (e.g., using the TCP-AO option), requiring reset segments to have one particular sequence number instead of one from a range, requiring particular values in the Timestamps option, and using other forms of cookies in which otherwise noncritical data values are arranged to depend on more exact knowledge of the connection or a secret value.

There are spoofing attacks that are not part of the TCP protocol yet can affect TCP's operation. For example, ICMP can be used to modify PMTUD behavior. It can also be used to indicate that a port or host is not available, and this often causes a TCP connection to be terminated. Many of these attacks are described in [RFC5927], which also suggests a number of ways of improving robustness against spoofed ICMP messages. The suggestions amount to validating not only the ICMP message but also as much of the contained TCP segment as possible. For example, the contained segment should have an appropriate 4-tuple and sequence number.

13.9 Summary

Before two processes can exchange data using TCP, they must establish a connection between themselves. When they are done, they terminate the connection. This chapter has provided a detailed look at how connections are established using a three-way handshake, and how they are terminated using four segments. We also saw how TCP can handle simultaneous open and close operations and how various options, including the Selective ACK, Timestamps, MSS, TCP-AO, and UTO options, are handled.

We used tcpdump and Wireshark to show TCP's behavior and its use of the fields in the TCP header. We also saw how connection establishment can time out, how resets are sent and interpreted, what happens with a half-open connection, and how TCP provides a half-close. TCP bounds both the number of connection attempts it will try when performing an active open and also the number of connection attempts it will service after performing a passive open.

Fundamental to understanding the operation of TCP is its state transition diagram. We followed through the steps involved in connection establishment and termination, and the state transitions that take place. We also looked at the implications of TCP's connection establishment for the design of concurrent TCP servers.

A TCP connection is uniquely defined by a 4-tuple: the local IP address, local port number, foreign IP address, and foreign port number. Whenever a connection is terminated, one end must maintain knowledge of the connection, and we saw that the TIME_WAIT state handles this. The rule is that the end that does the active close enters this state for twice the implementation's MSL, which helps protect TCP from processing segments from an older instantiation of the same connection. Using the Timestamps option can shorten the waiting time when new connections attempt to use the same 4-tuple, and it has other benefits for detecting wrapped sequence numbers and performing better RTT measurements.

TCP can be vulnerable to both resource exhaustion and spoofing attacks, but a number of methods have been developed to resist such issues. In addition, TCP can be affected by other protocols such as ICMP. Additional protection for ICMP is possible by carefully processing the original datagram returned by ICMP messages. Finally, TCP can be used in combination with protocols that provide security at other layers (e.g., IPsec and TLS/SSL, described in Chapter 18), which is now standard practice.

13.10 References

[CERTISN] http://www.cert.org/advisories/CA-2001-09.html

[ITP] http://www.iana.org/assignments/service-names-port-numbers

[LS10] M. Luckie and B. Stasiewicz, "Measuring Path MTU Discovery Behavior," *Proc. ACM IMC*, Nov. 2010.

[RFC0793] J. Postel, "Transmission Control Protocol," Internet RFC 0793/STD 0007, Sept. 1981.

[RFC0854] J. Postel and J. K. Reynolds, "Telnet Protocol Specification," Internet RFC 0854/STD 0008, May 1983.

[RFC0879] J. Postel, "The TCP Maximum Segment Size and Related Topics," Internet RFC 0879, Nov. 1983.

[RFC1025] J. Postel, "TCP and IP Bake Off," Internet RFC 1025, Sept. 1987.

[RFC1122] R. Braden, ed., "Requirements for Internet Hosts—Communication Layers," Internet RFC 1122/STD 0003, Oct. 1989.

[RFC1191] J. C. Mogul and S. E. Deering, "Path MTU Discovery," Internet RFC 1191, Nov. 1990.

[RFC1323] V. Jacobson, R. Braden, and D. Borman, "TCP Extensions for High Performance," Internet RFC 1323, May 1992.

[RFC1337] R. Braden, "TIME-WAIT Assassination Hazards in TCP," Internet RFC 1337 (informational), May 1992.

[RFC1948] S. Bellovin, "Defending against Sequence Number Attacks," Internet RFC 1948 (informational), May 1996.

[RFC1981] J. McCann, S. Deering, and J. Mogul, "Path MTU Discovery for IP Version 6," Internet RFC 1981, Aug. 1996.

[RFC2018] M. Mathis, J. Mahdavi, S. Floyd, and A. Romanow, "TCP Selective Acknowledgment Options," Internet RFC 2018, Oct. 1996.

[RFC2385] A. Heffernan, "Protection of BGP Sessions via the TCP MD5 Signature Option," Internet RFC 2385 (obsolete), Aug. 1998.

[RFC2675] D. Borman, S. Deering, and R. Hinden, "IPv6 Jumbograms," Internet RFC 2675, Aug. 1999.

[RFC2883] S. Floyd, J. Mahdavi, M. Mathis, and M. Podolsky, "An Extension to the Selective Acknowledgement (SACK) Option for TCP," Internet RFC 2883, July 2000.

[RFC2923] K. Lahey, "TCP Problems with Path MTU Discovery," Internet RFC 2923 (informational), Sept. 2000.

[RFC4254] T. Ylonen and C. Lonvick, ed., "The Secure Shell (SSH) Connection Protocol," Internet RFC 4254, Jan. 2006.

[RFC4727] B. Fenner, "Experimental Values in IPv4, IPv6, ICMPv4, ICMPv6, UDP, and TCP Headers," Internet RFC 4727, Nov. 2006.

[RFC4821] M. Mathis and J. Heffner, "Packetization Layer Path MTU Discovery," Internet RFC 4821, Mar. 2007.

[RFC4953] J. Touch, "Defending TCP against Spoofing Attacks," Internet RFC 4953 (informational), July 2007.

[RFC4987] W. Eddy, "TCP SYN Flooding Attacks and Common Mitigations," Internet RFC 4987 (informational), Aug. 2007.

[RFC5482] L. Eggert and F. Gont, "TCP User Timeout Option," Internet RFC 5482, Mar. 2009.

[RFC5925] J. Touch, A. Mankin, and R. Bonica, "The TCP Authentication Option," Internet RFC 5925, June 2010.

[RFC5926] G. Lebovitz and E. Rescorla, "Cryptographic Algorithms for the TCP Authentication Option (TCP-AO)," Internet RFC 5926, June 2010.

[RFC5927] F. Gont, "ICMP Attacks against TCP," Internet RFC 5927 (informational), July 2010.

[RFC5961] A. Ramaiah, R. Stewart, and M. Dalal, "Improving TCP's Robustness to Blind In-Window Attacks," Internet RFC 5961, Aug. 2010.

[RFC6056] M. Larsen and F. Gont, "Recommendations for Transport-Protocol Port Randomization," Internet RFC 6056/BCP 0156, Jan. 2011.

[RFC6146] M. Bagnulo, P. Matthews, and I. van Beijnum, "Stateful NAT64: Network Address and Protocol Translation from IPv6 Clients to IPv4 Servers," Internet RFC 6146, Apr. 2011.

[RFC6191] F. Gont, "Reducing the TIME-WAIT State Using TCP Timestamps," Internet RFC 6191/BCP 0159, Apr. 2011.

[RFC6298] V. Paxson, M. Allman, J. Chu, and M. Sargent, "Computing TCP's Retransmission Timer," Internet RFC 6298, June 2011.

[S96] B. Schneier, *Applied Cryptography* (Wiley, 1996).

[TPARAMS] http://www.iana.org/tcp-parameters

14

TCP Timeout and Retransmission

14.1 Introduction

Efficiency and performance are issues that we have not discussed much so far. We have primarily been concerned with correctness of operation. In this chapter and the next two, we will be focusing not only on the basic tasks TCP performs, but also on how well it performs them. The TCP protocol provides a reliable data delivery service between two applications using an underlying network layer (IP) that may lose, duplicate, or reorder packets. In order to provide an error-free exchange of data, TCP resends data it believes has been lost. To decide what data it needs to resend, TCP depends on a continuous flow of acknowledgments from receiver to sender. When data segments or acknowledgments are lost, TCP initiates a *retransmission* of the data that has not been acknowledged. TCP has two separate mechanisms for accomplishing retransmission, one based on time and one based on the structure of the acknowledgments. The second approach is usually much more efficient than the first.

TCP sets a timer when it sends data, and if the data is not acknowledged when the timer expires, a *timeout* or *timer-based retransmission* of data occurs. The timeout occurs after an interval called the *retransmission timeout* (RTO). It has another way of initiating a retransmission called *fast retransmission* or *fast retransmit*, which usually happens without any delay. Fast retransmit is based on inferring losses by noticing when TCP's cumulative acknowledgment fails to advance in the ACKs received over time, or when ACKs carrying selective acknowledgment information (SACKs) indicate that out-of-order segments are present at the receiver. Generally speaking, when the sender believes that the receiver might be missing some data, a choice needs to be made between sending new (unsent) data and retransmitting. In this chapter we look closely at how TCP determines that a segment is lost and what to send in response. The issue of how *much* to send is deferred until Chapter 16, where we discuss TCP's congestion control procedures that are commonly invoked when packet loss is suspected. Here, we investigate how the RTO is set based on measurements of a connection's round-trip time (RTT), the mechanics of a timer-based retransmission, and how TCP's fast retransmission mechanism works. We also look at how SACKs are used to help a TCP sender determine what data is missing at the receiver, the effect of reordering and duplication of IP packets on TCP's behavior, and the way TCP can change its packet size when retransmitting. We also look briefly at some attacks that can be mounted to fool TCP into behaving more aggressively or more passively.

14.2 Simple Timeout and Retransmission Example

We have already seen some examples of timeout and retransmission. (1) In the ICMP Destination Unreachable (Port Unreachable) example in Chapter 8 we saw the TFTP client using UDP employing a simple (and poor) timeout and retransmission strategy: it assumed 5s was an adequate timeout period and retransmitted every 5s. (2) In the attempted connection to a nonexistent host in Chapter 13, we saw that when TCP tried to establish the connection it retransmitted its SYN segment using a longer and longer delay between each successive retransmission. (3) In Chapter 3, we saw what happens when Ethernet encounters a collision. All of these mechanisms are initiated by the expiration of a timer.

We shall first look at the timer-based retransmission strategy used by TCP. We will establish a connection, send some data to verify that everything is OK, isolate one end of the connection, send some more data, and watch what TCP does. In this case, we will use Wireshark to see how the connection progresses (see Figure 14-1).

Segments 1, 2, and 3 correspond to the normal TCP connection establishment handshake. When the Web server completes the connection establishment, it remains silent, awaiting a Web request. Before we provide the request, we isolate (disconnect) the server host. The input at the client side is as follows:

```
Linux% telnet 10.0.0.10 80
Trying 10.0.0.10...
Connected to 10.0.0.10.
Escape character is '^]'.
GET / HTTP/1.0
Connection closed by foreign host.
```

This request cannot be delivered to the server, so it remains in TCP's queue at the client for quite some time. During this period, the netstat command on the client indicates that the queue is not empty:

```
Active Internet connections (w/o servers)
Proto Recv-Q Send-Q  Local Address       Foreign Address  State
tcp        0     18   10.0.0.9:1043       10.0.0.10:www    ESTABLISHED
```

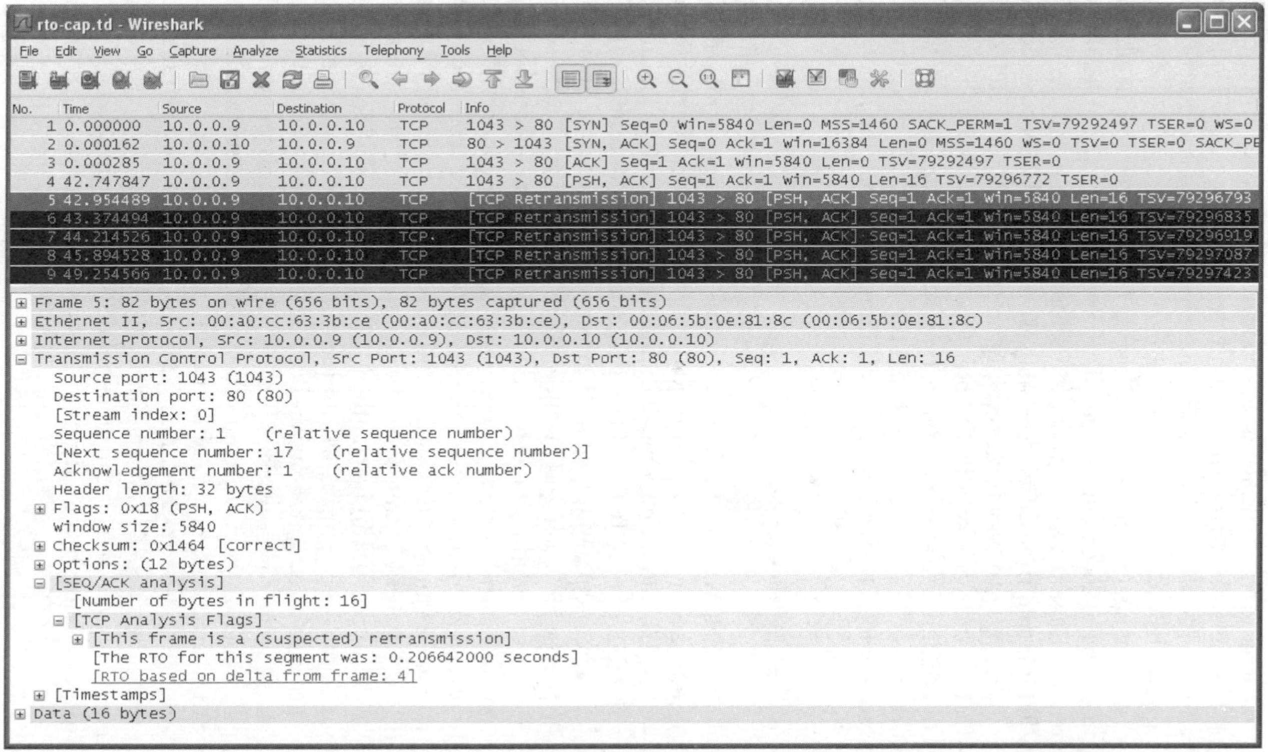

File Edit View Go Capture Analyze Statistics Telephony Tools Help

No.	Time	Source	Destination	Protocol	Info
1	0.000000	10.0.0.10	10.0.0.9	TCP	1043 > 80 [SYN] Seq=0 Win=5840 Len=0 MSS=1460 SACK_PERM=1 TSV=7292497 TSER=0 WS=0
2	0.000162	10.0.0.9	10.0.0.10	TCP	80 > 1043 [SYN, ACK] Seq=0 Ack=1 Win=16384 Len=0 MSS=1460 WS=0 TSV=0 TSER=0 SACK_PE
3	0.000285	10.0.0.10	10.0.0.9	TCP	1043 > 80 [ACK] Seq=1 Ack=1 Win=5840 Len=0 TSV=7292497 TSER=0
4	42.747847	10.0.0.10	10.0.0.9	TCP	1043 > 80 [PSH, ACK] Seq=1 Ack=1 Win=5840 Len=16 TSV=79296772 TSER=0
5	42.954489	10.0.0.9	10.0.0.10	TCP	[TCP Retransmission] 1043 > 80 [PSH, ACK] Seq=1 Ack=1 Win=5840 Len=16 TSV=79296793
6	43.374494	10.0.0.9	10.0.0.10	TCP.	[TCP Retransmission] 1043 > 80 [PSH, ACK] Seq=1 Ack=1 Win=5840 Len=16 TSV=79296835
7	44.214526	10.0.0.9	10.0.0.10	TCP.	[TCP Retransmission] 1043 > 80 [PSH, ACK] Seq=1 Ack=1 Win=5840 Len=16 TSV=79296919
8	45.894528	10.0.0.9	10.0.0.10	TCP	[TCP Retransmission] 1043 > 80 [PSH, ACK] Seq=1 Ack=1 Win=5840 Len=16 TSV=79297087
9	49.254566	10.0.0.9	10.0.0.10	TCP	[TCP Retransmission] 1043 > 80 [PSH, ACK] Seq=1 Ack=1 Win=5840 Len=16 TSV=7929723

Frame 5: 82 bytes on wire (656 bits), 82 bytes captured (656 bits)
Ethernet II, Src: 00:a0:cc:63:3b:ce (00:a0:cc:63:3b:ce), Dst: 00:06:5b:0e:81:8c (00:06:5b:0e:81:8c)
Internet Protocol, Src: 10.0.0.9 (10.0.0.9), Dst: 10.0.0.10 (10.0.0.10)
Transmission Control Protocol, Src Port: 1043 (1043), Dst Port: 80 (80), Seq: 1, Ack: 1, Len: 16
  Source port: 1043 (1043)
  Destination port: 80 (80)
  [Stream index: 0]
  Sequence number: 1   (relative sequence number)
  [Next sequence number: 17   (relative sequence number)]
  Acknowledgement number: 1   (relative ack number)
  Header length: 32 bytes
  Flags: 0x18 (PSH, ACK)
  Window size: 5840
  Checksum: 0x1464 [correct]
  Options: (12 bytes)
  [SEQ/ACK analysis]
    [Number of bytes in flight: 16]
    [TCP Analysis Flags]
      [This frame is a (suspected) retransmission]
      [The RTO for this segment was: 0.206642000 seconds]
      [RTO based on delta from frame: 4]
  [Timestamps]
Data (16 bytes)

Figure 14-1 A simple example of TCP's timeout and retransmission mechanism. The first retransmit occurs at time 42.954, followed by other retransmissions at times 43.374, 44.215, 45.895, and 49.255, respectively. The intervals between successive retransmissions are 206ms, 420ms, 841ms, 1.68s, and 3.36s, respectively. These times represent a doubling of the timeout between successive retransmissions of the same segment.

Here we see that 18 bytes are in the send queue, waiting to be delivered to the Web server. The 18 bytes consist of the characters displayed in the preceding request, plus two sets of carriage-return and newline characters. Details of the rest of the output, including addresses and state information, are described in the following paragraphs.

Segment 4 is the client's first attempt to send the Web request, at 42.748s. The next try is at 42.954, 0.206s later. Then it launches another try at 43.374, which is 0.420s later. Additional retries (retransmissions) occur at 44.215, 45.895, and 49.255s. These represent time differences of 0.841, 1.680, and 3.360s, respectively.

This doubling of time between successive retransmissions is called a *binary exponential backoff*, and we saw it in Chapter 13 during a failed TCP connection establishment attempt. We shall explore it in more detail later. If we measure the elapsed time between the initial request and the time at which the connection is finally aborted, the total time is about 15.5 minutes. After that, the following error message is displayed at the client:

```
Connection closed by foreign host.
```

Logically, TCP has two thresholds to determine how persistently it will attempt to resend the same segment. These thresholds are described in the Host Requirements RFC [RFC1122], and we mentioned them briefly in Chapter 13. Threshold R1 indicates the number of tries TCP will make (or the amount of time it will wait) to resend a segment before passing "negative advice" to the IP layer (e.g., causing it to reevaluate the IP route it is using). Threshold R2 (larger than R1) dictates the point at which TCP should abandon the connection. These thresholds are suggested to be at least three retransmissions and 100s, respectively. For connection establishment (sending SYN segments), these values may be different from those for data segments, and the R2 value for SYN segments is required to be at least 3 minutes.

In Linux, the R1 and R2 values for regular data segments are available to be changed by applications or can be changed using the system-wide configuration variables `net.ipv4.tcp_retries1` and `net.ipv4.tcp_retries2`, respectively. These are measured in the number of retransmissions, and not in units of time. The default value for `tcp_retries2` is 15, which corresponds roughly to 13–30 minutes, depending on the connection's RTO. The default value for `net.ipv4.tcp_retries1` is 3. For SYN segments, `net.ipv4.tcp_syn_retries` and `net.ipv4.tcp_synack_retries` bounds the number of retransmissions of SYN segments; their default value is 5 (roughly 180s). Windows also has a number of variables that affect the overall behavior of TCP, including values for R1 and R2. These are all available by modifying values under the following registry keys [WINREG]:

```
HKLM\System\CurrentControlSet\Services\Tcpip\Parameters
HKLM\System\CurrentControlSet\Services\Tcpip6\Parameters
```

Of immediate interest is the value called `TcpMaxDataRetransmissions`. This corresponds to the value of `tcp_retries2` in Linux. It has a default value of 5. Even in the simple retransmission example we have seen so far, TCP is required to assign some timeout value to its retransmission timer to dictate how long it should await an ACK for data it sends. If TCP were only ever used in one static environment, it would be possible to determine one particular correct value for the timeout value. Because TCP needs to operate in a large variety of environments, which themselves may change over time, TCP needs to determine this timeout value based on the current situation. For example, if a network link failed and traffic were rerouted, the RTT would change (possibly in a major way). In other words, TCP needs to *dynamically* determine its RTO. We consider this problem next.

14.3 Setting the Retransmission Timeout (RTO)

Fundamental to TCP's timeout and retransmission procedures is how to set the RTO based upon measurement of the RTT experienced on a given connection. If TCP retransmits a segment earlier than the RTT, it may be injecting duplicate traffic into the network unnecessarily. Conversely, if it delays sending until much longer than one RTT, the overall network utilization (and single-connection throughput) drops when traffic is lost. Knowing the RTT is made more complicated because it can change over time, as routes and network usage vary. TCP must track these changes and modify its timeout accordingly in order to maintain good performance.

Because TCP sends acknowledgments when it receives data, it is possible to send a byte with a particular sequence number and measure the time required to receive an acknowledgment that covers that sequence number. Each such measurement is called an RTT *sample*. The challenge for TCP is to establish a good estimate for the range of RTT values given a set of samples that vary over time. The second step is how to set the RTO based on these values. Getting this "right" is very important for TCP's performance.

The RTT is estimated for each TCP connection separately, and one retransmission timer is pending whenever any data is in flight that consumes a sequence number (including SYN and FIN segments). The proper way to set this timer has been a subject of research for years, and improvements are made on an occasional basis. In this section, we will explore some of the more important milestones in the evolution of the method used to compute the RTO. We begin with the first ("classic") method, as detailed in [RFC0793].

14.3.1 The Classic Method

The original TCP specification [RFC0793] had TCP update a *smoothed RTT estimator* (called *SRTT*) using the following formula:

$$SRTT \leftarrow \alpha(SRTT) + (1 - \alpha)\, RTT_s$$

Here, *SRTT* is updated based on both its existing value and a new sample, *RTT*ₛ. The constant α is a smoothing or scale factor with a recommended value between 0.8 and 0.9. *SRTT* is updated every time a new measurement is made. With the original recommended value for α, it is clear that 80% to 90% of each new estimate is from the previous estimate and 10% to 20% is from the new measurement. This type of average is also known as an *exponentially weighted moving average* (EWMA) or *low-pass filter*. It is convenient for implementation reasons because it requires only one previous value of *SRTT* to be stored in order to keep the running estimate.

Given the estimator *SRTT*, which changes as the RTT changes, [RFC0793] recommended that the RTO be set to the following:

$$RTO = \min(ubound, \max(lbound,(SRTT)\beta))$$

where β is a delay variance factor with a recommended value of 1.3 to 2.0, *ubound* is an upper bound (suggested to be, e.g., 1 minute), and *lbound* is a lower bound (suggested to be, e.g., 1s) on the RTO. We shall call this assignment procedure the *classic method*. It generally results in the RTO being set either to 1s, or to about twice *SRTT*. For relatively stable distributions of the RTT, this was adequate. However, when TCP was run over networks with highly variable RTTs (e.g., early packet radio networks in this case), it did not perform so well.

14.3.2 The Standard Method

In [J88], Jacobson detailed problems with the classic method further—basically, that the timer specified by [RFC0793] cannot keep up with wide fluctuations in the RTT (and in particular, it causes unnecessary retransmissions when the real RTT is much larger than expected). Unnecessary retransmissions add to the network load, when the network is already loaded, as indicated by the increasing sample RTT.

To address this problem, the method used to assign the RTO was enhanced to accommodate a larger variability in the RTT. This is accomplished by keeping track of an estimate of the variability in the RTT measurements in addition to the estimate of its average. Setting the RTO based on both a mean and a variability estimator provides a better timeout response to wide fluctuations in the round-trip times than just calculating the RTO as a constant multiple of the mean.

Figures 5 and 6 in [J88] show a comparison of the [RFC0793] RTO values for some actual round-trip times, versus the RTO calculations we show next, which take into account the variability of the round-trip times. If we think of the RTT measurements made by TCP as samples of a statistical process, estimating both the mean and variance (or standard deviation) helps to make better predictions about the possible future values the process may take on. A good prediction for the range of possible values for the RTT helps TCP determine an RTO that is neither too large nor too small in most cases.

As described by Jacobson, the *mean deviation* is a good approximation to the standard deviation, but it is easier and faster to compute. Calculating the standard deviation requires executing a square root mathematical operation on the variance, which was considered to be too expensive for a fast TCP implementation. (This is not the whole story, really. See the fascinating history of "the debate" in [G04].) We therefore need running estimates of both the average as well as the mean deviation. This leads to the following equations that are applied to each RTT measurement M (called RTT_s earlier):

$$srtt \leftarrow (1 - g)(srtt) + (g)M$$

$$rttvar \leftarrow (1 - h)(rttvar) + (h)(|M - srtt|)$$

$$RTO = srtt + 4(rttvar)$$

Here, the value $srtt$ effectively replaces the earlier value of $SRTT$, and the value $rttvar$, which becomes an EWMA of the mean deviation, is used instead of β to help determine the RTO. This set of equations can also be written in a form that requires a smaller number of operations when implemented on a conventional computer:

$$Err = M - srtt$$

$$srtt \leftarrow srtt + g(Err)$$

$$rttvar \leftarrow rttvar + h(|Err| - rttvar)$$

$$RTO = srtt + 4(rttvar)$$

As suggested, $srtt$ is the EWMA for the mean and $rttvar$ is the EWMA for the absolute error, $|Err|$. Err is the difference between the measured value M and the current RTT estimator $srtt$. Both $srtt$ and $rttvar$ are used to calculate the RTO, which varies over time. The gain g is the weight given to a new RTT sample M in the average $srtt$ and is set to 1/8. The gain h is the weight given to a new mean deviation sample (absolute difference of the new sample M from the running average $srtt$) for the deviation estimate $rttvar$ and is set to 1/4. The larger gain for the deviation makes the RTO go up faster when the RTT changes. The values for g and h are chosen as (negative) powers of 2, allowing the overall set of computations to be implemented in a computer using fixed-point integer arithmetic with shift and add operations instead of multiplies and divides.

Note

[J88] specified 2 * *rttvar* in the calculation of RTO, but after further research, [J90] changed the value to 4 * *rttvar*, which is what appeared in the BSD Net/1 implementation and ultimately in the standard [RFC6298].

Comparing the classic method with Jacobson's, we see that the calculations of the RTT average are similar (α is 1 minus the gain g) but a different gain is used. Also, Jacobson's calculation of the RTO depends on both the smoothed RTT and the smoothed deviation, whereas the classic method used a simple multiple of the smoothed RTT. This is the basis for the way many TCP implementations compute their RTOs to this day, and because of its adoption as the basis for [RFC6298] we shall call it the *standard method*, although there are slight refinements in [RFC6298], which we shall now discuss.

14.3.2.1 Clock Granularity and RTO Bounds

TCP has a continuously running "clock" that is used when taking RTT measurements. As with initial sequence numbers, real TCP connections do not start their clocks at zero and the clock does not have infinite precision. Rather, the TCP clock is usually the value of a variable that is updated as the system clock advances, not necessarily one-for-one. The length of the TCP's clock "tick" is called its *granularity*. Traditionally, this value was relatively large (about 500ms), but more recent implementations use finer-granularity clocks (e.g., 1ms for Linux).

The granularity can affect the details of making RTT measurements and also how the RTO is set. In [RFC6298], the granularity is used to refine how updates to the RTO are made. In addition, a lower bound is placed on the RTO. The equation used is as follows:

$$\text{RTO} = \max(srtt + \max(G, 4(rttvar)), 1000)$$

where G is the timer granularity and 1000ms represents a lower bound on the total RTO (recommended by rule (2.4) of [RFC6298]). Consequently, the RTO is always at least 1s. An optional upper bound is also allowed, provided it has a value of at least 60s.

14.3.2.2 Initial Values

We have seen how the estimators are updated as time progresses, but we also need to know how to set their initial values. Before the first SYN exchange, TCP has no good idea what value to use for setting the initial RTO. It also does not know what to use as the initial values for its estimators, unless the system has provided hints at this information (some systems cache this information in the forwarding table; see Section 14.9). According to [RFC6298], the initial setting for the RTO should be 1s, although 3s is used in the event of a timeout on the initial SYN segment. When the first RTT measurement M is received, the estimators are initialized as follows:

$$srtt \leftarrow M$$

$$rttvar \leftarrow M/2$$

We now have enough detail to see how the estimators are initialized and maintained. The procedures depend on obtaining RTT samples, which would appear to be straightforward. We now look at why this might not always be the case.

14.3.2.3 Retransmission Ambiguity and Karn's Algorithm

A problem measuring an RTT sample can occur when a packet is retransmitted. Say a packet is transmitted, a timeout occurs, the packet is retransmitted, and an acknowledgment is received for it. Is the ACK for the first transmission or the second? This is an example of the *retransmission ambiguity problem*. It happens because unless the Timestamps option is being used, an ACK provides only the ACK number with no indication of which copy (e.g., first or second) of a sequence number is being ACKed.

The paper [KP87] specifies that when a timeout and retransmission occur, we cannot update the RTT estimators when the acknowledgment for the retransmitted data finally arrives. This is the "first part" of Karn's algorithm. It eliminates the acknowledgment ambiguity problem by removing the ambiguity for purposes of computing the RTT estimate. It is a requirement in [RFC6298].

If we were to simply ignore retransmitted segments entirely when setting the RTO, however, we would be failing to take into account some useful information being provided by the network (i.e., that it is probably experiencing some form of inability to deliver packets quickly). In such cases, it would be beneficial to reduce the load on the network by decreasing the retransmission rate, at least until packets are no longer being lost. This reasoning is the basis for the exponential backoff behavior we saw in Figure 14-1.

TCP applies a *backoff factor* to the RTO, which doubles each time a subsequent retransmission timer expires. Doubling continues until an acknowledgment is received for a segment that was not retransmitted. At that time, the backoff factor is set back to 1 (i.e., the binary exponential backoff is canceled), and the retransmission timer returns to its normal value. Doubling the backoff factor on subsequent retransmissions is the "second part" of Karn's algorithm. Note that when TCP times out, it also invokes congestion control procedures that alter its sending rate. (Congestion control is discussed in detail in Chapter 16.) Karn's algorithm, then, really consists of two parts. As quoted directly from the 1987 paper [KP87]:

> When an acknowledgement arrives for a packet that has been sent more than once (i.e., is retransmitted at least once), ignore any round-trip measurement based on this packet, thus avoiding the retransmission ambiguity problem. In addition, the backed-off RTO for this packet is kept for the next packet. Only when it (or a succeeding packet) is acknowledged without an intervening retransmission will the RTO be recalculated from SRTT.

This algorithm has been a required procedure in a TCP implementation for some time (since [RFC1122]). There is an exception, however, when the TCP Timestamps option is being used (see Chapter 13). In that case, the acknowledgment ambiguity problem can be avoided and the first part of Karn's algorithm does not apply.

14.3.2.4 RTT Measurement (RTTM) with the Timestamps Option

The TCP Timestamps option (TSOPT), in addition to providing a basis for the PAWS algorithm we saw in Chapter 13, can be used for *round-trip time measurement* (RTTM) [RFC1323]. The basic format of the TSOPT was described in Chapter 13. It allows the sender to include a 32-bit number in a TCP segment that is returned in a corresponding acknowledgment.

The timestamp value (TSV) is carried in the TSOPT of the initial SYN and returned in the TSER part of the TSOPT in the SYN + ACK, which is how the initial values for *srtt*, *rttvar*, and RTO are determined. Because the initial SYN "counts" as data (i.e., it is retransmitted if lost and consumes a sequence number), its RTT is measured. TSOPTs are also carried in other segments, so the connection's RTT can be estimated on an ongoing basis. This seems straightforward enough but is made more complex because TCP does not always provide an ACK for each segment it receives. For example, TCP often provides one ACK for every other segment (see Chapter 15) when large volumes of data are transferred. In addition, when data is lost, reordered, or successfully retransmitted, the cumulative ACK mechanism of TCP means that there is not necessarily any fixed correspondence between a segment and its ACK. To handle these challenges, TCPs that use this option (most of them today—Linux and Windows included), employ the following algorithm for taking RTT samples:

1. The sending TCP includes a 32-bit timestamp value in the TSV portion of the TSOPT in each TCP segment it sends. This field contains the value of the sender's TCP "clock" when the segment is transmitted.

2. A receiving TCP keeps track of the received TSV value to send in the next ACK it generates (in a variable typically named *TsRecent*) and the ACK number in the last ACK that it sent (in a variable named *LastACK*). Recall that ACK numbers represent the next in-order sequence number the receiver (i.e., sender of the ACK) expects to see.

3. When a new segment arrives, if it contains the sequence number matching the value in *LastACK* (i.e., it is the next expected segment), the segment's TSV is saved in *TsRecent*.

4. Whenever the receiver sends an ACK, a TSOPT is included such that the timestamp value contained in *TsRecent* is placed in the TSER part of the TSOPT in the ACK.

5. A sender receiving an ACK that advances its window subtracts the TSER from its current TCP clock and uses the difference as a sample value to update its RTT estimators.

Timestamps are enabled by default in FreeBSD, Linux, and in response to systems that use them for later versions of Windows. In Linux, the system configuration variable net.ipv4.tcp_timestamps dictates whether or not they are used (value 0 for not used, value 1 for used). In Windows, their use is controlled by the `Tcp1323Opts` value in the registry area mentioned earlier. If it has the value 0, timestamps are disabled. If its value is 2, timestamps are enabled. This key has no default value (it is not in the registry by default). The default behavior is to use timestamps if a peer uses them when initiating a connection.

14.3.3 The Linux Method

The Linux RTT estimation procedure works somewhat differently from the standard method. It uses a clock granularity of 1ms, which is finer than that of many other implementations, along with the TSOPT. The combination of frequent measurements of the RTT and the fine-grain clock contributes to a more accurate estimate of the RTT but also tends to minimize the value of *rttvar* over time [LS00]. This happens because when a large enough number of mean deviation samples are accumulated, they tend to cancel each other out. This is one consideration for setting the RTO that differs somewhat from the standard method. Another relates to the way the standard method increases *rttvar* when an RTT sample is significantly *below* the existing RTT estimate *srtt*.

To understand the second issue better, recall that the RTO is usually set to the value *srtt* + 4(*rttvar*). Consequently, any large change in *rttvar* causes the RTO to increase, whether the latest RTT sample is greater or less than *srtt*. This is counterintuitive—if the actual RTT has dropped significantly, it is not desirable to have the RTO increase as a consequence. Linux deals with this issue by limiting the impact of significant downward drops in RTT sample values on the value of *rttvar*. We will now look at the details for the procedure Linux uses to set its RTO; the procedure addresses both of the issues just discussed.

Linux keeps the variables *srtt* and *rttvar*, as with the standard method, but also two new ones called *mdev* and *mdev_max*. The value *mdev* keeps the running estimate of the mean deviation using the standard algorithm for *rttvar* described before. The value *mdev_max* holds the maximum value of *mdev* seen over the last measured RTT and is never allowed to be less than 50ms. In addition, *rttvar* is regularly updated to ensure that it is at least as large as *mdev_max*. Consequently, the RTO never dips below 200ms.

Note

The minimum RTO can be changed. TCP_RTO_MIN, which is a kernel configuration constant, can be changed prior to recompiling and installing the kernel. Some Linux versions also allow it to be changed using the `ip route` command. When TCP is used in data-center networks where RTTs may be a few microseconds, 200ms minimum RTO can lead to severe performance degradations due to slow TCP recovery after packet loss in local switches. This is the so-called TCP "incast" problem. Various solutions exist to this problem, including modification of the TCP timer granularity and minimum RTO to be on the order of microseconds [V09]. Such small minimum RTO values are not recommended for use on the global Internet.

Linux updates *rttvar* to the value of *mdev_max* whenever the maximum increases. It always sets the RTO to be the sum of *srtt* and 4(*rttvar*) and ensures that the RTO never exceeds TCP_RTO_MAX, which defaults to 120s. See [SK02] for more details. We can see how the details of all of this work in Figure 14-2. This figure also shows how the Timestamps option operates.

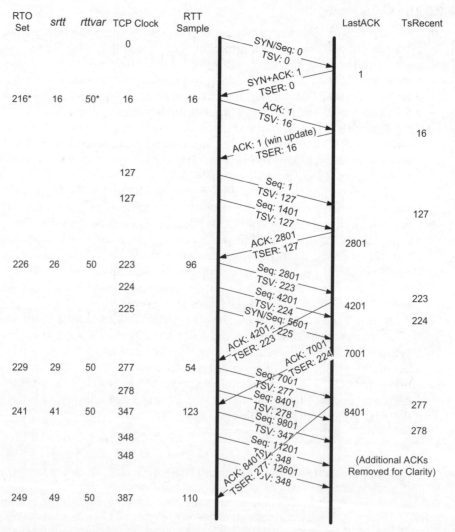

Figure 14-2   The TCP Timestamps option carries a copy of the TCP clock at the sender. ACKs return this value to the sender, which uses the difference (current clock - returned timestamp) to update its srtt and rttvar estimates. For clarity, only one set of timestamps is depicted. In this Linux system, the rttvar value is constrained to be at least 50 (millisecond) units, and the RTO has a lower bound of 200ms.

In Figure 14-2 we see a TCP connection using the Timestamps option as it starts up. The sender is a Linux 2.6 system and the receiver is a FreeBSD 5.4 system. Sequence numbers and timestamp values are depicted as relative values for clarity. In addition, only the sender's timestamps are shown. The figure is not drawn exactly to temporal scale, in order to make the numerical values easier to read. Based on the initial RTT measurement in this example, Linux makes the following updates:

- $srtt = 16$ms

- $mdev = (16/2)$ms $= 8$ms

- $rttvar = mdev\_max = \max(mdev, \text{TCP\_RTO\_MIN}) = \max(8, 50) = 50$ms

- RTO $= srtt + 4(rttvar) = 16 + 4(50) = 216$ms

After the initial SYN exchange, the sender supplies an ACK for the receiver's SYN and the receiver responds with a window update. As neither of these packets contains data (or *SYN* or *FIN* bit fields, which are counted as data), they are not timed, and no RTT estimator update is performed when the window update arrives back at the sender. Segments that do not contain data are not reliably delivered by TCP, meaning they are not retransmitted if lost. These types of segments do not require a retransmission timer to be set, because they are never retransmitted.

Note

It is worth mentioning that TCP options, by themselves, are also not retransmitted or reliably delivered. Only when options are specifically arranged to be present in data segments (including SYN and FIN segments) will options be retransmitted if lost, and then only as a side effect.

When the application performs its first write, the sending TCP emits two segments, each with a TSV value equal to 127. The values are identical in these two segments because the TCP clock has advanced less than 1ms (the sending TCP's clock granularity) between the first and second transmission. It is not unusual to see the clock fail to advance, or advance by small amounts, when the sender is sending multiple segments "back-to-back" in this fashion.

The *LastACK* variable at the receiver holds the ACK number last sent by the receiver. In this example, *LastACK* starts with the value 1 because the last ACK sent was the SYN + ACK packet sent during connection establishment. When the first full-size segment arrives, its sequence number matches the *LastACK* value, so the *TsRecent* variable is updated to contain the value 127 from the arriving segment's TSV. The arrival of the second segment does not update the *TsRecent* variable because its *Sequence Number* field does not match the value in *LastACK*. The ACK sent in response to the arriving packets includes the value of *TsRecent* in its TSER, and its transmission also causes the receiver to update the *LastACK* variable to the ACK number, 2801.

When this ACK arrives, TCP is able to make its second RTT measurement. It takes the current TCP clock and subtracts the TSER value from the arriving packet, forming the measurement m: $m = 223 - 127 = 96$. With this measurement, the Linux TCP updates the connection variables as follows:

- $mdev = mdev\,(3/4) + |m\text{-}srtt|\,(1/4) = 8(3/4) + |80|(1/4) = 26$ms

- $mdev\_max = \max(mdev\_max, mdev) = \max(50, 26) = 50$ms

- $srtt = srtt\,(7/8) + m(1/8) = 16(7/8) + 96(1/8) = 14 + 12 = 26$ms

- $rttvar = mdev\_max = 50$ms

- RTO $= srtt + 4(rttvar) = 26 + 4(50) = 226$ms

As mentioned previously, Linux TCP has several special modifications to the classic RTT estimation algorithm that merit discussion. At the time the classic algorithms were developed, the typical granularity of the TCP clock was 500ms and the Timestamps option was not in widespread use. It was typical to take only one RTT sample per window and update the estimators accordingly. This is still used if timestamps are not available or not enabled.

If only one RTT sample is taken per window, the *rttvar* term changes relatively slowly. With timestamps and per-packet timestamp measurements, many more measurements can take place. Because it is common for the RTT to vary little from one packet to the next in the same window of data, taking so many measurements in a small period of time (e.g., when the window is large) can lead to the mean deviation estimate being small (near zero, thanks to the law of large numbers [F68]). To address this issue, Linux maintains the *mdev* variable as the running mean deviation estimate but sets the RTO based on the *rttvar*, which is increased to the maximum value of *mdev* during one window of data and also clamped to be at least 50ms. *Rttvar* is allowed to decrease only one time, from one window to the next.

The standard approach uses a heavy weight (factor of 4) given to the *rttvar* term, and consequently the RTO tends to increase, even when the RTT is decreasing. With a coarse-granularity clock (e.g., 500ms) this may have relatively little effect because there are so few values the RTO can take on. However, with a finer-granularity clock, such as the 1ms used by Linux, this can be of concern. To address this issue, Linux handles the case where the RTT is decreasing by giving less weight to the new sample if it is below the "lower end" of the estimated RTT range (*srtt - mdev*). The complete relationship is as follows:

$$\text{if } (m < (srtt - mdev))$$

$$mdev = (31/32) * mdev + (1/32) * |srtt - m|$$

$$\text{else}$$

$$mdev = (3/4) * mdev + (1/4) * |srtt - m|$$

The conditional determines if the new RTT sample is below the bottom of the range of what an RTT measurement is expected to be. If so, the new sample indicates that the connection may be experiencing a significantly reducing RTT. To avoid increasing *mdev* (and consequently *rttvar* and RTO) in such cases, the new mean deviation sample, |srtt - m|, is given an 8x reduced weight versus its normal weighting. Overall, this results in avoiding the problem of increasing the RTO in cases where the RTT is decreasing. For an in-depth discussion of these issues, please see [LS00] and [SK02]. In [RKS07], the authors evaluated the TCP RTT estimation algorithms with various operating systems on 2.8 million TCP flows. They conclude that the Linux estimator is the most effective among those studied, largely because of its relatively quick convergence, but that it can also be tuned most effectively by reducing the influence of RTT variance on setting the RTO.

Returning now to Figure 14-2, when ACK 7001 is generated at the receiver, we see that its TSER contains a copy of a TSV value, not from the most recently arriving segment, but instead from the oldest segment that has not been ACKed. When returned to the sender, this ACK causes the RTT sample to be measured from the first of the two segments, rather than from the last one sent. This is how the timestamp algorithm works with delayed or otherwise erratic ACKs. When the RTT sample from the oldest packet is measured, the RTT sample is taken to be the time the sender should wait to expect an ACK, rather than the actual network RTT. This is important because the sender needs to base its RTO on the rate at which it can expect ACKs from the receiver, which may be less than the packet sending rate.

14.3.4 RTT Estimator Behaviors

As we have seen, substantial innovation and engineering have been invested in how to set TCP's RTO and how to estimate the RTT. Figure 14-3 shows how the more popular estimators work, based on applying the standard and Linux algorithms to a synthetic data set. The 1s RTO minimum recommended by [RFC6298] has been removed for the standard method for illustration. Most real-world TCP implementations today violate this directive anyhow [RKS07].

The graph shows a time-series plot of 200 synthetic values drawn from two Gaussian probability distributions, $N(200, 50)$ and $N(50, 50)$. The first distribution is used for the first 100 points, and the second is used for the second 100 points. Any negative samples were made positive by sign inversion (applicable only to the second distribution). Each plus (+) indicates a specific sample value. The significant drop in sample values after sample 100 is apparent, and it is easy to see how the Linux approach drops the RTO almost immediately after sample 100, while the standard approach requires another 20 samples.

If we focus now on the Linux *rttvar* line, we can see that it remains relatively constant. This is because of the 50ms minimum on the *mdev_max* value (and consequently the *rttvar* value). This has the effect of making the Linux RTO value always at least 200ms, and all unnecessary retransmissions are avoided (although the timer may not fire as quickly, leading to reduced performance when packets

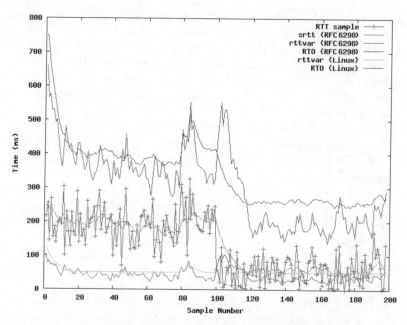

Figure 14-3   The Linux and standard RTO assignment and RTT estimation algorithms applied to synthetic (pseudorandom) sample points. The first 100 points are drawn from an $N(200, 50)$ distribution, and the second 100 are drawn from an $N(50, 50)$ distribution with negative values turned positive. Linux avoids the increase in RTO when the mean drops after sample 100. With Linux, the minimum RTO is effectively set to 200ms, so after sample 120, the standard method is tighter. Linux avoids setting the RTO too low in all cases for this example. The standard approach runs into potential problems at samples 78 and 191.

are lost). The standard approach runs into potential problems at samples 78 and 191, where a *spurious retransmission* could take place. We shall discuss this problem later.

14.3.5   RTTM Robustness to Loss and Reordering

The TSOPT has been shown to work properly when packets are not lost, whether or not the receiver delays some ACKs. The algorithm also operates correctly in the following cases:

- **Out-of-order segments**: When a receiver receives an out-of-order segment, typically because of the loss of a previous segment, an ACK is supposed to be generated immediately to help the fast retransmit algorithm (see Section 14.5) operate. This ACK includes as its TSER value the TSV value from the most recent in-order segment that arrived at the receiver (i.e., the most recent one to advance the window, which is generally *not* the arriving out-of-order segment). This tends to cause the sender's RTT sample values to increase, leading to a corresponding increase in the sender's RTO. When packets are being reordered, this is beneficial because it tends to allow the sender a bit more time to realize that packets are reordered rather than lost before initiating a retransmission.

- **Successful retransmissions**: When a receiver receives a segment that fills a hole in its receive buffer (e.g., because of the successful arrival of a retransmission), the window generally jumps forward. In this case, the value carried in the TSER of the corresponding ACK is from the most recently arriving segment. This is useful because if an older segment's TSV were used, it might be more than one RTO's worth of time old, leading to a large unwanted bias in the sender's RTT estimate.

The example in Figure 14-4 illustrates these points. Assume that three segments, each containing 1024 bytes, are received in the following order: segment 1 with bytes 1–1024, segment 3 with bytes 2049–3072, and then segment 2 with bytes 1025–2048.

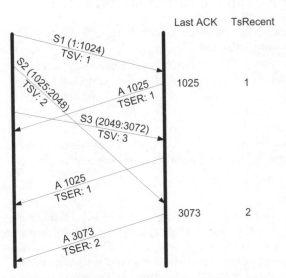

Figure 14-4   When segments are reordered, the returned timestamp is that of the last segment to advance the receiver's window (not the largest timestamp to arrive at the receiver). This biases the sender's RTO toward overestimating the RTT during periods of packet reordering and reduces its aggressiveness.

The ACKs sent back in Figure 14-4 are ACK 1025 with the timestamp from segment 1 (a normal ACK for data that was expected), ACK 1025 with the timestamp from segment 1 (a duplicate ACK in response to the in-window but out-of-sequence segment), then ACK 3073 with the timestamp from segment 2 (not the timestamp from segment 3). This has the effect of overestimating the RTT when segments are reordered (or lost). A larger RTT estimate leads to a larger RTO, making the sender less aggressive to retransmit. This is especially desirable in cases where packet reordering occurs, because aggressive retransmissions are likely to be spurious.

So, we have seen that the Timestamps option allows the sender to make estimates of the RTT even when there are packet delays, losses, and reorderings. The sender can measure the RTT using whatever values it wishes to in the option, but these units must at least be proportional to real time and of a reasonable granularity to be compatible with TCP sequence numbers and plausible link rates (see [RFC1323] for more details on this). In particular, to be useful to the sender, the TCP clock must "tick" at least once for any plausible RTT. On the other hand, it should not change faster than once every 59ns. If it did, the 32-bit TSV value holding the TCP clock value could wrap around within the maximum time permitted by the IP layer for a single packet to exist (255s) [ID1323b]. Assuming all this to be correct, the RTO value can now be used to trigger retransmissions.

14.4 Timer-Based Retransmission

Once a sending TCP has established its RTO based upon measurements of the time-varying values of effective RTT, whenever it sends a segment it ensures that a retransmission timer is set appropriately. When setting a retransmission timer, the sequence number of the so-called timed segment is recorded, and if an ACK is received in time, the retransmission timer is canceled. The next time the sender emits a packet with data in it, a new retransmission timer is set, the old one is canceled, and the new sequence number is recorded. The sending TCP therefore continuously sets and cancels one retransmission timer per connection; if no data is ever lost, no retransmission timer ever expires.

Note

This observation proved somewhat of a surprise to the designers of the host operating systems. In a typical operating system, timers are used to signal a wide variety of events, and the implementation of the timer facility is tuned to efficiently set up and expire timers (which invoke system functions). For TCP, however, the requirement is for efficient setting and resetting or canceling of timers; if TCP is working well, timers never expire.

When TCP fails to receive an ACK for a segment it has timed on a connection within the RTO, it performs a timer-based retransmission. We have seen this already in Figure 14-1. TCP considers a timer-based retransmission as a fairly major event; it reacts very cautiously when it happens by quickly reducing the rate at which it sends data into the network. It does this in two ways. The first way is to reduce its sending window size based on congestion control procedures (see Chapter 16). The other way is to keep increasing a multiplicative backoff factor applied to the RTO each time a retransmitted segment is again retransmitted. This is implemented in the "second part" of Karn's algorithm mentioned previously. In particular, the RTO value is (temporarily) multiplied by the value γ to form the backed-off timeout when multiple retransmissions of the same segment occur:

$$RTO = \gamma RTO$$

In ordinary circumstances, γ has the value 1. On subsequent retransmissions, γ is doubled: 2, 4, 8, and so forth. There is typically a maximum backoff factor that γ is not allowed to exceed (Linux ensures that the used RTO never exceeds the value TCP_RTO_MAX, which defaults to 120s). Once an acceptable ACK is received, γ is reset to 1.

14.4.1 Example

We can see the action of the retransmission timer by creating a connection similar to the one we looked at in Figures 14-1 and 14-2, but where we purposely drop the segment with sequence number 1401 twice (see Figure 14-5).

For this example, we send the TCP segments through a special function that is able to drop them a certain number of times based on their TCP sequence numbers. This adds a bit of extra delay to the RTT as compared with Figure 14-2. The connection starts out as before, except when the pair of segments with sequence numbers 1 and 1401 is sent, the second packet is dropped. Presumably the first of these segments reaches the receiver, but the receiver is delaying ACKs and does not respond immediately. Lacking a response in 219ms, the sender's retransmission timer expires, causing the packet with sequence number 1 to be resent (this time with TSV value 577). Its arrival elicits an ACK from the receiver, which returns to the sender. Because this ACK acknowledges data and moves the sender's window forward, its TSER value is used to update the *srtt* and RTO values to 34 and 234, respectively.

The next three ACKs are generated in response to packets that arrive at the receiver. The ACKs with the asterisks (*) are all duplicate ACKs and contain SACK information. We will discuss the effect of duplicate ACKs and SACKs in Sections 14.5 and 14.6. For now, because these ACKs do not move the sender's window forward, their TSER values are not used.

With the eventual retransmission and arrival of segment 1401 (at TCP clock time 911) at the receiver, the repair period is complete, and the receiver responds with ACK number 7001, indicating that all data has been received.

The retransmission timer provides a form of "last-resort restart" for a TCP connection that has ceased to move data through the network regularly. In most cases it is unnecessary (and undesirable) to have retransmission timers trigger retransmissions because the RTO is generally established to be larger than the

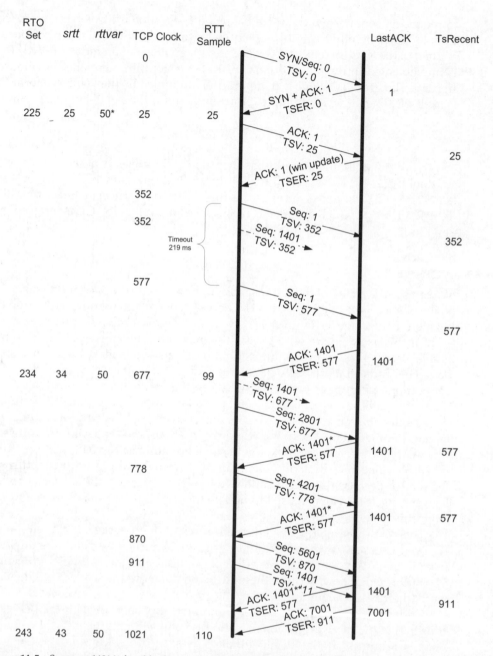

Figure 14-5   Segment 1401 is forcibly dropped twice. This results in a timer-based retransmission at the sender. The *srtt*, *rttvar*, and RTO values are updated only by a returning ACK that advances the sender's window. ACKs with asterisks (*) include SACK information.

typical RTT (by about a factor of 2 or more), so a timer-based retransmission often leads to underutilization of the network capacity. Fortunately, TCP has another method for detecting and repairing lost packets, which is almost always more efficient than timer-based retransmissions. It is called fast retransmit because it does not require the expiration of a retransmission timer to be invoked.

14.5 Fast Retransmit

Fast retransmit [RFC5681] is a TCP procedure that can induce a packet retransmission based on feedback from the receiver instead of requiring a retransmission timer to expire. As a result, packet loss can often be more quickly and efficiently repaired using fast retransmit than with timer-based retransmission. A typical TCP implements both fast retransmit and timer-based retransmission. Before we describe fast retransmit in more detail, it is important to realize that TCP is required to generate an immediate acknowledgment (a "duplicate ACK") when an out-of-order segment is received, and that the loss of a segment implies out-of-order arrivals at the receiver when subsequent data arrives. When this happens, a hole is created at the receiver. The sender's job then becomes filling the receiver's holes as quickly and efficiently as possible.

The duplicate ACKs sent immediately when out-of-order data arrives are not delayed. The reason is to let the sender know that a segment was received out of order, and to indicate what sequence number is expected (i.e., where the hole is). When SACK is used, these duplicate ACKs typically contain SACK blocks as well, which can provide information about more than one hole.

A duplicate ACK (with or without SACK blocks) arriving at a sender is a potential indicator that a packet sent earlier has been lost. As we discuss in Section 14.8 in more detail, duplicate ACKs can also appear when there is packet reordering in the network—if a receiver receives a packet for a sequence number beyond the one it is expecting next, the expected packet could be either missing or merely delayed. Because we generally do not know which one, TCP waits for a small number of duplicate ACKs (called the *duplicate ACK threshold* or *dupthresh*) to be received before concluding that a packet has been lost and initiating a fast retransmit. Traditionally, *dupthresh* has been a constant (with value 3), but some nonstandard implementations (including Linux) alter this value based on the current measured level of reordering (see Section 14.8).

A TCP sender observing at least *dupthresh* duplicate ACKs retransmits one or more packets that appear to be missing without waiting for a retransmission timer to expire. It may also send additional data that has not yet been sent. This is the essence of the fast retransmit algorithm. Packet loss inferred by the presence of duplicate ACKs is assumed to be related to network congestion, and congestion control procedures (discussed in Chapter 16) are invoked along with fast retransmit. Without SACK, no more than one segment is typically retransmitted until an acceptable ACK is received. With SACK, ACKs contain additional information allowing the sender to fill more than one hole in the receiver per RTT. We explore the use of SACK with fast retransmit after illustrating an example of the basic fast retransmit algorithm.

14.5.1 Example

In the following example, we create a TCP connection similar to the one from Figure 14-4, except this time we drop segments 23801 and 26601 and SACK is disabled. We will see how TCP uses the basic fast retransmit algorithm to repair these holes. The sender is a Linux 2.6 system and the receiver is a FreeBSD 5.4 system. The plot in Figure 14-6 from Wireshark's Statistics | TCP Stream Graph | Time-Sequence Graph (`tcptrace`) screen shows fast retransmit in action.

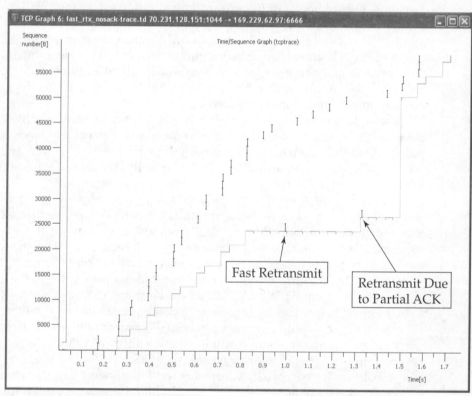

Figure 14-6   In this plot, TCP sequence numbers are on the *y*-axis and time is on the *x*-axis. Outgoing segments are displayed as darker line segments, and the incoming ACK numbers appear as lighter gray segments. Fast retransmit is triggered by the arrival of the third duplicate ACK at time 0.993s. This connection does not use SACK, so it is able to repair at most only one hole per RTT. Additional duplicate ACKs arriving after the third cause the sender to send new segments (not retransmissions). A "partial ACK" arriving at time 1.32 causes the next retransmission.

This plot indicates the relative sending sequence number on the y-axis and the elapsed time on the x-axis. The black vertical I-shaped extents indicate the span of sequence numbers present in the transmitted segment. The blue lines in Wireshark (lower light gray line in Figure 14-6) indicate ACK numbers in returning packets. At approximately time 1.0, sequence number 23801 is retransmitted because of the fast retransmit algorithm (the initial transmission is not visible because it was dropped by the process at the sender below the TCP protocol layer). The retransmission is triggered by the arrival of the third duplicate ACK, as illustrated by the repeated lower line segments. The retransmit can also be seen using the basic analysis screen of Wireshark (see Figure 14-7).

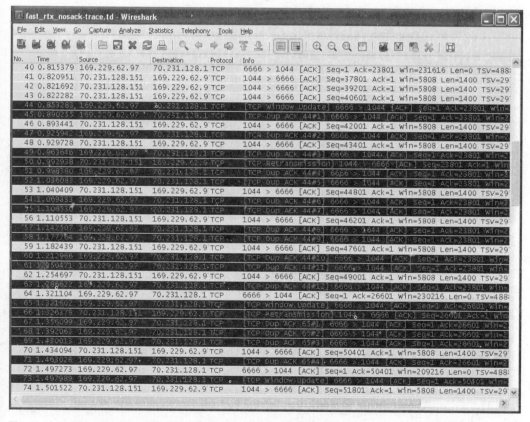

Figure 14-7 The TCP exchange showing relative sequence numbers. Packets 50 and 66 are retransmissions. Packet 50 is retransmitted because of the fast retransmit algorithm, which triggers as a result of three duplicate ACKs. No retransmission timer is required, so recovery is relatively quick.

The first line of Figure 14-7 (number 40) indicates the first time ACK 23801 is received. Wireshark highlights (in red, appearing as black in Figure 14-7) other "interesting" TCP packets. Such packets differ from what would be expected for a TCP transfer with no losses or other anomalies. We see window updates, duplicate ACKs, and retransmissions. The window update at time 0.853 is an ACK with a duplicate sequence number (because no data is being carried) but contains a change to the TCP flow control window. The window changes from 231,616 bytes to 233,016 bytes. Thus, it is not counted toward the three-duplicate-ACK threshold required to initiate a fast retransmit. Window updates merely provide a copy of the window advertisement. We will look at these in more detail in Chapter 15.

The packets arriving at times 0.890, 0.926, and 0.964 are all duplicate ACKs for sequence number 23801. The arrival of the third of these duplicate ACKs triggers the fast retransmit of segment 23801 at time 0.993. This can also be seen using Wireshark's Statistics | Flow Graph feature (see Figure 14-8).

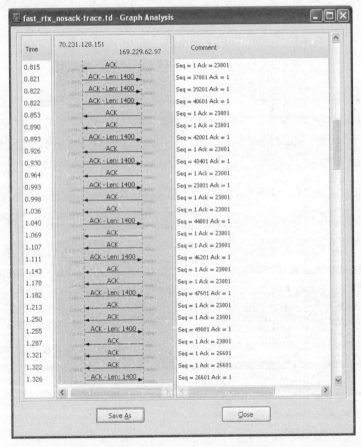

Figure 14-8 The retransmission at time 0.993 is triggered by the fast retransmit algorithm after receiving duplicate ACKs at times 0.890, 0.926, and 0.964. The ACK at time 0.853 is not considered a duplicate ACK because it contains a window update.

Here we see, in a slightly different way, the same fast retransmit at time 0.993. We can also see the second retransmission that takes place at time 1.326. This second retransmission takes place because of the arrival of the ACK at time 1.322.

The second retransmission is somewhat different from the first. When the first retransmission takes place, the sending TCP notes the highest sequence number it had sent just before it performed the retransmission (43401 + 1400 = 44801). This is called the *recovery point*. TCP is considered to be recovering from loss after a retransmission until it receives an ACK that matches or exceeds the sequence number of the recovery point. In this example, the ACKs at times 1.322 and 1.321 are not for 44801, but instead for 26601. This number is larger than the previous highest ACK value seen (23801), but not enough to meet or exceed the recovery point (44801). This type of ACK is called a *partial ACK* for this reason. When partial ACKs arrive, the sending TCP immediately sends the segment that appears to be missing (26601 in this case) and continues this way until the recovery point is matched or exceeded by an arriving ACK. If permitted by congestion control procedures (see Chapter 16), it may also send new data it has not yet sent.

This example illustrates the behavior of a TCP not using SACKs, when using fast retransmit, and when performing additional retransmits during recovery based on the "NewReno" sending algorithm [RFC3782]. Because no SACKs are being used, the sender can learn of at most one receiver hole per round-trip time, indicated by the increase in the ACK number of returning packets, which can only occur once a retransmission filling the receiver's lowest-numbered hole has been received and ACKed.

The precise behavior during recovery varies, depending on the type and configuration of the TCP sender and receiver. This example illustrates a non-SACK sender using the NewReno algorithm, a fairly common arrangement. With NewReno, partial ACKs keep the sender in recovery as described. With older TCP variants (plain Reno), there is no such concept, and any acceptable ACK brings the TCP out of recovery. Doing so can present some performance problems for TCP, and these are discussed in detail in Chapter 16. NewReno and SACK, which we discuss next, are sometimes called "advanced loss recovery" techniques to distinguish them from the older approaches.

14.6 Retransmission with Selective Acknowledgments

With the standardization of the Selective Acknowledgment options in [RFC2018], a SACK-capable TCP receiver is able to describe data it has received with sequence numbers beyond the cumulative *ACK Number* field it sends in the primary portion of the TCP header. As we mentioned before, gaps between the ACK number and other in-window data cached at the receiver are called holes. Data with sequence numbers beyond the holes are called out-of-sequence data because that data is not contiguous, in terms of its sequence numbers, with the other data the receiver has already received.

The job of a sending TCP is to fill the holes in the receiver by retransmitting any data the receiver is missing, yet to be as efficient as possible by not resending data the receiver already has. In many circumstances, the properly operating SACK sender is able to fill these holes more quickly and with fewer unnecessary retransmissions than a comparable non-SACK sender because it does not have to wait an entire RTT to learn about additional holes. When the SACK option is being used, an ACK can be augmented with up to three or four SACK blocks that contain information about out-of-sequence data at the receiver. Each SACK block contains two 32-bit sequence numbers representing the first and last sequence numbers (plus 1) of a continuous block of out-of-sequence data being held at the receiver.

A SACK option that specifies n blocks has a length of $8n + 2$ bytes, so the 40 bytes available to hold TCP options can specify a maximum of four blocks. It is expected that SACK will often be used in conjunction with the TSOPT, which takes an additional 10 bytes (plus 2 bytes of padding), meaning that SACK is typically able to include only three blocks per ACK.

With three distinct blocks, up to three holes can be reported to the sender. If not limited by congestion control (see Chapter 16), all three could be filled within one round-trip time using a SACK-capable sender. An ACK packet containing one or more SACK blocks is sometimes called simply a "SACK."

14.6.1 SACK Receiver Behavior

A SACK-capable receiver is allowed to generate SACKs if it has received the SACK-Permitted option during the TCP connection establishment (see Chapter 13). Generally speaking, a receiver generates SACKs whenever there is any out-of-order data in its buffer. This can happen either because data was lost in transit, or because it has been reordered and newer data has arrived at the receiver before older data. We consider the first case here and discuss the second one later.

The receiver places in the first SACK block the sequence number range contained in the segment it has *most recently received*. Because the space in a SACK option is limited, it is best to ensure that the most recent information is always provided to the sending TCP, if possible. Other SACK blocks are listed in the order in which they appeared as first blocks in previous SACK options. That is, they are filled in by repeating the most recently sent SACK blocks (in other segments) that are not subsets of another block about to be placed in the option being constructed.

The purpose of including more than one SACK block in a SACK option and repeating these blocks across multiple SACKs is to provide some redundancy in the case where SACKs are lost. If SACKs were never lost, [RFC2018] points out that only one SACK block would be required per SACK for full SACK functionality. Unfortunately, SACKs and regular ACKs are sometimes lost and are not retransmitted by TCP unless they contain data (or the *SYN* or *FIN* control bit fields are turned on).

14.6.2 SACK Sender Behavior

Although it is necessary for a SACK-capable receiver to generate proper SACK information to make full use of SACK, it is not sufficient for a TCP connection to benefit from SACKs. A SACK-capable sender must be used that treats the SACK blocks appropriately and performs *selective retransmission* by sending only those segments missing at the receiver, a process also called *selective repeat*. The SACK sender keeps track of any cumulative ACK information it receives (like any TCP sender), plus any SACK information it receives. It uses the SACK information it receives in ACKs generated at the receiver to avoid retransmitting data the receiver reports that it already has. One way it can do this is to keep a "SACKed" indication for each segment in its retransmission buffer that is set whenever a corresponding range of sequence numbers arrives in a SACK.

When a SACK-capable sender has the opportunity to perform a retransmission, usually because it has received a SACK or seen multiple duplicate ACKs, it has the choice of whether it sends new data or retransmits old data. The SACK information provides the sequence number ranges present at the receiver, so the sender can infer what segments likely need to be retransmitted to fill the receiver's holes. The simplest approach is to have the sender first fill the holes at the receiver and then move on to send more new data [RFC3517] if the congestion control procedures allow. This is the most common approach.

There is one exception to this behavior. In [RFC2018], the current specification for SACK options, SACK blocks are considered *advisory*. This means that a receiver could provide a SACK to the sender indicating that some sequence numbers have been received successfully and then change its mind later ("renege"). Because of this, the SACK sender is not able to free its retransmission buffer of data it has received only a SACK for; it is permitted to free a block of data only once the regular TCP ACK number of the receiver has passed by the highest sequence number of this data. The rule also affects what TCP is supposed to do when a retransmission timer expires. When a sending TCP initiates a timer-based retransmission, any information regarding out-of-sequence data at the receiver derived from SACKs is supposed to be forgotten. If out-of-sequence data remains at the receiver, the ACK for the retransmitted segment contains additional SACK blocks the sender can then use. Fortunately, reneging is rare and discouraged.

14.6.3 Example

To understand how the use of SACK alters the sender and receiver behaviors, we repeat the preceding fast retransmit experiment with the same setup (dropping sequence numbers 23601 and 28801), but this time the sender and receiver are using SACK. To get an immediate idea of what happens, we again use Wireshark's TCP sequence number (`tcptrace`) plot function (see Figure 14-9).

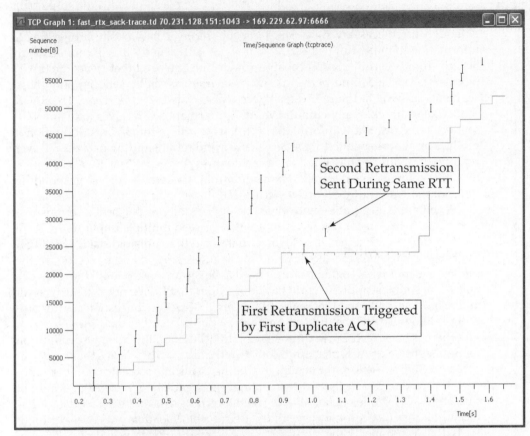

Figure 14-9   Fast retransmit is triggered by the arrival of the first duplicate ACK containing SACK information. The arrival of the next ACK allows the sender to learn of the second missing segment and
retransmit it within the same RTT.

Figure 14-9 is similar to Figure 14-6, but the SACK sender has not had to wait
an RTT to retransmit lost segment 28801 after retransmitting segment 23601. This
is a result of the SACK information contained in the arriving ACKs. We will look
at those in detail later, but first we verify the negotiation of the SACK-Permitted
option during connection setup. This can be seen in Figure 14-10.

As expected, the receiver indicates its ability to use SACKs with the SACK-
Permitted option. The SYN packet from the sender, the first packet of the trace,
also contains an identical option. These options are present only at connection
setup, and thus they only ever appear in segments with the *SYN* bit field set.

Once the connection is permitted to use SACKs, packet loss generally causes
the receiver to start producing SACKs. For example, Wireshark shows the contents
of the SACK options when the first SACK is selected (see Figure 14-11).

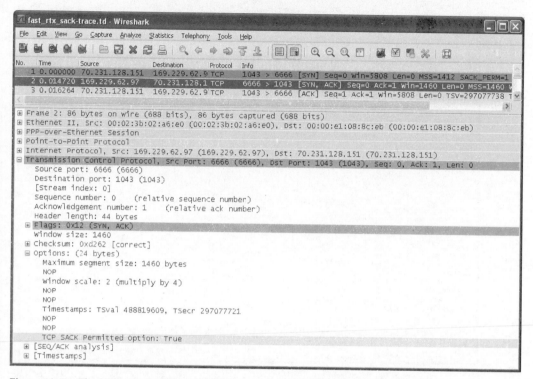

Figure 14-10   The SACK-Permitted option is exchanged in SYN segments to indicate the capability to generate and process SACK information. Most modern TCPs support the MSS, Timestamps, Window
Scale, and SACK-Permitted options during connection establishment.

Figure 14-11 shows the series of events after the first SACK is received. Wireshark indicates SACK information by indicating the left edge and right edge of
the SACK range. Here we see that the ACK for 23801 contains a SACK block of
[25201,26601], indicating a hole at the receiver. The receiver is missing the sequence
number range [23801,25200], which corresponds to the single 1400-byte packet
starting with sequence number 23801. Note that this SACK is a window update
and is not counted as a duplicate ACK for the reasons discussed earlier. It does not
trigger fast retransmit.

The SACK arriving at time 0.967 contains two SACK blocks: [28001,29401] and
[25201,26601]. Recall that the first SACK blocks from previous SACKs are repeated
in later positions in subsequent SACKs for robustness against ACK loss. This SACK
is a duplicate ACK for sequence number 23801 and suggests that the receiver now
requires two full-size segments starting with sequence numbers 23801 and 26601.
The sender reacts immediately by initiating fast retransmit, but because of congestion control procedures (see Chapter 16), the sender sends only one retransmission, for segment 23801. With the arrival of two additional ACKs, the sender is
permitted to send its second retransmission, for segment 26601.

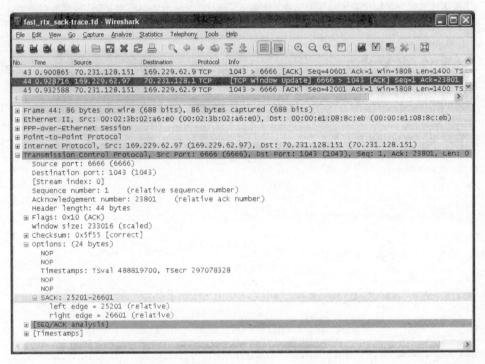

Figure 14-11   The first ACK containing SACK information indicates an out-of-order block with sequence number range 25201 to 26601.

A TCP SACK sender uses the recovery point idea introduced with NewReno. In this example, the highest sequence number sent prior to the retransmission is 43400, which is lower than in the NewReno example from Figure 14-5. For this implementation of SACK fast retransmit, three duplicate ACKs are not required; the TCP initiates its retransmission earlier. The recovery exit is essentially the same, though. Once the ACK for sequence number 43401 is received at time 1.3958, recovery is complete.

It is interesting to note that the potential for better control of the sender using SACKs does not always lead to increased overall throughput performance. This fact is suggested by looking at the two examples we have seen. The NewReno (non-SACK) sender completes the data transfer of 131,074 bytes in 3.592s. The SACK sender completes it in 3.674s. These two measurements are not directly comparable, however, because they did not face precisely the same network conditions (this was not a simulation but rather a live test), although the conditions were largely similar. The benefits of SACKs are more pronounced when the RTT is large and packet loss is severe. Under such circumstances, the benefits of being able to fill more than one hole per RTT are likely to be more significant.

14.7   Spurious Timeouts and Retransmissions

Under a number of circumstances, TCP may initiate a retransmission even when no data has been lost. Such undesirable retransmissions are called *spurious retransmissions* and are caused by *spurious timeouts* (timeouts firing too early) and other reasons such as packet reordering, packet duplication, or lost ACKs. Spurious timeouts can occur when the real RTT has recently increased significantly, beyond the RTO. This happens more frequently in environments where lower-layer protocols have widely varying performance (e.g., wireless) and was a concern mentioned in [KP87]. Here we focus primarily on spurious retransmissions caused by spurious timeouts. The effects of reordering and duplication on TCP are deferred until the following section.

A number of approaches have been suggested to deal with spurious timeouts. They generally involve a *detection* algorithm and a *response* algorithm. The detection algorithm attempts to determine whether a timeout or timer-based retransmission was spurious. The response algorithm is invoked once a timeout or retransmission is deemed spurious. Its purpose is to undo or mitigate some action that is otherwise normally performed by TCP when a retransmission timer expires. In this chapter we discuss only the segment retransmission behavior. The response algorithms typically involve congestion control changes as well, and those aspects are discussed in Chapter 16.

Figure 14-12 illustrates a highly simplified exchange that shows what happens to a basic TCP when a spurious retransmission occurs because of a delay spike in the ACK path after segment 8 is sent. After the retransmission of segment 5 occurs because of a timeout, there are still ACKs in flight from the original transmissions of segments 5 through 8. In this illustration, sequence and ACK numbers are based on packets instead of bytes, with ACKs indicating what has already arrived instead of what is expected next, for simplicity. When they arrive, TCP begins to retransmit additional segments that have already been received, starting with the segment following the ACKed segment. This causes TCP to behave in an undesirable "go-back-N" behavior pattern and in turn causes a collection of duplicate ACKs to be generated and returned to the sender, possibly triggering fast retransmit as well. Several techniques have been developed to mitigate these problems. We now have a look at some of the more popular ones.

14.7.1   Duplicate SACK (DSACK) Extension

With a non-SACK TCP, an ACK can indicate only the highest in-sequence segment back to the sender. With SACK, it can signal other (out-of-order) segments as well. The basic SACK mechanism we discussed previously does not say what happens when a receiver receives duplicate data segments. Such segments can be the result of spurious retransmissions, duplication within the network, or other reasons.

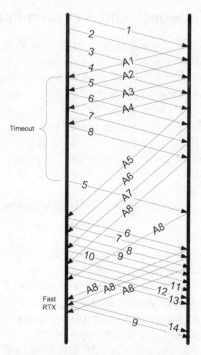

Figure 14-12   A delay spike occurs after the transmission of packet 8, causing a spurious retransmission timeout and retransmission of packet 5. After retransmission, an ACK for the first copy of 5 arrives. The retransmission for 5 creates a duplicate packet at the receiver, followed by an undesirable "go-back-N" behavior whereby packets 6, 7, and 8 are retransmitted even though they are already present at the receiver.

DSACK or D-SACK, which stands for *duplicate SACK* [RFC2883], is a rule, applied at the SACK receiver and interoperable with conventional SACK senders, that causes the first SACK block to indicate the sequence numbers of a duplicate segment that has arrived at the receiver. The main purpose of DSACK is to determine when a retransmission was not necessary and to learn additional facts about the network. With it, a sender has at least the possibility of inferring whether packet reordering, loss of ACKs, packet replication, and/or spurious retransmissions are taking place.

The implementation of DSACK is compatible with conventional SACK in the sense that no separate negotiation is required to make use of it. For it to work properly, a change is made to the content of SACKs sent from the receiver and a corresponding change to the logic at the sender. If a non-DSACK TCP shares a connection with a DSACK TCP, they will interoperate, but without any of the benefits of DSACK.

The change to the SACK receiver is to allow a SACK block to be included even if it covers sequence numbers *below* (or equal to) the cumulative *ACK Number* field.

This was not the original intent of SACK, but its capability is well matched to this purpose. (It applies equally well in cases where the DSACK information is above the cumulative *ACK Number* field; this happens for duplicated out-of-order segments.) DSACK information is included in only a single ACK, and such an ACK is called a DSACK. DSACK information is not repeated across multiple SACKs as conventional SACK information is. As a consequence, DSACKs are less robust to ACK loss than regular SACKs.

Exactly what a sender given DSACK information is supposed to do with it is not specified by [RFC2883]. An experimental algorithm is given in [RFC3708] for detecting spurious retransmissions using DSACK but does not provide any response algorithm. One option it mentions is to use the Eifel Response Algorithm, which we investigate in Section 14.7.4 after introducing a few other detection algorithms.

14.7.2 The Eifel Detection Algorithm

At the beginning of this chapter, we discussed the retransmission ambiguity problem. The experimental *Eifel Detection Algorithm* [RFC3522] deals with this problem using the TCP TSOPT to detect spurious retransmissions. After a retransmission timeout occurs, Eifel awaits the next acceptable ACK. If the next acceptable ACK indicates that the first copy of a retransmitted packet (called the *original transmit*) was the cause for the ACK, the retransmission is considered to be spurious.

The Eifel Detection Algorithm is able to detect spurious behavior earlier than the approach using only DSACK because it relies on ACKs generated as a result of packets arriving *before* loss recovery is initiated. DSACKs, conversely, are able to be sent only after a duplicate segment has arrived at the receiver and able to be acted upon only after the DSACK is returned to the sender. Detecting spurious retransmissions early can offer advantages, because it allows the sender to avoid most of the go-back-N behavior mentioned earlier.

The mechanics of the Eifel Detection Algorithm are simple. It requires the use of the TCP TSOPT. When a retransmission is sent (either a timer-based retransmission or a fast retransmit), the TSV value is stored. When the first acceptable ACK covering its sequence number is received, the incoming ACK's TSER is examined. If it is smaller than the stored value, the ACK corresponds to the original transmission of the packet and not the retransmission, implying that the retransmission must have been spurious. This approach is fairly robust to ACK loss as well. If an ACK is lost, any subsequent ACKs still have TSER values less than the stored TSV of the retransmitted segment. Thus, a retransmission can be deemed spurious as a result of any of the window's worth of ACKs arriving, so a loss of any single ACK is not likely to cause a problem.

The Eifel Detection Algorithm can be combined with DSACKs. This can be beneficial in the situation where an entire window's worth of ACKs are lost but both the original transmit and retransmission have arrived at the receiver. In this particular case, the arriving retransmit causes a DSACK to be generated. The Eifel

Detection Algorithm would by default conclude that the retransmission is spurious. It is thought, however, that if so many ACKs are being lost, allowing TCP to believe the retransmission was *not* spurious is useful (e.g., to induce it to start sending more slowly—a consequence of the congestion control procedures we discuss in Chapter 16). Thus, arriving DSACKs cause the Eifel Detection Algorithm to conclude that the corresponding retransmission is *not* spurious.

14.7.3   Forward-RTO Recovery (F-RTO)

Forward-RTO Recovery (F-RTO) [RFC5682] is a standard algorithm for detecting spurious retransmissions. It does not require any TCP options, so when it is implemented in a sender, it can be used effectively even with an older receiver that does not support the TCP TSOPT. It attempts to detect only spurious retransmissions caused by expiration of the retransmission timer; it does not deal with the other causes for spurious retransmissions or duplications mentioned before.

F-RTO makes a modification to the action TCP ordinarily takes after a timer-based retransmission. These retransmissions are for the smallest sequence number for which no ACK has yet been received. Ordinarily, TCP continues sending additional adjacent packets in order as additional ACKs arrive. This is the go-back-N behavior described previously.

F-RTO modifies the ordinary behavior of TCP by having TCP send new (so far unsent) data after the timeout-based retransmission when the first ACK arrives. It then inspects the second arriving ACK. If either of the first two ACKs arriving after the retransmission was sent are duplicate ACKs, the retransmission is deemed OK. If they are both acceptable ACKs that advance the sender's window, the retransmission is deemed to have been spurious. This approach is fairly intuitive. If the transmission of new data results in the arrival of acceptable ACKs, the arrival of the new data is moving the receiver's window forward. If such data is only causing duplicate ACKs, there must be one or more holes at the receiver. In either case, the reception of new data at the receiver does not harm the overall data transfer performance (provided there are sufficient buffers at the receiver).

14.7.4   The Eifel Response Algorithm

The *Eifel Response Algorithm* [RFC4015] is a standard set of operations to be executed by a TCP once a retransmission has been deemed spurious. Because the response algorithm is logically decoupled from the Eifel Detection Algorithm, it can be used with any of the detection algorithms we just discussed. The Eifel Response Algorithm was originally intended to operate for both timer-based and fast retransmit spurious retransmissions but is currently specified only for timer-based retransmissions.

Although the Eifel Response Algorithm can be used with any of the detection algorithms, it behaves somewhat differently based on whether a spurious timeout was detected early (e.g., by the Eifel or F-RTO detection algorithms) or later (e.g., by DSACKs). The former cases are called spurious timeouts and operate by inspecting ACKs for original transmissions. The latter are called *late* spurious timeouts and are based on ACKs for retransmissions invoked as a result of (spurious) timeouts.

The response algorithm operates on the first retransmission timer event only. It is not executed if a subsequent timeout occurs before recovery is complete. After the retransmission timer expires, it takes a snapshot of the values in *srtt* and *rttvar* and records them in new variables *srtt_prev* and *rttvar_prev* as follows:

$$srtt\_prev = srtt + 2(G)$$

$$rttvar\_prev = rttvar$$

These variables are assigned on any timer expiration but are used only when the timeout is determined to be spurious. If so, they help form the basis for setting the new RTO. In the formula, the value G represents the TCP clock granularity. *srtt_prev* is set to *srtt* plus twice the timer granularity based on the following chain of reasoning: The spurious timeout may have been invoked because the value of *srtt* is just a tad too small. If it were just a bit larger, no timeout would have happened. Adding the term $2(G)$ to *srtt* deals with this situation by storing a slightly increased value into *srtt_prev*, which is used later for setting the RTO.

After the *srtt_prev* and *rttvar_prev* values are stored, one of the detection algorithms is invoked. The result of running the algorithm produces a value assigned to a special variable called *SpuriousRecovery*. If the algorithm detects a spurious timeout, *SpuriousRecovery* is set to SPUR_TO. If it detects a late spurious timeout, it sets *SpuriousRecovery* to LATE_SPUR_TO. Otherwise, the timeout is not spurious, and ordinary TCP timeout processing continues.

If *SpuriousRecovery* is SPUR_TO, TCP can take action before recovery is complete. It does this by adjusting the sequence number of the next segment it is about to send (called SND.NXT) to the first new, unsent segment (called SND.MAX). This avoids the undesirable go-back-N behavior after the initial retransmission discussed previously. If the detection algorithm detects a late spurious timeout, an ACK for the initial retransmission has already taken place, so SND.NXT is not changed. In either case, however, the congestion control state is reset (see Chapter 16). In addition, once an acceptable ACK is received for a segment transmitted after the retransmission timer expires, the values of *srtt*, *rttvar*, and RTO can be updated as follows:

$$srtt \leftarrow max(srtt\_prev, m)$$

$$rttvar \leftarrow max(rttvar\_prev, m/2)$$

$$RTO = srtt + max(G, 4(rttvar))$$

Here, m is a sample of the RTT of the connection based on the arrival of the first acceptable ACK for data sent after the timeout. The motivation for these modifications is that the real RTT may have changed so significantly that the RTT history in the current estimators is no longer a valid basis for setting the RTO. If the real path RTT has increased abruptly (e.g., because of wireless handoff to a new base station), the current *srtt* and *rttvar* values are likely to be too small and should be reinitialized. On the other hand, an increase in path RTT could be only temporary, implying that reinitializing *srtt* and *rttvar* might not be such a good idea because they are likely to be approximately correct.

These equations try to balance between the two situations by reassigning the moving averages *srtt* and *rttvar* only if the new RTT samples are larger. Doing so effectively throws out the previous history of the RTT (and RTT variance). The values of *srtt* and *rttvar* can only increase as a result of the response algorithm. If the RTT does not appear to be increasing, the running estimators remain unchanged, essentially ignoring the fact that a timeout has occurred. The RTO is reassigned in the conventional way in any case, and a new retransmission timer is set for this timeout value.

14.8   Packet Reordering and Duplication

Most of the issues discussed so far relate to how TCP handles packet loss. This is a relatively common issue, and a great deal of work has gone into making TCP robust to packet drops. As we began to see in the last section, other packet delivery anomalies such as duplication and reordering can also affect TCP's operation. In both of these cases, we wish TCP to be able to distinguish between packets that are reordered or duplicated and those that are lost. As we shall now see, this is sometimes not so simple.

14.8.1   Reordering

Packet reordering can occur in an IP network because IP provides no guarantee that relative ordering between packets is maintained during delivery. This can be beneficial (to IP at least), because IP can choose another path for traffic (e.g., that is faster) without having to worry about the consequences that doing so may cause traffic freshly injected into the network to pass ahead of older traffic, resulting in the order of packet arrivals at the receiver not matching the order of transmission at the sender. There are other reasons packet reordering may occur. For example, some high-performance routers employ multiple parallel data paths within the hardware [BPS99], and different processing delays among packets can lead to a departure order that does not match the arrival order.

Reordering may take place in the forward path or the reverse path of a TCP connection (or in some cases both). The reordering of data segments has a somewhat different effect on TCP as does reordering of ACK packets. Recall that because of asymmetric routing, it is frequently the case that ACKs travel along different network links (and through different routers) from data packets on the forward path.

When traffic is reordered, TCP can be affected in several ways. If reordering takes place in the reverse (ACK) direction, it causes the sending TCP to receive some ACKs that move the window significantly forward followed by some evidently old redundant ACKs that are discarded. This can lead to an unwanted *burstiness* (instantaneous high-speed sending) behavior in the sending pattern of TCP and also trouble in taking advantage of available network bandwidth, because of the behavior of TCP's congestion control (see Chapter 16).

If reordering occurs in the forward direction, TCP may have trouble distinguishing this condition from loss. Both loss and reordering result in the receiver receiving out-of-order packets that create holes between the next expected packet and the other packets received so far. When reordering is moderate (e.g., two adjacent packets switch order), the situation can be handled fairly quickly. When reorderings are more severe, TCP can be tricked into believing that data has been lost even though it has not. This can result in spurious retransmissions, primarily from the fast retransmit algorithm.

Recall from previous discussions that the fast retransmit algorithm relies on observing duplicate acknowledgments from a TCP receiver in order to infer the loss of a packet and to initiate a retransmission without having to wait for a retransmission timer to expire. Because a TCP receiver is supposed to immediately ACK any out-of-sequence data it receives in order to help induce fast retransmit to be triggered on packet loss, any packet that is reordered within the network causes a receiver to produce a duplicate ACK. If fast retransmit were to be invoked whenever any duplicate ACK is received at the sender, a large number of unnecessary retransmissions would occur on network paths where a small amount of reordering is common. To handle this situation, fast retransmit is triggered only after the duplicate threshold (*dupthresh*) has been reached.

The effect is illustrated in Figure 14-13. The left portion of the figure indicates how TCP behaves with light reordering, where *dupthresh* is set to 3. In this case, the single duplicate ACK does not affect TCP. It is effectively ignored and TCP overcomes the reordering. The right-hand side indicates what happens when a packet has been more severely reordered. Because it is three positions out of sequence, three duplicate ACKs are generated. This invokes the fast retransmit procedure in the sending TCP, producing a duplicate segment at the receiver.

The problem of distinguishing loss from reordering is not trivial. Dealing with it involves trying to decide when a sender has waited long enough to try to fill apparent holes at the receiver. Fortunately, severe reordering on the Internet is not common [J03], so setting *dupthresh* to a relatively small number (such as the default of 3) handles most circumstances. That said, there are a number of research projects that modify TCP to handle more severe reordering [LLY07]. Some of these adjust *dupthresh* dynamically, as does the Linux TCP implementation.

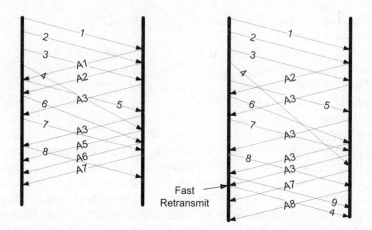

Figure 14-13 Mild reordering (left) is overcome by ignoring a small number of duplicate ACKs. When reordering is more severe (right), as in this case where packet 4 is three places out of sequence, a spurious fast retransmit can be triggered.

14.8.2 Duplication

Although rare, the IP protocol may deliver a single packet more than one time. This can happen, for example, when a link-layer network protocol performs a retransmission and creates two copies of the same packet. When duplicates are created, TCP can become confused in some of the ways we have seen already. Consider the case shown in Figure 14-14 in which packet number 3 has been duplicated three times.

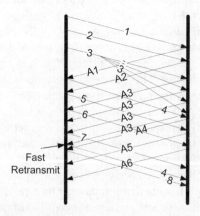

Figure 14-14 Packet duplication in the network has caused a spurious fast retransmission due to the presence of duplicate ACKs.

As we can see, the effect of packet 3 being duplicated is to produce a series of duplicate ACKs from the receiver. This is enough to trigger a spurious fast retransmit, as the non-SACK sender may mistakenly believe that packets 5 and 6 have arrived earlier. With SACK (and DSACK, in particular) this is more easily diagnosed at the sender. With DSACK, each of the duplicate ACKs for A3 contains DSACK information that segment 3 has already been received. Furthermore, none of them contains an indication of any out-of-order data, meaning the arriving packets (or their ACKs) must have been duplicates. TCP can often suppress spurious retransmissions in such cases.

14.9 Destination Metrics

As we have seen, TCP "learns" the characteristics of the network path between the sender and the receiver over time. The learning is kept in state variables at the sender such as *srtt* and *rttvar*. Some TCP implementations also keep track of an estimate of the amount of packet reordering that has occurred recently along a path. Historically, this learning is lost once the connection is closed. That is, if a new TCP connection is opened to the same receiver, it must start to determine values for the state variables from scratch.

Newer TCP implementations maintain many of the metrics that we have described in this chapter in a routing or forwarding table entry or other system-wide data structure that exists even after TCP connections are closed. When a new connection is created, TCP consults the data structure to see if there is any preexisting information regarding the path to the destination host with which it will be communicating. If so, initial values for *srtt*, *rttvar*, and so on can be initialized to some value based on previous, relatively recent experience. When a TCP connection closes down, it has the opportunity to update the statistics. This can be accomplished by replacing the existing statistics or updating them in some other way. In the case of Linux 2.6, the values are updated to be the maximum of the existing values and those measured by the most recent TCP. These values can be inspected using the ip program available from the iproute2 suite of tools [IPR2]:

```
Linux% ip route show cache 132.239.50.184
132.239.50.184 from 10.0.0.9 tos 0x10 via 10.0.0.1 dev eth0
    cache  mtu 1500 rtt 29ms rttvar 29ms cwnd 2 advmss 1460 hoplimit 64
```

This command shows information cached about previous connections with a particular DSCP value (16, indicating CS2 but represented using the older "ToS" byte terminology with value 0x10) between the local system and 132.239.50.184 using the IPv4 next hop 10.0.0.1 and accessed using the network device eth0. We can see packet size information (the path MTU learned with PMTUD, the MSS advertised by the remote side), the maximum number of hops to use (for IPv6; not applicable here), values of *srtt* and *rttvar*, along with congestion control information such as `cwnd` that we discuss in Chapter 16.

14.10 Repacketization

When TCP times out and retransmits, it does not have to retransmit the identical segment. Instead, TCP is allowed to perform *repacketization*, sending a bigger segment, which can increase performance. (Naturally, this bigger segment cannot exceed the MSS announced by the receiver and should not exceed the path MTU.) This is allowed in the protocol because TCP identifies the data being sent and acknowledged by its byte number, not its segment (or packet) number.

TCP's ability to retransmit a segment with a different size from the original segment provides another way of addressing the retransmission ambiguity problem. This has been the basis of an idea called STODER [TZZ05] that uses repacketization to detect spurious timeouts.

We can easily see repacketization in action. We use our `sock` program as a server and connect to it with Telnet. First we type the line `hello there`. This produces a segment of 13 data bytes, including the carriage-return and newline characters produced when the Enter key is pressed. We then disconnect the network and type `line number 2` (14 bytes, including the newline). We then wait about 45s, type `and 3`, and terminate the connection:

```
Linux% telnet 169.229.62.97 6666
hello there                    (first line gets sent OK)
                               (then we disconnect the Ethernet cable)
line number 2                  (this line gets retransmitted)
and 3                          (reconnect Ethernet)
^] telnet> quit
```

We can see the results using `tcpdump`:†

```
1 19:51:47.674418 IP 10.0.0.7.1029 > 169.229.62.97.6666:
    P 1:14(13) ack 1 win 5840  ◄──────────────────  "hello there\r\n"
    <nop,nop,timestamp 2343578137 596377728>

2 19:51:47.788992 IP 169.229.62.97.6666 > 10.0.0.7.1029:
    . ack 14 win 58254 <nop,nop,timestamp 596378252 2343578137>

3 19:52:35.130837 IP 10.0.0.7.1029 > 169.229.62.97.6666:
    FP 29:36(7) ack 1 win 5840  ◄──────────────────  "and 3\r\n"
    <nop,nop,timestamp 2343602439 596378252>

4 19:52:35.146358 IP 169.229.62.97.6666 > 10.0.0.7.1029:
    . ack 14 win 58254
    <nop,nop,timestamp 596382987 2343578137,nop,nop,
    sack sack 1 {29:36}>
```

```
5 19:52:39.414253 IP 10.0.0.7.1029 > 169.229.62.97.6666:
    FP 14:36(22) ack 1 win 5840  ◄──────────
    <nop,nop,timestamp 2343604633 596382987>
```
> "line number2\r\n and 3\r\n"

```
6 19:52:39.429228 IP 169.229.62.97.6666 > 10.0.0.7.1029:
    . ack 37 win 58248 <nop,nop,timestamp 596383416 2343604633>
```

```
7 19:52:39.429696 IP 169.229.62.97.6666 > 10.0.0.7.1029:
    F 1:1(0) ack 37 win 58254
    <nop,nop,timestamp 596383416 2343604633>
```

```
8 19:52:39.430119 IP 10.0.0.7.1029 > 169.229.62.97.6666:
    . ack 2 win 5840 <nop,nop,timestamp 2343604641 596383416>
```

In this trace, the initial SYN exchange has been removed. The first two segments contain the data strings `hello there` and its acknowledgment. The next packet in the trace is not in sequence: it starts with sequence number 29 and contains the string `and 3` (7 bytes). Its returning ACK contains ACK number 14 but a SACK block with relative sequence numbers {29,36}. The middle sequence of characters has been lost. TCP retransmits this but uses a larger packet, containing sequence numbers `14:36`. Thus, we can see how the retransmission for sequence number 14 resulted in a repacketization to form a larger packet of size 22 bytes. Interestingly, this packet overlaps the data present in the SACK block and also carries the *FIN* bit field, indicating that it is the last data of the connection.

14.11 Attacks Involving TCP Retransmission

There is a class of DoS attack called *low-rate* DoS attacks [KK03]. In such an attack, an attacker sends bursts of traffic to a gateway or host, causing the victim system to experience a retransmission timeout. Given an ability to predict when the victim TCP will attempt to retransmit, the attacker generates a burst of traffic at each retransmission attempt. As a consequence, the victim TCP perceives congestion in the network, throttles its sending rate to near zero, keeps backing off its RTO according to Karn's algorithm, and effectively receives very little network throughput. The proposed mechanism to deal with this type of attack is to add randomization to the RTO, making it difficult for the attacker to guess the precise times when a retransmission will take place.

A related but distinct form of DoS attack involves slowing a victim TCP's segments down so that the RTT estimate is too high. Doing so causes the victim TCP to be less aggressive in retransmitting its own packets when they are lost. The opposite attack is also possible: an attacker forges ACKs when data has been transmitted but has not actually arrived at the receiver yet. In this case, the attacker can cause the victim TCP to believe that the connection RTT is significantly smaller than it really is, leading to an overaggressive TCP that creates numerous unwanted retransmissions.

14.12 Summary

This chapter provided a detailed look at TCP's timeout and retransmission strategy. Our first example illustrated a case in which we simply unplugged the network when a TCP had a packet to send. This resulted in a retransmission timer initiating a timeout-based retransmission. Each successive retransmit took place at an interval twice as long as the previous transmission, the result of the second part of Karn's algorithm that incorporates binary exponential backoff.

TCP measures the RTT and then uses these measurements to keep track of a smoothed RTT estimator and a smoothed mean deviation estimator. These two estimators are then used to calculate the next retransmission timeout value. Without the Timestamps option, a TCP measures only a single RTT per window of data. Karn's algorithm removes the retransmission ambiguity problem by preventing the use of RTT measurements for segments that have been lost. Today, most TCPs use the Timestamps option, which permits each segment to be individually timed. The Timestamps option operates correctly even in the face of packet reordering or packet duplication.

We looked at the fast retransmit algorithm, which can be triggered without requiring a timer to expire. This is the most efficient method (and the most frequently used one) for TCP to fill holes at the receiver caused by missing packets. Fast retransmit can be improved with the use of selective ACKs. These carry additional information in the ACKs and permit the SACK-capable TCP sender to repair more than one hole per RTT. Doing so can lead to improved performance under some circumstances.

If the RTT estimate is below the actual RTT of the connection, a spurious retransmission may take place. In such cases, if TCP waited a little longer, the (unnecessary) retransmission would not happen. A number of algorithms have been developed to detect when a TCP has experienced a spurious timeout. The DSACK approach requires the arrival of a duplicate segment at the receiver. The Eifel Detection Algorithm depends on TCP timestamps but can react faster than DSACKs because it detects spurious timeouts based on ACKs returning from segments that were sent prior to the timeout. F-RTO is another algorithm that behaves similarly to Eifel but does not require timestamps. It also changes the sender to send new data after a timeout that is deemed to be spurious. All of these detection algorithms can be combined with a response algorithm. The main one described so far is the Eifel Response Algorithm, which can reset RTT and RTT variance estimates if the delay has increased substantially (and otherwise "undoes" any changes TCP would otherwise perform on a timeout).

We also looked at how TCP state can be cached across connections, how TCP is allowed to repacketize its data, and some attacks that can be mounted to fool TCP into behaving in undesired ways such as being too passive or aggressive. We shall see more about the consequences of these attacks in Chapter 16, where we investigate TCP's congestion control procedures.

14.13 References

[G04] S. Gorard, "Revisiting a 90-Year-Old Debate: The Advantages of the Mean Deviation," Department of Educational Studies, University of York, paper presented at the British Educational Research Association Annual Conference, University of Manchester, September 16–18, 2004.

[BPS99] J. Bennett, C. Partridge, and N. Shectman, "Packet Re-ordering Is Not Pathological Network Behavior," *IEEE/ACM Transactions on Networking*, 7(6), Dec. 1999.

[F68] W. Feller, *An Introduction to Probability Theory and Its Applications, Volume 1* (Wiley, 1968).

[ID1323b] V. Jacobson, B. Braden, and D. Borman, "TCP Extensions for High Performance" (expired), Internet draft-jacobson-tsvwg-1323bis-01, work in progress, Mar. 2009.

[IPR2] http://www.linuxfoundation.org/collaborate/workgroups/networking/iproute2

[J88] V. Jacobson, "Congestion Avoidance and Control," *Proc. ACM SIGCOMM*, Aug. 1988.

[J90] V. Jacobson, "Berkeley TCP Evolution from 4.3-Tahoe to 4.3 Reno," *Proc. 18th IETF*, Sept. 1990.

[J03] S. Jaiswal et al., "Measurement and Classification of Out-of-Sequence Packets in a Tier-1 IP Backbone," *Proc. IEEE INFOCOM*, Apr. 2003.

[KK03] A. Kuzmanovic and E. Knightly, "Low-Rate TCP-Targeted Denial of Service Attacks," *Proc. ACM SIGCOMM*, Aug. 2003.

[KP87] P. Karn and C. Partridge, "Improving Round-Trip Time Estimates in Reliable Transport Protocols," *Proc. ACM SIGCOMM*, Aug. 1987.

[LLY07] K. Leung, V. Li, and D. Yang, "An Overview of Packet Reordering in Transmission Control Protocol (TCP): Problems, Solutions and Challenges," *IEEE Trans. Parallel and Distributed Systems*, 18(4), Apr. 2007.

[LS00] R. Ludwig and K. Sklower, "The Eifel Retransmission Timer," *ACM Computer Communication Review*, 30(3), July 2000.

[RFC0793] J. Postel, "Transmission Control Protocol," Internet RFC 0793/STD0007, Sept. 1981.

[RFC1122] R. Braden, ed., "Requirements for Internet Hosts," Internet RFC 1122/STD 0003, Oct. 1989.

[RFC1323] V. Jacobson, R. Braden, and D. Borman, "TCP Extensions for High Performance," Internet RFC 1323, May 1992.

[RFC2018] M. Mathis, J. Mahdavi, S. Floyd, and A. Romanow, "TCP Selective Acknowledgment Options," Internet RFC 2018, Oct. 1996.

[RFC2883] S. Floyd, J. Mahdavi, M. Mathis, and M. Podolsky, "An Extension to the Selective Acknowledgement (SACK) Option for TCP," Internet RFC 2883, July 2000.

[RFC3517] E. Blanton, M. Allman, K. Fall, and L. Wang, "A Conservative Selective Acknowledgment (SACK)-Based Loss Recovery Algorithm for TCP," Internet RFC 3517, Apr. 2003.

[RFC3522] R. Ludwig and M. Meyer, "The Eifel Detection Algorithm for TCP," Internet RFC 3522 (experimental), Apr. 2003.

[RFC3708] E. Blanton and M. Allman, "Using TCP Duplicate Selective Acknowledgement (DSACKs) and Stream Control Transmission Protocol (SCTP) Duplicate Transmission Sequence Numbers (TSNs) to Detect Spurious Retransmissions," Internet RFC 3708 (experimental), Feb. 2004.

[RFC3782] S. Floyd, T. Henderson, and A. Gurtov, "The NewReno Modification to TCP's Fast Recovery Algorithm," Internet RFC 3782, Apr. 2004.

[RFC4015] R. Ludwig and A. Gurtov, "The Eifel Response Algorithm for TCP," Internet RFC 4015, Feb. 2005.

[RFC5681] M. Allman, V. Paxson, and E. Blanton, "TCP Congestion Control," Internet RFC 5681, Sept. 2009.

[RFC5682] P. Sarolahti, M. Kojo, K. Yamamoto, and M. Hata, "Forward RTO-Recovery (F-RTO): An Algorithm for Detecting Spurious Retransmission Timeouts with TCP," Internet RFC 5682, Sept. 2009.

[RFC6298] V. Paxson, M. Allman, and J. Chu, "Computing TCP's Retransmission Timer," Internet RFC 6298, June 2011.

[RKS07] S. Rewaskar, J. Kaur, and F. D. Smith, "Performance Study of Loss Detection/Recovery in Real-World TCP Implementations," *Proc. IEEE ICNP*, Oct. 2007.

[SK02] P. Sarolahti and A. Kuznetsov, "Congestion Control in Linux TCP," *Proc. Usenix Freenix Track*, June 2002.

[TZZ05] K. Tan and Q. Zhang, "STODER: A Robust and Efficient Algorithm for Handling Spurious Timeouts in TCP," *Proc. IEEE Globecomm*, Dec. 2005.

[V09] V. Vasudevan et al., "Safe and Fine-Grained TCP Retransmissions for Datacenter Communication," *Proc. ACM SIGCOMM*, Aug. 2009.

[WINREG] TCP/IP Registry Values for Microsoft Windows Vista and Windows Server 2008, Jan. 2008. See http://www.microsoft.com/download/en/details.aspx?id=9152

15

TCP Data Flow and Window Management

15.1 Introduction

Chapter 13 dealt with the establishment and termination of TCP connections, and Chapter 14 examined how TCP ensures reliable delivery using retransmissions of data that has been lost. We now examine the dynamics of TCP data transfers, focusing initially on interactive connections and then introducing flow control and associated window management procedures that are used in conjunction with congestion control (see Chapter 16) for bulk data transfers.

An "interactive" TCP connection is one in which user input such as keystrokes, short messages, or joystick/mouse movements need to be delivered between a client and a server. If small segments are used to carry such user input, the protocol imposes more overhead because there are fewer useful payload bytes per packet exchanged. On the other hand, filling packets with more data usually requires them to be delayed, which can have a negative impact on delay-sensitive applications such as online games and collaboration tools. We shall investigate techniques with which the application can trade off between these two issues.

After discussing interactive communications, we discuss the methods used by TCP for achieving flow control by dynamically adapting the window size to ensure that a sender does not overrun a receiver. This issue primarily impacts bulk data transfer (i.e., noninteractive communications) but can also affect interactive applications. In Chapter 16 we will explore how the concept of flow control can be extended to protect not only the receiver, but also the network between the sender and the receiver.

15.2 Interactive Communication

The amount of network traffic carried in a particular portion of the Internet over a certain amount of time is usually measured in terms of bytes or packets. There is considerable variation in these numbers. For example, local area traffic differs from wide area traffic, and traffic between different sites tends to vary. Studies of TCP traffic [P05][F03] usually find that 90% or more of all TCP segments contain *bulk data* (e.g., Web, file sharing, electronic mail, backups) and the remaining portion contains *interactive data* (e.g., remote login, network games). Bulk data segments tend to be relatively large (1500 bytes or larger), while interactive data segments tend to be much smaller (tens of bytes of user data).

TCP handles both types of data using the same protocol and packet format, but different algorithms come into play for each. In this section, we will look at how interactive data is transferred by TCP, using the ssh (secure shell) application as one example. Secure shell [RFC4251] is a remote login protocol that provides strong security (privacy and authentication based on cryptography). It has mostly replaced the earlier UNIX rlogin and Telnet programs that provide remote login service but without strong security.

As we investigate ssh, we will see how delayed acknowledgments work and how the *Nagle algorithm* reduces the number of small packets across wide area networks. The same algorithms apply to other applications supporting remote login capability such as Telnet, rlogin, and Windows Terminal Services.

Let us look at the flow of data when we type an interactive command on an ssh connection. The client captures what the user types and ships it over to the server to be interpreted, and the server ships any responses back to the client. The client encrypts the data it sends, meaning that the characters typed by the user are encoded before being transferred over the connection (see Chapter 18). The encoding makes determining the typed keys difficult for an eavesdropper. The client supports several encryption algorithms and different authentication methods. It also supports several other advanced features such as tunneling other protocols (see Chapter 3 and [RFC4254]).

Many newcomers to TCP/IP are surprised to find that each interactive keystroke normally generates a separate data packet. That is, the keystrokes are sent from the client to the server individually (one character at a time rather than one line at a time). Furthermore, ssh invokes a shell (command interpreter) on the remote system (the server), which echoes the characters that are typed at the client. A single typed character could thus generate four TCP segments: the interactive keystroke from the client, an acknowledgment of the keystroke from the server, the echo of the keystroke from the server, and an acknowledgment of the echo from the client back to the server (see Figure 15-1(a)).

Normally, however, segments 2 and 3 are combined—in Figure 15-1(b), the acknowledgment of the keystroke is sent along with the echo of the characters typed. We describe the technique that combines these (called *delayed acknowledgments* with *piggybacking*) in the next section.

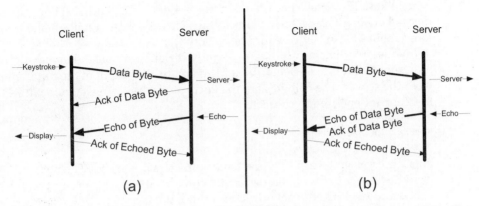

Figure 15-1 One possible way to remotely echo an interactive keystroke is a separate ACK and echo packet (a). A typical TCP coalesces the ACK for the data byte and the echo of the byte into a single packet (b).

We purposely use ssh for this example because it generates a packet for each character typed from the client to the server. If the user types especially fast, however, more than one character might be carried in a single packet. Figure 15-2 shows the flow of data using Wireshark when we type the date command across an active ssh connection to a Linux server.

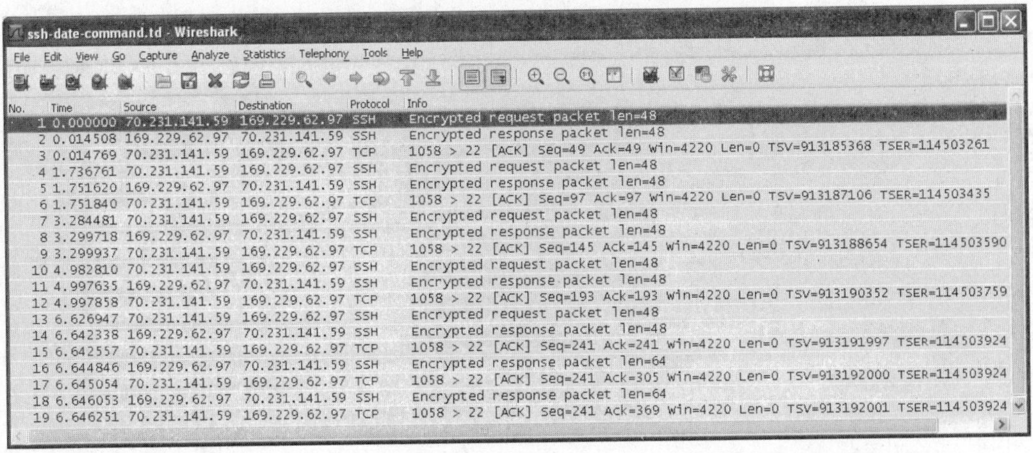

```
ssh-date-command.td - Wireshark                                                                    _ □ ×
File  Edit  View  Go  Capture  Analyze  Statistics  Telephony  Tools  Help

No.  Time       Source          Destination     Protocol  Info
  1 0.000000 70.231.141.59  169.229.62.97   SSH       Encrypted request packet len=48
  2 0.014508 169.229.62.97  70.231.141.59   SSH       Encrypted response packet len=48
  3 0.014769 70.231.141.59  169.229.62.97   TCP       1058 > 22 [ACK] Seq=49 Ack=49 Win=4220 Len=0 TSV=913185368 TSER=114503261
  4 1.736761 70.231.141.59  169.229.62.97   SSH       Encrypted request packet len=48
  5 1.751620 169.229.62.97  70.231.141.59   SSH       Encrypted response packet len=48
  6 1.751840 70.231.141.59  169.229.62.97   TCP       1058 > 22 [ACK] Seq=97 Ack=97 Win=4220 Len=0 TSV=913187106 TSER=114503435
  7 3.284481 70.231.141.59  169.229.62.97   SSH       Encrypted request packet len=48
  8 3.299718 169.229.62.97  70.231.141.59   SSH       Encrypted response packet len=48
  9 3.299937 70.231.141.59  169.229.62.97   TCP       1058 > 22 [ACK] Seq=145 Ack=145 Win=4220 Len=0 TSV=913188654 TSER=114503590
 10 4.982810 70.231.141.59  169.229.62.97   SSH       Encrypted request packet len=48
 11 4.997635 169.229.62.97  70.231.141.59   SSH       Encrypted response packet len=48
 12 4.997858 70.231.141.59  169.229.62.97   TCP       1058 > 22 [ACK] Seq=193 Ack=193 Win=4220 Len=0 TSV=913190352 TSER=114503759
 13 6.626947 70.231.141.59  169.229.62.97   SSH       Encrypted request packet len=48
 14 6.642338 169.229.62.97  70.231.141.59   SSH       Encrypted response packet len=48
 15 6.642557 70.231.141.59  169.229.62.97   TCP       1058 > 22 [ACK] Seq=241 Ack=241 Win=4220 Len=0 TSV=913191997 TSER=114503924
 16 6.644846 169.229.62.97  70.231.141.59   SSH       Encrypted response packet len=64
 17 6.645054 70.231.141.59  169.229.62.97   TCP       1058 > 22 [ACK] Seq=241 Ack=305 Win=4220 Len=0 TSV=913192000 TSER=114503924
 18 6.646053 169.229.62.97  70.231.141.59   SSH       Encrypted response packet len=64
 19 6.646251 70.231.141.59  169.229.62.97   TCP       1058 > 22 [ACK] Seq=241 Ack=369 Win=4220 Len=0 TSV=913192001 TSER=114503924
```

Figure 15-2 TCP segments sent when the date command is typed on an already-established ssh connection.

In Figure 15-2, packet 1 carries the character d from the client to the server. Packet 2 is the acknowledgment of this character and its echo (combining the middle two segments as in Figure 15-1). Packet 3 is the acknowledgment of the echoed character. Packets 4–6 correspond to the character a, packets 7–9 to the character t, and packets 10–12 to the character e. Packets 13–15 correspond to the Enter (carriage return) key. The delays between packets 3–4, 6–7, 9–10, and 12–13 are the human delays between typing each character, which were intentionally made unusually long (about 1.5s) in this case for illustration.

Notice that packets 16–19 are slightly different because they have grown in size from 48 bytes to 64 bytes. Packet 16 contains the output of the `date` command from the server. The 64 bytes are the encrypted version of the following 28 clear-text (not-yet-encrypted) characters:

```
Wed Dec 28 22:47:16 PST 2005
```

plus the carriage-return and line-feed characters at the end. The next packet sent from the server to the client (packet 18) contains the client's prompt on the server host: `Linux%`. Packet 19 acknowledges this data.

Figure 15-3 is the same trace as in Figure 15-2, except now more of the TCP-layer information is shown, indicating how TCP acknowledgments operate and the packet sizes used by `ssh`. Packet 1 (containing the `d` character) starts with the relative sequence number 0. Packet 2 ACKs the packet from line 1 by setting the ACK number to 48, the sequence number of the last successfully received byte plus 1. Packet 2 also sends the data byte with a sequence number of 0 from the server to the client, containing the echo of the `d` character. The echoed `d` is ACKed by the client in packet 3 by setting the ACK number to 48. We see that the connection has two streams of sequence numbers in use—one from the client to the server, and one in the reverse direction. We shall explore this in more detail when we discuss window advertisements.

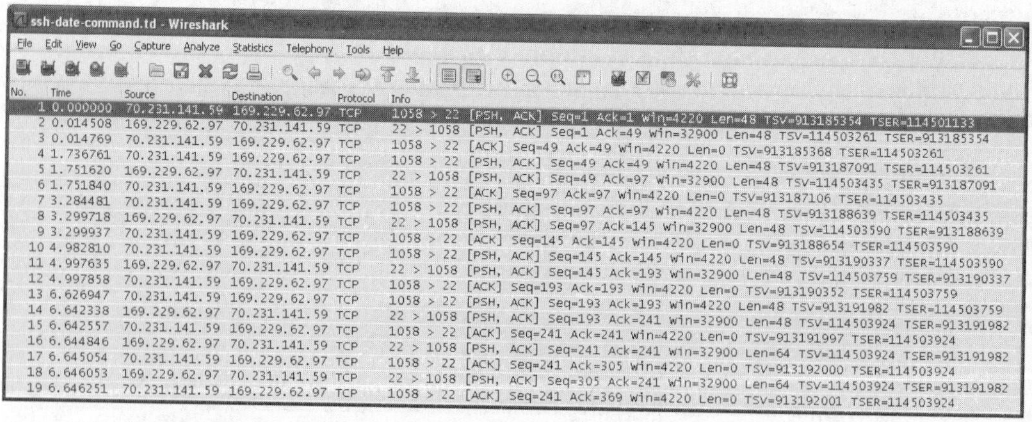

Figure 15-3 The same trace as in Figure 15-2, except the protocol decode for `ssh` has been disabled, revealing the TCP sequence number information. Note that all data packets are 48 bytes in size except the last two. The size of 48 bytes relates to the cryptography used in `ssh` (see Chapter 18).

One other observation we can make about this trace is that each packet with data in it (not zero length) also has the *PSH* bit field set. As mentioned earlier, this flag is conventionally used to indicate that the buffer at the side sending the packet has been emptied in conjunction with sending the packet. In other words, when the packet with the *PSH* bit field set left the sender, the sender had no more data to send.

15.3 Delayed Acknowledgments

In many cases, TCP does not provide an ACK for every incoming packet. This is possible because of TCP's cumulative *ACK* field (see Chapter 12). Using a cumulative ACK allows TCP to intentionally *delay* sending an ACK for some amount of time, in the hope that it can combine the ACK it needs to send with some data the local application wishes to send in the other direction. This is a form of *piggybacking* that is used most often in conjunction with bulk data transfers. Obviously a TCP cannot delay ACKs indefinitely; otherwise its peer could conclude that data has been lost and initiate an unnecessary retransmission.

Note

The Host Requirements RFC [RFC1122] states that TCP should implement a delayed ACK but the delay must be less than 500ms. Many implementations use a maximum of 200ms.

Delaying ACKs causes less traffic to be carried over the network than when ACKs are not delayed because fewer ACKs are used. A ratio of 2 to 1 is fairly common for bulk transfers. The use of delayed ACKs and the maximum amount of time TCP is allowed to wait before sending an ACK can be configured, depending on the host operating system. Linux uses a dynamic adjustment algorithm whereby it can change between ACKing every segment (called "quickack" mode) and conventional delayed ACK mode. On Mac OS X, the system variable `net.inet.tcp.delayed_ack` determines how delayed ACKs are to be used. The values work as follows: disable delay (0), always delay (1), ACK every other packet (2), and autodetect when to respond (3). The default is 3. On recent versions of Windows, the registry entries under

`HKLM\SYSTEM\CurrentControlSet\Services\Tcpip\Parameters\Interfaces\IG`

(where *IG* refers to the GUID of the particular network interface being referenced) for each interface GUID work a bit differently. The value for `TcpAckFrequency` (which needs to be added) can range from 0 to 255 and defaults to 2. It determines the number of ACKs outstanding before the delayed ACK timer is ignored. Setting the value to 1 effectively causes ACKs to be generated for every segment received. The ACK timer, when used, can be controlled with the `TcpDelAckTicks` registry entry. This value can be set in the range from 2 to 6 and defaults to 2. It is the number of hundreds of milliseconds to wait before sending a delayed ACK.

For the reasons mentioned earlier, TCP is generally set up to delay ACKs under certain circumstances, but not to delay them too long. We will see extensive use of delayed ACKs in Chapter 16, when we look at how TCP's congestion control behaves during bulk transfers with large packets. When smaller packets are used, such as for interactive applications, another algorithm comes into play. The combination of this algorithm with delayed ACKs can lead to poor performance if not handled carefully, so we will now look at it in more detail.

15.4 Nagle Algorithm

We saw in the previous section that as little as one keystroke at a time often flows from the client to the server across an ssh connection. When using IPv4, sending one single key press generates TCP/IPv4 packets of about 88 bytes in size (using the encryption and authentication from the example): 20 bytes for the IP header, 20 bytes for the TCP header (assuming no options), and 48 bytes of data. These small packets (called *tinygrams*) have a relatively high overhead for the network. That is, they contain relatively little useful application data compared to the rest of the packet contents. Such high-overhead packets are normally not a problem on LANs, because most LANs are not congested and such packets would not need to be carried very far. However, these tinygrams can add to congestion and lead to inefficient use of capacity on wide area networks. A simple and elegant solution was proposed by John Nagle in [RFC0896], now called the *Nagle algorithm*. First we will describe how it operates, and then we will discuss some pitfalls and problems that can occur as a result of using it with delayed ACKs.

The Nagle algorithm says that when a TCP connection has outstanding data that has not yet been acknowledged, small segments (those smaller than the SMSS) cannot be sent until all outstanding data is acknowledged. Instead, small amounts of data are collected by TCP and sent in a single segment when an acknowledgment arrives. This procedure effectively forces TCP into *stop-and-wait* behavior—it stops sending until an ACK is received for any outstanding data. The beauty of this algorithm is that it is *self-clocking*: the faster the ACKs come back, the faster the data is sent. On a comparatively high-delay WAN, where reducing the number of tinygrams is desirable, fewer segments are sent per unit time. Said another way, the RTT controls the packet sending rate.

We saw in Figure 15-3 that the RTT for a single byte to be sent, acknowledged, and echoed can be small (under 15ms). To generate data faster than this we would have to type more than 60 characters per second. This means that we rarely encounter any observable effects of this algorithm when sending data between two hosts with a small RTT, such as when they are on the same LAN.

To illustrate the effect of the Nagle algorithm, we can compare the behaviors of an application using TCP with the Nagle algorithm enabled and disabled. We modify a version of the ssh client for this purpose. Using a connection with a relatively large RTT of about 190ms, we can see the differences. First, we examine the case when Nagle is disabled (the default for ssh), as shown in Figure 15-4.

```
ssh-nagle-off.td - Wireshark
File  Edit  View  Go  Capture  Analyze  Statistics  Telephony  Tools  Help

No.  Time       Source           Destination       Protocol  Info
  1  0.000000   70.231.143.234   193.10.133.128    TCP       1055 > 22 [PSH, ACK] Seq=1 Ack=1 Win=8320 Len=48 TSV=134534
  2  0.069366   70.231.143.234   193.10.133.128    TCP       1055 > 22 [PSH, ACK] Seq=49 Ack=1 Win=8320 Len=48 TSV=1345
  3  0.189457   193.10.133.128   70.231.143.234    TCP       22 > 1055 [PSH, ACK] Seq=1 Ack=49 Win=10880 Len=48 TSV=213
  4  0.189706   70.231.143.234   193.10.133.128    TCP       1055 > 22 [ACK] Seq=97 Ack=49 Win=8320 Len=0 TSV=134535023
  5  0.202758   70.231.143.234   193.10.133.128    TCP       1055 > 22 [PSH, ACK] Seq=97 Ack=49 Win=8320 Len=48 TSV=134
  6  0.232567   70.231.143.234   193.10.133.128    TCP       1055 > 22 [PSH, ACK] Seq=145 Ack=49 Win=8320 Len=48 TSV=134
  7  0.260124   193.10.133.128   70.231.143.234    TCP       22 > 1055 [PSH, ACK] Seq=49 Ack=97 Win=10880 Len=48 TSV=21
  8  0.300289   70.231.143.234   193.10.133.128    TCP       1055 > 22 [ACK] Seq=193 Ack=97 Win=8320 Len=0 TSV=134535134
  9  0.377729   70.231.143.234   193.10.133.128    TCP       1055 > 22 [PSH, ACK] Seq=193 Ack=97 Win=8320 Len=48 TSV=134
 10  0.393425   193.10.133.128   70.231.143.234    TCP       22 > 1055 [PSH, ACK] Seq=97 Ack=145 Win=10880 Len=48 TSV=2
 11  0.393647   70.231.143.234   193.10.133.128    TCP       1055 > 22 [ACK] Seq=241 Ack=145 Win=8320 Len=0 TSV=13453527
 12  0.421981   193.10.133.128   70.231.143.234    TCP       22 > 1055 [PSH, ACK] Seq=145 Ack=193 Win=10880 Len=48 TSV=
 13  0.422435   70.231.143.234   193.10.133.128    TCP       1055 > 22 [ACK] Seq=241 Ack=193 Win=8320 Len=0 TSV=13453529
 14  0.567368   193.10.133.128   70.231.143.234    TCP       22 > 1055 [PSH, ACK] Seq=193 Ack=241 Win=10880 Len=48 TSV=
 15  0.567784   70.231.143.234   193.10.133.128    TCP       1055 > 22 [ACK] Seq=241 Ack=241 Win=8320 Len=0 TSV=13453540
 16  0.572460   193.10.133.128   70.231.143.234    TCP       22 > 1055 [PSH, ACK] Seq=241 Ack=305 Win=10880 Len=0 TSV=13453540
 17  0.572797   70.231.143.234   193.10.133.128    TCP       1055 > 22 [ACK] Seq=241 Ack=305 Win=10880 Len=112 TSV
 18  0.581490   193.10.133.128   70.231.143.234    TCP       22 > 1055 [PSH, ACK] Seq=241 Ack=305 Win=8320 Len=0 TSV=13453541
 19  0.581905   70.231.143.234   193.10.133.128    TCP       1055 > 22 [ACK] Seq=241 Ack=417 Win=8320 Len=0 TSV=13453541
```

Figure 15-4   An ssh trace showing a TCP connection with approximately a 190ms RTT. The Nagle algorithm is disabled. Transmissions and ACKs are intermingled, and the exchange takes 0.58s using 19 packets. Many packets are relatively small (48 bytes of user data). Pure ACKs (segments with no data) indicate that command output at the server has been processed by the client.

The trace in Figure 15-4 begins after the initial authentication protocol has completed and the login session has begun. The date command is then typed. We see that 19 packets are captured, and the entire exchange lasts 0.58s. There are five ssh request packets, seven ssh response packets, and seven TCP-level pure ACKs (no data). If we repeat this measurement soon after (i.e., in similar network conditions), but instead leave the Nagle algorithm enabled, we see the behavior shown in Figure 15-5.

We can see immediately that the number of packets in Figure 15-5 is smaller than in Figure 15-4 (by eight). The other striking difference is the regularity of how the requests and responses are ordered and separated by time. Recall that the Nagle algorithm forces TCP to operate in a stop-and-wait fashion, so that the TCP sender cannot proceed until ACKs are received. If we look at the times for each request/response pair—0.0, 0.19, 0.38, and 0.57—we see that they follow a pattern; each is separated by almost exactly 190ms, which is very close to the RTT of the connection. The consequence of having to wait one RTT for each request/response adds to the overall time to complete the exchange (0.80s instead of the 0.58s when Nagle was disabled). This is the trade-off the Nagle algorithm makes: fewer and larger packets are used, but the required delay is higher. The different behaviors can be seen even more clearly in Figure 15-6.

The effect of the Nagle algorithm's stop-and-wait behavior can be seen clearly in Figure 15-6. The exchange on the left side keeps both directions of the connection busy, while with the Nagle algorithm enabled only one direction of the connection is busy at any given time.

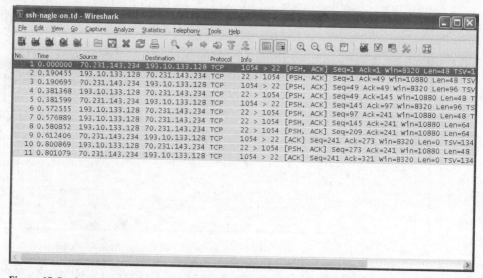

Figure 15-5 An ssh trace showing a TCP connection with a 190ms RTT and the Nagle algorithm in operation. Requests are followed in lockstep with responses, and the exchange takes 0.80s using 11 packets.

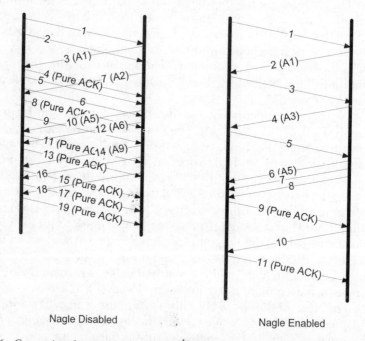

Nagle Disabled   Nagle Enabled

Figure 15-6 Comparing the use of the Nagle algorithm for TCP connections with a similar operating environment. With Nagle enabled, at most one packet is allowed to be outstanding at any given time. This reduces the number of small packets but increases delay.

15.4.1 Delayed ACK and Nagle Algorithm Interaction

If we consider what happens when the delayed ACK and Nagle algorithms are used together, we can construct an undesirable scenario. Consider a client using delayed ACKs that sends a request to a server, and the server responds with an amount of data that does not quite fit inside a single packet (see Figure 15-7).

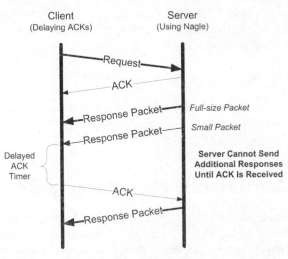

Figure 15-7   The interaction between the Nagle algorithm and delayed ACKs. A temporary form of deadlock can occur until the delayed ACK timer fires.

Here we see that the client, after receiving two packets from the server, withholds an ACK, hoping that additional data headed toward the server can be piggybacked. Generally, TCP is required to provide an ACK for two received packets only if they are full-size, and they are not here. At the server side, because the Nagle algorithm is operating, no additional packets are permitted to be sent to the client until an ACK is returned because at most one "small" packet is allowed to be outstanding. The combination of delayed ACKs and the Nagle algorithm leads to a form of *deadlock* (each side waiting for the other) [MMSV99][MM01]. Fortunately, this deadlock is not permanent and is broken when the delayed ACK timer fires, which forces the client to provide an ACK even if the client has no additional data to send. However, the entire data transfer becomes idle during this deadlock period, which is usually not desirable. The Nagle algorithm can be disabled in such circumstances, as we saw with ssh.

15.4.2 Disabling the Nagle Algorithm

As we might conclude from the previous example, there are times when the Nagle algorithm needs to be turned off. Typical examples include cases where as little delay as possible is required, for example, when a mouse movement or keystroke must be delivered without delay to provide real-time feedback for a user whose display is handled remotely. Another example is in multiplayer online games, where character movements must be delivered as quickly as possible so as to not interfere with proper causality in the game (and to not delay it too much for other players).

The Nagle algorithm can be disabled in a number of ways. The ability to disable it is required by the Host Requirements RFC [RFC1122]. An application can specify the TCP_NODELAY option when using the Berkeley sockets API. In addition, it is possible to disable the Nagle algorithm on a system-wide basis. In Windows, this can be accomplished using the following registry key:

```
HKLM\SOFTWARE\Microsoft\MSMQ\Parameters\TCPNoDelay
```

This DWORD value, which must be added by the user, should be set to the value 1 in order to disable the Nagle algorithm. Message Queuing may have to be installed for this change to be effective [MMQ].

15.5   Flow Control and Window Management

Recall from Chapter 12 that a variable sliding window can be used to implement flow control. In Figure 15-8, a TCP client and server are interacting, providing each other with information about the data flow, including segment sequence numbers, ACK numbers, and window sizes (i.e., available space at the receiver).

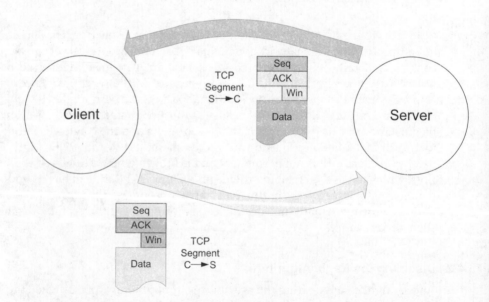

Figure 15-8   Each TCP connection is bidirectional. Data going in one direction causes the peer to respond with ACKs and window advertisements. The same is true for the reverse direction.

The two large arrows in Figure 15-8 indicate the direction of data flow (the direction in which TCP segments are sent). Recalling that every TCP connection has data flowing in both directions, we have two arrows, one in the client-to-server direction (C→S) and another in the server-to-client direction (S→C). Every segment contains ACK and window information and may also contain some user data. The fields used in the TCP header are shaded based on the direction of data flow they describe. For example, data flowing in the C→S direction is included in segments flowing along the bottom arrow, but the ACK number and window advertisement for this data are returned in segments following the top arrow. Every TCP segment (except those exchanged during connection establishment) includes a valid *Sequence Number* field, an *ACK Number* or *Acknowledgment* field, and a *Window Size* field (containing the window advertisement).

In each of the `ssh` examples in this chapter so far, we have seen an unchanging window advertisement conveyed from one TCP peer to the other. Examples include 8320 bytes, 4220 bytes, and 32,900 bytes. These sizes represent the amount of space the sender of the segment has reserved for storing incoming data the peer sends. When TCP-based applications are not busy doing other things, they are typically able to consume any and all data TCP has received and queued for them, leading to no change of the *Window Size* field as the connection progresses. On slow systems, or when the application has other things to accomplish, data may have arrived for the application, been acknowledged by TCP, and be sitting in a queue waiting for the application to read or "consume" it. When TCP starts to queue data in this way, the amount of space available to hold new incoming data decreases, and this change is reflected by a decreasing value of the *Window Size* field. Eventually, if the application does not read or otherwise consume the data at all, TCP must take some action to cause the sender to cease sending new data entirely, because there would be no place to put it on arrival. This is accomplished by sending a window advertisement of zero (no space).

The *Window Size* field in each TCP header indicates the amount of empty space, in bytes, remaining in the receive buffer. The field is 16 bits in TCP, but with the Window Scale option, values larger than 65,535 can be used (see Chapter 13). The largest sequence number the sender of a segment is willing to accept in the reverse direction is equal to the sum of the *Acknowledgment Number* and *Window Size* fields in the TCP header (scaled appropriately).

15.5.1   Sliding Windows

Each endpoint of a TCP connection is capable of sending and receiving data. The amount of data sent or received on a connection is maintained by a set of *window structures*. For each active connection, each TCP endpoint maintains a *send window structure* and a *receive window structure*. These structures are similar to the conceptual window structures described in Chapter 12, but here we describe them in more detail. Figure 15-9 shows a hypothetical TCP send window structure.

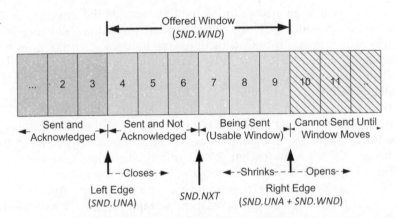

Figure 15-9   The TCP sender-side sliding window structure keeps track of which sequence numbers have already been acknowledged, which are in flight, and which are yet to be sent. The size of the offered window is controlled by the *Window Size* field sent by the receiver in each ACK.

TCP maintains its window structures in terms of bytes (not packets). In Figure 15-9 we have numbered the bytes 2 through 11. The window advertised by the receiver is called the *offered window* and covers bytes 4 through 9, meaning that the receiver has acknowledged all bytes up through and including number 3 and has advertised a window size of 6. Recall from Chapter 12 that the *Window Size* field contains a byte offset relative to the ACK number. The sender computes its *usable window*, which is how much data it can send immediately. The usable window is the offered window minus the amount of data already sent but not yet acknowledged. The variables SND.UNA and SND.WND are used to hold the values of the left window edge and offered window. The variable SND.NXT holds the next sequence number to be sent, so the usable window is equal to (SND.UNA + SND.WND – SND.NXT).

Over time this sliding window moves to the right, as the receiver acknowledges data. The relative motion of the two ends of the window increases or decreases the size of the window. Three terms are used to describe the movement of the right and left edges of the window:

1. The window *closes* as the left edge advances to the right. This happens when data that has been sent is acknowledged and the window size gets smaller.

2. The window *opens* when the right edge moves to the right, allowing more data to be sent. This happens when the receiving process on the other end reads acknowledged data, freeing up space in its TCP receive buffer.

3. The window *shrinks* when the right edge moves to the left. The Host Requirements RFC [RFC1122] strongly discourages this, but TCP must be able to cope with it. Section 15.5.3 on silly window syndrome shows an example where one side would like to shrink the window by moving the right edge to the left but cannot.

Because every TCP segment contains both an ACK number and a window advertisement, a TCP sender adjusts the window structure based on both values whenever an incoming segment arrives. The left edge of the window cannot move to the left, because this edge is controlled by the ACK number received from the other end that is cumulative and never goes backward. When the ACK number advances the window but the window size does not change (a common case), the window is said to advance or "slide" forward. If the ACK number advances but the window advertisement grows smaller with other arriving ACKs, the left edge of the window moves closer to the right edge. If the left edge reaches the right edge, it is called a zero window. This stops the sender from transmitting any data. If this happens, the sending TCP begins to *probe* the peer's window (see Section 15.5.2) to look for an increase in the offered window.

The receiver also keeps a window structure, which is somewhat simpler than the sender's. The receiver window structure keeps track of what data has already been received and ACKed, as well as the maximum sequence number it is willing to receive. The TCP receiver depends on this structure to ensure the correctness of the data it receives. In particular, it wishes to avoid storing duplicate bytes it has already received and ACKed, and it also wishes to avoid storing bytes that it should not have received (any bytes beyond the sender's right window edge). The receiver's window structure is illustrated in Figure 15-10.

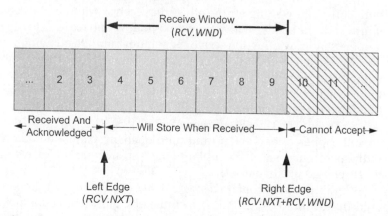

Figure 15-10   The TCP receiver-side sliding window structure helps the receiver know which sequence numbers to expect next. Sequence numbers in the receive window are stored when received. Those outside the window are discarded.

This structure also contains a left and right window edge like the sender's window, but the in-window bytes (4–9 in this picture) need not be differentiated as they are in the sender's window structure. For the receiver, any bytes received with sequence numbers less than the left window edge (called RCV.NXT) are discarded as duplicates, and any bytes received with sequence numbers beyond the right window edge (RCV.WND bytes beyond RCV.NXT) are discarded as out of scope. Bytes arriving with any sequence number in the receive window range are accepted. Note that the ACK number generated at the receiver may be advanced only when segments fill in directly at the left window edge because of TCP's cumulative ACK structure. With selective ACKs, other in-window segments can be acknowledged using the TCP SACK option, but ultimately the ACK number itself is advanced only when data contiguous to the left window edge is received (see Chapter 14 for more details on SACK).

15.5.2 Zero Windows and the TCP Persist Timer

We have seen that TCP implements flow control by having the receiver specify the amount of data it is willing to accept from the sender: the receiver's advertised window. When the receiver's advertised window goes to zero, the sender is effectively stopped from transmitting data until the window becomes nonzero. When the receiver once again has space available, it provides a *window update* to the sender to indicate that data is permitted to flow once again. Because such updates do not generally contain data (they are a form of "pure ACK"), they are not reliably delivered by TCP. TCP must therefore handle the case where such window updates that would open the window are lost.

If an acknowledgment (containing a window update) is lost, we could end up with both sides waiting for the other: the receiver waiting to receive data (because it provided the sender with a nonzero window and expects to see incoming data) and the sender waiting to receive the window update allowing it to send. To prevent this form of deadlock from occurring, the sender uses a *persist timer* to query the receiver periodically, to find out if the window size has increased. The persist timer triggers the transmission of *window probes*. Window probes are segments that force the receiver to provide an ACK, which also necessarily contains a *Window Size* field. The Host Requirements RFC [RFC1122] suggests that the first probe should happen after one RTO and subsequent problems should occur at exponentially spaced intervals (i.e., similar to the "second part" of Karn's algorithm, which we discussed in Chapter 14).

Window probes contain a single byte of data and are therefore reliably delivered (retransmitted) by TCP if lost, thereby eliminating the potential deadlock condition caused by lost window updates. The probes are sent whenever the TCP persist timer expires, and the byte included may or may not be accepted by the receiver, depending on how much buffer space it has available. As with the TCP retransmission timer (see Chapter 14), the normal exponential backoff can be used when calculating the timeout for the persist timer. An important difference, however, is that a normal TCP never gives up sending window probes, whereas it may eventually give up trying to perform retransmissions. This can lead to a certain resource exhaustion vulnerability that we discuss in Section 15.7.

15.5.2.1 Example

To illustrate the use of the dynamic window size adjustment and flow control in TCP, we create a TCP connection and cause the receiving process to pause before consuming data from the network. For this experiment, we use a Mac OS X 10.6 sender and a Windows 7 receiver. The receiver runs our sock program with the –P flag as follows:

```
C:\> sock -i -s -P 20 6666
```

This arranges for the receiver to pause 20s prior to consuming data from the network. The result is that eventually the receiver's advertised window begins to close, as shown with packet 125 in Figure 15-11.

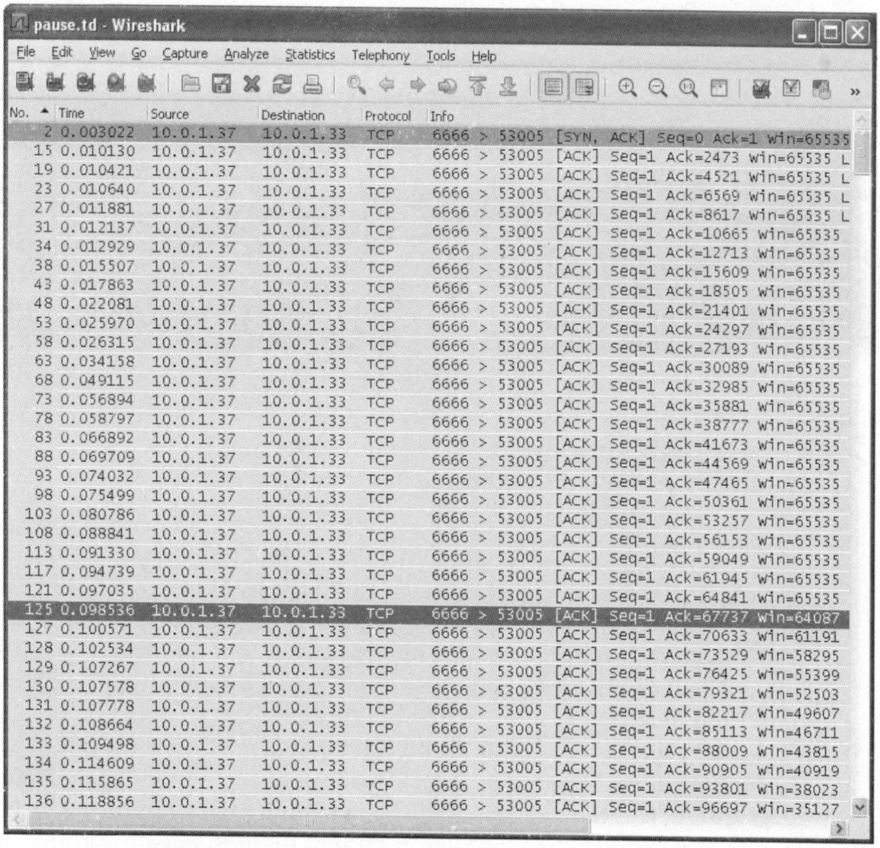

```
pause.td - Wireshark                                                    _ □ X

File  Edit  View  Go  Capture  Analyze  Statistics  Telephony  Tools  Help

No. ▲ Time      Source       Destination   Protocol  Info
    2 0.003022  10.0.1.37    10.0.1.33     TCP       6666 > 53005 [SYN, ACK] Seq=0 Ack=1 Win=65535
   15 0.010130  10.0.1.37    10.0.1.33     TCP       6666 > 53005 [ACK] Seq=1 Ack=2473 Win=65535 L
   19 0.010421  10.0.1.37    10.0.1.33     TCP       6666 > 53005 [ACK] Seq=1 Ack=4521 Win=65535 L
   23 0.010640  10.0.1.37    10.0.1.33     TCP       6666 > 53005 [ACK] Seq=1 Ack=6569 Win=65535 L
   27 0.011881  10.0.1.37    10.0.1.33     TCP       6666 > 53005 [ACK] Seq=1 Ack=8617 Win=65535 L
   31 0.012137  10.0.1.37    10.0.1.33     TCP       6666 > 53005 [ACK] Seq=1 Ack=10665 Win=65535
   34 0.012929  10.0.1.37    10.0.1.33     TCP       6666 > 53005 [ACK] Seq=1 Ack=12713 Win=65535
   38 0.015507  10.0.1.37    10.0.1.33     TCP       6666 > 53005 [ACK] Seq=1 Ack=15609 Win=65535
   43 0.017863  10.0.1.37    10.0.1.33     TCP       6666 > 53005 [ACK] Seq=1 Ack=18505 Win=65535
   48 0.022081  10.0.1.37    10.0.1.33     TCP       6666 > 53005 [ACK] Seq=1 Ack=21401 Win=65535
   53 0.025970  10.0.1.37    10.0.1.33     TCP       6666 > 53005 [ACK] Seq=1 Ack=24297 Win=65535
   58 0.026315  10.0.1.37    10.0.1.33     TCP       6666 > 53005 [ACK] Seq=1 Ack=27193 Win=65535
   63 0.034158  10.0.1.37    10.0.1.33     TCP       6666 > 53005 [ACK] Seq=1 Ack=30089 Win=65535
   68 0.049115  10.0.1.37    10.0.1.33     TCP       6666 > 53005 [ACK] Seq=1 Ack=32985 Win=65535
   73 0.056894  10.0.1.37    10.0.1.33     TCP       6666 > 53005 [ACK] Seq=1 Ack=35881 Win=65535
   78 0.058797  10.0.1.37    10.0.1.33     TCP       6666 > 53005 [ACK] Seq=1 Ack=38777 Win=65535
   83 0.066892  10.0.1.37    10.0.1.33     TCP       6666 > 53005 [ACK] Seq=1 Ack=41673 Win=65535
   88 0.069709  10.0.1.37    10.0.1.33     TCP       6666 > 53005 [ACK] Seq=1 Ack=44569 Win=65535
   93 0.074032  10.0.1.37    10.0.1.33     TCP       6666 > 53005 [ACK] Seq=1 Ack=47465 Win=65535
   98 0.075499  10.0.1.37    10.0.1.33     TCP       6666 > 53005 [ACK] Seq=1 Ack=50361 Win=65535
  103 0.080786  10.0.1.37    10.0.1.33     TCP       6666 > 53005 [ACK] Seq=1 Ack=53257 Win=65535
  108 0.088841  10.0.1.37    10.0.1.33     TCP       6666 > 53005 [ACK] Seq=1 Ack=56153 Win=65535
  113 0.091330  10.0.1.37    10.0.1.33     TCP       6666 > 53005 [ACK] Seq=1 Ack=59049 Win=65535
  117 0.094739  10.0.1.37    10.0.1.33     TCP       6666 > 53005 [ACK] Seq=1 Ack=61945 Win=65535
  121 0.097035  10.0.1.37    10.0.1.33     TCP       6666 > 53005 [ACK] Seq=1 Ack=64841 Win=65535
  125 0.098536  10.0.1.37    10.0.1.33     TCP       6666 > 53005 [ACK] Seq=1 Ack=67737 Win=64087
  127 0.100571  10.0.1.37    10.0.1.33     TCP       6666 > 53005 [ACK] Seq=1 Ack=70633 Win=61191
  128 0.102534  10.0.1.37    10.0.1.33     TCP       6666 > 53005 [ACK] Seq=1 Ack=73529 Win=58295
  129 0.107267  10.0.1.37    10.0.1.33     TCP       6666 > 53005 [ACK] Seq=1 Ack=76425 Win=55399
  130 0.107578  10.0.1.37    10.0.1.33     TCP       6666 > 53005 [ACK] Seq=1 Ack=79321 Win=52503
  131 0.107778  10.0.1.37    10.0.1.33     TCP       6666 > 53005 [ACK] Seq=1 Ack=82217 Win=49607
  132 0.108664  10.0.1.37    10.0.1.33     TCP       6666 > 53005 [ACK] Seq=1 Ack=85113 Win=46711
  133 0.109498  10.0.1.37    10.0.1.33     TCP       6666 > 53005 [ACK] Seq=1 Ack=88009 Win=43815
  134 0.114609  10.0.1.37    10.0.1.33     TCP       6666 > 53005 [ACK] Seq=1 Ack=90905 Win=40919
  135 0.115865  10.0.1.37    10.0.1.33     TCP       6666 > 53005 [ACK] Seq=1 Ack=93801 Win=38023
  136 0.118856  10.0.1.37    10.0.1.33     TCP       6666 > 53005 [ACK] Seq=1 Ack=96697 Win=35127
```

Figure 15-11   After a period when the advertised window does not change, acknowledgments continue but the window size grows smaller as the receiver's buffer fills up. If the receiving application fails to consume any data and the sender continues, the window eventually reaches zero.

In this trace we see that for more than 100 packets the receiver's window remains pegged at 64KB. This is because of an automatic window adjustment algorithm (see Section 15.5.4) that allocates memory to the receiving TCP even if not requested by the application. However, this eventually runs short, so we see the window begin to reduce starting with packet 125. A large number of ACKs follow, each reducing the window further while increasing the ACK number by 2896 bytes per ACK. This indicates that the receiving TCP is storing the data, but the application is not consuming it. If we look further into the trace, we see that eventually the receiver has no more space to hold the incoming data (see Figure 15-12).

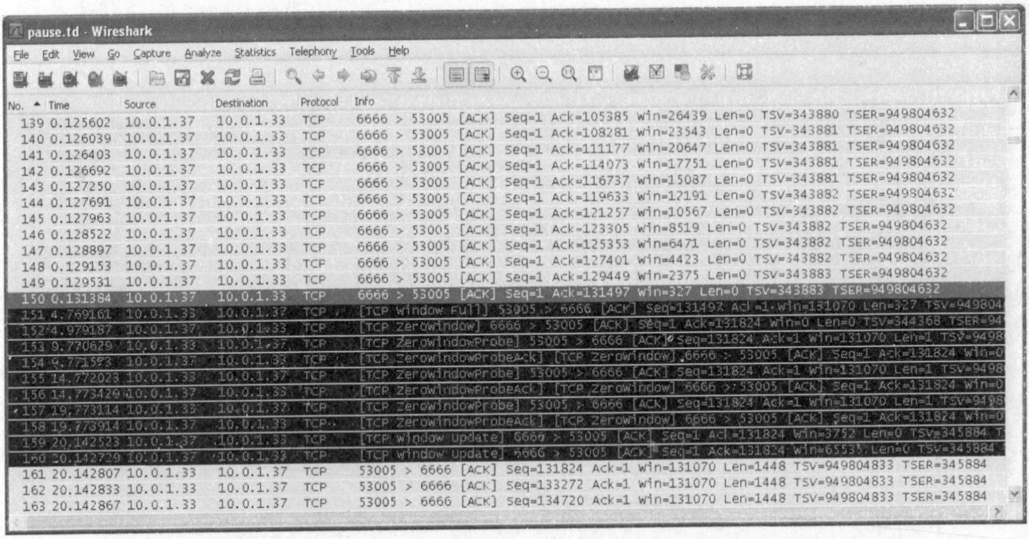

Figure 15-12   The receiver's buffer has filled up. When the receiving application starts reading again, a window update tells the sender that there is now an opportunity to transfer more data.

Here we can see that packet 151 fills the small 327-byte window, as indicated by the TCP Window Full comment provided by Wireshark. After about 200ms, at time 4.979, a zero window advertisement is produced, indicating that no more data can be received. This is no surprise, given that the sender has filled the last known available window and the receiving application will not consume any data until time 20.143.

After receiving the zero window advertisement, the sending TCP tries to probe the receiver three times at 5s intervals to see if the window has opened. At time 20, as instructed, the receiver begins to consume the data present in TCP's queue. This causes two window updates to be sent to the sender, indicating that further data transmission (up to 64KB) is now possible. Such segments are called window updates because they do not acknowledge any new data—they just advance the right edge of the window. At this point, the sender is able to resume normal data transmission and complete the transfer.

There are numerous points that we can summarize using Figures 15-11 and 15-12:

1. The sender does not have to transmit a full window's worth of data.

2. A single segment from the receiver acknowledges data and slides the window to the right at the same time. This is because the window advertisement is relative to the ACK number in the same segment.

3. The size of the window can decrease, as shown by the series of ACKs in Figure 15-11, but the right edge of the window does not move left, so as to avoid window shrinkage.

4. The receiver does not have to wait for the window to fill before sending an ACK.

In addition to these points, it is instructive to look at the throughput this connection achieves as a function of time. Using Wireshark's Statistics | TCP Stream Graph | Throughput Graph function, we observe the time series as shown in Figure 15-13.

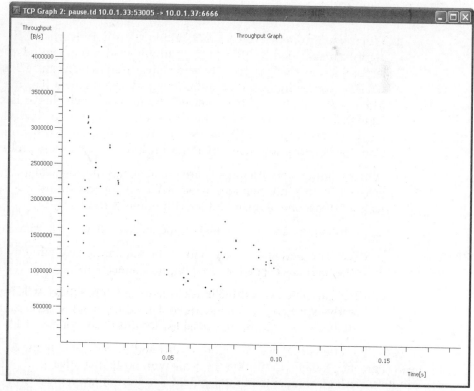

Figure 15-13 With a relatively large receive buffer, a significant amount of data can be transferred even before the receiving application reads any data from the network.

Here we see an interesting behavior. Even before the receiving application has consumed *any* data, the connection still achieves a throughput of approximately 1.3MB/s. This continues until approximately time 0.10. After that, the throughput is essentially zero until the receiver begins consuming data much later (after time 20).

15.5.3 Silly Window Syndrome (SWS)

Window-based flow control schemes, especially those that do not use fixed-size segments (such as TCP), can fall victim to a condition known as the *silly window syndrome* (SWS). When it occurs, small data segments are exchanged across the connection instead of full-size segments [RFC0813]. This leads to undesirable inefficiency because each segment has relatively high overhead—a small number of data bytes relative to the number of bytes in the headers.

SWS can be caused by either end of a TCP connection: the receiver can advertise small windows (instead of waiting until a larger window can be advertised), and the sender can transmit small data segments (instead of waiting for additional data to send a larger segment). Correct avoidance of silly window syndrome requires a TCP to implement rules specifically for this purpose, whether operating as a sender or a receiver. TCP never knows ahead of time how a peer TCP will behave. The following rules are applied:

1. When operating as a receiver, small windows are not advertised. The receive algorithm specified by [RFC1122] is to not send a segment advertising a larger window than is currently being advertised (which can be 0) until the window can be increased by either one full-size segment (i.e., the receive MSS) or by one-half of the receiver's buffer space, whichever is smaller. Note that there are two cases where this rule can come into play: when buffer space has become available because of an application consuming data from the network, and when TCP must respond to a window probe.

2. When sending, small segments are not sent and the Nagle algorithm governs when to send. Senders avoid SWS by not transmitting a segment unless at least one of the following conditions is true:

   a. A full-size (send MSS bytes) segment can be sent.

   b. TCP can send at least one-half of the maximum-size window that the other end has ever advertised on this connection.

   c. TCP can send everything it has to send and either (i) an ACK is not currently expected (i.e., we have no outstanding unacknowledged data) or (ii) the Nagle algorithm is disabled for this connection.

Condition (a) is the most straightforward and directly avoids the high-overhead segment problem. Condition (b) deals with hosts that always advertise tiny windows, perhaps smaller than the segment size. Condition (c) prevents TCP from sending small segments when there is unacknowledged data waiting to be ACKed and the Nagle algorithm is enabled. If the sending application is doing small writes (e.g., smaller than the segment size), condition (c) avoids silly window syndrome.

These three conditions also let us answer the following question: If the Nagle algorithm prevents us from sending small segments while there is outstanding unacknowledged data, how small is small? From condition (a) we see that "small" means that the number of bytes is less than the SMSS (i.e., the largest packet size that does not exceed the PMTU or the receiver's MSS). Condition (b) comes into play only with older, primitive hosts or when a small advertised window is used because of a limited receive buffer size.

Condition (b) of step 2 requires that the sender keep track of the maximum window size advertised by the other end. This is an attempt by the sender to guess the size of the other end's receive buffer. Although the size of the receive buffer could decrease while the connection is established, in practice this is rare. Furthermore, recall that TCP avoids window shrinkage.

15.5.3.1 Example

We will now present a detailed example to see silly window syndrome avoidance in action; this example also involves the persist timer. We will use our sock program with a Windows XP sending host and a FreeBSD receiver, doing three 2048-byte writes to the network. The command at the sender is as follows:

```
C:\> sock -i -n 3 -w 2048 10.0.0.8 6666
```

The corresponding command at the receiver is

```
FreeBSD% sock -i -s -P 15 -p 2 -r 256 -R 3000 6666
```

This fixes the receive buffer at 3000 bytes, causes an initial delay of 15s before reading from the network, injects 2s of delay between each read, and sets each read amount to be 256 bytes. The reason for the initial pause is to let the receiver's buffer fill, ultimately forcing the transmitter to stop. By having the receiver then perform small reads from the network, we expect to see it perform silly window syndrome avoidance. Figure 15-14 is the trace as displayed by Wireshark.

The contents of the entire connection are displayed in the figure. Packet lengths are described in terms of how many TCP payload bytes are included in each segment. During connection establishment, the receiver advertises a window of 3000 bytes with an MSS of 1460 bytes. The sender sends a 1460-byte packet (packet 4) at time 0.052 and 588 bytes (packet 5) at time 0.053. The sum of these sizes equals the 2048-byte write size used by the application. Packet 6 acknowledges both data packets from the sender and provides a window advertisement of 952 bytes (3000 − 1460 − 588 = 952).

The 952-byte window (packet 6) is not as large as a full MSS, so the Nagle algorithm at the sender prevents filling it immediately. Instead, we see a delay

```
sws-demonstrate.td - Wireshark

File  Edit  View  Go  Capture  Analyze  Statistics  Telephony  Tools  Help

No.  Time       Source      Destination  Protocol  Info
  1  0.000000   10.0.0.100  10.0.0.8     TCP   3699 > 6666 [SYN] Seq=0 Win=65535 Len=0 MSS=1460 SACK_PERM=1
  2  0.000332   10.0.0.8    10.0.0.100   TCP   6666 > 3699 [SYN, ACK] Seq=0 Ack=1 Win=3000 Len=0 MSS=1460 SACK_PERM=1
  3  0.001106   10.0.0.100  10.0.0.8     TCP   3699 > 6666 [ACK] Seq=1 Ack=1 Win=65535 Len=0
  4  0.052667   10.0.0.100  10.0.0.8     TCP   3699 > 6666 [ACK] Seq=1 Ack=1 Win=65535 Len=1460
  5  0.053057   10.0.0.100  10.0.0.8     TCP   3699 > 6666 [PSH, ACK] Seq=1461 Ack=1 Win=65535 Len=588
  6  0.053145   10.0.0.8    10.0.0.100   TCP   6666 > 3699 [ACK] Seq=1 Ack=2049 Win=952 Len=0
  7  5.066108   10.0.0.100  10.0.0.8     TCP   3699 > 6666 [ACK] Seq=2049 Ack=1 Win=65535 Len=952
  8  5.160715   10.0.0.8    10.0.0.100   TCP   [TCP ZeroWindow] 6666 > 3699 [ACK] Seq=1 Ack=3001 Win=0 Len=0
  9  6.970589   10.0.0.100  10.0.0.8     TCP   [TCP ZeroWindowProbe] 3699 > 6666 [ACK] Seq=3001 Ack=1 Win=65535 Len=1
 10  6.970734   10.0.0.8    10.0.0.100   TCP   [TCP ZeroWindowProbeAck] [TCP ZeroWindow] 6666 > 3699 [ACK] Seq=1 Ack=3001 Win=0
 11 10.782520   10.0.0.100  10.0.0.8     TCP   [TCP ZeroWindowProbe] 3699 > 6666 [ACK] Seq=3001 Ack=1 Win=65535 Len=1
 12 10.782692   10.0.0.8    10.0.0.100   TCP   [TCP ZeroWindowProbeAck] [TCP ZeroWindow] 6666 > 3699 [ACK] Seq=1 Ack=3001 Win=0
 13 18.408217   10.0.0.100  10.0.0.8     TCP   [TCP ZeroWindowProbe] 3699 > 6666 [ACK] Seq=3001 Ack=1 Win=65535 Len=1
 14 18.408384   10.0.0.8    10.0.0.100   TCP   [TCP ZeroWindow] [TCP ACKed lost segment] 6666 > 3699 [ACK] Seq=1 Ack=3002 Win=0
 15 25.061290   10.0.0.8    10.0.0.100   TCP   [TCP window Update] 6666 > 3699 [ACK] Seq=1 Ack=3002 Win=1535 Len=0
 16 25.064378   10.0.0.100  10.0.0.8     TCP   3699 > 6666 [PSH, ACK] Seq=3002 Ack=1 Win=65535 Len=1460
 17 25.161232   10.0.0.8    1).0.0.100   TCP   6666 > 3699 [ACK] Seq=1 Ack=4462 Win=75 Len=0
 18 30.043950   10.0.0.100  10.0.0.8     TCP   3699 > 6666 [ACK] Seq=4462 Ack=1 Win=65535 Len=75
 19 30.141368   10.0.0.8    10.0.0.100   TCP   [TCP ZeroWindow] 6666 > 3699 [ACK] Seq=1 Ack=4537 Win=0 Len=0
 20 31.548523   10.0.0.100  10.0.0.8     TCP   [TCP ZeroWindowProbe] 3699 > 6666 [ACK] Seq=4537 Ack=1 Win=65535 Len=1
 21 31.548698   10.0.0.8    10.0.0.100   TCP   [TCP ACKed lost segment] 6666 > 3699 [ACK] Seq=1 Ack=4538 Win=767 Len=0
 22 36.574538   10.0.0.100  10.0.0.8     TCP   3699 > 6666 [ACK] Seq=4538 Ack=1 Win=65535 Len=767
 23 36.671539   10.0.0.8    10.0.0.100   TCP   [TCP ZeroWindow] 6666 > 3699 [ACK] Seq=1 Ack=5305 Win=0 Len=0
 24 37.667677   10.0.0.100  10.0.0.8     TCP   [TCP ZeroWindowProbe] 3699 > 6666 [ACK] Seq=5305 Ack=1 Win=65535 Len=1
 25 37.667854   10.0.0.8    10.0.0.100   TCP   [TCP ACKed lost segment] 6666 > 3699 [ACK] Seq=1 Ack=5306 Win=767 Len=0
 26 42.784930   10.0.0.100  10.0.0.8     TCP   3699 > 6666 [ACK] Seq=5306 Ack=1 Win=65535 Len=767
 27 42.881712   10.0.0.8    10.0.0.100   TCP   [TCP ZeroWindow] 6666 > 3699 [ACK] Seq=1 Ack=6073 Win=0 Len=0
 28 43.485876   10.0.0.100  10.0.0.8     TCP   [TCP ZeroWindowProbe] 3699 > 6666 [ACK] Seq=6073 Ack=1 Win=65535 Len=1
 29 43.486016   10.0.0.8    10.0.0.100   TCP   [TCP ACKed lost segment] 6666 > 3699 [ACK] Seq=1 Ack=6074 Win=767 Len=0
 30 43.486822   10.0.0.100  10.0.0.8     TCP   3699 > 6666 [PSH, ACK] Seq=6074 Ack=1 Win=65535 Len=71
 31 43.581711   10.0.0.8    10.0.0.100   TCP   6666 > 3699 [ACK] Seq=1 Ack=6145 Win=696 Len=0
 32 43.711676   10.0.0.100  10.0.0.8     TCP   3699 > 6666 [FIN, ACK] Seq=6145 Ack=1 Win=65535 Len=0
 33 43.711806   10.0.0.8    10.0.0.100   TCP   6666 > 3699 [ACK] Seq=1 Ack=6146 Win=695 Len=0
 34 55.212068   10.0.0.8    10.0.0.100   TCP   [TCP window Update] 6666 > 3699 [ACK] Seq=1 Ack=6146 Win=2232 Len=0
 35 63.252390   10.0.0.8    10.0.0.100   TCP   6666 > 3699 [FIN, ACK] Seq=1 Ack=6146 Win=3000 Len=0
 36 63.253356   10.0.0.100  10.0.0.8     TCP   3699 > 6666 [ACK] Seq=6146 Ack=2 Win=65535 Len=0
```

Figure 15-14 Trace of a TCP transfer illustrating silly window syndrome avoidance. The sender avoids filling the offered window at time 0.053 because of sender-side SWS avoidance. Instead, it waits until time 5.066, also acting effectively as a window probe. Receiver-side SWS avoidance can be seen by looking at packet 14, which advertises a zero window even though the receiver has consumed some data.

of 5s before any further action is taken. The sender waits for 5s, until the persist timer expires, before sending a window probe. Given that the sender is sending a packet anyhow, the sending TCP adds the permitted 952 bytes to fill the available window. This fills the window, as confirmed by the zero window advertisement contained in packet 8.

The next event in the trace is when TCP sends a window probe at time 6.970, about 2s after receiving the first zero window advertisement. The probe itself contains a single data byte and is labeled "TCP ZeroWindowProbe" by Wireshark, but the ACK for this does not move the ACK number forward (Wireshark labels this a "TCP ZeroWindowProbeAck"), so the byte has not been kept at the receiver. Another 1-byte probe is produced at time 10.782 (about 4s later), and another at time 18.408 (about 8s later), showing the characteristic exponential timeout back-off. Note that for this latter window probe, the single byte is acknowledged by the receiver.

At time 25.061, after the application has had a chance to perform six 256-byte reads (spaced 2s apart), a window update indicates that 1535 bytes (plus 1 for the ACK number) are now free in the receiver's buffer. This is "large enough" according to receiver-side SWS avoidance. The sender begins to fill the window, starting with a 1460-byte packet at time 25.064, resulting in an ACK at time 25.161 for byte 4462 with a window advertisement of only 75 bytes (packet 17). This advertisement appears to violate our rule that the amount advertised should be at least an MSS or (in the case of FreeBSD) one-quarter of the total buffer. The reason is to avoid window shrinkage. With the last window update (packet 15), the receiver advertises a right window edge of byte (3002 + 1535) = 4537. If the present ACK (packet 17) were to advertise less than 75 bytes, as would be required by receiver-side SWS avoidance, the right window edge would move left, a condition TCP is not supposed to allow. Consequently the 75-byte advertisement represents a form of override: avoiding window shrinkage is preferred to avoiding SWS.

We see the effect of sender-side SWS avoidance once again with the 5s delay between packets 17 and 18. The sender is forced to send the 75-byte packet and the receiver responds with another zero window advertisement. Packet 20, which appears a second later, is another window probe, which results in a window of 767 bytes. Another round of sender-side SWS avoidance results in a 5s delay; the sender fills the window, again resulting in a zero window; and the pattern repeats. The pattern is eventually broken because the sender has no more data to send. Packet 30 represents the last data sent, and the connection is eventually closed some 20s later (because of the 2s delays between each read at the receiving application).

To understand the relationships among the application behavior, the advertised window, and SWS avoidance, we can capture the connection's dynamics in tabular form. Table 15-1 gives the action at the sender and the receiver, as well as an estimated time when the receiving application performs its reads.

Table 15-1 Dynamics of the window advertisement and application to avoid silly window syndrome

Time	Packet Number	Action			Receive Buffer	
		TCP Sender	TCP Receiver	Application	Data	Available
0.000	1	SYN			0	3000
0.000	2		SYN + ACK 1 win 3000		0	3000
0.001	3	ACK			0	3000
0.052	4	1:1460(1460)			1460	1539
0.053	5	1461:2049(588)			2048	952
0.053	6		ACK 2049 win 952		2048	952
5.066	7	2049:3000(952)			3000	0
5.160	8		ACK 3001 win 0		3000	0

(continues)

Table 15-1   Dynamics of the window advertisement and application to avoid silly window syndrome (*continued*)

Time	Packet Number	Action			Receive Buffer	
		TCP Sender	TCP Receiver	Application	Data	Available
6.970	9	3001:3001(1)			3000	0
6.970	10		ACK 3001 win 0		3000	0
10.782	11	3001:3001(1)			3000	0
10.782	12		ACK 3001 win 0		3000	0
15				256 byte read	2744	256
17				256 byte read	2488	512
18.408	13	3001:3001(1)			2489	511
18.408	14		ACK 3002 win 0		2489	511
19				256 byte read	2233	767
21				256 byte read	1977	1023
23				256 byte read	1721	1279
25				256 byte read	1465	1535
25.061	15		ACK 3002 win 1535		1465	1535
25.064	16	3002:4461(1460)			2925	75
25.161	17		ACK 4462 win 75		2925	75
27				256 byte read	2669	331
29				256 byte read	2413	587
30.043	18	4462:4536(75)			2488	512
30.141	19		ACK 4537 win 0		2488	512
31				256 byte read	2232	768
31.548	20	4537:4537(1)			2233	767
31.548	21		ACK 4538 win 767		2233	767
33				256 byte read	1977	1023
35				256 byte read	1721	1279
36.574	22	4538:5304(767)			2488	512
36.671	23		ACK 5305 win 0		2488	512
37				256 byte read	2232	768
37.667	24	5305:5305(1)			2233	767
37.667	25		ACK 5306 win 767		2233	767
39				256 byte read	1977	1023

Table 15-1 Dynamics of the window advertisement and application to avoid silly window syndrome (*continued*)

Time	Packet Number	Action			Receive Buffer	
		TCP Sender	TCP Receiver	Application	Data	Available
41				256 byte read	1721	1279
42.784	26	5306:6073(767)			2488	512
42.881	27		ACK 6074 win 0		2488	512
43				256 byte read	2232	768
43.485	28	6073:6073(1)			2233	767
43.485	29		ACK 6074 win 767		2233	767
43.486	30	6074:6144(71)			2304	696
43.581	31		ACK 6145 win 696		2304	696
43.711	32	6145 (FIN)				
43.711	33		ACK 6146 win 695		2305	695
45,47,49,51 53,55				6x256 byte read	769	2231
55.212	34		ACK 6146 win 2232		768	2232
57,59,61				3x256 byte read	0	3000
63				0 byte read	0	3000
63.252	35		FIN		0	3000

In Table 15-1, the first column is the relative point in time for each action if it appears in the trace. Those times with three digits to the right of the decimal point are taken from the Wireshark output (refer to Figure 15-16). Those times with no digits to the right of the decimal point are the inferred times of the action on the receiving host, which are not represented in the trace.

The amount of data in the receiver's buffer (labeled "Data" in the table) increases when data arrives from the sender and decreases as the application reads (consumes) data from the buffer. What we want to follow are the window advertisements sent by the receiver to the sender, and what those window advertisements contain. This lets us see how the receiver avoids SWS.

As discussed previously, the first evidence of SWS avoidance is the 5s delay between segments 6 and 7, where the sender avoids trying to send with a 952-byte window until it is forced to. When this happens, the receiver fills up, causing a series of zero window advertisements and window probe exchanges. We can see the exponential backoff on the persist timer in action: probes are sent at times 6.970, 10.782, and 18.408. These are approximately 2, 4, and 8s from when the sender first received the zero window advertisement at time 5.160.

Although the application reads data at times 15 and 17, it has read only 512 bytes by time 18.408. The receiver-side SWS avoidance rules dictate that no window update should be provided to the sender because the available 512 bytes of buffer are neither half the size of the total buffer (3000 bytes) nor at least one MSS (1460 bytes). Lacking a window update, the sender sends a window probe at time 18.408 (segment 13). This probe is received and the byte is kept by the receiver, because some buffer space is available, as verified by the increasing ACK number between segments 12 and 14.

Although 511 bytes are available in the receiver's buffer, receiver-side SWS avoidance kicks in once again. The FreeBSD implementation of receiver SWS avoidance differentiates between when to send a window update and how to respond to a window probe. Although it follows the rules in [RFC1122] and sends a window update only when at least half of the total receive buffer (or an MSS) can be advertised, when responding to a window probe it advertises a larger window when the window is either at least an MSS size or when at least *one-fourth* of the total receive buffer size can be advertised. In either case, the 511 bytes are less than a full MSS and also less than 3000/4 = 750 bytes, so this form of receiver-side SWS avoidance dictates that the window advertisement included in the ACK for segment 13 must contain the value 0.

By the time the application completes its sixth read at time 25, the receive buffer has 1535 bytes free (more than half of the total 3000-byte size), so a window update is sent (segment 15). The sender continues with a full-size segment (segment 16), for which it receives an ACK but a window advertisement of only 75 bytes. In the next 5s, both sender- and receiver-side SWS avoidance takes place. The sender waits for a larger window advertisement, and the application performs reads at times 27 and 29, but the 587 bytes of free receive buffer space are not enough to allow a window update to be sent. The sender therefore has to wait the entire 5s and eventually sends its 75 bytes, forcing the receiver again into SWS avoidance.

With the receiver not providing a window update, the sender's persist timer causes a window probe to be sent at time 31.548. In this case, the FreeBSD receiver responds with a nonzero window, of size 767 bytes (larger than one-fourth of the total receive buffer). This window is not large enough for the sender's SWS avoidance procedure, however, so the sender waits another 5s and the process repeats. Finally, at time 43.486, the last 71 bytes are sent and acknowledged. The acknowledgment contains a window advertisement of 696 bytes. Although it is less than one-quarter of the receiver's total buffer size, the advertisement is not made zero by receiver-side SWS avoidance in order to avoid window shrinkage.

The connection termination begins with segment 32, which contains no data. It is acknowledged immediately with a window advertisement of 695 bytes (the FIN consumed a sequence number at the receiver). After the application completes another six reads, the receiver provides a window update, but the sender is done sending and remains silent. The application performs another four reads, three of which return 256 bytes and the final one of which returns nothing, indicating the end of arriving data. At this point, the receiver closes the connection, causing the FIN to be sent to the sender. The sender responds with the final ACK, completing the bidirectional closing of the connection.

Because the sending application issues a close operation after performing its three 2048-byte writes, the sender's end of the connection goes from the ESTAB-LISHED state to the FIN_WAIT_1 state after sending segment 32 (see Chapter 13). It then goes to the FIN_WAIT_2 state after receiving segment 33. Although it receives a window update while in this state, no action is taken, because it has already sent a FIN that has been acknowledged (there is no timer in this state). Instead, it merely sits in this state until receiving a FIN from the other end. This is why we see no further transmissions by the sender until it receives the FIN (segment 35).

15.5.4 Large Buffers and Auto-Tuning

In this chapter, we have seen that an application using a small receive buffer size may be doomed to significant throughput degradation compared to other applications using TCP in similar conditions. Even if the receiver specifies a large enough buffer, the sender might specify too small a buffer, ultimately leading to bad performance. This problem became so important that many TCP stacks now decouple the allocation of the receive buffer from the size specified by the application. In most cases, the size specified by the application is effectively ignored, and the operating system instead uses either a large fixed value or a dynamically calculated value.

In newer versions of Windows (Vista/7) and Linux, receive window *auto-tuning* [S98] is supported. With auto-tuning, the amount of data that can be outstanding in the connection (its bandwidth-delay product, an important concept we discuss in Chapter 16) is continuously estimated, and the advertised window is arranged to always be at least this large (provided enough buffer space remains to do so). This has the advantage of allowing TCP to achieve its maximum available throughput rate (subject to the available network capacity) without having to allocate excessively large buffers at the sender or receiver ahead of time. In Windows, the receiver's buffer size is auto-sized by the operating system by default. However, the behavior can be modified using the `netsh` command:

```
C:\> netsh interface tcp set heuristics disabled
```

```
C:\> netsh interface tcp set global autotuninglevel=X
```

where X is one of the following: `disabled`, `highlyrestricted`, `restricted`, `normal`, or `experimental`. The setting affects the automatic selection of the receiver's advertised window. In the disabled state, auto-tuning is not used, and the window size uses a default value. The restricted modes slow the window growth, and the normal setting allows it to grow relatively quickly. The experimental mode allows the window to grow very aggressively but is not recommended for normal use because many Internet sites and some firewalls interfere with or fail to implement the TCP Window Scale option properly.

With Linux 2.4 and later, sender-side auto-tuning is supported. With version 2.6.7 and later, both receiver- and sender-side auto-tuning is supported. However, auto-tuning is subject to limits placed on the buffer sizes. The following Linux sysctl variables control the sender and receiver maximum buffer sizes. The values after the equal sign are the default values (which may vary depending on the particular Linux distribution), which should be increased if the system is to be used in high bandwidth-delay-product environments:

```
net.core.rmem_max = 131071
net.core.wmem_max = 131071
net.core.rmem_default = 110592
net.core.wmem_default = 110592
```

In addition, the auto-tuning parameters are given by the following variables:

```
net.ipv4.tcp_rmem = 4096 87380 174760
net.ipv4.tcp_wmem = 4096 16384 131072
```

Each of these variables contains three values: the minimum, default, and maximum buffer size used by auto-tuning.

15.5.4.1 Example

To demonstrate the behavior of receiver auto-tuning, we use a Windows XP sender (set to use large windows and window scaling) and a Linux 2.6.11 receiver that includes auto-tuning. At the sender, we issue the following command:

```
C:\> sock -n 512 -i 10.0.0.1 6666
```

At the receiver, we do not specify any setting for the receive buffer, but we do arrange for an initial delay of 20s before the application performs any reads:

```
Linux% sock -i -s -v -P 20 6666
```

To illustrate the growth of the receiver's advertised window, we can use Wireshark to sort the displayed packets based on the receiver's address (see Figure 15-15). During connection establishment, the receiver begins with an initial window size of 1460 bytes and an initial MSS of 1412 bytes. It is using window scaling, with a shift amount of 2 (not shown), leading to a maximum usable window of 256KB. We can see that after the initial packets, the window increases, which corresponds to the sender's increase in the data sending rate. We explore the sender's data rate control when we investigate TCP congestion control in Chapter 16. For now, we need only know that when the sender starts up, it typically starts by sending one packet and then increases the amount of outstanding data by one MSS packet for

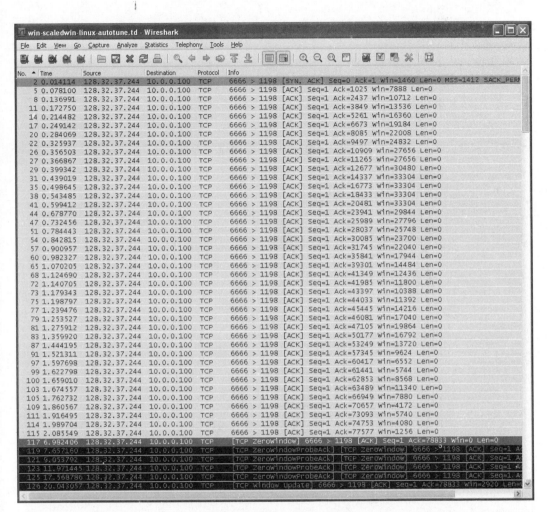

Figure 15-15 The Linux receiver performs receiver-side auto-tuning by increasing the window as more data is received. Because the application does not read for 20s, the window eventually closes.

each ACK it receives that indicates progress. Thus, it typically sends two MSS-size segments for each ACK it receives.

Looking at the pattern of the window advertisements—10712, 13536, 16360, 19184, . . .—we can see that the advertised window is increased by twice the MSS on each ACK, which mimics the way the sender's congestion control scheme operates, as we shall see in Chapter 16. Provided enough memory is available at the receiver, the advertised window is always larger than what the sender is permitted to send according to its congestion control limitations. This is the best case—the minimal amount of buffer space is being used and advertised by the receiver that keeps the sender sending as fast as possible.

If the receiver exhausts its buffers, auto-tuning is compromised. In this example, by time 0.678 the pattern of window growth reverses, having achieved a maximum of 33,304 bytes. The window size is no longer increasing, but instead the buffer is filling up while the application pauses. When the application begins reading at time 20, the window size again increases and goes beyond the point where it was previously (see Figure 15-16).

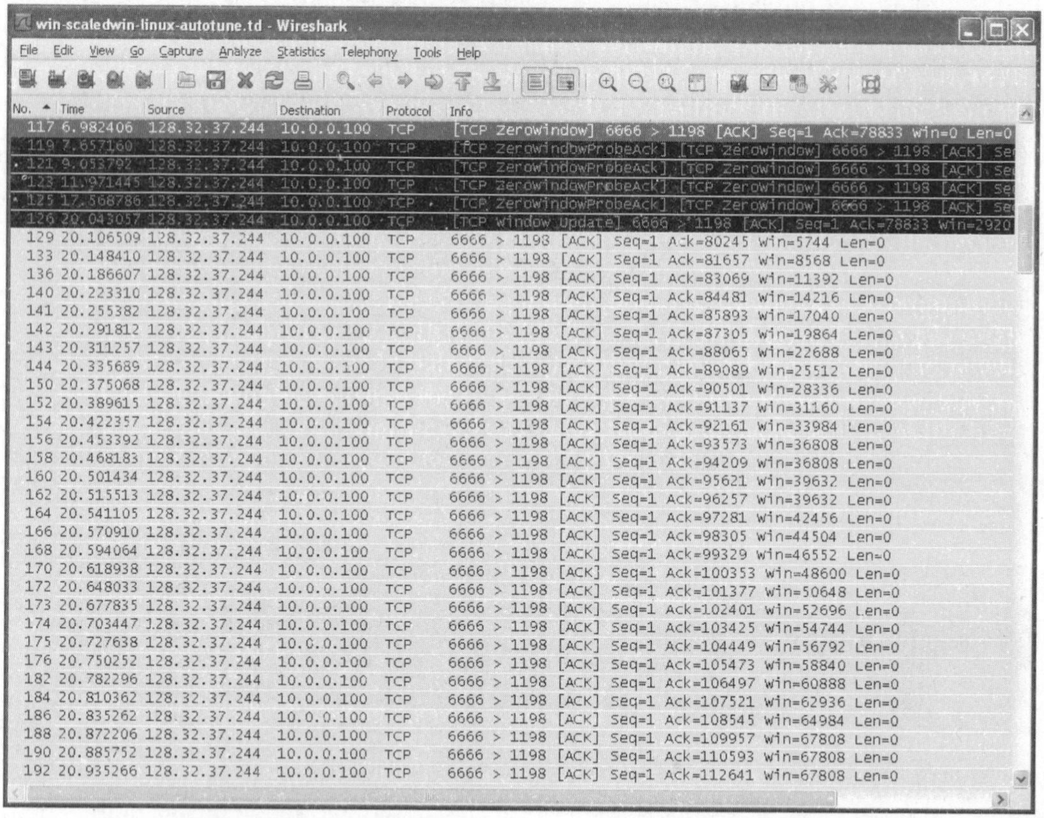
win-scaledwin-linux-autotune.td - Wireshark
File Edit View Go Capture Analyze Statistics Telephony Tools Help
No. Time Source Destination Protocol Info
117 6.982406 128.32.37.244 10.0.0.100 TCP [TCP ZeroWindow] 6666 > 1198 [ACK] Seq=1 Ack=78833 Win=0 Len=0
119 7.657160 128.32.37.244 10.0.0.100 TCP [TCP ZeroWindowProbeAck] [TCP ZeroWindow] 6666 > 1198 [ACK] Se
121 9.053792 128.32.37.244 10.0.0.100 TCP [TCP ZeroWindowProbeAck] [TCP ZeroWindow] 6666 > 1198 [ACK] Se
123 11.971445 128.32.37.244 10.0.0.100 TCP [TCP ZeroWindowProbeAck] [TCP ZeroWindow] 6666 > 1198 [ACK] Se
125 17.568786 128.32.37.244 10.0.0.100 TCP [TCP ZeroWindowProbeAck] [TCP ZeroWindow] 6666 > 1198 [ACK] Se
126 20.043057 128.32.37.244 10.0.0.100 TCP [TCP Window Update] 6666 > 1198 [ACK] Seq=1 Ack=78833 Win=2920
129 20.106509 128.32.37.244 10.0.0.100 TCP 6666 > 1198 [ACK] Seq=1 Ack=80245 Win=5744 Len=0
133 20.148410 128.32.37.244 10.0.0.100 TCP 6666 > 1198 [ACK] Seq=1 Ack=81657 Win=8568 Len=0
136 20.186607 128.32.37.244 10.0.0.100 TCP 6666 > 1198 [ACK] Seq=1 Ack=83069 Win=11392 Len=0
140 20.223310 128.32.37.244 10.0.0.100 TCP 6666 > 1198 [ACK] Seq=1 Ack=84481 Win=14216 Len=0
141 20.255382 128.32.37.244 10.0.0.100 TCP 6666 > 1198 [ACK] Seq=1 Ack=85893 Win=17040 Len=0
142 20.291812 128.32.37.244 10.0.0.100 TCP 6666 > 1198 [ACK] Seq=1 Ack=87305 Win=19864 Len=0
143 20.311257 128.32.37.244 10.0.0.100 TCP 6666 > 1198 [ACK] Seq=1 Ack=88065 Win=22688 Len=0
144 20.335689 128.32.37.244 10.0.0.100 TCP 6666 > 1198 [ACK] Seq=1 Ack=89089 Win=25512 Len=0
150 20.375068 128.32.37.244 10.0.0.100 TCP 6666 > 1198 [ACK] Seq=1 Ack=90501 Win=28336 Len=0
152 20.389615 128.32.37.244 10.0.0.100 TCP 6666 > 1198 [ACK] Seq=1 Ack=91137 Win=31160 Len=0
154 20.422357 128.32.37.244 10.0.0.100 TCP 6666 > 1198 [ACK] Seq=1 Ack=92161 Win=33984 Len=0
156 20.453392 128.32.37.244 10.0.0.100 TCP 6666 > 1198 [ACK] Seq=1 Ack=93573 Win=36808 Len=0
158 20.468183 128.32.37.244 10.0.0.100 TCP 6666 > 1198 [ACK] Seq=1 Ack=94209 Win=36808 Len=0
160 20.501434 128.32.37.244 10.0.0.100 TCP 6666 > 1198 [ACK] Seq=1 Ack=95621 Win=39632 Len=0
162 20.515513 128.32.37.244 10.0.0.100 TCP 6666 > 1198 [ACK] Seq=1 Ack=96257 Win=39632 Len=0
164 20.541105 128.32.37.244 10.0.0.100 TCP 6666 > 1198 [ACK] Seq=1 Ack=97281 Win=42456 Len=0
166 20.570910 128.32.37.244 10.0.0.100 TCP 6666 > 1198 [ACK] Seq=1 Ack=98305 Win=44504 Len=0
168 20.594064 128.32.37.244 10.0.0.100 TCP 6666 > 1198 [ACK] Seq=1 Ack=99329 Win=46552 Len=0
170 20.618938 128.32.37.244 10.0.0.100 TCP 6666 > 1198 [ACK] Seq=1 Ack=100353 Win=48600 Len=0
172 20.648033 128.32.37.244 10.0.0.100 TCP 6666 > 1198 [ACK] Seq=1 Ack=101377 Win=50648 Len=0
173 20.677835 128.32.37.244 10.0.0.100 TCP 6666 > 1198 [ACK] Seq=1 Ack=102401 Win=52696 Len=0
174 20.703447 128.32.37.244 10.0.0.100 TCP 6666 > 1198 [ACK] Seq=1 Ack=103425 Win=54744 Len=0
175 20.727638 128.32.37.244 10.0.0.100 TCP 6666 > 1198 [ACK] Seq=1 Ack=104449 Win=56792 Len=0
176 20.750252 128.32.37.244 10.0.0.100 TCP 6666 > 1198 [ACK] Seq=1 Ack=105473 Win=58840 Len=0
182 20.782296 128.32.37.244 10.0.0.100 TCP 6666 > 1198 [ACK] Seq=1 Ack=106497 Win=60888 Len=0
184 20.810362 128.32.37.244 10.0.0.100 TCP 6666 > 1198 [ACK] Seq=1 Ack=107521 Win=62936 Len=0
186 20.835262 128.32.37.244 10.0.0.100 TCP 6666 > 1198 [ACK] Seq=1 Ack=108545 Win=64984 Len=0
188 20.872206 128.32.37.244 10.0.0.100 TCP 6666 > 1198 [ACK] Seq=1 Ack=109957 Win=67808 Len=0
190 20.885752 128.32.37.244 10.0.0.100 TCP 6666 > 1198 [ACK] Seq=1 Ack=110593 Win=67808 Len=0
192 20.935266 128.32.37.244 10.0.0.100 TCP 6666 > 1198 [ACK] Seq=1 Ack=112641 Win=67808 Len=0

Figure 15-16 With the application pausing before reading, auto-tuning is compromised because the receive buffer becomes full. As the application begins reading, the advertised window increases, exceeding its previous value.

The zero window advertisement (packet 117) forces the sender to perform a series of window probes, resulting in a series of zero window advertisements. After the application begins reading at time 20.043, a window update is sent to the sender. The window begins to grow once again, twice the MSS in bytes for each ACK. As the sender continues to send additional data and the receiver consumes it, the receiver continues to increase the advertised window until the value

67808 is reached, which is the largest value the receiver ever advertises on this connection. This version of Linux also measures the time between adjacent application read completions and compares this value against the estimated connection round-trip time. If the RTT estimate increases, the buffer size is also increased (it is not decreased if the RTT becomes smaller). This helps auto-tuning keep the receiver's advertised window ahead of the sender's window even when the connection's bandwidth-delay product is increasing.

The problem of TCP applications using too-small buffers became a significant one as faster wide area Internet connections became available. In the United States, with cross-country round-trip times of approximately 100ms, using a 64KB window over a 1Gb/s network limits TCP throughput to about 640KB/s instead of the calculated maximum of about 130MB/s (a 99% waste of bandwidth). Practically speaking, it is not uncommon to see a factor of 100 increase in throughput performance when moving from a TCP with limited buffers to one with larger buffers on such networks. Significant credit should be given to the Web100 project [W100]. It created a set of tools and software patches in an effort to maximize the available throughput performance an application can obtain from various TCP implementations.

15.6 Urgent Mechanism

We saw in Chapter 12 that the TCP header has a special *URG* bit field to indicate "urgent data." An application is able to mark data as urgent by specifying a special option to the Berkeley sockets API (MSG_OOB) when it performs a write operation, although the use of urgent data is no longer recommended [RFC6093]. When the sender's TCP receives such a write request, it enters a special state called *urgent mode*. Upon entering urgent mode, it records the last byte the application specified as urgent data. This is used to set the *Urgent Pointer* field in each subsequent TCP header the sender generates until the application ceases writing urgent data and all the sequence numbers up to the urgent pointer have been acknowledged by the receiver. According to [RFC6093], the urgent pointer points to the sequence number of the byte of data following the last byte of urgent data. This resolves a longstanding ambiguity in various RFCs that included contradictory statements about the semantics of the *Urgent Pointer* field. When an IPv6 jumbogram is used, the *Urgent Pointer* value of 65535 may be used to indicate the end of urgent data is to be found at the end of the TCP data area [RFC2675], beyond the 64K byte offset expressible using the conventional 16-bit *Urgent Pointer* field.

A receiving TCP enters urgent mode when it receives a segment with the *URG* bit field set. The receiving application can discover whether its TCP has entered urgent mode using a standard socket API call (`select()`). The operation of the urgent mechanism has been a source of confusion because the Berkeley sockets API and documentation use the term *out-of-band* (OOB) data, although in reality TCP does not implement any true OOB capability. Instead, virtually all TCP implementations deliver the last byte of urgent data to an application using a distinct API call parameter at the receiver. The receiver must specify either the MSG_OOB option to retrieve the special byte or specify MSG_OOBINLINE to have the special byte remain in the regular data stream (this is now the required method, assuming the urgent mechanism is used at all).

15.6.1 Example

To get a better understanding of the urgent mechanism, we use a Mac OS X sender and Linux receiver to show how urgent mode behaves, including what happens during a zero window event. To achieve this, we first limit receive window auto-tuning on the Linux receiver:

```
Linux# sysctl -w net.ipv4.tcp_rmem='4096 4096 174760'

Linux% sock -i -v -s -p 1 -P 10 5555
```

The first command ensures that any receive window automatic adjustment does not exceed 4KB. This will be useful to us in order to see what happens when the window closes. The second command invokes the server and instructs it to wait 10s before performing any reads, and to wait 1s between each read operation it does perform. At the client, we execute the following command:

```
Mac% sock -i -n 7 -U 7 -p 1 -S 8192 10.0.1.1 5555
SO_SNDBUF = 8192
connected on 10.0.1.33.51101 to 10.0.1.1.5555
TCP_MAXSEG = 1448
wrote 1024 bytes
wrote 1024 bytes
wrote 1024 bytes
wrote 1024 bytes
wrote 1024 bytes
wrote 1024 bytes
wrote 1 byte of urgent data
wrote 1024 bytes
```

This command creates a client that performs seven 1024-byte writes spaced 1s apart but also performs a write of 1 byte of urgent data prior to the last write. The client's buffer is sufficiently large (set to 8192 bytes) that this application completes execution immediately because all the data it sends is buffered by the sending TCP.

In Figure 15-17, we can see how the initial right window edge advertised by the receiver is 2800 and is quickly increased to 5121. At time 1.0 the application performs a write, and the right window edge advances to about 6145. From then on the receiver's window increases no more because auto-tuning has been effectively disabled above 4192 bytes and the receiving application has not performed any reads. Until time 10.0, the sender probes the receiver but no additional window

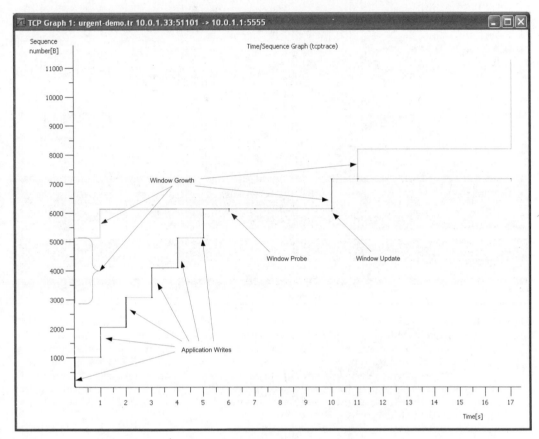

Figure 15-17 After six write operations, the receiver's window has not advanced. The sending TCP stops transmitting until the window opens at time 10.

growth occurs. Finally, when the receiver starts performing read operations after time 10.0, the window opens and the sender completes the transfer. The packets exchanged are shown in Figure 15-18.

The "exit point" for urgent mode is defined to be the sum of the *Sequence Number* field and the *Urgent Pointer* field in a TCP segment. Only one urgent "point" (a sequence number offset) is maintained per TCP connection, so a packet arriving with a valid *Urgent Pointer* field causes the information contained in any previous urgent pointer to be lost. Segment 16 is the first segment containing a valid urgent pointer, resulting in an exit point relative sequence number of 6146. Note that this sequence number may not be contained in the segment providing the indication but could instead be in some later segment. This is the case with segment 17, for example, which contains no data but includes the urgent pointer (with value 1).

As mentioned before, there has been some historical confusion about whether the exit point indicates the last byte of urgent data or the following first byte of

```
urgent-demo.tr - Wireshark
File  Edit  View  Go  Capture  Analyze  Statistics  Telephony  Tools  Help

No.  Time       Source      Destination  Protocol  Info
  1  0.000000   10.0.1.33   10.0.1.1     TCP       51101 > 5555 [SYN] Seq=0 Win=65535 Len=0 MSS=1460 WS=1 TSV=953549666 TSER=0 SACK_PERM=1
  2  0.002394   10.0.1.1    10.0.1.33    TCP       5555 > 51101 [SYN, ACK] Seq=0 Ack=1 Win=2896 Len=0 MSS=1460 SACK_PERM=1 TSV=4113124 TSER
  3  0.003797   10.0.1.33   10.0.1.1     TCP       51101 > 5555 [ACK] Seq=1 Ack=1 Win=65535 Len=0 TSV=953549666 TSER=4113124
  4  0.006090   10.0.1.33   10.0.1.1     TCP       51101 > 5555 [PSH, ACK] Seq=1 Ack=1 Win=65535 Len=1024 TSV=953549666 TSER=4113124
  5  0.008139   10.0.1.1    10.0.1.33    TCP       5555 > 51101 [ACK] Seq=1 Ack=1025 Win=4096 Len=0 TSV=4113131 TSER=953549666
  6  1.008635   10.0.1.33   10.0.1.1     TCP       51101 > 5555 [PSH, ACK] Seq=1025 Ack=1 Win=65535 Len=1024 TSV=953549676 TSER=4113131
  7  1.010700   10.0.1.1    10.0.1.33    TCP       5555 > 51101 [ACK] Seq=1 Ack=2049 Win=4096 Len=0 TSV=4114133 TSER=953549676
  8  2.008774   10.0.1.33   10.0.1.1     TCP       51101 > 5555 [PSH, ACK] Seq=2049 Ack=1 Win=65535 Len=1024 TSV=953549686 TSER=4114133
  9  2.012223   10.0.1.1    10.0.1.33    TCP       5555 > 51101 [ACK] Seq=1 Ack=3073 Win=3072 Len=0 TSV=4115135 TSER=953549686
 10  3.009696   10.0.1.33   10.0.1.1     TCP       51101 > 5555 [PSH, ACK] Seq=3073 Ack=1 Win=65535 Len=1024 TSV=953549696 TSER=4115135
 11  3.013135   10.0.1.1    10.0.1.33    TCP       5555 > 51101 [ACK] Seq=1 Ack=4097 Win=2048 Len=0 TSV=4116136 TSER=953549696
 12  4.010208   10.0.1.33   10.0.1.1     TCP       51101 > 5555 [PSH, ACK] Seq=4097 Ack=1 Win=65535 Len=1024 TSV=953549706 TSER=4116136
 13  4.012250   10.0.1.1    10.0.1.33    TCP       5555 > 51101 [ACK] Seq=1 Ack=5121 Win=1024 Len=0 TSV=4117135 TSER=953549706
 14  5.010332   10.0.1.33   10.0.1.1     TCP       51101 > 5555 [PSH, ACK] Seq=5121 Ack=1 Win=65535 Len=1024 TSV=953549716 TSER=4117135
 15  5.012424   10.0.1.1    10.0.1.33    TCP       [TCP ZeroWindow] 5555 > 51101 [ACK] Seq=1 Ack=6145 Win=0 Len=0 TSV=4118136 TSER=9535497
 16  6.011280   10.0.1.33   10.0.1.1     TCP       [TCP ZeroWindowProbe] 51101 > 5555 [PSH, ACK, URG] Seq=6145 Ack=1 Win=65535 Urg=1 Len=1
 17  6.011413   10.0.1.1    10.0.1.33    TCP       [TCP Dup ACK 16#1] 51101 > 5555 [ACK, URG] Seq=6145 Ack=1 Win=65535 Urg=1 Len=0 TSV=9535497
 18  6.013894   10.0.1.1    10.0.1.33    TCP       [TCP ZeroWindow] 5555 > 51101 [ACK] Seq=1 Ack=6145 Win=0 Len=0 TSV=4119136 TSER=9535497
 19  7.011514   10.0.1.33   10.0.1.1     TCP       [TCP Dup ACK 16#2] 51101 > 5555 [ACK, URG] Seq=6145 Ack=1 Win=65535 Urg=1 Len=0 TSV=953
 20  7.011921   10.0.1.33   10.0.1.1     TCP       [TCP Dup ACK 16#3] 51101 > 5555 [ACK, URG] Seq=6145 Ack=1 Win=65535 Urg=1 Len=0 TSV=953
 21  10.006001  10.0.1.1    10.0.1.33    TCP       [TCP Window Update] 5555 > 51101 [ACK] Seq=1 Ack=6145 Win=1024 Len=0 TSV=4123130 TSER=9
 22  10.006087  10.0.1.33   10.0.1.1     TCP       51101 > 5555 [ACK, URG] Seq=6145 Ack=1 Win=65535 Urg=1 Len=1024 TSV=953549766 TSER=4123130
 23  10.009394  10.0.1.1    10.0.1.33    TCP       [TCP ZeroWindow] 5555 > 51101 [ACK] Seq=1 Ack=7169 Win=0 Len=0 TSV=4123133 TSER=9535497
 24  10.010167  10.0.1.33   10.0.1.1     TCP       [TCP Dup ACK 22#1] 51101 > 5555 [ACK] Seq=7169 Ack=1 Win=65535 Len=0 TSV=953549766 TSER
 25  11.006855  10.0.1.1    10.0.1.33    TCP       [TCP Window Update] 5555 > 51101 [ACK] Seq=1 Ack=7169 Win=1024 Len=0 TSV=4124131 TSER=9
 26  11.006922  10.0.1.33   10.0.1.1     TCP       51101 > 5555 [FIN, PSH, ACK] Seq=7169 Ack=1 Win=65535 Len=1 TSV=953549776 TSER=4124131[
 27  11.048791  10.0.1.1    10.0.1.33    TCP       5555 > 51101 [ACK] Seq=1 Ack=7171 Win=1022 Len=0 TSV=4124173 TSER=953549776
 28  11.048878  10.0.1.33   10.0.1.1     TCP       [TCP Dup ACK 26#1] 51101 > 5555 [ACK] Seq=7171 Ack=1 Win=65535 Len=0 TSV=953549777 TSER
 29  17.012282  10.0.1.1    10.0.1.33    TCP       5555 > 51101 [FIN, ACK] Seq=1 Ack=7171 Win=4096 Len=0 TSV=4130137 TSER=953549777
 30  17.012373  10.0.1.33   10.0.1.1     TCP       51101 > 5555 [ACK] Seq=7171 Ack=2 Win=65535 Len=0 TSV=953549836 TSER=4130137
```

Figure 15-18 The entire data transfer showing a zero window advertisement from the receiver at time 5.012. When the application performs its next writes, the sending TCP enters urgent mode, resulting in the *URG* bit being set starting at time 6.0113 on a window probe segment containing one sequence number. At time 7 the application performs its final write and closes, producing two empty segments. A window update at time 10.006 restarts the data transfer. A zero window advertisement at time 10.009 again stops the transfer but also indicates that urgent mode can now be exited because the urgent pointer has been acknowledged. The FIN at time 11.007 contains the final data byte.

nonurgent data. In [RFC1122], the pointer is declared to point to the last byte of urgent data. However, essentially all TCP implementations do not follow this specification, so [RFC6093] recognizes this fact and changes various specifications to make the pointer indicate the first byte of nonurgent data. In this example, the byte with sequence number 6145 contains the 1 byte of urgent data produced by the sock client, but in all the segments we have seen the urgent pointer has a value of 1 when the sequence number field is 6145. Consequently, we can see that with this implementation of TCP, as with most, the exit point is the sequence number of the first byte of nonurgent data.

As we can see from this example, TCP carries urgent data inline with the data stream (not "out of band"). If an application really wants a separate out-of-band channel, a second TCP connection is the easiest way to accomplish this. (Some transport-layer protocols do provide what most people consider OOB data: a logically separate data path using the same connection as the normal data path. This is not what TCP provides.)

15.7 Attacks Involving Window Management

The window management procedures for TCP have been the subject of various attacks, primarily forms of resource exhaustion. In essence, advertising a small window slows a TCP transfer, tying up resources such as memory for a potentially long time. This has been used as a form of attack on bad traffic (i.e., worms). The LaBrea *tarpit* [L01], for example, arranges to complete the TCP three-way handshake and then either does nothing or produces minimal responses that simply cause the sending TCP to continually slow down. This keeps the sending TCP busy and essentially slows down worm propagation. Tarpits are thus attacks on attacking traffic.

A more recent attack was published in 2009 [I09], based on a known vulnerability of the persist timer. It uses a client-side variety of the "SYN cookies" technique (see Chapter 13). All the necessary connection state can thus be offloaded onto the victim machine, minimizing the amount of resources consumed at the attacker's machine. The attack itself is similar to the LaBrea idea, except it focuses specifically on the persist timer. Multiple such attacks can be mounted on the same server, which can lead to resource exhaustion (e.g., running out of system memory). The "solution" to this attack, as suggested by [C723308], is to allow some other process to terminate TCP connections when resource exhaustion appears to be taking place.

15.8 Summary

Interactive data is normally transmitted in segments smaller than the SMSS. Delayed acknowledgments may be used by the receiver of these small segments to see if the acknowledgment can be piggybacked along with data going back to the sender. This often reduces the number of segments, especially for interactive traffic, where the server is echoing the characters typed at the client. However, it may introduce additional delay.

On connections with relatively large round-trip times, such as WANs, the Nagle algorithm is often used to reduce the number of small segments. This algorithm limits the sender to a single small packet of unacknowledged data at any time. While this can reduce the number of high-overhead small packets in the network and reduce the total number of packets carried during a connection, it adds delay that is sometimes unacceptable to applications. In addition, the interaction between delayed ACKs and the Nagle algorithm can lead to an undesirable form of temporary deadlock. Because of these issues, the Nagle algorithm can be disabled by applications, and most interactive applications take advantage of this capability.

TCP implements flow control by including a window advertisement on every ACK it sends. Such window advertisements signal the peer TCP how much buffer space is left at the endpoint that sent the window advertisement ACK. The maximum window advertisement is 65,535 bytes unless the Window Scale TCP option is used. In that case, the maximum window advertisement can be much larger (about 1GB).

The window advertisement can be as small as 0 bytes, indicating that the receiver is completely full. When this happens, the sender stops sending data and instead begins probing the closed window using a retransmission interval with a backoff scheme similar to timer-based retransmissions (see Chapter 14). This probing of the closed window continues indefinitely, until either an ACK is returned indicating a larger window or the receiver sends an unsolicited window advertisement (a window update) because buffer space has become available. This indefinite behavior has been used to create a resource exhaustion attack against TCP.

During the development of TCP, a curious phenomenon was observed. When a small window was advertised, the sender would immediately fill it. This behavior, which causes the connection to use a large number of high-overhead small packets, would continue until the connection became idle and was dubbed "silly window syndrome." Techniques were created to avoid it, applying to both the TCP send and receive logic. The sender avoids sending small segments when a small window is advertised; receivers try to avoid ever sending small window advertisements.

The size of the receiver's window is limited by the size of the receiver's buffer. Historically, applications that failed to specify their receive buffers would be allocated a relatively small buffer that would cause throughput performance to suffer over network paths with high bandwidth and high delay. In more recent operating systems, auto-tuning sets the buffer size allocated automatically in an efficient way, causing such concerns to largely be a thing of the past.

15.9 References

[C723308] US-CERT Vulnerability Note VU#723308, Nov. 2009.

[F03] C. Fraleigh et al., "Packet-Level Traffic Measurements from the Sprint IP Backbone," *IEEE Network Magazine*, Nov./Dec. 2003.

[I09] F. Hantzis (ithilgore), "Exploiting TCP and the Persist Timer Infiniteness," *Phrack*, 66(9), June 2009.

[L01] T. Liston, "LaBrea: 'Sticky' Honeypot and IDS," http://labrea.sourceforge.net

[MM01] J. Mogul and G. Minshall, "Rethinking the TCP Nagle Algorithm," *ACM Computer Communication Review*, 31(6), Jan. 2001.

[MMQ] http://technet.microsoft.com/en-us/library/cc730960.aspx

[MMSV99] G. Minshall, J. Mogul, Y. Saito, and B. Verghese, "Application Performance Pitfalls and TCP's Nagle Algorithm," *Proc. Workshop on Internet Server Performance*, May 1999.

[P05] R. Pang, M. Allman, M. Bennett, J. Lee, V. Paxson, and B. Tierney, "A First Look at Modern Enterprise Traffic," *Proc. Internet Measurement Conference*, Oct. 2005.

[RFC0813] D. Clark, "Window and Acknowledgment Strategy in TCP," Internet RFC 0813, July 1982.

[RFC0896] J. Nagle, "Congestion Control in IP/TCP Internetworks," Internet RFC 0896, Jan. 1984.

[RFC1122] R. Braden, ed., "Requirements for Internet Hosts—Communication Layers," Internet RFC 1122/STD 0003, Oct. 1989.

[RFC2675] D. Borman, S. Deering, and R. Hinden, "IPv6 Jumbograms," Internet RFC 2675, Aug. 1999.

[RFC4251] T. Ylonen and C. Lonvick, "The Secure Shell (SSH) Protocol Architecture," Internet RFC 4251, Jan. 2006.

[RFC4254] T. Ylonen and C. Lonvick, ed., "The Secure Shell (SSH) Connection Protocol," Internet RFC 4254, Jan. 2006.

[RFC6093] F. Gont and A. Yourtchenko, "On the Implementation of the TCP Urgent Mechanism," Internet RFC 6093, Jan. 2011.

[S98] J. Semke, J. Mahdavi, and M. Mathis, "Automatic TCP Buffer Tuning," *Proc. ACM SIGCOMM*, Oct. 1998.

[W100] http://www.web100.org

16

TCP Congestion Control

16.1   Introduction

In this chapter we investigate how TCP approaches the issue of *congestion control*, which is most important in the context of bulk data transfers. Congestion control is a set of behaviors determined by algorithms that each TCP implements in an attempt to prevent the network from being overwhelmed by too large an aggregate offered traffic load. The basic approach is to have TCP slow down when it has reason to believe the network is about to be congested (or is already so congested that routers are discarding packets). The challenge is to determine exactly when and how TCP should slow down, and when it can speed up again.

TCP is a protocol designed to provide reliable delivery of data from one system to another. We have already seen in Chapter 15 how a sending TCP can be made to slow down if its peer (receiving) TCP cannot keep up. This is accomplished by TCP's procedures for *flow control* and is realized by a sender adapting its sending rate based on the advertised *Window Size* field provided by a receiver in its ACKs. This provides explicit information about the state of the receiver back to the sender and allows it to avoid overrunning the receiver's buffers.

Consider what happens when the network between a collection of senders and receivers is asked to carry more traffic than it can handle. Either the senders must slow down or the network must ultimately throw some data away (or some combination thereof). This fact arises from the most basic observation from queuing theory as applied at a router: even if the router can store some data, if the long-term data arrival rate exceeds the long-term departure rate, any amount of intermediate storage will grow without bound. Stated more simply, if a router receives more data per unit time than it can send out, it must store that data. If this situation persists, eventually the storage will run out and the router will be forced to drop some of the data.

This situation, when a router is forced to discard data because it cannot handle the arriving traffic rate, is called *congestion*. The router is said to be *congested* when it is in this state, and even a single connection can drive one or more routers into congestion. Left unaddressed, congestion can cause the performance of a network to be reduced so badly that it becomes unusable. In the very worst cases, it is said to be in a state of *congestion collapse*. To either avoid or at least react effectively to mitigate this situation, each TCP implements *congestion control procedures*. Different versions or variants of TCP (and the operating systems that host the TCP/IP stack) have somewhat different procedures and behaviors. We will discuss most of the better-known ones in this chapter.

16.1.1 Detection of Congestion in TCP

As we have seen, the primary mechanism TCP has available to combat packet loss is retransmission, induced either by a retransmission timer expiring, or by the fast retransmit algorithm (see Chapter 14). Consider, for a moment, the consequence of many TCP connections that share an Internet path simply retransmitting more packets while the network is in a state of congestion collapse. As you can imagine, this only makes the situation worse. It has been called the analog of pouring gasoline on a fire and is something to be avoided.

In order to deal with congestion, we would like to have sending TCPs slow down when congestion is present (or about to be) and, if the congestion has subsided, detect and use an appropriate amount of new bandwidth when it becomes available. In the Internet, this can be quite challenging, as there has traditionally been no explicit way for a sending TCP to learn about the state of the intermediate routers. In other words, there is no *explicit signaling* about congestion. Instead, if a typical TCP is to react somehow to congestion, it must first conclude that congestion is occurring. This is usually accomplished by detecting that one or more packets have been lost. In TCP, an assumption is made that a lost packet is an indicator of congestion, and that some response (i.e., slowing down in some way) is required. We shall see that TCP has been this way since the late 1980s. Other methods for detecting congestion, including measuring delay and network-supported *Explicit Congestion Notification* (ECN), which we discuss in Section 16.11, allow TCP to learn about congestion even before it has become so bad as to cause dropped packets. We discuss these approaches after studying the "classic" algorithms.

Note

In today's wired networks, packet loss is caused primarily by congestion in routers or switches. With wireless networks, transmission and reception errors become a significant cause of packet loss. Determining whether loss is due to congestion or transmission errors has been an active research topic since the mid-1990s when wireless networks started to attain widespread use.

In Chapter 14 we saw how TCP can use timers, acknowledgments, and selective acknowledgments to detect and recover from dropped packets. When packets are detected as lost, it is TCP's responsibility to resend them. We are now concerned with what else TCP does when it observes a lost packet. In particular, we are interested in how it interprets this as a signal that congestion has occurred, and that it should slow down. Just *how* it slows down and *when* (and how it speeds back up again) are the main subjects of the following sections. We begin with the classic algorithm used on a new connection to establish the base data rate and continue with another classic algorithm that is used by TCP during its steady-state operation when performing large data transfers. We will also incorporate the recommended variations on these algorithms into the discussion and discuss other modifications that have been made over the years. We will also examine an extended trace in detail. We conclude with a discussion of some of the security issues related to TCP congestion control and summarize the most important points. The area of congestion control has been a fertile area for networking researchers [RFC6077], and several new papers on this subject tend to appear each year.

16.1.2 Slowing Down a TCP Sender

One detail we need to address right away is just how to slow down a TCP sender. We saw in Chapter 15 that the *Window Size* field in the TCP header is used to signal a sender to adjust its window based on the availability of buffer space at the receiver. We can go a step further and arrange for the sender to slow down if either the receiver is too slow or the network is too slow. This is accomplished by introducing a window control variable at the sender that is based on an estimate of the network's capacity and ensuring that the sender's window size never exceeds the minimum of the two. In effect, a sending TCP then sends at a rate equal to what the receiver or the network can handle, whichever is less.

The new value used to hold the estimate of the network's available capacity is called the *congestion window*, written more compactly as simply *cwnd*. The sender's actual (usable) window W is then written as the minimum of the receiver's advertised window *awnd* and the congestion window:

$$W = \min(cwnd, awnd)$$

With this relationship, the TCP sender is not permitted to have more than W unacknowledged packets or bytes outstanding in the network. The total amount of data a sender has introduced into the network for which it has not yet received an acknowledgment is sometimes called the *flight size*, which is always less than or equal to W. In general, W can be maintained in either packet or byte units.

Note

When TCP does not make use of selective acknowledgment, the restriction on W means that the sender is not permitted to send a segment with a sequence number greater than the sum of the highest acknowledged sequence number and the value of W. A SACK TCP sender treats W somewhat differently, using it as an overall limit to the flight size.

This all seems logical but is far from the whole story. Because both the state of the network and the state of the receiver change with time, the values of both *awnd* and *cwnd* change over time. In addition, because of the lack of explicit signals (see the preceding section), the "correct" value of *cwnd* is generally not directly available to the sending TCP. Thus, all of the values *W*, *cwnd*, and *awnd* must be empirically determined and dynamically updated. In addition, as we said before, we do not want *W* to be too big or too small—we want it to be set to about the *bandwidth-delay product* (BDP) of the network path, also called the *optimal* window size. This is the amount of data that can be stored in the network in transit to the receiver. It is equal to the product of the RTT and the capacity of the lowest capacity ("bottleneck") link on the path from sender to receiver. Generally, the sending strategy is to keep the network busy by arranging to have an amount of data at least as large as the BDP in the network. Using an outstanding limit that substantially exceeds the BDP, however, is usually undesirable as it can lead to unwanted delays (see Section 16.10). On the Internet, determining the BDP for a connection can be challenging, given that routes, delay, and the level of statistical multiplexing (i.e., sharing of capacity) change as a function of time.

Note

Although handling congestion at the TCP sender is our primary area of interest, work has been done on handling the cases where congestion occurs on the reverse path, because of ACKs. In [RFC5690] a method is introduced to inform a TCP receiver of the ACK ratio it should use (i.e., how many packets it should receive before sending an ACK).

16.2 The Classic Algorithms

When a new TCP connection first starts out, it usually has no idea what the initial value for *cwnd* should be, as it has no idea how much network capacity is available for it to send its data. (There are some exceptions, such as systems that cache performance values that were determined earlier. These were called destination metrics in Chapter 14.) TCP learns the value for *awnd* with one packet exchange to the receiver, but without any explicit signaling, the only obvious way it has to learn a good value for *cwnd* is to try sending data at faster and faster rates until it experiences a packet drop (or other congestion indicator). This could be accomplished by either sending immediately at the maximum rate it can (subject to the value of *awnd*), or it could start more slowly. Because of the detrimental effects on the performance of other TCP connections sharing the same network path that could be experienced when starting at full rate, a TCP generally uses one algorithm to avoid starting so fast when it starts up to get to steady state. It uses a different one once it is in steady state.

The operation of TCP congestion control at a sender is driven or "clocked" by the receipt of ACKs. If a TCP is operating at steady state (with an appropriate value of *cwnd*), receipt of an ACK indicates that one or more packets have been removed from the network, and consequently that an opportunity to send more has arisen. Following this line of reasoning, the TCP congestion behavior in steady state attempts to achieve a *conservation of packets* in the network (see Figure 16-1). The term conservation here is used in the sense it is in physics—that some quantity (e.g., momentum, energy) going into a system does not simply disappear or appear but rather can be found as long as proper accounting is performed.

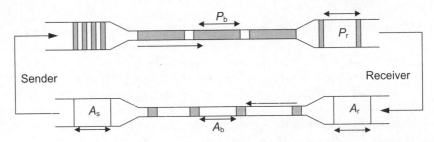

Figure 16-1   TCP congestion control operates on a principle of conservation of packets. Packets (P_b) are "stretched out" in time as they are sent from sender to receiver over links with constrained capacity. As they are received at the receiver spaced apart (P_r), ACKs are generated (A_r), which return to the sender. ACKs traveling from receiver to sender become spaced out (A_b) in relation to the inter-packet spacing of the packets. When ACKs reach the sender (A_s), their arrivals provide a signal or "ACK clock," used to tell the sender it is time to send more. In steady state, the overall system is said to be "self-clocked." The figure is adapted from [J88] and copied from S. Seshan's CMU Lecture Notes dated March 22, 2005.

This idea is illustrated in Figure 16-1. We shall call the top and bottom objects "funnels." The top funnel holds (larger) data packets traveling along the path from the sender to the receiver. The comparatively narrow width of the funnel depicts how packets are "stretched out" in time as they travel through a relatively slow link. The ends of the funnels (at sender and receiver) show the queues where packets are held before or after they travel along the path. The bottom funnel holds the ACKs sent by the receiver back to the sender that correspond to the data packets in the top funnel. When operating efficiently at steady state, there are no bunches of packets in the top or bottom funnels. In addition, there is no significant extra space between packets in the top funnel. Note that an arrival of an ACK at the sender "liberates" another data packet to be sent into the top funnel, and that this happens at just the right time (i.e., when the network is able to accept another packet). This relationship is sometimes called *self-clocking*, because the arrival of an ACK, called the *ACK clock*, triggers the system to take the action of sending another packet.

We now turn to the main two algorithms of TCP: slow start and congestion avoidance. These algorithms, based on the principles of packet conservation and ACK clocking, were first formally described in the classic paper by Jacobson [J88].

An update to the congestion avoidance algorithm was given by Jacobson a couple of years later [J90]. These algorithms do not operate at the same time—TCP executes only one at any given time, but it may switch back and forth between the two. We now explore these in more detail and examine what determines when each of them is used. We also look at how they have been modified and extended since they were initially implemented. Each TCP connection is able to individually execute these algorithms.

16.2.1 Slow Start

The slow start algorithm is executed when a new TCP connection is created or when a loss has been detected due to a retransmission timeout (RTO). It may also be invoked after a sending TCP has gone idle for some time. The purpose of slow start is to help TCP find a value for *cwnd* before probing for more available bandwidth using congestion avoidance and to establish the ACK clock. Typically, a TCP begins a new connection in slow start, eventually drops a packet, and then settles into steady-state operation using the congestion avoidance algorithm (Section 16.2.2). To quote from [RFC5681]:

> Beginning transmission into a network with unknown conditions requires TCP to slowly probe the network to determine the available capacity, in order to avoid congesting the network with an inappropriately large burst of data. The slow start algorithm is used for this purpose at the beginning of a transfer, or after repairing loss detected by the retransmission timer.

A TCP begins in slow start by sending a certain number of segments (after the SYN exchange), called the *initial window* (IW). The value of IW was originally one SMSS, although with [RFC5681] it is allowed to be larger. The formula works as follows:

$IW = 2*(SMSS)$ and not more than 2 segments (if $SMSS > 2190$ bytes)

$IW = 3*(SMSS)$ and not more than 3 segments (if $2190 \geq SMSS > 1095$ bytes)

$IW = 4*(SMSS)$ and not more than 4 segments (otherwise)

While this assignment for IW may allow several packets (e.g., three or four) in the initial window, we shall discuss the case where IW = 1 SMSS for simplicity. A TCP just starting out begins its connection, then, with *cwnd* = 1 SMSS, meaning the initial usable window W is also equal to SMSS. Note that in most cases SMSS is equal to the smaller of the receiver's MSS and the path MTU (less header sizes).

Assuming no packets are lost and each packet causes an ACK to be sent in response, an ACK is returned for the first segment, allowing the sending TCP to send another segment. However, slow start operates by incrementing *cwnd* by min(N, SMSS) for each good ACK received, where N is the number of previously unacknowledged bytes ACKed by the received "good ACK." A good ACK is one that returns a higher ACK number than has been seen so far.

Note

The number of bytes ACKed is used to support *Appropriate Byte Counting* (ABC) [RFC3465], an experimental specification recommended by [RFC5681]. It can be used to counter an "ACK division" attack, described in Section 16.12, where many small ACKs are used in an attempt to cause a TCP sender to send faster than normal. Linux uses the Boolean system configuration variable net.ipv4.tcp_abc to determine if ABC is enabled (default no). In recent versions of Windows, ABC defaults to on.

Thus, after one segment is ACKed, the *cwnd* value is ordinarily increased to 2, and two segments are sent. If each of those causes new good ACKs to be returned, 2 increases to 4, 4 to 8, and so on. In general, assuming no loss and an ACK for every packet, the value of W after k round-trip exchanges is $W = 2^k$. Rewriting, we can say that $k = \log_2 W$ RTTs are required to reach an operating window of W. This growth seems quite "fast" (increasing as an exponential function) but is still "slower" than what TCP would do if it were allowed to send immediately a window of packets equal in size to the receiver's advertised window. (Recall that W is still never allowed to exceed *awnd*.)

If we imagine a TCP connection where the receiver's advertised window is very large (say, infinitely large), *cwnd* is the primary governor of the sending rate (provided there is something for the sender to send). As we saw, this value grows exponentially fast in the RTT of the connection. So, eventually, *cwnd* (and thus W) could become so large that the corresponding window of packets sent overwhelms the network (recall that TCP's throughput rate is proportional to W/RTT). When this happens, *cwnd* is reduced substantially (to half of its former value). In addition, this is the point at which TCP switches from operating in slow start to operating in congestion avoidance. The switch point is determined by the relationship between *cwnd* and a value called the *slow start threshold* (or *ssthresh*).

Figure 16-2 (left) illustrates the operation of slow start. The numbers are in units of the RTT of the connection. Assuming the connection starts out with one packet (top), one ACK is returned, allowing two packets to be sent during the second RTT. These packets cause two ACKs to be returned. The TCP sender increments *cwnd* by one segment for each ACK returned, so the process continues. The exponential growth of *cwnd* as a function of time is illustrated on the right. The second line shows how *cwnd* grows when every other packet is acknowledged, which is common when delayed ACKs are being used. In this case, the growth is still exponential but not as rapid. For this reason, some TCPs arrange to delay ACKs only after the connection has completed slow start. In Linux, this is called *quick acknowledgments* ("quickack mode") and has been part of the basic TCP/IP stack since kernel version 2.4.4.

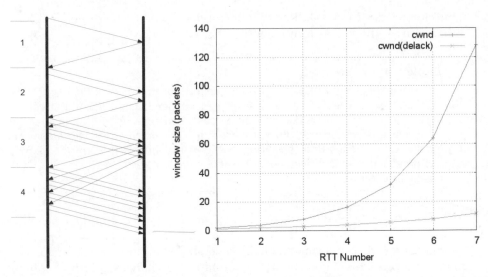

Figure 16-2   Operation of the classic slow start algorithm. In the simple case where ACKs are not delayed, every arriving good ACK allows the sender to inject two new packets (left). This leads to an exponential growth in the size of the sender's window as a function of time (right, upper line). When ACKs are delayed, such as when an ACK is produced for every other packet, the growth is still exponential but slower (right, lower line).

16.2.2 Congestion Avoidance

Slow start, just described, is used when initiating data flow across a connection or after a loss event invoked by a timeout. It increases *cwnd* fairly rapidly and helps to establish a value for *ssthresh*. Once this is achieved, there is always the possibility that more network capacity may become available for a connection. If such capacity were to be immediately used with large traffic bursts, other TCP connections with packets sharing the same queues in routers would likely experience significant packet drops, leading to overall instability in the network as many connections simultaneously experience packet drops and react with retransmissions.

To address the problem of trying to find additional capacity that may become available, but to not do so too aggressively, TCP implements the *congestion avoidance* algorithm. Once *ssthresh* is established and *cwnd* is at least at this level, a TCP runs the congestion avoidance algorithm, which seeks additional capacity by increasing *cwnd* by approximately one segment for each window's worth of data that is moved from sender to receiver successfully. This provides a much slower growth rate than slow start: approximately linear in terms of time, as opposed to slow start's exponential growth. More precisely, *cwnd* is usually updated as follows for each received nonduplicate ACK:

$$cwnd_{t+1} = cwnd_t + SMSS * SMSS/cwnd_t$$

Looking at this relationship briefly, assume $cwnd_0 = k*SMSS$ bytes were sent into the network in k segments. After the first ACK arrives, $cwnd$ is updated to be larger by a factor of $(1/k)$:

$$cwnd_1 = cwnd_0 + SMSS * SMSS/cwnd_0 = k*SMSS + SMSS * (SMSS/(k*SMSS)) = k*SMSS + (1/k) * SMSS = (k + (1/k))*SMSS = cwnd_0 + (1/k)*SMSS$$

Because the value of $cwnd$ grows slightly with each new ACK arrival, and this value is in the denominator of the expression in the first equation above, the overall growth rate of $cwnd$ is slightly sublinear. Nonetheless, we generally think of congestion avoidance growing the window linearly with respect to time (Figure 16-3), whereas slow start grows it exponentially with respect to time (Figure 16-2). This function is also called *additive increase* because a particular value (about one packet in this case) is added to $cwnd$ for each successfully received window's worth of data.

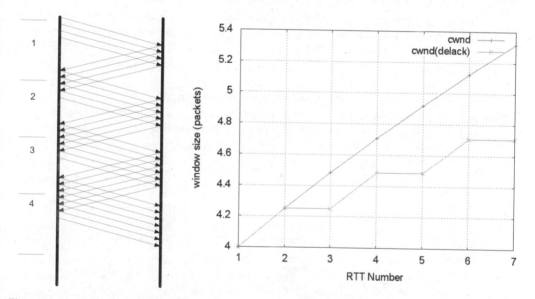

Figure 16-3   Operation of the congestion avoidance algorithm. In the simple case where ACKs are not delayed, every arriving good ACK allows the sender to inject approximately 1/W fraction of a new packet. This leads to approximately linear growth in the size of the sender's window as a function of time (right, upper line). When ACKs are delayed, such as when an ACK is produced for every other packet, the growth is still approximately linear but somewhat slower (right, lower line).

Figure 16-3 (left) illustrates the operation of congestion avoidance. Once again, the numbers are in units of the RTT of the connection. Assuming the connection sends four packets (top), four ACKs are returned, allowing $cwnd$ to grow slightly. By the second RTT period, the growth is enough to overcome the integer rounding and cause an increase of one SMSS to $cwnd$, allowing one additional packet to be sent. The growth of *cwnd* as a nearly linear function of time is illustrated on the right, on a linear-linear plot. The second line to the right shows how *cwnd* grows when every other packet is acknowledged, simulating the use of delayed ACKs. In this case, the growth is still about linear, but not as rapid.

The assumption of the algorithm is that packet loss caused by bit errors is very small (much less than 1%), and therefore the loss of a packet signals congestion somewhere in the network between the source and destination. If this assumption is false, which it sometimes is for wireless networks, TCP slows down even when no congestion is present. In addition, many RTTs may be required for the value of *cwnd* to grow large, which is required for efficient use of networks with high capacity. Fixing these issues with TCP has been a popular area for research, and we discuss some of the various approaches later.

16.2.3 Selecting between Slow Start and Congestion Avoidance

In normal operations, a TCP connection is always running either the slow start or the congestion avoidance procedure, but never the two simultaneously. We now turn to the question, What determines the algorithm TCP uses at any given time? We already know that slow start is used when a new connection is created or when a timeout-based retransmission occurs. We now turn to what controls the selection between slow start and congestion avoidance.

We mentioned *ssthresh* earlier. This threshold is a limit on the value of *cwnd* that determines which algorithm is in operation, slow start or congestion avoidance. When *cwnd* < *ssthresh*, slow start is used, and when *cwnd* > *ssthresh*, congestion avoidance is used. When they are equal, either can be used. The most important distinction between slow start and congestion avoidance, as we have seen, is how each modifies the value of *cwnd* when new ACKs arrive. What makes TCP somewhat tricky and interesting is that the value of *ssthresh* is not fixed but instead varies over time. Its main purpose is to remember the last "best" estimate of the operating window when no loss was present. Said another way, it holds the lower bound on TCP's best estimate of the optimal window size.

The initial value of *ssthresh* may be set arbitrarily high (e.g., to *awnd* or higher), which causes TCP to always start with slow start. When a retransmission occurs, caused by either a retransmission timeout or the execution of fast retransmit, *ssthresh* is updated as follows:

$$ssthresh = \max(\textit{flight size}/2, 2{*}SMSS) \tag{1}$$

Note

In Microsoft's most recent ("Next Generation") TCP/IP stack, this equation is reportedly changed to the somewhat more conservative relationship: *ssthresh* = max(min(*cwnd*, *awnd*)/2, 2*SMSS) [NB08].

Here we see that if a retransmission is required, TCP assumes that the operating window must have been too large for the network to handle. Reducing the estimate of the optimal window size is accompanied by altering *ssthresh* to be about half of what the current window size is (but not ever below twice the SMSS). This usually results in lowering *ssthresh*, but it can also result in increasing *ssthresh*. If we examine the congestion avoidance procedure for TCP, we recall that if an entire window's worth of data is successfully exchanged, the value of *cwnd* is allowed to increase by approximately 1 SMSS. Thus, if *cwnd* has grown large over a considerable amount of time, setting *ssthresh* to half of the flight size could cause it to increase. This happens when TCP has discovered more usable bandwidth. The interplay between *ssthresh* and *cwnd*, in conjunction with the operation of slow start and congestion avoidance, gives TCP its characteristic behavior in the face of congestion. We now explore the complete, combined algorithms.

16.2.4 Tahoe, Reno, and Fast Recovery

The algorithms discussed so far, slow start and congestion avoidance, constitute the first congestion control algorithms applied to TCP. They were introduced in the late 1980s with the 4.2 release of UC Berkeley's version of UNIX, called the *Berkeley Software Distribution*, or BSD UNIX. Thus began the convention of naming various versions of TCP after U.S. cities, especially those where gambling is permitted.

The 4.2 release of BSD (called Tahoe) included a version of TCP that started connections in slow start, and if a packet was lost, detected by either a timeout or the fast retransmit procedure, the slow start algorithm was reinitiated. Tahoe was implemented by simply reducing *cwnd* to its starting value (1 SMSS at that time) upon any loss, forcing the connection to slow start until *cwnd* grew to the value *ssthresh*.

One problem with this approach is that for large BDP paths, this can cause the connection to significantly underutilize the available bandwidth while the sending TCP goes through slow start to get back to the point at which it was operating before the packet loss. To address this problem, the reinitiation of slow start on any packet loss was reconsidered. Ultimately, if packet loss is detected by duplicate ACKs (invoking fast retransmit), *cwnd* is instead reset to the last value of *ssthresh* instead of only 1 SMSS. (Slow start is still initiated on a timeout, which is generally the case for most TCP variants.) This approach allows the TCP to slow down to half of its previous rate without reverting to slow start.

In exploring the issue of large BDP paths further and thinking back to the conservation of packets principle mentioned before, it has been observed that any ACKs that are received, even while recovering after a loss, still represent opportunities to inject new packets into the network. This became the basis of the *fast recovery* procedure, which was released in conjunction with the popular 4.3 BSD Reno version of BSD UNIX. Fast recovery allows *cwnd* to (temporarily) grow by 1 SMSS for each ACK received while recovering. The congestion window is therefore *inflated* for a period of time, allowing an additional new packet to be sent for each ACK received, until a good ACK is seen. Any nonduplicate ("good") ACK causes TCP to exit recovery and reduces the congestion back to its pre-inflated value. TCP Reno became very popular and ultimately the basis for what might reasonably be called "standard TCP."

16.2.5 Standard TCP

Although what constitutes "standard" TCP is subject to some debate, the algorithms we have discussed so far constitute the primary procedures identified with standard TCP operation. The slow start and congestion avoidance algorithms are usually implemented together, and the baseline overall behavior is given in [RFC5681]. This specification does not require the use of these exact algorithms, but a requirement is imposed that any TCP implementation not be more aggressive than these algorithms would allow.

To summarize the combined algorithm from [RFC5681], TCP begins a connection in slow start ($cwnd = IW$) with a large value of $ssthresh$, generally at least the value of $awnd$. Upon receiving a good ACK (one that acknowledges new data), TCP updates the value of $cwnd$ as follows:

$$cwnd \mathrel{+}= SMSS \qquad \text{(if } cwnd < ssthresh) \qquad \text{Slow start}$$

$$cwnd \mathrel{+}= SMSS*SMSS/cwnd \qquad \text{(if } cwnd > ssthresh) \qquad \text{Congestion avoidance}$$

When fast retransmit is invoked because of receipt of a third duplicate ACK (or other signal, if conventional fast retransmit initiation is not used), the following actions are performed:

1. *ssthresh* is updated to no more than the value given in equation [1].

2. The fast retransmit algorithm is performed, and *cwnd* is set to (*ssthresh* + 3*SMSS*).

3. *cwnd* is temporarily increased by *SMSS* for each duplicate ACK received.

4. When a good ACK is received, *cwnd* is reset back to *ssthresh*.

The actions in steps 2 and 3 constitute *fast recovery*. Step 2 first adjusts *cwnd*, which usually causes it to be reduced to half of its former value, and then temporarily inflates it to take into account the fact that the receipt of each duplicate ACK indicates that some packet has left the network (and thus should permit another to be inserted). This step is also where *multiplicative decrease* occurs, as *cwnd* is ordinarily multiplied by some value (0.5 here) to form its new value. Step 3 continues the inflation process, allowing the sender to send additional packets (assuming *awnd* is not exceeded). In step 4, the TCP is assumed to have recovered, so the temporary inflation is removed (and so this step is sometimes called "deflation").

Slow start is always used in two cases: when a new connection is started, and when a retransmission timeout occurs. It can also be invoked when a sender has been idle for a relatively long time or there is some other reason to suspect that *cwnd* may not accurately reflect the current network congestion state (see Section 16.3.5). In this case, the initial value of *cwnd* is set to the *restart window* (RW). In [RFC5681], the recommended value of $RW = min(IW, cwnd)$. Other than this case, when slow start is invoked, *cwnd* is set to IW.

16.3 Evolution of the Standard Algorithms

The classic and standard TCP algorithms made a tremendous contribution to the operation of TCP, essentially addressing the major problem of Internet congestion collapse.

Note

The problem of Internet congestion collapse was a serious concern during the years 1986–1988. In October 1986 the NSFNET backbone, an important component of the early Internet, had been observed to operate with an effective capacity some 1000 times less than it should have (called the "NSFNET meltdown"). The primary reason for the problem was aggressive retransmissions during times of loss without any controls. This behavior drove the network into a persistently congested state where packet loss was massive (causing more retransmissions) and throughput was low. Adoption of the classic congestion control algorithms effectively eliminated this problem.

However, there remained several areas for improvement. Given TCP's popularity, a growing amount of effort was put into ensuring that TCP could be made to work well under a wider range of conditions. We now mention several of these that are found in many TCP implementations today.

16.3.1 NewReno

One problem with fast recovery is that when multiple packets are dropped in a window of data, once one packet is recovered (i.e., successfully delivered and ACKed), a good ACK can be received at the sender that causes the temporary window inflation in fast recovery to be erased before all the packets that were lost have been retransmitted. ACKs that trigger this behavior are called *partial ACKs*. A Reno TCP reacting to a partial ACK by reducing its inflated congestion window can go idle until a retransmission timer fires. To understand why this happens, recall that (non-SACK) TCP depends on the signal of three (or *dupthresh*) duplicate ACKs to trigger its fast retransmit procedure. If there are not enough packets in the network, it is not possible to trigger this procedure on packet loss, ultimately leading to the expiration of the retransmission timer and invocation of the slow start procedure, which drastically impacts TCP throughput performance.

To address this problem with Reno, a modification called *NewReno* [RFC3782] has been developed. This procedure modifies fast recovery by keeping track of the highest sequence number from the last transmitted window of data (the recovery point, which we first saw in Chapter 14). Only when an ACK with an ACK number at least as large as the recovery point is received is the inflation of fast recovery removed. This allows a TCP to continue sending one segment for each ACK it receives while recovering and reduces the occurrence of retransmission time-outs, especially when multiple packets are dropped in a single window of data. NewReno is a popular variant of modern TCPs—it does not suffer from the problems of the original fast recovery and is significantly less complicated to implement than SACKs. With SACKs, however, a TCP can perform better than NewReno when multiple packets are lost in a window of data, but doing this requires careful attention to the congestion control procedures, which we discuss next.

16.3.2 TCP Congestion Control with SACK

With the introduction of SACKs and selective repeat to TCP, a sender is able to make better decisions about what segments to send in order to fill holes at the receiver (see Chapter 14). In filling the receiver's holes, the sender generally sends each of the missing segments, in order, until all of the retransmissions for the lost segments have been received successfully. This procedure differs from the basic fast retransmit/recovery procedure mentioned previously in a somewhat subtle way.

In the case of fast retransmit/recovery, when a packet is lost, the sending TCP transmits only the segment it believes is lost and is able to send new data if the window W allows. Because the window is inflated for each arriving ACK during fast recovery, with larger windows TCP typically is able to send some additional data after performing its retransmission. With SACK TCP, the sender can be informed of multiple missing segments and would theoretically be able to send them all immediately because they would all be in the valid window. However, this might involve sending too much data into the network at once, thereby compromising the congestion control. The following issue arises with SACK TCP: using only *cwnd* as a bound on the sender's sliding window to indicate how many (and which) packets to send during recovery periods is not sufficient. Instead, the selection of *which* packets to send needs to be decoupled from the choice of *when* to send them. Said another way, SACK TCP underscores the need to separate the congestion management from the selection and mechanism of packet retransmission. Conventional (non-SACK) TCP mixes these together.

One way to implement this decoupling is to have a TCP keep track of how much data it has injected into the network separately from the maintenance of the window. In [RFC3517] this is called the *pipe* variable, an estimate of the flight size. Importantly, the pipe variable counts bytes (or packets, depending on the implementation) of transmissions *and* retransmissions, provided they are not known to be lost. Assuming a large value of *awnd*, a SACK TCP is permitted to send a segment anytime the following relationship holds true: *cwnd - pipe* ≥ SMSS. In other words, *cwnd* is still used to place a limit on the amount of data that can be outstanding in the network, but the amount of data estimated to be in the network is accounted for separately from the window itself. How SACK TCP using this approach to congestion control compares with conventional TCP was first explored in detail with a series of simulations in [FF96].

16.3.3 Forward Acknowledgment (FACK) and Rate Halving

For TCP variants based on Reno (including NewReno), the typical behavior is that when *cwnd* is reduced after a fast retransmit, ACKs for at least one-half of the current window's outstanding data must be received before the sending TCP is allowed to continue transmitting. This is an expected consequence of reducing the congestion window by half immediately when a loss is detected. It causes the sending TCP to wait for about half of an RTT and then send any new data during the second half of the same RTT, a more bursty behavior than is really required.

In an effort to avoid the initial pause after loss but not violate the convention of emerging from recovery with a congestion window set to half of its size on entry, *forward acknowledgment* (FACK) was described in [MM96]. It consists of two algorithms called "overdamping" and "rampdown." Since the initial proposal, the authors updated their approach to form a unified and improved algorithm they call *rate halving*, based on earlier work by Hoe [H96]. To ensure that it works as effectively as possible, they further govern its behavior by adding bounding parameters, resulting in the complete algorithm being called *Rate-Halving with Bounding Parameters* (RHBP) [PSCRH].

The basic operation of RHBP allows the TCP sender to send one packet for every two duplicate ACKs it receives during one RTT. This causes the recovering TCP to have sent the appropriate amount of data by the end of the recovery period, but it spaces or *paces* this data evenly, rather than bunching all the transmissions into the second half of the RTT period. Avoiding the bunching or burstiness is advantageous because bursts tend to persist across multiple RTTs, stressing router buffers more than required.

To keep an accurate estimate of the flight size, RHBP uses information from SACKs to determine the FACK: the highest sequence number known to have reached the receiver, plus 1. Taking the difference between the highest sequence number about to be sent by the sender (SND.NXT in Figure 15-9) and the FACK gives an estimate of the flight size, not including retransmissions.

With RHBP, a distinction is made between the *adjustment interval* (the period when *cwnd* is modified) and the *repair interval* (when some segments are retransmitted). The adjustment interval is entered immediately upon a loss or congestion indicator. The final value for *cwnd* when the interval completes is half of the correctly delivered portion of the window of data in the network at the time of detection. The following expression allows the RHBP sender to transmit, if satisfied:

$$(SND.NXT - fack + retran\_data + len) < cwnd$$

This expression captures the flight size, including retransmissions, and ensures that if injecting another packet of length *len*, *cwnd* will not be exceeded. Provided all the data prior to the FACK is indeed no longer in the network (i.e., is lost or stored at the receiver), this causes the SACK sender to be appropriately controlled by *cwnd*. However, it can be overly aggressive if packets have been reordered in the network because the holes indicated by SACK have not been lost.

In Linux, FACK and rate halving are implemented and enabled by default. FACK is activated only when SACK is enabled and the Boolean configuration variable net.ipv4.tcp_fack is set to 1. When reordering is detected in the network, the more aggressive behavior of FACK is disabled.

Rate halving is one of several ways of pacing TCP's sending procedure to avoid or limit burstiness. Although it offers a number of benefits, it also has a few problems. In [ASA00], the authors analyze TCP pacing in some detail using simulations, concluding that in many cases it offers inferior performance to TCP Reno. Furthermore, rate-halving TCP has been known to exhibit poor performance when the connection may become limited by the receiver's advertised window [MM05].

16.3.4 Limited Transmit

In [RFC3042], the authors propose *limited transmit*, a small modification to TCP designed to help it perform better when the usable window is small. Recall from the experience with Reno TCP that when operating with a small window, there may not be enough packets in the network to trigger the fast retransmit/recovery algorithms when loss occurs, as these algorithms typically require three duplicate ACKs to be observed prior to initiation.

With limited transmit, a TCP with unsent data is permitted to send a new packet for each pair of consecutive duplicate ACKs it receives. Doing this helps to keep at least a minimal number of packets in the network—enough so that fast retransmit can be triggered upon packet loss. This is advantageous to TCP because waiting for an RTO (which can be a relatively large amount of time—several hundred milliseconds) can degrade throughput performance considerably. As of [RFC5681], limited transmit is now a recommended TCP behavior. Note that rate halving is one form of limited transmit.

16.3.5 Congestion Window Validation (CWV)

One of the issues with congestion management in TCP arises when the TCP sender stops sending for a period of time, either because it has no more data to send, or because it has been prevented from sending when it wants to for some other reason. If all goes well, a sender never pauses, and it continues sending data and receiving ACKs from its peer. This continuous feedback enables it to keep a reasonably current (within one RTT) estimate of what *cwnd* and *ssthresh* should be.

If the TCP sender has been sending for some time, its *cwnd* may have grown to a substantial size. If it then fails to send for some time but resumes later, the large *cwnd* may allow the sender to inject an undesirably large number of packets (i.e., a high-rate burst) into the network without delay. Furthermore, if the pause is sufficiently long, its last *cwnd* value may no longer be appropriate for the path and congestion state.

In [RFC2861], the authors propose an experimental *Congestion Window Validation* (CWV) mechanism. Essentially, the sender's current value of *cwnd* decays over a period of nonuse, and *ssthresh* maintains the "memory" of it prior to the initiation of the decay. To understand the scheme, a distinction is made between an *idle* sender and an *application-limited* sender. The idle sender has stopped producing data it wants to send into the network; ACKs for all the data it has sent so far have been received. Thus, the connection is truly quiescent—no data is flowing, so no ACKs are either, except for occasional window updates (see Chapter 15). The application-limited sender does have more data to send but has been unable to for some reason. This could be because the sending computer is busy doing other tasks, or because some mechanism or protocol layer below TCP is preventing data from being sent. This case results in underutilization of the allowed congestion window, but the connection is not completely quiescent. In particular, ACKs may still be returning for previously sent data.

The CWV algorithm work as follows: Whenever a new packet is to be sent, the time since the last send event is measured to determine if it exceeds one RTO. If so,

- *ssthresh* is modified but not reduced—it is set to max(*ssthresh*, (3/4)*cwnd*).

- *cwnd* is reduced by half for each RTT of idle time but is always at least 1 SMSS.

For application-limited periods that are not idle, the following similar behavior is used:

- The amount of window actually used is stored in *W_used*.

- *ssthresh* is modified but not reduced—it is set to max(*ssthresh*, (3/4)*cwnd*).

- *cwnd* is set to the average of *cwnd* and *W_used*.

Both of these changes decay the value of *cwnd* while "remembering" it in *ssthresh*. The first case can dramatically affect *cwnd* in one operation, if the application has been idle for a long time. Handling the congestion window in this way can lead to better performance under some circumstances. As the authors report, reducing the burst of packets that can arise after an idle period eases the pressure on potentially limited buffer space in routers, ultimately leading to fewer dropped packets. Note that because *cwnd* is decayed and *ssthresh* is not, the typical consequence of applying this algorithm is to place the sender into slow start after a long enough pause. CWV is enabled by default in Linux TCP implementations.

16.4 Handling Spurious RTOs—the Eifel Response Algorithm

As we saw in Chapter 15, when TCP encounters a large delay spike, it can experience a retransmission timeout even if no packet has been lost. Such spurious retransmissions arise in a number of circumstances relating to changes in the underlying link layer (such as cellular handoff) or sudden onset of severe congestion contributing to a large increase in RTT. When this happens, the TCP adjusts *ssthresh* and enters slow start by setting *cwnd* to *IW*. If no packets have been lost, ACKs arriving after the RTO cause *cwnd* to grow relatively quickly, but TCP still sends unnecessary retransmissions and underutilizes the capacity until *cwnd* and *ssthresh* resettle.

To avoid the performance problems associated with spurious retransmissions, several methods have been proposed to detect them. We discussed some of them (e.g., DSACK, Eifel, F-RTO) in Chapter 14. Any one of these, or possibly others that may be developed, can be coupled with a *response algorithm* used to "undo" the changes TCP makes to its congestion control variables after a timeout. One popular (i.e., in the IETF standards track) response algorithm is the *Eifel Response Algorithm* [RFC4015].

Eifel comprises both a detection and a response algorithm, which are logically disjoint. Any TCP implementation using the Eifel Response Algorithm is compelled to use some detection algorithm specified in a standards-track or experimental RFC (i.e., one that is documented).

The Eifel Response Algorithm is aimed at handling the retransmission timer and congestion control state after a retransmission timer has expired. Here we discuss only the congestion-related portions of the response algorithm. It is initiated after the first timeout-based retransmission is sent. Its purpose is to undo a change to *ssthresh* when a retransmission is deemed to be spurious. In all cases, before *ssthresh* is modified as a result of the RTO, it is captured in a special variable as follows: *pipe_prev* = min(*flight size*, *ssthresh*). Once this has been accomplished, a detection algorithm, such as one of those mentioned previously, is invoked in order to determine if the RTO is spurious. If it is, the following steps are executed when an ACK arrives after the retransmission:

1. If a received good ACK includes an ECN-Echo flag, stop (see Section 16.11).

2. *cwnd* = *flight size* + min(*bytes_acked*, *IW*) (assuming *cwnd* is measured in bytes).

3. *ssthresh* = *pipe_prev*.

The *pipe_prev* variable is set before *ssthresh* is changed in the ordinary way. It provides a memory for *ssthresh*, so that it can be reinstantiated in step 3 if necessary. Step 1 deals with the case of an arriving ACK carrying the ECN flag. (We discuss ECN more in Section 16.11.) When this happens, it is considered unsafe to avoid undoing the reduction of *ssthresh*, so the algorithm terminates. Steps 2 and 3 constitute the important part of the algorithm (with respect to *cwnd*). Step 2 restores *cwnd* to a point where it may be able to inject some additional traffic into the network, but not more than *IW* new data. *IW* is considered a safe amount of data to inject into a network path with unknown congestion state. Step 3 restores *ssthresh* to its value before the RTO occurred, completing the undo operation.

16.5 An Extended Example

We now turn to an extended example to demonstrate most of the behaviors described in the preceding sections. Using the `sock` program, we arrange to send about 2.5MB of data from a Linux (2.6) sender to a FreeBSD (5.4) receiver over a DSL line. The DSL line is rate-limited in this direction to approximately 300Kb/s. The FreeBSD receiver is attached to a high-bandwidth connection. The minimum RTT between sender and receiver is 15.9ms, and there are 17 hops in the path. The systems are configured to use the baseline algorithms (i.e., slow start and congestion avoidance) for most of their processing. This avoids many of the operating-system-specific details. (We cover some of these later.) To set up this experiment, we run the following command at the receiver:

```
FreeBSD% sock -i -r 32768 -R 233016 -s 6666
```

This command arranges for the `sock` program to use a fairly large socket receive buffer (228KB) and perform fairly large application reads (32KB). For the path used, this is an adequate size of buffer for the receiver. At the sender we run the `sock` program in sending mode, as follows:

```
Linux% sock -n20 -i -w 131072 -S 262144 128.32.37.219 6666
```

This selects a large send buffer and sends 20*131,072 bytes (2.5MB) of data. The packet trace is captured using `tcpdump` on the sender. The command used to capture this trace is as follows:

```
Linux# tcpdump -s 128 -w sack-to-free-12.td port 6666
```

This ensures that at least 128 bytes of each packet are captured, plenty to capture all interesting TCP and IP header information. After the trace is collected, we can use the `tcptrace` tool [TCPTRACE] to get a number of useful summary statistics regarding the connection:

```
Linux% tcptrace -Wl sack-to-free-12.td
```

This command requests the program to provide information on the congestion window and output using a long (verbose) format. It produces the following output:

```
1 arg remaining, starting with 'sack-to-free-12.td'
Ostermann's tcptrace -- version 6.6.7 -- Thu Nov  4, 2004

3175 packets seen, 3175 TCP packets traced
elapsed wallclock time: 0:00:00.167213, 18987 pkts/sec analyzed
trace file elapsed time: 0:01:40.475872
TCP connection info:
1 TCP connection traced:
TCP connection 1:
        host a:          adsl-63-203-72-138.dsl.snfc21.pacbell.net:1059
        host b:          dwight.CS.Berkeley.EDU:6666
        complete conn: yes
        first packet:  Wed Sep 28 22:15:29.956897 2005
        last packet:   Wed Sep 28 22:17:10.432769 2005
        elapsed time:  0:01:40.475872
        total packets: 3175
        filename:      sack-to-free-12.td
    a->b:                                    b->a:
    total packets:          1903             total packets:          1272
    ack pkts sent:          1902             ack pkts sent:          1272
    pure acks sent:            2             pure acks sent:         1270
    sack pkts sent:            0             sack pkts sent:           79
    dsack pkts sent:           0             dsack pkts sent:           0
    max sack blks/ack:         0             max sack blks/ack:         2
    unique bytes sent:   2621440             unique bytes sent:         0
    actual data pkts:       1900             actual data pkts:          0
    actual data bytes:   2659240             actual data bytes:         0
    rexmt data pkts:          27             rexmt data pkts:           0
    rexmt data bytes:      37800             rexmt data bytes:          0
    zwnd probe pkts:           0             zwnd probe pkts:           0
    zwnd probe bytes:          0             zwnd probe bytes:          0
    outoforder pkts:           0             outoforder pkts:           0
    pushed data pkts:         44             pushed data pkts:          0
    SYN/FIN pkts sent:       1/1             SYN/FIN pkts sent:       1/1
    req 1323 ws/ts:          Y/Y             req 1323 ws/ts:          Y/Y
    adv wind scale:            2             adv wind scale:            2
    req sack:                  Y             req sack:                  Y
    sacks sent:                0             sacks sent:               79
    urgent data pkts:          0 pkts        urgent data pkts:          0 pkts
    urgent data bytes:         0 bytes       urgent data bytes:         0 bytes
    mss requested:          1412 bytes       mss requested:          1460 bytes
    max segm size:          1400 bytes       max segm size:             0 bytes
    min segm size:           640 bytes       min segm size:             0 bytes
    avg segm size:          1399 bytes       avg segm size:             0 bytes
    max win adv:            5808 bytes       max win adv:          233016 bytes
    min win adv:            5808 bytes       min win adv:          170016 bytes
    zero win adv:              0 times       zero win adv:              0 times
    avg win adv:            5808 bytes       avg win adv:          232268 bytes
```

max owin:	137201 bytes	max owin:		1 bytes
min non-zero owin:	1 bytes	min non-zero owin:		1 bytes
avg owin:	37594 bytes	avg owin:		1 bytes
wavg owin:	33285 bytes	wavg owin:		0 bytes
initial window:	2800 bytes	initial window:		0 bytes
initial window:	2 pkts	initial window:		0 pkts
ttl stream length:	2621440 bytes	ttl stream length:		0 bytes
missed data:	0 bytes	missed data:		0 bytes
truncated data:	2556640 bytes	truncated data:		0 bytes
truncated packets:	1900 pkts	truncated packets:		0 pkts
data xmit time:	99.631 secs	data xmit time:	0.000 secs	
idletime max:	7778.8 ms	idletime max:	7930.4 ms	
throughput:	26090 Bps	throughput:		0 Bps

From this useful tool we can learn quite a bit about the connection. We are primarily interested in the left portion of the output (a->b). First of all, we see that 1903 packets were sent in the a->b direction and 1902 of them were ACKs. This is expected, as the very first packet is normally a SYN—the only packet without the ACK flag turned on. Pure ACKs refer to packets containing no data. The sender produces one of these early in the connection, when providing an ACK to its peer's SYN + ACK and when producing the final ACK when the connection is closed, so this is also expected. In the second column (b->a direction), we find that the receiver sent 1272 packets, all of which are ACKs. Of these, 1270 were pure ACKs, and 79 SACK packets (i.e., ACKs containing the SACK option) were sent. The two "non-pure" ACKs are the SYN + ACK and the FIN + ACK sent at the beginning and end of the connection, respectively.

The next five values indicate the proportion of data that was retransmitted. As we can see, 2,621,440 unique bytes were sent (i.e., not retransmitted), but 2,659,240 bytes were sent in total, meaning some 2,659,240 − 2,621,440 = 37,800 bytes must have been sent more than once. The next two fields confirm this and indicate that these retransmitted bytes were contained in 27 retransmitted packets, for an average retransmitted segment size of 1399 bytes. Because this connection transferred 2,659,240 bytes in 100.476s, its average throughput is 26,466 bytes/s (about 212Kb/s). Its average goodput, the amount of unretransmitted data transferred per unit time, is 2,621,440/100.476 = 26,090 B/s, about 209Kb/s. As we shall see, this connection experiences a number of significant disruptions to its normal operation. We shall use Wireshark's analysis capabilities and our own analysis to follow TCP's behavior when such events occur.

To get a visual image of the trace, we can use the Statistics | TCP Stream Graph | Time-Sequence Graph (tcptrace) function in Wireshark's Statistics menu to obtain the image shown in Figure 16-4 (enhanced with arrows for the discussion that follows).

The y-axis of Figure 16-4 represents the relative TCP sequence number. Each small tick mark represents 100,000 sequence numbers. The x-axis is time, in seconds. The dark solid line comprises many smaller I-shaped line segments, each of which represents the range of sequence numbers contained in a TCP segment.

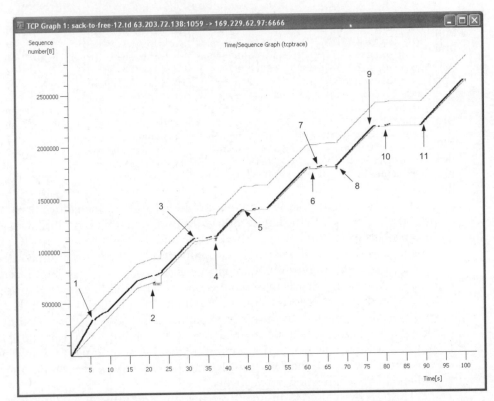

Figure 16-4 Wireshark trace of a 2.5MB file upload executed by a Linux 2.6.10 TCP sender over a DSL line rate-limited to approximately 300Kb/s. The dark line represents sent sequence numbers. The top line is the highest sequence number advertised by the receiver (its right window edge), and the lower line represents the highest segment acknowledged by the receiver so far seen at the sender. The 11 events labeled represent cases where the congestion window has been modified.

The height of the I indicates the user-data payload size, in bytes. The slope of the "line" formed by these I-shaped characters is the data rate achieved by the connection. Any movement to the lower right indicates a retransmission. The slope of the line for any given time range provides the average throughput over that time. As we can see, the highest sequence number sent was about 2600000 at time 100, which provides for a rough average goodput rate of 26,000 bytes/s, quite close to the numeric value from the preceding `tcptrace` output.

The top line is the largest sequence number the receiver is willing to accept (its highest advertised window) so far. As we can see, at the beginning of the time series, this line is at about 250000, with the actual value being 233016, as indicated in the `tcptrace` output, in the b→a column. The bottom line represents the highest ACK number received at the sender so far. As discussed previously, TCP searches for additional bandwidth while it operates, by increasing its congestion window. It does not violate the receiver's advertised window. We see this in operation in this graph as the solid line moves from the lower line toward the upper line over time. If the upper line is never reached, either the sender or the usable network capacity is the limiting factor for the throughput of the connection. If the upper line is always reached, the receiver's window is the likely limiting factor.

16.5.1 Slow Start Behavior

We begin our analysis by observing the operation of the slow start algorithm described earlier. In Wireshark, we select the first packet of the trace and then use its Statistics | Flow graph function to illustrate the packets exchanged at the beginning of the connection (see Figure 16-5).

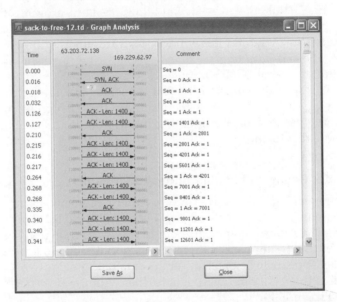

Figure 16-5 The Wireshark analysis shows the sequence and ACK numbers exchanged when the connection is first established. Each ACK received at the sender liberates two or three packets. This characteristic is typical of a sender in slow start.

Here we see the initial SYN and SYN + ACK exchange. The ACK at time 0.032 is a window update (see Chapter 15). The first two data packets are sent at times 0.126 and 0.127. The ACK at time 0.210 is not for a single packet. Its ACK number is 2801 and thus ACKs both of the previously sent data packets because of the cumulative property of TCP ACKs. This is an example of delayed ACKs, which are often generated for every other data packet (or more frequently, as recommended by [RFC5681]). As we shall see for this particular (FreeBSD 5.4) receiver, it alternates between ACKing one packet and two packets. This means there are two

ACKs returned for every three data packets sent on average (assuming no errors or retransmissions). We discussed delayed ACKs and window updates in Chapter 15.

An ACK arriving that covers two packets allows the sliding window at the sender to move forward by two packets and therefore permits two additional packets to be sent into the network. However, because this connection is just starting out and it is still executing slow start, the arrival of a good ACK causes the sender to increase its congestion window by one packet (this Linux TCP manages its congestion window in packet units). In this case, the *cwnd* grows from 2 to 3. This has effect of allowing *three* packets to be sent overall as a result of the arriving ACK. They are sent at times 0.215, 0.216, and 0.217.

The ACK arriving at time 0.264 ACKs a single packet and indicates that the receiver next expects to see sequence number 4201. That packet, however, and the one after it with sequence number 5601, have already been sent and are still outstanding. Thus, the ACK arrival allows *cwnd* to grow from 3 to 4, but because two packets are already outstanding, only two more are allowed to be sent (one because the ACK slid the window forward, another because the received good ACK allowed *cwnd* to grow by one packet). They are sent at times 0.268 and 0.268 (within the same 1/1000s).

This startup behavior is typical of a sender executing slow start with a receiver delaying ACKs. The process continues in this fashion (each ACK liberating two or three packets) until something interesting occurs at about time 5.6. We now explore this further.

16.5.2 Sender Pause and Local Congestion (Event 1)

Looking at Figure 16-4, we find that after a segment is sent at time 5.512, a pause occurs until the next data segment is set at time 6.162. This can be better seen by using Wireshark's graphical zoom-in feature as shown in Figure 16-6.

In this figure we see that the sender has stopped sending, no retransmitted packet appears to be present, yet the data rate appears to decrease after the pause. Why is this? We can investigate further with the flow trace function once again (see Figure 16-7).

The sending TCP has evidently ceased its sending demand at time 5.559. This is supported by the fact that the last transmitted data segment before the pause has the *PSH* flag turned on, which typically indicates that the sending buffer has been emptied. There could be several reasons for this, including the possibility that the host system is busy doing something else, preventing the sending application from initiating its next write of data into the network.

We can observe that this pause is not the beginning of a retransmission recovery period, yet the slope of the line decreases after the pause, indicating a reduced sending rate. Let us explore this behavior more closely to figure out why.

The last sequence number sent before the pause is $343001 + 1400 - 1 = 344400$, which has never been sent before and is therefore not a retransmission. After the segment is sent at time 5.486 (highlighted), this connection will have its greatest amount of outstanding data: $341,601 + 1400 - 205,801 = 137,200$ bytes (98 packets).

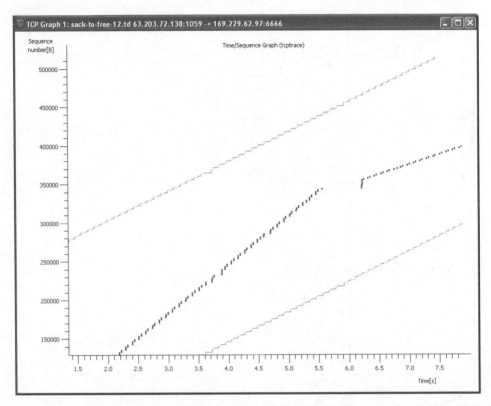

Figure 16-6 After starting using the slow start procedure, the connection pauses for about 512ms, at time 5.512, and then continues by sending a burst.

This tells us that the value of *cwnd* is 98 packets. The arrival of the ACK at time 5.556 indicates that two more packets have been received at the receiver. The last packet to be sent before the pause contains sequence number 344400, so 97 packets are outstanding.

While the application is paused, 11 ACKs arrive (each alternating between ACKing either one or two full-size segments as mentioned before). The last one indicates that sequence number 233800 has been received, meaning 110,600 bytes (79 packets) now remain outstanding. At this point, the sender wakes up and continues to transmit. As a result of receiving this ACK at time 6.204, it should be able to inject 98 – 79 = 19 more packets at this point but is able to send only 8. The last sequence number it is able to send is 354201 + 1400 – 1 = 355600 at time 6.128.

What happens to the TCP at this point is not immediately obvious from the trace. We would have expected 19 packets to be sent, but only 8 were. The reason is that the sender filled a local (lower-layer) queue with its burst of packets and the subsequent ones were unable to be sent. Using the following command in Linux, and knowing that our transfer takes place over the **ppp0** network interface, we can try to determine if some lower layer has caused TCP to have problems:

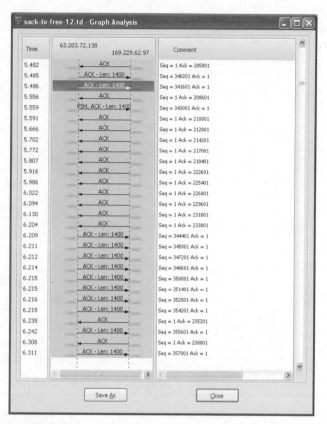

Figure 16-7   The sender pauses at time 5.559. In addition, the burst of packets at time 6.209 is limited to eight because of local congestion. Some TCP implementations such as this one limit the sending rate to avoid congesting queues on the sending host.

```
Linux% tc -s -d qdisc show dev ppp0
qdisc pfifo_fast 0: bands 3 priomap  1 2 2 2 1 2 0 0 1 1 1 1 1 1 1 1
Sent 122569547 bytes 348574 pkts (dropped 2, overlimits 0 requeues 0)
```

The tc program is used to administer the *packet scheduling and traffic control subsystem* in Linux [LARTC]. The −s and −d options provide detailed statistics. The directive qdisc show dev ppp0 means the *queuing discipline* for device ppp0 should be displayed, which is the method used to hold and prioritize the order in which packets are sent. Notice the two dropped packets. These packets were not dropped in the network but rather in the sending computer in a protocol layer below TCP. Furthermore, because they were dropped in a layer below TCP but above the layer where the packet capture facility operates, these packet transmission attempts are not visible in the trace. Dropping transmitted TCP packets at the sending system is sometimes called *local congestion*, and it arises because TCP is producing data faster than the underlying local queues can be emptied.

Note

The Linux traffic control subsystem and other priority or QoS features supported in routers and operating systems (e.g., Microsoft's qWave API [WQOS]) support different queuing disciplines that may order packets differently based on features in the packets (e.g., the IP DSCP value or TCP port number). Placing priority on some packets (e.g., multimedia data packets, TCP pure ACKs) may improve the user experience for interactive applications in networks that support priority. Much of the Internet does not support such priorities, but many LANs and some enterprise IP networks do.

Local congestion is one of several reasons the Linux TCP implementation may be placed in the *Congestion Window Reducing* (CWR) state [SK02]. It starts by setting *ssthresh* to *cwnd*/2, and by setting *cwnd* to min(*cwnd, flight size* + 1). In the CWR state, the sender reduces *cwnd* by one packet for every two ACKs received until *cwnd* reaches the new *ssthresh* or the CWR state is exited for some other reason such as a loss event. It is essentially the rate-halving algorithm we mentioned previously. It is also invoked when the sending TCP receives an ECN-Echo indication in the received TCP header (see Section 16.1.1).

With this knowledge, we can now understand what happened. When TCP continues after the pause, it is able to send only 8 packets. Any additional packets cannot be sent because of local congestion and instead place the TCP into the CWR state. Immediately, *ssthresh* is reduced to 98/2 = 49 packets and *cwnd* is set to 79 + 8 = 87 packets. It then remains in the CWR state where it reduces *cwnd* by 1 for every two ACKs it receives, leading to a reduction in sending rate, until *cwnd* reaches 66 packets at time 8.364.

The reduction in sending rate can also be observed as follows: Looking at Figure 16-6, before time 5.5 the slope of the line gives an effective data rate of approximately 500Kb/s. This is higher than the capacity of the link in the direction of the data transfer, so this extra apparent capacity is the result of one or more queues being filled up in the path, leading to an increased RTT because of queuing delay. We can use the Statistics | TCP Stream Graph | Round Trip Time Graph to visualize this effect (see Figure 16-8).

In this figure, the *y*-axis represents the estimated RTT in seconds and the *x*-axis represents the sequence number. We can see that at approximately sequence number 340000, the RTT begins to decrease. This sequence number corresponds closely to the last sequence number sent before the pause described earlier (344400). The decreasing RTT corresponds to the fact that as the sender slows down, the network is becoming less loaded (i.e., the rate at which data is draining from the network exceeds the rate at which new traffic is arriving). This causes queues within network routers to empty, leading to a smaller wait time and a consequentially lower RTT.

The sending rate reduction continues while TCP remains in the CWR state. Eventually, if this continued, the RTT would decrease to its bare minimum value of about 17ms. In general, TCP avoids allowing this to happen because it wants to

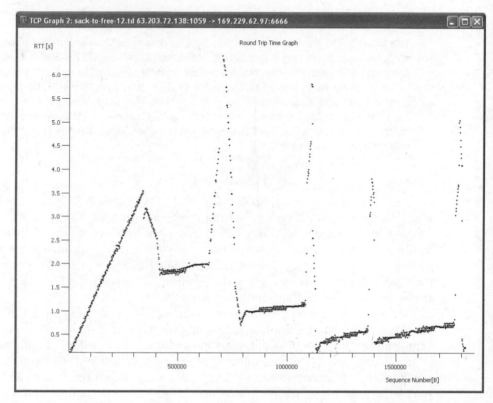

Figure 16-8   The sender's estimated connection round-trip time. Periods of increasing RTT (dense groupings of increasing values) correspond to buffers filling because of an excess of sending rate over forwarding rate at a router along the path. Decreasing RTTs represent the opposite effect, resulting from the sender slowing down and the queues draining.

"keep the pipe full" to ensure that it is using the maximum amount of network capacity currently available to it.

16.5.3 Stretch ACKs and Recovery from Local Congestion

At time 8.364, following the gradual reduction in *cwnd* initially caused by the TCP entering the CWR state, the TCP appears to start decreasing more quickly. This is a consequence of a change in the relationship of *cwnd* and the amount of outstanding data indicated by the ACK at time 8.362 (highlighted in Figure 16-9).

The ACK at time 8.362 is for sequence number 317801, but the previously received ACK is for sequence number 313601, meaning this new ACK is for 317,801 – 313,601 = 4200 bytes (three packets). This is commonly called a *stretch ACK*, meaning it ACKs more than twice the largest segment sent so far. It could be caused by a number of possibilities, the simplest of which is a lost ACK. It is usually difficult to determine with certainty the cause of the stretch ACK, but the precise reason

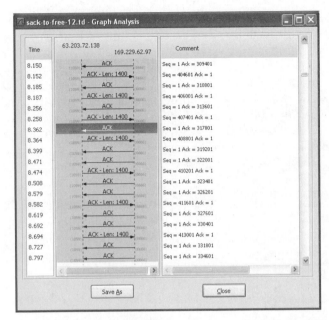

Figure 16-9   A "stretch ACK" acknowledges three packets' worth of sequence numbers. Such ACKs can cause the sender to act in a bursty manner and can occur when other ACKs are lost in transit.

is not usually important. In this example, we can assume that an earlier ACK was lost and continue to investigate how the sender behaves. Its arrival causes *cwnd* to drop from 68 to 66.

The Linux TCP implementation attempts to revise its estimate of the number of outstanding packets whenever it receives an ACK. (It also attempts to validate the congestion window whenever it sends segments, according to the Congestion Window Validation algorithm described previously, but this does not have an effect here.) When in CWR state, if the outstanding packet count estimate is reduced for some reason, as it is here after receiving the stretch ACK, *cwnd* is adjusted to be the estimate plus 1. Note that this is in addition to its ordinary behavior in CWR, where it reduces *cwnd* by 1 for each pair of ACKs received. Generally, *cwnd* is reduced by either 1 or 0 for each ACK, and then *cwnd* is set to min(*flight size* + 1, [possibly reduced] *cwnd*). The CWR state remains operating until *cwnd* reaches *ssthresh* or some other event, such as a loss and retransmission, occurs.

Prior to receiving the stretch ACK, at time 8.258, 407,401 + 1400 − 313,601 = 95,200 bytes (68 packets) are outstanding. After the stretch ACK is received, the number of outstanding packets is reduced to 65 and *cwnd* is set to 66.

Because the flight size estimate and *cwnd* are closely coupled in the CWR state, and the TCP receiver in this example delays ACKs, the result of a pair of ACKs arriving is to reduce *cwnd* by 2 and to liberate one packet. The reason for this is as follows: Assume that before the arrival of any ACKs, *cwnd* is c_0 and the flight size estimate is $f_0 = c_0$. When the first ACK arrives (i.e., for one packet), $f_1 = f_0 - 1$ and *cwnd* is updated to $c_1 = \min(c_0 - 1, f_1 + 1) = c_0 - 1$. When the second ACK arrives (for two packets, because of delayed ACKs), $f_2 = f_1 - 2 = c_0 - 3$ and *cwnd* is set to $c_2 = \min(c_1, f_2 + 1) = \min(c_0 - 1, c_0 - 2) = c_0 - 2$. Because the congestion window has shrunk by two packets, but three packets have been ACKed during this period, a single packet is liberated after the receipt of the second ACK.

The sender exits the CWR state at time 9.37 when *cwnd* reaches *ssthresh* at 49 packets. TCP now returns to normal behavior and continues in congestion avoidance (see Figures 16-10 and 16-11).

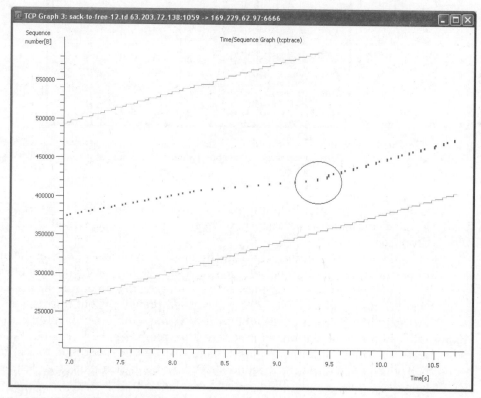

Figure 16-10   By time 9.369, the sender reverts to normal and sends either one or two packets per received ACK.

In Figure 16-10, the circled packets indicate where the sender's state changes from CWR back to normal, where the congestion avoidance algorithm takes over. Figure 16-11 shows this behavior in more detail.

The sender continues in congestion avoidance, achieving relatively stable throughput until time 17.232. At this point, severe network congestion begins to

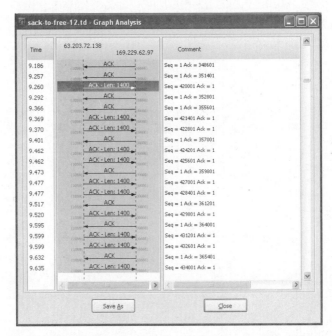

Figure 16-11   TCP has completed its recovery and is back in the normal (congestion avoidance) state. It sends one or two packets for each ACK received.

form, contributing to a large increase in the RTT. In Figure 16-8, this happens at sequence number 720000, where the RTT grows to about 6.5s—a more than three-fold increase from its previously stable value of about 2s. This effect is common with the onset of severe congestion. Eventually, the network congestion is sufficiently severe so as to cause a packet to be dropped. The sending TCP responds with its first retransmission.

16.5.4 Fast Retransmission and SACK Recovery (Event 2)

At time 21.209, after the dramatic increase in measured RTT, we observe the first retransmission. We can see this in more detail by zooming in as shown in Figure 16-12. The first retransmission (circled) is for the packet starting with sequence number 690201, matching the highest ACK received so far (also 690201). It is triggered by the receipt of a single duplicate ACK carrying the SACK block [698601,700001]. Recall that these numbers indicate the sequence number range already received at the receiver. In this case, it is a single packet.

At time 21.209, when the retransmission takes place, the largest sequence number sent so far is $761601 + 1400 - 1 = 763000$, and *cwnd* is 52. In conjunction with this fast retransmit, *ssthresh* is reduced from 49 to 26, and TCP enters the Recovery state. This TCP remains in Recovery state until it receives a cumulative ACK for the recovery point: sequence number 763000 (or higher). In addition,

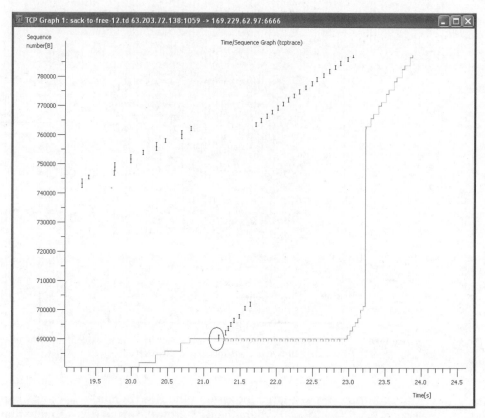

Figure 16-12   The first retransmission (circled) occurs at time 21.209. SACK blocks are used to guide the sender as to what packets to retransmit. Eight retransmissions in total occur between times 21.0 and 22.0.

cwnd is reduced to (*flight size* + 1) packets. However, because data has likely been lost, determining the flight size is not so straightforward. It is accomplished using the following relationship:

$$flight\ size = packets\_outstanding + packets\_retransmitted - packets\_removed$$

The first term on the right-hand side represents all the packets sent once by the sender and not yet ACKed with the regular TCP cumulative *ACK* field. The second term represents any that have been resent (and not ACKed), and the final term represents any packets that are no longer in the network but also have not been ACKed by the basic TCP cumulative ACK. The value of *packets_removed* must be estimated because TCP has no reliable way to directly learn it. It represents the sum of any (out-of-order) packets cached at the receiver plus any packets that have been lost in the network. With SACK, it is possible to learn the number of packets cached at the receiver, but the number of lost packets must still be estimated.

The value of *packets_outstanding* here is (763,001 − 690,201)/1400 = 72,800/1400 = 52 and the number of packets cached in the receiver is (700,001 − 698,601)/1400 = 1400/1400 = 1 (derived from the sequence numbers in the SACK block). With FACK enabled, as it is here by default, holes in the receiver inferred by SACK information are considered to be lost. Thus, in this case, TCP estimates that 698,601 − 690,201 = 8400 (6 packets) have been lost. The *flight size* is therefore 52 + 1 - (1 + 6) = 46 packets, and *cwnd* is set to 47. While in the Recovery state, TCP reduces *cwnd* by one packet for every two packets it receives, similar to the CWR state. After the first retransmission, another seven retransmissions take place, followed by transmission of new data, based on SACK option data carried in each of the arriving ACKs between times 21.2 and 21.7 (see Figure 16-13).

In this figure, much of the normal Wireshark information has been removed to more clearly see the SACK options on each ACK. By looking at the SACK sequence numbers (SLE and SRE), we can see that most of the time there are two active blocks at the receiver: [698601,700001], which holds one packet, and another [702801,763001] (at its largest), that grows to be 43 packets. During the recovery period, the general rate-halving algorithm applicable to the CWR and Recovery states reduces *cwnd* by at least one packet for every pair of ACKs received. Because each received ACK effectively ACKs one packet in this case (through an increase in the SACK block size by one packet), *flight size* reduces by 1, which would permit another packet to be sent. However, because *cwnd* is also reduced by 1 for every other ACK, it takes two ACKs to liberate a new packet. Note how this differs from the CWR case. In that case, some ACKs provided acknowledgment for two packets, whereas here only one packet is ACKed (SACKed) per arriving ACK. Thus, for each of the transmissions and retransmissions shown in the plot, *cwnd* is reduced by 1 after each pair of ACKs has been received. During this recovery period, overall, *cwnd* shrinks from 47 to 20.

Most ACKs containing SACK options are duplicate ACKs for sequence number 690201 (44 of them), as Wireshark points out. There are five good ACKs that contain the SACK blocks [702801,763001] and [698601,700001]. Two more contain only the SACK block [702801,763001]. These good ACKs do not take the sender out of recovery, because their ACK numbers are all below the sequence number of the recovery point at 763000; they are partial ACKs, as discussed earlier.

TCP recovers from fast retransmit at time 23.301 with the arrival of a good ACK equal to a sequence number (765801) larger than the recovery point. At this point, *cwnd* is 20 and *ssthresh* is 26, meaning TCP is in slow start. By time 23.659, after several round trips, *cwnd* reaches the value 27, TCP is in the normal operating state, and the congestion avoidance algorithm takes over. This completes the sender's first fast retransmit recovery period.

16.5.5 Additional Local Congestion and Fast Retransmit Events

The next four events consist of local congestion, a fast retransmit, and two more local congestion episodes. They are very similar to the types of events we have seen already, so they are summarized here only briefly.

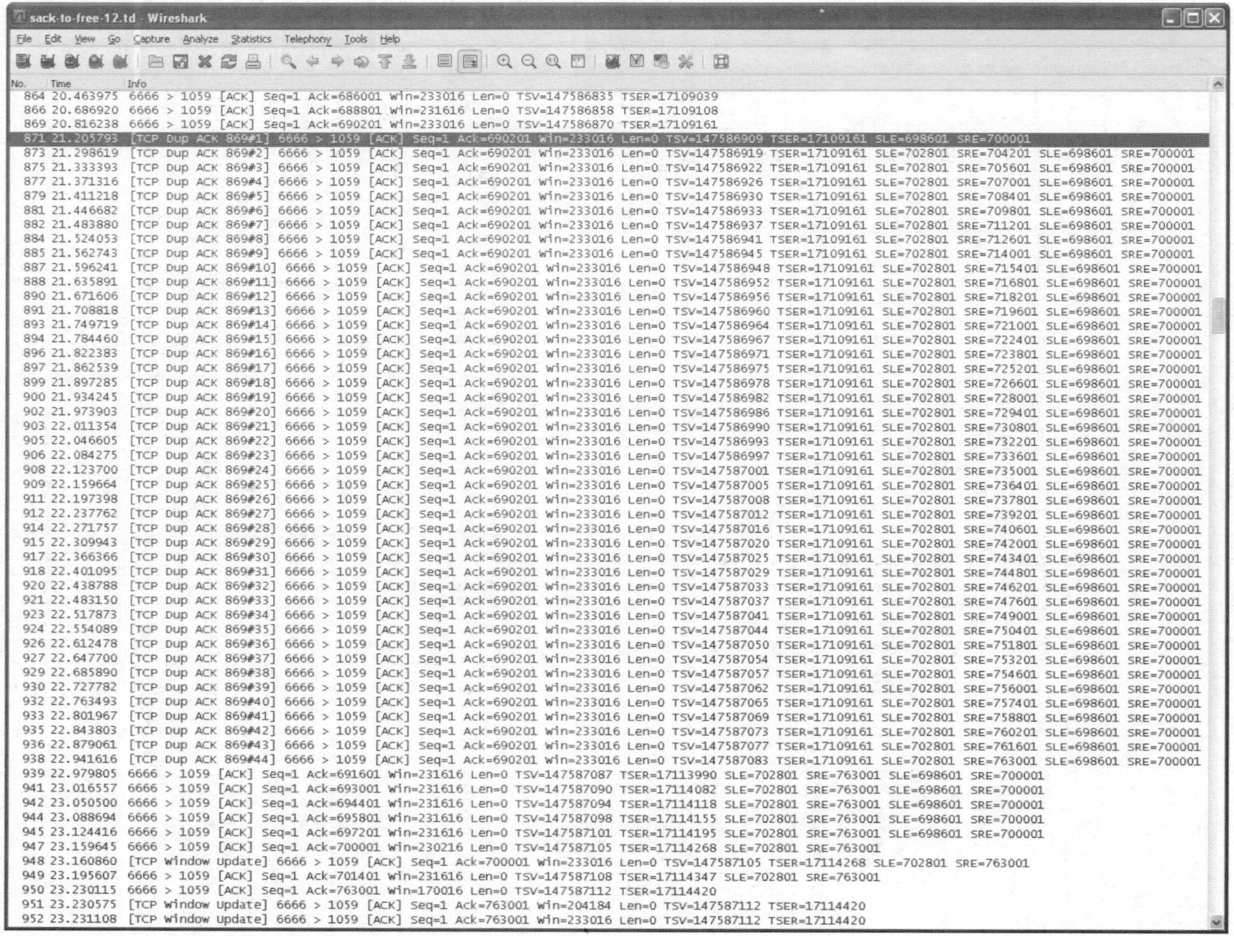

Figure 16-13 SACK recovery after fast retransmission. Packet 871 contains the first SACK option used on the connection. Subsequent ACKs contain SACK information until packet 950.

16.5.5.1 CWR Again (Event 3)

A CWR event due to local congestion occurs at time 30.745. At this point, 1,090,601 + 1400 − 1,051,401 = 40,600 (29 packets) are outstanding, and *cwnd* is 31. This should allow two additional packets to be injected, but none are, because of local congestion. In this particular case, *cwnd* is set to *flight size* + 1 = 30, and *ssthresh* is reduced to 15. TCP exits the CWR state when *cwnd* reaches *ssthresh*. This happens at time 34.759, after another significant increase in the connection's RTT.

16.5.5.2 Second Fast Retransmit (Event 4)

At time 36.914, there is another fast retransmit when *cwnd* = 16. Using the basic display from Wireshark, such retransmissions are easy to spot (see Figure 16-14).

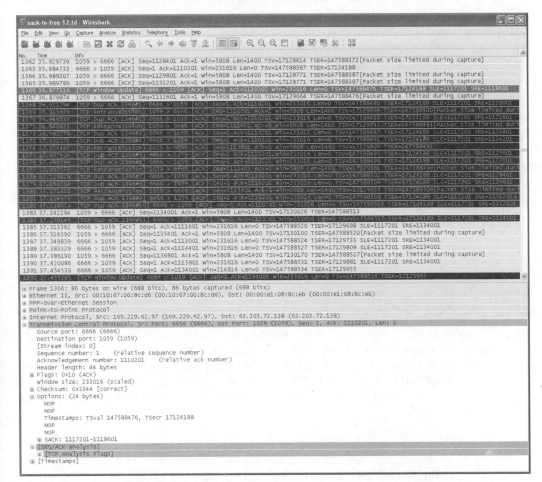

Figure 16-14 A Linux TCP sender enters the Disorder state upon receiving a duplicate ACK or an ACK with SACK information. Packets arriving while in this state trigger transmissions of new data. Subsequent duplicate ACKs (or presence of SACK information) place the sender into the Recovery state where retransmissions take place.

Here, the ACK arriving at time 36.878 (packet 1366) carries the SACK block [1117201,1118601] and ACK number 1110201. This places Linux TCP in the Disorder state, where arriving packets liberate one packet each (similar to limited transmit) of new data. Packet 1367 is the packet liberated in this case.

With the arrival of the ACK at time 36.912 (packet 1368), containing SACK block [1117201,1120001] and a duplicate ACK, TCP enters the Recovery state and triggers the fast retransmit at time 36.914 (packet 1369). The highest sequence number sent so far is $1132601 + 1400 - 1 = 113400$. Recovery is eventually completed at time 37.455, with the arrival of the ACK containing sequence number 1134001 (packet 1391). Note that immediately following this ACK is a window update. For bulk data transfers such as the present example, where the receiver's window is large relative to the bandwidth-delay product of the network, such updates are not usually of much consequence. When we have interactive traffic, small windows, or servers that only occasionally read from the network, these updates can become quite important, as we saw in Chapter 15. When the first retransmission takes place, *ssthresh* is reduced from 16 to 8. Eventually, when recovery completes, *cwnd* = 4 and *ssthresh* = 8. This leaves the sender in slow start because *cwnd* is smaller than *ssthresh*.

16.5.5.3 CWR Again (Events 5 and 6)

After the arrival of the ACK for sequence number 1359401 at time 43.356, TCP once again enters the CWR state because of local congestion when it tries to send subsequent packets. This ultimately reduces *ssthresh* to 8 and *cwnd* becomes 15. A second transmission failure, while in the CWR state, brings *ssthresh* down to 12. The CWR state is exited with *cwnd* = 7 and *ssthresh* = 8.

Another round of local congestion at time 59.652 forces TCP into CWR when *cwnd* = 19 and *ssthresh* = 10. In this case, the CWR state is interrupted by a timeout that places TCP into the Loss state. This represents a new type of event for us to investigate.

16.5.6 Timeouts, Retransmissions, and Undoing *cwnd* Changes

Although TCP keeps a retransmission timer in case fast retransmit is unable to repair a loss, we have not yet seen it in operation. This is fortunate, because generally when a timeout occurs, the connection is experiencing significant congestion and performance problems. In the next portion of the trace, shown in Figure 16-15, we see how the sending TCP handles the situation when its retransmission timer expires.

16.5.6.1 First Timeout (Event 7)

A retransmission occurs at time 62.486 (packet 2157) for sequence number 1773801 (highlighted in Figure 16-15). Immediately prior to this, there is no evidence of duplicate ACKs or SACKs.

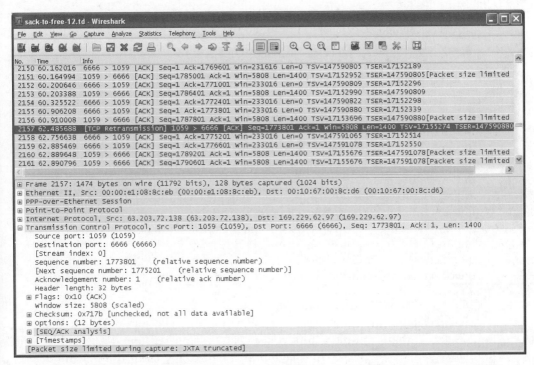

Figure 16-15   The sender experiences its first timeout when RTO = 1.57s. In this case, the sender declares the timeout to be spurious and undoes the modifications it made to its congestion control state.

In Figure 16-15, at time 62.486, about 1.58s have elapsed since the last ACK was received, but according to Figure 16-8, the estimated RTT at this point is only about 800ms. Thus, we may conclude this retransmission to be the result of a retransmission timer expiration. This places TCP into the Loss state, which ordinarily causes a drastic reduction of *cwnd* and effectively restarts the TCP in slow start. Here, TCP sets *cwnd* = 1 and *ssthresh* = 5, placing TCP in slow start, as expected. The timeout also forces any stored SACK information to be discarded. However, the receiver continues to send SACK information, so the sender can still make use of new SACK information it receives.

Note

TCP is supposed to "forget" its knowledge about received SACK information when experiencing a timeout because of the possibility that a receiver may renege on SACK information it provided earlier. This is suggested by [RFC2018] because of the (obscure) possibility that a receiver may wish to adjust its buffering so as to delete out-of-order data it has accumulated. Although not common, such behavior is permitted. When a receiver reneges, it is required to include the most recently received data blocks in the first SACK block of ACKs generated, even if it is discarded. Except for this block, additional blocks must cease to report data no longer being held at the receiver.

Most interestingly here, this congestion action is *undone*. As discussed earlier, the Eifel Response Algorithm can be invoked when TCP believes a retransmission timeout to be erroneous. In this case, it is declared erroneous because of evidence in the timestamp. The ACK received at time 62.757 for sequence number 1775201 (packet 2158) carries a TSOPT with TSV of 17152514. However, the retransmission has the TSV of 17155274. Because the TSER field in the ACK covering the retransmitted segment is *earlier* than the retransmission, the hole the retransmission was attempting to fill was not really a hole at all. Instead, the expiration of the retransmission timer must have been erroneous.

By declaring the retransmission timer expiration to be erroneous and invoking an Eifel-like response algorithm, TCP restores *cwnd* and *ssthresh* to their former values of 10 and immediately shifts to a normal operating state. This activates the congestion avoidance algorithm, and TCP continues without much fuss.

16.5.6.2 Fast Retransmit (Event 8)

The arrival of a duplicate ACK for sequence number 1789201 carrying SACK block [1792001,1793401] at time 67.510 (packet 2179) places TCP into the Disorder state once again. The largest sequence number sent so far when this state is entered is 1806000. Additional arriving SACKs trigger entry into the Recovery state and sending of another fast retransmit at time 67.550 for sequence number 1789201 (packet 2182). This reduces *ssthresh* to 5 and *cwnd* begins shrinking until it also reaches 5. Recovery is complete with the arrival of an ACK at time 67.916 containing sequence number 1806001 (packet 2197).

16.5.6.3 CWR Again (Event 9)

There is another local congestion event at time 77.121 when *cwnd* = 18. This sets *ssthresh* = 9 and places TCP into the CWR state once again. However, the reduction of *cwnd* in the CWR state this time is interrupted early by a timeout, when *cwnd* has been reduced by only 1, to 8.

16.5.6.4 Second Timeout (Event 10)

Another retransmission timeout triggers a retransmission at time 78.515 for sequence number 2175601 (not pictured). This sets *cwnd* = 1; *ssthresh* is still 9 and the retransmitted segment carries the TSOPT TSV value of 17171306. As with timeout event 7, this congestion action is also undone, by the arrival of the ACK at time 80.093 for sequence number 2179801 (packet 2641) containing the TSOPT TSER value of 17169948. When this happens, the *flight size* estimate is 2,184,001 + 1400 − 2,179,801 = 5600 bytes (four packets). If *cwnd* were immediately restored to its pre-timeout condition (8), this would allow four packets to be immediately injected into the network. Doing so is considered undesirable because it may lead to increased changes of dropped packets because of burstiness.

To prevent this bursty behavior, this Linux TCP implementation has a *congestion window moderation* procedure, which limits the maximum number of packets generated in response to a single ACK to *maxburst*, with a value of 3 packets in this example. In this case, *cwnd* is therefore set to (*flight size* + *maxburst*) = 4 + 3 = 7. This regulation is related to the parameter of the same name proposed for TCP and evaluated using the NS-2 network simulator. This simulator has been used extensively in the exploration and development of new TCP algorithms [NS2].

16.5.6.5 Timeout and Final Recovery (Event 11)

At time 88.929 a retransmission timer has expired and a retransmission for sequence number 2185401 occurs, as depicted in Figure 16-16.

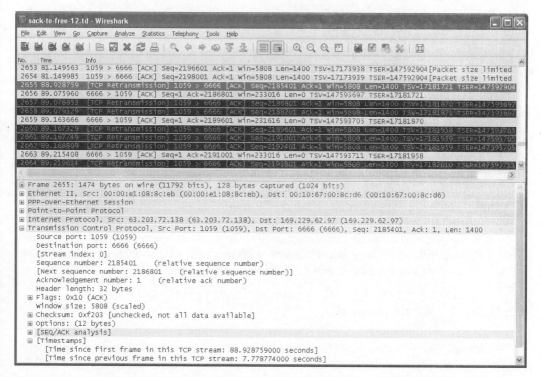

Figure 16-16   A retransmission timer expires, initiating a timeout-based retransmission that cannot be undone. TCP continues in slow start.

The expiring timer places the sender into slow start with *ssthresh* = 5. This time, TCP is not able to undo the timeout, so *cwnd* is set to 1 and slow start progresses. This can be seen more clearly from the flow trace (see Figure 16-17).

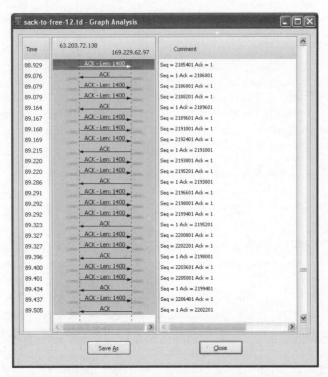

Figure 16-17 In Wireshark, the slow start behavior is apparent after a retransmission timeout. Each arriving ACK liberates two or three packets.

The retransmission for sequence number 2185401 is highlighted. Following the retransmission, we see the typical slow start behavior we saw during the beginning of the connection, when each arriving ACK liberates two or three packets, depending on how many packets were covered by the ACK. By time 89.434, when *cwnd* has reached *ssthresh* at 5, TCP continues in congestion avoidance.

16.5.7 Connection Completion

The final exchange of packets commences with the sender's transmission of a FIN at time 99.757. Following this transmission, 13 ACKs arrive followed by the receiver's FIN. The very last packet (a final ACK) is sent at time 100.476. This exchange is depicted in Figure 16-18.

The largest sequence number sent is 2620801 + 640 − 1 = 2621440, equivalent to the size of the overall transfer, 2.5MB. At time 99.757, (2,619,401 + 1400 − 2,594,201)/1400 + 1 = 20 packets are outstanding. The arrival of 13 ACKs (7 of which ACK two packets each) covers the whole window of (2*7) + (13 − 7) = 20 packets. Note that the ACK arriving at time 100.474 ACKs the final two packets of sizes 1400 and 640 bytes, respectively: 2,621,442 − 2,619,401 = 1400 + 640.

Figure 16-18   During the connection closing procedure, the receiver produces 13 pure ACKs to indicate that it has received all of the data the sender has produced. The final FIN-ACK exchange completes closure of the other half of the connection. Note that the FIN segments contain valid ACK numbers.

This extended example illustrates most of the algorithms described so far and includes aspects of the basic TCP algorithms (slow start, congestion avoidance), selective acknowledgment, rate halving, as well as some newer procedures such as spurious RTO detection. We now discuss some modifications and capabilities that are less widespread, more speculative, or more recent. The Linux TCP stack implements many of these procedures, but not all of them are enabled by default. Frequently, a small change using the `sysctl` program is sufficient to experiment with them. More recent versions of the Windows stack (i.e., Windows Vista and later) also implement improvements beyond the features discussed so far.

16.6   Sharing Congestion State

The discussion so far and the example we have just seen have focused on how a single TCP connection adapts to congestion along the path. If other connections between the same hosts are made later, these subsequent connections typically have to establish their own values for *ssthresh* and *cwnd* over time as described previously. In many cases, subsequent connections could possibly learn of these values from earlier connections to the same hosts or from other currently active connections to the same hosts. This idea involves sharing the congestion state across multiple connections in the same machine. An early description in [RFC2140], entitled "TCP Control Block Interdependence," describes how this might be accomplished. This work notes the difference between *temporal sharing* (new connections share information with others that are now CLOSED) and *ensemble sharing* (new connections share state with other active connections).

In an effort to generalize this idea and extend it to protocols and applications other than TCP, [RFC3124] describes the *Congestion Manager*, which provides a local operating system service available to protocol implementations to learn information such as path loss rate, estimated congestion, RTT, and so forth to destination hosts.

In Linux, this idea is made available in the same subsystem that contains routing information and is known as destination metrics, which we saw in Chapter 15. These metrics are enabled (but they were disabled for the extended example by setting the `sysctl` variable `net.ipv4.tcp_no_metrics_save` to 1). When a TCP connection goes to the CLOSED state, the following information is saved: RTT measurements (*srtt* and *rttvar*), an estimate of reordering, and the congestion control variables *cwnd* and *ssthresh*. These are used when new connections to the same destination start to help initialize the corresponding measurements.

16.7 TCP Friendliness

TCP being the dominant transport protocol on the Internet, it is commonplace for several TCP connections to be sharing one or more routers along their delivery paths. While they do not always share bandwidth equally in such circumstances, they do at least react to the dynamics of other TCP connections as they come and go over time. This is not guaranteed to be the case, however, when TCP competes for bandwidth with other (non-TCP) protocols, or when it competes with a TCP using some alternative set of controls on its congestion window.

To provide a guideline for protocol designers to avoid unfairly competing with TCP flows when operating cooperatively on the Internet, researchers have developed an *equation-based rate control* limit that provides a bound of the bandwidth used by a conventional TCP connection operating in a particular environment. This method is called *TCP Friendly Rate Control* (TFRC) [RFC5348][FHPW00]. It is designed to provide a sending rate limit based on a combination of connection parameters and with environmental factors such as RTT and packet drop rate. It also gives a more stable bandwidth utilization profile than conventional TCP, so it is expected to be appropriate for streaming applications that use moderately large packets (e.g., video transfer). TFRC uses the following equation to determine a sending rate:

$$X = s / \left(R\sqrt{2bp/3} \right) + 3pt_{RTO}\left(1 + 32p^2\right)\sqrt{3bp/8} \qquad [2]$$

Here, X is the throughput rate limit (bytes/second), s is the packet size (bytes, excluding headers), R is the RTT (seconds), p is the number of loss events as a fraction of packets sent [0,1.0], t_{RTO} is the retransmission timeout (seconds), and b is the maximum number of packets acknowledged by a single ACK. The value of t_{RTO} is recommended to be $4R$, and the recommended value of b is 1.

The TCP sending rate can be expressed another way, based on how it adjusts its window in response to receiving a good ACK during congestion avoidance. Recall from the earlier discussion that standard TCP, when using the congestion avoidance algorithm, increases *cwnd* by an additive amount of 1/*cwnd* for each arriving good ACK and decreases it by a multiplicative factor of one-half on a loss event. This is called *additive increase/multiplicative decrease* (AIMD) congestion control, and we can produce a generalized AIMD congestion avoidance equation by replacing the values of 1/*cwnd* and ½ with variables a and b as follows:

$$cwnd_{t+1} = cwnd_t + a / cwnd_t$$

$$cwnd_{t+1} = cwnd_t - b^* cwnd_t$$

Based on results from [FHPW00], this equation gives TCP the following sending rate, in packets per RTT:

$$T = \frac{\sqrt{\dfrac{a(2-b)}{2b}}}{\sqrt{p}} \qquad [3]$$

For regular TCP, where $a = 1$ and $b = 0.5$, this simplifies to $T = 1.2/\sqrt{p}$, known as the *simplified standard TCP response function*. It relates the speed of TCP (regulation of *cwnd*) to the packet drop rate the TCP experiences, without accounting for retransmission timeouts. When TCP is not limited by other factors (sender's or receiver's buffers, window scaling, etc.), this relationship governs TCP's performance in benign operating environments.

Any alteration to TCP's response function obviously affects the way it (or another protocol implementing a similar congestion control scheme) competes with standard TCP. Therefore, new proposed congestion control schemes are typically analyzed using a measure of *relative fairness*. Relative fairness gives the ratio of the speed of the protocol using a modified congestion control scheme relative to standard TCP, as a function of the packet drop rate. This is a strong indicator of how fair any such modified schemes are with respect to sharing bandwidth across a common Internet path.

Note that understanding these equations is only the first step in creating a speed regulation regime that competes fairly with standard TCP. The details of implementing TFRC for any particular protocol can be subtle and include how to correctly measure the RTT, loss event rate, and packet size. These issues are discussed in some detail in [RFC5348].

16.8 TCP in High-Speed Environments

In high-speed networks with large BDPs (e.g., WANs of 1Gb/s or more), conventional TCP may not perform well because its window increase algorithm (the congestion avoidance algorithm, in particular) takes a long time to grow the window large enough to saturate the network path. Said another way, TCP can fail to take advantage of fast networks even when no congestion is present. This issue arises primarily from the fixed additive increase behavior of congestion avoidance. If we consider a TCP using 1500-byte packets operating over a 10Gb/s long-distance link, some 83,000 segments are required to be outstanding in order to fully utilize the available bandwidth, assuming no packet drops or errors in five billion packets. For an RTT of 100ms, this takes about 1.5 hours to achieve. In order to address this deficiency, a number of researchers and developers have explored ways to alter TCP in order for it to perform better in such networks, while retaining a degree of fairness to standard TCP, especially for more common lower-speed environments.

16.8.1 HighSpeed TCP (HSTCP) and Limited Slow Start

The experimental HighSpeed TCP (HSTCP) specifications [RFC3649][RFC3742] propose to alter the standard TCP behavior when the congestion window is larger than a base value *Low_Window*, suggested to be 38 MSS-size segments. This value corresponds to a packet drop rate of 10^{-3} based on the simplified TCP response function given previously. This function is linear on a log-log plot of sending rate versus packet loss rate, so it is really a *power law* function.

Note

Functions that form a line on a log-log plot are called *power law functions*. They have equations of the form $y = ax^k$, meaning $\log y = \log a + k \log x$ (a and k are constants). This equation forms a line with slope k on a log-log plot.

To construct the type of power law function required, we select two points and create the equation that describes the line passing between them. Consider two such points as (p_1, w_1) and (P_0, W_0) where $w_1 > W_0 > 0$ and $0 < p_1 < P_0$. On a linear plot, this would form a line with slope $(w_1 - W_0)/(p_1 - P_0)$, but on a log-log plot it forms a line with slope $S = (\log w_1 - \log W_0)/(\log p_1 - \log P_0)$. Then, based on the equation in the Note, we have $w = Cp^S$, and we require some point, say (P_0, W_0), to determine C. After some algebra, we find that $C = P_0^{-S} W_0$, meaning $w = p^S P_0^{-S} W_0$.

In Figure 16-19, we see a plot of both the conventional TCP response function and a proposed response function for HSTCP based on the point $(P_0, W_0) = (.0015, 31)$ and $S = -0.82$. Note that for larger packet drop rates (over about .001) the response functions are the same, so these equations apply only for a certain maximum value of p. Comparing the two lines, when the packet drop rate is small enough, HSTCP is allowed to send more aggressively.

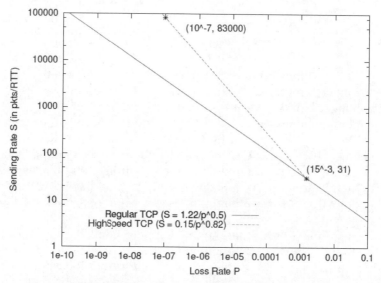

Figure 16-19   With HighSpeed TCP, the TCP response function is altered to be more aggressive for low packet drop rates and large windows, leading to higher throughputs for high bandwidth-delay-product networks. Image from presentation by Sally Floyd to IETF TWVWG, Mar. 2003.

To have TCP achieve this response function, the congestion avoidance procedure is modified to take into account the current size of the window when making changes. This takes place, as with conventional TCP, upon the arrival of a good ACK. The response for a good arriving ACK is generalized as follows:

$$cwnd_{t+1} = cwnd_t + \mathbf{a}(cwnd_t)/cwnd_t$$

When responding to a congestion event (e.g., packet loss, ECN indication), it responds as follows:

$$cwnd_{t+1} = cwnd_t - \mathbf{b}(cwnd_t)* cwnd_t$$

Here, $a()$ is the additive increase function and $b()$ is the multiplicative decrease function. In this generalization of standard TCP, they are functions of the current window size. To achieve the desired response function, we start by generalizing from equation [3]:

$$W_0 = \frac{\sqrt{\dfrac{\mathbf{a}(w)(2 - \mathbf{b}(w))}{2\mathbf{b}(w)}}}{\sqrt{P_0}}$$

This gives:

$$\mathbf{a}(w) = 2P_0 W_0^2\, \mathbf{b}(w)/(2 - \mathbf{b}(w))$$

This relationship does not have a unique solution—that is, there are many combinations of $a()$ and $b()$ that satisfy the relationship, even though some of them may not be practical or desirable for deployment.

Additional details of the changes proposed to the congestion avoidance procedure for TCP suggested by HSTCP are available in [RFC3649]. A companion document [RFC3742] describes how slow start can be modified to help TCP obtain a working congestion window in such environments. This is called *limited slow start* and is designed to slow down slow start, so that a TCP operating with large windows (thousands or tens of thousands of packets) does not double its window in one RTT.

With limited slow start, a new parameter called *max_ssthresh* is introduced. This value is not the maximum value of *ssthresh* but instead a threshold for *cwnd* that works as follows: If *cwnd* <= *max_ssthresh*, slow start proceeds as normal. If *max_ssthresh* < *cwnd* <= *ssthresh*, then *cwnd* is increased by at most (*max_ssthresh*/2) SMSS per RTT. This is accomplished by modifying the management of *cwnd* during slow start as follows:

```
if (cwnd <= max_ssthresh) {
        cwnd = cwnd + SMSS          (regular slow start)
} else {
        K = int(cwnd / (0.5 * max_ssthresh))
        cwnd = cwnd + int((1/K)*SMSS)     (limited slow start)
}
```

A suggested possible initial value for *max_ssthresh* is 100 packets, or 100*SMSS in bytes.

16.8.2 Binary Increase Congestion Control (BIC and CUBIC)

HSTCP is one of several proposals for modifying TCP to provide higher throughput for large BDP networks. While it considers throughput and fairness with respect to conventional TCPs in similar circumstances, and elects to be more aggressive than standard TCP under certain circumstances, it does not attempt to directly control what happens when HSTCP connections with differing RTTs compete with each other (called "RTT fairness"). This was studied for standard TCP some years back, revealing that TCPs with shorter RTTs obtain a larger share of the bandwidth on shared links as compared to those having larger RTTs, when using the same packet size and ACK strategy [F91]. For TCPs that increase *cwnd* as a function of its size (so-called *bandwidth-scalable* TCPs), this unfairness can be even more severe. Whether RTT fairness should be considered desirable is subject to debate. Although RTT fairness would seem attractive from first principles, connections with larger RTTs are likely to be using more network resources (e.g., passing through more routers), so it may be reasonable for them to receive somewhat less throughput. In any case, knowing just how RTT (un)fairness behaves is a driving factor behind the popular TCP variants we explore next.

16.8.2.1 BIC-TCP

In an effort to create a scalable TCP and deal with the issue of RTT fairness, BIC-TCP (formerly called BI-TCP) [XHR04] was developed and deployed in Linux kernels starting with version 2.6.8. The main goal of BIC TCP is to provide *linear RTT fairness* even though congestion windows may be quite large (which is required to use high-bandwidth links). Linear RTT fairness means that connections receive a bandwidth share inversely proportional to their RTTs, rather than some more complicated or unknown function.

The approach modifies a standard TCP sender with two algorithms: *binary search increase* and *additive increase*. These algorithms are invoked after a congestion indication (e.g., packet loss), but only one of the algorithms is in operation at any given point in time. The binary search increase algorithm operates as follows: The *current minimum window* is the last point at which the connection experienced no packet loss during an entire RTT. The *maximum window* is the window size at which the connection last experienced loss, if known. The desired window ies somewhere between the two. Using a binary search technique, BIC-TCP selects a *trial window* in the midpoint of these two values and tries again recursively. If this point shows continued packet loss, it becomes the new maximum and the process repeats. If not, it becomes the new minimum and the process repeats. The process terminates when the difference between the minimum and maximum windows is less than a predefined threshold called the *minimum increment*, or S_{min}.

The algorithm tends to find the desirable window, also called the *saturation point*, in a logarithmic number of trials, whereas a standard TCP would require a linear number (half of the difference in window sizes, on average). Thus, this approach makes BIC-TCP more aggressive than standard TCP during certain periods of operation, but this is desired in order to take advantage of high-speed environments without unwanted delay. The protocol is unusual, relative to other proposals, because its increase function is *concave* at some points—that is, its increase gets smaller as it gets closer to the saturation point. Most other algorithms use large change increments nearest the saturation point.

The additive increase algorithm works as follows: When using binary search increase, the situation can arise where the distance from the current window size to the midpoint (in the sense of the binary search described previously) is large. Increasing the window to the midpoint in one RTT may be ill advised because of the potential for injecting large packet bursts into the network. This is prevented by the additive increase algorithm, which is invoked when the distance to the midpoint from the current window is more than some amount S_{max}. When this happens, the increment is limited to S_{max} per RTT, called *window clamping*. Once the midpoint is closer than S_{max} to the trial window, binary search increase takes over. Overall, upon detection of a loss, the window is reduced by a multiplicative factor β, and its growth starts again with additive increase and switches to binary search once the desired increase amount is less than S_{max}. The authors call the combined algorithms *binary increase*, or BI.

When the window grows beyond the current maximum, or no maximum is yet known because no loss event has occurred, it must be established. This is accomplished by a procedure known as *max probing*. The purpose of max probing is to use bandwidth when it becomes available. It proceeds in a way symmetric to the additive increase and binary increase algorithms. It starts in small initial increments, followed by larger increments if no congestion is indicated. The approach shows good stability because small changes are made near the saturation point, where the network is believed to be operating near its greatest capacity.

Linux (kernels 2.6.8 through 2.6.17) includes an implementation of BIC-TCP that is enabled by default. Four `sysctl` parameters control its operation: `net.ipv4.tcp_bic`, `net.ipv4.tcp_bic_beta`, `net.ipv4.tcp_bic_low_window`, and `net.ipv4.tcp_bic_fast_convergence`. The first Boolean variable controls whether BIC is used (as opposed to the conventional fast retransmit/recovery procedures). The next contains a scaling factor for *cwnd* to determine S_{max} (default 819). The next parameter controls the minimum size of the congestion window before the BIC-TCP control algorithms take over. Its default value is 14, meaning that for small window values standard TCP congestion control is used. The last parameter is a flag, enabled by default. When set, it affects the way the new maximum and target windows are selected when the binary increase algorithm is in a downward trend. During a window reduction, the new maximum and minimum windows are set to the current and scaled (down by a factor of beta) values of *cwnd*, respectively. If fast convergence is enabled and the value of the new maximum is less than its previous value before it was set to *cwnd*, the value of the maximum window is further reduced between the average of it and the minimum window. After this, whether or not fast convergence is enabled, the target window is the average of the maximum and minimum values. This helps to achieve even bandwidth sharing more quickly when multiple BIC-TCP flows are sharing the same router.

16.8.2.2 CUBIC

The authors of BIC-TCP revised their basic algorithms to form a new control algorithm called *CUBIC* [HRX08]. It has been the default congestion control algorithm used in Linux TCP since kernel version 2.6.18. It addresses concerns raised that BIC-TCP may be too aggressive under some circumstances. It also simplifies the window growth procedures. Instead of using a threshold (S_{max}) to decide when to invoke the binary search increase versus additive increase, an odd-degree polynomial function, in particular a cubic function, is used instead to control the window increase function. Cubic functions can have both convex and concave portions, meaning that they can grow more slowly in some portions (concave) and more quickly in others (convex). Until BIC and CUBIC, virtually all of the TCP literature advocated convex window growth functions. The specific window growth function, used by CUBIC to set *cwnd*, is as follows:

$$W(t) = C(t - K)^3 + W_{max}$$

In this equation, $W(t)$ is the window at time t. C is a constant parameter (default 0.4), t is the elapsed time in seconds since the last window reduction, and K is the time period the function takes to increase W to W_{max} when there is no further loss event. W_{max} is the last window size prior to the last window adjustment. K can be calculated as follows:

$$K = \sqrt[3]{\frac{\beta W_{max}}{C}}$$

where β is the multiplicative decrease constant (default 0.2). An illustration of the CUBIC window growth function for $K = 2.71$, $W_{max} = 10$, and $C = 0.4$ on the interval $t = [0, 5]$ is shown in Figure 16-20.

This figure illustrates how the CUBIC window growth function contains both a concave portion and convex portion. When a fast retransmit occurs, W_{max} is set to *cwnd*, and new values of *cwnd* and *ssthresh* are set to β*cwnd*. CUBIC uses a default value of 0.8 for β. The value $W(t + RTT)$ gives the next target congestion window value. When an additional ACK arrives during congestion avoidance, *cwnd* is increased by $(W(t + RTT) - cwnd)/cwnd$.

It is worth noting that having t be the amount of elapsed time since the last window reduction event helps to ensure RTT fairness. Instead of changing the window by some fixed amount when ACKs arrive, the window change amount is a function of the elapsed time since the last window change. This decouples the window change operations from the particular pattern of ACK arrivals.

In addition to the cubic operating region, CUBIC also has a "TCP-friendly" region that operates when the window is small to ensure that CUBIC is not

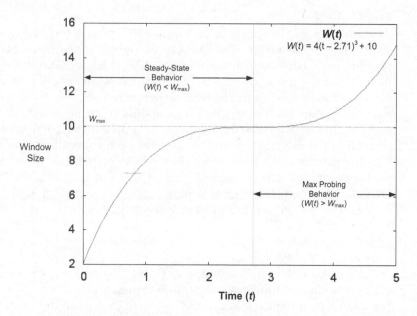

Figure 16-20 The CUBIC window growth function is a cubic function of t. It has a concave portion in the area where $W(t) < W_{max}$. In this region, CUBIC searches for the saturation point by growing *cwnd* with decreasing aggressiveness. After W_{max} is reached, the growth function becomes convex, where it searches by growing *cwnd* with increasing aggressiveness.

penalized relative to regular TCP. More specifically, the window size of standard TCP in terms of the elapsed time t, $W_{tcp}(t)$, is given by

$$W_{tcp}(t) = 3\frac{t}{RTT}\frac{(1-\beta)}{(1+\beta)} + W_{max}\beta$$

So if *cwnd* is less than $W_{tcp}(t)$ when an ACK arrives during congestion avoidance, CUBIC sets *cwnd* = $W_{tcp}(t)$. This ensures TCP friendliness in common low- to moderate-speed networks, where CUBIC would otherwise be disadvantaged.

As mentioned earlier, CUBIC has been the default congestion control algorithm for Linux kernels since 2.6.18. Since kernel version 2.6.13, however, Linux supports *pluggable congestion avoidance modules* [P07], allowing the user to pick which algorithm to use. The variable `net.ipv4.tcp_congestion_control` contains the current default congestion control algorithm (default: `cubic`). The variable `net.ipv4.tcp_available_congestion_control` contains the congestion control algorithms loaded on the system (in general, additional ones can be loaded as kernel modules). The variable `net.ipv4.tcp_allowed_congestion_control` contains those algorithms permitted for use by applications (either selected specifically or by default). The default supports CUBIC and Reno.

16.9 Delay-Based Congestion Control

The approaches to congestion control we have seen so far are usually triggered by packet loss, detected using some combination of ACKs or SACKs, ECN (if available), and expiration of a retransmission timer. ECN (see Section 16.11) allows a sending TCP to be informed about congestion prior to the need for the network to drop packets, but this requires participation from routers within the network that may not be available. However, even without ECN it is still possible to try to determine from a host whether congestion is about to occur within the network. One clue that congestion may be forming is an increase in measured RTT as the sender injects more packets into the network. We saw this situation in Figure 16-8, where additional packets were being queued rather than delivered, contributing to a higher measured RTT (until packets were ultimately discarded). Several congestion control techniques depend on this observation. They are called *delay-based* congestion control algorithms, as opposed to the *loss-based* congestion control algorithms we have seen so far.

16.9.1 Vegas

In 1994, *TCP Vegas* was introduced [BP95]. It was the first delay-based congestion control approach for TCP published and tested by the community of TCP developers. Vegas operates by estimating the amount of data it expects to transfer in a certain amount of time and comparing this with the amount of data it is actually able to transfer. If the requisite amount of data is not transferred, it is likely to be held up in a router queue along the path. If this condition persists, the Vegas sender slows down. This is in contrast to the standard TCP approach, which forces a packet drop to occur in order to determine the point at which the network is congested.

While in its congestion avoidance phase, during each RTT, Vegas measures the amount of data transferred and divides this number by the minimum delay observed across the connection. It maintains two thresholds, α and β (where $\alpha < \beta$). When the difference in expected throughput (window size divided by the smallest RTT observed) versus achieved throughput is less than α, the congestion window is increased; when it is greater than β, the congestion window is decreased. Otherwise, it is left as is. All changes to the congestion window are linear, meaning the scheme is an *additive increase/additive decrease* (AIAD) congestion control scheme.

The authors describe α and β in terms of buffer utilization at a bottleneck link. The smallest values of interest are 1 for α and 3 for β. The reasoning behind these values is as follows: At least one packet buffer should be occupied in the network path (i.e., at the queue in the router incident with the minimum-bandwidth link on the path) to keep the network busy. If extra bandwidth becomes available, occupying two additional buffers (up to 3, the value for α) obviates the need to wait an extra RTT in order to inject more, which would be required if Vegas tried to maintain only one buffer full. Furthermore, having the region (β–α) as the operating range leaves some room for minor changes in throughput without causing an immediate change in the window, a form of damping that aims to reduce rate oscillations.

With a slight modification, this approach can also be applied to the slow start period. Here, increasing *cwnd* by 1 for each good ACK is allowed only every *other* RTT. For those RTTs when it is not increased, a measurement is made to ensure that throughput is increasing. If not, the sender switches to the Vegas congestion avoidance scheme.

Under certain circumstances, Vegas can be "fooled" into believing that the forward-direction delay is higher than it really is. This happens when there is significant congestion in the reverse direction (recall that the paths in the two directions of a TCP connection may be different and have different states of congestion). In such cases, packets (ACKs) returning to the sending TCP are delayed, even though the sender is not really contributing to the (reverse-path) congestion. This causes Vegas to reduce the congestion window even though such an adjustment is not really necessary. This is a potential pitfall for most techniques based on measuring RTT as a basis for congestion control decisions. Indeed, significant traffic in the reverse direction can cause the ACK clock (Figure 16-1) to be significantly perturbed [M92].

Vegas is fair relative to other Vegas TCPs sharing the same path because each pushes the network to hold only a minimal amount of data. However, Vegas and standard TCP flows do not share paths equally. A standard TCP sender tends to fill queues in the network, whereas Vegas tends to keep them nearly empty. Consequently, as the standard sender injects more packets, the Vegas sender sees increased delay and slows down. Ultimately, this leads to an unfair bias in favor of the standard TCP. Vegas is supported by Linux but not enabled by default. For kernels prior to 2.6.13, the Boolean `sysctl` variable `net.ipv4.tcp_vegas_cong_avoid` determines whether it is used (default 0). The variables `net.ipv4.tcp_vegas_alpha` (default 2) and `net.ipv4.tcp_vegas_beta` (default 6) correspond to the alpha and beta described previously but are expressed in half-packet units (i.e., 6 corresponds to 3 packets). The variable `net.ipv4.tcp_vegas_gamma` (default 2) configures how many half-packets Vegas should attempt to keep outstanding during slow start. For kernels after 2.6.13, Vegas must be loaded as a separate kernel module and enabled by setting `net.ipv4.tcp_congestion_control` to `vegas`.

16.9.2 FAST

FAST TCP was developed with particular attention to operations in high-speed environments with large bandwidth-delay products [WJLH06]. Similar to Vegas in spirit, it adjusts the window based on the difference between an expected throughput rate and an experienced rate. It differs from Vegas by adjusting the window based not only on the window size, but also on the difference between the current and expected performance. It updates the sending rate every other RTT using a rate-pacing technique. If the measured delay is significantly below a threshold, the window is updated aggressively followed by a period when the increase is less aggressive. When the delay increases, the reverse takes place. FAST differs from the other approaches we have discussed because it is the subject of several patents and is being commercialized independently. It has received somewhat less scrutiny from the research community, but an independent evaluation [S09] has shown it to have good stability and fairness properties.

16.9.3 TCP Westwood and Westwood+

TCP Westwood (TCPW) and *TCP Westwood+* (TCPW+) aim at handling large bandwidth-delay-product paths by modifying a conventional TCP NewReno sender. TCPW+ is a correction to the original TCPW algorithm, so we will just refer to either as TCPW. In TCPW, the sender's *eligible rate estimate* (ERE) is an estimate of the bandwidth available on the connection. It is continuously computed in a fashion somewhat similar to Vegas (based upon the difference between an expected and an achieved rate), but with a variable measurement interval for the rates based on the dynamics of ACK arrivals. When congestion is low, the measurement interval is small, and vice versa. When a packet loss is detected, instead of reducing *cwnd* by half, TCPW computes an estimated BDP (ERE times the minimum RTT observed) and uses this as the new value for *ssthresh*. *Agile probing* [WYSG05] adaptively and repeatedly sets *ssthresh* when a connection would otherwise operate in slow start. This causes *cwnd* to grow exponentially in cases where *ssthresh* has been increased (by initiating slow start). Westwood can be enabled in Linux kernels after 2.6.13 by loading a TCPW module and setting `net.ipv4.tcp_congestion_control` to `westwood`.

16.9.4 Compound TCP

Starting with Windows Vista, it is possible to choose which congestion control procedure ("provider") TCP should use, in a way similar to Linux's pluggable congestion avoidance modules. One such option (but not the default, except for Windows Server 2008) is called *Compound TCP* (CTCP) [TSZS06]. CTCP makes window adjustments based upon packet loss, but also based on measured delays. In some sense it is a combination of standard TCP and Vegas, but with the scalability features of HSTCP.

The authors begin by recounting a number of results shown in the Vegas and FAST research that suggest that delay-based congestion control schemes tend to have better utilization, less self-induced packet loss, faster convergence (to the correct operating point), plus better RTT fairness and stabilization. However, as mentioned previously, delay-based approaches tend to lose bandwidth when competing with loss-based congestion control approaches. CTCP attempts to address this situation by combining a delay-based approach with a loss-based approach.

To do this, CTCP introduces a new window control variable called *dwnd* (the "delay window"). The usable window *W* then becomes

$$W = \min(cwnd + dwnd, awnd)$$

The handling of *cwnd* is similar to that of standard TCP, but the addition of *dwnd* may allow additional packets to be sent if the delay conditions are appropriate. When ACKs arrive during congestion avoidance, *cwnd* is updated as follows:

$$cwnd = cwnd + 1/(cwnd + dwnd)$$

The management of *dwnd* is based on Vegas and is nonzero only during congestion avoidance (CTCP uses conventional slow start). As a connection operates, the minimum RTT measured is maintained in the variable *baseRTT*. Then, the difference in expected data outstanding versus the actual amount, *diff*, is computed as follows: *diff* = $W*(1 - (baseRTT/RTT))$, where *RTT* is the estimated (smoothed) RTT estimate. The value of *diff* estimates the number of packets (or bytes) queued in the network. CTCP, like most delay-based schemes, attempts to keep *diff* at a certain threshold, called γ, in order to ensure that the network remains utilized but not congested. Given this goal, the control process for *dwnd* is then expressed as follows:

$$dwnd(t + 1) = \begin{cases} dwnd(t) + (\alpha * win(t)^k - 1)^+, & \text{if } diff < \gamma \\ (dwnd(t) - \zeta * diff)^+, & \text{if } diff \geq \gamma \\ (win(t) * (1 - \beta) - cwnd/2)^+, & \text{if loss detected} \end{cases}$$

where $(x)^+$ means $\max(x, 0)$. Note that *dwnd* can never be negative. Rather, it may be zero, in which case CTCP behaves like standard TCP.

In the first case, where the network may be underutilized, CTCP grows *dwnd* according to the polynomial $\alpha * win(t)^k$. This is a form of binomial increase and accounts for the way CTCP can be made more aggressive (similar to HSTCP) when the buffer occupancy is estimated to be less than γ. In the second case, where the buffer occupancy appears to be growing beyond the desired threshold γ, the constant ζ dictates how quickly the delay-based component should be reduced (but recall that *dwnd* is always added to *cwnd*). This is what contributes to CTCP's RTT and TCP fairness. When loss is detected, *dwnd* has its own multiplicative decrease factor β applied.

As can be seen, CTCP can be tuned using the parameters *k*, α, β, γ, and ζ. The value of *k* affects the level of aggressiveness. A value of about 0.8 was desired to be similar to HSTCP, but 0.75 was chosen for implementation reasons. The values of α and β affect smoothness and responsiveness. The default values are 0.125 and 0.5, respectively. For γ, the authors suggest a default value of 30 packets based on empirical evaluation. If this value is too small, there may not be enough packets outstanding to obtain good delay measurements. Conversely, values that are too large could result in undesirable persistent congestion.

CTCP is relatively new, so further experimentation and evaluation will no doubt be performed to see how well and fairly it competes with standard TCP, and how well it is able to adapt to significant changes in available bandwidth. In a simulation study, the author of [W08] noted that CTCP can perform poorly when network buffers are small (i.e., smaller than γ). They also suggest that CTCP can fall victim to some of the problems with Vegas, including rerouting (adapting to new paths with different delays) and persistent congestion. Finally, they observe that if many CTCP flows, each trying to keep γ packets in flight, share the same bottleneck link, performance can be poor.

As mentioned previously, CTCP is not enabled by default on most versions of Windows. However, the following command can be used to select CTCP as the congestion provider:

```
C:\> netsh interface tcp set global congestionprovider=ctcp
```

It can be disabled by selecting a different provider (or **none**). CTCP has also been ported to Linux as a pluggable congestion avoidance module but is not included by default.

16.10 Buffer Bloat

Although memory has traditionally been expensive (and remains so for high-end routers), it is now commonplace to find commodity networking equipment that contains a significant amount of memory, potentially multiple megabytes of packet buffers. Perhaps ironically, this large amount of memory (as compared to traditional networking devices) can actually lead to degraded performance for protocols such as TCP. This problem has been termed *buffer bloat* [G11][DHGS07]. It relates to high amounts of latency introduced by queuing delay, primarily at the uplink side of residential gateways and access points in homes and small offices. The standard TCP congestion control algorithms, which tend to keep buffers full at bottleneck links, do not operate well when a large amount of buffering occurs between the sender and receiver because the congestion indicator (a packet drop) takes a long time to be delivered to a sender.

In [KWNP10], the authors find that upload bandwidth in the United States over cable and DSL ranges from about 256Kb/s to 4Mb/s. They also inferred buffer sizing on commodity routers in the range from 16KB to 256KB. Figure 16-21 shows how latency relates to data rate for several buffer sizes to help provide a perspective on these findings.

In this figure, the log-log graph displays the amount of latency experienced by data required to queue for various buffer sizes (1KB–2MB). Residential Internet upload bandwidth rates (typically 250Kb/s to 10Mb/s) can lead to latencies in the

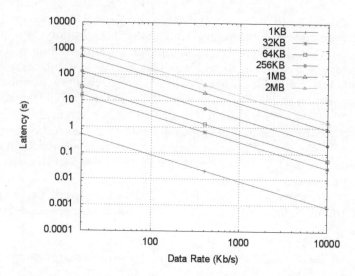

Figure 16-21   The log-log plot shows the latency due to queuing delay experienced by data in fully congested queues of various sizes. When large buffers remain full ("buffer bloat"), interactive applications can experience unacceptable latencies in the multiple-second range.

multiple-second range if buffers are sized to be a few hundred kilobytes or more. Interactive applications generally require one-way delays to be below 150ms to provide a good quality of experience to users [G114]. Thus, if buffers remain filled to capacity because of one or more large competing uploads (e.g., BitTorrent file sharing), interactive applications can be adversely affected.

Buffer bloat is not a problem in all networking equipment. Indeed, the primary concern appears to be in overbuffered end-user access devices. There are multiple potential ways to deal with the issue, including protocol modifications (e.g., delay-based congestion control such as Vegas, but it may be negatively affected by high jitter [DHGS07]), dynamic buffer sizing at the access devices (suggested in [KWNP10]), or a combination of the two. We next turn to a combination approach that may help the buffer bloat problem but also has a number of other benefits.

16.11 Active Queue Management and ECN

The discussion of TCP's congestion response so far has assumed that the only way a TCP infers that congestion is happening is observation of packet drops. In particular, routers (the things that are mostly likely to become congested) do not ordinarily help inform the TCP at each host that congestion is imminent. Instead, they simply drop arriving packets when no more buffer space is available (called "drop tail") and send packets that have already arrived in a first-in-first-out (FIFO) manner. When Internet routers are *passive* like this (that is, they simply discard packets when overloaded and provide no feedback regarding their congestion state), there is little a TCP can do other than react after the fact. If, however, these routers had a way to more actively manage their queues (i.e., by using a more sophisticated scheduling and buffer management policy than FIFO/drop tail), perhaps the situation could be improved. If they could also signal their congestion state to TCP endpoints, so much the better.

Routers that apply scheduling and buffer management policies other than FIFO/drop tail are usually said to be *active*, and the corresponding methods they use to manage their queues are called *active queue management* (AQM) mechanisms. The authors of [RFC2309] provide a discussion of the potential benefits of AQM. Although AQM can be useful independently, it becomes more useful when routers and switches implementing AQM have a common method for conveying their status to the end systems. For TCP, this is described in [RFC3168] and extended with additional security in an experimental specification [RFC3540]. These RFCs describe Explicit Congestion Notification (ECN), which is a way for routers to *mark* packets (by ensuring both of the ECN bits in the IP header are set) to indicate the onset of congestion.

Random Early Detection (RED) gateways [FJ93] are one mechanism suggested as being capable of detecting the onset of congestion and controlling the marking of packets. These gateways implement a queue management discipline that measures the average queue occupancy over time. If the occupancy exceeds the minimum (called *minthresh*) and is less than the maximum (called *maxthresh*), a packet is marked with an increasing probability. If the average queue occupancy exceeds *maxthresh*, packets are marked with a configurable maximum probability (called *MaxP*), which could be 1.0. RED can also be configured to drop packets instead of marking them.

Note

The RED algorithm is the basis for a number of variants (e.g., Cisco's WRED, which uses different RED instances based on IP DSCP or precedence values) that are supported on many routers and switches.

When received by a TCP, a congestion mark indicates that the packet has passed through a congested router. Of course, it is the *sender* (rather than the receiver) that really needs this information in order to react by slowing down. Thus, the receiver echoes this indication back to the sender in a series of ACK packets.

The ECN mechanism operates partially at the IP layer and so is potentially applicable to transport protocols other than TCP, although most of the work on ECN has been with TCP, and it is what we discuss here. When an ECN-capable router experiencing persistent congestion receives an IP packet, it looks in the IP header for an *ECN-Capable Transport* (ECT) indication (currently defined as either of the two ECN bits in the IP header being set). If set, the transport protocol responsible for sending the packet understands ECN. At this point, the router sets a *Congestion Experienced* indication in the IP header (by setting both ECN bits to 1) and forwards the datagram. Routers are discouraged from setting a *CE* indication when congestion does not appear to be persistent (e.g., upon a single recent packet drop due to queue overrun) because the transport protocol is supposed to react given even a *single* CE indication.

The TCP receiver observing an incoming data packet with a *CE* set is obliged to return this indication to the sender (there is an experimental extension to add ECN to SYN + ACK segments as well [RFC5562]). Because the receiver normally returns information to the sender by using (unreliable) ACK packets, there is a significant chance that the congestion indicator could be lost. For this reason, TCP implements a small reliability-enhancing protocol for carrying the indication back to the sender. Upon receiving an incoming packet with *CE* set, the TCP receiver sets the *ECN-Echo* bit field in each ACK packet it sends until receiving a *CWR* bit field set to 1 from the TCP sender in a subsequent data packet. The *CWR* bit field being set indicates that the congestion window (i.e., sending rate) has been reduced.

Note

Although RED and ECN have been known for nearly two decades, they have not seen widespread Internet deployment. A variety of reasons have been asserted as to why (e.g., difficulty in setting RED parameters, a perception of limited benefits). In 2005, a "reexamination" of ECN [K05] pointed out that using ECN on only data packets limits its benefits substantially. An experimental extension [RFC5562] defines the use of ECN in SYN + ACK packets with the possibility of greatly increasing the utility of ECN for certain workloads (e.g., Web traffic).

A sending TCP receiving an ECN-Echo indicator in an ACK reacts the same way it would when detecting a single packet drop by adjusting *cwnd*, and it also arranges to set the *CWR* bit field in a subsequent data packet. The prescribed congestion response of the fast retransmit/recovery algorithms is invoked (of course, without the packet retransmission), causing the TCP to slow down prior to suffering packet drops. Note that the TCP should not overreach; in particular, it should not react more than once for the same window of data. Doing so would overly penalize an ECN TCP relative to others.

In Windows Vista and later, ECN needs to be enabled to be used:

```
C:\> netsh int tcp set global ecncapability=enabled
```

In Linux, ECN is enabled if the Boolean `sysctl` variable `net.ipv4.tcp_ecn` is nonzero. The default varies based on which Linux distribution is used, with off being most common. On Mac OS 10.5 and later, the variables `net.inet.tcp.ecn_initiate_out` and `net.inet.tcp.ecn_negotiate_in` control whether ECN is enabled for outgoing traffic and for incoming traffic with ECN flags set, respectively. Of course, without cooperation from routers or switches, the utility of ECN is limited in any case. Only time will tell if the vision for AQM will ever be fully realized in the global Internet.

Note

RED and ECN have been used successfully in a radically different operating environment from that for which they were designed. Microsoft and Stanford have developed *Data Center TCP* (DCTCP) [A10], which uses RED implemented in layer 2 switches with simplified parameters to mark packets when instantaneous congestion is experienced. They also modify the TCP receiver behavior to set ECN-Echo in ACKs only when the last received packet contains a CE mark. They report a 90% reduction in buffer occupancy for comparable TCP throughput, allowing a tenfold increase in background traffic to be supported.

16.12 Attacks Involving TCP Congestion Control

We have seen already how TCP can be attacked by generating packets that cause TCP's connection state machine to terminate the connection. TCP can also be attacked (or at least induced to behave in peculiar ways) when operating in the ESTABLISHED state. Most attacks on TCP congestion control attempt to force a TCP to send faster or slower than it would under ordinary circumstances.

Perhaps the earliest attack involves the fabrication of ICMPv4 Source Quench messages. When these are delivered to a host running TCP, any connection to the IP address contained in the offending datagram inside the ICMP message slows down. While this may have been a vulnerability some years back, using Source Quench messages for congestion control has been deprecated for use by routers since about 1995 (via [RFC1812], Section 5.3.6). On the other hand, for end hosts, [RFC1122] stated that a TCP must react to a Source Quench by slowing down. Combining these two facts, the simplest solution is to block ICMP Source Quench traffic at the router or host, and this is now common.

A more sophisticated and more recent set of attacks have been considered by looking at *misbehaving receivers* [SCWA99]. The authors describe three types of attacks that can cause a TCP sender to inject data at a rate faster than intended. Such attacks could be used, for example, to cause a Web client to have an unfair advantage over competing clients. The attacks are named *ACK division*, *DupACK spoofing*, and *Optimistic ACKing* and are implemented in a TCP variant the authors (jokingly) call "TCP Daytona."

ACK division operates by producing more than one ACK for the range of bytes being acknowledged. Because the TCP congestion control typically operates based on the arrival of ACK packets (rather than the *ACK* field contained in the ACK itself), a sending TCP can be induced to increase *cwnd* faster than it would otherwise. This problem can be mitigated by basing the congestion control computations on the amount of data acknowledged rather than the arrival of a packet, as is done with ABC.

DupACK spoofing causes a sender to increase its congestion window during fast recovery. Recall from the previous discussion that during standard fast recovery, *cwnd* is incremented for each duplicate ACK received. The attack involves creating extra duplicate ACKs that cause this to happen more quickly than intended. This attack is more difficult to defend against, because there is no clean way to map received duplicate ACKs to the segments they acknowledge (a *nonce*, an associated value that changes with time, which we discuss in Chapter 18, would solve this problem). While the Timestamps option relates to this problem, it is an option and can be disabled on a per-connection basis. The best approach to addressing this problem appears to be modification of the sender side to limit the amount of outstanding data during recovery.

Optimistic ACKing involves producing ACKs for segments that have *not yet arrived*. Because TCP's congestion control computations are based on end-to-end RTTs, ACKing data that has not yet arrived causes the sender to react faster than it would because it is fooled into believing the actual RTT is smaller. Furthermore, there is little penalty for doing this, as a sender typically ignores ACKs for data it has not yet sent. While this approach does not preserve data reliability at the TCP layer as the other attacks do (i.e., ACKed data could still be lost), it is frequently the case (e.g., in HTTP/1.1) that missing data can be reconstructed by an application- or session-layer protocol. The authors describe a *cumulative nonce* that can address this problem and a way to alter the sizes of sent segments over time to better match up ACKs with sent segments. When the ACKs do not correspond, the sender can take action.

The problems described for misbehaving receivers have also received attention with respect to ECN by some of the same authors. Recall that with AQM using ECN, the TCP receiver returns the ECN indication to the sender in an ACK. The sender is then supposed to respond by slowing down. If the receiver fails to return the ECN indications to the sender (or routers in the network clear the indicators), the sender would never be informed of congestion and would not slow down. In [RFC3540], the authors describe an experimental way to use the *ECT* bit field of the *ECN* field (2 bits) of an IP packet as a form of nonce. The sender places a random binary value in the field, and the receiver returns a 1-bit sum (an XOR operation) of the values of this field over time. When generating an ACK, the receiver places the sum bit 7 of the TCP header (currently reserved as zero). A misbehaving receiver has a 50/50 chance of guessing the sum. Because each packet represents an independent trial and a successful misbehaving receiver must have every sum correct, its chance of doing so is $1/2^k$ for k packets (vanishingly small for a connection of any reasonable duration).

16.13 Summary

TCP was designed as the primary reliable transport protocol for the Internet. Although its initial design included a flow control capability, used to cause a sender to slow down when a receiver could not keep up, no provision was made initially for preventing the sender from overwhelming the network in between. In the late 1980s, the slow start and congestion avoidance algorithms were developed to regulate a TCP sender's aggressiveness so as to avoid losing packets because of congestion in the network. These algorithms depend on using an implicit signal, packet loss, and an indicator of congestion. They are triggered when loss is detected, either by the fast retransmit algorithm or by retransmission timeouts.

Slow start and congestion avoidance regulate a sender's operation by introducing a congestion window at the sender. This is used in conjunction with the conventional window (based on window advertisements provided by the receiver). A standard TCP limits its window to the minimum of the two. Slow start grows the value of the congestion window exponentially with time, and congestion avoidance grows it about linearly with time. Only one of the two algorithms is in operation at any one time, and this decision is made by comparing the current value of the congestion window to the slow start threshold: if the congestion window exceeds the threshold, congestion avoidance takes control; otherwise, slow start is used. Slow start is used initially when TCP establishes its connection and after restart conditions due to timeouts. It can also be used when a connection has gone idle for a significant amount of time. The slow start threshold is adjusted dynamically during the course of the connection.

Congestion control has been a significant focus of the networking research community over the years. After more experience was gained with TCP and its slow start and congestion avoidance procedures, a number of improvements have been suggested, implemented, and standardized. By keeping track of when TCP is recovering from a collection of lost packets, the NewReno variant of TCP avoids some of the stalls that can occur with Reno variants when multiple packets are dropped in a single window of data. SACK TCP can improve upon NewReno's behavior by permitting the sender to intelligently repair more than one packet drop per RTT. With SACK TCP, careful accounting must be established to ensure that the sender is not overly aggressive with respect to other TCPs with which it may be sharing an Internet path.

Some of the more recent changes to TCP congestion management include rate halving, congestion window validation and moderation, and "undo" procedures. The rate-halving algorithm causes the congestion window to reduce gradually after detected loss events instead of reducing it immediately. Congestion window validation tries to ensure that the congestion window is not overly large if a sending application has been idle or unable to send for some time. Congestion window moderation limits the size of a burst in response to the receipt of a single ACK. The "undo" procedures, such as the Eifel Response Algorithm, undo congestion window modifications if the packet loss signal is deemed to be spurious, a condition detectable using a number of techniques. In such cases, the negative impact on performance by reducing the congestion window is minimized by restoring the congestion state to its condition prior to the reduction of the congestion window.

After significant experience with TCP, it was observed that the congestion avoidance procedure can take a long time to find and exploit additional bandwidth that becomes available. As a result, numerous proposals for "bandwidth-scalable" TCP variants have been made. One of the better-known versions (within the IETF) is HSTCP, which allows the congestion window to grow much more aggressively in operating regimes where few packets are dropped and windows are large, as compared with conventional TCP. Subsequent suggestions have included FAST and CTCP, which base their window growth procedures on packet loss and latency measures. Widely deployed in Linux, the BIC-TCP and CUBIC algorithms use growth functions that are convex in some portions and concave in others. This supports small window changes during the saturation point, leading to enhanced stability at the possible cost of somewhat sluggish response to new available bandwidth (but still faster than standard TCP).

A significant change to the operation of TCP and Internet routers has been proposed with the specification of Explicit Congestion Notification (ECN), which would allow TCP to detect the onset of congestion before a packet loss is experienced. Although simulations and research results have shown this to be desirable, it requires a moderate change to TCP implementations and a significant change to the way Internet routers operate. The extent to which this capability is deployed remains to be seen.

Although TCP provides the most widely used method for reliably moving data on the Internet, it does not implement much in the way of its own security. It is generally vulnerable to packet-forging attacks that can cause disruptions of connections; an attacker need only have a good guess at a viable (in-window) sequence number to launch such attacks. In addition, modification of the ACK stream (or ECN bits, if they are supported) can induce a sender to behave in ways that are unfair to other TCP connections. Furthermore, nothing physically prevents an overly aggressive sender from simply violating all congestion control rules.

Combining all of the various algorithms and techniques developed for TCP into a single TCP implementation is not an easy task (Linux 2.6.38 TCP/IPv4 is about 20,000 lines of C code), and analyzing traces of a real-world TCP in action can be time-consuming. Tools such as `tcpdump`, Wireshark, and `tcptrace` make this job considerably easier. Because of its dynamic adaptation to the performance of the network, understanding TCP's behavior is most easily accomplished with visualization techniques based on time-series plots, such as those used in this chapter.

16.14 References

[A10] M. Alizadeh et al., "Data Center TCP (DCTCP)," *Proc. ACM SIGCOMM*, Aug./Sept. 2010.

[ASA00] A. Aggarwal, S. Savage, and T. Anderson, "Understanding the Performance of TCP Pacing," *Proc. INFOCOM*, Mar. 2004.

[BP95] L. Brakmo and L. Peterson, "TCP Vegas: End to End Congestion Avoidance on a Global Internet," *IEEE JSAC*, 13(8), Oct. 1995.

[DHGS07] M. Dischinger, A. Haeberlen, K. Gummadi, and S. Saroiu, "Characterizing Residential Broadband Networks," *Proc. ACM IMC*, Oct. 2007.

[F91] S. Floyd, "Connections with Multiple Congested Gateways in Packet-Switched Networks, Part 1: One-Way Traffic," *ACM Computer Communication Review*, 21, 1991.

[FF96] S. Floyd and K. Fall, "Simulation-Based Comparisons of Tahoe, Reno, and SACK TCP," *ACM Computer Communications Review*, July 1996.

[FHPW00] S. Floyd, M. Handley, J. Padhye, and J. Widmer, "Equation-Based Congestion Control for Unicast Applications," *Proc. ACM SIGCOMM*, Aug. 2000.

[FJ93] S. Floyd and V. Jacobson, "Random Early Detection Gateways for Congestion Avoidance," *IEEE/ACM Transactions on Networking*, 1(4), Aug. 1993.

[G11] J. Gettys, "Bufferbloat: Dark Buffers in the Internet," *Internet Computing*, May/June 2011.

[G114] International Telecommunication Union Recommendation G.114, "One-Way Transmission Time," May 2003.

[H96] J. Hoe, "Improving the Start-up Behavior of a Congestion Control Scheme for TCP," *Proc. ACM SIGCOMM*, Aug. 1996.

[HRX08] S. Ha, I. Rhee, and L. Xu, "CUBIC: A New TCP-Friendly High-Speed TCP Variant," http://netsrv.csc.ncsu.edu/export/cubic_a_new_tcp_2008.pdf

[J88] V. Jacobson, "Congestion Avoidance and Control," *Proc. ACM SIGCOMM*, Aug. 1988. This paper was later updated in 1992 to include M. Karels as coauthor. The update is available at http://www-nrg.ee.lbl.gov/papers/congavoid.pdf

[J90] V. Jacobson, "Modified TCP Congestion Avoidance Algorithm," posting to the end2end-interest group mailing list, Apr. 1990, available at ftp://ftp.ee.lbl.gov/email/vanj.90apr30.txt

[K05] A. Kuzmanovic, "The Power of Explicit Congestion Notification," *Proc. ACM SIGCOMM*, Aug. 2005.

[KWNP10] C. Kreibich, N. Weaver, B. Nechaev, and V. Paxson, "Netalyzr: Illuminating Edge Network Neutrality, Security and Performance," *Proc. ACM IMC*, Nov. 2010.

[LARTC] http://lartc.org

[M92] J. Mogul, "Observing TCP Dynamics in Real Networks," *Proc. ACM SIGCOMM*, Aug. 1992.

[MM05] M. Mathis, personal communication, Sept. 2005.

[MM96] M. Mathis and J. Mahdavi, "Forward Acknowledgment: Refining TCP Congestion Control," *Proc. ACM SIGCOMM,* Aug. 1996.

[NB08] J. Nievelt and V. Bhanu, "Developing TCP Chimney Drivers for Windows 7," presentation at Microsoft Windows Drivers Developer Conference, 2008.

[NS2] http://www.isi.edu/nsnam/ns (also see NS3 at http://www.nsnam.org)

[P07] http://lwn.net/Articles/128681

[PSCRH] M. Mathis, J. Mahdavi, and J. Semke, "TCP Rate Halving," http://www.psc.edu/networking/projects/rate-halving

[RFC1122] R. Braden, ed., "Requirements for Internet Hosts—Communication Layers," Internet RFC 1122/STD 0003, Oct. 1989.

[RFC1812] F. Baker, ed., "Requirements for IP Version 4 Routers," Internet RFC 1812, June 1995.

[RFC2018] M. Mathis, J. Mahdavi, S. Floyd, and A. Romanow, "TCP Selective Acknowledgment Options," Internet RFC 2018, Oct. 1996.

[RFC2140] J. Touch, "TCP Control Block Interdependence," Internet RFC 2140, Apr. 1997.

[RFC2309] B. Braden et al., "Recommendations on Queue Management and Congestion Avoidance in the Internet," Internet RFC 2309 (informational), Apr. 1998.

[RFC2861] M. Handley, J. Padhye, and S. Floyd, "TCP Congestion Window Validation," Internet RFC 2861 (experimental), June 2000.

[RFC3042] M. Allman, H. Balakrishnan, and S. Floyd, "Enhancing TCP's Loss Recovery Using Limited Transmit," Internet RFC 3042, Jan. 2001.

[RFC3124] H. Balakrishnan and S. Seshan, "The Congestion Manager," Internet RFC 3124, June 2001.

[RFC3168] K. Ramakrishnan, S. Floyd, and D. Black, "The Addition of Explicit Congestion Notification (ECN) to IP," Internet RFC 3168, Sept. 2001.

[RFC3465] M. Allman, "TCP Congestion Control with Appropriate Byte Counting (ABC)," Internet RFC 3465 (experimental), Feb. 2003.

[RFC3517] E. Blanton, M. Allman, K. Fall, and L. Wang, "A Conservative Selective Acknowledgment (SACK)-Based Loss Recovery Algorithm for TCP," Internet RFC 3517, Apr. 2003.

[RFC3540] N. Spring, D. Wetherall, and D. Ely, "Robust Explicit Congestion Notification (ECN) Signaling with Nonces," Internet RFC 3540 (experimental), June 2003.

[RFC3649] S. Floyd, "HighSpeed TCP for Large Congestion Windows," Internet RFC 3649 (experimental), Dec. 2003.

[RFC3742] S. Floyd, "Limited Slow-Start for TCP with Large Congestion Windows," Internet RFC 3742 (experimental), Mar. 2004.

[RFC3782] S. Floyd, T. Henderson, and A. Gurtov, "The NewReno Modification to TCP's Fast Recovery Algorithm," Internet RFC 3782, Apr. 2004.

[RFC4015] R. Ludwig and A. Gurtov, "The Eifel Response Algorithm for TCP," Internet RFC 4015, Feb. 2005.

[RFC5348] S. Floyd, M. Handley, J. Padhye, and J. Widmer, "TCP Friendly Rate Control (TFRC): Protocol Specification," Internet RFC 5348, Sept. 2008.

[RFC5562] A. Kuzmanovic, A. Mondal, S. Floyd, and K. Ramakrishnan, "Adding Explicit Congestion Notification (ECN) Capability to TCP's SYN/ACK Packets," Internet RFC 5562 (experimental), June 2009.

[RFC5681] M. Allman, V. Paxson, and E. Blanton, "TCP Congestion Control," Internet RFC 5681, Sept. 2009.

[RFC5690] S. Floyd, A. Arcia, D. Ros, and J. Iyengar, "Adding Acknowledgement Congestion Control to TCP," Internet RFC 5690 (informational), Feb. 2010.

[RFC6077] D. Papadimitriou, ed., M. Welzl, M. Sharf, and B. Briscoe, "Open Research Issues in Internet Congestion Control," Internet RFC 6077 (informational), Feb. 2011.

[S09] B. Sonkoly, *Fairness and Stability Analysis of High Speed Transport Protocols*, Ph.D. Thesis, Budapest University of Technology and Economics, 2009.

[SCWA99] S. Savage, N. Cardwell, D. Wetherall, and T. Anderson, "TCP Congestion Control with a Misbehaving Receiver," *ACM Computer Communication Review*, Apr. 1999.

[SK02] P. Sarolahti and A. Kuznetsov, "Congestion Control in Linux TCP," *Proc. Usenix Freenix Track*, June 2002.

[TCPTRACE] http://jarok.cs.ohiou.edu/software/tcptrace/index.html

[TSZS06] K. Tan, J. Song, Q. Zhang, and M. Sridharan, "A Compound TCP Approach for High-Speed and Long-Distance Networks," *Proc. INFOCOM*, Apr. 2006.

[W08] X. Wu, "A Simulation Study of Compound TCP," http://www.comp.nus .edu.sg/~wuxiucha/research/reactive/publication/ctcp_study.pdf

[WJLH06] D. Wei, C. Jin, S. Low, and S. Hegde, "FAST TCP: Motivation, Architecture, Algorithms, Performance," *IEEE/ACM Trans. on Networking*, Mar. 2006.

[WQOS] http://technet.microsoft.com/en-us/network/bb530836.aspx

[WYSG05] R. Wang, K. Yamada, M. Sanadidi, and M. Gerla, "TCP with Sender-Side Intelligence to Handle Dynamic, Large, Leaky Pipes," *IEEE JSAC*, 23(2), Feb. 2005.

[XHR04] L. Xu, K. Harfoush, and I. Rhee, "Binary Increase Congestion Control for Fast Long-Distance Networks," *Proc. INFOCOM*, Mar. 2004.

17

TCP Keepalive

17.1 Introduction

Many newcomers to TCP/IP are surprised to learn that no data whatsoever flows across an idle TCP connection. That is, if neither process at the ends of a TCP connection is sending data to the other, nothing is exchanged between the two TCP endpoints. There is no polling, for example, as you might find with other networking protocols. This means that we can start a client process that establishes a TCP connection with a server and walk away for hours, days, weeks, or months, and the connection should remain up. In theory, intermediate routers can crash and reboot, data lines may go down and back up, but as long as neither host at the ends of the connection reboots (or changes its IP address), the connection remains established. This is how TCP/IP was designed.

> **Note**
> The previous statement assumes that neither application—neither the client nor the server—has application-level timers to detect inactivity, causing either application to terminate. It also assumes that no intermediate router is keeping state about the connection (such as a NAT box) that is required for proper operation that it might delete because of inactivity or lose because of system failure. In today's Internet, these are big assumptions.

Under some circumstances, it is useful for a client or server to become aware of the termination or loss of connection with its peer. In other circumstances, it is desirable to keep a minimal amount of data flowing over a connection, even if the applications do not have any to exchange. TCP *keepalive* provides a capability useful for both cases. Keepalive is a method for TCP to probe its peer without affecting the content of the data stream. It is driven by a *keepalive timer*. When the timer fires, a *keepalive probe* (*keepalive* for short) is sent, and the peer receiving the probe responds with an ACK.

Note

Keepalives are not part of the TCP specification. The Host Requirements RFC [RFC1122] says that this is because they could (1) cause perfectly good connections to break during transient Internet failures, (2) consume unnecessary bandwidth, and (3) cost money for an Internet path that charges for packets. Nevertheless, most implementations provide the keepalive capability.

TCP keepalive is a controversial feature. Many feel that polling of the other end has no place in TCP and should be done by the application, if desired. On the other hand, if many applications require such functionality, it is convenient to place it in TCP so that its implementation can be shared. The keepalive is an optionally enabled feature that can cause an otherwise good connection between two processes to be terminated because of a temporary loss of connectivity in the network joining the two end systems. For example, if the keepalive probes are sent during the time that an intermediate router has crashed and is rebooting, TCP incorrectly thinks its peer host has crashed.

The keepalive feature was originally intended for server applications that might tie up resources on behalf of a client and want to know if the client host crashes or goes away. Using TCP keepalive to detect dead clients is most useful for servers that expect to have a relatively short-duration dialogue with a noninteractive client (e.g., Web servers, POP and IMAP e-mail servers). Servers implementing more interactive-style services that last for a long time (e.g., remote login such as ssh and Windows Remote Desktop) might wish to avoid using keepalives.

A common example showing the utility of the keepalive feature nowadays is when a user uses the ssh (secure shell) remote login program to log in to a remote host through a NAT router. If the user were to establish the connection, do some work, then just power off the computer at the end of the day, without logging off, a half-open connection would be left. In Chapter 13 we showed that sending data across a half-open connection causes a reset to be returned, but that was from the server end, where the client was sending the data. If the client disappears, leaving the half-open connection on the server's end, and the server is waiting for some data from the client, the server will wait forever. The keepalive feature is intended to detect these half-open connections from the server side.

Another reason for using keepalives is somewhat the reverse. If the user does not power off the computer but instead leaves a connection open all night (and wishes to continue using it the next day), the connection goes idle for many hours. In Chapter 7 we discussed how most NAT routers include a timeout mechanism that flushes the state of a connection after some period of inactivity. If the NAT timeout is less than the several hours before the user returns to use the login session, and the NAT is not smart enough to probe the end station to make sure it is still active, or the NAT crashes, the connection is terminated. To avoid this common problem, ssh can be configured to use TCP keepalives. ssh also has the ability to use *application-managed* keepalives, and the two behave differently, especially with respect to their security properties. (Please see Section 17.3 for more on this.)

17.2 Description

Either end of a TCP connection may request keepalives, which are turned off by default, for their respective direction of the connection. A keepalive can be set for one side, both sides, or neither side. There are several configurable parameters that control the operation of keepalives. If there is no activity on the connection for some period of time (called the *keepalive time*), the side(s) with keepalive enabled sends a keepalive probe to its peer(s). If no response is received, the probe is repeated periodically with a period set by the *keepalive interval* until a number of probes equal to the number *keepalive probes* is reached. If this happens, the peer's system is determined to be unreachable and the connection is terminated.

A keepalive probe is an empty (or 1-byte) segment with sequence number equal to one less than the largest ACK number seen from the peer so far. Because this sequence number has already been ACKed by the receiving TCP, the arriving segment does no harm, but it elicits an ACK that is used to determine whether the connection is still operating. Neither the probe nor its ACK contains any new data (it is "garbage" data), and neither is retransmitted by TCP if lost. [RFC1122] dictates that because of this fact, the lack of response for a single keepalive probe should not be considered sufficient evidence that the connection has stopped operating. This is the reason for the *keepalive probes* parameter setting mentioned previously. Note that some (mostly older) TCP implementations do not respond to keepalives lacking the "garbage" byte of data.

Anytime it is operating, a TCP using keepalives may find its peer in one of four states:

1. The peer host is still up and running and reachable. The peer's TCP responds normally and the requestor knows that the other end is still up. The requestor's TCP resets the keepalive timer for later (equal to the value of the *keepalive time*). If there is application traffic across the connection before the next timer expires, the timer is reset back to the value of *keepalive time*.

2. The peer's host has crashed and is either down or in the process of rebooting. In either case, its TCP is not responding. The requestor does not receive a response to its probe, and it times out after a time specified by the *keepalive interval*. The requestor sends a total of *keepalive probes* of these probes, *keepalive interval* time apart, and if it does not receive a response, the requestor considers the peer's host as down and terminates the connection.

3. The client's host has crashed and rebooted. In this case, the server receives a response to its keepalive probe, but the response is a reset segment, causing the requestor to terminate the connection.

4. The peer's host is up and running but is unreachable from the requestor for some reason (e.g., the network cannot deliver traffic and may or may not

inform the peers of this fact using ICMP). This is effectively the same as state 2, because TCP cannot distinguish between the two. All TCP can tell is that no replies are received to its probes.

The requestor does not have to worry about the peer's host being shut down gracefully and then rebooting (as opposed to crashing). When the system is shut down by an operator, all application processes are terminated (i.e., the peer's process), which causes the peer's TCP to send a FIN on the connection. Receiving the FIN would cause the requestor's TCP to report an end-of-file to the requestor's process, allowing the requestor to detect this scenario and exit.

In the first state the requestor's application has no idea that keepalive probes are taking place (except that it chose to enable keepalives in the first place). Everything is handled at the TCP layer. It is transparent to the application until one of states 2, 3, or 4 is determined. In these three cases, an error is returned to the requestor's application by its TCP. (Normally the requestor has issued a read from the network, waiting for data from the peer. If the keepalive feature returns an error, it is returned to the requestor as the return value from the read.) In scenario 2 the error is something like "Connection timed out," and in scenario 3 we expect "Connection reset by peer." The fourth scenario may look as if the connection timed out, or may cause another error to be returned, depending on whether an ICMP error related to the connection is received and how it is processed (see Chapter 8). We look at all four scenarios in the next section.

The values of the variables *keepalive time, keepalive interval,* and *keepalive probes* can usually be changed. Some systems allow these changes on a per-connection basis, while others allow them to be set only system-wide (or both in some cases). In Linux, these values are available as `sysctl` variables with the names `net.ipv4``.tcp_keepalive_time`, `net.ipv4.tcp_keepalive_intvl`, and `net.ipv4``.tcp_keepalive_probes`, respectively. The defaults are 7200 (seconds, or 2 hours), 75 (seconds), and 9 (probes).

In FreeBSD and Mac OS X, the first two values are also available as `sysctl` variables called `net.inet.tcp.keepidle` and `net.inet.tcp.keepintvl`, with default values 7,200,000 (milliseconds, or 2 hours) and 75,000 (milliseconds, or 75s), respectively. These systems also have a Boolean variable called `net.inet``.tcp.always_keepalive`. If this value is enabled, all TCP connections have the keepalive function enabled, even if the application did not request it. In these systems, the number of probes is a fixed default value: 8 (FreeBSD) or 9 (Mac OS X).

In Windows, these values are available for modification via registry entries under the system key:

`HKLM\SYSTEM\CurrentControlSet\Services\Tcpip\Parameters`

The value `KeepAliveTime` defaults to 7,200,000ms (2 hours); `KeepAlive-Interval` defaults to 1000ms (1s). If there is no response to ten keepalive probes, Windows terminates the connection.

Note that [RFC1122] places certain restrictions on the use of keepalives. In particular, the *keepalive time* must be configurable and must not default to less than 2 hours. In addition, keepalives must not be enabled unless an application requests one (although this behavior is violated if the `net.inet.tcp.always_ keepalive` variable is set). Linux does not provide a native facility for adding keepalives to applications that do not request it, but a special library can be *preloaded* (i.e., loaded prior to ordinary shared libraries) to get this effect [LKA].

17.2.1 Keepalive Examples

We shall now go through states 2, 3, and 4 from the previous section, to see the packets exchanged using the keepalive mechanism. The operation in state 1 will be illustrated in the course of looking at the others.

17.2.1.1 Other End Crashes

Let us see what happens when the server host crashes and does not reboot. To simulate this we will do the following steps:

1. Using the `regedit` program on a Windows client, modify the registry key, and set `KeepAliveTime` to 7000ms (7s). This may require the system to be rebooted to accept the new value.

2. Establish an `ssh` connection between the Windows client and a Linux server using an option that enables TCP keepalives.

3. Verify that data can go across the connection.

4. Watch the client's TCP send keepalive packets every 7s, and see them acknowledged by the server's TCP.

5. Disconnect the network cable from the server, and leave it disconnected until the example is complete. This makes the client think the server host has crashed.

6. We expect the client to send ten keepalive probes, 1s apart, before declaring the connection dead.

Here is the interactive output on the client:

```
C:\> ssh -o TCPKeepAlive=yes 10.0.1.1
(password prompt and login continues)
Write failed: Connection reset by peer (about 15 seconds after disconnect)
```

Figure 17-1 shows the results using Wireshark. In this example, the connection has already been established. The Wireshark output begins with a keepalive (packet 1) that is not identified as such. At this point, Wireshark has not processed enough packets to determine that the one sequence number in packet 1 is below

Figure 17-1   TCP keepalives are generated every 7s after the connection becomes idle. Each contains a below-window sequence number that is ACKed by the peer. A cable disconnection after 1 minute causes subsequent keepalives to not be ACKed. The client tries ten times before giving up and terminating the connection. The termination is signaled to the server by the final reset segment (which the server cannot hear). This example also illustrates the use of DSACKs at the server and a spurious retransmission caused by the client delaying ACKs.

the receiver's left window edge and is therefore a keepalive. Packet 2 contains an ACK number that allows Wireshark to process the sequence numbers in subsequent packets appropriately.

Most of this connection consists of keepalives and corresponding ACKs. Packets 1, 3, 5, 7, 14, 16, 18, 20, and 22–31 are all keepalives. Packets 2, 4, 6, 8, 15, 17, 19, and 21 are the corresponding ACKs. Keepalives are sent periodically every 7s provided they are ACKed. When no ACK is returned for a keepalive, the sender switches to a 1s interval for sending keepalives, according to the default value of `KeepAliveInterval`. This starts with packet 23 at time 62.120. The sender produces ten unacknowledged keepalives in total (packets 22–31). After that, it terminates the connection, which results in the final reset segment (packet 32) that is never received by the disconnected receiver. The user receives the following output when the connection terminates:

```
Write failed:  Connection reset by peer
```

This is a clear indication that the connection has terminated, but it is not entirely accurate. It was really the sender that terminated the connection, but it did so based on the lack of response from the receiver.

Apart from the use of keepalive segments, there are some other interesting features of this connection we will mention briefly. First, the server uses DSACKs (see Chapter 14). Each ACK contains the sequence number range of the previously received in-window segment. Next, a small bit of data is exchanged at time 26.09. The data represents a single key press. It is sent to the server, ACKed by the server, and echoed back. The data is encrypted, causing the packets containing data to be 48 bytes in user data size (see Chapter 18).

Interestingly, the echoed character is sent twice. We can see that packet 11, which contains the echoed character is not ACKed immediately. Recall from Chapter 14 that Linux uses an RTO of at least 200ms. Here we see that the Linux server retransmits the echoed character 200ms later, which produces an immediate response from the client. Because this test was performed on an uncongested LAN, it is highly unlikely that segment 11 was dropped. Instead, it appears that Linux produced a spurious retransmission due to the client delaying ACKs. This is a similar sort of hazard we saw when exploring the poor interaction between the Nagle algorithm and delayed ACKs we discussed in Chapter 15. Here, the dynamic results in an unnecessary delay of about 200ms.

17.2.1.2 Other End Crashes and Reboots

In this example we will see what happens when the peer crashes and reboots. The initial scenario is the same as the previous one, except this time we set `KeepAliveTime` to 120,000 (2 minutes). We establish a connection and then wait just over 2 minutes to allow a keepalive message to be sent and ACKed. Then we disconnect the server from the network, reboot it, and then reconnect it. We expect the next keepalive probe to generate a reset·from the server, because the server now knows nothing about this connection. Figure 17-2 presents the trace as displayed by Wireshark.

In this example, the connection has been established and small amounts of data are exchanged starting at seconds 0.00 and 3.46. Then the connection goes idle. After 2 minutes have elapsed (the *keepalive time*), the client sends the first keepalive probe at time 123.47, containing the "garbage" byte below the receiver's

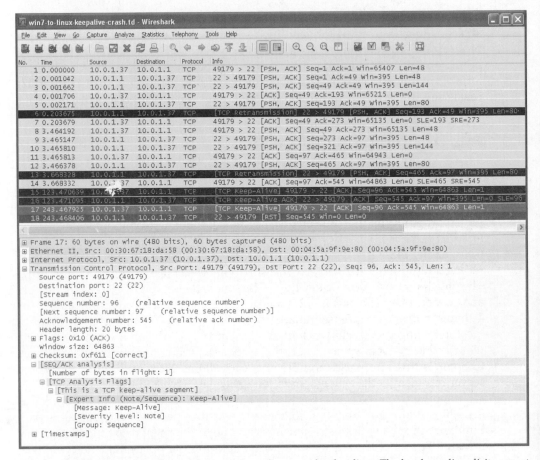

Figure 17-2 The server has rebooted between keepalives sent by the client. The last keepalive elicits a reset segment because the server no longer knows anything about the connection.

left window edge. It is acknowledged, and the server is disconnected, rebooted, and reconnected. At time 243.47, 120s later, the client sends its second keepalive probe. Although this reaches the server, the server no longer has any knowledge about the connection and responds with a reset segment (packet 18). This informs the client that the connection is no longer active, and the user is provided the same "Connection reset by peer" error message we saw before.

17.2.1.3 Other End Is Unreachable

In this case, the server has not crashed but becomes unreachable during the interval when the keepalive probes are sent. An intermediate router may have crashed, a phone line may be temporarily out of order, or something similar. To simulate this example we will use our sock program with the keepalive option set to establish a connection to a Web server. We will use a Mac OS X client and an LDAP server (port 389) running on `ldap.mit.edu`. After shortening the client's *keepalive time* (for convenience) and opening the connection, we disconnect the network to see the effects. Here are the command lines and output at the client:

```
Mac# sysctl -w net.inet.tcp.keepidle=75000
Mac% sock -K ldap.mit.edu 389
recv error: Operation timed out          about 14 minutes later
```

The trace is displayed using Wireshark (see Figure 17-3).

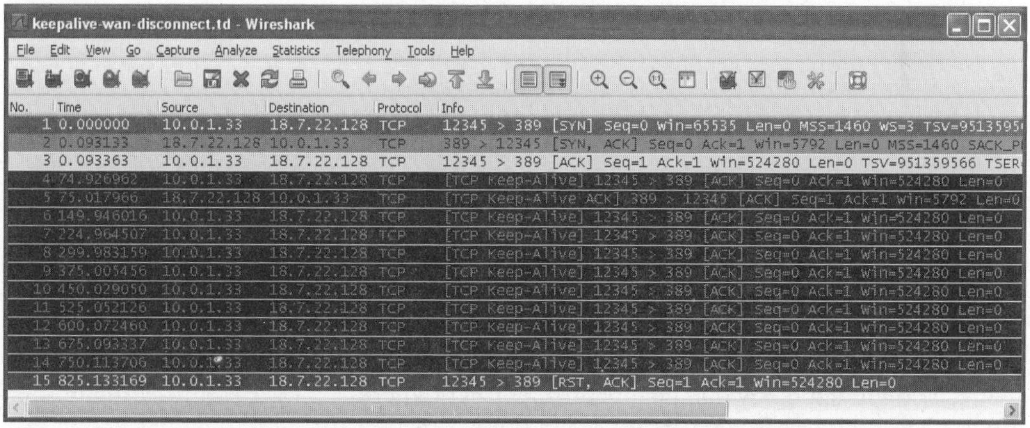

Figure 17-3   The WAN connection is taken down after the first keepalive probe is acknowledged. Another probe is sent every 75s. After nine keepalives are sent without a response, the connection is terminated and the client sends a reset to its peer. For the client, the situation is very similar to when the server crashes, as illustrated in Figure 17-1.

In this figure we can see the entire connection. After the initial three-way handshake, the connection remains idle and a keepalive is sent and acknowledged at about time 75 (packet 4). This first keepalive is triggered by the value of the `net.inet.tcp.keepidle` variable. Shortly thereafter, the network is severed. Neither end of the connection produces data, so the next event is another keepalive sent by the client at time 150 (75s later, the value of the `net.inet.tcp.keepintvl` variable). This pattern repeats with packets 7–14, with no ACKs present, even though the server is up and running. Finally, the client gives up 75s after its ninth unacknowledged keepalive probe. The connection termination is indicated to the server by a reset segment at the end (packet 15). Of course, the server is unable to receive this packet because the network is not operating.

When a client TCP using keepalives is unable to communicate across the network with its peer, as this example shows, it retries some number of times before giving up. This is essentially the same behavior we saw when the other end crashed. In most cases, the sending TCP cannot tell the difference. There are some exceptions, such as when ICMP indicates that the destination has become unreachable or otherwise unavailable because of problems in the network, but these conditions are relatively rare because ICMP is often blocked. As a result, mechanisms such as TCP keepalive (or similar mechanisms implemented by applications) are used to detect disconnection periods.

17.3 Attacks Involving TCP Keepalives

As we mentioned before, `ssh` (version 2) has an application-level form of keep-alive called *server alive messages* and *client alive messages*. These are different from TCP keepalive messages because they are sent over an encrypted channel at the application layer and contain data. TCP keepalives contain no user-level data, so the use of encryption is limited at best. The consequence is that TCP keepalives may be spoofed. When TCP keepalives are spoofed, the victim can be coerced into keeping resources allocated for a period longer than intended.

Although it may be a relatively minor concern, TCP keepalives are driven off a timer based on the various configuration parameters discussed earlier, and not off the dynamically adjusted retransmission timer used to retransmit segments with data. A passive observer could notice the existence of keepalives and their inter-arrival times to conceivably learn information about the configuration parameters (possibly identifying the type of sending system, called *fingerprinting*) or about the network topology (i.e., whether downstream routers are forwarding traffic or not). These issues could be of concern in some environments.

17.4 Summary

As we said earlier, the keepalive feature has been somewhat controversial. Protocol experts continue to debate whether it belongs in the transport layer or should be handled entirely by the application. All popular TCP implementations now include the keepalive feature, which applications may optionally use to establish a "heartbeat" of traffic moving across a connection. Doing so can help a server by allowing it to detect nonresponsive clients and can help clients by keeping connections active (e.g., to keep NAT state active) even if no application-layer data is flowing.

Keepalives operate by sending a probe packet (usually containing a "garbage" byte, although zero-length probes are also possible) across a connection after the connection has been idle for some relatively long period of time, often 2 hours. Four different scenarios can occur: the other end is still there, the other end has crashed, the other end has crashed and rebooted, or the other end is currently unreachable. We saw each of these scenarios with an example.

In the first two keepalive examples that we examined, had keepalives not been used, and without any application-level timer or activity, TCP would never have known that the other end had crashed (or crashed and rebooted). In the final example, however, nothing was wrong with the other end; the connection was temporarily down. We must be aware of this limitation when using keepalives and consider whether or not such behavior is desired.

Attacks against the keepalive mechanism include causing a system to keep resources allocated longer than intended and possibly learning some otherwise hidden information about the end systems (although such information may be of limited use to an attacker). In addition, by default TCP does not use its own encryption, so keepalives and keepalive ACKs can be spoofed, whereas application-level keepalives that employ encryption (e.g., `ssh`) cannot.

17.5 References

[LKA] http://libkeepalive.sourceforge.net

[RFC1122] R. Braden, ed., "Requirements for Internet Hosts," Internet RFC 1122, Oct. 1989.

18

Security: EAP, IPsec, TLS, DNSSEC, and DKIM

18.1 Introduction

In this chapter we will take a look at several forms of security used with TCP/IP. Security is a very broad and interesting topic, and covering it comprehensively is far beyond the scope of this book. Consequently, we will be interested to know about the various types of security threats on the Internet, and we will delve into some detail on those security mechanisms aimed at countering them that are applicable to the operation of various protocols such as IP, TCP, and the important e-mail and DNS application protocols.

Although our partitioning is not really formal, security threats can be broken down into attacks that target implementation problems by trying to subvert processes into running code that was not intended, trying to get users to run programs that do bad things, and using network protocols in compliant but unauthorized ways. We have already seen forms of these attacks in other chapters. For example, one of the earliest *worms* (self-propagating software) on the Internet used a *buffer overflow* that overwrites the server process's memory. Doing so allows a client program to inject software into a server that ultimately runs this injected code. The injected code then performs the same action, thereby causing the program to self-propagate. Naturally, such code could perform more malicious activities than simply self-propagation.

The various types of attacks and techniques can be combined, and complicated software and security analysis tools have been developed as the value of the information on the Internet has increased. A variety of texts, including [MSK09], discuss the tools and techniques in more detail. Today, essentially any software executed by a user or as a user against the user's intentions is known by the general term *malware*, short for "malicious software." Entire industries have been developed to both create and reduce the effects of malware. Malware can be delivered in e-mail messages or attachments (e.g., in spam), picked up while visiting a Web site (*drive-by* attacks), or acquired when using portable media such as portable USB drives.

In some cases, malware is used to take control of a large number of computers in the Internet (*botnets*). Botnets are controlled by individuals or organizations (*bot herders*) and can be used on a wide scale for a number of purposes such as sending spam, compromising other computers, exfiltrating information from the compromised system (e.g., credit card and bank account information, and the user's logged keystrokes), and launching DoS attacks by sending a large aggregate volume of Internet traffic to one or more victims. Botnets are now commonly offered as a service on a rental basis—a client can hire a bot herder to perform one or more nefarious tasks. One common task is to generate e-mails in hopes of inducing the recipient(s) to visit a particular Web site or purchase a particular product (*phishing*). When a specific victim is targeted in this way, the activity is usually called *spear phishing*.

Our interest is in understanding how secure communication protocols on the Internet work. Ironically, perhaps, many worms or viruses implement secure communication protocols. In most cases, we will see how the types of protocols we have already studied such as IP, TCP, e-mail, and DNS have been augmented with security extensions (sometimes in the form of additional protocols) to enhance security. We need to be somewhat precise in defining what "security" means in terms of a communication protocol, in order to understand if the techniques available to us are sufficient to provide our desired level of protection. Therefore, we shall begin by studying the properties of information protection considered desirable in the field of *information security*.

18.2 Basic Principles of Information Security

There are three primary properties of information, whether in a computer network or not, that may be desirable from an information security point of view: confidentiality, integrity, and availability (the *CIA triad*) [L01], summarized here:

- **Confidentiality** means that information is made known only to its intended users (which could include processing systems).

- **Integrity** means that information has not been modified in an unauthorized way before it is delivered.

- **Availability** means that information is available when needed.

These are core properties of information, yet there are other properties we may also desire, including *authentication*, *nonrepudiation*, and *auditability*. Authentication means that a particular identified party or *principal* is not impersonating another principal. Nonrepudiation means that if some action is performed by a principal (e.g., agreeing to the terms of a contract), this fact can be proven later (i.e., cannot successfully be denied). Auditability means that some sort of trustworthy log or accounting describing how information has been used is available. Such logs are often important for forensic (i.e., legal and prosecuritorial) purposes.

These principles are applicable to information in physical (e.g., printed) form, for which mechanisms such as safes, secured facilities, and guards have been used for thousands of years to enforce controlled sharing, storage, and dissemination. When information is to be moved through an unsecured environment, additional techniques are required. To see why, let us examine the types of threats to which information can be exposed when it travels through an unsecured communication channel.

18.3 Threats to Network Communication

When considering the design and operation of network protocols, ensuring that information has the desired properties of integrity, availability, and confidentiality can be quite a challenge because of the wide range of possible attacks that can be carried out in an otherwise uncontrolled network such as the Internet. Attacks can generally be categorized as either *passive* or *active* [VK83]. Identifying the category is useful because different techniques are required to provide security depending on the particular category. Passive attacks are mounted by monitoring or eavesdropping on the contents of network traffic, and if not handled they can lead to unauthorized release of information (loss of confidentiality). Active attacks can cause modification of information (with possible loss of integrity) or denial of service (loss of availability). Logically, such attacks are carried out by an "intruder" or adversary. This is often depicted using the scenario shown in Figure 18-1.

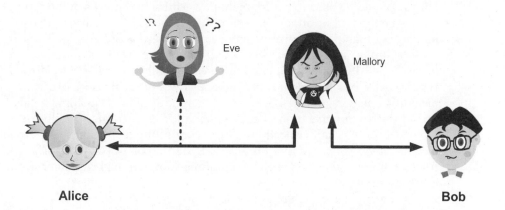

Figure 18-1   The principals, Alice and Bob, attempt to communicate securely, but Eve may eavesdrop and Mallory may modify messages in transit.

The figure depicts the principals, Alice and Bob, trying to communicate. However, there are two attackers, Eve and Mallory. Eve (eavesdropper) is only able to monitor the traffic exchanged between Alice and Bob and thus can carry out only passive attacks. Mallory (malicious attacker) can store, modify, and replay traffic passing between Alice and Bob, so she can carry out active and passive attacks. Table 18-1 summarizes the major categories of passive and active attacks that Alice and Bob may face.

Table 18-1   Attacks on communication are broadly classified as passive or active. Passive attacks are ordinarily more difficult to detect, and active attacks are ordinarily more difficult to prevent.

Passive		Active	
Type	Threats	Type	Threats
Eavesdropping	Confidentiality	Message stream modification	Authenticity, integrity
Traffic analysis	Confidentiality	Denial of service (DoS)	Availability
		Spurious association	Authenticity

From an attacker's perspective, Table 18-1 gives a quick summary of the passive attacks available to Eve and the active (and passive) attacks available to Mallory. Eve is able to *eavesdrop* (listen in on, also called *capture* or *sniff*) and perform *traffic analysis* on the traffic passing between Alice and Bob. Capturing the traffic could lead to compromise of confidentiality, as sensitive data may be available to Eve without Alice or Bob knowing. In addition, traffic analysis can determine the features of the traffic, such as its size and when it is sent, and possibly identify the parties to a communication. This information, although it does not reveal the exact contents of the communication, could also lead to disclosure of sensitive information and could be used to mount more powerful active attacks in the future.

While the passive attacks are essentially impossible for Alice or Bob to detect, Mallory is capable of performing more easily noticed active attacks. These include *message stream modification* (MSM), *denial-of-service* (DoS), and *spurious association* attacks. MSM attacks (including so-called called *man-in-the-middle* or MITM attacks) are a broad category and include any way traffic is modified in transit, including deletion, reordering, and content modification. DoS might include deletion of traffic, or generation of such large volumes of traffic so as to overwhelm Alice, Bob, or the communication channel connecting them. Spurious associations include *masquerading* (Mallory pretends to be Bob or Alice) and *replay*, whereby Alice or Bob's earlier (authentic) communications are replayed later, from Mallory's memory.

Two major methods are available to prevent the passive and active attacks we have just described. One method would be to ensure through physical security that only trusted parties have access to the communication infrastructure connecting Alice and Bob. This approach is used in limited circumstances but is effectively impractical for any network spanning a large geographical distance. Of course, if the communication channel is wireless, securing it using only physical methods is effectively impossible. Given these considerations, some mechanism is needed to allow information to pass through unsecured communication channels in such a way that adversaries like Eve and Mallory are, for the most part at least, thwarted. This mechanism is *cryptography*. With effective and careful use of cryptography, passive attacks are rendered ineffective, and active attacks are made detectable (and to some degree preventable).

18.4 Basic Cryptography and Security Mechanisms

Cryptography evolved from the desire to protect the confidentiality, integrity, and authenticity of information carried through unsecured communication channels. Such a capability is clearly of significant importance in protecting confidential information such as military orders, intelligence, and recipes for creating especially dangerous or valuable materials. The use of cryptography, at least in a primitive form, dates back to at least 3500 BCE. The earliest systems were usually *codes*. Codes involve substitutions of groups of words, phrases, or sentences with groups of numbers or letters as given in a *codebook*. Codebooks needed to be kept secret in order to keep communications private, so distributing them required considerable care.

More advanced systems used *ciphers*, in which both substitution and rearrangement are used. Several codes were used in the Middle Ages, and by the late 1800s large code and cipher systems were commonly use for diplomatic and military communications. By the early twentieth century, cryptography was well established but would not take its major leap forward until World War II. During this period, electromechanical cryptographic machines such as the German ENIGMA and Lorenz machines posed a challenge to Allied *cryptanalysts* (code breakers). One of the first digital computers, Colossus, was developed by the British to decipher Lorenz-enciphered messages. A functioning Colossus Mark 2 machine was created in 2007, after a 14-year effort, by Tony Sale of the National Museum of Computing at Bletchley Park, UK [TNMOC].

18.4.1 Cryptosystems

While the historical basis for cryptography is primarily for preserving confidentiality, other desirable properties such as integrity and authentication can also be achieved using cryptographic and related mathematical techniques. To help understand the basics, Figure 18-2 illustrates how the two most important types of cryptographic algorithms, called *symmetric key* and *public (asymmetric) key* ciphers, work.

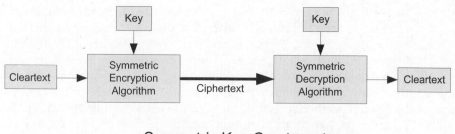

Symmetric Key Cryptosystem

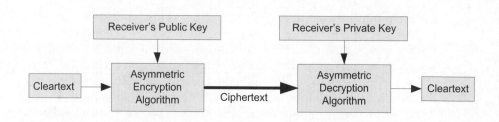

Asymmetric (Public Key) Cryptosystem

Figure 18-2   The unencrypted (cleartext) message is passed through an encryption algorithm to produce an encrypted (ciphertext) message. In a symmetric cryptosystem, the same (secret) key is used for encryption and decryption. In an asymmetric or public key cryptosystem, confidentiality is achieved by using the recipient's public key for encryption and private (secret) key for decryption.

This figure shows the high-level operation of symmetric and asymmetric key cryptography. In each case, a *cleartext* message is processed by an encryption algorithm to produce *ciphertext* (scrambled text). The *key* is a particular sequence of bits used to drive the *encryption algorithm* or cipher. With different keys, the same input produces different outputs. Combining the algorithms with supporting protocols and operating methods forms a *cryptosystem*. In a *symmetric cryptosystem*, the encryption and decryption keys are typically identical, as are the encryption and decryption algorithms. In an *asymmetric cryptosystem*, each principal is generally provided with a *pair* of keys consisting of one public and one private key. The public key is intended to be known to any party that might want to send a message to the key pair's owner. The public and private keys are mathematically related and are themselves outputs of a *key generation* algorithm. One of the major benefits of asymmetric key cryptosystems is that secret key material does not have to be securely distributed to every party that wishes to communicate.

Without knowing the symmetric key (in a symmetric cryptosystem) or the private key (in a public key cryptosystem), it is (believed to be) effectively impossible for any third party that intercepts the ciphertext to produce the corresponding cleartext. This provides the basis for confidentiality. For the symmetric key cryptosystem, it also provides a degree of authentication, because only a party holding the key is able to produce a useful ciphertext that can be decrypted to something sensible. A receiver can decrypt the ciphertext, look for a portion of the resulting cleartext to contain a particular agreed-upon value, and conclude that the sender holds the appropriate key and is therefore authentic. Furthermore, most encryption algorithms work in such a way that if messages are modified in transit, they are unable to produce useful cleartext upon decryption. Thus, symmetric cryptosystems provide a measure of both authentication and integrity protection for messages, but this approach alone is weak. Instead, special forms of checksums are usually coupled with symmetric cryptography to ensure integrity. We discuss these later, after the cryptographic preliminaries.

A symmetric encryption algorithm is usually classified as either a *block cipher* or a *stream cipher*. Block ciphers perform operations on a fixed number of bits (e.g., 64 or 128) at a time, and stream ciphers operate continuously on however many bits (or bytes) are provided as input. For years, the most popular symmetric encryption algorithm was the *Data Encryption Standard* (DES), a block cipher that uses 64-bit blocks and 56-bit keys. Eventually, the use of 56-bit keys was felt to be insecure, and many applications turned to *triple-DES* (also denoted 3DES or TDES—applying DES three times with two or three different keys to each block of data). Today, DES and 3DES have been largely phased out in favor of the Advanced Encryption Standard (AES) [FIPS197], also known occasionally by its original name the *Rijndael algorithm* (pronounced "rain-dahl"), in deference to its Belgian cryptographer inventors Vincent Rijmen and Joan Daemen. Different variants of AES provide key lengths of 128, 192, and 256 bits and are usually written with the corresponding extension (i.e., AES-128, AES-192, and AES-256).

Asymmetric cryptosystems have some additional interesting properties beyond those of symmetric key cryptosystems. Assuming we have Alice as sender and Bob as intended recipient, any third party is assumed to know Bob's public key and can therefore send him a secret message—only Bob is able to decrypt it because only Bob knows the private key corresponding to his public key. However, Bob has no real assurance that the message is authentic, because *any* party can create a message and send it to Bob, encrypted in Bob's public key. Fortunately, public key cryptosystems also provide another function when used in reverse: authentication of the sender. In this case, Alice can encrypt a message using her private key and send it to Bob (or anyone else). Using Alice's public key (known to all), anyone can verify that the message was authored by Alice and has not been modified. However, it is not confidential because everyone has access to Alice's public key. To achieve authenticity, integrity, *and* confidentiality, Alice can encrypt a message using her private key and encrypt the result using Bob's public key. The result is a message that is reliably authored by Alice and is also confidential to Bob. This process is illustrated in Figure 18-3.

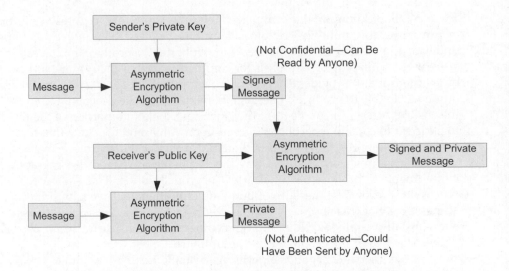

Asymmetric (Public Key) Cryptosystem

Figure 18-3   The asymmetric cryptosystem can be used for confidentiality (encryption), authentication (digital signatures or signing), or both. When used for both, it produces a signed output that is confidential to the sender and the receiver. Public keys, as their name suggests, are not kept secret.

When public key cryptography is used in "reverse" like this, it provides a *digital signature*. Digital signatures are important consequences of public key cryptography and can be used to help ensure authenticity and nonrepudiation. Only a party possessing Alice's private key is able to author messages or carry out transactions as Alice.

In a *hybrid* cryptosystem, elements of both public key and symmetric key cryptography are used. Most often, public key operations are used to exchange a randomly generated confidential (symmetric) *session key*, which is used to encrypt traffic for a single transaction using a symmetric algorithm. The reason for doing so is performance—symmetric key operations are less computationally intensive than public key operations. Most systems today are of the hybrid type: public key cryptography is used to establish keys used for symmetric encryption of individual sessions.

18.4.2 Rivest, Shamir, and Adleman (RSA) Public Key Cryptography

We have seen how public key cryptography can be used for both digital signatures and confidentiality. The most common approach is called RSA in deference to its authors' names, Rivest, Shamir, and Adleman [RSA78]. The security of this system hinges on the difficulty of factoring large numbers into constituent primes.

To initialize RSA, two large prime numbers p and q are generated, which usually involves checking a number of large odd numbers that are randomly generated until two primes are found. The product of these primes $n = pq$ is called the *modulus*. The length of n, p, and q is usually measured in bits, with n often being 1024 bits and the others being about 512, although larger sizes such as 2048 are now recommended. The value $\Phi(v)$ is known in number theory as the *Euler totient* of the integer v. It gives the number of positive integers less than v that are also coprime to v (i.e., whose greatest common divisor is 1). Because of the way n is constructed for RSA, $\Phi(n) = (q - 1)(p - 1)$.

Using the defnition for $\Phi(n)$, we can choose the RSA public exponent (called e for "encryption") and derive a private exponent (called d for "decryption") as multiplicative inverses using the relation $d = e^{-1} \pmod{\Phi(n)}$. In practice, e is often some value with a fairly small population count (i.e., has a small number of 1 bits) such as 65,537 (10000000000000001 binary), for faster computations. To form an encrypted ciphertext c from a cleartext message m, the value $c = m^e \pmod{n}$ is computed. To form the value m from c, decryption is performed: $m = c^d \pmod{n}$. An RSA public key consists of the public exponent e and modulus n. The corresponding private key consists of the private exponent d and the modulus n.

As suggested earlier, public key algorithms such as RSA can also be used to produce digital signatures by essentially running RSA "in reverse." To create an RSA signature of a message m, the value $s = m^d \pmod{n}$ can be produced as a signed version of m. Anyone receiving the value s can apply the public exponent e to produce $m = s^e \pmod{n}$, which provides the basis for verifying that whatever produced the value s was in possession of the private value d (otherwise the value m produced would not be sensible).

The security of RSA is based on the difficulty of factoring large numbers. In the context of RSA and our scenario of Figure 18-1, Eve is able to obtain n and e but does not know p, q, or $\Phi(n)$. If she could determine any of these last three values, it would be trivial to determine d using the relation we have described. However, doing so appears to involve factoring n, and factoring numbers of 1000 or more bits is currently believed to be out of reach for even the best factorization algorithms. Indeed, factoring semiprimes (numbers that are a product of two primes) appears to represent the most difficult case for such algorithms.

18.4.3 Diffie-Hellman-Merkle Key Agreement (aka Diffie-Hellman or DH)

A common requirement in security protocols is to have two parties agree on a common set of secret bits that can be used as a symmetric key. Doing so in a network that may contain eavesdroppers (such as Eve) is a challenge, because it is not immediately obvious how to have two principals (such as Alice and Bob) agree on a common secret number without Eve knowing. The *Diffie-Hellman-Merkle Key Agreement protocol* (more commonly called simply Diffie-Hellman or DH) provides a method for accomplishing this task, based on the use of finite field arithmetic

[DH76].[1] DH techniques are used in many of the Internet-related security protocols [RFC2631] and are closely related to the RSA approach for public key cryptography. We shall have a brief look at how they work.

With the same cast of characters (Alice, Bob, etc.), let us assume that all parties are aware of two integers p and g. Let p be a (large) prime number and $g < p$ be a primitive root mod p. With these assumptions, every integer in the group $\mathbf{Z}_p = \{1, ..., p - 1\}$ can be generated by raising g to some power. Said another way, for every n, there exists some k for which $g^k \equiv n$ (mod p). Finding the value (or values) of k given g, n, and p (called the *discrete log problem*) is considered to be difficult, resulting in the belief that DH is secure. Finding the value of n given g, k, and p is easy, resulting in the approach being practical.

For Alice and Bob to establish a shared secret key, they can use the following protocol: Alice chooses a secret random number a and computes A = g^a (mod p), which she sends to Bob. Bob chooses a secret random number b and computes B = g^b (mod p), which he sends to Alice. Alice and Bob arrive at the same shared secret K = g^{ab} (mod p). Alice computes this value this way:

$$K = B^a \pmod{p} = g^{ba} \pmod{p}$$

and Bob computes it this way:

$$K = A^b \pmod{p} = g^{ab} \pmod{p}$$

Given that g^{ba} is equal to g^{ab} (because $\mathbf{Z}_p$ is so-called *power associative* and we assumed all parties are aware of the group $\mathbf{Z}_p$ being used), both Alice and Bob know K. Note that Eve has access only to g, p, A, and B so cannot determine K without solving the discrete log problem [MW99]. However, this basic protocol is vulnerable to an attack from Mallory. Mallory can pretend to be Bob when communicating with Alice and vice versa by supplying her own A and B values. However, the basic DH protocol can be extended to protect from this man-in-the-middle attack if the public values for A and B are authenticated [DOW92]. The classic approach, called the *Station-to-Station protocol* (STS), involves Alice and Bob signing their public values.

18.4.4 Signcryption and Elliptic Curve Cryptography (ECC)

When using RSA, additional security is provided with larger numbers. However, the basic mathematical operations required by RSA (e.g., exponentiation) can be computationally intensive and scale as the numbers grow. Reducing the effort of combining digital signatures and encryption for confidentiality, a class of *signcryption* schemes [Z97] (also called *authenticated encryption*) provides both features

---

1. The technique was described in a then-classified reference in 1973 by C. Cocks, "A Note on 'Non-Secret Encryption.'" See http://www.cesg.gov.uk/publications/media/notense.pdf.

at a cost less than the sum of the two if computed separately. However, even greater efficiency can sometimes be achieved by changing the mathematical basis for public key cryptography.

In a continuing search for security with greater efficiency and performance, researchers have explored other public key cryptosystems beyond RSA. An alternative based on the difficulty of finding the discrete logarithm of an *elliptic curve* element has emerged, known as *elliptic curve cryptography* (ECC, not to be confused with error-correcting code) [M85][K87][RFC5753]. For equivalent security, ECC offers the benefit of using keys that are considerably smaller than those of RSA (e.g., by about a factor of 6 for a 1024-bit RSA modulus). This leads to simpler and faster implementations, issues of considerable practical concern. ECC has been standardized for use in many of the applications where RSA still retains dominance, but adoption has remained somewhat sluggish because of patents on ECC technology held by the Certicom Corporation. (The RSA algorithm was also patented, but patent protection lapsed in the year 2000.)

18.4.5 Key Derivation and Perfect Forward Secrecy (PFS)

In communication scenarios where multiple messages are to be exchanged, it is common to establish a short-term session key to perform symmetric encryption. The session key is ordinarily a random number (see the following section) generated by a function called a *key derivation function* (KDF), based on some input such as a master key or a previous session key. If a session key is compromised, any of the data encrypted with the key is subject to compromise. However, it is common practice to change keys (*rekey*) multiple times during an extended communication session. A scheme in which the compromise of one session key keeps future communications secure is said to have *perfect forward secrecy* (PFS). Usually, schemes that provide PFS require additional key exchanges or verifications that introduce overhead. One example is the STS protocol for DH mentioned earlier.

18.4.6 Pseudorandom Numbers, Generators, and Function Families

In cryptography, random numbers are often used as initial input values to cryptographic functions, or for generating keys that are difficult to guess. Given that computers are not very random by nature, obtaining true random numbers is somewhat difficult. The numbers used in most computers for simulating randomness are called *pseudorandom numbers*. Such numbers are not usually truly random but instead exhibit a number of statistical properties that suggest that they are (e.g., when many of them are generated, they tend to be uniformly distributed across some range).

Pseudorandom numbers are produced by an algorithm or device known as a *pseudorandom number generator* (PRNG) or *pseudorandom generator* (PRG), depending on the author. Simple PRNGs are deterministic. That is, they have a small amount of internal state initialized by a *seed* value. Once the internal state is known, the sequence of PNs can be determined. For example, the common *Linear Congruential Generator* (LCG) algorithm produces random-appearing values that are entirely predictable if the input parameters are known or guessed. Consequently, LCGs are perfectly fine for use in certain programs (e.g., games that simulate random events) but insufficient for cryptographic purposes.

A *pseudorandom function family* (PRF) is a family of functions that appear to be algorithmically indistinguishable (by polynomial time algorithms) from truly random functions [GGM86]. A PRF is a stronger concept than a PRG, as a PRG can be created from a PRF. PRFs are the basis for *cryptographically strong* (or secure) pseudorandom number generators, called CSPRNGs. CSPRNGs are necessary in cryptographic applications for several purposes, including session key generation, for which a sufficient amount of randomness must be guaranteed [RFC4086].

18.4.7 Nonces and Salt

A *cryptographic nonce* is a number that is used once (or for one transaction) in a cryptographic protocol. Most commonly, a nonce is a random or pseudorandom number that is used in authentication protocols to ensure *freshness*. Freshness is the (desirable) property that a message or operation has taken place in the very recent past. For example, in a *challenge-response* protocol, a server may provide a requesting client with a nonce, and the client may need to respond with authentication material as well as a copy of the nonce (or perhaps an encrypted copy of the nonce) within a certain period of time. This helps to avoid replay attacks, because old authentication exchanges that are replayed to the server would not contain the correct nonce value.

A *salt* or salt value, used in the cryptographic context, is a random or pseudorandom number used to frustrate *brute-force* attacks on secrets. Brute-force attacks usually involve repeatedly guessing a password, passphrase, key, or equivalent secret value and checking to see if the guess was correct. Salts work by frustrating the checking portion of a brute-force attack. The best-known example is the way passwords used to be handled in the UNIX system. Users' passwords were encrypted and stored in a password file that all users could read. When logging in, each user would provide a password that was used to double encrypt a fixed value. The result was then compared against the user's entry in the password file. A match indicated that a correct password was provided.

At the time, the encryption method (DES) was well known and there was concern that a hardware-based *dictionary attack* would be possible whereby many words from a dictionary were encrypted with DES ahead of time (forming a *rainbow table*) and compared against the password file. A pseudorandom 12-bit salt was added to perturb the DES algorithm in one of 4096 (nonstandard) ways for each password in an effort to thwart this attack. Ultimately, the 12-bit salt was determined to be insufficient with improved computers (that could guess more values) and was expanded.

18.4.8 Cryptographic Hash Functions and Message Digests

In most of the protocols we have studied, including Ethernet, IP, ICMP, UDP, and TCP, we have seen the use of a frame check sequence (FCS, either a checksum or a CRC) to determine whether a PDU has likely been delivered without bit errors. Such mathematical functions tend to trade off the likelihood of detecting random errors against the amount of overhead required to carry the FCS value. When considering security, however, we are interested in ensuring message integrity not only against random, infrequent errors, but also against intentional message stream modification attacks. We are worried about Mallory modifying messages as they travel through the network. Ordinary FCS functions are not sufficient for this purpose.

A checksum or FCS can be used to verify message integrity against an adversary like Mallory if properly constructed using special functions. Such functions are called *cryptographic hash functions* and often resemble portions of encryption algorithms. The output of a cryptographic hash function H, when provided a message M, is called the *digest* or *fingerprint* of the message, $H(M)$. A message digest is a type of strong FCS that is easy to compute and has the following important properties:

- **Preimage resistance**: Given $H(M)$, it should be difficult to determine M if not already known.

- **Second preimage resistance**: Given $H(M1)$, it should be difficult to determine an $M2 \neq M1$ such that $H(M1) = H(M2)$.

- **Collision resistance**: It should be difficult to find any pair $M1$, $M2$ where $H(M1) = H(M2)$ when $M2 \neq M1$.

If a hash function has all of these properties, then if two messages have the same cryptographic hash value, they are, with negligible doubt, the same message. The two most common cryptographic hash algorithms are at present the *Message Digest Algorithm 5* (MD5, [RFC1321]), which produces a 128-bit (16-byte) digest, and the *Secure Hash Algorithm 1* (SHA-1), which produces a 160-bit (20-byte) digest. More recently, a family of functions based on SHA called SHA-2 [RFC6234] produce digests with lengths of 224, 256, 384, or 512 bits (28, 32, 48, and 64 bytes, respectively). Others are under development.

Notes

Cryptographic hash functions are often based on a *compression function f*, which takes an input of length L and produces a collision-resistant but deterministic output of size less than L. The *Merkle-Damgård construction*, which essentially breaks an arbitrarily long input into blocks of length L, pads them, passes them to f, and combines the results, produces a cryptographic hash function capable of taking a long input and producing an output with collision resistance.

MD5 had been in widespread use with Internet protocols until it was reported broken in 2005 (i.e., two different 128-byte sequences were shown to have the same MD5 value) [WY05]. SHA-1 was used as an alternative, but it was also thought to possibly have weaknesses, so a SHA-2 family of algorithms was developed. Given SHA-2's similarity to SHA-1, there is concern that it, too, may have weaknesses. In December 2010, the National Institute of Standards and Technology (NIST) in the United States announced that five algorithms had been selected as final candidates for a new "SHA-3" cryptographic hash algorithm [CHP]. The selection of the final winning algorithm is scheduled for sometime after spring 2012.

18.4.9 Message Authentication Codes (MACs, HMAC, CMAC, and GMAC)

A message authentication code (unfortunately abbreviated MAC or sometimes MIC but unrelated to the link-layer MAC addresses we discussed in Chapter 3) can be used to ensure message integrity and authentication. MACs are usually based on *keyed* cryptographic hash functions. Such functions are like message digest algorithms (see Section 18.4.8) but require a private key to produce or verify the integrity of a message and may also be used to verify (authenticate) the message's sender.

MACs require resistance to various forms of *forgery*. For a given keyed hash function $H(M,K)$ taking input message M and key K, resistance to *selective forgery* means that it is difficult for an adversary not knowing K to form $H(M,K)$ given a specific M. $H(M,K)$ is resistant to *existential forgery* if it is difficult for an adversary lacking K to find any previously unknown valid combination of M and $H(M,K)$. Note that MACs do not provide exactly the same features as digital signatures. For example, they cannot be a solid basis for nonrepudiation because the secret key is known to more than one party.

A standard MAC that uses cryptographic hash functions in a particular way is called the *keyed-hash message authentication code* (HMAC) [FIPS198][RFC2104]. The HMAC "algorithm" uses a generic cryptographic hash algorithm, say $H(M)$. To form a t-byte HMAC on message M with key K using H (called *HMAC-H*), we use the following definition:

$$HMAC\text{-}H\,(K, M)^t = \Lambda_t\,(H((K \oplus opad)\,||\,H((K \oplus ipad)\,||\,M)))$$

In this definition, *opad* (outer pad) is an array containing the value 0x5C repeated |K| times, and *ipad* (inner pad) is an array containing the value 0x36 repeated |K| times. $\oplus$ is the vector XOR operator, and || is the concatenation operator. Normally the HMAC output is intended to be a certain number t of bytes in length, so the operator $\Lambda_t(M)$ takes the left-most t bytes of M.

The careful reader will observe that the definition of HMAC is a hash around another hash, of the form $H(K1\,||\,H(K2\,||\,M))$ using keys $K1$ and $K2$. This structure resists so-called *extension attacks* in which a selected pad value can be combined (e.g., by Mallory) with an intercepted message and digest value to form a new, valid message and digest value (not sent by Alice). The values of *ipad* and *opad* are not critical but tend to produce *K1* and *K2* values with few bits in common (i.e., they have a large *hamming distance*). Certain extension attacks have been shown to be effective against naively constructed MACs such as those of the form $H(K \parallel M)$ or $H(M \parallel K)$ but ineffective against the HMAC construct (or NMAC construct [BCK96], of which HMAC is a derivative)[B06].

More recently, other forms of MACs have been standardized, called the *cipher-based MAC* (CMAC) [FIPS800-38B] and GMAC [NIST800-38D]. Instead of using a cryptographic hash function such as HMAC, these use a block cipher such as AES or 3DES. CMAC is envisioned for use in environments where it is more convenient or efficient to use a block cipher in place of a hash function. Details of CMAC using AES-128, called *AES-CMAC*, are provided in [RFC4493]. In essence, it works by encrypting a message block using AES-128 with a key *K*, taking the result and XORing it with the subsequent block, encrypting the result, and repeating the process until no more message blocks remain, with the output value being the result of the final encryption operation. If the final message block's length is an even multiple of the algorithm's block size, one *subkey*, derived from *K* using a special subkey-generating algorithm [IK03], is used in performing the final encryption. If not, the final message block is first padded and a second subkey, also generated from *K*, is used to perform the final encryption. GMAC uses a special mode of AES called *Galois/Counter Mode* (GCM). It also uses a keyed hash function (called *GHASH*, which is not a cryptographic hash function). We will see more about cryptographic operating modes in the next section.

18.4.10 Cryptographic Suites and Cipher Suites

At this point we have seen mechanisms to ensure confidentiality, authenticity, and integrity of information sent across an unsecured communication network. There are other capabilities (e.g., nonrepudiation) that can also be achieved by selecting the appropriate mathematical or cryptographic techniques. The combination of techniques used in a particular system, especially those we see used with Internet protocols, are called a *cryptographic suite* or sometimes a *cipher suite*, although the first term is more accurate. A cryptographic suite defines not only an enciphering (encryption) algorithm but may also include a particular MAC algorithm, PRF, key agreement algorithm, signature algorithm, and associated key lengths and parameters.

Many cryptographic suites are defined for use with the security protocols we shall discuss. Usually, an encryption algorithm is specified by its name and description, how many bits are used for its keys (often a multiple of 128 bits), along with its operating *mode*. Encryption algorithms that have been standardized for use with Internet protocols include AES, 3DES, NULL [RFC2410], and CAMELLIA [RFC3713]. The NULL encryption algorithm does not modify the input and is used in certain circumstances where confidentiality is not required.

The operating mode of an encryption algorithm, especially a block cipher, describes how to use the encryption function for a single block repeatedly (e.g., in a cascade) to encrypt or decrypt an entire message with a single key. Common modes today include *cipher block chaining* (CBC) and *counter* (CTR) mode, although many others have been defined. When performing encryption using CBC mode, a cleartext block to be encrypted is first XORed with the previous ciphertext block (the first block is XORed with a random *initialization vector* or IV). Encrypting in CTR mode involves first creating a value combining a nonce (or IV) and a *counter* that increments with each successive block to be encrypted. The combination is then encrypted, the output is XORed with a cleartext block to produce a ciphertext block, and the process repeats for successive blocks. In effect, this approach uses a block cipher to produce a *keystream*. A keystream is a sequence of (random-appearing) bits that are combined (e.g., XORed) with cleartext bits to produce a ciphertext. Doing so essentially converts a block cipher into a stream cipher because no explicit padding of the input is required.

CBC requires a serial process for encryption and a partly serial process for decryption, whereas counter mode algorithms allow more efficient fully parallel encryption and decryption implementations. Consequently, counter mode is gaining popularity. In addition, variants of CTR mode (e.g., counter mode with CBC-MAC (CCM), Galois Counter Mode, or GCM) can be used for authenticated encryption [RFC4309], and possibly to authenticate (but not encrypt) additional data (called *authenticated encryption with associated data* or AEAD) [RFC5116]. When authenticated encryption algorithms are used, separate MACs are generally not necessary. In the degenerate case of an AEAD algorithm operating on data that does not require confidentiality, a form of MAC is effectively produced (e.g., GMAC). When an encryption algorithm is specified as part of a cryptographic suite, its name usually includes the mode, and the key length is often implied. For example, ENCR_AES_CTR refers to AES-128 used in CTR mode.

When a PRF is included in the definition of a cryptographic suite, it is usually based on a cryptographic hash algorithm family such as SHA-2 [RFC6234] or a cryptographic MAC such as CMAC [RFC4434][RFC4615]. Constructions of this type generally include the name of the function serving as the basis. For example, the algorithm AES-CMAC-PRF-128 refers to a PRF constructed using a CMAC based on AES-128. It is also written as PRF_AES128_CMAC. The algorithm PRF_HMAC_SHA1 refers to a PRF based on HMAC-SHA1.

Key agreement parameters, when included with an Internet cryptographic suite definition, refer to DH group definitions, as no other key agreement protocol is in widespread use. When DH key agreement is used in generating keys for a particular encryption algorithm, care must be taken to ensure that the keys produced are of sufficient length (strength) to avoid compromising the security of the encryption algorithm. Consequently, more than 16 groups for use with DH in different contexts have been standardized [RFC5114]. The first 5 have become known as the "Oakley Groups" because they were specified by the Oakley protocol [RFC2409], an early component of IPsec that has since been deprecated. The *modular exponential* or MODP groups are based on exponentiation and modular arithmetic. The *elliptic curve groups modulo a prime* or ECP groups [RFC5903] are based on curves over the Galois field $GF(P)$ for a prime P, and the *elliptic curve groups modulo a power of two* or EC2N are based on curves over the field $GF(2^N)$ for some N.

A signature algorithm is sometimes included in the definition of a cryptographic suite. It may be used for signing a variety of values including data, MACs, and DH values. The most common is to use RSA to sign a hashed value for some block of data, although the *digital signature standard* (written as DSS or DSA to indicate the *digital signature algorithm*) [FIPS186-3] is also used in some circumstances. With the advent of ECC, signatures based on elliptic curves (e.g., ECDSA [X9.62-2005]) are also now supported in many systems.

The concept of a cryptographic suite evolved in the context of Internet security protocols because of a need for modularity and decoupled evolution. As computational power has improved, older cryptographic algorithms and smaller key lengths have fallen victim to various forms of brute-force attacks. In some cases, more sophisticated attacks have revealed flaws that necessitate the replacement of the underlying mathematical and cryptographic methods, but the basic protocol machinery is otherwise sound. As a result, the choice of a cryptographic suite can now be made separately from the communication protocol details and depends on factors such as convenience, performance, and security. Protocols tend to make use of the components of a cryptographic suite in a standard way, so an appropriate cryptographic suite can be "snapped in" when deemed appropriate. It is now common practice in protocol design to "outsource" the security processing to a separately defined set of cryptographic suites that have been analyzed by a large community with the necessary cryptographic and mathematical expertise. Although the ability to "snap in" a new cipher suite is appealing, it can still take years to standardize on acceptable suites and get them deployed. For interoperability, each participant in a communication exchange must usually employ the same suite. This can be a significant hurdle when cipher suites may be implemented in a wide range of software and hardware systems.

18.5 Certificates, Certificate Authorities (CAs), and PKIs

The tools provided by cryptography and related mathematics, including digital signatures and enciphering algorithms, provide a sound basis for constructing secure systems, but a great deal of additional work is required to create an entire system from these parts. Among the items of particular concern are the construction of secure protocols that use cryptographic methods in safe ways, and how keys are created, exchanged, and revoked (called *key management*). Key management remains one of the greatest challenges in deploying cryptographic systems on a widespread basis across multiple administrative domains.

One of the challenges with public key cryptosystems is to determine the correct public key for a principal or identity. In our running example, if Alice were to send her public key to Bob, Mallory could modify it in transit to be her own public key, and Bob (called the *relying party* here) might unknowingly be using Mallory's key, thinking it is Alice's. This would allow Mallory to effectively masquerade as Alice. To address this problem, a *public key certificate* is used to bind an identity to a particular public key using a digital signature. At first glance, this presents a certain "chicken-egg" problem: How can a public key become signed if the digital signature itself requires a reliable public key? There are two ways this is accomplished today.

One model, called a *web of trust*, involves having a certificate (identity/key binding) *endorsed* by a collection of existing users (called *endorsers*). An endorser signs a certificate and distributes the signed certificate. The more endorsers for a certificate over time, the more reliable it is likely to be. An entity checking a certificate might require some number of endorsers or possibly some particular endorsers to trust the certificate. The web of trust model is decentralized and "grassroots" in nature, with no central authority. This has mixed consequences. Having no central authority suggests that the scheme will not collapse because of a single point of failure, but it also means that a new entrant may experience some delay in getting its key endorsed to a degree sufficient to be trusted by a significant number of users. Some groups hold "key signing parties" to hasten this process. The web of trust model was first described as part of the *Pretty Good Privacy* (PGP) encryption system for electronic mail [NAZ00], which has evolved to support a standard encoding format called *OpenPGP*, defined by [RFC4880].

A more formal approach, which has the added benefit of being provably secure under certain theoretical assumptions in exchange for more dependence on a centralized authority, involves the use of a public key infrastructure (PKI). A PKI is a service responsible for creating, revoking, distributing, and updating key pairs and certificates. It operates with a collection of *certificate authorities* (CAs). A CA is an entity and service set up to manage and attest to the bindings between identities and their corresponding public keys. There are several hundred commercial CAs. A CA usually employs a *hierarchical* signing scheme. This means that a public key may be signed using a parent key which is in turn signed by a grandparent key, and so on. Ultimately a CA has one or more *root certificates* upon which many subordinate certificates depend for trust. An entity that is authoritative for certificates and keys (e.g., a CA) is called a *trust anchor*, although this term is also used to describe the certificates or other cryptographic material associated with such entities [RFC6024], which we discuss next.

18.5.1 Public Key Certificates, Certificate Authorities, and X.509

While several types of certificates have been used in the past, the one of most interest to us is based on an Internet profile of the ITU-T X.509 standard [RFC5280]. In addition, any particular certificate may be stored and exchanged in a number of file or encoding formats. The most common ones include DER, PEM (a Base64 encoded version of DER), PKCS#7 (P7B), and PKCS#12 (PFX). We also saw the use of PKCS#1 [RFC3447] in Chapter 8. Today, Internet PKI-related standards tend to use the *cryptographic message syntax* [RFC5652], which is based on PKCS#7 version 1.5. In the following example, we use an X.509 certificate in PEM format, which is the default format for many Internet applications and has the added advantage of being easily displayed as ASCII.

Certificates are primarily used in identifying four types of entities on the Internet: individuals, servers, software publishers, and CAs. One popular commercial CA, Verisign, assigns a "class" to each certificate, in the range 1 through 5. Class 1 certificates are intended for individuals, class 2 for organizations, class 3 for servers and software signing, class 4 for online transactions between companies, and class 5 for private organizations and governments. Certificate classes are primarily a convenience for grouping and naming types of certificates and for defining different security policies associated with them. Generally speaking, a higher class number is supposed to indicate more rigorous controls on the process required to validate an identity (called *identity proofing*) prior to issuing the associated certificate.

This still does not totally solve the chicken-egg PKI bootstrapping problem mentioned before. In practice, systems requiring public key operations have root certificates for popular CAs installed at configuration time (e.g., Microsoft Internet Explorer, Mozilla's Firefox, and Google's Chrome are all capable of accessing a preconfigured database of root certificates). To see how this works, we can use a command that gives information about certificates. The `openssl` command, available for most common platforms including Linux and Windows, allows us to see the certificates for a Web site (some lines are wrapped for clarity):

```
Linux% CDIR=`openssl version -d | awk '{print $2}'`
Linux% openssl s_client -CApath $CDIR \
              -connect www.digicert.com:443 > digicert.out 2>1
^C  (to interrupt)
```

The first command determines where the local system stores its preconfigured CA certificates. This is usually a directory that varies by system. In this case, the name of the directory is stored in the shell variable `CDIR`. We next make a connection to the HTTPS port (443) on the `www.digicert.com` server and redirect the output to the `digicert.out` file. The `openssl` command[2] takes care to print the entity identified by each of the certificates, and at what depth they are in the certificate hierarchy relative to the root (depth 0 is the server's certificate, so the depth numbers are counted bottom to top). It also checks the certificates against the stored CA certificates to see if they verify properly. In this case, they do, as indicated by "verify return" having value 0 (`ok`).

---

2. Note that a similar command unique to Windows called `certutil` is available with Windows 2003 Server and the Windows Server 2003 Administration Tools Pack.

```
Linux% grep "return code" digicert.out
    Verify return code: 0 (ok)
```

The file digicert.out contains not only a trace of the connection to the server but also a copy of the server's certificate. To get the certificate into a more usable form, we can extract the certificate data, convert it, and place the result into a PEM-encoded certificate file:

```
Linux% openssl x509 -in digicert.out -out digicert.pem
```

Given the certificate in PEM format, we can now use a variety of openssl functions to manipulate and inspect it. At the highest level, the certificate includes some data to be signed (called the "TBSCertificate") followed by a signature algorithm identifier and signature value. To see the server certificate, we can use the following command (some lines are wrapped or removed for clarity):

```
Linux% openssl x509 -in digicert.pem -text
Certificate:
    Data:
        Version: 3 (0x2)
        Serial Number:
            02:c7:1f:e0:1d:70:41:4b:8b:a7:e2:9e:5e:58:42:b9
        Signature Algorithm: sha1WithRSAEncryption
        Issuer: C=US, O=DigiCert Inc, OU=www.digicert.com,
                CN=DigiCert High Assurance EV CA-1
        Validity
            Not Before: Oct  6 00:00:00 2010 GMT
            Not After : Oct  9 23:59:59 2012 GMT
        Subject: 2.5.4.15=V1.0, Clause 5.(b)/
                 1.3.6.1.4.1.311.60.2.1.3=us/
                 1.3.6.1.4.1.311.60.2.1.2=Utah/
                 serialNumber=5299537-0142,
                 C=US, ST=Utah, L=Lindon, O=DigiCert, Inc.,
                 CN=www.digicert.com
        Subject Public Key Info:
            Public Key Algorithm: rsaEncryption
            RSA Public Key: (2048 bit)
                Modulus (2048 bit):
                    00:d1:76:0b:1e:4e:96:d2:08:c1:b8:75:bd:20:9c:
                    66:7f:42:6b:54:8b:7f:7a:4a:f8:3e:df:70:68:1f:
                    ...
                    25:7b:40:e9:e3:cc:a2:0d:95:29:f4:08:ed:50:16:
                    52:11:6f:de:a0:bb:34:bc:8b:b5:60:c1:ab:e4:78:
                    75:9f
                Exponent: 65537 (0x10001)
        X509v3 extensions:
            X509v3 Authority Key Identifier:
                keyid:4C:58:CB:25:F0:41:4F:52:F4:
                28:C8:81:43:9B:A6:A8:A0:E6:92:E5
```

```
X509v3 Subject Key Identifier:
    4F:E0:97:FF:C1:AE:06:53:03:19:F7:
    0A:37:4B:9F:F0:13:E2:88:D8
X509v3 Subject Alternative Name:
    DNS:www.digicert.com, DNS:content.digicert.com
Authority Information Access:
    OCSP - URI:http://ocsp.digicert.com
    CA Issuers - URI:
        http://www.digicert.com/CACerts/
        DigiCertHighAssuranceEVCA-1.crt
Netscape Cert Type:
    SSL Client, SSL Server
X509v3 Key Usage: critical
    Digital Signature, Key Encipherment
X509v3 Basic Constraints: critical
    CA:FALSE
X509v3 CRL Distribution Points:
    URI:http://crl3.digicert.com/ev2009a.crl
    URI:http://crl4.digicert.com/ev2009a.crl
X509v3 Certificate Policies:
    Policy: 2.16.840.1.114412.2.1
      CPS: http://www.digicert.com/ssl-cps-repository.htm
      User Notice:
        Explicit Text:

X509v3 Extended Key Usage:
    TLS Web Server Authentication,
    TLS Web Client Authentication
Signature Algorithm: sha1WithRSAEncryption
    e1:e6:dd:0e:23:5f:08:9a:63:63:c7:a1:f3:95:f0:ca:7e:3c:
    57:81:2c:2a:19:2b:24:fe:e4:26:bd:91:27:7c:11:50:35:e7:
    ...
    fd:64:6f:97:8b:15:fb:d1:7a:f7:67:80:da:da:41:d8:e3:f9:
    e4:bd:92:97
-----BEGIN CERTIFICATE-----
MIIHLTCCBhWgAwIBAgIQAscf4BlwQUuLp+KeXlhCuTANBgkqhkiG9w0BAQUFADBp
MQswCQYDVQQGEwJVUzEVMBMGA1UEChMMRGlnaUNlcnQgSW5jMRkwFwYDVQQLExB3
...
8+qQ0wF/xY9rHM0+eIqy3da4AFhfW4sAmyafs7hcEMjUAkS6Yb0qIw8ud/1kb5eL
FfvRevdngNraQdjj+eS9kpc=
-----END CERTIFICATE-----
```

Looking at the command's output, we see a decoded version of the certificate followed by an ASCII (PEM) representation of the certificate (between the BEGIN CERTIFICATE and END CERTIFICATE indicators). The decoded certificate shows a data portion and a signature portion. Within the data portion is some metadata including a *Version* field, indicating the particular X.509 certificate type (3, the most recent, is encoded using hex value 0x02), a *Serial Number* of the particular certificate, a number assigned by the CA unique to each certificate, and a *Validity* field that gives the time during which the certificate should be treated as legitimate, starting with the *Not Before* subfield and ending with the *Not After* subfield. The certificate metadata also indicates which signature algorithm is used to sign the data portion. In this case, it is signed by computing a hash using SHA-1 and signing the result using RSA. The signature itself appears at the end of the certificate.

The *Issuer* field indicates the *distinguished name* (jargon from the ITU-T X.500 standard) of the entity that issued the certificate and may have these special subfields (based on X.501): *C* (country), *L* (locale or city), *O* (organization), *OU* (organizational unit), *ST* (state or province), *CN* (common name). Other subfields have also been defined. In this case, we can see that an *extended validation* (EV) [CABF09] CA certificate has been used to sign the server's certificate.

EV certificates represent an industry response to certain phishing attacks involving malicious Web sites that were issued certificates without rigorous identity proofing. Issuing of an EV certificate takes place only under an agreed-upon set of stringent criteria, and a user visiting a Web site using EV certificates and a modern browser typically sees a green title bar and CA information to indicate the enhanced level of rigor. One of the requirements for EV certificates placed upon each CA is to provide a *certification practice statement* (CPS), which outlines the practices used in issuing certificates. Considerations for authors of CPSs (and *certificate policies* or CPs that apply on a per-certificate basis) are given in [RFC5280]. Note that although EV certificates may provide higher assurance (e.g., for some Web sites), most users do not pay careful attention to the cues provided by Web browsers that reveal this fact [BOPSW09].

The *Subject* field identifies the entity this certificate is about, and the owner of the public key contained in the subsequent *Subject Public Key Info* field. In this example, the *Subject* field is a somewhat complex structure like the *Issuer* field and contains multiple *object IDs* (OIDs) [ITUOID]. Most are decoded with names (e.g., *O, C, ST, L, CN*), but some are not because the particular version of `openssl` that printed the output did not understand them. The OID 1.3.6.1.4.1.311.60.2.1.3 is also called jurisdictionOfIncorporationCountryName, and 1.3.6.1.4.1.311.60.2.1.2 is called jurisdictionOfIncorporationStateOrProvinceName, both with obvious meanings. The OID 2.5.4.15 is businessCategory (see [CABF09] for details). Note that the *CN* subfield tends to be an important one when identifying subjects and issuers for certificates used on the Internet. For this certificate, it gives the correct matching name for the server (along with any names included in the *Subject Alternative Name* (SAN) extension). Nonmatching names or URLs (e.g., `https://digicert.com` instead of `https://www.digicert.com`) referring to the same server, when accessed, result in an error. Note that *CN* is not really the field for holding a DNS name; SANs are intended for this purpose.

When a certificate needs to be validated, a recursive process works up the certificate hierarchy to a root CA certificate by matching the issuer distinguished name in one certificate with the subject name in another. In this case, the certificate was issued by `DigiCert High Assurance EV CA-1` (the issuer's *CN* subfield). Assuming all certificates are current in their validity periods and are being used in appropriate ways, some parent certificate (immediate parent, grandparent, etc., but usually a root CA certificate) to the *Subject* field of the certificate we are evaluating must be trusted for validation to be successful.

The *Subject Public Key Info* field gives the algorithm and public key belonging to the entity specified in the *Subject* field. In this case, the public key is an RSA public key with a 2048-bit modulus and public exponent of 65537. The subject is in possession of the matching RSA private key (modulus plus private exponent) that is paired to the public key. If the private key is compromised, or if the public key needs to be changed for other reasons, the public and private keys must be regenerated and a new certificate issued. The old certificate is then revoked (see Section 18.5.2).

Version 3 X.509 certificates may include zero or more *extensions*. Extensions are either *critical* or *noncritical,* and some are required by the Internet profile in [RFC5280]. If critical, an extension must be processed and found acceptable by the relying party's (CPS jargon) policy. Noncritical extensions are processed if supported but do not otherwise cause errors. In the present example, there are ten X.509v3 extensions. Although many extensions have been defined, those we shall discuss tend to fall into two informal categories. The first category includes information about the subject and how the certificate in question can be used. The second category relates to items describing the issuer and may include key identification and URIs indicating locations of additional information related to the issuing CA that is not included elsewhere. The certificate in our example is an *end entity* (not CA) certificate. CA certificates often have somewhat different extensions or values for their extensions.

The *Basic Constraints* extension, a critical extension, indicates whether the certificate is a CA certificate. In this case it is not, so it cannot be used for signing other certificates. A certificate indicating that it is a CA certificate may be used in a certificate validation chain at a location other than a leaf. This is common for root CA certificates or for other certificate-signing certificates ("intermediate" certificates, such as the `DigiCert High Assurance EV CA-1` certificate referenced in this example).

The *Subject Key Identifier* extension identifies the public key in the certificate. It allows different keys owned by the same subject to be differentiated. The *Key Usage* extension, a critical extension, determines the valid usage for the key. Possible usages include digital signature, nonrepudiation (content commitment), key encipherment, data encipherment, key agreement, certificate signing, CRL signing (see Section 18.5.2), encipher only, and decipher only. Because server certificates of this kind are primarily used for identifying the two endpoints of a connection and encrypting a session key (see Section 18.9), the possible usages may be somewhat limited, as in this case. The *Extended Key Usage* extension, which may be critical or noncritical, may provide further restrictions on the key use. Possible values of this extension when used in the Internet profile include the following: TLS client and server authentication, signing of downloadable code, e-mail protection (nonrepudiation and key agreement or encipherment), various IPsec operating modes (see Section 18.8), and timestamping. The SAN extension allows a single certificate to be used for multiple purposes (e.g., for multiple Web sites with distinct DNS names). This alleviates the need to have a separate certificate for each Web site, which can significantly reduce cost and administrative burden. In this case, the certificate can be used for either of the DNS names www.digicert.com or content.digicert.com (but not digicert.com, as mentioned before). The *Netscape Cert Type* extension is now deprecated but was used to indicate key usage to Netscape software.

The remaining extensions in our example certificate relate to the management and status of the certificate and its issuing CA. The *CRL Distribution Points* (CDP) extension gives a list of URLs for finding the CA's *certificate revocation list* (CRL), a list of revoked certificates used to determine if a certificate in a validation chain has been revoked (see Section 18.5.2). The *Certificate Policies* (CP) extension includes certificate policies applicable to the certificate [RFC5280]. In this example, the CP extension contains a policy with two *qualifiers*. The *Policy* value of 2.16.840.1.114412.2.1 indicates that the certificate complies with an EV policy. The *CPS* qualifier gives a pointer to the URI where the particular applicable CPS for the policy may be found. The *User Notice* qualifier may contain text intended to be displayed to a relying party. In this case it contains the following string:

> Any use of this Certificate constitutes acceptance of the DigiCert EV CPS and the Relying Party Agreement which limit liability and are incorporated herein by reference.

The *Authority Key Identifier* identifies the public key corresponding to the private key used to sign the certificate. It is useful when an issuer has multiple private keys used for generating signatures. The *Authority Information Access* (AIA) extension indicates where information may be retrieved from the CA. In this case, it indicates a URI used to determine if the certificate has been revoked using an online query protocol (see Section 18.5.2). It also indicates the list of CA issuers, which includes a URL containing the CA certificate responsible for signing the example server certificate.

Following the extensions, the certificate contains the signature portion. It contains the identification of the signature algorithm (SHA-1 with RSA here), which must match the *Signature Algorithm* field we encountered earlier. In this case, the signature itself is a 256-byte value, corresponding to the 2048-bit modulus used for this use of RSA.

18.5.2 Validating and Revoking Certificates

We have already encountered the idea that a certificate may have to be revoked and possibly replaced with a freshly issued certificate. Within the IETF, [RFC5280] defines the use of X.509 version 3 certificates with X.509 version 2 CRLs for the Internet. This brings up the question of how a certificate is revoked and how this fact is made known to relying parties that need to know that the certificates on which they depend are no longer trustworthy.

To validate a certificate, a *validation* or *certification path* must be established that includes a set of validated certificates, usually up to some trust anchor (e.g., root certificate) that is already known to the relying party. One of the key steps involves determining if one or more of the certificates in a chain have been revoked. If so, the path validation fails. We saw some of this in Section 8.5.5.

There are several reasons why a certificate may need to be revoked, such as when a certificate's subject (or issuer) changes affiliations or name. When a certificate is revoked, it may no longer be used. The challenge is to ensure that entities that wish to use a certificate become aware if it has been revoked. In the Internet, there are two primary ways this is accomplished: CRLs and the *Online Certificate Status Protocol* (OCSP) [RFC2560]. When the *CRL Distribution Point* extension includes an HTTP or FTP URI scheme, as it does in the preceding example, the complete URL gives the name of a file encoded in DER format containing an X.509 CRL. In our example, we can retrieve the CRL corresponding to the certificate using the following command:

```
Linux% wget http://crl3.digicert.com/ev2009a.crl
```

and print it out as follows:

```
Linux% openssl crl -inform der -in ev2009a.crl -text
Certificate Revocation List (CRL):
        Version 2 (0x1)
        Signature Algorithm: sha1WithRSAEncryption
        Issuer: /C=US/O=DigiCert Inc/OU=www.digicert.com/
                CN=DigiCert High Assurance EV CA-1
        Last Update: Jan  2 06:20:13 2011 GMT
        Next Update: Jan  9 06:20:00 2011 GMT
        CRL extensions:
            X509v3 Authority Key Identifier:
                keyid:4C:58:CB:25:F0:41:4F:52:F4:
                28:C8:81:43:9B:A6:A8:A0:E6:92:E5

            X509v3 CRL Number:
                732Revoked Certificates:
    Serial Number: 0119BF8D1A24460EBE59355A11AD7B1C
        Revocation Date: Jul 29 19:25:40 2009 GMT
        CRL entry extensions:
            X509v3 CRL Reason Code:
            Unspecified
    ...
    Serial Number: 0D2ED685A9A828A21067D1826C5015A9
        Revocation Date: Dec 17 17:18:40 2010 GMT
        CRL entry extensions:
            X509v3 CRL Reason Code:
            Superseded
    Signature Algorithm: sha1WithRSAEncryption
        d4:a3:50:07:1b:b8:17:ff:e2:83:3d:b9:6a:3e:22:8d:e4:22:
        40:12:0b:cf:26:d9:16:99:b1:96:5a:86:ea:3e:8a:3f:f9:39:
    ...
```

```
        c7:e0:92:f6:66:72:7e:a4:f0:fd:16:d4:ec:2f:10:35:ea:2d:
        45:06:19:4b
-----BEGIN X509 CRL-----
MIIHeDCCBmACAQEwDQYJKoZIhvcNAQEFBQAwaTELMAkGA1UEBhMCVVMxFTATBgNV
BAoTDERpZ21DZXJ0IEluYzEZMBcGA1UECxMQd3d3LmRpZ21jZXJ0LmNvbTEoMCYG
...
hzcRf+ITVZ76LtHdzWDDPFujPyqPzMnkbGqGVsve9Gd4NcQiozOyoCDvaLezgO69
EYmMayk9zXFSaBVdEZ5Tgekrj0fFnsfgkvZmcn6k8P0W1OwvEDXqLUUGGUs=
-----END X509 CRL-----
```

Here we can see the format of an X.509 v2 CRL. The format is very similar to that of a certificate, and the entire message is signed by a CA as certificates are. This is useful because CRLs can be distributed like certificates: using otherwise untrusted communication channels and servers. In comparison with a certificate, the validity period is replaced by a list of the previous and next CRL updates. There is no subject and no public key but instead a list of serial numbers for revoked certificates plus the time and reason for revocation. There may also be CRL extensions that are unique to CRLs. In this example, the *Authority Key Identifier* extension gives a number identifying the key used by the CA in signing the CRL. The *CRL Number* extension gives the sequence number of the CRL. Other values are given in [RFC5280].

The other primary method for determining if a certificate has been revoked is OCSP. OCSP is an application-level request/response protocol usually operated over HTTP (i.e., using the HTTP protocol with TCP/IP on TCP port 80). An OCSP request includes information identifying a particular certificate, plus some optional extensions. A response indicates whether the certificate is not revoked, unknown, or revoked. An error may be returned if the request cannot be parsed or otherwise acted upon. The key used for signing the OCSP response need not necessarily match the key used to sign the original certificate. This is possible if the issuer included a *Key Usage* extension indicating an alternate OCSP provider.

To see an OCSP request/response exchange, we can execute the following commands once we have obtained the appropriate Class 1 certificate in the file DigiCertHighAssuranceEVCA-1.pem (not shown). In the following example, some lines are wrapped for clarity:

```
Linux% CERT=DigiCertHighAssuranceEVCA-1.pem
Linux% openssl ocsp -issuer $CERT -cert digicert.pem \
-url http://ocsp.digicert.com -VAfile $CERT -no_nonce -text
OCSP Request Data:
    Version: 1 (0x0)
    Requestor List:
        Certificate ID:
            Hash Algorithm: sha1
            Issuer Name Hash: B8A299F09D061DD5C1588F76CC89FF57092B94DD
            Issuer Key Hash: 4C58CB25F0414F52F428C881439BA6A8A0E692E5
            Serial Number: 02C71FE01D70414B8BA7E29E5E5842B9
```

```
OCSP Response Data:
    OCSP Response Status: successful (0x0)
    Response Type: Basic OCSP Response
    Version: 1 (0x0)
    Responder Id: 4C58CB25F0414F52F428C881439BA6A8A0E692E5
    Produced At: Jan  2 08:03:24 2011 GMT
    Responses:
    Certificate ID:
      Hash Algorithm: sha1
      Issuer Name Hash: B8A299F09D061DD5C1588F76CC89FF57092B94DD
      Issuer Key Hash: 4C58CB25F0414F52F428C881439BA6A8A0E692E5
      Serial Number: 02C71FE01D70414B8BA7E29E5E5842B9
    Cert Status: good
    This Update: Jan  2 08:03:24 2011 GMT
    Next Update: Jan  9 08:18:24 2011 GMT

Response verify OK
digicert.pem: good
        This Update: Jan  2 08:03:24 2011 GMT
        Next Update: Jan  9 08:18:24 2011 GMT
```

As we can see, the OCSP transaction has indicated that the certificate is good. The request included the identification of a hash algorithm (SHA-1), a hash of the issuer name, a number identifying the issuer's key (the same as the *Key ID* extension in the certificate), plus the certificate's serial number. The responder, identified by the responder ID, identifies itself and signs the response. The response includes the hashes and numbers from the request, as well as the certificate status of "good" (i.e., not revoked). The OCSP protocol alleviates the client from having to download the latest CRL to check but still requires the client to form and verify the entire certification path. In some cases, this can be a considerable burden for the client.

To help address the burden of certificate chain formation and validation imposed on client systems, the *Server-Based Certificate Validation Protocol* (SCVP) has been defined in [RFC5055] but is not widely used. With SCVP, formulation of a certification path (called *delegated path discovery* or DPD) and, optionally, validation (called *delegated path validation* or DPV) of it can be offloaded to a server. Validation is offloaded only to a trusted server. Not only does this provide a method to reduce the load on clients, but it also offers a method for helping to ensure that a common validation policy is used consistently throughout an enterprise.

18.5.3 Attribute Certificates

In addition to public key certificates (PKCs) used to bind names to public keys, X.509 defines another type of certificate called an *attribute certificate* (AC). ACs are similar in structure to PKCs but lack a public key. They are used to indicate other information, including authorization information that may have a lifetime different from (e.g., shorter than) a corresponding PKC [RFC5755]. ACs contain other structures similar to PKCs, including extensions and AC policies.

18.6   TCP/IP Security Protocols and Layering

We have seen that cryptography provides a basis for building communication systems that have a number of desirable security properties. Protocols involving cryptography can (and do) exist at a number of different layers in the protocol stack. Consistent with our understanding of the OSI reference model we discussed in Chapter 1, we now see that encryption, and thus various forms of strong security, can be supported at essentially every layer.

As we might expect, security services at the link layer protect information only as it flows across a single communication hop, security at the network layer protects information flowing between hosts, security at the transport layer protects process-to-process communication, and security at the application layer protects information manipulated by applications. It is also possible to protect the data manipulated by applications independently of the communication layers (e.g., files can be encrypted and sent as e-mail attachments). Figure 18-4 illustrates the most common security protocols used in conjunction with TCP/IP.

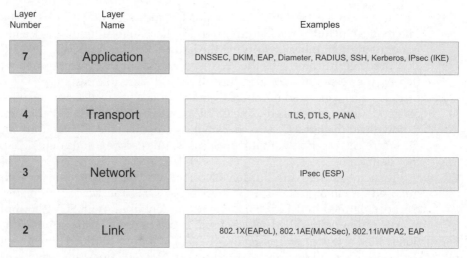

Layer Number	Layer Name	Examples
7	Application	DNSSEC, DKIM, EAP, Diameter, RADIUS, SSH, Kerberos, IPsec (IKE)
4	Transport	TLS, DTLS, PANA
3	Network	IPsec (ESP)
2	Link	802.1X(EAPoL), 802.1AE(MACSec), 802.11i/WPA2, EAP

Figure 18-4   Security protocols exist at essentially every OSI stack layer, plus some "in-between" layers. Selecting the appropriate protocols for the threats to be addressed requires attention to detail.

In Figure 18-4, we can see that there are many security protocols, and the ones we care about at any given time depend on what scope of functionality we require. We shall discuss most of the protocols in Figure 18-4 in what follows, with particular emphasis on IPsec (machine-to-machine security at layer 3), TLS (Transport Layer Security designed for supporting applications), and DNSSEC. TLS and IPsec are the most prevalent, as TLS is used with all secure Web communications (HTTPS) and IPsec is used with most network-layer security, including VPNs.

DNSSEC, which secures the DNS (see Chapter 11), is being introduced slowly, but the perceived demand is significant. Security of the DNS will help to limit *DNS hijacking* attacks, in which client systems are redirected to bogus DNS servers that supply incorrect information. Two of the fairly popular protocols we do not discuss in detail are Kerberos [RFC4120]—a trusted third-party authentication system now used in Windows enterprise environments—and SSH [RFC4251]—the secure shell remote login and tunneling protocol used most often with UNIX-like systems. These protocols tend to be used among computers running particular operating systems, although this is by no means required. We have elected to use the detailed protocol descriptions in this chapter to cover the protocols that we believe will apply to an even broader Internet audience over time.

Although virtually every modern networking technology has some associated security approach, we shall move up the layers in the OSI stack from the bottom, starting with the link layer. We have already seen (see Chapter 3) that some of the link-layer protocols have their own security mechanisms (e.g., 802.11-2007 has WPA2 included in the specification, based on the earlier 802.11i specification). We shall be especially concerned with protocols that apply to more than one specific type of link layer network.

18.7 Network Access Control: 802.1X, 802.1AE, EAP, and PANA

Network Access Control (NAC) refers to methods used to authorize or deny network communications to particular systems or users. Defined by the IEEE, the 802.1X *Port-Based Network Access Control* (PNAC) standard is commonly used with TCP/IP networks to support LAN security in enterprises, for both wired and wireless networks. The purpose of PNAC is to provide access to a network (e.g., intranet or the Internet) only if a system and/or its user has been authenticated based on the system's network attachment point. Used in conjunction with the IETF standard Extensible Authentication Protocol (EAP) [RFC3748], 802.1X is sometimes called *EAP over LAN* (EAPoL), although the 802.1X standard covers more than just the EAPoL packet format.

The most common variant of 802.1X is based on the standard as published in 2004, however, [802.1X-2010] includes compatibility with 802.1AE (IEEE standard LAN encryption called MACSec) and 802.1AR (X.509 certificates for secure device identities). It also includes a somewhat complex *MACSec key agreement* protocol called MKA that we do not discuss further. In 802.1X, a system being authenticated implements a function known as a *supplicant*. The supplicant interacts with an *authenticator* and a *backend authentication server* to perform authentication and gain network access. VLANs (see Chapter 3) are often used in helping to enforce the access control decisions made by 802.1X.

EAP can be used with multiple link-layer technologies and supports multiple methods for implementing *authentication, authorization,* and *accounting* (AAA). EAP does not perform encryption itself, so it must be used in conjunction with some other cryptographically strong protocol to be secure. When used with link-layer encryption such as WPA2 on wireless networks or 802.1AE on wired networks, 802.1X is relatively secure. EAP uses the same concepts of supplicant and authentication server as does 802.1X, but with different terminology (EAP uses the terms *peer*, *authenticator*, and *AAA server* although even in EAP-related literature *backend authentication server* is sometimes used). An example setup is shown in Figure 18-5.

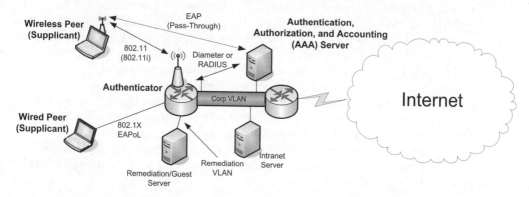

Figure 18-5   EAP, supported by 802.11i and 802.1X, allows for a peer (supplicant) to be authenticated by an authenticator that is separate from an AAA server. The authenticator can operate in "pass-through" mode in which it does little more than forward EAP packets. It can also participate more directly in the EAP protocol. The pass-through mode allows authenticators to avoid having to implement a large number of authentication methods.

In this figure we see a hypothetical enterprise network including wired and wireless peers, a protected network that includes the AAA server and another intranet server on a particular VLAN, and an unauthenticated or "remediation" VLAN. The authenticator's job is to interact with unauthenticated peers and the AAA server (via AAA protocols such as RADIUS [RFC2865][RFC3162] or Diameter [RFC3588]) to determine if each peer should be granted access to the protected network. If so, this can be accomplished in several ways. The most common approach is to make a VLAN mapping adjustment so that the authenticated peer is assigned to the protected VLAN or to another VLAN that provides connectivity to the protected VLAN using a router (layer 3). An authenticator may use VLAN trunking (IEEE 802.1AX link aggregation; see Chapter 3) and may be capable of assigning VLAN tags based on port number or forwarding VLAN tagged frames sent by the peer.

Note

In some EAP deployments, the authenticator is used without an AAA server, and the authenticator must evaluate the peer's credentials on its own. When referring to the location where authentication is determined, the term *EAP server* is used in the EAP literature. Generally, the EAP server is the AAA server (backend authentication server) when the authenticator acts in pass-through mode and is the authenticator otherwise.

In 802.1X, the protocol between the supplicant and the authenticator is divided into a lower and upper sublayer. The lower layer is called the *port access control protocol* (PACP). The higher layer is ordinarily some variant of EAP. For use with 802.1AR, the variant is called EAP-TLS [RFC5216]. PACP uses EAPoL frames for communication, even if EAP authentication is not used (e.g., when MKA is used). EAPoL frames use an *Ethertype* field value of 0x888E (see Chapter 3).

Moving to IETF standards, EAP is not a single protocol but rather a framework for achieving authentication using a combination of other protocols, some of which we discuss throughout the chapter, including TLS and IKEv2. The baseline EAP packet format is shown in Figure 18-6.

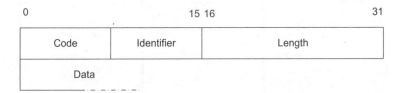

Figure 18-6 The EAP header includes a *Code* field for demultiplexing packet types (Request, Response, Success, Failure, Initiate, Finish). The *Identifier* helps match requests to responses. For request and response messages, the first data byte is a *Type* field.

The EAP packet format is simple. In Figure 18-6, the *Code* field contains one of six EAP packet types: Request (1), Response (2), Success (3), Failure (4), Initiate (5), and Finish (6). The last two are defined by the EAP Re-authentication Protocol (see Section 18.7.2); the official field values are maintained by the IANA [IEAP]. The *Identifier* field contains a number chosen by the sender and is used to match requests with replies. The *Length* field gives the number of bytes in the EAP message, including the *Code*, *Identifier*, and *Length* fields. Requests and responses are used to perform identification and authentication with the peer, ultimately resulting in a Success or Failure indication. The protocol is capable of carrying an informative message so that human users can be given some instructions about what to do if their system is unable to authenticate. It is a reliable protocol that runs on a lower-layer protocol that is assumed to preserve order but is not assumed to be reliable. EAP itself does not implement other features such as congestion or flow control but may use protocols that do.

The typical EAP exchange starts with the authenticator sending a Request message to the peer. The peer responds with a Response message. Both messages use the same format, as shown in Figure 18-6. An overview of the exchange is shown in Figure 18-7.

The primary purpose of the Request and Response messages is to exchange whatever information is required to allow an authentication *method* to succeed. Numerous methods are defined within [RFC3748], and several are defined in other standards. The particular method being used is encoded in the *Type* field of

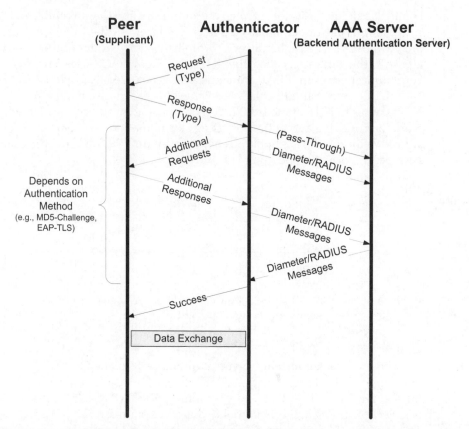

Figure 18-7   The baseline EAP messages carry authentication material between the peer and the authenticator. In many deployments, the authenticator is a relatively simple device that acts in a "pass-through" mode. In such cases, most of the protocol processing takes place on the peer and AAA server. IETF standard AAA-specific protocols such as RADIUS or Diameter may be used to encapsulate EAP messages carried between the AAA server and authenticator.

Request and Response messages using values of 4 or greater. Other special *Type* field values include Identity (1), Notification (2), Nak ("Legacy Nak") (3), and an Expanded Type extension (254). The Identity type is used by an authenticator to ask the peer its identifying information and provide a method for the peer to respond. The Notification type is used to display a message or notification to a user or log file (not for errors, but for notifications). When a peer does not support a method requested by the authenticator, it replies with a negative ACK (either a Legacy Nak or an Extended Nak). Extended Naks include a vector of implemented authentication methods not present in Legacy Naks.

EAP is a layered architecture that supports its own multiplexing and demultiplexing. Conceptually, it consists of four layers: the lower layer (for which there are multiple protocols), EAP layer, EAP peer/authenticator layer, and EAP methods layer (for which there are many methods). The lower layer is responsible for transporting EAP frames in order. Perhaps ironically, some of the protocols used to transport EAP are actually higher-layer protocols, many of which we have discussed already. Examples of EAP "lower-layer" protocols include 802.1X, 802.11 (802.11i) (see Chapter 3), UDP with L2TP (see Chapter 3), UDP with IKEv2 (see Section 18.8.1), and TCP (see Chapters 12–17). Figure 18-8 shows how the layers are implemented in conjunction with a pass-through authenticator. A pass-through server would be the opposite but is not supported by RADIUS or Diameter.

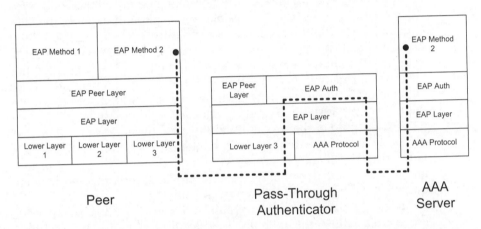

Figure 18.8 The EAP stack and implementation model. In the pass-through mode, the peer and AAA server are responsible for implementing the EAP authentication methods. The authenticator need only implement EAP message processing, the authenticator processing, and enough of an AAA protocol (e.g., RADIUS, Diameter) to exchange information with the AAA server.

In the "EAP stack" depicted in Figure 18-8, the *EAP layer* implements reliability and duplicate elimination. It also performs demultiplexing based on the code value in EAP packets. The *peer/authenticator layer* is responsible for implementing the peer and/or authenticator protocol messages, based on demultiplexing of the *Code* field. The *EAP methods layer* consists of all the specific methods to be used for authentication, including any required protocol operations to handle large messages. This is necessary because the rest of the EAP protocol does not implement fragmentation and some methods may require large messages (e.g., containing certificates or certificate chains).

18.7.1 EAP Methods and Key Derivation

Given its architecture, many EAP authentication and encapsulation methods are available for use (more than 50). Some are specified by IETF standards, and others have evolved separately (e.g., from Cisco or Microsoft). Some of the more common methods include TTLS [RFC5281], TLS [RFC5216], FAST [RFC4851], LEAP (Cisco proprietary), PEAP (EAP over TLS, Cisco proprietary), IKEv2 (experimental) [RFC5106], and MD5. Of these, only MD5 is specified in [RFC3748], but it is no longer recommended for use. Unfortunately, the complexity does not end when specifying one of these methods alone. Within each method there are sometimes different options for cryptographic suites or identity verification. With PEAP, for example, some versions of Microsoft Windows support MSCHAPv2 and TLS.

The reasons for having so many options are partly historical. As security and operational experience have evolved over time, some methods were found to be too insecure or insufficiently flexible. Some authentication methods require an operating PKI that can provide client certificates (e.g., EAP-TLS), while others (e.g., PEAP, TTLS) do not require such infrastructure. Older protocols (e.g., LEAP) were designed at a time when other standards such as 802.11 (incorporating 802.11i) were not yet mature. Consequently, depending on the particular environment, various combinations of smart cards or tokens, passwords, or certificates may be required to use EAP.

The purpose of the EAP methods is to establish authentication, and possibly authorization for network access. In some cases (e.g., EAP-TLS), the methods provide bidirectional authentication, whereby each end acts as both an authenticator and a peer. The type of authentication provided by a method is often a consequence of the cryptographic primitives it employs.

Some methods provide more than authentication. Those that provide *key derivation* are able to agree upon and export keys in a key hierarchy [RFC5247] and must provide for mutual authentication between the EAP peer and EAP server. The *master session key* (MSK, also called AAA-key) is used in deriving other keys using a KDF, either at an EAP peer or authenticator. MSKs are at least 64 bytes in length and are typically used to derive *transient session keys* (TSKs) that are used to enforce access control between a peer and an authenticator, often at lower layers. *Extended MSKs* (EMSKs) are also provided along with MSKs but are made available only to the EAP server or peer, not to pass-through authenticators, and are used in deriving *root keys* [RFC5295]. Root keys are keys associated with particular *usages* or *domains*. A *usage-specific root key* (USRK) is a key derived from an EMSK in the context with a particular usage. A *domain-specific root key* (DSRK) is a key derived from an EMSK for use in a particular domain (i.e., collection of systems). Child keys derived from a DSRK are known as *domain-specific usage-specific root keys* (DSUSRKs).

During an EAP exchange, multiple peer and server identities may be used, and a session identifier is allocated. On completion of an EAP-based authentication where key derivation is supported, the MSK, EMSK, peer identifier(s), server identifier(s), and a session ID are made available to lower layers. (A now-deprecated initialization vector might also be provided.) Keys generally have an associated lifetime (8 hours is recommended), after which EAP re-authentication is required. For an in-depth discussion of EAP's key management framework and an accompanying detailed security analysis, please see [RFC5247].

18.7.2 The EAP Re-authentication Protocol (ERP)

In cases where EAP authentication has completed successfully, it is often desirable to reduce latency if a subsequent authentication exchange is required (e.g., a mobile node moves from one access point to another). The *EAP Re-authentication Protocol (ERP)* [RFC5296] provides the ability to do this independent of any particular EAP method. EAP peers and servers that support ERP are called ER peers and servers, respectively. ERP uses a re-authentication root key (rRK) derived from a DSRK (or the EMSK, but [RFC5295] suggests avoiding this) along with a re-authentication integrity key (rIK) derived from the rRK used to prove knowledge of the rRK.

ERP operates in a single round-trip time, which is consistent with its goal of reducing re-authentication latency. ERP begins with a full conventional EAP exchange, assumed to be in the "home" domain. The MSK generated is distributed to the authenticator and peer as usual. However, the rIK and rRK values are also determined at this time and shared only between the peer and EAP server. These values can be used in the home domain, along with rMSKs generated for each authenticator. When the ER peer moves to a different domain, different values (DS-rIK and DS-rRK, which are DSUSRKs) are used. The domain of the ER server is contained in a TLV area in ERP messages, allowing peers to determine the domain of the server with which they are communicating. Details of the protocol are given in [RFC5296].

18.7.3 Protocol for Carrying Authentication for Network Access (PANA)

While combinations of EAP, 802.1X, and PPP have all been used to support authentication of the client (and network, in some cases), they are not entirely link-independent. EAP tends to be implemented for particular links, 802.1X applies to IEEE 802 networks, and PPP uses a point-to-point network model. To address this concern, the *Protocol for Carrying Authentication for Network Access* (PANA) has been defined in [RFC5191], [RFC5193], and [RFC6345] based on requirements set out in [RFC4058] and [RFC4016]. It acts as an EAP lower layer, meaning it acts as a "carrier" for EAP information. It uses UDP/IP (port 716) and is therefore applicable to more than a single type of link, and it is not limited to a point-to-point network model. In effect, PANA allows EAP authentication methods to be used on any link-layer technology for determining network access.

The PANA framework includes three main functional entities: the PANA Client (PaC), PANA Authentication Agent (PAA), and the PANA Relay Element (PRE). Normal usage also involves an Authentication Server (AS) and Enforcement Point (EP). The AS may be a conventional AAA server accessed using access protocols such as RADIUS or Diameter. The PAA is responsible for conveying authentication material from a PaC to the AS, and for configuration of the EP when network access is approved or revoked. Some of these entities may be colocated. The PaC and associated EAP peer are always colocated, as are the EAP authenticator and PAA. A PRE can be used to relay communications between a PaC and PAA when direct communication is not otherwise possible.

The PANA protocol consists of a set of request/response messages including an extensible set of attribute-value pairs managed by the IANA [IPANA]. The primary payloads are EAP messages, sent in UDP/IP datagrams as part of a PANA session. There are four phases in a PANA session: authentication/authorization, access, re-authentication, and termination. The re-authentication phase is really a portion of the access phase wherein the session lifetime is extended by re-executing EAP-based authentication. The termination phase is entered either explicitly or as the result of the session timing out (either because of lifetime exhaustion or failure of liveness detection). PANA sessions are identified by a 32-bit session identifier included in each PANA message.

PANA also provides a form of reliable transport protocol. Each message contains a 32-bit sequence number. The sender keeps track of the next sequence number to send, and receivers keep track of the next expected sequence number. Answers contain the same sequence number as the corresponding request. Initial sequence numbers are randomly selected by the sender of the message (i.e., PaC or PAA). PANA also implements time-based retransmission. PANA is a weak transport protocol—it operates in a stop-and-wait fashion, does not use an adaptive retransmission timer, and cannot perform repacketization. It does, however, perform exponential backoff on its retransmission timer when faced with multiple packet losses.

18.8 Layer 3 IP Security (IPsec)

IPsec is an architecture and collection of standards that provide data source authentication, integrity, confidentiality, and access control at the network layer for IPv4 and IPv6 [RFC4301], including Mobile IPv6 [RFC4877]. It also provides a way to exchange cryptographic keys between two communicating parties, a recommended set of cryptographic suites, and a method for signaling the use of compression. Each communicating party may be an individual host or a *security gateway* (SG) that provides a boundary between a protected and an unprotected portion of a network. Thus, IPsec can be used in applications such as remote access to a corporate LAN (forming a VPN), to interconnect different portions of an enterprise securely across the open Internet, or to secure the communications of hosts or routers acting as hosts when exchanging routing information. When choosing a security approach for newly developed protocols, IPsec is sometimes selected [RFC5406].

Figure 18-9 indicates the types of deployments that can be accomplished using IPsec. A host implementation of IPsec may be integrated within the IP stack itself or may act as a driver sitting "below" the rest of the network stack (called the "Bump in the Stack" or BITS implementation). Alternatively, it may reside inside an inline SG, which is sometimes called the "Bump in the Wire" or BITW implementation approach. For BITW implementations, both host and SG functionality is generally required, as the device typically needs to be managed remotely. This is similar to the reasons we see applications and transport protocols implemented in routers that would otherwise be pure layer 3 devices (see Chapter 1). IPsec can support multicast communications, but we focus first on the simpler and more common unicast case.

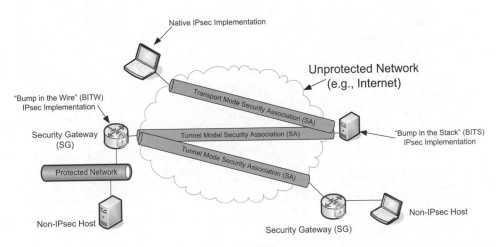

Figure 18-9   IPsec is applicable to securing host-to-host communications, host-to-gateway communications, and gateway-to-gateway communications. It also supports multicast distribution and mobility.

The operation of IPsec can be divided into the establishment phase, where key material is exchanged and a *security association* (SA) is built, followed by the data exchange phase, where different types of encapsulation schemes, called the *Authentication Header* (AH) and *Encapsulating Security Payload* (ESP), may be used in different modes such as *tunnel mode* or *transport mode* to protect the flow of IP datagrams. Each of these IPsec components uses a cryptographic suite, and IPsec is designed to support a wide range of suites. A complete IPsec implementation includes the SA establishment protocol, AH (optionally), ESP, and a collection of appropriate cryptographic suites, configuration information, and setup tools. An overview that summarizes the evolution and current specifications for all IPsec components is given in [RFC6071].

Although an IPsec implementation may be present in a system (it is required to be present for IPv6 implementations), IPsec operates only selectively on certain packets based on policies set by administrators. The policies are contained in a *security policy database* (SPD), logically resident with each IPsec implementation. IPsec also requires two additional databases called the *security association database* (SAD) and *peer authorization database* (PAD). These are consulted when determining how packets are to be handled, as illustrated in Figure 18-10.

Taking the (somewhat simplified) SG of Figure 18-10 as an example, particular fields of an arriving packet (*traffic selectors*) are inspected to determine whether

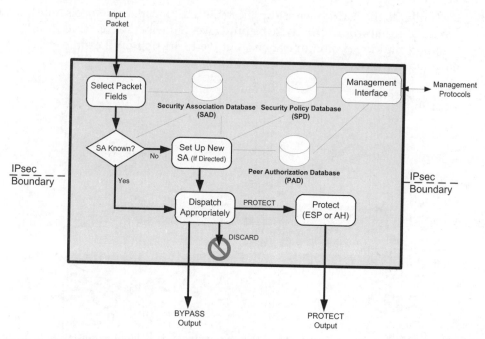

Figure 18-10   In a security gateway, IPsec packet processing takes place at layer 3 in a logical entity separating a protected and an unprotected network. The security policy database dictates the disposition of packets: bypass, discard, or protect. Protection generally involves applying or validating integrity protection or encryption. An administrator configures the SPD to achieve desired security goals.

the arriving packet is using IPsec and has a preexisting SA. If so, processing is relatively simple and usually involves applying either ESP or AH, as described in Sections 18.8.2 and 18.8.3. If not, the SPD is used to determine what type of SA should be established, if any, and the SAD is populated to contain information on the new SA. If a new SA needs to be established, the simplest way is using some automated key establishment protocol. Although IPsec mandates the support of manual keying, where keys are simply typed in by hand, this method does not scale well and is error-prone. Therefore, it is expected that normally a key establishment protocol is used in establishing SAs. For IPsec, the most recent version of this protocol is what we explore next.

18.8.1   Internet Key Exchange (IKEv2) Protocol

The first step in using IPsec is to establish an SA. An SA is a simplex (one-direction) authenticated association established between two communicating parties, or between a sender and multiple receivers if IPsec is supporting multicast. Most frequently, communication is bidirectional between two parties, so a pair of SAs is required to use IPsec effectively. A special protocol called the *Internet Key Exchange*

(IKE) is used to accomplish this task automatically. The current version of the protocol is called IKEv2 [RFC5996]. We will refer to it simply as IKE. Note that IKE is one of the more complicated pieces of IPsec, so once we understand it, the rest is comparatively straightforward. Note, however, that we will discuss only the major points of how IKE operates as a protocol. For particular details, such as the myriad cryptographic suites and configuration parameters supported, the reader should consult [RFC5996] directly.

To establish an SA, IKE begins with a simple request/response message pair that includes a request to establish the following parameters: an encryption algorithm, an integrity protection algorithm, a Diffie-Hellman group, and a PRF that gives a random-appearing output given any input bit string. In IKE, a PRF is used for generation of session keys. IKE first establishes an SA for itself (called an IKE_SA) and can subsequently establish SAs for either AH or ESP (called CHILD_SAs). IKE is also capable of negotiating the use of *IP Payload Compression* (IPComp) [RFC3173] with each CHILD_SA, because applying compression at other layers after performing encryption is ineffective. We discuss the details of AH and ESP in Sections 18.8.2 and 18.8.3.

IKE operates using pairs of messages called *exchanges* that are sent between an *initiator* and a *responder*. The first two exchanges, called IKE_SA_INIT and IKE_AUTH, establish an IKE_SA and a single CHILD_SA. Subsequently, CREATE_CHILD_SA exchanges, used to establish additional CHILD_SAs, and INFORMATIONAL exchanges, used to initiate changes in or gather status information about an SA, may occur. In most cases, a single IKE_SA_INIT and IKE_AUTH exchange (a total of four messages) is sufficient. Messages used in an exchange contain *payloads* identified by type numbers that identify the type of information carried in each payload. Multiple payloads per message are common, and some long messages may require IP fragmentation.

IKE messages are sent encapsulated in UDP using port number 500 or 4500. However, because IKE traffic may pass through a NAT where the port number is rewritten, an IKE receiver should be prepared to receive traffic originating from any port. Port 4500 is reserved for UDP-encapsulated ESP and IKE [RFC3948]. IKE messages appearing on port 4500 are required to have their initial 4 data bytes set to 0 (the "non-ESP marker") to differentiate them from other (i.e., ESP or WESP) messages.

IKE initiators perform timer-based retransmissions when IKE messages appear to have been lost. Responders perform retransmissions only when triggered by an incoming request. An exponentially increasing retransmission timer is used for retransmissions, but the total number of retransmissions is left unspecified. Both initiators and responders keep track of their last transmitted messages and corresponding sequence numbers. Sequence numbers are used to match requests with responses, and to identify message retransmissions. This makes IKE a window-based protocol with a maximum window size given by a responder that is initialized when an SA is first set up but can be increased later. The maximum window size limits the total number of outstanding requests.

18.8.1.1 IKEv2 Message Formats

IKE messages contain a header followed by zero or more *IKE payloads*. The header structure is shown in Figure 18-11.

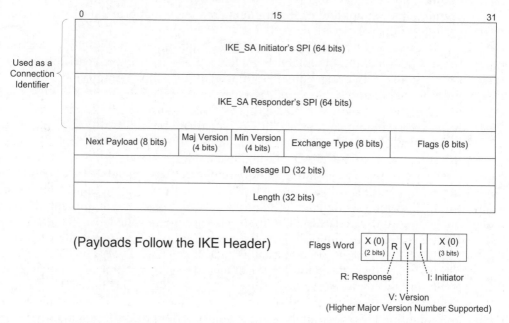

Figure 18-11   The IKE v2 header. All IKE messages contain a header followed by zero or more payloads. IKE uses 64-bit SPI values. The *Exchange Type* gives the purpose of the exchange and the payloads that may be expected in the message. The *Flags* field indicates whether the message was sent from an initiator or a responder. The *Message ID* associates requests with responses and is used for detecting replay attacks.

In the headers of IKE messages, as shown in Figure 18-11, the *Security Parameter Index* (SPI) is a 64-bit number that identifies a particular IKE_SA (other IPsec protocols use a 32-bit SPI value). Both the initiator and the responder have an SA for their peer, so each provides the SPI it is using, and this pair of values, combined with the IP addresses of the endpoints, can be used to form an effective connection identifier. The *Next Payload* field is discussed later in this section. The *Major Version* and *Minor Version* fields are set to 2 and 0, respectively, for this version of IKE. The major version number is changed when interoperability cannot be maintained between versions. The *Exchange Type* field gives the type of exchange of which the message is part: IKE_SA_INIT (34), IKE_AUTH (35), CREATE_CHILD_SA (36), INFORMATIONAL (37), and IKE_SESSION_RESUME (38; see [RFC5723]). Other values are reserved; the range 240–255 is reserved for private use. Three bit fields are defined for the *Flags* field (bits are labeled right to left, starting from 0): *I* (*Initiator*, bit 3), *V* (*Version*, bit 4), and *R* (*Response*, bit 5). The *I* bit field is set by the original initiator and cleared by the recipient for return messages. The *V* bit field indicates that the sender supports a higher major version number of the protocol than is currently being used. The *R* bit field indicates that the message is a response to a previous message using the same message ID.

The *Message ID* field in IKE acts somewhat like the *Sequence Number* field in TCP (see Figure 12-3 in Chapter 12), except the message ID starts with 0 for the initiator and 1 for the responder. The field is incremented by 1 for each subsequent transmission, and responses use the same message ID as the requests. The *I* and *R* bit fields differentiate requests from responses. Message IDs are remembered when sent or received. Doing so allows each end to perform *replay detection*. Old message IDs are not processed. Wrapping of the *Message ID* field (possible, but not likely with 4 billion IKE messages) is handled by reinitiating the IKE_SA_INIT exchange.

The other fields (*Next Payload* and *Length*) help describe what the IKE message contains. Each message contains zero or more payloads, and each payload has its own particular structure. The *Length* field gives the size (in bytes) of the header plus all payloads in the message. The *Next Payload* field gives the type of the following payload. At present, 16 nontrivial types are defined (value 0 indicates no next payload), as shown in Table 18-2. The official current list can be found in [IKEPARAMS], which contains all standardized field values for IKEv2.

Table 18-2   IKEv2 payload types. A value of 0 indicates no next payload.

Value	Notation	Purpose	Value	Notation	Purpose
33	SA	Security association	41	N	Notify
34	KE	Key exchange	42	D	Delete
35	IDi	Identification (initiator)	43	V	Vendor ID
36	IDr	Identification (responder)	44	TSi	Traffic selector (initiator)
37	CERT	Certificate	45	TSr	Traffic selector (responder)
38	CERTREQ	Certificate request (indicates trust anchors)	46	SK { }	Encrypted and authenticated (contains other payloads)
39	AUTH	Authentication	47	CP	Configuration
40	Ni, Nr	Nonces (initiator, responder)	48	EAP	Extensible authentication (EAP)

The ranges 1–32 and 49–255 are reserved; the range 128–255 is reserved for private use. Each IKE payload begins with an IKE *generic payload header*, shown in Figure 18-12.

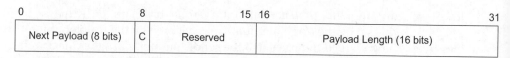

Figure 18-12   A "generic" IKEv2 payload header. Each payload begins with a header of this form.

The generic payload header is fixed at 32 bits, and the *Next Payload* and *Payload Length* fields provide for a "chain" of variable-size payloads (up to 65,535 bytes each, including the 4-byte payload header) to be present in a single IKE message. Each payload type has its own set of special headers. The C (critical) bit field indicates that the current payload (not the one identified by the *Next Payload* field) is deemed "critical" for a successful IKE exchange. Receivers of critical payloads that do not understand the type code (provided in the previous payload's *Next Payload* field or in the IKE header's *Next Payload* field) must abort the IKE exchange. Note that this capability provides the ability to create new payload types that may not be understood by all implementations.

18.8.1.2 The IKE_SA_INIT Exchange

To get a better idea of how IKE operates, we will start by describing the IKE_SA_INIT exchange. It is the first of two exchanges, IKE_SA_INIT and IKE_AUTH, constituting the "initial exchanges" of IKE shown in Figure 18-13. The initial exchanges were formerly known as Phase 1 in earlier versions of IKE. Other exchanges (CREATE_CHILD_SA and INFORMATIONAL) may be initiated by either party only after the initial exchanges have completed, and they are always secured (encrypted and integrity-protected) based on the parameters established using the first two exchanges.

As shown in Figure 18-13, IKE_SA_INIT negotiates the choice of cryptographic suite, exchanges nonces, and performs a DH key agreement. It may also include additional information, depending on the particular implementation and deployment scenario. It begins when the initiator sends an IKE message containing its set of supported cryptographic suites, DH information, and nonce using three payloads (SA, KE, and Ni). Details of each payload type are given in Section 3 of [RFC5996], and we discuss some of them in Section 18.8.1.3; note that in some implementations additional payloads are also included. A lack of response to this message triggers retransmissions at the initiator.

Upon receiving the first message, the responder becomes aware that an IKE transaction is requested by the initiator, the initiator's supported cryptographic suites, and configuration parameters. The responder selects an acceptable cryptographic suite and expresses this in the SAr1 payload (see Section 18.8.1.3). It also provides its portion of the DH key agreement parameters in KEr, its nonce in Nr, and an optional request for the initiator's certificate in the CERTREQ payload. CERTREQ payloads include an indication of CAs the responder finds acceptable for validating certificates that may be used in subsequent exchanges (i.e., it indicates the responder's trust anchors). A message containing the responder's IKE

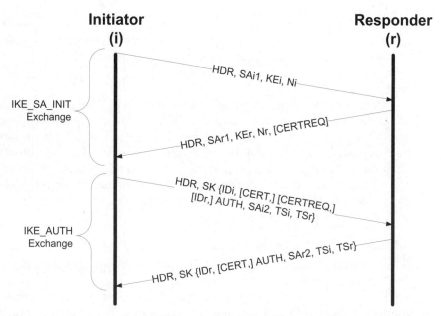

Figure 18-13   The IKE_SA_INIT and IKE_AUTH exchange involves payloads used to establish the first two security associations (IKE_SA and one CHILD_SA). Certificates and certificate request payloads (with trust anchors) may also be included, as may Notification and Configuration payloads (not shown).

header and all of these payloads is then sent in response to the initiator, completing the IKE_SA_INIT exchange. In some implementations, extra payloads (e.g., Notify and Configuration payloads; see Section 18.8.1.5) are also included. To better understand how IKE_SA_INIT operates, we shall begin by discussing its most important payloads: SA, KE, Ni, and Nr.

18.8.1.3 Security Association (SA) Payloads and Proposals

SA payloads contain an SPI value and a set of *proposals* (often one). Proposals are built using proposal structures that are somewhat complex. Each proposal structure is numbered and contains an IPsec protocol ID. A protocol ID indicates one of the following IPsec protocols: IKE, AH, or ESP (see Sections 18.8.2 and 18.8.3). Multiple proposal structures using the same proposal number are considered to be part of the same proposal (an "AND" of the specified protocols). Proposal structures with different proposal numbers are considered different proposals (an "OR" of the specified protocols).

Each proposal/protocol structure contains one or more *transform* structures that describe algorithms to be used with the specified protocols. Typically, AH has a single transform (integrity check algorithm), ESP has two (integrity check and encryption algorithms), and IKE has four (DH group number, PRF, integrity check, and encryption algorithms). Combined encryption/integrity algorithms (e.g., authenticated encryption algorithms) are expressed solely as encryption algorithms with no separate integrity protection specification. A special extended sequence number "transform," which is really just a Boolean value, indicates whether sequence numbers used with the SA (i.e., for AH or ESP) should be computed using 32 or 64 bits.

If there are multiple transforms of the same type, the proposal is the union of the transforms (i.e., any are acceptable). If there are multiple transforms with different types, the proposal is the intersection. An individual transform may have zero or more *attributes*. These are necessary when a transform can be used in more than one way (e.g., a transform capable of processing keys of differing lengths would have an associated attribute with the particular key length to be used for the proposal). Most transforms do not require attributes, but the relatively common AES encryption transform does.

18.8.1.4 Key Exchange (KE) and Nonce (Ni, Nr) Payloads

In addition to SA payloads, IKE_SA_INIT messages include a KE (Key Exchange) and Nonce payload (written as Ni, Nr, or sometimes No). The KE payload contains the DH group number and key exchange data representing the public numbers used in forming an ephemeral Diffie-Hellman key (initial shared secret). The DH group number gives the group in which the public value was computed. The Nonce payload contains a recently generated nonce between 16 and 256 bytes in length. It is used in generating key material to ensure freshness and protect against replay attacks.

Once the DH exchange completes, each side can compute its SKEYSEED value, which is used for all subsequent key generation associated with the IKE_SA (unless a key-generating EAP method is used for this purpose; see Section 18.8.1.9), a total of seven secret values: SK_d, SK_ai, SK_ar, SK_ei, SK_er, SK_pi, and SK_pr. These values are computed as follows:

$$\text{SKEYSEED} = \text{prf}(\text{Ni} \mid \text{Nr}, g^{\wedge}ir)$$

$$\{\text{SK\_d}|\text{SK\_ai}|\text{SK\_ar}|\text{SK\_ei}|\text{SK\_er}|\text{SK\_pi}|\text{SK\_pr}\} = \text{prf+}(\text{SKEYSEED}, \text{Ni}|\text{Nr}|\text{SPIi}|\text{SPIr})$$

Here, | is the concatenation operator. The cascading PRF function prf+ (K,S) = T1 | T2 | ..., where T1 = prf(K, S|0x01), T2 = prf(K, T1|S|0x03), T3 = prf(K, T2|S|0x03), T4 = prf(K, T3|S|0x04),.... . The value $g^{\wedge}ir$ is the shared secret established during the DH exchange. Ni and Nr are nonces (stripped of any payload headers). Note that each direction of each SA uses different keys, which explains why so many keys are required. The SK_d key is used for deriving keys for CHILD_SAs. The SK_a and SK_e keys are for authentication and encryption, respectively. The SK_p keys are used in generating AUTH payloads during the IKE_AUTH exchange.

18.8.1.5 Notification (N) and Configuration (CP) Payloads

The N payload is a Notification or Notify payload. Although this type of payload is not shown in Figure 18-13, we shall see it used in the examples later. It can be used for conveying error messages and indications of various processing capabilities with most of the IKE exchange types. It contains a variable-length *SPI* field and a 16-bit field to indicate the notification type [IKEPARAMS]. Values below 8192 are used for standard errors, and values above 16383 are used for status indicators. For example, when requesting the creation of a transport mode SA instead of the default tunnel mode, a Notify payload containing the USE_TRANSPORT_ MODE value (16391) is used. If IP compression [RFC3173] is supported, this fact can be indicated by the IPCOMP_SUPPORTED value (16387). If Robust Header Compression (ROHC) [RFC5857] is supported, this can be indicated using the ROHC_SUPPORTED value (16416), which also includes ROHC parameters used to establish a so-called ROHCoIPsec SA. A desire to use the "wrapped ESP" mode (see Section 18.8.3.2) is indicated using the USE_WESP_MODE value (16415). Notify payloads may contain a variable-length data portion whose content depends on the notification type.

A CP or Configuration payload also contains additional information like a Notify payload but is used primarily for initial system configuration. For example, obtaining information that might ordinarily be conveyed using DHCP (see Chapter 6) can be carried over IKE using a CP. Configuration payloads are of the following major types: CFG_REQUEST, CFG_REPLY, CFG_SET, and CFG_ACK. CPs use attribute-value (ATV) pairs that contain a variable-length associated data area. Some 20 ATV pairs are defined [IKEPARAMS]. Most involve methods to learn about IPv4 or IPv6 addresses, subnet masks, or DNS server addresses. IPv6 configuration requires special attention because of the way IPv6 ordinarily employs ICMPv6 for stateless autoconfiguration and Neighbor Discovery (see Chapter 8). An experimental specification [RFC5739] explores how IKEv2 can be used in configuring an IPv6 node across an IPsec association in a VPN configuration.

18.8.1.6 Algorithm Selection and Application

IKE divides the set of transforms forming a cryptographic suite into four types: encryption (type 1, used with IKE and ESP), PRF (type 2, used with IKE), integrity protection (type 3, used with IKE and AH and optional in ESP), and DH group (type 4, used with IKE and optional in AH and ESP). Although IKE is capable of negotiating which particular cryptographic suite is to be used for each direction of an SA, support for a baseline set of algorithms (transforms) is deemed mandatory for any implementation. In addition, several algorithms have been chosen as recommended, with the strong possibility that they will be mandatory in the future. These algorithms are provided in [RFC4307] (see Table 18-3).

The IANA also keeps an official registry of values [IKEPARAMS], and although the list here includes the mandatory algorithms at the time of writing, many other algorithms, groups, and techniques have been proposed and published, including options for ECC-based digital signatures (see [RFC4754]).

Table 18-3 Mandatory-to-implement algorithms for use with IKEv2, grouped by type number

Purpose	Name	Number	Status	Original Defining RFC/ Reference
IKE Transform Type 1 (encryption)	ENCR_3DES	3	Required	[RFC2451]
	ENCR_NULL	11	Optional	[RFC2410]
	ENCR_AES_CBC	12	Recommended	[RFC3602]
	ENCR_AES_CTR	13	Recommended	[RFC3686]
IKE Transform Type 2 (for PRFs)	PRF_HMAC_MD5	1	Optional	[RFC2104]
	PRF_HMAC_SHA1	2	Required	[RFC2104]
	PRF_AES128_CBC	4	Recommended	[RFC4434]
IKE Transform Type 3 (integrity)	AUTH_HMAC_MD5_96	1	Optional	[RFC2403]
	AUTH_HMAC_SHA1_96	2	Required	[RFC2404]
	AUTH_AES_XCBC_96	5	Recommended	[RFC3566]
IKE Transform Type 4 (DH groups)	1024 MODP (Group 2)	2	Required	[RFC2409]
	2048 MODP (Group 14)	14	Recommended	[RFC3526]

18.8.1.7 The IKE_AUTH Exchange

As mentioned earlier, the SKEYSEED value is used to derive encryption and authentication keys that are in turn used to secure payloads during the IKE_AUTH exchange. These keys are called SK_e and SK_a, respectively. The notation $SK\{P1, P2, ..., PN\}$ indicates that payloads P1, ..., PN are encrypted and integrity-protected using these keys. The primary purpose of the IKE_AUTH exchange is to provide identity validation for each peer. It also exchanges sufficient information to establish the first CHILD_SA.

To begin the IKE_AUTH exchange, the initiator sends the payload SK{IDi, AUTH, SAi2, TSi, TSr}. Given the proper decryption key, it provides the initiator's identity, authentication information validating the initiator's identity, another SA payload for the first CHILD_SA called SAi2, and a pair of *traffic selectors* (payloads TSi and TSr, discussed in Section 18.8.1.8). The initiator may also include its certificate in a CERT payload, a certificate request in a CERTREQ payload that identifies its trust anchors, and identification of the responder in the IDr payload. Sending the responder's identity is useful in the case where the responder has multiple identities associated with the same IP address and needs to ensure that the proper SA is set up. Several different identity types are supported for ID payloads, including IP address, FQDN, e-mail address, and distinguished name (to be used with X.509 certificates). The various types are maintained in the IKEv2 Identification Payload ID Types registry [IKEPARAMS].

The final message of the exchange includes the responder's identity (IDr), authentication material to prove the responder's identity (AUTH), the other SA constituting the CHILD_SA (SAr2), and a set of traffic selectors (TSi and TSr), which may be subsets of the original TSi and TSr values. All payloads in the IKE_AUTH exchange are encrypted and integrity-protected. A certificate payload (CERT) containing one or more certificates may also be sent at this point. If so, any public key required to validate the AUTH payload appears first in the certificate list. The specific contents vary depending on the cryptographic suite selected. During the exchanges, both sides must check all applicable signatures in order to be safe from compromise, including MITM attacks.

18.8.1.8 Traffic Selectors and TS Payloads

Traffic selectors indicate the fields and corresponding values of an IP datagram that cause it to be "selected" for IPsec processing. They are used in combination with an IPsec SPD to determine whether the containing datagram should be protected using IPsec. As mentioned previously, datagrams that are not protected are either bypassed or dropped by IPsec processing.

The contents of a TS payload may include IPv4 or IPv6 address ranges, port number ranges, and an IPv4 protocol ID or IPv6 header value. Ranges are sometimes denoted with wildcard notation. For example, the notation 192.0.2.* or 192.0.2.0/24 would represent the range 192.0.2.0–192.0.2.255. Traffic selectors can be used to help implement policies such as which cryptographic suite is required to establish an SA to a particular host or port range. Most of these details are handled in the management interface to the SPD. During an IKE_AUTH exchange, each party specifies a TSi and TSr payload containing TS values. When one range is smaller than another, the smaller range is selected for use in a process called "narrowing."

18.8.1.9 EAP and IKE

Although IKE includes its own authentication methods (see Section 2.15 of [RFC5996]), it can also make use of EAP (see Sections 2.16 and 3.16 of [RFC5996]). With EAP, a wide array of authentication methods can be used beyond the relatively limited set of pre-shared keys or public key certificates otherwise required by IKE. Indeed, these limited sets of options for keying are one reason for the relatively limited success of IPsec more generally.

A desire to use EAP is indicated by omitting the first AUTH payload from the IKE_AUTH exchange in message 3 (Figure 18-1). By including the IDi payload but no AUTH payload, the initiator asserts an identity but does not prove it. If EAP is acceptable, the responder returns an EAP payload and defers sending the SAr2, TSi, and TSr payloads until the EAP-based authentication is complete. This happens once the initiator has finally sent an EAP-acceptable AUTH payload that can be verified by the responder after one or more EAP payloads have been exchanged.

One issue regarding EAP with IKE involves a possible inefficiency due to double authentication. In particular, older EAP methods provided only one direction of authentication (peer to authenticator), so IKE requires certificate-based authentication to perform authentication in the other direction. Recognizing that deploying the necessary key infrastructure is sometimes difficult, and that newer EAP methods support mutual authentication and key derivation, [RFC5998] provides a way to use *only* EAP for authentication. Using an EAP_ONLY_AUTHEN-TICATION Notification payload sent by the initiator, the responder is able to suppress sending the AUTH and CERT payloads carried in message 4 (in Figure 18-1). In this case, subsequent AUTH payloads use the key generated by EAP instead of SK_pi and SK_pr.

Performing EAP-only authentication relies on EAP methods that are sufficiently secure so as to obviate the need for IKE authentication. These are called *safe* EAP methods. To be safe, an EAP method must provide mutual authentication, be capable of generating keys, and be resistant to dictionary attacks. Some 13 methods are given in [RFC5998], including EAP-TLS, EAP-FAST, and EAP-TTLS, that are believed to be safe.

18.8.1.10 Better-than-Nothing Security (BTNS)

A relatively recent development with IKE and IPsec is called *better-than-nothing security* (BTNS, pronounced "buttons"). BTNS aims to address some of the usability and ease of deployment issues with IPsec, especially the need to establish a PKI or other deployed authentication system [RFC5387] to use certificates. Technically, BTNS is essentially unauthenticated IPsec [RFC5386], and it can be supported when IKE is used to establish an SA. With BTNS, public keys are used, but their containing certificates are not checked against a chain or root certificate. Consequently, an SA can ensure that the same entity is communicating over time but cannot ensure that any particular, validated entity established the SA. This form of authentication is called *continuity of association* and is weaker than the *data origin authentication* present in ordinary IPsec. BTNS makes no other substantive changes to IPsec; the formats of IKE, AH, and ESP messages remain the same.

18.8.1.11 The CREATE_CHILD_SA Exchange

The CREATE_CHILD_SA exchange is used to create CHILD_SAs for ESP or AH, or to rekey existing SAs (either IKE_SAs or CHILD_SAs) once the initial exchanges have completed. It uses a single exchange of packets and may be initiated by either side of the IKE_SA established during the initial exchanges. There are two variants, depending on whether a CHILD_SA or IKE_SA is being modified. Figure 18-14 shows the variants, where the initiator is the entity initiating the CREATE_CHILD_SA exchange and not necessarily the original initiator of the IKE_SA.

In Figure 18-14, the first exchange depicts a CREATE_CHILD_SA used to create a new CHILD_SA or rekey an existing one. Rekeying is indicated by the presence of an N(REKEY_SA) Notification payload sent by the initiator. To complete the rekey operation, a new SA is first created, and the old one is subsequently deleted (see the next section). The new SA and traffic selector (TS) information allows most of the connection parameters to be altered. If desired, new DH values can also be exchanged at this point using KE payloads. This provides better

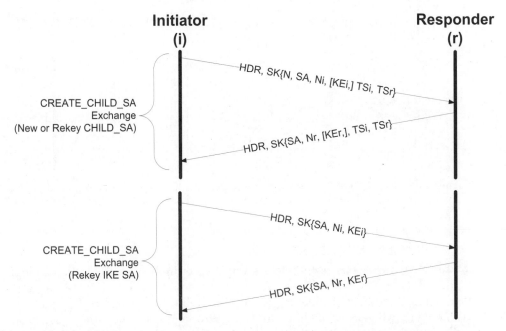

Figure 18-14 The CREATE_CHILD_SA exchange can be used to create or rekey a CHILD_SA, or to rekey an IKE_SA. A Notification payload is used when modifying a CHILD_SA to indicate the SPI of the SA to modify.

forward secrecy for the new SA. Rekeying an IKE_SA uses a similar exchange, except the KE payloads are required and the TS payloads are not used, as shown in the second part of Figure 18-14.

18.8.1.12 The INFORMATIONAL Exchange

The INFORMATIONAL exchange is used for conveying status and error information, usually using Notify (N) payloads. It is also used for deleting SAs using a Delete (D) payload and therefore constitutes one portion of the SA rekeying procedure. The exchange is shown in Figure 18-15.

An INFORMATIONAL exchange can take place only after successful completion of the initial exchanges. It includes an optional set of notifications, Delete (D) payloads that specify SAs to delete by SPI value, and Configuration (CP) payloads. Some response is always required for any message received from an initiator, even if it is an empty IKE message (i.e., contains only a header). Otherwise, the initiator would retransmit its message unnecessarily. In unusual cases, INFORMATIONAL messages may be sent outside the context of an INFORMATIONAL exchange, usually to signal the receipt of an IPsec message containing an unrecognized SPI value or unsupported IKE major version number.

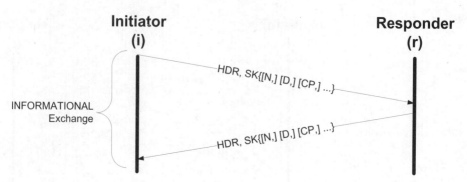

Figure 18-15   The INFORMATIONAL exchange is used to convey status information and delete SAs. It makes use of Notification (N), Delete (D), and Configuration (CP) payloads.

18.8.1.13 Mobile IKE (MOBIKE)

Once the IKE_SA has been established, it is ordinarily used until no longer required. However, when IPsec operates in an environment where IP addresses may change because of mobility or interface failure, a variant of IKE has been specified in [RFC4555] called MOBIKE. MOBIKE augments the basic IKEv2 protocol to include additional "address change" options available in INFORMATIONAL exchanges. MOBIKE specifies what to do when the changed addresses are known. It does not address the discovery problem of how to determine these addresses.

18.8.2 Authentication Header (AH)

Defined in [RFC4302], the IP *Authentication Header* (AH), one of the three major components of IPsec, is an optional portion of the IPsec protocol suite that provides a method for achieving origin authentication and integrity (but not confidentiality) of IP datagrams. By providing only integrity and not confidentiality (and not working with NAT; see the remainder of this section), AH is the (far) less popular of the two primary IPsec data-securing protocols. In transport mode, AH uses a header placed between the layer 3 (IPv4, IPv6 base, or IPv6 extension) header and the following protocol header (e.g., UDP, TCP, ICMP). With IPv6, AH may appear immediately before a Destination Options extension header, if present. In tunnel mode, the "inner" IP header carries the original IP datagram, containing the ultimate IP source and destination information, and a newly created "outer" IP header contains information describing the IPsec peers. In this mode, AH protects the entire inner IP datagram. Generally speaking, transport mode is used between end hosts that are directly connected, and tunnel mode is used between SGs or between a single host and an SG (e.g., for supporting a VPN). The IPv4 and IPv6 encapsulations for transport-mode AH, using TCP as an example, are shown in Figure 18-16.

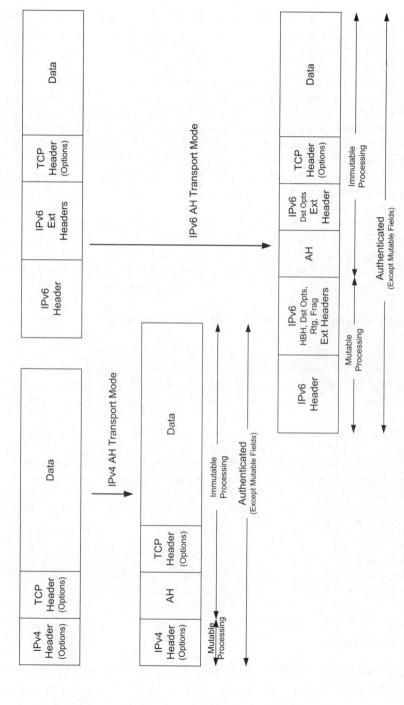

Figure 18-16 The IPsec Authentication Header is used to provide authentication and integrity protection for IPv4 and IPv6 datagrams. In transport mode (depicted here with TCP), a conventional IP datagram is modified to include the AH.

In the figure, the IPv4 encapsulation uses a special IPv4 protocol number (51). For IPv6, the AH is placed between the destination and other options. In either case, the resulting datagram has a *mutable* portion of its header and an *immutable* portion of its header. The mutable portion is changed as the datagram moves through the network. Modifications include changing the IPv4 *TTL* or IPv6 *Hop Limit* field, IPv6 *Flow Label* field, *DS Field*, and *ECN* bits. The immutable portion, containing the source and destination IP addresses, is not changed by the network and is integrity-protected using fields in the AH. This prevents transport mode AH datagrams from being rewritten by NATs, a potential problem for many deployments. Transport mode cannot be used with fragments (IPv4 or IPv6).

An alternative to transport mode is AH tunnel mode, shown in Figure 18-17. In this mode, the original datagram is untouched and instead is inserted inside an integrity-protecting new IP datagram.

In tunnel mode, the entire original IP datagram is encapsulated and protected with the AH. The "inner" header is unmodified, and the "outer" header is created using the source and destination IP addresses associated with an SG or host. In such cases, AH protects all of the original datagram, plus some portions of the new header (which prevents it being modified by a NAT).

Both modes of AH use the same AH shown in Figure 18-18. It identifies the datagram length and associated SA and includes integrity check information The *Payload Length* specifies the length of the AH in 32-bit-word units minus 2. The *Security Parameters Index* (*SPI*) field contains a 32-bit identifier of an SA at the receiver that contains SA-derived information relating to the association. For multicast SAs, the SPI value is handled in a special way (see Section 18.8.4). The *Sequence Number* is a 32-bit field that increments by 1 for each packet sent on the SA. This field is used for replay protection if enabled by the receiver (but it is always included by the sender, even if not checked by the receiver). An *extended sequence number* (ESN) operating mode is also defined and recommended and is negotiated during the IKE_SA_INIT exchange. If enabled, the sequence number is calculated using 64 bits, but only the lower-order 32 bits are included in the *Sequence Number* field. The length of the *Integrity Check Value* (*ICV*) field is variable and depends on the cryptographic suite used. This field is always an integral multiple of 32 bits in length.

The algorithm used for integrity protection is specified in the corresponding SA as a type 3 transform and can be established manually or by using some automatic method such as IKE. The optional, recommended, and mandatory algorithms for AH (and ESP, later) are provided in [RFC4835] and include HMAC-MD5-96 (optional), AES-XCBC-MAC-96 (recommended), and HMAC-SHA1-96 (mandatory). The integrity check is computed over the following portions of the datagram: header fields before the AH that are either immutable in transit or predictable in value when arriving at the destination AH SA endpoint, the AH, everything after the AH, high-order bits of the ESN (if employed, even though they are not sent), plus any padding.

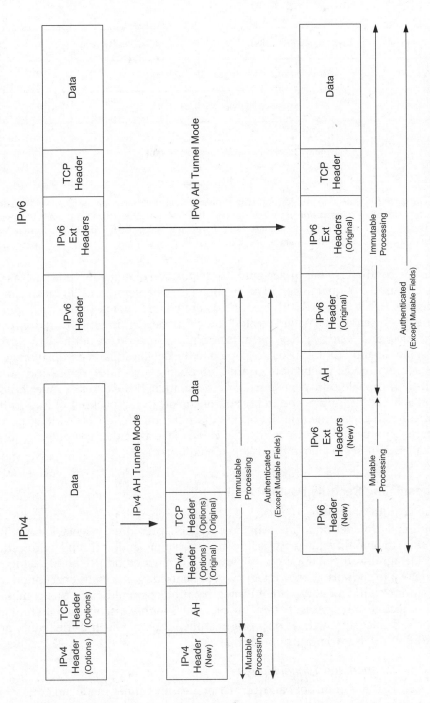

Figure 18-17 The IPsec tunnel mode AH encapsulations provide authentication and integrity protection for IPv4 and IPv6 datagrams. In tunnel mode (depicted here carrying TCP), a conventional IP datagram is encapsulated inside a new "outside" IP datagram that carries the original datagram.

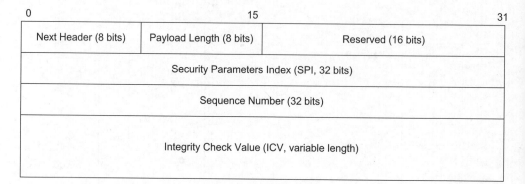

Figure 18-18   The IPsec AH is used to provide authentication and integrity protection for IPv4 and IPv6 datagrams in either transport or tunnel mode. The SPI value indicates which SA the AH belongs to. The *Sequence Number* field is used for countering replay attacks. The *ICV* provides a form of MAC over the immutable portions of the payload.

Some controversy has arisen over the disposition of mutable fields such as the ECN bits used to signal incipient congestion (see Chapters 5 and 16) when tunnel modes are used. In [RFC4301], such fields are simply copied to the corresponding fields present in the newly created "outer" IP header. In [RFC6040], however, *normal mode* and *compatibility mode* for tunnel encapsulation are defined. In normal mode, the *CE* and *ECT* bit fields are copied to the new header on encapsulation. In compatibility mode, the bits are cleared, producing an "outer" packet indicating a non-ECN-capable transport. During decapsulation, if the outer or inner header contains a CE indication, the indication is copied to the packet produced after decapsulation unless the original packet did not indicate ECT (in which case the packet is dropped). In addition, if ECT is indicated by either the outer or inner headers, ECT is set to true in the decapsulated packet.

18.8.3 Encapsulating Security Payload (ESP)

The ESP protocol of IPsec, defined in [RFC4303] (where it is called ESP (v3) even though ESP provides no formal version numbers), provides a selectable combination of confidentiality, integrity, origin authentication, and anti-replay protection for IP datagrams. It can employ a NULL encryption method [RFC2410], which is mandatory to support, if only integrity is to be used. Conversely, encryption can be used for confidentiality without integrity protection, although this combination is effective only against passive attacks and is highly discouraged. In the context of ESP, integrity includes data origin authentication. Given its flexibility and feature set, ESP is (far) more popular than AH.

18.8.3.1 Transport and Tunnel Modes

Like AH, ESP has transport and tunnel modes. In tunnel mode, an "outer" IP packet includes an "inner" IP packet that may be entirely encrypted. This provides for a limited form of *traffic flow confidentiality* (TFC) because the "inner" datagram's size and contents can be hidden using encryption. ESP may be used in combination with AH, if desired, and supports both IPv4 and IPv6. Using ESP in "integrity-only" mode may be preferable to AH in some cases for performance reasons (ESP may be more amenable to pipelining) and is a required configuration option for IPsec implementations. The encapsulations for ESP transport mode are shown in Figure 18-19.

The transport mode structure is similar to AH transport mode, except ESP trailer structures are used in support of ESP's encryption and integrity protection methods (see Section 18.8.3). As with AH, ESP transport mode cannot be used with fragments. The tunnel mode encapsulations for ESP, similar to those for AH, are shown in Figure 18-20.

ESP does not use a strict header in the same way AH does. Instead, there is an overall ESP structure that includes a header and trailer portion. There is an optional (second) trailer structure if ESP is used with an integrity protection mechanism that requires space for additional check bits (labeled ESP ICV). The ESP structure is shown in Figure 18-21.

ESP-encapsulated IP datagrams use the value 50 in the *Protocol* (IPv4) or *Next Header* (IPv6) header fields. The ESP payload structure, shown in Figure 18-21, includes the SPI and sequence numbers, used in the same way as with AH. The primary difference is in the payload area. This area may be confidentiality-protected (encrypted) and can include a variable-length pad portion required by some encryption algorithms.

The payload is required to end on a 32-bit boundary (64 for IPv6) and have the last two 8-bit fields identify the *Pad Length* and *Next Header* (*Protocol*) field values. The *Pad*, *Pad Length*, and *Next Header* fields constitute the ESP trailer shown in Figures 18-19 and 18-20. Certain cryptographic algorithms may employ an IV. If present, the IV appears at the beginning of the payload area (not shown). Additional padding for TFC purposes (called *TFC padding*) is permitted to appear within the payload area in front of the ESP trailer (see Figure 2 of [RFC4303] for details). It is used to disguise the length of the datagram to help resist traffic analysis attacks, although this features does not appear to be widely used. The *Next Header* field contains values chosen from the same space used in the IPv4 *Protocol* field or IPv6 *Next Header* field (e.g., 4 for IPv4, 41 for IPv6). It may contain the value 59, indicating "no next header," when carrying a dummy packet that is to be discarded. Dummy packets are another method sometimes used for resisting traffic analysis attacks.

The ESP ICV is a variable-length trailer used if integrity support is enabled and required by the integrity-checking algorithm. It is computed over the ESP header, payload, and ESP trailer. Implicit values (e.g., high-order ESN bits) are also included. The length of the ICV is known as a consequence of selecting the particular integrity-checking method. It is therefore established at the time the corresponding SA is set up and not changed as long as the SA exists.

Anti-replay is supported provided integrity protection is enabled. This is accomplished using a sequence number derived from a running counter. The

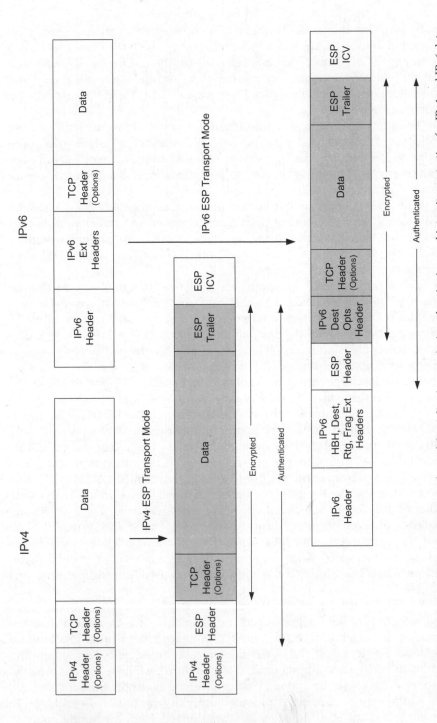

Figure 18-19 The IPsec ESP is used to provide confidentiality (encryption), authentication, and integrity protection for IPv4 and IPv6 datagrams. In transport mode (depicted here with TCP), a conventional IP datagram is modified to include the ESP head er. ESP in transport mode allows the transport payload to be encrypted, authenticated, and integrity-protected.

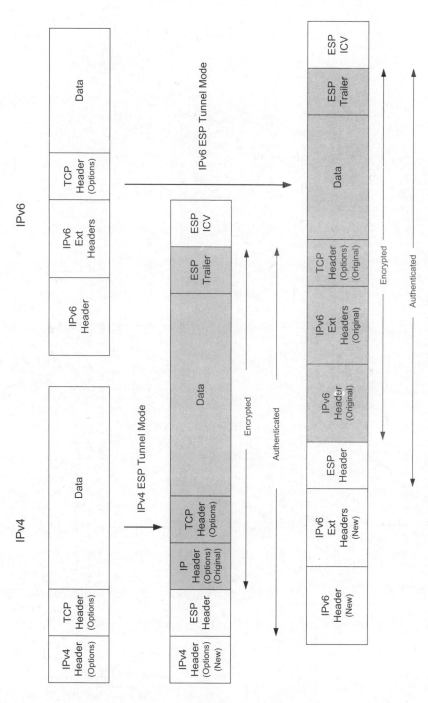

Figure 18-20 In tunnel mode (depicted here with TCP), ESP encapsulates a conventional IP datagram inside a new "outside" IP datagram that carries the original datagram. ESP allows the outer datagram to be modified (e.g., for NAT traversal) while the inner datagram remains intact. ESP is more popular than AH for most applications.

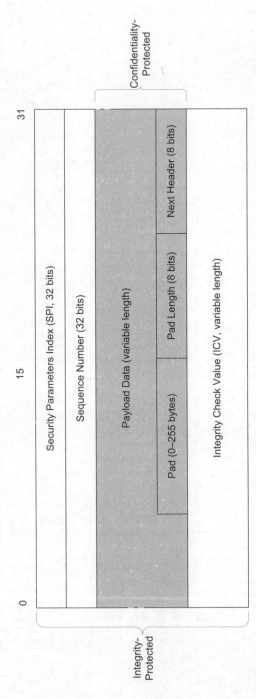

Figure 18-21 The ESP message structure includes the encrypted payload in the middle. The *SPI* and *Sequence Number* constitute the ESP header, and the combination of the *Pad*, *Pad Length*, and *Next Header* fields constitutes the ESP trailer. An optional ESP ICV trailer is also used when integrity protection is employed.

counter is initialized to 0 when an SA is first set up and incremented before being copied into each datagram sent on the SA. When anti-replay is enabled (the normal default), the sender checks to see that the counter has not wrapped and creates a new SA if wrapping is about to occur. The receiver implementing anti-replay keeps a valid window of sequence numbers (similar in some ways to the TCP receiver's window). Datagrams containing out-of-window sequence numbers are dropped.

For systems that implement auditing, ESP processing can result in one or more *auditable events*. These events include the following: no valid SA exists for a session, the datagram given to ESP for processing is a fragment, the anti-replay counter is about to wrap, a received packet was out of the valid anti-replay window, the integrity check failed. Auditable events are recorded in a logging system. These events include metadata such as the SPI value, current date and time, source and destination IP addresses, sequence number, and IPv6 flow ID (if present).

18.8.3.2 ESP-NULL, Wrapped ESP (WESP), and Traffic Visibility

As mentioned previously, ESP ordinarily provides privacy using encryption, but it can also operate in an integrity-only mode using the NULL encryption algorithm. Integrity-only mode (also called ESP-NULL) may be desirable in some circumstances, especially in enterprise environments where sophisticated packet inspection takes place within the network and confidentiality may be addressed in other ways. For example, some network infrastructure devices inspect packets for unwanted content (e.g., malware signatures) and are capable of providing alerts or shutting down network access when policy is violated. Such devices are essentially disabled if ESP is used with encryption in an end-to-end fashion (i.e., the way it was designed). Said another way, unless they have *traffic visibility*, they cannot do their jobs.

When a packet inspection device is faced with ESP traffic, it needs to make a decision about whether the traffic is encrypted (i.e., whether NULL encryption is being used or not). Given that the negotiation of an IPsec cryptographic suite is handled outside ESP (e.g., manually or using a protocol such as IKE), there are two current methods for doing so. The first is simply to use a set of nonstandard heuristics to make a guess [RFC5879]. Use of these has the benefit of not requiring any modification to ESP for supporting traffic visibility. The other method is to add a special description to ESP to indicate whether encryption is used. *Wrapped ESP* (WESP) [RFC5840], a standards-track RFC, defines a header that is placed ahead of the ESP packet structure. WESP uses a different protocol number (141) from ESP and can be negotiated with IKE using the USE_WESP_MODE (value 16415) Notify payload. The variable-length WESP header includes fields to indicate the location of payload information, along with a *Flags* field (maintained by the IANA [IWESP]) containing a bit indicating whether ESP-NULL is being used. Although WESP makes the job of determining whether ESP-NULL is being used or not easier for network infrastructure, its utility also depends on end hosts using the WESP header appropriately. Given that WESP is relatively new, this is not yet the case today. On the other hand, the WESP format is extensible, so once implemented it could be adapted for other purposes in the future.

18.8.4 Multicast

IPsec optionally supports multicast operations [RFC5374], although this capability is not often used. The most basic form involves using manual key configuration, but there are also multicast group key establishment methods called *group key management* (GKM) protocols managed by *group controller/key servers* (GCKSs). These are used to produce *group security associations* (GSAs), which include one or more IPsec SAs plus one or more GKM SAs used to provide parameters for establishing the IPsec SAs [RFC3740]. Given that members may dynamically join or leave a group, GKM protocols must deal with rekeying more frequently and carefully than regular two-party key establishment protocols, and such protocols have been a favorite topic for security researchers [AKNT04]. We shall not explore the details of how GKMs operate (such an explanation would be lengthy), but the interested reader may consult documentation for GDOI [RFC3547] or GSAKMP [RFC4535].

At present, multicast IPsec operation requires all members of a group to be homogeneous in their algorithmic and protocol processing capabilities. Both any-source and single-source multicast (ASM and SSM) operations are supported (see Chapter 9), and the same procedures are used for IPv4 local broadcast addresses and for IPv6 anycast addresses. Host IPsec implementations may use any combination of tunnel and transport mode, but SGs must use tunnel mode where the tunnel destination addresses are multicast addresses.

Multicast IP datagrams present a challenge for IPsec when a tunnel mode is used because the outer IP datagram's addressing needs to be a multicast destination address in order to be routed efficiently using a multicast-capable infrastructure. This requires a special procedure, known as *tunnel mode with address preservation*, to be applied when placing datagrams into AH or ESP tunnels. In short, this procedure involves choosing the outer IP source and destination addresses to match the inner addresses (assuming the same version of IP is being used). The purposes of doing so are (1) to ensure that multicast routing is invoked on the datagram and (2) to ensure that the reverse path forwarding (RPF) check used in computing multicast routes works properly (see Chapter 9).

Introduction of multicast requires modification of some of the low-level IPsec machinery we saw in Figure 18-10. For example, the SPD and SAD are modified to include an "address preservation" flag used in implementing the address-preserving tunnel modes. In addition, a directionality flag in the SPD is used to determine under what circumstances SAs should be automatically created. This ensures that no SAs are created that would use prohibited multicast source addresses as a consequence of simply reversing source and destination IP addresses (as with unicast SAs). The SPD may need to include state as to when a GKM protocol needs to be invoked (e.g., for obtaining a needed group key), and a group PAD (GPAD) holds the information specific to each GCKS, including for which traffic selectors each GCKS is able to produce SAs and authentication information that may be required to engage in a particular GKM protocol with a particular GCKS. GPAD material is not consulted by non-GKM protocols such as IKE, but the PAD and GPAD structures might be implemented together.

18.8.5 L2TP/IPsec

The Layer 2 Tunneling Protocol (L2TP) (see Chapter 3) supports tunneling of layer 2 traffic such as PPP through IP and non-IP networks. It relies on authentication methods that provide some authentication during connection initiation, but no subsequent per-packet authentication, integrity protection, or confidentiality. To address this concern, L2TP can be combined with IPsec [RFC3193]. The combination, called L2TP/IPsec, provides a recommended method to establish remote layer 2 VPN access to enterprise (or home) networks. L2TP can be secured with IPsec using either a direct L2TP-over-IP encapsulation (protocol number 115) or a UDP/IP encapsulation that eases NAT traversal.

L2TP/IPsec uses IKE by default, although other keying methods are possible. It uses an ESP SA in either transport mode (support required) or tunnel mode (support optional). The SA is used to secure the L2TP traffic, which is then responsible for establishing the layer 2 tunnel. Because it is really a combination of two protocols, both of which involve authentication, L2TP/IPsec often requires two distinct authentication procedures: one for the machine (using IPsec with pre-shared keys or certificates) and another for the user (e.g., using a name and password or access token).

L2TP/IPsec is supported on most modern platforms. On Windows, creating a new connection with the "Connect to a workplace" option can be used to enable L2TP and L2TP/IPsec. Some smartphones (e.g., Android, iPhone) support L2TP in their networking configuration setup screens. Mac OS X includes an L2TP/IPsec network adapter type that can be added using the system preferences. On Linux, it may be necessary to configure both IPsec and L2TP for them to work together. If L2TP is not required on such systems, direct IPsec may be preferable.

18.8.6 IPsec NAT Traversal

Using NATs with IPsec can present something of a challenge, primarily because IP addresses have traditionally been used in identifying communication endpoints and are assumed to not change. These assumptions were not entirely avoided (or obviated) when IPsec was first designed, so NAT has posed a problem. This is one factor contributing to the relatively slow deployment of IPsec. However, today IPsec supports both changing addresses (with MOBIKE) and NAT traversal.

To have a complete NAT traversal solution, we must take into account IKE, AH, and ESP in both transport and tunnel modes. As we shall see, when NATs must be accommodated, not all combinations of IPsec may be usable with all applications.

Guidance for what a solution requires is given in [RFC3715]. We shall first discuss a variety of issues that highlight fundamental incompatibilities between NATs and IPsec and then describe the methods that have been adopted to handle the problems.

One fundamental problem arises with AH and how NATs update the addresses in datagrams. Because the AH includes a MAC computation covering the datagram's IP addresses, a NAT is unable to rewrite addresses without invalidating the AH. Note that ESP does not share this issue, as its integrity protection mechanism does not include the IP addresses in its MAC.

Another problem arises with the UDP and TCP transport protocols because of the pseudo-header checksum, which incorporates IP addresses in its computation. When the transport-layer checksum is integrity-protected or encrypted, the NAT is unable to update the checksum without forming an invalid packet. A similar situation can arise for NAPT when changing port numbers, or for other protocols that perform layering violations.

A third major problem relates to the ID payloads in IKE. There are several ways to identify an IKE peer, one of which is to use IP addresses. As these addresses are embedded within an encrypted IKE payload, they are not able to be modified by a conventional NAT, leading to failure. Alternative methods for identifying peers may be available, however (e.g., FQDN or the distinguished name from an X.509 certificate).

A fourth significant concern is how a NAT or NAPT demultiplexes incoming traffic to the proper host. In protocols such as TCP and UDP, the port number is used for this purpose. However, IPsec AH and ESP act like transport protocols that carry no port numbers but instead use an SPI value. While some NATs can make use of the SPI value for demultiplexing, these values are chosen by an IPsec responder as a local matter and multiple independent hosts may choose the same value. Because a NAT cannot easily modify these values, it is possible for a NAT to improperly demultiplex incoming (returning) traffic, with a potential for erroneous delivery.

There are other potential problems for NATs that become more acute when IPsec is employed. For example, application protocols that carry IP addresses (e.g., SIP), if integrity-protected or encrypted, cannot be modified by a conventional NAT. In addition, configuration and analysis are more difficult because traffic that could otherwise be decoded for analysis is now obscured because of encryption. Fortunately, some network analysis tools (e.g., Wireshark) can process encrypted traffic if provided the necessary key material.

The primary approach to dealing with most of the NAT traversal concerns is to encapsulate IPsec ESP and IKE traffic using UDP/IP, which can be modified by conventional NATs when necessary. (There is no supported solution for NAT traversal of AH.) An IKE initiator can use UDP port 500 or 4500 for sending IKE and then transition to using port 4500 for UDP-encapsulated ESP and IKE, whether or not a NAT is present. UDP ESP encapsulation is prohibited on port 500 according to [RFC5996]. The purpose of using port 4500 is to avoid some NATs that improperly process IPsec traffic on port 500.

NAT traversal for IKE is an optional feature of an IKE implementation. If supported, the following two Notification payloads can be included with the IKE_SA_INIT exchange: NAT_DETECTION_DESTINATION_IP and NAT_DETECTION_SOURCE_IP. If present, these appear after the Ni and Nr payloads and before CERTREQ payloads. The data associated with these payloads includes a SHA-1 hash of the SPIs for the SA, the source or destination IP address, and the source or destination port number. Such information is preserved as the IKE messages are passed through NATs. When receiving IKE messages that suggest a NAT is present, IKE processing continues using a UDP/IP encapsulation on port 4500, which tends to pass through NATs unimpeded.

After having traversed one or more NATs, arriving IKE traffic being used to set up a transport-mode SA may contain traffic selectors (TS payloads) with IP addresses or ranges that are not meaningful (i.e., they are private IP addresses "behind" a NAT) and that do not match the IP addresses contained in the addressing fields of the IKE datagram arriving at the responder. This is handled by first storing the addresses in TSi and TSr IKE payloads for later use and later replacing them with the source and destination IP addresses present in the received datagram. In essence, this is a form of "delayed NAT" on TS payloads performed by the recipient. The resulting datagram and TS payloads are used to query the SPD in order to determine the security policy for the requested SA. If transport mode is used, the responder completes the exchange and the initiator performs similar TS payload substitution processing (see Section 2.23.1 of [RFC5996] for more details).

18.8.7 Example

There are several open-source and proprietary IPsec implementations. Windows 7 supports IKEv2 and MOBIKE in Microsoft's Agile VPN subsystem. Linux includes kernel-level IPsec support in kernel version 2.6 and later, and the OpenSwan and StrongSwan packages can be used to implement complete VPN solutions. In the following example, we use a Linux server running StrongSwan (IPv4 address 10.0.0.3) with a Windows 7 client (IPv4 address 10.0.1.48) using RSA-based machine certificates we have created for authentication to demonstrate IKE. The IKE initial exchanges are shown in Figure 18-22.

Looking at this figure, we can see that Wireshark decodes the IKE exchange using ISAKMP as the protocol name. This is the now-deprecated *Internet Security Association and Key Management Protocol* and is the historical name of what ultimately became IKE. The IKE header contains the initiator's SPI (labeled "Initiator cookie") and the responder's SPI, which has not yet been established. The version number is 2, indicating that this packet contains IKEv2, and the exchange type is IKE_SA_INIT.

Looking closer, we can see this is an IKE_SA_INIT message containing five payloads: one SA, one KE, one Nonce, and two of type Notify. The SA payload includes six proposals, each of which contains a list of transforms. The proposals

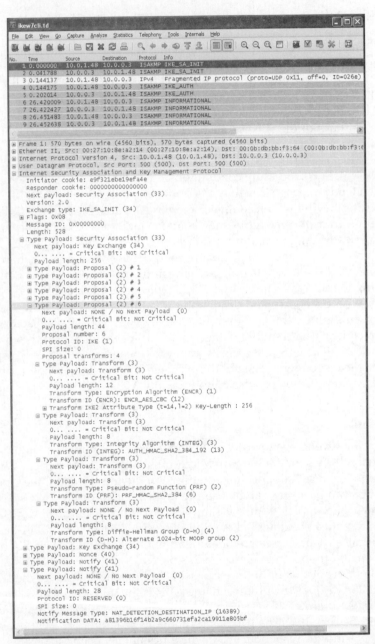

Figure 18-22 A trace of the initial IKE exchanges, highlighting the first packet. The IKE_SA_INIT exchange is carried on UDP port 500 and includes the initiator's SPI, proposals for cryptographic suite algorithms, DH key exchange material, a nonce, and Notify payloads used to indicate addresses for NAT traversal. Each proposal in the SA payload requests the establishment of an IKE_SA using a set of transforms for encryption, integrity protection, a PRF used for generation of random numbers, and DH group parameters used in key agreement.

represent sets of algorithms the initiator is willing to use. Proposal 6 (the last one) has been expanded to show more detail. It suggests AES in CBC mode with a 256-bit key length for encryption, HMAC with SHA-256 for integrity protection, a PRF based on SHA-384, and the alternate 1024-bit MODP group for DH key agreement. The other proposals (not detailed) include suggestions for 3DES encryption, AES encryption with different key lengths, SHA-1 for integrity protection, and other SHA variants for the PRF. Following the SA payload, the Key Exchange payload contains the public information required to perform a DH exchange using the "alternate 1024-bit MODP group." In the other payloads, we find a nonce containing a 48-byte random bit string and two Notify payloads used for NAT traversal. The first Notify payload is of type NAT_DETECTION_SOURCE_IP, and the second contains NAT_DETECTION_DESTINATION_IP. The value in the first contains a 20-byte SHA-1 hash over these values: 8 bytes of the initiator's SPI, 8 bytes of the responder's SPI (0 here), 4 bytes of source IPv4 address, and 2 bytes of UDP source port number. The value in the second covers the same as the first, except the destination port is used in place of the source port. Figure 18-23 illustrates the response to the first IKE_SA_INIT message.

In this figure, the IKE_SA_INIT message contains the following payloads: SA, KE, Nonce, three of type Notify, and a Certificate Request. The SA payload contains only one proposal, comprising the following transforms: 3DES for encryption, HMAC_SHA1_96 for integrity, HMAC_SHA1 for the PRF, and group 2 for the DH exchange. The KE payload contains a 128-byte value from the 1024-bit MODP group. The Nonce payload contains a 32-byte random value for freshness. The next two Notify payloads contain NAT_DETECTION_SOURCE_IP and NAT_DETECTION_DESTINATION_IP, as described earlier. Following these are new payloads we have not yet encountered: CERTREQ and MULTIPLE_AUTH_SUPPORTED.

The Certificate Request (CERTREQ) payload indicates the responder's preferred certificates. In this case, the responder indicates that any certificates later supplied by the initiator should be associated with a particular certificate authority. The encoding used to express the CA is one of several defined in Section 3.6 of [RFC5996], but only the values 4, 12, and 13 are currently standardized. Here, the payload contains the value 4, meaning the *Certificate Authority Data* subfield contains a concatenation of SHA-1 hashes of the public keys (X.509 *Subject Public Key Info* element) of trusted CAs. Given that the length of this subfield is only 20 bytes in this example, we can see that only a single CA is listed. It happens to be the SHA-1 hash of the DER encoding of the public key of the sample root certificate for the "Test CA" we created for this example.

Note

The binary *Distinguished Encoding Rules* (DER) format is a subset of the ASN.1 standard *Basic Encoding Rules* (BER). DER permits values to be encoded in only a single, unambiguous way. DER is one of the two most popular ways to encode X.509 certificates. The other is PEM, an ASCII format, which we showed earlier. Various utilities, including `openssl`, may be used to convert between the two formats.

Figure 18-23   The completion of the IKE_SA_INIT exchange includes the responder's SPI (labeled "cookie"), a single proposal with transforms, DH parameters, a nonce value, and NAT traversal address parameters. This message also includes a CERTREQ payload to indicate and request acceptable certificates, and a notification indicating that multiple authentication methods (in series) are supported.

The final payload in Figure 18-23 is a Notify payload containing the MULTIPLE_ AUTH_SUPPORTED indication and no associated data. Defined as an experimental extension to IKE in [RFC4739], it indicates the ability to use more than one authentication method. Such a situation may arise, for example, when using an IKE_AUTH exchange based on certificates to establish IKE SAs to a service provider, followed by some form of EAP-based authentication for the individual user.

The remaining packets shown in Figure 18-23 contain IKE_AUTH messages that are encrypted. They are carried using source and destination port number 4500 instead of 500, and the encapsulation uses the special "non-ESP marker" containing 4 bytes of 0 [RFC3947], indicating that the traffic is IKE and not ESP. The marker and port numbers are also used for the INFORMATIONAL exchanges we discussed previously.

Wireshark has the capability to decrypt encrypted IKE traffic if provided with the proper keys and SPI values. By providing a copy of the log trace file from the IKE server to Wireshark (located under Edit | Preferences | Protocols | ISAKMP), we can see the decrypted IKE payload information. (The Wireshark developers tend to prefer the original names of protocols such as ISAKMP and SSL instead of IKE and TLS, so that is what we see when looking at Wireshark output.)

The third packet in Figure 18-22 is the first fragment of a UDP/IP datagram that Wireshark reassembles when it receives the second fragment (packet 4). The decrypted and reassembled result is shown in Figure 18-24.

Here we can see the contents of the reassembled and decrypted UDP/IPv4 fragments constituting the first packet of the IKE_AUTH exchange. The client provides the following IKE payloads: IDi, CERT, CERTREQ, AUTH, N(MOBIKE_ SUPP), CP, SA, TSi, and TSr. The IDi payload contains the name of the initiator, test client. The CERT payload contains a client certificate for test client signed by the Test CA certificate authority that we know the corresponding server should accept (because it was configured to). The CERTREQ payload contains requests for Test CA as well as 21 other CAs (not shown) known by this Windows 7 client. The AUTH payload contains a data block signed using the RSA private key of the initiator (see Section 2.15 of [RFC5996]), which provides origin authentication. The N(MOBIKE_SUPPORTED) indicates the client's willingness to follow the MOBIKE protocol. The CP(CFG_REQUEST) payload (not detailed) contains the following attributes: INTERNAL_IP4_ADDRESS, INTERNAL_IP4_DNS, INTERNAL_IP4_NBNS, and a PRIVATE_USE type (23456). These are used to help in configuring VPN access and serve a similar purpose to the configuration information typically provided locally by DHCP (see Chapter 6). NBNS refers to a NetBIOS name server. NetBIOS is an API that can be implemented on a number of networking protocols and is common in Microsoft Windows environments.

The SA payload in Figure 18-24 represents the information required to form a CHILD_SA. There are two proposals (not detailed), each for ESP using 32-bit SPI values (note that IKE uses 64-bit SPI values) with AUTH_HMAC_SHA1_96 as the integrity algorithm and not using extended sequence numbers (indicated using a proposal transform). The first proposal suggests the use of ENCR_AES_CBC

Figure 18-24   The IKE_AUTH exchange contains encrypted information and operates on UDP port 4500. The reassembly of two fragments produces an IKE message with an Encrypted/Authenticated data payload containing the following payloads: Identification initiator (IDi), Certificate (CERT), Certificate Request (CERTREQ), Authentication (AUTH), Notify (N), Configuration (CP), Security Association (SA), Traffic Selector initiator (TSi), and Traffic Selector responder (TSr).

(256-bit keys) for encryption, and the second suggests ENCR_3DES. Because there is no N(USE_TRANSPORT_MODE) payload present, we conclude that each of the proposals involves using ESP in the default tunnel mode.

The Traffic Selector (TSi and TSr) payloads in Figure 18-24 indicate the IPv4 and IPv6 address ranges that are permitted to be associated with the forming SA. The TSi has both a TS_IPv6_ADDR_RANGE and TS_IPv4_ADDR_RANGE that contain their entire address and port number ranges. TSr (not detailed) contains the same values.

The first IKE_AUTH message we just discussed is fairly complicated and requires more than a single 1500-byte UDP/IPv4 datagram to hold it. After processing by the responder, the final message in the exchange is produced. It is shown in Figure 18-25.

In this figure, the server sends a response with the following payloads: IDr, CERT, AUTH, CP(CFG_REPLY), SA, TSi, TSr, N(AUTH_LIFETIME), N(MOBIKE_ SUPPORTED), and N(NO_ADDITIONAL_ADDRESSES). The IDr payload contains a DER-encoded name of the server. The CERT payload contains the matching (server) certificate, and the AUTH payload indicates knowledge of the corresponding private key. The CP(CFG_REPLY) payload includes an INTERNAL_IP4_ADDRESS attribute, which is useful for VPN configuration. The SA payload is similar to the client's SA payload from Figure 18-24 and includes a single proposal with transforms ENCR_AES_CBC (256-bit keys), AUTH_HMAC_SHA1_96, and no ESNs.

The TSi and TSr values in this packet have been "narrowed" to be much smaller ranges than in the client's IKE_AUTH message. In this case, the TSi is narrowed to the single IPv4 address 10.100.0.1. The TSr has been narrowed to 10.0.0.0/16. Each uses the full port range 0–65535. This is a relatively simple case of narrowing. In cases where more than one discontinuous subset of the range specified by the initiator is acceptable, an N(ADDITIONAL_TS_POSSIBLE) payload may be generated. Narrowing is used to achieve mutually agreeable address ranges for an SA.

The N(AUTH_LIFETIME) payload indicates that the authentication is going to last at most only 2.8 hours (10,154s, expressed as 000027aa in the trace). The N(MOBIKE_SUPPORTED) payload indicates the responder's support for MOBIKE. The N(NO_ADDITIONAL_ADDRESSES) payload (not detailed) is used with MOBIKE to indicate that no additional IP addresses other than those used in the exchange are being used.

At this point, a tunnel mode ESP CHILD_SA has been set up and traffic can flow. We do not detail the traffic flow containing ESP packets (they are comparatively straightforward) but instead jump to the point where the SAs are to be torn down. This is accomplished using two sets of INFORMATIONAL exchanges containing Delete payloads—one for the ESP SA and one for the IKE SA. Figure 18-26 shows the request to close the ESP SA.

We can see in this figure the SA being deleted based on a close request at the client. Like other IKE traffic, it includes an encrypted and authenticated payload. The encrypted payload in turn includes a single Delete payload. The Delete payload can indicate that more than one SPI is to be deleted, but in this case it

Figure 18-25 Completing the IKE_AUTH exchange, the responder produces an Encrypted/Authenticated data payload containing the following payloads: Identification responder (IDr), CERT, AUTH, CP(CFG_REPLY), SA, narrowed TSi and TSR, along with N(AUTH_LIFETIME), N(MOBIKE_SUPPORTED), and N(NO_ADDITIONAL_ADDRESSES). The first CHILD_SA can now commence.

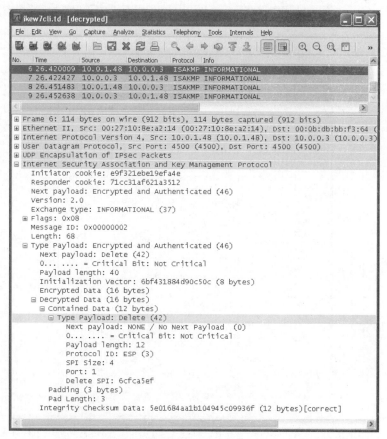

Figure 18-26   A request to delete the child ESP SA with SPI 6cfca5ef is carried on the IKE SA. The Delete payload shows Port: 1, which is mislabeled by Wireshark. (It should be Number of SPIs: 1.)

indicates only the one with SPI value 0x6cfca5ef. Packet 7 from the responder is essentially the same but contains a different setting in the *Flags* field (responder instead of initiator and response instead of request), a different encryption IV and integrity checksum data, and specification of a different SPI (c348faf2) in the Delete payload.

To close the IKE_SA, another exchange of INFORMATIONAL messages is required. The initiator begins with the packet shown in Figure 18-27. We can see here a request to close the IKE SA. Encrypted like other traffic, the Delete payload does not need to include an SPI value because it is implied to be the IKE SA carrying the deletion request. To complete the IKE SA deletion, the responder replies with an IKE message containing only an empty encrypted/authenticated payload type in packet 9. Its *Next Payload* type field is NONE (zero). This indicates the completion of the IKE SA deletion.

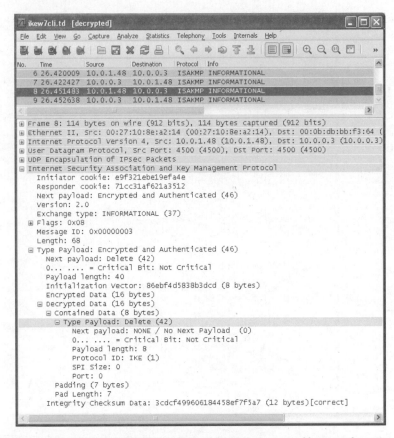

Figure 18-27   A request to delete the IKE SA. SPI values are not required because the entire message is carried on the IKE SA and there is no ambiguity.

18.9 Transport Layer Security (TLS and DTLS)

So far we have discussed security protocols at layers 2 and 3. The most widely used protocol for security operates just above the transport layer and is called *Transport Layer Security* (TLS). TLS is used for securing Web communications and for several other popular protocols, including POP and IMAP (which are called POP3S and IMAPS, respectively, when protected with TLS). One reason for TLS's popularity is that it can be implemented within or underneath applications that ride on top of the lower layers, whereas protocols such as EAP and IPsec usually require capabilities within the operating systems and protocol implementations of hosts and embedded devices.

There are several versions of TLS and its predecessor, the *Secure Sockets Layer* (SSL) [RFC6101]. We shall focus on TLS version 1.2 [RFC5246], which is the most recent at the time of writing. TLS 1.2 can support backward compatibility with most older versions of TLS and SSL (e.g., TLS 1.0, 1.1, and SSL 3.0). However, SSL 2.0 is weaker, and while interoperability with it is possible, it is now prohibited [RFC6176]. After discussing TLS 1.2, which operates over a stream-oriented protocol (usually TCP), we will look at the datagram-oriented variant called the *Datagram Transport Layer Security* (DTLS) [RFC4347]. DTLS is slowly gaining popularity for some applications such as VPN implementations that do not use IPsec. Its current specification is based on TLS 1.1 [RFC4346], but updates are under way [IDDTLS].

18.9.1 TLS 1.2

The security goals of TLS are not unlike those for IPsec, but TLS operates at a higher layer. Confidentiality and data integrity are provided based on a variety of cryptographic suites that use certificates that can be provided by a PKI. TLS can also establish secure connections between two anonymous parties (without using certificates), but this application is vulnerable to a MITM attack (not surprising, given that each end is not even strongly identified). The TLS protocol has two layers of its own, called the *record layer* and the *upper layer*. The Record protocol implements the record (lower) layer and is assumed to be layered on a reliable underlying protocol (e.g., TCP). Figure 18-28 shows the basic organization.

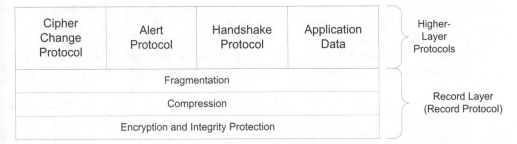

Figure 18-28   The TLS protocol "stack" has a lower record layer and three of its own upper-layer protocols called handshaking protocols. A fourth upper-layer protocol is the application protocol using TLS. The record layer provides fragmentation, compression, integrity protection, and encryption. The handshaking protocols perform many of the same tasks for TLS that IKE does for IPsec.

TLS is a client/server protocol, designed to support security for a connection between two applications. The Record protocol provides fragmentation, compression, integrity protection, and encryption for data objects exchanged between clients and servers, and the handshake protocols establish identities, perform authentication, indicate alerts, and provide unique key material for the Record protocol to use on each connection. The handshaking protocols comprise four specific protocols: the Handshake protocol, the Alert protocol, the Change Cipher Spec protocol, and the application data protocol. Like IPsec, TLS is extensible and can accommodate existing or future cryptographic suites, which TLS calls *cipher suites* (CS). Many such combinations have been defined, and the IANA maintains a registry of the current set [TLSPARAMS]. Modern variants of TLS are based on SSL 3.0, originally developed by Netscape. TLS and SSL do not directly interoperate, but there are negotiation mechanisms that allow clients and servers to dynamically discover which protocol to use when a connection is first established.

The Change Cipher Spec protocol is used to change the current operating parameters. This is accomplished by first using the Handshake protocol to set up a "pending" state, followed by an indication to switch from the current state to the pending state (which then becomes the current state). Such switching is allowed only after the pending state has been readied. TLS depends on five cryptographic operations: digital signing, stream cipher encryption, block cipher encryption, AEAD, and public key encryption. For integrity protection, the TLS record layer uses HMAC. For key generation, TLS 1.2 uses a PRF based on HMAC with SHA-256. TLS also integrates an optional compression algorithm that is negotiated when a connection is first established.

18.9.1.1 TLS Record Protocol

The Record protocol uses an extensible set of record content type values to identify which message type (i.e., which of the higher-layer protocols) is being multiplexed. At any given point in time, the Record protocol has an active *current connection state* and another set of state parameters called the *pending connection state*. Each connection state is further divided into a read state and a write state. Each of these states specifies a compression algorithm, encryption algorithm, and MAC algorithm to be used for communication, along with any necessary keys and parameters. When a key is changed, the pending state is first set up using the Handshake protocol, and then a synchronization operation (usually accomplished using the Cipher Change protocol) sets the current state equal to the pending state. When first initialized, all states are set up with NULL encryption, no compression, and no MAC processing.

The Record protocol's processing flow is shown in Figure 18-29. It divides (fragments) higher-layer information blocks into records called *TLSPlaintext records*, which can be at most 2^{14} bytes in length (but are usually much less). The choice of record size resides within TLS; higher-layer message boundaries are not preserved. Once formed, TLSPlaintext records are compressed using a compression algorithm [RFC3749] identified in the current connection state. There is always one compression protocol active, although it may be (and usually is) the NULL compression protocol (which, not surprisingly, provides no compression gain). The compression algorithm converts a TLSPlaintext record into a *TLSCompressed* structure. Compression algorithms are required to be lossless and may not produce an output that is larger than the input by more than 1KB. To protect the payload from disclosure and modification, encryption and integrity protection algorithms convert a TLSCompressed structure into a *TLSCiphertext* structure, which is then sent on the underlying transport connection.

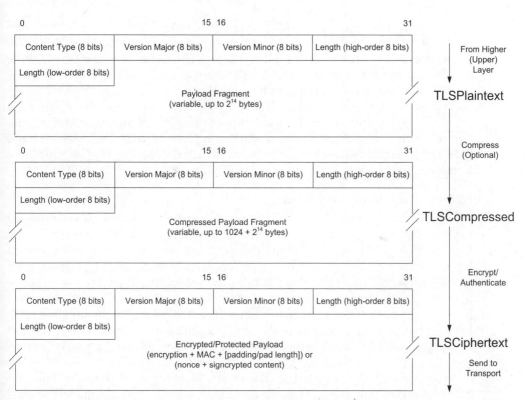

Figure 18-29   The TLS record layer starts with a TLSPlaintext record, which is compressed by a lossless compression algorithm to form a TLSCompressed record. The TLSCompressed record is encrypted (and has a MAC applied) to form a TLSCiphertext record, which is sent for transmission. Conventional stream and block ciphers require a MAC, and block ciphers may include padding. When using AEAD ciphers, a nonce is included with the encrypted and integrity-protected content, but no separate MAC is used.

Referring to Figure 18-29, when producing a TLSCiphertext structure, a sequence number is first computed (but not placed in the message), then a MAC is computed if necessary, and finally symmetric encryption is performed. Prior to encryption, the message may be padded (up to 255 bytes) to meet any block length requirements imposed by the encryption algorithm (e.g., for block ciphers). A MAC is not required for AEAD algorithms that provide both integrity and encryption (e.g., CCM, GCM), but a nonce is used in such cases.

Keys for the Record protocol are derived from a *master secret* provided by some method outside the Record protocol, most often by the Handshake protocol. Using the master secret, along with random values provided by the client and server applications at the beginning of the connection, the following keys are generated:

$$M_c \mid M_s \mid D_c \mid D_s \mid IV_c \mid IV_s = \text{PRF}(\text{master\_secret}, \text{"key expansion"},$$
$$\text{server\_random} + \text{client\_random})$$

In this assignment, | is the splitting operator and + is the concatenation operator. M_c denotes the MAC write key for the client, M_s denotes the MAC write key for the server, D_c denotes the client's data write key, D_s denotes the server's data write key, IV_c denotes the client's IV, and IV_s denotes the server's IV. With the | operator, each key uses however many bytes from the PRF function are required. MAC, encryption, and IV keys, if used, have a fixed length based on the cipher suite selected. The last two values are used only in cases where implicit nonce generation takes place with AEAD ciphers (see Section 3.2.1 of [RFC5116]). According to [RFC5246], the cipher suite requiring the most material is AES_256_CBC_SHA256. It requires four 32-byte keys, for a total of 128 bytes.

18.9.1.2 TLS Handshaking Protocols

There are three subprotocols to TLS, which perform tasks roughly equivalent to those performed by IKE in IPsec. More specifically, these other protocols are identified by numbers used for multiplexing and demultiplexing by the record layer and are called the Handshake protocol (22), Alert protocol (21), and Cipher Change protocol (20). The Cipher Change protocol is very simple. It consists of one message containing a single byte that has the value 1. The purpose of the message is to indicate to the peer a desire to change from the current to the pending state. Receiving such a message moves the read pending state to the current state and causes an indication to the record layer to transition to the pending write state as soon as possible. This message is used by both client and server.

The Alert protocol is used to deliver status information from one end of a TLS connection to another. This can include terminating conditions (either fatal errors or controlled shutdowns) or nonfatal error conditions. As of the publication of [RFC5246], 24 alert messages were defined in standards. More than half of them are always fatal (e.g., bad MACs, missing or unknown messages, algorithm failures).

The Handshake protocol sets up the relevant connection operating parameters. It allows the TLS endpoints to achieve six major objectives: agree on algorithms and exchange random values used in forming symmetric encryption keys, establish algorithm operating parameters, exchange certificates and perform mutual authentication, generate a session-specific secret, provide security parameters to the record layer, and verify that all of these operations have executed properly. Figure 18-30 shows the messages required.

The handshake shown in Figure 18-30 begins with Hello messages. The ClientHello message is usually the first message sent from client to server. It contains a session ID, proposals for the cryptographic suite number (CS in Figure 18-30), and a set of acceptable compression algorithms (which are usually just NULL, although [RFC3749] also defines DEFLATE). TLS supports in excess of 250 cipher suite options [TLSPARAMS].

The ClientHello message also contains the TLS version number and a random number called *ClientHello.random*. Upon receiving the ClientHello message, the server checks to see if the session ID is present in its cache. If so, the server

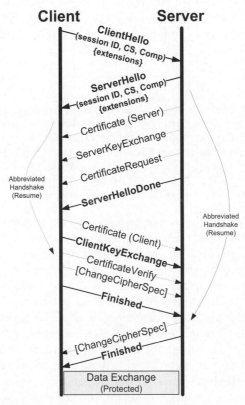

Figure 18-30   The normal TLS connection initiation exchange consists of several messages that may be pipelined. Required messages have solid arrows and are shown in boldface type. An abbreviated exchange takes place if a previously existing connection can be restarted. This avoids endpoint authentication, which can be costly for systems with limited processing capabilities.

may agree to continue a previously existing connection (called a "resume") by performing an *abbreviated handshake*. The abbreviated handshake is key to TLS performance and avoids having to repeatedly verify the authenticity of each end-point, but it does require synchronization with respect to the cipher specification. The ServerHello message completes the first part of the exchange by carrying the server's random number (*ServerHello.random*) to the client. This message also contains a session ID value. If the value is the same as that provided by the client, it indicates the server's willingness to resume. If not, it has the value 0 and a full handshake is required.

    If a full (nonabbreviated) handshake is executed, the exchange of Hello messages results in each end becoming aware of the cipher suites, compression algorithms, and random values of its peer. The server selects among the cryptographic suites specified by the client and may be required to provide its certificate chain in a Certificate message if it is to be authenticated (which is the typical case for secure Web traffic or HTTPS). The server may also send a ServerKeyExchange message if its certificate is not valid for signing, it has no certificate, or a temporary or ephemeral key is to be used to generate session keys.

Note

The ServerKeyExchange message is used only in cases where the Certificate (server) message does not contain enough information to establish a premaster secret. Such cases include anonymous or ephemeral DH key agreement (i.e., cipher suites starting with TLS_DHE_anon, TLS_DHE_DSS, TLS_ DHE_RSA). The ServerKeyExchange message is *not* used for other suites, including those starting with TLS_RSA, TLS_DH_DSS, or TLS_DH_RSA.

At this point, the server may require client authentication. If so, it generates a CertificateRequest message. Once this message is sent, the server completes the second portion of the exchange by sending the mandatory ServerHelloDone message. Upon receiving this (possibly pipelined) message from the server, the client may be required to prove its identity (i.e., knowledge of an appropriate private key corresponding to a certificate). If so, it first sends its certificate using a Certificate message in the same format used by the server. It then sends the mandatory ClientKeyExchange message. The contents of this message depend on the cryptographic suite used, but it generally contains either an RSA-encrypted key or Diffie-Hellman parameters that may be used to create a type of seed for creating new keys (called the *premaster secret*). Finally, it sends a CertificateVerify message to demonstrate that it possesses the private key corresponding to the previously provided certificate, if the server requested client authentication. This message contains a signature on the hash of all of the handshake messages the client has received and sent up to this point.

The final portion of the exchange includes a ChangeCipherSpec message, which is an independent TLS protocol content type (i.e., technically not a Handshake protocol message). However, the mandatory Handshake protocol Finished messages can be exchanged only after a successful exchange of ChangeCipherSpec messages. The Finished messages are the first ones to be protected using the parameters exchanged up to this point. The Finished message themselves contain "verify data," which consists of the following value:

verify_data = PRF(master_secret, finished_label, Hash(handshake_messages))

where finished_label has the value "client finished" for the client and "server finished" for the server. The particular hash function Hash is associated with the selection of the PRF made during the initial Hello exchange. TLS 1.2 provides the ability to have variable-length verify data, but all previous versions and current cipher suites produce 12 bytes of verify data. The 48-byte master_secret value is computed as follows:

$$master\_secret = PRF(premaster\ secret, \texttt{"master secret"},$$
$$ClientHello.random + ServerHello.random)$$

where + is the concatenation operator. The Finished message is important because it can be used to know with a high degree of certainty that the Handshake protocol has completed successfully and subsequent data exchange can take place.

18.9.1.3 TLS Extensions

If we compare the capabilities of IKE and TLS we have discussed so far, we can see that IKE includes the ability to carry information beyond that required for basic SA establishment. This is accomplished using IKE Notify and Configuration payloads. To provide a similar extensible mechanism for TLS, various *extensions* can be included with TLS 1.2 messages in a standard way. The baseline specification for TLS 1.2 [RFC5246] includes a "signature algorithms" extension that a client uses to specify to a server what types of hash and signature algorithms it supports (MD5, SHA-1, SHA-224, SHA-256, SHA-384, SHA-512 for hashes and RSA, DSA, ECDSA for digital signatures are defined). They are indicated in descending order of preference by pairs, as some systems allow only certain combinations. The current list of extensions is given in [TLSEXT].

Previous versions of TLS had about a half-dozen extensions, and [RFC6066] updates these extensions for TLS 1.2. It defines the following extensions: server_name (DNS-style name of the server being contacted), max_fragment_length (maximum length of a message as 2^n bytes for n having values 9–12), client_certificate_url (indicates support for the CertificateURL handshake message used to send the URL of a certificate instead of a complete certificate), trusted_ca_keys (hashes or the names of trusted CA public keys and/or certificates), truncated_hmac (use the first 80 bits of HMAC calculations only), and status_request (requests that a server invoke OCSP and provide the DER-encoded response in a CertificateStatus handshake message to check a certificate). Each of these extensions may be present in an (extended) ClientHello message and in some circumstances may appear in the ServerHello message to indicate agreement. Aside from these extensions and the two handshake messages already mentioned, [RFC6066] also defines four alert messages: certificate_unobtainable, unrecognized_name, bad_certificate_status_response, and bad_certificate_hash_value. These are self-explanatory and are not sent unless the peer has demonstrated understanding of the extended ClientHello type message.

Several other extensions have been defined or are reserved. The user_mapping extension [RFC4681] provides a method for providing context for the user identifier (e.g., Windows domain). Another expands the cert_type extension to include not only X.509 certificates but also OpenPGP certificates [RFC6091]. Elliptic curve cipher suites are described by the informational document [RFC4492]. The *Secure Remote Password protocol* (SRP) can be integrated with TLS according to the methods defined in the informational document [RFC5054]. A use_srtp extension designed to produce a version of the *Secure Real-Time protocol* (SRTP) based on DTLS (see Section 18.9.2) is given in [RFC5764]. A method to eliminate the state a server must store to perform session resumption is given by the SessionTicket TLS extension [RFC5077]. It involves placing the necessary state in an encrypted form in the client. Finally, an important renegotiation_info extension is used to combat a renegotiation vulnerability. We shall describe it in more detail next.

18.9.1.4 Renegotiation

TLS supports the ability to renegotiate cryptographic connection parameters while maintaining the same connection. This can be initiated by either the server or the client. If the server wishes to renegotiate the connection parameters, it generates a HelloRequest message, and the client responds with a new ClientHello message, which begins the renegotiation procedure. The client is also able to generate such a ClientHello message spontaneously, without prompting from the server.

Support for renegotiation is optional but "highly recommended" and is used, for example, when sequence numbers are about to wrap. Renegotiation can be refused by generating a "no_renegotiation" (type 100) warning alert. Although this type of alert is not required to be terminal, receiving such an alert may, by local policy, result in connection termination.

In 2009, a successful attack on TLS was demonstrated using the renegotiation capability. We describe it in more detail in Section 18.12. The vulnerability allows an attacker to establish a malicious TLS session with a server that can later be spliced into a subsequent legitimate session by a client using a MITM attack. The server believes that only a standards-compliant renegotiation has taken place. A solution to the problem, given in [RFC5746], involves binding any renegotiation more closely with the existing session using a TLS extension called renegotiation_info (type 0xff01). When creating a new connection, renegotiation_info is empty. When client renegotiation takes place, it contains "client_verify_data," and when server renegotiation takes place it contains a concatenation of "client_verify_data" and "server_verify_data." The client_verify_data is defined to be the same verify_data used with the Finished message sent by the client on the completion of the last handshake. This is a 12-byte value in TLS (36 for SSLv3). The server_verify_data is defined to be the verify_data used with the Finished message sent by the server on completion of the last handshake.

Some deployed TLS (and SSL) servers abort a connection when unknown extensions are present. To handle this issue when deploying the (relatively new) renegotiation_info extension, an alternative is available. The TLS cipher suite TLS_EMPTY_RENEGOTIATION_INFO_SCSV can be used during connection establishment to indicate the equivalent of an empty renegotiation_info extension. This is using a *signaling cipher suite value* (SCSV) not to encode a real cipher suite, but instead to indicate a certain set of functions. (A similar trick is used in DNSSEC for NSEC3 records; see Section 18.10.1.3.)

18.9.1.5 Example

In the example shown in Figure 18-31, we see the messages exchanged during a connection setup with TLS 1.2 using TCP/IP on the local loopback interface. The client and server have RSA certificates, which each provides to its peer. The initial

TCP handshake and window update, as well as the 127.0.0.1 source and destination IPv4 addresses, are not shown. The trace has been annotated with right and left arrows for additional clarity. The arrows pointing to the right indicate TCP segments containing at least one TLS message sent by the client headed for the server. Left-pointing arrows indicate messages from the server to the client. To see this output, Wireshark was told to decode the trace by first choosing SSL under the Analyze | Decode As ... menu.

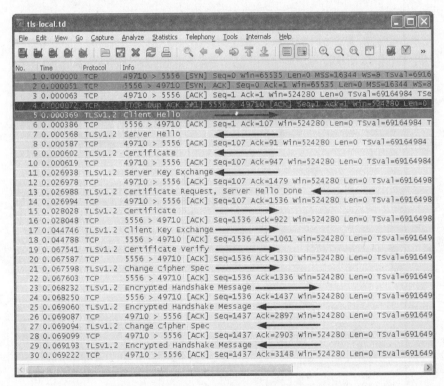

Figure 18-31   A normal TLS 1.2 connection establishment as shown by Wireshark. The server runs on port 5556. Client messages sent to the server are highlighted by arrows pointing to the right. Server messages sent to the client are shown with left-pointing arrows. TCP ACKs are interspersed with the TLS messages. After the Change Cipher Spec message (segment 21), other messages are encrypted and authenticated. Segment 13 also includes the ServerHelloDone message.

In Figure 18-31, after the initial TCP-level handshake, the TLS exchange begins with a ClientHello message. TCP pure ACKs are seen interspersed with the TLS messages. After the ChangeCipherSpec message has been processed, the subsequent information is encrypted. To see what is happening in more detail, we shall expand the first few TLS messages. Figure 18-32 shows the detailed contents of the ClientHello message.

Figure 18-32 A ClientHello message in TLS 1.2 contains version information, supported cipher suites and compression algorithms, random data, and a number of extensions. Here, the client supports Diffie-Hellman key agreement as well as key exchange using RSA. It uses AES-256 in CBC mode for encryption and SHA-256 for integrity protection.

The ClientHello message detailed in Figure 18-32 is a Record protocol message carrying the ClientHello handshake message. It contains a 32-bit UNIX timestamp counting seconds since midnight, January 1, 1970, plus a random 28-byte value (*ClientHello.random*) used in forming keys. As this is a brand-new connection, its session ID is 0. Six bytes are devoted to carrying the client's three supported cipher suites in preference order (most preferred first). Each suite is encoded using a 16-bit value specified by the TLS Cipher Suite Registry in [TLSPARAMS]. Only a single compression method is supported—the NULL method, which achieves no compression gain and is typical. Also, 50 bytes are included for extensions. The cert_type extension indicates that either X.509 or OpenPGP certificates are understood. The server_name extension contains 127.0.0.1, which was the name of the server provided to the client application. The renegotiation_info is empty, as this is the first handshake, as is the SessionTicket TLS extension. The signature_algorithms extension indicates that the following combinations can be processed by the client: sha1-rsa, sha1-dsa, sha256-rsa, sha384-rsa, and sha512-rsa.

In this sample exchange, the server has been configured with only one cipher suite, TLS_DHE_RSA_WITH_AES_256_CBC_SHA256 (0x006b). The server indicates this fact when responding to the ClientHello by using the ServerHello message shown in Figure 18-33.

In this figure, the server responds with a ServerHello message to the client's ClientHello. The server provides its copy of the current time and its 28-byte random value. It also includes a random 32-byte session ID. The server supports only a single cipher suite (DH key agreement using RSA certificates with AES-256 encryption in CBC mode for encryption and SHA-256 for integrity protection). Like the client, it does not support any compression methods. It includes an empty renegotiation_info extension and an empty SessionTicket TLS extension. Following this first message, the server continues with a Certificate message, as shown in Figure 18-34.

The message in Figure 18-34 carries the server's 841-byte X.509v3 certificate to the client, which has been signed by a sample certificate authority called Test CA shown in the *Issuer* field. The field called *SubjectPublickeyInfo* contains the server's 270-byte public RSA key, which the client will use in authenticating the server. There are six extensions in the certificate: *basicConstraints* (critical), *subjectAltName* (contains a DNS name for the server using the certificate), *extKeyUsage* (extended key usage, indicating that the purpose of the key is for authenticating a server), *keyUsage* (critical; indicates that the enclosed key may be used for key encipherment or for generating digital signatures), *subjectKeyIdentifier* (a 20-byte number identifying the signed public key), and the *authorityKeyIdentifier* (a 20-byte number identifying the key used by the certificate authority to produce this certificate).

The ClientKeyExchange message is not detailed as it mostly includes binary information used in forming the DH exchange. The next message of interest is segment 13, which is a single TCP segment containing both a CertificateRequest message and a ServerHelloDone message. Figure 18-35 shows the contents.

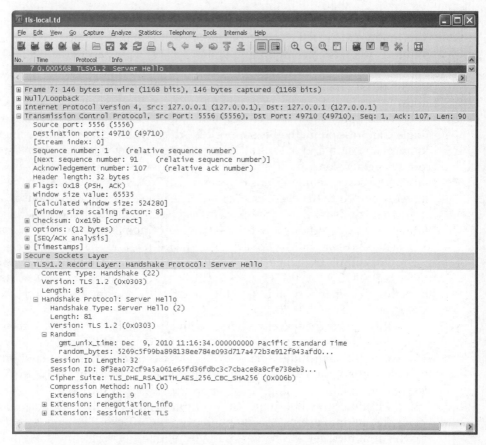

Figure 18-33   A ServerHello message in TLS 1.2 contains version information, supported cipher suites and compression algorithms, and a number of extensions. Here, the client supports Diffie-Hellman key agreement. It uses AES-256 for encryption and SHA-256 for integrity protection.

Figure 18-35 shows a TCP segment containing both a CertificateRequest message and a ServerHelloDone message. The CertificateRequest is requesting the client to provide its certificate and to verify its authenticity using a subsequent CertificateVerify message. The type of certificate requested should be signed using either RSA or DSS from the Test CA certificate authority. The signature algorithms listed are sha1-rsa, sha1-dsa, sha256-rsa, sha384-rsa, and sha512-rsa.

Packet 15 (not detailed) contains the Certificate message that has the certificate chain for the client and its public key. In this case, the subject field contains "test client" and the issuer is Test CA. Thus, the client's and server's certificates were signed by the same CA and the chain is a single certificate. For the client to prove that it possesses the corresponding private key, it generates the CertificateVerify

Figure 18-34 Following the ServerHello, the server generates a Certificate message to carry its certificate. The client can use the certificate to authenticate the server. The same message format is used when the server authenticates the client.

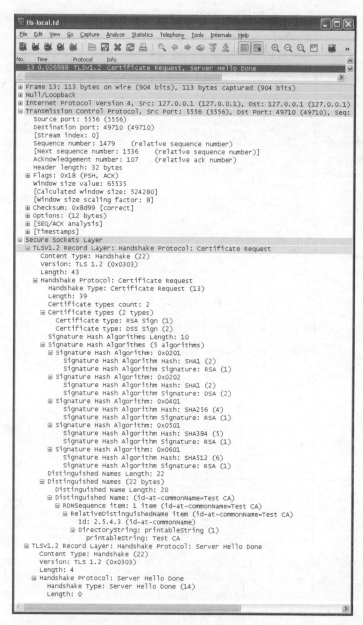

Figure 18-35 The server's CertificateRequest and ServerHelloDone messages are contained in the same TCP segment. The client can use the certificate to authenticate the server. The same message format is used when the server authenticates the client.

message (packet 19). The CertificateVerify message contains a signature on a hash of all the session's handshake messages sent or received so far, signed using the private key of the client. This proves not only that the client is authentic, but that it has participated appropriately in the TLS exchanges up to this point and not lost or reordered any messages. After the CertificateVerify message, the Change Cipher message begins the subsequent (encrypted) communication.

18.9.2 TLS with Datagrams (DTLS)

The TLS protocol assumes a stream-based underlying transport protocol for delivering its messages. A datagram version (DTLS) relaxes this assumption but aims to otherwise achieve the same security goals as TLS using essentially all the same message formats. It was originally motivated by protocols such as SIP that run on UDP but do not care to use IPsec [RFC5406]. DTLS has also been adapted for use with DCCP [RFC5238] and SCTP [RFC6083]. The current version at the time of writing is DTLS 1.0 [RFC4347], based on TLS 1.1. An update, based on TLS1.2, is in the works [IDDTLS]. It uses the same protocol layering shown in Figure 18-28 and most of the same message exchanges.

The main challenge of providing TLS-like service without a reliable transport is that datagrams may get lost, reordered, or duplicated. These problems can affect encryption and the Handshake protocol, both of which have ordering dependencies in TLS. To handle them, DTLS adds an explicit sequence number to each record carried by the record layer (they were implicit with regular TLS) and a timeout-based retransmission scheme with (different) sequence numbers from those used by the Handshake protocol.

18.9.2.1 DTLS Record Layer

In TLS, the ordering of records is important because the MAC computation of one record depends on its predecessor. More specifically, the MAC computation depends on an implicit 64-bit sequence number for each record that is incorrect in the presence of datagram reordering or loss. To remedy this problem, DTLS uses explicit sequence numbers at the record layer. These sequence numbers are reset to the value 0 after each ChangeCipherSpec message is sent. They are used in combination with an additional 16-bit *epoch number* incorporated into each record's header. The epoch number is incremented by 1 for each change of cipher state. This handles the situation where multiple messages containing the same sequence number, generated as a result of multiple proximate handshakes, might be in flight simultaneously.

The MAC computation in DTLS is modified from its TLS counterpart to include the 64-bit concatenation of the two new fields (epoch first, followed by sequence number). This allows each record to be handled independently. Note that with TLS, a bad MAC results in connection termination. With DTLS, a full connection abort is not necessary, and a receiver may choose to simply discard the record containing the invalid MAC or send an alert message (which, if generated, must be terminal).

Duplicates are simply dropped or are optionally considered as a replay and possible attack. Replay detection, if supported, is based on keeping a window of current sequence numbers at the receiver. The window is required to be at least 32 messages but is suggested to be at least 64. The scheme is similar to that used in IPsec for AH and ESP. Records arriving with sequence numbers less than the left window edge are silently discarded as old or duplicative. Those within the window are checked as possible duplicates. A message within the window carrying a valid MAC is kept, even if out of order. Those with invalid MACs are discarded. Those with valid MACs that exceed the right window edge cause the right window edge to be advanced. Thus, the right window edge represents the validated message with the highest sequence number.

A single datagram may contain multiple DTLS records, but no single record may span multiple datagrams. The record layer allows applications to implement a PMTUD process similar to TCP's (see Chapter 15) and avoids sending datagrams it believes are likely to be fragmented. Indeed, applications are supposed to receive an error indication if they attempt to send application messages that exceed the PMTU or maximum application datagram size (PMTU minus DTLS overhead). An exception to this rule is how DTLS handles the Handshake protocol, which can involve relatively large messages.

18.9.2.2 DTLS Handshake Protocol

Handshake protocol messages can be as large as 2^{24} - 1 bytes but in practice are several kilobytes. This can exceed a typical maximum UDP datagram size of 1.5KB. To handle this situation, a Handshake protocol message may span multiple DTLS records using a fragmentation procedure. Each fragment is contained in a record, which is contained in an underlying datagram. To implement fragmentation, each Handshake message contains a 16-bit *Sequence Number* field, a 24-bit *Fragment Offset* field, and a 24-bit *Fragment Length* field.

To perform fragmentation, the original message's content is divided into multiple contiguous data ranges. Each range is required to be less than the maximum fragment size. Each range is placed in a message fragment. Each fragment contains the same sequence number as the original message. The *Fragment Offset* and *Fragment Length* fields are expressed in bytes. Senders avoid overlapping data ranges, but receivers are required to handle this possibility because senders may be required to adjust their record size over time and retransmissions may be necessary.

To handle message loss, DTLS implements a simple timeout and retransmission capability that operates on groups of messages called *flights*. Figure 18-36 shows both the full (left) and abbreviated (right) establishment exchanges, along with the DTLS Handshake protocol state machine.

In Figure 18-36, flight numbers are given in the area between the full and abbreviated exchanges. The full exchange is very similar to the full TLS exchange

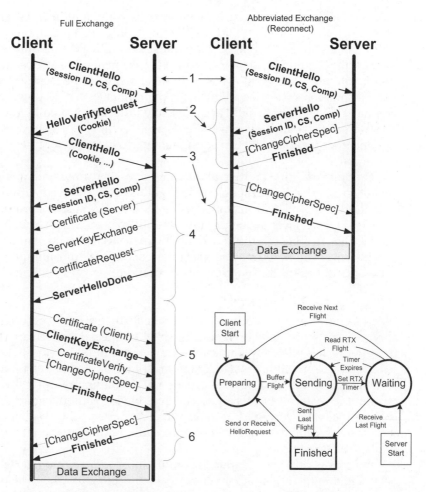

Figure 18-36 In DTLS, the possibility of lost datagrams must be handled. The initial full exchange (left) comprises six "flights" of information, each of which can be retransmitted. The DTLS abbreviated exchange (top right) uses only three and differs slightly from TLS. DTLS maintains a three-state finite state machine (bottom right) when processing the protocol.

shown in Figure 18-30, except for the additional HelloVerifyRequest and second ClientHello messages (which now contain cookies). The abbreviated exchange is different, however. In DTLS the server sends the first Finished message, whereas in TLS the client sends the first Finished message.

The lower right portion of Figure 18-36 depicts the state machine used by DTLS implementations when performing the Handshake protocol. There are three primary states: Preparing, Sending, and Waiting. The client starts in the Preparing state as it creates its ClientHello message. The server begins in the Waiting state with no buffered messages or active retransmission timer. When sending, a retransmission timer is set and the Waiting state is entered upon completion of the transmission. Expiration of the retransmission (RTX) timer brings the protocol back to the Sending state to perform a retransmission, as does the receipt of a retransmitted flight from the peer. In this latter case the local system performs a retransmission of its own flight with the rationale that its previous transmission must have been partially or completely lost, as indicated by the presence of peer retransmission. If everything goes well, a flight is received, and the local system either finishes or returns to the Preparing state to form its next flight for transmission.

The state machine is driven by a retransmission timer with a recommended default value of 1s. If no response for a flight has been received within the timeout duration, the flight is retransmitted using the same Handshake protocol sequence numbers; record-layer sequence numbers still advance. Subsequent retransmissions without a response result in doubling of the RTX timeout value, up to a value of at least 60s. This value may be reset after a successful transmission or a long idle period (ten times the current timer value or more).

18.9.2.3 DTLS DoS Protection

When datagrams are used instead of a reliable byte stream protocol, some additional security considerations come into play. Of special concern are two potential DoS attacks. It is relatively simple for an attacker to forge a source IP address when sending a ClientHello message. Many such messages could cause a DoS attack at the DTLS server because of exhaustion of processing resources when forming responses. A variant of this attack involves having multiple attacking machines include the same forged source (victim) IP address. The responding server(s) then send(s) responses to the victim's IP address, causing the victim machine to undergo a DoS attack.

A stateless cookie validation procedure incorporated into the Hello exchange helps resist both DoS attacks. When a server receives a ClientHello message, it generates a new HelloVerifyRequest message containing a 32-bit cookie (which may be a function of a secret, the client's IP addresses, and the connection parameters). A subsequent ClientHello message must contain a copy of the appropriate cookie. Otherwise, the server refuses the exchange. This allows the server to quickly dispense with requests that do not provide valid cookies. It does not protect against coordinated attacks from multiple legitimate IP addresses that can complete the cookie exchange.

18.10 DNS Security (DNSSEC)

Now that we have discussed popular security protocols at the link, network, and transport layers, we move to the application layer. Although it is not yet widely deployed at the time of writing, we shall focus on how to provide enhanced security for the Domain Name System (DNS). Security for DNS covers both data within the DNS (resource records or RRs) as well as security of transactions that synchronize or update contents of DNS servers. Given its important role in the operation of the Internet, a major effort has been undertaken to deploy these security mechanisms. The mechanisms are called the *Domain Name System Security Extensions* (DNSSEC) and are discussed in a family of RFCs [RFC4033][RFC4034] [RFC4035]. These RFCs are sometimes referred to as *DNSSECbis* because they replace an earlier set of specifications for DNSSEC. As we explore DNSSEC in further detail, it may be worthwhile to review the description of basic DNS (see Chapter 11).

The extensions provide origin authentication and integrity assurance for DNS data, along with a (limited) key distribution facility. That is, the extensions provide a cryptographically secure way to determine what entity has authored a block of DNS information and that the information has been received unaltered. DNSSEC also provides *authenticated nonexistence*. DNS responses indicating the nonexistence of a particular domain name include protection similar to that of responses for existing domain names. DNSSEC does not provide privacy (confidentiality) of DNS information, DoS protection, or access control. Transaction security, used with DNSSEC, is defined separately, and we will mention it briefly after discussing the core DNSSEC data security capabilities.

DNSSEC accommodates resolvers with varying levels of security "awareness." A *validating security-aware resolver* (also called *validating resolver*) checks cryptographic signatures to ensure that the DNS data it handles is secure. Other resolvers, including stub resolvers on hosts and the "resolver side" of recursive name servers, may be security-aware but may not perform cryptographic validation. Instead, such resolvers should establish secure associations with validating resolvers. We shall focus on the validating resolvers, as they are the most sophisticated and interesting. When operating, they are able to ascertain whether DNS information is *secure* (valid with all signatures checked), *insecure* (valid signatures indicate that something should not be present but is), *bogus* (proper data appears to be present but cannot be validated for some reason), or *indeterminate* (veracity cannot be determined, usually because of lack of signatures). The indeterminate case is the default case when no other information is available.

DNSSEC works securely only when a zone is signed by a domain administrator, there is some basis for trust, and both server and resolver software participate. Validating resolvers check signatures to ensure that DNS information is secure, and they must be configured with one or more initial trust anchors that are similar to root certificates in a PKI. Note, however, that DNSSEC is not a PKI; in particular, it provides only limited signing and key revocation. It does not implement an analog to certificate revocation lists [RFC5011].

When performing a DNS query with DNSSEC, a security-aware resolver uses EDNS0 and enables the *DO* (DNSSEC OK) bit in an OPT meta-RR present in the request. This bit indicates the client's interest in and ability to process DNSSEC-related information along with its support for EDNS0. The *DO* bit is the first (high-order) bit of the second 16-bit field in the "extended RCODE and flags" portion of the EDNS0 meta-RR (see Section 3 of [RFC3225] and Section 4 of [RFC2671]). Servers that receive requests in which the *DO* bit is not set (or present) are prohibited from returning most of the RRs discussed in Section 18.10.1 unless such records are explicitly asked for in the request. This helps to improve DNS performance because it avoids having to carry security-related RRs that are never processed by security-unaware resolvers. This can be especially beneficial because DNS typically uses relatively small UDP packets and falls back to using TCP, which increases latency due to its three-way handshake, for large responses.

When a server processes a request from a DNSSEC-enabled resolver, it checks the *CD* (checking disabled) bit in the DNS request (see Chapter 11). If set, this indicates that the client is willing to accept nonvalidated data in a response. When preparing a response, a server ordinarily validates the data it is returning cryptographically. Successful validation results in the *AD* (authentic data) bit being set in the response [RFC4035]. A security-aware but nonvalidating resolver can in principle trust this information if it has a secure path to the server. However, the arguably best case is to use validating stub resolvers that perform cryptographic validation and consequently set the *CD* bit on queries. This provides end-to-end security of the DNS (i.e., an intermediate resolver need not be trusted), and it reduces the computational load on the intermediate servers that would otherwise have to perform cryptographic validation.

18.10.1 DNSSEC Resource Records

As specified in [RFC4034], DNSSEC uses four new resource records (RRs) and two message header bits (*CD* and *AD*). It also requires EDNS0 support and uses the *DO* bit field we mentioned previously. Two of the four RRs are used to contain signatures for portions of the DNS name space, and the other two are used in helping to distribute and validate keys. A change in [RFC5155] created two additional new RRs, intended to replace one of the original four.

18.10.1.1 DNS Security (DNSKEY) Resource Records

We begin by looking at how DNSSEC stores and distributes keys. DNSSEC uses the DNSKEY resource record to hold public keys. The keys are intended for use with DNSSEC only; other RRs (e.g., the CERT RR [RFC4398]) may be useful for holding keys or certificates for other purposes. The format of the RDATA portion of a DNSKEY RR is shown in Figure 18-37.

The *Flags* field in Figure 18-37 has 3 bits currently defined. Bit 7 is the *Zone Key* bit field. If set, the DNSKEY RR owner's name must be the name of a zone and the included key is called either a *Zone Signing Key* (ZSK) or a *Key Signing Key* (KSK). If not set, the record holds some other kind of DNS key that cannot be used for validating signatures for zones. Bit 15 is called the *Secure Entry Point* (SEP) bit. It is a hint that can be used by debugging or signing software to make an informed guess as to the purpose of the key. Signature validation does not interpret the *SEP*

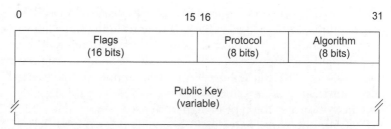

Figure 18-37   The RDATA portion of the DNSKEY RR contains a public key used only for DNSSEC. The *Flags* field includes a *Zone Key* indicator (bit 7), a *Secure Entry Point* indicator (bit 15), and *Revoked* indicator (bit 8). Generally, the zone key is set for all DNSSEC keys. If the advisory *SEP* bit is also set, the key is typically called a key signing key and is used for validating delegations to child zones. If not, the key is usually a zone signing key, has a shorter validity period, and is typically used to sign zone contents and not delegations. The included key is to be used with the algorithm specified in the *Algorithm* field.

bit, but keys with this bit set are usually KSKs and are used to secure the DNS hierarchy by validating keys in child zones (via DS records; see Section 18.10.1.2). Bit 8 is the Revoked bit [RFC5011] if set the key cannot be used for validation. The *Protocol* field holds the value 3 for this version of DNSSEC. The *Algorithm* field indicates the signing algorithm [DNSSECALG]. Only DSA and RSA with SHA-1 (values 3 and 5, respectively) are defined for use with DNSKEY RRs according to [RFC4034], but additional specifications support other algorithms (e.g., see [RFC5933] for ECC-GOST (value 12), [RFC5702] for SHA-256 (value 8)). These values are also used with several of the other DNSSEC RRs. The *Public Key* field holds a public key whose format depends on the *Algorithm* field.

18.10.1.2 Delegation Signer (DS) Resource Records

A *delegation signer* (DS) resource record is used to refer to a DNSKEY RR, usually from a parent zone to a descendant zone. These records are used during the authentication process to verify a public key (see Section 18.10.2). The DS RR format is shown in Figure 18-38.

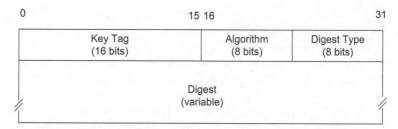

Figure 18-38   The RDATA portion of the DS RR contains a nonunique reference to a DNSKEY RR in the *Key Tag* field. It also contains a message digest of the DNSKEY RR and its owner, plus indications of the type of digest and algorithm.

The *Key Tag* field in Figure 18-38 is a reference to a DNSKEY RR. However, it is not unique. Multiple DNSKEY RRs may have the same tag value, so the field is used only as a search hint (confirming that validation is still necessary). The value for this field is computed as the 16-bit unsigned sum of data comprising the referenced DNSKEY RR RDATA area (carries are ignored) as shown in Figure 18-37. The *Algorithm* field uses the same values as the DNSKEY RR *Algorithm* field. The *Digest Type* field indicates the type of signature used. Only value 1 (SHA-1) is defined by [RFC4034], but SHA-256 (value 2) is specified for use by [RFC4509]. The current list is contained in the DS RR Type Digest Algorithms registry [DSRRTYPES]. The *Digest* field contains the digest of the DNSKEY RR being referenced. More specifically, the digest is computed as follows:

digest = digest_algorithm(DNSKEY owner name | DNSKEY RDATA)

where | is the concatenation operator and the DNSKEY RDATA value is computed from the referenced DNSKEY RR as follows:

DNSKEY RDATA = *Flags* | *Protocol* | *Algorithm* | *Public Key*

For the case of SHA-1, the digest is 20 bytes in length. For SHA-256 it is 32 bytes. The DS RR is used to provide a downward link in the authentication chain across zone boundaries, so the referenced DNSKEY RR must be a zone key (i.e., bit 7 of the *Flags* field in the DNSKEY RR must be set).

Note

At the time of writing, a variant of the DS RR called DS2 is under consideration [IDDS2]. It introduces a Canonical Signer Name to the DS RR so that multiple zones with identical content can be named differently and signed by multiple (different) signers. In addition, there is a DLV RR [RFC4431] that has been used to provide delegations in cases where a parent zone is not signed or has not published DS RRs. The format of a DLV RR is identical to that of a DS RR; only the interpretation differs.

18.10.1.3 NextSECure (NSEC and NSEC3) Resource Records

Now that we have seen the RRs needed to hold and securely refer to keys, we move on to the records used to validate the structure of a zone and the resource records it contains. The NextSECure (NSEC) RR is used to hold the "next" RRset owner's domain name in the canonical ordering of names (see Section 18.10.2.1) or a delegation point NS type RRset. (Recall, an RRset is a set of RRs with the same owner, class, TTL, and type but with different data.) It also holds a list of RR types present at the NSEC RR owner's name. This provides authentication and integrity verification for the zone structure. The format of an NSEC RR is shown in Figure 18-39.

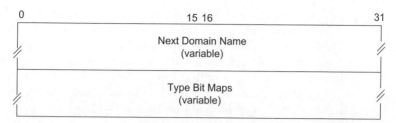

Figure 18-39   The RDATA portion of the NSEC RR contains the name of the next RRset owner for the zone in canonical order. It also contains an indication of which RR types were present at the NSEC RR owner's domain name.

The NSEC RR is used to form a chain of names corresponding to RRsets within a zone. Consequently, an RRset *not* present in the chain can be shown to not exist. This provides the authenticated denial of existence feature mentioned previously. The *Next Domain Name* field holds the next entry in the canonically ordered domain name chain for the zone without using the domain name compression technique described in Chapter 11. The value of this field for the last NSEC record of the chain is the zone apex (the owner name of the zone's SOA RR).

The *Type Bit Maps* field of the NSEC RR holds a bitmap of RR types present at the NSEC RR owner's domain name. There is a maximum of 64K possible types, about 100 of which have been defined to date [DNSPARAMS]. Only a fraction of these are in widespread use. For example, the Internet's root zone (domain name "."), which became operational with DNSSEC on July 15, 2010, contains a *Next Domain Name* field of ac (a ccTLD) and a bitmap indicating the presence of records of the following types: NS, SOA, RRSIG, NSEC, and DNSKEY.

To encode the presence of a type, the whole space of RR types is divided into 256 "window blocks," numbered 0 through 255. For each block number, the presence of up to 256 RR types can be encoded using a bit mask. Given a block number N and bit position P, the corresponding RR type number is ($N*256 + P$). For example, in block 1, bit position 2 corresponds to RR type 258 (a type not currently defined). The field is encoded as follows:

Type Bit Maps = (window block number | bitmap length | bitmap)*

where | is the concatenation operator and * represents Kleene closure (i.e., zero or more). Each instance of the window block number contains a value in the range 0–255, and the bitmap length contains the length of the corresponding bitmap in bytes (maximum value 32). The window block number and bitmap length are each single bytes, and the bitmap can be as long as 32 bytes (256 bits, one for each possible RR type in the window). Blocks in which no RR type is present are not included. The encoding is optimized for a sparse presence of types across blocks. For example, if only RR types 1 (A) and 15 (MX) were present, the encoding for the field would be as follows: 0x00024001 = (0x00 | 0x02 | 0x4001).

The original structure of NSEC records defined in [RFC4034] creates a situation in which anyone is able to enumerate the authority records in a zone by walking the NSEC chain, called *zone enumeration*. This is an unwanted opportunity for "leakage" of information for many deployments. As a result, a pair of RRs, intended to replace NSEC, is defined in [RFC5155]. The first is called NSEC3. It uses cryptographic hashes of RR owner domain names rather than unencoded domain names. The format is shown in Figure 18-40.

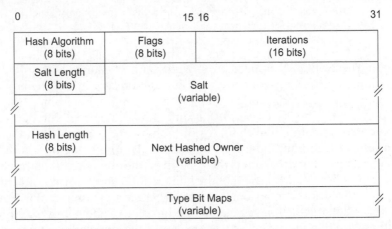

Figure 18-40   The RDATA portion of the NSEC3 RR contains a hash of the name of the next RRset owner for the zone in canonical order. The hash function has been applied the number of times specified in the *Iterations* field. The variable-length *Salt* value is appended to the name prior to applying the hash function to provide dictionary attack resistance. The *Type Bit Maps* field uses the same structure as NSEC RRs. NSEC3PARAM records are similar but contain only the hash parameters (not the *Next Hashed Owner* or *Type Bit Maps* fields).

In the NSEC3 record, the *Hash Algorithm* field identifies the hash function applied to the next owner name to produce the *Next Hashed Owner* field. Only SHA-1 (value 1) is defined to date [NSEC3PARAMS]. The low-order bit of the *Flags* field contains an *opt-out* flag. If set, it indicates that the NSEC3 record may cover unsigned delegations. This is used in cases where a delegation (NS RRset) refers to a child zone that is not required to be or is not desired to be signed. The *Iterations* field indicates how many times the hash function has been applied. A larger number of iterations may help to protect against finding the owner names corresponding to hash values found in NSEC3 records (dictionary attacks). The *Salt Length* field gives the length of the *Salt* field in bytes. The *Salt* field contains a value appended to the original owner name prior to computing the hash function. Its purpose is to help thwart dictionary attacks.

The second RR specified by [RFC5155] is called the NSEC3PARAM RR (not shown separately). It uses the same format as the NSEC3 RR, except the *Hash*

Length, Next Hashed Owner, and *Type Bit Maps* fields are not present. It is used by an authoritative name server when choosing NSEC3 records to use in a negative response. The NSEC3PARAM RR provides the parameters needed for computing a hashed owner name.

To obtain the hash value for the *Next Hashed Owner* field, the following computation is performed:

$$IH(0) = H(\text{owner name} \mid Salt)$$

$$IH(k) = H(IH(k - 1) \mid Salt) \text{ if } k > 0$$

$$Next\ Hashed\ Owner = H(IH(Iterations) \mid Salt)$$

where H is the hash function specified in the *Hash Algorithm* field and the owner name is in canonical form. The iterations and salt values are taken from the corresponding fields of the NSEC3 RR.

To avoid confusion between NSEC and NSEC3 RR types, [RFC5155] allocates and requires the use of special security algorithm numbers 6 and 7 as aliases for identifiers 3 (DSA) and 5 (SHA-1) in zones employing NSEC3 RRs. Resolvers unaware of the NSEC3 record type receiving these values treat the resulting records as insecure. This provides a certain limited form of backward compatibility (i.e., failing, but doing so without incorrectly interpreting RR data).

18.10.1.4 Resource Record Signature (RRSIG) Resource Records

Moving from the DNS structure to its contents, we require a way to provide origin authentication and integrity protection for RRs. DNSSEC signs and validates signatures on RRsets using the *Resource Record Signature* (RRSIG) RR, and every authoritative RR in a zone must be signed (glue records and delegation NS records present in parent zones aren't). An RRSIG RR contains a digital signature for a particular RRset, along with information to identify which public key can be used to validate the signature, as shown in Figure 18-41.

The *Type Covered* field indicates the type of the RRset to which the signature applies. The value is taken from the standard set of RR types in [DNSPARAMS]. The *Algorithm* field indicates the signing algorithm. Only DSA and RSA with SHA-1 (values 3 and 5, respectively) are defined for use with RRSIG RRs according to [RFC4034], but [RFC5702] covers SHA-2 algorithms and [RFC5933] covers GOST algorithms (from the Russian Federation). The *Labels* field gives the number of labels in the original owner's name of the RRSIG RR. The *Original TTL* field holds a copy of the TTL from the RRset as it appears in the authoritative zone (caching name servers may reduce the TTL). The *Signature Expiration* and *Signature Inception* fields indicate the starting and ending validity times for the signature, expressed in seconds since January 1, 1970, 00:00:00 UTC. The *Key Tag* field helps to identify the DNSKEY RR that can be used to obtain the public key necessary to validate the signature contained in the *Signature* field, using the format described previously for the DS RR.

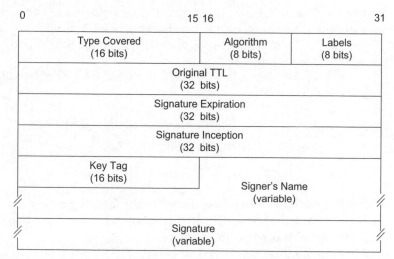

Figure 18-41   The RDATA portion of the RRSIG RR contains a signature for an RRset. The *TTL* of the RRset as it appears in the authoritative zone is also included, along with indicators of the algorithm and signature validity period. The *Key Tag* field refers to a DNSKEY RR containing a public key that can be used to validate the signature. The *Labels* field indicates how many labels constitute the original owning name of the RR.

18.10.2 DNSSEC Operation

Now that we have covered all the RRs required by DNSSEC, we can see how to use DNSSEC to secure zones. We shall first require the definition of a *canonical ordering*, mentioned earlier when defining the NSEC and NSEC3 record types. The purpose of a defined canonical ordering for a zone is to be able to enumerate a zone's contents in a reproducible way that can be signed (different orders of the same contents would produce different values for any good hash function). Once we are familiar with the ordering, we look at how a zone is signed and how signed records describing a zone are validated.

18.10.2.1 Canonical Orderings and Forms

There are three canonical orderings of interest to us: the canonical name order within a zone, the canonical form for a single RR, and the canonical ordering of an RRset [RFC4034]. Recall from Chapter 11 that each RR has an owner name (owner's domain name) consisting of labels. By treating each label in a name as a left-justified string of bytes and treating uppercase US-ASCII letters as lowercase, we can form a list of names. We first sort the names by their most significant (right-most) label, then by the next most significant label, and so on. The absence of a byte sorts before a zero-value byte. A valid canonical ordering would be com, company.com, *.company.com, UK.company.COM, usa.company.com. Wildcards can be used.

For a particular RR, there is a well-defined canonical form. This form requires the RR to adhere to the following rules:

1. Every domain name is an FQDN and fully expanded (no compression labels).

2. All uppercase US-ASCII letters in the owner name are replaced by the corresponding lowercase versions.

3. All uppercase US-ASCII letters are replaced by their lowercase versions for any domain names present in the RDATA portion of records with type numbers 2–9, 12, 14, 15, 17, 18, 21, 24, 26, 33, 35, 36, 39, and 38.

4. Any wildcards (*) are not substituted.

5. The TTL is set to its original value as it appeared in the originating authoritative zone or the *Original TTL* field of the covering RRSIG RR.

Note

A number of clarifications and important changes are being applied to the baseline DNSSECbis family of documents. The reader is encouraged to consult the most recent version of [IDDCIN] for further details.

The canonical order of the RRs within an RRset follows essentially the same rule as for owner names but applies to an RR's RDATA contents in canonical form treated as a left-justified byte string.

18.10.2.2 Signed Zones and Zone Cuts

DNSSEC depends on signed zones. Such zones include RRSIG, DNSKEY, and NSEC (or NSEC3) RRs and may contain DS RRs if there is a signed delegation point. Signing makes use of public key cryptography where the public keys are stored in and distributed by the DNS. Figure 18-42 shows an abstract delegation point between a parent and child zone.

In the figure, the parent zone contains its own DNSKEY RR, which provides the public key corresponding to the private key used to sign all authoritative RRsets in the zone using RRSIG RRs (multiple DNSKEYs are possible). A DS RR in the parent provides a hash of one of the DNSKEY RRs in the child's apex. This establishes a chain of trust from the parent to the child. A validating resolver that trusts the parent's DS RR can validate the child's DNSKEY RR and ultimately the RRSIGs and signed RRsets within the child zone. This happens only if the validator has a root of trust that can be connected to the parent's DNSKEY RR.

18.10.2.3 Resolver Operation Example

Given a chain of signed zones and a security-aware validating resolver, we can see how the contents of a DNS response can be validated. In the best case, a zone

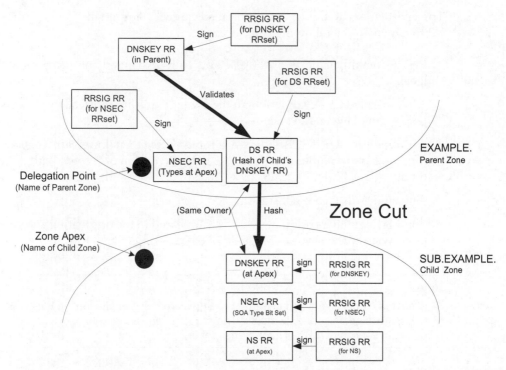

Figure 18-42 A zone cut for an authenticated delegated zone includes a DS RR in the parent containing a hash of the DNSKEY RR(s) in the child. All RRsets are signed with corresponding RRSIG RRs except the delegation NS RRs (and glue records) in the parent. NSEC RRs can be used to verify the types present in the zone and include an SOA RR type indication at the apex in the child zone.

can be reached through a chain of trust from the root zone. ICANN keeps a list of which zones have been enabled for DNSSEC by having DS records present in the root zone and signed DNSKEY RRs [TLD-REPORT].

Assume that we wish to resolve and verify an A RR type for the domain name `www.icann.org`. Proceeding from the root downward, we shall at first require the root's trust anchor (i.e., DNSKEY RRs), DS records for `org.` contained in one of the root name servers, and perhaps RRSIG and NSEC (NSEC3) records. We then repeat the process using the `org.` and `icann.org.` domain names and corresponding DNS servers. We begin with the root zone:

```
Linux% dig @a.root-servers.net. . dnskey +noquestion +nocomments \
+nostats +multiline
;; Truncated, retrying in TCP mode.
; <<>> DiG 9.7.2-P3 <<>> @a.root-servers.net. . dnskey
        +noquestion +nocomments +nostats +multiline
; (1 server found)
;; global options: +cmd
.       86400 IN    DNSKEY         257 3 8 ( AwEAAagAIKl ... ) ; key id = 19036
```

```
.  86400  IN    DNSKEY     256 3 8 ( AwEAAb5gVAz ... ) ; key id = 21639
.  86400  IN    DNSKEY     256 3 8 ( AwEAAcAPhPM ... ) ; key id = 40288
```

Here we can see the trust anchor for the root zone, which constitutes the root of trust for all DNSSEC in the Internet. The first key is a KSK, indicated by the value 257 (*SEP* bit is 1), which is the preferred one used in forming trust chains. The others are marked as ZSKs. Next, we would like to ensure that all the records we have just seen are supposed to be present and have appropriate signatures. The root's RRSIG records of interest can be seen as follows:

```
Linux% dig @a.root-servers.net. . rrsig +noquestion +nocomments \
+nostats +noauthority +noadditional
;; Truncated, retrying in TCP mode.

; <<>> DiG 9.7.2-P3 <<>> @a.root-servers.net. . rrsig +noquestion
       +nocomments +nostats +noauthority +noadditional
; (1 server found)
;; global options: +cmd
. 86400 IN  RRSIG NSEC 8 0 86400 20101228000000 20101220230000
                       40288 . RyoGB1dxxX...
. 86400 IN  RRSIG DNSKEY 8 0 86400 20110105235959 20101221000000
                       19036 . f8bzNvPmHR...

...
```

The RRSIG covering the DNSKEY record uses key tag 19036, which matches the KSK contained in the root zone's DNSKEY RR. The root contains other RRSIG records (for its SOA and NS records), but we are more concerned with the RRSIGs for the DNSKEY and NSEC RRs. Just to be extra-sure that the DNSKEY RR should be present, we can inspect the root's NSEC RR to verify that its type is present:

```
Linux% dig @a.root-servers.net. . nsec +noquestion +nocomments \
+nostats +noauthority +noadditional
; <<>> DiG 9.7.2-P3 <<>> @a.root-servers.net. . nsec +noquestion
       +nocomments +nostats +noauthority +noadditional
; (1 server found)
;; global options: +cmd
.                86400 IN    NSEC  ac. NS SOA RRSIG NSEC DNSKEY
```

This confirms that the root zone officially contains RRset types NS, SOA, RRSIG, NSEC, and DNSKEY, so we are in good shape so far. (Note also that `ac.` is the first TLD in the canonical ordering of the root zone.) Next we need to check out the signatures on the delegation from the root to `org.`. This can be done as follows:

```
Linux% dig @a.root-servers.net. org. rrsig +noquestion +nocomments \
+nostats +noadditional +dnssec
; <<>> DiG 9.7.2-P3 <<>> @a.root-servers.net. org. rrsig +noquestion
       +nocomments +nostats +noadditional +dnssec
```

```
; (1 server found)
;; global options: +cmd
org. 172800      IN    NS    d0.org.afilias-nst.org.
org. 172800      IN    NS    b2.org.afilias-nst.org.
org. 172800      IN    NS    a0.org.afilias-nst.info.
org. 172800      IN    NS    b0.org.afilias-nst.org.
org. 172800      IN    NS    a2.org.afilias-nst.info.
org. 172800      IN    NS    c0.org.afilias-nst.info.
org. 86400       IN    DS    21366 7 2 96EEB2FFD9 ...
org. 86400       IN    DS    21366 7 1 E6C1716CFB ...
org. 86400 IN    RRSIG DS 8 1 86400 20101228000000 20101220230000
                       40288 . jpcJOGclvvlnx9Kvz5 ...
```

The presence of the DS RRset and its associated RRSIG suggests that indeed there is a DNSSEC secured delegation. The RRSIG RR contains the key tag 40288, which refers to the third DNSKEY RR we saw earlier for the root zone (the ZSK). The NS records provide us with the names of the next servers to use in the next steps for our query. We can proceed by repeating the queries we made for the root, but this time using org.. We direct such queries at one of the servers specified in the NS RR for org. in the root:

```
Linux% dig @d0.org.afilias-nst.org. org. dnskey +dnssec +nostats \
+noquestion +multiline
; <<>> DiG 9.7.2-P3 <<>> @d0.org.afilias-nst.org. org. dnskey +dnssec
       +nostats +noquestion +multiline
; (1 server found)
;; global options: +cmd
;; Got answer:
;; ->>HEADER<<- opcode: QUERY, status: NOERROR, id: 8061
;; flags: qr aa rd; QUERY: 1, ANSWER: 6, AUTHORITY: 0, ADDITIONAL: 1
;; WARNING: recursion requested but not available

;; OPT PSEUDOSECTION:
; EDNS: version: 0, flags: do; udp: 4096
;; ANSWER SECTION:
org.   900 IN  DNSKEY   256 3 7 ( AwEAAZTErUF ... ) ; key id = 1743
org.   900 IN  DNSKEY   256 3 7 ( AwEAAazTpnm ... ) ; key id = 43172
org.   900 IN  DNSKEY   257 3 7 ( AwEAAYpYfj3 ... ) ; key id = 21366
org.   900 IN  DNSKEY   257 3 7 ( AwEAAZTjbIO ... ) ; key id = 9795
org.   900 IN  RRSIG DNSKEY 7 1 900 20101231154644
                       20101217144644 21366 org.
                       aIZgEsoJO+Q8ZXM ...
org.   900 IN  RRSIG DNSKEY 7 1 900 20101231154644
                       20101217144644 43172 org. MWWosWBdEmM8CiM ...
```

Here we can see that four DNSKEY RRs exist, two of which are KSKs (value 257) and two of which are ZSKs (value 256). The third one listed (21366) corresponds to the DS RR we found located in the root zone. The RRSIG RRs use this key, plus the ZSK with ID 43172. To verify their presence as legitimate, we can look for NSEC or NSEC3 records that may be present for org.:

```
Linux% dig @d0.org.afilias-nst.org. org. nsec +dnssec +nostats \
+noquestion
; <<>> DiG 9.7.2-P3 <<>> @d0.org.afilias-nst.org. nsec org. +dnssec
      +nostats +noquestion
; (1 server found)
;; global options: +cmd
;; Got answer:
;; ->>HEADER<<- opcode: QUERY, status: NOERROR, id: 61632
;; flags: qr aa rd; QUERY: 1, ANSWER: 0, AUTHORITY: 4, ADDITIONAL: 1
;; WARNING: recursion requested but not available

;; OPT PSEUDOSECTION:
; EDNS: version: 0, flags: do; udp: 4096
;; AUTHORITY SECTION:
h9p7u7tr2u91d0v0ljs9llgidnp90u3h.org. 86400 IN NSEC3 1 1 1
                                       D399EAAB
                                       H9RSFB7FPF2L8HG35CMPC765TDK23RP6
                                       NS SOA RRSIG DNSKEY NSEC3PARAM
h9p7u7tr2u91d0v0ljs9llgidnp90u3h.org. 86400 IN RRSIG NSEC3 7 2
                                       86400 20110105003654
                                       20101221233654
                                       43172 org. eBtna4fok ...
```

Here we see an NSEC3 record with owner name equal to the hashed version of org.. It indicates the presence of a DNSKEY and RRSIG record, as well as NS and NSEC3PARAM records. Following the last type, we can determine the NSEC3 information:

```
Linux% ./dig @a0.org.afilias-nst.info. org. nsec3param +dnssec \
+nostats +noadditional +noauthority +noquestion
; <<>> DiG 9.7.2-P3 <<>> @a0.org.afilias-nst.info. org. nsec3param
      +dnssec +nostats +noadditional +noauthority +noquestion
; (1 server found)
;; global options: +cmd
;; Got answer:
;; ->>HEADER<<- opcode: QUERY, status: NOERROR, id: 38602
;; flags: qr aa rd; QUERY: 1, ANSWER: 2, AUTHORITY: 7, ADDITIONAL: 13
;; WARNING: recursion requested but not available

;; OPT PSEUDOSECTION:
; EDNS: version: 0, flags: do; udp: 4096
;; ANSWER SECTION:
org.             900    IN     NSEC3PARAM 1 0 1 D399EAAB
org.             900    IN     RRSIG NSEC3PARAM 7 1 900 20101231154644
                               20101217144644 43172 org. fS2kFw53e1Y ...
```

We can see that this NSEC3PARAM RR matches the NSEC3 RR because of the match of the value D399EAAB (signature). We can also see that the signature in the RRSIG RR came from the private key associated with DNSKEY having ID 43172. If all signatures match, so far we have a valid chain of trust. To complete the chain, we need information about icann.org.:

```
Linux% dig @a0.org.afilias-nst.info. icann.org. any +dnssec +nostats \
+noadditional
; <<>> DiG 9.7.2-P3 <<>> @a0.org.afilias-nst.info. icann.org. any
        +dnssec +nostats +noadditional
; (1 server found)
;; global options: +cmd
;; Got answer:
;; ->>HEADER<<- opcode: QUERY, status: NOERROR, id: 61234
;; flags: qr rd; QUERY: 1, ANSWER: 0, AUTHORITY: 8, ADDITIONAL: 3
;; WARNING: recursion requested but not available

;; OPT PSEUDOSECTION:
; EDNS: version: 0, flags:; udp: 4096
;; QUESTION SECTION:
;icann.org.              IN      ANY

;; AUTHORITY SECTION:
icann.org.        86400 IN    NS      a.iana-servers.net.
icann.org.        86400 IN    NS      b.iana-servers.org.
icann.org.        86400 IN    NS      c.iana-servers.net.
icann.org.        86400 IN    NS      d.iana-servers.net.
icann.org.        86400 IN    NS      ns.icann.org.
icann.org.        86400 IN    DS      41643 7 1 93358DB ...
icann.org.        86400 IN    DS      41643 7 2 B8AB67D ...
icann.org.        86400 IN    RRSIG DS 7 2 86400 20101231154644
                                      20101217144644 43172 org. cZ1Z30w// ...
```

We can see the DS RR indicating the signed delegation for icann.org. from org.. The RRSIG for the DS RRset is signed based on the ZSK with ID 43172. Using one of the servers present in the NS records, we can look at the final server:

```
Linux% dig @a.iana-servers.net. icann.org. dnskey +dnssec +nostats \
+noquestion +multiline

; <<>> DiG 9.7.2-P3 <<>> @a.iana-servers.net. icann.org. dnskey +dnssec
        +nostats +noquestion +multiline
; (1 server found)
;; global options: +cmd
;; Got answer:
;; ->>HEADER<<- opcode: QUERY, status: NOERROR, id: 22065
;; flags: qr aa rd; QUERY: 1, ANSWER: 5, AUTHORITY: 0, ADDITIONAL: 1
;; WARNING: recursion requested but not available

;; OPT PSEUDOSECTION:
; EDNS: version: 0, flags:; udp: 4096
;; ANSWER SECTION:
icann.org. 3600 IN   DNSKEY 256 3 7 ( AwEAAbDmrVc ... ) ; key id = 41295
icann.org. 3600 IN   DNSKEY 256 3 7 ( AwEAAbgrYZd ... ) ; key id = 55469
icann.org. 3600 IN   DNSKEY 257 3 7 ( AwEAAZuSdr4 ... ) ; key id = 7455
icann.org. 3600 IN   DNSKEY 257 3 7 ( AwEAAcyguBH ... ) ; key id = 41643
icann.org. 3600 IN   RRSIG DNSKEY 7 2 3600 20101229153632
                             20101222042536 41643 icann.org.
                             UxR/5vyOIS ...
```

Here we can see that four DNSKEY RRs exist—two KSKs and two ZSKs. The fourth one listed (41643) corresponds to the DS RR we found located in the org. zone. The RRSIG RR uses this key. To find the answer to our ultimate query, we request the A record:

```
Linux% dig @a.iana-servers.net. www.icann.org. a +dnssec +nostats \
+noquestion  +noauthority +noadditional
; <<>> DiG 9.7.2-P3 <<>> @a.iana-servers.net. www.icann.org. a +dnssec
      +nostats +noquestion +noauthority +noadditional
; (1 server found)
;; global options: +cmd
;; Got answer:
;; ->>HEADER<<- opcode: QUERY, status: NOERROR, id: 56258
;; flags: qr aa rd; QUERY: 1, ANSWER: 2, AUTHORITY: 6, ADDITIONAL: 3
;; WARNING: recursion requested but not available

;; OPT PSEUDOSECTION:
; EDNS: version: 0, flags:; udp: 4096
;; ANSWER SECTION:
www.icann.org.          600   IN    A      192.0.32.7
www.icann.org.          600   IN    RRSIG A 7 3 600 20101229143630
                                    20101222042536 55469 icann.org.
                                    YRhlL/RA ...
```

We have finally reached the end of the chase for the A RR for www.icann. org.. It contains the IP address 192.0.32.7, signed by an RRSIG RR using key ID 55469. This is the key from the fourth DNSKEY RR we saw at the apex of the icann.org. zone. So at this point it would appear that all is order. However, we have not demonstrated that all the signature values are actually correct. To do this validation, the following command may be executed:

```
Linux% dig @a.root-servers.net. www.icann.org. a +sigchase +topdown \
+trusted-key=trusted-keys
```

This command works if the dig program has been compiled with the —DDIG_SIGCHASE=1 compile-time option and the file trusted-keys contains the root's DNSKEY RRset. After many lines of output, we find that it does indicate success. A simpler method for checking the validity can be achieved using a DNS/DNS-SEC-checking Web site such as http://dnsviz.net. Output from such a query is shown in Figure 18-43.

Here we can see a successful validation for the A and AAAA RR types for the domain name www.icann.org.. Each rectangle represents a zone and contains its name and the time it was analyzed. Within each zone are ovals representing elements in the chain of trust, either DNSKEY or DS RRs. Dashed ovals indicate that the keys are not being used for signatures of interest. Arrows between ovals indicate RRSIG or DS digests. Two types of algorithms are represented. In the root

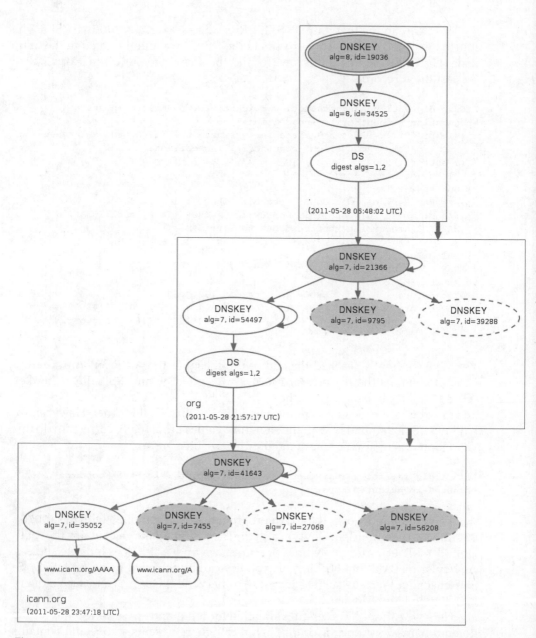

Figure 18-43 A visualization of a DNSSEC chain of trust. Rectangles represent zones. Ovals represent chain
nodes, and shaded ovals have the *SEP* bit set. Arrows indicate valid RRSIG records or DS digests.
The double-circle oval indicates a trust anchor.

zone, "alg = 8" indicates that RSA/SHA-256 [RFC5702] signatures are in use. In other zones, "alg = 7" indicates RSA/SHA-1 that permits the use of NSEC3 records [RFC5155]. For the DS RR in the root zone, "digest algs = 1,2" indicates that SHA-1 [RFC4034] and SHA-256 [RFC4509] are supported.

18.10.3 Transaction Authentication (TSIG, TKEY, and SIG(0))

Some transactions in DNS, such as zone transfers and dynamic updates, could compromise the DNS structure or contents if improperly used. Consequently, they require some form of authentication. Even conventional DNS resolution may require authentication if a resolver expects to depend on validated DNS resolutions but does not implement full DNSSEC processing. With transaction authentication, the exchange between a particular resolver and server (or between servers) is protected. Note, however, that transactional security does not directly protect the contents of the DNS, as does DNSSEC. As a result, DNSSEC and transaction authentication are complementary and can be deployed together. DNSSEC provides data origin authentication and integrity of zone data, while transaction authentication provides integrity and authentication for a particular transaction between a client and a server without checking the correctness of the content being exchanged.

There are two primary methods for authenticating DNS transactions: TSIG and SIG(0). TSIG uses shared keys and SIG(0) uses public/private key pairs. To help ease the burden of deployment, a TKEY RR type can be used to help form keys (e.g., by holding public DH values) for either TSIG or SIG(0). We will begin by discussing TSIG, the more common of the transaction security mechanisms.

18.10.3.1 TSIG

Secret Key Transaction Authentication for DNS or *Transaction Signatures* (TSIG) [RFC2845] adds transactional authentication for DNS exchanges using signatures based on shared secret keys. TSIG makes use of a TSIG pseudo-RR that is computed on demand and is used only to secure a single transaction. The format of the RDATA portion of a TSIG pseudo-RR is shown in Figure 18-44.

The figure shows the format of a TSIG pseudo-RR. Such RRs are sent in the additional data section of a DNS request or response. The original MAC algorithm specified in [RFC2845] was based on HMAC-MD5, but newer GSS-API (Kerberos) [RFC3645] and SHA-1- and SHA-256-based algorithms have since been specified in [RFC4635]; the current list is available at [TSIGALG]. The algorithm names were envisioned to be encoded as domain names (e.g., HMAC-MD5.SIG-ALG. REG.INT), but now most use descriptive strings (e.g., hmac-sha1, hmac-sha256). The 48-bit *Signed Time* field is in UNIX time format (seconds since January 1, 1970, UTC) and gives the time the message contents were signed. This field is covered in the digital signature and is designed to detect and prevent replay attacks. The consequence of using an absolute time here is that peers using TSIG must agree on the time to within the number of seconds specified by the *Fudge* field. The *MAC*

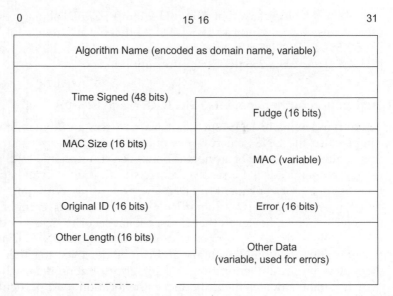

Figure 18-44   The TSIG pseudo-RR RDATA area contains a signature algorithm ID, signature time and time fudge factor, and a MAC. Originally, only an MD5-based signature was used, but now SHA-1- and SHA-2-based signatures have been standardized. TSIG peers must be time-synchronized to within the number of seconds in the *Fudge* field. TSIG RRs are carried in the additional data section of a DNS message.

Size field gives the number of bytes required to contain the MAC in the *MAC* field and depends on the particular MAC algorithm. The *Other Length* field gives the size of the *Other Data* field in bytes, which is used only in carrying error messages.

To see TSIG in action, we can construct a sample zone called `dynzone.` and perform a signed dynamic update. We use the `nsupdate` program supplied with BIND9 to perform the update:

```
Linux% nsupdate
> zone dynzone.
> server 127.0.0.1
> key tsigkey.dynzone. 1234567890abcdef
> update delete two.dynzone.
> send
```

This series of instructions forms a DNS update message signed using TSIG that is sent to the server once the `send` instruction is issued. The request is shown in Figure 18-45.

In this figure, a dynamic DNS update request has been signed using the HMAC-MD5 signature algorithm. The signing key's name is `tsigkey.dynzone.`. The request is to update the zone `dynzone.` by removing the entry `two.dynzone.`. The name of the signature algorithm is HMAC-MD5.SIG-ALG.REG.INT, which is

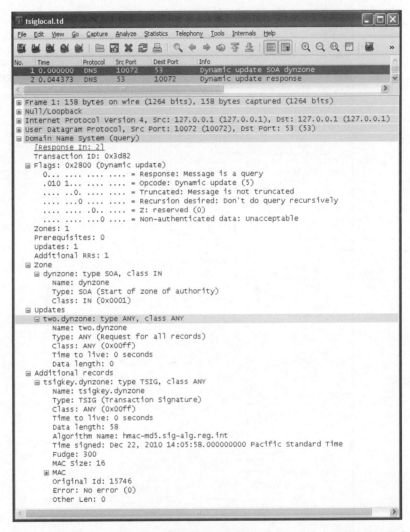

Figure 18-45 A DNS dynamic update signed using TSIG. The request is to delete the RR for two.
dynzone.. The request is signed using the key with name tsigkey.dynzone.. The
signature algorithm is HMAC-MD5, which produces a 128-bit (16-byte) signature.

the only signature algorithm supported by this particular software package. Note
that the *Original ID* field (15746 decimal) matches the value of the *Transaction ID*
field (0x3d82). The response confirms that the update was successful, as shown in
Figure 18-46.

Figure 18-46 show a successful response to a DNS dynamic update request
signed using TSIG. The *Flags* field indicates that a dynamic update response contains no errors. Once again, the TSIG pseudo-RR is contained in the additional
information area.

Figure 18-46   A DNS dynamic update response signed using TSIG. The RRset two.dynzone. has
been successfully removed using dynamic update.

18.10.3.2 SIG(0)

Early versions of DNSSEC included signature (SIG) resource records that correspond to the modern RRSIG RRs discussed previously. However, a particular kind
of SIG RR called SIG(0) [RFC2931] does not cover static records in the DNS but
instead is generated dynamically for transactions. The 0 part of SIG(0) refers to the
length of data within an RR covered by the signature. As a result, SIG(0) records

can in principle be used instead of TSIG RRs to achieve the same result. However, they are implemented in different ways. Most importantly, SIG(0) places its basis of trust in public keys instead of shared keys. SIG(0) appears to be shrinking in popularity in favor of TSIG, so we do not discuss it further.

18.10.3.3 TKEY

The TKEY meta-RR type is intended to simplify the deployment of DNS transaction security such as TSIG and SIG(0) [RFC2930]. To do this, TKEY RRs are dynamically created and sent in the additional information section of DNS requests and responses. They can contain either keys or material used to form keys such as DH public values. It may be useful in local deployments but is not in widespread use.

18.10.4 DNSSEC with DNS64

In Chapter 11 we described DNS64, which translates IPv6 DNS requests into IPv4 DNS requests and can synthesize AAAA records based on A records found in the IPv4 DNS. The scheme is useful for allowing IPv6-only hosts to access IPv4 servers and services. DNS64 works by synthesizing AAAA records. With DNSSEC, however, DNS RRs need to be signed by the signing authority (typically the domain name owner or zone administrator). This presents a challenge: How can DNS64 synthesize RRs if it lacks the keys to produce DNSSEC-compatible signatures? The answer is, essentially, that it does not (see Sections 5.5 and 6.2 in [RFC6147]).

To operate DNS64 in conjunction with DNSSEC, the validation function is performed either in the host (where DNS64 could be implemented) or by the DNS64 device, assuming there exists a secure channel between a stub resolver and the DNS64 acting as a recursive name server. A validating DNS64 is known as *vDNS64*. A vDNS64 interprets the *CD* and *DO* bits in an incoming query. If neither is set, the vDNS64 performs synthesis and validation but does not set the *AD* bit in the (validated) response. If the *DO* bit is set and the *CD* bit is not, the vDNS64 performs validation and synthesis and returns a validated response with the *AD* bit set (which the client presumably interprets as meaning that the returned RRs are authentic). Note that the DNS64 first requests AAAA records on the IPv4 side and synthesizes A records only when it can validate that no AAAA records with the same owner exist. If both the *DO* and *CD* bits are set, the DNS64 may perform validation but not synthesis. In this case, it is presumed that the client will perform validation. This case represents a potential problem because if the client is security-aware but translation-oblivious, the returned RRs will probably not be usable in the IPv6 addressing realm.

18.11 DomainKeys Identified Mail (DKIM)

DomainKeys Identified Mail (DKIM) [RFC5585] is intended to provide an association between an entity and a domain name that can be used to help determine the party responsible for originating a message, especially in the e-mail context.

It provides a method to help authenticate the signer of a message, which is not necessarily the sender, and this can be used in helping to fight spam at the e-mail distribution level (i.e., between mail agents). This is accomplished by adding a *DKIM-Signature* field to the basic Internet message format [RFC5322]. This field contains a digital signature of the header and body of the message. DKIM replaces an earlier standard called DomainKeys, which uses the *DomainKey-Signature* field.

18.11.1 DKIM Signatures

To produce a digital signature for a message, a *Signing Domain Identifier* (SDID) uses RSA/SHA-1 or RSA/SHA-256 and an associated private key. SDIDs are domain names from the DNS and are used to retrieve public keys stored as TXT RRs. A DKIM signature is encoded as a message header field using Base64 (such as PEM) that signs an explicitly listed set of message fields and the message body. When receiving an e-mail, for example, a mail transfer agent uses the SDID to perform a DNS query to find the corresponding public key, which it then uses to verify the signature. This avoids requiring a PKI. The owning domain name is constructed from the domain itself along with the *selector* (public key selector). For example, the public key for the selector `key35` in domain `example.com` would be a TXT RR owned by `key35._domainkey.example.com`.

The *DKIM-Signature* field [RFC6376] is added to a message header and may contain several subfields (see [DKPARAMS] for the complete list). The operation of DKIM is conceptually similar to the DNS Sender Policy Framework (SPF; see Chapter 11) but is stronger because of the cryptographic digital signature. DKIM and SPF can be used together.

DKIM-enabled domains may elect to participate in *Author Domain Signing Practices* (ADSP) [RFC5617]. ADSP involves the creation of a machine-readable *signing practices statement* for a domain. Such records are placed in the DNS using TXT RRs with owner name equal to `_adsp._domainkey.domain.`. At present ADSP records are simple and indicate only how the authoring domain uses DKIM signatures. The values may be `unknown`, `all`, or `discardable`. These are really hints as to what a receiving agent might do with a received message. The value `unknown` indicates no particular statement, `all` indicates that the author signs all messages but unsigned ones may still be worthwhile, and `discardable` indicates that unsigned messages should be considered subject to discarding. `discardable` is the most stringent level.

18.11.2 Example

To get an idea of how a DKIM signature appears in an e-mail, we can simply extract the *DKIM-Signature* field from an e-mail message generated from a large e-mail provider such as Google's Gmail:

```
DKIM-Signature: v=1; a=rsa-sha256; c=relaxed/relaxed;
        d=gmail.com; s=gamma;
```

```
h=domainkey-signature:mime-version:received:
   sender:received:date
  :x-google-sender-auth:message-id:subject:from:to:content-type;
bh=PU2XIErWsXvhvt1W96ntPWZ2VImjVZ3vBY2T/A+wA3A=;
b=WneQe6kpeu/BfMfa2RS1AllTvYKfIKmoQRXNc
   IQJDIVoE38+fGDaj0uhNm8vXp/8kJ
   I8HqtkV4/P6/QVPMN+/5bS5dsnlhz0S/YoP
   bZx0Lt2bD67G4HPsvm6eLsaIC9rQECUSL
   MdaTBK3BgFhYo3nenq3+8GxTe9I+zBcqWAVPU=
```

This indicates a version 1 signature and digest algorithm of SHA-256 signed using RSA. The header and body *canonicalization algorithms* are both "relaxed," as shown by the `c=` field. Canonicalization algorithms are used to rewrite messages in a consistent form. The current options are "simple" (the default), which does not alter the text, and "relaxed," which can rewrite the input in common ways such as altering whitespace and wrapping long header lines. The selector (`s=`) is called `gamma` and the domain (`d=`) is `gmail.com`. We shall use these later to retrieve the appropriate public key. The header fields used in computing the signature (indicated by `h=`) include `domainkey-signature` (predecessor to DKIM), version of MIME, `received`, sender date, `x-google-sender-auth`, `message-id`, `subject`, `from`, and `content-type`. The `bh=` subfield indicates the hash value on the message body expressed in Base64. The `b=` value contains the RSA signature on the hash of the headers listed in the `h=` subfield.

To retrieve the public key to validate the signature, we can form the following query:

```
Linux% dig gamma._domainkey.gmail.com. txt +nostats +noquestion
; <<>> DiG 9.7.2-P3 <<>> gamma._domainkey.gmail.com. txt
       +nostats +noquestion
;; global options: +cmd
;; Got answer:
;; ->>HEADER<<- opcode: QUERY, status: NOERROR, id: 17372
;; flags: qr rd ra; QUERY: 1, ANSWER: 1, AUTHORITY: 0, ADDITIONAL: 0

;; ANSWER SECTION:
gamma._domainkey.gmail.com. 296     IN    TXT    "k=rsa\; t=y\; p=MIGfMA0GCS
qGSIb3DQEBAQUAA4GNADCBiQKBgQDIhyR3oItOy22ZOaBrIVe9m/iME3RqOJeasANSpg2YTHTYV
+Xtp4xwf5gTjCmHQEMOs0qYu0FYiNQPQogJ2t0Mfx9zNu06rfRBDjiIU9tpx2T+NGlWZ8qhbiLo
5By8apJavLyqTLavyPSrvsx0B3YzC63T4Age2CDqZYA+OwSMWQIDAQAB"
```

This result indicates that the key is an RSA public key. The `t=y` entry denotes that the domain is testing DKIM, meaning that the results of any DKIM validation should not ultimately affect the message delivery process. To see an example of an ADSP, we can execute the following command:

```
Linux% host -t txt _adsp._domainkey.paypal.com.
_adsp._domainkey.paypal.com descriptive text "dkim=discardable"
```

Here we can see that Paypal has elected to use the most stringent DKIM signing policy, suggesting that messages failing DKIM validation should be subject to being discarded. The use of ADSP statements at present is fairly rare because of the wide variety of e-mail systems and the ways that various mail agents rewrite messages.

18.12 Attacks on Security Protocols

Attacks on security protocols are somewhat different from the attacks on protocols we have seen in other chapters. Attacks discussed in other chapters tend to compromise some protocol that was never really designed with security in mind by taking advantage of some design or implementation flaw. Attacks against security protocols not only take these forms but may also involve cryptographic attacks that somehow subvert the mathematical basis upon which the security depends. Attacks can be successful against poor algorithms, weak or too-short keys, or poor combinations of various components that render an otherwise secure system much weaker. (A classic and fascinating example can be seen in the cryptanalysis of the VENONA system [VENONA].)

To understand some of the types of attacks targeting security protocols, we will begin from the lowest layer and work our way up. A number of attacks have been waged against 802.11 and EAP. Early security in 802.11 (e.g., WEP and WPA-TKIP) has been shown to be easily compromised cryptographically [TWP07] [OM09], and WPA2-AES is believed to be substantially more resilient, although use of poorly selected pre-shared keys (PSKs) can represent a significant vulnerability to dictionary attacks.

EAP does not have its own authentication method but can inherit vulnerabilities of the authentication methods on which it depends. Once again, systems based on EAP using keys derived from user passwords (e.g., EAP-GSS, EAP-LEAP, EAP-SIM) are often vulnerable to dictionary attacks. 802.1X/EAP is vulnerable to MITM attacks involving tunneled authentication protocols as discussed in [ANN02]. The problem relates to deriving a session key after only one side of a two-party connection has been authenticated. For example, if a server authenticates to a client and this exchange is used as the basis to form a tunnel secured by a derived session key where another protocol that authenticates in the reverse direction operates inside, a MITM attack involving impersonation of the legitimate client becomes possible.

A number of attacks have been published against IPsec, including a class of attacks that exploit the use of encryption without integrity protection [PY06], a configuration option supported but discouraged by the IPsec documentation. In essence, the ability to modify the ciphertext undetected using a *bit flipping attack* can cause encrypted datagrams to be decrypted into datagrams that have been corrupted in predictable ways. For example, a tunnel mode ESP datagram with its bits flipped appropriately may decrypt to a datagram with an artificially increased *Internet Header Length* (*IHL*) field that causes the payload to be processed as (invalid) IP options, ultimately generating an ICMP message that may be of use to an attacker.

At the transport layer, SSL 2.0 was shown to be vulnerable to a *cipher suite rollback attack*, in which a MITM could cause each end of an SSL connection to conclude that the peer is capable of only weak encryption. Doing so causes the peers to adopt an insecure cipher suite, which the attacker can exploit. A more sophisticated attack on SSL/TLS took advantage of the order of operations performed at a receiver: decrypt, remove padding, and check MAC. If the padding length or MAC is incorrect, an SSL error message is generated. By observing the timing of these error messages, it was possible to create a *padding oracle* [CHVV03] to recover plaintext from OpenSSH. A padding oracle tells whether the plaintext used to create a ciphertext had a valid amount of padding. As mentioned previously, a more recent attack (on TLS 1.2) involves a MITM attack whereby a prefix of arbitrary length is injected into a TLS association, which is then renegotiated (but continued) when a legitimate client arrives [RD09]. The solution involves binding the previous channel parameters to the subsequent channel parameters using a TLS extension. The issue of channel binding and security is covered more broadly in [RFC5056].

Securing the DNS has been a long time coming, but the importance was underscored by the Kaminsky cache poisoning attack we described in Chapter 11. One of the original problems was the *enumeration attack* made available (actually required) by the use of NSEC records and countered by the use of NSEC3 records, if used properly [BM09]. At the end of 2009, Dan Bernstein mentioned a number of problems with DNSSEC in his keynote talk at a workshop [B09]: it can be used as a basis for amplification of DoS attacks, it leaks zone data even with NSEC3, its implementations contain exploitable bugs, signatures cannot be revoked, the cryptography may be subject to cryptanalysis, and some NS and A records pose vulnerabilities. At the time of writing, the root zone has been signed only recently, and few organizations have fully adopted DNSSEC. It is therefore likely that a variety of improvements and modifications will be implemented in the years to come.

18.13 Summary

The subject of security is broad and interesting, and we have only scraped the surface in this chapter. We desire several important properties of communication security, and typically these consist of some combination of confidentiality, authentication, integrity, and nonrepudiation. Cryptography is our most important tool for achieving these information security properties. It involves a set of algorithms and keys. The two most important forms are symmetric or "secret key" cryptography, which has good computational performance but requires keys to be kept secret, and public key (asymmetric key) cryptography whereby each principal has a key pair and one key is made public. Public key cryptography supports both authentication and confidentiality and can be combined with symmetric key cryptography for better performance. Other algorithms that involve mathematics closely related to cryptography include Diffie-Hellman key agreement used to establish symmetric keys, pseudorandom functions for selecting random components to form keys, and MACs used to check message integrity. Protocols that use random nonces attempt to ensure freshness and resist replay attacks by requiring queries and responses to hold a common recently generated value. Salt (in the cryptographic sense) is used to perturb algorithms or input to algorithms in order to make dictionary attacks more difficult to mount.

When relying on a public key, we ordinarily want the public key to be signed or authenticated by some entity or group that we trust. A public key infrastructure or PKI that involves one or more certificate authorities is commonly used for this purpose, but web of trust models are also available. The most common format for holding PKI public keys (and other material) is based on the ITU-T X.509 standard for PKI and certificates. Certificates are usually signed recursively forming a tree, culminating at some top-level root of trust or trust anchor. To ensure that the trust chain is in place, certificates must be validated to ensure that the trust chain is unbroken and each chain element has not been revoked. Certificate status can be evaluated using widely distributed certificate revocation lists (CRLs) or using an online protocol such as OCSP. The entire certificate validation process can also be delegated to another party using SCVP, a protocol developed for this specific purpose.

There are a variety of file formats for holding certificates and keys. The DER or CER format is a binary encoding based on ASN.1. The PEM format expresses the DER encoding in ASCII, so such files are easily edited and inspected. The PKCS#12 (successor to Microsoft's PFX) format can hold both certificates and private keys and is ordinarily encrypted for protection of the private key material. A variety of programs such as `openssl` are capable of converting between formats.

There are security protocols at every protocol layer, and some between layers. Working from layer 2 up, some link technologies include their own encryption and authentication protocols, although these are not ordinarily considered TCP/IP protocols. In TCP/IP, EAP is used to establish authentication with a wide variety of mechanisms such as machine certificates, user certificates, smart cards, passwords, and so on. EAP is most often used in enterprise settings that have a backend authorization or AAA server. EAP can also be used for authentication in other protocols such as IPsec.

IPsec is a collection of protocols that provide security at layer 3: IKE, AH, and ESP. IKE establishes and manages security association between two parties. Security associations can involve authentication (AH) or encryption (ESP) and can operate in either transport or tunnel mode. In transport mode, the IP header is modified for authentication or encryption, while in tunnel mode an IP datagram in its entirety is placed inside a new IP datagram. ESP is the most popular. All IPsec protocols can use different algorithms and parameters (cryptographic suites) for encryption, integrity protection, DH key agreement, and authentication.

Moving up the stack, transport-layer security (current version TLS 1.2) protects information moved between applications. It has its own internal layering consisting of a record-layer protocol and three handshaking protocols called the Cipher Change protocol, Alert protocol, and Handshake protocol. In addition, the Record protocol supports application data. The record layer is responsible for encrypting and integrity-protecting data based on parameters supplied by the Handshake protocol. The Cipher Change protocol is invoked to change from a previously set-up pending protocol state to an active protocol state. The Alert protocol indicates errors or connection problems. TLS with TCP/IP is the most widely used security protocol and supports encrypted Web browser connections (HTTPS). A variant of TLS called DTLS adapts TLS for use with datagrams and protocols such as UDP and DCCP.

To help secure host names and the Web better, DNSSEC is targeted at providing security for the DNS. On July 15, 2010, the Internet's signed root zone was put into operation, satisfying a prerequisite for worldwide deployment. DNS-SEC works by employing several new resource records in the DNS: DNSKEY, DS, NSEC/NSEC3/NSEC3PARAM, and RRSIG. The first two hold and refer to public keys used for signing the structure and contents of a zone. The NSEC or NSEC3/NSEC3PARAM records help provide a canonical ordering of names and list of types present for a domain name. This allows a query to reliably determine the nonexistence of a domain name or presence of a particular type for a particular domain name. RRSIG records hold signatures on other records, and for a zone to be signed, all authoritative RRs within the zone must have associated RRSIG RRs. Once set up, security of DNS queries is checked by a validating resolver or name server that requires a trust anchor. Such systems check to ensure that digital signatures match the public keys supplied by the DNS. This allows for errors to be generated when some record is found to be inconsistent, and it is hoped it can thwart domain name hijacking attacks in which attackers masquerade as legitimate hosts. In some cases, DNS transactions are also secured. The TSIG and SIG(0) protocols provide a form of channel authentication, but only in the scope of DNS transactions. These protocols are used for transactions such as DNS dynamic updates and zone transfers.

Attacks on security protocols include not only the common exploitation of implementation bugs and insecure designs but also mathematical compromises and "side channel" attacks that are used to discover secret information (e.g., bits of keys). Over the years it has become clear that flexibility is needed in the strength of the cryptography used to secure communications, so most of the protocols we have discussed provide for cryptographic suites that can evolve as computational power improves and additional experience is gained. Many seemingly secure protocols, even those that have received extensive scrutiny by experts, have fallen prey to an energetic set of analysts who seek exploitable flaws, especially when MITM and other active attacks are possible. Extreme care is required in designing new security protocols and operating existing protocols in a secure fashion.

18.14 References

[802.1X-2010] "IEEE Standard for Port-Based Network Access Control," IEEE Std 802.1X-2010, Feb. 2010.

[AKNT04] Y. Amir, Y. Kim, C. Nita-Rotaru, and G. Tsudik, "On the Performance of Group Key Agreement Protocols," *ACM Transactions on Information and System Security*, 7(3), Aug. 2004.

[ANN02] N. Asokan, V. Niemi, and K. Nyberg, "Man-in-the-Middle in Tunneled Authentication Protocols (Extended Abstract)," *Proc. 11th Security Protocols Workshop/LNCS 3364* (Springer, 2003).

[B06] M. Bellare, "New Proofs for NMAC and HMAC: Security without Collision-Resistance" (preliminary version in *CRYPTO 06*), June 2006.

[B09] D. Bernstein, "Breaking DNSSEC," keynote talk at Workshop on Offensive Technologies (WOOT), Aug. 2009.

[BCK96] M. Bellare, R. Canetti, and H. Krawczyk, "Keying Hash Functions for Message Authentication" (abridged version in *CRYPTO 96/LNCS 1109*), June 1996.

[BM09] J. Bau and J. Mitchell, "A Security Evaluation of DNSSEC with NSEC3," Network and Distributed System Security Symposium (NDSS), Feb.–Mar. 2010.

[BOPSW09] R. Biddle et al., "Browser Interfaces and Extended Validation SSL Certificates: An Empirical Study," *Proc. ACM Cloud Security Workshop*, Nov. 2009.

[CABF09] CA/Browser Forum, "Guidelines for the Issuance and Management of Extended Validation Certificates (v1.2)," 2009, http://www.cabforum.org/Guidelines_v1_2.pdf

[CHP] National Institute of Standards and Technology, Cryptographic Hash Project, *Computer Security Division—Computer Security Resource Center*, http://csrc.nist.gov/groups/ST/hash

[CHVV03] B. Canvel, A. Hiltgen, S. Vaudenay, and M. Vuagnoux, "Password Interception in a SSL/TLS Channel," *CRYPTO 2003/LNCS 2729*.

[DH76] W. Diffie and M. Hellman, "New Directions in Cryptography," *IEEE Transactions on Information Theory*, IT-22, Nov. 1976.

[DKPARAMS] http://www.iana.org/assignments/dkim-parameters

[DNSSECALG] http://www.iana.org/assignments/dns-sec-alg-numbers

[DOW92] W. Diffie, P. Oorschot, and M. Wiener, "Authentication and uthenticated Key Exchanges," *Designs, Codes and Cryptography*, 2, June 1992.

[DSRRTYPES] http://www.iana.org/assignments/ds-rr-types

[FIPS186-3] National Institute for Standards and Technology, "Digital Signature Standard (DSS)," FIPS PUB 186-3, June 2009.

[FIPS197] National Institute for Standards and Technology, "Advanced Encryption Standard (AES)," FIPS PUB 197, Nov. 2001.

[FIPS198] National Institute for Standards and Technology, "The Keyed-Hash Message Authentication Code (HMAC)," FIPS PUB 198, Mar. 2002.

[FIPS800-38B] National Institute for Standards and Technology, "Recommendation for Block Cipher Modes of Operation: The CMAC Mode for Authentication," NIST Special Publication 800-38B, May 2005.

[GGM86] O. Goldreich, S. Goldwasser, and S. Micali, "How to Construct Random Functions," *Journal of the ACM*, 33(4), Oct. 1986.

[IDDCIN] S. Weiler and D. Blacka, "Clarifications and Implementation Notes for DNSSECbis," Internet draft-ietf-dnsext-dnssec-bis-updates, work in progress, July 2011.

[IDDS2] B. Dickson, "DNSSEC Delegation Signature with Canonical Signer Name," Internet draft-dickson-dnsext-ds2 (expired), work in progress, Nov. 2010.

[IDDTLS] E. Rescorla and N. Modadugu, "Datagram Transport Layer Security Version 1.2," Internet draft-ietf-tls-rfc4347-bis, work in progress, July 2011.

[IEAP] http://www.iana.org/assignments/eap-numbers

[IK03] T. Iwata and K. Kurosawa, "OMAC: One-Key CBC MAC," *Proc. Fast Software Encryption*, Mar. 2003.

[IKEPARAMS] http://www.iana.org/assignments/ikev2-parameters

[IPANA] http://www.iana.org/assignments/pana-parameters

[ITUOID] http://www.itu.int/ITU-T/asn1

[IWESP] http://www.iana.org/assignments/wesp-flags

[K87] N. Koblitz, "Elliptic Curve Cryptosystems," *Mathematics of Computation*, 48, 1987.

[L01] C. Landwehr, "Computer Security," Springer-Verlag Online, July 2001.

[M85] V. Miller, "Uses of Elliptic Curves in Cryptography," *Advances in Cryptology: CRYPTO '85*, Lecture Notes in Computer Science, Volume 218 (Springer-Verlag, 1986).

[MSK09] S. McClure, J. Scambray, and G. Kurtz, *Hacking Exposed, Sixth Edition* (McGraw-Hill, 2009).

[MW99] U. Maurer and S. Wolf, "The Relationship between Breaking the Diffie-Hellman Protocol and Computing Discrete Logarithms," *Siam Journal on Computing*, 28(5), 1999.

[NAZ00] Network Associates and P. Zimmermann, *Introduction to Cryptography*, Part of PGP 7.0 Documentation, available from http://www.pgpi.org/doc/guide/7.0/en

[NIST800-38B] National Institute for Standards and Technology, "Recommendation for Block Cipher Modes of Operation: Galois/Counter Mode (GCM) and GMAC," NIST Special Publication 800-38D, Nov. 2005.

[NSEC3PARAMS] http://www.iana.org/assignments/dnssec-nsec3-parameters

[OM09] T. Ohigashi and M. Morii, "A Practical Message Falsification Attack on WPA," Joint Workshop on Information Security, Aug. 2009.

[PY06] K. Paterson and A. Yau, "Cryptography in Theory and Practice: The Case of Encryption in IPsec," *EUROCRYPT 2006/LNCS 4004*.

[RD09] M. Ray and S. Dispensa, "Renegotiating TLS," PhoneFactor Technical Report, Nov. 2009.

[RFC1321] R. Rivest, "The MD5 Message-Digest Algorithm," Internet RFC 1321 (informational), Apr. 1992.

[RFC2104] H. Krawczyk, M. Bellare, and R. Canetti, "HMAC: Keyed-Hashing for Message Authentication," Internet RFC 2104 (informational), Feb. 1997.

[RFC2403] C. Madson and R. Glenn, "The Use of HMAC-MD5-96 within ESP and AH," Internet RFC 2403, Nov. 1998.

[RFC2404] C. Madson and R. Glenn, "The Use of HMAC-SHA-1-96 within ESP and AH," Internet RFC 2404, Nov. 1998.

[RFC2409] D. Harkins and D. Carrel, "The Internet Key Exchange (IKE)," Internet RFC 2409 (obsolete), Nov. 1998.

[RFC2410] R. Glenn and S. Kent, "The NULL Encryption Algorithm and Its Use with IPsec," Internet RFC 2410, Nov. 1998.

[RFC2451] R. Pereira and R. Adams, "The ESP CBC-Mode Cipher Algorithms," Internet RFC 2451, Nov. 1998.

[RFC2560] M. Myers, R. Ankney, A. Malpani, S. Galperin, and C. Adams, "X.509 Internet Public Key Infrastructure Online Certificate Status Protocol—OCSP," Internet RFC 2560, June 1999.

[RFC2631] E. Rescorla, "Diffie-Hellman Key Agreement Method," Internet RFC 2631, June 1999.

[RFC2671] P. Vixie, "Extension Mechanisms for DNS (EDNS0)," Internet RFC 2671, Aug. 1999.

[RFC2845] P. Vixie, O. Gudmundsson, D. Eastlake 3rd, and B. Wellington, "Secret Key Transaction Authentication for DNS (TSIG)," Internet RFC 2845, May 2000.

[RFC2865] C. Rigney, S. Willens, A. Rubens, and W. Simpson, "Remote Authentication Dial In User Service (RADIUS)," Internet RFC 2865, June 2000.

[RFC2930] D. Eastlake 3rd, "Secret Key Establishment for DNS (TKEY RR)," Internet RFC 2930, Sept. 2000.

[RFC2931] D. Eastlake 3rd, "DNS Request and Transaction Signatures (SIG(0)s)," Internet RFC 2931, Sept. 2000.

[RFC3162] B. Aboba, G. Zorn, and D. Mitton, "RADIUS and IPv6," Internet RFC 3162, Aug. 2001.

[RFC3173] A. Shacham, B. Monsour, R. Pereira, and M. Thomas, "IP Payload Compression Protocol (IPComp)," Internet RFC 3173, Sept. 2001.

[RFC3193] B. Patel, B. Aboba, W. Dixon, G. Zorn, and S. Booth, "Securing L2TP Using IPsec," Internet RFC 3193, Nov. 2001.

[RFC3225] D. Conrad, "Indicating Resolver Support of DNSSEC," Internet RFC 3225, Dec. 2001.

[RFC3447] J. Jonsson and B. Kaliski, "Public-Key Cryptography Standards (PKCS) #1: RSA Cryptography Specifications Version 2.1," Internet RFC 3447 (informational), Feb. 2003.

[RFC3526] T. Kivinen and M. Kojo, "More Modular Exponential (MODP) Diffie-Hellman Groups for Internet Key Exchange (IKE)," Internet RFC 3526, May 2003.

[RFC3547] M. Baugher, B. Weis, T. Hardjono, and H. Harney, "The Group Domain of Interpretation," Internet RFC 3547, July 2003.

[RFC3566] S. Frankel and H. Herbert, "The AES-XCBC-MAC-96 Algorithm and Its Use with IPsec," Internet RFC 3566, Sept. 2003.

[RFC3588] P. Calhoun, J. Loughney, E. Guttman, G. Zorn, and J. Arkko, "Diameter Base Protocol," Internet RFC 3588, Sept. 2003.

[RFC3602] S. Frankel, R. Glenn, and S. Kelly, "The AES-CBC Cipher Algorithm and Its Use with IPsec," Internet RFC 3602, Sept. 2003.

[RFC3645] S. Kwan, P. Garg, J. Gilroy, L. Esibov, J. Westhead, and R. Hall, "Generic Security Service Algorithm for Secret Key Transaction Authentication for DNS (GSS-TSIG)," Internet RFC 3645, Oct. 2003.

[RFC3686] R. Housley, "Using Advanced Encryption Standard (AES) Counter Mode with IPsec Encapsulating Security Payload (ESP)," Internet RFC 3686, Jan. 2004.

[RFC3713] M. Matsui, J. Nakajima, and S. Moriai, "A Description of the Camellia Encryption Algorithm," Internet RFC 3713 (informational), Apr. 2004.

[RFC3715] B. Aboba and W. Dixon, "IPsec-Network Address Translation (NAT) Compatibility Requirements," Internet RFC 3715 (informational), Mar. 2001.

[RFC3740] T. Hardjono and B. Weis, "The Multicast Group Security Architecture," Internet RFC 3740 (informational), Mar. 2004.

[RFC3748] B. Aboba, L. Blunk, J. Vollbrecht, J. Carlson, and H. Levkowetz, ed., "Extensible Authentication Protocol (EAP)," June 2004.

[RFC3749] S. Hollenbeck, "Transport Layer Security Protocol Compression Methods," Internet RFC 3749, May 2004.

[RFC3947] T. Kivinen, B. Swander, A. Huttunen, and V. Volpe, "Negotiation of NAT-Traversal in the IKE," Internet RFC 3947, Jan. 2005.

[RFC3948] A. Huttunen, B. Swander, V. Volpe, L. DiBurro, and M. Stenberg, "UDP Encapsulation of IPsec ESP Packets," Internet RFC 3948, Jan. 2005.

[RFC4016] M. Parthasarathy, "Protocol for Carrying Authentication and Network Access (PANA) Threat Analysis and Security Requirements," Internet RFC 4016 (informational), Mar. 2005.

[RFC4033] R. Arends, R. Austein, M. Larson, D. Massey, and S. Rose, "DNS Security Introduction and Requirements," Internet RFC 4033, Mar. 2005.

[RFC4034] R. Arends, R. Austein, M. Larson, D. Massey, and S. Rose, "Resource Records for the DNS Security Extensions," Internet RFC 4034, Mar. 2005.

[RFC4035] R. Arends, R. Austein, M. Larson, D. Massey, and S. Rose, "Protocol Modifications for the DNS Security Extensions," Internet RFC 4035, Mar. 2005.

[RFC4058] A. Yegin, ed., Y. Ohba, R. Penno, G. Tsirtsis, and C. Wang, "Protocol for Carrying Authentication for Network Access (PANA) Requirements," Internet RFC 4058 (informational), May 2005.

[RFC4086] D. Eastlake 3rd, J. Schiller, and S. Crocker, "Randomness Requirements for Security," Internet RFC 4086/BCP 0106, June 2005.

[RFC4120] C. Neuman, T. Yu, S. Hartman, and K. Raeburn, "The Kerberos Network Authentication Service (V5)," Internet RFC 4120, July 2005.

[RFC4251] T. Ylonen and C. Lonvick, ed., "The Secure Shell (SSH) Protocol Architecture," Internet RFC 4251, Jan. 2006.

[RFC4301] S. Kent and K. Seo, "Security Architecture for the Internet Protocol," Internet RFC 4301, Dec. 2005.

[RFC4302] S. Kent, "IP Authentication Header," Internet RFC 4302, Dec. 2005.

[RFC4303] S. Kent, "IP Encapsulating Security Payload (ESP)," Internet RFC 4303, Dec. 2005.

[RFC4307] J. Schiller, "Cryptographic Algorithms for Use in the Internet Key Exchange Version 2 (IKEv2)," Internet RFC 4307, Dec. 2005.

[RFC4309] R. Housley, "Using Advanced Encryption Standard (AES) CCM Mode with IPsec Encapsulating Security Payload (ESP)," Internet RFC 4309, Dec. 2005.

[RFC4346] T. Dierks and E. Rescorla, "The Transport Layer Security (TLS) Protocol Version 1.1," Internet RFC 4346 (obsolete), Apr. 2006.

[RFC4347] E. Rescorla and N. Modadugu, "Datagram Transport Layer Security," Internet RFC 4347, Apr. 2006.

[RFC4398] S. Josefsson, "Storing Certificates in the Domain Name System (DNS)," Internet RFC 4398, Mar. 2006.

[RFC4431] M. Andrews and S. Weiler, "The DNSSEC Lookaside Validation (DLV) DNS Resource Record," Internet RFC 4431 (informational), Feb. 2006.

[RFC4434] P. Hoffman, "The AES-XCBC-PRF-128 Algorithm for the Internet Key Exchange Protocol (IKE)," Internet RFC 4434, Feb. 2006.

[RFC4492] S. Blake-Wilson, N. Bolyard, V. Gupta, C. Hawk, and B. Moeller, "Elliptic Curve Cryptography (ECC) Cipher Suites for Transport Layer Security (TLS)," Internet RFC 4492 (informational), May 2006.

[RFC4493] JH. Song, R. Poovendran, J. Lee, and T. Iwata, "The AES-CMAC Algorithm," Internet RFC 4493 (informational), June 2006.

[RFC4509] W. Hardaker, "Use of SHA-256 in DNSSEC Delegation Signer (DS) Resource Records (RRs)," Internet RFC 4509, May 2006.

[RFC4535] H. Harney, U. Meth, A. Colegrove, and G. Gross, "GSAKMP: Group Secure Association Key Management Protocol," Internet RFC 4535, June 2006.

[RFC4555] P. Eronen, "IKEv2 Mobility and Multihoming Protocol (MOBIKE)," Internet RFC 4555, June 2006.

[RFC4615] J. Song, R. Poovendran, J. Lee, and T. Iwata, "The Advanced Encryption Standard-Cipher-Based Message Authentication Code-Pseudo-Random Function-128 (AES-CMAC-PRF-128) Algorithm for the Internet Key Exchange Protocol (IKE)," Internet RFC 4615, Aug. 2006.

[RFC4635] D. Eastlake 3rd, "HMAC SHA (Hashed Message Authentication Code, Secure Hash Algorithm) TSIG Algorithm Identifiers," Internet RFC 4635, Aug. 2006.

[RFC4681] S. Santesson, A. Medvinsky, and J. Ball, "TLS User Mapping Extension," Internet RFC 4681, Oct. 2006.

[RFC4739] P. Eronen and J. Korhonen, "Multiple Authentication Exchanges in the Internet Key Exchange (IKEv2) Protocol," Internet RFC 4739 (experimental), Nov. 2006.

[RFC4754] D. Fu and J. Solinas, "IKE and IKEv2 Authentication Using the Elliptic Curve Digital Signature Algorithm (ECDSA)," Internet RFC 4754, Jan. 2007.

[RFC4835] V. Manral, "Cryptographic Algorithm Implementation Requirements for Encapsulating Security Payload (ESP) and Authentication Header (AH)," Internet RFC 4835, Apr. 2007.

[RFC4851] N. Cam-Winget, D. McGrew, J. Salowey, and H. Zhou, "The Flexible Authentication via Secure Tunneling Extensible Authentication Protocol Method (EAP-FAST)," Internet RFC 4851 (informational), May 2007.

[RFC4877] V. Devarapalli and F. Dupont, "Mobile IPv6 Operation with IKEv2 and the Revised IPsec Architecture," Internet RFC 4877, Apr. 2007.

[RFC4880] J. Callas, L. Donnerhacke, H. Finney, D. Shaw, and R. Thayer, "Open-PGP Message Format," Internet RFC 4880, Nov. 2007.

[RFC5011] M. StJohns, "Automated Updates of DNS Security (DNSSEC) Trust Anchors," Internet RFC 5011, Sep. 2007.

[RFC5054] D. Taylor, T. Wu, N. Mavrogiannopoulos, and T. Perrin, "Using the Secure Remote Password (SRP) Protocol for TLS Authentication," Internet RFC 5054 (informational), Nov. 2007.

[RFC5055] T. Freeman, R. Housley, A. Malpani, D. Cooper, and W. Polk, "Server-Based Certificate Validation Protocol (SCVP)," Internet RFC 5055, Dec. 2007.

[RFC5056] N. Williams, "On the Use of Channel Bindings to Secure Channels," Internet RFC 5056, Nov. 2007.

[RFC5077] J. Salowey, H. Zhou, P. Eronen, and H. Tschofenig, "Transport Layer Security (TLS) Session Resumption without Server-Side State," Internet RFC 5077, Jan. 2008.

[RFC5106] H. Tschofenig, D. Kroeselberg, A. Pashalidis, Y. Ohba, and F. Bersani, "The Extensible Authentication Protocol-Internet Key Exchange Protocol Version 2 (EAP-IKEv2) Method," Internet RFC 5106 (experimental), Feb. 2008.

[RFC5114] M. Lepinski and S. Kent, "Additional Diffie-Hellman Groups for Use with IETF Standards," Internet RFC 5114 (informational), Jan. 2008.

[RFC5116] D. McGrew, "An Interface and Algorithms for Authenticated Encryption," Internet RFC 5116, Jan. 2008.

[RFC5155] B. Laurie, G. Sisson, R. Arends, and D. Blacka, "DNS Security (DNSSEC) Hashed Authenticated Denial of Existence," Internet RFC 5155, Mar. 2008.

[RFC5191] D. Forsberg, Y. Ohba, ed., B. Patil, H. Tschofenig, and A. Yegin, "Protocol for Carrying Authentication for Network Access (PANA)," Internet RFC 5191, May 2008.

[RFC5193] P. Jayaraman, R. Lopez, Y. Ohba, ed., M. Parthasarathy, and A. Yegin, "Protocol for Carrying Authentication for Network Access (PANA) Framework," Internet RFC 5193 (informational), May 2008.

[RFC5216] D. Simon, B. Aboba, and R. Hurst, "The EAP-TLS Authentication Protocol," Internet RFC 5216, Mar. 2008.

[RFC5238] T. Phelan, "Datagram Transport Layer Security (DTLS) over the Datagram Congestion Control Protocol (DCCP)," Internet RFC 5238, May 2008.

[RFC5246] T. Dierks and E. Rescorla, "The Transport Layer Security (TLS) Protocol Version 1.2," Internet RFC 5246, Aug. 2008.

[RFC5247] B. Aboba, D. Simon, and P. Eronen, "Extensible Authentication Protocol (EAP) Key Management Framework," Internet RFC 5247, Aug. 2008.

[RFC5280] D. Cooper, S. Santesson, S. Farrell, S. Boeyen, R. Housley, and W. Polk, "Internet X.509 Public Key Infrastructure Certificate and Certificate Revocation List (CRL) Profile," Internet RFC 5280, May 2008.

[RFC5281] P. Funk and S. Blake-Wilson, "Extensible Authentication Protocol Tunneled Transport Layer Security Authenticated Protocol Version 0 (EAP-TTLSv0)," Internet RFC 5281 (informational), Aug. 2008.

[RFC5295] J. Salowey, L. Dondeti, V. Narayanan, and M. Nakhjiri, "Specification for the Derivation of Root Keys from an Extended Master Session Key (EMSK)," Internet RFC 5295, Aug. 2008.

[RFC5296] V. Narayanan and L. Dondeti, "EAP Extensions for EAP Re-authentication Protocol (ERP)," Internet RFC 5296, Aug. 2008.

[RFC5322] P. Resnick, ed., "Internet Message Format," Internet RFC 5322, Oct. 2008.

[RFC5374] B. Weis, G. Gross, and D. Ignjatic, "Multicast Extensions to the Security Architecture for the Internet Protocol," Internet RFC 5374, Nov. 2008.

[RFC5386] N. Williams and M. Richardson, "Better-than-Nothing Security: An Unauthenticated Mode of IPsec," Internet RFC 5386, Nov. 2008.

[RFC5387] J. Touch, D. Black, and Y. Wang, "Problem and Applicability Statement for Better-than-Nothing Security (BTNS)," Internet RFC 5387 (informational), Nov. 2008.

[RFC5406] S. Bellovin, "Guidelines for Specifying the Use of IPsec Version 2," Internet RFC 5406/BCP 0146, Feb. 2009.

[RFC5585] T. Hansen, D. Crocker, and P. Hallam-Baker, "DomainKeys Identified Mail (DKIM) Service Overview," Internet RFC 5585 (informational), July 2009.

[RFC5617] E. Allman, J. Fenton, M. Delany, and J. Levine, "DomainKeys Identified Mail (DKIM) Author Domain Signing Practices (ADSP)," Internet RFC 5617, Aug. 2009.

[RFC5652] R. Housley, "Cryptographic Message Syntax (CMS)," Internet RFC 5652/STD 0070, Sept. 2009.

[RFC5702] J. Jansen, "Use of SHA-2 Algorithms with RSA in DNSKEY and RRSIG Resource Records for DNSSEC," Internet RFC 5702, Oct. 2009.

[RFC5723] Y. Sheffer and H. Tschofenig, "Internet Key Exchange Protocol Version 2 (IKEv2) Session Resumption," Internet RFC 5723, Jan. 2010.

[RFC5739] P. Eronen, J. Laganier, and C. Madson, "IPv6 Configuration in Internet Key Exchange Protocol Version 2 (IKEv2)," Internet RFC 5739 (experimental), Feb. 2010.

[RFC5746] E. Rescorla, M. Ray, S. Dispensa, and N. Oskov, "Transport Layer Security (TLS) Renegotiation Indication Extension," Internet RFC 5746, Feb. 2010.

[RFC5753] S. Turner and D. Brown, "Use of Elliptic Curve Cryptography (ECC) Algorithms in Cryptographic Message Syntax (CMS)," Internet RFC 5753 (informational), Jan. 2010.

[RFC5755] S. Farrell, R. Housley, and S. Turner, "An Internet Attribute Certificate Profile for Authorization," Internet RFC 5755, Jan. 2010.

[RFC5764] D. McGrew and E. Rescorla, "Datagram Transport Layer Security (DTLS) Extension to Establish Keys for the Secure Real-Time Transport Protocol (SRTP)," Internet RFC 5764, May 2010.

[RFC5840] K. Grewal, G. Montenegro, and M. Bhatia, "Wrapped Encapsulating Security Payload (ESP) for Traffic Visibility," Internet RFC 5840, Apr. 2010.

[RFC5857] E. Ertekin, C. Christou, R. Jasani, T. Kivinen, and C. Bormann, "IKEv2 Extensions to Support Robust Header Compression over IPsec," Internet RFC 5857, May 2010.

[RFC5879] T. Kivinen and D. McDonald, "Heuristics for Detecting ESP-NULL Packets," Internet RFC 5879 (informational), May 2010.

[RFC5903] D. Fu and J. Solinas, "Elliptic Curve Groups Modulo a Prime (ECP Groups) for IKE and IKEv2," Internet RFC 5903 (informational), June 2010.

[RFC5933] V. Dolmatov, ed., A. Chuprina, and I. Ustinov, "Use of GOST Signature Algorithms in DNSKEY and RRSIG Resource Records for DNSSEC," Internet RFC 5933, July 2010.

[RFC5996] C. Kaufman, P. Hoffman, Y. Nir, and P. Eronen, "Internet Key Exchange Protocol Version 2 (IKEv2)," Internet RFC 5996, Sept. 2010.

[RFC5998] P. Eronen, H. Tschofenig, and Y. Sheffer, "An Extension for EAP-Only Authentication in IKEv2," Sept. 2010.

[RFC6024] R. Reddy and C. Wallace, "Trust Anchor Management Requirements," Internet RFC 6024 (informational), Oct. 2010.

[RFC6040] B. Briscoe, "Tunnelling of Explicit Congestion Notification," Internet RFC 6040, Nov. 2010.

[RFC6066] D. Eastlake 3rd, "Transport Layer Security (TLS) Extensions: Extension Definitions," Internet RFC 6066, Jan. 2011.

[RFC6071] S. Frankel and S. Krishnan, "IP Security (IPsec) and Internet Key Exchange (IKE) Document Roadmap," Internet RFC 6071 (informational), Feb. 2011.

[RFC6083] M. Tuexen, R. Seggelmann, and E. Rescorla, "Datagram Transport Layer Security (DTLS) for Stream Control Transmission Protocol (SCTP)," Internet RFC 6083, Jan. 2011.

[RFC6091] N. Mavrogiannopoulos and D. Gillmor, "Using OpenPGP Keys for Transport Layer Security (TLS) Authentication," Internet RFC 6091 (informational), Feb. 2011.

[RFC6101] A. Freier, P. Karlton, and P. Kocher, "The Secure Socket Layer (SSL) Protocol Version 3.0," Internet RFC 6101, Aug. 2011.

[RFC6147] M. Bagnulo, A. Sullivan, P. Matthews, and I. van Beijnum, "DN64: DNS Extensions for Network Address Translation from IPv6 Clients to IPv4 Servers," Internet RFC 6147, Apr. 2011.

[RFC6176] S. Turner and S. Polk, "Prohibiting Secure Sockets Layer (SSL) Version 2.0," Internet RFC 6176, Mar. 2011.

[RFC6234] D. Eastlake 3rd and T. Hansen, "US Secure Hash Algorithms (SHA and SHA-based HMAC and HKDF)," Internet RFC 6234 (informational), May 2011.

[RFC6345] P. Duffy, S. Chakrabarti, R. Cragie, Y. Ohba, ed., and A. Yegin, "Protocol for Carrying authentication for Network Access (PANA) Relay Element," Internet RFC 6345, Aug. 2011.

[RFC6376] D. Crocker, ed., T. Hansen, ed., M. Kucherawy, ed., "DomainKeys Identified Mail (DKIM) Signatures," Internet RFC 6376, Sep. 2011.

[RSA78] R. Rivest, A. Shamir, and L. Adleman, "A Method for Obtaining Digital Signatures and Public Key Cryptosystems," *Communications of the ACM*, 21(2), Feb. 1978.

[TLD-REPORT] http://stats.research.icann.org/dns/tld_report

[TLSEXT] http://www.iana.org/assignments/tls-extensiontype-values

[TLSPARAMS] http://www.iana.org/assignments/tls-parameters

[TNMOC] The National Museum of Computing, http://www.tnmoc.org

[TSIGALG] http://www.iana.org/assignments/tsig-algorithm-names

[TWP07] E. Tews, R. Weinmann, and A. Pyshkin, "Breaking 104 Bit WEP in Less than 60 Seconds," *Proc. 8th International Workshop on Information Security Applications* (Springer, 2007).

[VENONA] R. L. Benson, National Security Agency Center for Cryptologic History, "The VENONA Story," http://www.nsa.gov/public_info/declass/venona

[VK83] V. Voydock and S. Kent, "Security Mechanisms in High-Level Network Protocols," *ACM Computing Surveys*, 15, June 1983.

[WY05] X. Wang and H. Yu, "How to Break MD5 and Other Hash Functions," *EUROCRYPT*, May 2005.

[X9.62-2005] American National Standards Institute, "Public Key Cryptography for the Financial Services Industry: The Elliptic Curve Digital Signature Standard (ECDSA)," ANSI X9.62, 2005.

[Z97] Y. Zheng, "Digital Signcryption or How to Achieve Cost(Signature & Encryption) << Cost(Signature) + Cost(Encryption)," *Proc. CRYPTO*, Lecture Notes in Computer Science, Volume 1294 (Springer-Verlag, 1997).

Glossary of Acronyms

3GPP   3rd Generation Partnership Project (cellular SDO responsible for GSM, W-CDMA, LTE, etc.)

3GPP2   3rd Generation Partnership Project 2 (cellular SDO responsible for CDMA2000, EV-DO, etc.)

6rd   IPv6 Rapid Deployment (an IPv6 transition mechanism in which IPv6 traffic is carried over IPv4 networks, similar to 6to4 but using IPv6 prefix assignments based on unicast address assignments)

6to4   Six to Four (carrying IPv6 traffic in IPv4 tunnels, some operational challenges have occurred)

A   Address (IPv4) (DNS RR carrying an IPv4 address)

AAA   Authentication, Authorization and Accounting (management capabilities associated with certain access protocols such as RADIUS and Diameter)

AAAA   Address (IPv6) (DNS RR carrying an IPv6 address)

ABC   Appropriate Byte Counting (in TCP congestion control, a method to account for the number of bytes ACKed instead of a constant factor when performing CWND computations; can mitigate the slow window growth associated with delayed ACKs)

AC   Attribute Certificate (a type of certificate used to carry attributes such as authorizations, but does not include a public key and therefore differs from a PKC)

ACCM   Asynchronous Control Character Map (in PPP, indicates which bytes need to be escaped to avoid having unwanted effects)

ACD   Automatic Collision Detection (procedure to detect and avoid IP address assignment collisions)

ACFC   Address and Control Field Compression (in PPP, eliminating the address and control fields to reduce overhead)

ACK   Acknowledgment (an indication that data has arrived at a receiver successfully; applicable to multiple layers of the protocol stack)

ACL   Access Control List (list of filtering rules determining which traffic is permitted, e.g., through a firewall)

ADSP   Author Domain Signing Practices (with DKIM, a policy statement pertaining to how DKIM is used or deployed within a particular domain)

AEAD   Authenticated Encryption with Associated Data (algorithms that perform encryption and authentication on one portion of their input and authentication on another portion)

AES   Advanced Encryption Standard (current-generation U.S. encryption standard)

AF   Assured Forwarding (a PHB offering priority classes and prioritization within classes)

AFTR   Address Family Transition Router element (in DS-Lite, a SPNAT used to share a small number of IPv4 addresses with multiple customers)

AH   Authentication Header (optional IPsec protocol providing for authentication of IP traffic, including header information, which is incompatible with NATs)

AIA   Authority Information Access (an X.509 certificate extension indicating resources useful in validating a certificate)

AIAD   Additive Increase Additive Decrease (in TCP, methods that moderate CWND by adding to its value when congestion appears to be low and subtracting from it when congestion appears to be increasing; not the standard TCP algorithm)

AIMD   Additive Increase Multiplicative Decrease (in TCP, methods that moderate CWND by adding to its value when congestion appears to be low and multiplying it by a fraction less than one when congestion appears to be increasing)

ALG   Application Layer Gateway (an agent, usually software, that converts protocols at the application layer)

A-MPDU   Aggregated MPDU (frame containing multiple MPDUs, part of IEEE 802.11n)

A-MSDU   Aggregated MSDU (frame containing multiple MSDUs, part of IEEE 802.11n)

ANDSF   Access Network Discovery and Selection Function (a portion of MoS indicating information about networks that may be used to influence handoff and network selection)

AODV   Ad-hoc On-Demand Distance Vector routing protocol (early ad-hoc on-demand routing protocol using distance vectors)

AP   Access Point (802.11 STA usually used to interconnect wireless and wired network segments)

API   Application Programming Interface (functions invoked by applications to obtain effects such as sending and receiving network traffic)

APIPA   Automatic Private IP Addressing (a mechanism whereby a node self-configures its own IP address from a particular range; usually applies to IPv4 nodes)

APSD   Automatic Power Save Delivery (periodic batch processing of 802.11 frames in support of PSM)

AQM   Active Queue Management (queue management methods that react to the traffic dynamics, not including "drop-tail" typical of FCFS/FIFO queue management)

ARP   Address Resolution Protocol (a protocol above the link layer that resolves IPv4 addresses to MAC layer addresses, uses link layer broadcast addressing)

ARQ   Automatic Repeat Request (the retransmission of information; usually after inferred loss)

AS   Authentication Server (with PANA, server where authentication checks are performed)

AS   Autonomous System (a 16- or 32-bit number used in connection with inter-ISP routing to identify a collection of network prefixes and their owner)

ASM   All-Source Multicast (multicast wherein any party can source traffic)

ASN.1   Abstract Syntax Notation One (an ISO standard defining the abstract syntax for information but not the corresponding encoding format; BER and DER are encodings for ASN.1 information)

AUS   Application Unique String (input string to the DDDS algorithm)

AUTH   Authentication (with IKE, payload containing information required to perform authentication of the sender)

AXFR   Zone Transfer (full exchange of DNS zone information; uses TCP)

B4   Bridging Broadband element (in DS-Lite, a router which encapsulates IPv4 traffic in IPv6 tunnels terminated at an AFTR, a B4 does not perform NAT functions)

BACP   Bandwidth Allocation Control Protocol (with PPP, a protocol for configuring BoD)

BAP   Bandwidth Allocation Protocol (a protocol used to configure links in a bundle for MPPP)

BCMCS   Broadcast and Multicast Service Controller (in cellular networks, manages multicast)

BER   Basic Encoding Rules (an ITU standard encoding syntax; a subset of ASN.1)

BER   Bit Error Rate (number of bit errors expected per number of bits in transit)

BGP   Border Gateway Protocol (inter-domain routing protocol with policy support)

BIND9   Berkeley Internet Name Domain (version 9) (a name server software implementation popular on UNIX-like systems)

BITS   Bump In the Stack (option for implementing IPsec in the host)

BITW Bump In the Wire (option for implementing IPsec in the network)

BL Bulk Leasequery (in DHCP, a request/response protocol to convey current lease information)

BoD Bandwidth on Demand (ability to dynamically adjust available link bandwidth)

BOOTP Bootstrap Protocol (precursor to DHCP; used to configure hosts)

BPDU Bridge PDU (PDUs used by STP; exchanged by switches and bridges)

BPSK Binary Phase Shift Keying (modulating binary using two signal phases)

BSD Berkeley Software Distribution (UC Berkeley's version of UNIX, included the first widely used implementation of TCP/IP)

BSDP Boot Server Discovery Protocol (an extension to DHCP developed by Apple to discover a boot image server)

BSS Basic Service Set (IEEE 802.11 terminology for an access point and associated stations)

BTNS Better Than Nothing Security (with IPsec, an option for using certificates without a full PKI but which is vulnerable to MITM attacks)

BU Binding Update (in MIP, establishes the mapping between a MN's CoA and HoA)

CA Certificate Authority (organization responsible for generating and issuing public/private key pairs and signing and distributing signed public keys and CRLs)

CALIPSO Common Architecture Label IPv6 Security Option (security labels for IP packets; not widely used)

CBC Cipher Block Chaining (an encryption mode that uses the XOR operation to chain encrypted blocks together in an effort to resist re-arrangement attacks)

CBCP Callback Control Protocol (in PPP, establishes a callback number)

CCA Clear Channel Assessment (802.11 PHY-layer mechanism that detects channel usage)

CCITT Comité Consultatif International Téléphonique et Télégraphique (now ITU-T)

CCM Counter mode with CBC Message Authentication Code (an authenticated encryption mode combining CTR mode encryption with CBC-MAC)

CCMP Counter Mode with CBC-MAC Protocol (encryption used with WPA2; from IEEE 802.11i; successor to WPA)

CCP Compression Control Protocol (in PPP, established the compression methods to use)

ccTLD   Country Code TLD (a TLD based on the ISO3661-2 country code list)

CDP   CRL Distribution Point (a location where a CA's current CRL may be obtained)

CERT   Certificate (with IKE, payload containing a certificate)

CERT   Computer Emergency Response Team (groups that handle computer security incidents, including the first CERT at Carnegie Mellon University and U.S. Government's US-CERT)

CERTREQ   Certificate Request (with IKE, payload indicating trust anchor as an indication of acceptable certificates)

CGA   Cryptographically Generated Address (address generated based on a hash on a public key)

CHAP   Challenge-Handshake Authentication Protocol (protocol requiring a challenge to match a response; vulnerable to MITM attacks)

CIA   confidentiality, integrity, and availability (principles of information security; the "CIA triad")

CIDR   Classless Inter-Domain Routing (a move to address the ROAD problem by removing the IP address class boundaries but requiring an associated CIDR mask to be used with inter-domain routing)

CMAC   Cipher-based Message Authentication Code (a particular way of using encryption algorithms as a MAC)

CN   Correspondent Node (an MN's conversation peer in MIP scenario)

CNAME   Canonical Name (DNS RR providing an alias for another domain name)

CoA   Care-of Address (MN's address assigned while visiting non-home network)

CoS   Class of Service (general term referring to differentiated services based on different classes of traffic; a concept supported by the Diff Serv architecture)

CoT   Care-of Test (in a RR check, message sent to MN via its CoA resulting in MN obtaining a portion of a key used to secure BUs)

CoTI   Care-of Test Init (in a RR check, triggers receiver to send a CoT message)

CP   Configuration Payload (with IKE, extensible structure for conveying configuration parameters)

CPS   Certification Practice Statement (a CA's policy statement about how certificates are issued or managed)

CRC   Cyclic Redundancy Check (mathematical functions used to check for bit errors)

CRL   Certificate Revocation List (a list of invalid certificates issued by a CA)

CS   Cipher Suite (in TLS, the choice of cryptographic algorithm suite)

CS   Class Selector (in IP, a DSCP value designed to be compatible with the bit values associated with the now-deprecated "Type of Service" and "Traffic Class" IP header fields)

CSMA/CA   Carrier-Sense Multiple Access/Collision Avoidance (WiFi's MAC protocol, which involves sending when a link is idle and backing off if it is not)

CSMA/CD   Carrier-Sense Multiple Access/Collision Detection (Ethernet's classic MAC protocol, which involves sending when a link is idle and backing off if collisions are detected)

CSPRNG   Cryptographycially Secure Preudo-Random Number Generator (a PRNG suitable for cryptographic use)

CSRG   Computer Systems Research Group (developers of BSD UNIX at UC Berkeley)

CTCP   Compound TCP (a "scalable" TCP variant implemented in modern Windows systems that combines both delay-based and packet-loss based window adjustments)

CTR   Counter (an encryption mode that uses a counter value to impose a required order on encrypted blocks while permitting parallel execution of encryption or decryption on multiple blocks)

CTS   Clear To Send (message authorizing sender of RTS to send)

CW   Contention Window (range of time an 802.11 station will wait before sending under DCF)

CWND   Congestion Window (in TCP, a limit placed on the sender's window size to avoid or reduce congestion)

CWR   Congestion Window Reducing (or Reduced) (in TCP, reduction of the sender's usable window size)

CWV   Congestion Window Verification (in TCP, a method to check and update the current value of CWND when deemed necessary)

DAD   Duplicate Address Detection (with IPv6 ND and SLAAC, DAD helps determine whether a candidate IPv6 address is already in use by sending an NS message for the proposed address)

DCCP   Datagram Congestion Control Protocol (a protocol that provides best-effort datagram service to applications and also controls congestion)

DCF   Distributed Coordination Function (CSMA/CA MAC for 802.11 networks)

DDDS   Dynamic Delegation Discovery System (methods to support lazy binding of strings to data; usually used with DNS for discovery of servers for various application protocols)

DDoS   Distributed DoS (a network-based attack often launched by botnets)

DER   Distinguished Encoding Rules (an ITU standard encoding syntax; a subset of BER for ASN.1 that requires a unique representation to be used for each value)

DES   Data Encryption Standard (an older U.S. standard for symmetric data encryption using 56-bit keys)

DF   Don't Fragment (an IPv4 header bit indicating no fragmentation should be performed; important for PMTUD)

DH   Diffie-Hellman (mathematical protocol to establish a secret value between two parties even in the presence of an evesdropper)

DHCP   Dynamic Host Configuration Protocol (evolved from BOOTP; sets up systems with configuration information such as leased IP addresses, default router, and DNS server IP address)

DIFS   DCF Inter-Frame Space (time between frames under 802.11 DCF)

DIX   Digital, Intel, Xerox (creators and name of early Ethernet standard)

DKIM   Domain Keys Identified Mail (a protocol for cryptographically binding the sending domain of e-mail with the associated originating mail servers)

DLNA   Digital Living Network Alliance (an industry group focused on interoperability and protocols for consumer media devices such as TVs, DVD players, DVRs, etc.)

DMZ   De-Militarized Zone (a network segment outside an organization's inside firewall, usually used for hosts providing services to customers or the public)

DNA   Detecting Network Attachment (procedures to detect a change in connection state)

DNAME   Non-Terminal Name Redirection (DNS RR supporting generation of multiple CNAME records using a DNS subtree aliasing mechanism)

DNS   Domain Name System (maps names to IP addresses and more)

DNS64   DNS IPv4/IPv6 translation (a mechanism for IPv4/IPv6 coexistence to translate IPv4 DNS information for IPv6 DNS use)

DNSKEY   Key for DNS (DNS RR used with DNSSEC to hold a public key)

DNSSEC   DNS Security (original authentication and integrity assurance for DNS data)

DNSSL   DNS Search List (used with RAs, indicates list of default domain extensions)

DOI   Digital Object Identifier (a method for naming content objects and associating them with information records)

DoS   Denial of Service (a type of resource exhaustion attack)

DPD   Delegated Path Discovery (method for delegating the collection of all information required to validate a certificate path)

DPV   Delegated Path Validation (method for delegating the entire validation procedure for a certificate)

DS   Delegation Signer (in DNS, an RR used with DNSSEC to secure a delegation)

DS   Differentiated Services (in IP traffic management, methods to provide performance differentiation for traffic delivery)

DS   Distribution Service (in 802.11 LANs, the network or service used to interconnect APs, which is most often a wired 802.3/Ethernet network)

DSA   Digital Signature Algorithm (an algorithm for generating digital signatures based on the discrete logarithm problem)

DSACK   Duplicate SACK (in TCP, a SACK variant that includes description of received duplicated segments)

DSCP   DS Code Point (field value in packet indicating a particular forwarding behavior is desired)

DSL   Digital Subscriber Line (dedicated broadband data link over POTS line)

DS-Lite   Dual Stack Lite (a framework for IPv6-based service providers to provide access to dual stack or single stack clients using a combination of IPv4-in-IPv6 tunneling and NAT)

DSRK   Domain-Specific Root Key (key derived from an EMSK intended for use by systems under a single administrative authority)

DSS   Digital Signature Standard (a U.S. standard for digital signatures based on DSA)

DSUSRK   Domain-Specific USRK (a key combining the usage policies of a USRK and DSRK)

DTLS   Datagram TLS (variant of TLS used with datagram protocols such as UDP)

DUID   DHCP Unique Identifier (value placed in DHCP request to match responses)

DUP   Duplicate (used in multiple context—e.g., DUP ACKs)

EAP   Extensible Authentication Protocol (framework supporting various authentication methods)

EAP-FAST   EAP-Flexible Authentication via Security Tunneling (Cisco's EAP method using TLS that replaces its earlier LEAP EAP method)

EAPOL   EAP over LAN (e.g., EAP over Ethernet as used in IEEE 802.1X)

EAP-TTLS   EAP-Tunneled Transport Layer Security (an EAP method based on earlier TLS EAP method, but requires only server side to obtain certificate)

EC2N   Elliptic Curve groups modulo a power of 2 (groups based on elliptic curves, in the abstract algebra sense, over the Galois Field $GF(2^N)$)

ECC   Error Correcting Code (redundant bits added to information bits usable to correct errors)

ECDSA   Elliptic Curve Digital Signature Algorithm (a variant of DSA using ECC)

ECE   ECN Echo (in TCP with ECN, the reflection of ECN information to a TCP sender)

ECN   Explicit Congestion Notification (direct method of indicating congestion—e.g., by routers to hosts)

ECP   Elliptic Curve groups modulo a Prime (groups based on elliptic curves, in the abstract algebra sense, over the Galois Field $G(P)$ for a prime P)

ECT   ECN-Capable Transport (a transport protocol capable of interpreting ECN indicators)

EDCA   Enhanced Distributed Channel Access (802.11 coordinating function supporting QoS, from 802.11e)

EDNS0   Extension mechanisms for DNS (version 0) (a method to extend DNS RRs, version 0, needed by DNSSEC)

EF   Expedited Forwarding (a PHB offering a service class as if no congestion were present, generally implying it is the highest priority and requiring admission control to avoid oversubscription)

EFO   Expanded Flags Option (used with DHCP, indicates presence of additional options)

EIFS   Extended IFS (extended IFS used when receiving unrecognized frame under 802.11 DCF)

EMSK   Extended MSK (a secondary key generated in addition to the MSK by EAP after key derivation)

ENUM   E.164 to URI DDDS Application (a particular DDDS used to map E.164 telephony-style addresses to URIs)

EP   Enforcement Point (with PANA, point where access control policies are enforced)

EQM   Equal Modulation (using the same modulation scheme on different data streams simultaneously)

ERE   Eligible Rate Estimate (part of TCP Westwood+; estimate of the amount of bandwidth that could be used by a connection)

ERP   EAP Re-authentication Protocol (an EAP extension to reduce the latency when re-establishing authentication)

ESN   Extended Sequence Number (in IPsec, an extended sequence number of 64 bits used to combat replay attacks; normal sequence numbers are 32 bits)

ESP   Encapsulating Security Payload (required IPsec protocol providing for authentication and/or confidentiality of traffic)

ESSID   Extended Service Set Identifier (IEEE 802.11 network name)

EUI   Extended Unique Identifier (MAC-layer address prefix format defined by IEEE, extended from OUI)

EV   Extended Validation (a form of certificate with enhanced identity validation performed prior to issuance)

EV-DO   Evolution, Data Optimized (or Only) (3GPP2 wireless broadband standard; an evolution of CDMA2000)

FACK   Forward Acknowledgment (in TCP, one more than the highest sequence number known to have reached the receiver; determined using SACK)

FCFS   First Come, First Served (scheduling discipline with in-order service; no priority)

FCS   Frame Check Sequence (general term for bits used to check for bit errors)

FEC   Forward Error Correction (using redundant bits to correct errors in data bits)

FIFO   First In, First Out (queue management discipline with in-order service; no re-arrangements)

FIN   Finish (a TCP header bit and last segment type sent on a TCP connection)

FMIP   Mobile IP with Fast Handovers (modification to MIPv6 with early handovers)

FQDN   Fully Qualifies Domain Name (a domain name with full domain extension included)

F-RTO   Forward RTO (in TCP, a method to infer whether a retransmission was spurious and if so facilitate the avoidance of unnecessary retransmissions)

FTP   File Transfer Protocol (a TCP-based file transfer protocol using separate control and data connections)

GCKS   Group Controller/Key Server (in IPsec, used with GKM; holds and issues keys for GSAs)

GCM   Galois/Counter Mode (an authenticated encryption mode combining CTR mode encryption with Galois mode authentication)

GDOI   Group Domain of Interpretation (in IPsec, a group key management protocol based on ISAKMP and IKE)

GENA   General Event Notification Architecture (an XML-based notification framework using HTTP over multicast UDP; used with UPnP)

GI   Guard Interval (in communications engineering, minimum time between transmissions used to avoid inter-symbol interference)

GKM Group Key Management (in IPsec, methods to distribute key material to a group in order to support group SA formation)

GMAC Galois Message Authentication Code (an authentication-only variant of GCM)

GMI Group Membership Interval (in IGMP and MLD, the amount of time a multicast router waits before deciding there is no particular source or no more group members; set to QRV * QI + QRI)

GMRP Generic Multicast Registration Protocol (replaced by MMRP)

GPAD Group PAD (with IPsec, abstraction of a database containing authentication data for all GCKS entities)

GRE Generic Routing Encapsulation (generic encapsulation within IP datagrams)

GSA Group Security Association (in IPsec, an SA established among group members using a multicast protocol)

GSAKMP Group Secure Association Key Management Protocol (a framework for creating groups with common cryptographic information, distributing policy, performing access control, generating group keys, and recovering from group dynamic changes)

GSPD Group SPD (in IPsec, an SPD capable of holding information for both SAs and GSAs)

GSS-API Generic Security Services API (an API to access myriad security services such as authentication, confidentiality, etc.; typically used with the Kerberos authentication system)

gTLD Generic TLD (a TLD—such as COM, EDU, MIL—not based based on country code)

GVRP Generic Attribute Registration Protocol (replaced by MRP)

HA Home Agent (system offering MIP helper service to an MN)

HAIO Home Agent Information Option (in ICMPv6, an option supporting MIPv6 to indicate address of an HA)

HCF Hybrid Coordination Function (coordinating function supporting both priority and contention-based 802.11 channel access)

HDLC High-level Data Link Control (a popular ISO standard data link protocol, the basis for the most popular variant of PPP)

HELD HTTP-Enabled Location Delivery (a protocol for delivering LCI using HTTP/TCP/IP)

HIP Host Identity Protocol (a research protocol architecture focusing on mobility and security)

HMAC Hash-based Message Authentication Code (a particular way of using hashing algorithms as a MAC)

HoA   Home Address (in MIP, a MN's address from its home network)

HOPOPT   IPv6 Hop-by-Hop Option (an IPv6 option type applicable to each hop in a path)

HoT   Home Test (in an RR check, message sent to MN via HA resulting in MN obtaining a portion of a key used to secure BUs)

HoTI   Home Test Init (in an RR check, triggers receiver to send a HoT message)

HSPA   High-Speed Packet Access (3GPP wireless broadband standard; an evolution of WCDMA)

HSTCP   Highspeed TCP (a "scalable" TCP variant in which CWND is adjusted based in part on its current value; designed to operate more effectively in high capacity environments)

HT   High Throughput (higher speeds associated with the IEEE 802.11n standard)

HTML   Hyper-Text Markup Language (the basic language of the WWW)

HTTP   Hyper-Text Transfer Protocol (primary protocol of the WWW; often carries HTML)

HTTPMU   HTTP using UDP (a method for carrying HTTP traffic on UDP using multicast addressing; used to carry SSDP messages in UPnP)

HTTPS   HTTP over SSL/TLS (standard for secure WWW exchange)

HWRP   Hybrid Wireless Routing Protocol (routing protocol proposed for IEEE 802.11s)

IA   Identity Association (in DHCP, a collection of addresses)

IAB   Internet Architecture Board (one of IETF's governing bodies; responsible for architectural oversight and apppointment of liasons to other SDOs)

IAID   IA Identifier (in DHCP, an ID referring to a particular IA)

IANA   Internet Assigned Numbers Authority (maintains protocol numbers and field values)

IBSS   Independent Basic Service Set (802.11 ad-hoc network)

ICANN   Internet Corporation for Assigned Names and Numbers (non-profit governing body for domain names and related policy)

ICE   Interactive Connectivity Establishment (a framework for performing NAT traversal, which entails trying direct connections, STUN, and finally TURN to enable communication in the presence of NATs)

ICMP   Internet Control Message Protocol (an information and error reporting protocol considered part of IP)

ICS   Internet Connection Sharing (alternative name for NAT; used with Microsoft Windows)

ICV   Integrity Check Value (a value used to check the integrity of a message—e.g., cryptographic hash)

ID   Identification (in IKE, payload indicating identity of sender)

IDN   Internationalized Domain Name (domain name encoding non-ASCII characters)

IEEE   Institute of Electrical and Electronics Engineers (SDO for link-layer protocols and more)

IESG   Internet Engineering Steering Group (IETF's governing body with RFC approval authority)

IETF   Internet Engineering Task Force (SDO for Internet standards)

IGD, IGDDC   Internet Gateway Device/Discovery and Control (a UPnP protocol for discovering and configuring gateway devices such as home NATs)

IGMP   Internet Group Message Protocol (a protocol to manage IPv4 multicast groups; used by routers and end hosts)

IHL   Internet Header Length (IPv4 header field indicating the header length in 32-bit words)

IID   Interface Identifier (numeric identifier usually based on MAC address; used when choosing IPv6 addresses, but not used for this purpose when privacy extensions are enabled)

IKE   Internet Key Exchange (part of IPsec; a protocol to dynamically establish security associations including keys and operating parameters)

IMAP   Internet Message Access Protocol (used to retrieve e-mail headers and messages from servers)

IMAPS   IMAP over SSL/TLS (a secure protocol for fetching e-mail, supported by most e-mail programs)

IN   Internet (in DNS, the class name indicating Internet information)

IND   Inverse Neighbor Discovery (provides RARP-like function for IPv6)

IP   Internet Protocol (standard best-effort Internet packet protocol implementing a common abstract datagram on any link layer network)

IPCP   IP Control Protocol (in PPP, an NCP used to configure an IPv4 network link)

IPG   Inter-Packet Gap (minimum spacing between frames in a MAC protocol)

IPsec   IP Security (a framework for securing IP traffic, including the IKE, AH, and ESP protocols)

IPV6CP   IPv6 Control Protocol (in PPP, an NCP used to configure an IPv6 network link)

IRIS Internet Registry Information Service (database containing information relating address ranges, associated AS numbers, contact information, and name servers)

IRTF Internet Research Task Force (research groups affiliated with IETF via the IAB)

ISAKMP Internet Security Association and Key Management Protocol (in IPsec, SA establishment protocol pre-dating IKE)

ISATAP Intra-Site Automatic Tunnel Addressing Protocol (an automatic IPv6-to-IPv4 tunneling technology supported by Microsoft)

ISDN Integrated Services Digital Network (combination circuit/packet switched data service)

IS-IS Intermediate System to Intermediate System (ISO link-state routing protocol)

ISL Cisco's Inter-Switch Protocol (Cisco's protocol for maintaining VLAN information among switches)

ISM Industrial, Scientific, and Medical (licence-free frequency bands in much of the world, used by Wi-Fi)

ISN Initial Sequence Number (in TCP, the first sequence number for a connection; assigned to the SYN)

ISO International Organization for Standardization (SDO responsible for defining various protocols and encodings once considered for replacing TCP/IP)

ISOC Internet Society (Internet standards leadership nonprofit corporation)

ISP Internet Service Provider (an entity, often a business, that allocates addresses, provides DNS and routing, and works with other ISPs)

ITU International Telecommunications Union (SDO for radio and telephony standards)

ITU-T ITU Telecommunication Standardization Sector (formerly CCITT; one of the three "sectors" of ITU responsible for standards or "recommendations" such as ASN.1, X.25, DSL)

IW Initial Window (in TCP, the initial value of CWND)

IXFR Incremental Zone Transfer (incremental exchange of DNS zone information, uses TCP)

KE Key Exchange (with IKE, payload used for establishing keys; generally uses DH)

KSK Key Signing Key (a key used with DNSSEC for signing other keys; typically has the SEP bit set)

L2TP Layer 2 Tunneling Protocol (IETF standard link layer tunneling protocol)

LACP Link Aggregation Control Protocol (part of IEEE 802.1AX for managing link aggregates)

LAG Link Aggregation Group (set of links acting together as one virtual higher-performance link)

LAN Local Area Network (a network within a small geographic area such as a single site, office, or home)

LCG Linear Congruential Generator (a deterministic type of popular PRNG, which is not a CSPRNG)

LCI Location Configuration Information (data representing the location—geographical or civic—of a system)

LCI Logical Channel Identifier (in circuit switching, identifier for a virtual channel)

LCN Logical Channel Number (in circuit switching, number of a virtual channel)

LCP Link Control Protocol (in PPP, used to establish a link)

LDAP Lightweight Directory Access Protocol (a lookup protocol based on the ISO X.500 DAP protocol)

LDRA Lightweight DHCP Relay Agent (mechanisms to allow layer 2 devices to act as DHCP relay agents)

LEAP Lightweight Extensible Authentication Protocol (Cisco's EAP method using WEP or TKIP keys; now known to have vulnerabilities)

LLA Link Layer Address (in FMIPv6, a mobility header option to indicate link layer address)

LLC Logical Link Control (sublayer of the MAC layer related to link control)

LLMNR Link Local Multicast Name Resolution (a multicast variant of DNS designed for on-link use and that runs on a different port number than DNS; used for local service and node discovery)

LMQI Last Member Query Interval (in IGMP and MLD, the time between group-specific query messages)

LMQT Last Member Query Time (in IGMP and MLD, the total spent after sending a last member query and possible transmissions; represents the "leave latency")

LNP Local Network Protection (a collection of techniques suggested for use in IPv6 deployments making NATs unnecessary)

LoST Location-to-Service Translation (a framework for offering services based on location—e.g., indication of the nearest hospital)

LQR Link Quality Reports (in PPP, reports of link quality measurements including number of packets received, sent, and rejected due to errors)

LTE   Long-Term Evolution (3GPP wireless broadband standard; an evolution of HSPA)

LW-MLD   Lightweight MLD (variant of MLD with simpler join/leave semantics)

MAC   Media Access Control (controls for mediating access to a shared network medium, usually a portion of the link layer protocol)

MAC   Message Authentication Code (a mathematical function used to help verify the integrity of a message)

MAN   Metropolitan Area Network (a network spanning a modest geographical extent, such as a city or region)

MCS   Modulation and Coding Scheme (combination of modulation and coding, many combinations are available in 802.11n)

MD   Message Digest Algorithms (mathematical functions giving a short numeric "fingerprint" for a larger message)

mDNS   Multicast DNS (local variant of name service developed by Apple)

MIH   Media-Independent Handoff (mechanisms to support change of network attachment point between heterogeneous networks; the IEEE 802.21 standard covers MIH for 802.3, 802.11, 802.15, 802.16, 3GPP, and 3GPP2 network types)

MII   Media-Independent Interface (in hardware, the interface between the MAC implementation and PHY protocol implementation, which is PHY-independent)

MIME   Multipurpose Internet Mail Extensions (method for labeling and encoding various object types in electronic mail)

MIMO   Multiple Input, Multiple Output (wireless antenna scheme with multiple antennas offering performance superior to single-antenna systems but requiring more sophisticated signal processing)

MIP   Mobile IP (IP addressing and routing extensions to support movement of network attachment point without address change)

MITM   Man-in-the-Middle attack (the typical form of an MSM attack, carried out by an interposer)

MLD   Multicast Listener Discovery (used by IPv6 routers to discover multicast receivers on a link; provides similar capabilities as IGMP for IPv4)

MLPP   Multilevel Precedence and Preemption (telephone scheme to prioritize calls—e.g., for military use)

MMRP   Multiple MAC Registration Protocol (part of MRP used for registering multicast interest)

MN   Mobile Node (the moving node in a MIP scenario)

MOBIKE   Mobile version of IKE (enhancements to IKE to support mobility and change of addressing information)

MODP   Modulo-P groups (groups based on modular arithmetic, in the abstract algebraic sense, used with key establishment protocols)

MoS   Mobility Services (portion of the IEEE 802.21 standard supporting media-independent handoff services)

MP   Mesh Point (name of a node in IEEE 802.11s operating in a mesh configuration)

MP, MPPP, MLP, MLPPP   Multi-link PPP (using PPP over multiple links simultaneously)

MPDU   MAC Protocol Data Unit (name of the frame used in 802.11 standards)

MPE   Manchester Phase Encoding (bit encoding scheme where a voltage transition indicates one bit)

MPLS   Multi-Protocol Label Switching (architecture that switches frames based on tag values, not IP addresses)

MPPC   Microsoft's Point-to-Point Compression (used with PPP)

MPPE   Microsoft's Point-to-Point Encryption (used with PPP)

MPV   Maximum Pad Value (in PPP, maximum number of pad bytes)

MRD   Multicast Router Discovery (protocol to discover on-link multicast router neighbors)

MRP   Multiple Registration Protocol (IEEE 802.1ak standard for registering attributes)

MRRU   Multilink Maximum Received Reconstructed Unit (MRU after reconstruction from parts on multiple MP links)

MRU   Maximum Receive Unit (largest packet/message size a receiver will accept)

MS-CHAP   Microsoft's Challenge-Handshake Authentication Protocol (an authentication protocol involving a request/replay and validated response, with two versions: MS-CHAPv1 and MS-CHAPv2)

MSDU   MAC Services Data Unit (802.11 frame type available to layers above MAC)

MSK   Master Session Key (a key derived after an EAP session using methods supporting key derivation)

MSL   Maximum Segment Lifetime (in TCP, the maximum time a segment can exist in the network before being determined invalid)

MSM   Message Stream Modification (active modification of messages; usually a type of attack)

MSS   Maximum Segment Size (in TCP, the largest segment a receiver is willing to receive; usually provided in an option during connection establishment)

MTU   Maximum Transmission Unit (maximum frame size a network will transport)

MVRP   Multiple VLAN Registration Protocol (part of MRP used for registering VLANs)

MX   Mail Exchanger (DNS RR indicating a priority order of hosts willing to use SMTP to exchange mail)

NAC   Network Access Control (process employed to determine whether a device should receive access rights to use a network)

NACK   Negative Acknowledgment (an indication of non-receipt or non-acceptance)

NAP   Network Access Protection (Microsoft's variant of NAC; first available with Windows Server 2008)

NAPT   NAT with Port Translation (NAT with port re-writing, the most common form of NAT)

NAPTR   Name Authority Pointer (DNS RR used with a DNS-based DDDS for holding re-writing rules)

NAR   New Access Router (in FMIPv6, router that is expected to be used soon)

NAT   Network Address Translation (mechanism to re-write addresses in IP datagrams; used primarily to reduce the usage of globally routable IP addresses; usually used in conjunction with private IP addresses; also supports a type of firewall capability)

NAT64   IPv6/IPv6 NAT (a NAT that translates between IPv4/ICMPv4 and IPv6/ICMPv6 and vice versa; proposed for IPv6/IPv4 interoperability and coexistence)

NAT-PMP   NAT Port Mapping Protocol (an alternative to IGD developed by Apple for configuring some NAT devices; provides the ability to remotely set up port forwarding)

NAT-PT   NAT with Protocol Translation (now-deprecated approach to IPv4/IPv6 translation)

NAV   Network Allocation Vector (time delay before sending due to other stations' channel use in 802.11 DCF)

NBMA   Non-Broadcast Multiple Access (multi-user networks lacking broadcasting capability)

NCoA   New Care-of Address (in FMIPv6, CoA to be obtained from NAR)

NCP   Network Control rotocol (in PPP, used to establish the network-layer protocol)

ND, NDP Neighbor Discovery (IPv6 method to discovery and obtain MAC address of on-link neighbors; works like ARP; implemented as part of ICMPv6)

NEMO Network Mobility (mobility where a router and network changes attachment point)

NIC Network Interface Card (the device interfacing a computer with a network)

NONCE number used once (a random value used in many cryptographic protocols to combat replay attacks)

NPT66 IPv6-to-IPv6 NAPT (NAT with algorithmic address and port translation)

NRO Number Resource Organization (the Address Supporting Organization to ICANN)

NS Name Server (DNS RR carrying the name of another name server)

NS Neighbor Solicitation (part of IPv6 ND; similar to an IPv4 ARP request but uses IPv6 multicast addressing; implemented using ICMPv6)

NSCD Name Services Cache Daemon (process to provide caching for DNS and other resolutions popular on UNIX systems)

NSEC Next Secure (DNS RR used with DNSSEC to indicate the next RR in an ordered list; used for authenticated denial of existence)

NSEC3 Next Secure (version 3) (DNS RR like NSEC but including hash function to resist DNS name enumeration attacks)

NSEC3PARAM NSEC Parameters (DNS RR used with DNSSEC holding NSEC3 hash function parameters)

NTN Non-Terminal NAPTR (in DNS, a NAPTR pointing to another domain with records)

NTP Network Time Protocol (a protocol for synchronizing clocks)

NUD Neighbor Unreachability Detection (in IPv6 ND, to determine if a neighbor can still be reached)

OCSP Online Certificate Status Protocol (a protocol for checking the validity of a certificate; an alternative to obtaining a CRL)

OFDM Orthogonal Frequency Division Multiplexing (a sophisticated modulation scheme in which subcarriers of multiple frequences are simultaneously modulated in a specified bandwidth to achieve high throughput; used by DSL, 802.11a/g/n, 802.16e, and advanced cellular data standards including LTE)

OID Object Identifier (numeric identifier of a digital object; used in certificate encodings)

OLSR Optimized Link State Routing (a standard protocol for on-demand routing in ad-hoc networks)

OOB Out Of Band (information delivered outside a primary communication channel)

ORO Option Request Option (in DHCP, an option indicating a systems interest in knowing which options are supported)

OSI Open System Interconnect (an abstract reference model specified by ISO for open systems that helped form the basis of layered design in protocols)

OUI Organizationally Unique Identifier (original MAC-layer address prefix format defined by IEEE)

P2P Peer-to-Peer (participating systems are both clients and servers)

PA Provider-Aggregatable (IP address space where a customer's prefix is given by their provider)

PAA PANA Authentication Agent (PANA agent performing authentication, such as an AAA server)

PaC PANA Client (PANA agent requesting authentication)

PAD Peer Authentication Database (with IPsec, abstraction of database containing authentication information for each peer such as use of IKE or PSK and associated authentication data)

PANA Protocol for Carrying Authentication for Network Access (UDP/IP carrier for EAP)

PAP Password Authentication Protocol (protocol that carries cleartext password; vulnerable to MITM or eavesdroppers)

PAWS Protection Against Wrapped Sequence Numbers (in TCP, method using TSOPT values to notice sequence number wrapping)

PCF Point Coordinating Function (combined contention-free and contention-based MAC protocol for 802.11; not widely used)

PCO Phased Coexistence Operation (method for an 802.11 AP to switch channel widths for less negative impact on legacy equipment)

PCoA Previous Care-of Address (in FMIPv6, current or previous CoA obtained from PAR)

PCP Port Control Protocol (current-generation draft IETF protocol for configuring NATs including SPNATs and NAT64)

PDU Protocol Data Unit (describes a message at some protocol layer; sometimes used interchangeably and informally with packet, frame, datagram, segment, or message)

PEAP Protected Extensible Authentication Protocol (a popular method to encapsulate EAP in TLS; similar to EAP-TTLS)

PEN Private Enterprise Number (numbers assigned by IANA usable by an enterprise in forming OIDs)

PFC   Protocol Field Compression (in PPP, eliminating the *Protocol* field to reduce overhead)

PFS   Perfect Forward Secrecy (in public key cryptography, the property by which compromise of one key leads at most to the compromise of data encrypted with that key and not other data or keys)

PHB   Per-Hop Behavior (abstract behavior at router used to implement DS)

PHY   Physical (a layer in the OSI; usually describes connectors, frequencies, coding, and modulation)

PI   Provider-Independent (IP address space owned by a customer; not derived from an ISP's address prefix)

PIM   Protocol Independent Multicast (non-local multicast routing protocol that can leverage unicast routing protocols' data and operations)

PIO   Prefix Information Option (in ICMPv6, an option carrying an IP address prefix)

PKC   Public Key Certificate (a digital object including a public key and signature from a CA, along with various usage policies and parameters)

PKCS   Public Key Cryptography Standards (methods to encode and represent public key and related material)

PKI   Public Key Infrastructure (system for managing and distributing public keys)

PLCP   Physical Layer Convergence Procedure (802.11 method for encoding and determining frame type and radio parameters)

PMTU   Path MTU (minimum MTU across links on the path from sender to receiver)

PMTUD   PMTU Discovery (process of determining the PMTU; usually depends on ICMP PTB messages)

PNAC   Port-Based NAC (a version of NAC wherein the physical port of attachment is used in making an authorization decision)

PoE   Power over Ethernet (carries device power over Ethernet wiring)

POTS   Plain Old Telephone Service (conventional analog telephone service)

PPP   Point-to-Point Protocol (a link-layer configuration and data encapsulating protocol capable of carrying multiple network layer protocols and using multiple underlying physical links)

PPPoE   PPP over Ethernet (methods to establish a PPP association over an Ethernet link)

PPTP   Point-to-Point Tunneling Protocol (Microsoft's link layer tunneling protocol)

PRF   Pseudorandom Function Family (a set of functions that cannot be distinguished from truly random functions using a polynomial-time algorithm; also sometimes used less formally to refer to a single such function)

PRNG, PRG   Pseudo-Random Generator (a mathematical function used to compute a series of random-appearing values)

PSK   Pre-Shared Key (pre-placing encryption keys; no dynamic key exchange protocol used)

PSM   Power Save Mode (a mode of 802.11 where devices may "sleep" when not busy and poll to receive their information from an AP at a later time)

PSMP   Power-Save Multi-Poll (bi-directional version of APSD, part of 802.11n)

PTB   Packet Too Big (a ICMP Destination Unreachable Fragmentation Required or IPv6 Packet Too Big message indicating a packet is too large for the next-hop MTU size)

QAM   Quadrature Amplitude Modulation (combination of phase and amplitude modulation)

QBSS   QoS BSS (an 802.11 BSS enhanced with 802.11e or 802.11n QoS features)

QI   Query Interval (in IGMP and MLD, time between general queries)

QoS   Quality of Service (general term describing how traffic can be handled differently, usually with better or worse latency or drop precedence, based on configuration parameters)

QPSK   Quadrature Phase Shift Keying (typically, modulating two bits per symbol typically using four signal phases, although more advanced versions with more bits per symbol are possible)

QQI   Querier's Query Interval (in IGMP and MLD, time between sending general query messages; current non-querier multicast routers adopt the most recently received QQI value as their QI value)

QQIC   Querier's Query Interval Code (in IGMP and MLD messages, encoding of the QQI value)

QRI   Query Response Interval (in IGMP and MLD, the maximum amount of time a receiver is permitted to send a response to a query)

QRV   Querier Robustness Variable (in IGMP and MLD, sets number of retransmissions)

QS   Quick Start (in TCP, an experimental modification for faster startup behavior provided devices on the path agree)

QSTA   QoS STA (an 802.11 STA supporting QoS capabilities)

RA   Router Advertisement (message indicating presence of an on-link router neighbor; uses ICMP)

RADIUS   Remote Authentication Dial-In User Service protocol (a popular protocol for carrying AAA data)

RAIO   Relay Agent Information Option (in DHCPv6, an option used by relays to insert various bits of information)

RARP   Reverse ARP (protocol providing network layer to MAC layer address mappings)

RAS   Remote Access Server (a server that handles remote users—authentication, access control, etc.)

RC4   Rivest Cipher #4 (a popular symmetric key encryption scheme designed by Ron Rivest)

RD   Router Discovery (procedure to locate a proximal router; uses ICMP)

RDATA   Returned Data (part of the DNS protocol used to hold returned data)

RDNSS   Recursive DNS Server (used in RAs; indicates address of DNS server)

RED   Random Early Detection (an AQM scheme that marks or drops packets with increasing probability when persistent congestion appears to be growing)

RFC   Request for Comments (documents published by IETF; some are standards)

RGMP   Router-port Group Management Protocol (Cisco's protocol to enable IGMP snooping)

RH   Routing Header (an IPv6 extension header that alters traffic delivery path)

RHBP   Rate Halving with Bounded Pacing (in TCP, an evolved version of the FACK algorithm to help spread retransmissions more evenly across an RTT period after inferred packet loss)

RIP   Routing Information Protocol (small organization routing protocol; the original version does not support subnet masks)

RIR   Regional Internet Registry (allocates address space for some region of the world)

RO   Route Optimization (improving routes from indirect "dogleg" paths used in simple MIP)

ROAD   Running Out of Address Space (a problem motivating the creation of IPv6 and resulting in the creating of CIDR)

ROHC   Robust Header Compression (current-generation standards for protocol header compression)

RP   Rendezvous Point (used with multicast routing to exchange group information)

RPC   Remote Procedure Call (a framework supporting a program's procedure calls to be handled remotely)

RPF Reverse Path Forwarding (to avoid loops, an RPF check is performed by multicast routers to ensure a multicast datagram arrives on the same interface used to reach the sender)

RPSL Routing Policy Specification Language (a language used to express routing policies such as which network prefix corresponds to which owning AS)

RR Resource Record (a typed information block owned by a domain name and distributed via DNS)

RRP, RR Return Routability/Procedure (a check used with MIPv6 to ensure a mobile node is authentic, and includes a HoA check and CoA check)

RRset Resource Record Set (a collection of DNS RRs with same domain name owner and class)

RRSIG Resource Record Signature (DNS RR used with DNSSEC holding a signature on an RRset)

RS Router Solicitation (an ICMP message that induces a router to produce a response)

RSA Rabin, Shamir, Adelman (the most popular public key cryptography algorithm)

RSN Robust Security Network (improved security in IEEE 802.11i/WPA; included in 802.11 standard)

RSNA RSN Association (full use/implementation of RSN)

RST Reset (a TCP header bit and segment type that causes a TCP connection abort)

RSTP Rapid Spanning Tree Protocol (decreased latency version of STP)

RTO Retransmission Timeout (time before retransmitting data thought to be lost)

RTS Request To Send (message indicating desire to send a subsequent message)

RTT Round Trip Time (minimum time to expect a response from a communication peer)

RTTM RTT Measurement (an instantaneous estimate of the RTT)

RTTVAR RTT Variance (in TCP, time-averaged estimate of a connection's RTT deviation)

RTX Retransmission (re-sending of data)

RW Restart Window (in TCP, CWND value when TCP restarts sending after an idle period)

SA Security Association (in IPsec, state pertaining to a unidirectional association between peers; includes agreed-upon keys, algorithms, etc.; an SA can be unicast or multicast)

SACK   Selective Acknowledgment (in TCP, an option indicating correctly received out-of-sequence data)

SAD   Security Association Database (in IPsec, abstraction of database containing information on each active SA; logically indexed by SPI)

SAE   Simultaneous Authentication of Equals (form of authentication used with 802.11s)

SAP   Session Announcement Protocol (carries experimental multicast session announcements; *see also* SDP)

SCSV   Signaling Cipher Suite Value (in TLS, a CS value that indicates not a CS but a particular set of alternative functions or options)

SCTP   Stream Control Transport Protocol (a reliable transport protocol alternative to TCP that does not enforce strict ordering and supports multiple substreams and endpoint address changes)

SCVP   Server-Based Certificate Verification Protocol (a protocol supporting DPD and DPV for certificates)

SDID   Signing Domain Identifier (with DKIM, name for the domain of the signer)

SDLC   Synchronous Data Link Control (a precursor to HDLC, the link layer of SNA)

SDO   Standards-Defining Organization (including IEEE, IETF, ISO, ITU, 3GPP, 3GPP2)

SDP   Session Description Protocol (a protocol that describes multimedia sessions)

SEND   Secure Neighbor Discovery (a secure variant of ND using CGAs)

SEP   Secure Entry Point (in DNSSEC, indicates a DNSKEY RR contains a KSK)

SFD   Start Frame Delimiter (bit pattern indicating the starting portion of frame in a link PDU)

SG   Security Gateway (with IPsec, system terminating IPsec protocols, often at network edge)

SHA   Secure Hash Algorithm (one of a set of hashing algorithms suitable for ensuring message integrity)

SIFS   Shorts Inter-Frame Space (smallest amount of time between an 802.11 frame and its ACK)

SIIT   Stateless IP/ICMP Translation (a framework for translation between IPv4 and IPv6, including special rules for ICMP translation, NAT64, and DNS64)

SIP   Session Initiation Protocol (general signaling protocol; used with VoIP)

SLAAC   Stateless Address Autoconfiguration (a mechanism whereby a node self-configures its own IP address; usually applies to IPv6 nodes)

SLLAO Source Link-Layer Address Option (in ICMPv6, an option carrying the sender's link layer address)

SMSS Sender's MSS (the MSS for a connection as viewed by the sender)

SMTP Simple Mail Transfer Protocol (a protocol to carry e-mail in transit among mail transfer agents)

SNA Systems Network Architecture (IBM's network architecture)

SNAP Subnetwork Access Protocol (IEEE terminology for 802.2 encapsulation; rare for TCP/IP networks)

S-NAPTR Straightforward NAPTR (simplified NAPTR where AUS maps directly to result without regular expression substitution)

SNMP Simple Network Management Protocol (status reporting and configuration settings for network equipment; usually used with UDP/IP)

SOA Start of Authority (DNS RR indicating meta-data about a zone)

SOAP (formerly) Simple Object Access Protocol (a web services application protocol using XML, which provides RPC-like capabilities; SOAP is no longer an acronym)

SPD Security Policy Database (with IPsec, abstraction of database containing security policies applying to how traffic is handled—e.g., discard, bypass, or protect)

SPI Security Parameter Index (in IPsec, a logical index into the SAD to indicate security parameters, either 32 or 64 bits)

SPNAT, CGN, LSN Service-Provider ("large scale") NAT (a NAT deployment arrangement where address translation is performed by a service provider instead of a customer)

SRP Secure Remote Password (a strong key agreement protocol based on passwords; being supported by various security protocols such as TLS and EAP)

SRTP Secure Real-Time Protocol (a secure variant of the UDP/IP based real-time protocol; typically used to carry multimedia information)

SRTT Smoothed RTT (in TCP, time-averaged estimate of a connection's RTT)

SSDP Simple Service Discovery Protocol (an IETF-specified distributed service discovery protocol designed for LANs and residential networks used by UPnP)

SSH Secure Shell Protocol (secure remote login/execution protocol; also supports tunneling of other protocols)

SSID Service Set Identifier (802.11 network name)

SSL Secure Sockets Layer (encrypted and integrity-protected layer above TCP; precursor to TLS)

SSM   Single-Source Multicast (multicast wherein only a single party can source traffic to a particular group)

STA   Station (IEEE 802.11 terminology for an access point or associated wireless host)

STP   Spanning Tree Protocol (protocol used among bridges and switches to avoid loops)

STUN   Session Traversal Utilities for NAT (a client/server protocol for helping to fix the address and port number of a traffic flow when passing through a NAT)

SWS   Silly Window Syndrome (in protocols using window-based flow control, an undesirable situation where small amounts of data are exchanged due to the use of small window sizes)

SYN   Synchronize (a TCP header bit and first segment type sent on a TCP connection)

TCP   Transmission Control Protocol (a connection-oriented reliable stream protocol lacking message boundaries, which includes flow and congestion control)

TCP-AO   TCP Authentication Option (in TCP, an algorithm-agile mechanism to combat MSM attacks)

TDES, 3DES   Triple DES (encryption using three rounds of DES encipherment, resulting in an effective key length of 112 bits)

TDM   Time Division Multiplexing (sharing by allocation of separate usage time slots)

TFC   Traffic Flow Confidentiality (in IPsec, methods to disguise the traffic flow even when encrypted, including padding and generation of dummy packets)

TFRC   TCP Friendly Rate Control (methods to control the sending rate of a protocol so as to not compete unfairly with a TCP flow in a similar operating environment)

TFTP   Trivial File Transfer Protocol (UDP/IP-based simple transfer protocol)

TKIP   Temporal Key Integrity Protocol (replaced the WEP encryption algorithm for WPA)

TLD   Top-Level Domain (a top-level domain name such as EDU, COM, UK, ZA)

TLS   Transport Layer Security (based on the SSL protocol developed by Netscape)

TLV   Type/Length Value (used in protocols; indicates a type, length of variable-length value, and the value)

ToS   Type of Service (older name for the IPv4 header byte indicating type of service; replaced with DS Field and ECN bits)

TS   Traffic Selector (with IKE, specifications for identifying traffic such as IP address range, port number, etc.)

TSER, TSecr   Timestamp Echo Reply (in TCP, portion of TSOPT used to echo TSV value to peer)

TSF   Time Synchronization Function (establishes a common time in an 802.11 BSS)

TSIG   Transaction Signatures (signatures used to secure individual DNS transactions, not content from its origin)

TSOPT   Timestamps Option (in TCP, an option including the TSV and TSER values)

TSPEC   Traffic Specification (a structure indicating traffic parameters for 802.11 QoS)

TSV   Timestamp Value (in TCP, portion of TSOPT used to identify the sender's time—used in RTTM and PAWS)

TTL   Time-to-Live (IPv4 header field indicating number of remaining router hops allowed for a datagram)

TURN   Traversal Using Relay NAT (a protocol in which a third party relays information between hosts that are otherwise unable to communicate due to the presence of one or more NATs)

TWA   Time-Wait Assassination (in TCP, an erroneous condition caused by receiving certain segments during TIME-WAIT state)

TXOP   Transmission Opportunity (in 802.11, a form of "credit" allowing a station to send one or more frames)

TXT   Text (DNS RR carrying descriptive text; used by DKIM)

UBM   Unicast Prefix-based Multicast addressing (deriving multicast addresses based on assigned unicast prefixes)

UDL   Unidirectional Link (link providing communication in only one direction)

UDP   User Datagram Protocol (a best-effort message protocol with message boundaries and lacking congestion or flow control)

UEQM   Unequal Modulation (using different modulation schemes on different data streams simultaneously)

ULA   Unique Local IPv6 Unicast Addresses (private addresses used with IPv6, allocated from the fc00::/7 prefix)

U-NAPTR   URI-enabled NAPTR (simplified NAPTR allowing limited regular expression substitution)

U-NII   Unlicensed National Information Infrastructure (unlicensed radio spectrum in much of the world)

UNSAF   Unilateral Self-Address Fixing (heuristics used in an attempt to determine how a traffic flow is identified after passing through a NAT; a fragile process for which techniques like ICE are recommended alternatives)

UP   User Priority (802.11 priorities; based on same terminology from 802.1d)

UPnP   Universal Plug and Play (a protocol framework for device and service discovery aimed at the residential user; standardized by the UPnP Forum)

URG   Urgent Mechanism (in TCP, a method for marking and indentifying information as "urgent"; not recommended for use)

URI   Universal Resource Identifier (string of characters identifying a name or resource on the Internet, including URLs and URNs)

URL   Uniform Resource Locator (informally, a "WWW address")

URN   Universal Resource Name (a URI using the urn scheme not implying availability of resource)

USRK   Usage-Specific Root Key (key derived from an EMSK intended to be used for certain purposes)

UTC   Coordinated Universal Time (standard time used by NTP and other protocols; effectively interchangeable with GMT but with some technical differences)

UTO   User Timeout (in TCP, the maximum time a TCP sender will wait attempting to retransmit before abandoning a connection)

VC   Virtual Circuit (a simulated dedicated communication path)

VLAN   Virtual LAN (used most often to simulate multiple distinct LANs on shared wiring)

VLSM   Variable-Length Subnet Masks (proximal use of subnet masks of differing lengths in same environment)

VoIP   Voice over IP (the carriage of voice traffic over IP networks, usually involves SIP signaling)

VPN   Virtual Private Network (virtually isolated network; often encrypted)

W3C   World Wide Web Consortium (SDO defining web standards such as XML)

WAN   Wide Area Network (a network connecting geographically distributed sites; usually involving multiple administrative authorities)

WEP   Wired Equivalent Privacy (original WiFi encryption; found to be catastrophically weak)

WESP   Wrapped ESP (in IPsec, a method to prepend ESP with a header to indicate if the following traffic is encrypted or only authenticated; useful for inspection by middleboxes)

Wi-Fi Wireless Fidelity (IEEE 802.11 wireless LAN standard)

WiMAX Worldwide Interoperability for Microwave Access (IEEE 802.16 wireless broadband standard)

WKP Well-Known Prefix (a checksum neutral IPv6 prefix, 64:ff9b::/96, used in algorithmic mappings between IPv4 and IPv6 addresses)

WLAN Wireless LAN (a wireless LAN such as WiFi)

WMM Wi-Fi Multimedia (subset of 802.11e QoS functions now available in 802.11n)

WoL Wake on LAN (method to remain in "sleep" mode until a particular packet is received)

WPA WiFi Protected Access (802.11 encryption method)

WPAD Web Proxy Autodiscovery Protocol (a protocol to discover the presence of a proximate WWW proxy)

WRED Weighted RED (RED where the mark/drop probablity is a function of traffic class and weight assignment)

WSCALE, WOPT, WSOPT Window Scale Option (in TCP, an option indicating a scaling factor is to be applied to the Window Size field)

WWW World Wide Web (networked data environment using the HTTP/TCP/IP protocol suite)

X.25 ITU-T recommendation X.25 (an ITU-T standard packet switched network standard covering OSI layers 1-3; the most popular packet switched technology until widespread use of TCP/IP)

XML Extensible Markup Language (a set of rules for encoding documents in machine-readable form; extensively used by web services)

XMPP Extensible Messaging and Presence Protocol (an open, extensible, HTML-based protocol for the exchange of messages, presence, and contact list information)

ZSK Zone Signing Key (a key used with DNSSEC for signing zone contents, usually signed by a KSK)

Index

Symbols

* (Wildcard)
    domain names and, 526
    local IP address restrictions in server design,
        500–501
.in-addr.arpa
    classless delegation, 539
    special domain for IPv4, 537–538
.ip6.arpa, 537–538

Numbers

2.4GHz band, Wi-Fi, 124–126
3DES. *See* Triple-DES
3GPP (3rd Generation Partnership Project), 275, 933
5GHz band, Wi-Fi, 124–126
6rd (IPv6 Rapid Deployment), 339, 933
6to4
    definition of, 933
    IPv4 to IPv6 transition, 482

A

A (address) records
    definition of, 529, 933
    overview of, 529–530
    querying, 531
    translating DNS from IPv4 to IPv6, 569
A-MPDU (aggregated MAC protocol data unit)
    definition of, 934
    frame aggregation support, 118–119
A-MSDU (aggregated MAC service data unit)
    definition of, 934
    frame aggregation support, 118
AAA (authentication, authorization, and account-
    ing), 833–834, 933
AAAA (address) records
    definition of, 933
    DNS resource record types, 529–530
    translating DNS from IPv4 to IPv6, 569
Abbreviated handshake, TLS, 881
ABC (Appropriate Byte Counting), in TCP, 733, 933
Abortive release, of TCP connections, 627
Abstract Syntax Notation One (ASN.1), 935
Access categories (ACs), in EDCA, 123

Access control
    NAC (Network Access Control), 833–837
    RADIUS server for, 141
Access control lists. *See* ACLs (access control lists)
Access Network Discovery and Selection Function
    (ANDSF), 275, 934
Access points. *See* APs (access points)
ACCM (Asynchronous Control Character Map), in
    PPP
    definition of, 933
    escaping characters and, 134–135
ACD (Address Conflict Detection), 176–177, 933
ACFC (Address and Control Field Compression), in
    PPP, 132, 933
ACK clock, in TCP, 731
ACK division, attack against TCP, 785
Acknowledge Number field, in GRE tunnels, 150
ACKs (acknowledgement)
    clocking congestion via, 730–731
    combined with SYN segments (SACK), 607
    cumulative in TCP, 586–587
    definition of, 933
    duplicate ACK threshold in fast retransmit, 667
    establishing TCP connections and, 597, 602–603
    NAT and TCP and, 307–308
    requesting connection to nonexistent TCP port,
        626
    retransmission and, 580–581
    retransmission timeout settings, 584
    stretch ACKs in recovery from local congestion,
        754–757
    TCP header field, 588–589
    TCP segments and, 701
    in Wi-Fi control frames, 116
    window update and, 583
ACLs (access control lists)
    definition of, 933
    in packet-filtering firewalls, 300
    rules in, 335
ACs (access categories), in EDCA, 123
ACs (attribute certificates)
    as alternative to public key certificates, 831
    definition of, 933

ACSII characters, escaping in PPP operations, 134–135

Actions, in ACL rules, 335

Active attacks, threats to network communication, 807–809

Active closer, FIN segments and, 597

Active open, in TCP connections, 597

Active opener (client)
RST segments, 631
simultaneous open and, 600
in TCP connections, 596, 599

Active queue management (AQM), 782–785, 935

Ad hoc mode, Wi-Fi, 112

Ad-Hoc On-Demand Distance Vector (AODV)
definition of, 934
Wi-Fi mesh and, 130

Additive increase/additive decrease (AIAD)
congestion control and, 777
definition of, 934

Additive increase/multiplicative decrease (AIMD)
congestion control and, 769
definition of, 934

Address (A) records. See A (address) records

Address (AAAA) records. See AAAA (address) records

Address (Addr) field, in PPP frames, 132

Address and Control Field Compression (ACFC), in PPP, 132, 933

Address autoconfiguration. See SLAAC (stateless address autoconfiguration)

Address behavior, in NAT, 311–313

Address Conflict Detection (ACD), 176–177, 933

Address Family Transition Router (AFTR), in DS-Lite, 340, 934

Address management, DHCP for, 235

Address pools, DHCP, 235–236

Address realms
IP addresses, 299
proxy firewalls supporting private address realms, 301

Address Resolution Protocol (ARP), 165

Address selection, in IP host models
destination address selection algorithm, 224–225
overview of, 222–223
source address selection algorithm, 223–224

Address unreachable message, ICMPv6, 364

Admin-scope boundaries, in router configuration, 53

Administrative prohibition, ICMP messages and, 365

Administrative scope, in multicast addresses, 53

ADSP (Author Domain Signing Practices), in DKIM, 916–917, 933

Advanced Encryption Standard. See AES (Advanced Encryption Standard)

ADVERTISE message, DHCPv6, 262–264

Advertised window. See awnd (advertised window)

Advertisement Interval option, neighbor discovery in IPv6, 412

Advertisement messages, in MRD, 394–395

AEAD (authenticated encryption with associated data), 820, 934

AES (Advanced Encryption Standard)
definition of, 934
standardized for Internet use, 819
as symmetric encryption algorithm, 811
in Wi-Fi security, 129

AES-MAC, 819

AF (Assured Forwarding), 190, 934

AFTR (Address Family Transition Router), in DS-Lite, 340, 934

Aggregated MAC service data unit. See A-MSDU (aggregated MAC service data unit)

Aggregation
route aggregation, 50
of Wi-Fi frames, 116–119

Agile probing, in TCP, 779

AH (Authentication Header)
authentication and integrity protection with, 856, 858
definition of, 934
fields in, 856
in IPSec, 841
NAT updates and, 866
overview of, 454–455
transport and tunnel modes, 856–857

AIA (Authority Information Access)
certificate extension, 828
definition of, 934

AIAD (additive increase/additive decrease)
congestion control and, 777
definition of, 934

AIMD (additive increase/multiplicative decrease)
congestion control and, 769
definition of, 934

Alert protocol, TLS handshaking, 880

ALGs (application layer gateways). See also Gateways
definition of, 934
IP routers, 20
IPv4/IPv6 translation, 340–345
NAT Traversal as alternative to, 316
proxy firewalls and, 301

Allocation of IP addresses
multicast addresses, 65
overview of, 62
unicast addresses, 62–65
to users and organizations, 31

Alternate ports
    RSTP, 110
    STP, 104–105
Amplification attacks, DNS-related attacks, 571
ANDSF (Access Network Discovery and Selection
    Function), 275, 934
Answer, authority, and additional information sec-
    tion, of DNS message, 526–527
Any-source multicast (ASM)
    definition of, 935
    as multicast service model, 54
Anycast addresses, 62
AODV (Ad-Hoc On-Demand Distance Vector)
    definition of, 934
    Wi-Fi mesh and, 130
APIPA (Automatic Private IP Addressing)
    definition of, 934
    SLAAC and, 276, 284
APIs (Application Programming Interfaces)
    definition of, 934
    design and, 22
Application design
    APIs in, 22
    client/server design pattern, 20–21
    peer-to-peer design pattern, 21–22
Application layer
    full-duplex TCP service to, 587
    of OSI model, 10
    TCP and UDP services for, 585
Application-managed keepalives, 794
Application Programming Interfaces. *See* APIs
    (Application Programming Interfaces)
Application protocols, NAT and, 304
Application-unique strings. *See* AUS (application-
    unique strings)
Appropriate Byte Counting (ABC), in TCP, 733, 933
APs (access points)
    definition of, 934
    ICMP fast handover messages and, 388
    Wi-Fi, 112
APSD (automatic power save delivery), 120, 935
AQM (active queue management), 782–785, 935
Architecture, protocol
    end-to-end argument, 6
    error control and flow control, 7–8
    fate sharing, 6–7
    packets, connections, and datagrams, 3–6
    principles of, 2–3
    of protocol suite, 1
ARM (ARPANET Reference Model), 1–2, 13–16
ARP (Address Resolution Protocol)
    ACD (Adddress Conflict Detection), 176–177
    announcement packets, 176

`arp` command, 177–178
    attacks related to, 178–179
    cache, 169–170
    cache timeout, 174
    definition of, 935
    determining MAC addresses, 442
    direct delivery and, 167–169
    example of use, 166–167
    frame format, 170–171
    gratuitous ARP, 175–176
    interaction between IP fragmentation and
        ARP/ND, 496–497
    introduction to, 165–166
    IPv4 and, 13
    operation of, 171–173
    Proxy ARP, 174–175
    request to nonexistent host, 173–174
    setting IPv4 address for embedded device, 178
    summary and references, 179–180
    TCP connection timeouts and, 604
`arp` command
    ARP cache timeout and, 174
    examining ARP cache, 169–170
    options, 177–178
ARP hack, 175
ARP poisoning, attacks on ICMP, 429
ARP probe, ACD defining, 176
ARP reply frames, 168
ARP request frames
    direct delivery and, 167
    Proxy ARP and, 174–175
    request to nonexistent host, 173–174
ARPANET Reference Model (ARM), 1–2, 13–16
ARQ (Automatic Repeat Request), 579–581, 935
AS (Authentication Server), in PANA, 935
AS (autonomous system)
    definition of, 935
    multicast addresses based on, 55
ASM (any-source multicast)
    definition of, 935
    as multicast service model, 54
ASN.1 (Abstract Syntax Notation One), 935
Assignment of unicast addresses
    to devices, 32
    multiple providers/multiple networks/multiple
        addresses, 68–70
    overview of, 65–66
    single provider/multiple networks/multiple
        addresses, 67–68
    single provider/no network/single address, 66–67
    single provider/single network/single address, 67
Assignment policies, IA (Identity Association) based
    on, 255–256

Assured Forwarding (AF), 190, 934
Asymmetric (public) key ciphers. *See also* Public key
        cryptography, 809–812
Asynchronous Control Character Map (ACCM)
    definition of, 933
    escaping characters and, 134–135
Attacks
    ARP, 178–179
    DNS, 571–572
    ICMP, 428–429
    Internet architecture, 25–26
    IP address, 70–71
    IP protocol, 226
    link layer, 154–156
    on NAT and firewall, 345–346
    system configuration, 292
    TCP, 640–643
    TCP congestion control and, 785–786
    TCP keepalive and, 802
    TCP timeout/retransmission and, 687
    TCP window management and, 723
    UDP, 507–508
Attribute certificates (ACs)
    as alternative to public key certificates, 831
    definition of, 933
Attribution, of datagrams, 26
Auditability, ESP and, 863
Augmented message, CRC, 86
AUS (application-unique strings)
    definition of, 935
    ENUM records and, 551–552
    NAPTR records and, 549
AUTH (authentication packets), in IKE, 935
Authenticated encryption, 814–815
Authenticated encryption with associated data
        (AEAD), 820, 934
Authenticated nonexistence, DNSSEC, 895
Authentication
    AH (Authentication Header). *See* AH (Authenti-
        cation Header)
    basic principles of security, 806–807
    DHCP and, 271–273
    EAP methods for, 838
    PPP and, 140–141
    PSKs (preshared keys) for, 129–130
    SAE (Simultaneous Authentication of Equals),
        130
    SHA-1 algorithm in, 268
    spoofing attacks and, 226
    TCP-AO (Authentication Option), 612
Authentication, authorization, and accounting
        (AAA), 833–834, 933

Authentication Header. *See* AH (Authentication
        Header)
Authentication Option (TCP-AO)
    definition of, 959
    TCP header, 612
Authentication Server (AS), in PANA, 55, 935
Author Domain Signing Practices (ADSP), 916–917, 933
Authorities, in allocation of IP addresses, 62
Authority Information Access (AIA)
    certificate extension, 828
    definition of, 934
Authority Key Identifier, for identifying public keys,
        828, 830
Auto-proxy ARP, 175
Automatic power save delivery (APSD), 120, 935
Automatic Repeat Request (ARQ), 579–581, 935
Autonegotiation, in Ethernet
    duplex mismatch and, 96
Autonomous system (AS)
    definition of, 935
    multicast addresses based on, 55
Autotuning TCP receive windows, 715–716
Availability, in CIA triad, 806
awnd (advertised window) in TCP
    overview of, 729–730
    slow start algorithm and, 733–734, 736
AXFR (full zone transfer) messages, in DNS,
        559–561, 935

B
B4 (Bridging Broadband), 340, 935
Backoff factor, RTO and, in TCP, 655
Backoff time, in MAC, 121–122
Backup ports, STP, 104–105
BACP (Bandwidth Allocation Control Protocol), 139,
        935
Bandwidth Allocation Protocol (BAP), 139
Bandwidth (capacity)
    allocating in MP, 139
    buffer bloat and, 781
    connections and, 3
Bandwidth-delay product. *See* BDP (bandwidth-
        delay product)
Bandwidth on demand (BOD), 139, 936
Bandwidth-scalable TCPs, 773
Bank teller's algorithm, 138
BAP (Bandwidth Allocation Protocol), 139
Baran, Paul, 1
Basic Encoding Rules (BER), 935
Basic service set. *See* BSS (basic service set)
BCMCS (Broadcast and Multicast Service Control-
        ler), 935

BCP (best current practice) category, RFCs and, 23
BDP (bandwidth-delay product)
   congestion control and, 730
   high-speed networks and, 770
   HSTCP (HighSpeed TCP) and, 772
BER (Basic Encoding Rules), 935
BER (bit error rate)
   data frame fragmentation, 117–118
   definition of, 935
Berkeley Internet Name Domain v. 9 (BIND9), 935
Berkeley sockets
   half-close support, 598
   incoming connection queue and, 636, 639–640
   popular APIs, 22
   restrictions on foreign endpoints, 635
   state transitions, 618
   TCP ports, 588
   TCP_NODELAY option for disabling Nagle
      algorithm, 700
Berkeley Software Distribution. *See* BSD (Berkeley
      Software Distribution)
Best current practice (BCP) category, RFCs and, 23
Best-effort delivery, of packets, 7
Better-than-Nothing Security (BTNS), 852, 936
BGP (Border Gateway Protocol), 935
BI (binary increase), 774
BIC (Binary Increase Congestion Control)
   BIC-TCP, 773–774
   overview of, 772–773
Bidirectional tunneling, in mobile IP, 216–217
Big endian byte ordering, 183
Binary additive increase algorithm, 773–774
Binary exponential backoff, retransmission and, 650
Binary increase (BI), 774
Binary Increase Congestion Control (BIC)
   BIC-TCP, 773–774
   overview of, 772–773
Binary notation
   expressing IP addresses in, 32–33
   prefixes, 48
   of subnet masks, 39
Binary phase shift keying (BPSK)
   definition of, 936
   higher throughput (802.11n) support and, 128
Binary search increase algorithm, BIC-TCP and,
      773–774
BIND9 (Berkeley Internet Name Domain v. 9), 935
Binding method, in STUN, 321
Binding, MNs (mobile nodes), 216–217
Binding Update (BU), in MIP, 936
Bit error rate (BER)
   data frame fragmentation, 117–118
   definition of, 935

Bit flipping attack, 918
Bit stuffing, in PPP frames, 132
BITS (Bump in the Stack), in IPsec, 840, 935
BITW (Bump in the Wire), in IPsec, 840, 936
Bitwise AND operation, used with subnet masks, 40
BL (Bulk Leasequery)
   DCHP relay agents, 269–270
   definition of, 936
Black hats, attacks related to Internet architecture, 26
Black holes, in PMTUD, 613
Blackhole route messages, ICMPv6, 372
Block ciphers, 811
Blocking route messages, ICMPv6, 372
Bloop attacks, 429
BOD (bandwidth on demand), 139, 936
Bombs, ICMP attacks, 428
Bonding, link aggregation and, 92–93
Boot Server Discovery Protocol (BSDP), 246, 936
BOOTP (Internet Bootstrap Protocol)
   compatibility with DHCP, 236–238
   definition of, 936
   DHCP based on, 235
   options, 238–239
   relay agents, 268
BOOTREQUEST, 239, 242
Border Gateway Protocol (BGP), 209, 935
Bot attacks, 26
Bot herders, 806
Botnets
   attacks related to Internet architecture, 26
   taking control of computers, 806
BPDUs (Bridge PDUs)
   building the spanning tree, 107
   definition of, 936
   RSTP (Rapid Spanning Tree Protocol), 110–111
   STP and, 104
   structure of, 105–107
   viewing with Wireshark, 109
BPSK (binary phase shift keying)
   definition of, 936
   higher throughput (802.11n) support and, 128
Bridge PDUs. *See* BPDUs (Bridge PDUs)
Bridges
   layer 2 relay agents, 270
   overview of, 98–102
   STP. *See* STP (Spanning Tree Protocol)
Bridging Broadband (B4), in DS-Lite, 340, 935
Broadcast addresses
   overview of, 15
   setting/finding, 437–439
   structure of, 42–43
Broadcast and Multicast Service Controller
      (BCMCS), in cellular networks, 239, 935

Broadcast domain, link-layer broadcast, 167
Broadcasting
    introduction to, 435–436
    overview of, 436–437
    sending broadcast datagrams, 439–441
    setting/finding broadcast addresses, 437–439
Brute-force attacks, 816
BSD (Berkeley Software Distribution)
    definition of, 936
    standards and, 24
    Tahoe release, 737
BSDP (Boot Server Discovery Protocol), 246, 936
BSS (basic service set)
    definition of, 936
    QoS BBS, 122
    Wi-Fi, 112
BTNS (Better-than-Nothing Security), in IPsec, 852,
    936
BU (Binding Update), in MIP, 936
Buffer bloat, TCP congestion control and, 781–782
Buffer overflow, worms, 805
Buffers
    large buffers and auto-tuning, 715–719
    packets stored in, 4
Bulk data, in TCP communication, 692
Bulk Leasequery (BL)
    DCHP relay agents, 269–270
    definition of, 936
Bump in the Stack (BITS), in IPsec, 840, 935
Bump in the Wire (BITW),in IPsec, 840, 936
Bundles, of PPP links, 137, 139
Byte stuffing, in PPP frames, 132

C
Cache
    ARP cache, 169–170
    ARP cache timeouts, 174
Cache poisoning, DNS-related attacks, 572
Caching servers, DNS, 517–518
CALIPSO (Common architecture Label IPv6 Secu-
    rity Option), 199, 936
Callback Control Protocol (CBCP), in PPP
    definition of, 936
    negotiation of callbacks in LCP, 136
Callback, PPP supporting, 136
CAMELLIA, standardized for Internet use, 819
Candidate sets (CS), in source address selection,
    223–224
Candidate transport addresses, in ICE, 333
Canonical name records. See CNAME (canonical
    name) records
Canonical ordering, of RRset in DNSSEC, 902–903
Capture, network communication, 808

Capturing portals, link layer attacks, 155
Care-of address (CoA)
    definition of, 937
    in Mobile IP, 216–217
Care-of Test (CoT)
    definition of, 937
    mobility messages in RRP, 218–219
Care-of Test Init (CoTI)
    definition of, 937
    mobility messages in RRP, 218–219
Carrier-grade NAT (CGN), 315
Carrier sense, 120
Carrier sense, multiple access with collision avoid-
    ance. See CSMA/CA (carrier sense, multiple
    access with collision avoidance)
Carrier sensed, multiple access with collision detec-
    tion (CSMA/CD)
    definition of, 938
    Ethernet interface and, 80–81
CAs (certification authorities). See also Certificates
    (public key)
    definition of, 936
    PKI (Public Key Infrastructure) and, 821–822
Catenet. See also Internetwork, 1
CBC (cipher block chaining)
    block ciphers in encryption algorithms, 820
    definition of, 936
CBC-MAC (cipher block chaining message authenti-
    cation code), 129
CBCP (Callback Control Protocol)
    definition of, 936
    negotiation of callbacks in LCP, 136
CCA (clear channel assessment), in Wi-Fi
    definition of, 936
    for physical carrier sense, 121
CCITT (Comité Consultatif International Télé-
    graphique), 24, 936
CCM (counter mode)
    CCMP algorithm based on, 129
    definition of, 936
CCMP (counter mode with CBC Message Authenti-
    cation Code)
    definition of, 936
    in Wi-Fi security, 129–130
CCP (Compression Control Protocol), in PPP,
    definition of, 936
    MPPE and, 145
    overview of, 139–140
ccTLDs (country code TLDs)
    definition of, 937
    in DNS name space, 512–514
CDN (content delivery networks), 535
CDP (CRL Distribution Point), 828–829, 937

CE (Congestion Experienced) bit, in IP header, 783–784
CERT (Computer Emergency Response Team), 937
Certificate Policies (CP), 828
Certificate Request (CERTREQ) payload
    definition of, 937
    in IKE, 869–870
Certificate revocation lists. *See* CRLs (certificate revocation lists)
Certificates, ACs (attribute certificates), 831
Certificates option, in ND, 417
Certificates (public key)
    CAs and PKIs and, 821–822
    extensions, 827–828
    for identifying four types of Internet entities, 823
    validating, 826
    validating and revoking certificates, 828–831
    viewing preconfigured, 823–826
Certificates, SEND, 403
Certification authorities. *See* CAs (certification authorities)
Certification Path Advertisement message, ICMP Send messages, 407
Certification Path Solicitation message, ICMP Send messages, 406–407
Certification Practice Statement (CPS), 937
CERTREQ (Certificate Request) payload
    definition of, 937
    in IKE, 869–870
CGAs (cryptographically generated addresses)
    definition of, 937
    Handover Key Request/Reply options, 422–423
    neighbor discovery options in IPv6, 414–415
    RSA Signature option, 415–416
    securing IPv6 Neighbor Discovery, 292
    SEND (Secure Neighbor Discovery) and, 403–406
    verification of, 405
CGN (carrier-grade NAT), 315
Chaddr (Client Hardware Address) field
    DHCP/BOOTP message format, 238
    MAC addresses in, 244
Challenge-response protocols, 816
Change Cipher Spec protocol, 878
Channels
    in SSM multicast service model, 54
    TURN, 327
    Wi-Fi, 124
CHAP (Challenge-Handshake Authentication Protocol)
    definition of, 937
    for PPP authentication, 140–141
Character stuffing, in PPP frames, 132
Checkpointing, saving work, 10

Checksums
    (Generic Routing Encapsulation), 150
    applying at application layer, 601
    for detecting packet errors, 580
    IP header fields, 185
    TCP, 586, 590
    UDP, 475–478
    UDP-Lite, 487–488
    verifying message integrity, 817
    WKP checksum neutrality, 341
CIA (confidentiality, integrity, and availability)
    AH and, 856, 858
    definition of, 937
    ESP and, 860
    overview of, 806
ciaddr (Client IP address) field, 237
CIDR (Classless Inter-Domain Routing)
    definition of, 937
    developed to alleviate pressure on available IPv4 addresses, 47–48
    masks, 47
    routing scalability addressed by, 303
Cipher-based MAC (CMAC), 819–820, 937
Cipher block chaining (CBC)
    block ciphers in encryption algorithms, 820
    definition of, 936
Cipher block chaining message authentication code (CBC-MAC), 129
Cipher Change protocol, TLS handshaking, 880
Cipher suite rollback attacks, 919
Cipher suites. *See* CS (cipher suites)
Ciphertext
    encrypting cleartext message, 810
    TLS, 878–879
Civic location, location information in DHCP, 274
Clark, D., 3
Class of Service (CoS), 937
Class selector code points, 190
Class Selector (CS), 938
Classes, IP address
    Class D addresses reserved for IPv4 multicast, 54–55
    overview of, 34–36
    prefix length and, 47–48
Classic RTO method, 651–652
Classless Inter-Domain Routing. *See* CIDR (Classless Inter-Domain Routing)
Classless routes, DHCP and, 246
Classless Static Route (CSR) parameter, 246
Clear channel assessment (CCA)
    definition of, 936
    for physical carrier sense, 121
Clear to send. *See* CTS (clear to send)

Client alive messages, 802
Client Hardware Address (Chaddr) field
    DHCP/BOOTP message format, 238
    MAC addresses in, 244
Client IP address (Ciaddr) field, in DHCP, 237
Client/server design pattern, 20–21
Client state machine, DHCP, 251–252
ClientHello message, in TLS, 887
Clients
    keepalives detecting state of client host, 795
    setting keepalive time for Windows client,
        797–799
Clock granularity, RTO bounds and, 654
Clock recovery, Ethernet frames, 84
CLOSED state, in TCP,
    sharing connection state, 768
    simultaneous open and close transitions, 625
    TCP state transitions, 618
CLOSE_WAIT state, TCP state transitions, 618
CMAC (cipher-based MAC), 819–820, 937
CNAME (canonical name) records
    definition of, 937
    DNS resource record types, 534–536
    translating DNS from IPv4 to IPv6, 569
CNs (correspondent nodes), in MIP, 216–218, 937
CoA (care-of address)
    definition of, 937
    in Mobile IP, 216–217
Coding theory, 579
Collision Count field, CGAs, 404–405
Comité Consultatif International Télégraphique
        (CCITT), 24, 936
Common architecture Label IPv6 Security Option
        (CALIPSO), 199, 936
Communication protocols
    ARQ (Automatic Repeat Request), 579–581
    congestion control, 583–584
    flow control, 583
    introduction to, 579
    retransmission settings, 584
    sliding windows, 582
    TCP. See TCP (Transmission Control Protocol)
    windows of packets, 581–582
Compound TCP (CTCP) algorithm, 779–781, 938
Compression
    ACFC (Address and Control Field Compression),
        132
    CCP (Compression Control Protocol), 139–140
    header compression, 139, 142–143
    MPPC (Microsoft Point-to-Point Compression
        Protocol), 140
    PFC (Protocol Field Compression), 133

VJ (Van Jacobson) compression, 141
Compression Control Protocol. See CCP (Compres-
        sion Control Protocol)
Compression labels, DNS names and, 523–524
Compression-optional attributes, STUN, 321
Computer Emergency Response Team (CERT), 937
Computer Systems Research Group (CSRG), 24, 938
Concurrent servers, 21
Confidentiality, in CIA triad, 806
Confidentiality, integrity, and availability. See CIA
        (confidentiality, integrity, and availability)
Configuration data delivery, DHCP for, 235
Configuration Payload (CP)
    definition of, 937
    IKE, 849
Congestion avoidance algorithm
    classic algorithms for TCP congestion, 734–736
    comparing with slow start, 736–737
Congestion collapse state, 728
Congestion control. See also Flow control
    in communication protocols, 583–584
    in TCP. See TCP congestion control
    in UPD server design, 505
Congestion Experienced (CE) indicator, in IP header,
        783–784
Congestion indicator, ECN, 188
Congestion Manager, 768
Congestion window. See cwnd (congestion window)
Congestion Window Reducing. See CWR (Conges-
        tion Window Reducing)
Congestion Window Validation (CWV), in TCP,
        742–744, 938
Connection completion, TCP congestion control,
        766–767
Connection-oriented networks, 5
Connection-oriented protocols, 595
Connection-oriented service, 585
Connection refused error, in TCP and UDP, 626
Connection state, TCP, 595
Connectionless networks, 5, 181
Connectionless protocols, 595
Connections, in protocol architecture, 3–6
Connections, TCP
    aborting, 627–628
    attacks related to, 640–643
    establishing and terminating, 595–598
    example of PMTUD with, 613–616
    example showing packet-level details, 602–604
    FIN_WAIT_2 state, 625
    half-close operation, 598–599
    half-open connections, 628–630
    header options, 605–606

incoming connection queue, 636–640
introduction to, 595
ISN (initial sequence number), 601–602
MSS (Maximum Segment Size) option, 606–607
PAWS (Protection against Wrapped Sequence
        Numbers), 610–611
PMTUD (Path MTU Discovery) and, 612–613
port numbers and, 632–634
quiet time concept, 624
requesting connection to nonexistent port, 626
reset segments, 625–626
restrictions on foreign endpoints, 635–636
restrictions on local IP addresses, 634–635
SACK (selective acknowledgement) option, 607
server operation and, 631–632
simultaneous open and close, 599–601
simultaneous open and close transitions, 625
state transition diagrams, 617–618
summary and references, 643–645
TCP-AO (Authentication Option), 612
timeout settings, 604–605
Timestamps option, 608–610
TIME_WAIT state (2MSL), 618–624
translating addresses and port numbers, 605
TWA (TIME-WAIT Assassination), 630–631
UTO (User Timeout) option, 611–612
WSCALE (Window Scale) option, 608
Conservation of packets, 731
Content delivery networks (CDN), 535
Content filters, web proxies operating as, 302
Contention window (CW)
    definition of, 938
    in MAC, 122
Control field, in PPP frames, 132
Control frames, Wi-Fi, 115–116
Cooks, C., 814
Coordinated Universal Time (UTC), 961
Correspondent nodes (CNs), in MIP, 216–218, 937
Correspondent registration, in RO, 218
CoS (Class of Service), 937
CoT (Care-of Test)
    definition of, 937
    mobility messages in RRP, 218–219
CoTI (Care-of Test Init)
    definition of, 937
    mobility messages in RRP, 218–219
Counter (CTR) mode
    definition of, 938
    operating modes of encryption algorithms, 820
Counter mode (CCM)
    CCMP algorithm based on, 129
    definition of, 936

Counter mode with CBC Message Authentication
        Code (CCMP)
    definition of, 936
    in Wi-Fi security, 129–130
Counters, IGMP/MLD, 467–468
Country code TLDs (ccTLDs)
    definition of, 937
    in DNS name space, 512–514
CP (Certificate Policies), 828
CP (Configuration Payload)
    definition of, 937
    IKE, 849
CPS (Certification Practice Statement), 937
CRCs (Cyclic Redundancy Checks)
    applying at application layer, 601
    compared with Internet checksum, 186
    definition of, 937
    for detecting errors in packets, 580
    host address filtering and, 449, 451
    integrity checking in Ethernet frames, 86–88
    TCP reliability and, 586
CREATE_CHILD_SA exchange, IKE protocol, 852–853
CRL Distribution Point (CDP), 828–829, 937
CRLs (certificate revocation lists)
    definition of, 937
    distribution point for, 828–829
    extensions, 830
Cryptographic suites, 819–821
Cryptographically generated addresses. See CGAs
        (cryptographically generated addresses)
Cryptographically strong PRNGs (CSPRNGs), 816,
        938
Cryptography. See also Encryption
    attacks, 918
    cryptographic and cipher suites, 819–821
    cryptosystems, 809–812
    DH (Diffie-Hellman-Merkle Key Agreement),
        813–814
    ECC (Elliptic Curve Cryptography), 815
    hash functions and message digests, 817–818
    message authentication codes, 818–819
    message syntax, 823
    nonces and salt, 816
    overview of, 809
    PFS (Perfect Forward Secrecy), 815
    pseudorandom numbers, generators, and func-
        tion families, 815–816
    RSA (Rivest, Shamir, and Adleman) public key
        cryptography, 812–813
    signcryption, 814–815
CS (candidate sets), in source address selection,
        223–224

CS (cipher suites)
    definition of, 938
    overview of, 819–821
    in TLS, 878
CS (Class Selector), 938
CSMA/CA (carrier sense, multiple access with colli-
        sion avoidance)
    DCF as form of, 120
    definition of, 938
    WLANs (wireless LANs), 84
CSMA/CD (carrier sensed, multiple access with col-
        lision detection)
    definition of, 938
    Ethernet interface and, 80–81
CSPRNGs (cryptographically strong PRNGs), 816, 938
CSR (Classless Static Route) parameter, 246
CSRG (Computer Systems Research Group), 24, 938
CTCP (Compound TCP) algorithm, 779–781, 938
CTR (Counter) mode
    definition of, 938
    operating modes of encryption algorithms, 820
CTS (clear to send)
    carrier sense and, 121
    definition of, 938
    Wi-Fi control frames, 115
CUBIC algorithm, for
        TCP congestion control, 775–776
Current-state records, IGMP/MLD group member-
        ship reports, 457
CW (contention window)
    definition of, 938
    in MAC, 122
cwnd (congestion window) in TCP
    comparing slow start with congestion avoidance,
        736–737
    congestion avoidance algorithm and, 734–736
    CWV (Congestion Window Validation), 742–744
    definition of, 938
    Eifel Response Algorithm and, 744–745
    FACK (forward acknowledgment) and, 741
    overview of, 729–730
    SACK congestion control and, 740–741
    slow start algorithm and, 732–734
    standard TCP algorithm and, 738
    Tahoe, Reno, and Fast Recovery and, 737
    undoing changes in, 762–766
CWR (Congestion Window Reducing)
    CWR bit, 784
    definition of, 938
    fast retransmit events, 761–762
    local congestion events, 764
    sender pause and, 753

CWV (Congestion Window Validation), 742–744, 938
Cyclic Redundancy Checks. See CRCs (Cyclic
        Redundancy Checks)

D
DAD (duplicate address detection)
    definition of, 938
    DHCPv6, 259–260
    IPv6 addresses and, 277–278
    MLD messages and, 457
    Neighbor Discovery protocol and, 253
    RA and RS messages and, 280–282
Daemen, Joan, 811
Data Encryption Standard. See DES (Data Encryp-
        tion Standard)
Data flow, TCP. See TCP data flow
Data frames
    fragmentation and aggregation, 94–95
    Wi-Fi, 116–119
Data labels, DNS names and, 523
Data-link layer, of OSI model, 9
Data types, resource record categories, 528
Datagram Congestion Control Protocol. See DCCP
        (Datagram Congestion Control Protocol)
Datagram TLS. See DTLS (Datagram TLS)
Datagrams
    attribution of, 26
    fragmenting, 148
    important concepts in development of network
        architecture, 5–6
    in protocol architecture, 3–6
    receiving multicast, 447–449
    sending multicast, 446–447
    spoofing attacks and, 25–26
    TLS with. See DTLS (Datagram TLS)
Datagrams, IP
    direct delivery of, 167
    DNS messages using IPv4 datagrams, 525
    fragmentation of, 488
    of ICMP messages within, 354–355
    IPv4, 182
    TCP encapsulation in, 587
Datagrams, UDP
    DNS messages using, 525
    encapsulation, 474
    fragmentation of, 488–492
    maximum size, 497–498
    translating UDP/IPv4 and UDP/IPv6 datagrams,
        505–506
    truncation of, 498
Davies, Donald, 1
Day, J., 2

DCCP (Datagram Congestion Control Protocol)
    definition of, 938
    NAT and, 309
    transport protocols in TCP/IP suite, 16
DCF (distributed coordinating function), in Wi-Fi
    collision avoidance/backoff procedure, 121–122
    definition of, 938
    options for controlling sharing of wireless
        medium, 120
DDDS (Dynamic Delegation Discovery System)
    definition of, 938
    ENUM records and, 551–552
    DNS NAPTR records and, 549
    URI/URN resolution and, 553
DDNS (Dynamic DNS)
    mapping DNS to DHCP addresses, 286
    supporting DNS Update, 567
DDoS (distributed DoS)
    attacks related to Internet architecture, 26
    definition of, 939
Deadlock, Nagle algorithm resulting in, 699
Decimal notation, expressing IP addresses in, 32
Default router, IP forwarding, 208
Deferred authentication, in DHCP, 272
Defragmentation, of data frames. See also Fragmen-
    tation, 117
Delay-based congestion control
    buffer bloat and, 782
    CTCP (Compound TCP) algorithm, 779–781
    FAST TCP algorithm, 778–779
    overview of, 777
    TCPW (TCP Westwood) algorithm, 779
    Vegas TCP algorithm, 777–778
Delayed ACKs
    interaction with Nagle algorithm, 699
    with piggybacking, 692
    in TCP data flow, 695–696
Delegated path discovery (DPD)
    certificate validation and, 831
    definition of, 940
Delegated path validation (DPV)
    certificate validation and, 831
    definition of, 940
Delegation
    classless .in-addr.arpa delegation, 539
    DNS zones and, 516
Delegation signer (DS) resource record
    definition of, 940
    DNSSEC, 897–898
Delivery to multiple locations, broadcasting and
    multicasting for, 435
Demilitarized zones. See DMZ (demilitarized zones)

Demultiplexing
    identifiers in, 11
    implementation and design and, 10–13
    TCP/IP suite and, 16–17
Denial-of-service. See DoS (denial-of-service)
DER (Distinguished Encoding Rules), 869, 939
DES (Data Encryption Standard). See also Triple-DES
    definition of, 939
    dictionary attacks and, 816
    as symmetric encryption algorithm, 811
Destination address selection algorithm, in IP host
    models, 224–225
Destination cache, 403
Destination (DST) address, in Ethernet frame for-
    mat, 85
Destination IP address
    host processing of IP datagrams, 220–221
    in IP datagrams, 186
    in IP forwarding, 209
    IPv6 header fields, 196
    Routing header fields, 201
    selection by hosts, 222–223
    Teredo tunneling and, 485
Destination metrics, TCP timeout/retransmission,
    685–686
Destination Options, IPv6, 196
Destination unreachable messages, ICMP
    overview of, 364
    PTB (Packet Too Big), 612
    requesting connection to nonexistent ports, 626
    UDP datagram and, 480
Detecting Network Attachment (DNA), 241, 939
Detection algorithm, for spurious timeouts and
    retransmissions, 677
Detection, of congestion, 728–729
DF (Don't Fragment), 939
DH (Diffie-Hellman-Merkle Key Agreement),
    813–814, 939
DHCP (Dynamic Host Configuration Protocol)
    address pools and leases, 235–236
    attacks related to, 292
    authentication, 271–273
    automatic address assignment, 67
    BOOTP message format, 236–238
    BOOTP options, 238–239
    definition of, 939
    DHCP/DNS interaction, 285–286
    DHCPACK message, 250
    DHCPDISCOVER message, 244–247
    DHCPNAK message, 243
    DHCPOFFER message, 247–248
    DHCPREQUEST message, 241–243, 248–249

DHCP (Dynamic Host Configuration Protocol), *continued*
    location information, 274–275
    manual configuration, 265–266
    mobility and handoff information, 275
    operation of, 239–241
    overview of, 234–235
    PPPoE (PPP over Ethernet) and, 286–291
    Rapid Commit option, 273–274
    reconfigure extension, 273
    relays, 267–271
    snooping, 276
    state machine, 251–252
    subnet mask configuration, 39
    summary and references, 292–298
DHCP Unique Identifier. *See* DUID (DHCP Unique Identifier)
DHCPACK message, 241, 250
DHCPDECLINE message, 241
DHCPDISCOVER message, 240, 244–247
DHCPINFORM message, 241
DHCPLEASEQUERY message, 269
DHCPNAK message, 241, 243
DHCPOFFER message, 240, 247–248
DHCPRELEASE message, 241
DHCPREQUEST message, 239–243, 248–249
DHCPv6
    DAD (Neighbor Solicitation), 259–260
    DUID (DHCP Unique Identifier), 256–257
    IA (Identity Association), 255–256
    IPv6 address lifecycle, 252–253
    manual configuration, 250–251
    message format, 253–255
    operation of, 257–258
    overview of, 252
    prefix delegation, 266–267
    REQUEST message, 264–265
    router solicitation and advertisement, 260–263
Dictionary attacks
    DES and, 816
    security protocol-related, 918
Differentiated Services Code Point (DSCP), 188–190, 940
Differentiated Services field. *See* DS (Differentiated Services) field
Diffie-Hellman-Merkle Key Agreement (DH), 813–814, 939
DIFS (distributed inter-frame space), in Wi-Fi
    carrier sense and, 120–121
    definition of, 939
Digest challenge, STUN mechanisms and, 325
Digests, message digests, 817–818

Digital, Intel, Xerox (DIX)
    definition of, 939
    Ethernet, 82
Digital Living Network Alliance (DLNA), 939
Digital Object Identifier (DOI), 939
Digital Signature Algorithm (DSA), 821, 940
Digital Signature Standard (DSS), 821, 940
Digital signatures
    in cipher suites, 821
    in public key cryptography, 812
    RSA Signature option, 416
Digital subscriber line. *See* DSL (digital subscriber line)
Direct delivery
    IP forwarding, 210–212
    with IPv4, 167–169
Directed broadcast, 43
Direction specification, in firewall rules, 335
Discard Request messages, in LCP operation, 134
Discovery problem, in p2p networks, 22
Discrete log problem, in DH (Diffie-Hellman) encryption, 814
Distinguished Encoding Rules (DER), 869, 939
Distributed coordinating function. *See* DCF (distributed coordinating function)
Distributed DoS (DDoS)
    attacks related to Internet architecture, 26
    definition of, 939
Distributed inter-frame space (DIFS)
    carrier sense and, 120–121
    definition of, 939
Distribution service (DS)
    definition of, 940
    Wi-Fi, 112
Distributions, TCP/IP suite, 24–25
DIX (Digital, Intel, Xerox)
    definition of, 939
    Ethernet, 82
DKIM (DomainKeys Identified Mail)
    definition of, 939
    DKIM signatures, 916
    example using, 916–918
    overview of, 915–916
DLNA (Digital Living Network Alliance), 939
DMZ (demilitarized zones)
    definition of, 939
    DNS queries and, 565–567
    packet-filtering firewalls and, 300
    unicast addresses and, 67–68
DNA (Detecting Network Attachment), 241, 939
DNAME resource records, DNS, 536, 939
DNS-0x20, 572

DNS (Domain Name System)
   address and name server records, 529–530
   answer, authority, and additional information
      section formats, 526–527
   attacks related to, 571–572
   AXFR (full zone transfer) messages, 559–561
   caching and, 517–518
   CNAME (canonical name) records, 534–536
   definition of, 939
   DHCP and, 233, 285–286
   DNS notify, 564–565
   dynamic updates, 555–558
   ENUM records, 551–552
   example using resource record types, 530–534
   extension format (EDNSO), 524–525
   introduction to, 511–512
   IXFR (incremental zone transfer) messages,
      561–563
   LDAP and, 570–571
   LLMNR and mDNS, 569–570
   mDNS (Multicast DNS), 444–445
   message format, 520–524
   MX (mail exchanger) records, 544–545
   name resolution process, 518–520
   name servers and zones, 516–517
   name space, 512–514
   naming syntax, 514–516
   NAPTR (name authority pointer) records, 549–551
   open DNS servers and DDNS, 567
   OPT (option) pseudo records, 547–548
   PTR (pointer) records, 536–541
   question (query) and zone section format, 526
   resource record types, 527–529
   S-NAPTR and U-NAPTR, 554–555
   security. *See* DNSSEC (DNS Security)
   SIP records, 552
   SOA (start of authority) records, 541–544
   sort lists, round-robin, and split DNS, 565–567
   SPF (sender policy framework) and TXT records,
      545–547
   SRV (service) records, 548–549
   summary and references, 572–578
   TCP/IP suite and, 19
   translating DNS from IPv4 to IPv6, 568–569
   transparency and extensibility, 567–568
   URI/URN resolution, 553–554
   well-known ports, 18, 525–526
   zone transfers, 558–559
DNS Notify
   initiating zone transfers, 525
   necessity of zone transfers, 518
DNS proxy, 568
DNS Security. *See* DNSSEC (DNS Security)

DNS servers
   caching, 517–518
   gTLD servers, 519–520
   primary and secondary, 517
   response to DNS queries, 565–567
   root servers, 518
   zones, 516–517
DNS Update, DDNS support for, 567
DNS64
   definition of, 939
   DNSSEC with, 915
   translating DNS from IPv4 to IPv6, 568–569
DNSKEY resource record
   definition of, 939
   DNSSEC and, 896–897
   signed zones and zone cuts, 903
DNSSEC (DNS Security)
   canonical orderings and forms, 902–903
   definition of, 939
   DNS-related attacks and, 571
   DNS64 and, 915
   DNSKEY resource record in, 896–897
   DS (delegation signer) resource record in,
      897–898
   NSEC (NextSECure) resource record in, 898–901
   operation of, 902
   overview of, 894–896
   resolver operation example, 903–911
   resource records, 896
   RRSIG (Resource Record Signature) resource
      record in, 901–902
   signed zones and zone cuts, 903
   transaction authentication, 911–915
DNSSL (DNS Search List) option, in ND, 422–423
DOI (Digital Object Identifier), 939
Domain hacks, 514
Domain Keys Identified Mail. *See* DKIM (Domain
   Keys Identified Mail)
Domain Name System. *See* DNS (Domain Name
   System)
Domain names, DNS Search List option, 422–423
Domain-specific keys (DSRK)
   definition of, 940
   key derivation in EAP, 838
Domain-specific usage-specific root keys
   (DSUSRKs)
   definition of, 940
   key derivation in EAP, 838
Domains
   DNS and, 19
   in DNS name space, 512
Done message, ICMP, 388–390
Don't Fragment (DF), 939

DoS (denial-of-service)
definition of, 939
DNS attacks, 571
DTLS (Datagram TLS) protection, 894
IGMP or MLD attacks, 469–470
Internet architecture attacks, 26
system configuration attacks, 292
TCP attacks, 640
TCP timeout/retransmission attacks, 686
types of threats to network communication, 808
UDP attacks, 506
Dotted-decimal notation
IP addresses in, 32, 537
of subnet masks, 39
DPD (delegated path discovery)
certificate validation and, 831
definition of, 940
DPV (delegated path validation)
certificate validation and, 831
definition of, 940
Drive-by attacks, 806
Drop precedence, assigned to datagrams, 191
DS (delegation signer) resource record
definition of, 940
DNSSEC, 897–898
DS (Differentiated Services) field
definition of, 940
ICMP Parameter Problem and, 379
in IP header, 183
in IP protocol, 188–192
DS (distribution service)
definition of, 940
Wi-Fi, 112
DS-Lite (Dual-Stack Lite)
definition of, 940
IPv4/IPv6 translation, 339–340
DSA (Digital Signature Algorithm), 821, 940
DSACK (duplicate SACK) extension
definition of, 940
Eifel Detection Algorithm and, 679
Eifel Response Algorithm and, 681
overview of, 677–679
DSCP (Differentiated Services Code Point), 188–190, 940
DSL (digital subscriber line)
buffer bloat and, 781
definition of, 940
overview of, 4
PPPoE and, 286–287
DSRK (domain-specific keys)
definition of, 940
key derivation in EAP, 838

DSS (Digital Signature Standard), 821, 940
DST (Destination) address, in Ethernet frame format, 85
DSUSRKs (domain-specific usage-specific root keys)
definition of, 940
key derivation in EAP, 838
DTCP (Dynamic Tunnel Configuration Protocol), 154
DTLS (Datagram TLS)
definition of, 940
DoS protection, 894
example of use of, 884–891
handshake protocol, 892–894
overview of, 876–877
record layer, 891–892
Dual-Stack Lite (DS-Lite)
definition of, 940
IPv4/IPv6 translation, 339–340
DUID (DHCP Unique Identifier)
definition of, 940
DHCPDISCOVER message and, 246
types of, 256–257
DupACK spoofing, TCP congestion control attacks, 785–786
Duplex modes
duplex mismatch, 96
overview of, 94–96
Duplicate ACK threshold (dupthresh), in TCP
in fast retransmit, 667
NewReno algorithm and, 739
packet reordering and, 683
Duplicate acknowledgements, congestion control and, 589
Duplicate address detection. See DAD (duplicate address detection)
Duplicate SACK. See DSACK (duplicate SACK) extension
Dupthresh. See Duplicate ACK threshold (dupthresh)
Duration field, in frame transmission, 121
DWORD value, 518
Dynamic Delegation Discovery System. See DDDS (Dynamic Delegation Discovery System)
Dynamic DNS (DDNS)
mapping DNS to DHCP addresses, 286
supporting DNS Update, 567
Dynamic Host Configuration Protocol. See DHCP (Dynamic Host Configuration Protocol)
Dynamic/private ports, 18
Dynamic Tunnel Configuration Protocol (DTCP), 154
Dynamic updates, DNS, 555–558

E

E-mail, PGP (Pretty Good Privacy) encryption for, 822

EAP (Extensible Authentication Protocol)
attacks related to, 918
definition of, 940
ERP (EAP Re-authentication Protocol), 839
IKE protocol and, 851–852
key derivation, 838
layers of, 836–837
methods, 837–838
network security and, 833–834
packet format, 835
for PPP authentication, 141
request/response messages, 835–836
in Wi-Fi security, 129

EAP-FAST (EAP-Flexible Authentication via Security Tunneling), 940

EAP Re-authentication Protocol (ERP), 839, 941

EAP-TTLS (EAP-Tunneled Transport Layer Security), 838, 940

EAPoL (EAP over LAN), 833–834, 940

Eavesdropping
link layer attacks, 155
types of threats to network communication, 808

EC2N (Elliptic Curve groups modulo a power 2), 821, 941

ECC (Elliptic Curve Cryptography), 815, 821

ECC (Error Correcting Code), 579, 941

ECDSA (Elliptic Curve Digital Signature Algorithm), 941

ECE (ECN Echo), 589, 941

Echo Request/Reply (ping) messages
example of broadcasting, 438–439
ICMP, 380–383
in LCP operation, 134
Redirect message and, 374
sending from link-local unicast address, 445
translating ICMPv6 to ICMPv4, 426

ECN-Capable Transport (ECT), 783, 941

ECN Echo (ECE), 589, 941

ECN (Explicit Congestion Notification)
delay-based congestion control and, 777
detecting congestion, 728
ECN-Echo bit, 784
ICMP Parameter Problem and, 379
IP header fields, 183, 188–192
TCP congestion control attacks and, 786
TCP header fields, 782–785

ECP (Elliptic Curve groups modulo a Prime), 821, 941

EDCA (enhanced DCF channel access)
definition of, 941

UPs (user priorities), 123
Wi-Fi mesh and, 130

Edge ports, RSTP (Rapid Spanning Tree Protocol), 110

Editors, NAT, 315

EDNS0 (Extension format for DNS)
definition of, 941
DNS (Domain Name System), 524–525
DNSSEC, 895–896

EF (Expedited Forwarding), 191, 941

EFO (Extended Flags option)
definition of, 941
Router Advertisement Flags Extension option, 420–421

Eifel Detection Algorithm, 679–680

Eifel Response Algorithm
handling spurious RTOs in congestion control, 744–745
responding to spurious transmissions, 680–682

EIFS (extended interframe space), in Wi-Fi carrier sense and, 121
definition of, 941

Eligible rate estimate (ERE)
definition of, 941
in TCPW congestion control, 779

Elliptic Curve Cryptography (ECC), 815, 821

Elliptic Curve Digital Signature Algorithm (ECDSA), 941

Elliptic Curve groups modulo a power 2 (EC2N), 821, 941

Elliptic Curve groups modulo a Prime (ECP), 821, 941

Elliptic curves, 815

Embedded devices, setting IPv4 addresses for, 178

EMSKs (extended MSKs)
definition of, 941
key derivation in EAP, 838

Encapsulating Security Payload. See ESP (Encapsulating Security Payload)

Encapsulation
definition of, 10
of ICMP messages within IP datagrams, 354–355
IGMP/MLD, 453–454
implementation and design and, 10–13
TCP encapsulation in IP datagrams, 587
TCP/IP suite and, 16–17
tunnel encapsulation limits in IPv6, 198
of UDP datagram, 474

Encryption. See also Cryptography
MPPE (Microsoft Point-to-Point Encryption), 145
spoofing attacks and, 226
TCP-AO (Authentication Option), 612
in Wi-Fi security, 129

End system, for protocol suites, 12
End-to-end argument, in protocol architecture, 6
End-to-end checksum, in UDP, 473, 475
Endpoint discriminator, LCP options, 138
Endpoints, TCP, 588, 595–596
Enforcement Point (EP), in PANA, 839, 941
Enhanced DCF channel access. *See* EDCA (enhanced
        DCF channel access)
ENUM records
    definition of, 941
    DNS resource record types, 551–552
Enumeration attacks, 919
EOL (End of List), TCP header options, 605
EP (Enforcement Point), in PANA, 941
Ephemeral port numbers, 18
EQM (equal modulation)
    definition of, 941
    higher throughput (802.11n) support and, 127
Equation-based rate control, 768
ERE (eligible rate estimate)
    definition of, 941
    in TCPW congestion control, 779
ERP (EAP Re-authentication Protocol), 839, 941
Error control, in protocol architecture, 7–8
Error Correcting Code (ECC), 579, 941
Error messages, ICMP
    destination unreachable, 364–372
    extended and multipart messages, 363–364
    overview of, 309, 361–363
    Parameter Problem message, 379–380
    Redirect message, 372–375
    time exceeded message, 375–378
    translating ICMPv4 to ICMPv6, 424–425
    translating ICMPv6 to ICMPv4, 427
ESN (Extended Sequence Number), in IPsec, 856, 942
ESP (Encapsulating Security Payload)
    definition of, 942
    ESP-NULL, WESP, and traffic visibility, 863–864
    in IPSec, 217, 841
    overview of, 858
    transport and tunnel modes, 858–863
ESP-NULL, 863–864
ESS (extended service set), Wi-Fi, 112
ESSID (extended service set identifiers)
    definition of, 942
    Wi-Fi, 112
Established connections, TCP, 596
ESTABLISHED state in TCP
    half-open connections and, 628
    incoming connection queue and, 636
    simultaneous open and close transitions, 625
    TCP port numbers and, 632–634
    TCP state transitions, 618

Ethernet (IEEE 802.3)
    autonegotiation in, 95
    converting IP multicast addresses to MAC
            addresses, 442–444
    flow control, 98
    frames, 84–86
    frames sizes, 88–89
    integrity checking on frames, 86–88
    LAN/MAN standards, 82–84
    MAC addresses, 16
    MTU (maximum transmission unit), 506
    overview of, 80–82
    power saving, 96–97
    speeds, 81
    supporting broadcasting at link layer, 437
Ethernet interfaces, Promiscuous mode, 155
Ethernet type field, 16
ethtool, Linux program for checking full duplex
        support, 94
EUI (extended unique identifier)
    definition of, 942
    formats of IPv6 addresses, 44–45
EV-DO (Evolution, Data Optimized (or Only)), 942
EV (Extended Validation), 942
Exchange of database records. *See* Zone transfers
Expedited Forwarding (EF), 191, 941
Experimental category, RFCs and, 23
Experimental Values, neighbor discovery in IPv6,
        423
Explicit Congestion Notification. *See* ECN (Explicit
        Congestion Notification)
Explicit sending, in congestion control, 583
Explicit signaling, in congestion control, 728
Exponential backoff
    binary, 650
    SWS (silly windows syndrome) and, 713
    in TCP connection timeout, 604
Extended and multipart messages, ICMP, 363–364
Extended Flags option (EFO)
    definition of, 941
    Router Advertisement Flags Extension option,
            420–421
Extended interframe space (EIFS)
    carrier sense and, 121
    definition of, 941
Extended MSKs (EMSKs)
    definition of, 941
    key derivation in EAP, 838
Extended Sequence Number (ESN), in IPsec, 856, 942
Extended service set (ESS), Wi-Fi, 112
Extended service set identifiers (ESSID)
    definition of, 942
    Wi-Fi, 112

Extended unique identifier (EUI)
    definition of, 942
    formats of IPv6 addresses, 44–45
Extended Validation (EV), certificates, 942
Extensibility, DNS, 567–568
Extensible Authentication Protocol. *See* EAP (Extensible Authentication Protocol)
Extensible Markup Language (XML)
    common use with Web pages, 338
    definition of, 962
Extensible Messaging and Presence Protocol (XMPP), 333, 962
Extension data structure, appended to ICMP messages, 363–364
Extensions
    DNS. *See* EDNS0
    identifiers, 44
    IP header, 182–183
    IPv6 header, 194–196
    TLS, 883–884
Extranets, 20

F

F-RTO (Forward-RTO Recovery), in TCP
    definition of, 942
    for detecting spurious transmissions, 680
FACK (forward acknowledgment), in TCP
    definition of, 942
    for TCP congestion control, 741–742
Fast Recovery algorithm, 737–738
Fast retransmit
    event, 761
    example of, 668–671
    introduction to, 647
    local congestion and, 759–762
    overview of, 667–668
    SACK recovery and, 757–759
FAST TCP algorithm, 778–779
Fate sharing, in protocol architecture, 6–7
FCFS (first-come-first-served)
    definition of, 942
    packet processing, 4
FCS (Frame Check Sequence)
    definition of, 942
    integrity checking in Ethernet frames, 88
    verifying message integrity, 817
FEC (forward error correction)
    definition of, 942
    higher throughput (802.11n) support and, 128
FIFO (first-in-first-out)
    definition of, 942
    queue management and, 782
    scheduling packets, 4

File (Boot File Name) field, DHCP/BOOTP message format, 238–239
File Transfer Protocol. *See* FTP (File Transfer Protocol)
Filter-mode-change records, IGMP/MLD group membership reports, 457
Filters
    host address filtering, 449–451
    IGMP/MLD processing and, 456
    `iptables`, 335
    NAT, 312–313
    packet-filtering firewalls, 300
    web proxies operating as content filters, 302
FIN segments, in TCP
    active and passive closers and, 597–598
    connection completion and, 766
    definition of, 942
    half-close operation and, 598–599
    half-open connections and, 628
    sequence numbers in, 603
Fingerprinting, TCP keepalive attacks, 802
Fingerprints, or digest of message, 817–818
FIN_WAIT_1 state, TCP state transitions, 618, 625
FIN_WAIT_2 state, TCP state transitions, 618, 625
Firewalls
    attacks related to, 345–346
    configuring, 334
    direct interaction with, 338–339
    IP addresses and, 67
    overview of, 300
    packet-filtering firewalls, 300–301
    proxy firewalls, 301–303
    rules for packet-filtering, 335–336
    summary and references, 345–346
First-come-first-served (FCFS)
    definition of, 942
    packet processing, 4
First-in-first-out. *See* FIFO (first-in-first-out)
Flags
    DHCP/BOOTP message format, 236
    GRE tunnels and, 150
    IPv6 multicast addresses, 57, 58
Flooding attacks, 102, 428
Flow control. *See also* Congestion control
    link layer and, 98
    in protocol architecture, 7–8
    rate-based and window-based, 583
    in UPD server design, 505
Flow control, in TCP
    example of dynamic window size adjustment and flow control, 705–708
    large buffers and auto-tuning, 715–719
    overview of, 700–701

Flow control, in TCP, *continued*
  sliding window protocol, 701–704
  SWS (silly windows syndrome), 708–715
  TCP header and, 590
  zero windows and TCP persistent timer, 704–705
FMIP (Mobile IP with Fast Handovers), 388, 942
Foreign IP addresses
  TCP port numbers and, 632
  TCP server restrictions on foreign endpoints, 635–636
Forgery, message authentication codes protecting against, 818
Forward acknowledgment (FACK), in TCP
  definition of, 942
  for TCP congestion control, 741–742
Forward error correction (FEC)
  definition of, 942
  higher throughput (802.11n) support and, 128
Forward-RTO Recovery (F-RTO)
  definition of, 942
  for detecting spurious transmissions, 680
Forwarding actions, IP forwarding, 209–210
Forwarding datagrams, 14
Forwarding tables, IP forwarding, 208–209
Four-message exchange operations, of DHCPv6, 265–266
FQDN (fully qualified domain names)
  definition of, 942
  DHCPv6 and, 260
  vs. unqualified domain names, 515
Fraggle attacks, UDP-related attacks, 506
Fragment header, IPv6 protocol, 203–208
Fragment number, data frame fragmentation, 117
Fragment Offset field
  in IPv6 Fragment header, 203–205
  in UDP fragmentation, 489
Fragmentation
  of datagrams, 14
  of IGMP packets, 470
  of Internet traffic, 506
  IP fragmentation. *See* IP fragmentation
  UDP/IPv4, 488–492
  of Wi-Fi frames, 116–119
Frame Check Sequence. *See* FCS (Frame Check Sequence)
Frame Control Word
  in MPDU, 113
  PSM (power save mode) and, 119
  Retry bit and, 116
Frame Relay, best-effort delivery, 7
Frames, Ethernet
  802.3 standard, 84–86
  ARP frame format, 170–171

ARP reply frames, 168
ARP request frames, 167, 173–174
integrity checking on, 86–88
link-layer PDUs, 14
payload of, 16
sizes, 88–89
Frames, PPP, 131–132
Frames, Wi-Fi
  control frames, 115–116
  data frames, 116–119
  management frames, 113–115
  overview of, 113
FreeBSD
  broadcast addresses, 441
  incoming connection queue and, 638
  standards and, 24
Frequencies, Wi-Fi, 124
Freshness property, authentication protocols and, 816
FTP (File Transfer Protocol)
  definition of, 942
  NAT and, 304
  TCP/IP suite and, 13
Full duplex
  support, 94–95
  TCP service to application layer, 587
Fully qualified domain names. *See* FQDN (fully qualified domain names)

G

Galois/Counter Mode. *See* GCM (Galois/Counter Mode)
Galois MAC (GMAC), 819–820, 943
Gateway or Router IP Address (Giaddr) field
  DHCP/BOOTP message format, 238
  LDRAs and, 271
Gateways
  application layer. *See* ALGs (application layer gateways)
  between packet-switching networks, 1
  between protocols, 20
  RED (Random Early Detection) gateways, 783–785
GCKSs (group controller/key servers)
  definition of, 942
  multicast support in IPSec, 864–865
GCM (Galois/Counter Mode)
  AES and, 819
  definition of, 942
  operating modes of encryption algorithms, 820
GDOI (Group Domain of Interpretation), 942
GENA (General Event Notification Architecture), 338, 942
Generator polynomial, CRC and, 86–87
Generic Attribute Registration Protocol (GVRP), 943

Generic Multicast Registration Protocol (GMRP), 943
Generic Routing Encapsulation. *See* GRE (Generic Routing Encapsulation)
Generic Security Services API (GSS-API), 943
Generic top-level domains (gTLD), 512–514, 943
GI (guard interval)
   definition of, 942
   higher throughput (802.11n) support and, 127
Giaddr (Gateway or Router IP Address) field
   DHCP/BOOTP message format, 238
   LDRAs and, 271
GKM (group key management)
   definition of, 943
   multicast support in IPSec, 864
Global Internet. *See* Internet
Global scope
   configuring global addresses with SLAAC, 278
   of IPv6 addresses, 43
   of multicast addresses, 53
GLOP addressing, IP multicast, 54–56
GMAC (Galois MAC), 819–820, 943
GMRP (Generic Multicast Registration Protocol), 943
GPAD (Group PAD), 864, 943
Granularity, of TCP clock, 654
Gratuitous ARP, 175–176
GRE (Generic Routing Encapsulation)
   definition of, 943
   establishing tunneling with, 149–153
   link layer attacks and, 156
   NAT and tunneled packets, 310
Greenfield mode, 802.11n operating modes, 128
Group addresses. *See* Multicast addresses
Group controller/key servers (GCKSs)
   definition of, 942
   multicast support in IPSec, 864–865
Group Domain of Interpretation (GDOI), 942
Group key management (GKM)
   definition of, 943
   multicast support in IPSec, 864
Group members (Group Member Part), IGMP/MLD processing by, 454–457
Group membership
   displaying IP group membership, 446–447
   IGMP membership reports, 455
Group PAD (GPAD), 864, 943
Group Secure Association Key Management (GSAKMP), 943
Group security associations (GSAs)
   definition of, 943
   multicast support in IPSec, 864
Group SPD (GSPD), 943
GSAKMP (Group Secure Association Key Management), 943

GSAs (group security associations)
   definition of, 943
   multicast support in IPSec, 864
GSPD (Group SPD), 943
GSS-API (Generic Security Services API), 943
gTLD (generic top-level domains), 512–514, 943
Guard interval (GI)
   definition of, 942
   higher throughput (802.11n) support and, 127
GVRP (Generic Attribute Registration Protocol), 943

H

HAIO (Home Agent Information Option), 943
Hairpinning (HP), 314, 486
Half-close operation, TCP connections, 598–599
Half-open connections, keepalives detecting, 794
Handoff information, DHCP, 275
Handover Key Request/Reply options, in ND, 422–423
Handshaking protocols
   DTLS (Datagram TLS), 892–894
   three-way handshake in TCP, 597, 640
   TLS, 880–883
HAs (home agents)
   definition of, 943
   Home Agent Information option in ND, 412–413
   ICMP Home Agent Discovery Request message, 386
   ICMP Mobile Prefix Solicitation message, 387–388
   in Mobile IP, 216–217
Hash-based addresses (HBAs), 405
Hash functions
   CGAs (cryptographically generated addresses) and, 404–405
   cryptographic, 817–818
   initial sequence numbers in TCP and, 601–602
   TCP-AO (Authentication Option), 612
HBAs (hash-based addresses), 405
HC (hybrid coordinator), in HCCA, 123
HCCA (HFCA-controlled channel access), 123
HCF (hybrid coordination function)
   definition of, 943
   options for controlling sharing of wireless medium, 120
   QoS and, 122–123
HDLC (High-Level Data Link Control)
   Address and Control fields, 132
   definition of, 943
   LCP links based on, 131
Header compression, in PPP
   CCP (Compression Control Protocol), 139
   PPP (Point-to-Point Protocol), 142–143

Header, ICMP
    ICMP Parameter Problem and, 379–380
    Redirected Header option in ND, 411
Header, IP
    CE (Congestion Experienced) indicator in,
        783–784
    Checksum field, 186–188
    DS and ECN fields, 188–192
    extensions, 182–183
    header compression, 142–143
    IPv6 extensions, 194–196
    IPv6 Fragment header, 203–208
    IPv6 RH (Router header), 200–203, 955
    Mobile IP, 216
    overview of, 183–186
Header, TCP
    connection options, 605–606
    fields in, 588–590
    MSS (Maximum Segment Size) option, 606–607
    PAWS (Protection against Wrapped Sequence
        Numbers), 610–611
    SACK (selective acknowledgement) option, 607
    TCP-AO (Authentication Option), 612
    Timestamps option, 608–610
    UTO (User Timeout) option, 611–612
    WSCALE (Window Scale) option, 608
Header, UDP, 474–476, 481–482
HELD (HTTP-enabled Location Delivery)
    definition of, 943
    location information in DHCP, 274
Hexadecimal notation
    expressing IP addresses in, 32–33
    IPv6 addresses in, 537
HFCA-controlled channel access (HCCA), 123
Hierarchical routing, 48
High-Level Data Link Control. See HDLC (High-
        Level Data Link Control)
High-speed environments, congestion control in, 770
High-Speed Packet Access (HSPA), 944
High Throughput (HT), 128, 944
HighSpeed TCP (HSTCP), 770–772, 944
Hijacking attacks
    firewalls and NATs and, 345
    TCP-related attacks, 641
HIP (Host Identity Protocol)
    definition of, 943
    Identifier/locator separating protocols, 70
Historic category, RFCs and, 23
HK-LIFETIME, Handover Keys, 422–423
Hlen (HW Len) field, DHCP/BOOTP message
        format, 236
HMAC (keyed-hash message authentication code),
        818–819, 943

HoA (home address)
    definition of, 944
    of IPv6 node, 199
    in Mobile IP, 216–218
Hole punching, in NAT traversal, 317
Home address. See HoA (home address)
Home Agent Discovery Request message, ICMP, 386
Home Agent Information Option (HAIO), 943
Home Agent Information option, in ND, 412–413
Home agents. See HAs (home agents)
Home Test (HoT)
    definition of, 944
    mobility messages in RRP, 218–219
Home Test Init (HoTI)
    definition of, 944
    mobility messages in RRP, 218–219
Hop-by-hop
    IP forwarding, 209
    protocols, 12
Hop-by-hop options (HOPOPTs)
    definition of, 944
    IPv6, 196
Hop Limit field
    ICMP Time Exceeded message, 375
    IPv6, 199
    MRD (Multicast Router Discovery) and, 394
    ND messages and, 396
HOPOPTs (hop-by-hop options)
    definition of, 944
    IPv6, 196
Hops field, DHCP/BOOTP message format, 236
Host addresses, 35
Host fields, in IP addresses, 37
Host Identity Protocol (HIP)
    definition of, 943
    Identifier/locator separating protocols, 70
Host models, IP
    address selection, 222–223
    destination address selection algorithm, 224–225
    overview of, 220–222
    source address selection algorithm, 223–224
Host names, 19
Host number, in IP addresses, 35
Host Requirements RFCs, 23
Host unreachable message, ICMP, 364
Hosts
    ARP request to nonexistent, 173–174
    host address filtering, 449–451
    keepalives detecting state of peer host, 795
    server host crashes and does not reboot (keepal-
        ive scenarios), 796
    server host crashes and reboots (keepalive sce-
        narios), 797–799

server host unreachable (keepalive scenarios), 799–800
in small networks, 11–13
HoT (Home Test)
definition of, 944
mobility messages in RRP, 218–219
HoTI (Home Test Init)
definition of, 944
mobility messages in RRP, 218–219
HP (Hairpinning), 314, 486
HSPA (High-Speed Packet Access), 944
HSTCP (HighSpeed TCP), 770–772, 944
HT (High Throughput), 128, 944
HTML (Hyper-Text Markup Language), 944
HTTP-enabled Location Delivery (HELD)
definition of, 943
location information in DHCP, 274
HTTP (Hypertext Transfer Protocol)
definition of, 944
proxy firewalls, 302–303
well-known port for, 18
HTTP over SSL/TLS (HTTPS), 944
HTTP using UDP (HTTPMU), 338, 944
HTTPMU (HTTP using UDP), 338, 944
HTTPS (HTTP over SSL/TLS), 944
Htype (HW Type) field, DHCP/BOOTP message format, 236
HWRP (Hybrid Wireless Routing Protocol)
definition of, 944
Wi-Fi mesh and, 130
Hybrid coordination function. *See* HCF (hybrid coordination function)
Hybrid coordinator (HC), in HCCA, 123
Hybrid cryptosystems, 812
Hybrid Wireless Routing Protocol (HWRP)
definition of, 944
Wi-Fi mesh and, 130
Hyper-Text Markup Language (HTML), 944
Hypertext Transfer Protocol. *See* HTTP (Hypertext Transfer Protocol)

I

IA (Identity Association)
definition of, 944
in DHCPv6, 255–256
IAB (Internet Architecture Board), 22, 944
IAID (Identity Association Identifier)
definition of, 944
in DHCP, 246, 255–256
IANA (Internet Assigned Numbers Authority)
allocation of IP addresses and, 62
allocation of IPv6 multicast addresses, 58
definition of, 944

IKE registry of values, 849
OUI (Organizationally Unique Identifier), 442–444
port number assignments, 18, 632
registry for Sec values, 405
registry for SRV values, 548–549
URI, 553
IANA Service Name and Transport Protocol Port Number (ISPR), 548
IBSS (independent basic service set)
definition of, 944
Wi-Fi, 112
ICANN (Internet Corporation for Assigned Names and Numbers)
definition of, 944
DNSSEC zones list, 904
TLD management, 512
ICE (Interactive Connectivity Establishment), 332–334, 944
ICMP fix-up, 309
ICMP (Internet Control Message Protocol)
Advertisement Interval option in ND, 412
attacks related to, 428–429
Certificate option in ND, 417
CGA options in ND, 414–415
definition of, 944
destination unreachable, 364–372
DNS Search List option in ND, 422–423
Echo Request/Reply messages, 380–383
encapsulation of messages within IP datagrams, 354–355
error messages, 361–363
Experimental Values in ND, 423
extended and multipart messages, 363–364
Handover Key Request/Reply options in ND, 422–423
Home Agent Discovery Request message, 386
Home Agent Information option in ND, 412–413
ICMPv4 messages, 356–357
ICMPv6 messages, 358–360
IND (Inverse Neighbor Discovery), 401–402
introduction to, 353–354
IP Address/Prefix option in ND, 417–418
Link-Layer Address (LLA) option in ND, 418–419
MIPv6 fast handover messages, 388
MLD extension messages, 390–394
Mobile Prefix Solicitation message, 387–388
MRD (Multicast Router Discovery), 394–395
MTU option in ND, 411–412
NAT and, 309
ND options, 407–409
ND support, 395–396
Nonce option in ND, 416–417
NS (Neighbor Solicitation) message, 398–401

ICMP (Internet Control Message Protocol), *continued*
  NUD (Neighbor Unreachability Detection),
      402–403
  Parameter Problem message, 379–380
  Prefix Information option in ND, 410–411
  processing messages, 360–361
  queries/informational messages, 380
  Recursive DNS Server option in ND, 420
  Redirected Header option in ND, 411
  redirection of messages, 372–375
  Route Information option in ND, 420
  Router Advertisement Flags Extension option in
      ND, 420–421
  router solicitation and advertisement messages
      in ICMPv4, 383–385
  router solicitation and advertisement messages
      in ICMPv6, 396–398
  RSA Signature option in ND, 415–416
  SEND (Secure Neighbor Discovery), 403–407
  sending broadcast datagrams, 439
  Source Link-Layer Address option in ND,
      409–410
  Source Quench messages, 785
  Source/Target Address List options in ND,
      413–414
  summary and references, 430–434
  TCP-related attacks, 641–642
  time exceeded message, 375–378
  Timestamp option in ND, 416
  translating ICMPv4 to ICMPv6, 424–426
  translating ICMPv6 to ICMPv4, 426–428
  Trust Anchor option in ND, 417
  use in layers of TCP/IP suite, 15
ICS (Internet Connection Sharing)
  assignment of unicast addresses, 67
  definition of, 944
  NAT in Windows OS context, 337
ICV (Integrity Check Value), 856, 945
ID (identification payload), in IKE, 945
Id/loc split protocols, 70
Identification field
  IP header fields, 185, 203–204
  in UDP fragmentation, 489
Identification (ID payload), in IKE, 945
Identification messages, in LCP operation, 134
Identifier/locator separating protocols, 70
Identifiers
  in demultiplexing, 11
  IP addresses as, 70
  in multiplexing, 10
Identity Association (IA)
  definition of, 944
  in DHCPv6, 255–256

Identity Association Identifier (IAID)
  definition of, 944
  in DHCP, 246, 255–256
IDN ccTLS (Internationalized ccTLDs), 512
IDNs (internationalized domain names), 512, 945
IEEE (Institute of Electrical and Electronics
      Engineers)
  definition of, 945
  Ethernet. *See* Ethernet (802.3)
  interface standards, 44
  LAN/MAN standards (802), 82–84
  link aggregation (802.1AX), 92–93
  Logical Link Control (802.2), 84
  Multiple Registration Protocol (802.1ak), 111
  network security (802.1x), 833–834
  quality of service (802.1p), 90
  standards of, 24
  for VLANs (802.1q), 89–92
  wireless (802.11). *See* Wi-Fi (wireless
      fidelity-802.11)
IESG (Internet Engineering Steering Group), 22–23,
      945
IETF (Internet Engineering Task Force)
  definition of, 945
  for Internet standards, 22–23
  ROAD (ROuting and ADdressing) group, 47
  securing IPv6 Neighbor Discovery, 292
ifconfig command, in UNIX and Linux
  setting/finding broadcast addresses, 437
  viewing active multicast addresses, 66
  viewing format of link-local IPv6 address, 45–46
IGD (Internet Gateway Device), in UPnP
  definition of, 945
  NAT and, 338–339
IGDDC (Internet Gateway Device Discovery and
      Control), 337
IGMP (Internet Group Management Protocol)
  attacks related to, 469–470
  counters and variables, 467–468
  definition of, 945
  examples, 459–464
  lightweight IGMP3, 464–465
  MLD as translation of IGMPv3 to IPv6, 390
  MRD (Multicast Router Discovery) and, 394
  in multicast addressing, 15
  overview of, 451–453
  processing by group members (Group Member
      Part), 454–457
  processing by multicast routers (Multicast Router
      Part), 457–459
  robustness of, 465–467
  snooping, 468–469
  summary and references, 470–472

IHL (Internet Header Length), in IPv4
   attacks related to, 919
   definition of, 945
   ICMP Parameter Problem and, 379
   IP header and, 183
IIDs (interface identifiers)
   as basis for unicast IPv6 addresses, 43–46
   definition of, 945
   for link-scoped IPv6 addresses, 58
IKE (Internet Key Exchange), in IPsec
   algorithm selection and application, 849–850
   BTNS (Better-than-Nothing Security), 852
   CREATE_CHILD_SA exchange, 852–853
   definition of, 945
   EAP and, 851–852
   example using, 867–876
   IKE_AUTH exchange, 850–851
   IKE_SA_INIT exchange, 846–847
   INFORMATIONAL exchange, 853–854
   KE (Key Exchange) and Ni, Nr (Nonce) payloads,
      848
   message formats, 844–846
   MOBIKE (Mobile IKE), 854
   N (Notification) and CP (Configuration) pay-
      loads, 849
   NAT updates and, 866
   overview of, 842–843
   SA (Security Association) payloads and propos-
      als, 847–848
   traffic selectors, 851
IKE_AUTH exchange, 850–851, 871–874
IKE_SA_INIT exchange, 846–847, 867–870
IMAP (Interactive Mail Access Protocol)
   definition of, 945
   SRV record providing IMAP service, 549
   well-known port for, 18
IMAPS (IMAP over SSL/TLS), 18, 945
Implementation architecture
   design and, 8
   layering, 8–10
   multiplexing, demultiplexing, and encapsula-
      tion, 10–13
Implementations, TCP/IP suite, 24–25
Implicit sending, in congestion control, 583
IN (Internet class name), 945
Incoming connection queue, TCP servers, 636–640
Incremental zone transfer (IXFR) messages, in DNS,
   561, 946
IND (Inverse Neighbor Discovery)
   definition of, 945
   neighbor discovery in IPv6, 401–402
   Source/Target Address List options in ND,
      413–414

Independent basic service set (IBSS)
   definition of, 944
   Wi-Fi, 112
Indication transactions, STUN, 320
Indirect delivery, example of IP forwarding, 212–215
Industrial, Scientific, and Medical (ISM), 124
Information disclosure attacks, ICMP and, 428
Information security. See also Security, 806
Information theory, 579
Informational category, RFCs and, 23
INFORMATIONAL exchange, IKE protocol,
   853–854, 873, 875
Informational messages, ICMP, 309
Initial sequence number. See ISN (initial sequence
   number)
Initial window (IW) value
   definition of, 946
   in slow start algorithm, 732
Institute of Electrical and Electronics Engineers
   (IEEE). See IEEE (Institute of Electrical and
   Electronics Engineers)
Integrated Services Digital Network (ISDN), 946
Integrity Check Value (ICV), 856, 945
Integrity, in CIA triad, 806
Integrity protection, AH (Authentication Header),
   856, 858
Inter-Packet Gap (IPG), in Ethernet, 89, 945
Inter-Switch Link (ISL)
   definition of, 946
   VLAN trunking, 90
Interactive communication, TCP data flow, 692–695
Interactive Connectivity Establishment (ICE),
   332–334, 944
Interactive data, in TCP communication, 692
Interactive keystrokes, TCP and, 692–693
Interactive Mail Access Protocol. See IMAP (Interac-
   tive Mail Access Protocol)
Interface address, IP addresses and, 35
Interface identifiers. See IIDs (interface identifiers)
Interface, in IP forwarding, 209
Intermediate system, for protocol suites, 12
Intermediate System to Intermediate System (IS-IS),
   946
International Organization for Standardization
   (ISO), 8–9
International Telecommunication Union. See ITU
   (International Telecommunication Union)
Internationalized ccTLDs (IDN ccTLS), 512
Internationalized domain names (IDNs), 512, 945
Internet
   attacks related to Internet architecture, 25–26
   internationalization of, 512
   overview of, 19–20

Internet, *continued*
    TCP/IP suite forming basis of, 2
    UDP in, 506–507
    WWW compared to, 2–3
Internet Architecture Board (IAB), 22, 944
Internet Assigned Numbers Authority. *See* IANA
        (Internet Assigned Numbers Authority)
Internet checksum
    algorithm for computing Internet-related check-
        sum, 185
    mathematics of, 187–188
    overview of, 186–187
Internet class name (IN), 945
Internet Connection Sharing. *See* ICS (Internet Con-
        nection Sharing)
Internet Control Message Protocol. *See* ICMP (Inter-
        net Control Message Protocol)
Internet Corporation for Assigned Names and Num-
        bers. *See* ICANN (Internet Corporation for
        Assigned Names and Numbers)
Internet Engineering Steering Group (IESG), 22–23,
        945
Internet Engineering Task Force. *See* IETF (Internet
        Engineering Task Force)
Internet Gateway Device Discovery and Control
        (IGDDC), 337
Internet Gateway Device (IGD)
    definition of, 945
    NAT and, 338–339
Internet Group Management Protocol. *See* IGMP
        (Internet Group Management Protocol)
Internet Header Length. *See* IHL (Internet Header
        Length)
Internet Key Exchange. *See* IKE (Internet Key
        Exchange)
Internet Protocol Control Protocol (IPCP)
    MPPE and, 145
    types of NCPs used on PPP links, 141
Internet Registry Information Service (IRIS), 554, 946
Internet Research Task Force (IRTF), 23, 946
Internet Security Association and Key Management
        Protocol (ISAKMP), 867, 946
Internet Service Providers. *See* ISPs (Internet Service
        Providers)
Internet Society (ISOC), 23, 946
Internetwork layer. *See* Network (internetwork) layer
Intra-Site Automatic Tunnel Addressing Protocol
        (ISATAP), 440, 946
Intranets, 20
Inverse Neighbor Discovery. *See* IND (Inverse
        Neighbor Discovery)
IP address pooling behavior, NAT and, 312
IP Address/Prefix option, in ND, 417–418

IP addresses
    Address realms, 299
    allocation of, 62
    allocation of multicast addresses, 65
    allocation of unicast addresses, 62–65
    anycast addresses, 62
    assigning unicast addresses, 65–66
    attacks involving, 70–71
    broadcast addresses, 42–43
    CIDR, 47–48
    classful addressing, 34–36
    converting IP multicast addresses to MAC
        addresses, 442–444
    definition of, 14
    in DHCP/BOOTP message format, 237–238
    expressing, 32–34
    foreign IP address restrictions in server design,
        502–503
    host names and, 19
    introduction to, 31–32
    IPv4/IPv6 translators, 52–53
    IPv4 multicast addresses, 54–57
    IPv6 addresses and interface identifiers, 43–46
    IPv6 multicast addresses, 57–61
    multicast addresses, 53–54
    multiple addresses in UDP server design,
        501–502
    multiple providers/multiple networks/multiple
        addresses, 68–70
    route aggregation, 48–50
    single provider/multiple networks/multiple
        addresses, 67–68
    single provider/no network/single address,
        66–67
    single provider/single network/single address, 67
    spanning IP address families in server design,
        504
    special use addresses, 50–52
    spoofing attacks and, 226
    structure of, 34
    subnet addressing, 36–39
    subnet masks, 39–41
    summary and references, 71–77
    TCP/IP suite and, 19
    TCP server restrictions on local, 634–635
    unicast and broadcast, 15
    in UPD server design, 499–501
    VSLM (variable-length subnet masks), 41–42
IP datagrams. *See also* Packets
    fragmenting, 184
    of ICMP messages within IP datagrams, 354–355
    LCP (Link Control Protocol) and, 131–137
    PPP and, 130–131

source and destination IP addresses in, 186
in TCP/IP suite, 14
IP forwarding
    direct delivery, 210–212
    forwarding actions, 209–210
    forwarding table, 208–209
    indirect delivery, 212–215
    overview of, 208
IP fragmentation
    example of UPD/IPv4 fragmentation, 488–492
    interaction between IP fragmentation and ARP/
        ND, 496–497
    of IP datagrams, 184
    IP performing, 148
    IPv6 Fragment header, 203–208
    overview of, 488
    reassembly timeout, 492
    UDP-related attacks, 506
IP (Internet Protocol)
    address selection by hosts, 222–223
    attacks, 226
    best-effort delivery, 7
    bidirectional tunneling in mobile IP, 216–217
    destination address selection algorithm, 224–225
    discussion of issues in mobile IP, 220
    DS field and ECN, 188–192
    examples of forwarding, 210–215
    forwarding. See IP forwarding
    Fragment header, 203–208
    header. See Header, IP
    host models, 220–222
    ICMP addressing limits in, 353
    Internet checksum, 186–188
    introduction to, 181–183
    IPv6 extension headers, 194–196
    IPv6 options, 196–199
    mobile IP. See MIP (Mobile IP)
    options, 192–194
    RO (route optimization) in mobile IP, 217–219
    Routing header, 200–203
    source address selection algorithm, 223–224
    summary and references, 226–231
IP masquerading
    ipchains command for configuring, 345
    NAT in Linux context, 337
IP routers, 20
ipchains command, configuring IP masquerading
    in Linux, 345
ipconfig command in Windows
    manual management of DHCP information,
        250–251
    manual management of DHCPv6 information,
        265–266

IPCP (Internet Protocol Control Protocol), in PPP
    MPPE and, 145
    types of NCPs used on PPP links, 141
IPG (Inter-Packet Gap), in Ethernet, 89, 945
IPSec (IP Security)
    attacks related to, 918
    Authentication Header. See AH (Authentication
        Header)
    definition of, 945
    Encapsulating Security Payload. See ESP (Encap-
        sulating Security Payload)
    example using IKE, 867–876
    GRE tunnels and, 150
    Internet Key Exchange protocol. See IKE (Internet
        Key Exchange)
    L2TP/IPSec, 865
    layer 3 security with, 840–842
    multicast support, 864
    NAT traversal, 865–867
iptables, 335
IPv4 addresses
    allocation of multicast addresses, 65
    allocation of unicast addresses, 62–65
    configuring with SLAAC, 276
    example of subnet addressing, 37
    examples of subnet masks, 39
    expressing, 32–33
    foreign IP address restrictions in server design,
        502–503
    IPv4-converted addresses, 341
    IPv4-embedded IPv6 address, 52
    IPv4/IPv6 translators, 52–53
    IPv4-translatable addresses, 341
    local address restrictions in UDP server design,
        500–501
    multicast addresses, 54–57
    multiple addresses in UDP server design,
        501–502
    multiple servers per port in UPD server design,
        503–504
    setting for embedded devices, 178
    spanning IP address families in UDP server
        design, 504
    special-use addresses, 50–51
    tunneling IPv6 packets over UDP/IPv4 packets,
        154
    using ARP to map to hardware addresses, 165
IPv4/IPv6 translation
    DS-Lite (Dual-Stack Lite), 339–340
    IPv4-converted and IPv4 translatable addresses,
        341–342
    NAT and ALG for, 340–345
    overview of, 340–341

IPv4/IPv6 translation, *continued*
    stateful translation, 344–345
    stateless translation, 342–344
IPv4 protocol
    ARP and, 13
    Checksum field, 186–188
    computing Internet checksum, 186–187
    direct delivery with, 167–169
    DS and ECN fields, 188–192
    encapsulation of ICMP messages in, 354–355
    header, 182–183
    header fields, 183–186
    ICMP messages related to, 356–357
    ToS (Type of Service) byte in, 188–189
    translation to/from IPv6. *See* IPv4/IPv6
        translation
    tunneling IPv6 through, 482–487
IPv6 addresses
    allocation of multicast addresses, 65
    allocation of unicast addresses, 62–65
    configuring global addresses with SLAAC, 278
    configuring with SLAAC, 276–277
    DAD (Duplicate Address Detection), 277–278
    examples of subnet masks, 40
    expressing, 32–34
    interface identifiers and, 43–46
    IPv4/IPv6 translators, 52–53
    lifecycle of, 252–253
    multicast addresses, 57–61
    multiple servers per port in UPD server design,
        503–504
    spanning IP address families in UDP server
        design, 504
    special-use addresses, 51–52
    tunneling IPv6 packets over UDP/IPv4 packets, 154
    ULAs (Unique Local IPv6 Unicast Addresses), 225
    wildcard address, 632
IPv6 protocol
    Checksum field, 186–188
    DS and ECN fields, 188–192
    encapsulation of ICMP messages in, 354–355
    extension headers, 194–196
    Fragment header, 203
    header, 182–183
    header fields, 183–186
    ICMP messages related to, 358–360
    jumbogram support, 481
    NAT and, 310–311
    neighbor discovery. *See* ND (Neighbor Discovery
        Protocol)
    options, 196–199
    Rapid Deployment (6rd), 339, 933
    Routing header, 200–203

    Traffic Class byte in, 188–189
    translating to/from IPv4. *See* IPv4/IPv6
        translation
    tunneling through IPv4 networks, 482–487
    UDP and, 481–482
IPv6 Remote-ID, DCHP relay agents, 268
IPV6CP (IPv6 Control Protocol), in PPP, 141, 945
IRIS (Internet Registry Information Service), 554, 946
IRTF (Internet Research Task Force), 23, 946
IS-IS (Intermediate System to Intermediate System),
    946
ISAKMP (Internet Security Association and Key
    Management Protocol), 867, 946
ISATAP (Intra-Site Automatic Tunnel Addressing
    Protocol), 440, 946
ISDN (Integrated Services Digital Network), 946
ISL (Inter-Switch Link)
    definition of, 946
    VLAN trunking, 90
ISM (Industrial, Scientific, and Medical), 124
ISN (initial sequence number)
    definition of, 946
    SYN segment containing, 597
    in TCP connection establishment, 601–602
    TCP header and, 589
ISO (International Organization for Standardiza-
    tion), 8–9
ISOC (Internet Society), 23, 946
ISPR (IANA Service Name and Transport Protocol
    Port Number), 548
ISPs (Internet Service Providers)
    ACs (access concentrator), 287
    allocation of IP addresses and, 32, 62–63
    definition of, 946
    MTU (maximum transmission unit), 494
Iterative servers, 21
ITU (International Telecommunication Union)
    definition of, 946
    standards organizations, 24
    X.509 standard. *See* X.509 standard
IW (initial window) value, in TCP
    definition of, 946
    in slow start algorithm, 732
iwconfig command, setting Wi-Fi control frame
    variables, in UNIX and Linux, 115
IXFR (incremental zone transfer) messages, in DNS,
    561–563, 946

J
Jacobson, V., 652–654, 731
Jumbograms
    IPv6 options for, 198
    IPv6 supporting, 481

K

Kaminsky attacks, DNS-related, 572
Kamoun, F., 48
Karn's algorithm, 655
KDF (key derivation function), 815
KE (Key Exchange)
    definition of, 946
    IKE payloads, 848
Keepalive interval
    changing values of, 796
    definition of, 795
Keepalive probes
    changing values of, 796
    definition of, 795
    overview of, 793
Keepalive time
    changing values of, 796–797
    definition of, 795
    server host crashes and reboots, 799–800
    server host unreachable, 800–802
Keepalive timers, 793
Keepalives, TCP. *See* TCP keepalive
Key derivation function (KDF), 815
Key Exchange (KE)
    definition of, 946
    IKE payloads, 848
Key Hash field, RSA Signature option, 416
Key management, in cryptography, 821
Key signing keys. *See* KSKs (key signing keys)
Keyed-hash message authentication code (HMAC),
        818–819, 943
Keys, cryptographic, 810
Kleinrock, Leonard, 1, 48
KSKs (key signing keys)
    definition of, 946
    DNSSEC, 897, 905

L

L2TP/IPSec, 865
L2TP (Layer 2 Tunneling Protocol)
    definition of, 946
    establishing tunneling with, 149
LaBrea tarpit, attacks related to window manage-
        ment, 723
LACP (Link Aggregation Control Protocol), 92–93,
        947
LAGs (link aggregation groups), 93, 947
Land attacks, ICMP attacks, 428
LANs (local area networks)
    definition of, 947
    Ethernet standards, 82–84
    virtual. *See* VLANs (virtual LANs)
Large-scale NAT (LSN), IPv6 transition, 315

Last Member Query Interval (LMQI), in IGMP/
        MLD, 468, 947
Last Member Query Time (LMQT), 466–467, 947
LAST_ACK state
    simultaneous open and close transitions, 625
    TCP state transitions, 618
Latency, connections and, 4
Layer 2 devices, DCHP relay agents, 270–271
Layer 2 Tunneling Protocol (L2TP)
    definition of, 946
    establishing tunneling with, 149
Layering
    implementation and design and, 8–10
    security protocols, 832–833
    TCP/IP suite and, 14
Layering violation, transport layer, 476
LCG (Linear Congruential Generator), 816, 947
LCI (Location Configuration Information), 274, 947
LCI (logical channel identifier), 5
LCN (logical channel number), 5, 947
LCP (Link Control Protocol)
    definition of, 947
    operation of, 133–134
    options, 134–137
    overview of, 131–134
LDAP (Lightweight Directory Access Protocol)
    definition of, 947
    DNS and, 570–571
    SRV record providing LDAP service, 548–549
    well-known port for, 18
LDRAs (lightweight DHCP relay agents), 271, 947
LEAP (Lightweight EAP), 947
Leasequery, DCHP relay agents, 269–270
Leases
    in BOOTP, 235
    duration of DHCP leases, 235–236
Length field
    in Ethernet frame format, 85–86
    UDP header, 475, 481–482
    Payload Length field, in IPv6 header, 184, 198,
        204–205
    Total Length field, in IPv4 header, 183–184, 207
Licklider, J.C.R., 2
Lightweight DHCP relay agents (LDRAs), 271, 947
Lightweight Directory Access Protocol. *See* LDAP
        (Lightweight Directory Access Protocol)
Lightweight EAP (LEAP), 947
Lightweight IGMP3, 464–465
Lightweight MLD (LW-MLD), 394, 948
Lightweight MLDv2, 464–465
Limited slow start, 772
Limited transmit approach, to congestion control in
        TCP, 742

Linear Congruential Generator (LCG), 816, 947
Link Address field, in DHCPv6 message format, 254
Link aggregation (802.1AX), 92–93
Link Aggregation Control Protocol (LACP), 92–93, 947
Link aggregation groups (LAGs), 93, 947
Link Control Protocol. *See* LCP (Link Control Protocol)
Link discriminator, LCP options, 139
Link layer
    address resolution and, 165–166
    attacks on, 154–156
    autonegotiation in Ethernet interface, 95
    bridges and switches, 98–102
    broadcasting ARP frames, 167
    duplex mismatch, 96
    Ethernet (802.3) frames, 84–86
    Ethernet frame sizes, 88–89
    Ethernet supporting broadcasting at, 437
    flow control (802.1X) in Ethernet interface, 98
    full duplex Ethernet, 94–95
    IEEE 802 LAN/MAN standards for, 82–84
    integrity checking on Ethernet frames, 86–88
    introduction to, 79
    link aggregation (802.1AX), 92–93
    MRP (Multiple Registration Protocol), 111
    MTU (maximum transmission unit), 148
    Point-to-Point Protocol. *See* PPP (Point-to-Point Protocol)
    standards, 80–82
    STP (Spanning Tree Protocol). *See* STP (Spanning Tree Protocol)
    summary and references, 156–163
    tunneling, 149–153
    UDLs (unidirectional links), 153–154
    VLANs and QoS tagging, 89–92
    wireless LANs. *See* Wi-Fi (wireless fidelity-802.11)
    WoL (Wake-on LAN), power saving, and magic packets, 96–97
Link-Layer Address. *See* LLA (Link-Layer Address)
Link Local Multicast Name Resolution (LLMNR), 445, 569–570, 947
Link-local scope
    configuring IPv4 addresses with SLAAC, 276
    configuring IPv6 addresses with SLAAC, 276–277
    of IPv6 addresses, 43
    IPv6 multicast addresses, 58–59
    multicast addresses, 53
    viewing format of link-local IPv6 address, 45
Link Quality Reports (LQRs)
    definition of, 947
    in PPP operations, 136

Links, unidirectional, 153–154
Linux OSs
    autotuning TCP receive windows, 715
    `ethtool` program for checking full duplex support, 94
    IP masquerading, 337
    IPSec implementations, 867
    quick acknowledgments, 733
    rate limiting of ICMP messages, 369–370
    RTT estimation, 657–661
    standards and, 24
    vconfig command for manipulating 802.1p/q information, 90–91
LISTEN state, in TCP
    TCP port numbers and, 632–633
    TCP state transitions and, 618
LLA (Link-Layer Address)
    definition of, 947
    Link-Layer Address (LLA) option in ND, 418–419
    Source Link-Layer Address option in ND, 409–410
    Source/Target Address List options in ND, 413–414
LLC (Logical Link Control)
    802.2 standard defining, 84
    definition of, 947
    relationship of link layer frames to data frames, 116
LLMNR (Link Local Multicast Name Resolution), 445, 569–570, 947
LMQI (Last Member Query Interval), in IGMP/MLD, 468, 947
LMQT (Last Member Query Time), 466–467, 947
LNP (Local Network Protection), 310, 947
Local area networks. *See* LANs (local area networks)
Local congestion, in Linux TCP example,
    fast retransmit and, 759–762
    sender pause and, 750–754
    stretch ACKs and recovery from, 754–757
Local IP addresses
    restrictions in UDP server design, 500–501
    TCP server restrictions on local, 634–635
Local net (limited) broadcast, 43
Local Network Protection (LNP), 310, 947
Location Configuration Information (LCI), 274, 947
Location-to-Service Translation (LoST), 274–275
Locators, IP addresses as, 70
Logical channel identifier (LCI), 5
Logical channel number (LCN), 5, 947
Logical Internet addresses, translating to physical hardware addresses, 167
Logical Link Control. *See* LLC (Logical Link Control)
Long options, DHCP/BOOTP options, 239

Long-term credential mechanism, STUN, 325–326
Long-Term Evolution (LTE), 948
Longest matching prefix algorithm, 69, 209–210
Lookup, IP addresses form host names, 19
Loopback
    hairpinning (NAT loopback), 314, 486
    implementing loopback capacity, 145–148
    PPP issues and, 134
LoST (Location-to-Service Translation), 274–275
Low-rate DoD attacks, TCP timeout/retransmission
    attacks, 686
LQRs (Link Quality Reports), in PPP
    definition of, 947
    in PPP operations, 136
LSN (large-scale NAT), IPv6 transition, 315
LTE (Long-Term Evolution), 948
LW-MLD (Lightweight MLD), 948

M

MAC layer, sublayer of link layer, 84
MAC (Media Access Control)
    addresses in Ethernet frames, 16
    chaddr (Client Hardware Address) field, 244
    DCF collision avoidance/backoff procedure,
        121–122
    definition of, 948
    HCF (hybrid coordination function), 122–123
    multicast addresses, 437
    overview of, 120–121
    protocols, 81
    virtual carrier sense and physical carrier sense, 121
MAC (message authentication codes), 818–820, 948
MAC PDU (MPDU), 113, 949
MAC Services Data Unit (MSDU), in 802.11n, 949
Magnification attacks, UDP-related attacks, 506
Mail exchanger (MX) records, in DNS
    definition of, 950
    DNS resource record types, 544–545
Mailboxes, port numbers as, 474
Malware (malicious software)
    attacks related to Internet architecture, 26
    definition of, 805–806
Man-in-the-middle attacks. See MITM (man-in-the-
        middle) attacks
Management frames, Wi-Fi, 113–115
Manchester Phase Encoding (MPE)
    clock recovery in Ethernet frames, 85
    definition of, 949
MANs (metropolitan area networks)
    cable TV and DSL, 79
    definition of, 948
    Ethernet standards, 82–84
Mapping timer, clearing NAT state, 308–309

MAPs (mesh APs), 130
Masks, in IP forwarding, 209
Masquerading attacks
    firewalls and NATs and, 345
    ICMP attacks and, 429
    link layer attacks, 155
    types of threats to network communication, 808
Master session keys (MSK), in EAP
    definition of, 949
    key derivation in EAP, 838
Maximum pad value (MPV), 137, 949
Maximum probing, 774
Maximum received unit (MRU)
    definition of, 949
    length of LCP packet and, 134
Maximum segment life (MSL). See also TIME_WAIT
        state (2MSL)
    SYN segments, 610
    TIME_WAIT state (2MSL) and, 618
Maximum Segment Size. See MSS (Maximum Seg-
        ment Size)
Maximum transmission unit. See MTU (maximum
        transmission unit)
MCS (Modulation and coding scheme)
    definition of, 948
    higher throughput (802.11n) support and, 127
MD (Message Digest Algorithms)
    definition of, 948
    MD-5 (Message Digest Algorithm 5), 817–818
    TLS extensions, 883
mDNS (Multicast DNS), 444–445, 570, 948
Mean deviation, in RTT estimation, 653
Mechanisms
    DNS TXT records and DKIM, 546
    STUN, 325–326
Media Access Control. See MAC (Media Access
        Control)
Media independent handoff (MIH)
    definition of, 948
    mobility and handoff information in DHCP, 275
Member links, in PPP bundles, 137
Mesh (802.11s), Wi-Fi, 130
Mesh APs (MAPs), 130
Mesh deterministic access, 130
Mesh Point (MP), 949
Mesh points (MPs), 130, 949
Mesh STAs (mesh stations), 130
Message authentication codes (MAC), 818–820, 948
Message boundaries, datagrams and, 5–6
Message digests
    Message Digest Algorithms. See MD (Message
        Digest Algorithms)
    overview of, 817–818

Message formats
  DHCP and BOOTP, 236–238
  DHCPv6, 253–255
  DNS, 520–524
  ESP, 862
  IKE protocol, 844–846
  STUN, 320
Message stream modification (MSM)
  definition of, 949
  types of threats to network communication, 808
Meta types, resource record categories, 528
Metcalfe's Law, 19
Metropolitan area networks. See MANs (metropolitan area networks)
MF (More Fragments) field, in UDP fragmentation, 489
Michael, for message integrity checking, 129
Microsoft CHAP (MS-CHAP), 949
Microsoft Point-to-Point Compression Protocol (MPPC), 140, 949
Microsoft Point-to-Point Encryption (MPPE), 145, 150
MIH (media independent handoff)
  definition of, 948
  mobility and handoff information in DHCP, 275
MIME (Multipurpose Internet Mail Extensions), 948
MIMO (multiple input, multiple output)
  definition of, 948
  higher throughput (802.11n) support, 126–127
MIP (Mobile IP)
  bidirectional tunneling, 216–217
  definition of, 948
  DHCP and, 233
  discussion of issues in, 220
  handling IP nodes, 199
  ICMP fast handover message in MIPv6, 388
  ICMP Home Agent Discovery Request message, 386
  ICMP Mobile Prefix Solicitation message, 387–388
  Mobile IP with Fast Handovers (FMIP), 942
  Mobile IPv6, 70
  overview of, 215–216
  RO (route optimization), 217–219
  Routing header and, 200
Misbehaving receivers, TCP congestion control attacks, 785
MITM (man-in-the-middle) attacks
  ICMP attacks and, 428
  security protocol-related, 918–919
  types of threats to network communication, 808
MLD (Multicast Listener Discovery)
  attacks related to, 469–470
  counters and variables, 467–468

DAD and, 278
definition of, 948
examples, 459–464
ICMP extension messages, 390–394
lightweight MLDv2, 464–465
overview of, 15, 451–453
processing by group members (Group Member Part), 454–457
processing by multicast routers (Multicast Router Part), 457–459
query/report/done messages in ICMP, 388–390
robustness of, 465–467
snooping, 468–469
summary and references, 470–472
MLPP (Multilevel Precedence and Preemption), 189, 948
MMRP (Multiple MAC Registration Protocol), 111, 948
MNs (mobile nodes)
  definition of, 948
  in Mobile IP, 216–218
MOBIKE (Mobile IKE), 854, 865, 949
Mobile IP. See MIP (Mobile IP)
Mobile nodes (MNs)
  definition of, 948
  in Mobile IP, 216–218
Mobile Prefix Advertisement messages, ICMP, 410–411
Mobile Prefix Solicitation message, ICMP, 387–388
Mobility header, 216
Mobility messages, in RRP, 218–219
Mobility Services (MoS)
  definition of, 949
  mobility and handoff information in DHCP, 275
Modifiers, DNS TXT records, 546
MODP (Modulo-P groups), in DH, 821, 949
Modulation and coding scheme (MCS), in 802.11n
  definition of, 948
  higher throughput (802.11n) support and, 127
Modulo-P groups (MODP), in DH, 821, 949
More Frag field, data frame fragmentation, 117
MoS (Mobility Services)
  definition of, 949
  mobility and handoff information in DHCP, 275
MP (Multilink PPP)
  definition of, 949
  overview of, 137–139
MPDU (MAC PDU), 113, 949
MPE (Manchester Phase Encoding)
  clock recovery in Ethernet frames, 85
  definition of, 949
MPLS (Multi-Protocol Label Switching), 215, 949
MPPC (Microsoft Point-to-Point Compression Protocol), 140, 949

MPPE (Microsoft Point-to-Point Encryption), 145, 150
MPs (mesh points), 130, 949
MPV (maximum pad value), 137, 949
MRD (Multicast Router Discovery)
    definition of, 949
    designing location of multicast routers, 469
    overview of, 394–395
MRP (Multiple Registration Protocol)
    802.1ak, 111
    definition of, 949
MRRU (multilink maximum received reconstructed
    unit), 138, 949
MRU (maximum received unit)
    definition of, 949
    length of LCP packet and, 134
MS-CHAP (Microsoft CHAP), 949
MSDU (MAC Services Data Unit), in 802.11n, 949
MSK (master session keys)
    definition of, 949
    key derivation in EAP, 838
MSL (maximum seqment life), in TCP. *See also*
    TIME_WAIT state (2MSL)
    SYN segments, 610
    TIME_WAIT state (2MSL) and, 618
MSM (message stream modification) attack
    definition of, 949
    types of threats to network communication, 808
MSS (Maximum Segment Size), in TCP
    definition of, 950
    SWS (silly windows syndrome) and, 709
    TCP header, 590, 605–607
MSTP (Multiple Spanning Tree Protocol), in bridges,
    111
MTU (maximum transmission unit)
    definition of, 950
    for Ethernet, 86, 506
    frame formats and, 79
    ISPs (Internet Service Providers) and, 494
    link layer and, 148
    neighbor discovery options in IPv6, 411–412
    PPPoE (PPP over Ethernet) and, 614
    preventing fragmentation of TCP datagrams,
        612–613
    PTB messages in ICMPv6, 370–371
Multi-access networks, 9
Multi-Protocol Label Switching (MPLS), 215, 949
Multi6 architecture, 70
Multicast addresses
    allocation of, 65
    IPv4 multicast addresses, 54–57
    IPv6 multicast addresses, 57–61
    NAT and, 310
    overview of, 53–54

Multicast DNS (mDNS), 444–445, 570, 948
Multicast groups
    overview of, 15
    RP (rendezvous point), 60
Multicast Listener Discovery. *See* MLD (Multicast
    Listener Discovery)
Multicast Listener Query, Report, and Done mes-
    sages, ICMP messages, 388–390
Multicast Router Discovery. *See* MRD (Multicast
    Router Discovery)
Multicast routers
    designing location of, 469
    IGMP/MLD processing by, 457–459
    overview of, 452–454
    querier election, 466
    query message options, 459
Multicast state, 441
Multicasting
    converting IP multicast addresses to MAC
        addresses, 442–444
    example of, 444–446
    host address filtering, 449–451
    introduction to, 435–436
    IPSec supporting, 864–865
    overview of, 441–442
    receiving multicast datagrams, 447–449
    sending multicast datagrams, 446–447
Multihomed systems
    IPv6 and, 70
    overview of, 12–13
    unicast addresses and, 67–68
Multilevel Precedence and Preemption (MLPP), 189,
    948
Multilink maximum received reconstructed unit
    (MRRU), 138, 949
Multilink PPP (MP), 137–139, 949
Multiple input, multiple output (MIMO)
    definition of, 948
    higher throughput (802.11n) support, 126–127
Multiple MAC Registration Protocol (MMRP), 948
Multiple Registration Protocol (MRP)
    802.1ak, 111
    definition of, 949
Multiple Spanning Tree Protocol (MSTP), 111
Multiple VLAN Registration Protocol (MVRP), 111, 950
Multiplexing
    implementation and design and, 10–13
    important concepts in development of network
        architecture, 4
    TCP/IP suite and, 16–17
Multipurpose Internet Mail Extensions (MIME), 948
MVRP (Multiple VLAN Registration Protocol), 111,
    950

MX (mail exchanger) records, in DNS
  definition of, 950
  DNS resource record types, 544–545

N

N (Notification), IKE payloads, 849, 873
NA (Neighbor Advertisement)
  ICMPv6 messages, 277
  IND (Inverse Neighbor Discovery), 401
  main components of ND, 396
  neighbor discovery in IPv6, 398–401
NAC (Network Access Control), 833–837, 950
NACK (Negative ACKs), 111, 950
Nagle algorithm, in TCP
  Delayed ACK interaction with, 699
  disabling, 699–700
  overview of, 696–698
  reducing number of packets across WANs, 692
Nagle, John, 696
Name authority pointer records. See NAPTR (name
    authority pointer) records
Name resolution. See also DNS (Domain Name
    System)
  of host names into IP addresses, 511
  process of, 518–519
Name server (NS) records
  definition of, 951
  DNS resource record types, 529–530
Name servers
  caching, 517–518
  DNS, 516–517
Name Service Caching Daemon (NSCD), 518, 951
Name space, DNS, 512–514
Naming syntax, DNS, 514–516
NAP (Network Access Protection)
  definition of, 950
  DHCP leases and, 246
NAPT (Network Address Port Translation), 305–306,
    950
NAPTR (name authority pointer) records
  definition of, 950
  DNS resource record types, 549–551
  NTN (non-terminal NAPTR), 551–552
  S-NAPTR and U-NAPTR, 554–555
  URI/URN resolution and, 553–554
NAR (New Access Router), 417, 950
NAT (network address translation)
  address and port translation behavior, 311–313
  address pools, 312
  attacks related to, 345–346
  configuring, 334
  definition of, 950
  direct interaction with, 338–339
  DS-Lite (Dual-Stack Lite) and, 339–340

  editors, 315
  filtering behavior, 312–313
  firewall rules, 335–336
  hairpinning (NAT loopback), 314, 486
  ICE and, 332–334
  ICMP and, 309
  IPSec NAT traversal, 865–867
  IPv4/IPv6 translation, 340–345
  IPv6 and, 310–311
  mapping, 307
  multicast and, 310
  NAPT (Network Address Port Translation),
    305–306
  other transport protocols and, 309
  overview of, 303–305
  pinholes and hole punching, 317
  port forwarding and port mapping and, 314
  private addresses and, 51
  rules, 337–338
  session, 307–308
  SPNAT (service provider NAT), 315–316
  STUN (Session Traversal Utilities for NAT),
    319–326
  summary and references, 346–352
  TCP and, 306–308
  Teredo tunneling and, 485–486
  translating TCP and UDP addresses and port
    numbers, 605
  traversal, 316
  tunneled packets and, 310
  TURN (Traversal Using Relays around NAT),
    326–332
  UDP and, 308–309
  UNSAF (unilateral self-address fixing), 317–319
NAT-PMP (NAT Port Mapping Protocol)
  definition of, 950
  direct interaction with NAT and firewalls,
    338–339
NAT Port Mapping Protocol (NAT-PMP)
  definition of, 950
  direct interaction with NAT and firewalls,
    338–339
NAT-PT (NAT with Port Translation), 950
NAT Traversal
  ICE (Interactive Connectivity Establishment),
    332–334
  overview of, 316
  pinholes and hole punching, 317
  STUN (Session Traversal Utilities for NAT),
    319–326
  TURN (Traversal Using Relays around NAT),
    326–332
  UNSAF (unilateral self-address fixing), 317–319
NAT with Port Translation (NAT-PT), 950

NAT64, IPv6/IPv4 translation, 344, 950
NAV (Network Allocation Vector), 121, 950
NBMA (non-broadcast multiple access)
    ICMP Redirect message used with, 375
    ND and, 396
    overview of, 167
NCoA (New Care-of Address), 419, 950
NCPs (Network Control Protocols), 131, 141–142,
    950
ND (Neighbor Discovery Protocol)
    Advertisement Interval option, 412
    Certificate option, 417
    CGA options, 414–415
    definition of, 951
    DNS Search List option, 422–423
    Experimental Values in, 423
    Handover Key Request/Reply options, 422–423
    Home Agent Information option, 412–413
    IND (Inverse Neighbor Discovery), 401–402
    interaction between IP fragmentation and ARP/
        ND, 496–497
    IP Address/Prefix option, 417–418
    Link-Layer Address (LLA) option, 418–419
    MTU option in, 411–412
    Nonce option, 416–417
    NS (Neighbor Solicitation) message, 398–401
    NUD (Neighbor Unreachability Detection),
        402–403
    options, 407–409
    overview of, 395–396
    Prefix Information option, 410–411
    Recursive DNS Server option, 420
    Redirected Header option, 411
    Route Information option, 420
    Router Advertisement Flags Extension option,
        420–421
    router solicitation and advertisement messages
        in ICMPv6, 396–398
    RSA Signature option, 415–416
    SEND (Secure Neighbor Discovery), 403–407
    Source Link-Layer Address option, 409–410
    Source/Target Address List options, 413–414
    Teredo tunneling and, 486–487
    Timestamp option, 416
    Trust Anchor option, 417
NDP. See ND (Neighbor Discovery Protocol)
Negative ACKs (NACK), 133, 950
Negative caching, DNS servers and, 517
Neighbor Advertisement. See NA (Neighbor
    Advertisement)
Neighbor Discovery Protocol. See ND (Neighbor
    Discovery Protocol)
Neighbor Solicitation messages, ICMPv6, 277

Neighbor Unreachability Detection (NUD)
    definition of, 951
    neighbor discovery in IPv6, 402–403
NEMO (Network Mobility), 216, 951
Net number, in IP addresses, 35
NetBoot service, from Apple, 246
netsh command, viewing in-use multicast groups
    in Windows OSs, 447–448
netstat command
    displaying IP group membership, 446–447
    restricting local IP addresses, 634
    viewing active multicast addresses, 66
    viewing forwarding table with, 446–447
    viewing IPv4 UDP servers, 500–501
Network Access Control (NAC), 833–837, 950
Network Address Port Translation (NAPT), 305–306,
    950
Network address translation. See NAT (network
    address translation)
Network Allocation Vector (NAV), in Wi-Fi, 121, 950
Network architecture
    APIs, 22
    ARM (ARPANET Reference Model), 1–2, 13–16
    attacks related to Internet architecture, 25–26
    client/server design pattern, 20–21
    end-to-end argument, 6
    error control and flow control, 7–8
    fate sharing, 6–7
    implementation and design, 8
    implementations and distributions, 24–25
    Internet, intranets, extranets, 19–20
    layering, 8–10
    multiplexing, demultiplexing, and encapsula-
        tion, 10–13, 16–17
    names, addresses, and DNS, 19
    packets, connections, and datagrams, 3–6
    peer-to-peer design pattern, 21–22
    port numbers, 17–19
    principles of, 2–3
    standardization of, 22–24
    summary and references, 26–30
    TCP/IP suite, 13
Network byte order, TCP/IP headers, 183
Network communication, threats to, 807–809
Network Control Protocols (NCPs), 131, 141–142, 950
Network File System (NFS), 478
Network interface cards. See NICs (network inter-
    face cards)
Network (internetwork) layer
    address resolution and, 165–166
    of OSI model, 9
    passing datagram to transport layer, 17
    TCP and UDP in, 585

Network Mobility (NEMO), 216, 951
Network Time Protocol. *See* NTP (Network Time Protocol)
New Access Router (NAR), 417, 950
New Care-of Address (NCoA), 419, 950
NewReno algorithm, 739–740
Next Header field
    ICMP Parameter Problem and, 379–380
    IPv6, 194–195
    Mobile IP, 216
    UDP header, 476
    UDP-Lite, 487
Next-hop, in IP forwarding, 209
Next Server IP Address (Siaddr) field, DHCP/BOOTP message format, 238, 246
NextSECure resource record. *See* NSEC (NextSECure) resource record
NFS (Network File System), 478
NICs (network interface cards)
    definition of, 951
    host address filtering, 449–451
    overview of, 92
No Route to Destination, ICMPv6 messages, 365
Node-local scope
    of IPv6 addresses, 43
    multicast addresses, 53
Node Requirements RFCs, 23
Nominees, in ICE, 333
Non-broadcast multiple access. *See* NBMA (non-broadcast multiple access)
Non-HT mode, 802.11n operating modes, 128
Non-terminal NAPTR (NTN), 551, 951
Nonce (number used once)
    cryptographic nonces and, 816
    definition of, 951
    IKE payloads, 848
    in ND, 416–417, 486–487
Nonportable addresses, allocation of IP addresses and, 62
Nonrepudiation, basic principles of security, 806–807
NOP (No Operation), TCP header options, 605
Notification (N), IKE payloads, 849, 873
NPTv6, 310, 951
NRO (Number Resource Organization)
    allocation of IP addresses and, 62–63
    definition of, 951
NS (name server) records
    definition of, 951
    DNS resource record types, 529–530
NS (Neighbor Solicitation)
    definition of, 951
    IND (Inverse Neighbor Discovery), 401–402

main components of ND, 396
    neighbor discovery in IPv6, 398–401
NSCD (Name Service Caching Daemon), 518, 951
NSEC (NextSECure) resource record
    canonical ordering of, 902
    definition of, 951
    DNSSEC, 898–901
    signed zones and zone cuts, 903
NSEC Parameters (NSEC3PARAM), in DNSSEC, 898, 951
NSEC3PARAM (NSEC Parameters), in DNSSEC, 900, 951
NTN (non-terminal NAPTR), 551, 951
NTP (Network Time Protocol)
    definition of, 951
    multicast group in, 54
    variable-scope IPv6 multicast addresses, 58
NUD (Neighbor Unreachability Detection)
    definition of, 951
    neighbor discovery in IPv6, 402–403
Nuke class, bombs attacks on ICMP, 428
NULL encryption algorithm, 819
Number Resource Organization (NRO)
    allocation of IP addresses and, 62–63
    definition of, 951
Number used once. *See* Nonce (number used once)

O

Object Identifier (OID), 951
OCSP (Online Certification Status Protocol)
    definition of, 951
    validating and revoking certificates, 829–831
OFDM (Orthogonal frequency division multiplexing)
    definition of, 951
    MIMO and, 127
OID (Object Identifier), 951
OLSR (Optimized Link State Routing)
    definition of, 951
    Wi-Fi mesh and, 130
Online Certification Status Protocol (OCSP)
    definition of, 951
    validating and revoking certificates, 829–831
OOB (Out of Band), 719, 952
Op field, DHCP/BOOTP message format, 236
Open DNS servers, 567
Open Systems Interconnection (OSI)
    definition of, 952
    layering and, 8
Open systems, TCP/IP suite as, 2
OpenPGP, 822, 883
OPT (option) pseudo records, DNS resource record types, 547–548

Optimal window size, 730
Optimistic ACKing, TCP congestion control attacks, 785–786
Optimistic DAD, 253
Optimistic state, IPv6 addresses, 253
Optimized Link State Routing (OLSR)
    definition of, 951
    Wi-Fi mesh and, 130
Option overloading, DHCP/BOOTP, 239
Option Request Option (ORO), in DHCP, 952
Orderly release, aborting TCP connections, 627
Organizationally Unique Identifier. *See* OUI (Organizationally Unique Identifier)
ORO (Option Request Option), in DHCP, 952
Orthogonal frequency division multiplexing (OFDM)
    definition of, 951
    MIMO and, 127
OSI (Open Systems Interconnection)
    definition of, 952
    layering and, 8
OUI (Organizationally Unique Identifier)
    definition of, 952
    formats of IPv6 addresses, 44–45
    IP multicasting and, 442–444
Out of Band (OOB), 719, 952
Overlay networks
    p2p and, 22
    tunneling allowing formation of, 149

P

P2P (Peer-to-Peer)
    definition of, 952
    design pattern, 21–22
    discovery problem in, 22
PA (provider-aggretable) addresses
    allocation of IP addresses and, 62
    definition of, 952
PAA (PANA Authentication Agent), 839, 952
PaC (PANA client), 839, 952
Packet duplication, TCP timeout/retransmission, 684–685
Packet-filtering firewalls
    overview of, 300–301
    rules, 335–336
Packet-filtering, NAT functions, 305
Packet reordering, TCP timeout/retransmission, 682–684
Packet size threshold, in Wi-Fi control frames, 115
Packet sniffing, 26, 156
Packet-switching, 4
Packet-switching networks, 1
Packet Too Big. *See* PTB (Packet Too Big)

Packetization, TCP reliability and, 586
Packets
    AQM (active queue management), 782–783
    conservation of, 731
    IEEE, 84
    in protocol architecture, 3–6
    retransmission and, 580–581
    sliding window protocol, 582
    in TCP/IP suite, 14
    windows of packets, 581–582
PACP (port access control protocol), 835
PAD (peer authorization database)
    definition of, 952
    in IPSec, 841
PAD (PPPoE Activity Discovery) messages, 288
Padded payload, in Ethernet frame format, 86
Padding
    block size in PPP, 136–137
    IPv6 options for, 197–198
Padding oracle, security protocol-related attacks and, 919
PANA Authentication Agent (PAA), 839, 952
PANA client (PaC), 839, 952
PANA (Protocol for Carrying Authentication for Network Access), 839–840, 952
PAP (Password Authentication Protocol)
    definition of, 952
    for PPP authentication, 140
Parameter Problem messages
    ICMP, 379–380
    translating ICMPv4 to ICMPv6, 426
    translating ICMPv6 to ICMPv4, 426–427
Partial ACKs, in TCP, 739
Passive attacks, types of threats to network communication, 807–809
Passive closer, FIN segments and, 597
Passive open, in TCP connections, 597
Passive opener (server)
    RST segments, 631
    in TCP connections, 599
Password Authentication Protocol (PAP)
    definition of, 952
    for PPP authentication, 140
Path MTU, 148
Path MTU Discovery. *See* PMTUD (Path MTU Discovery)
Path MTU (PMTU), 953
Pattern-match-criteria, in ACL rules, 335
PAWS (Protection against Wrapped Sequence Numbers)
    definition of, 952
    TCP header, 610–611

Payloads
    of frames, 16, 86
    IKE protocol, 847–849
    IP header, 184–185, 203–206
    jumbogram options, 198
    UDP header, 475, 482
PCF (point coordination function), in Wi-Fi
    definition of, 952
    options for controlling sharing of wireless
        medium, 120
PCO (phased coexistence operation)
    definition of, 952
    higher throughput (802.11n) support and, 128
PCoA (Previous Care-of Address), 419, 952
PCP (Port Control Protocol)
    definition of, 952
    direct interaction with NAT and firewalls, 339
PD (prefix delegation), 266–267
PDUs (protocol data units)
    definition of, 952
    encapsulation and, 10
    link layer. See Frames, Ethernet
PEAP (Protected EAP), 838, 952
Peer Address field, in DHCPv6 message format, 254
Peer authorization database (PAD)
    definition of, 952
    in IPSec, 841
Peer-to-Peer (P2P)
    definition of, 952
    design pattern, 21–22
    discovery problem in, 22
PEN (Private Enterprise Number), 257, 952
Per-association (per-connection) basis, for NAT con-
        nections, 303–304
Per-flow state, LCI and LCN and, 5
Per-hop behavior (PHB)
    definition of, 953
    forwarding and, 189
Perfect Forward Secrecy (PFS), 815, 953
PFC (Protocol Field Compression)
    definition of, 953
    PPP and, 133
PFS (Perfect Forward Secrecy), 815, 953
PGP (Pretty Good Privacy), 822
Phased coexistence operation (PCO)
    definition of, 952
    higher throughput (802.11n) support and, 128
PHB (per-hop behavior)
    definition of, 953
    forwarding and, 189
Phishing attacks, 806
PHY (physical) layer, 953

Physical addresses, translating logical addresses to,
    167
Physical carrier sense, 121
Physical layer
    802.11 standard describing, 123–124
    channels and frequencies, 124–126
    of OSI model, 9
PI (provider-independent) addresses
    allocation of IP addresses and, 63
    definition of, 953
Piggybacking, Delayed ACKs and, 692, 695
PIM (Protocol Independent Multicast), 953
ping. See Echo Request/Reply (ping) messages
Ping of death attacks
    ICMP attacks, 428
    UDP attacks, 506–507
Pinholes, in NAT traversal, 317
PIO (Prefix Information option)
    definition of, 953
    neighbor discovery options in IPv6, 410–411
PKCs (public key certificates). See also Certificates,
    831, 953
PKCS (Public Key Cryptography Standards), 953
PKI (Public Key Infrastructure)
    CGAs not requiring, 404
    definition of, 953
    overview of, 822
Plain old telephone service (POTS)
    definition of, 953
    DSL and, 287
Plaintext
    encrypting cleartext message, 810
    TLS, 878
PLCP (Physical Layer Convergence Procedure), 113,
    953
PLPMTUD (Packetization Layer Path MTU Discov-
        ery), 612–613
Plug and Play, 337–339
PMTU (Path MTU), 148, 953
PMTUD (Path MTU Discovery)
    definition of, 953
    example of use with TCP, 613–616
    example using UDP, 493–496
    link layer and, 148
    PTB messages in ICMPv6, 370–371
    TCP connections and, 612–613
    TCP-related attacks, 641–642
    using UDP for, 493
PNAC (Port-Based Network Access Control), 833, 953
PoE (power-over-Ethernet)
    definition of, 953
    higher throughput (802.11n) support and, 128

Point coordination function (PCF), in Wi-Fi
    definition of, 952
    options for controlling sharing of wireless
        medium, 120
Point-to-Point Protocol. *See* PPP (Point-to-Point
    Protocol)
Point-to-Point Tunneling Protocol. *See* PPTP (Point-
    to-Point Tunneling Protocol)
Pointer (PTR) records, DNS resource record types,
    536–541
POP3, SRV record providing POP3 service, 549
Port access control protocol (PACP), 835
Port-Based Network Access Control (PNAC), 833, 953
Port Control Protocol (PCP)
    definition of, 952
    direct interaction with NAT and firewalls, 339
Port forwarding, in NAT, 314
Port mapping, in NAT, 314
Port numbers
    binding options available to TCP server, 635
    as mailboxes, 474
    TCP/IP suite and, 17–19
    TCP servers, 632–634
    in UPD server design, 499–500
Port overloading, in NAT, 313
Port parity, in NAT, 313
Port preservation, NAT and TCP and, 307
Port-Preserving Symmetric NAT (PP), 486
Port states, STP, 104–105
Port translation behavior, in NAT, 311–313
Port unreachable message, ICMP, 365–370
Ports
    multiple UDP servers per port, 503–504
    requesting connection to nonexistent TCP port,
        626
    in TCP header, 588
POTS (plain old telephone service)
    definition of, 953
    DSL and, 287
Pouzin, Louis, 1
Power-over-Ethernet (PoE)
    definition of, 953
    higher throughput (802.11n) support and, 128
Power save mode (PSM), 119–120, 954
Power Save Multi-Poll (PSMP), 120, 954
Power saving, Ethernet (802.3) and, 96–97
PP (Port-Preserving Symmetric NAT), 486
PPP over Ethernet. *See* PPPoE (PPP over Ethernet)
PPP (Point-to-Point Protocol)
    authentication, 140–141
    CCP (Compression Control Protocol) and,
        139–140

definition of, 953
example of, 143–145
header compression, 142–143
MP (Multilink PPP), 137–139
NCPs (Network Control Protocols), 141–142
overview of, 130–131
PPPMux, 137
PPPMuxCP (PPP Mux Control Protocol), 137
PPPoE Activity Discovery (PAD) messages, 288
PPPoE (PPP over Ethernet)
    definition of, 953
    Discovery and PPP Session phases, 288
    DSL and, 287
    example of use of, 289–291
    message format, 288–289
    MTU (maximum transmission unit) and, 614
    overview of, 286
PPTP (Point-to-Point Tunneling Protocol)
    definition of, 953
    establishing sessions, 151–153
    establishing tunneling with, 149–153
    NAT editors and, 315
Preamble, of Ethernet frame, 84
Preferred lifetime
    IA (Identity Association) and, 255
    IPv6 addresses, 252
Prefix delegation (PD), 266–267
Prefixes
    in IPv4 and IPv6 address management, 47–48
    route aggregation and, 50
    subnet mask formats, 39
Presentation layer, of OSI model, 10
Preshared keys. *See* PSKs (preshared keys)
Pretty Good Privacy (PGP), 822
Previous Care-of Address (PCoA), 419, 952
PRFs (pseudorandom functions), 816, 954
PRGs (pseudorandom generators), 815–816, 954
Primary DNS servers, 517
Priority fields, QoS 802.1p, 90
Private Enterprise Number (PEN), 257, 952
PRNGs (pseudorandom numbers)
    definition of, 954
    overview of, 815–816
Probing, NAT session, 308
Promiscuous ARP, 175
Promiscuous mode, Ethernet interfaces, 155
Protected EAP (PEAP), 838, 952
Protection against Wrapped Sequence Numbers
        (PAWS)
    definition of, 952
    TCP header, 610–611
Protocol data units. *See* PDUs (protocol data units)

Protocol field
  IP header, 185
  in PPP frames, 132–133
  UDP header, 476
Protocol Field Compression (PFC)
  definition of, 953
  PPP and, 133
Protocol for Carrying Authentication for Network
      Access (PANA), 839–840, 952
Protocol identifiers, in multiplexing, 10
Protocol Independent Multicast (PIM), 953
Protocol multiplexing, 10
Protocol suites
  definition of, 1
  end and intermediate systems, 12
Protocols, 1
Provider-aggregatable (PA) addresses
  allocation of IP addresses and, 62
  definition of, 952
Provider-independent (PI) addresses
  allocation of IP addresses and, 63
  definition of, 953
Proxy ARP, 174–175
Proxy firewalls
  overview of, 301–303
  types of firewalls, 300
Proxy Router Solicitation (RtSolPr), 388
Proxy routers, 388
PrRtAdv (Proxy Router Advertisement), 388
Pseudorandom functions (PRFs), 816, 954
Pseudorandom generators (PRGs), 815–816, 954
Pseudorandom numbers. *See* PRNGs (pseudoran-
      dom numbers)
PSH bit
  sender pause and local congestion (event 1), 750
  in TCP communication, 694–695
PSKs (preshared keys)
  definition of, 954
  encryption and, 129–130
  vulnerability to dictionary attacks, 918
PSM (power save mode), 119–120, 954
PSMP (Power Save Multi-Poll), 120, 954
PTB (Packet Too Big)
  definition of, 954
  destination unreachable and, 612
  ICMP attacks and, 429
  ICMPv6 messages, 364, 370–371
  TCP-related attacks, 641
PTR (pointer) records, DNS resource record types,
      536–541
Public key certificates. *See also* Certificates
  DNSKEY resource record and, 896
  overview of, 822

Public key cryptography
  asymmetric (public) key ciphers, 809–812
  Handover Key Request/Reply options, 422–423
  RSA (Rivest, Shamir, and Adleman), 812–813
Public Key Infrastructure. *See* PKI (Public Key
      Infrastructure)
Pure ACK, TCP header, 590

Q

QAM (quadrature amplitude modulation), 128, 954
QAPs (QoS access points), 122
QBSS (QoS BSS), 122, 954
QI (Query Interval), in IGMP and MLD, 468, 954
QoS access points (QAPs), 122
QoS BSS (QBSS), 122, 954
QoS (quality of service)
  802.1p standard, 90
  APSD and, 120
  definition of, 954
  HCF (hybrid coordination function) and, 122–123
  tagging, 89–92
  in VLANs, 86
QoS stations (QSTAs), 122–123, 954
QPSK (quadrature phase shift keying), 128, 954
QQI (Querier's Query Interval), in IGMP/MLD, 954
QQIC (Querier's Query Interval Code)
  definition of, 954
  in MLD, 390
  MLD and, 459
QRI (Query Response Interval), in IGMP/MLD, 468,
      954
QRV (querier robustness variable), in IGMP/MLD,
      466–467, 954
QS (Quick-Start)
  definition of, 954
  IPv6 options for, 199
QSTAs (QoS stations), 122–123, 954
Quadrature amplitude modulation (QAM), 128, 954
Quadrature phase shift keying (QPSK), 128, 954
Qualifiers, DNS TXT records, 546
Quality of service. *See* QoS (quality of service)
Querier election, multiple multicast routers and, 466
Querier robustness variable (QRV), 466–467, 954
Querier Robustness Variable (QVR), 390
Querier's Query Interval Code. *See* QQIC (Querier's
      Query Interval Code)
Querier's Query Interval (QQI), in IGMP/MLD, 954
Queries, DNS, 526
Queries/informational messages, ICMP
  Echo Request/Reply messages, 380–383
  Home Agent Discovery Request message, 386
  MIPv6 fast handover messages, 388
  MLD extension messages, 390–394

MLD query/report/done messages, 388–390
Mobile Prefix Solicitation message, 387–388
MRD (Multicast Router Discovery), 394–395
overview of, 380
router solicitation and advertisement messages
    in ICMPv4, 383–385
Query Interval (QI), in IGMP and MLD, 468, 954
Query message
    ICMP, 388–390
    IGMP, 457–459
Query/response, in DNS protocol, 518
Query Response Interval (QRI), in IGMP/MLD, 468,
    954
Query types, resource record categories, 528
Question (query) and zone section format, 526
Queueing theory, in congestion control, 583
Queues
    packets stored in, 4
    TCP server incoming connection queue, 636–640
Quick acknowledgments, Linux, 733
Quick-Start (QS)
    definition of, 954
    IPv6 options for, 199
Quiet time concept, TCP state transitions, 624
QVR (Querier Robustness Variable), 390

R

RA (Router Advertisement)
    Advertisement Interval option in ND, 412
    definition of, 954
    DHCPv6, 260–263
    Home Agent Information option in ND, 412–413
    ICMP attacks and, 429
    ICMP messages, 383–385
    ICMPv6 messages, 280–281
    link with NA (Neighbor Advertisement), 396
    MTU option in ND, 411–412
    neighbor discovery in IPv6, 396–398
    Prefix Information option, 410–411
    Route Information option in ND, 420
    Router Advertisement Flags Extension option,
        420–421
    Trust Anchor option, 417
RADIUS (Remote Authentication Dial-In User
    Service)
    for access control, 141
    definition of, 955
RAIO (Relay Agent Information Option)
    definition of, 955
    DHCP, 268
Random Early Detection (RED) gateways
    AQM (active queue management) and, 783–785
    definition of, 955

Random numbers, in ND, 416–417
Rapid Commit option, DHCP/BOOTP message
    format, 273–274
Rapid Spanning Tree Protocol (RSTP), 103, 110–111,
    956
RARP (reverse ARP), 166, 955
RASs (remote access servers)
    control decisions by, 141
    definition of, 955
Rate-based flow control, 583
Rate halving, for TCP congestion control, 741–742
Rate-Halving with Bounding Parameters (RHBP)
    definition of, 955
    for TCP congestion control, 741–742
Rate limiting, of ICMP messages in Linux server,
    369–370
RC4 algorithm
    definition of, 955
    in Wi-Fi security, 129–130
RD (Router Discovery)
    definition of, 955
    overview of, 383–385
RDATA, in DNS resource record, 527, 955
RDNSS (Recursive DNS Server)
    definition of, 955
    neighbor discovery in IPv6, 420
Real-Time Protocol (RTP), 313
Reassembly
    fragmentation and, 488
    of fragmented datagrams, 14, 205
    timeout, 492
Rebinding time (T2), for DHCP messages, 240
Receive window structure, sliding window protocol,
    701
Reconfigure extension, DHCP, 273
Record layer, in TLS
    DTLS (Datagram TLS), 891–892
    TLS (Transport Layer Security), 877
Record markers, datagrams, and, 5–6
Record protocol, TLS, 878–880
Recovery point, in TCP retransmission, 671
Recur field, GRE tunnels and, 150
Recursive DNS Server (RDNSS)
    definition of, 955
    neighbor discovery in IPv6, 420
RED (Random Early Detection) gateways
    AQM (active queue management) and, 783–785
    definition of, 955
Redirect messages, ICMP
    ICMP attacks and, 428
    overview of, 372–375
    Redirected Header option in ND, 411
Reference model, of protocol suite, 1

Referenced connections, TCP reset segments and, 625

`regedit` program in Windows, setting keepalive time with, 797

Regional Internet registries (RIRs)
  allocation of IP addresses and, 62–63
  definition of, 955

Registered ports, 18

Reject route message, ICMPv6, 372

Relative fairness, congestion control schemes and, 769

Relay Agent Information Option (RAIO)
  definition of, 955
  DHCP, 268

Relay agents, DHCP
  layer 2 devices, 270–271
  leasequery and bulk leasequery, 269–270
  overview of, 267
  RAIO (Relay Agent Information Option), 268
  Remote-ID and IPv6 Remote-ID, 268
  Server Identifier Override, 268–269

Relayed transport address, TURN, 326

Reliability, TCP, 586–587

Remote access servers (RASs)
  control decisions by, 141
  definition of, 955

Remote Authentication Dial-In User Service (RADIUS)
  for access control, 141
  definition of, 955

Remote-ID, DCHP relay agents, 268

Remote procedure call (RPC)
  definition of, 955
  SOAP and, 338

Rendezvous point (RP)
  definition of, 955
  for multicast groups, 60

Renegotiation, of cryptographic connection parameters in TLS, 884

Renewal time (T1), for DHCP messages, 240

Reno algorithm, 737–738

Renumbering, allocation of IP addresses and, 63

Repacketization, in TCP
  overview of, 586
  TCP timeout/retransmission, 686–687

Replay attacks
  Nonce option in ND countering, 416–417
  types of threats to network communication, 808

Report message, ICMP, 388–390

REQUEST message, DHCPv6, 264–265, 269

Request/response transactions, in STUN, 320

Request to send. See RTS (request to send)

Reserved addresses, IPv6 multicast, 61

Reserved field, in IPv6 Fragment header, 203–204

Reset (RST) segments, TCP
  aborting connections, 627–628
  definition of, 956
  half-open connections, 628–630
  incoming connection queue and, 637
  overview of, 625–626
  requesting connection to nonexistent port, 626
  TWA (TIME-WAIT Assassination), 630–631

Resolver
  accessing DNS with, 511
  DNSSEC example of operation, 903–911
  UDP and, 525–526
  validating security aware resolver, 895

Resource Record Set. See RRSet (Resource Record Set)

Resource Record Signature resource record. See RRSIG (Resource Record Signature) resource record

Resource records. See RRs (resource records)

Resource utilization attacks
  attacks related to IGMP or MLD, 469–470
  UDP-related attacks, 506

Response algorithm, for spurious timeouts and retransmissions, 677

Restart Window (RW), 739, 956

Retransmission
  ARQ and, 580
  of packets, 7
  in TCP. See TCP timeout/retransmission
  timeout settings in communication protocols, 584

Retransmission ambiguity problem, 655, 679

Retransmission (RTX), 894, 956

Retransmission timeout. See RTO (retransmission timeout)

Retry bit, Frame Control Word, 116

Return Routability Procedure (RRP), in MIP
  definition of, 956
  in RO, 218–219

Reverse ARP (RARP), 166, 955

Reverse DNS queries, 536

Reverse lookup, host names from IP addresses, 19

Reverse Path Forwarding (RPF), 956

RFC (Request for Comments), 23–24, 955

RGMP (Router-port Group Management Protocol), 469, 955

RH (Routing Header)
  definition of, 955
  in IPv6, 200–203

RHBP (Rate-Halving with Bounding Parameters)
  definition of, 955
  for TCP congestion control, 741–742

RIID field, IPv6 multicast addresses, 60–61

Rijmen, Vincent, 811

Rijndael algorithm. *See* AES (Advanced Encryption Standard)
RIP (Router Information Protocol), 955
RIRs (regional Internet registries)
    allocation of IP addresses and, 62–63
    definition of, 955
Rivest, Shamir, and Adleman. *See* RSA (Rivest, Shamir, and Adleman)
`rlogin` (UNIX), precursor to SSH, 692
RO (route optimization), in MIP
    definition of, 955
    in mobile IP, 217–219
ROAD (Running Out of Address Space), 955
Robust Header Compression (ROHC), 143, 955
Robust Security Network access (RSNA)
    definition of, 956
    in Wi-Fi security, 129
Robust Security Network (RSN)
    definition of, 956
    in Wi-Fi security, 129
Robustness/reliability, of IGMP and MLD, 465–467
ROHC (Robust Header Compression), 143, 955
Roles, STP, 104–105
Root bridge, building the spanning tree in STP, 107
Root certificates, 822
Root ports, STP, 104–105
Rouge RAs, ICMP attacks and, 429
Round-robin, DNS, 565–567
Round-trip time. *See* RTT (round-trip time)
Round-trip-time
    estimation, 584
    `traceroute` measuring, 377
Route aggregation, 48–50
Route Information option, in ND, 420
Route optimization (RO), in MIP
    definition of, 955
    in mobile IP, 217–219
Route Type identifiers, 201
Router Advertisement. *See* RA (Router Advertisement)
Router Alert, IPv6 options for, 198
Router Discovery (RD)
    definition of, 955
    overview of, 383–385
Routing Header (RH)
    definition of, 955
    IPv6, 200–203
Router Information Protocol (RIP), 955
Router Requirements RFC, 23
Router Solicitation. *See* RS (Router Solicitation)
Router solicitation and advertisement messages in ICMPv4, ICMP, 383–385

Routers
    congestion of, 727–728
    crashes, 226
    default router, 208
    IGMP/MLD processing by multicast routers, 457–459
    IP routers, 20
    multicast routing, 452–454
    between packet-switching networks, 1
    in small networks, 11–13
Routing Policy Specification Language (RPSL), 65, 956
Routing protocols, 209
Routing tables, 208, 439–441
RP (rendezvous point), in IP Multicast
    definition of, 955
    for multicast groups, 60
RPC (remote procedure call)
    definition of, 955
    SOAP and, 338
    Reverse Path Forwarding (RPF), 956
RPSL (Routing Policy Specification Language), 65, 956
RRP (Return Routability Procedure), in MIP
    definition of, 956
    in RO, 218–219
RRs (resource records), in DNS
    address and name server records, 529–530
    CNAME (canonical name) records, 534–536
    definition of, 956
    in DNS message format, 520–521
    dynamic DNS updates and, 555–557
    ENUM records, 551–552
    example using resource record types, 530–534
    MX (mail exchanger) records, 544–545
    NAPTR (name authority pointer) records, 549–551
    OPT (option) pseudo records, 547–548
    overview of, 527–529
    PTR (pointer) records, 536–541
    S-NAPTR and U-NAPTR, 554–555
    SIP records, 552
    SOA (start of authority) records, 541–544
    SPF (sender policy framework) and TXT records, 545–547
    SRV (service) records, 548–549
    translating DNS from IPv4 to IPv6, 569
    transparency and, 568
    URI/URN resolution, 553–554
RRs (resource records), DNSSEC
    DNSKEY resource record, 896–897
    DS (delegation signer) resource record, 897–898
    NSEC (NextSECure) resource record, 898–901

RRs (resource records), DNSSEC, *continued*
  overview of, 896
  RRSIG (Resource Record Signature) rescource
    record, 901–902
RRset (Resource Record Set)
  canonical ordering of, 902–903
  definition of, 956
  dynamic DNS updates and, 555–557
  overview of, 527
RRSIG (Resource Record Signature) resource record
  definition of, 956
  DNSSEC, 901–902
  signed zones and zone cuts, 903
RS (Router Solicitation)
  definition of, 956
  DHCPv6, 260–263
  ICMP attacks and, 429
  ICMP messages, 383–385
  ICMPv6 messages, 280
  link with NS (Neighbor Solicitation), 396
  neighbor discovery in IPv6, 396–398
RSA (Rivest, Shamir, and Adleman)
  in cipher suites, 821
  definition of, 956
  ECC as alternative to, 815
  overview of, 812–813
  TLS extensions, 883
RSA Signature option, in ND, 415–416
RSN (Robust Security Network)
  definition of, 956
  in Wi-Fi security, 129
RSNA (Robust Security Network access)
  definition of, 956
  in Wi-Fi security, 129
RST. *See* Reset (RST) segments, TCP
RSTP (Rapid Spanning Tree Protocol), 103, 110–111,
    956
RTO (retransmission timeout), in TCP
  classic method, 651–652
  clock granularity and RTO bounds, 654
  definition of, 956
  initial values, 654
  introduction to, 647
  Linux RTT estimation, 657–661
  retransmission ambiguity and Karn's algorithm,
    655
  robustness of RTTM to loss and reordering,
    662–664
  RTT estimation behaviors, 661–662
  RTTM (RTT Measurement) with Timestamps
    option, 656–657
  setting, 651
  slow start algorithm and, 732

spurious. *See* Spurious timeouts and retransmis-
    sions, in TCP
  standard method, 652–654
  TCP connections and, 611
RTP (Real-Time Protocol), 313
RTS (request to send)
  carrier sense and, 121
  definition of, 956
  Wi-Fi control frames, 115
RtSolPr (Proxy Router Solicitation), 388
RTT (round-trip time)
  classic method of RTT estimation, 651–652
  clock granularity and RTO bounds, 654
  definition of, 956
  estimation behaviors, 661–662
  HSTCP (HighSpeed TCP) and, 773
  initial values in RTO, 654
  Linux estimation of, 657–661
  Nagle algorithm and, 696–697
  retransmission timeout settings and, 584–585
  RTO based on, 648, 651
  standard method of estimating, 652–654
  "stop and wait' protocol and, 581
  STUN messages, 320
  TCP Timestamp option and, 610
RTTM (RTT Measurement)
  robustness to loss and reordering, 662–664
  with Timestamps option, 656–657, 956
RTTVAR (RTT Variance), in TCP, 685–686, 956
RTX (Retransmission), 894, 956
RW (Restart Window), in TCP, 739, 956

S
S-NAPTR (straightforward NAPTR)
  definition of, 958
  DNS resource record types, 554
SACK (selective acknowledgement)
  definition of, 957
  DSACK (duplicate SACK) extension, 677–679
  example of retransmission with, 673–676
  fast retransmit and SACK recovery, 757–759
  receiver behavior, 672
  retransmission with, 647, 671–672
  sender behavior, 673
  for TCP congestion control, 740–741
  in TCP header, 589, 607
SAD (security association database)
  definition of, 957
  in IPSec, 841–842
SAE (Simultaneous Authentication of Equals)
  definition of, 957
  Wi-Fi mesh and, 130
Salt, in cryptography, 816

SAP (Session Announcement Protocol)
    definition of, 957
    for multicast sessions, 55
SAs (Security Associations), in IPsec
    CREATE_CHILD_SA exchange, 852–853
    definition of, 956
    GSAs (group security associations), 864
    in IPSec, 841
    payloads and proposals, 847–848
    proposed algorithms, 867–869
Scalability, of DNS, 516
Scope
    ICMPv6 error (Beyond Scope of Source Address),
        371
    of IPv6 addresses, 43
    IPv6 multicast addresses, 57–58
    of multicast addresses, 53
SCSV (Signaling Cipher Suite Value), 884, 957
SCTP (Stream Control Transmission Protocol)
    definition of, 957
    NAT and, 309
    transport protocols in TCP/IP suite, 16
SCVP (Server-Based Certificate Validation Protocol)
    certificate validation and, 831
    definition of, 957
SDID (Signing Domain Identifier), 916, 957
SDLC (Synchronous Data Link Control)
    based on HDLC, 131
    definition of, 957
SDOs (standards-defining organizations), 23, 957
SDP (Session Description Protocol)
    definition of, 957
    ICE and, 332–333
    IP multicast and, 55
Secondary DNS servers, 517
Secret Key Transaction Authentication for DNS
    (TSIG), 911–914
Secs field, DHCP/BOOTP message format, 236
Secure Entry Point (SEP) bit, DNSSEC, 896, 905, 957
Secure Hash Algorithm 1. See SHA 1 (Secure Hash
    Algorithm 1)
Secure hash function, 404
Secure Neighbor Discovery. See SEND (Secure
    Neighbor Discovery)
Secure Real-Time Protocol (SRTP), 883, 958
Secure Remote Password (SRP), 883, 958
Secure Shell. See SSH (Secure Shell)
Secure Sockets Layer (SSL). See also TLS (Transport
    Layer Security), 876–877, 958
Security
    ACs (attribute certificates), 831
    basic principles, 806–807

certificates, CAs, and PKIs, 821–822
    cryptographic and cipher suites, 819–821
    cryptographic nonces and salt, 816
    cryptosystems, 809–812
    DH (Diffie-Hellman-Merkle Key Agreement),
        813–814
    ECC (Elliptic Curve Cryptography), 815
    hash functions and message digests, 817–818
    introduction to, 805–806
    message authentication codes, 818–819
    PFS (Perfect Forward Secrecy), 815
    protocols. See Security protocols
    pseudorandom numbers, generators, and func-
        tion families, 815–816
    public key certificates, CAs, and X.509, 822–828
    RSA (Rivest, Shamir, and Adleman) public key
        cryptography, 812–813
    signcryption, 814–815
    summary and references, 919–932
    threats to network communication, 807–809
    validating and revoking certificates, 828–831
    Wi-Fi, 129–130
Security association database (SAD)
    definition of, 957
    in IPSec, 841–842
Security Associations. See SAs (Security
    Associations)
Security Gateway (SG), in IPsec, 840, 957
Security Parameter Index (SPI), in IPsec
    definition of, 958
    IKE protocol, 844
Security policy database (SPD), in IPsec
    definition of, 958
    in IPSec, 841–842
Security protocols
    attacks on, 918–919
    DKIM (Domain Keys Identified Mail), 915–918
    DNS. See DNSSEC (DNS Security)
    EAP methods, 837–838
    ERP (EAP Re-authentication Protocol), 839
    Internet Key Exchange. See IKE (Internet Key
        Exchange)
    IPSec (IP Security), 840–842
    IPSec NAT traversal, 865–867
    L2TP/IPSec, 865
    layering and, 832–833
    NAC (Network Access Control), 833–837
    PANA (Protocol for Carrying Authentication for
        Network Access), 839–840
    transport layer. See TLS (Transport Layer
        Security)
Segments Left field, in Routing header, 201–202

Segments, TCP, 586

Selective acknowledgement. *See* SACK (selective acknowledgement)

Selective retransmission, 673

Self-clocking
  ACKs and, 731
  Nagle algorithm and, 696

Self-describing padding, 137

Send maximum segment size. *See* SMSS (send maximum segment size)

SEND (Secure Neighbor Discovery)
  Certificate option, 417
  certification path solicitation/advertisement, 406–407
  CGAs (cryptographically generated addresses), 403–406
  definition of, 957
  Handover Key Request/Reply options, 422–423
  ICMP attacks and, 429
  neighbor discovery options in IPv6, 414–415
  Nonce option in ND, 416–417
  overview of, 403
  RSA Signature option, 415–416
  securing IPv6 Neighbor Discovery, 292
  Timestamp option, 416
  Trust Anchor option, 417
  as variant on ND, 396

Send window structure, sliding window protocol, 701

Sender pause and local congestion (event 1), TCP congestion control, 750–754

Sender policy framework (SPF) records, DNS resource record types, 545–547

SEP (Secure Entry Point) bit, DNSSEC, 896, 905, 957

Sequence Control field, data frame fragmentation, 117

Sequence numbers
  for avoiding duplicate packets, 580
  data frame fragmentation and, 117
  GRE, 150
  PPP, 138
  TCP, 587–588
  TCP-related attacks, 641
  TCP segments, 701
  URG, 590

Sequencing header, in MP, 138

Sequential Port-Symmetric NAT (SP), 486

Server alive messages, TCP keepalive attacks, 802

Server-Based Certificate Validation Protocol (SCVP), 831

Server Identifier Override, DCHP relay agents, 268–269

Server Load Reduction (SLR), 486

ServerHello message, in TLS, 887–889

Servers
  accessing servers behind NAT, 314
  iterative and concurrent, 21
  server host crashes and does not reboot (keepalive scenarios), 796
  server host crashes and reboots (keepalive scenarios), 797–799
  server host unreachable (keepalive scenarios), 799–800

Service model, TCP, 585–586

Service provider NAT. *See* SPNAT (service provider NAT)

Service set identifiers (SSID)
  definition of, 958
  Wi-Fi, 112

Service sets, Wi-Fi, 112

Service (SRV) records, DNS resource record types, 548–549

Session Announcement Protocol (SAP)
  definition of, 957
  for multicast sessions, 55

Session Description Protocol. *See* SDP (Session Description Protocol)

Session Initiation Protocol (SIP)
  definition of, 957
  ENUM records and, 551–552

Session keys, in public key cryptography, 812

Session layer, of OSI model, 10

Session timers, NAT, 307–308

Session Traversal Utilities for NAT. *See* STUN (Session Traversal Utilities for NAT)

SFD (start frame delimiter), in link layer protocols
  clock recovery in Ethernet frames, 84
  definition of, 957

SG (Security Gateway), in IPsec, 840, 957

SHA 1 (Secure Hash Algorithm 1)
  for authentication in DHCP, 268
  definition of, 957
  overview of, 817–818
  TLS extensions, 883

Shannon, Claude, 579

Sharing connection state, 767–768

Shim6 protocol, 70

Short Interframe Space (SIFS), in Wi-Fi
  definition of, 957
  in MAC, 122

Short sequence number, LCP options, 138

Short-term credential mechanism, STUN, 325

Siaddr (Next Server IP Address) field, DHCP/BOOTP message format, 238, 246

SIFS (Short Interframe Space), in Wi-Fi
    definition of, 957
    in MAC, 122
Signaling Cipher Suite Value (SCSV), 884, 957
Signature verification, CGAs for, 405–406
Signed zones, DNSSEC, 903
Signing Domain Identifier (SDID), 916, 957
SIIT (Stateless IP/ICMP Translation)
    definition of, 957
    IPv4/IPv6 translation, 342–344
Silly windows syndrome. *See* SWS (silly windows
        syndrome)
Simple Mail Transfer Protocol. *See* SMTP (Simple
        Mail Transfer Protocol)
Simple Network Management Protocol (SNMP)
    definition of, 958
    well-known port for, 18
Simple Object Access Protocol (SOAP)
    definition of, 958
    GENA using, 338
Simple Service Discovery Protocol. *See* SSDP (Simple
        Service Discovery Protocol)
Simple Tunneling of UDP through NATs, 319
Simultaneous Authentication of Equals (SAE)
    definition of, 957
    Wi-Fi mesh and, 130
Simultaneous close, in TCP connections
    overview of, 600–601
    state transition, 625
Simultaneous open, in TCP connections
    defined, 597
    overview of, 599–600
    state transition, 625
SIP Outbound mechanism, in ICE, 333
SIP records, DNS resource record types, 552
SIP (Session Initiation Protocol)
    definition of, 957
    ENUM records and, 551–552
SLAAC (stateless address autoconfiguration)
    configuring IPv4 link-local addresses, 276
    configuring IPv6 link-local addresses, 276–277
    deciding whether to use, 244
    definition of, 957
    example of, 278–283
    IPv6 DAD (Duplicate Address Detection), 277–278
    IPv6 global addresses, 278
    overview of, 276
    stateless DHCP and, 283–284
    utility/benefit of, 284–285
Sliding window protocol
    movement of windows, 702–704
    in packet communication, 582
    send and receive structures, 701

TCP as, 589
SLLAO (Source Link-Layer Address Option),
        409–410, 958
Slot time, in MAC, 122
Slow start algorithm, in TCP
    classic algorithms for TCP congestion, 732–734
    comparing with congestion avoidance, 736–737
    limited, 772
    viewing slow start behavior with Wireshark,
        749–750
slow start threshold. *See* ssthresh (slow start
        threshold)
SLR (Server Load Reduction), 486
Smack attacks, ICMP attacks and, 429
Smoothed RTT. *See* SRTT (smoothed RTT)
SMSS (send maximum segment size)
    definition of, 958
    SWS (silly windows syndrome) and, 709
    TCP connections and, 613
SMTP (Simple Mail Transfer Protocol)
    definition of, 958
    MX (mail exchanger) records and, 544
    SRV record providing SMTP service, 549
    well-known port for, 18
Smurf attacks, ICMP, 428
SNA (System Network Architecture)
    definition of, 958
    SDLC in, 131
Sname (Server Name) field, DHCP/BOOTP message
        format, 238–239
SNAP (Subnetwork Access Protocol), 958
Sniffing, 808
SNMP (Simple Network Management Protocol)
    definition of, 958
    well-known port for, 18
Snooping
    DHCP, 276
    IGMP/MLD, 468–469
SNS (Symmetric NAT Support), 486
SOA (start of authority) records
    definition of, 958
    DNS resource record types, 541–544
SOAP (Simple Object Access Protocol)
    definition of, 958
    GENA using, 338
sock program
    creating UDP datagram, 493, 496
    generating UDP datagram with, 478–481
    restricting local IP addresses, 634
Sockets
    popular APIs, 22
    in TCP connections, 595–596
    TCP ports, 588

SOCKS proxy firewalls, 302–303
Soft state
    ARP cache timeout and, 174
    multicast information and, 441
SOLICIT message, DHCPv6, 260, 269
Solicitation messages, in MRD, 394–395
Solicitation of servers, by clients, 435
Sort lists, DNS, 565–567
Source address selection algorithm, in IP host models, 223–224
Source IP addresses
    address selection by hosts, 222–223
    host processing of IP datagrams, 220–221
    ICMPv6 errors, 371–372
    in IP datagrams, 186
Source Link-Layer Address Option (SLLAO), 409–410, 958
Source Quench messages, TCP congestion control attacks, 785
Source/Target Address List options, in ND, 413–414
SP (Sequential Port-Symmetric NAT), 486
Spam
    DNS resource record for fighting, 545–547
    as malware, 806
Spanning tree, building, 107
Spanning Tree Protocol. *See* STP (Spanning Tree Protocol)
Spatial multiplexing, power save mode, 120
Spatial streams, higher throughput (802.11n) support, 126
SPD (security policy database)
    definition of, 958
    in IPSec, 841–842
Spear phishing attacks, 806
Special-use IP addresses
    for IPv4, 50–51
    for IPv6, 51–52
    local net (limited) broadcast, 43
SPF (sender policy framework) records, DNS resource record types, 545–547
SPI (Security Parameter Index)
    definition of, 958
    IKE protocol, 844
Split DNS, 565–567
SPNAT (service provider NAT)
    definition of, 958
    DS-Lite and, 339
    overview of, 315–316
Spoofing attacks
    ICMP, 429
    Internet architecture, 25
    IP addresses, 70, 226
    TCP, 640–642
    TCP keepalive attacks, 802

Spurious association attacks, 808
Spurious timeouts and retransmissions, in TCP congestion control and, 744–745
    DSACK (duplicate SACK) extension, 677–679
    Eifel Detection Algorithm, 679–680
    Eifel Response Algorithm, 680–682
    F-RTO (Forward-RTO Recovery), 680
    overview of, 677
SRC (Source) address, in Ethernet frame format, 85
SRP (Secure Remote Password), 883, 958
SRTP (Secure Real-Time Protocol), 883, 958
SRTT (smoothed RTT)
    classic method of RTT estimation, 651–652
    definition of, 958
    destination metrics and, 685–686
SRV (service) records, DNS resource record types, 548–549
SSDP (Simple Service Discovery Protocol)
    definition of, 958
    direct interaction with NAT and firewalls, 338
    viewing in-use multicast groups in Windows OSs, 448
SSH (Secure Shell)
    for application-managed keepalives, 794
    definition of, 958
    TCP data flow and, 692
    tracing RTT of TCP connection, 697–698
    well-known port for, 18
    well-known ports for, 632
SSID (service set identifiers)
    definition of, 958
    Wi-Fi, 112
SSL (Secure Sockets Layer). *See also* TLS (Transport Layer Security), 876–877, 958
SSM (source-specific multicast)
    attacks related to IGMP or MLD, 470
    definition of, 959
    IGMP and MLD supporting, 452
    MLD supporting, 390
    as multicast service model, 54
ssthresh (slow start threshold), in TCP congestion control
    comparing slow start with congestion avoidance, 736
    Eifel Response Algorithm and, 744–745
    overview of, 733
    standard TCP algorithm and, 738
Standard RTO method, in TCP, 652–654
Standard TCP congestion control algorithm, 728–739
Standards
    IETF (Internet Engineering Task Force) in, 22–23
    link layer, 80–82
    other organizations in, 23–24
    RFC (Request for Comments) and, 23–24

Standards-defining organizations (SDOs), 23, 957
Standards-track category, RFCs and, 23
Start frame delimiter (SFD)
    clock recovery in Ethernet frames, 84
    definition of, 957
Start of authority (SOA) records, in DNS
    definition of, 958
    DNS resource record types, 541–544
STAs (stations), in Wi-Fi
    definition of, 959
    Wi-Fi, 112
State-change records, IGMP/MLD group member-
        ship reports, 457
State machine, DHCP, 251–252
State, storing in connection switches, 5
State transitions, TCP
    FIN_WAIT_2 state, 625
    overview of, 616
    quiet time concept, 624
    simultaneous open and close transitions, 625
    state transition diagrams, 617–618
    TIME_WAIT state (2MSL), 618–624
Stateful translation, IPv4/IPv6, 344–345
Stateless address autoconfiguration. See SLAAC
        (stateless address autoconfiguration)
Stateless IP/ICMP Translation (SIIT)
    definition of, 957
    IPv4/IPv6 translation, 342–344
Stateless mode, DHCPv6, 283–284
Static multiplexing, 4
Station-to-Station (STS) protocol, relation to DH
        (Diffie-Hellman), 814
Statistical multiplexing, 4
STODER, repacketization and, 686
"Stop and wait" protocol
    communication protocols and, 581
    Nagle algorithm and, 697
    TCP and, 696
STP (Spanning Tree Protocol), in bridges
    BPDU structure, 105–107
    building the spanning tree, 107
    definition of, 959
    example of, 107–109
    handling topology changes, 107
    overview of, 102–104
    port states and roles, 104–105
    RSTP (Rapid Spanning Tree Protocol), 110–111
Straightforward NAPTR (S-NAPTR)
    definition of, 958
    DNS resource record types, 554
Stream ciphers, symmetric key ciphers, 811
Stream Control Transmission Protocol. See SCTP
        (Stream Control Transmission Protocol)

Stretch ACKs, 754–757
Strong host model, 220
STS (Station-to-Station) protocol, relation to DH
        (Diffie-Hellman), 814
STUN (Session Traversal Utilities for NAT)
    attributes defined by TURN, 328
    binding method, 321
    definition of, 959
    ICE making use of, 332–334
    mechanisms, 325–326
    message formats, 320
    Teredo servers compared with, 482
Subdomains, in DNS hierarchy, 514
Subnet addressing, 36–39
Subnet broadcast addresses. See Broadcast
        addresses
Subnet fields, in IP addresses, 37
Subnet masks
    overview of, 39–41
    VLSM (variable-length subnet masks), 41–42
Subnetwork Access Protocol (SNAP), 105, 958
Subnetworks, 37
Switches and bridges
    attacks on, 155
    layer 2 relay agents and, 270
    link layer and, 98–102
    in small networks, 11–13
    VLAN, 90
SWS (silly windows syndrome)
    definition of, 959
    example of avoiding, 709–715
    overview of, 708
    rules for avoiding, 708–709
Symmetric key encryption
    cryptographic algorithms, 809–811
    KDF (key derivation function) in, 815
Symmetric NAT Support (SNS), 486
SYN bit field, TCP header, 589–590
SYN cookies, in TCP
    attacks related to window management and, 723
    TCP-related attacks, 640–641
SYN floods, TCP-related attacks, 640
SYN segments, in TCP
    combined with ACKs (SACK), 607
    definition of, 959
    establishing TCP connections and, 602–603
    MSL (maximum seqment life), 610
    NAT and TCP, 307–308
    requesting connection to nonexistent TCP port,
        626
    in TCP connections, 596–597
    TCP header and, 589
    WSCALE (Window Scale) option and, 608

Synchronous Data Link Control (SDLC)
based on HDLC, 131
definition of, 957
SYN_RCVD state, in TCP
incoming connection queue and, 636
simultaneous open and close transitions, 625
TCP state transitions, 618
SYN_SENT state, in TCP
simultaneous open and close transitions, 625
TCP state transitions, 618
System configuration options
attacks related to system configuration, 292
autoconfiguration. *See* SLAAC (stateless address autoconfiguration)
DHCP (Dynamic Host Configuration Protocol). *See* DHCP (Dynamic Host Configuration Protocol)
introduction to, 233–234
summary and references, 292–298
System Network Architecture (SNA) from IBM
definition of, 958
SDLC in, 131

T

T1 (Renewal time), for DHCP messages, 240
Tahoe algorithm, TCP congestion control, 737–738
Tarpits, attacks related to window management, 723
Tayor, Bob, 2
tc program, for packet scheduling and traffic control subsystem in Linux, 752
TC (Topology Change), in BPDU structure, 106
TCA (Topology Change Acknowledgment), 106
TCN (topology change notification), 107
TCP-AO (Authentication Option)
definition of, 959
TCP header, 612
TCP congestion control
active queue management and ECN, 782–785
attacks related to, 785–786
BIC (Binary Increase Congestion Control), 772–774
buffer bloat, 781–782
classic algorithms for, 730–732
comparing slow start with congestion avoidance, 736–737
congestion avoidance algorithm, 734–736
connection completion and, 766–767
CTCP (Compound TCP) algorithm, 779–781
CUBIC, 775–776
CWV (Congestion Window Validation), 742–744
delay-based, 777
example of handling, 745–749

FACK (forward acknowledgment) and rate halving for, 741–742
fast retransmit and local congestion, 759–762
fast retransmit and SACK recovery, 757–759
FAST TCP algorithm, 778–779
handling spurious RTOs, 744–745
in high-speed environments, 770
HSTCP (HighSpeed TCP), 770–772
introduction to, 727–728
limited transmit approach to, 742
NewReno algorithm for, 739–740
SACK (selective acknowledgement) for, 740–741
sender pause and local congestion (event 1), 750–754
sharing connection state, 767–768
slow start algorithm, 732–734
slow start behavior, 749–750
slowing down TCP senders, 729–730
standard TCP algorithm, 728–739
stretch ACKs and recovery from local congestion, 754–757
summary and references, 786–792
Tahoe, Reno, and Fast Recovery algorithms, 737–738
TCPW (TCP Westwood) algorithm, 779
TFRC (TCP Friendly Rate Control), 768–770
timeouts, retransmissions, and undoing cwnd changes, 762–766
Vegas TCP algorithm, 777–778
TCP data flow
attacks related to window management, 723
delayed ACK interaction with Nagle algorithm, 699
delayed ACKs, 695–696
disabling Nagle algorithm, 699–700
example of dynamic window size adjustment and flow control, 705–708
example using urgent mechanism, 720–722
flow control, 700–701
interactive communication, 692–695
introduction to, 691
large buffers and auto-tuning, 715–719
Nagle algorithm, 696–698
sliding window protocol, 701–704
summary and references, 723–725
SWS (silly windows syndrome), 708–715
urgent mechanism, 719–720
zero windows and TCP persistent timer, 704–705
TCP Friendly Rate Control (TFRC), 768–770, 959
TCP/IP suite
ARPANET Reference Model, 13–16
based on ARPANET, 1

implementations and distributions, 24–25
layering, 14
multiplexing, demultiplexing, and encapsulation, 16–17
names, addresses, and DNS, 19
OSI model compared with, 8–9
overview of, 13
port numbers, 17–19
TCP keepalive
  attacks related to, 802
  description of, 795–797
  introduction to, 793–794
  server host crashes and does not reboot, 797–799
  server host crashes and reboots, 799–800
  server host unreachable, 800–802
  summary and references, 802–803
TCP segments, 15
TCP servers
  incoming connection queue, 636–640
  overview of, 631–632
  port numbers and, 632–634
  restrictions on foreign endpoints, 635–636
  restrictions on local IP addresses, 634–635
TCP timeout/retransmission
  attacks related to, 687
  classic RTO method, 651–652
  clock granularity and RTO bounds, 654
  congestion control and, 762–766
  connection establishment and, 604–605
  destination metrics, 685–686
  DSACK (duplicate SACK) extension, 677–679
  Eifel Detection Algorithm, 679–680
  Eifel Response Algorithm, 680–682
  example of, 648–651
  example of fast retransmit, 668–671
  example of retransmission with SACK, 673–676
  example of timer-based retransmission, 665–667
  F-RTO (Forward-RTO Recovery), 680
  fast retransmit, 667–668
  introduction to, 647–648
  Linux RTT estimation, 657–661
  packet duplication, 684–685
  packet reordering, 682–684
  repacketization, 686–687
  retransmission ambiguity and Karn's algorithm, 655
  retransmission with SACK, 671–672
  robustness of RTTM, 662–664
  RTO (retransmission timeout) setting, 651
  RTT estimation behaviors, 661–662
  RTTM (RTT Measurement) with Timestamps option, 656–657

SACK receiver behavior, 672
SACK sender behavior, 673
spurious timeouts and retransmissions, 677
standard RTO method, 652–654
summary and references, 688–690
timer-based retransmission, 664–665
TCP (Transmission Control Protocol)
  ARQ as basis of, 579
  connection management. *See* Connections, TCP
  definition of, 959
  encapsulation in IP datagrams, 587
  flow control and, 7–8
  header fields, 588–590
  introduction to, 584–585
  NAT and, 306–308
  reliability, 586–587
  service model, 585–586
  STUN and, 320
  summary and references, 591–593
  transport protocols in TCP/IP suite, 15
  well-known ports for, 525–526
TCP Westwood+ (TCPW+) algorithm, 777
TCP Westwood (TCPW) algorithm, 779
`tcpdump` command
  connecting to Web server on host, 171
  ICMP destination unreachable messages, 480
  not converting IP addresses to machine names, 479
  viewing UDP fragmentation, 490–491
TCP_NODELAY option, for disabling Nagle algorithm, 700
`tcptrace`, connection statistics with, 745–747
TCPW+ (TCP Westwood+) algorithm, 777
TCPW (TCP Westwood) algorithm, 779
TDM (time-division multiplexing), 4, 959
Teardrop attacks
  ICMP, 428
  UDP, 506
`telnet` command
  connecting to Web server on host, 171
  establishing TCP connections, 602
Telnet program
  SSH replacing, 692
  well-known port for, 18
Temporal Key Integrity Protocol (TKIP), in Wi-Fi, 129–130
Temporary addresses, in DHCPv6, 255–256
Tentative state, IPv6 addresses, 253
Teredo, tunneling IPv6 over IPv4
  IPv4/IPv6 translation, 339
  relays and servers, 482
  tunneling, 154, 482–487

Termination messages
    in LCP operation, 134
    in MRD, 394–395
Termination, of TCP connections, 595–598
TFC (Traffic Flow Confidentiality), 858
TFN (Tribe Flood Network), 429
TFRC (TCP Friendly Rate Control), 768–770, 959
TFTP (Trivial File Transfer Protocol)
    definition of, 959
    ICMP port unreachable messages and, 366–370
Threats, to network communication, 807–809
Three-way handshake, 597, 640
Throughput (802.11n), Wi-Fi, 126–128
Time-division multiplexing (TDM), 4, 959
Time exceeded message, ICMP, 375–378
Time-Remaining messages, in LCP operation, 134
Time sync function. See TSF (time sync function)
Time-to-live. See TTL (Time-to-live)
TIME-WAIT Assassination (TWA), 630–631, 960
Timed wait (MSL), 618
Timeouts, TCP. See TCP timeout/retransmission
Timer-based retransmission
    example of, 665–667
    introduction to, 647
    overview of, 664–665
Timestamp Echo Reply. See TSER (Timestamp Echo
        Reply)
Timestamp Request/Replay message, ICMP attacks
        and, 429
Timestamp Value. See TSV (Timestamp Value)
Timestamps option. See also TSOPT (timestamps
        option)
    neighbor discovery in IPv6, 416
    TCP header, 608–610
TIME_WAIT state (2MSL), in TCP
    overview of, 618–624
    TCP state transitions, 624
    TWA (TIME-WAIT Assassination), 630–631
Tinygrams, 696
TKIP (Temporal Key Integrity Protocol), in Wi-Fi,
        129–130
TLDs (top-level domains)
    definition of, 959
    in DNS name space, 512
    name servers for, 517
TLS (Transport Layer Security)
    with datagrams (DTLS), 884–891
    definition of, 959
    DTLS DoS protection, 894
    DTLS handshake protocol, 892–894
    DTLS record layer, 891–892
    example of use of, 884–891

extensions, 883–884
handshaking protocols, 880–883
HTTP/HTTPS and, 18
overview of, 876–877
Record protocol, 878–880
renegotiation of cryptographic connection
        parameters, 884
TCP with, 320
TLS 1.2, 877–878
TLV (type-length-value) sets
    definition of, 959
    IPv6 options held as, 196–197
Top-level domains. See TLDs (top-level domains)
Topology Change Acknowledgment (TCA), 106
Topology change notification (TCN), 107
Topology Change (TC), in BPDU structure, 106
Topology changes, STP handling, 107
ToS (Type of Service) byte
    definition of, 959
    ICMP Parameter Problem and, 379
    in IPv4, 183, 188–189
    redefined as DSCP/ECN fields, 379
Total Length field
    ICMP Parameter Problem and, 379
    in IP header, 183–184
TPDU (transport PDU), 10
traceroute, for determining routing path,
        376–378
Traffic analysis, types of threats to network com-
        munication, 808
Traffic Class byte, in IPv6, 183, 188–189
Traffic Flow Confidentiality (TFC), 858
Traffic selectors (TS)
    definition of, 960
    IKE, 851, 873
Traffic specification (TSPEC), in Wi-Fi QoS
    definition of, 960
    in HCCA, 123
traffic visibility, ESP (Encapsulating Security Pay-
        load), 863–864
Transacation authentication, in DNS, 911–915
Transaction Signatures (TSIG), in DNS
    definition of, 960
    transaction authentication in DNSSEC, 911–914
Transient session keys (TSKs), 838
Translating
    DNS from IPv4 to IPv6, 568–569
    ICMPv4 to ICMPv6, 424–426
    ICMPv6 to ICMPv4, 426–428
    IPv4 to IPv6, 482
    UDP/IPv4 and UDP/IPv6 datagrams, 505–506
Translation behavior, NAT, 312

Translation functions, NAT, 305
Translators, TCP connections, 605
Transmission Control Protocol. *See* TCP (Transmission Control Protocol)
Transmit opportunities (TXOPs), in Wi-Fi QoS
   in DCF, 123
   definition of, 960
Transparency, DNS, 567–568
Transport layer
   layering violation, 476
   of OSI model, 9–10
   security. *See* TLS (Transport Layer Security)
   transport protocols in TCP/IP suite, 15–16
   UDP checksum, 475–476
Transport Layer Security. *See* TLS (Transport Layer Security)
Transport PDU (TPDU), 10
Transport protocols, 309
Traversal, NAT, 316
Traversal Using Relays around NAT. *See* TURN (Traversal Using Relays around NAT)
Tribe Flood Network (TFN), 429
Triple-DES (3DES)
   definition of, 959
   standardized for Internet use, 819
   as symmetric encryption algorithm, 811
Trivial File Transfer Protocol (TFTP)
   definition of, 959
   ICMP port unreachable messages and, 366–370
Trunking, VLAN switches and, 90
Trust anchors
   CAs (certification authorities) and, 822
   in ND, 417
   SEND (Secure Neighbor Discovery), 403
TS (traffic selectors), in IPsec
   definition of, 960
   IKE, 851, 873
TSER (Timestamp Echo Reply), in TCP
   definition of, 960
   Eifel Detection Algorithm and, 679
   TCP Timestamp option and, 609
   timer-based retransmission and, 665–666
TSF (time sync function), in Wi-Fi
   in 802.11 specification, 119–120
   definition of, 960
   Wi-Fi frames and, 114
TSIG (Transaction Signatures), in DNS
   definition of, 960
   transaction authentication in DNS, 911–914
TSKs (transient session keys), 838
TSOPT (timestamps option), in TCP
   definition of, 960

Eifel Detection Algorithm using, 679
Linux RTT estimation and, 657
robustness of RTTM to loss and reordering, 662–664
RTTM (RTT Measurement) with, 656–657
TCP header, 608–610
TSPEC (traffic specification), in Wi-Fi QoS
   definition of, 960
   in HCCA, 123
TSV (Timestamp Value), in TCP
   definition of, 960
   Eifel Detection Algorithm and, 679
   RTTM with Timestamps option, 656
   TCP Timestamp option and, 608–609
TTL (Time-to-live)
   definition of, 960
   ICMP Time Exceeded message, 375, 378
   IP header fields, 184
   MRD (Multicast Router Discovery) and, 394
   name servers, 517
   QS (Quick-Start) TTL, 199
   SYN segments, 611
Tunnel endpoint, IPv6 traffic and, 46
Tunneled packets, NAT and, 310
Tunneling
   IPv4/IPv6 translation, 339
   IPv6 options for, 198
   link layer and, 149–153
   link layer attacks and, 156
Tunneling proxy servers, 302
TURN (Traversal Using Relays around NAT)
   definition of, 960
   ICE making use of, 332–334
   overview of, 326–332
   Teredo relays compared with, 482
TWA (TIME-WAIT Assassination), 630–631, 960
TXOPs (transmit opportunities), in Wi-Fi QoS
   in DCF, 123
   definition of, 960
TXT records
   definition of, 960
   DNS resource record types, 545–547
Type field, in Ethernet frame format, 85–86
Type-length-value (TLV) sets
   definition of, 959
   IPv6 options held as, 196–197
Type of Service byte. *See* ToS (Type of Service) byte

U

U-NAPTR (URI-enabled NAPTR)
   definition of, 960
   DNS resource record types, 555

U-NII (Unlicensed National Information
      Infrastructure)
   5GHz band for, 124
   definition of, 960
UBM (unicast-prefix-based multicast)
   allocation of IPv4 addresses, 56
   definition of, 960
UDLs (unidirectional links)
   definition of, 960
   link layer and, 153–154
UDP-Lite, 487–488
UDP servers
   designing, 498–499
   flow control and congestion control in server
      design, 505
   foreign IP address restrictions in server design,
      502–503
   IP addresses and port numbers in server design,
      499–500
   local IP address restrictions in server design,
      500–501
   multiple addresses in server design, 501–502
   multiple servers per port, 503–504
   spanning IP address families in server design,
      504
UDP (User Datagram Protocol)
   attacks related to, 507–508
   broadcast overhead and, 451
   checksum, 475–478
   connection refused error, 626
   as connectionless protocols, 595
   definition of, 960
   examples, 478–481
   flow control and congestion control in server
      design, 505
   foreign IP address restrictions in server design,
      502–503
   header, 474–475
   ICE and, 332
   interaction between IP fragmentation and ARP/
      ND, 495–497
   in the Internet, 506–507
   introduction to, 473–474
   IP addresses and port numbers in server design,
      499–500
   IP fragmentation and, 488–492
   IPv6 and, 481–482
   local IP address restrictions in server design,
      500–501
   maximum UDP datagram size, 497–498
   multiple addresses in server design, 501–502
   multiple servers per port, 503–504
   NAT and, 308–309

   PMTUD (Path MTU Discovery) with, 493–496
   reassembly timeout, 492
   sending broadcast datagrams, 439
   server design, 498–499
   spanning IP address families in server design, 504
   STUN and, 320
   summary and references, 508–510
   Teredo tunneling and, 482–487
   translating UDP/IPv4 and UDP/IPv6 datagrams,
      505–506
   transport protocols in TCP/IP suite, 15
   UDP-Lite, 487–488
   well-known ports for, 525–526
UEQM (unequal modulation), in 802.11n
   definition of, 960
   higher throughput (802.11n) support and, 127
ULAs (Unique Local IPv6 Unicast Addresses)
   definition of, 960
   NAT and, 310
   overview of, 225
Unauthorized access attacks, 26
Unequal modulation (UEQM), in 802.11n
   definition of, 960
   higher throughput (802.11n) support and, 127
Unicast addresses
   allocation of, 62–65
   anycast addresses, 62
   assigning, 65–66
   C class spaces for, 35
   definition of, 34
   Echo Request message sent from link-local uni-
      cast address, 445–446
   IIDs as basis for unicast IPv6 addresses, 43–46
   multiple providers/multiple networks/multiple
      addresses, 68–70
   overview of, 15
   single provider/multiple networks/multiple
      addresses, 67–68
   single provider/no network/single address,
      66–67
   single provider/single network/single address,
      67
Unicast-prefix-based IPv6 multicast addresses, 58
Unicast-prefix-based multicast (UBM)
   allocation of IPv4 addresses, 56
   definition of, 960
Unicode, internationalization of Internet, 512
Unidirectional links (UDLs)
   definition of, 960
   link layer and, 153–154
Uniform Resource Locator (URL), 961
Unilateral self-address fixing. See UNSAF (unilateral
      self-address fixing)

Unique Local IPv6 Unicast Addresses. *See* ULAs
        (Unique Local IPv6 Unicast Addresses)
Universal Plug and Play (UPnP) framework
        definition of, 961
        direct interaction with NAT and firewalls,
            337–339
Universal Resource Identifier. *See* URI (Universal
        Resource Identifier)
UNIX
        Berkeley version. *See* BSD (Berkeley Software
            Distribution)
        rlogin, 692
Unlicensed National Information Infrastructure
        (U-NII)
        5GHz band for, 124
        definition of, 960
Unreachable hosts, keepalives detecting, 795–796
UNSAF (unilateral self-address fixing)
        definition of, 961
        overview of, 317–319
        STUN (Session Traversal Utilities for NAT), 319–326
Updates
        DNS Update, 567
        dynamic DNS updates, 555–558
UPnP (Universal Plug and Play) framework
        definition of, 961
        direct interaction with NAT and firewalls, 337–339
Upper layer, TLS (Transport Layer Security), 877
UPs (user priorities), in Wi-Fi QoS, 123, 961
URG (Urgent Mechanism), in TCP
        definition of, 961
        example working with urgent data, 720–722
        overview of, 719–720
        TCP header, 590
URI-enabled NAPTR (U-NAPTR)
        definition of, 960
        DNS resource record types, 555
URI (Universal Resource Identifier)
        definition of, 961
        ENUM records and, 551–552
        NAPTR records and, 549
        URI/URN resolution, 553–554
URL (Uniform Resource Locator), 961
URN resolution, 553–554
Usage-specific keys (USRK), in EAP
        definition of, 961
        key derivation in EAP, 838
User Datagram Protocol. *See* UDP (User Datagram
        Protocol)
User priorities (UPs), in Wi-Fi QoS, 123, 961
User Timeout (UTO) option, in TCP
        definition of, 961
        TCP header, 611–612

USRK (usage-specific keys)
        definition of, 961
        key derivation in EAP, 838
UTC (Coordinated Universal Time), 961
UTO (User Timeout) option, in TCP
        definition of, 961
        TCP header, 611–612

V

Valid lifetime
        IA (Identity Association) and, 255
        IPv6 addresses, 252
Validating certificates, 828–831
Validating security aware resolver, in DNSSEC,
        895
Variable-length subnet masks (VLSM), 41–42, 961
Variable-scope addresses, IPv6 multicast, 58
Variables, IGMP/MLD, 467–468
vconfig command, for manipulating 802.1p/q
        information in Linux, 90–91
VCs (virtual circuits)
        definition of, 961
        multiplexing and, 4
Vegas TCP algorithm, 777–778
Vendor Extension field, DHCP/BOOTP message
        format, 238, 246
VENONA system, 918
Virtual carrier sense, 121
Virtual circuits (VCs)
        definition of, 961
        multiplexing and, 4
Virtual LANs. *See* VLANs (virtual LANs)
Virtual private networks. *See* VPNs (virtual private
        networks)
Viruses, 806
VJ (Van Jacobson) compression, 141–142
VLAN identifier, 90
VLAN tag, 90
VLANs (virtual LANs)
        definition of, 961
        multicast routing, 452
        overview of, 89–92
        QoS tagging and, 145–148
VLSM (variable-length subnet masks), 41–42, 961
VoIP (Voice over IP), 961
VPNs (virtual private networks)
        connecting to Internet via, 20
        definition of, 961
        tunneling, 149

W

W3C (World Wide Web Consortium), 24, 961
Wake-on LAN (WoL), 96–97, 962

WANs (wide area networks)
  definition of, 961
  Internet as, 2
  PPPoE and, 286–287
War driving, link layer attacks, 155
Weak host model, 220
Web caches, web proxies operating as, 302
Web of trust, public key certificates and, 822
Web proxies, 302
Web Proxy Auto-Discovery Protocol (WPAD), 302, 962
Web Proxy Autodiscovery Protocol (WRED), 962
Weighted RED (WRED), 783, 962
Well-known ports
  overview of, 18
  for SSH (Secure Shell), 632
  for UDP or TCP, 525–526
Well-Known Prefix (WKP), in algorithmic address translation, 341, 962
WEP (wired equivalent privacy) in Wi-Fi
  attacks related to, 918
  definition of, 961
  Wi-Fi attacks and, 155
  for Wi-Fi security, 129–130
WESP (Wrapped ESP), in IPsec, 863–864, 961
White hats, 26
WHOIS service, 63–64
Wi-Fi Multimedia (WMM), in Wi-Fi QoS, 122, 962
Wi-Fi Protected Access. See WPA (Wi-Fi Protected Access)
Wi-Fi (wireless fidelity- IEEE 802.11)
  attacks, 155
  attacks related to, 918
  channels and frequencies (802.11b/g), 124–125
  control frames, 115–116
  CSMA/CA and, 84
  data frames, fragmentation, and aggregation, 116–119
  definition of, 962
  frames, 113–115
  higher throughput (802.11n), 126–128
  mesh (802.11s), 130
  overview of, 111–112
  physical layer, 123–124
  physical layer channels and frequencies, 124–126
  power save mode and time sync function, 119–120
  RSTP (Rapid Spanning Tree Protocol), 120–123
  security, 129–130
  throughput (802.11n), 116, 126–128
Wide area networks. See WANs (wide area networks)

Wildcard (*)
  domain names and, 526
  local IP address restrictions in server design, 500–501
Wildcard address, IPv6 addresses, 632
WiMAX (Worldwide Interoperability for Microwave Access), 79, 82–83, 962
Window advertisement (window update)
  in window-based flow control, 583
  WSCALE (Window Scale) option in TCP, 608
Window-based flow control, 583
Window management, TCP
  example of dynamic window size adjustment and flow control, 705–708
  flow control and, 700–701
  large buffers and auto-tuning, 715–719
  sliding window protocol, 701–704
  SWS (silly windows syndrome), 708–715
  zero windows and TCP persistent timer, 704–705
Window probes, in TCP window management, 704
Window Size field
  cwnd (congestion window), 729
  flow control and, 727
  TCP segments, 701
Window update
  SWS (silly windows syndrome) and, 711
  TCP header and, 590
  window management and, 706
Windows of packets, in communication protocols, 581–582
Windows OS (Microsoft)
  autotuning TCP receive windows, 715
  ICS (Internet Connection Sharing), 337
  IPSec implementations, 867
Wired equivalent privacy. See WEP (wired equivalent privacy)
Wireless fidelity. See Wi-Fi (wireless fidelity-802.11)
Wireless LANs (WLANs). See also Wi-Fi (wireless fidelity-802.11), 962
Wireshark
  Flow graph, 749
  monitoring TCP keepalives, 797–798
  TCP Stream Graph, 707, 747–748
  TCP ZeroWindowProbe, 710
  viewing BPDUs with, 109
WKP (Well-Known Prefix), 341, 962
WLANs (wireless LANs). See also Wi-Fi (wireless fidelity-802.11), 962
WMM (Wi-Fi Multimedia), in Wi-Fi QoS, 122, 962
WoL (Wake-on LAN), 96–97, 962
WOPT. See WSOPT (Window Scale Option)
World Wide Web Consortium (W3C), 24, 961

World Wide Web (WWW)
    definition of, 962
    Internet compared to, 2–3
Worldwide Interoperability for Microwave Access
        (WiMAX), 79, 82–83, 962
Worms
    attacks related to window management, 723
    buffer overflow and, 805
    types of malware, 806
WPA (Wi-Fi Protected Access)
    attacks related to, 918
    definition of, 962
    Wi-Fi attacks and, 155
    for Wi-Fi security, 129–130
WPAD (Web Proxy Auto-Discovery Protocol), 302, 962
Wrapped ESP (WESP), in IPsec, 863–864, 961
WRED (Weighted RED), 783, 962
WSOPT (Window Scale Option)
    definition of, 962
    TCP header, 608, 610
WWW (World Wide Web)
    definition of, 962
    Internet compared to, 2–3

X

X.25 protocol
    definition of, 962
    VCs (virtual circuits) and, 4–5
X.509 standard
    certificate extensions, 827–828
    file or encoding formats in, 822–823
    TLS extensions, 883
    validating and revoking certificates, 828–831
    viewing preconfigured certificates, 823–826
XML (Extensible Markup Language)
    common use with Web pages, 338
    definition of, 962

XMPP (Extensible Messaging and Presence Proto-
        col), 333, 962

Y

Yiaddr (Your IP address) field, DHCP/BOOTP mes-
        sage format, 237, 247
Your IP address (Yiaddr) field, DHCP/BOOTP mes-
        sage format, 237, 247

Z

Zero window advertisement
    example of dynamic window size adjustment
        and flow control, 705–708
    large buffers and auto-tuning, 717–719
    probes, 710
    SWS (silly windows syndrome) and, 711–713
    TCP persistent timer and, 704–705
Zombie attacks, 26
Zone cuts, DNS and DNSSEC, 903
Zone enumeration, NSEC chain and, 900
Zone signing key (ZSK)
    definition of, 962
    DNSSEC, 896, 905
Zone transfers, in DNS
    AXFR (full zone transfer) messages, 559–561
    DNS notify and, 558–559, 564–565
    initiating, 525
    IXFR (incremental zone transfer) messages,
        561–563
    overview of, 517–518
Zones, DNS
    dynamic updates, 555–558
    overview of, 516–517
Zones, DNSSEC, 903
ZSK (zone signing key)
    definition of, 962
    DNSSEC, 896, 905

IPv4 Header

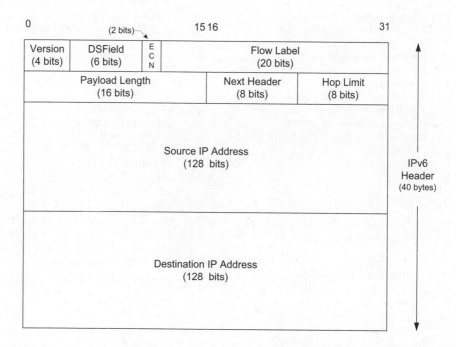

IPv6 Header

UDP Header

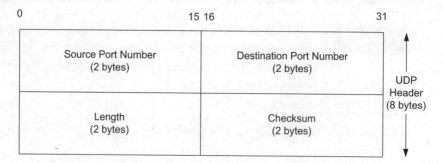

TCP Header

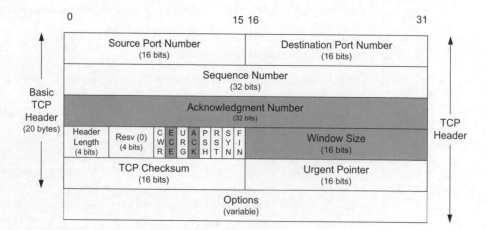